W9-CRK-041

THE DC COMICS ENCYCLOPEDIA

THE DEFINITIVE GUIDE TO THE CHARACTERS OF THE DC UNIVERSE

SENIOR EDITOR: Cefn Ridout
SENIOR DESIGNER: Robert Perry
EDITORS: Kate Berens, Kathryn Hill, Nick Jones, Laura Palosuo
DESIGNERS: Nick Avery, Simon Murrell, Anna Pond
ORIGINAL COVER ARTWORK: Carlo Pagulayan, Elmer Santos
SENIOR PRE-PRODUCTION PRODUCER: Rebecca Fallowfield
SENIOR PRODUCER: Zara Markland
MANAGING EDITOR: Sadie Smith
MANAGING ART EDITOR: Ron Stobbart
ART DIRECTOR: Lisa Lanzarini
PUBLISHER: Julie Ferris
PUBLISHING DIRECTOR: Simon Beecroft

Dorling Kindersley would like to thank:
Josh Anderson at Warner Bros. Global Publishing;
Joe Daley, Jim Hancock, Kevin Kiniry, Hank Manfra,
Leah Tuttle, Erin Vanover at DC Comics
Many thanks also to: Alastair Dougall, David Fentiman, Elizabeth Dowsett,
Emma Grange, Lauren Nesworthy, Tina Jindal, Joel Kempson for editorial assistance;
Ros Bird, Kathryn Boynton, Mabel Chan, Jo Connor, Jon Hall,
Guy Harvey, Gema Salamanca, Anna Sander, Clive Savage,
Rhys Thomas, Pallavi Kapur for design assistance;
John Wells for fact checking; Simon Hugo for proofreading;
Helen Peters for the index

First American Edition, 2016
Published in the United States by DK Publishing
345 Hudson Street, New York, New York 10014
16 17 18 19 20 10 9 8 7 6 5 4 3 2 1
001-283106-Nov/2016

Published in Great Britain by Dorling Kindersley Limited.
A catalog record for this book is available
from the Library of Congress.

ISBN: 978-1-4654-5357-0

Printed and bound in China

A WORLD OF IDEAS:
SEE ALL THERE IS TO KNOW

WWW.DK.COM

THE DC COMICS ENCYCLOPEDIA

THE DEFINITIVE GUIDE TO THE CHARACTERS OF THE DC UNIVERSE

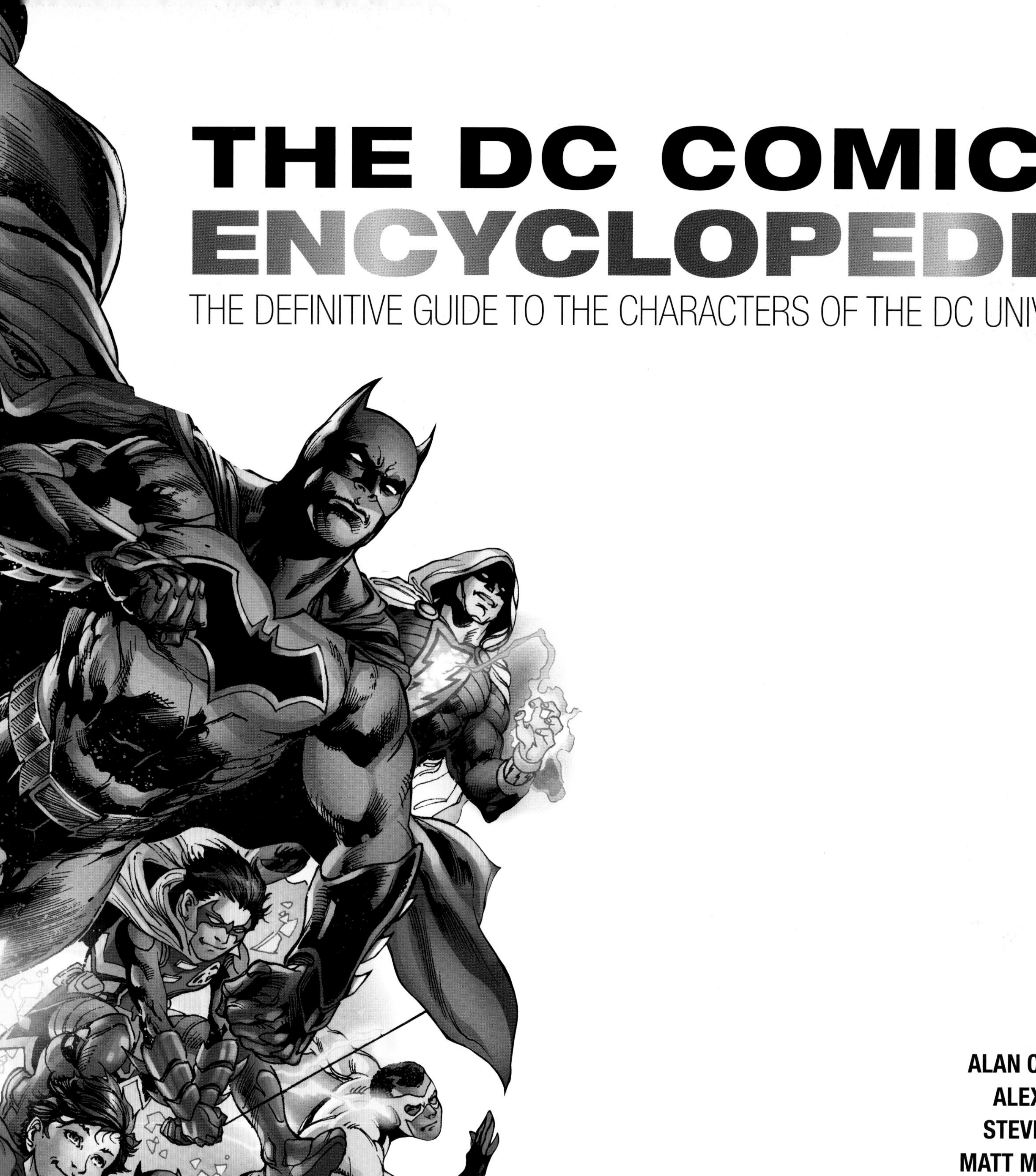

Text by

ALAN COWSILL
ALEX IRVINE
STEVE KORTE
MATT MANNING
STEPHEN (WIN) WIACEK
SVEN WILSON

Additional text by

SCOTT BEATTY
ROBERT GREENBERGER
PHIL JIMINEZ
NICK JONES
DAN WALLACE

CONTENTS

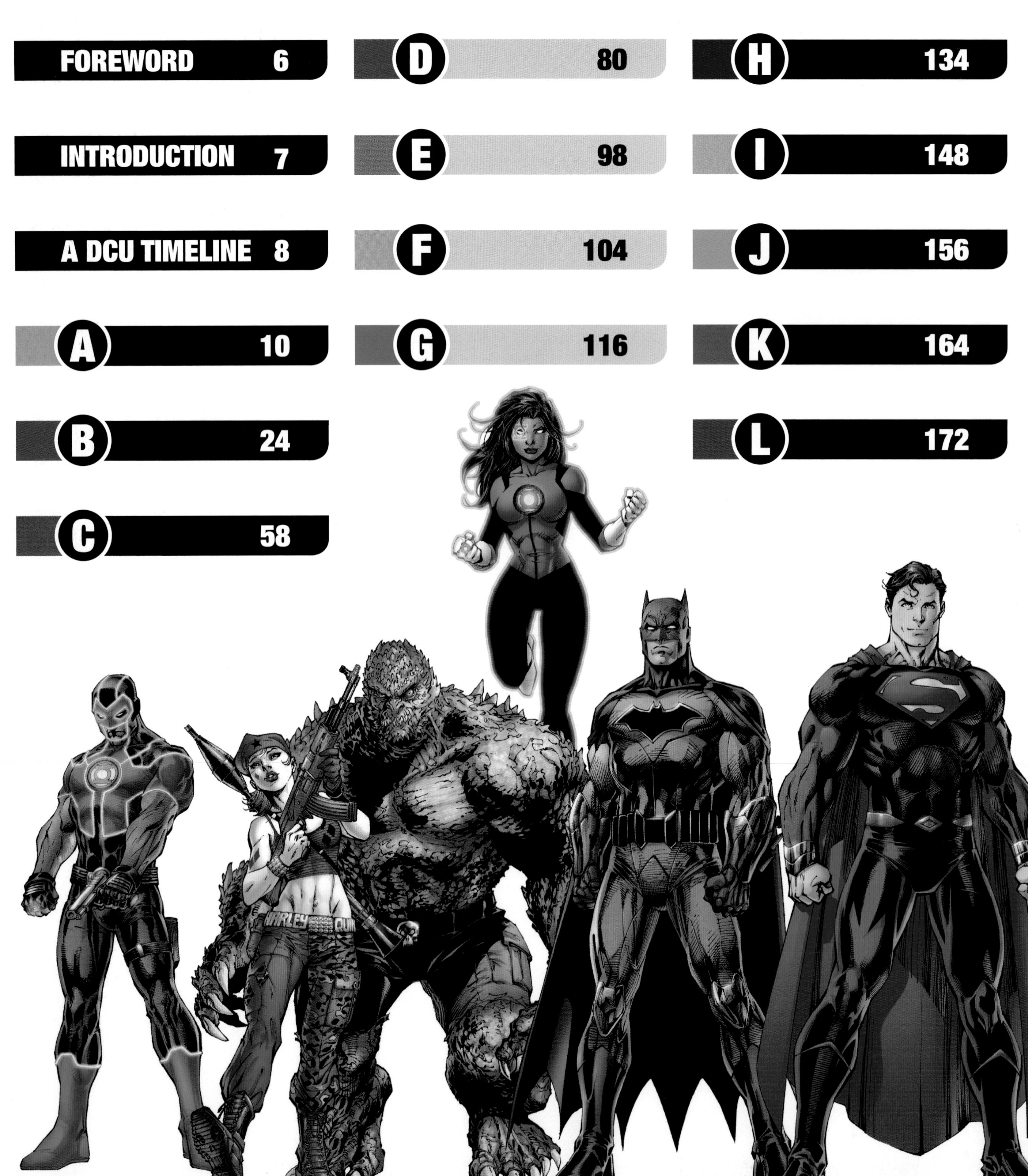

FOREWORD

This book is a celebration, a modern age tome to the amazing universe of Super Heroes and super-villains of the DC universe. You'll find characters that you've known your whole life like Batman and Catwoman, and others you may have never heard of like Blue Devil and Element Woman.

You may ask yourself, why would I be interested in obscure characters on the fringes of the DC Universe? I'd answer because every single character in here is full of limitless potential, most of which has been realized in stories published over the decades of comics, film, television, animation, and games. And then you'll also find the really obscure, the ones that have potentially been forgotten for awhile. Those are my favorite characters. The creative underdogs. Sometimes those are heroes as well known as Aquaman or as obscure as Mera became for awhile. Sometimes the reason they became popular in the first place has been lost and we need to get back to it, which is what the thematic for the REBIRTH relaunch across DC Comics in 2016 has been about.

As a writer who has worked with these characters for over 17 years now, I always found myself drawn to the obscure and forgotten because it was the unlocked potential that grabbed my imagination and attention. That's why books like this have always been my favorite to spend time with. There is a legacy here worth our time, our energy, and our passion.

Generations of writers and artists have built upon the foundation of those first creators. New writers and artists celebrate DC's iconic characters, and they allow those characters to grow. They add new ones. And then other creators continue their stories. This book is the culmination of that up to today.

This newly updated edition of the *DC Comics Encyclopedia* celebrates the entire timeline of the DC Universe: past, present, and future. It explores the mythology of more than 1,000 classic characters and many of their most iconic storylines. I'm sure you will find a few surprises in this volume. And I hope you will stick around to join us for the ongoing saga of the DC Universe. The next chapter awaits.

Geoff Johns
Chief Creative Officer, DC Entertainment

INTRODUCTION

Everyone knows the icons: Batman, Superman, and Wonder Woman. They have adorned bed sheets, T-shirts, action figures, and lunch boxes for decades. They have enthralled successive generations of cinema-goers and television viewers. And they have become synonymous with the words "Super Hero" and even "pop culture." In 2016, it's hard to imagine that the comic books in which they first appeared came about almost by accident, thanks to a fortuitous meeting of commerce and creativity.

The company known today as DC Comics officially began publishing with February 1935's *New Fun* #1, subtitled "The Big Comic Magazine." While the word "comic book" was not yet a household term, *New Fun* joined a growing number of comic magazines on newsstands at the time. From the start of the 20th century, syndicated comic strips had proved to be the most popular section of newspapers. Seizing the opportunity to reach a wider, generally younger, readership and keep their printing presses busy, publishers began reprinting collections of these strips on cheap paper, bound by a flimsy cover. *New Fun*, however, tried something different. It featured all-new strips, which served as proof that readers were hungry for original material in this new format.

In March 1937, *Detective Comics* debuted as an anthology of detective and crime stories that would later inspire the DC Comics name. However, it wasn't until June 1938 that *Action Comics* #1 hit the stands, introducing the world to the first official Super Hero—Superman. The Man of Steel caught on with young fans "faster than a speeding bullet," and soon Batman, his youthful sidekick Robin, and Wonder Woman followed him to four-color fame. Super Heroes quickly became the dominant genre of these fledgling comics books, and have yet to relinquish their hold on a still-fascinated audience.

Over the next eight decades, DC Comics built their stable of characters to include now famous heroes like the Flash, Green Lantern, Aquaman, Shazam, and Hawkman, and villains such as Lex Luthor, the Joker, Darkseid, and a relatively new favorite, Harley Quinn. DC Comics has itself evolved into DC Entertainment, attracting new comic fans every day through their blockbuster movies, TV shows, and video games. In the process, the DC Universe has expanded from a handful of members in the first Super Hero team, the Justice Society of America, to a vast multiverse populated by thousands of denizens, each with a dramatic story to tell.

The *DC Comics Encyclopedia* is a road map to that universe. It's a guide to the best and the brightest, and the most corrupt and notorious. It not only reveals to new readers the rich and detailed landscape of the DC Universe and its characters, but also reminds longtime fans of their favorite storylines and moments, providing even the most die-hard reader with a tantalizing new fact or 20.

The characters in this volume were hand-picked by DC Comics, and thoroughly researched by a team of passionate comic book historians. The Encyclopedia contains all the need-to-know background of each hero, villain, group, or supporting character, and many extra tidbits along the way. Every entry is accompanied with stunning visuals pulled from the DC Comics archive to showcase the work of countless writers, pencillers, inkers, and colorists who have lent their talents to make DC Comics the popular and well-respected creative powerhouse it is today.

The entries in this Encyclopedia range from substantial spreads on DC Comics' biggest names, to smaller profiles on the lesser-knowns and up-and-comers. Each entry provides a "Data Box" presenting essential information such as the character's debut issue, secret identity, vital stats, and powers and abilities. Larger entries feature an "At a Glance" section that summarizes a hero's or villain's defining characteristics and life events; a "Classic Stories" box that points readers toward further essential reading; and "Key Storylines" that spotlight some of their most memorable adventures.

Things change, adapt, evolve. DC Comics is no exception, and often leads by example. The company not only invented Super Heroes in the 1930s, but redefined them for new generations: The Flash ushered in the Silver Age in the 1950s, while *Batman: The Dark Knight* did the same for the Dark Age in the 1980s. Both landmark comics showcased innovative storytelling that not only captivated an older readership, but also inspired the comics writers and artists of the future, paving the way for the Modern Age. That progressive thinking has also changed the status quo on more than one occasion, most notably after the continuity-altering events Crisis on Infinite Earths, Flashpoint, and Rebirth. In the face of these changes, it is worth bearing in mind that while continuities may be overwritten, characters updated, and histories reimagined, the core of what makes DC Comics unique remains. The legacy abides.

To reflect this, the *DC Comics Encyclopedia* focuses on the most current version of a given character's backstory, with larger entries including an "On the Record" section that captures telling moments from the character's life prior to the Flashpoint reboot. The Encyclopedia also sketches out, where practicable, the changes to high-profile characters wrought by the recent Rebirth event. This ensures the Encyclopedia is as comprehensive and up-to-date as possible, while remaining user-friendly to those readers unfamiliar with the myriad of astonishing tales that make up the DC Comics Universe.

Everyone knows something about the icons of DC Comics. Now, thanks to the *DC Comics Encyclopedia*, they have the opportunity to know virtually everything.

Matt Manning, Contributing Author
Cefn Ridout, Senior Editor

A BRIEF HISTORY OF THE DC COMICS UNIVERSE

The DC Comics Universe (DCU), with its multitude of characters, stories, and events, may seem a little daunting to new readers and fans alike. To aid travelers on their journey through this universe, this timeline highlights major turning points in DC Comics' long and dynamic history—from birth to Rebirth.

GOLDEN AGE

***Action Comics* #1 (Jun. 1938)**
The world's first-ever Super Hero debuts in the mighty form of Superman, the Man of Steel. His immediate success kick-starts the Golden Age of comic books.

***Detective Comics* #27 (May 1939)**
Batman swings into comic book action, inspired by both Superman and the masked-man pulp fiction popular at the time.

***All-Star Comics* #3 (Winter 1940)**
The DC Comics Universe takes shape as some of the most successful Super Heroes band together for the first time to start the Justice Society of America (JSA). Members include the recently created Flash, Green Lantern, and Hawkman.

***All-Star Comics* #8 (Dec. 1941–Jan. 1942)**
The first truly iconic female Super Hero is torn from myth and transported to modern times—the Amazing Amazon, Wonder Woman.

SILVER AGE

***Showcase* #4 (Sep.–Oct. 1956)**
The Silver Age of Comics dawns as the Flash is reinvented for a new era with the debut of Barry Allen.

***The Brave and the Bold* #28 (Feb.–Mar. 1960)**
The concept behind the Justice Society of America—a high-profile group of Super Heroes—is rekindled with DC Comics' modern icons teaming up to form the Justice League of America (JLA).

***The Flash* #123 (Sep. 1961)**
The multiverse is created when the Golden Age Flash comes face to face with his Silver Age counterpart. The Golden Age Flash's reality would become known as Earth-2, while the Silver Age Flash's world would eventually be designated Earth-1.

***Justice League of America* #21 (Aug. 1963)**
The DC Comics Universe has its first interdimensional crisis when the JLA meets the JSA for the first time, in what will become a yearly team-up tradition.

***Detective Comics* #359 (Jan. 1967)**
Batgirl, Barbara Gordon, bursts onto the scene in her debut appearance; an independent, capable hero who fast became one of DC Comics' most popular characters.

BRONZE AGE

***Detective Comics* #395 (Jan. 1970)**
Batman is taken back to his darker roots in "The Secret of the Waiting Graves," a momentous issue that helped usher in the Bronze Age of comics.

***Green Lantern* #76 (Apr. 1970)**
The pairing of Green Lantern and Green Arrow brings comics up to speed with the problems of the modern world, serving up a healthy dose of social commentary.

***New Gods* #1 (Mar. 1971)**
The DC Comics Universe gains a pantheon of New Gods in an epic space saga set in a Fourth World on the fringes of Superman's reality.

***DC Comics Presents* #26 (Oct. 1980)**
The "junior Justice League" known as the Teen Titans comes into its own in a preview to their ongoing title, *The New Teen Titans*.

***Crisis on Infinite Earths* #1 (Apr. 1985)**
To streamline the various multiple Earths that had formed in their 50-year history, DC Comics launches a 12-issue series that sees many worlds perish at the hands of the Anti-Monitor. When the villain is finally dispatched, only one Earth remains.

In this new reality, most Earth-2 heroes are established as having been active during World War II, while the adventures of Earth-1's heroes take place in the present day. In the wake of *Crisis on Infinite Earths*, the origin stories for icons such as Superman, Batman, and Wonder Woman are retold, with major continuity corrections that match the reality of their new Earth.

1938–1955 | 1956–1969 | 1970–1983

DARK AGE

***Batman: The Dark Knight* #1 (1986)**
In a dystopian near-future, an aging, embittered Batman steps over the thin blue line to battle foe and friend alike to bring rough justice to Gotham City. This landmark miniseries connected with a mature readership and set the content, tone, and style for the coming of comics' Modern Age.

***Watchmen* #1 (Sep. 1986)**
Another watershed miniseries, Watchmen put the "meta" into metahumans, updating Silver Age Super Heroes for adult readers. Set on the brink of armageddon, this elaborate murder mystery unfolds into a sprawling, literary epic that would have a significant impact on the DCU and beyond.

***Legends* #1 (Nov. 1986)**
When Darkseid, the tyrannical lord of Apokolips, attacks the world's heroes by turning the common man against them, a new incarnation of the Justice League forms to oppose him, alongside government-run super-villain team the Suicide Squad.

***Superman* (Vol. 2) #75 (Jan. 1993)**
The Man of Steel is killed while subduing a murderous alien beast known as Doomsday. Superman later finds his way back to the land of the living after a tumultuous year for Metropolis.

***The Batman Adventures* #12 (Sep. 1993)**
Making the transition from screen to page, Harley Quinn arrived in the DCU from the acclaimed *Batman: The Animated Series* and became a permanent fixture in Batman's rogue's gallery.

***Zero Hour* #4 (Sep. 1994)**
While the DCU's various Earths were merged into one during *Crisis on Infinite Earths*, some lingering continuity issues are neatly tied up in the miniseries *Zero Hour*, which tells of power-mad former Green Lantern Hal Jordan's attempts to remake the world in his image. Ongoing tie-in titles, each with their own issue #0, relate the title character's newly revised origin.

MODERN AGE

***Identity Crisis* #1 (Aug. 2004)**
Dark secrets from the Justice League of America's storied history come to light in this murder mystery miniseries that reveals a time when the League resorted to wiping the minds of its villains.

***Infinite Crisis* #1 (Dec. 2005)**
Survivors of some of the lost realities from the original *Crisis on Infinite Earths* return to the DCU. In this miniseries, the crazed Superboy-Prime and the manipulative Alexander Luthor of Earth-3 instigate a new Crisis to retrieve their respective Earths. The result is New Earth, as continuity is again tweaked to update the DCU.

***52* #1 (May 2006)**
As DCU titles jump a year ahead in the wake of *Infinite Crisis*, the weekly 52-issue maxiseries, simply dubbed *52*, fills in the gaps, culminating with the villainous Mr. Mind altering multiple worlds and creating a new multiverse of 52 Earths.

***Final Crisis* #1 (Jul. 2008)**
Evil wins as Darkseid's forces conquer the Earth, succeeding in "killing" Batman, until Superman leads a revolt to stop the tyrant. By the end of the series, it is revealed that Bruce Wayne is merely displaced in time; he eventually finds his way home in 2010, while Dick Grayson, as Batman, protects Gotham City.

***Blackest Night* #1 (Sep. 2009)**
Undead DCU heroes and villains are recruited as Black Lanterns, due to the machinations of the villain Nekron. Several Lanterns from across the Emotional Spectrum work together to stop this Blackest Night. The result is the Brightest Day maxiseries that sees the rebirth of many characters, including Swamp Thing.

Flashpoint #1 (Jul. 2011)
The most significant continuity-altering event since *Crisis on Infinite Earths*, *Flashpoint* establishes an alternate world that a stranded Barry Allen must fight his way back from. However, when the Flash manages to return the world to its proper status quo, the result is Earth-0, a universe similar to the former New Earth, yet different in many ways.

MODERN AGE

***The New 52* (Nov. 2011)**
The universe of Earth-0 is introduced with the launch of 52 separate titles. Long-running mainstay titles like *Action Comics* and *Detective Comics* restart from issue #1, as the world discovers a fresh reality where iconic heroes are in the prime of their lives. Superman's origin is retold in *Action Comics*, Wonder Woman's past is reevaluated in the pages of her own title, and Batman embarks on a "Zero Year" that reveals a modern take on his familiar history.

***Forever Evil* #1 (Nov. 2013)**
Spinning out of the pages of the crossover "Trinity War" that featured in the three Justice League titles of the time, *Forever Evil* tells how Earth-3's Crime Syndicate arrives on Earth-0, forcing Batman and Lex Luthor to team up to stop them.

***Convergence* #0 (Jun. 2015)**
Readers are treated to the adventures of characters from a variety of past continuities as Brainiac tries to converge the worlds of the multiverse. When the heroes rebel, a newly updated multiverse is formed, with worlds similar to the ones that came before, yet modernized for a new audience.

***DC You* (Aug. 2015)**
A series of new titles is launched, while many of DC Comics' icons get a facelift. Commissioner Gordon temporarily assumes Batman's mantle when the Dark Knight goes missing, Superman briefly loses his powers due to Vandal Savage's manipulations, and Wonder Woman sports a new costume and mission.

***Justice League* #40 (Jun. 2015)**
In an initial, prologue chapter, "The Darkseid War" begins, pitting the all-powerful Anti-Monitor against Darkseid in a clash that briefly grants godlike powers to members of the Justice League.

DC Universe: Rebirth #1 (May 2016)
In a one-shot special that leads to a series of character-specific Rebirth specials, the DCU takes its next step in evolution when Wally West (the Flash) returns. While some major titles restart at issue #1, two flagship books, *Action Comics* and *Detective Comics*, return to their old issue numbering prior to the New 52. The pre-Flashpoint Superman picks up where his recently deceased successor left off, the forgotten original Teen Titans form the Titans, and Wonder Woman's history is again revised. All the while, the cast of the Watchmen wait in the wings, surveying their handiwork.

1984–1998 **1999–PRESENT**

A.R.G.U.S.

DEBUT *Justice League* (Vol. 2) #7 **(May 2012)**
BASE Mobile
OFFICIAL NAME Advanced Research Group Uniting Super-Humans
ALLIES Justice League, Killer Frost
ENEMIES Secret Society of Super-Villains
AFFILIATIONS Justice League of America

Officially, A.R.G.U.S. was created by the US President as America's official government liaison to the Justice League. With Steve Trevor in command, the agency provided financial support and clean-up services, but its real purpose was to spy on seemingly all-powerful Super Heroes.

Over a period of five years, Trevor expanded the organization's remit to include the monitoring of all metahuman and unnatural threats. A.R.G.U.S. agents confiscated mystical artifacts and advanced technologies, policed extra-dimensional incursions, and covertly battled monsters, villains, and Super Heroes acting against the perceived interests of the US and humanity. These threats were neutralized deposited in classified research vaults known as the Black Room, Red Room, and Circus.

When Amanda Waller replaced Trevor, she created the Justice League of America as a secret weapon in case the original heroes should ever go rogue.

Unproven stories persist that the A.R.G.U.S. organization has effectively existed ever since the Revolutionary War. When Civil War divided the country several decades later, it became known as the Anonymous Ranger Group of the United States. **WW**

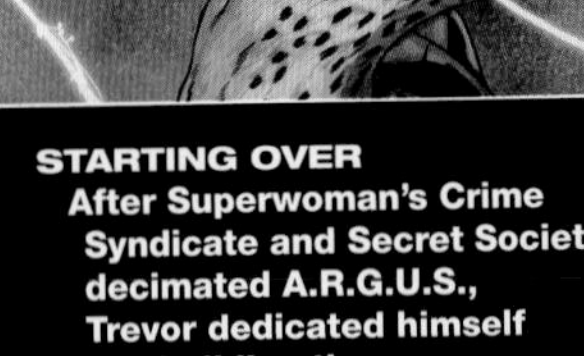

STARTING OVER
After Superwoman's Crime Syndicate and Secret Society decimated A.R.G.U.S., Trevor dedicated himself to rebuilding the agency.

EYES ON THE PRIZE
As long as Steve had a few good men and women to back him up, A.R.G.U.S. could never be counted out.
1 Steve Trevor
2 Agent Dale Gunn
3 Director Amanda Waller
4 Etta Candy

ALL-STAR SQUADRON

DEBUT *Justice League of America* (Vol. 1) #193 (free preview insert) **(Aug. 1981)**; *All Star Squadron* (Vol. 1) #1 **(Sep. 1981)**
UNIVERSE Earth-2
BASE The Trylon and Perisphere, New York City
POWERS/ABILITIES Many and various, employed by every World War II American hero and mystery man united in defense of liberty and democracy against the Axis powers.
ALLIES Blackhawks
ENEMIES Adolf Hitler, Nazi Germany, Imperial Japan, Baron Blitzkrieg, Ultra-Humanite, Per Degaton, enemy spies
AFFILIATIONS Federal Bureau of Investigation, U.S. War Department

IN TIMES OF CRISIS...
The All-Star Squadron was shaken to its core when the crisis instigated by the cosmic destroyer the Anti-Monitor reconfigured the multiverse. As a result, history was rewritten and heroes such as Superman, Batman, Wonder Woman, and Green Arrow ceased to exist on Earth-2. This left a leaner, meaner Squadron to battle Hitler's hordes.

ALL-STARS AND STRIPES
When Earth-2 needed them most, America's mystery men and masked heroes banded together to answer the call.

When President Franklin Delano Roosevelt received warning of an imminent Japanese attack on Pearl Harbor, he sent out an urgent call to the newly constituted Justice Society of America (JSA). Unfortunately, the JSA had been ambushed by an association of enemies from their own future and were unable to respond.

However, with the heroic "big guns" unavailable for duty, a number of other patriots who had recently begun fighting as masked heroes acted upon the President's desperate pleas. Coming together in the wake of the Japanese attack and led by Liberty Belle and Hawkman, a battalion of these new heroes formed the All-Star Squadron. This loose umbrella organization comprised the Justice Society, Seven Soldiers of Victory, and Freedom Fighters, as well as various non-aligned "mystery men." Their joint mission was to defend America until victory was finally achieved. When World War II ended, the All-Star Squadron was duly disbanded.

The costumed champions' overwhelming firepower may well have ended World War II early but for a mystic barrier that covered every inch of Axis-controlled territory. This arcane curtain served to enthrall any magic-based or susceptible hero, turning them into slaves of the aggressor nations. **WW**

ALL CASTE

DEBUT *Red Hood and the Outlaws* (Vol. 1) #1 (Nov. 2011)
BASE Acres of All
POWERS/ABILITIES Martial arts, advanced meditative techniques.
ALLIES S'aru the Protector, Jason Todd
ENEMIES The Untitled

Millennia ago, a family of nine warriors formed the Untitled, a cult dedicated to absolute evil, and gained vast power and immortality. Eventually, one sister, Ducra, broke away to form her own faction—the All Caste—and fight her malign siblings.

For 3,000 years, Ducra the Instructor led this clandestine order of warrior-monks in a secret war against her own family. Cloistered in the Chamber of All, deep within the Himalayan mountains, the monks toiled tirelessly, forging links with the outside world while still managing to remain largely independent from it.

On the recommendation of Talia Al Ghūl, the warrior-monks trained Jason Todd after his resurrection from death. When he returned to the Acres of All many years later, he discovered that Ducra and her All Caste had been brutally exterminated. As he apologized to Ducra's body for having failed her, Ducra's spirit appeared and told Todd that they had been murdered by their sworn enemies the Untitled. Alongside the sole survivor, Essence, Todd avenged the All Caste's deaths, ending the Untitled's depredations forever. **WW**

ARMY OF THE DEAD
When Todd returned to the All Caste, he found that they had been slaughtered. Their reanimated corpses then attacked him and his allies, Arsenal and Starfire.

AMAZING MAN

DEBUT *All Star Squadron* (Vol. 1) #23 (Jul. 1983)
CURRENT VERSION *O.M.A.C.* (Vol. 4) #2 (Dec. 2011)
REAL NAME Rocker Bonn
BASE Wayne, Texas
HEIGHT Variable **WEIGHT** Variable
EYES Brown **HAIR** Black
POWERS/ABILITIES Matter absorption, body transmutation and regeneration; can discharge absorbed matter as blasts of energy.
ENEMIES Brother Eye, O.M.A.C.

Rocker Bonn was an operative of the intelligence agency Checkmate before being transferred to its public subsidiary Cadmus Industries. Subjected to genetic experiments as part of Project Cadmus, he gained the power to explosively incorporate mass and matter, while also taking on their physical properties. Given the codename Amazing Man, Bonn escaped rather than become Cadmus' tool.

Sometime later, while Bonn was in hiding working at a Texas diner, the rogue sentient satellite Brother Eye manipulated him into battling Kevin Kho, the unwilling host of the Eye's One Machine Attack Construct (O.M.A.C.). Caught in a confusing three-way battle between the police, O.M.A.C., and himself, Amazing Man was held at bay and, after being tricked into absorbing some of O.M.A.C.s circuitry, was ultimately absorbed into Brother Eye, who deemed the transmorph useful to its own plans. **WW**

GO FOR THE EYES
Tricked into combat with O.M.A.C., Amazing Man initially had the upper hand until O.M.A.C. temporarily blinded him.

ALPHA CENTURION

DEBUT *Zero Hour* (Vol. 1) #3 (Sept. 1994)
CURRENT VERSION *Convergence: Superman* Vol. 1 #2 (Jul. 2015)
REAL NAME Roman
BASE Metropolis
HEIGHT 5ft 8ins **WEIGHT** 165 lbs
EYES Brown **HAIR** Black
POWERS/ABILITIES Superhuman strength, flight, durability, speed; can manifest a personal pantheon of alien warriors called the Pax Galactica.
ALLIES Superman, Supergirl, Eradicator, Steel
ENEMIES Lex Luthor, Cyborg Superman

College student Roman was gravely wounded during an attack by Lexus terrorists at the Metropolis Museum of History. Bleeding profusely, he used an ancient belt as a tourniquet and was instantly possessed by a minor Roman god trapped inside the strap. Alpha Centurion took over and transformed Roman's body. Blessed with superhuman abilities, he easily defeated the terrorists.

Since that moment, Alpha Centurion has repeatedly commandeered Roman's body, leaving his host terrified that one day the warrior-hero will decide to possess him for good. The Centurion seems able to sense imminent danger before it arises and force the change without warning. Alpha Centurion has possessed many hosts over the centuries, destroying monsters and carrying out the edicts of the mystical Pantheon of Grace. He is compelled to save lives and maintain order at all costs. **WW**

QUO VADIS?
Roman never knew when his body would be suddenly taken over by Alpha Centurion, or where the latest usurpation would take him.

ALPHA LANTERNS

DEBUT *Green Lantern* (Vol. 4) #26 (Feb. 2008)
CURRENT VERSION *Green Lantern Corps* (Vol. 3) #8 (Jun. 2012)
BASE Oa
POWERS/ABILITIES Cyborg bodies, incorporating Manhunter technology, able to drain Green Lantern rings of charge.
ENEMIES Sinestro Corps, Cyborg Superman, Guardians of the Universe
AFFILIATIONS Green Lantern Corps

When the Guardians of the Universe rewrote the Green Lanterns' rules of conduct, they created a new rank to police the Corps. Alpha Lanterns were loyal veterans converted into cyborgs incorporating Manhunter technology, with an inbuilt Battery of Power able to drain Lanterns' rings.

This "Internal Affairs" division was disliked by rank-and-file officers, as was their chilling Oath of Intent:

"In days of peace, in nights of war,
Obey the laws forever more
Misconduct must be answered for
Swear us, the chosen...
The Alpha Corps!"

On deciding Green Lanterns were a failed experiment, the Guardians manipulated their Alpha Lanterns into triggering a civil war within the Corps. By maneuvering Guy Gardner and an army of Emerald Warriors into destroying their cyborg overseers, the Oans were simply removing an obstacle to the introduction of their remorseless, emotionless "Third Army." **WW**

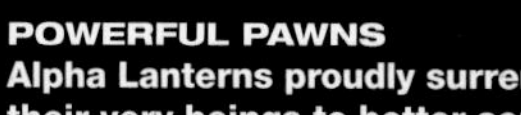

POWERFUL PAWNS
Alpha Lanterns proudly surrendered their very beings to better serve the Corps, but were betrayed without qualm by their callous masters.

AMBUSH BUG

DEBUT *DC Comics Presents* #52 (Dec. 1982)
CURRENT VERSION *Channel 52* #1 (Apr. 2013)
BASE Metropolis
REAL NAME Irwin Schwab
HEIGHT 5ft 10in **WEIGHT** 145 lbs
HAIR None **EYES** Green
POWERS/ABILITIES Interviewing, consciousness of fourth wall.
AFFILIATION Channel 52

Channel 52 news reporter Ambush Bug is your arthropod-on-the-scene when there are heroes (and villains) to be interviewed about their latest exploits. He was there for Trinity War; he was there for Darkseid's invasion; he has been there for nearly every crisis and every convergence, getting a microphone in the faces of the people who matter most, whether they're on Earth-1 or Earth-31, the 21st century or the year 3000.

For updates on recent shake-ups in the Teen Titans, or the real story on Superwoman's baby, or insights into the ongoing dramas up on Mount Olympus, Ambush Bug's your insectoid. He has the stories the *Daily Planet* won't touch, and is right on the spot when Galaxy Broadcasting hides out in the studio. If you want the latest on the big events affecting your world and beyond, tune in to Channel 52 and trust Ambush Bug to bring you the news you can use! **AI**

ANTENNAE FOR NEWS
Ambush Bug always seems to know when there's a story brewing, and he's not afraid to rake a little muck or ruffle a few feathers to get at the truth.

AMAZO

DEBUT *The Brave and the Bold* #30 **(Jun.–Jul. 1960)**
CURRENT VERSION (As android) *Justice League* (Vol. 2) #8 **(Jun. 2012)**; (As Ikarus) *Justice League* (Vol. 2) #36 **(Jan. 2015)**
BASE New York City
REAL NAME Armen Ikarus
HEIGHT 8ft **WEIGHT** 485 lbs
HAIR Red **EYES** Yellow
POWERS/ABILITIES Synthetic absorption cells granting powers of any metahuman within close proximity; unpredictable creation and recombination of those powers.
ALLIES Professor Ivo
ENEMIES Justice League
AFFILIATIONS Secret Society of Super-Villains

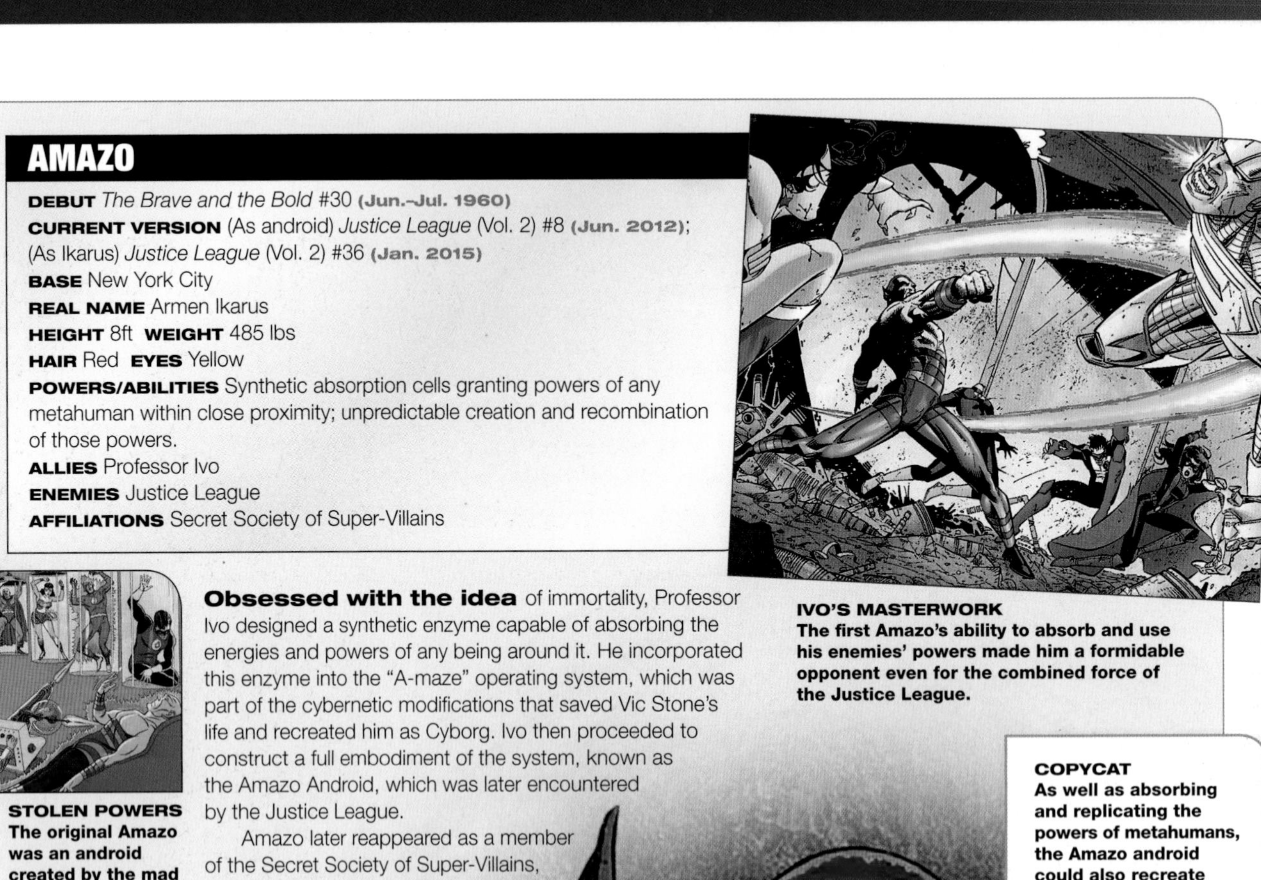

IVO'S MASTERWORK
The first Amazo's ability to absorb and use his enemies' powers made him a formidable opponent even for the combined force of the Justice League.

STOLEN POWERS
The original Amazo was an android created by the mad scientist Professor Ivo. He gifted it with powers stolen from Earth's greatest heroes, in hopes of using it to conquer the world.

Obsessed with the idea of immortality, Professor Ivo designed a synthetic enzyme capable of absorbing the energies and powers of any being around it. He incorporated this enzyme into the "A-maze" operating system, which was part of the cybernetic modifications that saved Vic Stone's life and recreated him as Cyborg. Ivo then proceeded to construct a full embodiment of the system, known as the Amazo Android, which was later encountered by the Justice League.

Amazo later reappeared as a member of the Secret Society of Super-Villains, created by Professor Ivo in league with the Outsider. Lex Luthor subsequently used the Amazo system as the basis of his deadly Amazo Virus, which spread via LexCorp's Dr. Armen Ikarus—the first casualty of the virus—to infect dozens of people. The virus also mutated Ikarus into the new Amazo, giving him the ability not just to mimic and replicate powers, but to suppress them. However, its unpredictability made it a dire threat when unleashed in Metropolis. Luthor and the Justice League stopped Ikarus from dispersing the virus worldwide, and quickly created a vaccine, but not before a number of new metahumans were created, who kept their newfound powers even after the virus was purged from their systems. **AI**

COPYCAT
As well as absorbing and replicating the powers of metahumans, the Amazo android could also recreate their equipment, such as Green Lantern power rings.

IKARUS ASCENDING
Dr. Armen Ikarus became the new Amazo, and nearly provided a vector for the new Amazo virus to spread worldwide, with catastrophic results.

AMAZONS

DATA

DEBUT *All-Star Comics* #8 **(Dec. 1941–Jan. 1942)**
CURRENT VERSION *Wonder Woman* (Vol. 4) #1 **(Nov. 2011)**
BASE Themyscira/Paradise Island
NOTABLE MEMBERS Diana; Hippolyta; Derinoe; Dessa; Hessia; Aleka; Donna Troy
POWERS/ABILITIES Superhuman strength, peerless combat and tactical abilities; some magical powers in certain individuals.
ALLIES Sons of Hephaestus
ENEMIES First Born
AFFILIATIONS Olympian Gods

PEACEFUL WARRIORS
The Amazon way is to train mind, body, and spirit, ensuring that war is only undertaken for the right reasons.

A race of superhuman warrior women created by Olympian goddesses from the spirits of women who had died at the hands of men, the Amazons inhabit Paradise Island. There they stand guard over the ancient evil buried deep beneath the island.

For thousands of years the Amazons lived on Paradise Island—Themyscira—guarding Pandora's Box, which was buried deep below their homeland. Occasionally they added to their number by abducting hapless sailors who passed too close. While the male offspring from union with these captive seafarers would be consigned to the care of Hephaestus, the girls would grow up to become Amazons.

The Amazonian princess Diana, daughter of Queen Hippolyta and Zeus, grew up believing she had been created from clay, but this was a ruse by Hippolyta to protect her daughter from the wrath of Zeus's wife, Hera. Later, the discovery of Diana's origins caused a schism among the Amazons, many of whom felt Diana had already abandoned them to undertake her missions in Patriarch's World as Wonder Woman. This rebellion came to a head when Hippolyta was killed and her rival Derinoe used sorcerous means to create a new Amazon champion, named Donna Troy, from the queen's clay remains, echoing the cover story of Diana's own origins.

The rebel Amazons, led by Donna Troy, massacred the Sons of Hephaestus, setting the stage for a showdown between Wonder Woman and Donna Troy—in which Wonder Woman triumphed, asserting herself as Queen of the Amazons and her mother's true heir. Now the Amazons are unified once more under Diana's leadership, although the underlying tensions that caused the rebellion have not completely disappeared. **AI**

INTERNAL TREACHERY
Derinoe presented Donna Troy as a true champion of the Amazons.

ON THE RECORD

In their 1940s comics debut, the Amazons were a group of immortal warrior women who were compelled by the goddess Aphrodite to leave the world of men for the isolated Paradise Island. Over time, the Amazons reestablished diplomatic relations with the outside world and even reconstructed their island home after it was destroyed.

Hippolyta had been present since comics Golden Age, and her death forced the Amazons into a new era, with Diana as their Queen. From the late 1960s, the Amazons' fearsome fighting abilities made them the frequent target of various Olympian gods and worldly forces who wanted to control them.

UNITED FRONT
Notable women from the history of the Amazons of Themyscira.

UNPROVOKED MASSACRE
Donna Troy led the rebellious Amazons in a bloody incursion against the Sons of Hephaestus, who had historically been granted refuge on Themyscira. This betrayal of their principles brought the Amazons to the brink of civil war.

AMETHYST

DEBUT *Legion of Super-Heroes* (Vol. 2) #298 **(Apr. 1983)**
CURRENT VERSION *Sword of Sorcery Featuring Amethyst* #0 **(Nov. 2012)**
REAL NAME Amy Winston
BASE Nilaa
HEIGHT 5ft 8in **WEIGHT** 122 lbs
EYES Violet **HAIR** Blonde
POWERS/ABILITIES Expert swordfighter; wields the magical forces of House Amethyst.
ALLIES Princess Ingvie, John Constantine
ENEMIES Lady Mordiel, Eclipso
AFFILIATIONS House Amethyst, Justice League Dark

Amy Winston didn't fit in at high school. She lived in a trailer with her mother, Graciel, who insisted Amy train at sword fighting in her spare time. She promised to take Amy to her true home on her 17th birthday and, when the time came, she took her to a remote area and activated a portal gem. Amy walked through it, and emerged in the mystical world of Nilaa as Princess Amaya of House Amethyst.

On Nilaa, she found her mother was the target of her corrupt aunt, Lady Mordiel. Mordiel desired the death of Graciel so she could secure the full power of the House of Amethyst. (In fact, it was Lady Mordiel's lust for power that had caused Graciel to flee Nilaa all those years ago.) As it transpired, when Amaya later fought for her life against the deadly super-villain Eclipso, her mother and aunt gave all their power to her, allowing Amaya to triumph. **MM**

ON THE RECORD

Amy Winston and her alter ego Amethyst debuted in an insert story in the pages of *Legion of Super-Heroes* in 1983. However, her story had little to do with the Legion's 31st century adventures and was instead set in the present.

Amy fought the forces of Dark Opal and, unlike the current version, the reality she was transported to was usually referred to as Gemworld rather than Nilaa. Amethyst would go on to star in her own 12-issue maxi-series, followed by a slightly longer series in 1985.

GROWING PAINS
When she debuted, Amy Winston was just 13 years old. In Gemworld, she became an adult and had to face villains, including Flaw and the Child.

ANGEL AND THE APE

DEBUT *Showcase* (Vol. 1) #77 (Sep. 1968)
BASE New York City
HEIGHT 5ft 10in (Angel); 5ft 9in (Sam)
WEIGHT 140 lbs (Angel); 550 lbs (Sam)
EYES Blue (Angel); Hazel (Sam)
HAIR Blonde (Angel); Black (Sam)
POWERS/ABILITIES **Angel**: Adept detective; linguist; martial artist; skilled fencer. **Sam**: Mind control powers.

While exploring Africa with her father, Professor Theo O'Day, Angel discovered a talking gorilla. When she returned to the US with the ape, he adopted the name Sam Simeon and lived with the O'Days, including Theo's wife, former crime fighter Princess Power, and their other daughter, the super-strong Athena, who would later gain notoriety of a sort as the Inferior Five member Dumb Bunny.

Sam originally hailed from Gorilla City and was relate to one of the Flash's fiercest adversaries, Gorilla Grodd, though he possessed only a fraction of Grodd's formidable mental powers. While Sam pursued a career as a cartoonist, Angel honed her intellectual and physical skills, which she put to good use as a private investigator. The two shared an office and their subsequent adventures provided ample inspiration for Sam's comic book tales. **MM**

ON THE RECORD

The original Anarky was Lonnie Machin, an anarchist out to cause trouble in Gotham City. During his first encounter with the Dark Knight, he spray-painted his logo on Batman's cape. His moniker was later usurped by another of Batman's young enemies, the General, who wore a variation on the classic red Anarky costume. After the reality-altering Flashpoint event, Lonnie was known only as Moneyspider, but may become the new Anarky.

INTERGALACTIC ANARCHY
Anarky fused the two halves of his brain, become incredibly smart and an effective vigilante. He even became a Green Lantern for a brief time after securing a power ring.

ANARKY

DEBUT *Detective Comics* (Vol. 1) #608 **(Nov. 1989)**
CURRENT VERSION *Green Lantern Corps* (Vol. 3) #25 **(Jan. 2014)** (Anarky I); *Detective Comics* (Vol. 2) #37 **(Feb. 2015)** (Anarky II)
REAL NAME Sam Young
BASE Gotham City
HEIGHT 6ft 2in **WEIGHT** 215 lbs
EYES Blue **HAIR** Blond
POWERS/ABILITIES Highly intelligent and a keen strategist; usurped the Mad Hatter's mind-control technology to serve his own ends; powerful connections in Gotham City's high society.
ALLIES Cult of followers
ENEMIES Batman, Mad Hatter, Harvey Bullock
AFFILIATIONS Gotham City Council

When a human trafficker named Jeb Lester was set on fire and thrown from Wayne Tower in downtown Gotham City, Batman and Harvey Bullock began investigating the case. They discovered that Lester's killer was a new vigilante calling himself Anarky, using the persona of a figure seen during the Zero Year. After attempting to blow up Wayne Tower itself, Anarky went public with a video, exhorting Gotham City's citizens to break free from their self-imposed prisons and participate in citywide chaos. To enable people to do so anonymously, he arranged for Anarky masks to be delivered to everyone's doorsteps.

In truth, Anarky was city councilman Samuel Young, who was using his Anarky movement as a smokescreen to hide his real activities and motives. Several years previously, when Sam was younger, his sister had been abused and murdered by the Mad Hatter. Now an adult, Sam wanted revenge, so he kidnapped the villain. He planned to murder the Mad Hatter and also use the Mad Hatter's mind-controlling technology to command an army of innocent citizens, all wearing Anarky masks. He even went so far as to model his Anarky masks after his sister's face!

It took the joint efforts of Batman and Detective Harvey Bullock of the G.C.P.D. to foil Anarky's plans. **MM**

ANIMAL MAN

DEBUT *Strange Adventures* (Vol. 1) #180 **(Sep. 1965)**
CURRENT VERSION *Animal Man* (Vol. 2) #1 **(Nov. 2011)**
REAL NAME Bernhard "Buddy" Baker
BASE San Diego, California
HEIGHT 5ft 11in **WEIGHT** 172 lbs
EYES Blue **HAIR** Blond
POWERS/ABILITIES Able to connect to the mystical and powerful Red life force, which enables him to use the abilities of any animal; charismatic; talented stunt man; peak physical fitness.
ALLIES Swamp Thing, Adam Strange
ENEMIES Anton Arcane, Brother Blood
AFFILIATIONS Justice League United

Over five years ago in the Congo, a hero named Animal Man pursued a group of poachers. The chosen avatar for the Red, a mystical force that connects all animals, Animal Man was surprised when one of the men he was pursuing turned out to be Anton Arcane, an agent for a rival force of death and decay known as the Rot. Arcane murdered this Animal Man; as a result, the Red sought to create a new avatar. They chose movie stunt man Buddy Baker to serve their needs.

While driving home from work, Buddy saw what appeared to be an alien spaceship crash in nearby woods. He went to investigate—and passed out. Buddy never suspected that the Red was simply creating an origin scenario for him that he could easily comprehend, rather than reveal its true properties. So, when he awoke in the woods, Buddy came to believe that he had been kidnapped by aliens and operated on. Finding a costume the Red had left for him, he decided to become a Super Hero, just as the Red had planned all along. Buddy later learned the true secret of his transformation after he had already embraced his heroic role as Animal Man. **MM**

RED POWER
Animal Man's adventures have seen him battle the forces of the Rot, as well as the twisted villain Brother Blood.

ON THE RECORD

Debuting in the mid-1960s, Animal Man was born after an alien visitation. After a stint as a member of the Forgotten Heroes, Buddy was given his own series, and became a founding member of Justice League Europe. In his own title, he discovered his true origins and even broke the fourth wall, meeting the writer of his exploits. Animal Man became an ambassador of the Red, at one point changing his look with long black-and-white hair.

STRANGE BEDFELLOWS
Animal Man became a close ally with Adam Strange and Starfire when the three embarked on an outer-space adventure together in the pages of the maxiseries *52*.

ANTI-MONITOR

DEBUT *Crisis on Infinite Earths* #2 **(May 1985)**
CURRENT VERSION *Forever Evil* #7 **(Jul. 2014)**
REAL NAME Mobius
BASE Mobile
HEIGHT Variable **WEIGHT** Variable
EYES Red **HAIR** None
POWERS/ABILITIES Near-omnipotent when merged with Anti-Life Equation; superhuman strength, endurance, durability; energy projection; commands army of Shadow Demons; can absorb life-force of victims.
ALLIES Grail
ENEMIES Darkseid, Justice League, Crime Syndicate

On the distant planet Qward many years ago, a man named Mobius built a sophisticated device called the Mobius Chair. On a quest to glimpse the forbidden, Mobius attempted to view the source of the Anti-Matter universe, hoping to discover what sparked its creation. What he found was the Anti-Life Equation, an infamous truth the tyrant Darkseid had spent a lifetime trying to locate. The equation merged with Mobius, transforming him into the immensely powerful Anti-Monitor. Meanwhile, the Mobius Chair came into the possession of the New God Metron, who used it to explore the universe.

The Anti-Monitor became a destroyer, traveling from one universe to the next, consuming worlds. He caused the Crisis on Infinite Earths, destroying the multiverse, an event only a few, including Metron, recall. But Mobius soon grew tired of his destructive life and hatched an elaborate plan with Darkseid's daughter, Grail, to rid him of this burden. Waging war on Grail's father, he murdered five billion people on Earth-3 to absorb their energies and then attacked and killed Darkseid. This act released his energies and allowed Mobius to free himself of the curse of living as the Anti-Monitor. **MM**

ON THE RECORD

In his original incarnation, the Anti-Monitor looked different, but was just as powerful as his reinvented form after the Flashpoint event. While Crisis on Infinite Earths altered reality in the 1980s and Flashpoint changed it again in 2011, the Anti-Monitor's multiverse reshaping role remained the same—though few characters could recall fighting the super-villain.

Destroyed during Crisis, the Anti-Monitor was reborn when 52 new realities formed, and became guardian of the Sinestro Corps.

WORLDS IN CRISIS
The Anti-Monitor's devastating attempts to create a pure anti-matter multiverse only ended when the surviving heroes of different Earths sacrificed their lives to stop him.

AQUAMAN

DATA

DEBUT *More Fun Comics* #73 **(Nov. 1941)**
CURRENT VERSION *Aquaman* (Vol. 7) #1 **(Nov. 2011)**
REAL NAME Arthur Curry
BASE Boston; Amnesty Bay; Atlantis
HEIGHT 6ft 1in **WEIGHT** 325 lbs **EYES** Blue **HAIR** Blond
POWERS/ABILITIES Superhuman strength, reflexes, and stamina due to hybrid Atlantean physiology; telepathic control over all marine organisms; water-breathing and pressure resistance; energy and heat resistance; wields the Trident of Poseidon.
ALLIES Stephen Shin, Mera, Batman
ENEMIES Orm, Chimera, Black Manta
AFFILIATIONS Justice League, the Others

Raised by lighthouse keeper Tom Curry after his Atlantean mother Atlanna returned to the oceans, Arthur Curry was called back to fulfill his royal destiny before he reached adulthood in the small coastal town of Amnesty Bay, Maine. His kingdom spans nearly 70 percent of the Earth's surface, and he commands the allegiance of all creatures that swim in salt water. Ruler of Atlantis and Poseidon's designated guardian of the oceans, Aquaman is also a founding member of the Justice League.

AT A GLANCE...

City under the sea
The legendary city of Atlantis has spawned myths for centuries. Behind them all lies a reality even more extraordinary than the myths. This fantastic seafloor city is home to an advanced civilization whose citizens guard the oceans and mistrust anyone who lives on land.

Mera
A fearless and powerful hero in her own right, the Xebel princess Mera was trained from childhood to kill Atlanteans. Her love for Aquaman has superseded Xebel teachings, however.

Aquatic influence
Aquaman has the ability to influence the behavior of marine organisms. It isn't exactly telepathy, since most sea creatures don't have enough of a mind to respond to telepathic commands, but he can create desires within them and rely on their own natures to do the rest.

Disillusioned with the life of a Super Hero—and with being mocked by the public—Aquaman abandoned both the Justice League and the throne of Atlantis for a quieter life in Boston with his wife Mera, Princess of Xebel. But when ravenous aquatic monsters attacked a small town near his childhood home of Amnesty Bay, the pair tracked them to the Marianas Trench on the advice of Aquaman's former mentor Dr. Stephen Shin. There they discovered a dying alien civilization that hunted surface creatures in order to stay alive, and buried them with a seafloor volcanic explosion.

IN HIS ELEMENT
Aquaman as a toddler with his human father and Atlantean mother. He would always suffer conflicting loyalties toward the land and sea.

They also found an Atlantean artifact that appeared to hold a clue about the destruction of Atlantis. Consulting with Dr. Shin, Aquaman was interrupted by Ya'Wara, who revealed that his old nemesis Black Manta was hunting the Others, a team Aquaman had created to protect ancient Atlantean artifacts. Black Manta had captured artifacts including the scepter that belonged to Atlantis's ancient ruler, known only as the Dead King. Black Manta headed for the Dead King's tomb in Antarctica, with Aquaman and the Others on his trail, while Mera went on a mission to Xebel.

The exiled Atlantean Vulko told Aquaman the story of how his parents met, hinting at its significance. The Others intercepted Black Manta and Aquaman defeated him, but an unknown party seized the scepter and used it to release the Trench creatures from their volcanic prison. As Aquaman's brother Orm started a war with the surface when a military missile test went wrong and threatened Atlantis, Aquaman discovered Vulko had betrayed him, stealing the scepter and awakening the Dead King.

TRENCH WARFARE
Aquaman and Mera face a horde of the ravenous Trench.

The Dead King attacked the surface world with snow and froze the undersea kingdom of Xebel with Mera inside, while Aquaman's old adversary the Scavenger attacked Atlantis. Aquaman freed Mera and repelled the Scavenger, but the Dead King took his trident and told him that his family were not true royals, but usurpers. To Aquaman's shame, he discovered that his ancestor was the Dead King's brother, who murdered the rest of his family. In revenge, the Dead King had created the relics and used the scepter to sink Atlantis.

Locating the scepter in a shipwreck, Aquaman tapped its powers to lead the Trench in an attack against the Dead King

CLASSIC STORIES

***Aquaman* (Vol. 5) #42–46 (Mar.–Jul. 1998)** Olympian dynastic wars come to Atlantis in "Triton Wars," as Poseidon's son seeks to rule the seven seas.
***Aquaman* (Vol. 6) #15–20 (Apr.–Sep. 2004)** "American Tidal" sees the spontaneous sinking of San Diego kill thousands… but gives thousands more a new aquatic life. Who is behind it?
***Aquaman: Sword of Atlantis* (Vol. 1) #40–45 (May–Oct. 2006)** Young Arthur Curry falls into a series of undersea intrigues involving King Shark, the history of his namesake, and the destiny of Atlantis.
***Aquaman* (Vol. 7) #14–17 (Jan.–Apr. 2013)** A missile drill gone awry starts a war between Atlantis and the surface world, with Aquaman caught in the middle.

GIANT BORN
Archaeologist Daniel Evans stole Aquaman's trident, believing a rune inscribed on it would open a gateway to Atlantis. Unfortunately he had been tricked, and the word meant not "gate," but "Hell"—so when he opened the gateway, a long-imprisoned and insane Hercules burst through, accompanied by the Giant Born, four horrific beasts not seen since ancient times.

HERCULEAN TASK
Aquaman can only watch as Hercules tears his way out of Hell and into the world again.

TRIDENT OF POSEIDON
A talisman of the sea god's favor, the trident symbolizes Aquaman's role as protector of the world's oceans. Granting vast powers over the oceans and weather, it can also create solid objects, project force fields, and transform into a sword.

and then destroyed the weapon once the Dead King was defeated. Aquaman became King of Atlantis again, but his brother Orm, in the wake of the peace settlement between Atlantis and surface dwellers, was now searching for other lost undersea kingdoms that existed during the Dead King's rule.

A new adversary appeared: the Chimera, created from the mangled body of a diver Aquaman had saved. At the same time, earthquakes struck Atlantis, and after a combative misunderstanding with the Swamp Thing, his investigation led Aquaman again into the tangled mystery of his heritage. Searching for his mother Atlanna through dimensional portals, Aquaman and Mera found her—only to have her deny he was her son. It seemed Atlantis itself was rejecting Aquaman due to his false ancestry. With the help of the Martian Manhunter and Gorilla Grodd, Aquaman and Mera convinced Atlanna of the truth—but not before she tried to sacrifice them to the volcano god Karaku. **AI**

REBIRTH

MAN OF TWO WORLDS
After years ruling Atlantis while simultaneously striving to be hero to the surface world, Aquaman now takes on his most challenging role: mediator and peacemaker.

With tensions between water-worlders and air-breathers mounting, the King of the Seas strives to forge lasting peace and understanding among powerful factions on both sides who are intent on remaining distrustful, natural enemies. Unless his deadliest foe, the vengeful Black Manta, doesn't kill him and everyone he holds dear first.

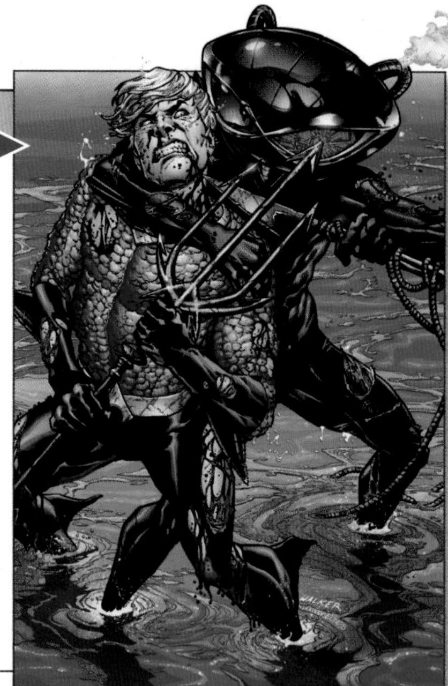

ON THE RECORD

Aquaman's origin has been told and retold over the years, like any good sea story. For years he was Arthur Curry, half-human son of Tom Curry and an Atlantean woman, Atlanna. His brother Orm, later the Ocean Master, was introduced, as young Arthur discovered Atlantis, his powers, and his destiny to become the Sea King.

Atlantean origins
This Silver Age story of Tom Curry succeeded a Golden Age tale of exploration and scientific experimentation, in which Aquaman's father made the boy fit for a life under the sea. Following Crisis on Infinite Earths, the hero was recast as Orin, son of Queen Atlanna and the wizard Atlan, abandoned due to the Atlantean belief that his blond hair was the mark of a curse. Atlantean scientist Vulko tried to save him, and later became Aquaman's guide to Atlantean ways after the nearly feral boy had grown up on the periphery of the surface world.

STEALTH SUIT
Vulko designed Aquaman a new blue and violet suit, designed to hide him from pursuing enemies.

Post-Crisis
Following Crisis on Infinite Earths, Aquaman appeared in a 1986 miniseries wherein he briefly wore a different costume design, deep blue and purple to camouflage him in the ocean depths. Ocean Master immersed himself in the lore of Atlantean magic as he fought his half-brother for the throne of Atlantis and later sold his soul to Neron for more sorcerous power. Orin's wife, Mera, has also transformed over time, becoming a powerful hero in her own right and acquiring a backstory that puts her on an equal footing with Aquaman.

Magic hand
The villain Charybdis cost Aquaman a hand in the 1990s, after which he had implanted a cybernetic harpoon designed by S.T.A.R. Labs. This was later replaced by a shape-changing golden hand, courtesy of Atlantean science. Later this too was destroyed, and the Arthurian Lady of the Lake gave Aquaman a hand composed of mystical living water. Murdered by Black Manta shortly before Final Crisis, Aquaman was resurrected—and his hand restored to its original state—at the conclusion of Blackest Night.

"I am Aquaman. King of the Seven Seas. This is my birthright. This is my responsibility. And I will embrace it!"

ARTHUR CURRY

ANTHRO

DEBUT *Showcase* (Vol. 1) #74 (May 1968)
BASE Prehistoric Earth
HEIGHT 5ft 2in **WEIGHT** 137 lbs
EYES Brown **HAIR** Brown
POWERS/ABILITIES Skilled hunter and tracker with exceptional leadership skills.
ALLIES Lart, D-Ahn, Doctor Thirteen, Embra
ENEMIES Vandal Savage
AFFILIATIONS Bear tribe

Anthro was the first Cro-Magnon man, precursor to the human race. His father, Ne-ahn, was a Neanderthal from the Bear tribe, while his mother was from another tribe. Restless and thrill-seeking, Anthro often got into trouble. When he was young, he was given the gift of fire by the New God Metron and used this to fight immortal villain Vandal Savage.

His family included brother Lart, step-mother Emba, and uncle D-Ahn. Anthro married another Cro-Magnon, Embra. In time, he became the chief of the Bear tribe. Anthro taught his people compassion and, in alternate realities, met several of Earth's present-day Super Heroes via time travel. When Bruce Wayne was stranded in the past after being blasted by Darkseid's Omega Sanction, he met Anthro and laid his utility belt on the old man's body as he passed away. **AC**

ANTON ARCANE

DEBUT *Swamp Thing* (Vol. 1) #2 (Dec. 1972–Jan. 1973)
CURRENT VERSION *Swamp Thing* (Vol. 5) #3 (Jan. 2012)
BASE Blestemat
EYES Black **HAIR** Bald
POWERS/ABILITIES As an Avatar of the Rot, he can control decay and the dead.
ALLIES Un-Men
ENEMIES Swamp Thing, Animal Man

Anton Arcane was an evil sorcerer and scientist who became the avatar of the Rot, an unworldly force that was at war against the life-forces known as the Red and the Green (which empowered Animal Man and Swamp Thing respectively).

Arcane was born in the late 1800s and was obsessed with decay from an early age. When the Parliament of Rot appointed him its avatar, he was tasked with destroying the Green's avatars. When he killed Alec Holland, who was destined to be a Green avatar, he brought about the coming of the Swamp Thing. Arcane and Swamp Thing fought each other numerous times. When Swamp Thing was lost in the Rot, Arcane took the opportunity to spread his influence over the whole world. He was eventually defeated by the Swamp Thing, leading him to flee back in time. Seeking balance, the Parliament of Rot sent Swamp Thing back to face Arcane. Ultimately, Arcane's niece Abigail helped Swamp Thing defeat her uncle and took his place as the Avatar of the Rot. **AC**

MONSTER OF DECAY
Arcane's deadly relationship with living things extends to his niece, Abigail. She is also an avatar of the Rot, but nowhere near as rotten as he is.

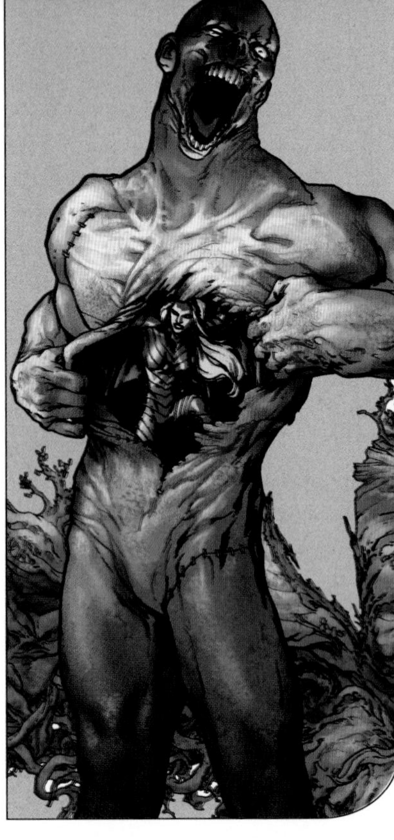

ARAK

DEBUT *The Warlord* (Vol. 1) #48 (Aug. 1981)
CURRENT VERSION (As Telos) *Convergence* (Vol. 1) #0 (Jun. 2015)
REAL NAME Bright Sky After Storm
BASE Eighth-century Europe
HEIGHT 6ft **WEIGHT** 190 lbs
EYES Brown **HAIR** Black
POWERS/ABILITIES Expert fighter with a sword and an otomahuk; shamanistic powers.
ALLIES Vikings
ENEMIES Angelica of Albracca

Native American Arak was born in the eighth century, and later in life learned his father was He-No, the Quontauka god of thunder. He survived the massacre of his tribe, escaping in a canoe into the Atlantic where he was found and adopted by Vikings. He became a fearsome warrior and favored his native otomahuk ax in battle. When the Vikings he fought with were killed, he became a wanderer before joining the court of Emperor Charlemagne in western Europe. He traveled in time to fight alongside the All-Star Squadron, and at some point was taken by Brainiac and transformed into the creature known as Telos. As Telos, he watched over some of the cities taken from various realities by the Collector of Worlds before turning against his master after regaining his memories. **AC**

ARCHITECT, THE

DEBUT *Batman: Gates of Gotham* (Vol. 1) #1 (Jul. 2011)
CURRENT VERSION *Batman Eternal* #21 (Oct. 2014)
REAL NAME Zachary Gate
EYES Blue **HAIR** Blond
POWERS/ABILITIES Explosives expert, wears heavily-armored, protective suit.
ENEMIES Batman

Zachary Gate is a direct descendant of Nicholas Anders, one of the brothers who crafted Gotham City's great bridges. When his stepbrother died in a bridge collapse, Nicholas sought revenge on Gotham City's founding families—the Kanes, Waynes, and Cobblepots—eventually killing Robert Kane. He was sent to jail, swearing vengeance an all children of Gotham City's forefathers.

Decades later, Zachary found Nicholas's tell-all diary and decompression suit, and began blowing up Gotham City's main bridges to avenge his ancestor. Zachary was caught by Batman (Dick Grayson) who had worked out that the suit had driven both men insane. He was later freed from Arkham by Jason Bard as part of a plan to destroy Gotham City and Batman. As the Architect, Zachary tried to demolish the Beacon—a new building funded by Bruce Wayne—but was defeated by Batman. **AC**

ARES

DEBUT *Wonder Woman* (Vol. 1) #1 (Summer 1942) (as Mars); *Wonder Woman* (Vol. 1) #183 (Jul.–Aug. 1969) (as Ares)
CURRENT VERSION *Wonder Woman* (Vol. 4) #4 (Feb. 2012)
BASE Mount Olympus
POWERS/ABILITIES Godlike strength; ability to summon and lead armies; superb martial skills.
ENEMIES First Born
AFFILIATIONS Gods of Olympus

Ares was the Greek God of War, was almost immortal, and could often be found near conflict. He was Wonder Woman's older brother and taught the young Diana the ways of war, training her in secret on every full moon. He was protective of Wonder Woman and stood by her against the First Born, Zeus's first son who sought to kill all his kin.

When First Born and Wonder Woman had their final confrontation in London, the then-aging Ares fought by her side. The heroes seemed outmatched until Ares called on an army of soldiers from across time. At the height of the battle, Ares took on the First Born himself. Then Wonder Woman speared both Ares and First Born. The First Born was defeated and Ares killed. Hades claimed him as Wonder Woman became the new God of War. **AC**

ARION

DEBUT *Warlord* #55 (Mar. 1982)
REAL NAME Ahri'ahn
BASE Ancient Atlantis
HEIGHT 6ft 3in **WEIGHT** 190 lbs
EYES Green **HAIR** Brown, white
POWERS/ABILITIES Immortality, vast range of magical abilities.
ALLIES Wyynde
ENEMIES Garn Daanuth
AFFILIATIONS Lords of Order

Arion was the greatest mage of ancient Atlantis, more than 45,000 years ago. His father was Calculhah, a force for good, while his mother was Dark Majistra, a force for strife. She raised Arion's twin brother, Garn Daanuth, who became his sworn enemy. Arion prevented his mother and brother from destroying Atlantis, but at the cost of his own life. His lifeforce survived, however, and he returned to help Atlantis many times before its eventual destruction. He then led some of its survivors into new homes across the globe.

Regaining corporeal form, Arion eventually came into conflict with Superman when he believed the Man of Steel's morality and heroics would prevent humanity surviving an attack by the super-villain Khyber. Arion was killed helping the Justice Society of America fight the evil Mordru. **AC**

ARISIA

DEBUT *Tales of Green Lantern Corps* (Vol. 1) #1 (May 1981)
CURRENT VERSION *Green Lantern Corps: Edge of Oblivion* #1 (Mar. 2016)
REAL NAME Arisia Rrab
BASE Space Sector 2815
HEIGHT 5ft 9in **WEIGHT** 136 lbs
EYES Gold **HAIR** Blonde
POWERS/ABILITIES Ring creates energy constructs; physiology enhances healing; flight.
ALLIES Hal Jordan, Guy Gardner

Born on Graxos IV, Arisia Rrab was at least the fifth member of her family to serve as a Green Lantern, following on from her father, Fentara, and uncle, Blish. When Blish was killed in action, his ring sought out the then-teenage Arisia, making her the Green Lantern of Sector 2815. She was rapidly aged while a member of the Corps, and became close to Hal Jordan while spending time on Earth.

Seemingly killed by Major Force, Arisia was later found in suspended animation. She rejoined the Green Lantern Corps and was tasked with watching over Green Lantern Sodam Yat. She fought in the Sinestro Corps Wars and, during Nekron's attack on Earth and Oa, faced Black Lantern versions of her family. Arisia later died, trying to save the doomed planet Perduron. **AC**

ARSENAL

DATA

DEBUT (As Speedy) *More Fun Comics* #73 **(Nov. 1941)**
CURRENT VERSION *Red Hood and the Outlaws* #1 **(Nov. 2011)**
REAL NAME Roy Harper
BASE Formerly Seattle
HEIGHT 5ft 11in **WEIGHT** 185 lbs
EYES Green **HAIR** Red
POWERS/ABILITIES Expert archer and fighter; gifted mechanic; computer hacker; and engineer.
ALLIES Green Arrow
ENEMIES Cheshire
AFFILIATIONS Teen Titans, The Outlaws

TOOLED UP
While Roy is an expert archer, he is more than willing to utilize other weaponry, which he straps to his back. He wears a variety of baseball caps.

WILD CHILD
Computer genius Roy was taken in by Oliver Queen and helped Oliver's alter ego the Green Arrow fight crime.

Arsenal was once the teen sidekick of the Green Arrow, helping the hero fight crime one arrow at a time—with Roy creating trick arrows for his mentor. After falling out with Oliver Queen, Roy's life took a dark path and he became an alcoholic. He eventually managed to deal with his personal demons to become a hero again. Calling himself Arsenal, he now fights alongside the Red Hood.

Roy Harper first met Oliver Queen 12 months after Oliver had become the Green Arrow. Roy was a wild teenager, but also a computer expert who managed to hack into Queen Industries R&D hub before his arrest. Oliver bailed him out of jail and offered him a job at his company, Q-Core. He was given his own lab and crew to create new tech for Q-Core. Six months after starting, a shooting at a party resulted in Roy finding out that Oliver was also the Green Arrow. Roy helped the Green Arrow fight crime alongside expert marksman John Diggle and later became a member of the original Teen Titans.

He eventually fell out with Oliver and was kicked off the team. Roy started to drink to excess while also trying to die fighting. He reached a new low when he tried to commit suicide by attacking Killer Croc. The villain not only refused to kill Roy but became his sponsor in Alcoholics Anonymous. Roy still sought danger and one adventure left him imprisoned in a Middle Eastern jail. He was freed by Red Hood (Jason Todd) and Starfire, the three becoming a team and close friends. Roy also started a relationship with Starfire. The three heroes thought of themselves as outlaws and helped others—as well as protecting each other when their turbulent pasts caught up with them. While Starfire left, Jason and Roy remained a team, and were joined by the Joker's Daughter. **AC**

ON THE RECORD

Roy Harper has changed a great deal since his first appearance as Speedy, the Green Arrow's young sidekick with a slightly garish red Robin Hood-style costume. The fall-out from the classic *Green Lantern/Green Arrow #85* saw him portrayed as a recovering drug addict. While a Teen Titan, he had a relationship and child with the assassin known as Cheshire. His evolution into Arsenal saw him move away from his role as Green Arrow's sidekick and start to favor more high-tech weaponry. When he later joined the JLA as Red Arrow, he returned to his roots but turned more brutal following the murder of his daughter and loss of his arm, which was replaced by a robotic version.

CYBERNETIC ARM
Roy's arm was cut off by villain Prometheus. It was replaced by an advanced, cybernetic limb, but he would experience phantom pain.

CLASSIC STORIES

***Green Lantern* (Vol. 2) #85 (Aug.-Sep. 1971)** Roy Harper is revealed to be a drug addict in one of the most controversial stories of the era.

***New Teen Titans* #99 (Jul. 1993)** Roy assumes the name and identity of Arsenal for the first time.

***Justice League of America* (Vol. 2) #7 (May 2007)** Roy is the Red Arrow and becomes a member of the Justice League of America.

THE OUTLAWS
Roy joined forces with the Red Hood and Starfire to form the Outlaws. He also began a relationship with teammate Starfire.

ARKHAM, AMADEUS

DEBUT *Arkham Asylum* (1989)
CURRENT VERSION *All-Star Western* (Vol. 3) #1 (Nov. 2011)
BASE Gotham City
HEIGHT 6ft 3in **WEIGHT** 175 lbs
EYES Brown **HAIR** Black
POWERS/ABILITIES Expert in psychiatry.
ALLIES Jonah Hex
ENEMIES John Cromwell

During the late 19th century, Gotham City physician Amadeus Arkham developed a specialty in the emerging sciences of psychology and psychiatry, lending his expertise to the Gotham City Police Department. He also founded the asylum that still bears his name, and which later became the notorious home of Gotham City's most depraved criminals.

Detective Lofton of the Gotham City police brought Arkham in on their investigation of a series of brutal murders committed by the Gotham Butcher. After encountering some resistance, Arkham himself brought in bounty hunter Jonah Hex to help his inquiry, and they discovered that Gotham was home to the Religion of Crime sect. Their subsequent endeavors uncovered the identity of the Gotham Butcher and the existence of the villainous cabal the Court of Owls. **AI**

ARKILLO

DEBUT *Green Lantern* (Vol. 4) #10 (May 2006)
CURRENT VERSION *Green Lantern: New Guardians* #1 (Nov. 2011)
BASE Vorn
HEIGHT 6ft 6in **WEIGHT** 370 lbs
EYES Black **HAIR** None
POWERS/ABILITIES Power ring grants flight, energy control, and construct creation.
ALLIES Sinestro
ENEMIES Guardians
AFFILIATIONS New Guardians, Sinestro Corps

Recruited by Sinestro to join his Corps in the antimatter universe of Qward, Arkillo traveled to Earth when he learned that one of the Corps had died there. While on Earth, he discovered the New Guardians, a team led by Green Lantern Kyle Rayner that boasted ring bearers from across the Emotional Spectrum who had rallied behind Rayner.

Arkillo joined them on the journey to Oa, where the Guardians of the Universe attacked them. They then battled the Archangel Invictus before Arkillo learned that Sinestro and Hal Jordan had cooperated to destroy the Sinestro Corps' Power Battery. With a new battery powered by fear, Arkillo rejoined the fight against Invictus before leaving the New Guardians—though he rejoined the team to face the growing threat of the old Guardians. **AI**

ARTEMIS

DEBUT *Wonder Woman* (Vol. 1) #5 (Jul. 1943)
CURRENT VERSION *Wonder Woman* (Vol. 4) #11 (Sep. 2012)
BASE Olympus
HEIGHT 5ft 8in **WEIGHT** 125 lbs
EYES White **HAIR** White
POWERS/ABILITIES Divinely enhanced strength and speed; regenerative abilities.
ALLIES Apollo
ENEMIES First Born
AFFILIATIONS Olympian Gods

Goddess of the Hunt and twin sister of Apollo, Artemis allied herself with her brother's claim to the throne after the disappearance of their ruler, Zeus. Artemis fought Wonder Woman and Hermes, as well as her half-brother Lennox—another of Zeus' bastard children—before Apollo assumed the throne. Then, during another battle, she discovered the true extent of Wonder Woman's powers, being beaten unconscious after Diana removed her protective bracers.

Apollo sent her to kill the baby Zeke, who was Zeus reborn, but Diana prevented this. The humiliated Artemis demanded Diana submit to her before she would assist in the search for Zeke. She also manipulated Diana into adopting the title Goddess of War so she could fight First Born, whom Artemis hated because he caused her brother's death. In this way Artemis—despite her animosity toward Wonder Woman—paved the way for Diana's defeat of First Born and her assumption of her new destiny. **AI**

HUNTRESS
With a doggedness befitting her status as Goddess of the Hunt, Artemis backed Apollo's claim to the throne, even though it put her at odds with Diana.

ARKHAM, JEREMIAH

DEBUT *Batman: Shadow of the Bat* #1 (Jun. 1992)
CURRENT VERSION *Detective Comics* (Vol. 2) #1 (Nov. 2011)
BASE Arkham Asylum
HEIGHT 5ft 9in **WEIGHT** 170 lbs
EYES Brown **HAIR** Brown
POWERS/ABILITIES Advanced medical and physiological knowledge.
AFFILIATIONS Arkham Asylum

Head doctor at Arkham Asylum, which was founded by his great-uncle Amadeus, Jeremiah was known for his unorthodox approach to psychiatric care. However, Jeremiah, himself, was mysteriously driven insane and disguised himself as the Joker. He entered the asylum, freed the inmates, and filled it with Joker Gas, giving him control over many of the inmates.

He then led a brief campaign of terror, ordering the killing of Arkham's guards until one of the last survivors punched him and knocked off the Joker mask. Having discovered he wasn't the Joker, the angry inmates would have killed him, save for the intervention of Gotham City police. It is not known whether the Joker engineered his breakdown, or whether it had another cause. Ultimately, he was locked in the asylum that bears his name. **AI**

ARROWETTE

DEBUT *Impulse* #28 (Aug. 1997)
CURRENT VERSION *The Multiversity: The Just* #1 (Dec. 2014)
BASE Earth-16
REAL NAME Cissie King-Hawke
HEIGHT 5ft 6in **WEIGHT** 125 lbs
EYES Blue **HAIR** Blonde
POWERS/ABILITIES Archery, acrobatics.
ALLIES Menta
ENEMIES Gentry, League of Sivanas
AFFILIATIONS The Just

Daughter of Earth-16's Green Arrow, Arrowette grew up in a world purged of evil and danger by the last generation of heroes; a utopia that left her hungry for a way to make her mark as her father had. When the threat of the Gentry loomed, she fought with her father over her desire to follow in his footsteps and start up a super-team called The Just with her friend Menta, daughter of Mento and Elasti-Girl. A superb archer and athlete like her father, Cissie had the skills and desire to do good; all she needed was the arrows. He gave her five trick arrows and a stern warning about the dangers of getting involved in heroic endeavors. A true teenager, she ignored her father's advice, getting tangled up in the Gentry's attempt to conquer the multiverse in concert with the threat of the League of Sivanas. **AI**

ATLAN

DEBUT *Atlantis Chronicles* #5 (Jul. 1990)
CURRENT VERSION *Aquaman* (Vol. 7) #17 (Apr. 2013)
BASE Atlantis
HEIGHT 6ft 3in **WEIGHT** 220 lbs
EYES Blue **HAIR** Blond
POWERS/ABILITIES Vast magical abilities e.g. cryokinesis; arsenal of magical weaponry.
ALLIES Vulko
ENEMIES Orin, Aquaman

Centuries in the past, Atlan ruled Atlantis, which grew to include seven lands under his reign. His brother Orin (Aquaman's ancestor) quarreled with Atlan over his inclusive policies and plotted against Atlan to protect the purity of the Atlantean bloodline. War followed, during which Atlan went into hiding and Orin murdered his family. Stricken with grief, Atlan forged six magical weapons to retake Atlantis. He used one of them to sink the kingdom, destroying four of its lands and transforming the other three: Atlantis, Xebel, and the Trench. He then fell into a long magical sleep deep under the ocean.

Atlan was revived in the present day by Atlantean advisor Vulko, who wanted to restore Atlantis's true king. Still angry, Atlan tried to permanently destroy Atlantis, but was stopped by Aquaman. The old king melted away, presumably for good. **AI**

ATLAS

DEBUT *1st Issue Special* #1 (Apr. 1975)
BASE Metropolis
HEIGHT 6ft 5in **WEIGHT** 250 lbs
EYES Blue **HAIR** Brown
POWERS/ABILITIES Superhuman strength and stamina
ALLIES Chagra
ENEMIES King Hyssa, Superman
AFFILIATIONS Project 7734

In ancient times, a despotic king named Hyssa sent raiders to Atlas's village on the Crystal Mountain, killing Atlas's family and enslaving him along with the rest of the village's survivors. Wearing a mystical crystal talisman struck from the Crystal Mountain, Atlas escaped and found a new home with a good-hearted man named Chagra. It was not long before Chagra realized the boy had jaw-dropping strength and stamina. He became Atlas's manager and accompanied him on his journeys, watching the hero rescue citizens and defeat evil princes, eventually toppling King Hyssa himself.

After coming to Earth, Atlas ended up working for the mysterious Project 7734, a government investigation into the possibility of using magic to fight Kryptonians. Atlas often battled Superman, stating his goal to replace him as champion of Metropolis. **AI**

ATOM

DATA

DEBUT *All-American Comics* (Vol. 1) #19 **(Oct. 1940)** (Al Pratt); *Showcase* (Vol. 1) #34 **(Sep.–Oct. 1961)** (Ray Palmer); *Brave New World* (Vol. 1) #1 **(Aug. 2006)** (Ryan Choi)
CURRENT VERSION *Frankenstein, Agent of S.H.A.D.E.* #1 **(Nov. 2011)** (Ray Palmer); *DC Universe Rebirth* #1 **(Jul. 2016)** (Ryan Choi)
REAL NAMES Raymond Palmer; Ryan Choi
BASE Ant Farm (Ray Palmer); Ivy Town (Ryan Choi)
HEIGHT Variable **WEIGHT** Variable
EYES Brown (Palmer, Choi); **HAIR** Brown (Palmer); Black (Choi)
POWERS/ABILITIES Shrinking to any size including subatomic; acrobatics; advanced knowledge of biomechanics and physics.
ALLIES Superman, Frankenstein, Kyle Rayner, Wonder Woman
ENEMIES Vandal Savage, Chronos, M'nagalah
AFFILIATIONS Justice League of America, S.H.A.D.E.

SUITED UP
The Atom's suit features life-support systems for Ray Palmer when he is riding through someone's bloodstream—or when he can't breathe regular air because the molecules are too big.

Science liaison to S.H.A.D.E. and a hero in his own right as the Atom, Ray Palmer is the creator of the Ant Farm, a pioneer in miniaturization technology, and a recent welcome addition to the Justice League of America.

BLOOD TEST
Called in by the JLA for his expertise, Ray Palmer found a microscopic metropolis built inside Batman's brain.

Ray Palmer became science advisor to S.H.A.D.E., the Super-Human Advanced Defense Executive, and built the Ant Farm, a self-contained miniaturized base for S.H.A.D.E. Agents that included S.H.A.D.E. City. The Ant Farm was a technological marvel, with an independent power source, atmosphere, and artificial gravity, accessible only via simultaneous teleportation and shrinking using a process Palmer created. Knowing of Palmer's work, Superman sought his help after Batman contracted a mysterious illness. Diving into a sample of Batman's blood, Palmer discovered that the Dark Knight was suffering from the effects of a microscopic city having been constructed in a blood vessel in his brain. Miniaturizing Superman, he took the Man of Steel inside Batman's brain, finding the tiny city and trapping it inside a globe similar to the Ant Farm.

Palmer came to the heroes' aid again, helping Superman locate the Bottle City of Kandor and devising an armored suit of Kryptonite that the Man of Steel could use against Vandal Savage after the immortal villain had stolen his powers. Encouraged by these successes, Palmer followed through on his plan to embrace the Super Hero life and called himself the Atom. **AI**

REBIRTH

LITTLE VICTORIES, BIG DREAMS

In *DC Universe Rebirth* #1, Ryan Choi returns as Ray Palmer's teaching assistant at Ivy University. With Palmer lost in the microverse, Choi inherits his size-altering belt after receiving a desperate, if garbled, warning from his mentor. The part-time Super Hero is confident his protégé will rise to every challenge to save him as a new Atom.

Though Palmer's message is abruptly cut off, one thing is certain. To find him, Choi must finally live up to the huge potential everyone else feels he possesses. Now all he has to do is believe it himself.

ON THE RECORD

UP AND ATOM
Ray Palmer was the best-known Atom, remaining in the role for over five decades, and counting.

Since his creation in 1940, many heroes have been the Atom. The original was super-strong student Al Pratt, who lived a long heroic life and perished during the Zero Hour event. College Professor Ray Palmer then became the Atom in 1961 after inventing miniaturization technology that allowed him and later Atoms to alter their size, weight, and mass. Using an Atom belt confiscated from Palmer, covert operative Adam Cray succeeded him and died while working with the Suicide Squad.

In 2006, Palmer's friend and former student Ryan Choi inherited his technology and his position as Physics Professor at Ivy University. A reluctant hero at first, Choi soon carved his own legend as the All-New Atom, saving Earth from invasion by microscopic aliens, the Waiting, and thwarting a time-bending conspiracy involving his employer Dean Macy and Chronos. Choi next freed the eccentric size-shifting super-villain Giganta from cancer-god M'nagalah's control, and then dated her. However, he faced his greatest trials after accidentally bringing back a microbial carnivore from the microverse. This predator shrunk its prey, storing them in a sub-atomic realm, and it took all Choi's bravery and brilliance to rescue the surviving victims. Ryan was murdered by Deathstroke, but returned during the Convergence event to help Ray Palmer bring the assassin to justice.

BITE-SIZED HERO
Under the malign influence of cancer-god M'nagalah, Giganta bit off more than she could chew when she swallowed Ryan whole.

BIG BOOTS TO FILL
Initially plagued with self-doubt, Ryan Choi became a true hero using the Atom suit to save lives, defeat villains, and explore the farthest and strangest corners of the microverse.

CLASSIC STORIES

***Showcase* (Vol. 1) #34 (Sep.–Oct. 1961)** Scientist Ray Palmer devises a way to shrink himself using matter from a white dwarf star. He dubs himself the Atom and frees an alien named Kulan Dar, who has had to commit crimes for a local thief.

***Sword of the Atom* #1–4 (Sep. 1983)** With his marriage to Jean Loring on the rocks, Ray Palmer finds himself frozen at a six-inch stature. He discovers a society of miniature people in the Amazon, and becomes the leader of a rebel faction.

***All-New Atom* (Vol 1.) #5 (Jan. 2007)** Rookie Atom Ryan Choi faces demonic corrupter M'nagalah, and is briefly swallowed by his possessed new colleague Professor Doris (Giganta) Zuel.

***Titans* (Vol. 2) #38 (Oct. 2011)** Ray Palmer investigates the disappearance of his successor, Ryan Choi. He hunts down Deathstroke, sparking a battle between the Justice League and the Titans.

ATOM SMASHER

DEBUT *All-Star Squadron* #25 (Sep. 1983)
REAL NAME Albert Julian Rothstein
BASE New York City
HEIGHT 7ft 6in (15ft at full height) **WEIGHT** 297 lbs (700 lbs at full size)
EYES Blue **HAIR** Red
POWERS/ABILITIES Superhuman strength, endurance, and durability; able to increase size, gaining weight simultaneously; wears S.T.A.R. Labs-designed suit that can change size with him.
ALLIES Obsidian, Jade, Black Adam **ENEMIES** Extant, Kobra
AFFILIATIONS Infinity, Inc., Conglomerate, Justice Society of America, Justice League America, Suicide Squad

NEW WAVE NUKLON Atom Smasher struggled hard to live down his old look as Nuklon, when he sported a once trendy Mohican haircut.

A true example of a legacy hero, Albert Rothstein is the godson to the original Golden Age hero Atom, as well as the grandson of the super-villain Cyclotron. Albert decided to use his inherited powers for good, calling himself Nuklon and becoming a founding member of the young Super Hero team Infinity, Inc. After the team disbanded, Albert continued to move up in Super Hero circles, joining the Conglomerate and then Justice League America, the latter alongside another former Infinity, Inc. member, Obsidian. Following an attack on the JLA's satellite headquarters, Nuklon left the team when many of its members decided to form a new Justice League America incarnation.

It wouldn't take long for Nuklon to find a new team of Super Heroes to fight alongside. He joined the reformed Justice Society of America. This JSA was made up of many legacy heroes, including Black Canary (Dinah Laurel Lance), Starman (Jack Knight), Stargirl (Courtney Whitmore), and even his god-brother and Atom's son, Damage (Grant Emerson). Prolonged exposure to thorium radiation had given Albert the ability to change his size and density. This inspired him to adopt the name Atom Smasher, to better honor both his godfather and grandfather. **MM**

FISTS OF FURY After his mother died at the hands of the villain Kobra, Albert was consumed with vengeance. Growing to a dangerously unstable size he flew into a murderous rage against his Kobra's forces.

ATOMICA

DEBUT *The New 52: Free Comic Book Day Special* #1 (Jun. 2012)
REAL NAME Rhonda Pineda
HEIGHT 5ft 2in **WEIGHT** 107 lbs
EYES Brown **HAIR** Brown
POWERS/ABILITIES Able to shrink to microscopic size.
ALLIES Johnny Quick, the Outsider
ENEMIES Justice League, Justice League of America, Anti-Monitor, Lex Luthor

The Earth-3 equivalent of Bonnie from the infamous duo of Bonnie and Clyde, Rhonda Pineda was the partner of Jonathan Allen, both of whom enjoyed careers as criminals and killers. But the law eventually caught up with them and they were surrounded by police on the roof of S.T.A.R. Labs. A lightning strike caused the duo to be exposed to Ray Palmer's equipment, housed inside the S.T.A.R. facility. Rhonda gained shrinking powers, while Johnny gained super-speed.

Joining Earth-3's Crime Syndicate as Atomica, Rhonda ventured to Earth-0. Here she became a double-agent for both the Justice League and the Justice League of America as the Atom, before she revealed herself as the Syndicate's mole. During a battle with Batman and his allies, she was crushed beneath Lex Luthor's boot. **MM**

ATOMIC KNIGHT

DEBUT *Strange Adventures* (Vol.1) #117 (Jun. 1960)
CURRENT VERSION *Batman Beyond* (Vol. 5) #1 (Aug. 2015)
REAL NAME Gardner Grayle
BASE Blüdhaven
HEIGHT 6ft 1in **WEIGHT** 189 lbs
EYES Blue **HAIR** Blond
POWERS/ABILITIES Weaponized armor can form around him from out of nowhere.

Gardner Grayle lived in a reality in which the Atomic War of 1986 had left the Earth in ruins. There he served alongside several other heroes as an Atomic Knight, fighting injustice in a post-apocalyptic landscape. Waking up in S.T.A.R. Labs, he realized that his Atomic Knight life had been just a simulation to test how people would adapt after an Atomic War. Donning a S.T.A.R. Labs hi-tech battle suit, he set out as the Atomic Knight, later joining the Outsiders hero team.

Following Infinite Crisis, Gardner's history was altered. This time he woke up in Blüdhaven alongside other Atomic Knights with visions of a horrible future. As leader, he did his best to defend the city from threats, working with the Roundtable organization. After the events of Flashpoint, the Atomic Knights were relocated to the post-apocalyptic future of Batman Beyond. **MM**

ATOMIC SKULL

DEBUT *Superman* (Vol. 1) #323 (May 1978)
CURRENT VERSION *Action Comics* (Vol. 2) *Annual* #1 (Dec. 2012)
REAL NAME Joseph Martin
BASE Metropolis
HEIGHT 6ft **WEIGHT** 185 lbs
EYES Purple **HAIR** None
POWERS/ABILITIES: Absorbs and projects nuclear energy; superhuman strength; flight.
ENEMIES Superman, Wonder Woman, Steel

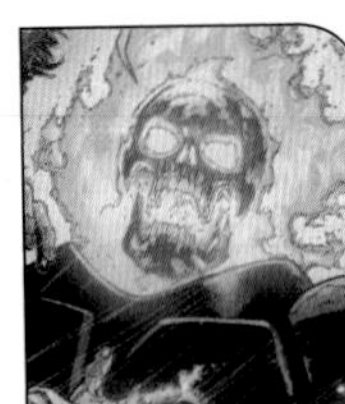

Scientist Joseph Martin was deeply in love with a coworker, but was an extremely jealous man. When their relationship began to fall apart and he caught her dancing with another man, Martin killed her, burying her in a shallow grave. Sometime later, while aboard an experimental S.T.A.R. Labs submarine, he was exposed to a blast of nuclear energy when the ship crashed at the bottom of the ocean. Shipwrecked on a desert island, he survived by releasing deadly blasts of nuclear energy via his mouth.

After exploiting this newfound power several times, his skin and muscles literally peeled off of his face, inspiring him to create a new identity for himself—super-villain-for-hire Atomic Skull. He rapidly became a regular foe of Superman, fighting the Man of Steel alongside criminals such as Major Disaster and the Royal Flush Gang. **MM**

AXIS AMERIKA

DEBUT *Young All-Stars* #1 (Jun. 1987)
NOTABLE MEMBERS Ubermensch, Horned Owl, Fledermaus, Hel, Gudra, Sea Wolf, Usil, Kamikaze, Fleshburn, Baron Blitzkrieg, Zaladin, Ubermensch II, Great White

During World War II, the super-villain squad Axis Amerika was created to serve the Axis Powers against Super Hero teams based in the US, such as the All-Star Squadron. Axis Amerika's leader was usually Ubermensch, who possessed superhuman strength, durability, and speed; however the infamous Baron Blitzkrieg was also known to lead the team.

Other prominent members included: The Horned Owl, who was the German equivalent of Batman, partnering with his son, Fledermaus; Gudra, a powerful Valkyrie brought to Earth from another dimension thanks to Hitler's Spear of Destiny; Sea Wolf, an aquatic werewolf; Usil, an expert archer; and Kamikaze, known as the "living missile," who was equipped with rocket-powered armor. Together, the group battled the offshoot of the All-Star Squadron, the Young All-Stars.

Decades later, a new Axis America team, comprised of American supremacists, clashed with the JLA. They were led by an American taking the name Übermensch II, and included his wife Hel, a flying swordswoman; Fleshburn, a fire-wielder; Great White, who wielded an energized bullwhip; and Zaladin, a mystic swordsman. **MM**

EXTREME PREJUDICE Übermensch II enlisted like-minded villains Hel, Zaladin, Great White, and Fleshburn to a new Axis America to take on the JLA.

ATROCITUS

DEBUT *Green Lantern* (Vol. 4) #28 **(Apr. 2008)**
CURRENT VERSION *Red Lanterns* (Vol. 1) #1 **(Nov. 2011)**
REAL NAME Atros
BASE Ysmault
HEIGHT 7ft 9in **WEIGHT** 438 lbs
EYES Yellow **HAIR** None
POWERS/ABILITIES Superhuman strength, endurance, and durability; Red Lantern Ring enables flight, formation of rage-fueled energy constructs, projection of force-fields, and an acid-like plasma.
ALLIES Dex-Starr
ENEMIES Guardians of the Universe, Guy Gardner
AFFILIATIONS Red Lanterns, Five Inversions

Long ago, on the planet Ryutt, an alien named Atros lived with his wife and children. Policed by the Guardians of the Universe's Manhunter androids, the people lived in peace, until the Manhunters malfunctioned and razed the planet. Atros' family was killed, leaving him alone in his rage. After destroying many Manhunters with his bare hands, Atros was found by Qull, Roixaeume, Orphram, and Dal-Xauix, beings banished from their home world and considered demons. Atros fell in with them, and the group became known as the Five Inversions, using blood-magick to battle the Guardians of the Universe for centuries.

Eventually, the Guardians' new servants, the Green Lanterns, bested the Five Inversions. Atros killed his teammates, using their blood to build a Red Lantern power battery, empowered by his own rage. He took the name Atrocitus and created his own Red Lantern Corps. **MM**

ON THE RECORD

A pivotal flashback in *Green Lantern* (Vol. 4) #30 (Jun. 2008) revealed that Atrocitus had murdered Hal Jordan's predecessor, Abin Sur, which makes Atrocitus responsible for Hal acquiring a power ring and becoming a Green Lantern.

Atrocitus fought against Nekron in the Blackest Night event and briefly gave a Red Lantern ring to Aquaman's longtime love interest, Mera, during that conflict.

BLOOD OATH
Like the Green Lantern Corps, the Red Lanterns have their own oath:
"With blood and rage of crimson red,
Ripped from a corpse so freshly dead,
Together with our hellish hate,
We'll burn you all—that is your fate!"

AZTEK

DEBUT *Aztek* #1 **(August 1996)**
REAL NAME Uno, Dr. Curtis Falconer (alias)
BASE Vanity
HEIGHT 6ft 2in **WEIGHT** 185 lbs
EYES Blue **HAIR** Blond
POWERS/ABILITIES Weaponized suit includes wings; helmet enhances senses.
ALLIES Joy Page, Green Lantern (Kyle Rayner), Batman
ENEMIES Death-Doll, the Lizard King, the Joker, Heatsnap, Parasite, Mageddon

The Brotherhood of the Q raised Uno to wear the helmet of Quetzalcoatl and to defend the city of Vanity and the world against the shadow god Tezcatlipoca. When Uno arrived in Vanity, however, he encountered a vigilante named Bloodtype, in reality Dr. Curtis Falconer. Bloodtype died after their battle, but not before he told Uno that he was about to start work at St. Bartholomew's Hospital that very day.

Deciding that he needed a civilian identity, Uno impersonated Falconer. He also began protecting the city as a Super Hero who was later dubbed Aztek by the press. After team-ups with Green Lantern and Batman, Aztek briefly joined the JLA. He was killed attacking the living planet Mageddon, the supposed second coming of Tezcatlipoca. **MM**

AZRAEL

DEBUT *Batman: Sword of Azrael* #1 **(Oct. 1992)**
CURRENT VERSION *Batman and Robin Eternal* #9 **(Feb. 2016)**
REAL NAME Jean-Paul Valley
BASE Mobile
HEIGHT 6ft 2in **WEIGHT** 210 lbs **EYES** Blue **HAIR** Blond
POWERS/ABILITIES Expert hand-to-hand combatant and swordsman; underwent Mother's traumatic conditioning, making him a near-perfect warrior; possesses a so-called "Wrath of God" ability that produces awe and visions in the minds of his victims.
ALLIES Red Robin, Red Hood
ENEMIES St. Dumas, Mother
AFFILIATIONS Church of St. Dumas

During the early years of Batman's career, when he first started working with Dick Grayson as his partner, Robin, the Dark Knight learned of a criminal calling herself Mother. Mother offered a bizarre specialty service that would deliver a perfect partner or soldier for the right price. To create that perfect companion, Mother first traumatized her innocent victims at an early age, which then enabled her to imprint the desired qualities on them.

Jean-Paul Valley was one of those innocents. Mother used a new technique on him while working with the Church of St. Dumas. Utilizing a combination of awe and pain, Jean-Paul was forged into a near-perfect warrior—Azrael.

On the trail of the villain Orphan, Red Robin and Red Hood ventured to Peña Duro, the infamous prison on the corrupt island nation of Santa Prisca. There they teamed with an unlikely ally, Bane, as they stormed Peña Duro, which had been converted into a church called the Crusade of St. Dumas. They then encountered Azrael, who defeated Bane by showing him a religious vision that seemed to confirm the Church of St. Dumas' philosophy. **MM**

ON THE RECORD

Pre-Flashpoint, Jean-Paul Valley's discovery of his dying father dressed as Azrael changed his life forever. Brainwashed by the System to become the Church of St. Dumas' assassin, Jean-Paul worked with Batman instead, standing in for the Dark Knight when Bane broke the hero's back.

Unbalanced by his upbringing, Valley became a more violent Batman, and wore heavier armor. He later surrendered the mantle to a newly healed Bruce Wayne and set out on his own adventures as Azrael.

THE RETURN OF AZRAEL
After Jean-Paul Valley's death at the hands of his greatest enemies, Biis and Scratch, a new Azrael emerged. Michael Lane, a former cop, had been trained to become the G.C.P.D.'s equivalent of Batman.

BANE

DATA

DEBUT *Batman: Vengeance of Bane* #1 **(Jan. 1993)**
CURRENT VERSION *Batman: The Dark Knight* (Vol. 2) #6 **(Apr. 2012)**
BASE Gotham City
HEIGHT 6ft 8in **WEIGHT** 350 lbs (425 lbs with Venom)
EYES Brown **HAIR** Brown
POWERS/ABILITIES Enhanced strength, weight, durability, and endurance due to use of a super-steroid called Venom; extremely intelligent; master strategist; possesses indomitable will; expert fighter and natural leader.
ALLIES Santa Prisca mercenaries; prison inmates Bird, Trogg, and Zombie
ENEMIES Batman, the Batman Family, Batwoman, Killer Croc
AFFILIATIONS Santa Prisca inmates

BREAKING THE BAT
When Bane snapped Batman's back, he triumphed over the hero by using not just his strength, but also his cunning.

CLASSIC STORIES

***Batman: Vengeance of Bane* #1 (Jan. 1993)** Bane's origin is revealed in a powerful tale of one man's struggle to the top of the criminal heap.

***Batman* (Vol. 1) #492–500, *Detective Comics* (Vol. 1) #659–666, *Showcase '93* #7–8 (May 1992–Oct. 1993)** Bane not only plans a way to triumph over Batman, but he breaks the crime fighter's back in the memorable saga, "Knightfall."

***Batman: Vengeance of Bane* #2 (Dec. 1995)** After his defeat to Azrael's Batman, Bane escapes prison once again to reclaim his greatness without Venom.

***Batman: Bane of the Demon* #1–4 (Mar.–Jun. 1998)** Bane becomes Rā's al Ghūl's heir apparent, setting the stage for the epic "Legacy" crossover.

BORN LEADER
Bane presents a huge physical threat and, unfortunately for Batman, is also a charismatic leader who can enlist others in his quest for domination.

Despite his impressive physique and prodigious strength, the man known only as Bane is far from a simple physical threat for Batman. An unjustly imprisoned inmate, Bane trained his mind and body to near perfection. With the help of the super-steroid known as Venom, Bane has become one of the most dangerous men the Dark Knight has ever faced, a perfect combination of brain and brawn.

Little is known about the past of the man who is simply known as Bane. With his true name lost somewhere to legend—if he ever had one at all—the story of Bane begins in a prison complex called Peña Dura in the corrupt Caribbean island nation of Santa Prisca. While it has never been proven, many legends state that Bane was born inside the prison's walls, and was forced to live his life there, serving the sentence his mysterious father avoided by escaping "justice."

When he was just a boy, Bane was forced into solitary confinement, nearly drowning each night when water would flood his cell. Surviving off the sea creatures that came in with the tide, Bane began to focus his mind and body, training himself for a war to come. That war would loom ever closer when, as an adult, Bane was chosen for an experimental program that saw his body injected with the super-steroid Venom. Now even more of a powerhouse, he escaped and headed to Gotham City to claim it as his own. A genius strategist, Bane challenged and triumphed over Batman, only to have Gotham City subsequently ripped from his grasp by its protector.

After experimenting with various forms of Venom, Bane once more set his sights on Batman's hometown, choosing to strike when the Dark Knight had been temporarily taken out of action by the Crime Syndicate. He adopted a Batman-like costume and bested Killer Croc for territory, but Bane was once again defeated by the city's true Dark Knight. **MM**

ON THE RECORD

Prior to the reality-altering miniseries *Flashpoint*, Bane's past was explored along with his memorable defeat of Batman. After escaping Peña Dura with the help of three fellow inmates, Bird, Trogg, and Zombie, Bane freed many of the Dark Knight's worst enemies from Arkham Asylum. Exhausted, Batman refused to rest until they were once again caged. Meanwhile, Bane broke into Wayne Manor to confront the hero in a brutal fight that saw the villain snap Batman's back.

A NEW KNIGHT
As Bruce Wayne and his allies worked towards a permanent cure for his broken back, Batman's successor, Azrael, took up the mantle and finally managed to beat Bane.

BANE OF GOTHAM
The super-steroid Venom is fed into Bane's bloodstream via tubes. The Venom temporarily gives the villain superhuman strength, speed, and endurance.

BARD, JASON

DEBUT *Detective Comics* (Vol. 1) #392 (Oct. 1969)
CURRENT VERSION *Batman Eternal* #1 (Jun. 2014)
BASE Gotham City
HEIGHT 6ft **WEIGHT** 175 lbs
EYES Brown **HAIR** Brown
ABILITIES Highly intelligent and cunning.
ALLIES Vicki Vale, Hush, Jim Gordon
ENEMIES Mayor Sebastian Hady, Carmine Falcone, Batman
AFFILIATIONS G.C.P.D. (former)

Jason Bard was a hard-working, respected police officer in Detroit whose partner was killed when a Batman imitator interfered in police business. Blaming the real Dark Knight for the mistakes of his copycat, Bard traveled to Gotham City, seeking out the villain Hush.

After Police Commissioner James Gordon was framed and imprisoned, Bard manipulated reporter Vicki Vale at the *Gotham Gazette*, and rose to the position of commissioner before seeing the error of his ways after an encounter with Batman. He then began to work against the very criminals he had partnered with. He freed Gordon, resigned from the force, and gave a tell-all confession to Vale. **MM**

BARON BLITZKRIEG

DEBUT *World's Finest Comics* (Vol. 1) #246 (Aug.–Sep. 1977)
REAL NAME Reiter (first name unknown)
BASE Nazi Germany
HEIGHT 6ft 6in **WEIGHT** 245 lbs (in armor)
EYES Blue **HAIR** Black
POWERS/ABILITIES Psychic power to control metabolism; eyes emit heat.
ALLIES Adolf Hitler, Atomic Skull
ENEMIES Wonder Woman, All-Star Squadron, Damage, Iron Munro
AFFILIATIONS Third Reich, the Society, Shadowspire, Axis Amerika

The man who would later become known as Baron Blitzkrieg was originally a Prussian nobleman whom Adolf Hitler favored. Heading up a concentration camp, this commandant was scarred when acid was thrown in his face. This prompted Hitler to attempt to unlock the man's latent psychic powers, realizing the Baron was of little other use to him.

Transformed into a super soldier for the Third Reich, Baron Blitzkrieg became a staunch opponent of the wartime heroes in the All-Star Squadron, and later Wonder Woman (Hippolyta). His untimely death occurred at the hands of Superboy Prime who killed the Baron with his heat vision. **MM**

BAT LASH

DEBUT *Showcase* (Vol. 1) #76 (Aug. 1968)
CURRENT VERSION *All-Star Western* (Vol. 3) #10 (Aug. 2012)
REAL NAME Bartholomew Aloysius Lash
BASE American Southwest (late 19th century)
HEIGHT 5ft 11in **WEIGHT** 167 lbs
EYES Blue **HAIR** Reddish blond
POWERS/ABILITIES Expert gunfighter, bar brawler, and card player; razor-keen wit.
ALLIES Jonah Hex, Cinnamon, Scalphunter, Enemy Ace
ENEMIES Hundreds of card players
AFFILIATIONS Rough Bunch

An adorable baby, Bartholomew Aloysius Lash grew up learning how to use his good looks and charm to his benefit. After his parents were swindled out of their farm, Bartholomew sought justice, but found himself killing a corrupt police deputy. Branded an outlaw, Bat Lash began a journey across the old west, making his living thanks to his knack at poker and his ability to talk himself out of any bad situation. **MM**

TONGUE LASHING
While he's no stranger to a barroom brawl, Batlash is an even better talker, and often maintains a smile on his face and flower in his hat.

BASILISK

DEBUT *Suicide Squad* (Vol. 4) #4 (Feb. 2012)
BASE The Andes
MEMBERS/ABILITIES
Regulus: Tactical analysis, weapons expert; **Grey Lora**: Enhanced reflexes; **Red Orchid**: Chlorokinesis; **Black Spider**: Hand-to-hand combat, marksmanship; **Hammerdown**: Invulnerability, super-strength; **Whipcrack**: Energy whip; **Tsiklon**: Wind manipulation; **Uplink**: Telepathy; **Dr. Elisa Visyak**: Scientific genius.
ENEMIES Suicide Squad, Team 7, Birds of Prey

Basilisk is a powerful terrorist organization that has several metahuman men and women at its disposal. It is led by Regulus, a super-villain formed from a psychic and physical merger between Dean Higgins—a former member of the special ops group Team 7—and Kaizen, the insane ruler of the outlaw nation of Gamorra.

Part cult group drawing power from a mythic snake, part conspiracy collective preparing for a war against super-powered threats, Basilisk has had numerous clashes with the Suicide Squad. At one point the terror cell planted one of its members, Black Spider, in the Squad's ranks in an attempt to destroy the Squad from within. Basilisk also tangled with the Birds of Prey when Black Canary discovered Basilisk was holding her husband, Kurt Lance, hostage. **MM**

BAT-MITE

DEBUT *Detective Comics* (Vol. 1) #267 (May 1959)
CURRENT VERSION *Convergence: Supergirl Matrix* #2 (Jul. 2015)
BASE Gotham City
HEIGHT 2ft 11in **WEIGHT** 47 lbs
EYES Black **HAIR** Unknown
POWERS/ABILITIES Flight; teleportation; can alter reality including the ability to change clothing of others; weapons include Utility Belt filled with gadgets together with a bat-shaped cellphone, Bat-shield, and Bat-laser.
ALLIES Batman, the Batman Family, Booster Gold
ENEMIES Gridlock, Dr. Trauma
AFFILIATIONS Justice Mites of America

An imp hailing from an unnamed dimension, the pint-sized provocateur known as Bat-Mite is a perpetual thorn in Batman's side.

Declaring himself Batman's biggest fan and clad in a Batsuit that resembles his hero's current look, the troublesome Bat-Mite has the unerring knack of popping up at the most inopportune times to assist Batman with his own brand of mischievous heroics. The result is invariably mayhem, making the Dark Knight work twice as hard to resolve the situation.

Recently, Bat-Mite's otherworldly antics led him to be banned from his own dimension. Stranded in Batman's reality, but still possessing his magical abilities, Bat-Mite stole the Batmobile to engage in a spot of crime fighting, but promptly crashed it off a cliff. Not content with "helping" the Dark Knight, Bat-Mite has also managed to make life difficult for other Super Heroes, including Hawkman, Robin, and Booster Gold. **MM**

ON THE RECORD

Bat-Mite has remained essentially the same bothersome imp since his debut in 1959. After aiding and/or annoying the Silver Age Batman, Bat-Mite faded into obscurity after the events of *Crisis on Infinite Earths*. A modern incarnation of the "Dark Mite" reemerged in *Batman: Legends of the Dark Knight* #38 in 1992, when the mighty Mite appeared as the probable hallucination of a drug addict named Overdog. The imp returned in the 2000s as a delusion of Batman himself.

MITE OR FLIGHT?
During a mental meltdown caused by the villain Dr. Hurt, Batman became the only person who could see Bat-Mite.

BATGIRL

DATA

DEBUT *Detective Comics* (Vol. 1) #359 **(Jan. 1967)**
CURRENT VERSION *Batgirl* (Vol. 4) #1 **(Nov. 2011)**
REAL NAME Barbara Joan Gordon **BASE** Burnside, Gotham City
HEIGHT 5ft 11in **WEIGHT** 135lbs **EYES** Blue **HAIR** Red
POWERS/ABILITIES Expert martial artist and gymnast trained in part by Batman; extremely athletic and agile; eidetic memory; very intelligent with advanced knowledge of computers; natural leader; weapons include fully stocked Utility Belt, protective suit, and compact Batcycle.
ALLIES Batman, The Batman Family, Black Canary, Frankie Charles, James Gordon
ENEMIES The Joker, James Gordon Jr., Knightfall, Velvet Tiger
AFFILIATIONS Birds of Prey, Justice League United, Batman, Inc.

A presence in Batman's world ever since she forcibly inserted herself into it, the tenacious Barbara Gordon has spent her life following in the footsteps of her hero father, Commissioner James "Jim" Gordon. While James Gordon has done much to help Gotham City as one of the few honorable cops on the Gotham City Police force, Barbara has done even more as Batgirl. Originally starting her career by imitating Gotham City's legendary Dark Knight, Batgirl has since become her own woman, fighting crime in an original style, and putting her years of training and brilliant mind to work protecting the Gotham City borough of Burnside.

AT A GLANCE...

Commissioner's daughter
Barbara Gordon grew up a police "brat," idolizing her father James Gordon and wanting to follow in his footsteps. Her father introduced her to judo and gymnastics, and imbued her with a strong moral character. These skills all came into play when Barbara first donned a Batsuit and became the Super Hero known as Batgirl.

Expanded wardrobe
Batgirl has worn several costumes over the course of her relatively short career. First donning a police Batsuit, Barbara soon adopted an official Batgirl costume, complete with domino-style mask. After an injury at the hands of the Joker, she wore a more armored Batgirl suit.

Team player
Batgirl met and teamed with vigilantes Black Canary and Starling to form the Birds of Prey—a team that later brought crime fighters like Katana, Strix, and Condor into its lineup. While considering herself a solo act, Batgirl has always fought well alongside others.

Barbara Gordon grew up in the shadow of Gotham City's white knight, James Gordon. Rightfully idolizing her father, she used to paper her walls with news articles detailing Gordon's fight against the city's corruption and criminal element. Intense and driven, Barbara wanted to follow her dad's example, but did so in her own unique way. She mastered ballet and judo, and put her photographic memory to good use studying criminology.

It was during a trip to the Gotham City Police Department as part of her research for "Intro to Criminology" that Barbara caught her first glimpse of her life's calling. Visiting the precinct alongside her little brother James Jr., Barbara saw her true reason for touring the GCPD, a mock-up of the Batsuit crafted by the S.W.A.T. team based on eyewitness sightings of the elusive Batman. As interested as she was in her father's line of work, Barbara had become truly fascinated by Gotham City's Dark Knight, and wanted to learn everything she could about the vigilante. But little did she know she would get a chance to take a trial run at filling the Batman's shoes that very same day.

After police escorted a hulking criminal called Harry X past Barbara, the villain escaped with the help of a few armed accomplices. Barbara used the chaos as cover, and donned the GCPD's Batsuit in order to best Harry X in combat without exposing her identity. When she met Batman face-to-face immediately afterwards, her actions were praised by the hero. The entire event proved too irresistible for Barbara, and soon she was wearing her own blue-and-gray Batsuit, and learning the ins and outs of crime fighting firsthand as Batgirl.

DADDY DEAREST
Barbara idolized her father, Commissioner Gordon, and plastered her bedroom walls with news stories of his heroic efforts.

AFFAIRS OF THE HEART

Barbara Gordon and Dick Grayson, the original Robin, have shared a longstanding romance that began when Barbara first started out as Batgirl. From the outset, Grayson noticed the young vigilante's grace and skill, and soon developed a crush on the heroine. While their romance never truly got off the ground, the two understood they shared a mutual attraction. But when Grayson faked his own death to join the spy network Spyral, Barbara moved on with her life and began a romance with Luke Fox, aka Batwing. When she finally learned that Dick was still alive, Barbara had grown accustomed to life without him, and chose to stay with Luke, considering Grayson to be just a friend.

MOVING ON
Dick Grayson wasn't happy about Barbara's decision to end their years-long flirtation, but he realized that she was happy, and did his best to be happy for her.

CLASSIC STORIES

***Detective Comics* (Vol. 1) #359 (Jan. 1967)** Batgirl makes her debut by proving herself in combat against the longtime Batman foe, Killer Moth.

***Batgirl Special* #1 (Jan. 1988)** In her first solo self-titled comic, Batgirl ends an old score and retires from the Super Hero life, setting the stage for the monumental *Batman: The Killing Joke* special.

***Batgirl: Year One* #1–9 (Feb.–Oct. 2003)** Barbara Gordon's origin is retold for the modern era, explaining how she made the transition from lone vigilante to a member of Batman's inner circle.

***Batgirl* (Vol. 4) #35 (Dec. 2014)** Batgirl opts for independence and moves to the Gotham City borough of Burnside, adopting a new look and perspective on life.

"...for the first time in a long while, I know who I am..."

BATGIRL

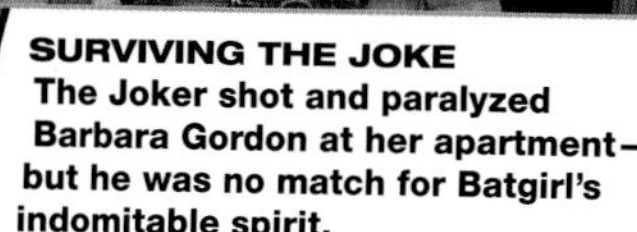

SURVIVING THE JOKE
The Joker shot and paralyzed Barbara Gordon at her apartment—but he was no match for Batgirl's indomitable spirit.

However, the first chapter of Batgirl's life as a Super Hero was about to come to a crashing halt. When super-villain the Joker broke into her apartment in his latest scheme against Jim Gordon, he shot Batgirl in the spine, leaving her wheelchair-bound. Through the use of cutting-edge technology, however, and with an unwavering desire to overcome adversity, Barbara regained her ability to walk. She was soon back in prime fighting form, adopting a new Batgirl costume that better matched Batman's armored counterpart.

Back as a Super Hero, Batgirl's life did not slow down in the slightest. Initially reluctant to commit herself to a team, Barbara became a member of the female vigilantes called the Birds of Prey. She met a host of new adversaries including Grotesque and Gretel, and an arch foe in the form of Knightfall. Perhaps her most disturbing case involved the return of the Joker and the manipulation by her own psychotic brother, James Gordon Jr., who wanted nothing more than the death of their mother, Barbara Kean Gordon. **MM**

FAMILY CRISIS
Barbara Gordon finally got the answers she had been wanting when her mother, Barbara Kean Gordon, came back to Gotham City following a long absence. As it turned out, Barbara's mother was terrified of her own son, James Gordon Jr., and had fled the city after he had threatened her daughter's life. When Barbara Sr. returned, James Jr. continued his deadly old tricks, and attempted to kill his mother. Barbara Sr. shot James Jr., but it was Batgirl who knocked him off the side of a dock. She believed herself responsible for her brother's death, but would later discover that James Jr. had survived the fall.

WANTED
Commissioner Gordon witnessed James Jr.'s plummet off the dock, and blamed Batgirl for his son's death. Unwilling to reveal her double identity to her father, Batgirl was forced to live as a fugitive for a time.

NEW LOOK
After losing her Bruce Wayne-funded costume in a fire. Barbara hand crafted a replacement which had a button-on cape.

REBIRTH

CLASS ACT
Always an overachiever and hungry to be the best she can be, Barbara Gordon starts a global odyssey to hone her crime-fighting combat skills to the maximum. Unfortunately, even before completing her first lessons in Japan, Batgirl is drawn into a deadly game of murder and mystery.

ON THE RECORD

While Barbara Gordon has remained the iconic version of Batgirl since her debut, the original Batgirl, Betty Kane, first appeared in 1961 in *Batman (Vol. 1) #139*. The niece of Kathy Kane (aka Batwoman), Betty launched the long and eventful history of Batgirl.

Enter Batgirl
Before the reality-altering event "Crisis on Infinite Earths," Barbara Gordon was introduced as a librarian who had designed a Batman-like costume to attend a policeman's ball. On the way to the event, however, she encountered Killer Moth and quickly leapt to Batman and Robin's aid in defeating the villain. Sold on a life of fighting crime, Barbara became Batgirl. A breath of fresh air in Gotham City, she was soon found driving her Batgirl cycle around the city, establishing her own crime-busting credentials.

MAKING HER MARK
When Batgirl moved to Washington, D.C., Barbara became a congresswoman. Despite her busy schedule, she still kept her late night appointments as Batgirl.

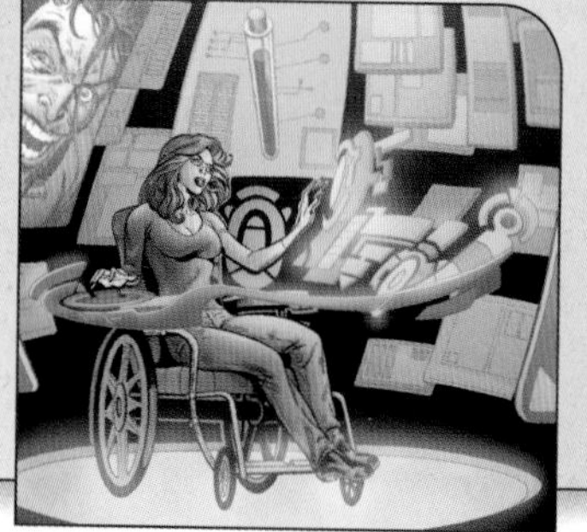

The Origins of Oracle
Soon after "Crisis on Infinite Earths," Batgirl's story was streamlined. In this incarnation, a retired Batgirl was injured by the Joker and would never walk again. However, rather than give up, Barbara changed the way she fought crime, becoming Oracle, a computer guru able to find any information on the Internet. As Oracle, Barbara was an invaluable aide to the Batman Family, became a member of the Justice League of America, a mentor for the new Batgirl, Cassandra Cain, and helped form the Birds of Prey.

BATMAN

DATA

DEBUT *Detective Comics* (Vol. 1) #27 **(May 1939)**
CURRENT VERSION *Flashpoint* (Vol. 2) #5 **(Oct. 2011)**
REAL NAME Bruce Wayne **BASE** Gotham City
HEIGHT 6ft 2in **WEIGHT** 210 lbs **EYES** Blue **HAIR** Black
POWERS/ABILITIES Martial arts expert; skilled acrobat, gymnast, and athlete; escape artist; highly intelligent with advanced knowledge of technologies; natural leader; master strategist; weapons include Utility Belt and armored suit; owns customized land, air, and water vehicles.
ALLIES Batman Family, Alfred Pennyworth, James Gordon, Superman
ENEMIES Arkham Asylum inmates, Blackgate Penitentiary inmates, Rā's al Ghūl
AFFILIATIONS Justice League, Justice League of America, Justice League International, Batman, Inc.

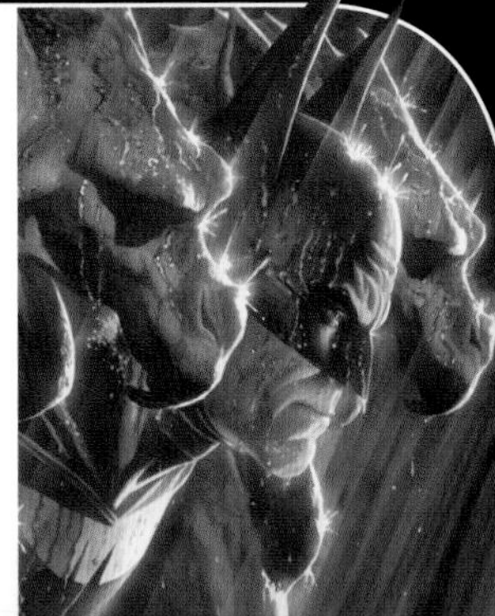

The Dark Knight. The World's Greatest Detective. Gotham City's Guardian. The hero known as Batman goes by many titles, the result of a life in the shadows building an urban legend that is as revered by the innocent as much as it is feared by Gotham City's cowardly and superstitious criminal lot. In a world full of Super Heroes and super-villains, Batman fights crime using his intellect, physical and mental training, and an arsenal developed with his family's fortune. Moreover, Bruce Wayne has an unrelenting need to prevent the kind of tragedy that he suffered from happening to any of Gotham City's innocents.

AT A GLANCE...

The Mark of Zorro
After attending a viewing of *The Mark of Zorro* film with his parents in the Gotham City neighborhood called Park Row, a young Bruce Wayne watched as his mother and father were gunned down before his eyes by a common criminal. It was on this night that the Batman was truly born.

The Batman Family
While he considers himself a loner, Batman has many allies in his war on crime. These include several young heroes who each served as his partner, Robin, and other allies inspired by his career, such as Batgirl and Batwoman. He even organized an international fighting force under the name Batman, Inc., taking Batman's mission to a global level.

The wonders of the Batcave
Batman operates from the large caverns below Wayne Manor. He is constantly developing new technologies, vehicles, and weapons to aid in his never-ending crusade against crime in Gotham City. From the dozens of models of his Batmobile, Batplane, and Batboat, to the simple gadgets in his Utility Belt, Batman is always ahead of the technological curve.

CLASSIC STORIES

***Detective Comics* (Vol. 1) #395 (Jan. 1970)** Batman is brought back to his noir roots in "The Secret of the Waiting Graves," where he tangles with a mysterious couple in Central Mexico.

***Batman* (Vol. 1) #404-407 (Feb.–May 1987)** Batman's origin is brought to life for a modern audience in the Year One storyline following the events of Crisis on Infinite Earths, which seemed to wipe away much of his original continuity.

***Batman* (Vol. 1) #492-500, *Detective Comics* (Vol. 1) #659-666, *Showcase '93* #7-8 (May-Oct. 1993)** In Knightfall, Batman is forced to run a gauntlet of his most dangerous foes before finally facing super-villain Bane in a climactic fight that sees the Dark Knight's true breaking point.

***Batman* (Vol. 2) #21-33 (Aug. 2013-Sep. 2014)** After the events of Flashpoint altered reality again, Batman's origin story was given a facelift in Zero Year. Bruce Wayne sets up a base of operations in a cave beneath Wayne Manor and the concept of the Batman is born.

When Bruce Wayne pressured his parents to take him to see the film *The Mark of Zorro*, he had no idea that his life was about to change forever. As his family walked from the movie theater down a dark Park Row street in Gotham City, an armed thug stepped from the shadows pointing his gun at the Waynes. In a simple mugging gone wrong, criminal Joe Chill shot and killed both Thomas and Martha Wayne, making young Bruce an orphan in a split second. Reeling from the shock of the traumatic loss, Bruce made a vow on his parents' grave to wage a lifetime of war against criminals who would prey on the innocent. Although he wasn't aware of it yet, on that night, Bruce truly became Batman.

After brief stints at a few schools, including Gotham Academy, Bruce Wayne traveled the world learning the tools of the crime-fighting trade he fully intended to ply. When he was 21 years old, he studied the ins and outs of technological gadgetry under the guidance of the brilliant inventor, Sergei Alexandrov. He learned from Brazilian criminal Don Miguel how to race cars in life-or-death situations, and spent much of his time studying martial arts with masters like Shihan Matsuda in the Himalayas. But Bruce didn't stop there. He delved into criminology, chemistry, and even acting, understanding that his future would require the mastery of a vast number of specialized skills. All the while, he trained his mind and body to near perfection, often practicing his fighting techniques on dozens of opponents at one time. And while he knew he would still require a lifetime of practice to reach a level of perfection he could be satisfied with, Bruce Wayne nevertheless returned to Gotham City in order to begin his mission to clean up the corrupted town.

UTILITY PATENT
Alexandrov's teachings were instrumental in enabling Bruce to create Batman's famed Utility Belt.

Bruce Wayne was fortunate enough to have been born into a wealthy family. The natural heir to the Wayne fortune and its main corporation, Wayne Enterprises, the idealistic Bruce represented a threat to the company's established ways of doing business. And while he had not intended to make his return to Gotham City a publicized event, his uncle Philip Kane managed to do that for him, both happy to see his nephew's return from his mysterious journeys, yet also dubious of the young man, immediately plotting against him.

Away from his corporate obligations, Bruce began his campaign against crime, taking steps to combat the city's worst scourge, the Red Hood Gang. Led by the mysterious Red Hood One, the criminal organization seemed to have its claws in everything from illegal weapons deals to politics. Disguising himself as the criminal known as the Penguin, Bruce managed to break up one of those weapons deals, only narrowly escaping with his life.

THE COURT OF OWLS
Batman uncovered an underground criminal society in Gotham City, discovering that this clandestine organization dated back to the very origins of the city itself. Called the Court of Owls, the secret society maintained an army of assassins named Talons. Batman was not only forced to escape the Court's elaborate labyrinth located underneath the city streets, but he also faced a small army of Talons when the Court unleashed them on some of Gotham City's most powerful political figures. Batman and his allies defeated the assassins, forcing the Court even further underground.

THOMAS WAYNE, JR.
An acquaintance of Bruce Wayne, Lincoln March, proved to be an agent of the Court of Owls. Batman defeated March, but he could not shake off the villain's claim that he was Bruce's younger brother Thomas, abandoned by the family at a young age.

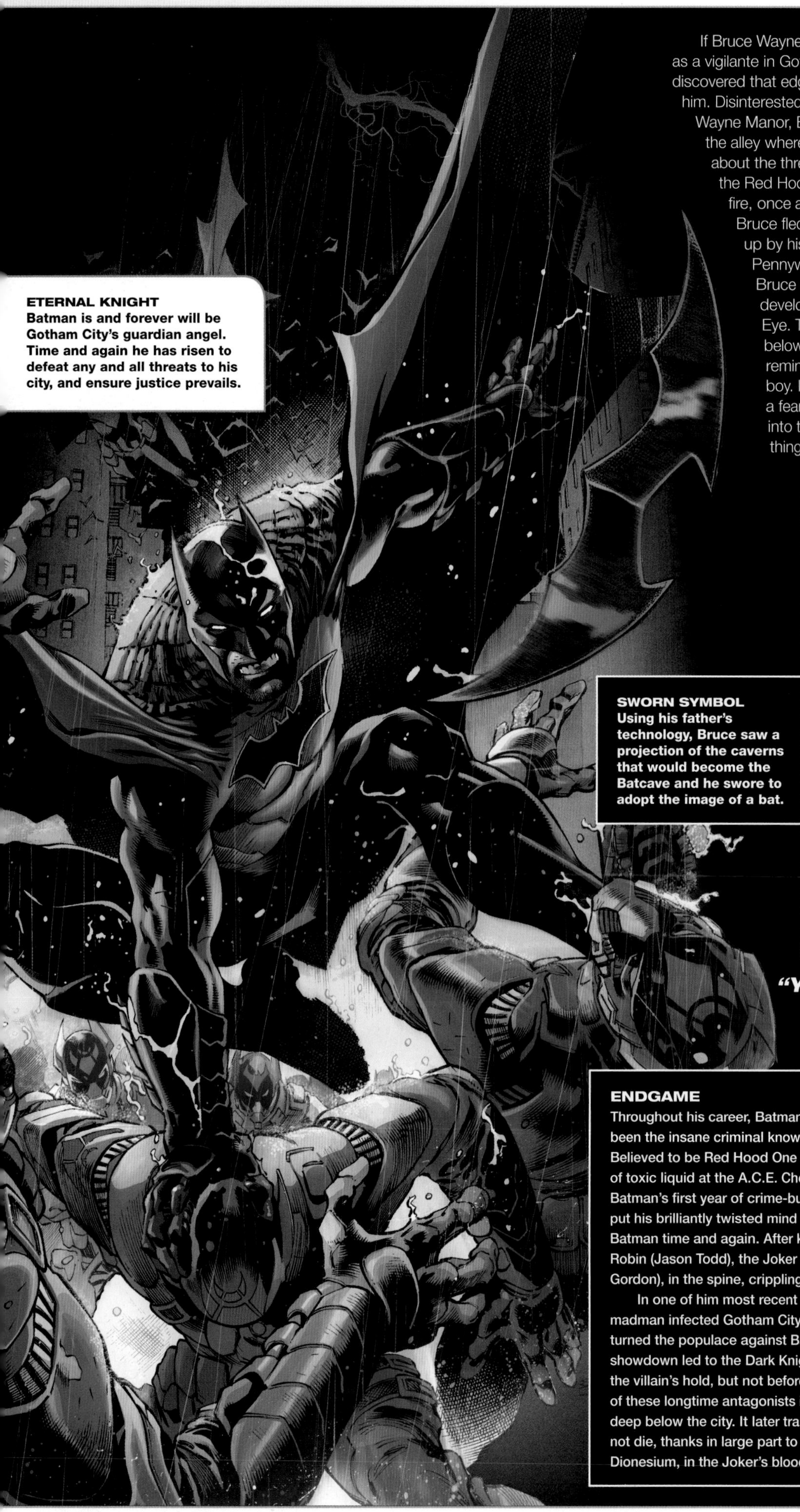

If Bruce Wayne was going to continue to operate as a vigilante in Gotham City, he would need an edge. Wayne discovered that edge the night the Red Hood Gang came for him. Disinterested in the Wayne legacy or his family home, Wayne Manor, Bruce set up operations in a townhouse on the alley where his parents had been killed. Worried about the threat Bruce represented to their organization, the Red Hood Gang invaded the house and set it on fire, once again nearly killing Bruce in the process. Bruce fled to Wayne Manor, where he was patched up by his longtime family friend and butler, Alfred Pennyworth. Later venturing to his father's study, Bruce discovered a piece of technology developed by Thomas Wayne called a Witch's Eye. The Eye projected the image of the caverns below Wayne Manor onto the walls of the study, reminding Bruce of the day he fell into those very caves as a young boy. It made Bruce remember the thing that haunted his childhood, a fear of bats. It was then that Bruce Wayne realized that to strike fear into the hearts of Gotham City's criminals, he had to become the very thing that had terrified him as a boy—a bat.

BECOMING BATMAN
Injured from his fight with the Red Hood Gang, Bruce Wayne knew he needed to tackle crime fighting from a different angle.

ETERNAL KNIGHT
Batman is and forever will be Gotham City's guardian angel. Time and again he has risen to defeat any and all threats to his city, and ensure justice prevails.

SWORN SYMBOL
Using his father's technology, Bruce saw a projection of the caverns that would become the Batcave and he swore to adopt the image of a bat.

"Yes, father. I shall become a bat."

Bruce Wayne

ENDGAME

Throughout his career, Batman's greatest foe has been the insane criminal known simply as the Joker. Believed to be Red Hood One after falling into a vat of toxic liquid at the A.C.E. Chemical Plant during Batman's first year of crime-busting, the Joker has put his brilliantly twisted mind to work tormenting Batman time and again. After killing the second Robin (Jason Todd), the Joker shot Batgirl (Barbara Gordon), in the spine, crippling her.

In one of him most recent schemes, the madman infected Gotham City with a virus that turned the populace against Batman. The final brutal showdown led to the Dark Knight freeing the city of the villain's hold, but not before the apparent death of these longtime antagonists in a cave collapse deep below the city. It later transpired that they did not die, thanks in large part to the regenerative fluid, Dionesium, in the Joker's bloodstream entering the pool of blood in which they both lay. However, the event profoundly changed Bruce, threatening the end of Batman's career forever.

LAST LAUGH?
The so-called Clown Prince of Crime released a deadly Joker virus across Gotham City, to create an army of zombie-like Jokerized victims.

BATMAN

BREAKING UP THE BAND
The Batman costume was as effective and dramatic as Bruce had hoped when he appeared before the Red Hood Gang.

REBIRTH

DARK KNIGHT DISCIPLES
To reinforce his resources for protecting Gotham City while he's ferreting out the secret of Wally West's return from outside reality, Batman recalls Red Robin (Tim Drake) and Orphan (Cassandra Cain). He assigns them, alongside Spoiler (Stephanie Brown) and raw recruit Basil "Clayface" Karlo, to his drill sergeant Kate (Batwoman) Kane, who will turn them into a unit capable of defending Gotham City when and if he cannot.

With these disciples forming the core of a new, consolidated group, the Dark Knight hopes he can mold them into highly trained, battle-ready army to effectively counter the threat of a new covert force bringing military justice to his city.

RIOT GEAR
The Batsuit—armored especially at the knees, forearms, and around the cowl—came in handy when the Dark Knight faced a riot at Arkham Asylum.

Donning his first version of a Batsuit, Bruce Wayne became the Batman, taking the fight directly to the Red Hood Gang. His campaign was immediately successful, defeating the criminals during a showdown with Red Hood One at the A.C.E. Chemical Factory—a conflict that tragically cost the life of his uncle Philip Kane, a secret member of the Red Hood Gang.

Batman would soon be put to the ultimate test when a super-villain known as the Riddler took control of Gotham City, shutting off its power just as a super storm approached. The result was an isolated metropolis ruled by a criminal who planned to wipe the entire city off the map. Working directly with police captain James Gordon and Wayne Enterprises scientist Lucius Fox, Batman overcame the eccentric super-villain, earning his fabled reputation as Gotham City's Dark Knight.

As Batman's career continued, he adjusted his Batsuit to better serve his needs, and soon became a founding member of the Justice League alongside other legendary heroes such as Superman and Wonder Woman. He partnered with a talented former circus performer named Dick Grayson, who became the first of four young men to adopt the title of Robin and be personally trained by the Dark Knight. Grayson was succeeded by the headstrong Jason Todd, who was in turn succeeded by the computer genius Tim Drake, who adopted the name Red Robin to set himself apart from Batman's former partners. Batman's current partner is Damian Wayne, the fourth Robin and Bruce Wayne's own son.

Building a small army of allies over the years inspired Batman to take his work onto a global scale, and he soon introduced Batman, Inc., a Wayne Enterprises-sponsored organization that placed a Batman representative in many countries. While Batman, Inc. eventually folded in Gotham City, Batman's legacy remains far-reaching and his heroics are known throughout the world. The Dark Knight has become the creature of the night he set out to be, feared by criminals in Gotham City and beyond. **MM**

REBIRTH

STRANGERS IN TOWN
Gotham's tenuous balance of power is disrupted by newcomers Gotham City and Gotham Girl. They have the strength to pluck crashing planes from the sky and a heroic, take-charge attitude, but can the Dark Knight afford to believe they are as benevolent as they claim?

ON THE RECORD

When he debuted in 1939, Batman was intended to be a "creature of the night," a hero inspired by the often dark and shadowy world of pulp magazines of the time. That brooding vigilante would soon be brightened by a child partner, Robin, and then lightened further throughout the 1950s and '60s. Batman returned to his role as a true Dark Knight Detective in the 1970s, and grew grim and gritty in the 1980s and '90s. Able to thrive in almost any incarnation, Batman has been a hero for the ages, one often reflective of the real world that inspires his creators.

THE ICONIC LOOK
Since his 1939 debut, Batman's look has included a bat-eared cowl and cape. In the 1960s, he adopted the yellow oval around his Bat-Symbol—an iconic logo that lasted into the 1990s.

Dark Knight Detective
After embracing light-hearted sci-fi romps in the 1950s and the offbeat adventures of the 1960s, Batman returned to his darker roots with a vengeance in *Detective Comics* #395 (January 1970), in a story entitled "The Secret of the Waiting Graves." While not as grim as he'd emerge in the 1980s after the miniseries *Batman: The Dark Knight*, the 'Caped Crusader' of the 1970s was once again a creature of the night, as a new generation of writers and artists recaptured the original Batman magic.

MENACE TO SOCIETY?
Batman was often targeted as a dangerous vigilante by many in Gotham City's corrupt police force, before proving he was a hero.

Year One
The modern incarnation of the Dark Knight truly emerged after the world-shattering events of Crisis on Infinite Earths. Given a realistic overhaul, Batman struggled to find his footing in a corrupted Gotham City, finally finding an ally in the form of James Gordon, the city's future police commissioner. Batman saved the life of Gordon's son, forever cementing their partnership.

The broken bat
Bruce Wayne wouldn't be the only Batman in Gotham City during the course of his career. When criminal mastermind Bane unleashed the inmates of Arkham Asylum onto Gotham City, he forced an exhausted Batman to capture them one by one. Bane then broke into Wayne Manor and crippled Batman, breaking his back. Temporarily out of action, Batman promoted Jean Paul Valley—a vigilante formerly called Azrael—into the role. Bruce was forced to recover on his own with the aid of Alfred and Robin, before finally training his body back to near physical perfection and reclaiming his mantle as the true Dark Knight.

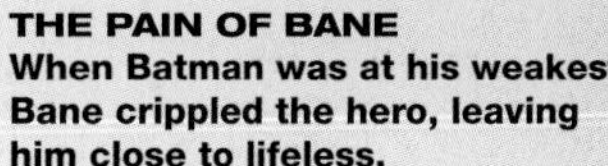

THE PAIN OF BANE
When Batman was at his weakest, Bane crippled the hero, leaving him close to lifeless.

Out of the past
As well as facing a mysterious new villain in Thomas Elliot's Hush, Batman ran the gauntlet of his most famous foes in the memorable "Hush" storyline. Introducing a threat from Bruce Wayne's past, this series saw the return of Jason Todd (in a fashion), the death of Batman's longtime inventor friend Harold Allnut, and the villainous Riddler discovering Batman's secret identity.

IDENTITY ISSUES
Batman was forced to encounter his old foes as he deduced Hush's identity and the man behind the villain's rise to power, the Riddler.

BATMAN BEYOND

DATA

DEBUT *Batman Beyond* (Vol. 1) #1 **(Mar. 1999)**
CURRENT VERSION *The New 52: Future's End* #47 **(May 2015)**
UNIVERSE Earth-12 **REAL NAME** Timothy Drake (formerly Terry McGinnis)
BASE Neo-Gotham
HEIGHT 6ft **WEIGHT** 198 lbs **EYES** Blue **HAIR** Black
POWERS/ABILITIES Computer expert with near genius IQ; natural leader and expert strategist; expert gymnast and martial artist trained directly by Batman (Bruce Wayne); weapons include high-tech armored suit that can fly with the aid of glider wings and rocket boots, turn practically invisible, and shoot a grappling hook, Batarangs, and/or explosive discs.
ALLIES Commissioner Barbara Gordon, Max Gibson, Matt McGinnis
ENEMIES Blight, Shriek, Spellbinder, Rewire, Inque, Jokerz
AFFILIATIONS Justice League Beyond, Teen Titans (formerly)

BEYOND THE BATSUIT
The Batman Beyond suit contains rocket boots, wings, a Utility Belt, a built-in grapnel, and a cowl that greatly improves Batman's vision and hearing.

BEHIND THE VEIL
Much of Neo-Gotham was protected from Brother Eye thanks to technology called the Veil. As such, it was one of the only remaining cities left standing in the future reality of Batman Beyond.

A few decades into the future, Gotham City has evolved into Neo-Gotham, a metropolis of tremendous skyscrapers, flying cars, and sleek technology. In that brave new world, a new kind of Batman is required to keep the peace, he is an armored hero capable of flight and invisibility. There have been two of these protectors taking on Bruce Wayne's old role: Terry McGinnis and now Tim Drake, the newest Batman Beyond.

Bruce Wayne retired as Batman. He felt he was growing too old for the job, even with the hi-tech flight suit he had made with help from Wayne Enterprises. Now an old man living alone in Wayne Manor, Bruce came to the aid of a teenager named Terry McGinnis when Terry was being terrorized by a group of gang members called the Jokerz—pale imitations of the original Clown Prince of Crime. Terry returned to Wayne Manor with Bruce and discovered that Bruce Wayne and Batman were one and the same. After a testy start, Terry was eventually accepted by the Dark Knight as his heir following the death of McGinnis' own father. With Bruce helping Terry on his missions via communication from the Batcave, a new Batman was born, suited for the times.

After a brief period where Dick Grayson took over for Wayne, Terry and Bruce fought their most destructive enemy, an artificial intelligence called Brother Eye. The Eye had conquered the world, and to combat it, Terry traveled back in time to a future five years before the events of the present day. There he battled Brother Eye, but was killed for his efforts. His mantle was passed to former Red Robin, Tim Drake. Tim fought the Eye and was shot back into Terry's future in the process. Now in Neo-Gotham, Drake defeated Brother Eye with the help of Terry's old enemy, Inque, truly earning the title of Batman. **MM**

ON THE RECORD

Batman Beyond originally debuted in cartoon form in his self-titled animated series in 1999. While a tie-in comic came soon after, Batman Beyond didn't make his way into the DC Universe until a storyline in the pages of *Superman/Batman* showcased the hero living in an alternate universe. However that hero was oddly Tim Drake under the Batsuit, not Terry McGinnis.

In 2010, McGinnis was given his own miniseries that soon led to an ongoing series, tying in Terry's life more closely to the future of the DCU by having him fight not just threats from the animated series, but comic book villains like Hush.

A DIFFERENT BEYOND
Tim Drake debuted as Batman Beyond, tangling with a time-displaced Bizarro Superman during a deadly reality-hopping game being played by the Joker and Mr. Mxyzptlk.

CITY OF YESTERDAY
Outside the realm of Neo-Gotham, the world had been left in tatters in Batman Beyond's new future. The ruins of Metropolis were overrun by genetic monstrosities.

CLASSIC STORIES

***Batman Beyond* (Vol. 1) #1–6 (Mar.–Aug. 1999)** Batman Beyond's origin is adapted from the cartoon series before the hero goes on new adventures.

***Batman Beyond* (Vol. 3) #1–6 (Aug. 2010–Jan. 2011)** Batman Beyond faces a threat from Bruce Wayne's past when a new Hush debuts and begins killing minor super-villains like Signalman.

***The New 52: Future's End* (Vol. 1) #0–48 (Jun. 2014–Jun. 2015)** Terry McGinnis heads back in time to thwart Brother Eye, eventually handing over the reins to a new Batman Beyond, Tim Drake.

***Batman Beyond* (Vol. 5) #1–6 (Aug. 2015–Jan. 2016)** Tim Drake, clad as Batman Beyond, finally triumphs over the forces of the seemingly unstoppable Brother Eye.

BATMAN, INC.

DATA

DEBUT *Batman and Robin* (Vol. 1) #16 **(Jan. 2011)**
CURRENT VERSION *Batman, Incorporated* (Vol. 2) #1 **(Jul. 2012)**
BASE Gotham City and various countries around the globe
NOTABLE MEMBERS **BATMAN** (Bruce Wayne); **ROBIN** (Damian Wayne); **RED ROBIN** (Tim Drake); **CATWOMAN** (Selina Kyle); **DICK GRAYSON**; **BATGIRL** (Barbara Gordon); **BATWING** (David Zavimbe); **BATWING** (Luke Fox); **NIGHTRUNNER** (Bilal Asselah); **BATMAN JAPAN** (Jiro Osamu); **WINGMAN** (Jason Todd); **KNIGHT (FORMERLY SQUIRE)** (Beryl Hutchinson); **EL GAUCHO** (Santiago Vargas); **MAN-OF-BATS** (Dr. William Great Eagle); **HOOD** (George Cross); **RAVEN RED** (Charles Great Eagle); **DARK RANGER (FORMERLY SCOUT)** (Johnny Riley); **TALON** (Calvin Rose).
ALLIES Commissioner Barbara Gordon, Max Gibson, Matt McGinnis
ENEMIES Leviathan, Talia al Ghūl

CLASSIC STORIES

***Batman: The Return* #1 (Jan. 2011)** After journeying through time due to the machinations of the villain Darkseid, Batman returns to the present and begins to lay the groundwork for Batman, Inc.

***Batman, Incorporated* (Vol. 1) #1 (Jan. 2011)** Batman heads to Japan with Catwoman to kick start his global Batman, Inc. effort.

***Batman, Incorporated: Leviathan Strikes* #1 (Feb. 2012)** The first half of the Batman, Inc. saga comes to a climax in an oversized special that sees the Dark Knight discover that Talia is the face behind Leviathan.

***Batman, Incorporated* (Vol. 2) #13 (Sep. 2013)** Batman successfully brings down Leviathan with the help of an old ally, Kathy Kane, the original Batwoman.

GOING PUBLIC
Bruce Wayne publicized his funding of the Batman's operations when he introduced the concept of Batman, Incorporated.

The idea came to Batman in something akin to a dream: a global team of Batmen, working together for the common safety of the world. When Batman introduced Batman, Incorporated to the world, he did so knowing that this particular team of international heroes would all use the Batman's methods, and would answer solely to him.

After catching a glimpse of his future and the global threat of the evil and clandestine organization called Leviathan, Batman decided he needed to step-up his crime-fighting game, and formed a new team of Super Hero operatives under the name Batman, Incorporated. Fully and publicly funded by Wayne Enterprises, Batman, Inc. united not just his allies in the Batman Family, but also saw new heroes adopt costumed identities to follow in the Dark Knight's footsteps and uphold his brand of justice.

Batman had briefly fought with a group of international crime fighters called the Club of Heroes, so it only made sense that he recruited some of those old allies into his new operation, or in cases like the Knight, Batman recruited the heir to the original hero's mantle. Newcomers like the French crimefighter Nightrunner and Batman Japan were also welcomed into the fold, and soon, Batman had a veritable army of skilled and like-minded heroes to command against the rising threat of Leviathan.

Led by Talia al Ghūl, Leviathan proved to be as dangerous as the Dark Knight had feared. Not only did the cult of villains kill the Knight, they also ended the life of Batman's partner and son, Robin (Damian Wayne), causing the Dark Knight to be enraged like never before. Gotham City became a battle zone, waging a war that culminated in a fight between Batman and Talia in the Batcave. Talia al Ghūl, did not walk away from that particular fight, but was shot and killed by another of the enemies she had made in her bid for world conquest. **MM**

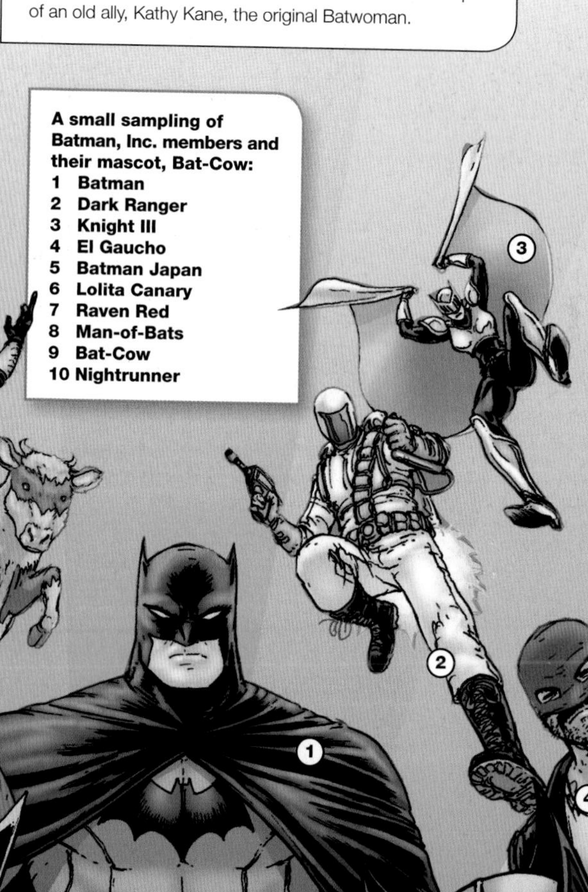

A small sampling of Batman, Inc. members and their mascot, Bat-Cow:
1 Batman
2 Dark Ranger
3 Knight III
4 El Gaucho
5 Batman Japan
6 Lolita Canary
7 Raven Red
8 Man-of-Bats
9 Bat-Cow
10 Nightrunner

ON THE RECORD

The first volume of Batman, Inc. formed the epic final chapter in the sweeping Batman saga that began with the "Batman and Son" storyline in *Batman* (Vol. 1) #655.

The second volume appeared after the reality-altering Flashpoint event, which led to some elements of the series, such as Batman's costume, being changed. New heroes like Black Bat (Cassandra Cain) joined up, while others, such as the original Batwoman (Kathy Kane) reemerged with significantly revised personal histories.

GONE IN A FLASH
Some characters in the first incarnation of Batman, Inc., like Batgirl Stephanie Brown, would not return in the second volume.

BATWOMAN

DATA

DEBUT *Detective Comics* #233 **(Jul. 1956)**
CURRENT VERSION *Batwoman* (Vol. 1) #1 **(Nov. 2011)**
REAL NAME Katherine (Kate) Kane
BASE Gotham City
HEIGHT 5ft 11in **WEIGHT** 141 lbs **EYES** Green **HAIR** Red
POWERS/ABILITIES Skilled martial artist, detective, and gymnast; highly trained soldier; additional training with operatives known as the Murder of Crows; equipment and resources include protective suit, fully stocked Utility Belt, and hi-tech command center.
ALLIES Hawkfire, Batman, the Batman Family, Maggie Sawyer, Red Alice
ENEMIES Nocturna, Ceto, Mr. Bones, Wolf Spider
AFFILIATIONS The Unknowns

DADDY'S LITTLE GIRL
Jacob Kane supported Kate's decision to become Batwoman, helping her set up a secret HQ as well as finding allies to train her in non-lethal techniques.

To the general public, Kate Kane seems to have everything. Like her cousin, Bruce Wayne, Kate has never wanted for money, and has been known to frequent the most exclusive nightclubs. However, Kate has lived a tragic life—one that has shaped her into a crime fighter and sworn protector of the innocent: Batwoman.

As a young girl, Kate Kane was very interested in athletics. Like her twin sister Beth, she enjoyed gymnastics and soccer. The two girls were the quintessential "military brats," moving around the country whenever their parents were stationed at a new location. They always had each other, were the best of friends, and assumed they would be lifelong confidantes.

On their 12th birthday, Kate and Beth realized just how wrong their assumptions had been. Their mother was taking the two girls out to celebrate when they were abducted and held prisoner. Their father ultimately assembled and led a squad of elite soldiers to come to their rescue. However, the damage was done: Kate's mother had been shot and killed, and it appeared that Beth had suffered the same fate. From that day forward, Kate Kane would live a lonely life, with only her doting father for support.

Jacob Kane did his best as a single father. He supported Kate, and taught her to live a disciplined and honorable life. When Kate was kicked out of the United States Military Academy at West Point for being gay, her father stood by her, realizing her honesty and integrity were more important than a career with the military. Kate had been an excellent cadet, and without school, there was a void in her life—one she filled with excessive partying. She lacked direction, and only found it when she saved herself from a mugging, meeting Batman in the process. With her father's training and support, Kate transformed herself into Batwoman, enrolling into a new kind of service to the public. **MM**

COLORS OF WAR
Batwoman's father designed her costume. Col. Kane made sure the suit was stab resistant, bullet proof, and dramatic with its black and red color scheme.

ON THE RECORD

Kate Kane first appeared just five years before the Flashpoint event that altered the DC Universe. While much of her backstory has stayed the same, one aspect that has only lightly been touched on is her relationship with Renee Montoya, the second hero to adopt the name of the Question.

Kate had a romantic relationship with Renee before the couple became Super Heroes. However, in the current continuity, Renee's career as the Question is yet to begin. The two have dated, but their shared past remains something of a mystery.

NIGHT AND DAY
Before Flashpoint, Kate and Renee had a serious relationship, despite their different backgrounds. Kate was born into money, while Renee was a cop.

CLASSIC STORIES

***52* #7–52 (Jun. 2006–May 2007)**
Kate Kane is introduced, together with her tumultuous relationship with Renee Montoya, the new Question.

***Detective Comics* (Vol. 1) #854–857 (Aug.–Nov. 2009)**
Batwoman temporarily takes over as the star of *Detective Comics* when she finds her sister has become her worst enemy.

***Detective Comics* (Vol. 1) #858–860 (Dec. 2009–Feb. 2010)**
Batwoman's origin is told, from the family's kidnapping to her first meeting with Batman.

***Batwoman* (Vol. 1) #17 (Apr. 2013)**
Kate reveals her identity as Batwoman as she proposes to girlfriend Maggie Sawyer.

BATS OF A FEATHER
As part of the D.E.O. (Department of Extranormal Operations) was instructed to take down Batman. She soon left the organization, realizing that the Dark Knight was her true ally.

BATWING

DEBUT *Batman Inc.* (Vol. 1) #5 **(May 2011)** (David Zavimbe)
CURRENT VERSION *Batwing* #19 **(Jun. 2013)**
REAL NAME Lucas "Luke" Fox
BASE Gotham City
HEIGHT 5ft 9in **WEIGHT** 170 lbs **EYES** Brown **HAIR** Black
POWERS/ABILITIES Highly skilled mixed martial artist; brilliant designer and engineer much like his father Lucius Fox; able to think fast on his feet; near unlimited access to Wayne Enterprises' technology; weapons include bulletproof suit equipped with hi-tech weaponry and defense systems, his suit also enables flight and limited invisibility.
ALLIES Batgirl, Lucius Fox, Batman, the Batman Family
ENEMIES Lady Vic, Ratcatcher, Charlie Caligula, Menace
AFFILIATIONS Batman, Inc.

Luke Fox had no intention of following his father, Lucius Fox, into a career with Wayne Enterprises. Despite having a knack for technology the equal of his fathers, Luke preferred to go his own way in life, a decision that constantly frustrated Lucius, who felt his son was squandering both his intelligence and his opportunities. Despite clashing with his father on a near daily basis, Luke became extremely interested in the fighting arts, participating in a variety of mixed martial arts events. Luke's intelligence, strong will, and skills in the ring soon attracted Batman's attention, and the Dark Knight offered Luke the role of his agent Batwing, after the original Batwing, David Zavimbe, retired from life as a Super Hero. Wearing a new suit designed by his father, Luke has become a valued ally to Batman, despite often upsetting his family due to his many unexplained absences while on duty. **MM**

GOING HIS OWN WAY
Much to his father's relief, Luke has recently created his own company called FoxTek. He has also begun a relationship with fellow tech-minded hero, Batgirl.

BATWINGING IT
Batwing's suit is highly advanced and a true work in progress. Luke inherited his love for technology from his father, constantly updating his suit.

ON THE RECORD

While Luke Fox as Batwing debuted just months before the continuity changing Flashpoint event, a few characters existed in the past that bore a striking similarity to the hero. In *Batman* (Vol. 1) #250 (Jul. 1973), a child's interpretation of Batman, nicknamed "Batwings" appeared in "The Batman Nobody Knows!" Later, on Earth-2, a hero that went by the name Blackwing fought alongside the Huntress.

However, it wasn't until Crisis on Infinite Earths, and later events, that the first true Batwing was introduced in the form of David Zavimbe, the Batman Incorporated representative for Africa.

BATTLE READY
David Zavimbe lived a hard life as a child soldier in Africa. But Batman saw promise in him, promoting him to Batwing after learning of his amateur crime fighting.

BAZ, SIMON

DEBUT ***The New 52 Free Comic Book Day Special Edition* #1 (Jun. 2012)**
REAL NAME Simon Baz
BASE Dearborn, Michigan
HEIGHT 5ft 11in **WEIGHT** 183 lbs
EYES Brown **HAIR** Black
POWERS/ABILITIES Ability to overcome fear; carries handgun and power ring, which permits flight, force fields, and space travel; precognition.
ALLIES Green Lantern (Hal Jordan), Power Ring (Jessica Cruz)
ENEMIES Black Hand, Sinestro
AFFILIATIONS Green Lantern Corps, JLA

As a young Muslim boy growing up in Dearborn, Michigan, Simon Baz was often the target of bigotry, especially after the tragic events of September 11, 2001.

Years of bullying gave Simon a serious chip on his shoulder, and after he lost his job at an automotive plant he took up illegal street racing, only narrowly avoiding jail time. Financially desperate, Simon started stealing cars to make ends meet. One night he stole a van, only to discover a ticking bomb inside the vehicle, and after a high-speed chase he was taken into custody as a suspected terrorist. Amid a harsh interrogation by federal agents, a power ring found its way to Baz, gifting him with the abilities of a Green Lantern, jump starting his Super Hero career.

Recently he reluctantly joined Jessica Cruz as the new Green Lanterns of Earth, both being trained by Hal Jordan to take his place on the Justice League. **MM**

EMERALD VISION
Simon has manifested a very rare ability among Green Lanterns—The Emerald Sight. This grants him visions of the near future.

BEAUTIFUL DREAMER

DEBUT ***Forever People* (Vol. 1) #1 (Feb.–Mar. 1971)**
CURRENT VERSION ***Infinity Man and the Forever People* #1 (Aug. 2014)**
BASE New Genesis; Venice Beach, California
HEIGHT 5ft 6in **WEIGHT** 128 lbs
EYES Blue **HAIR** Black
POWERS/ABILITIES Able to create lifelike illusions; precognitive dreams; can resurrect the dead using the Anti-Life equation.
ALLIES Infinity Man
ENEMIES Darkseid, Mantis, Femmes Fatales

A student at the Academy of Higher Conscience on the planet New Genesis, Beautiful Dreamer was with Vykin Baldaur when he touched a non-functioning Mother Box and it bonded with him as its host. Soon Dreamer found herself traveling through a Boom Tube to Earth with her friend Vykin, his sister Serafina, and Mark Moonrider for an academy assignment to help advance humankind.

After meeting fellow Academy member Big Bear, the group set up camp in Venice Beach, California. During a fight with the villain Mantis, they touched the Mother Box in unison and were replaced by Infinity Man. Together the team became the Forever People.

Pre-Flashpoint, Beautiful Dreamer was kidnapped by Darkseid and taken to Earth, where she was rescued by Superman and the Forever People. The team were ultimately killed by Infinity Man on his campaign for the Source to destroy all New Gods. **MM**

DREAM WEAVER
Dreamer's strong connection to the Anti-Life Equation gives her the ability to manipulate the powerful mind-controlling formula.

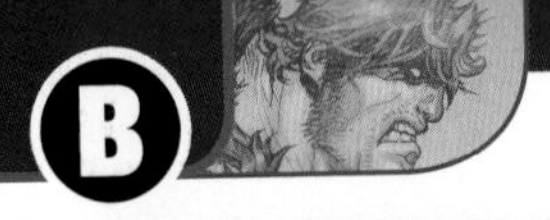

B

BENNETT, ANDREW

DEBUT *House of Mystery* (Vol. 1) #290 **(Mar. 1981)**
CURRENT VERSION *I, Vampire* #1 **(Nov. 2011)**
EYES Red
HAIR Black (with white streak)
POWERS/ABILITIES Like all vampires, can assume wolf or mist form and hypnotize humans, but is weakened by sunlight; skilled sorcerer and has shown the ability to bring dead vampires back to life.
ENEMIES Cain, Mary Seward, the Blood Red Moon

In Elizabethan England, young Andrew Bennett was attacked by Cain, the first of the vampires. Cain's bite passed the curse of vampirism to Bennett, and he awoke with an unholy thirst for blood. Bennett turned his lover, Mary, into a vampire too, but she came under demonic influence and became obsessed with taking over the world. Taking the title of the Blood Red Queen, Mary founded a vicious vampire cult called the Blood Red Moon and led them on a 'holy war' against mankind.

However, Andrew refused to give up his humanity by feeding on people, and was determined to stop Mary and her followers. When she attacked Gotham City, Andrew teamed up with Batman, Professor John Troughton, and teen tearaway Tig to take on the horde. Tig killed Andrew, hoping to destroy Mary's vampires by eliminating her sire, but that caused Cain to arise again. After being resurrected by Madame Xanadu, Bennett slew Cain and continued his war against Mary and her followers, ultimately absorbing their evil into himself to save them. **SW**

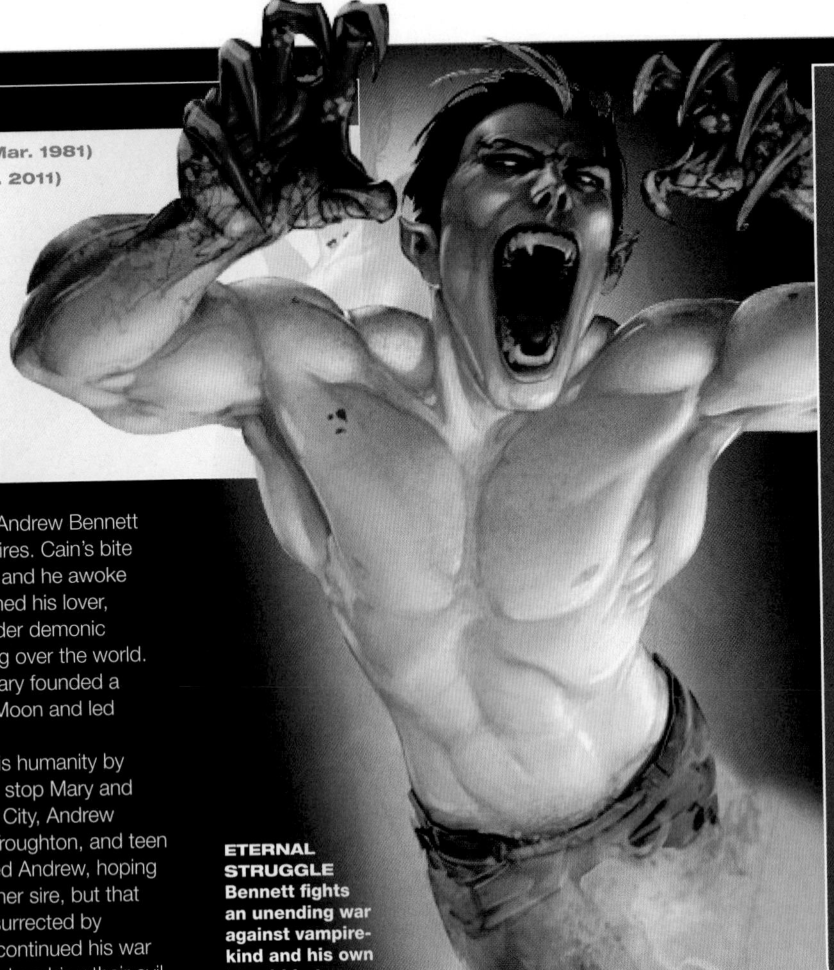

ETERNAL STRUGGLE Bennett fights an unending war against vampire-kind and his own bloodthirsty impulses.

ON THE RECORD

Pre-Flashpoint, Andrew Bennett was a nobleman at Queen Elizabeth I's court, before being bitten by a vampire. He clashed with his former lover Mary, who had become the vampiric Queen of Blood, and regained his humanity and witnessed her destruction before he himself died.

However, Andrew could not escape the vampiric curse; after rising from the grave, he attempted suicide, but returned to unlife. Bennett joined occult group Team 13 and intervened in the infernal war between the demons Satanus and Neron.

UNDEAD HERO Despite his menacing appearance, Andrew Bennett is a tormented soul who has spent centuries protecting humanity from his own kind.

BEKKA

DEBUT *DC Graphic Novel: The Hunger Dogs* #4 (1985)
CURRENT VERSION *Green Lantern/New Gods: Godhead* #1 (Dec. 2014)
BASE New Korugar, Sector 3567
HEIGHT 5ft 7in **WEIGHT** 132 lbs
EYES Blue **HAIR** Auburn/red
POWERS/ABILITIES Increased strength, speed and durability of a New God; can make others fall in love with her.
ENEMIES Darkseid, Mongul, Apex League

Bekka is a New God from New Genesis, the daughter of the scientist Himon. Born with an innate power to make people fall in love with her made her a formidable general—her besotted troops would die for her, and enemies would surrender without fighting.

New Genesis' ruler, Highfather, made Bekka a member of his Council of Eight and dispatched her to New Korugar, headquarters of the Sinestro Corps. She battled the Corps and brought back one of their yellow power rings, but also attracted the attention of Sinestro himself. He saw that Bekka possessed the capacity to inspire fear as well as love and offered to make her a member of the Corps. She ultimately accepted, forsaking her allegiance to New Genesis and going into action to save Sinestro from the warlord Mongul. **SW**

BERNADETH

DEBUT *Mister Miracle* (Vol. 1) #6 (Jan.–Feb. 1972)
BASE Apokolips
HEIGHT 5ft 10in **WEIGHT** 140 lbs
EYES Brown **HAIR** Black
POWERS/ABILITIES Superhuman physical capabilities and immortality due to New Gods heritage.
ALLIES Granny Goodness, Darkseid, Desaad
ENEMIES Big Barda, Mister Miracle, Lashina

Bernadeth is a member of the Female Furies, Darkseid's elite female fighting unit. She is the sister of Darkseid's torturer Desaad and shares his sadistic tendencies. Her signature weapon is the fahren-knife, which can slice through rock and roast anyone it pierces from the inside.

Bernadeth was Big Barda's second-in-command in the Furies, but when Barda betrayed Darkseid, Lashina, not Bernadeth, was made the new leader. Bernadeth took her revenge by leaving Lashina behind on Earth when the Furies were sent to rescue Glorious Godfrey. Lashina returned to Apokolips with members of the Suicide Squad and killed Bernadeth, but Darkseid punished Lashina for bringing humans to Apokolips by slaying her and returning Bernadeth to life. Bernadeth has remained in Darkseid's service, clashing with Supergirl, Wonder Woman, and Hawkgirl. **SW**

BIBBO

DEBUT *Adventures of Superman* (Vol. 1) #428 (May 1987)
REAL NAME Bo Bibbowski
BASE The Ace O'Clubs bar
HEIGHT 6ft 3in **WEIGHT** 250 lbs
EYES Gray **HAIR** Gray
ALLIES Superman, Jimmy Olsen, Lobo, Professor Emil Hamilton
ENEMIES Doomsday

Metropolis native Bibbo Bibbowski is a longshoreman, former boxer, and one of Superman's biggest fans. He has also been known to hang out with another super-tough guy: Lobo. Bibbo and the Man of Steel first met when Superman came to the Ace O'Clubs looking for information. Bibbo mistook him for a troublemaker in a Superman costume and punched him, but only injured his own hand! Impressed, Bibbo decided on the spot that Superman was his "fav'rit" hero.

Later, Bibbo bought the bar after finding a winning lottery ticket and helped Superman on numerous occasions, most notably when Doomsday attacked Metropolis. Bibbo and Professor Hamilton used a laser cannon against the monstrous alien (to no effect) and after Superman was killed by Doomsday, Bibbo tried to revive the fallen hero with an improvised defibrillator. **SW**

BIG BEAR

DEBUT *The Forever People* (Vol. 1) #1 (Feb.–Mar. 1971)
CURRENT VERSION *Infinity Man and the Forever People* #1 (Aug 2014)
BASE New Genesis HQ, Venice Beach, CA.
HEIGHT 6ft 8in **WEIGHT** 598 lbs
EYES Brown **HAIR** Red-brown
POWERS/ABILITIES New God with superhuman strength; wields claw-like blades.
ENEMIES Mantis, Femmes Fatales, Guy Gardner, Highfather

Burly New God Big Bear came from Apokolips, but turned his back on his bleak, oppressive home world and joined the Academy of Higher Conscience on New Genesis. He was put in charge of New Genesis' outpost on Earth, finding its easy-going ways preferable to New Genesis' rigid order. He welcomed New God students Serafina, Dreamer Beautiful, Vykin, and Mark Moonrider when they visited the planet.

The group was contacted by the Infinity Man, who called on them to reject both New Genesis and Apokolips. Big Bear and his friends took the name the Forever People and discovered that they could merge to form a massively powerful incarnation of the Infinity Man. They soon clashed with the Green Lanterns, the Femmes Fatales, and Highfather, ruler of New Genesis. **SW**

BIG BARDA

DATA

DEBUT *Mister Miracle* (Vol. 1) #4 **(Sep.-Oct. 1971)**
CURRENT VERSION *Earth 2* #11 **(Jun. 2013)**
REAL NAME Barda
HEIGHT 7ft **WEIGHT** 197 lbs
EYES Blue **HAIR** Black
POWERS/ABILITIES Immortal with superhuman mental and physical attributes as part of her New God heritage; she is also exceptionally strong and tough even for her kind; arsenal includes formidable Aegis armor and a rod which fires energy blasts.
ALLIES Mister Miracle, Darkseid, Justice League
ENEMIES Darkseid, Fury
AFFILIATIONS New Gods of Apokolips, Female Furies

HAMMER OF THE GODS
After becoming Doyenne of the Furies, Barda received a battle-maul that served as both a powerful weapon and a symbol of her authority.

ON THE RUN
After escaping Apokolips with Mister Miracle, Barda found herself pursued by Darkseid's forces and the World Army of Earth-2.

Big Barda was once a Female Fury who served Darkseid, the evil overlord of Apokolips, enforcing his will with her fearsome Mega-Rod. However, when Barda fell in love with rebel and escape-artist Mister Miracle, she changed her allegiance. Now this fierce New God fights for freedom against her former master.

Barda and Mister Miracle fled to Earth-2 just as Apokolips attacked the planet, and were captured by Earth-2's World Army. The couple agreed to take part in a desperate mission to save Earth-2 from Apokolips. They found a vulnerable Darkseid in stasis at Apokolips' core, but at this point Barda betrayed her companion. She urged Mister Miracle to use Stasis Bombs to kill the super-villain, knowing that this would in fact release him from stasis. A revived Darkseid attacked Mister Miracle, though the hero later escaped.

Barda was rewarded for her loyalty and made Doyenne of the Furies—Darkseid's elite female shock troops—and led Apokolips' armies as they scourged Earth-2. However, her Aegis armor was removed by Jimmy Olsen, who had been granted the cosmic powers of the Source by a Mother Box. Stripped of her symbol of office, she was turned on by Parademons and Darkseid's son Kalibak. She escaped and met up with K'li, Apokolips' former Fury of War. Keen to conquer new worlds for Darkseid, the pair sneaked aboard one of the spacecraft fleeing the planet.

Later, in a surprise turn of events, Mister Miracle was attacked by Kanto on Earth, when Barda suddenly appeared from a Boom Tube to save him. After a passionate reunion, it turned out that the two had been married all along and had just pretended to be enemies. **SW**

HELL HATH NO FURY
Barda was locked in a cycle of conflict with fellow warrior Fury, who was sometimes her ally, sometimes her rival—and often her foe.

ON THE RECORD

Big Barda's early history tread a familiar path. Trained to be a warrior on Apokolips, she taught other female fighters. She later rejected Darkseid and Apokolips, married Mr. Miracle, and traveled to Earth.

On Earth, Mister Miracle joined Justice League International. When he was captured by trader Manga Khan, Barda embarked on an interstellar mission to rescue him.

Barda then proved her value as a team player in a succession of groups. She mentored Fire while in the JLA, became a mother figure for Sin in Birds of Prey, and even started her own pro-wrestling crew.

HOUSEWIFE WARRIOR
When Big Barda first moved to Earth, she enjoyed life as a "domestic goddess," often resenting her routine being interrupted by adventures with her husband Mister Miracle!

CLASSIC STORIES

***Mister Miracle* (Vol. 1) #18 (Feb.-Mar. 1974)** Big Barda and Mister Miracle celebrate their love when they are married by Highfather on New Genesis.

***The Death of the New Gods* #1 (Dec. 2007)** When a mysterious killer begins slaying the New Gods, Big Barda is one of his first victims.

***Earth-2* #28 (Jan. 2015)** Chronicles how Barda found and trained the ruthless New God K'li, who would rise through the ranks to become Darkseid's Fury of War.

BEAST BOY

DATA

DEBUT *Doom Patrol* (Vol. 1) #99 **(Nov. 1965)**
CURRENT VERSION *Superboy* (Vol. 6) #8 **(Jun. 2012)**
REAL NAME Garfield Logan
HEIGHT 5ft 8in **WEIGHT** 150 lbs
HAIR Green (formerly red) **EYES** Red
POWERS/ABILITIES Genetic code provides a link with the Red, enabling transformation into any desired animal form.
ALLIES Terra, Animal Man
ENEMIES The Rot, N.O.W.H.E.R.E.
AFFILIATIONS Ravagers, Teen Titans

TEEN HERO
Beast Boy may look young, but he has got a long track record of heroism with the Teen Titans and the Ravagers—even if he doesn't remember all of it.

Better known as Beast Boy, young Garfield Logan is able to transform himself into any animal shape. He is a deeply loyal friend with an instinctive distrust of authority and a tendency to do the opposite of what he is told—a quality that led him to break away from the Ravagers and make his own way as an independent hero.

Garfield Logan was one of a large number of young metahumans captured by N.O.W.H.E.R.E. and experimented upon in the underground base know as the Colony. With his memory compromised, he fought as Beast Boy in the Culling, a gladiatorial tournament N.O.W.H.E.R.E. used to winnow its captives down to the strongest, who were known as Ravagers. Beast Boy, together with members of the Teen Titans and the time-displaced Legion of Super-Heroes, escaped. While on the run, he fought Brother Blood, from whom Garfield learned of his connection to the Red, the cosmic force inherent in all animal life. Brother Blood wanted to exploit that connection to access the Red Kingdom and the powers there, but Beast Boy escaped to Los Angeles and teamed up with Superboy, determined to find N.O.W.H.E.R.E.'s other Colonies and destroy them.

Before that mission could be carried out, Beast Boy was drawn into the elemental battle in Rotworld after Anton Arcane unleashed the Rot into the world. The Red and Green Kingdoms, representing animal and vegetable energies, united to combat the Rot, which corrupted and possessed a number of other heroes—including Beast Boy's friends in the Teen Titans. Teaming up with Black Orchid and Steel, he rescued Animal Man and they traveled to the last stronghold of the Red, the Parliament of Limbs. From there they journeyed through the Rotworld versions of New Gorilla City and Metropolis to Arcane's fortress where, with the Swamp Thing's help, they defeated Arcane and restored the balance between Red and Green.

The Rotworld events also transformed Beast Boy's appearance. Dating from his captivity in the Colony, his skin and hair—as well as his animal forms—were turned red, due to his bond with the animal force, the Red. Following a battle against the Rotlings, Garfield's skin turned green, possibly because Animal Man drained his link to the Red in a last-ditch battle against Arcane and the Rotlings. **AI**

CLASSIC STORIES

***Doom Patrol* (Vol. 1) #99 (Nov. 1965)** Garfield Logan makes his first appearance, breaking into the Doom Patrol's headquarters. He is given the moniker Beast Boy by Robotman.

***New Titans* (Vol. 1) #97-102 (May-Oct. 1993)** Beast Boy—going by the name of Changeling—makes a devil's bargain with the Brotherhood of Evil to save Cyborg's life.

***Beast Boy* (Vol. 1) #1-4 (Jan.-Apr. 2000)** Beast Boy's Super Hero and TV careers collide following the breakup of Titans West. A doppelgänger frames him for several crimes—he finds out it is the villain Gemini, and defeats her.

ANIMAL MAGIC
Beast Boy's laid-back charm and wit belied his true animal instincts, fearsome powers and tenacious spirit.

ANI-MORPH
Beast Boy can change into any animal form, whether it's an existing creature or one he's made up himself.

ON THE RECORD

Before becoming a mentor to later versions of the Teen Titans, Beast Boy had his own struggles, particularly when his adoptive father Steve Dayton—also known as Mento—suffered paranoid delusions. Trying to save him, Garfield stole the Mento Helmet, which affected him as it had its creator, giving his animal transformations a more violent edge.

Historically, Beast Boy was always green due to a side effect of the experimental process his scientist father used to save his life from a rare tropical disease. His appearance helped him carve out a brief career as a television actor in the series *Space Trek: 2022*.

SNAKE IN THE GRASS
Attempting to give his girlfriend Terra a "cobra kiss" during a playful training session, Gar Logan never suspected that she secretly conspired to destroy the Teen Titans.

BIRDS OF PREY

DATA

DEBUT *Black Canary/Oracle: Birds of Prey* #1 **(Jun. 1996)**
CURRENT VERSION *Birds of Prey* (Vol. 3) #1 **(Nov. 2011)**
BASE Gotham City
NOTABLE MEMBERS POWERS **BLACK CANARY** Martial arts; Canary Cry sonic attack; **BATGIRL** Unarmed combat, computer whiz, photographic memory; **HUNTRESS** Martial arts, superalative archery skills; **STARLING** Firearms, martial arts; **KATANA** Soultaker sword traps souls of opponents; **POISON IVY** Plant manipulation and pheromonal powers; **STRIX** Superior combat skills, stealth; **CONDOR** Telekinesis, psionic ability
ALLIES Mother Eve
ENEMIES Choke, Basilisk, Rā's al Ghūl

REBIRTH

NEW BIRDS
Barbara Gordon (aka Batgirl) unites her sisterly allies to defeat a new threat to Gotham City, a criminal who has hijacked her old identity—Oracle.
1 Batgirl (Barbara Gordon)
2 Black Canary (Dinah Drake)
3 Huntress (Helena Bertinelli)

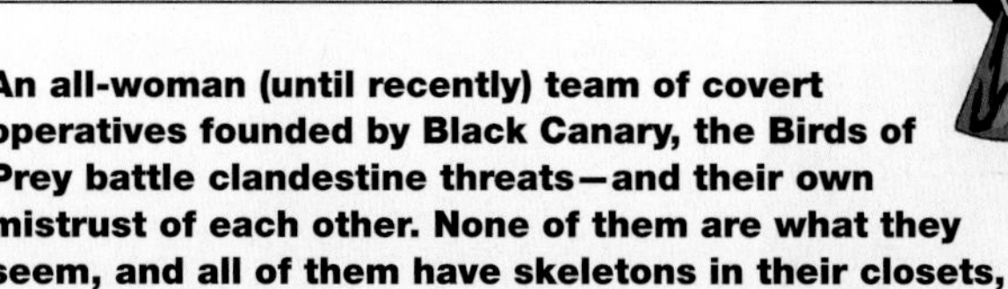

An all-woman (until recently) team of covert operatives founded by Black Canary, the Birds of Prey battle clandestine threats—and their own mistrust of each other. None of them are what they seem, and all of them have skeletons in their closets, but when they band together they are more than any villain can handle.

COURT APPEARANCE
The Birds met their first real test as a group against the mysterious Court of Owls, which was later revealed to have corrupted the Birds of Prey team from within.

The Birds of Prey came together when Amanda Waller manipulated Team 7's Black Canary and Starling into cooperating on a string of covert missions. The pair then began investigating a series of break-ins at research facilities, adding Poison Ivy, Katana, and Batgirl to their team. They traced the crimes to a villain calling himself Choke, and ended his scheme to transform people into human bombs using nanotechnology, .

They next fought the Court of Owls, a battle in which Poison Ivy was badly hurt. They took her to heal in the Heart of the Green, where she revealed she had poisoned the team to force them to join her war against environmental criminals. Katana killed Poison Ivy and then left the team following the theft of her Soultaker sword. Strix and Condor joined to replenish the team's numbers, which took a hit again when Starling betrayed them to Mr. Freeze and the Court of Owls.

Black Canary later discovered the group called Basilisk was holding her comatose husband Kurt—whom she had thought dead—hostage, and its leader was her former Team 7 partner Dean Higgins. After defeating Basilisk, Black Canary quit the Birds, furious at Amanda Waller, who had known Kurt was alive. Rā's al Ghūl offered her a vial of healing serum from his Lazarus Pits in exchange for her promise not to interfere with his plot against the mysterious Mother Eve. Torn, she fought al Ghūl's League of Assassins before learning that he had planned to betray her all along. Chastened, Black Canary rejoined the Birds just in time for Waller to reveal one last secret that finally broke the team—though Mother Eve, who was observing events, suggested that the future held more for the Birds of Prey. **AI**

ON THE RECORD

Originally a partnership between Oracle and the Black Canary, the Birds of Prey did not start calling themselves by that name until they had added other members: first Huntress, and later Lady Blackhawk. Other female heroes rotated through the team, but its core membership remained that first quartet.

Barbara Gordon's transformation from Oracle back to Batgirl also remade the fundamental dynamic of the Birds of Prey. Originally Oracle brought in Black Canary on operations because Oracle could not undertake missions herself while confined to her wheelchair.

SOUL SISTERS
The Birds of Prey, with Oracle and Black Canary front and center, after the Canary's return to the team.

SUICIDE PREVENTION
The Birds tangled with the Suicide Squad after Mother Eve sent them on a rescue mission to the Democratic Republic of Congo.

CLASSIC STORIES

***Black Canary/Oracle: Birds of Prey* #1 (Jun. 1996)** Black Canary is hired by Oracle to be a bodyguard to businessman Nick Devine. She soon learns that he is a terrorist and takes him down, establishing a partnership with Oracle.

***Birds of Prey* (Vol. 1) #56-59 (Aug.-Nov. 2003)** Black Canary is trapped and tortured by Savant and Creote in an attempt to make Oracle divulge Batman's identity. Huntress is brought in to rescue Black Canary.

***Birds of Prey* (Vol. 1) #75 (Dec. 2004)** Big changes are in the air as Oracle's original Gotham Clock Tower headquarters are destroyed and Lady Blackhawk is added to the team as pilot of its new mobile base, Aerie One.

BIZARRO SUPERMAN

DATA

DEBUT *Superboy* (Vol. 1) #68 **(Nov. 1958)**
CURRENT VERSION *Superman* (Vol. 3) #23.1 *Bizarro* **(Nov. 2013)**
REAL NAME Subject B-Zero, B-0
BASE LexCorp Labs, Metropolis
HEIGHT 6ft 3in **WEIGHT** 345 lbs
EYES Black **HAIR** Black
POWERS/ABILITIES Super-strength, speed, flight, invulnerability, flame breath, and Arctic vision.
ALLIES Lex Luthor
ENEMIES The Crime Syndicate, Mazahs/Alexander Luthor, Ultraman
AFFILIATIONS Injustice League

WORK IN PROGRESS
When he was forced to curtail B-0's gestation, Luthor had no idea how powerfully his experiment would affect his own feelings and conscience.

CLASSIC STORIES

***Superman* (Vol. 1) #140 (Oct. 1960)** Bizarro #1 leads a backwards battalion of imperfect Superman doppelgangers in a war against Earth to reclaim his misplaced first-born son.

***World's Finest Comics* (Vol. 1) #156 (Mar. 1966)** When Bizarro-Superman and Bizarro-Batman visit Earth to act as helpful fill-ins for the absent heroes, they become the unwitting pawns of the ever crafty Joker.

***Action Comics* (Vol. 1) #855–857 (Oct.–Dec. 2007)** Experimented upon by Lex Luthor, a psychologically wounded and existentially lonely Bizarro flees Earth. He then creates his own square planet in space and populates it with warped copies of Superman's friends and family.

TEETHING TROUBLE
When Subject A-0 proved to be a dead end, Luthor swiftly moved from nanobots and gene-splicing to cloning in his search for a super-slave.

The insidious experiment that named itself Bizarro was not the first of its kind and, thanks to the perseverance of his creator, will not be the last. Possessing many Kryptonian abilities—albeit warped and twisted—the creature's purpose was simple and clear-cut. As Earth seemed destined to be plagued by superhumans, billionaire businessman Lex Luthor was going to have his own personal army of them...

When Luthor first mapped Superman's genome, he spliced it with genetically modified human DNA, hoping to create a superpowered creature superior to both. The result of over two years' work was then injected into frail, simple-minded volunteer Bobby, whose greatest dream was to be stronger.

Unfortunately when "Subject A-0" was bathed in yellow solar rays, he experienced catastrophic cell division and multiplication, and went completely berserk. Forced to destroy his aberrant super-servant, Luthor went back to the drawing board. He realized that human DNA was too fragile for his purposes and opted for a fully Kryptonian clone. Setting Subject B-0's creation in motion, Luthor deemed the many years it would take to be an acceptable cost if the end result was an army of Supermen he could control.

Luthor's plan changed significantly when Earth was conquered by the Crime Syndicate of Earth-3, who had convinced most of the world's criminal metahumans to work for them. Refusing to acknowledge anyone as his master and with almost all Super Heroes vanquished, Luthor could only recruit a few fellow malcontents to his cause. As such, he was forced to unleash his latest experimental subject far too early in its development phase to supplement his strike power.

The shambling, incoherent, unfinished creature was like an adoring child, delighted to fight or kill for Luthor, and was instrumental in defeating the Syndicators. When Lex was brutally attacked by his own Earth-3 iteration, Alexander Luthor—aka Mazahs—Bizarro valiantly saved his "father" at the cost of his own unnatural life. **WW**

ON THE RECORD

Bizarro first appeared as a misunderstood copy of Superboy. Thanks to the Silver Age Luthor, he returned to bedevil Superman, but became a popular humor-oriented adversary of the Man of Steel. He even had his own comedic series in *Adventure Comics*.

However, the bludgeoning beast revived in the 1980s was far from funny. An anti-Superman weapon created by Luthor, he self-destructed in combat, but returned three more times. The longest-lived version of Bizarro was created by the Joker using Mr. Mxyzptlk's purloined magic as the 21st century began.

A MIRROR CRACK'D
Each iteration of Bizarro was more tragically misunderstood than malign, but his overwhelming power and limited intellect always made him dangerous.

CHILDLIKE DEVOTION
A terrifying, superpowered titan with the mind of a confused child, Bizarro was utterly devoted to his creator.

BLACK ALICE

DEBUT *Birds of Prey* (Vol. 1) #76 (Jan. 2005)
CURRENT VERSION *Secret Six* (Vol. 4) #1 (Feb. 2015)
REAL NAME Lori Zechlin
HEIGHT 5ft 5in **WEIGHT** 110 lbs
EYES Blue **HAIR** Black
POWERS/ABILITIES Able to tap into and steal the powers of any mystical beings.
ALLIES Zatanna, Big Shot
ENEMIES Most of Earth's sorcerers, mystics
AFFILIATIONS Secret Six

Troubled teen Lori Zechlin wasn't aware that she died in the accident which killed her parents. The rebellious, death-obsessed Goth-girl had been messing around with pagan magic for months, and in the moment of her death, called out instinctively to the great beyond.

Something dark answered, moving quietly into her head where it lurks unobserved. Now "Black Alice" only knows that since the accident she can instinctively manifest the powers of any supernatural entity in the world, known or unknown.

She reluctantly joined other outcasts in the Secret Six, but has become a true trouble-magnet. Her powers trigger at random, endangering everyone around her. Who knows what will happen when she learns she cannot age or die? **WW**

LOOKS ARE DECEIVING
Despite her youth and appearance, her powerful and unpredictable abilities make Black Alice one of the most dangerous teenagers on Earth.

BLACK ADAM

DEBUT *Marvel Family* (Vol. 1) #1 (Dec. 1945)
CURRENT VERSION *Justice League* (Vol. 2) #10 (Aug. 2012)
REAL NAME Teth-Adam
BASE Kahndaq; Philadelphia
HEIGHT 6ft 3in **WEIGHT** 250 lbs
EYES Brown **HAIR** Black
POWERS/ABILITIES Immortality, super-speed, strength, endurance, invulnerability, flight; magically-enhanced perceptions and intellect; teleportation; self-healing and the ability to instantly heal others.
ALLIES Lex Luthor, Injustice League
ENEMIES Shazam
AFFILIATIONS Council of Eternity

LIGHTNING WAR
Arrogant Black Adam could never accept that a mere child could wield the power of Shazam, or match his wisdom.

Four thousand years ago, the wizard Shazam granted the pure-of-heart Khandaqui youth Aman the power of the gods to avenge his murdered family and save his nation from an invading oppressor. The noble, selfless hero requested the power be shared with his dying uncle Teth-Adam. It was a fatal mistake.

Adam killed his nephew and, after liberating the occupied Kahndaq and capturing the infamous Seven Sins, slaughtered the immortal Council of Eternity before Shazam finally imprisoned him.

More recently, Black Adam was accidentally freed and went after the young Billy Batson who had recently inherited Shazam's mantle and extraordinary powers. Seeking them for his own, Adam was tricked by the boy into resuming his mortal form and four millennia instantly caught up with the rapidly aging villain.

Billy returned Black Adam's remains to Kahndaq, where a freedom-fighter who venerated this legend sacrificed herself to restore him. Adam returned in time to battle the Crime Syndicate and subsequently vanished to work on his own plans. **MM**

ON THE RECORD

The original Black Adam was an outright villain and bully, but after his reintroduction in the mid-1990s was re-imagined as a more nuanced—if still extremely ruthless—character.

Adam even joined the Justice Society of America (JSA) where his hard-line views swayed many of the younger recruits. Obsessed with his ancient homeland of Kahndaq, he and his disciples eventually broke away from the JSA, sparking a civil war in the team's ranks.

ANCIENT, MY ENEMY
Hawkman had been Adam's trusted ally and comrade in ancient Egypt, but knew his old-world solutions could never work in a complex modern society.

NO REST FOR THE WICKED
Empowered by Egyptian gods, the former slave Teth-Adam dealt harshly with all forms of oppression and those who stood in the way of his dark justice.

BLACK CANARY

DATA

DEBUT *Flash Comics* #86 **(Aug. 1947)**
CURRENT VERSION *Birds of Prey* (Vol. 3) #1 **(Nov. 2011)**
REAL NAME Dinah Drake
BASE Gotham City
HEIGHT 5ft 7in **WEIGHT** 130 lbs
EYES Blue **HAIR** Blond
POWERS/ABILITIES Expert in martial arts with extensive military training; metahuman ability allows her to emit a piercing sound—"the canary cry"—that can shatter metal.
ALLIES Batman
ENEMIES Basilisk, Ocean Master
AFFILIATIONS Team 7, Birds of Prey, Justice League

CLASSIC STORIES

***Flash Comics* #92 (Feb. 1948)**
Black Canary gets her first strip. Dinah Drake is a mild-mannered florist before she adopts her Black Canary persona in order to fight crime.

***Justice League* #1 (May 1987)**
Black Canary sported a new look as she joined the Justice League International, becoming a key member of the Martian Manhunter's new line-up.

***Black Canary/Oracle: Birds of Prey* (Jun. 1996)**
Dinah starts working for Oracle, not realizing to begin with that Oracle is former acquaintance Barbara Gordon.

CANARY CRY
Black Canary can emit a powerful sound wave—her "Canary Cry"—that is able to stop large opponents in their tracks.

KICK START
The young Dinah was taken in and trained in martial arts by the master Desmond Lamar. She would eventually inherit his dojo.

Black Canary has been many things—black ops agent, fugitive, Super Hero, and rock star. She has trained with some of the best martial artists in the world, while her "canary cry" gives her an edge in combat. She was a key member of Team 7 and later founded the Birds of Prey, fighting alongside heroines such as Starling, Poison Ivy, and Batgirl. She has also been a member of the Justice League.

Dinah Drake raised herself on the streets of Gotham City after being abandoned by her mother. Martial arts teacher and ex-special forces agent Desmond Lamar took her in and became a father figure to the ten-year-old Dinah. He trained her in the martial arts and she eventually inherited his dojo. During a blackout in Gotham City, the dojo was burnt down by rioters. With nothing left for her in Gotham City, she accepted John Lynch's offer to join Team 7 (a covert military special ops unit). While part of the team, Dinah's metahuman ability was unleashed. She fought alongside and married Kurt Lance, but he was apparently killed when Dinah's cry destroyed the island base where Team 7 was conducting a mission.

On the run after quitting the team, she briefly worked undercover at the Penguin's Iceberg Lounge as part of the security team, trying to bring the metahuman terrorists of Basilisk to justice. After meeting Evelyn Crawford (later known as Starling) and Batgirl (Barbara Gordon) at the Lounge, she formed the Birds of Prey. Dinah remained good friends with Barbara after the team split. Seeking a new challenge, Dinah formed a band—calling herself D.D.—and was soon fronting a new group called Black Canary. Although she started to make a name for herself as a rock star, her crime-fighting past was never far behind, with fights often breaking out at her shows when villains attacked. **AC**

ON THE RECORD

Before the reality-changing events of Flashpoint, Dinah Lance was the daughter of the original Black Canary—a hero in the 1940s and a member of the JSA. Young Dinah had a superpower her mother had lacked—her "Canary Cry"—and was taught to fight by Ted Grant (Wildcat in the JSA). She gained a new outfit (without her iconic fishnets) when she joined the Justice League International. Her long, tempestuous relationship with Oliver Queen (the Green Arrow) eventually led to their marriage.

SIDE-BY-SIDE
Black Canary and Green Arrow formed a long-running crime-fighting partnership.

D.D. ROCKS
Dinah tried to turn her back on violence and embarked on a career as a rock singer in her band Black Canary.

B

THE BLACK GLOVE

DEBUT *Batman* (Vol. 1) #667 (Aug. 2007)
MEMBERS Dr. Simon Hurt, Jezebel Jet, Cardinal Maggi, Al-Khidr, Sir Anthony, General Malenkov, Senator Vine

The Black Glove was a criminal organization formed by Thomas Wayne in the 1700s and later led by Dr. Simon Hurt, who used the group to target Batman. Its membership comprised wealthy men and women, often in positions of power. But its connections ran through all levels of society, from the actors the group used in their schemes through to high-ranking officials.

The group came close to defeating Batman, almost driving him insane, before the Dark Knight and his allies defeated them and Hurt was seemingly killed in a helicopter explosion. The Black Glove were counting on the fact that even if their scheme failed, Batman wasn't a killer. They hadn't counted on Batman's links to Talia al Ghūl. Within six months, Talia's League of Assassins had eliminated most of the Black Glove's members. **AC**

BLACK HAND

DEBUT *Green Lantern* (Vol. 2) #29 (Jun. 1964)
CURRENT VERSION *Green Lantern* (Vol. 5) #7 (Mar. 2012)
REAL NAME William Hand
BASE Ryut, Sector 666; Coast City
HEIGHT 5ft 7in **WEIGHT** 165 lbs **EYES** Brown **HAIR** Black
POWERS/ABILITIES Using his black power ring, can reanimate the dead and steal energy by killing his victims and tearing out their hearts.
ALLIES Nekron
ENEMIES Green Lantern (Hal Jordan), Green Lantern Corps

William Hand was raised in a funeral parlor. Obsessed with death, he was chosen by Nekron, Lord of the Unliving, as his avatar. Nekron continually whispered to the boy, slowly driving him insane. Hand killed his parents, took his own life, and was reborn as a Black Lantern. Soon he commanded a vast army of the risen dead—the Black Lantern Corps.

During the Blackest Night, the Green Lanterns teamed up with other Corps to fight Nekron and the Black Lanterns as they tried to destroy the White Entity hidden on Earth. Hand was eventually defeated and returned to life by the White Entity. Taken in by the Indigo Tribe, he escaped and killed himself. A black power ring emerged from his body and he was raised from the dead as a Black Lantern. Seeking revenge, Hand replaced his own hand with that of Green Lantern Hal Jordan's dead father, swearing to kill Jordan with his father's own hand. He failed, and Jordan imprisoned him in the Source Wall at the end of the universe. **AC**

ON THE RECORD

Black Hand may be one of the Green Lantern's deadliest foes, but it wasn't always that way. The original Black Hand was a minor Green Lantern villain who would sometimes break the fourth wall to talk directly to the reader.

Shortly before Hal Jordan's "rebirth" as a Green Lantern, the Spectre (then Jordan) turned one of the villain's hands to coal dust as punishment when he tried to steal Hal's green power ring from the Green Arrow.

PRELUDE TO BLACKEST NIGHT
Death-obsessed William Hand was the doorway to absolute darkness for the demonic alien Atrocitus. After using Atrocitus' cosmic rod to take his own life, Hand would rise from the dead to become the grimmest reaper of all.

BLACK LANTERN CORPS

DEBUT *Green Lantern* (Vol. 4) #25 (Jan. 2008)
BASE Ryut, Sector 666
POWERS/ABILITIES Members are reanimated dead, able to infect the living with their bite and regenerate damaged flesh. They recharge their central power battery by removing the hearts from their victims.
ENEMIES Green Lantern (Hal Jordan), Green Lantern Corps
AFFILIATIONS Nekron

The Black Lanterns are an undead army brought back to the land of the living by Nekron, Lord of the Unliving, to wage war against the various Corps of the Emotional Spectrum. They use black power rings, which reanimate the dead and also symbolize the absence of emotion and life. Using Black Hand as his avatar, Nekron unleashed a full-on assault on Earth with countless numbers of the dead—including many heroes—returning as Black Lanterns.

Black Lanterns often sought to consume the heart of those who cared for them most—this emotional pain helping to empower Nekron. While the Black Lantern Corps was defeated during the "Blackest Night," Black Hand subsequently returned as his master's avatar on several occasions, each time threatening to bring more death and destruction into existence. Even Green Lantern Hal Jordan briefly became a Black Lantern, when the path seemed to be the only way to defeat Volthoom, the First Lantern. Hal raised an army of the undead and even Nekron himself before defeating Volthoom. He was then returned to life by a Green Lantern power ring. **AC**

ON THE RECORD

While Black Hand was the first member of the Black Lantern Corps, others soon followed. Among them were a number of long-dead heroes, including Elongated Man and Sue Dibny, Hawkman, Hawkgirl, and Aquaman. The Black Lanterns often attacked those closest to them to gain greater impact from their deaths. The dead parents of both Tim Drake (Robin) and Dick Grayson (Batman) returned as Black Lanterns, as did the clone of Bruce Wayne.

DARKEST KNIGHT
Batman's clone was raised from the dead as a Black Lantern.

BLACK LIGHTNING

DATA

DEBUT *Black Lightning* #1 **(Apr. 1977)**
CURRENT VERSION *DC Universe Presents* #13 **(Dec. 2012)**
BASE Los Angeles
REAL NAME Jefferson Pierce
HEIGHT 6ft 1in **WEIGHT** 182 lbs **EYES** Brown **HAIR** Black
POWERS/ABILITIES Olympic-level athlete; creation and control of lightning and electromagnetic fields.
ALLIES Blue Devil
ENEMIES Tobias Whale, Nebiros
AFFILIATIONS Outsiders, JLA

ARMY OF DARKNESS
Black Lightning had to take on a demonic army of addicts corrupted by the supernatural drug Nebiros created with crime lord Tobias Whale.

BLACK AND BLUE
Following an initial misunderstanding, Black Lightning teamed up with Blue Devil to take on the drug lord, Tobias Whale.

Former Olympic decathlete Jefferson Pierce is a committed teacher at Los Angeles' Grassland High School by day. At night, he becomes the vigilante Black Lightning and protects the city's children from threats the L.A.P.D. could not—or would not—handle themselves.

Hunting down drug dealers responsible for selling in the high school where he teaches, Black Lightning ran into the Blue Devil, who was also tracking the same drug dealers. The two initially clashed because Pierce suspected the Blue Devil of being in league with the oversized crime lord Tobias Whale.

After their misunderstanding, the pair banded together to bring down "the Whale" and his operation, while Pierce's journalist father, Alvin, worked to expose Whale's operation. After they disrupted a major drug deal, the gangster struck back by drawing the two heroes out into the open, where his thugs could attack them. He also threatened their families, killing Blue Devil's grandfather and turning his sights on Alvin Pierce. At the same time, Black Lightning discovered that Tobias Whale had made a deal with the demon Nebiros to use Blue Devil to provide Nebiros with a supply of souls. Whale would then use the souls to create a supernaturally addictive drug.

As the new drug began to hit the streets and Nebiros' demonic army grew, Black Lightning and Blue Devil prepared for a final showdown, given special urgency because Jefferson's father, Alvin, was now squarely in Whale's crosshairs. Black Lightning appeared to be killed, saving his father in the final battle against Whale and Nebiros' forces. However, he was later seen mulling over an offer to join the Justice League of America—suggesting that at least part of that story has yet to come to light. **AI**

ELECTRIC POWERHOUSE
Thanks to his Olympic training, Black Lightning is in peak physical condition. He can generate and manipulate electricity at will.

ON THE RECORD

Black Lightning was DC Comics' first African-American hero to have his own solo series. Jefferson Pierce was a teacher at Garfield High School in Metropolis' notorious Suicide Slum. Pierce tried to clear out mob-connected drug pushers from his school and was driven to vigilantism as Black Lightning after one of his students was murdered by Tobias Whale and the crime organization, the 100.

Pierce didn't realize the full extent of his powers until his first term of duty with the Outsiders, when a latent metagene enabled him to internalize and amplify his lightning powers. Previous to that, he used an electronic belt to generate shock attacks and disguised himself using a costume created by his childhood mentor, tailor Peter Gambi.

LIGHTNING STRIKES
Black Lightning defended the inhabitants of Metropolis' Suicide Slum and kept them safe from drug dealers.

CLASSIC STORIES

***Black Lightning* #3–5 (Jul.–Nov. 1977)** Hunting down Tobias Whale, Black Lightning runs afoul of Superman when the Man of Steel thinks Pierce has hurt Jimmy Olsen.

***Amazons Attack* (Vol. 1) #1 (Jun. 2007)** As a founding member of a new Justice League, Black Lightning saves the President's life when the Amazons of Themyscira invade Washington, DC.

***Black Lightning: Year One* #1–6 (Mar.–Aug. 2009)** Black Lightning's origin is retold as he crosses paths with Superman and Lois Lane during his quest to avenge the death of student Earl Clifford.

BLACK MANTA

DATA

DEBUT *Aquaman* (Vol. 1) #35 **(Sep.–Oct. 1967)**
CURRENT VERSION *Aquaman* (Vol. 7) #7 **(May 2012)**
HEIGHT 6ft 2in **WEIGHT** 205 lbs
EYES Black **HAIR** Bald
POWERS/ABILITIES Engineering and technological expertise; skilled with knives; armored suit tailored for underwater use; enhanced strength; energy blasts projected from helmet's lenses.
ALLIES Vulko
ENEMIES Aquaman, the Others
AFFILIATIONS Secret Society of Super-Villains, Suicide Squad

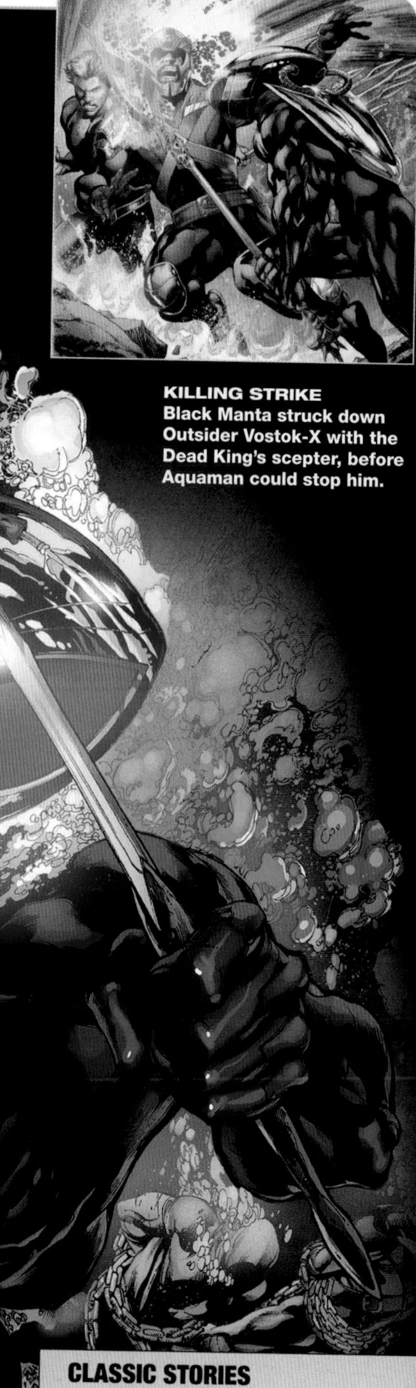

KILLING STRIKE
Black Manta struck down Outsider Vostok-X with the Dead King's scepter, before Aquaman could stop him.

VIOLENT OBSESSION
From the outset Black Manta was driven by a homicidal mania for revenge against Aquaman.

Prone to violence from childhood, Black Manta was driven by an obsessive hatred for Aquaman and desire to avenge the killing of his father. He devoted his adult life to killing the King of the Seven Seas and destroying everything he cared about, whether his family or the kingdom of Atlantis itself.

Black Manta's origin and real name are unknown, but he swore revenge on Aquaman after the Atlantean king accidentally killed his father following Manta's attack on Aquaman's own father, Tom Curry. Possessing a variety of high-tech devices and weapons—though he favored a pair of long daggers—he became an accomplished treasure hunter. After killing two of Aquaman's teammates in the Others—Kahina and Vostok-X—Manta stole Atlantean artifacts, including an enchanted scepter, for the traitorous Atlantean Vulko, who planned to use it to resurrect the Dead King. Defeated by Aquaman and the Others while delivering the scepter, Black Manta dared Aquaman to kill him. Despite his desire to avenge his dead friends, Aquaman refused.

Black Manta was imprisoned in Belle Reve, where he rejected Amanda Waller's offer to join the Suicide Squad. He was freed when the Outsider gathered the Secret Society of Super-Villains to help the Crime Syndicate of America take over Earth. When Ultraman moved the Moon to block the sun, the resulting tidal wave broke open Black Manta's father's grave. This violation turned Black Manta against the Crime Syndicate, and after locating Black Adam's body, formed an alliance with other defecting members of the Secret Society, including Lex Luthor and Captain Cold. They brought Black Adam back to life and teamed up with the Justice League in an alliance of convenience to fight the Crime Syndicate. Black Manta killed the Outsider and then, refusing an offer of amnesty, disappeared, though he has recently resurfaced to resume his vendetta against Aquaman. **AI**

ON THE RECORD

Earlier versions of Black Manta revealed slightly more of the character's origin, telling the story of a boy kidnapped and forced into abusive servitude aboard a ship. Spotting Aquaman, he signaled for help, but when the hero did not see him, the boy grew to hate him and the sea he represented. This led to him creating the Black Manta persona and a deadly arsenal of marine weapons and vehicles.

Black Manta's uncontrollable rage ultimately caused the death of Aquababy, turning a one-sided obsession into a mutual blood feud. Ultimately Aquaman defeated the villain, but refused to compromise his ideals by exacting vengeance. This act further enraged Black Manta and he went on to sell his soul to the demon Neron.

DEATH OF AQUABABY
The infant son of Aquaman and Queen Mera, Arthur Curry, Jr. was murdered by Black Manta and buried at Mercy Reef.

DEADLY PREDATOR
In his water- and pressure-resistant suit, Black Manta can hunt Aquaman relentlessly throughout the undersea realms.

CLASSIC STORIES

***Aquaman* (Vol. 1) #35 (Sep.–Oct. 1967)** Black Manta's attempt to kidnap Aquababy is thwarted when the Ocean Master frees the baby from Black Manta's ship.

***Adventure Comics* (Vol. 1) #452 (Aug.–Sep. 1977)** Black Manta forces Aquaman and Aqualad to fight each other to the death, or Aquababy will die in a globe filled with air. Aquaman shatters the globe, but too late to save him.

***Brightest Day* #19–20 (Apr.–May 2011)** Black Manta goes hunting for his son, Jackson Hyde, who has been protected by Mera since infancy. He battles Aquaman and Jackson, before Mera seals Manta away in the Bermuda Triangle.

BLACK MASK

DEBUT *Batman* (Vol. 1) #386 (Aug. 1985)
CURRENT VERSION *Detective Comics* (Vol. 2) #9 (Jul. 2012)
REAL NAME Roman Sionis
BASE Gotham City
EYES Brown **HAIR** None
POWERS/ABILITIES Skilled combatant and marksman; mask enables mind-control.
ALLIES Dr. Jeremiah Arkham
ENEMIES Batman, Catwoman, the Mad Hatter

Criminal Roman Sionis carved his signature black mask from his father's coffin. It gave Sionis the ability to control others, and he started his own gang, the False Face Society. While incarcerated at Arkham Asylum, Sionis was separated from his mask, but when the Talons of the Court of Owls attacked the asylum, its director, Dr. Jeremiah Arkham, returned it so that Black Mask could protect him. In the event, Black Mask used the mask to escape.

He then battled the Mad Hatter, who wanted the power of the False Face Society's masks for himself. Batman cracked the mask with a kick, driving Black Mask/Sionis insane. Returned to Arkham Asylum, he was broken out and joined the Secret Society when the Crime Syndicate invaded Earth. He later turned his sights on ruling Gotham City's underworld, but clashed with Catwoman. **SW**

BLACK ORCHID

DEBUT *Adventure Comics* (Vol. 1) #428 (Jul.-Aug. 1973)
CURRENT VERSION *Justice League Dark* #9 (Jul. 2012)
REAL NAME Alba Garcia
EYES Brown **HAIR** Black
POWERS/ABILITIES Her link to the Red and the Green gives her shape-changing abilities that make her a master of disguise.
ALLIES Dr. Mist, A.R.G.U.S., Animal Man
ENEMIES Felix Faust, the Demons Three, Nick Necro
AFFILIATIONS Justice League Dark

Private Alba Garcia was transformed into shapeshifter Black Orchid by A.R.G.U.S.'s Project Ascension, which linked her to the primal forces of the Green and the Red, and gave her superpowers. She joined occult task force Justice League Dark and helped them to keep the Books of Magic out of the hands of sorcerer Felix Faust. The team then traveled to the World of Epoch, where they helped lead a magical rebellion to free the world from the Network.

In this realm, Black Orchid became a Swamp Thing-like monster. She helped Animal Man to fight the malevolent forces of the Rot and, when the Crime Syndicate invaded Earth, she was one of the heroes captured and used to power the magic-channeling Thaumaton weapon. Rescued by Justice League Dark, she briefly joined the group on a mind-bending journey during the war between the House of Mystery and the House of Secrets. **SW**

ON THE RECORD

The original Black Orchid was a mistress of disguise who used her powers to fight crime. She was once a human woman called Susan Linden-Thorne, but when she was killed by her husband, the botanist Philip Sylvain used her DNA to create a human/plant hybrid called Black Orchid. The heroine was killed while investigating LexCorp, but two other plant/human hybrids with her DNA survived and continued the Black Orchid legacy.

DEADLY BLOSSOMING
After being murdered, Linden-Thorne returned as a human/plant hybrid that drew power from the Green, the force created by all plant life on Earth.

BLACK RACER

DEBUT *New Gods* (Vol. 1) #3 (Jun.-Jul. 1971)
CURRENT VERSION *Justice League* (Vol. 2) #44 (Nov. 2015)
EYES Red **HAIR** None
POWERS/ABILITIES Immortal avatar of Death who flies on cosmic skis; can possess other beings; turn intangible at will, and kill with his lightning scythe.
ALLIES Anti-Monitor, the Flash
ENEMIES Darkseid
AFFILIATIONS New Gods

For the New Gods of Apokolips and New Genesis, the mysterious Black Racer is the avatar of Death, relentlessly pursuing those doomed to die. He takes over other beings, using them as vessels while he carries out his forbidding task; Mister Miracle once served as one of his hosts.

Darkseid summoned the deadly Black Racer during his battle with the Anti-Monitor, bonding the Racer with the Flash (Barry Allen). However, the Anti-Monitor used his mastery of Anti-Life to turn the Racer against Darkseid, seemingly killing the dark lord of Apokolips.

Barry attempted to free himself from the Black Racer's control, but the grim entity explained that death was essential to the proper functioning of the universe, showing Barry visions of his dead mother Nora and of Central City reduced to a mausoleum. The Flash tried to slay the Racer with his own scythe, but he was subjected to horrifying visions of what would befall the universe if he refused to become an avatar of Death. This convinced Barry to accept his role as the Black Racer's host.

The Flash and the Black Racer were finally separated by the child of Earth-3's Superwoman and Alexander Luthor, who used his father's power absorption abilities. The Racer then claimed the life of Volthoom before disappearing on his never-ending journey of death. **SW**

IMPLACABLE PURSUIT
The Black Racer chases his prey across time and space to carry out his dark duty.

ON THE RECORD

The Black Racer was a legendary figure in pre-Flashpoint reality, and made his first recorded appearance on Earth after he was diverted there by the New God Metron. He chose handicapped veteran Sgt. Willie Walker as his host and attempted to claim the lives of several heroes, notably Steel. The Black Racer was one of the first victims killed by Infinity Man during the Death of the New Gods event.

FINAL RECKONING
Black Racer could phase through solid objects, fly on cosmically charged skis, and deliver death with a touch. He occasionally used a lethal staff to mete out justice.

BLACKBRIAR THORN

DEBUT *DC Comics Presents* (Vol. 1) #66 (Feb. 1984)
CURRENT VERSION *Justice League Dark* #12 (Oct. 2012)
REAL NAME Blackbriar Thorn
EYES Brown **HAIR** White
POWERS/ABILITIES A powerful magician; can create a treelike body around his frail form; controls plant matter and regenerates.
ENEMIES Superman, the Demon, Justice League Dark

When the Romans invaded Britain, the druid Blackbriar Thorn cast a spell that turned him into a towering, treelike being. Inadvertently buried, he returned to life in the 20th century when dug up and exposed to moonlight. After clashing with Superman and the Demon, Thorn went to live in the Amazon rainforest, where Deadman and Zatanna encountered him. Thorn attacked them, but Deadman possessed him and returned him to human form.

Following this defeat, Thorn allied himself with Felix Faust, Nick Necro, and Dr. Mist against Justice League Dark, but was struck down by Andrew Bennett and turned into inanimate wood. When anti-life force the Rot threatened Earth, Thorn returned and took over Metropolis, but Animal Man defeated him by taking termite form. **SW**

BLACKHAWK

DEBUT *Military Comics* #1 (Aug. 1941)
CURRENT VERSION *Blackhawks* #1 (Nov. 2011)
REAL NAME Andrew Lincoln
EYES Blue **HAIR** White
POWERS/ABILITIES Expert pilot and military veteran with excellent combat and leadership skills.
ALLIES Priscilla Kitaen
ENEMIES Mother Machine, Titus, Voodoo
AFFILIATIONS The Blackhawks, the Black Razors

Andrew Lincoln is a military officer with extensive special operations experience. His personal details remain classified, and he has faked his death more than once, adopting another identity. A skilled pilot and leader, he commanded the UN's secret multinational strike force the Blackhawks. Operating out of their secret base, the Eyrie, the team took on Mother Machine, who plotted to use nanotechnology to transform the world. The Blackhawks destroyed Mother Machine's base, but when team member Kunoichi was taken over by Mother Machine's nanobots, Blackhawk had to destroy the Eyrie to finally take her down.

Lincoln then disbanded the Blackhawks and faked his death, resurfacing in command of the Black Razors, a covert force that impounded alien technology. He sent agents Black Jack and Jessica Fallon to capture human-alien hybrid Voodoo, but the villain killed them. Blackhawk then recruited Priscilla Kitaen, the woman whose DNA was used to create Voodoo, and trained her to take on her clone-sister. Blackhawk and Kitaen tracked Voodoo to the dead city of the Daemonites on Europa, Jupiter's sixth moon, where Priscilla confronted Voodoo in an epic battle that ended in a stalemate. **SW**

ON THE RECORD

The post-Crisis Blackhawk was Janos Prohaska, a Polish fighter pilot who fought in the Spanish Civil War. Following the fall of Poland, he traveled to the UK, where he became the commander of the secret Allied Blackhawk Squadron. Blackhawk's team stayed together after World War II and battled communists and super-villains. They subsequently served as both a courier service (Blackhawk Express) and as part of the Checkmate organization.

FLYING INTO DANGER
Blackhawk led his squadron in thrilling adventures across the globe, where they battled many exotic foes, including the Winged Death cult.

BLACK SPIDER

DEBUT *Detective Comics* (Vol. 1) #463 (Sept. 1976)
CURRENT VERSION *Suicide Squad* (Vol. 4) #1 (Nov. 2011)
REAL NAME Eric Needham
BASE Belle Reve Penitentiary
EYES Brown **HAIR** Black
POWERS/ABILITIES Amazing reflexes; multi-optic helmet with breath mask; wields twin sickles with devastating skill.
ENEMIES Resurrection Man, Amanda Waller

While serving a 60-year term in Belle Reve Penitentiary, masked vigilante Black Spider was selected by Administrator Amanda Waller for her Suicide Squad—a penal unit of villains secretly working for the US government. Black Spider joined Harley Quinn, Deadshot, King Shark, and El Diablo on the team.

He was sidelined by a back injury but soon recovered, and earned a reputation as perhaps the team's most heroic member. Waller even offered to have him released, but he elected to stay with the Suicide Squad. However, Black Spider had an ulterior motive: he was in reality an agent of the Basilisk organization, sent to infiltrate the Suicide Squad and kill Waller. He attacked Waller and her mother, but was captured and imprisoned by his teammates. **SW**

BLACKHAWKS

DEBUT *Military Comics* #1 (Aug. 1941)
CURRENT VERSION *Blackhawks* #1 (Nov. 2011)
BASE The Eyrie
POWERS/ABILITIES Highly experienced elite military personnel with a wide variety of skills; Kunoichi possesses super-strength.
ENEMIES Mother Machine, Titus, Steig Hammer
AFFILIATIONS United Nations

The Blackhawks are a covert multinational force sanctioned by the United Nations to combat hi-tech threats. The team is led by Blackhawk and includes the Irishman, Canada, Kunoichi, Attila, and the mysterious Lady Blackhawk, with Wildman acting as team doctor. The Blackhawks operate out of the secret Eyrie base, which is staffed by androids and serves as a base for a fleet of hi-tech aircraft.

On a mission to Kazakhstan, Kunoichi was infected by nanocites developed by Mother Machine. Canada and Wildman were captured and taken to Mother Machine's HQ, but they escaped and destroyed it. Wildman died in a bomb attack by arms manufacturer Steig Hammer, and when Mother Machine's consciousness took over the Eyrie's systems, Blackhawk had to destroy the base. The Blackhawks then split up. **SW**

BLACKFIRE

DEBUT *Tales of the New Teen Titans* #4 (Sep. 1982)
CURRENT VERSION *Red Hood and the Outlaws* #11 (Sep. 2012)
REAL NAME Komand'r
BASE Tamaran
EYES Green **HAIR** Black
POWERS/ABILITIES Trained in combat and leadership.
ALLIES Koriand'r, Red Hood and the Outlaws
ENEMIES The Blight, the Citadel, Lord Helspont

Komand'r was the eldest child of the rulers of the planet Tamaran, but then the Citadel and their Dominator allies invaded and killed her parents. In the aftermath of the attack, Komand'r agreed to become the conquerors' puppet ruler Blackfire and allow her little sister Koriand'r to be taken from Tamaran in chains.

Eventually, Koriand'r escaped from enslavement and found a home on Earth, joining Red Hood and the Outlaws. When she heard that Tamaran was besieged by the alien Blight she returned there with her friends and was reunited with Komand'r, who begged for forgiveness. The two joined forces to vanquish the Blight. Komand'r appeared to betray her sister and the Earth to the Citadel, but she ultimately helped Koriand'r to fight off the aliens. **SW**

BLASTERS, THE

DEBUT *Invasion!* #1 (Jan. 1989)
MEMBERS POWERS/ABILITIES
"Snapper" Carr Teleportation; **Churljenkins** Piloting; **Dust Devil** Tornado control, **Crackpot** Telepathy; **Frag** Energy projection; **Gunther** Enhanced intellect; **Looking Glass** Deflection; **Jolt** Force-field creation.
ALLIES L.E.G.I.O.N., Valor, Omega Men
ENEMIES The Dominators, Spider Guild, Doctor Bendorion

The alien Dominators invaded Earth and kidnapped 50 humans. As an experiment, they were placed in a kill zone called the Blaster. Most were eliminated, but a handful survived when the threat of death triggered a "metagene" that gave them superpowers. This international group became the Blasters: US conman Crackpot, Israeli kid Dust Devil, model Jolt, Austrian Frag, English author Looking Glass, and disgraced former JLA associate Lucas "Snapper" Carr.

The Blasters were interned in the galactic prison Starlag, but escaped with help from L.E.G.I.O.N., alien pilot Churljenkins and renegade Dominator Gunther. Back on Earth, they battled the Spider Guild and then tried to rescue the hero Valor from Starlag II, but were trapped inside the prison when it was destroyed. Their fate remains unknown, though "Snapper" Carr escaped. **SW**

BLEEZ

DEBUT *Final Crisis: Rage of the Red Lanterns* (Vol. 1) #1 (Dec. 2008)
CURRENT VERSION *Red Lanterns* (Vol. 1) #1 (Nov. 2011)
BASE Sector 33
EYES Blue, Yellow **HAIR** Black
POWERS/ABILITIES Seduction, magic-wielding, able to expel blazing bile; equipped with a Red Lantern ring affording flight, full environmental protection, intergalactic transportation, translation, violent energy projection solid-light constructions.
ALLIES Kyle Rayner
ENEMIES Atrocitus
AFFILIATIONS Red Lantern Corps, New Guardians

A pampered princess on a paradise world, Bleez was abducted by members of the Sinestro Corps. Abused and tortured for their amusement, she escaped, but filled with overwhelming fury and indignation, she was possessed by a red power ring. This suppressed her intellect, making her an explosive slave to boiling rage, and she joined the Red Lantern Corps.

When a series of cosmic catastrophes forced the Emotional Spectrum groups into tenuous alliances, Bleez was assigned to join Green Lantern Kyle Rayner's New Guardians by the Reds' leader Atrocitus. His dissatisfaction at leading a legion of functional fools compelled Atrocitus to restore her mind. Bleez then became his rival, rising to the top of the Red Lantern Corps, wielding every ring Atrocitus had created, but at the moment of her greatest triumph she was freed from her obsessive rage and restored to mortal form by Blue Lantern Guy Gardner. **WW**

ON THE RECORD

Red ring wearers are filled with a boiling, corrosive napalm-like substance that matches the constant feral fury gripping them. This anger, though invaluable in combat, also clouds the mind.

Eventually Corps founder Atrocitus used shamanistic blood magic to restore the intellect without quelling the rage of his subordinates. His mistake was starting with Bleez, who instantly challenged his authority and began plotting to replace him.

CALM BEFORE THE STORM
Her early life as a princess valued only as "marriage material" made Bleez determined that no one would ever control her again.

BIRD ON A WIRE
Harper's electronics genius quickly made her an invaluable asset in Batman's war on crime and defense of Gotham City.

BLIGHT

DEBUT *Justice League Dark* (Vol. 1) #24 (Dec. 2013)
CURRENT VERSION *Justice League Dark* (Vol. 1) #27 (Mar. 2014)
POWERS/ABILITIES Harnesses a mystical accumulation of pettiness and ill-feeling in mankind's collective unconsciousness, the embodiment of despair and evil.
ALLIES Seven Deadly Sins
ENEMIES John Constantine, Phantom Stranger, Pandora, Justice League Dark

Earth-3's Crime Syndicate invasion of Earth took place on a physical and psychic level. Their arrival boosted humanity's worst traits as people engaged in everything from petty transgressions to appalling atrocities. This growing ocean of sin expanded until mankind's collective unconsciousness manifested as a creature of infinite evil: Blight.

Achieving sentience, Blight occupied the body of the recently resurrected boy Chris Esperanza and began attacking Earth. John Constantine detected Blight as he searched for his missing Justice League Dark comrades and was forced to fight the corruption with a substitute team. But Blight was ultimately destroyed by Esperanza, who, having experienced the absolute worst of humanity, gained the knowledge to eradicate the beast from within. **WW**

BLOCKBUSTER

DEBUT *Detective Comics* (Vol. 1) #345 (Nov. 1965)
CURRENT VERSION *Hawk and Dove* (Vol. 5) #6 (Apr. 2012)
BASE Gotham City
POWERS/ABILITIES Superhuman strength, enhanced stamina
REAL NAME Mark Desmond
ALLIES Necromancer, Outsider
ENEMIES Batman, Hawk and Dove
AFFILIATIONS Secret Society of Super-Villains

Mark Desmond wanted to be smarter, and so became a willing subject of Dr. Phayne's radical experiments. One night, Mark was accidentally subjected to a massive overdose of Phayne's chemical compound and was transformed into a simple-minded behemoth of immense physical might and durability. But his power was no protection against psychic assaults, and he was promptly subjugated by the enigmatic Necromancer, who needed him to steal an arcane artifact from a Washington, DC museum. This brought Blockbuster into conflict with Batman and Robin, and Hawk and Dove.

Blockbuster later resurfaced with the Secret Society of Super-Villains, recruited by the Outsider to pave the way for the invasion of Earth-3's Crime Syndicate. **WW**

BLOODSPORT

DEBUT *Superman* (Vol. 2) #4 (Apr. 1987)
CURRENT VERSION *Superman* (Vol. 1) #652 (Jul. 2006)
BASE Metropolis
POWERS/ABILITIES Teleportation, instant inter-dimensional access to arsenal of advanced armaments and weapons
REAL NAME Robert DuBois; Alex Trent
ALLIES Riot, Hellgrammite
ENEMIES Superman

Bloodsport is the name used by a succession of fanatics who have battled Superman. Using technology provided by Lex Luthor, the deranged Robert DuBois repeatedly attempted to kill the Man of Steel with futuristic firearms teleported directly into his hands, many firing Kryptonite bullets.

Dubois died in battle and his gadgetry fell into the hands of the demon Bloodthirst, who bonded it to radical white supremacist Alex Trent. This Bloodsport began murdering minority citizens, but was defeated by Superman and killed in prison by his own Aryan Brotherhood colleagues. The third, unidentified Bloodsport took over the technology and costume but pursued no ideological agenda, acting as a super-powered mercenary for major criminals. **WW**

BLUEBIRD

DEBUT *Batman* (Vol. 2) #7 (May 2012)
CURRENT VERSION (As Bluebird) *Batman Eternal* (Vol. 1) #41 (May 2015)
REAL NAME Harper Row
BASE Gotham City
EYES Brown **HAIR** Purple
POWERS/ABILITIES Electrical engineering and computers, marksmanship, combat.
ALLIES Red Robin, Batman, Alfred Pennyworth
ENEMIES Tiger Shark, Mad Hatter

Streetwise Harper Row might have ended up very different had Batman not saved her brother Cullen from being beaten in a hate crime. From then on she was obsessed with the Dark Knight, resolving to help him make Gotham City a better, safer place. Her first overture was to locate the devices Batman used to avoid the city's surveillance cameras. Upgrading and improving them, she began to regularly insert herself into his cases. But having just lost his son Damian, Batman responded with uncharacteristic brutality. He had no desire to see more brave kids die. Harper quietly persisted, however, and eventually won him over after she saved his life during his battle against the Court of Owls.

Her graduation to costumed crime-fighter came after she joined Red Robin to save Cullen and other kids from the Mad Hatter. However, instead of becoming the latest Robin, Harper created her own masked persona: Bluebird. **WW**

BLUE DEVIL

DEBUT *Firestorm* (Vol. 2) #24 **(Jun. 1984)**
CURRENT VERSION *DC Universe Presents* (Vol. 1) #13 **(Dec. 2012)**
BASE Los Angeles
HEIGHT 6ft 8in **WEIGHT** 385 lbs
EYES Red **HAIR** None
POWERS/ABILITIES When wearing the demon skin, possesses enhanced strength, speed, durability, assorted magical tricks, and a mystic trident.
REAL NAME Daniel Cassidy
ALLIES Black Lightning
ENEMIES Nebiros, Tobias Whale
AFFILIATIONS The Enclave

Daniel Cassidy is an actor and stuntman. He is also the last son in an ancient line tasked with safeguarding the world's most potent supernatural relics. These were cunningly hidden in plain sight as movie props in his grandfather Liam's horror film studio. Daniel dreamed of being a Super Hero, and when he came upon a Blue Devil bodysuit on the shelves, he decided to "borrow" it. He began prowling the streets of Los Angeles, fighting thugs working for the unassailable crime overlord Tobias Whale. This crusade—which also involved his old schoolfriend Jeff Pierce in the guise of Black Lightning—resulted in Liam's murder, and the discovery that the suit was in fact the skin of a demon named Nebiros, and its special effects were genuinely magical.

As Blue Devil, Daniel became increasingly wild and uncontrollable, with new powers manifesting constantly. His war against the Whale eventually aroused Nebiros, who came to Earth to reclaim his hide. In the epic battle that followed, the skin rejected the arch-demon and instead helped Daniel imprison him. From those early exploits, Blue Devil rose to pre-eminence amongst Earth's arcane defenders, battling beside Justice League Dark, Pandora, and the Secret Six. **WW**

ON THE RECORD

Blue Devil was originally a light-hearted, irrepressible adventurer bonded into a mechanical outfit by demonic magic and cursed to be a magnet for weirdness. His constant battles against dark magic and supernatural menaces mutated his form even further.

He joined a succession of teams such as the Justice League and Sentinels of Magic and even briefly became the Prince of Hell before becoming the heavy hitter of mystical super-team Shadowpact.

LUCKY DEVIL
Cassidy's power came at a cost: his mystical enhancements attracted wild magic and triggered all manner of weird happenings.

BLUE LANTERN CORPS

DEBUT *Green Lantern* (Vol. 4) #25 **(Jan. 2008)**
CURRENT VERSION *Green Lantern: New Guardians* (Vol. 1) #1 **(Nov. 2011)**
BASE Odym, Elpis
POWERS/ABILITIES Power rings channel the blue light of Hope, powering flight, intergalactic travel, and self-defense.
CURRENT MEMBERS Saint Walker, Guy Gardner
ALLIES Hal Jordan, Kyle Rayner
ENEMIES Red Lantern Corps, Larfleeze, the Reach
AFFILIATIONS Green Lantern Corps

Following the war between the Green Lanterns and Sinestro Corps, maverick Guardians of the Universe Ganthet and Sayd were banished from Oa. They settled on Odym, building a Central Power Battery to harness the Emotional Spectrum's blue light of Hope. They were soon joined by wanderer Saint Walker, who became their first agent.

Blue rings are primarily defensive. Aggressive capabilities like energy-blasts only activate when they are in close proximity to a Green Lantern ring. The same connection automatically boosts an emerald warrior's ring up to 300 percent beyond its normal charge capacity.

Run like an order of monks, Blue Lanterns were recruited slowly, with each new member responsible for finding the next. When Odym was destroyed by the all-conquering Reach, the survivors relocated to Elpis, but were subsequently wiped out in an overwhelming attack by pre-Big Bang villain Relic. With only Saint Walker surviving, it is unlikely the universe will soon hear their comforting oath:

"In fearful day, in raging night,
With strong hearts full, our souls ignite,
When all seems lost in the War of Light,
Look to the stars—for hope burns bright!" **WW**

ON THE RECORD

Blue Lanterns made their first appearance saving their Green cousins from attack by Atrocitus's Red Lanterns. They remained a breed apart in the escalating conflicts of the War of Light, but played a major role in turning back the risen dead during the Blackest Night.

Sadly, Hope's promise and its azure emissaries' pacifist nature made them easy targets for colonial aggressors the Reach, who decimated their ranks and drove them from their base-world Odym.

LIGHT IN THE DARKNESS
Despite the increasing chaos and horror of a universe in conflict, Blue Lanterns always clung to the heartfelt belief that "All will be well."

BLUE BEETLE

DATA

DEBUT *Infinite Crisis* #3 **(Feb. 2006)**
CURRENT VERSION *Blue Beetle* #1 **(Nov. 2011)**
REAL NAME Jaime Reyes
BASE El Paso, Texas
HEIGHT 5ft 8in **WEIGHT** 145 lbs **EYES** Brown **HAIR** Black
POWERS/ABILITIES Sentient Blue Beetle armor provides protection, boosts physical capabilities, and can create blades, energy weapons, wings, or thrusters at will; onboard systems include sensors, life support, and a universal translator.
ALLIES Paco Testas, Brenda Del Vecchio, Booster Gold, Green Lantern (Kyle Rayner)
ENEMIES La Dama, Brotherhood of Evil, the Reach
AFFILIATIONS Justice League International

When Jaime Reyes stumbled upon a mysterious alien artifact that transformed him into a bio-armored hero, he became the latest champion to carry the name Blue Beetle. Continuing the legacy of Dan Garrett and Ted Kord, Jaime found himself thrust into the role of hero— but soon found the Scarab that gave him his powers was created to help conquer humanity. The teenager battled villains who were after the Scarab, while trying to conceal his identity and protect the people he loved from coming to harm.

AT A GLANCE...

Alien hybrid
When Jaime Reyes bonded with the Scarab, he was transformed into a symbiotic armored being that could deploy guns, wings, blades, or jets on command. He had gone from ordinary teenager to living weapons system—and the Scarab could not be removed.

Who's the boss?
The Scarab fed Jaime data and tactical advice, but it was designed for aggression and saw extreme violence as the solution to every problem. The Scarab's damage prevented it from taking over Jaime completely, but he had to constantly argue with it to keep it under control.

Swiss Army scarab
The Blue Beetle armor can change shape as required and deploy a vast arsenal of energy weapons. While on Scarabworld, Jaime learned that it could also enter different combat modes, focusing on strength, speed, or defense.

Teenager Jaime Reyes and his friend Paco were driving through their hometown of El Paso when they found themselves caught up in a battle between the villainous Brotherhood of Evil and superhuman mercenaries hired by local crime boss La Dama. Both groups were fighting over a backpack, and in the chaos Jaime managed to nab the bag. Inside the backpack, the sentient alien Scarab suddenly came to life and attached itself to Jaime's spine, encasing him in a suit of blue and black armor—and transforming him into the Blue Beetle.

He heard the voice of the Scarab within his head, telling him to exterminate the others, but Jaime refused. When the superpowered villains attacked him, Jaime discovered that the Blue Beetle armor endowed him with increased strength, speed, and protection, and offered tactical information, making him a match for his assailants. He grabbed Paco and flew him to safety using the suit's energy wings.

Jaime convinced the Scarab to stop trying to control him and retract the armor, but when Paco was attacked by the Brotherhood of Evil and their new leader—the apelike cyborg Silverback—Jaime used the armor's powers to defeat them. However, when Paco recognized Jaime in the suit with the faceplate open, the armor reacted to the Blue Beetle's identity being "compromised" by impaling Paco on a claw. A shocked Jaime forced the suit to use its medical capabilities to save Paco, but the incident left him thoroughly shaken.

PIERCING ANGUISH
When the Scarab lashes out at Paco and mortally wounds him, Jaime is devastated by the capabilities of the Blue Beetle armor.

The Blue Beetle was now hunted by both La Dama and the Brotherhood of Evil. Not wanting to put his loved ones at risk, Jaime decided to leave El Paso for New York City. Once in Manhattan, he was mistaken for a menace and attacked by publicity-hungry hero Booster Gold, who accused him of being an agent of an alien race called "the Reach."

When Booster Gold realized that Jaime was a hero, he offered him a job with Justice League International. But it was a role he never got the chance to play, as team member

BRIGHT LIGHTS, BLUE BEETLE
Jaime went to Manhattan looking for advice on how to be a proper "super-guy," but found life in the big city a huge challenge. When he tried to fight crime, he was mistaken for a bug-like bad guy, and footage of his bloopers got plenty of hits on the "Superfail" website. He briefly met a Green Lantern (Kyle Rayner), clashed with Booster Gold, and had to battle Paco when his friend was transformed into a "Blood Beetle" by Reach technology. Jaime quickly discovered that being a teen hero was far from easy.

IMAGE PROBLEM
Jaime was determined to be a hero, but his menacing armor saw him mistaken for a villain by both the public and hot-headed heroes like Kyle Rayner.

CLASSIC STORIES

***Infinite Crisis* #1–7 (Dec. 2005–Jun. 2006)** When Jaime Reyes finds the Scarab, Booster Gold recruits him to help attack the Brother Eye satellite during the multiverse-shaking Infinite Crisis event.

***Blue Beetle* Vol. 8 #22–25 (Feb.–May 2008)** Jaime discovers an insidious Reach plot to enslave humanity and leads an attack on the alien mothership.

***The New 52: Futures End* #0 (Jul. 2014)** In this grim tale of an alternate future, Jaime rebels against the all-seeing Brother Eye, but is captured and brutally assimilated into the AI's collective.

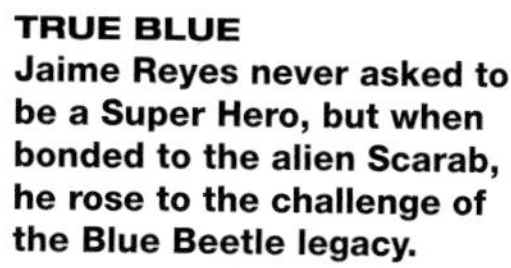

TRUE BLUE
Jaime Reyes never asked to be a Super Hero, but when bonded to the alien Scarab, he rose to the challenge of the Blue Beetle legacy.

"No! I don't wanna kill ANYONE!"

JAIME REYES

O.M.A.C. betrayed the League and teleported Blue Beetle to Reach space.

This was when the Scarab finally revealed its origins to Jaime. Named Khaji-Da, it was a living weapon created by the alien Reach. Scarabs were designed to travel to distant planets and bond with lifeforms there, creating warriors that would prepare the way for a Reach invasion. Fortunately for Jaime, Khaji-Da had been damaged and could no longer take control of its organic host.

Blue Beetle was then surrounded by a squad of Reach Beetles, who declared him a traitor. He went on the run on Reachworld, destroyed Scarabworld, the source of the Scarabs, and then crash-landed on the planet Tolerance. Here he found himself under constant siege on the all-too real glimmernet game show, *The Hunted*. **SW**

FIGHT FOR SURVIVAL
While being hunted on Tolerance as part of a deadly reality game show, Blue Beetle accidentally clashed with the hard-bitten Jediah Caul.

REBIRTH

TANGLED UP IN BLUE

Jaime Reyes has never been able to fully trust the alien scarab-symbiote grafted to his spine, even though it bestows on him the awesome firepower of the Blue Beetle and enables him to be a hero.

Now, however, the mystic master Doctor Fate is telling a dismayed Jaime that the living talisman has been lying to him all along. Doctor Fate suggests that the true secret of the teenager's abilities might end up costing him his sanity, his life, and his soul.

At least Jaime can trust his old mentor Ted Kord... or can he?

ON THE RECORD

The Silver Age Blue Beetle was Daniel Garrett, a brave archaeologist who found a glowing scarab in the tomb of the pharaoh Kha-Ef-Re. When he held it and uttered the words "Kaji-Dha," Dan was transformed into a mystically powered Super Hero who fought fantastical foes in Hub City and beyond.

A new beetle

When Dan was mortally wounded thwarting the maniacal Jarvis Kord and his army of robots from dominating the world, he passed on the role of Blue Beetle to his friend and student Ted Kord, Jarvis's nephew. However, the magical Scarab would not work for Ted, who relied on his agility and arsenal of non-lethal weapons and gadgets—including his iconic aerial vehicle the "Bug"—to combat crime in Hub City and later Chicago.

Ted also found time to set up the hi-tech corporation K.O.R.D. (Kord Omniversal Research and Development) and join the Justice League International, where he made a lifelong friend in the time-traveling Booster Gold. While investigating the spy agency Checkmate, Ted was shot in the head by its leader Maxwell Lord.

Lost and found

Ted had left the Scarab with Shazam at the Rock of Eternity. When the Rock exploded, the Scarab was thrown into space and eventually ended up in El Paso, Texas, where it was found by teenager Jaime Reyes. At this point, the Scarab was retconned to be a creation of the alien Reach that had been affected by the magical energies in the tomb of Kha-Ef-Re.

FAMILY MATTERS
Jaime Reyes tried to keep his Super Hero career secret from his parents and little sister Miagro, worried they might be targeted by his enemies.

BEETLE MANIA
Despite lacking any superpowers, Ted Kord took to the heroic life with gusto, quickly making a name for himself with his sense of adventure, quick wit, and steadfast bravery.

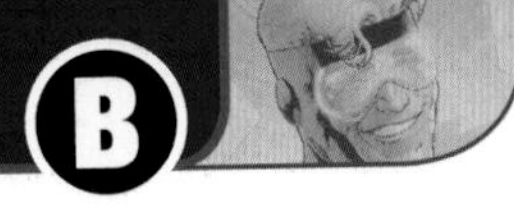

BOOSTER GOLD

DATA

DEBUT *Booster Gold* (Vol. 1) #1 **(Feb. 1986)**
CURRENT VERSION *Justice League International* (Vol. 3) #1 **(Nov. 2011)**
REAL NAME Michael Jon Carter
HEIGHT 6ft 2in **WEIGHT** 215 lbs
EYES Blue **HAIR** Blond
POWERS/ABILITIES Booster's powers come from his gear, which includes an armored strength-boosting suit, a thermal- and x-ray-vision visor, Brainiac 5's force-field projector belt, energy-blaster gauntlets, and a Legion of Super-Heroes' flight ring. He is assisted by his robot pal, Skeets, who provides data and communications.
ALLIES Batman, Batwing, Rip Hunter, Blue Beetle (Jaime Reyes), Godiva
ENEMIES Peraxxus, O.M.A.C., Brother Eye, the Burners
AFFILIATIONS Justice League International, A.R.G.U.S.

LEADERSHIP POTENTIAL
As leader of the JLI, Booster Gold had to deal with political interference and team infighting, but with some help from Batman, he proved his worth and forged an effective team.

CLASSIC STORIES

***Booster Gold* (Vol. 1) #8–9 (Sep.–Oct. 1986)** Michael Carter makes his mark as a Super Hero by saving President Reagan—who inadvertently gives the hero his codename!

***The OMAC Project* #1–6 (Jun.–Nov. 2005)** Booster Gold goes in search of his missing best friend, Ted Kord—and is devastated when he finds out he has been murdered.

***Convergence: Booster Gold* #1 (Jun. 2015)** In this time-twisting adventure, Booster meets Rip Hunter, the son of the pre-Flashpoint incarnation of Booster himself!

GRIEF-STRICKEN
Booster took his role seriously as Justice League International leader, and was traumatized when his beloved team was decimated by a bomb.

After making a mess of his life in the future, disgraced sportsman Michael Carter decided to make a new career in the 21st century as the hero Booster Gold. Though he loves a photo opportunity or a lucrative advertising deal, the brash and charming Booster has proven to be a true hero—as he demonstrated while leading the Justice League International team.

Michael Carter was born in Canada in the 25th century, and grew up dreaming of fame and fortune. After earning a football scholarship, brash and handsome Carter became a sports star, but he lost it all after taking money to fix matches. After being caught and serving his time in jail, he could only find work as a security guard at Metropolis' Space Museum.

Inspired by the museum's exhibits about 21st century Super Heroes, Carter decided to go back in time to become a champion of justice—and get money, fame, and girls along the way. He helped himself to a suit, various hi-tech gadgets, and a security bot called Skeets from the museum. Then he used a time machine that once belonged to chrononaut Rip Hunter and traveled back to the 21st century.

Carter used his futuristic gadgets and flair for showmanship to build a reputation as the hero Booster Gold. However, Booster was treated as something of a joke by other heroes because he also made money from commercial endorsements—he even appeared in beer commercials! Nevertheless, the United Nations chose him to lead their super-team, Justice League International. Booster had his hands full managing the group's multinational lineup, and the team finally collapsed after new member O.M.A.C. betrayed them.

Booster Gold was then contacted by an older, pre-Flashpoint incarnation of himself, who warned him that the time-guardian Rip Hunter was after him. Before he realized what was happening, Booster was swept into further adventures across time and space. **SW**

ON THE RECORD

In his pre-Flashpoint career, Booster served as a key member of many super-teams and stood in the front line during several cosmic events that reshaped the universe.

Booster really made his mark when he joined the Justice League International. He met Blue Beetle (Ted Kord) and they became best friends. Booster was devastated when Kord was murdered, and in *The O.M.A.C. Project*, he tracked down the killer: Maxwell Lord. Booster later joined Rip Hunter as one of the Time Masters. As a chrononaut, he could cross over to the post-Flashpoint universe.

FAMILY TIME
When Michael joined the enigmatic Rip Hunter in the *Time Masters*, he had no idea that he was actually working with his future son.

THE FACE THAT LAUNCHED A THOUSAND COMMERCIALS
Booster Gold combined courage with a flair for self-promotion, and proudly endorsed companies that paid him enough!

B

BOLT

DEBUT *Blue Devil* #6 (Nov. 1984)
CURRENT VERSION *Batgirl* (Vol. 4) #34 (Oct. 2014)
REAL NAME Larry Bolatinsky
HEIGHT 6ft 4in **WEIGHT** 220 lbs
EYES Blue **HAIR** Brown
POWERS/ABILITIES Teleportation; expert assassin and special effects coordinator.
ALLIES Deadshot, Merlyn, Chiller, Deadline
ENEMIES Blue Devil, Batgirl, Captain Atom
AFFILIATIONS Killer Elite, Suicide Squad

A mainstay assassin and mercenary for hire, Bolt is a former special effects expert who moved into the world of freelance killing. Facing foes as diverse as Blue Devil, Captain Atom, and Starman, Bolt demanded a high price, despite many failures to complete his contracts. At one point, he joined a group of assassins which included Deadshot and Merlyn, called the Killer Elite. Then he served briefly on the Suicide Squad.

Following years of work for hire, Bolt was killed by his son, Dreadbolt, when he was teleported into a brick wall. Dreadbolt continued his father's legacy as a member of the Terror Titans. Bolt briefly returned as a member of the undead Black Lantern Corps. After Flashpoint, Bolt lived again and took a contract for the villain Knightfall that led him into conflict with Batgirl. **SW**

BOODIKKA

DEBUT *Green Lantern* (Vol. 3) #20 (Jan. 1992)
CURRENT VERSION *Green Lantern Corps* (Vol. 3) #8 (Jun. 2012)
HEIGHT 5ft 8in **WEIGHT** 125 lbs
EYES White **HAIR** Black
POWERS/ABILITIES Ability to overcome great fear; expert fighter and hand-to-hand combatant; weapons include Green Lantern ring.
ALLIES Chaselon, Kilowog
ENEMIES Star Sapphire, Flicker, Cyborg Superman, Doomsday

A natural fighter with no qualms about showing off her skills, Boodikka hailed from the planet Bellatrix. After working as a member of the mercenary group Bellatrix Bombers, Boodikka joined Green Lantern Corps. With her aggressive attitude and problem with authority figures, she initially had a difficult time fitting in at the Corps, but she proved her worthiness in battle.

When Hal Jordan was corrupted by the being Parallax, Boodikka fought him, but had her hand severed by him in the process. After a brief time spent as a member of the Brotherhood of the Cold Flame, she was promoted into the Alpha Lanterns, a police force within the Green Lantern Corps. After valiant fights with villains including Cyborg Superman and Doomsday, Boodikka was killed by the Alpha Lantern Varix. **SW**

BORDEAUX, SASHA

DEBUT *Detective Comics* (Vol. 1) #751 (Dec. 2000)
BASE The Castle, Swiss Alps
HEIGHT 5ft 7in **WEIGHT** 135 lbs
EYES One red, one blue **HAIR** Black
POWERS/ABILITIES Expert bodyguard; highly adept martial artist; enhanced strength and speed.
ALLIES: Batman, Mr. Terrific, Jessica Midnight
ENEMIES Maxwell Lord, David Cain

Sasha Bordeaux would go from life as a bodyguard to becoming a leader within the world's most powerful spy organization. Sasha first entered Bruce Wayne's life when a worried Lucius Fox assigned her to be Batman's bodyguard. While Bruce kept her at arm's length, she discovered a hidden compartment in his briefcase where he stored his Batman weaponry. She was soon allowed into Batman's life, adopting a mask to help protect him on missions.

When Wayne was framed for murder, Sasha was sentenced to jail as his accomplice. While Wayne beat the charges against him, Sasha was recruited by spy agency Checkmate, and soon emerged as its Black Queen. Her body was augmented by O.M.A.C. technology, effectively changing her into a cyborg. **SW**

BOUNCING BOY

DEBUT *Action Comics* (Vol. 1) #276 (May 1961)
CURRENT VERSION *Legion of Super-Heroes* (Vol. 7) #5 (Mar. 2012)
REAL NAME Chuck Taine
BASE Legion Academy
HEIGHT 5ft 8in **WEIGHT** 227 lbs
EYES Blue **HAIR** Black
POWERS/ABILITIES Can inflate to shape of large, bouncing ball; possesses Legion flight ring.
ALLIES Legion of Super-Heroes
ENEMIES Dominators, Hunter, Computos
AFFILIATIONS Legion of Substitute Heroes

Growing up on Earth in the 31st century, Chuck Taine was an errand boy for a famous scientist. Tasked with delivering a super-plastic fluid to the Science Council, he took a break from his task, mistaking the fluid for his soda, and drank the experimental compound. Chuck's body soon expanded to a ball-like shape, and he found he could bounce around unharmed.

Happy to have a superpower, he applied for membership of the Legion of Super-Heroes as Bouncing Boy, but was rejected twice. Finally earning a place on the team, Chuck developed a crush on his teammate Duo Damsel, and she returned his affections. The two married, and left the team before finding true purpose supervising the Legion Academy. **SW**

BRADLEY, SLAM

DEBUT *Detective Comics* (Vol. 1) #1 (Mar. 1937)
REAL NAME Samuel Emerson Bradley
BASE Gotham City
HEIGHT 6ft 1in **WEIGHT** 205 lbs
EYES Gray **HAIR** Dark Brown (with gray temples)
POWERS/ABILITIES Excellent brawler and hand-to-hand combatant; expert marksman; adept detective with decades of experience; possesses a particular talent for disguise and mimicry for undercover work.
ALLIES Catwoman, Sam Bradley, Jr., Holly Robinson, Superman
ENEMIES Black Mask
AFFILIATIONS Gotham City Police Department (formerly)

Slam Bradley hails from Cleveland, Ohio, but has spent the majority of time in two of the United States' most famous cities, Gotham City and Metropolis. He earned his nickname on the streets of Cleveland, however, growing up in a fairly rough neighborhood. He was 12 years old when he challenged a local 17-year-old bully, knocking the boy out with a single punch.

As an adult, Slam tried stints in both the army and the police force before settling in for a life as private investigator, a job where he was his own boss. Slam worked in Metropolis, Keystone, and New York City, before opting to move to the East End of Gotham City, where he met and befriended Catwoman. Slam soon found himself falling in love with Catwoman, who had too much on her plate to ever significantly return Slam's feelings. However, the two remained allies, even after Catwoman had a child with Slam's son, Sam Bradley, Jr. **SW**

TO CATCH A CAT
Slam became a staunch ally of Catwoman after being hired by the Mayor of Gotham City to locate her. He grew to care for Selina and her circle of friends.

BRANDE, R. J.

DEBUT *Adventure Comics* (Vol. 1) #350 (Nov. 1966)
CURRENT VERSION *Legion: Secret Origin* #1 (Dec. 2011)
REAL NAME Ren Daggle
BASE 31st century, mobile
EYES Blue **HAIR** White
POWERS/ABILITIES Astute businessman.
ALLIES Legion of Super-Heroes
ENEMIES Leland McCauley IV
AFFILIATIONS United Planets Ruling Council

Flamboyant Sun-maker, Stargate builder, and politician, Rene Jacques Brande famously bankrolled the renowned Legion of Super-Heroes; unobtrusively steering a club for aspiring young do-gooders to its current position as a key component of United Planets' defense strategy. Nobody knew the universe's richest man was a fiction, a clever mask behind which Daggle hid for decades. Years earlier, Yorggian Fever had permanently locked the Durlan shapeshifter in human form and Daggle was forced into exile light-years away from him family.

The resourceful "R. J. Brande" thrived beyond his secretive homeworld. When some superpowered teens saved his life, funding a team of heroes offered a perfect opportunity to dispel some of the mistrust other races felt about Durlans. **WW**

BRAIN

DEBUT *Doom Patrol* (Vol. 1) #86 (Mar. 1964)
CURRENT VERSION *Teen Titans* (Vol. 5) #20 (Jul. 2016)
BASE Paris, France; Telistocc, Russia
POWERS/ABILITIES Genius-level intellect
ALLIES Monsieur Mallah
ENEMIES Doom Patrol, Teen Titans, Flash
AFFILIATIONS Brotherhood of Evil, Secret Society of Super-Villains

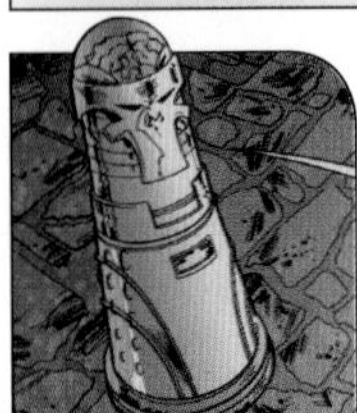

Very little is known about the anonymous French scientist known as the Brain. The infamous criminal mastermind claimed to have worked with Niles Caulder before the maverick researcher formed the Doom Patrol. Brain also believed Caulder, who was envious of his work, was behind the accident that nearly took his life.

The Brain's most important work was the radical course of treatments that elevated a gorilla's intelligence to a level beyond human genius. The grateful primate returned the favor by transplanting the dying man's brain into a cybernetically enhanced containment unit. A close intellectual relationship developed as the ape—dubbed Monsieur Mallah—kept the Brain alive, helping him orchestrate a campaign of vengeance against Caulder and the world. They went on to recruit villains to their Brotherhood of Evil. **WW**

BRAIN WAVE

DEBUT *All Star Comics* (Vol. 1) #15 (Feb.–Mar. 1943)
CURRENT VERSION *Earth 2: World's End* (Vol. 1) #8 (Jan. 2015) (as Brain Wave)
REAL NAME Henri Roy Jr., Henry King Jr.
BASE Arkham Base, Earth-2
EYES Brown **HAIR** Red
POWERS/ABILITIES Telepathy.
ALLIES Jonni Thunder, Obsidian
ENEMIES Batman
AFFILIATIONS John Constantine, World Army

When Apokolips invaded parallel world Earth-2, the entire planet became an armed camp awaiting Darkseid's inevitable return, with all metahuman activity strictly controlled. After Henri Roy Jr. turned in his arms-dealer father to the World Army, the boy was sent to Arkham Base in Gotham City to be treated for headaches. When his psychosis and psionic abilities manifested, he was hidden away with other dangerous superpowered youngsters.

They were freed by dimensionally-adrift John Constantine, who was seeking his own Earth. As Earth-2 was rocked by Apokolips' second assault, humanity prepared to flee and Brain Wave began mind-controlling the surviving refugees. His bid for domination of mankind's last survivors was foiled by aging Batman, Thomas Wayne. **WW**

BRIMSTONE

DEBUT *Legends* (Vol. 1) #1 (Nov. 1986)
BASE Apokolips
HEIGHT 50ft 6in **WEIGHT** 60,000 lbs
EYES Yellow **HAIR** None
POWERS/ABILITIES Pyrokinesis; incineration; flaming-energy construct creation.
ALLIES Glorious Godfrey, Darkseid
ENEMIES Suicide Squad, Firestorm, Cosmic Boy, Teen Titans
AFFILIATIONS Gods of Apokolips

The techno-seed that grew into Brimstone was created in the labs of Apokolips during Darkseid's campaign to destroy humanity's concept of heroism. When launched into a fusion reactor on Earth, it became a walking incinerator, targeting Super Heroes and terrorizing civilization.

The colossal monster was actually a semi-sentient artificial intelligence. Composed of super-heated hydrogen plasma wrapped around a core nexus of programming, its appearance was maintained by a delicate balance of magnetic fields. Though dangerous at full expansion, the construct was vulnerable to disruption of its magnetic shield. It carried a flaming sword and made declarations of being an "avenging angel" sent to destroy "false gods and graven images." **WW**

BRAINIAC 5

DEBUT *Action Comics* (Vol. 1) #276 **(May 1961)**
CURRENT VERSION *Legion of Super-Heroes* (Vol. 7) #1 **(Nov. 2011)**
REAL NAME Querl Dox
BASE Legion of Super-Heroes HQ, 31st-century Metropolis
HEIGHT 5ft 10in **WEIGHT** 160 lbs
EYES Green **HAIR** Blond
POWERS/ABILITIES Super intelligence; perfect memory; strategic skills; force-field belt; advanced unarmed combat training.
ALLIES Nura Nal, Imra Ardeen, Superman
ENEMIES Legion of Super-Villains, Fatal Five, Dark Circle
AFFILIATIONS Legion of Super-Heroes, Time Institute

Querl Dox is a 12th-level mind, the smartest son of a race of super-intellectual beings who only register as eighth-level thinkers. A direct descendant of Vril Dox, the infamous, self-styled Collector of Worlds, his brilliance counted as a unique superpower when he applied to the Legion of Super-Heroes. His inherited honorific as the fifth Brainiac became his codename.

Initially earnest and self-effacing, eventually "Brainy's" innate confidence—which looks exactly like impatience and arrogance—soon resurfaced as his hyper-fast mind made even his closest associates seem plodding, and tedious. His ferocious concentration, intransigence, and sarcastic irritability often border on mental instability. On some occasions he has descended into actual psychosis. However, thanks to 31st Century-psychiatric medicine and his own indomitable will, Brainy always fought his way back to sanity, better than ever.

Though an experienced combatant, Brainiac 5 fights best from his laboratory. As researcher, advisor, tactician, and support scientist, he has frequently saved the day, and the universe. As the inventor of the multi-functional Legion flight ring, he is the team's intellectual backbone, but cannot understand why he has not been elected its permanent leader. **WW**

ON THE RECORD

Brainiac 5 has supreme confidence in his mental strength but frequently shows appalling judgment. In a Silver Age tale, his Artificial Intelligence creation named Computo killed fellow Legionnaire Triplicate Girl and almost conquered Earth before he found a way to shut it down. That recklessness was still evident in a recent tale of his early years when he breached a vault containing the first Brainiac's cached inventions. They ran amok and would have decimated the planet Colu if not for his new-found Legion allies.

CLEAN-UP CREW Brainy's notions would often cause as much carnage as any marauding menace, if not for the diligent work of his Legionnaire allies.

BRAINIAC

DATA

DEBUT *Action Comics* (Vol. 1) #242 **(Jul. 1958)**
CURRENT VERSION *Action Comics* (Vol. 2) #4 **(Feb. 2012)**
REAL NAME Vril Dox
BASE Mobile
HEIGHT Variable **WEIGHT** Variable
EYES Red **HAIR** None
POWERS/ABILITIES 12th-level intellect; controls multiple bodies; possesses accumulated technologies from numerous destroyed worlds.
ALLIES Lex Luthor, Lady Styx
ENEMIES Superman, the Multitude
AFFILIATIONS The Twenty

MESSAGE FROM A BOTTLE
When Brainiac tried to 'collect' Metropolis, Jor-El's son Superman arrived to save the city's bottled citizenry.

The radically advanced intellect who calls himself Collector of Worlds began his cosmic campaign of acquisition for benevolent reasons. At least that is what Brainiac claims. In reality, he deploys automatons and miniaturization machines to infiltrate and erase civilizations, while harvesting and preserving their most advanced population centers. A 12th-level intellect, Vril Dox is a master of all physical sciences and has a deep and devious understanding of the mind.

Brainiac's collecting mania began on the super-scientific planet Yod-Colu, where researcher Vril Dox discovered a means of observing the uncanny and unstable Fifth Dimension. A gifted scientist, he was already acclaimed as designer of the supervisory Artificial Intelligence system C.O.M.P.U.T.O. and inventor of force-field generators and matter-reduction technology. After broaching the realm of incomprehensible chaos, however, Dox learned that a consequence of Fifth-Dimensional struggles was the unleashing of the deadly Multitude—a weapon also known as "The Spear-of-Infinite-Heads"—into the Third-Dimensional universe. This destructive horde was on an undeviating path, eradicating inhabited planets as it progressed through space. Brainiac hoped to preserve some fraction of the disappearing civilizations before they were lost forever.

Dox's preparations included experimenting on his son. For this atrocity he was exiled, but his access to C.O.M.P.U.T.O. enabled him to replicate himself: carrying out his salvation program without hindrance. Krypton was in the Multitude's path, but after harvesting the Kryptonian city of Kandor, Brainiac discovered that the brilliant scientist Jor-El had somehow turned back the Multitude. Before he could determine how, Krypton was destroyed by its own internal pressures. Initially defeated by Superman—Jor-El's son living on Earth—Brainiac withdrew, waiting for his contingency plan to bear fruit. Having seeded 20 Earthlings with psionic abilities, he waited until they attained a sufficient level of power before returning to Earth, where he was again thwarted by Superman. **WW**

ON THE RECORD

When Superman first met Brainiac he seemed to be an organic being intent on repopulating his dead world with Earthlings, but he was soon re-imagined as a devious construct spying for mechanical villains, the Computer Tyrants of Colu.

Brainiac was radically altered in the 1980s into a scarily remorseless and predatory mechanoid intent on subjugating all organic life. These and many other versions resurfaced in *Convergence*, when a Brainiac from beyond the multiverse began assimilating his parallel selves while collecting cities from all 52 alternate universes and their attendant or divergent timelines. These stolen cities were then pitted against each other, with Over-Brainiac's enslaved ringmaster Telos arranging the bouts.

ALIEN ENCOUNTER
For many years, Superman was unaware that his force-field shielded arch-foe was also a man of steel (and gears, tubes, plastic relays, and chemicals).

CLASSIC STORIES

***Action Comics* (Vol. 1) #242 (Jul. 1958)** Superman battles an alien city-stealer who is defeated when his own lab monkey turns off his force-field. There is no hint that Brainiac is an artificial foe.

***Superman* (Vol. 1) #141 (Nov. 1960)** Superman time-travels to Krypton and helps his father construct a massive space-ark. But the factory is in Kandor and is bottled with the city by Brainiac.

***Superboy and the Legion of Super-Heroes* (Vol. 1) #223-224 (Jan.-Feb. 1977)** Brainiac reappears in the 30th century as Pulsar Stargrave, impersonating Brainiac 5's father. He tries to trick the Legion of Super-Heroes into helping him conquer the universe.

WEAKNESS IN NUMBERS
A Brainiac threatened every world in the multiverse, but they were all just tasty morsels for the all-consuming, all-conquering Over-Brainiac.

COLLECTION MANIA
A ruthless master of mentality, Brainiac rebuilt, customized and mass-produced his body to ensure no region of the cosmos would be beyond his grasp.

BRONZE TIGER

DEBUT *Richard Dragon: Kung-Fu Fighter* (Vol. 1) #1 (Apr.–May 1975) (as Turner); *Richard Dragon: Kung-Fu Fighter* (Vol. 1) #18 (Nov.–Dec. 1977) (as Tiger)
CURRENT VERSION *Red Hood and the Outlaws* #20 (Jul. 2013)
REAL NAME Benjamin Turner
BASE 'Eth Alth'eban
HEIGHT 5ft 11in **WEIGHT** 196 lbs
EYES Brown **HAIR** None
POWERS/ABILITIES Superb martial artist; can shift into animalistic tiger form.

EYE OF THE TIGER
Bronze Tiger is a savage foe who often employs claw-like weapons; however, he's deadliest when he becomes a humanoid tiger.

Little is known about Bronze Tiger, one of the world's leading martial artists. He has been seen in the world of mercenaries for years now, having been an old drinking buddy of Slade Wilson, aka Deathstroke the Terminator. He worked with Rā's al Ghūl's infamous League of Assassins, and gained much power and influence within the group. So much so, that when the Red Hood was recruited to join the organization, it was Bronze Tiger who personally welcomed him to their fabled city 'Eth Alth'eban.

Bronze Tiger has a long history with fellow assassin Lady Shiva and reported ties to Richard Dragon. Aside from being a skilled fighter, proficient with a range of weapons, Bronze Tiger has an advantage in any fight, thanks to a talisman that transforms him into a primal tiger form. This talisman comes at a cost: it supposedly "burns away" a little piece of his soul every time he employs it. **MM**

BROTHERHOOD OF EVIL

DEBUT *Doom Patrol* (Vol. 1) #86 (Mar. 1964); *New Titans Annual* #6 (1990) (Society of Sin)
CURRENT VERSION *Blue Beetle* (Vol. 9) #1 (Nov. 2011)
MEMBERS/POWERS **Phobia**: Projection of illusions animating a foe's greatest fear; **Plasmus**: Protoplasmic burning touch; **Warp**: Teleportation; **Silverback**: Cybernetic enhancements, firearms expertise.
ENEMIES Blue Beetle, La Dama

MEETING THE BEETLE
The three original members of the Brotherhood of Evil decided that if they couldn't keep the alien Scarab away from the Blue Beetle, they would just have to take it back.
1 Phobia
2 Warp
3 Plasmus

The Brotherhood of Evil was formed many years ago by the Brain and his ape companion, Monsieur Mallah. It has been reformed with different members on several occasions, and has sometimes been known as the Society of Sin. Most recently, the group was tasked by parties unknown with hunting down the extraterrestrial Scarab that had fallen into the possession of Jaime Reyes and transformed him into the Super Hero Blue Beetle.

Three longstanding members—Phobia, Plasmus, and Warp—were later joined by the gun-toting cybernetic gorilla Silverback, who threatened the original trio with terrible consequences if the Scarab was not located—and soon. In this quest, they competed with the agents of La Dama and the soldiers of the Reach, both of whom had their own designs on the Scarab. Whether they will now ally with La Dama, or continue to fight both her and others seeking the Scarab remains to be seen. **AI**

BROTHER BLOOD

DEBUT *The New Teen Titans* (Vol. 1) #21 (Jul. 1982)
CURRENT VERSION *The Ravagers* #2 (Aug. 2012)
BASE Hollywood, California
HEIGHT 6ft 2in **WEIGHT** 193 lbs
EYES Red **HAIR** None
POWERS/ABILITIES Able to heal wounds; enslaves others by contact with their blood; charismatic leader with fanatical followers.
ENEMIES Ravagers, Animal Man, Animal Girl

BLOOD BATH
Brother Blood fully embraces his gory associations, often bathing in blood. The villain will stop at nothing to increase his powers and gain dominion over the Red.

The mysterious cult leader Brother Blood shares a connection to the Red, the intangible web that connects all animals and powers such heroes as Animal Man. Brother Blood first reared his demonic head in a dream experienced by then Ravager and current Teen Titan, Beast Boy. Through his connection to the Red, Beast Boy realized that Brother Blood was out to kill the Ravagers, a premonition that almost came true when he invaded Blood's church home, only to be captured by the villain. Brother Blood hoped to use Beast Boy's blood to create a doorway to the Red that he had been shown in a dream. However, he was defeated by the Ravagers and his temple was destroyed.

Blood next set his sights on Animal Man Buddy Baker, and soon was able to travel to the Red by drinking Buddy's blood. There he attempted a hostile takeover of the dimension, but was stopped by Animal Man and his daughter, Animal Girl. **MM**

BULLETEER

DEBUT *Seven Soldiers: Bulleteer* #1 (Jan. 2006)
REAL NAME Alix Harrower
HEIGHT 6ft **WEIGHT** 155 lbs
EYES White **HAIR** Red
POWERS/ABILITIES Skin bonded with Smartskin, making her nearly invulnerable and immune to pain; superhuman strength.
ALLIES Firestorm, Firehawk, Super-Chief
ENEMIES The Nebula Man, Sally Sonic
AFFILIATIONS Seven Soldiers of Victory, Justice League of America

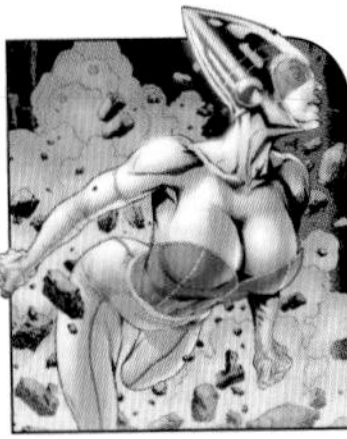

Alix Harrower's scientist husband Lance was working on a "Smartskin" project—turning soft tissue into a metal material stronger than steel. Obsessed with preserving not only his youth, but that of his 27-year-old wife, Lance tried the Smartskin on himself, and died by suffocation. Before he breathed his last, he touched Alix, passing his Smartskin on to her.

She survived the bonding process and then discovered that Lance had been obsessed with a Super Hero on the internet named Sally Sonic. In despair, Alix ran into the night, happening upon a building on fire and saved its residents. Realizing her calling, she became the Bulleteer, a Super Hero inspired by the World War II Bulletman. She later served with honor in the Seven Soldiers of Victory as well as the JLA. **MM**

BULLETMAN

DEBUT *Nickel Comics* (Vol. 1) #1 (May 1940)
REAL NAME James Barr
BASE Fawcett City
HEIGHT 6ft 4in **WEIGHT** 177 lbs
EYES Blue **HAIR** White
POWERS/ABILITIES Able to fly and repel bullets thanks to his Gravity Regular Helmet; superhuman strength and intelligence.
ALLIES Bulletgirl, Starman, Shazam
ENEMIES Weeper
AFFILIATIONS All-Star Squadron

The inspiration for the later crime fighter Bulleteer, Bulletman was a Super Hero active during World War II. The son of a police officer who was killed on duty, Jim Barr opted to become a crime fighter himself using his science smarts to increase his strength and to develop a Gravity Regulator Helmet that allowed him to fly. Taking the name Bulletman from the Gravity Regulator's appearance, he was soon joined by Bulletgirl, Susan Kent.

The two fought bravely during the war, and afterwards retired to live in Fawcett City. Later, as an older man who had made a good living from Bulletman merchandise, Jim was falsely accused of having committed treason back in 1942. However, Captain Marvel and Starman teamed up to prove he was innocent of all charges. **MM**

BUMBLEBEE

DEBUT *Teen Titans* (Vol. 1) #45 **(Dec. 1976)** (as Karen); *Teen Titans* (Vol. 1) #48 **(Jun. 1977)** (as Bumblebee)
CURRENT VERSION *Titans Hunt* #1 **(Dec. 2015)**
REAL NAME Karen Beecher-Duncan
BASE Metropolis
HEIGHT 5ft 7in **WEIGHT** 130 lbs
EYES Brown **HAIR** Black
ALLIES Malcolm Duncan, Jung-Mo
ENEMIES Mr. Twister, Neil Richards
AFFILIATIONS Teen Titans

MAD ABOUT YOU
While Karen didn't realize it at the time, Neil Richards, aka the fashion designer Mad Mod, had a history with the Teen Titans.

The past of Karen Beecher-Duncan and her role as the Super Hero Bumblebee is shrouded in mystery and memory loss. The wife of Malcolm Duncan, an award-winning composer known for his movie scores, Karen appears to have completely forgotten her Super Heroic adventures and battles as part of the Teen Titans.

Karen believes that she first met her husband Mal while he was scoring the movie *Crash Site*. As an air accident investigator, she was a technical consultant on the film. The two hit it off, and Mal affectionately nicknamed Karen "Bumblebee." After their marriage, Karen became pregnant, and then experienced the first flash of a possible previous life when she noticed a shadowy figure lurking behind Mal during his acceptance of a Golden Star Award for Best Score. Karen began investigating the people in a photo taken of her husband when he accepted his award, only to learn that Mal had collapsed while at work, and then disappeared after being driven away in an ambulance. Karen was visited in the hospital waiting room by a man named Neil Richards, who claimed that Mal had been a member of the original Teen Titans. **MM**

ON THE RECORD

Before Flashpoint, Karen Beecher-Duncan was the Super Hero Bumblebee. Involved in a relationship with Teen Titan Mal Duncan, better known as the hero Herald (and much later, Vox), Karen decided to be a crime fighter herself, and designed her flying Bumblebee costume and weaponry. She was welcomed into the first Teen Titans team, and after that version disbanded, Karen worked for S.T.A.R. Labs before becoming a member of the Doom Patrol.

BEE MINOR
During Infinite Crisis, Bumblebee's physiology was altered, reducing her size to around six inches tall.

BUNKER

DEBUT *Teen Titans* (Vol. 4) #1 (Nov. 2011)
REAL NAME Miguel Jose Barragan
HEIGHT 5ft 8in **WEIGHT** 132 lbs
EYES Brown **HAIR** Black
POWERS/ABILITIES Able to create bricks of psionic energy; infectiously positive disposition.
ALLIES Beast Boy, Red Robin, Skitter, Solstice, Wonder Girl
ENEMIES Harvest, Grymm
AFFILIATIONS Teen Titans

Raised in the Mexican village of El Chilar, Miguel Jose Barragan finally made his way to the US, in part by hitching a ride on a train. After discovering the giant cocoon of future Teen Titan Skitter in one of the cars, Miguel was attacked by a homeless man, who turned out to be Red Robin (Tim Drake) in disguise. Drake mistook Barragan for a villain working with the evil organization N.O.W.H.E.R.E., and a scuffle broke out between them. However, Miguel suddenly hugged Red Robin, citing him as his inspiration for leaving Mexico to become the Super Hero Bunker.

The two became allies and founding members of Red Robin's team of young Super Heroes, the Teen Titans. Openly gay, Miguel has remained on the Titans, often serving as the team's ray of positivity in troubled times. **MM**

BULLOCK, HARVEY

DEBUT *Batman* (Vol. 1) #361 **(Jul. 1983)**
CURRENT VERSION *Detective Comics* (Vol. 2) #1 **(Nov. 2011)**
REAL NAME Harvey Bullock
BASE Gotham City
HEIGHT 5ft 10in **WEIGHT** 248 lbs **EYES** Brown **HAIR** Black
POWERS/ABILITIES Excellent detective; able brawler with street smarts and years of experience; highly trained in police procedure; extremely loyal to his friends.
ALLIES James Gordon, Batman, the Batman Family, Renee Montoya
ENEMIES Anarky, Joker's Daughter, Dr. Death
AFFILIATIONS G.C.P.D., Batman Task Force

Sometimes the best cops in Gotham City are hard to spot in a lineup. While his uncouth attitude and slovenly appearance may suggest otherwise, Harvey Bullock is in truth one of the few good cops left in a city filled with corruption, and a steadfast supporter of James Gordon and the high ideals for which he stands.

While he may have been tempted by an amoral police department in the past, Harvey Bullock was inspired by the arrival of Lieutenant James Gordon to Gotham City, and stuck up for Gordon when the lieutenant was going after underworld boss Roman Sionis. Bullock also worked with Gordon on the case of Dr. Death during the city's Zero Year event. The two slowly became allies, as Gordon rose through the ranks to become Gotham City's Commissioner.

After years of dedicated service, James Gordon was briefly imprisoned for a murder he did not willingly commit. Bullock remained loyal to Gordon, and when he was finally released and became involved with the G.C.P.D. again as the city's official new Batman, Harvey remained by his side as a member of the Batman Task Force. **MM**

ON THE RECORD

In his early appearances, Harvey Bullock was a clumsy slob, who seemed to get in the way more often than he helped; he also clashed with Commissioner Gordon. In time, Harvey changed his ways, making friends with the second Robin, Jason Todd. He later began work at the government spy agency Checkmate. In the 1990s, he became the longtime partner of fellow officer Renee Montoya, but the infamously unorthodox cop finally crossed the line in 2000's "Officer Down" storyline and resigned from the G.C.P.D.

BAD NEWS BULLOCK
When he first appeared, Lt. Bullock wasn't a fan of either Batman or Commissioner Gordon, referring to Gordon as a "weak sister," and Batman as "fancy britches."

C.O.M.P.U.T.O.

DEBUT *Adventure Comics* (Vol. 1) #340 (Jan. 1966)
CURRENT VERSION *Action Comics* (Vol. 2) #4 (Feb. 2012)
REAL NAME Cyber-cerebral Overlapping Multiprocessor Transceiver Operator
BASE Robotica
POWERS/ABILITIES Incredible intelligence, ability to control machines, assumes energy form.
ALLIES Rā's al Ghūl
ENEMIES Legion of Super-Heroes

When the Legion of Super-Heroes was stranded in the 20th century, Brainiac 5 combined a Mother Box from New Genesis, Dr. Magnus' responsometer, and the Legion's own Omnicom communicator to create an artificial intelligence that could help get them back to the 31st century. The resulting Cyber-cerebral Overlapping Multiprocessor Transceiver Operator created a time portal, but then attacked the team. The Legion seemingly destroyed the AI, but it returned as Mr. Venge—an advisor to Rā's al Ghūl—and later as leader of the machine civilization known as Robotica. C.O.M.P.U.T.O. led Robotica in an attack on Earth, but Brainiac 5.1 managed to stop his violent tendencies.

Post Flashpoint, Vril Dox merged with C.O.M.P.U.T.O. to create the Collector of Worlds, also known as Brainiac. **SW**

CAIN AND ABEL

DEBUT *House of Mystery* (Vol. 1) #175 (Aug. 1968) (Cain); *DC Special* #4 (Jul–Sep. 1969) (Abel)
CURRENT VERSION (Abel) *Justice League United* #16 (Feb. 2016)
BASE House of Mystery (Cain); House of Secrets (Abel)
HEIGHT 6ft 2in (Cain); 5ft 7in (Abel)
WEIGHT 174 lbs (Cain); 396 lbs (Abel)
EYES Brown (Cain); Blue (Abel)
HAIR Brown (Cain); Black (Abel)
POWERS/ABILITIES Immortality.

Cain and Abel are two brothers who dwell in the Dreaming, the realm of Morpheus. They inhabit the House of Mystery and House of Secrets respectively, and tell chilling stories to visitors. While Abel is timorous and soft-hearted, Cain has a cruel streak. Though he loves his brother, Cain often loses his temper and murders Abel in a gruesome fashion. However, Abel always comes back to life, as per the terms of a contract the brothers signed with Morpheus.

When Abel was killed by the Furies of Greek Legend, his brother successfully petitioned Morpheus to resurrect him. They later ran the House of Mystery as a bar where customers paid for drinks by telling macabre stories. When the House of Mystery was destroyed, the brothers rebuilt it, but it soon became the Justice League Dark's HQ.

After Flashpoint, the Justice League United encountered Abel when they entered the House of Secrets. **SW**

BLOOD BROTHERS
Cain (left) and Abel are brothers bound together by fate, doomed to repeat a cycle of murder and resurrection.

CALENDAR MAN

DEBUT *Detective Comics* (Vol. 1) #259 (Sep. 1958)
CURRENT VERSION *Detective Comics Annual* #3 (Sep. 2014)
REAL NAME Julian Gregory Day
BASE Arkham Island
HEIGHT 5ft 11in **WEIGHT** 193 lbs
EYES Black **HAIR** Bald
POWERS/ABILITIES Hardened street fighter.
ALLIES The Squid, Arkham inmates
ENEMIES Batman, the Riddler

Julian Day was a happily married man with a son, Aiden. When his wife died in a blackout caused by the Riddler, Day went off the rails and began working for a drug dealer called the Squid. When Batman met Aiden, the boy said that his father abused and neglected him. Batman beat up Day, accusing him of forgetting his son's birthday.

Consequently, Day became obsessed with dates. Taking the name Calendar Man, he committed several date-themed crimes and was incarcerated on Arkham Island. He then threatened to cause a blackout across Gotham City unless the man he blamed for ruining his life surrendered to him. Batman coerced the Riddler into helping him infiltrate Arkham, then handed him over to Calendar Man, who exacted his brutal revenge on the villain. **SW**

CAIN, DAVID

DEBUT *Batman* #567 (Jul. 1999)
CURRENT VERSION *Batman and Robin Eternal* #1 (Dec. 2015)
BASE The Nursery, Prague, Czech Republic
EYES Brown **HAIR** Brown
POWERS/ABILITIES Highly trained killer, skilled in martial arts and swordsmanship.
ALLIES Mother
ENEMIES Batgirl (Cassandra Cain), Bluebird, Red Hood, Red Robin, Dick Grayson, Bruce Wayne
AFFILIATIONS Mother's organization

David Cain is a skilled and ruthless killer who works for the shadowy underworld figure known as "Mother." Mother kidnapped children, brainwashing them into becoming her obedient agents. Using the codename "Orphan," Cain faithfully served as Mother's assassin, and fought Batman when the Dark Knight hindered her schemes for world domination.

Over time, Cain himself became obsessed with turning a child into a perfect merciless killer. From a young age, he subjected his own daughter, Cassandra, to a brutal training regime: desensitizing her to violence, refusing to let her speak, and teaching her that sympathy was a sign of weakness. Cassandra later escaped her father's influence and fled to Gotham City, adopting the identity of Batgirl. When Cain came to Gotham City to kill the hero Bluebird, Batgirl intervened and cut off his hand. Orphan escaped to Mother's Nursery facility in Prague where his hand was replaced by a cybernetic one. **SW**

BLOODLUST
David Cain is obsessed with death and violence, and takes pleasure in the suffering of others.

CAPTAIN CARROT

DEBUT *New Teen Titans* (Vol. 1) #16 (Feb. 1982)
CURRENT VERSION *The Multiversity* #1 (Oct. 2014)
REAL NAME Rodney Rabbit
BASE House of Heroes satellite, Earth-26
HEIGHT Over 6ft **EYES** White **HAIR** White
POWERS/ABILITIES Eating cosmic carrots bestows Rodney with temporary superpowers.
ALLIES Superman
ENEMIES Starro the Conqueror, Frogzilla, Lord Havok, the Gentry
AFFILIATIONS The Zoo Crew, Multiversity

A rabbit Super Hero from an alternate reality populated by anthropomorphic cartoon animals, Rodney was just a mild-mannered cartoonist until he ate a cosmic carrot. He gained superpowers and became Captain Carrot, joining fellow heroes Pig-Iron, Alley-Kat-Abra, Fastback the turtle, Yankee Poodle, and Rubberduck in the Zoo Crew.

They embarked on a series of wacky adventures, encountering both Superman and Starro the Conqueror. When their world was threatened, the Zoo Crew took its inhabitants to New Earth, where they changed into ordinary animals. Captain Carrot became a stage rabbit, but later regained his powers and helped fight Darkseid during the Final Crisis. Rodney was later recruited into Operation Justice Incarnate, a team of pan-universal heroes. The team battled the Gentry, a group of cosmic entities that sought to destroy the multiverse with their Oblivion Machine. **SW**

ZOO-ILLOGICAL!
Captain Carrot and his pals in the Zoo Crew defended Earth-26 from other-worldly intruders as well as local menaces like the monstrous Hogzilla.

CAPTAIN ATOM

DATA

DEBUT *Space Adventures* #33 **(Mar. 1960)**
CURRENT VERSION *Captain Atom* (Vol. 3) #1 **(Nov. 2011)**
REAL NAME Nathaniel Adam
BASE The Continuum, Kansas
EYES Silver **HAIR** Silver
HEIGHT 6ft 4in **WEIGHT** 200 lbs
POWERS/ABILITIES Has control over the strong nuclear force that binds atomic nuclei together. Can fire energy blasts, absorb energy, and transform matter. Able to fly and pick up transmissions from across the electromagnetic spectrum.
ALLIES The Flash, Firestorm
ENEMIES Dr. Megala, Monarch
AFFILIATIONS USAF, Continuum research facility

NUCLEAR POWER
Captain Atom must use his control of the strong nuclear force to keep his structural integrity. Nate's atoms constantly undergo fission, so he has an almost infinite amount of energy.

INFORMATION OVERLOAD
As Captain Atom, Nate Adam discovered that he had become a human antenna—and was able to pick up broadcast information of all types.

Captain Atom is a hero with the ability to control the power of the atom, allowing him to shape matter and energy to his will. Though the US military wanted to use him as a living weapon of mass destruction, he has chosen to wield his devastating power for the good of all mankind. However, with almost infinite energy at his command, he must constantly struggle to hold onto his humanity.

Captain Nathaniel Adam was a USAF fighter pilot, but when his behavior became erratic following his father's death, he was grounded. Nate then found work at the Continuum, a scientific research facility where he participated in an experiment run by renowned quantum physicist Dr. Megala, author of the controversial "M-Theory." Megala believed that there were multiple parallel realities, and he wanted Nate to pilot an experimental capsule that was designed to travel to other dimensions.

When the capsule was activated, it imploded in a flash of light, destroying Nate at a subatomic level. Somehow his consciousness survived and created a new body for itself, molecule by molecule. One month after he had disappeared, the being that was once Nate Adam reappeared as a glowing silver form with a red atomic symbol emblazoned on his chest.

Nate discovered that he was now a living nuclear reactor that could also absorb energy and even transmute matter. However, when he used these powers his own body became unstable. General Wade Eiling approached Nate and told him that he was now a military asset—and a living weapon of mass destruction. Nate refused to cooperate and chose to serve the world as Captain Atom. He used his new-found powers to intervene in a Libyan insurrection, save New York City from a volcanic eruption, and help a child with cancer. When Dr. Megala took control of the nuclear hero Firestorm, Nate had to battle his mentor. Captain Atom defeated Megala, but an explosion hurled the hero into the 31st century. **SW**

SCIENCE GONE WRONG!
One of the first foes Captain Atom faced was a huge biological monstrosity that had originally been a lab rat used in one of Dr. Megala's experiments!

ON THE RECORD

The pre-Flashpoint Nate Adam was a decorated pilot framed for a crime he did not commit. To gain a pardon, Nate participated in an experiment involving an atomic bomb and a crashed alien spacecraft. Seemingly vaporized in the test, he reappeared 18 years later with a skin of alien metal and incredible powers.

Calling himself Captain Atom, Nate was forced to work for the government. Eventually, he cleared his name and left the Air Force. Nate battled villain Monarch in the *Armageddon* 2001 story arc and time-traveled to foil a plot by Super Hero-hating Maxwell Lord.

THE GOOD SOLDIER
As a military man, Captain Atom follows orders—even if it means having to arrest the Dark Knight himself!

CLASSIC STORIES

***Armageddon: The Alien Agenda* #1–4 (Nov. 1991–Feb. 1992)** In this time-traveling epic, Captain Atom and his nemesis Monarch fight an alien threat in the prehistoric era, in Imperial Rome, and during World War II.

***Countdown: Arena* #1–4 (Feb. 2008)** Nate Adam becomes the new incarnation of his main adversary, Monarch. He recruits an army to battle the Monitors, but is successfully opposed by a team of alternate Captain Atoms.

***Captain Atom* (Vol. 2) #7–10 (May–Aug. 2012)** Nate is contacted by a future version of himself. Captain Atom journeys into the timestream to face the consequences of his actions and to prevent the destruction of the world.

CAPTAIN BOOMERANG

DATA

DEBUT *Flash* (Vol. 1) #117 **(Dec. 1960)**
CURRENT VERSION *Suicide Squad* (Vol. 4) #3 **(Jan. 2012)**
REAL NAME George "Digger" Harkness
BASE Belle Reve Prison
HEIGHT 5ft 9in **WEIGHT** 167 lbs **EYES** Brown **HAIR** Brown
POWERS/ABILITIES Expert with throwing weapons; carries a number of boomerangs at all times, including some with special properties such as razor-sharp sides, and others that explode.
ALLIES Deadshot, Harley Quinn
ENEMIES Black Manta, the Flash
AFFILIATIONS Suicide Squad

CLASSIC STORIES

***The Flash* #117 (Dec. 1960)** Captain Boomerang makes his debut—and nearly kills the Flash by tying him to a giant boomerang that he catapults into space.

***Identity Crisis* #5 (Sep. 2004)** Captain Boomerang is hired to kill Tim Drake's father—but both men end up dead.

***The Flash* (Vol. 3) #7 (Jan. 2011)** Recently brought back to life, Digger escapes jail and recalls his early years as a villain.

OUTBACK
As a young child growing up in Australia, Digger was sent boomerangs by a mysterious benefactor. He quickly mastered their use.

George "Digger" Harkness is a mercenary and killer with an aptitude for boomerangs and other projectiles. Antagonistic and often annoying to those around him, he has fought the Flash and, since his incarceration, has become a member of Task Force X, aka the Suicide Squad.

Born in Australia, George "Digger" Harkness developed an aptitude for boomerangs and soon became deadly with them. An moving to the US, he turned to crime, battling the Flash and other heroes. After Harkness went to jail, Amanda Waller selected him for Task Force X (the Suicide Squad), along with new member Yo-Yo, to replace fallen members Voltaic and Savant. While Harkness claimed to be the new team leader—and was given a detonator to control the explosive devices buried inside his fellow teammates—this was later revealed to be a ruse by Waller. Harkness was captured on a mission against the terrorist group known as Basilisk, and seemed to betray the Suicide Squad—until he helped them break free. Waller had asked him to infiltrate Basilisk and get close to its leader, Regulus, to help the Suicide Squad defeat him.

Captain Boomerang went on several more missions with the Squad, including one to China to destroy a top-secret installation creating cloned super beings. Another mission saw him infiltrate a Middle Eastern death cult started by renegades from the League of Assassins. Harkness, Deadshot and Black Manta successfully joined the group, but when Harkness allowed some kids to play football, he was arrested by the cult and severely beaten by Manta, who had begun to follow the cult leader, Saladin. Task Force X managed to stop the terrorists and Manta was taken back as a prisoner. When Black Manta joined forces with Vic Sage during his attempt to take full control of Task Force X by killing Waller, Captain Boomerang got his revenge. He used his signature weapon to inflict further pain on Manta after the latter was shot in the wrist by Deadshot. **AC**

ON THE RECORD

Capitalizing on his Australian background, Captain Boomerang first came to fame as a toy spokesman before being exposed as a super-villain. A longtime member of the infamous Rogues—the Flash's recurring adversaries—Captain Boomerang developed a harder edge after joining the Suicide Squad.

He was later hired to kill Jack Drake, the father of Tim Drake (who would become Robin), but as he carried out the contract, he too was killed—by his target. Harkness' son, Owen Mercer, went on to become the new Captain Boomerang, while George returned as a Black Lantern during Nekron's attack on Earth and was reborn following Nekron's defeat.

LAST STAND
An aged, balding Captain Boomerang assassinated Jack Drake, but not before he was shot and killed by his victim.

LETHAL WEAPONRY
Digger Harkness has created a number of weaponized and trick boomerangs, which become deadly tools in his hands.

C

CAPTAIN COLD

DATA

DEBUT *Showcase* #8 **(May–Jun. 1957)**
CURRENT VERSION *The Flash* (Vol. 4) #3 **(Jan. 2012)**
REAL NAME Leonard Snart
BASE Central City
HEIGHT 6ft 2in **WEIGHT** 196 lbs **EYES** Blue **HAIR** Brown
POWERS/ABILITIES Captain Cold is an excellent tactician—especially when planning heists—and has a cold gun that can create absolute zero, super dense blocks of ice, form ice barriers, and other cold-related effects; goggles protect him from the glare caused by using his gun.
ALLIES Lex Luthor
ENEMIES The Flash, Crime Syndicate
AFFILIATIONS The Rogues

COLD COMFORT
They may be criminals, but Captain Cold and his fellow Rogues have a strict no-killing policy.

FLASH ON ICE
Captain Cold can freeze the Flash on the spot, making his super-speed useless.

Leonard Snart is Captain Cold, one of the Flash's main enemies and leader of the Rogues. While Snart has spent most of his life as a criminal, he has a strict code of honor.

Leonard Snart had a troubled childhood. His father was a drunken thug, and Snart's relationships with his sister, Lisa, and his grandfather were the only good things in his life. Following his father's death, Snart left home and soon turned to petty crime to survive. When working as part of a criminal gang, he was arrested by the Flash and sent to jail. While in jail, Snart created a special cold gun that he hoped would give him the edge in his next confrontation with the Flash. After he was released, he returned to a life of crime as Captain Cold, and soon teamed up with other villains to form the Rogues. After several defeats by Flash, Cold tried to upgrade the Rogues' powers by using a Genome Recorder, but it backfired and left his friends injured and Lisa in a coma. When Flash's enemy Mob Rule caused a blackout, it threatened Snart's sister's chances of survival. Snart blamed Flash and attacked the hero. In the end, Flash not only stopped Captain Cold but used his Speed Force to help Lisa survive. She joined the Rogues as Glider, having gained powers of her own.

The Rogues had their own strict code—one that brought them into conflict with more brutal evildoers, such as Gorilla Grodd and the Crime Syndicate. Captain Cold joined Lex's group of villains to attack the Syndicate, and after the Syndicate's defeat, found himself hailed a hero. Snart was hired by Lex as his bodyguard and saved his life when would-be assassin Bullet tried to kill him, and when people infected by the Amazo virus attacked. Only time will tell if Snart will return to his villainous ways. **AC**

ON THE RECORD

The original Captain Cold was older than his modern counterpart, and his costume far more like a snowsuit. During his criminal career, this version of Cold lost his sister when she was killed by fellow ice-themed villain Chillblaine; Cold then killed Chillblaine in revenge.

Alongside his fellow Rogues, Cold also took the life of Bart Allen's Flash, but expressed remorse at his actions on discovering that this incarnation of the Flash was just a kid.

ICED AGE
The original, older Captain Cold with a fur-trimmed parka-style costume, lacked superpowers, relying on his ice guns for his criminal work.

CLASSIC STORIES

***Showcase* #8 (May–Jun. 1957)** Leonard Snart makes his first appearance as Captain Cold—and comes close to defeating the Flash.

***The Flash: The Fastest Man Alive* #13 (Aug. 2007)** Bart Allen's short-lived era as the Flash ends in tragedy when Captain Cold and the Rogues kill him.

***Final Crisis: Rogues' Revenge* (Sep.–Nov. 2008)** On the run for killing the Flash, Captain Cold and his allies plan revenge against fellow villain Inertia, who they believe used them to kill the Flash.

CAPTAIN COMET

DEBUT *Strange Adventures* #9 (Jun. 1951)
CURRENT VERSION *Action Comics* (Vol. 2) #10 (Aug. 2012)
BASE Cairn **REAL NAME** Adam Blake
HEIGHT 6ft 2in **WEIGHT** 190 lbs
HAIR Brown **EYES** Brown
POWERS/ABILITIES Super-strength; super-speed; telepathy; telekinesis; flight; photographic memory; heightened intelligence.
ALLIES Superman
ENEMIES Doomsday

A comet passing over the Blake family home in Kansas during Adam's birth gave him latent superpowers. These manifested many years hence when he learned from Professor Emery Zackro that his body had evolved thousands of years ahead of normal human biology. Adam learned that his destiny lay in space as one of the first *Neo sapiens*, tasked with finding others who had evolved ahead of their species' timeline.

While on this quest he battled Superman, whom he mistook for Superdoomsday. Realizing his error, he teamed up with the Man of Steel and Lex Luthor to fight off Mr. Mxyzptlk and an army of alternate Supermen threatening Metropolis. He then disappeared in his spaceship with its crew of Wanderers, their destination unknown. He later turned up as a member of the Crucible Academy. **AI**

CAPTAIN STEEL

DEBUT *Steel, the Indestructible Man* #1 (Mar. 1978)
CURRENT VERSION *Earth 2 Annual* #1 (Jul. 2013)
REAL NAME Henry Heywood Jr.
UNIVERSE Earth-2
HEIGHT 6ft **WEIGHT** 378 lbs
HAIR Black **EYES** Brown
POWERS/ABILITIES Metallic alloy skeleton; super-strength; limited control over machinery.
ENEMIES Apokolips, Parademons

Born with a birth defect that would have killed him by causing his bones to crumble, Henry Heywood Jr. survived thanks to his scientist father, who bound his bones to a metal alloy that interacted with Henry's DNA. The alloy also replaced some of Henry's organs, making his body partly metallic and conferring on him superhuman powers. Henry's father planned to turn his research results over to the World Army, but Apokolips and his Parademons attacked, and Heywood destroyed the documents—and himself—to prevent them falling into their hands.

Following the Apokolips War, Henry Jr. became Captain Steel and a great asset to the World Army, forging a partnership with Atom. His father's untimely death and his powers' side effects have made Captain Steel emotionally distant. **AI**

CARR, SNAPPER

DEBUT *Brave and the Bold* #28 (Feb.–Mar. 1960)
BASE Happy Harbor
REAL NAME Lucas Carr
HEIGHT 5ft 10in **WEIGHT** 175 lbs
HAIR Brown **EYES** Blue
POWERS/ABILITIES Teleports by snapping his fingers.
ALLIES JLA, Young Justice
ENEMIES Joker

When Simon Carr bankrolled the Justice League of America and outfitted their mountain base, his nephew Lucas lent a hand. As a reward, the finger-popping teen, nicknamed "Snapper," was made an honorary member of the JLA. Years later, a "John Doe" charmed Snapper into revealing the location of the JLA's HQ. Doe turned out to be the Joker, and Snapper left the JLA ashamed he'd been tricked into betraying them.

Not long after, Snapper was captured by the alien Dominators and subjected to experiments that activated his teleporting metagene. Snapper and other survivors of the tests escaped and worked as the Blasters. During one of their adventures, the Khunds severed his hands, but Colu's Vril Dox replaced them with new ones. Snapper later became a mentor to the android Hourman III, made a fortune writing his JLA memoirs, and coached Young Justice. **AI**

CARSON, CAVE

DEBUT *The Brave and the Bold* #31 (Aug.–Sep. 1960)
REAL NAME Calvin Carson
HEIGHT 5ft 11in **WEIGHT** 178 lbs
HAIR Brown **EYES** Blue
POWERS/ABILITIES Cybernetic eye; expert in geology and related sciences.
ENEMIES Eclipso

Calvin Carson was a lab technician for E. Borsten & Co., which developed a digging machine, the Mighty Mole, for the government. When the project was axed, Carson stole the device and began to explore beneath the Earth's surface with the help of ex-convict Bulldozer Smith, geologist Christie Madison, and adventurer Johnny Blake.

After Cave's team found lost Nazi gold and time-travel technology, the Borsten family sued to regain the Mighty Mole, but instead settled for the time-travel equipment, letting Cave keep the Mole. Carson would later use his fortune to fund the Borsten's Rip Hunter-helmed time-travel experiments. When the US government banned his explorations, Carson joined the Forgotten Heroes, providing specialist help to Aquaman and the Sea Devils, the Time Masters, Amanda Waller, and the Justice Society of America. A true survivor, he even narrowly survived a brutal attack from Eclipso. **AI**

CATMAN

DEBUT *Detective Comics* #311 (Jan. 1963)
CURRENT VERSION *Secret Six* (Vol. 4) #1 (Feb. 2015)
BASE Gotham City
REAL NAME Thomas Blake
HEIGHT 6ft **WEIGHT** 179 lbs **HAIR** Brown **EYES** Green
POWERS/ABILITIES Talented inventor with high-level athletic ability; believed to have nine lives due to mystical cloth used in his costume.
ENEMIES The Riddler, Batman, Green Arrow
AFFILIATIONS Secret Six

BLACK MAGIC When a recovering Black Alice is threatened by dark mystics out to stop her full powers emerging, Catman had to team up with Etrigan to protect her.

On the run after breaking his way out of imprisonment by the mysterious Mockingbird, Thomas Blake found himself caught and confined again. This time, he and five others were trapped in a metal box under the ocean, and presented with a riddle to solve if they were to get out alive. Catman nearly panicked, since his feline affinities made him hate both water and confinement, but he kept his cool long enough for the group to escape—and thus the Secret Six were born. (Ventriloquist insists their actual number is seven because of her dummy.)

Working to discover who was manipulating them, Catman and his compatriots learned that Mockingbird was a cover identity for the Riddler, who had placed a mole in their team—Big Shot. The Riddler pursued the Secret Six, but Catman convinced his operatives—Scandal Savage, Ragdoll, and Jeannette—to turn on the Prince of Puzzles. The Secret Six then became embroiled in a war between rival arcane powers, with Catman joining forces with the Demon Etrigan to prevent Black Alice becoming the pawn of demonic forces. **AI**

ON THE RECORD

Previously Thomas Blake worked as a big-game hunter, tracking big cats and selling them to zoos. His cat obsession led him to a Pacific island, home to a cat cult, from whom he stole a sacred cat carving and the cloth that covered it.

Back in Gotham City, Blake became a costumed criminal and equipped himself with feline-themed accessories inspired by Catwoman and Batman, including catarangs and a turbocharged cat-car. He eventually joined the Secret Six, before being exiled during Salvation Run.

CAT MEETS BAT Catman, in his original Batman-mimicking regalia, grapples with the Dark Knight—the enemy who originally inspired him.

CATSEYE

DEBUT *Suicide Squad* (Vol.1) #53 (May 1991)
BASE Tokyo
HEIGHT 6ft 1in **WEIGHT** 195 lbs
HAIR Black **EYES** Brown
POWERS/ABILITIES Poison-tipped claws; enhanced speed and leaping ability.
ALLIES Yakuza, Outsiders
ENEMIES Suicide Squad

A ruthless killer, bioengineered as a metahuman agent of the Yakuza crime family, Catseye's real name and origin remain a mystery. He clashed with various members of the Suicide Squad when that covert agency went to Japan on a mission to recover a stolen cache of Russian weapons, known as the Dragon's Hoard. Several other rival groups came searching for the Dragon's Hoard as well, including the clandestine Russian Red Shadows and the Khmer Rouge.

Suicide Squad members Manhunter and Bronze Tiger were captured by the Yakuza, but freed by Katana from the Outsiders while Catseye fought Atom for possession of the stolen weapons. Later he attacked the Squad again, this time in an ancient temple, but was scratched by his own poison-tipped claws while fighting Bronze Tiger. Catseye met his end when he was incinerated in an explosion triggered by Deadshot. **AI**

CHAIN LIGHTNING

DEBUT *World's Finest Comics* #272 (Oct. 1981)
REAL NAME Amy
HEIGHT 5ft 4in **WEIGHT** 121 lbs
HAIR Blonde **EYES** Blue
POWERS/ABILITIES Absorption of electrical energy.
ALLIES Captain Marvel Jr.
ENEMIES Mary Marvel

Amy's metagene kicked in during her early teens, but she was unable to control it until an unknown person provided her with a bodysuit that housed containment circuitry. Unfortunately, Amy also began suffering from dissociative identity disorder. The dominant personality is the disturbed Amy, who tried to commit suicide in New York, but was rescued by Captain Marvel Jr., earning her lasting affection.

Her other three identities, however, are less benign. Amber is destructive; The Inner Child is a hulking brute; while Id is a small girl trapped inside the others. Together, they are known as Chain Lightning, and at different times Amy's powers appear as four distinct electrical beings. Shazam's magic lightning bolt gave all four personalities physical form, and Captain Marvel Jr. and Mister Scarlet had to subdue them before Fawcett City was reduced to rubble. Amy then underwent treatment at S.T.A.R. Labs. **AI**

CHAMELEON BOY

DEBUT *Adventure Comics* #267 (Dec. 1959)
CURRENT VERSION *Legion of Super-Heroes* (Vol. 7) #1 (Nov. 2011)
REAL NAME Reep Daggle
BASE Metropolis, 31st century
HEIGHT 5ft 9in **WEIGHT** 135 lbs
HAIR None **EYES** Yellow
POWERS/ABILITIES Duplication of the appearance of any object or being.
ENEMIES Daxamites

Reep Daggle is a Durlan—a race of hooded, tentacled aliens—that are feared and mistrusted throughout the galaxy for their shape-shifting abilities. Reep serves with the Legion of Super-Heroes in the 31st century. His strict Durlan upbringing leaves him ill-equipped to relate to his teammates' jokes, which is not helped by his abiding guilt at being forced to kill his brother Liggt during a Durlan ritual known as the Right of Survival.

Chameleon Boy prefers to appear as an androgynous figure, though he is capable of assuming almost any shape. However, as he is fond of reminding his fellow Legionnaires, he cannot duplicate the qualities of an object, only its appearance. Chameleon Boy has served the Legion well as an infiltrator and spy in their ongoing battle against the alien Daxamites. **AI**

CHARAXES

DEBUT *Batman* (Vol. 1) #63 (Feb. 1951) (as Killer Moth); *Underworld Unleashed* #1 (Nov. 1995) (as Charaxes)
REAL NAME Drury Walker
BASE Gotham City
HEIGHT 6ft 9in **WEIGHT** 202 lbs
HAIR Yellow **EYES** Red
POWERS/ABILITIES Insect form provides incredible strength, exoskeletal armor, as well as sticky, acidic secretions.
ENEMIES Batman, Robin, Superboy-Prime
AFFILIATIONS Black Lanterns

As Killer Moth, Drury Walker operated as a second-rate hood and paid protector to Gotham City's gangsters. Despite an arsenal of weapons, he was bested by Batman at every turn, leaving his clients irate and incarcerated. Finally, the demon Neron gave Walker his heart's desire: to be feared. Drury was transformed into a real Killer Moth—the man-eating Charaxes!

Charaxes repeatedly turned up in Gotham City seeking sustenance and crossing paths with Robin. During Infinite Crisis, Superboy-Prime tore Charaxes in half. He was reanimated as a Black Lantern but died again when Superboy-Prime—also a Black Lantern—overloaded his ring and exploded, killing Charaxes and a number of other Black Lanterns. **AI**

CHALLENGERS OF THE UNKNOWN

DEBUT *Showcase* #6 (Jan.-Feb. 1957)
CURRENT VERSION *DC Universe Presents* (Vol. 1) #6 (Apr. 2012)
BASE Challenger Mountain
MEMBERS/POWERS **Prof. Haley**: Skin diver and oceanographer; **Red Ryan**: Mountaineer and former circus acrobat; **June Robbins**: Computer and robotics expert; **Rocky Davis**: Wrestling champion and top strategist; **Ace Morgan**: Former test pilot and amateur sorcerer; **Clay Brody**: Former race-car driver; **Marlon Corbett**: Top-notch pilot; **Kenn Kawa**: Software and electronics specialist; **Brenda Ruskin**: Brilliant theoretical physicist.

The group of adventurers called Challengers were initially a reality TV phenomenon assembled by archaeologist presenter Clay Brody for his *Challengers* program. Things didn't go according to the script when, on a flight over the Himalayas, Clay, the contestants, producer June, and pilots Ace and Maverick crashed and went missing. All but Ace reappeared a few weeks later, remembering a recuperative period in Nanda Parbat, during which a high priest presented them a real-life mission: to beware the unknown, but also to challenge it and, in so doing, save the world.

After Clay sacrificed his life to provide cover for the Challengers' escape from a monster, the group examined a talisman that had led Clay to pick them, and discovered a note explaining that it was one of a set that the team had to recover before it fell into the wrong hands. The *Challengers* program was retooled to take advantage of this real-world quest. Their home base on a Metropolis soundstage was dubbed Challengers Mountain, and the group searched the world's most remote regions, encountering all manner of inexplicable phenomena, including animated statues and hordes of giant ants. More tragically they had to face the zombie return of their lost pilot and friend Ace, and the deaths of half their number: Lester, Brenda, Kenn, and Walter. **AI**

ON THE RECORD

The earliest version of the Challengers got their start when pilot "Ace" Morgan, wrestler "Rocky" Davis, circus daredevil "Red" Ryan, and diver "Prof." Haley survived an airplane crash on their way to appear on a radio program. Deciding that they were now "living on borrowed time," the four united as a team of adventurers-for-hire. They later learned that by cheating death, they no longer existed in the Book of Destiny, which led them to become caretakers of it.

INTO THE UNKNOWN
Fighting a cave-dwelling monster was just another day at the office for the Challengers, seen here shortly after June Robbins started to take a more active role in the group.

CATWOMAN

DATA

DEBUT *Batman* (Vol. 1) #1 **(Spring 1940)**
CURRENT VERSION *Catwoman* (Vol. 4) #1 **(Nov. 2011)**
REAL NAME Selina Kyle
BASE The East End, Gotham City
HEIGHT 5ft 7in **WEIGHT** 128lbs **EYES** Blue-green **HAIR** Black
POWERS/ABILITIES Master cat burglar; formidable fighter with expertise in boxing, acrobatics, and many martial arts disciplines; weapons include cat-o'-nine tails whip and gloves with diamond-tipped claws; wears protective goggles.
ALLIES Killer Croc, Alice Tesla, Batman (on occasion)
ENEMIES Joker's Daughter, Bone, Black Mask, Dollhouse
AFFILIATIONS Calabrese Crime Family, Justice League of America, Batman, Inc.

Catwoman is one of the great mysteries of Gotham City. Often switching from hero to villain in a single night, over the years Selina Kyle has been a help to Batman as often as she's been a thorn in his side. A capable leader, an intimidating fighter, and a savvy street-smart cat burglar, Catwoman has gone from being one of Gotham City's many forgotten children to one of its most powerful figures. After a stint as one of Gotham City's major crime bosses, Catwoman has returned to the rooftops, once again an independent creature of the night, answerable to no one except herself.

AT A GLANCE...

Hard knock life
Selina Kyle was a child of the system. But in a town like Gotham City, that system tended to be as corrupt as its elected officials. Selina grew up in Oliver's Group Home, coached in the ways of thievery by the institution's headmistress, Miss Oliver.

Getting organized
Catwoman became the leader of an organized crime family when she discovered that her father, Rex "the Lion" Calabrese, the former head of Gotham City's Mafia, was alive. He was residing in a cell in Blackgate Penitentiary, forgotten by the rest of Gotham City's criminals.

The Cat and the Bat
Despite often being on opposite sides of the law, Catwoman and Batman have shared a romantic interest in one another for years. While Catwoman isn't aware of Batman's double identity, that hasn't stopped the pair from having many intimate encounters and romantic flings.

Selina Kyle started life at a distinct disadvantage. As a child, she bounced around from foster home to foster home, before finding a more permanent residence at Oliver's Group Home, run by the unscrupulous Miss Oliver. The kids at the home were forced to break into jewelry stores and homes, stealing priceless treasures for the strict Miss Oliver. Learning the ins and outs of thievery at Oliver's, Selina retained a rebellious streak, often hiding expensive items in her teddy bear to invest in her future.

Years later, after leaving Miss Oliver's Home, Selina tried to build a better, legit future for herself and found gainful employment working for the city. She soon began using her access to Gotham City's computer files to research her history. When she dug too deep into her past, however, her boss promptly pushed her off a rooftop for her efforts. Her life was saved when she fell through a handily placed awning and awoke to find several cats attempting to rouse her from the city street. The incident spurred her to return to her thieving ways, and Selina fashioned a costume from the very awning that broke her fall, setting a single-minded course for a life of crime and cat burglary as Catwoman.

SIZE MATTERS
Young Selina Kyle realized the benefit of her small size when she was made to commit daring robberies for the head of her group home, Miss Oliver.

It wasn't long before she attracted the attention of Batman, and, as if to foreshadow the romance they would later share, the date of their auspicious first meeting was Valentine's Day. On that occasion, Batman stopped Catwoman from robbing the Sunnyside Housing Project. The night's events had a huge impact on Selina. She realized that while she couldn't give up her life of crime, she would choose to steal from the rich rather than the less fortunate.

Before long, Catwoman and Batman's rooftop flirtations and verbal and physical sparring would turn into a full-blown romance. While Batman learned about Selina's identity, Catwoman was never able to discover the Dark Knight's real name, despite the intimacy of their relationship. Catwoman's criminal acts, however, constantly caused a rift between the two, and they soon returned to their old status quo, with only the occasional team-up or confrontation.

CLASSIC STORIES

***Batman* (Vol. 1) #62 (Dec. 1950)** Catwoman's origin is revealed and tweaked for Earth-2's Catwoman.

***Batman* (Vol. 1) #404-407 (Feb.-May 1987)** In the groundbreaking *Batman: Year One*, Selina Kyle goes from call girl to vigilante after being inspired by the Dark Knight.

***Catwoman* (Vol. 1) #1-4 (Feb.-May 1989)** Catwoman's post-Crisis origin is explored in detail, including her training by the hero Wildcat.

***Catwoman: When in Rome* #1-6 (Nov. 2004-Apr. 2005)** Catwoman takes a trip to Italy with the Riddler by her side in a tale emerging out of the powerful "Batman: The Long Halloween" series.

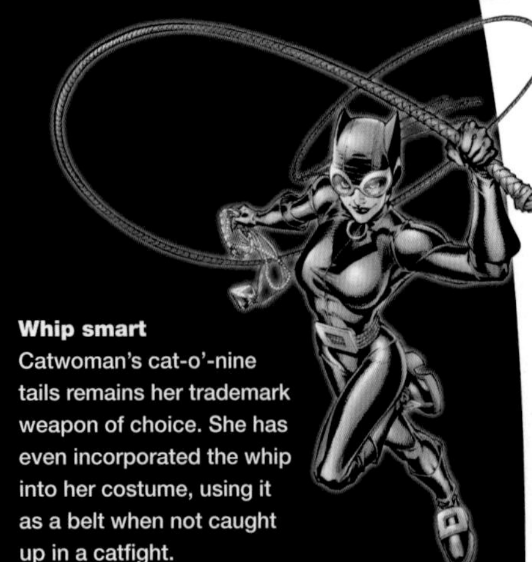

Whip smart
Catwoman's cat-o'-nine tails remains her trademark weapon of choice. She has even incorporated the whip into her costume, using it as a belt when not caught up in a catfight.

IN THE DOLLHOUSE

The daughter of the serial killer known as the Dollmaker, a twisted criminal called Dollhouse put herself in Catwoman's sights when she began kidnapping Gotham City's prostitutes and drug addicts. Afraid for the safety of those who had been taken, Catwoman investigated and discovered that Dollhouse used her victims to make macabre flesh-and-blood mannequins, positioning them like helpless living dolls, while selling their organs on the black market. With the timely help of Batman, Catwoman was able to shut down Dollhouse's sick operation.

ART ATTACK
Selina stumbled on Dollhouse's grisly handiwork, which the villain felt honored her family legacy and was also a form of artistic self-expression. Her victims felt quite differently.

THE GRIP OF GOTHTOPIA

In one his most ingenious "experiments" yet, the super-villain Scarecrow, aka Dr. Jonathan Crane, released a potent hallucinogen across Gotham City that made the entire populace believe their corrupt, shadowy metropolis had become a bright, crime-free utopia. In this world, Catwoman became Catbird, Batman's Super Hero partner. However, it wasn't long before the Dark Knight shook the influence of the drug, as did Catwoman, and brought about a dramatic end to the Scarecrow's elaborate scheme.

CATBIRD CALLS
In the faux world of Gothtopia, Catwoman became the equivalent of Robin. As Batman's partner and lover, the role was perfect for Selina, who was disappointed when the illusion shattered.

"My world is all just shades of gray, Batman. That's why you'll never understand me."

SELINA KYLE

While she considers herself a solo agent, Catwoman was at one point recruited into the government's own team of Super Heroes, the Justice League of America. Chosen for her criminal background, Catwoman was the perfect candidate to help the JLA infiltrate the Secret Society, a group of super-villains united under the leadership of the enigmatic Outsider.

When the Justice League of America failed to have the staying power of its inspiration—the Justice League—Catwoman found herself a part of a different type of organization altogether, the Calabrese crime family. After learning that her father—the imprisoned former mob boss Rex "the Lion" Calabrese—was still alive, Selina Kyle decided to take over the family business, believing that if she could control organized crime in Gotham City, she could actually make the city safer in the process. Ultimately, however, she couldn't betray her natural instincts, and soon handed over the crime syndicate's operation to her cousin Antonia, returning to her fulfilling full-time role as Catwoman. **MM**

OUT OF UNIFORM
Selina Kyle often proved as great a threat as her costumed alter ego. She mixed easily with Gotham City's elite, while always hiding her own personal agenda.

PICK AND CHOOSE
Never afraid to leap into battle, Catwoman picks her capers very carefully, often lashing out at injustices that affect her friends or her neighborhood.

ON THE RECORD

Catwoman has changed considerably since her debut in 1940. Originally simply called the Cat, Selina Kyle adopted a cat mask after her very first encounter with Batman. Since then, her costume and origin have evolved several times over the decades, but her role as Batman's chief femme fatale has remained constant.

Top Cat

In her original incarnation, Selina Kyle, aka Catwoman, was a former flight attendant-turned-thief. After dozens of clashes with the Dark Knight, she turned over a new leaf and became a trusted ally of Batman's. The two even formed a romantic relationship, learning each other's secret identities in the process.

After the cosmos-shattering events of Crisis on Infinite Earths, Catwoman gained a new backstory. A criminal who drifted into a life of prostitution, Selina Kyle was inspired by Batman to become a creature of the night. However, unlike the Dark Knight, Catwoman focused her night-time exploits on personal gain, becoming the quintessential cat burglar.

I LOVE PURPLE
After the events of *Batman: Year One*, Catwoman sported a gray bodysuit for a time before switching to a variation of her original purple look.

Changing ways

Having grown up in the troubled East End of Gotham City, Selina Kyle had remained very protective of her neighborhood, even as she spent most of her nights thieving from some of Gotham City's more well-heeled areas. After a visit to her old stomping grounds, Selina decided to turn around her career as Catwoman, becoming the East End's protector. She even retired from her life as a vigilante for a time when she had a baby. She briefly handed over the mantle of Catwoman to Holly Robinson, her loyal ally since her days as a prostitute. But Selina couldn't keep her true calling suppressed for long, and eventually returned to her life as Catwoman.

THE SACRIFICE
After having a daughter with her friend Sam Bradley Jr., Selina realized her lifestyle was too dangerous for a family. However, she was still devastated when she had to gave up her child, Helena, for adoption.

CHARYBDIS

DEBUT *Aquaman* (Vol. 5) #1 (Aug. 1994)
CURRENT VERSION *Aquaman* (Vol. 7) #42 (Sep. 2015)
BASE Seven Seas
HEIGHT 6ft 4in **WEIGHT** 237 lbs
EYES Black **HAIR** Black
POWERS/ABILITIES Absorbs talents and powers of others; breathes underwater as Piranha Man.
ENEMIES Aquaman

Charybdis and his wife Scylla were terrorists named after two horrific characters from Greek mythology (Charybdis was a deadly whirlpool, Scylla a multi-headed monster). Scylla died when a bomb exploded in her hands, and her death drove Charybdis insane. After this devastating incident, he was next seen displaying vast powers and a hatred for Aquaman. Defeating the Atlantean King in battle, Charybdis took his powers and caused the loss of Aquaman's hand, before the villain was shot by Dolphin. Close to death, Charybdis absorbed the essence of the piranhas that had eaten Aquaman's hand, preserving his life and allowing him to evolve into Piranha Man. He aimed to absorb every last shred of Aquaman's powers, leaving him for dead. The Sea King finally got the better of Piranha Man, but not before seeing his loved ones suffer.

Charybdis would later reappear as a member of the group Mera, assembled to hunt Aquaman when he took up arms against his former kingdom of Atlantis. **AI**

PIRANHA MAN
Charybdis transformed into Piranha Man when he was left for dead and was attacked by piranhas—he was then able to communicate with fish.

CHASE, CAMERON

DEBUT *Batman* #550 (Jan. 1998)
CURRENT VERSION *Batwoman* #1 (Nov. 2011)
BASE New York City
HEIGHT 5ft 5in **WEIGHT** 129 lbs
EYES Green **HAIR** Blonde
POWERS/ABILITIES Dampen superhuman powers; skilled investigator; firearms training.
ALLIES Manhunter
AFFILIATIONS Department of Extranormal Operations

Former private detective Cameron Chase is one of the top agents in the Department of Extranormal Operations, a branch of US intelligence that keeps tabs on the Earth's metahumans and supernatural beings.

Working under the skull-faced Director Bones, Chase was sent to Gotham City to unmask Batwoman, after Director Bones told her that hunting Batman's identity had turned out to be a dead end.

Cameron's dislike of costumed crime fighters stemmed from her childhood—her father was the little-known hero Acro-Bat whose throat was torn out by Dr. Trap. She followed Bones' orders even when he transformed her hunt for Batwoman into Operation Batfrack—in which dangerous villains were released into Gotham City as a plot to flush out Batman. Chase assisted in this operation, holding Gotham City under martial law on Bones' orders. When she learned Bones had gone rogue, she quit the D.E.O. and became a private investigator. **AI**

GIVING CHASE
Agent Cameron Chase had one thing on her mind: hunting down and exposing Batwoman, no matter what the cost.

CHECKMATE

DEBUT *Action Comics* #598 **(Mar. 1988)**
CURRENT VERSION *O.M.A.C.* (Vol. 4) #2 **(Dec. 2011)**
BASE Mount Rushmore
NOTABLE MEMBERS **Maxwell Lord, Maribel, Mokkari, Sarge Steel, Martin Welman, Anthony Jay, Rocker Bonn**
ALLIES S.H.A.D.E.
ENEMIES Brother Eye, O.M.A.C., Spyral

Checkmate is an international organization, led by Maxwell Lord, that cooperates with the needs of the world's governments while maintaining its independence from all of them. Characterized as a "global peace agency," the group is nevertheless noted for its sometimes questionable methods. Their most recent operations involved the pursuit of O.M.A.C.: a biotechnologically enhanced version of Project Cadmus scientist Kevin Kho. O.M.A.C. was created by the rogue sentient satellite Brother Eye who had turned on Project Cadmus, seeking to destroy it. A team of Checkmate agents—led by Sarge Steel and including Maribel and Little Knipper, and later, Mokkari—failed to capture O.M.A.C., after which Lord sought the assistance of S.H.A.D.E., over Sarge Steel's objections.

This escalation was answered by Brother Eye's attempt to assassinate Lord, against whom it held a previous grudge. Lord, however, destroyed Brother Eye in a final battle at Mount Rushmore, during which Sarge Steel lost a hand. Lord then decided to call off the hunt for O.M.A.C., deeming it no longer a threat to global interests because it was once again under the control of Kevin Kho's personality. **AI**

WHITE KNIGHTS?
Sarge Steele, Maribel, and Mokkari were members of Checkmate, with Maxwell Lord as their leader.

BACK IN TOUCH
Maxwell Lord received an unwelcome call from his old adversary, Brother Eye.

ON THE RECORD

Previous versions of Checkmate were organized by Amanda Waller as an independent arm of Task Force X, a quasi-governmental bureau overseeing black-ops missions deemed vital to US interests.

Task Force X also controlled the Suicide Squad, foreshadowing Waller's later work assembling the squad when she was in control of A.R.G.U.S.. Maxwell Lord later supplanted Waller and took control of Checkmate, killing the Blue Beetle along the way and then unleashing O.M.A.C.

KOBRA STRIKES
Checkmate's enemies were numerous, but none were more deadly—and persistent—than Kobra and his minions.

CHEETAH II

DATA

DEBUT *Wonder Woman* (Vol. 2) #7 **(Aug. 1987)**
CURRENT VERSION *Justice League* (Vol. 2) #10 **(Aug. 2012)**
REAL NAME Barbara Ann Minerva
HEIGHT 5ft 9in **WEIGHT** 140 lbs
EYES Brown **HAIR** Red
POWERS/ABILITIES Channeling the spirit of the Cheetah grants superhuman strength and agility, razor-sharp claws, as well as bloodlust.
ALLIES Circe
ENEMIES Wonder Woman, Amazons
AFFILIATIONS Secret Society of Super-Villains, Menagerie, Suicide Squad

CEREMONIAL SUICIDE
Aunt Lyta instructed Barbara to thrust the God-Slayer Knife into her own chest in order to become the avatar of the goddess of the hunt.

Raised in a cult called Amazonia, Barbara Minerva became Cheetah, mortal adversary of the real Amazon—Wonder Woman—after cutting herself with the God-Killer Knife. Whether with the Suicide Squad, the Secret Society of Super-Villains, or the Menagerie, she has a burning desire to put an end to the Amazon Queen.

Barbara Minerva grew up under the sway of a woman known as Aunt Lyta, who taught her charges that life was a hunt and every person on Earth was either a rival… or prey. Her final initiation into the cult of Amazonia was a fight to the death against her own brother, after which Aunt Lyta sent her out into the world to retrieve the God-Killer Knife. Barbara built a reputation as an expert in antiquities and was thrilled to meet Wonder Woman—until Diana mocked her cultish beliefs. Maintaining a friendly facade, Minerva convinced Wonder Woman to let her inspect A.R.G.U.S.' Black Room of magical artifacts. While there, she found the God-Killer Knife and stabbed herself with it, becoming the Cheetah.

Over the next six years, she went on a crime spree and tangled with Wonder Woman on several occasions. Spending time with the Suicide Squad after her capture, she was broken out by the Crime Syndicate and killed everyone in the Amazonia cult before receiving Wonder Woman's Lasso of Truth from the Crime Syndicate.

Gathering a group of animal-themed villains she called the Menagerie, Cheetah caught Steve Trevor in the Lasso only to discover that because she lacked Diana's purity of purpose the Lasso's powers would not work for her. Trevor then ensnared her in it and knocked her out. She was later hired to kill Green Arrow but was unable to do so, and lost her powers when a group of Elder Gods struck at the magical powers of Earth's metahumans. **AI**

FELINE PHYSIOLOGY
As well as exhibiting superhuman strength, speed, and stamina, Cheetah could "infect" others with feline traits by biting them.

ON THE RECORD

Two of the current Cheetah's aliases—Priscilla Rich and Sabrina Ballesteros—mirror the identities of previous Cheetahs. Priscilla Rich was a socialite and also the first Cheetah, a Golden Age adversary of Wonder Woman. Priscilla's niece Debbi Domaine succeeded her in 1980.

Corporate raider Sebastian Ballesteros was the fourth Cheetah. He usurped the powers of archaeologist Barbara Minerva after making a bargain with the African plant-god Urzkartaga. Ballesteros also made a pact with the sorceress Circe to turn Diana's friend Vanessa Kapatelis into a second Silver Swan, and became the witch's lover. Minerva later killed Ballesteros, and reclaimed the title of Cheetah.

A HOST FOR HUNTING
Ballesteros convinced Urzkartaga to abandon its female host and use him as the conduit for the ancient powers of the Cheetah.

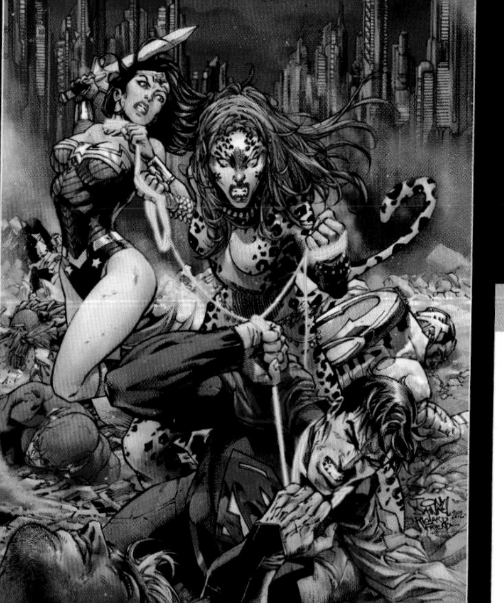

JUST ONE BITE
Wonder Woman, Superman, and the rest of the Justice League tracked down Cheetah in the Congo where Superman was attacked and bitten by the villain.

CLASSIC STORIES

***Wonder Woman* (Vol. 1) #6 (Fall 1943)** Priscilla Rich suffers from a split personality that leads her to become the first Cheetah out of jealousy toward Wonder Woman. She joins Villainy Inc.

***Wonder Woman* (Vol. 2) #206 (Sep. 2004)** After being outmaneuvered by Sebastian Ballesteros and losing her Cheetah powers, Barbara Minerva gets her revenge, killing him and becoming Cheetah.

***Final Crisis: Resist* #1 (Dec. 2008)** Unaffected by the Anti-Life Equation, Cheetah has a brief affair with Snapper Carr, who helps her join Checkmate and fight against Darkseid.

CHEMO

DEBUT *Showcase* (Vol. 1) #39 (Jul.–Aug. 1962)
CURRENT VERSION *Justice League* #28 (Apr. 2014)
HEIGHT 25ft or far taller **WEIGHT** 5,697 lbs
EYES Red **HAIR** None
POWERS/ABILITIES Can spew dangerous, extremely toxic, experimental chemicals from his mouth; enhanced strength and endurance; extremely limited intelligence.
ENEMIES Metal Men

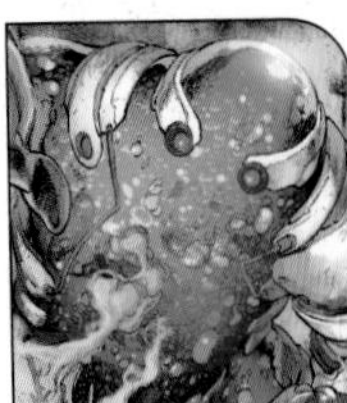

An expert in robotics, Dr. Will Magnus was working for the US Army when he developed the first significant step towards artificial intelligence in robotics: a responsometer. Placed into different vats of molten metal, the responsometer animated the material and brought about the creation of the robotic heroes called the Metal Men: Gold, Mercury, Lead, Iron, Tin, and Platinum.

When a mysterious saboteur stole a responsometer and threw it into a vat of hazardous waste, the gigantic monster Chemo was formed. Unlike the Metal Men, the villain did not seem to possess much of a conscience. Instead, it had an appetite for destruction, ejecting noxious chemicals from its mouth and causing untold havoc, until it was stopped by the valiant sacrifice of the original Metal Men. **MM**

CHESHIRE

DEBUT *The New Teen Titans* (Vol. 1) Annual #2 (Dec. 1983)
CURRENT VERSION *Red Hood and the Outlaws* #20 (Jul. 2013)
REAL NAME Jade Nguyen
BASE 'Eth Alth'eban
HEIGHT 5ft 9in **WEIGHT** 135 lbs
EYES Black **HAIR** Black
POWERS/ABILITIES Master martial artist and fighter; adept at utilizing poisons.
ALLIES Red Hood, Lady Shiva, Bronze Tiger
ENEMIES The Untitled, Aquaman, the Others

Little is known about the assassin called Cheshire, aside from her real name. As a member of both the League of Assassins and the terrorist organization Mayhem, Cheshire has earned a reputation as one of the most dangerous people on the planet. While viewed as cutthroat and evil, Cheshire has shown a conscience from time to time, especially when it comes to Arsenal. While working with the League of Assassins, Cheshire stole Arsenal's hat, appearing to flirt with the vigilante. She later freed Arsenal from imprisonment after feeling pity for him.

However, Cheshire is not to be trifled with. A martial arts expert, she uses a device to teleport during combat, as well as a variety of lethal poisons, some of which she uses to lace her sharp fingernails. **MM**

CHIEF, THE

DEBUT *My Greatest Adventure* (Vol. 1) #80 (Jun. 1963)
CURRENT VERSION *The Ravagers* #4 (Oct. 2012)
REAL NAME Dr. Niles Caulder
HEIGHT 5ft 10in **WEIGHT** 215 lbs
EYES Red **HAIR** Blue
POWERS/ABILITIES Genius level intellect; incredibly persuasive; uses experimental sciences.
ALLIES Beast Boy, A.R.G.U.S.
ENEMIES Crime Syndicate, Lex Luthor
AFFILIATIONS The Doom Patrol

A wheelchair-bound mad scientist, Dr. Niles Caulder has a shared past with Dr. Caitlin Fairchild, and even spent time helping her team of runaway metahumans, the Ravagers. But Caulder is also a man of secrets, and successfully hid the truth that his ally was not the true Caitlin Fairchild but a clone of the original.

Later, Caulder formed his own Super Hero team, known as the Doom Patrol. A metahuman support group, it made heroes out of people on the brink of death. After his original team was wiped out by the Crime Syndicate, Caulder recruited new members, including Robotman, Negative Man, Element Woman, and Elasti-Girl. They later battled with the Justice League over the fate of Power Ring (Jessica Cruz) before disappearing. **MM**

CHRONOS

DEBUT *The Atom* (Vol. 1) #3 (Oct.–Nov. 1962)
CURRENT VERSION *Justice League of America* (Vol. 3) #5 (Aug. 2013)
REAL NAME David Clinton
HEIGHT 5ft 10in **WEIGHT** 173 lbs
EYES Blue **HAIR** Black
POWERS/ABILITIES Highly intelligent; can teleport himself and others through time.
ENEMIES Justice League of america, Secret Society
AFFILIATIONS Secret Society

When the Outsider–Alfred Pennyworth of Earth-3–traveled to the dimension of the Justice League, he paved the way for the arrival of his master, Owlman, and his allies, the Crime Syndicate. To that end, he gathered together some of Earth's most dangerous super-villains to form the Secret Society. Desiring a HQ that could shift through time and space, the Outsider shackled and drained the energies of the time-traveling villain, Chronos. In so doing, he could use Chronos' temporal energy to fuel the hideout's leaps through time.

Little else is known about the modern-day incarnation of Chronos. However, before the reality-altering event Flashpoint, Chronos was a recurring thorn in the side of the size-changing Super Hero known as the Atom. **MM**

CIRCE

DEBUT *Wonder Woman* (Vol. 1) #37 (Sep.–Oct. 1949)
CURRENT VERSION *Men of War* (Vol. 2) #2 (Dec. 2011)
BASE The Island of Aiaia
HEIGHT 5ft 11in **WEIGHT** 135 lbs
EYES Yellow **HAIR** Red
POWERS/ABILITIES Extremely powerful sorceress; able to transform humans into superhumans or animal/human hybrids; can teleport at will; can produce illusions and alter physical objects around her; extremely long-lived.
ALLIES Magog, Ani-Men
ENEMIES Wonder Woman, Superman, Hippolyta

Stories of the nefarious witch Circe date back to the days of ancient civilization and legendary tales like "The Odyssey." While determining fact from fiction can sometimes be difficult when it comes to the sorceress' past, it is clear that Circe has had a very longstanding rivalry with Wonder Woman's mother, Hippolyta. When Hippolyta was a young queen, she accepted Circe's services of enchanting the Amazon's weapons in exchange for male Amazon heirs to serve as human fodder for Circe's army of animal/human hybrids called Ani-Men. When Hippolyta backed out of her deal, making an alternative agreement with the god Hephaestus instead, Circe was enraged and began plotting her revenge.

She took it out on Wonder Woman, lashing out at the Amazon by empowering a young man named David Reid with a hatred of Super Heroes. Circe transformed Reid into the powerful super-villain Magog, and unleashed him on Superman, while she personally attacked Wonder Woman. Neither succeeded in their attempt to take down the heroes. **MM**

BEAUTY AND THE BEAST
Circe is not above using her physical charms to get weak-willed men to do her bidding.

ON THE RECORD

Circe originally challenged the Golden Age Wonder Woman, then became a recurring figure in Diana's Rogues Gallery in the early 1980s. Following Circe's reinvention after the events of Crisis on Infinite Earths, this modern version of the sorceress fitted perfectly with a Wonder Woman more grounded in Greek mythology than ever before.

Replacing the Cheetah as Wonder Woman's most dangerous foe, Circe even earned a place in the Injustice Gang during the late 1990s reboot of the *JLA*.

GOADING THE GODS
One of Circe's most ambitious plots was to pit god against god in the miniseries *War of the Gods*. Even with an army of the undead behind her, Circe fell to Wonder Woman and her allies.

CLAYFACE

DATA

DEBUT *Detective Comics* (Vol. 1) #40 **(Jun. 1940)**
CURRENT VERSION *Batman* (Vol. 2) #1 **(Nov. 2011)**
REAL NAME Basil Karlo **BASE** Gotham City
HEIGHT Variable **WEIGHT** Variable **EYES** Yellow **HAIR** None
POWERS/ABILITIES Able to shift his clay-like form into a variety of weapons including giant mallets and blades; superhuman strength that increases in proportion to his size; can become an exact clone of someone simply by touching them; gifted actor able to mimic a variety of voices and mannerisms.
ALLIES Poison Ivy, Batwoman, Ragman, Penguin, Secret Society of Super-Villains
ENEMIES Batman, the Batman Family
AFFILIATIONS The Unknowns

MAN WITHOUT A FACE **Clayface's powers eventually caused him to lose his own DNA, becoming those he mimics right down to the cellular level.**

FEAT OF CLAY **Clayface briefly tried to reform his ways while suffering from amnesia. He joined the short-lived Super Hero team led by Batwoman called the Unknowns.**

Clayface is one of the most infamous and powerful super-villains in Gotham City, a rogue who has proven notoriously hard for Batman to defeat in combat. Able to transform his body into anything from a weapon to a perfect likeness of another human being or animal, Clayface can blend into any crowd, or choose to tower above it. An actor with delusions of grandeur, Clayface's most prized role is as an arch foe to the Dark Knight.

Basil Karlo never stood out in high school, being neither bullied nor lauded. After leaving, Karlo tried to distinguish himself by becoming a famous actor. However, his acting career mirrored his school days, and he had trouble landing major parts and distinguishing himself from the pack. Desperate for work, he went to the Penguin, who presented him with a rare block of clay-like material excavated from a Navajo reservation decades ago. The clay attached itself to Karlo and instantly gave him an acting range he'd never dreamed of. He landed a starring role in a film called *The Terror*, and his movie career finally took off.

Karlo was now handsome and charismatic, but he also had a nasty streak. His arrogance would often boil over into violence, and when his temper made him lash out at a director, he was fired from the job. To make matters worse, he began to forget his lines, preferring to improvise rather than go to the trouble of memorizing his movie scripts. But that was the least of his worries. The ever-shifting clay formula inside him began to make it impossible for him to hold his shape for an entire day's work.

As his star fell in the motion picture business, Karlo began to repay the Penguin with his developing Clayface abilities, committing crimes for the villain for years, until he finally grasped his own potential. Using his acting skills and newfound powers, Karlo found he could become anyone he wanted, or form giant weapons out of his massive body. During his criminal career, he clashed repeatedly with Batman. He became one of the Dark Knight's most powerful enemies—one who has even forced Batman to adopt specialized armor in order to combat him. **MM**

ON THE RECORD

In the long history of DC Comics, several villains have taken the name Clayface. The Golden Age Basil Karlo first adopted the villainous identity as a simple masked murderer. In the 1960s, the Clayface name was appropriated by Matt Hagen, who stumbled on a pool of unusual liquid that gave him shape-shifting abilities.

Hagen died during *Crisis on Infinite Earths*, but not before Preston Payne stole his name as a tortured Clayface with a melting touch. The villain Kobra even created his own Clayface in the form of Lady Clay, Preston's future lover and the mother of their son, Cassius, aka Clayface V.

COMPOSITE CLAYFACE **Basil Karlo injected himself with a mix of Hagen, Payne, and Fuller's blood, turning into the modern incarnation of Clayface.**

CLASSIC STORIES

***Detective Comics* (Vol. 1) #298 (Dec. 1961)** The second Clayface, Matt Hagen, employs fantastic shape-shifting powers that truly earn him his villainous title.

***Batman* (Vol. 1) Annual #11 (Nov. 1987)** The tragic life of the third Clayface, Preston Payne, is examined in detail, including his "romance" with a lifeless mannequin.

***Detective Comics* (Vol. 1) #604–607 (Sep.–Nov. 1989)** Batman and his ally Looker fight the combined might of the united Clayfaces, with Basil Karlo transforming himself into the Ultimate Clayface.

CLOCK KING

DEBUT *World's Finest Comics* #111 (Aug. 1960)
CURRENT VERSION *Green Arrow* (Vol. 5) #22 (Sep. 2013)
BASE Seattle
REAL NAME William "Billy" Tockman
HEIGHT 6ft 1in **WEIGHT** 235 lbs
HAIR Black **EYES** Brown
ABILITIES Exceptional criminal mind.
ENEMIES Green Arrow, Richard Dragon

Seattle crime boss Billy Tockman used a vintage-clock repair shop called Clock King as cover for his many illegal business enterprises. When the crime-fighting vigilante Green Arrow began complicating business for all of Seattle's gangs, Tockman proposed a truce between them to unite against their common enemy. His criminal counterparts were not keen on the idea, and shortly after two of them—Jin Fang and Jimmy MacGowan—were killed, but not by Green Arrow.

Their real enemy was Richard Dragon, as John Diggle informed Tockman, who cut a deal with Diggle to take down Dragon, in return for which Green Arrow would ignore Billy's operations. However, Dragon outfoxed them, forcing Tockman to try to kill Q-Core employees Naomi Singh and Henry Fyff. In the event, Green Arrow's daughter, Emiko, intervened and took Tockman down.

Pre-Flashpoint, the Clock King was a clock-faced costumed criminal living on borrowed time, who was seemingly killed on a mission with the Suicide Squad. **AI**

CRIME TIME
Billy Tockman was known by some as the Clock King, the name of the shop that fronted his criminal activities.

COBALT BLUE

DEBUT *Speed Force* #1 (Nov. 1997)
REAL NAME Malcolm Thawne
HEIGHT 5ft 11in **WEIGHT** 179 lbs
HAIR Blond **EYES** Blue
POWERS/ABILITIES Possesses a gem whose flame can steal the Flash's speed and displays a number of other magical powers.
ENEMIES The Flash

The identical twin brother of Barry Allen—the second Flash—Malcolm Thawne was stolen away and raised in secret by the Thawnes, an abusive family of crooks. Malcolm learned of Barry's existence and of the loving family that fate had decreed he would never know and used his gifts for sorcery to give vent to his jealous rage. Calling himself Cobalt Blue, he drew power from a mystic blue flame and a crystalline talisman that focused his anger—a Thawne legacy that was passed onto him—which was capable of stealing Barry Allen's super-speed.

Barry's death during the Crisis on Infinite Earths appeared to have cheated Thawne of his revenge, so instead he focused on Allen's descendants and traveled through time trying to exterminate them.

The third Flash, Wally West, finally ended the menace of Cobalt Blue by running at such tremendous speeds that Thawne's magical gem overloaded from the excess energy. Thawne was presumably destroyed, but his talisman—which also contained his consciousness—would be passed onto Thawne's hate-filled progeny. **AI**

SIBLING SORCERY
Cobalt Blue wore an enchanted gem in the center of his chest. The magic blue flame it generated had the power to steal the Flash's super-speed.

CLUEMASTER

DEBUT *Detective Comics* #351 (May 1966)
CURRENT VERSION *Batman Eternal* #3 (Jun. 2014)
REAL NAME Arthur Brown
BASE Gotham City
HEIGHT 5ft 11in **WEIGHT** 169 lbs
HAIR Blond **EYES** Blue
POWERS/ABILITIES Various weapons and defensive items built into suit.
ENEMIES Batman
AFFILIATIONS Injustice League, Suicide Squad

Celebrity game show host Arthur Brown lost his show after insulting a contestant and turned to crime as the Cluemaster, daring his pursuers to catch him by leaving behind clues at the scene of every crime.

Batman discovered his secret identity, but let him go as Brown was providing for his family. Soon after, Cluemaster proposed to Lincoln March that they work together to bring down the Dark Knight for good. They brought together a huge swath of Gotham City's criminal underground to run Batman to the point of exhaustion by executing several attacks at once. After this, Cluemaster confronted Batman on top of Beacon Tower. He taunted him, but then became enraged when Batman called him a second-rate Riddler who could never have pulled off the operation by himself.

Cluemaster was killed by Lincoln March just as he was about to shoot Batman, his ultimate plot foiled by an even more subtle schemer—proving Batman right. **AI**

CLUELESS
The Cluemaster thought he had gotten the better of Batman, unaware that Lincoln March was just waiting for his own moment to strike.

CONGLOMERATE, THE

DEBUT *Justice League Quarterly* #1 (Dec. 1990)
MEMBERS **Booster Gold** (Michael Carter); **Echo** (Terri Eckhart); **Gypsy** (Cindy Reynolds); **Jesse Quick** (Jesse Chambers); **Hardline** (Armando Ramone, formerly **Reverb**); **Maxi-Man** (Henry Hayes); **Nuklon** (Albert Rothstein); **Praxis** (Jason Praxis); **Vapor** (Carrie Donahue); **Templar** (Colin Brandywine).
ALLIES Justice League International (JLI)
ENEMIES Despero
AFFILIATIONS S.T.A.R. Labs

Lacking superpowers, the hero Booster Gold felt like a "second-stringer" with the JLA, so he formed his own team. With the help of businesswoman Claire Montgomery, he founded the corporate-sponsored super-team the Conglomerate.

The roster included "fledgling" Super Heroes such as Echo, Gypsy, and Praxis. They disbanded following a series of less-than-notable adventures. Montgomery formed a second Conglomerate, this time made up of the Qwardian villains Deadeye, Elasti-Man, Element Man, Frostbite, Fiero, Scarab, and Slipstream for a pay-per-view battle with the JLI.

Later, Claire hired British hero Templar to lead a short-lived, third version featuring both new and original employees. **AI**

HEROES' WELCOME
The Conglomerate received a warm welcome from the press and the public when they debuted as a team.
1 Reverb
2 Vapor
3 Echo
4 Maxi-Man
5 Booster Gold
6 Praxis
7 Gypsy

CONSTANTINE

DATA

DEBUT *Swamp Thing* (Vol. 2) #37 **(Jun. 1985)**
CURRENT VERSION *Justice League Dark* (Vol. 1) #1 **(Nov. 2011)**
BASE House of Mystery
REAL NAME John Constantine
HEIGHT 6ft **WEIGHT** 158 lbs
HAIR Blond **EYES** Blue
POWERS/ABILITIES Access to powerful mystical artifacts and vast knowledge of magical and arcane rituals.
ALLIES Zatanna, Swamp Thing
ENEMIES Cult of the Cold Flame
AFFILIATIONS Justice League Dark

UNHOLY SMOKE
Constantine works best behind the scenes manipulating other people. But, when the occasion calls for it, he can unleash his own formidable powers.

FAMILY SACRIFICE
Young John discovered that great power brought great sacrifice as he witnessed the death of his family.

Feared by most, trusted by few, needed by many, John Constantine wields both powerful magic and a devious mind. He is untroubled by social mores and will use anyone to get what he wants. Fortunately for his friends and the millions of people he has saved over the years, he usually wants the right thing. Usually.

A native of Liverpool, England, John Constantine has had many conflicting stories told about his childhood, but all end with the tragic loss of his family. He was drawn into the world of the occult as a young man and spent years traveling Europe to deepen his knowledge before going to New York City to study with Nick Necro and Baron Winters. Constantine fell in love with Necro's girlfriend Zatanna, also a magician. Together, they battled the Cult of the Cold Flame, but the alliance fractured when Nick's obsession with the Books of Magic brought John and Zatanna together.

In revenge, Nick bargained with the Cold Flame to consign Constantine to Hell in exchange for his help in finding the Books of Magic. John outsmarted Nick and sent him to Hell instead, but his romance with Zatanna was broken when Constantine's occult investigations resulted in the death of her father, Zatara. The pair did not see each other again until John tracked Zatanna down after learning of the Enchantress' separation from her human host, June Moone, and the threat she posed to the world. He was instrumental in bringing together a team that included Zatanna—the Justice League Dark—to fight the Enchantress, and reunited the villain with her host, despite the team's objections.

Constantine also tried to manipulate the race for Pandora's Box, temporarily borrowing Shazam's powers, but was unable to prevent the Crime Syndicate from coming to Earth. After their defeat, he renewed his battle with the Cold Flame and was magically transported to Earth-2. There, he eliminated the alternate version of himself to save a large group of people—including some of his family—from Darkseid and the rampaging Parademons. He brought these rescued souls to Earth and then teleported away, knowing he had—as always—done what was necessary. **AI**

ON THE RECORD

Constantine's cynicism, cigarettes, and trench coat are constants in his history across universes and storylines. However, his path to occult prominence differed in his first incarnations.

After a traumatic childhood and a stint with a touring punk-rock band, John tried magic in an ill-fated ritual that ended with a demon capturing the girl he had intended to help. Shell-shocked, he spent time in a mental institution before embarking on a career as a paranormal investigator. Mistrusted by friends and enemies, he has a solid partnership with the Swamp Thing, who has known him since his earliest days in the paranormal business.

BOYS ON FILM
When a US cable channel wanted to film a documentary on his old band Mucous Membrane, John found himself looking into strange goings-on in Newcastle.

CLASSIC STORIES

***Hellblazer* #11 (Nov. 1988)** The tragic story of the Newcastle Crew, a loose group of young occult investigators who try—and fail—to save the child Astra Logue from the demon Nergal.

***Swamp Thing* (Vol. 2) #46 (Apr. 1986)** Constantine introduces the Swamp Thing to the Parliament of Trees, setting the stage for the Swamp Thing's ascent into the role of Avatar of the Green.

***Hellblazer* #41-46 (May-Oct. 1991)** John's past and bad habits catch up with him all at once as he faces terminal lung cancer and a devil determined to collect his soul.

FIGHT FOR ZATANNA
Nick Necro and John Constantine battled each other. One of them had to be sacrificed if the woman they both loved, Zatanna, was to be saved.

COPPERHEAD

DEBUT *The Brave and the Bold* (Vol. 1) #78 **(Jun.–Jul. 1968)**
CURRENT VERSION *Justice League* (Vol. 2) #18 **(May 2013)**
HEIGHT 6ft 2in (human); variable (reptiloid)
WEIGHT 200 lbs (human); variable (reptiloid)
EYES Brown (human); green (reptiloid)
POWERS/ABILITIES Serpentine contortionist; enhanced speed, reflexes, and strength; venomous, fanged bite; near-frictionless movement; prehensile tail; scaling sheer surfaces; crushing prey.
ALLIES Hellgrammite
ENEMIES Batman, Black Canary, Nightwing
AFFILIATIONS Secret Society of Super-Villains, Black Lantern Corps

SNAKESKIN BOOTS
Copperhead's brutal bestiality, serpentine speed, and reptilian strength could never match Batman's cool thinking and unerring martial arts training.

Career criminal Copperhead utilized a technologically advanced snake-themed costume that mimicked the evolutionary advantages of many reptiles. However, his reputation for infallibility was ruined as soon as he came up against Super Heroes. A ruthless and dangerous adversary for the regular police, he became something of a joke among meta-criminals.

On a frustrating downward spiral, Copperhead sold his soul in return for increased power, and was mystically transformed into a snake-human hybrid. Sadly, although the transformation granted him lethal natural powers, it also greatly diminished his intellect. He became a brutish thug, enslaved to the carnivorous appetites of the reptiles he embodied, his body and mind gradually regressing to those of a savage beast.

No longer a schemer, but still ferociously dangerous, Copperhead became a professional enforcer and assassin in groups such as the Secret Society of Super-Villains. Arrogant and over-confident, he was an easy kill for Deathstroke the Terminator when the mercenary abruptly switched sides during the Crime Syndicate's invasion. **WW**

AMBUSH PREDATOR
For all his reptilian prowess and mystical augmentation, Copperhead was only a real threat when he could take his opponents by surprise.

ON THE RECORD

A thief and killer with an arsenal of tricks, Copperhead was always a second-rater. After being recreated by the demonic tempter Neron, he began a shocking descent into sheer bestiality.

When he started eating his victims, he was tried as a serial killer by District Attorney Kate Spencer, who subsequently eliminated him in her guise of Manhunter. The name of Copperhead was then taken by psychopathic murderer Nathan Prince of the Terror Titans.

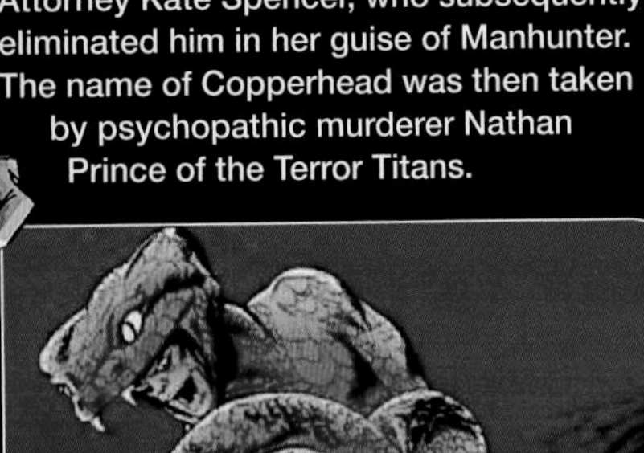

GETTING A GRIP
Copperhead's ambition, guile, and savage power initially helped him get the upper hand against heroes such as Batman, but the tables were soon turned.

COUNT VERTIGO

DEBUT *World's Finest Comics* (Vol. 1) #251 **(Jun.–Jul. 1978)**
CURRENT VERSION *Green Arrow* (Vol. 5) #22 **(Sep. 2013)**
REAL NAME Warren (formerly Werner) Zytle
BASE Vlatava
HEIGHT 5ft 11in **WEIGHT** 189 lbs
EYES Blue **HAIR** Blond
POWERS/ABILITIES Cybernetic brain augmentations that can produce disruption of equilibrium and even death by inducing cerebral hemorrhages.
ENEMIES Green Arrow, Shado
AFFILIATIONS Longbow Hunters, Crius

DIZZY WITH POWER
Werner Zytle believed that his ability to twist perceptions and to mangle minds put him beyond the reach of common heroes.

Decades ago, when the Eastern European kingdom of Vlatava fell to republican rebels, ruler Count Zytle was killed and his wife and child fled to Canada. She became a prostitute to survive, descending into drug addiction while constantly blaming her feeble son Werner for all her troubles. Eventually she sold little Werner to the Crius Mental Health and Research Hospital. The efficient, dispassionate scientists were seeking ways to selectively "improve" the children in their wards, and the frail boy—renamed Warren—seemed an ideal candidate for their radical theories and experiments.

Clinically abused and utterly abandoned, Warren spent his childhood under the cold tutelage of Doctor Witchell. For ten years his brain was systematically modified by electronic devices, and he developed the power to agonizingly disorient the minds of those around him. Werner escaped as a teenager, and after disabling Crius's failsafe mechanisms, used his abilities to kill his supervisors. Acquiring funds by working in organized crime, he returned to Vlatava and single-handedly reclaimed his country, installing himself as its ruler, Count Vertigo. Appearing to the world as a benevolent monarch, Vertigo covertly controls a criminal empire, bringing him into conflict with Green Arrow and Shado. **WW**

ON THE RECORD

Count Vertigo's first appearance was during his attempt to steal back the crown jewels Vlatava had sold off during the war. Confronted by Green Arrow, he unleashed his disorientation powers, which were a side-effect of technology used to correct a hereditary ear condition.

Following years of criminal activity Vertigo was finally imprisoned, and joined the Suicide Squad to reduce his sentence. He was eventually recruited to UN intelligence agency Checkmate, becoming Amanda Waller's White Knight.

POWER POLITICS
Count Vertigo understood how to use power, choosing allies for their immediate usefulness rather than any long-term potential.

COSMIC BOY

DATA

DEBUT *Adventure Comics* (Vol. 1) #247 **(Apr. 1958)**
CURRENT VERSION *Legion of Super-Heroes* (Vol. 7) #1 **(Nov. 2011)**
BASE Legion of Super-Heroes HQ, 31st-century Metropolis
HEIGHT 5ft 7in **WEIGHT** 145 lbs
EYES Blue **HAIR** Black
POWERS/ABILITIES Generation and manipulation of magnetic fields; unwavering dedication and devotion to the concept of the Legion.
REAL NAME Rokk Krinn
ALLIES Garth Ranzz, Imra Ardeen, Superman
ENEMIES Legion of Super-Villains, Fatal Five, Dark Circle
AFFILIATIONS Legion of Super-Heroes

CLASSIC STORIES

***Adventure Comics* (Vol. 1) #247 (Apr. 1958)**
History-loving Cosmic Boy leads his friends back in time to recruit Superboy and play a little joke on the mythic Boy of Steel.

***Legion of Super-Heroes* (Vol. 2) #297 (Mar. 1983)**
After his family are caught in a terrorist nuclear strike, the usually stable, stoic Cosmic Boy goes on a fury-fueled rampage of vengeance.

***Legion of Super-Heroes* (Vol. 3) #62 (Jul. 1989)**
With the Magic Wars devastating the laws of reality, Rokk's younger brother Pol—fresh out of the Legion Academy—sacrifices his life to save the universe.

HOME FOR HEROES
Fellow founders Saturn Girl and Lightning Lad created normal lives outside the team, but Cosmic Boy always considered the Legion his true home.

Possessing unparalleled strength and incomparable skill in manipulating magnetic fields and forces, founding Legionnaire Cosmic Boy is the backbone of the Legion of Super-Heroes: dependable, valiant, and coolly capable. He was unanimously voted the team's first leader by his colleagues and has served faithfully with dedication and distinction under each commander who followed his sterling example.

Rokk Krinn was born on Earth, just months before his parents returned to their homeworld Braal. Due to the intermingling of magnetic fields in his formative months, the infant developed his race's inherent magnetic manipulation abilities to an extraordinary degree. In his early teens he used these powers to became a champion of the sport Magno-ball.

During one of Braal's frequent economic recessions, the 15-year-old Rokk left his planet to find work elsewhere. En route to Earth he met Garth Ranzz from Winath and Imra Ardeen from Saturn's moon Titan, and together they foiled an assassination attempt on R.J. Brande. The wealthy technologist showed his gratitude by setting them up as a team of independent heroes, an offer that included a steady salary. Cool under pressure and strategically gifted, Rokk was elected leader and set about expanding the team through interviews and auditions. His astute management style did much to ensure the Legion's enduring independence and security.

Rokk brought his parents and younger brother to Earth and through the team met his eventual wife Lydda Jath (Night Girl). He suffered a major blow when his parents were caught in a nuclear terrorist attack, but after taking revenge and briefly quitting the team, Rokk returned, more determined than ever to protect the weak from the ruthless. **WW**

MAXIMUM OVERDRIVE
Life as a Legionnaire taught Cosmic Boy how to use his magnetic powers in ways—and with an intensity—other Braalians could not imagine or match.

FORCE OF NATURE
Rokk Krinn's most potent talent was his ability to attract valiant, idealistic youngsters to the Legion, and to reshape them into universe-saving heroes.

ON THE RECORD

Cosmic Boy has a unique bond with Garth, Imra, and Superboy; a deep, lasting connection that extends beyond even Legion camaraderie. When the adult Superman was captured by the Legion of Super-Villains, Rokk led his closest friends back in time to rescue him.

On a prior occasion, following the Crisis on Infinite Earths, Rokk learned history had changed, with Superboy now never becoming a Legionnaire. Cosmic Boy and his girlfriend, Night Girl, were catapulted to the End of Time, where their struggle against Time Trapper ended inconclusively; they never realized that they had been allowed to escape.

MAGNETIC INTERFERENCE
Cosmic Boy was always a hero who fought as much with his mind as his mighty magnetic powers.

COURT OF OWLS

DATA

DEBUT *Batman* (Vol. 2) #1 **(Nov. 2011)**
REAL NAME Court of Owls
BASE Originally Gotham City, now global
ALLIES Army of Talons and fellow secret Owl members
ENEMIES Batman, Talon (Calvin Rose), Bane, Mister Freeze
AFFILIATIONS High society around the globe
NOTABLE PAST MEMBERS Benjamin Orchard, John Wycliffe, Maria Powers, Joseph Powers, Sebastian Clark, Lincoln March, Robin (Damian Wayne), Dick Grayson

CLASSIC STORIES

***Batman* (Vol. 2) #1–10 (Nov. 2011–Sep. 2012)** Batman first discovers the Court of Owls, battles his way through their labyrinth, and learns Lincoln March's connection to both the Court and his past.
***Batman and Robin* (Vol. 2) #23.2 (Nov. 2013)** The Court's past is exposed, from the early days of Gotham City's rundown area the Narrows in 1862, through the 1970s to the present day.
***Batman* (Vol. 2) #39 (Apr. 2015)** The Dark Knight finds himself returning to the Court's labyrinth in order to attempt to recruit the Owls' help in defeating the Joker.

FOWL PLAY
The Court of Owls uses assassins known as Talons to do their bidding at night, killing their targets in an unseen fashion and covering up any signs of wrongdoing.

"Beware the Court of Owls, that watches all the time, ruling Gotham from a shadowed perch, behind granite and lime. They watch you at your hearth, they watch you in your bed, speak not a whispered word of them or they'll send the Talon for your head." That rhyme about the Court of Owls is as old as Gotham City itself, but as Batman has recently discovered, this supposedly urban legend is very real and very dangerous.

A secret society comprised of only the most elite and corrupt figures, the Court of Owls is a veritable who's who of Gotham's wealthy sociopaths. The Court believes they own the city, and enforce that idea with an army of assassins called Talons, ready to kill on command any person who gets in their way.

While the Dark Knight only recently found proof of the Court's existence, there have been tales of their activity as far back as 1862, when they unleashed a Talon called the Gotham Butcher on their political targets. Instead of killing his prey as intended and disappearing into the night, the Talon made a spectacle of his murders, even making the newspapers. In 1891, a photographer attempted to expose the Court of Owls' nefarious activities, and was hanged for his actions. And in 1914, Court member Benjamin Orchard punished Gotham City's mayor and imprisoned him in the Court's labyrinth that runs beneath the city streets.

Batman discovered that same labyrinth while investigating the Court of Owls, and was forced to run a gauntlet and fight off a powerful Talon determined to break him. Batman soon deduced that his associate Lincoln March was actually a member of the Court's ranks, and was attempting to make off with its fortune by betraying them. While the Dark Knight successfully defeated the crazed March—who insisted he was Bruce Wayne's brother—it was too late to prevent the villain from poisoning a roomful of the Court's most valuable members. March would later wheedle his way back into the Court of Owl's good graces when he recruited Dick Grayson into their clandestine organization. **MM**

COURTING THE YOUTH
The Court of Owls starts its members at a young age, welcoming them to their cause and desensitizing them to the violence inflicted by their Talon servants.

SIBLING RIVALRY?
Batman and Lincoln March battled over the rooftops of Gotham City when March tried to convince Bruce Wayne that he was Thomas Wayne Jr., his brother.

OWL-WOL
Calvin Rose was intended to be a Talon for the Court of Owls, but rebelled and was brutally shown the errors of his ways by Bane. Rose eventually secured his freedom and joined Batman, Inc.

CREATURE COMMANDOS

DEBUT *Weird War Tales* (Vol. 1) #93 **(Nov. 1980)**
CURRENT VERSION *Frankenstein: Agent of S.H.A.D.E.* #1 **(Nov. 2011)**
BASE The Ant Farm
ALLIES S.H.A.D.E., Father Time, Ray Palmer
ENEMIES Random monsters
NOTABLE MEMBERS Frankenstein, Lady Frankenstein, The Mermaid (Dr. Nina Mazursky), The Werewolf (Warren Griffith), The Vampire (Vincent Velcoro), G.I. Robot, G.I. Zombie, The Mummy (Khalis), Bogman, Dr. Medusa

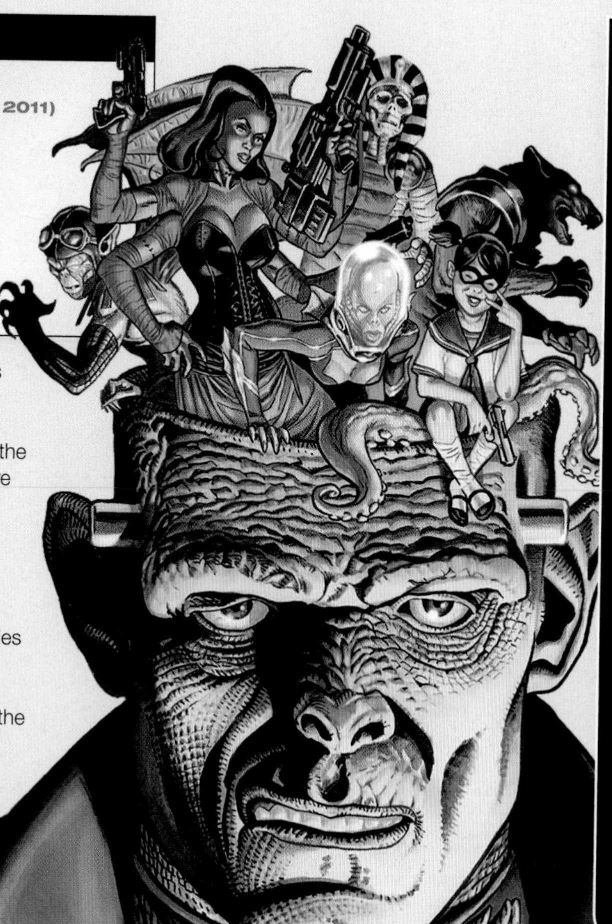

Hidden in a mobile, flying three-inch indestructible globe is the headquarters of S.H.A.D.E., The Super Human Advanced Defense Executive. Reached via a hybrid of teleportation and shrink technology designed by the S.H.A.D.E. science liaison Ray Palmer, the sphere serves as the base of operations for some of the most bizarre metahuman heroes on the planet: the Creature Commandos.

Led by Agent Frankenstein—the monster famed for being fictionalized in the pages of Mary Shelley's celebrated gothic tale—the Creature Commandos take their ultimate orders from Father Time, S.H.A.D.E.'s head of operations. While Father Time currently resembles a young girl, the natural born leader has taken many bodies over the course of his long life to ensure he remains a vital part of S.H.A.D.E.'s operations.

The Commandos are officially called Division M, and are mostly the results of S.H.A.D.E.'s science division experiments, except for the Mummy, who is reportedly thousands of years old and was simply discovered by S.H.A.D.E.. Frankenstein joined the team when his ex-wife went missing while investigating a monster attack. This led S.H.A.D.E. to travel to the so-called Monster Planet, a successful mission that warmed Frankenstein to the prospect of working with a field team. They have since become the first line of defense against things that go bump in the night. **MM**

ON THE RECORD

The original Creature Commandos first appeared in 1980 in *Weird War Tales*. Labeled Project "M," the unit was a World War II-era innovation, creating nightmare soldiers that would terrify the Axis.

This original team was led by Lt. Matthew Shrieve and included both the Werewolf and Vampire from the current roster, as well as a Frankenstein-like monster named Elliot Taylor. The team was then joined by female member Dr. Medusa. Two further versions of the Commandos were introduced prior to their post-Flashpoint reincarnation.

SEEING ACTION
Superman met the Creature Commandos when touring the restored city of Kandor in the Arctic. Kidnapped by Brainiac, this team had served in World War II and included G.I. Robot.

CREEPER, THE

DEBUT *Showcase* (Vol. 1) #73 **(Mar.–Apr. 1968)**
CURRENT VERSION *Katana* #3 **(Jun. 2013)**
REAL NAME Jack Ryder
HEIGHT 6ft **WEIGHT** 194 lbs
EYES Green **HAIR** Red
POWERS/ABILITIES Hosts a magical demon that possesses superhuman strength, endurance, and agility; able to leap far distances; weapons include chains used to generate artificial tornados.
ALLIES Killer Croc
ENEMIES Katana, Batman

The entity known as the Creeper is actually a mystical creature called the Oni Demon who hails from another reality. He first came to Earth through a so-called "crack in the world" in 16th-century Japan. In an era plagued with famines, tornados, and the like, the Oni Demon assumed the form of a little boy named Jakku.

After 20 years of causing mayhem, the Oni Demon was finally discovered by a samurai and imprisoned in the mystical Soultaker sword. Centuries passed and the sword fell into the possession of the hero Katana. However, during a battle with Killer Croc, the sword was broken—freeing its inhabitants, including the Creeper.

Meanwhile, Jack Ryder, the host of the talk show *You Don't Know Jack*, was killed while reporting on a giant monster. When Ryder's body was shipped to San Francisco, the Creeper took possession of it, resurrecting Ryder in the process. Ryder is now torn between two identities, his orderly civilian life, and the Creeper's chaotic existence. **MM**

ON THE RECORD

The original version of the Creeper debuted in the late 1960s. When talk show host Jack Ryder investigated a criminal organization, he gave himself yellow skin, green trunks, and red, boa-like fur.

When dying scientist Professor Yatz injected the Creeper with a formula to boost his powers, Ryder found he could alter between his civilian identity and his guise as the Creeper with the switch of an activator. He fought crime, using a manic laugh to instill fear into criminals' hearts.

KEEP 'EM LAUGHING
The Creeper's backstory was altered after a few reality-changing events. In this version, the concoction that turned Ryder into the Creeper was tainted with the Joker's venom.

CRIME SYNDICATE

DATA

DEBUT *Justice League of America* #29 **(Aug. 1964)**
CURRENT VERSION *Justice League* (Vol. 2) #23 **(Oct. 2013)**
BASE Earth-3
MEMBERS (EARTH SUPER HERO COUNTERPART)
ULTRAMAN (Superman); **SUPERWOMAN** (Wonder Woman); **OWLMAN** (Batman); **POWER RING** (Green Lantern); **DEATHSTORM** (Firestorm); **ATOMICA** (Atom); **JOHNNY QUICK** (The Flash); **SEA KING** (Aquaman); **GRID** (Cyborg); **OUTSIDER** (criminal mastermind).
ALLIES Secret Society of Super-Villains
ENEMIES Justice Leagues, Injustice League, Alexander Luthor, Teen Titans, Doom Patrol

ON THE DEFENSIVE
With many of its members imprisoned in a subatomic matrix, the Justice League was dangerously shorthanded when they faced down the Crime Syndicate in the wrecked Watchtower.

CLASSIC STORIES

***Justice League of America* #29–30 (Aug.–Sep. 1964)** The Crime Syndicate look for a new challenge—and bite off more than they can chew when the villains take on both the Justice League and the Justice Society of America.

***JLA* (Vol. 1) #107–114 (Dec. 2004 –Jul. 2005)** The Antimatter Universe version of the Crime Syndicate invades Earth, and brings with it the dire attentions of the alien Qwardians.

***JLA* (Vol. 2) #50–53 (Dec. 2010 –Mar. 2011)** The Syndicate reluctantly teams up with the JLA to battle the fearsome Omega Man, before Owlman betrays the JLA. Batman, anticipating this, executes a plan to resurrect Lex Luthor.

NEW ARRIVALS
As several members of the Crime Syndicate arrived in the Justice League Watchtower on Earth-1, Sea King seemed not to have survived the trip from Earth-3.

The tyrannical Earth-3 version of the Justice League, the Crime Syndicate of America, saw Earth-1 as a new frontier to conquer after the Anti-Monitor's devastating attack on the Syndicate's home planet. But first the team needed to defeat its Earth-1 counterparts, who received help from unexpected quarters...

The Crime Syndicate came together as the brutal overlords of Earth-3, a world where ideas of right and wrong were completely abandoned and only strength mattered. An attack by a mysterious entity (later revealed as the Anti-Monitor) laid waste to much of the planet, causing the Crime Syndicate to look for a new world to dominate. Its members set their sights on Earth-1, invading after two members—Atomica and the Outsider—laid the groundwork by gathering the Secret Society of Super-Villains and plotting with them to weaken the Justice League.

The Outsider had obtained Pandora's Box and used it to open a portal between the two Earths, sparking a brief reign of terror during which the Syndicate's members killed a number of Earth-1's heroes. Power Ring, The Outsider, Atomica, and Johnny Quick were killed in a fight against the combined forces of all three Justice Leagues and several defecting members of the Secret Society. In the aftermath of the conflict, the rest of the Syndicate either died or went their separate ways.

During the battle, the Earth-3 Shazam—a captive Alexander Luthor—was freed, but later killed by Earth-1's Lex Luthor. Sea King, presumed dead after the transit to Earth-1, reawakened and was briefly host to Deadman. Ultraman, a pregnant Superwoman, and Owlman were either imprisoned or disappeared. Grid was destroyed and Power Ring's Ring of Volthoom found a new host, Jessica Cruz. It used Cruz to recreate Grid from Cyborg. Cruz and Cyborg visited Superwoman in prison, while Owlman reappeared with a scheme to free Ultraman and work with the Justice League of America against the Anti-Monitor. **AI**

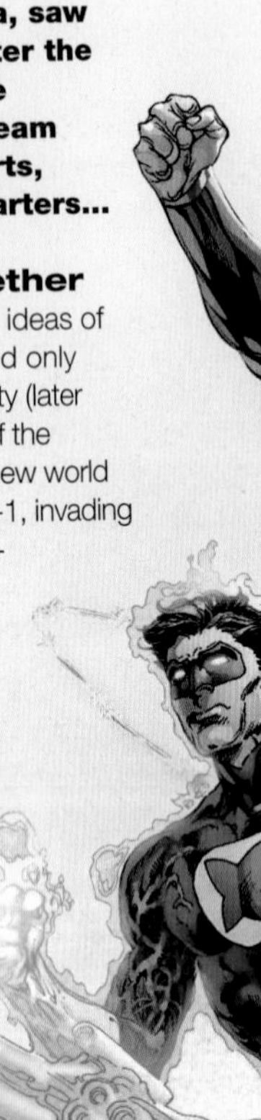

DEADLY DOPPLEGANGERS
Some of the original Crime Syndicate members:
1. Ultraman
2. Superwoman
3. Deathstorm
4. Power Ring
5. Grid
6. Owlman
7. Johnny Quick
8. Atomica

ON THE RECORD

The Crime Syndicate of America had plagued the Justice League and Justice Society for decades, since the second *Crisis* story in 1964 combined the histories of Earth-2 and Earth-3. This first version of Earth-3 did not have any heroes until the debut of a heroic counterpart to Lex Luthor. A later attempt at conquest by the antimatter universe version of the Syndicate was stopped by Martian Manhunter.

SURPRISE ATTACK!
The classic Crime Syndicate line-up launched an offensive on an unprepared JLA, who were expecting a visit from the JSA.

CRIMSON AVENGER

DEBUT *Detective Comics* (Vol. 1) #20 (Oct. 1938) (male Lee Travis)
CURRENT VERSION *Earth 2* (Vol. 1) #5 (Dec. 2012) (female Lee Travis)
BASE New York City, Earth-2
REAL NAME Lee Travis (female)
HEIGHT 5ft 7in **WEIGHT** 135 lbs
HAIR Black **EYES** Brown
ABILITIES Skilled investigative journalist.
ALLIES James Wing

MANY CRIMSON FACES
Jill Kyle (1), the male Lee Travis (2), and a female reporter of the same name (3), are all linked to the Crimson Avenger.

The first Crimson Avenger was Lee Travis, publisher of the *Daily Globe-Leader* and in his costumed guise the first known masked Super Hero, who was ably assisted by his valet, Wing. They joined the Seven Soldiers of Victory, and the Nebula Man sent Travis forward in time, where he learned how he died. Travis' twin Colt pistols later found their way to a young African-American lawyer—Jill Kyle—in Detroit, who discovered that the guns were cursed, and using them transformed her into a spirit of vengeance known as the Crimson Avenger.

Post-Flashpoint, another Lee Travis worked as a reporter for Earth-2's Global Broadcasting Corporation. She was present at the debut of the new Wonders of the World when they battled the life-draining Solomon Grundy. She later witnessed, alongside photographer James Wing, the apparent death of Alan Scott (Green Lantern) at the hands of Steppenwolf and his Hunger Dogs—perhaps hinting that a new Crimson Avenger may appear. **AI**

CRUX

DEBUT *Red Hood and the Outlaws* (Vol. 1) #1 (Nov. 2011)
REAL NAME Simon Amal
HEIGHT 7ft 7in **WEIGHT** 380 lbs
HAIR None **EYES** Yellow
POWERS/ABILITIES Flight; enhanced strength and durability; xenobiology expertise.
ALLIES Arsenal, Red Hood
ENEMIES Tamaraneans
AFFILIATIONS Outlaws

Simon Amal's parents, both researchers in extraterrestrial life, were killed when a Tamaranean spacecraft crashed into them. Driven to seek revenge against all aliens—but Tamaraneans in particular—he continued his parents' research and devised a way to splice alien DNA into his own genome. This gave him the ability to transform into a large, winged reptilian form.

When Simon saw a picture of Starfire, he recognized her as a Tamaranean and hatched a plot to kill her in his new guise as Crux. Attacking her in Colorado using remnant Tamaranean technology, he found himself facing Jason Todd and Roy Harper. He was overpowered and Jason Todd left him at Arkham Asylum. Later, with Starfire missing, Todd asked Crux to help find her. A penitent Crux agreed to join Arsenal and Red Hood in the search. **AI**

CUPID

DEBUT *Green Arrow and Black Canary* #15 (Feb. 2009)
CURRENT VERSION *Green Arrow* (Vol. 5) #39 (Apr. 2015)
REAL NAME Carrie Cutter
HEIGHT 5ft 8in **WEIGHT** 130 lbs
HAIR Red **EYES** Blue
POWERS/ABILITIES Special ops training; enhanced senses; expert archer and marksman.
ALLIES John King
ENEMIES Green Arrow

Special ops soldier Carrie Cutter was so deeply disturbed by what happened on one of her missions that she underwent experimental treatment with the organization C.O.B.A.L.T.. She emerged with enhanced physical and sensory abilities, but at the cost of her emotional stability. When Oliver Queen (Green Arrow) killed her husband in a case of mistaken identity, Carrie fell obsessively in love with him and became Cupid. With no moral compass, she viewed winning Green Arrow as the only worthwhile goal in her life, and would kill anyone—in particular Black Canary—to make it happen.

Cupid murdered many of Queen's enemies and then disappeared. She later emerged in Seattle, when Green Arrow's nemesis, John King, brought together a villainous gang to eliminate Oliver. **AI**

CYBORG SUPERMAN

DEBUT *Adventures of Superman* #465 **(Apr. 1990)** (As Henshaw); *Adventures of Superman* #500 **(Jun. 1993)** (As Cyborg)
CURRENT VERSION *Supergirl* (Vol. 6) #5 **(Mar. 2012)** (As Zor-El); *Supergirl* (Vol. 6) #21 **(Aug. 2013)** (As Cyborg)
BASE Mobile
REAL NAME Zor-El
HEIGHT Variable **WEIGHT** Variable
POWERS/ABILITIES Power over machinery and computers; physical strength and offensive powers mimicking those of Superman.
ALLIES Brainiac, Doomsday
ENEMIES Superman, Supergirl

Superman's uncle Zor-El, long thought lost in the destruction of Krypton, was in fact rescued by Brainiac and subjected to a series of cybernetic augmentations that deranged his personality and rebuilt him as the Cyborg Superman—Brainiac's scout for stronger species in the universe.

Wanting to reconstitute his physical body, Zor-El lured Supergirl to the planet I'noxia, which was composed of fragments of lost worlds. When he had gained her trust, he attacked, hoping to use Supergirl's Kryptonian body as material for his new form. She escaped, but Brainiac's schemes for Cyborg Superman continued.

Zor-El then undertook the next part of Brainiac's plan, helping to activate Doomsday and mount a full-scale invasion of Earth. He diverted Superman long enough for Brainiac's Doomsday fleet to reach Earth. Cyborg Superman then lay siege to the Fortress of Solitude, but was defeated. Superman then put an end to Brainiac's continued plotting by throwing the Collector of Worlds into a black hole. **AI**

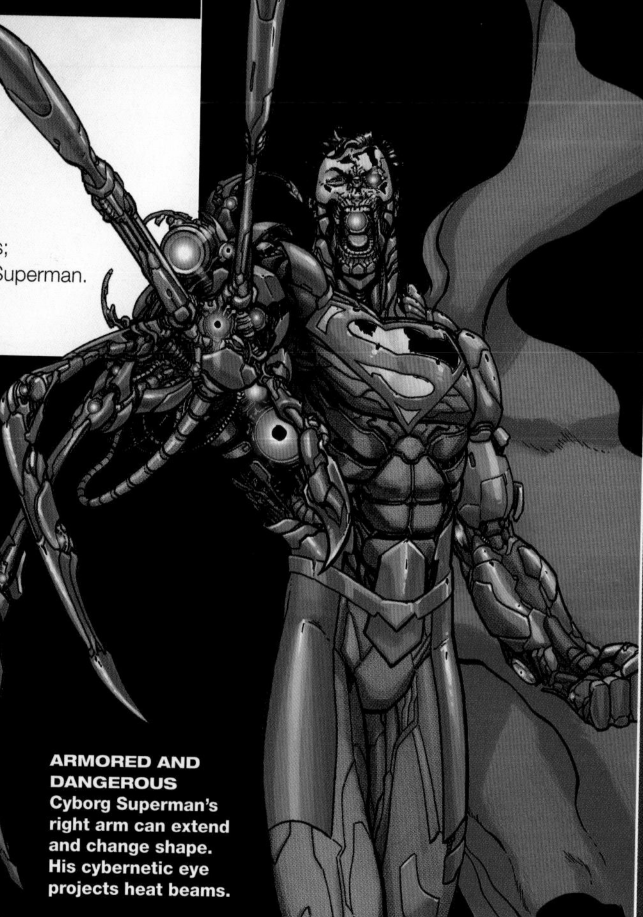

ARMORED AND DANGEROUS
Cyborg Superman's right arm can extend and change shape. His cybernetic eye projects heat beams.

ON THE RECORD

The former Cyborg Superman, astronaut Hank Henshaw, was onboard the LexCorp space shuttle *Excalibur* with his wife Terri and two other crew members when it crashed. At first, the accident was thought to have been caused by Superman who had created a solar flare—exposing the crew to a fatal dose of radiation.

With his physical form deteriorating, Hank transferred his consciousness into the LexCorp mainframe, recreating himself as a cyborg in Superman's image. When Terri later died, a deranged Hank blamed Superman for her death, and became one of the Man of Steel's fiercest foes.

ON TRIAL!
During the Trial of Superman, Cyborg Superman took on the Superman Rescue Squad and defeated them single-handedly.

CYBORG

DATA

DEBUT *DC Comics Presents* (Vol. 1) #26 **(Oct. 1980)**
CURRENT VERSION *Justice League* (Vol. 2) #1 **(Oct. 2011)**
REAL NAME Victor Stone
HEIGHT 6ft 6in **WEIGHT** 385 lbs **EYES** Brown **HAIR** Black
POWERS/ABILITIES Implants give him massively enhanced strength; armored chassis and promethium-impregnated flesh provide superb damage resistance; sensors and onboard processors intercept signals and hack systems remotely; can create Boom Tubes for transport, and fly using boot jets; arms can be reconfigured into energy or projectile weapons.
ALLIES Superman, Batman, Green Lantern, Flash, Wonder Woman
ENEMIES Darkseid, Crime Syndicate, Graves, Ohm
AFFILIATIONS Justice League

Vic Stone never wanted to be a Super Hero, but after he was wounded in an alien invasion, he was rebuilt as a half-machine, half-human entity: a cybernetic organism. As Cyborg, he became a founding member of the Justice League, where his combination of hi-tech systems and reconfigurable firepower made him an essential member of the superpowered lineup. However, despite his accomplishments and the friendship of his teammates, Cyborg remains haunted by the possibility of losing his humanity and becoming a mere machine.

AT A GLANCE...

Man vs. machine
The cybernetic enhancements implanted by his father saved Vic's life, but the experience proved traumatic. The young hero fears losing his humanity and becoming a machine that merely thinks it is human. As host to several advanced AI systems, he is also vulnerable to hacking—as became clear when his robotic parts were hijacked by Grid during the Crime Syndicate's attack on the Justice League.

Weapons systems
In addition to his other high-tech capabilities, Cyborg can reconfigure himself to create powerful arm cannons that suit a particular combat mode. In his first clash he deployed a sonic white-noise cannon to obliterate a Parademon; other variations include the twin-Gatling gun setup he used to fight the Spore creatures.

Killer apps
Cyborg integrates advanced tech that gives him access to vast databases of knowledge and allows him to hack enemy systems. He provides the Justice League with a hi-tech edge in their battles and serves as a vital source of intelligence.

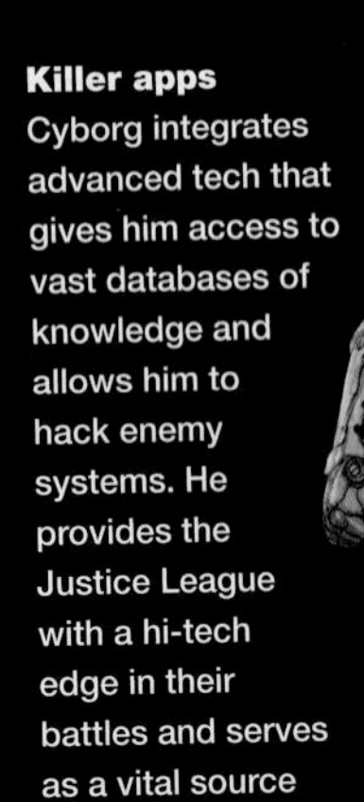

Vic Stone was a high school football star who wanted to play professionally, but this brought him into conflict with his father, scientist Silas Stone, who insisted that his son become an academic. Vic went to S.T.A.R. Labs to confront his father, who was working on reverse-engineering a "Mother Box," a sentient extraterrestrial computer.

Vic and Silas quarreled, but then the Mother Box pinged, generating a Boom Tube portal, out of which emerged a horde of Parademons serving Darkseid, the Warlord of Apokolips. Vic was struck by a blast of red energy that began to dissolve his body, so his father dragged him into the lab's Red Room, which contained experimental technology, and replaced the damaged parts of Vic's body with cybernetic systems and promethium skin grafts, incorporating the Mother Box's energies into Vic's new form. When a Parademon broke into the Red Room, Vic's arm automatically reconfigured into a white-noise cannon that vaporized his foe.

INTERFACED
As alien energy devoured Vic Stone's body, his quick-thinking father Silas implanted and activated advanced cybernetics, which saved his son's life.

The Parademon attack on S.T.A.R. Labs was not an isolated incident: Boom Tubes were opening all over the world, disgorging Parademons. Vic learned that his cybernetic system could pick up communications from the aliens' Mother Boxes and even generate its own Boom Tubes. His Mother Box then activated and transported him to Metropolis, where the world's Super Heroes had gathered to face Darkseid himself. In an epic battle, Cyborg generated a Boom Tube that carried Darkseid back to Apokolips and ended the invasion.

In the aftermath of the attack, Superman, Green Lantern, Wonder Woman, Aquaman, and the Flash decided to create a team to defend Earth, and Cyborg joined their ranks as a founding member of the Justice League. Cyborg's advanced systems and weapons proved useful when the team fought the biological villain Spore, but when they encountered the mysterious Graves in the Himalayas, the villain used psychic powers to make Vic experience his greatest fear: that he was losing his humanity as a result of having so much of his body replaced by artificial components.

THRONE OF ATLANTIS
When sub-aquatic warlord Ocean Master flooded Gotham City and led the forces of Atlantis against the surface world, the Justice League responded—but most were captured and imprisoned beneath the sea. Proving his heroism and leadership ability, Cyborg replaced his remaining lung with a module for underwater operations, recruited new Justice League members, and went to rescue his teammates.

TERROR FROM THE DEEP
Cyborg led the rescue mission after Aquaman's evil half-brother, Ocean Master, had captured several Justice League members.

CLASSIC STORIES

***The New Teen Titans* (Vol. 1) #1 (Nov. 1980)** Cyborg joins the Teen Titans on their first mission—to save the United Nations from invading aliens.

***DC Special: Cyborg* #1–6 (Jul.–Dec. 2008)** Vic Stone is forced to battle a cybernetically enhanced former friend and a version of himself from an alternate future.

***Teen Titans Spotlight* #13 (Aug. 1987)** Scarred villain Two-Face resents how Victor has managed to become a hero despite being maimed, and plots to destroy Cyborg's hard-won reputation.

***JLA/Titans* #1–3 (Dec. 1998–Feb. 1999)** When Vic returns from deep space as part of a Technis construct that absorbs the Moon, the Titans embark on a mission to restore their friend's humanity.

DISASSEMBLED
When the Crime Syndicate launched its attack on Earth, Vic Stone's systems were hijacked by an AI calling itself Grid.

When the evil Crime Syndicate attacked the Justice League, Vic's cybernetic systems were taken over by an artificial intelligence, creating a malign, separate entity called Grid. Vic was fitted with a new body and took down Grid, and the Crime Syndicate was ultimately defeated. Later, after having terrible nightmares about fighting techno-inorganic beings on an alien world, Vic was killed by power-armored figures, but his cybernetic systems revived him. These Tekbreakers, from an alternate dimension, wanted to destroy Cyborg before his advanced systems could draw the attention of the Techsapiens, aliens infected by cybernetic parasites. Cyborg and other heroes joined the Tekbreakers to protect Earth, and Vic defeated the Techsapien invaders by hacking their operating system. **SW**

CYBORG 2.0

Vic Stone bore a grudge against his emotionally distant father for opposing his sporting ambitions and then for transforming him into the half-machine Cyborg. However, when Cyborg had his cybernetics taken by Grid, Vic and his dad had a chance to reconcile. They made peace with each other, and Silas fitted his son with a sleek new cybernetic body. Upgraded and ready for action, Vic then launched an attack on Grid and took the AI menace off line for good.

STRIPPED DOWN
When Cyborg was stripped of his hardware, he and his father finally had an opportunity to set aside their differences.

CYBERNETIC CHAMPION
Cyborg gets his power from hi-tech upgrades, but it is his human heart and courage that make him a hero.

"If I could unplug, I would, but unlike you I can't take my costume off..."

CYBORG

ON THE RECORD

The pre-Flashpoint incarnation of Vic Stone was a star football player, but after he was mortally injured in a laboratory experiment gone wrong, his father turned him into a cyborg to save his life. This was the first of several transformations the young hero would undergo in his career.

Technis transformation

Vic joined the Teen Titans but was seriously damaged when Jericho, son of Deathstroke, betrayed the team. He was rebuilt by Soviet scientists, but had seemingly lost his memories. An alien cybernetic hive mind called the Technis restored him, absorbing him and assimilating his humanity into their sterile AI collective. Vic was then taken to the Technis' homeworld and transformed into a being called Cyberion.

Reintegration

Vic/Cyberion returned to the solar system as a herald of the Technis and transformed the moon into a Technis construct. The Justice League of America perceived Cyberion as a threat to be eliminated, but the Titans were determined to save their friend. The two teams clashed, but in the end the young heroes were able to build a rapport with Vic and channel his life energy into a cloned body, restoring his humanity.

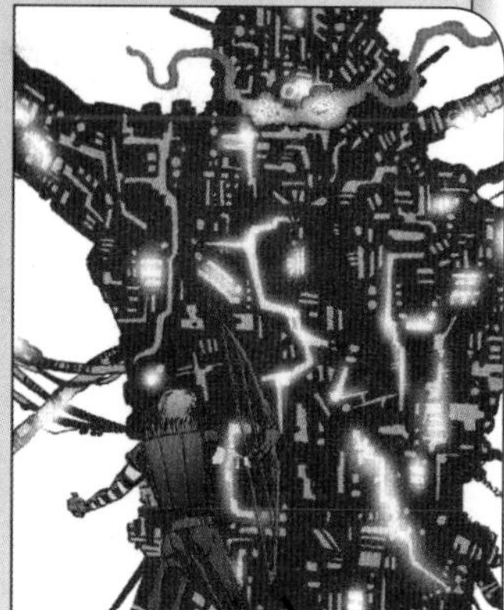

MACHINE CIVILIZATION
The artificial intelligences of the Technis collective chose to absorb Cyborg in order to learn about humanity.

Team player

When a new Teen Titans team was formed, Vic served as advisor and elder statesman. However, he left Earth during Infinite Crisis to help battle Alexander Luthor and sustained heavy damage. After undergoing repairs, Vic led a new Titans East squad and helped the other Titans battle their zombified former teammates during Blackest Night. He then joined the Justice League, providing tech support and forming a close bond with the android Red Tornado.

TITANS TOGETHER
Victor felt his cybernetics made him an outsider and a freak, but found a new family in the Teen Titans.

DAMAGE

DEBUT *Damage* **#1 (Apr. 1994)**
REAL NAME Grant Emerson
BASE New York City
EYES Brown **HAIR** Brown
POWERS/ABILITIES Biochemical fusion reactor in his body provides increased strength, durability, and energy projection.
ENEMIES Symbolix, Zoom
AFFILIATIONS New Titans, Justice Society of America

DAMAGE LIMITATION
The fires of Damage's biochemical reactor always burned, as did the trauma of his abusive upbringing.

The boy who grew up to be Damage was the product of an *in utero* genetic experiment overseen by Vandal Savage. Savage had provided an expatriate German scientist with funding on behalf of a company called Symbolix, together with cellular samples of other heroes.

The research bore fruit and when the child was born, Savage had his mother killed and placed the infant, who was called Grant Emerson, with an abusive surrogate family. Grant's powers manifested when he was 16 and Symbolix came to collect him. They killed Grant's foster family but he escaped, taking the name Damage and beginning to learn how to use his powers with the New Titans. Adopting a mask after his face was badly scarred in a fight with Zoom, he joined the Justice Society of America and was later killed and reanimated by Black Lanterns during Blackest Night. Retaining his own mind, he sacrificed himself to destroy other Black Lanterns before they breached the JSA stronghold. **AI**

DARKSTARS

DEBUT *Darkstars* **#1 (Oct. 1992)**
BASE Space
NOTABLE MEMBERS Ferrin Colos; Munchukk; Carla White; Medphyll; John Flint (dismissed); **Donna Troy** (retired); **John Stewart** (retired); **Hollika Rahn, Mo Douglas, Charlie Vicker, Galius Zed, K'ryssma, Threllian** (all deceased). Their exo-mantle battle suits provide super-strength, speed, and flight; they also carry force-field projectors and laser blasters.
ALLIES Green Lantern Corps
ENEMIES Grayven

The Controllers, an aggressive sect of the Guardians of the Universe, and N.E.M.O. (the Network for the Establishment and Maintenance of Order) formed the Darkstars to patrol space and destroy chaos. Ferrin Colos of Zamba, joined the group and was assigned to Earth. After the Darkstars, L.E.G.I.O.N., and the Green Lantern Corps saved the universe from the Triarch—a trinity of malign ancient deities—the three organizations agreed on their separate peacekeeping roles in the universe.

When the Green Lantern Corps was torn apart by Hal Jordan, the members of the Darkstars were left to patrol space themselves, recruiting former Green Lantern John Stewart and New Titan Troia to their ranks. Eventually, most Darkstars resigned or were killed by Darkseid's son, Grayven, leaving only Chaser Bron, Munchukk, and Ferrin Colos to carry out the Controllers' intergalactic mission of eradicating evil. **AI**

SHINING LIGHTS
Key Darkstars line-up for action.
1 Ferrin Colos
2 John Flint
3 Carla White
4 Mo Douglas

DARHK, DAMIEN

DEBUT *The Titans* **#1 (Mar. 1999)**
HEIGHT 6ft **WEIGHT** 160 lbs
EYES Blue **HAIR** Brown
POWERS/ABILITIES Highly intelligent, tech-savvy, ruthless; possibly immortal.
ALLIES Adeline Kane
ENEMIES Teen Titans
AFFILIATIONS H.I.V.E.

The mysterious, boyish-looking Damien Darhk has evaded all attempts to pin down his sketchy background, despite extensive investigations by the CIA and the FBI, as well as the Teen Titans. The latter had encountered him while battling H.I.V.E. and Grant Wilson—the son of Deathstroke who was also known at large as the Ravager. Darhk's role in H.I.V.E.'s machinations remains unclear, and it is also not understood how he came to occupy such a powerful, well connected position within H.I.V.E. at a relatively young age.

During the final confrontation between the Teen Titans and H.I.V.E., Darhk suffered a near-fatal gunshot wound courtesy of Vandal Savage, and survived only after receiving a blood transfusion from then-H.I.V.E. Mistress Adeline Kane, perhaps granting him immortality. Darhk's current whereabouts are unknown. **AI**

DARK OPAL

DEBUT *Legion of Super-Heroes* **(Vol. 2) #298 (Apr. 1983)**
BASE Gemworld
HEIGHT 6ft 4in **WEIGHT** 235 lbs
EYES Red **HAIR** Black
POWERS/ABILITIES Immense strength, expert swordsman, variety of mystical powers.
ENEMIES Child, Amethyst
AFFILIATIONS House of Opal

By making pacts with otherworldly forces, forging secret alliances with rival Houses, and mastering sorcery, Dark Opal became ruler of Gemworld. However, he failed to kill the infant heir of the House of Amethyst, who was hidden on Earth. After 20 years, that heir had grown up to be Amy Winston, a potent mystic known as Amethyst.

Amy went to Gemworld and thwarted Dark Opal's various attempts to forge a suit of armor containing slivers from each of Gemworld's 11 Houses. Amethyst ultimately deposed him, and went on to lead an alliance of all Gemworld's other Houses.

Dark Opal was presumed killed in a powerful backlash of mystical energies, but the sorcerer had only retreated into the enchanted clasp of his cloak. Dark Opal returned to retake Gemworld, but was destroyed by Child, a Lord of Chaos, and his servant, Flaw. **AI**

DAXAMITES

DEBUT *Adventure Comics* **#312 (Sep. 1963)**
CURRENT VERSION *Legion of Super-Heroes* **(Vol. 7) #2 (Dec. 2011)**
BASE Daxam
POWERS/ABILITIES Similar to Kryptonians when exposed to the rays of a yellow sun.
ALLIES Green Lantern Corps, Superman
ENEMIES Sinestro Corps, Dominators

A genetically variant race descended from exploring Kryptonians, Daxamites possess similar powers to their ancestors when in the presence of a yellow sun. They allied with a number of other alien races led by the Dominators to conquer Earth and control its unusual propensity to produce super-powered beings. They were initially relegated to a support and science role, but they soon discovered their extra abilities in the yellow radiation of Earth's sun.

A Daxamite detachment fought Superman, beating him badly before succumbing to Earth's dire air pollution. Superman saved their lives, spurring them to switch sides and turn against the rest of the Dominator invasion force. One of this rebel group, Lar Gand (also known as Mon-El and Jonathan Kent) was later instrumental in forming the United Planets consortium of worlds. Another Daxamite, Sodam Yat, would become a Green Lantern who turned Daxam's sun yellow so they could battle the Sinestro Corps. **AI**

MIGHTY DAXAMITES
The inhabitants of Daxam appeared to be like Earth's humans, but their solar-receptive biology was more advanced.

DEADMAN

DATA

DEBUT *Strange Adventures* #205 **(Oct. 1967)**
CURRENT VERSION *DC Universe Presents* #1 **(Nov. 2011)**
REAL NAME Boston Brand
BASE House of Mystery
HEIGHT 6ft **WEIGHT** 201 lbs
EYES White **HAIR** Bald
POWERS/ABILITIES Able to possess human bodies for limited periods of time, communicate with spirits, and travel across dimensional boundaries; flight, invisibility.
ALLIES Madame Xanadu
ENEMIES Felix Faust, Enchantress, Pantheon
AFFILIATIONS Justice League Dark

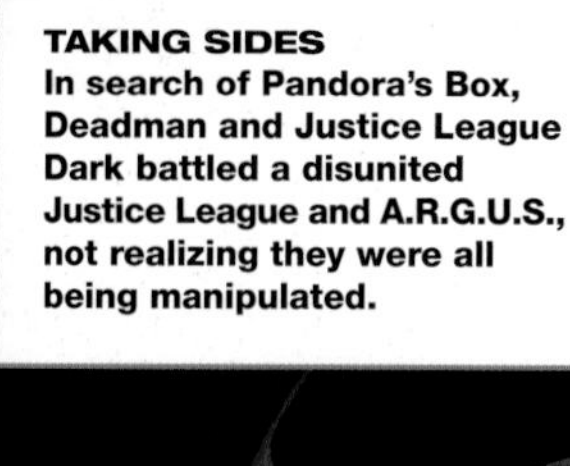

TAKING SIDES
In search of Pandora's Box, Deadman and Justice League Dark battled a disunited Justice League and A.R.G.U.S., not realizing they were all being manipulated.

CLASSIC STORIES

***Forever People* #9–10 (Jun.–Jul./Aug.–Sep. 1972)** Deadman's quest to track down the Hook gets help from an unexpected quarter: the Forever People, who also temporarily house Deadman's spirit in an artificial body.

***Brightest Day* #1–24 (Jun. 2010 –Jun. 2011)** A White Lantern Ring gives Boston Brand the chance to live again. He must protect the Star City forest from the Dark Avatar of Nekron. Mortally wounded in the forest, Brand is again condemned to a ghostly existence.

***Deadman: Dead Again* #1–5 (Oct. 2001)** As the Crisis on Infinite Earths rages around him, Deadman battles the sorcerous plot of Darius Caldera to provide heroic souls for the demon Neron.

DEAD RECKONING
After being shot and killed, Deadman found himself face to face with Rama Kushna in a place between life and death, sin and absolution.

Circus acrobat Boston Brand, traumatized by the anger and abuse he experienced as a child, was murdered and then given a new chance at life. As Deadman, he can inhabit the bodies of the living, always driven to atone for the selfish way he lived his life by bringing hope to the hopeless.

Brought up in a household bristling with anger, Boston Brand ran away to the circus, becoming a star, but also a selfish hedonist with violent tendencies. As Deadman, he was a star acrobat and aerialist, until a mysterious assassin shot him and made his circus moniker all too real. Brand was transformed into a spirit being by the Hindu goddess Rama Kushna and returned to the world of the living on the condition that he do good deeds to atone for his sins.

Deadman was approached by June Moone who asked him to help protect her from the Enchantress, who had been using June as a host. While trying to help her, Deadman was also recruited into the Justice League Dark by Madame Xanadu, who believed he would play a critical role in the League's battle against an oncoming occult threat. John Constantine—another of Xanadu's recruits—forcibly reunited June and the Enchantress, infuriating Deadman, who nevertheless joined Justice League Dark to face the menace of a risen Cain, progenitor of all vampires. Deadman continued to fight with the League against supernatural and magical dangers, the Crime Syndicate of America, and the Blight. Along the way, Constantine and Deadman clashed again after the former locked Deadman inside the body of the dead Sea King, Atlan.

Based with the rest of the Justice League Dark in the House of Mystery, Deadman led his teammates in a battle to protect the mystical city of Nanda Parbat, dying and being reborn in the body of his spirit guide, Brahma Dass. He subsequently combined the League's powers to remake the godlike Pantheon into a more joyful presence. **AI**

ON THE RECORD

In pre-Flashpoint stories, Boston Brand's assassin was discovered to be the Hook, an aspiring member of the League of Assassins who killed Boston Brand as his initiation into the group. This backfired when the League's leader, the Sensei, thought Brand was still alive due to Boston's twin brother, Cleveland, temporarily becoming the trapeze artist Deadman. The Sensei put an end to the Hook, but witnessing his killer's death gave Deadman no peace.

Previous versions of Deadman were invisible and intangible to humans who lacked some form of preternatural perception. This was an advantage to him, but it also reinforced how alienated he was from the living, and at times made it difficult for him to live up to his mission of helping people who would never know he existed.

BY HOOK OR BY CROOK
Deadman asked Batman to help him find his killer—whom he believed was a villain named the Hook.

DARKSEID

DATA

DEBUT *Superman's Pal, Jimmy Olsen* #134 **(Dec. 1970)**
CURRENT VERSION *Justice League* (Vol. 2) #3 **(Jan. 2012)**
REAL NAME Uxas **BASE** Apokolips
HEIGHT 8ft 9in **WEIGHT** 1,815 lbs **EYES** Red **HAIR** None
POWERS/ABILITIES Formidable intellect, godlike strength and endurance; eyes fire target-seeking 'Omega Beams;' access to advanced Apokoliptian technology, including Mother Boxes; projects 'Boom Tubes,' for interdimensional teleportation.
ALLIES Parademon legions, Desaad, Steppenwolf, Kanto, Female Furies
ENEMIES Mr. Miracle, Big Barda, Highfather and the inhabitants of New Genesis, the Justice League, the Anti-Monitor

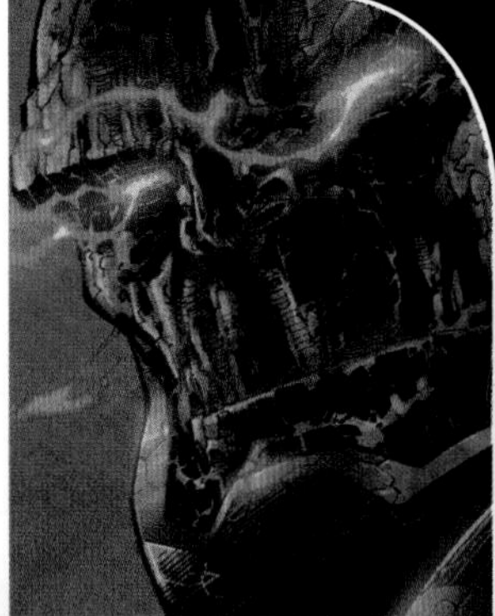

Darkseid is one of the most feared entities in the universe: a ruthless, unstoppable tyrant with godlike power and an all-consuming obsession with enslaving every being in existence. As the evil dread lord of the hellish planet Apokolips, Darkseid commands armies of henchmen and bizarre, lethal Parademons. He can access incredible technologies, such as the sentient Mother Boxes that serve as floating sensor drones. Moreover, as well as emitting deadly beams from his eyes, Darkseid has proved to be a formidable combatant, capable of taking on several mortal heroes at a time and emerging triumphant.

AT A GLANCE...

Lust for power
Darkseid's motivation is not wealth or revenge: he wants to control every being in the entire universe. When he confronts an enemy, Darkseid prefers to break their will and subjugate them, rather than destroy them outright. This has been seen in his confrontations with Superman, his estranged foster son Mister Miracle, and the mortals of Earth.

Omega Beams
Darkseid can kill with a glance by firing destructive Omega Beams from his eyes. These glowing red blasts change course to track their targets, though they can be evaded. Both the Flash and Supergirl were fast enough to avoid Omega Beams in battles with Darkseid.

Apokolips
Darkseid's homeworld is a hellish industrial planet with a surface cratered by fire pits. Slaves provide labor for its many armament production facilities, while its barracks and Parademon factories train hordes of faceless troopers for Darkseid's armies.

CLASSIC STORIES

The New Gods **(Vol. 1) #1-2 (Feb./Mar.-Apr./May 1971)** In one of his first-ever stories, Darkseid's deadly scheme is foiled by his estranged son, Orion.

New Gods **(Vol. 3) #8 (Sep. 1989)** This story tells of Darkseid's romance with the beautiful pacifist Suli. Tragically, she is murdered by Desaad, and the trauma helps turn Darkseid into a ruthless villain.

Final Crisis **#1-7 (Jul. 2008-Mar. 2009)** In this cosmos-altering event, Darkseid attempts to conquer reality by unleashing the power of the Anti-Life Equation on Earth.

The being who would become Darkseid was once called Uxas, the youngest son of Yuga Khan, one of the legendary Old Gods. Resenting their authority, the rebellious and cunning Uxas whispered lies and words of hate into the Old Gods' ears. Under his deceitful influence, the Old Gods fought and killed each other, and as they died Uxas stole their power to become a New God, Darkseid. Seizing his chance, Darkseid went to war against his weakened elders, persuading his benevolent older brother Izaya to reluctantly join him, and making an enemy of their father Yuga Khan. When father and sons finally clashed, Yuga Khan was slain by Uxas, ending the rule of the Old Gods.

GOD SLAYER
Uxas' hatred of the Old Gods saw him slaughter them—and seize their power for himself.

In the aftermath, the dying Sky God passed the last traces of his power to Izaya, also transforming him into a New God. Izaya tried to convince Darkseid that they should usher in a new age of enlightenment together, but Darkseid refused, destroying their world. Izaya then left to create a planet called New Genesis, which he presided over as Highfather, while Darkseid made Apokolips, an industrial hell-world populated by his engineered Parademon troopers and cruel New God minions.

Darkseid then embarked on a multidimensional campaign of conquest, seeking the Anti-Life Equation, the cosmic formula that would allow him to eliminate free will and control reality. World after world fell before him, their inhabitants enslaved or fed into flesh-recycling plants. However, the alternate world of Earth-2 managed to stave off an invasion, though its incarnations of Batman, Superman, and Wonder Woman sacrificed their lives in the process.

DARKSEID VS. THE JUSTICE LEAGUE
When the evil lord Darkseid launched his first attack on Earth-0, he initially inflicted heavy punishment on the planet's gathered Super Heroes—his mighty Omega Beams even knocked Superman out of action. However, Darkseid was then stabbed in the eyes by Wonder Woman and Aquaman. This act gave Superman the chance to recover and knock the villain into a Boom Tube portal summoned by Cyborg. This battle was one of Darkseid's most humiliating defeats, and it took him a long time to recover. The threat posed by Darkseid also served as the catalyst to unite Earth's heroes as the Justice League.

FOR GREAT JUSTICE
Even when they united, the Earth's most powerful Super Heroes—including Wonder Woman, Superman, and Batman—could barely defeat the almighty Darkseid.

"All hail Darkseid!"

STEPPENWOLF

Darkseid's armies then launched an attack on Earth-0 using Boom Tubes to create teleportation portals and attack multiple sites simultaneously. They were opposed by the world's champions, including Superman, Wonder Woman, Green Lantern (Hal Jordan), the Flash, Aquaman, and Cyborg. The heroes held their own against the attacking Parademons, but when Darkseid himself emerged from a Boom Tube, they found themselves outmatched. However, just as Darkseid was claiming victory, Earth's champions regrouped and launched a furious counterattack, grievously wounding the dark lord. Superman then forced Darkseid into a Boom Tube, sending him back to Apokolips.

Heavily weakened, Darkseid sealed himself in the Mobius Chamber at Apokolips' core, tapping into the planet's energies to heal himself. With Apokolips now deteriorating, he set it on a course for Earth 2, planning to drain its life energies to replenish his world. Meanwhile, Darkseid's estranged foster-son Mister Miracle launched a stealth attack on Apokolips and found his 'father' in the Mobius Chamber. Miracle tried to kill him with the Boom Spheres invented by Mister Terrific, but these merely freed Darkseid.

Darkseid used a Terraformer to begin harvesting Earth-2 to replenish Apokolips. A small force of Earth-2 heroes confronted him, but they proved no match for the villain. He declared war on Earth-1, but was opposed by Mister Miracle and Myrina Black—an Amazon who had secretly given birth to his daughter whom she had plotted to use against him. Naming her Grail, Myrina had sent her child to find a being who could defeat Darkseid, and Grail had returned with the cosmic force of annihilation, the Anti-Monitor.

Darkseid and the Anti-Monitor clashed on Earth, and their conflict threatened to destroy the planet. As the two fought, the Anti-Monitor revealed that the Anti-Life Equation—the ultimate power Darkseid had thirsted for—ran in his veins. With that, the Anti-Monitor used the Black Racer—the very embodiment of death itself—to slay Darkseid. **SW**

DEATH OF A GOD
The lord of Apokolips was killed by the Anti-Monitor and the Black Racer (who had possessed the Flash).

OMEGA POWER
The wielder of the power of the Old Gods, Darkseid proclaimed himself a New God. He can focus the Omega energy he possesses through his hands to generate huge shock waves.

THE WORLD'S END

If his clash with the Justice League marked an ignominious defeat for the evil Darkseid, his apocalyptic war against Earth-2 showed him at his most ruthless and powerful. As his forces inflicted a devastating defeat on this Earth's military, Darkseid personally defeated the planet's united heroes. The world was left in his grasp, to be consumed at his leisure.

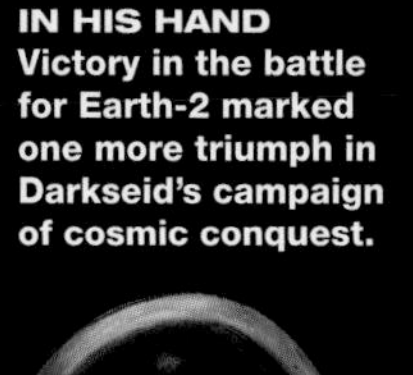

THE WHOLE WORLD IN HIS HAND
Victory in the battle for Earth-2 marked one more triumph in Darkseid's campaign of cosmic conquest.

ON THE RECORD

Darkseid was introduced as a godlike being obsessed with cosmic domination, and this would remain the defining nature of his character. In his time, the all-conquering super-villain has undergone several startling transformations.

Secret agents
In the 30th century, Darkseid secretly initiated a plan of conquest using cloned Super Heroes as his agents. Under his influence, the mighty Daxamites—whose powers were similar to Superman's—sculpted their planet's surface in Darkseid's own image, and began to transform it into a new Apokolips. The Legion of Super Heroes soon discovered the threat, and Darkseid was defeated.

His feminine side
On one occasion, Darkseid launched an attack on the Amazon island of Themyscira, and Wonder Woman punished him in a unique fashion. Using a mental link created by the Super Hero Raven, she imbued Darkseid with some of her compassion, sapping his power and tempering his darkness. Wonder Woman and the Amazons even allied with Darkseid to save Apokolips and Earth from the threat of Brainiac-13's Warworld.

Mob warfare
After Darkseid had his heart torn out by his son Orion, the villain found a human host on Earth: a mob boss called 'Boss Dark Side'. Operating out of the Dark Side Club in Blüdhaven, the Boss plotted to overtake reality. During the Final Crisis event, Darkseid seemingly killed Batman with his Omega Beams, but was defeated and slain by Earth's heroes.

KILL OR BE KILLED
Batman planned to shoot Darkseid with the same bullet that Darkseid had used to kill Orion, but he had to avoid the Cosmic Beams.

DEADSHOT

DATA

DEBUT *Batman* (Vol. 1) #59 **(Jun.–Jul. 1950)**
CURRENT VERSION *Suicide Squad* (Vol. 4) #1 **(Nov. 2011)**
REAL NAME Floyd Lawton
BASE Belle Reve Penitentiary
HEIGHT 6ft 1in **WEIGHT** 202 lbs **EYES** Brown **HAIR** Brown
POWERS/ABILITIES Expert marksman with extensive training in unarmed combat and use of other weapons; armored suit includes helmet with integral low-light, thermal, and targeting optics; wears gauntlets featuring built-in laser designators and submachine guns.
ALLIES Harley Quinn
ENEMIES Mad Dog, Captain Boomerang, Batman, Unknown Soldier, Deathstroke, Basilisk
AFFILIATIONS Suicide Squad

KILLER WITH A CODE
Even though he is a ruthless killer, Floyd Lawton lives by a strict code of honor: he would never kill for free, and he would never waste a bullet. For Lawton, every life has value—so he expects to get paid for each one he ends.

MAD LOVE
Deadshot had a brief fling with fellow Suicide Squad member Harley Quinn. He soon learned that his Joker-obsessed teammate was mad, bad, and very dangerous to know!

SUICIDAL TENDENCIES
Deadshot soon discovered that the only thing he and his four Suicide Squad teammates had in common was a propensity for extreme violence.

An expert marksman with a callous disregard for life, Deadshot worked as a professional hitman until he was imprisoned at Belle Reve Penitentiary, a notorious prison for superpowered criminals. The authorities then forced him to 'volunteer' for the Suicide Squad, a team of expendable super-villains used for dangerous black-ops missions by the US government. The lone-wolf sniper soon found himself leading a motley crew of dangerous and unpredictable bad guys on a series of near-impossible missions.

Floyd Lawton's family were indiscriminately gunned down by criminals when he was just a child, so he became obsessed with revenge and mastered the art of marksmanship. Lawton served in the Marines and then became a hitman, going by the name of Deadshot. A consummate professional, he prided himself on never missing a shot, though on one mission he was apprehended by Batman before he could kill his target.

Deadshot was later imprisoned on Death Row at Belle Reve Penitentiary in Louisiana, but was selected as a potential recruit for Task Force X, a penal squad of super-villains assembled by tough government agent Amanda Waller. After a brutal training period, Deadshot, Harley Quinn, Black Spider, King Shark, and El Diablo were inducted into Task Force X which became known as Suicide Squad. Each team member had a nanite bomb implanted in their neck to ensure obedience, and was sent into action.

Though he preferred to operate as a sole agent, Deadshot proved to be an effective leader, and when the Suicide Squad was captured by the secret terror group Basilisk, he even shot himself through the heart to kill the group's leader, Regulus. The doctors at Belle Reve resurrected him using an experimental process, and Waller told him even death could not get him out of the team. Later, Lawton was shot by new leader the Unknown Soldier, returned to life again, and then helped defend Belle Reve from a Crime Syndicate assault. He longs to escape the Suicide Squad and get revenge on Waller. **SW**

ON THE RECORD

The pre-Flashpoint Deadshot came from a wealthy family, and the pivotal moment in his childhood occurred when he accidentally shot his brother instead of his abusive father. When Lawton first embarked on his career as Deadshot, he wanted to replace Batman as Gotham City's hero and used non-lethal shots to take down criminals, but he turned to villainy after being defeated by the Dark Knight.

Deadshot worked as a solo assassin, taking on targets that included Deathstroke and the Joker, but spent most of his career as part of Amanda Waller's Suicide Squad and joined Lex Luthor's Secret Six for a time. As a member of the Six, he teamed up with his former Suicide Squad comrades to take on the undead Black Lanterns in the "Danse Macabre" crossover story.

SIX OF THE WORST
Deadshot experienced both comradeship and betrayal when he joined the Secret Six.

CLASSIC STORIES

***Detective Comics* (Vol. 1) #474 (Dec. 1977)** Deadshot embraces super-villainy and marks Batman for death, utilizing his distinctive targeting monocle and glove-mounted guns for the first time.

***Secret Six* (Vol. 3) #1–7 (Nov. 2008–May 2009)** The Secret Six is hired to protect Tarantula from a horde of super-villains who covet a mystical object in her possession: a card that entitles a sinner to get out of Hell.

***Justice League of America* (Vol. 3) #7.1 (Nov. 2013)** A moving chronicle of Floyd's tragic childhood—and a thrilling assassination mission in which Deadshot delivers a precision sniper shot while in free fall.

DEATHSTROKE

DATA

DEBUT *New Teen Titans* (Vol. 1) #2 **(Dec. 1980)**
CURRENT VERSION *Deathstroke* (Vol. 2) #1 **(Nov. 2011)**
REAL NAME Slade Wilson
HEIGHT 6ft 4in **WEIGHT** 225 lbs **EYES** Blue **HAIR** White-blond
POWERS/ABILITIES Master tactician with Special Forces training; experimental gene treatments boost strength, speed, toughness, mental acuity, and healing rate to superhuman levels; skills and enhancements allow him to anticipate and avoid enemy attacks.
ALLIES Team 7, the Crime Syndicate, Lex Luther
ENEMIES Lobo, Batman, Jericho, Majestic, Legacy, Jericho, Suicide Squad
AFFILIATIONS None (formerly Team 7, US Army, Injustice League, Secret Society of Super-Villains, Suicide Squad)

COUP DE GRACE
Deathstroke's favored weapon is a sword used in mid-air combat.

Deathstroke is the most feared and respected mercenary in the world. His elite military training and a genetically enhanced physique make him a very dangerous combatant, but his deadliest weapon is his mind. A master strategist and tactician, Deathstroke specializes in psychological warfare tactics that he uses to devastating effect.

Slade Wilson joined the US Army at the age of 16 and proved to be an exceptional soldier, earning decorations for valor in combat. He was then selected for the covert-operations unit Team 7, and received experimental genetic-enhancement treatments that boosted his physical capabilities to superhuman levels. He married his military trainer, Adeline Kane, and they had two sons, Grant and Joseph. Slade then quit the military to work as a mercenary. Adopting the codename Deathstroke, Slade earned a reputation for ruthless efficiency but also made many enemies. Adeline and Joseph were seemingly killed when gunmen attacked their home.

When Grant Wilson grew up, he fought alongside his father as Ravager, but tragedy struck on a mission in North Korea: Grant was gunned down in an ambush, while Slade lost an eye. Deathstroke later had a daughter, Rose, who became the new Ravager. Wilson then learned that Grant, Joseph, and Adeline were still alive. Joseph had gained mind-control powers as a result of the government's Majestic program, but the process had driven him insane. Now calling himself Jericho, Joseph used his powers to turn Adeline and Grant against Deathstroke. In the ensuing battle, Adeline was killed and Deathstroke had to eliminate Grant to defeat Jericho. Slade then served in the Suicide Squad, but betrayed them for money. The enigmatic Red Fury restored his youth, healed his eye, and revealed that Jericho was alive. **SW**

DEADLY ACCURACY
Slade's combat skills and preternatural reflexes make him an almost unstoppable force in battle.

ON THE RECORD

Prior to the "Flashpoint" storyline, Deathstroke was defined by his complex relationship with the Teen Titans and his tormented son, Jericho. The young man joined the Titans—whom Slade had earlier been contracted to kill—to oppose his father, but when Jericho was possessed by the evil Spirits of Azarath, he turned on his team.

Deathstroke helped the heroes and killed Jericho to save him from the torment of possession, but was later possessed by his son's spirit. Slade's daughter Rose (Ravager) initially became a mercenary like her father, but later joined the Titans, alongside a revived Jericho.

TEEN TERROR
Deathstroke was the Teen Titans' deadliest and most persistent foe. However, he was sometimes forced to help the team, and developed a grudging respect for the heroes.

CLASSIC STORIES

***Identity Crisis* #3 (Oct. 2004)** In this riveting story, Deathstroke accepts a contract to protect the villain Dr. Light from the Justice League—and almost defeats the heroic team single-handedly.

***The New Titans* (Vol. 1) #71–84 (Nov. 1990–Mar. 1992)** Deathstroke finds himself fighting to protect his foes, the Teen Titans, against his insane son Jericho in the classic "Titans Hunt" epic.

***Deathstroke* (Vol. 2) #7 (May 2012)** Slade Wilson is targeted by his estranged son Grant, as his offspring attempts to prove that he is a better warrior than his father.

DEMOLITION TEAM

DEBUT *Green Lantern* (Vol. 2) #176 (May 1984)
BASE Rosie's Bar, New Orleans, Louisiana
MEMBERS/ABILITIES **Rosie**: Team leader, who wields a rapid-fire hot rivet gun; **Hardhat**: Uses powered helmet and strength-boosting harness; **Jackhammer**: Deploys a jackhammer capable of untold destruction; **Scoopshovel**: Mechanical excavator arm can dig up anything; **Steamroller**: Drives steamroller that can flatten buildings.
ALLIES Congressman Bloch
ENEMIES Predator, Blood Pack, O.M.A.C.

The Demolition Team is a group of mercenaries armed with construction equipment that has been re-purposed for combat. The group all have blue-collar day jobs, but when leader Rosie lines up a contract, they drop everything and get tooled-up for action. Corrupt congressman Jason Bloch hired them to wreck Ferris Aircraft, but the team was stopped and easily beaten by the enigmatic Predator—the male alter ego of Carol Ferris.

When Coast City was reduced to rubble by Mongul, the Demolition Team decided to destroy threats to the planet. After upgrading their gear, they attacked a nuclear power plant in Germany, but were stopped by corporate-funded heroes Blood Pack. Rosie then briefly became part of the composite hero Enginehead, but soon reunited with the Demolition Team. Most of them were apparently killed when the O.M.A.C.s attacked Earth, though Hardhat survived. **SW**

DAY OF WRECKENING
Guaranteed to leave a trail of destruction, the Demolition Team used all manner of re-purposed tools and building equipment to provide cheap muscle for bad guys on a budget!
1 Scoopshovel
2 Steamroller
3 Rosie
4 Hardhat
5 Jackhammer

DEIMOS

DEBUT *1st Issue Special* #8 (Nov. 1975)
CURRENT VERSION *Convergence* (Vol. 1) #2 (Jun. 2015)
BASE Thera, Skartaris
HEIGHT 6ft 1in **WEIGHT** 193 lbs
EYES Black **HAIR** Black
POWERS/ABILITIES Immortal; used Atlantean computer to perform 'magic.'
ALLIES The Evil One
ENEMIES Warlord
AFFILIATIONS Thera

An inhabitant of Skartaris—the realm within Earth's core—High Priest Deimos used the knowledge he found in the Scrolls of Blood and his mastery of Atlantean computer technology to rule the kingdom of Thera. He then tried to conquer all of Skartaris, but was killed battling United States Air Force pilot Lt. Colonel Travis Morgan, better known as the hero Warlord. One of Deimos' minions resurrected him with the Mask of Life, which also gave Deimos magical powers and immortality. Warlord executed Deimos, throwing his head to the wolves, while Warlord's son Joshua trapped the sorcerer within a magic mirror, but Deimos always returned.

During the Convergence event, when Brainiac's servant Telos forced the heroes of alternate Earths to battle for their very existence, Deimos launched his master plan. He tapped into the power of the Time Masters in an attempt to conquer all reality, but was killed by the entity Parallax. **SW**

TAKEOVER
When worlds converged, Deimos used the power of the Time Masters to destroy Warlord—before attempting to take control of the multiverse.

DEMON KNIGHTS

DEBUT *Demon Knights* #1 (Nov. 2011)
MEMBERS POWERS **The Demon (Etrigan)**: Demonic physiology, sorcery; **Jason Blood**: Sorcery; **Madame Xanadu (Nimue Inwudu)**: sorcery; **The Horsewoman**: Archery, empathic link with horses; **Sir Ysrtin the Shining Knight**: Immortality, flying horse (Vanguard), magic sword (Caliburn); **Al Jabr**: Genius scientist; **Exoristos the Amazon**: Immortality, superhuman strength, agility, and stamina; **Vandal the Savage**: Immortality, tactical genius
ALLIES Alba Sarum denizens, Merlin, King Arthur
ENEMIES Questing Queen, Morgaine le Fey

In the Dark Ages, the evil Questing Queen attacked the village of Little Spring, but was opposed by a motley group of adventurers. Calling themselves the Demon Knights, this fractious team comprised Vandal Savage, Amazon warrior Exoristos, Moorish scientist Al Jabr, the archer Horsewoman, the Shining Knight, Madame Xanadu, and the demon Etrigan (and his human host Jason Blood). Together, they drove off the queen's armies.

The 'heroes' then searched for Avalon and clashed with Morgaine le Fey. Betrayed by Etrigan, they were taken to Hell, but were later freed by Jason Blood and the Shining Knight. In Avalon, they defeated the armies of the Questing Queen and Lucifer (with help from Merlin and King Arthur). Merlin named the group as the first-ever Stormwatch team, but they immediately disbanded. However, Al Jabr later reunited Demon Knights to battle vampires on Themyscira and embark on a quest for the Holy Grail. **SW**

DARK KNIGHTS
The dysfunctional members of the Demon Knights fought each other as well as their enemies, helping to protect civilization in a barbaric age.

DETECTIVE CHIMP

DEBUT *Adventures of Rex the Wonder Dog* #4 (Jul.–Aug. 1952)
REAL NAME Magnificent Finder of Tasty Grubs
BASE Oblivion Bar
HEIGHT 3ft 7in **WEIGHT** 76 lbs
EYES Black **HAIR** Black
POWERS/ABILITIES Highly intelligent, deductive skills; briefly had powers of Doctor Fate.
ALLIES Rex the Wonder Dog, Blue Devil, Batman
ENEMIES Spectre, Eclipso, Trickster
AFFILIATIONS Shadowpact, Bureau of Amplified Animals

The 'Magnificent Finder of Tasty Grubs' was a sideshow act until he drank from the Fountain of Youth. This bestowed him with a genius intellect and the ability to speak. He solved a murder and went into business as 'Detective Chimp.' Sadly, his status as a non-person caused several legal issues and his agency failed. It was a crushing blow and he began drinking heavily at the Oblivion Bar, a watering-hole for occult beings.

When the Spectre began eliminating all magic, Detective Chimp recruited some of the bar's patrons to fight the threat and Shadowpact was born. He briefly wore the Helmet of Doctor Fate, which gave him great power, but he found it overwhelming and very quickly relinquished it. **SW**

DEMON, THE

DATA

DEBUT *Demon* (Vol. 1) #1 **(Aug.–Sep. 1972)**
CURRENT VERSION *Demon Knights* (Vol. 1) #1 **(Nov. 2011)**
REAL NAME Etrigan
BASE Hell
HEIGHT 6ft 4in (as the Demon); 6ft (as Jason Blood)
WEIGHT 3,512 lbs (as the Demon); 182 lbs (as Jason Blood)
EYES White, green, or red (as the Demon); Brown (as Jason Blood)
HAIR None (as the Demon); Brown with white streak (as Jason Blood)
POWERS/ABILITIES Preternaturally strong, agile, and heat-resistant; fire breath; powerful claws and fangs; flight; precognition.
ALLIES Lucifer, Secret Six, Catwoman, the Unknowns, Merlin
ENEMIES Morgaine le Fey, Questing Queen, Stormwatch
AFFILIATIONS Demon Knights

INFERNAL FUSION
Merlin punished both his rebellious scribe Jason Blood and the demon Etrigan by binding them together—a union that would last for centuries.

Etrigan was a lesser demon of Hell who burned with rage and ambition. When he rebelled against his master Lucifer, the infernal lord allowed the magician Merlin to bind Etrigan to a human scribe named Jason Blood. When danger threatens, Jason switches with Etrigan, but is transported to Hell while the demon is in control. For his part, Etrigan resents being forced to act like a 'hero' for a human and plots to gain his freedom.

The spell that bound Etrigan, the Demon and Jason Blood together destroyed Camelot. Jason then wandered the world and rescued sorceress Madame Xanadu, who was about to be burned at the stake as a witch. They became lovers, and to help keep Etrigan under control, Xanadu romanced the jealous demon as well. When the demon hordes of the Questing Queen threatened the village of Little Spring, Jason joined a group of disparate warriors to fight her and her dragons. Etrigan, Xanadu, and their fellow Demon Knights fought off the Questing Queen's army.

Etrigan betrayed the Knights and sent them to Hell, but Blood saved them. They later split up, and former member Vandal Savage took Jason prisoner. He cast a mute spell to stop Jason summoning Etrigan and tortured him for damning him to Hell. Blood was then freed by his friends and dispelled the muting magic. Blood and Etrigan rejoined the Demon Knights on their quest to find the Holy Grail. Madame Xanadu then used a spell to imprison Etrigan beneath London, but he broke free in the 21st century. He clashed with Stormwatch (the modern incarnation of the Demon Knights) and then plotted to kill his former host. However, Blood was saved by Batwoman, and Etrigan teamed up with her to prevent the return of Arthurian villainess Morgaine Le Fey. He then found himself thrust into the role of hero once again as he helped the Secret Six battle invading Elder Gods. **SW**

DEMON WARRIOR, HOLY QUEST
As a member of the Demon Knights, Etrigan embarked on a quest for the Holy Grail and encountered many dangers—including the octopoid Archetheusis!

CLASSIC STORIES

***Swamp Thing* (Vol. 2) #49–50 (Jun.–Jul. 1986)** When Swamp Thing, Deadman, and the Phantom Stranger recruit Etrigan to take part in a battle to decide the fate of the world, the demon leads the assault on the Great Darkness.

***Hitman* #16–19 (Jul.–Oct. 1997)** Hitman Tommy Monaghan uses Etrigan to get his hands on the Ace of Winchesters—the one gun that can slay the firearms-demon Mawzir.

***Shadowpact* #11 (May 2007)** Etrigan tries to take the Trident of Lucifer, but is turned to stone by the Shadowpact (and used as a hat rack in the Oblivion Bar).

ON THE RECORD

The post-Crisis incarnation of Etrigan was the son of the demon Belial. In the Dark Ages, Merlin summoned him in a vain attempt to save Camelot from Morgaine le Fey's horde, binding him to a human host, the peasant Jason Blood. This made Jason immortal, and he studied demonology to better understand the entity within him.

In the 20th century, Blood came across an incantation that allowed him to transform into Etrigan, and used it to battle various occult foes. Later, during the "Blackest Night" storyline, he battled Black Lanterns after being possessed by Deadman.

GOING MEDIEVAL
After being released in the 20th century, Etrigan relished the opportunity to inflict some old-fashioned demonic mayhem! The modern-day minions of Morgaine le Fey discovered this to their cost!

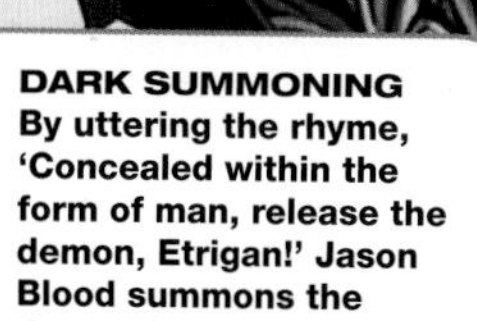
DARK SUMMONING
By uttering the rhyme, 'Concealed within the form of man, release the demon, Etrigan!' Jason Blood summons the demon from Hell.

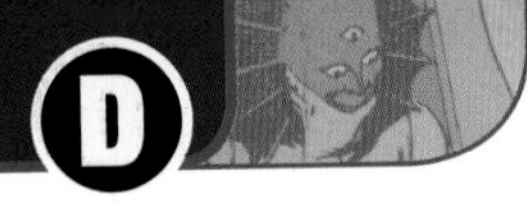

DESAAD

DEBUT *The Forever People* (Vol. 1) #2 **(Apr.–May 1971)**
CURRENT VERSION *Justice League* (Vol. 2) #6 **(Apr. 2012)**
BASE Apokolips
EYES Black **HAIR** Black
HEIGHT 5ft 11in **WEIGHT** 152 lbs
POWERS/ABILITIES New God physiology bestows immortality and superhuman physical capabilities; can take on illusionary appearances, mentally influence others, and gain power from others' pain.
ALLIES Darkseid, Steppenwolf
ENEMIES Mister Miracle, Power Girl, Huntress, Superman (Val-Zod), Batman (Earth-2), the Wonders of the World
AFFILIATIONS Apokolips

Desaad is a New God of Apokolips, and a henchman of its overlord Darkseid. On Apokolips cruelty is a way of life, but Desaad is infamous for his sadism, drawing power from others' agony. He became Darkseid's interrogator and took part in Steppenwolf's attack on Earth-2. When the forces of Darkseid invaded Earth, Desaad tortured the Man of Steel, planning to use his DNA to create more powerful Parademons. The invasion failed, leaving Desaad stranded on Earth, where he used his advanced technology and mind-control powers to spread strife, corruption, and suffering.

When businessman and hero Mister Terrific was exiled to Earth-2 in a quantum-tunneling mishap, Desaad stole his identity, and clashed with Terrific's girlfriend, Power Girl, and her companion Huntress, as he constantly tried to find his way back to Apokolips and his master. Desaad was summoned to take part in Apokolips's second attack on Earth-2. Working from a hidden lair beneath Geneva, he turned Huntress into a warped Fury called Famine and created a new breed of warriors that helped Darkseid conquer Earth-2: the Protofuries. **SW**

ON THE RECORD

The post-Crisis Desaad discovered his sadistic side when young Prince Uxas (the future Darkseid) tricked him into killing his own pet. Desaad became Uxas's minion, helping him to steal the Omega Force from his brother Drax. However, he did once betray his master by trying to steal the Omega Force with Highfather's staff. Desaad also displayed a flair for corrupting others, possessing the young Mary Marvel during the Final Crisis, before being banished.

PAIN AND PUNISHMENT
Desaad fed on the fear and pain of others, but when Darkseid caught him siphoning emotions from Orion and Kalibak, he destroyed Desaad with his Omega Beams.

DESPERO

DEBUT *Justice League of America* (Vol. 1) #1 **(Oct.–Nov. 1960)**
CURRENT VERSION *Justice League* (Vol. 2) #19 **(Jun. 2013)**
EYES Yellow **HAIR** None
HEIGHT 8ft 1in **WEIGHT** 850 lbs
POWERS/ABILITIES Third eye channels phenomenal psychic powers including telekinesis, telepathy, mind control, astral projection, and illusion creation; superhumanly strong; capable of interstellar flight; invulnerability and regenerative powers.
ALLIES Crime Syndicate
ENEMIES Martian Manhunter, Stargirl, Justice League
AFFILIATIONS Secret Society of Super-Villains

Despero was a member of a powerful alien race—the Klanorian—who became obsessed with conquest and made himself ruler of three planets inhabited by less powerful beings. The Justice League attempted to overthrow him on one of their very first missions, and after a close battle he was defeated by the Martian Manhunter. Despero became obsessed with revenge, and attacked the Justice League's Watchtower satellite while junior members Atom, Firestorm, and Element Woman were left in charge. He appeared unstoppable, but once again the Martian Manhunter managed to defeat him in a psychic battle and he was imprisoned.

When the evil Crime Syndicate from Earth-3 invaded Earth-0 and defeated the Justice League, they freed Despero and he joined the Syndicate. The alien then used his prodigious mental powers to imprison Justice League members within their own minds, and appeared to beat his nemesis Martian Manhunter to death—though this proved to be a very convincing illusion. Following the defeat of the Crime Syndicate, mastermind Manchester Black manipulated the Teen Titans into breaking Despero out of prison for his own purposes, but the "Despero" they were rescuing turned out to be an illusion created by Dr. Psycho. **SW**

ON THE RECORD

Despero was initially a psychic mastermind who preferred to defeat his foes using elaborate games. However, he later evolved a physical form powerful enough to battle the entire Justice League single-handed. In one battle at the United Nations building, he was only defeated when Martian Manhunter showed him a vision of the thing he most wanted: the destruction of the Justice League. At peace, Despero reverted (temporarily) to a harmless fetus.

GAMES MASTER
In his very first encounter with the Justice League, Despero captured the team and then forced the Flash to play against him in a game to win their freedom.

CONQUEROR
Despero's psychic and physical power enabled him to conquer entire planets.

DEVASTATION

DEBUT *Wonder Woman* (Vol. 2) #143 (Apr. 1999)
HEIGHT 4ft 6in **WEIGHT** 82 lbs
EYES Pale blue **HAIR** Red
POWERS/ABILITIES Superhuman abilities, tactical genius, supersonic flight; can cause earthquakes and manipulate emotions.
ALLIES Cronus, Dr. Poison, Agua Sin Gaaz, Lady Zand
ENEMIES Wonder Woman, Wonder Girl (Cassie Sandsmark), Young Justice
AFFILIATIONS The Titans

TINY TERROR
Devastation's divinely bestowed powers and bottomless appetite for destruction made her a fearsome opponent, despite her diminutive size.

Devastation was created by the Titan Cronus as a weapon to cause discord on Earth. When she raised havoc in a small South Carolina town, Wonder Woman arrived to confront her, but quickly discovered that Devastation was just as powerful as she was. Devastation spread rioting and destruction across the South and tried to detonate a nuclear weapon, but Wonder Woman buried it underground and Devastation was atomized in the blast.

Seeking revenge, Devastation reconstructed herself and used her mind-warping powers to turn Wonder Woman's protégé Wonder Girl against her. Wonder Woman used her love for Cassie to break Devastation's programming, though, and the villain fled. Cassie later joined Young Justice, and when the team invaded the super-villain haven of Zandia, Devastation agreed to help defend it on the condition that she got to take on Wonder Girl herself—but was beaten in a muddy brawl. **SW**

DEVILANCE THE PURSUER

DEBUT *Forever People* (Vol. 1) #11 (Oct.–Nov. 1972)
BASE Apokolips
EYES Blue
HEIGHT 7ft 1in **WEIGHT** 405 lbs
POWERS/ABILITIES Immortality, strength; energy lance tracks targets and allows flight.
ALLIES Darkseid
ENEMIES Forever People, Lobo, Starfire, Animal Man, Adam Strange, New Genesis

Devilance is the huntsman of Darkseid and the New God of Pursuit, dispatched to track down enemies of Apokolips. Darkseid sent Devilance to Earth to capture the Forever People of New Genesis, and the young heroes only escaped by switching places with Infinity Man, who was trapped in a pocket dimension. Infinity Man grabbed Devilance's weapon, and both were seemingly destroyed in an explosion.

Years later, however, Animal Man, Adam Strange, and Starfire encountered Devilance when they were stranded on a paradise planet. The Pursuer took the heroes prisoner, but they managed to escape, stealing his lance to power their ship. Devilance pursued them, but was attacked and killed by the alien bounty hunter Lobo, who impaled the New God's head on his own lance. **SW**

DEX-STARR

DEBUT *Final Crisis: Rage of the Red Lanterns* #1 (Dec. 2008)
CURRENT VERSION *Red Lanterns* #1 (Nov. 2011)
BASE Ysmault
POWERS/ABILITIES Red Lantern power ring gives speed, toughness, strength, interstellar flight; and can create Red Energy constructs.
ALLIES Atrocitus
ENEMIES Guy Gardner, Lobo
AFFILIATIONS Red Lanterns

Dexter was once an ordinary cat, but when he saw his master murdered he was overcome by anger and was chosen by a Red Lantern power ring. After exacting revenge on his master's killers, he joined the Red Lantern Corps as Dex-Starr and developed a close bond with its leader, Atrocitus. He also gained the ability to create energy constructs by licking up the blood of his fellow Lantern, Rankorr.

When Guy Gardner defeated Atrocitus and took over the Corps, the loyal Dex-Starr took Atrocitus to safety and helped him recruit an army to attack Gardner and his Red Lanterns. Gardner won the battle, but quit the Corps and Atrocitus took command again. Dex-Starr was later killed by the bounty hunter Lobo, but was reborn from a pool of Red Lantern blood as a being of pure rage. **SW**

DIAL H FOR HERO

DEBUT *House of Mystery* (Vol. 1) #156 (Jan. 1966)
CURRENT VERSION *Dial H* #1 (Jul. 2012)
REAL NAME Nelson Jent
BASE Littleville
EYES Brown **HAIR** Blond
POWERS/ABILITIES By using the H-Dial, Nelson receives a seemingly random Super Hero identity and corresponding powers, from causing despair (Captain Lachrymose) or disease (Human Virus) to pelican summoning (Pelican Army).
ALLIES Manteau, the Squid, the Dial Bunch
ENEMIES Ex Nihilo, Abyss, Centipede, the Fixer

When unemployed loser Nelson Jent witnessed his friend being beaten by thugs, he ran to a phone booth and tried to call for help. The phone was fitted with a strange "H-Dial," and when Nelson inadvertently dialed H-E-R-O, he was transformed into a pollution-powered Super Hero called Boy Chimney. In this form he defeated the criminals and saved his friend, later waking up as his normal self. He experimented with the H-Dial and discovered that it transformed him into a different hero each time he dialed H-E-R-O.

Jent then crossed paths with a ruthless nullomancer called Ex Nihilo, and met a heroine called Manteau, who possessed a dial similar to his own. Nelson and Manteau teamed up to stop Ex Nihilo and defeat the terrifying creature she had summoned: a sentient void called Abyss. Nelson and Manteau then embarked on a quest in search of the origin of their dials. On this bizarre interdimensional journey, they encountered the Dial Bunch (a group of heroic dial-wielders) and prevented the mysterious O the Lost Operator from destroying the multiverse—one randomly dialed reality at a time—with his Doom-Dial. **SW**

ON THE RECORD

The first known dial-user was teenager Robby Reed, who discovered an alien dial in a cavern. However, when he dialed S-P-L-I-T while battling Shirkon of the Many Eyes, he divided into two beings. The good Wizard and the evil Master became foes of Chris King and Vicki Grant, the next dial-wielders, until Robby's halves were reunited. A flashback later revealed that Robby had once used his dial to switch the JLA's powers, thus helping them to defeat the Injustice League.

DIAL P FOR PATRIOTISM!
In one of his early adventures, Robby Reed transformed into the star-spangled Yankee Doodle Kid and battled the villainous Cougar.

DIGGLE, JOHN

DEBUT *Green Arrow* (Vol. 5) #24 **(Dec. 2013)**
REAL NAME John Andrew Diggle
BASE Seattle, Washington
HEIGHT 6ft 1in **WEIGHT** 209 lbs
EYES Brown **HAIR** Black
POWERS/ABILITIES Special forces training and combat experience makes him a formidable opponent.
ALLIES Green Arrow, Green Lantern (Hal Jordan)
ENEMIES The Clock King, Richard Dragon and the Longbow Hunters, John King
AFFILIATIONS Team Arrow

Former Green Beret John Diggle was working as a bodyguard at Queen Industries when Green Arrow (Oliver Queen) showed up at his Seattle apartment. The bow-slinging vigilante offered Diggle a job as 'point man' in his war against crime, and Diggle accepted on the condition that he didn't have to wear tights or a mask. The duo fought crime for a year, but when Oliver's mother died of cancer and he went into mourning, Diggle put on the Green Arrow outfit without permission and took down crime lord Ricardo Diaz. Following an argument, Queen fired Diggle.

Four years later, when Green Arrow was fighting Komodo and the Outsiders in Prague, Diggle resurfaced to take on the crime boss Richard Dragon, who was assuming control of the Seattle underworld. Diggle was betrayed by the mobster the Clock King and captured by Dragon, who turned out to be Ricardo Diaz's son. Dragon knocked Diggle out of a window, but he was rescued by Green Arrow, and the two teamed up to best the villain. Diggle then joined Team Arrow to take down philanthropist and criminal mastermind John King. **SW**

THE FALL GUY
When Richard Dragon declared war on Green Arrow and his allies, he tortured John Diggle before kicking him out a window. Fortunately, Green Arrow broke his friend's fall with a foam arrow.

PARTNERS IN CRIME FIGHTING
Diggle was a practical and pragmatic counterpart to the flamboyant and idealistic Green Arrow.

DIRECTOR BONES

DEBUT *Infinity Inc.* #16 (Jul. 1985)
CURRENT VERSION *Batwoman* (Vol. 2) #1 (Nov. 2011)
BASE The Lipstick Building, NYC, New York
HEIGHT 5ft 10in **WEIGHT** 165 lbs
POWERS/ABILITIES Toxic 'cyanide touch;' is immune to cyanide.
ALLIES Agent Chase
ENEMIES Batwoman, Batman, Blue Beetle
AFFILIATIONS Department of Extranormal Operations

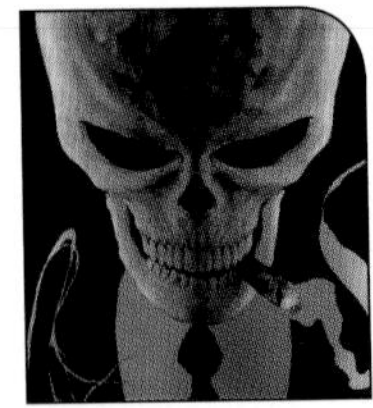

The skull-faced Director Bones led the Department of Extranormal Operations, a secret government agency that monitored superhuman activity. Bones focused on gathering intelligence on 'capes' and then utilizing this information to control them for his own ends.

After gaining information on Batwoman's secret identity, Bones convinced her to work for him by threatening to incarcerate her father. She teamed up with Wonder Woman to track down the Medusa. The director then forced her to help him uncover Batman's secret identity by revealing that her long-lost twin sister Beth was in custody. Batman and Batwoman teamed up to save Beth. Mounting concern over Director Bones' sociopathic behavior led to his eventual incarceration in a secure facility. **SW**

DIRECTOR ZITHER

DEBUT *The Fury of Firestorm: The Nuclear Men* (Vol. 1) #1 (Nov. 2011)
REAL NAME Candace Zither
BASE Zithertech Compound, Nevada
EYES Brown **HAIR** Black
POWERS/ABILITIES Ace strategist, resolute leader.
ALLIES Helix, Dog Squad, Hyena Squad
ENEMIES Firestorm, Pozhar
AFFILIATIONS Zithertech

Candace Zither was the ruthless director of Zithertech. When Professor Martin Stein invented the Firestorm Protocol—which transformed humans into living atomic weapons—Zithertech tried to duplicate the formula and sell it to rogue nations.

The first test subject was Candace's husband Roger, but it went wrong. Roger was transformed into the monster Helix, their children were killed, and Candace was badly burned. She sent a team to seize Stein's last sample, but he had given it to student Jason Rusch. Jason triggered the Protocol and merged with jock Ronnie Raymond to form Firestorm. Zither tried to co-opt the pair into working with her, but they went rogue after a battle with a suicidal Firestorm from Quarac. Following a congressional enquiry, Candace was seemingly vaporized by Firehawk. **SW**

DNANGELS

DEBUT *Superboy* (Vol. 4) #87 (Jul. 2001)
BASE Metropolis
MEMBERS POWERS/ABILITIES
Cherub: Taps into Speed Force; **Epiphany**: Flight, superhuman strength, speed, and durability; **Seraph**: Telekinesis enhanced strength; can fly, generate force fields, and hurl energy bolts.
ALLIES Superboy
ENEMIES Supergirl
AFFILIATIONS US Government, League of Assassins

The DNAngels are a superpowered team created by a secret $2 billion cloning program. Speedster Cherub was made by mixing the DNA of Impulse with that of Superboy's deceased girlfriend Tana Moon; Epiphany was based on the DNA of Wonder Girl (Cassie Sandsmark); and Seraph gained her powers from the genetic code of Superboy.

Their first mission was to recover an infant clone of Jim Harper (Guardian) from Superboy, but the hero outwitted them. Their bosses, Amanda Spence and General Good, captured Superboy, but he broke free. Cherub found the hero and admitted she liked him, then Spence gravely wounded her. The DNAngels saved Cherub while Superboy destroyed the clone-creation facilities. Later, the group worked for the League of Assassins. **SW**

DOC MAGNUS

DEBUT *Showcase* #37 (Mar.–Apr. 1962)
CURRENT VERSION *Justice League* (Vol. 2) #18 (May 2013)
REAL NAME William Magnus
BASE US Army Research Lab, Adelphi, Maryland
EYES Brown **HAIR** Brown
POWERS/ABILITIES Scientific genius and inventor with a talent for robotics.
ALLIES Cyborg
ENEMIES Chemo, Technosapiens
AFFILIATIONS Metal Men, US Army

Temperamental robotics genius Dr. William Magnus was hired by the US Army to create a robot suitable for search-and-rescue missions. He invented the Responsometer, a compact Artificial Intelligence that could shape metal around it. Magnus used it to make the 'Metal Men'—sentient robots formed from different metals: Gold, Tin, Platinum, Iron, Lead, and Mercury.

However, when ordered to assassinate an enemy in Kahndaq, the robots refused. They went AWOL and hid in Magnus' apartment before sacrificing themselves to defeat the villain Chemo. When the Crime Syndicate invaded Earth, Magnus rebuilt the Metal Men so they could help Cyborg take down the Syndicate's AI, Grid. Magnus and the Metal Men also helped Cyborg fight and defeat the Technosapien invaders. **SW**

DOCTOR FATE

DATA

DEBUT *More Fun Comics* #55 **(May 1940)**
CURRENT VERSION *Convergence Aquaman* #2 **(Jul. 2015)**
REAL NAME Khalid Nassour
BASE Brooklyn
EYES Brown **HAIR** Black
POWERS/ABILITIES Helmet of Fate bestows powers of flight and healing, and the ability to channel and redirect wind, fire, water, earth, and lightning, as well as to phase through walls; Staff of Power emits magical blasts.
ALLIES Nabu, Osiris, Bastet **ENEMIES** Anubis

HELMET OF DESTINY
As a descendant of the Pharaohs, med student Khalid was chosen to be the new Doctor Fate and heal the world.

Down the millennia, the gods of Egypt have chosen brave champions to put on Nabu's golden helmet and accept the sacred duty of protecting the world as Doctor Fate. When Khalid Nassour was chosen, his world changed forever. He discovered that he now possessed incredible element-controlling powers, and soon found himself locked in a spiritual and physical battle with Anubis, the evil God of the Dead.

When Egyptian-American med student Khalid Nassour went to Brooklyn Museum to find a gift for his girlfriend Shaya, a statue of the Egyptian goddess Bastet held out an ancient golden helmet to him. She told him that it was his destiny to oppose the dark god Anubis and heal the world. Khalid put on the golden helmet and transformed into the latest incarnation of Doctor Fate, Earth's mystic defender. He saw visions of the Egyptian gods, perceived hidden secrets of the universe, and discovered that he could fly and manipulate the elements. Khalid was advised by the spirit of Nabu—an ancient priest of Thoth that now inhabited the helmet—but he was also menaced by a feral dog that was an avatar of Anubis, who warned him that he would pay a price for defying him. As Fate, Khalid used his new elemental-control powers to land a damaged plane, protect New York from a storm, and rescue his father, who had been blinded in a traffic accident.

Anubis offered to restore the old man's sight, but when Khalid accepted, Anubis took his sight in return. However, Khalid discovered that he could still see when he put on the helmet of Doctor Fate, and when Anubis unleashed storms around the globe he faced the evil god at a local power facility. In the ensuing battle the jackal-god swallowed Khalid, who found himself trapped in the Ancient Egyptian afterlife, where Anubis prepared to judge him. Khalid prayed to Osiris for help, and the god appeared and gave him his Staff of Power. Wielding this weapon, Khalid defeated Anubis and returned to the land of the living. He then went to work repairing storm damage and defusing a riot at the United Nations. **SW**

SPIRITUAL ADVISOR
The Helmet of Fate is inhabited by the spirit of its original owner, the ancient priest Nabu, who instructs Khalid in the use of his new powers.

CLASSIC STORIES

***The Immortal Doctor Fate* #1–3 (Jan.–Mar. 1985)** A collection of the definitive adventures of the original Doctor Fate, Kent Nelson, as he clashes with the likes of Wotan, Khalis, and Anubis.

***Doctor Fate* (Vol. 1) #1–4 (Jul.–Oct. 1987)** Eric Strauss is chosen to wear the Helmet of Fate, merging with his stepmother Linda to become a new Doctor Fate.

***Countdown to Mystery* #1–8 (Nov. 2007–Jun. 2008)** Kent V. Nelson, the grandnephew of the original Doctor Fate, continues the family tradition by donning the Helmet of Fate as the world moves inexorably towards the Final Crisis.

***The Brave and the Bold* (Vol. 3) #30 (Feb. 2010)** Kent Nelson places part of his spirit in Green Lantern's (Hal Jordan) ring so that he might see into the future, only to discover how he will die.

ON THE RECORD

Several heroes have served as Nabu's host, assuming the role of Doctor Fate over the years. Kent Nelson found the Helmet of Fate in the 1920s on an Egyptian archaeological dig. After being trained by the spirit of Nabu the Wise, he began his career as Doctor Fate in the 1940s.

When Kent died 40 years later, the Helmet passed to Eric Strauss, who mystically merged with his stepmother Linda Strauss to become the second Doctor Fate. After Eric was killed, Linda continued as Doctor Fate and came into conflict with the God of Chaos-possessed Benjamin Stoner, the evil Anti-Fate. On Linda's death, Kent Nelson's wife Inza Kramer briefly succeeded her, after which smuggler Jared Stevens served as a reluctant Doctor Fate until the late 1990s. Hector Hall, son of the Golden Age Hawkman and Hawkgirl, took on the role next, and after he was depowered by the Spectre, Kent Nelson's grandnephew, Kent V. Nelson, became Nabu's host.

On Earth-2, Khalid Ben-Hassin donned a helmet that imbued him with Nabu's essence. He became that world's Doctor Fate, and joined the Super Hero team the Wonders of the World.

MYSTERY MAN
Kent Nelson was a proud member of the first generation of Super Heroes and a founding member of the JSA.

LEGACY OF FATE
Alcoholic former psychologist Kent V. Nelson was at rock-bottom when he found his great-uncle's helmet. Soon he rose to become the new Doctor Fate.

MYSTIC JOURNEY
When he put on the Helmet of Fate, Khalid gained the ability to see into the mystic realm, and discovered that the gods of his ancestors were all too real.

DOCTOR BEDLAM

DEBUT *Mister Miracle* (Vol. 1) #3 (Jul.–Aug. 1971)
CURRENT VERSION *Earth-2* (Vol. 1) #14 (Sep. 2013)
BASE Dherain
EYES Purple **HAIR** None
POWERS/ABILITIES Telepathy
ENEMIES Flash, Green Lantern, and other Earth-2 heroes.
AFFILIATIONS Hunger Dogs

Doctor Bedlam is a devoted follower of Darkseid, and now most commonly refers to himself simply as "Bedlam." His past is shrouded in mystery, but he was one of Steppenwolf's Hunger Dogs alongside Brutaal and Beguiler. He attacked Earth-2's heroes, but when Brutaal was revealed to be Superman, he used his telepathic powers to control several people, including Mister Terrific, forcing them to try and create a device that would move Earth-2 so that it could become a new home for his master, Darkseid.

Pre-Flashpoint, Doctor Bedlam could also manipulate people telepathically, but was a being of pure psionic energy which he housed in an android body. If this body was destroyed, Doctor Bedlam would simply move his consciousness into another one—although it seemed he was eventually killed by the Infinity Man. **AC**

DOCTOR DESTINY

DEBUT *Justice League of America* (Vol. 1) #5 (Jun.–Jul. 1961)
CURRENT VERSION *Justice League Dark* (Vol. 1) #19 (Jun. 2013)
EYES Red **HAIR** None
POWERS/ABILITIES Uses the Dreamstone to bring nightmares to life.
ENEMIES Justice League Dark, Madame Xanadu
AFFILIATIONS The Cold Flame

Doctor Destiny could make nightmares become real and trap people in their own dreams. He was the son of Madame Xanadu who had a vision when he was born of how evil he would become and was forced to abandon her child lest she destroy him as her vision had foretold. When Xanadu was part of the Justice League Dark alongside John Constantine and Swamp Thing, her son, now calling himself Doctor Destiny, attacked the team. He had been given the Dreamstone by agents of the Cold Flame and used it to steal the House of Mystery. The Swamp Thing was imprisoned in the House, but eventually broke free and helped to stop Doctor Destiny, who was then killed by Madame Xanadu.

In his pre-Flashpoint incarnation, Doctor Destiny gained his power from stealing the Dreamstone (known as the Materioptikon) from Dream of the Endless. **AC**

DOCTOR LIGHT II

DEBUT *Crisis on Infinite Earths* (Vol. 1) #4 (Jul. 1985)
REAL NAME Kimiyo Tazu Hoshi
BASE Japan
EYES Black **HAIR** Black
HEIGHT 5ft 3in **WEIGHT** 105 lbs
POWERS/ABILITIES Can control light in all its forms and fly.
ENEMIES Doctor Light (the original, villainous Arthur Light)

Kimiyo Tazu Hoshi was a Japanese scientist and astronomer who became the second Doctor Light during the first great Crisis. The Monitor, realizing he needed to recruit more Super Heroes, sent a beam of energy to Earth that struck Kimiyo, giving her the ability to control all forms of light.

As Doctor Light, Kimiyo used her powers for good, but her arrogant attitude annoyed other heroes at first—until she witnessed Supergirl's heroic death during the fight against the Anti-Monitor. After the battle, a more respectful Doctor Light fought alongside both the Doom Patrol and the Justice League, spending time with the League's European branch. As a single mother with two kids, she decided to put her family first and became a reserve member of the Justice League, but heeded the call when needed—returning to active duty to fight Eclipso, the Secret Six, and the Crime Syndicate.

In post-Flashpoint reality, Kimiyo was the wife of scientist hero Arthur Light. **AC**

SOLAR POWER
While Kimiyo's powers are very strong, she needs light energy to feed them. If she is trapped in darkness her abilities will simply fade away.

DOCTOR MID-NITE

DEBUT *Doctor Mid-Nite* #1 (1991) (Pieter Cross)
REAL NAME Pieter Anton Cross, M.D.
BASE Portsmouth City
EYES Blue **HAIR** Black **HEIGHT** 5ft 10in **WEIGHT** 175 lbs
POWERS/ABILITIES Able to see in the dark; carries inventions to aid his crime fighting, including blackout bombs; excellent medical and surgical skills.
ENEMIES Johnny Sorrow, Icicle, Ultra-Humanite, Mordru, Endless Winter, Mircea
AFFILIATIONS Justice Society of America

Pieter Anton Cross was the second person to take on the role of Doctor Mid-Nite. The original, Dr. Charles M. McNider, had saved Pieter's pregnant mother when she'd been attacked, and helped her give birth to Pieter. Cross grew up to be a physician himself, graduating from Harvard Medical School aged only 19, and worked with McNider, who became his mentor.

While investigating the origins of a dangerous drug called A39 (a variation of the Venom serum), Cross was knocked out and injected with the drug by the dealers, who placed him behind the wheel of a car. Cross regained consciousness just as the car struck a woman. The drug and accident left him blind but astonishingly allowed him to see during the night. He became Doctor Mid-Nite to bring the dealers to justice, and then continued in the role, joining a reformed Justice Society of America. When not crime fighting, he often used his medical skills to aid other Super Heroes and later mentored the young Blue Beetle (Jaime Reyes).

In the post-Flashpoint reality, Pieter Cross worked as a doctor in Seattle, and aided the Green Arrow after he was wounded. **AC**

"YOU'LL LIVE"
As the de facto team medic, Doctor Mid-Nite treated Mr. America's injuries when he received a nasty beating at the hands of the corrupted missionary William Matthews.

DOCTORS IN THE HOUSE
Two other heroes took on the role of Doctor Mid-Nite. The original, Dr. Charles McNider (top), lost his sight to a grenade, and fought crime alongside the original Justice Society of America. The second was Beth Chapel (above). She became a member of Infinity, Inc. but was killed by Eclipso soon after becoming a hero.

DOCTOR LIGHT

DATA

DEBUT *Justice League of America* (Vol. 1) #12 **(Jun. 1962)**
CURRENT VERSION *Justice League of America* (Vol. 3) #4 **(Jul. 2013)**
REAL NAME Arthur Light
BASE Rockville, Maryland.
EYES Black **HAIR** Black
HEIGHT 5ft 11in **WEIGHT** 171 lbs
POWERS/ABILITIES Can manipulate light—either to cause blinding brightness or powerful laser beams.
ENEMIES The Outsider, Crime Syndicate
AFFILIATIONS Justice League of America, A.R.G.U.S., Crimson Men

CLASSIC STORIES

***Secret Origins* (Vol. 3) #37 (Feb. 1989)** The truth about Doctor Light's origins are revealed—including details of the original Doctor Light.

***Identity Crisis* (Aug. 2004–Feb. 2005)** Doctor Light takes on a darker twist as secrets of his past are revealed, including his part in one of the most horrific attacks ever to take place on a member of the Justice League.

***Justice League* (Vol. 2) #22 (Sep. 2013)** The new, heroic Doctor Light—still a relative newcomer to the Super Hero world—is killed by Superman when the Man of Steel's powers misfire.

BROUGHT TO LIGHT
Caught in the Lasso of Truth, Doctor Light came to the terrible realization that he is in fact already dead.

ASHES TO ASHES
Doctor Light came to a horrific end. After he accidentally hit Wonder Woman with his powers, an enraged Superman inadvertently decapitated him with his heat vision.

Doctor Arthur Light was a dedicated scientist working for A.R.G.U.S. when an accident gave him amazing metahuman abilities. A married man with a family, Arthur Light had no intention of being a Super Hero, but was forced into the role as part of the Justice League of America—with fatal consequences.

Arthur Light was a scientist working for A.R.G.U.S. (Advanced Research Group Uniting Superhumans) and the Justice League of America. A married man with three daughters, Arthur lived an unremarkable life until tasked with studying a coin used for communication by agents of the Crime Syndicate. While investigating it, the coin received a signal and Arthur was engulfed in a blast of light that transformed him into a metahuman. While A.R.G.U.S. helped him come to terms with his new abilities, they also put him to work as a member of the Justice League of America.

On his very first mission his light powers seemed to set off Superman's heat vision and Doctor Light was killed. Batman (with the Phantom Stranger) later ventured to the afterlife to try and find out more about Doctor Light's death. When they met him, Light recalled nothing of his death and was at peace in the spirit world.

After the Crime Syndicate took over Earth-0, Light seemingly returned after his corpse was used to cause an explosion that destroyed A.R.G.U.S.' Washington, DC headquarters. An energy apparition of Doctor Light appeared and was taken in by the Crimson Men who promised to return him to a physical form if he gave them information on Steve Trevor. When Doctor Light was forced to attack Trevor, he found himself also fighting Killer Frost. Trevor used Wonder Woman's Lasso of Truth on Doctor Light, causing him to remember that he had died. Realizing he was just an echo of the real Doctor Light, the apparition vanished in a blast of energy. **AC**

ON THE RECORD

The original Doctor Light was a villain. Doctor Arthur Light worked at S.T.A.R. Labs where his colleague Jacob Finlay had created an energy-manipulating costume to become a Super Hero called Doctor Light. After accidentally killing Finlay, Arthur took the costume and name to fight the Justice League and Teen Titans.

A brief member of the Suicide Squad, Light was retroactively revealed to have assaulted the Elongated Man's wife Sue Dibny and later helped murder the Martian Manhunter. The Spectre eventually executed the villain in *Final Crisis: Revelations* #1 (Oct. 2008).

LIGHT GOES BLACK
Doctor Light returned as a Black Lantern to attack his successor, Kimiyo Hoshi, during the Blackest Night event.

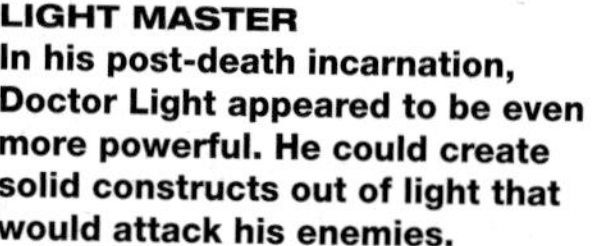

LIGHT MASTER
In his post-death incarnation, Doctor Light appeared to be even more powerful. He could create solid constructs out of light that would attack his enemies.

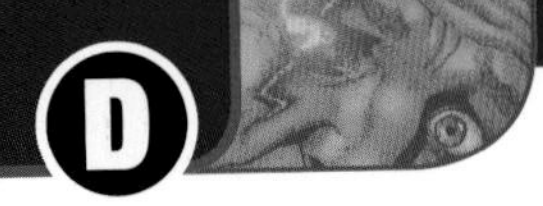

DOCTOR PHOSPHORUS

DEBUT *Detective Comics* #469 (May 1977)
CURRENT VERSION *Catwoman* (Vol. 4) #22 (Oct. 2013)
REAL NAME Alex Sartorius
BASE Gotham City
HEIGHT 5ft 11in **WEIGHT** 169 lbs
HAIR None **EYES** White
POWERS/ABILITIES Combusts in oxygen, emits toxic fumes; manipulates radiation.
ALLIES Neron
ENEMIES Starman, Batman

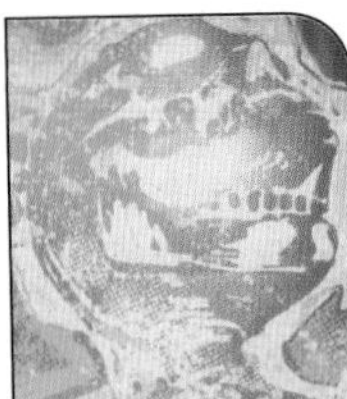

Doctor Phosphorus, eternally burning from millions of particles of phosphorus in his body, joined the Secret Society of Super-Villains and ended up in Arkham Asylum when the Crime Syndicate's invasion collapsed. He was later broken out as war loomed between the Penguin's costumed crew and the murderous Carmine Falcone.

Phosphorus vanished into Gotham Underground, taking over Charneltown with his daughter, Tinderbox. He wanted to control other parts of the Underground and strike at the surface, but he needed to change the surface environment, or his nature, in order to survive there. He found that if he could make the diamonds in the lava pits of Rock Bottom explode using the correct harmonic frequency, all of Gotham City would be engulfed in fire, thus allowing him to live on the surface. **AI**

DOCTOR PSYCHO

DEBUT *Wonder Woman* (Vol. 1) #5 (Jun.–Jul. 1943)
CURRENT VERSION *Superboy* (Vol. 6) #18 (May 2013)
REAL NAME Edgar Cizko
HEIGHT 3ft 9in **WEIGHT** 85 lbs
HAIR None **EYES** Brown
POWERS/ABILITIES Psionic ability; hallucination creation; astral projection.
ENEMIES Justice League
AFFILIATIONS Secret Society of Super-Villains

Doctor Psycho was a diminutive con man with psionic abilities. He carried out séances in New York City in order to telepathically steal his clients' identities and data, which he used to hide from H.I.V.E., who was hunting telepaths at the time.

Doctor Psycho astral projected into Superboy's mind while Superboy fought Plasmus, and then allied with him against H.I.V.E.. Escaping, Psycho vanished, until the Question saw evidence implicating him in the death of Arthur Light, for which Superman blamed himself. The JLA and the Question traced him and Martian Manhunter looked into his mind. He saw that the Secret Society had sent Psycho to Kahndaq on the day of Light's death, but he hadn't affected Superman's behavior. Psycho later battled the Metal Men with the Fearsome Five. **AI**

DOCTOR THIRTEEN

DEBUT *Star-Spangled Comics* #122 (Nov. 1951)
CURRENT VERSION *Phantom Stranger* (Vol. 4) #2 (Jan. 2013)
BASE Gotham City
REAL NAME Terrence Thirteen II
HEIGHT 5ft 11in **WEIGHT** 168 lbs
HAIR Brown **EYES** Brown
POWERS/ABILITIES Skilled chemist and supernatural investigator.
ALLIES Phantom Stranger
ENEMIES Haunted Highwayman
AFFILIATIONS Justice League Dark

Doctor Thirteen was a supernatural investigator in 1880s Gotham City. He was devoted to exposing those who used pseudo-science to defraud the gullible. He helped the police catch a thief known as the Haunted Highwayman, exposing him as Professor Jonathan Rood. In the ensuing fight, a stray bullet killed the thief's mother. Before he was hanged, Rood pronounced a curse on Thirteen and all his descendants.

One of those descendants, also named Terrence, used his investigative and medical talents during the Justice League Dark's battle against the Blight. He and Nightmare Nurse brought the team back to life before Thirteen went with the Phantom Stranger to locate Chris Esperanza, a boy the Blight was using as a human host. **AI**

DOLLMAKER

CURRENT VERSION *Detective Comics* (Vol. 2) #1 (Nov. 2011)
BASE Gotham City
REAL NAME Barton Mathis
HEIGHT 5ft 11in **WEIGHT** 160 lbs
HAIR Brown **EYES** Blue
POWERS/ABILITIES Skilled surgeon.
ALLIES The Joker
ENEMIES Batman

Young Barton Mathis' father Wesley was a cannibal serial killer, who took his son along on his hunts. Deranged by this experience, Barton was further unhinged when he witnessed his father's killing by a young Gotham City police officer named James Gordon. The orphaned boy was placed into foster care, but ran away, surfacing years later as the Dollmaker.

He wore a mask stitched together from other faces—one of which was his father's—and led several thugs with similar skin masks. Dollmaker conspired with the Joker to capture Batman and Commissioner Gordon, cutting off the Joker's face and providing a new one so he could escape Arkham Asylum while people believed he was dead. Their plot failed when Batman freed himself and went after Dollmaker, who escaped, leaving behind the Joker's face—which became an object of perverse worship for the Joker's minions. **AI**

DOCTOR POLARIS

DEBUT *Green Lantern* (Vol. 2) #21 (Jun. 1963)
BASE New Mexico
REAL NAME Neal Emerson
HEIGHT 6ft 1in **WEIGHT** 194 lbs
HAIR Brown **EYES** Blue
POWERS/ABILITIES Wields magnetic energy to levitate, move metallic objects, and make force fields.
ALLIES Neron
ENEMIES Green Lantern Corps

Neal Emerson's research into magnetic polarity resulted in several medical breakthroughs. However, his work also caused him to develop a personality disorder. Over time, his darker side became the villainous, power-hungry Doctor Polaris.

Polaris clashed with Hal Jordan, Earth's Green Lantern, several times, with Hal often coaxing out Neal's benevolent personality, and so ending Polaris' magnetic rampages.

Emerson originally used technology to control magnetism, but his body eventually internalized the power. After the Anti-Monitor attacked Earth, Polaris and other villains tried to destroy all Earth-based Green Lanterns. During the Infinite Crisis, Polaris joined the Secret Society of Super-Villains, but later perished in an explosion. His successor, John Nichol, was killed by the Black Lantern version of Emerson. **AI**

DOCTOR SIVANA

DEBUT *Whiz Comics* #2 (Feb. 1940)
CURRENT VERSION *Justice League* (Vol. 2) #7 (May 2012)
REAL NAME Thaddeus Bodog Sivana
HEIGHT 5ft 6in **WEIGHT** 123 lbs
HAIR Bald **EYES** Brown
POWERS/ABILITIES Wide-ranging mastery of scientific and technical disciplines.
ALLIES Mr. Mind, Black Adam
ENEMIES Justice League
AFFILIATIONS Secret Society of Super-Villains

When his scientific investigations failed to provide answers in his quest to save his family from a terrible threat, Doctor Sivana turned to magic. He learned the story of Teth-Adam becoming Black Adam, and went to the site in Iraq he thought contained his tomb to search for an entrance to the Rock of Eternity.

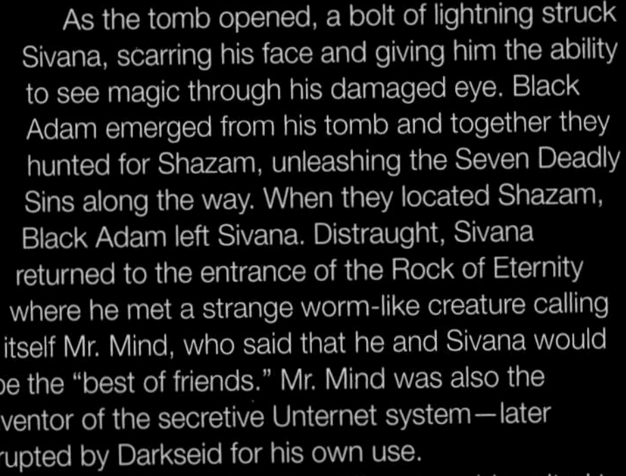

As the tomb opened, a bolt of lightning struck Sivana, scarring his face and giving him the ability to see magic through his damaged eye. Black Adam emerged from his tomb and together they hunted for Shazam, unleashing the Seven Deadly Sins along the way. When they located Shazam, Black Adam left Sivana. Distraught, Sivana returned to the entrance of the Rock of Eternity where he met a strange worm-like creature calling itself Mr. Mind, who said that he and Sivana would be the "best of friends." Mr. Mind was also the inventor of the secretive Unternet system—later corrupted by Darkseid for his own use.

A Legion of Sivanas from the different worlds united to destroy the Shazam Family and conquer the Multiverse, attempting to seize control of the Rock of Eternity. **AI**

ON THE RECORD

Doctor Sivana was originally a mad scientist but, during his pre-Flashpoint history, his feud with the Marvel Family got more personal. He was now a rogue scientist and corrupt billionaire implicated in the murders of archaeologists C.C. and Marilyn Batson.

Sivana attempted to steal the scarab necklace of the ancient wizard Shazam. He was thwarted by Captain Marvel, whom Sivana learned was young Billy Batson, and whom he mocked as "The Big Red Cheese."

GOLDEN AGE ADVERSARIES
Doctor Sivana and his family—which include Georgia and Sivana Jr.—have long been foes of the Shazam family.

DOLL GIRL AND DOLL MAN

DEBUT (Doll Man) *Feature Comics* #27 (Dec. 1939); (Doll Girl) *Doll Man* #37 (Dec. 1951)
CURRENT VERSION (Doll Man) *Phantom Lady* #1 (Oct. 2012)
REAL NAMES Dane Maxwell (Doll Man); Martha Roberts (Doll Girl)
BASE Metropolis
HEIGHT/WEIGHT Variable (Doll Man, Doll Girl)
HAIR Brown (Doll Man, Doll Girl)
EYES Blue (Doll Man); Brown (Doll Girl)
POWERS/ABILITIES Shrinking effect increases strength and physical abilities.
ENEMIES "Warlock" McGraw, Funerella

The original Doll Girl was Martha Roberts, at first a companion to her boyfriend Darrel Dane, the original Doll Man. Martha later acquired similar shrinking powers to his and embarked on adventures of her own. A second Doll Girl briefly became a member of the Teen Titans.

Much later, Doll Man returned to action in the form of Dane Maxwell, a longtime friend of Jennifer Knight (also known as the Phantom Lady). While helping Knight track down the people who killed her parents, Dane was trapped in an experimental apparatus and shrunk to a minuscule size.

He then teamed up with the Phantom Lady to fight crime in Suicide Slum, starting with gangster Frank "Warlock" McGraw and the mysterious Funerella. This crusade brought them to the attention of Uncle Sam, who offered them a position with his national security-focused hero team. **AI**

ORIGINAL DUO
The first Doll Man and Doll Girl battled villains and threats that would appear mundane to those of regular stature.

MIGHTY MITE
Dane Maxwell, aka Doll Man, at rest in the palm of the Phantom Lady's hand. He may look small, but he packs a very big punch.

DOLPHIN

DEBUT *Showcase* #79 (Dec. 1968)
BASE Atlantis
HEIGHT 5ft 10in **WEIGHT** 145 lbs
EYES Blue **HAIR** White
POWERS/ABILITIES Very fast swimmer who can breathe in air and water; able to withstand deep-sea pressures.
ALLIES Aquaman, Tempest
ENEMIES Spectre
AFFILIATIONS Forgotten Heroes

A woman nicknamed Dolphin is the sole surviving member of an alien experiment on humans. She was freed by the spirit of Kordax the Cursed—which hailed from Atlantis' earliest days—and then found by Navy officer Chris Landau and his crew.

Dolphin was initially the main attraction at Oceanworld, but eventually returned to the sea, where she discovered Atlantis and was made welcome. She met Aquaman during a battle with Charybdis and later fell in love with Aquaman's adopted son, Tempest.

Dolphin joined father and son on several missions until she and Tempest married. They had a child, during the war between Atlantis and Cerdia, and the baby was named Cerdian to help heal the conflict. Dolphin later insisted that Tempest leave the Teen Titans to devote his time to their family and home in Atlantis. **AI**

DOMINATORS

DEBUT *Adventure Comics* #361 (Oct. 1967)
CURRENT VERSION *Legion of Super-Heroes* (Vol. 7) #2 (Dec. 2011)
BASE Dominion
HEIGHT Variable **WEIGHT** Variable
EYES Black **HAIR** Bald
POWERS/ABILITIES Master geneticists with highly advanced technologies.
ENEMIES Legion of Super-Heroes

The Dominators were a highly advanced, technological civilization organized on rigid hierarchical lines. Collectively known as The Dominion, this alien race specialized in genetic manipulation. Using sampled metagenes, they created members of their civilization with a variety of powers and abilities.

They have a long and tangled history with the United Planets of the 30th century, including periods of conflict interrupted by an uneasy peace, and are one of the Legion of Super-Heroes' main enemies.

An encounter with Booster Gold led them to believe an attack on the Dominion was imminent, and they invaded Earth to stop it. Cosmic Boy and Mon-El led the fight against them, detonating a bomb that was thought to have destroyed the Dominators. It later emerged that it had only trapped them in the Phantom Zone. **AI**

DOOM PATROL

DEBUT *My Greatest Adventure* #80 (Jun. 1963)
CURRENT VERSION *Justice League* (Vol. 2) #24 (Dec. 2013)
BASE Los Angeles
CURRENT MEMBERS/POWERS The Chief (Dr. Niles Caulder): genius intellect; **Elasti-Girl** (Rita Farr): elasticity, size alteration; **Negative Man** (Lawrence Trainor): radioactive projection, can fly and become intangible; **Robotman** (Cliff Steele): nanomachine-created robot body with various powers; **Element Woman** (Emily Sung): metamorphosis, elemental manipulation.
ALLIES A.R.G.U.S., Justice League
ENEMIES Crime Syndicate of America

Dr. Niles Caulder—also known as the Chief—created the Doom Patrol from a group of ostracized and traumatized metahuman misfits, figuring they would have nothing to lose. The first roster, which included the likes of Scorch, Karma, Negative Woman, and Tempest, were all killed in a fight with Johnny Quick and Atomica of the Crime Syndicate of America when they invaded Earth. As a result, Dr. Caulder brought together a new team: Elasti-Girl, Negative Man, Robotman, and Element Woman, who was estranged from the Justice League.

The team went after the new Power Ring, Jessica Cruz, but during the mission the members of Doom Patrol learned that Caulder was not at all what he seemed, when they crossed paths with Justice League members also pursuing Cruz. Not only did Dr. Caulder try to lobotomize Jessica so that he could control her, but Lex Luthor informed the Doom Patrol that Caulder himself was also responsible for the freak accidents that gave the members their powers.
Celsius and Tempest, previous Doom Patrol members, had faked their own deaths to free themselves of his control. In the aftermath of these revelations, the future of the team is uncertain. **AI**

MOTLEY CREW
1 Robotman
2 The Chief
3 Element Woman
4 Negative Man
5 Elasti-Girl

ON THE RECORD

The first Doom Patrol—Elasti-Girl, Negative Man, and Robotman—was assembled by the wheelchair-bound Dr. Niles Caulder. He believed that his band of alienated outcasts would be willing to risk their lives as the world's strangest Super Heroes battling equally bizarre villains.

By contrast, the pre-Flashpoint Caulder manipulated and betrayed the trust of the team, even as he encouraged them to fight the Brotherhood of Evil and General Immortus. One especially odd later addition to the team was the sentient road, Danny the Street, who later helped the Teen Titans escape the evil Harvest.

TRUST ISSUES
Niles Caulder put the Doom Patrol together, but he wasn't sentimental about individual members whom he considered a threat.

DOOMSDAY

DATA

DEBUT *Superman: Man of Steel* (Vol. 1) #17 **(Nov. 1992)**
CURRENT VERSION *Batman/Superman* #3.1 *Doomsday* **(Nov. 2013)**
BASE Phantom Zone, mobile
HEIGHT 8ft 10in **WEIGHT** 915 lbs
EYES Red **HAIR** White
POWERS/ABILITIES Overwhelming strength, regeneration, invulnerability, teleportation, toxikinesis.
ALLIES None
ENEMIES Superman, Wonder Woman

UNENDING TORMENT
Doomsday's greatest triumph was infecting Superman with contaminating spores and slowly turning the Man of Steel into a monster as deadly as the original.

CLASSIC STORIES

***Superman* (Vol. 2) #75 (Jan. 1993)** Doomsday falls to Superman's ultimate efforts. The unconscious monstrosity is carted away into captivity as Earth mourns the death of its greatest hero.

***Superman/Doomsday: Hunter/Prey* (Vol. 1) #1–3 (Apr.–Jun. 1994)** Thrown into space, Doomsday landed on Apokolips and battled Darkseid. He was then transported to the planet of Calaton, with Superman in hot pursuit.

***Superman: The Doomsday Wars* (Vol. 1) #1–3 (Nov. 1998–Jan. 1999)** Doomsday is plucked from the End of Time and his body merged with Brainiac's intellect in a lethal experiment.

WORST NIGHTMARE
Earth's Super Heroes had never faced a more terrible foe; but they had yet to contend with Doomsday in his full-blown adult form.

Doomsday is an alien creature of overwhelming force and savage bloodlust whose appearance invokes terror. When it first arrived on Earth, the skies turned red and its rampage of mindless destruction devastated Metropolis. The carnage ended only after Superman seemingly lost his life fighting it. On Superman's return, the creature was exiled to the Phantom Zone and humanity breathed a collective sigh of relief.

The true origins of Doomsday are unknown, but the horrific juggernaut of destruction has tormented the House of El since before Krypton died. When it first appeared, Doomsday encountered Superman's future mother Lara Lor-Van—then a lieutenant of the elite Military Seminary. She was unable to stop it and only the steely determination of her superior officer Colonel Zod, wearing an ancient Warsuit, drove the unrelenting creature away and saved Krypton. Zod later claimed to Lara's niece, Kara Zor-El, that he had created the beast, needing it to shock the complacent, decadent Kryptonian society back into being the vibrant, ferocious, dominant race it had once been.

Exiling Doomsday to the Phantom Zone, Superman believed the threat over, but some years later it reappeared. Science wizard Dr. Shay Veritas concluded the monster had until now been in a juvenile stage, but was maturing with new and greater powers, such as the ability to teleport back and forth from the Phantom Zone. Terrifyingly, the creature now emitted toxic radiation and spread contaminating spores while absorbing the life-force of all around it. To defeat it, Superman had to tear apart Doomsday and inhale the spores.

More recently, after the death of Superman at the hands of an energy-draining doppelganger, an earlier version of Doomsday returned to torment Metropolis. The only force capable of standing in its way was a reluctant alliance between an alternate Earth Man of Steel and Lex Luthor in a war suit bearing Superman's symbol. **WW**

WALKING NIGHTMARE
Ruthless, relentless, unstoppable; the monolithic monster spread terror and death wherever he went.

ON THE RECORD

Doomsday debuted in 1992: a relentless, unreasoning juggernaut of destruction intent on invading Metropolis. Draped in a shroud with futuristic, broken shackles, it smashed its way across America and was only stopped at the cost of Superman's life.

In 2011, mere months before the Flashpoint event, Luthor unleashed a wave of Doomsday clones against every hero wearing Superman's symbol. The furious onslaught enveloped Superboy, Supergirl, Eradicator, Steel, and even Cyborg-Superman, the Outsiders, and the Justice League. None knew their true enemy was an intelligent and manipulative super-Doomsday clone called the Doomslayer.

REIGN OF THE DOOMSDAYS
Although no longer unique, the alien entity Doomsday was always an aptly named, serious threat.

DRAGON, RICHARD

DEBUT *Richard Dragon, Kung Fu Fighter* (Vol. 1) #1 (Apr.–May 1975)
CURRENT VERSION *Green Arrow* (Vol. 5) #23 (Oct. 2013)
REAL NAME Ricardo Diaz, Jr.
BASE Seattle
EYES Brown **HAIR** Bald
POWERS/ABILITIES Accomplished martial artist; strategic and tactical mastermind.
ALLIES Billy "The Clock King" Tockman, Count Vertigo, Red Dart, Brick, Killer Moth
ENEMIES Green Arrow, Shado, John Diggle
AFFILIATIONS The Longbow Hunters, League of Assassins

DRAGON'S HORDE
The merciless and deadly Crime King of Seattle took whatever he wanted and defended his treasures with an army of lethal metahuman killers.

Ricardo Diaz, Jr. is the son of criminal royalty. Until Green Arrow and John Diggle stopped him, Diaz Senior ruled Seattle's underworld, and when they destroyed the enterprise his son swore vengeance. He joined the League of Assassins and was trained by Richard Drakunovski in all aspects of the martial arts.

Ricardo readily absorbed the combat lore of the fabled "Richard Dragon" but rejected his sensei's attempts to instill a moral code or compassion. When he learned all he could, Diaz killed his mentor, taking his name.

Returning to Seattle, the new Dragon began reclaiming his inheritance, killing gang bosses and bringing together the fragmented groups to form an army of terror. He organized a super-villain task-force to collect a multi-million dollar bounty on Green Arrow and tried to force the hero into accepting him as Seattle's ultimate power. **WW**

DREAM GIRL

DEBUT *Adventure Comics* (Vol. 1) #317 (Feb. 1964)
CURRENT VERSION *Legion of Super-Heroes* (Vol. 7) #1 (Nov. 2011)
BASE LSH HQ, 1st-century Metropolis
REAL NAME Nura Nal
HEIGHT 5ft 5in **WEIGHT** 120 lbs
EYES Blue **HAIR** Silver
POWERS/ABILITIES Oneiromancy, preternaturally accurate precognitive dreams.
ALLIES High Seer of Naltor
ENEMIES Dominators
AFFILIATIONS Legion of Super-Heroes, Legion of Substitute Heroes

VISIONARY LEADER
Dream Girl's superpower was just a handy qualifying detail for Legion membership. Her true value is as an independent, inspirational commander.

Nura Nal was the most infallible seer of a race capable of glimpsing the future. Foreseeing a crisis where Legionnaires died, Nura acted to prevent the catastrophe by manipulating them into recruiting her. With the matter resolved she resigned and joined the Legion of Substitute Heroes, but was eventually asked to rejoin the main team.

Though her dreams are invariably accurate, interpretation is sometimes difficult and erratic. This is more than offset by her incisive mind, decisive nature, and diplomatic brilliance. Her sister Mysa is the sorceress Black Witch and Nura is often the only Legionnaire who understands what Brainiac 5 is saying.

Dream Girl led the Legion against Darkseid, expanded its Academy, and is a crucial component of its crisis management and political structure. **WW**

DRAK, LYSSA

DEBUT *Green Lantern* (Vol. 4) #18 (May 2007)
CURRENT VERSION *Green Lantern* (Vol. 5) #6 (Apr. 2012)
REAL NAME Lyssa Drak
BASE Talok V, Qward, Sector 3500
EYES Red **HAIR** Black
POWERS/ABILITIES Emotional empathy, prognostication, seduction through storytelling.
ALLIES Arkillo, Amon Sur
ENEMIES Green Lantern Corps, Guardians of the Universe, Sinestro
AFFILIATIONS Sinestro Corps, Black Lanterns

Purportedly recruited by Sinestro himself to haunt Space Sector 3500, the empath was one of his most effective Yellow Lanterns. Drak also recorded the Legion of Fear's atrocities in the Book of Parallax.

A gifted seer and raconteur who could seduce the unwary with horrific tales, she tested Yellow Corpsmen. When Arkillo finished their training in ring-wielding, Drak would make them confront their darkest terrors in her Fear Lodge. All who failed died horribly, their fates recorded in the Book.

After being captured by John Stewart and Guy Gardner, Drak was imprisoned in a Sciencell on Oa. When Blackest Night began, she tried to steal the Book of the Black, but was trapped in its pages before being released and becoming its keeper. **WW**

DURLANS

DEBUT *Action Comics* (Vol. 1) #283 (Dec. 1961)
CURRENT VERSION *Legion of Super-Heroes* (Vol. 7) #1 (Nov. 2011)
BASE Durla
HEIGHT Variable **WEIGHT** Variable
EYES Variable **HAIR** Variable
POWERS/ABILITIES Elastic physicality, able to instantly reshape their form.
ENEMIES Other Durlans
AFFILIATIONS United Planets

Durla was a wealthy, technologically advanced world until a "Six-Minute War" between its leading nations left the planet a radioactive ruin. The conflagration turned the planet into a desert husk where survivors mutated into physically unstable shape-shifters who chose a base shape—usually multi-tentacled and enshrouded. These Durlans gradually formed regressive anti-technology clans, perpetually at war with each other, but uniformly suspicious of—and xenophobic towards—off-worlders.

In time, a separate sub-group evolved out of the warring sects. Futurist Durlans resolved to regain control of their species' mutated genome, actively embraced science, and infiltrated Earth in the early 20th century to exploit its rapidly growing technological base. **WW**

DUCARD, HENRI

DEBUT *Detective Comics* (Vol. 1) #599 (Apr. 1989)
REAL NAME Henri Ducard
BASE Paris, France
HEIGHT 6ft 4in **WEIGHT** 215 lbs
EYES Brown **HAIR** Gray
POWERS/ABILITIES Keen deductive reasoning, expert marksman.
ALLIES Morgan Ducard
ENEMIES Bruce Wayne
AFFILIATIONS Interpol

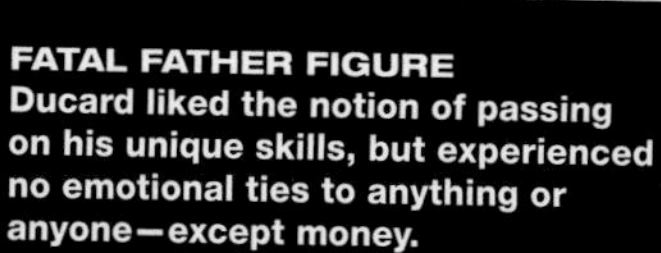

FATAL FATHER FIGURE
Ducard liked the notion of passing on his unique skills, but experienced no emotional ties to anything or anyone—except money.

Manhunter and mercenary, former French Interpol agent Henri Ducard was considered the world's greatest and most dependable tracker. As such he was sought out by young Bruce Wayne, who wanted to learn all his techniques and strategies for his own future role as a crime fighter. Although Henri was employed by government agencies, they usually needed his other—more discreet—services as a professional assassin.

When the implacable stalker at last agreed to teach the boy-millionaire, Ducard paired him with his own son, Morgan, to track a terrorist across Paris. Wayne was unaware Ducard had been hired to murder their target, or that his classmate was avidly learning all the tricks of a successful killer for hire.

As a deadly graduation test, the remorseless and utterly amoral tutor tasked Morgan with killing Bruce, but when the junior Ducard failed, Henri cut off all contact with his son. **WW**

ECHO

DEBUT *Batman: Legends of the Dark Knight* #119 (Jul. 1999)
REAL NAME Isabella Cheranova
EYES Hazel **HAIR** Red
HEIGHT 5ft 4in **WEIGHT** 110 lbs
POWERS/ABILITIES Espionage and combat training; Turing implant allows her to pick up electromagnetic signals (incl. radio waves) and read minds; holographic camouflage suit makes her invisible for short periods.
ENEMIES Batman

Echo was enigmatic Soviet agent Isabella Cheranova trained by G.R.U. (Soviet military intelligence) to be an assassin from age 10. She served in Afghanistan and was selected to be implanted with experimental organic "wetware" as part of the Turing Project—and was the only test subject to survive.

When Gotham City descended into anarchy after an earthquake, she was captured by Two-Face's forces. She was made to fight the monstrous Rhino, but saved by Batman. However, the Dark Knight was Echo's real target. She temporarily incapacitated him with a powerful sedative and revealed that it was her mission to keep him out of action while Two-Face and Penguin took over his territory. She then disappeared.

Several other people have adopted the codename Echo, including a foe of the first Crimson Avenger, a member of the 31st-century Legion of Super-Villains, and Terry Eckhart of Booster Gold's Conglomerate team. **SW**

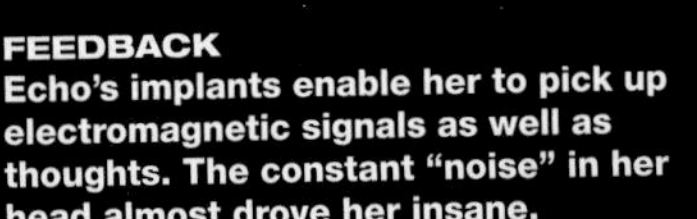

FEEDBACK
Echo's implants enable her to pick up electromagnetic signals as well as thoughts. The constant "noise" in her head almost drove her insane.

ECLIPSO

DEBUT *House of Secrets* (Vol. 1) #61 **(Jul.-Aug. 1963)**
CURRENT VERSION *Team 7* (Vol. 2) #2 **(Jan. 2013)**
REAL NAME Kaala
BASE The Black Diamond
HEIGHT Variable **WEIGHT** Variable
EYES Red **HAIR** None
POWERS/ABILITIES Can teleport through shadow, possess, or control other beings, and drain their memories; powers are magnified tenfold during an eclipse.
ALLIES Kaala, Alex Montez, Gordon Jacobs
ENEMIES Team 7, Lady Chandra, Princess Amaya
AFFILIATIONS House Onyx, House Diamond

Eclipso is the evil Spirit of God's Vengeance, created at the dawn of time. Over the eons he has taken over many hosts, and millennia ago he was incarnated on the magical world of Nilaa as Lord Kaala, scion of House Onyx and House Diamond. As Kaala, Eclipso launched a war to conquer Nilaa but was defeated by Lady Chandra of House Amethyst, who trapped him in a gem called the Black Diamond and took it to Earth.

The Black Diamond holding Eclipso was hidden on Sentinel Island until it was recovered in modern times by the US government's Team 7. The Black Diamond was locked in A.R.G.U.S.'s secret Black Room, but Catwoman stole it for Alex Montez, who became Eclipso's new host.

John Constantine offered Montez/Eclipso passage back to Nilaa, then sealed the portal after him. Eclipso used his powers to take control of House Onyx and House Diamond once more and led them against House Amethyst, but was trapped in the Black Diamond by Princess Amaya. The gem then reappeared on Earth, and Eclipso found a new host: disgraced scientist Gordon Jacobs. **SW**

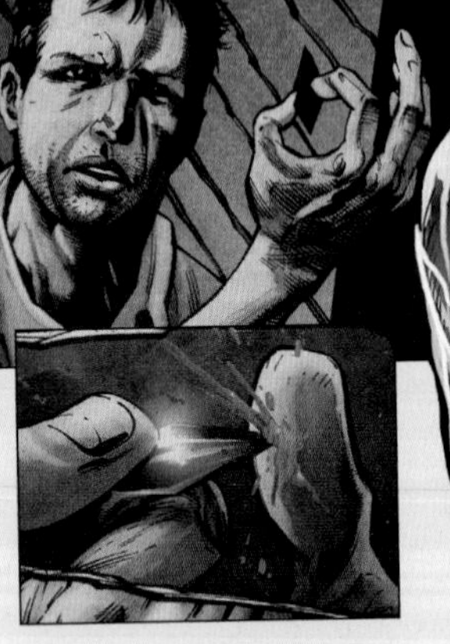

BLOOD SACRIFICE
Eclipso persuaded Gordon Jacobs to release him from the Black Diamond—by mutilating himself with the gem.

TAKING POSSESSION
Eclipso escaped the Black Diamond on Kalaa and possessed Deathstroke, but was imprisoned in the jewel again by Slade's Team 7 comrades.

ON THE RECORD

The pre-Flashpoint Eclipso was God's original Spirit of Vengeance, but when it turned evil it was replaced by the Spectre. Eclipso initially possessed solar-technology expert Bruce Gordon, though he later broke free. Alex Montez then used a set of mystic tattoos to harness Eclipso's power without surrendering control to the spirit.

During the Day of Vengeance, Eclipso possessed the Atom's ex-wife, Jean Loring, and drew Mary Marvel under his evil influence. When the Brightest Day event occurred, the villain plotted to kill God.

SPLIT PERSONALITY
When hosted by scientist Bruce Gordon, Eclipso found himself unwillingly forced into the role of hero.

DARK NEMESIS
Though Eclipso has been defeated multiple times, this relentless, malevolent villain always returns, seemingly more powerful than before.

EDGE, MORGAN

DEBUT *Superman's Pal, Jimmy Olsen* #133 (Oct .1970)
CURRENT VERSION *Superman* (Vol. 3) #1 (Nov. 2011)
REAL NAME Morgan Edge
BASE Metropolis
EYES Brown **HAIR** Bald (black)
HEIGHT 6ft 2in **WEIGHT** 235 lbs
POWERS/ABILITIES Ruthless but highly intelligent businessman.
ENEMIES Superman

Media baron Morgan Edge is the president and CEO of the Planet Global Network and owner of the PGN TV network and *The Globe* tabloid. He also acquired the *Daily Planet* newspaper replacing its iconic globe-topped building with a sleek modern office block. As CEO of PGS, he backed the *Challengers* adventure reality TV show (starring the Challengers of the Unknown) and shamelessly exploited the tragic deaths of three team members for publicity.

Edge also aired a report that (incorrectly) claimed to reveal Superman's secret identity—over the objections of PGN's executive producer, Lois Lane. Edge's cavalier approach to journalistic ethics led to Clark Kent and Jack Ryder quitting. However, when Metropolis was attacked by an alien monster, Edge displayed a gift for leadership. **SW**

NEW PLANET
Edge's new and more callous style of business management won him few friends among long-serving *Daily Planet* staff.

EL DIABLO (LAZARUS LANE)

DEBUT *All-Star Western* (Vol. 2) #2 (Oct.–Nov. 1970)
CURRENT VERSION *All-Star Western* (Vol. 3) #2 (Dec. 2011)
REAL NAME Lazarus Lane
EYES Blue **HAIR** Black with white streak
HEIGHT 6ft **WEIGHT** 182 lbs
POWERS/ABILITIES Rendered unconscious, Lane releases El Diablo, a Spirit of Vengeance armed with revolver, bolos, and flaming whip.
ENEMIES Black River

Old West bank teller Lazarus Lane survived a bank robbery, but was struck by lightning and sent into a coma . He was then cursed by an Apache shaman, Wise Owl, and when Lane awoke he found he was the host for El Diablo, a demonic masked vigilante. From then on, whenever Lane was knocked unconscious, El Diablo would appear to mete out harsh justice with his six-guns and fiery whip, soon becoming a feared figure on his trusted black stallion, Lucifer.

When El Diablo intervened to save a small town from a zombie curse, he confronted the villain behind the infestation, a Native American spirit warrior named Black River. Black River told him to punish the white men for killing Native American tribes and stealing their land. However, El Diablo refused, stating that more killing would not change the past, and undid the zombie curse. The legend of El Diablo would later inspire other heroes, including Rafael Sandoval and Chato Santana. **SW**

DESERT DEVIL
Native Americans who dared gaze into Lazarus Lane's eyes could see the terrible fury of the Spirit of Vengeance that dwelled within.

EFFIGY

DEBUT *Green Lantern* (Vol. 3) #110 (Mar. 1999)
REAL NAME Martin Van Wyck
BASE New York City, New York
EYES Blue **HAIR** Blond
HEIGHT 6ft 1in **WEIGHT** 195 lbs
POWERS/ABILITIES Flies through space, generates flame bursts, creates fiery energy constructs.
ENEMIES Green Lantern, Spectre

Disgruntled loser Martin Van Wyck was abducted by the alien Controllers and given fire-based superpowers before being deemed a "failed experiment" and sent back to Earth. When using his powers, Van Wyck transformed into a white-skinned, flame-headed being and took the name Effigy. With no other ambitions, he used his newfound abilities to wreak havoc in Los Angeles, setting fire to the Hollywood sign before being confronted by Green Lantern Kyle Rayner. After a brief battle he was reclaimed by the Controllers, who took him into space to serve them.

Effigy later returned to Earth, where he fell for cryogenic villainess Killer Frost—but when she was buried in an avalanche by Kyle Rayner, Effigy callously abandoned her. The villain then served in the Society and Libra's Secret Society of Super-Villains and was one of the evildoers briefly exiled to the planet of Salvation. Effigy suffered a gruesome death during Final Crisis, when Spectre burned him alive in a lantern. **SW**

FIRESTARTER
Effigy was no master criminal—this hot-headed hooligan only wanted to cause chaos and destruction, until his life was extinguished by the Spectre.

EL DIABLO (CHATO SANTANA)

DEBUT *El Diablo* (Vol. 3) #1 (Nov. 2008)
CURRENT VERSION *Suicide Squad* (Vol. 4) #1 (Nov. 2011)
REAL NAME Chato Santana
BASE Belle Reve Penitentiary
EYES Black **HAIR** Bald
POWERS/ABILITIES Tattoos provide flame generation powers; can also use these powers to heal by burning toxins from people's systems.
ENEMIES Basilisk, Resurrection Man, Bloodletter

Chato Santana was born in a deprived neighborhood and became a member of a notorious street gang. He developed a fearsome reputation as "El Diablo" and had his body tattooed with demonic designs, which gave him pyrotechnic powers. When a rival gang crossed him, he set their house ablaze, realizing too late that there were women and children in the building.

Overcome with remorse, El Diablo did not resist arrest when the police arrived and was imprisoned at the notorious Belle Reve Penitentiary. Administrator Amanda Waller chose him as a potential candidate for her Suicide Squad, a secret government-backed team of convicted super-villains. After surviving a potentially lethal training exercise, El Diablo saw serving in the Squad as a chance for redemption.

Recently, El Diablo received an unexpected pardon and left Belle Reve for his old neigborhood, only to come up against a heavily-armed local gang and their super-powered leader, Bloodletter. **SW**

REDEMPTION SEEKER
Driven by a desire to atone for murdering innocent people, Santana struggled with the fluid morality of his Suicide Squad teammates.

ELASTI-GIRL

DEBUT *My Greatest Adventure* (Vol. 1) #80 **(Jun. 1963)**
CURRENT VERSION *Justice League* (Vol. 2) #30 **(Jul. 2014)**
REAL NAME Rita Farr
BASE Los Angeles
HEIGHT 5ft 6in, variable **WEIGHT** 126 lbs, variable
EYES Brown **HAIR** Brown
POWERS/ABILITIES Unstable body structure allows her to change size and shape, but if she loses focus she is in danger of losing her human form and turning into a blob of protoplasm.
ALLIES Niles Caulder, Negative Man, Robot Man, Element Woman
ENEMIES Jessica Cruz's Power Ring
AFFILIATIONS Doom Patrol

Movie star Rita Farr (Rita Starr to her legion of fans) was filming on location in Africa when she was exposed to a mysterious gas that disrupted her cellular structure and caused it to break down. She discovered that she could now alter her size and shape at will. However, if she lost focus or relaxed that famous Rita Starr smile, she would lose her shape and start to turn into a formless mass. Traumatized by this accident, Rita suffered a nervous breakdown. Learning of her predicament, the reclusive and opportunistic mad scientist Niles Caulder approached her and asked Rita to join his oddball "super support group" for people with freakish superpowers: the Doom Patrol.

Using the codename Elasti-Girl, she joined Negative Man, Robotman, and Element Woman in the group. Caulder ("the Chief") led his team of "abnormals" on several missions, and they went into action after Jessica Cruz fell under the control of a malign Green Lantern power ring and caused havoc in Portland, Oregon. When Jessica fled, the callous Caulder ordered the Doom Patrol to ignore the plight of innocents caught up in Jessica's rampage and retrieve the ring—but the Justice League stepped in to stop them. In a brief clash, Rita almost lost control of her form, and the Justice League took Jessica into custody. **SW**

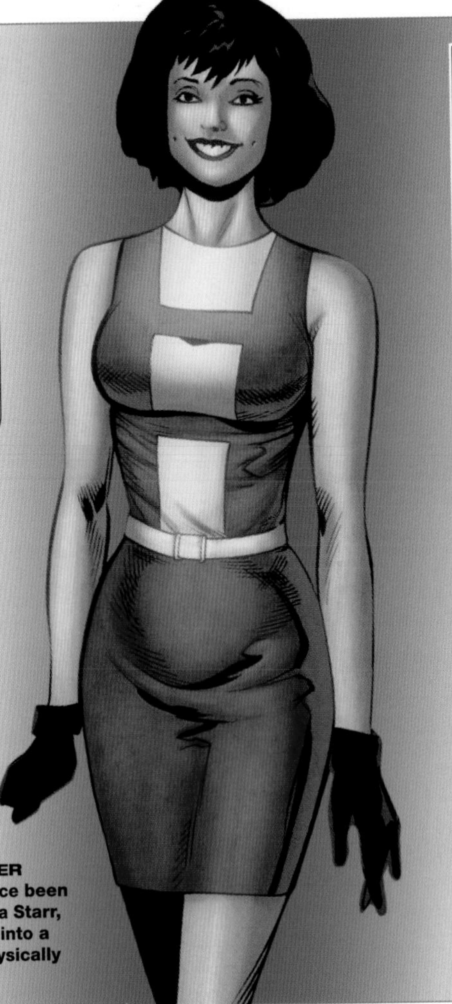

KEEPING IT TOGETHER
Elasti-Girl may have once been Hollywood celebrity Rita Starr, but her transformation into a metahuman left her physically and mentally unstable.

ON THE RECORD

The original Rita Farr joined Doom Patrol as Elasti-Girl and married the psychic hero Mento. While on a mission, Rita was seemingly killed in an explosion. The pre-Flashpoint heroine later reunited with Mento and the Doom Patrol with no memory of how she had cheated death. Years later, it was revealed that the returned Elasti-Girl (or Elasti-Woman, as she was now called) was actually a protoplasmic duplicate created by the Chief—and that Mento had been manipulating her mind.

ATTACK OF THE 50FT WOMAN
Elasti-Girl took center stage as the Doom Patrol were forced to team up with their arch-enemies, the Brotherhood of Evil, to defeat the cosmic criminal Zarox-13.

ELEMENT LAD

DEBUT *Adventure Comics* (Vol. 1) #307 (Apr. 1963)
CURRENT VERSION *Legion of Super-Heroes* (Vol. 7) #1 (Nov. 2011)
REAL NAME Jan Arrah
BASE Legion Headquarters, 31st-century Earth
EYES Hazel **HAIR** Blond
HEIGHT 5ft 7in **WEIGHT** 140 lbs
POWERS/ABILITIES As a Tromian, can transmute nearby elements; Legion flight ring.
ENEMIES Res-Vir, Dominators, Fatal Five

Jan Arrah was born in the 30th century on the planet Trom. After his race was wiped out in a devastating attack by the pirate Kivun Roxxas, Jan went to Earth and joined the Legion of Super-Heroes. When the ranks of the Legion were decimated by a disaster he was thrust into a leadership role, taking fresh recruits on various missions—though he found the burden of command heavy. He became a mentor to the inexperienced Chemical Kid, and the youngster saved his life after he was knocked out on a mission against Braalian raiders.

When the Legion and the United Planets were devastated by the Fatal Five (including the Promethean Giant), Element Lad was incapacitated by the Emerald Empress. The Legion finally triumphed, but was then disbanded by the UP. Jan accepted a position in the Science Police, but later joined a Legion team that went back to the 21st century to fight the cosmic menace Infinitus. **SW**

ELEMENTARY
Despite his youth, Element Lad took his duties as leader in the Legion seriously, and the burden of command weighed heavily on him.

ELEMENT WOMAN

DEBUT *Metamorpho* (Vol. 1) #10 (Feb. 1967)
CURRENT VERSION *DC Comics – The New 52 FCBD Special Edition* #1 (May 2012)
REAL NAME Emily Sung
BASE Justice League's Watchtower satellite
EYES Violet **HAIR** Purple
POWERS/ABILITIES Can metamorphose into any element found in the human body.
ALLIES Firestorm, Metamorpho
ENEMIES Despero, Crime Syndicate
AFFILIATIONS Justice League, Doom Patrol

Emily Sung used her extraordinary elemental-transformation abilities to fight villainy as Element Woman. During the short-lived war between America and Atlantis, Emily was invited to join the Justice League. She and fellow novices Firestorm and the Atom helped to defend the League's satellite from alien intergalactic conqueror Despero. She later used her powers to remove a sliver of deadly Kryptonite from Superman's brain.

When the Crime Syndicate invaded Earth and took on the Justice League, Element Woman was imprisoned within Firestorm; when released, she disappeared. Her molecules were found and contained by Dr. Niles Caulder of the Doom Patrol, who convinced her that the Justice League did not want her, and offered her a place in his own team. Emily accepted, and she briefly battled her former teammates when the two groups clashed over Jessica Cruz's Power Ring. **SW**

PERSONAL ISSUES
Element Woman has amazing powers, but is plagued by insecurity and fear of rejection—which makes her easily manipulated by Niles Caulder.

ELONGATED MAN

DEBUT *The Flash* (Vol. 1) #112 **(Apr.–May 1960)**
CURRENT VERSION *Secret Six* (Vol. 4) #1 **(Feb. 2015)**
REAL NAME Ralph Dibny **BASE** New York City
HEIGHT 6ft 1in (variable) **WEIGHT** 178 lbs **EYES** Blue **HAIR** Red (variable)
POWERS/ABILITIES Can alter his body to change his appearance, increase in size, stretch, or even turn into a parachute.
ALLIES Superman, Etrigan the Demon, Scandal Savage, Ragdoll, Jeanette
ENEMIES The Riddler (Mockingbird), Thrumm, League of Assassins
AFFILIATIONS Secret Six

Ralph Dibny gained his amazing contortion powers through unknown means and used them to begin his career as a 'detective with bonuses'. Working alongside his beloved wife Sue, he became a jet-setting investigator, but all that changed when the couple went on a mission to recover a priceless diamond during a party on the Riddler's yacht. As the Riddler brazenly propositioned Sue in front of Ralph, the lights suddenly went out. In the ensuing chaos the diamond vanished, explosions ripped through the ship—and Sue disappeared.

A shocked Ralph used his body-altering powers to change his identity to that of a size-altering detective called Big Shot to track Sue down. However, he was captured and imprisoned in a hi-tech underwater prison by the mysterious Mockingbird, along with Strix, Porcelain, Catman, Ventriloquist, and Black Alice. 'Big Shot' helped the group escape and provided sanctuary at his and Sue's home, where the misfit 'Secret Six' became a family of sorts, with Ralph as a father figure. After the group rescued an amnesiac Sue from the clutches of Mockingbird (who turned out to be the Riddler), Ralph revealed his true identity as the Elongated Man, and continued to work with the Secret Six. **SW**

ON THE RECORD

Pre-Flashpoint, young Ralph Dibny was fascinated by traveling contortionists and worked out that their abilities stemmed from Gingold, a soft drink containing juice from the gingo fruit. When Ralph drank a concentrated gingo extract it gave him amazing stretching powers.

He moved to Central City to start a career as a Super Hero: the Elongated Man. Initially mistaken for a villain by local champion, the Flash, Ralph quickly built a reputation as an eccentric hero, detective, and member of several Justice League teams. He also somehow found time to fall in love with Sue Dearbon, and after they were married the couple traveled the country, solving mysteries.

Ralph was devastated when Sue was murdered by Jean Loring. The sorcerer Felix Faust tried to trick Ralph into raising Sue from the dead, but the hero turned the tables on him, trapping the magician and his master, Neron, in Doctor Fate's tower—but at the cost of Ralph's own life. Ralph and Sue were finally reunited in the afterlife and became ghostly detectives. Their corpses were briefly animated during the Blackest Night.

'TIL DEATH DO US PART? **Reunited in the afterlife, Ralph and Sue became the world's foremost ghost detectives!**

ENCHANTRESS

DEBUT: ***Strange Adventures*** **(Vol. 1) #187 (Apr. 1966)**
CURRENT VERSION ***Justice League Dark*** **(Vol. 1) #1 (Nov. 2011)**
REAL NAME June Moone
BASE Washington, DC
EYES Blue
HAIR Blond (as Enchantress: Red)
HEIGHT 5ft 6in **WEIGHT** 126 lbs
POWERS/ABILITIES Powerful magician; can warp reality and create duplicates of herself.
ALLIES Deadman, Justice League Dark
ENEMIES Felix Faust

June Moone is the host for a magical entity called the Enchantress, which gave her amazing magical powers, but also affected her sanity. As the Enchantress, June was sometimes a troubled villain, and sometimes a heroine who tried to atone for her misdeeds. When Zatanna separated June from the Enchantress, June was reduced to near-madness, while the Enchantress-entity unleashed a storm of deadly magic across the country trying to reunite with her "bright half."

The Justice League tried to stop the Enchantress but were driven off by a surreal storm of teeth, and Zatanna was forced to assemble a team of occult heroes to meet this supernatural threat: Justice League Dark. In a climactic confrontation, June merged with the Enchantress once more and ended the threat. Later, the Enchantress was one of the occult beings captured by Felix Faust to power the Crime Syndicate's Thaumaton weapon project, but was freed by Justice League Dark. **SW**

EMOTIONAL TRAUMA **Bonding with the Enchantress took a heavy toll on June Moone's sanity.**

ENEMY ACE

DEBUT *Our Army At War* #151 **(Feb. 1965)**
CURRENT VERSION *Justice League (Vol. 1)* #13 **(Nov. 2013)**
REAL NAME Hans von Hammer
BASE Germany
POWERS/ABILITIES Superb aerial combatant.
ENEMIES The Hangman, Allied Forces

With the twin guns of his Fokker triplane blazing a trail of destruction, the Enemy Ace, Hans von Hammer, became a legendary German pilot during World War I. The "Hammer of Hell" was the son of aristocrats and grew up in the Black Forest in south-west Germany, where he became an expert fencer and a true man of honor. To the other pilots in his fighter squadron, he was a human killing machine with more than 70 enemy deaths to his name.

Although he was unhappy with the Nazi regime, he was persuaded to come out of retirement and piloted a jet-powered Messerschmitt Me 262 during World War II. In the waning moments of the war, von Hammer's plane was shot down, and he landed in the Dachau concentration camp. Facing the horrific mass genocide of the Nazis for the first time, the renowned fighter renounced the German regime and surrendered to the Americans.

One of von Hammer's most unusual adventures occurred when he teamed up with the present-day members of the Justice League United in the French town of Arracourt. That site became unmoored in time, due to the presence of an anomaly in the universe known as a "breaker." During that distortion in time, the Enemy Ace of 1940 shot down the high-flying Stargirl of the 21st century. The breaker had trapped von Hammer, Sgt. Rock, the Unknown Soldier, and the Creature Commandos within a jumbled timescape that included the past and future, leading them to fight over and over in that one location. **SK**

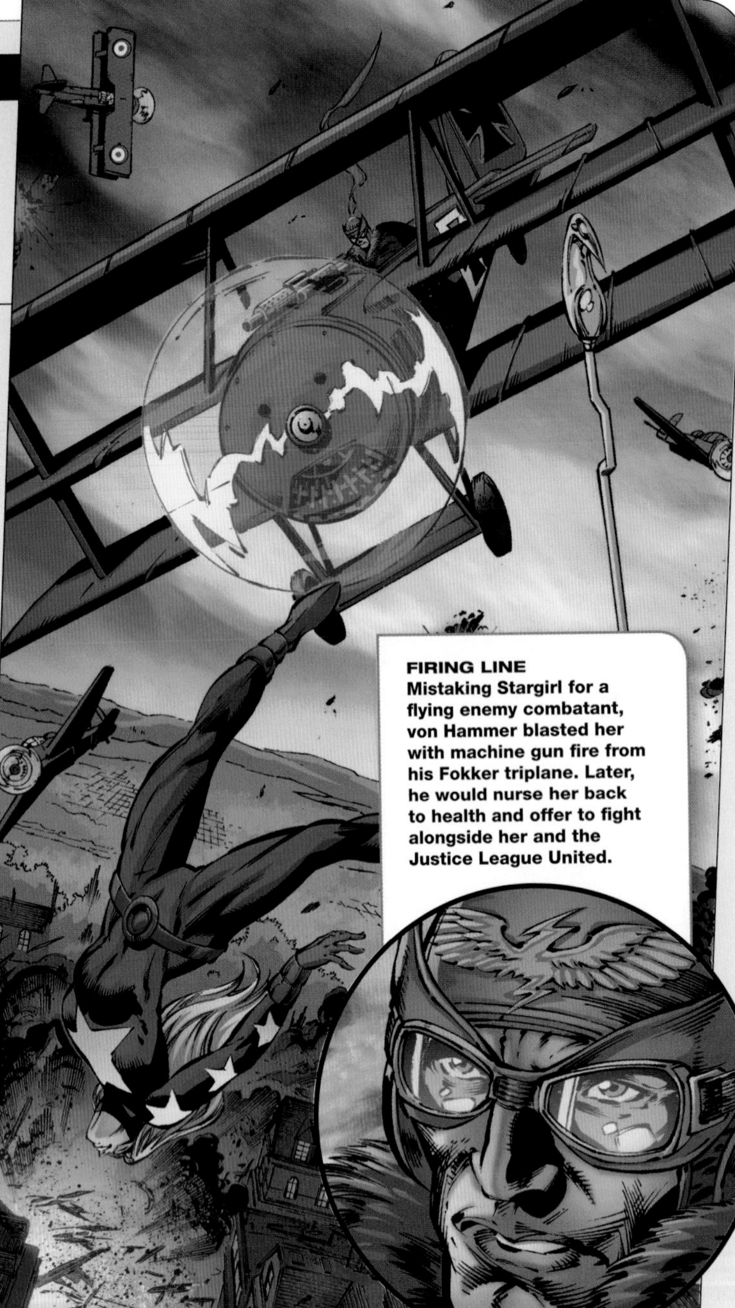

FIRING LINE
Mistaking Stargirl for a flying enemy combatant, von Hammer blasted her with machine gun fire from his Fokker triplane. Later, he would nurse her back to health and offer to fight alongside her and the Justice League United.

EQUINOX

DEBUT *Justice League United* #0 (Jun. 2014)
REAL NAME Miiyahbin "Mii" Marten
BASE Ontario, Canada
POWERS/ABILITIES Flight, ice control, wind bursts.
ALLIES Justice League United
ENEMIES The Whitago

Miiyahbin Marten was a native Canadian and a citizen of the Cree Nation. When she turned 16, she was threatened by the Whitago, a dangerous supernatural creature that took its power from the seven dark pillars of Cree life. Instinctively tapping into deeply buried ancient knowledge, Miiyahbin uttered the ancient word "Keewatin" and was transformed into the hero Equinox. In her new identity, she invokes the power of the Midayo, the embodiment of the seven heroic aspects of the Cree—love, humility, bravery, truth, respect, wisdom, and honesty. This power, inherited from her grandmother, enables Miiyahbin to continue to protect her people from the Whitago, which can never be fully destroyed.

Equinox has a deep, spiritual connection to her homeland and its weather, and her powers change with the four seasons. When she experienced trouble controlling those powers, she reached out to the Justice League United for help. Eventually, she joined as a full member of the team. **SK**

SEASONAL WARRIOR
Equinox utilizes the powers of the seasons to battle the deadly, unstoppable Whitago.

ON THE RECORD

Perhaps no story better distilled the essence of the Enemy Ace better than "Killer of the Skies," (Showcase #57, Aug. 1965). In that four- part epic, von Hammer ruefully admitted that he was trained to kill and took no pleasure in his victories or the deaths of his opponents.

The Enemy Ace and two other German pilots then took to the skies to battle a Canadian pilot he had nicknamed the 'Hunter.' Von Hammer was appalled by the cowardice of his comrades when they realized the skill of their quarry and turned tail—only to be shot down as they fled the fight.

The Enemy Ace then proposed a duel of honor, which the Hunter willingly accepted. As each man saluted the other, von Hammer confessed, "I will regret having to kill such a superb fighting man." After a thundering dogfight in the sky, both planes crashed to the ground. Refusing to be taken prisoner, the badly injured Hunter died in the field of battle, and von Hammer saluted his gallant foe one final time.

ACES HIGH
After a stunt pilot was murdered on the set of a movie about Enemy Ace, Batman investigated rumors that von Hammer's ghost was responsible. The culprit turned out to be a crew member, Heinrich Franz, an alleged descendent of Hans von Hammer.

ERADICATOR

DEBUT *Action Comics Annual* #2 (1989)
CURRENT VERSION *Supergirl* (Vol. 6) #20 (Jul. 2013)
BASE Sanctuary of Solitude
POWERS/ABILITIES Energy manipulation and projection; flight; super-strength; heat vision.
ENEMIES Supergirl, Superboy, Power Girl

The Eradicator is a highly advanced Artificial Intelligence that was originally developed as a superweapon on Krypton, designed to cleanse the planet of all alien influences.When it came into Superman's possession, the Eradicator built the Fortress of Solitude and even attempted to turn Earth into a replica of Krypton. The Eradicator later assumed Superman's form after the Man of Steel's death at the hands of Doomsday.

Following Superman's resurrection, the still-evolving Eradicator temporarily melded its techo-consciousness to the soul of S.T.A.R. Labs scientist David Connor. Most recently, the Eradicator program functioned as one component of Supergirl's Sanctuary of Solitude. After a malfunction caused the Sanctuary to determine that Power Girl was a clone of Supergirl, the program decided to eradicate Power Girl. The Sanctuary unveiled a sentient robot drone as the newest form of the Eradicator AI, and Supergirl battled the android to save her fellow hero. **SK**

KILLER PROGRAM
A destructive Eradicator emerged from Supergirl's Sanctuary of Solitude, determined to eliminate Power Girl.

EXTREME JUSTICE

DEBUT *Extreme Justice* #0 (Jan. 1995)
MEMBERS AND POWERS
Captain Atom: Atomic-based powers; **Amazing Man:** Transforms into any material; **Blue Beetle:** Wielder of hi-tech; **Booster Gold:** Superb athlete; **Maxima:** Super-strong and cunning alien queen.
BASE Mount Thunder, Nevada
ENEMIES Legion of Doom

Officially known as Justice League West, the Super Hero team Extreme Justice formed when Captain Atom decided the world needed crime fighters willing to play by tougher rules than the Justice League. The new team's mission was to deal out "extreme justice" and, unlike the Justice League, they chose not to be sanctioned by the United Nations. Instead, Extreme Justice worked alone, seeking out criminals rather than responding to threats.

One of their first successful missions was ending a military coup and preventing nuclear holocaust. The team later expanded to include the heroes Firestorm, Plastique, and Wonder Twins Zan and Jayna. Their most notable battle was with the Legion of Doom, an equally tough super-villian team. Extreme Justice disbanded after their final mission, in which they invaded the country of Bialya and destroyed an army of cyborgs. **SK**

EXTREME JUSTICE
1 Amazing Man, 2 Captain Atom, 3 Maxima, 4 Booster Gold, 5 Blue Beetle

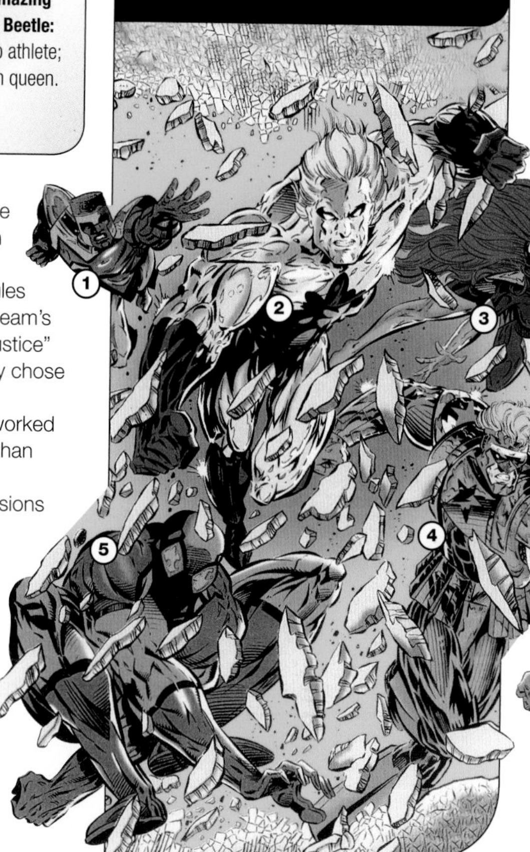

EXTANT

DEBUT *Showcase '94* #9 (Aug. 1994)
REAL NAME Henry "Hank" Hall
BASE Mobile
POWERS/ABILITIES Armor provides super-strength and invulnerability; can control and manipulate time.
ALLIES Dove
ENEMIES Monarch, Justice Society of America

Hank Hall has had several identities over the years, ranging from hot-headed hero to deadly villain. He and his brother Don gained superpowers when they were in their teens and fought crime together as Hawk and Dove. After Don was killed, Hank grew increasingly aggressive and assumed the role of a villain from the future known as Monarch. After he acquired Monarch's time-controlling abilities and powerful suit of armor, he renamed himself Extant and fought the Justice Society of America.

In addition to possessing super-strength and invulnerability, Extant displayed the ability to age or de-age his victims. He was destroyed in an airplane explosion, but was later resurrected as a zombie to join the Black Lantern Corps during their Blackest Night. After a violent battle with a new Hawk and Dove team, Hank was brought fully back to life by the Emotional Spectrum power of white light. **SK**

EXTREMISTS

DEBUT *Justice League Europe* #15 (Jun. 1990)
CURRENT VERSION *Countdown* #29 (Dec. 2007)
UNIVERSE Earth-8
MEMBERS AND POWERS
Lord Havok: Battlesuit can mutate on command;
Gorgon: Cybernetic hands and tentacles on his head;
Dreamslayer: Ability to manipulate matter and teleport;
Tracer: Deadly blades attached to his arms;
Doctor Diehard: Can control magnetism.
ALLIES Barracuda
ENEMIES Monarch, Challengers of the Unknown

On Earth-8, in the country of Angor, the newly elected president Tin Man authorized a law that required all metahumans to be registered by the government and operate as one unifying force to be known as the Meta Militia. An armor-clad villain known as Lord Havok assassinated the president, and Havok then formed a rebellious group of freedom fighters known as the Extremists. They were composed of the government worker Gorgon, the sorcerer Dreamslayer, the savage Tracer, and the master of magnetic force Doctor Diehard. One other member, the clown-like Carny, was murdered within seconds of the team's formation for daring to contradict Lord Havok.

The Extremists declared war on the governments of Earth-8 and formed an undercover alliance with Barracuda, the head of Angor's Meta Militia. When the Challengers of the Unknown traveled to Earth-8 in search of Ray Palmer, Jason Todd killed Barracuda. Later, the time-controlling villain Monarch enlisted the Extremists in his multiversal army, making Lord Havok his lieutenant. Together, they plotted to conquer or destroy worlds throughout the multiverse. **SK**

THE EXTREMISTS 1 Gorgon, 2 Dreamslayer, 3 Doctor Diehard, 4 Tracer, 5 Lord Havok, 6 Carny

FAITH

DEBUT *JLA* (Vol. 1) #69 (Oct. 2002)
HEIGHT 5ft 10in **WEIGHT** 148 lbs
EYES Brown **HAIR** Brown
POWERS/ABILITIES Telekinesis; emits positive vibrations that help calm those around her; flight; highly trained former government agent.
ALLIES Green Arrow, Nightwing, Nudge, Hawkgirl, Major Disaster
ENEMIES Kanjar Ro, Lord Crucifer, Crime Syndicate
AFFILIATIONS Justice League of America, Doom Patrol

It seems only Batman knows Faith's secrets, which he has largely kept to himself. It is known that Faith was raised by the military and worked with a black ops team under the nickname "the Fat Lady" (because she finished what others started, as per the saying "it's not over until the fat lady sings").

When the JLA needed replacements during the Obsidian Age event when they were sent thousands of years into the past, Faith stepped up to the role and stayed on as a member after the League returned. Soon after, she briefly joined the Doom Patrol, becoming a role model to the young hero Nudge. She later worked with the JLA when the Earth faced the threat of the Crime Syndicate. **MM**

FALCONE, CARMINE

DEBUT *Batman* (Vol. 1) #405 **(Mar. 1987)**
CURRENT VERSION *Batman Eternal* #2 **(Jun. 2014)**
REAL NAME Carmine Falcone
BASE Gotham City
HEIGHT 6ft 1in **WEIGHT** 205 lbs
EYES Brown **HAIR** Gray
POWERS/ABILITIES Powerful crime boss with many connections in the underworld; extremely wealthy; very intelligent strategist.
ALLIES Mayor Sebastian Hady, Jack Forbes, Tiger Shark
ENEMIES Batman, Catwoman, James Gordon, the Penguin, Professor Pyg
AFFILIATIONS Falcone Crime Family

When Batman first embarked on his crime-fighting career in Gotham City, it took his and James Gordon's combined efforts to drive the notorious mob leader Carmine "the Roman" Falcone out of their town. More than five years later, when Commissioner James Gordon was imprisoned after being falsely accused of murder, the Roman reemerged in Gotham City, realizing it was the opportune time to reestablish his criminal empire. He had spent years in Hong Kong and had been successful overseas, but he had been looking for the chance to retake his home turf.

One of Carmine's first actions was to take revenge on Catwoman for scarring his face. He kidnapped her, only to be attacked and taken hostage himself by one of Gotham City's newer super-villains, Professor Pyg. Carmine's illegal activities later caught up with him, and he was arrested and imprisoned by Detective Jason Bard. The Falcone family remains active in Gotham City, however, and played an integral part in corrupting Harvey Bullock's G.C.P.D. partner, Nancy Yip. **MM**

ON THE RECORD

Carmine Falcone first appeared in Gotham City in "Batman Year One," which retold Batman's origin after the Crisis on Infinite Earths.

A near-untouchable crime boss, Falcone's most obvious physical trait was a scratch on his face made by Catwoman. His past and family were further examined in *Batman: The Long Halloween*, a series where he met his end at the hands of a crazed Two-Face.

FAMILY TIES
In *Batman: Dark Victory*, the follow-up series to *The Long Halloween*, Catwoman revealed that she believed Carmine Falcone was her real father.

FAIRCHILD, CAITLIN

DEBUT *Deathmate Black* **(Sep. 1993)**
CURRENT VERSION *Superboy* (Vol. 6) #1 **(Nov. 2011)**
REAL NAME Dr. Caitlin Fairchild
HEIGHT 5ft 7in/6ft 4in (max. size) **WEIGHT** 133 lbs/300 lbs (max. size)
EYES Green **HAIR** Red
POWERS/ABILITIES Can increase in size and weight; superhuman strength, endurance, and durability; extremely intelligent with advanced knowledge of robotics and biology; psionic communication.
ALLIES Superboy, Dr. Niles Caulder, Ridge
ENEMIES Rose Wilson, Harvest, Deathstroke, Warblade
AFFILIATIONS Ravagers, N.O.W.H.E.R.E. (formerly)

Caitlin Fairchild was the daughter of Alex Fairchild, a member of the strategic task force called Team 7. Caitlin benefited from her father's connections, receiving an internship at the prestigious Advanced Prosthetic Research Center. However, that 'benefit' would turn out to seal her doom when the A.P.R.C.'s Project Spartan got out of hand. Caitlin was turned into a cyborg and was no longer in control of her own body, killing her father when he attempted to rescue her. In turn, she was eliminated by his Team 7 comrade Slade Wilson, aka Deathstroke.

However, the complex life of Caitlin Fairchild did not end there. Prior to her death at the A.P.R.C., Caitlin had been secretly cloned and her clone now worked for Harvest at the clandestine operation N.O.W.H.E.R.E., believing she was the original Fairchild. Initially lending her expertise to Harvest's Superboy project, Caitlin had a change of heart when she learned of the Culling process for N.O.W.H.E.R.E.'s metahumans, and helped a group of superpowered teenagers escape his horrific killing fields. The escapees became a short-lived Super Hero group called the Ravagers, but were ultimately defeated by Harvest and his employee Deathstroke. **MM**

ON THE RECORD

Caitlin Fairchild debuted in a different reality. The daughter of Alex Fairchild in this reality too, smart, quiet Caitlin attended Princeton University, where she was recruited into Project Genesis. As a result of her experimental work, she became "Gen-active," and developed superpowers. When she realized she was being used as a lab rat of sorts, she fled the project with a few other powered teens, and they formed the Super Hero group Gen-13, in which Caitlin served as the leader.

NEXT GEN
While Caitlin Fairchild had a different past in previous incarnations, she always retained her distinctive green and purple costume color scheme.

FAORA

DEBUT *Action Comics* (Vol. 1) #471 **(May 1977)**
CURRENT VERSION *Action Comics* (Vol. 2) #23.2 **(Nov. 2013)**
REAL NAME Faora Hu-Ul
HEIGHT 5ft 7in **WEIGHT** 150 lbs
EYES Brown **HAIR** Black
POWERS/ABILITIES As a Kryptonian exposed to Earth's yellow sun, Faora has all the powers of Superman including heat vision; freeze breath; superhuman strength; endurance and durability; enhanced senses; and the ability to fly; she is extremely proficient in fighting arts, a tactical expert, and a weapons expert.
ALLIES General Zod, Non
ENEMIES Superman, Wonder Woman

Hailing from the planet Krypton and born years before Kal-El—the hero who would become Superman—the notoriously cruel Faora Hu-Ul was a loyal lieutenant to Dru-Zod. Working alongside the rebel scientist Non, Faora was chosen from thousands of recruits to serve General Zod. Relishing her role in his quest for power and war, Faora helped Zod fabricate a conflict with the alien Char, even as Zod and Faora began a romantic relationship. However, their duplicity was eventually discovered by Kal-El's father, Jor-El, and the pair were sentenced, along with their accomplice Non, to the dreaded prison dimension known as the Phantom Zone.

Decades later, General Zod would escape the Phantom Zone and arrive on Earth, where he encountered Superman. He soon showed his true colors, tricking the Man of Steel into taking him to his Fortress of Solitude, where he freed Faora from the Zone and departed the Fortress with her. When Superman pursued them, they attacked him, causing Wonder Woman to also join the fray. After Zod and Faora narrowly won the battle, Superman and Wonder Woman adopted new armor, but were brutally dispatched when the Greek god Apollo came to the villains' aid. Zod and Faora then opened a portal to the Phantom Zone to access the Warworld and rain devastation down on Earth. However, their plans were thwarted when the portal was destroyed by a nuclear explosion set off by Superman and Wonder Woman, which trapped the evil Kryptonians in the Zone once more. **MM**

ON THE RECORD

Faora first appeared in Metropolis after having escaped the Phantom Zone. She had survived the destruction of Krypton, but had found a way to shift in and out of the Phantom Zone, making her a huge threat to the Man of Steel. Faora had been sentenced to the zone for causing the death of 23 Kryptonian men. After the Crisis on Infinite Earths, Faora reemerged as one of the fighters for a new version of General Zod.

PHANTOM MENACE
When Faora Hu-Ul first debuted, it was as a phantom form. When she caused havoc in the streets, Superman attacked her, not realizing that she was a woman.

FATALITY

DEBUT *Green Lantern* (Vol. 3) #82 (Jan. 1997)
CURRENT VERSION *Green Lantern New Guardians* #1 (Nov. 2011)
REAL NAME Yrra Cynril
HEIGHT 5ft 9in **WEIGHT** 125 lbs
EYES Brown **HAIR** Black
POWERS/ABILITIES Superhuman strength, durability, and endurance; expert fighter.
ALLIES Star Sapphire, Major Force
ENEMIES Green Lantern

Yrra Cynril was the oldest child of the planet Xanshi's ruling family. As such, she was sent off-world to study the fighting arts with the renowned Warlords of Okaara. However, soon after Yrra left, Xanshi was destroyed because of a terrible mistake made by Green Lantern John Stewart. Seemingly her world's only survivor, Yrra swore vengeance against all Green Lanterns. In defiance of the warlords, she left Okaara to became one of the fiercest warriors in the universe. Calling herself Fatality, Yrra concentrated her efforts on eliminating Earth's Green Lantern, Kyle Rayner, but was unsuccessful.

She later became a member of the Sinestro Corps, before being "rehabilitated" by the Star Sapphire's guardians, the Zamarons. She soon found herself partnering with Lanterns from all the different spectrums of light, forming the New Guardians in the process. However, when separated from her Star Sapphire ring, Fatality realized how she'd been manipulated by the Zamarons, and renewed her hatred for John Stewart. **MM**

LOVE CONQUERS ALL
During her time as a Star Sapphire, Fatality embraced the role, letting love overwhelm her and even falling for the destroyer of her world, John Stewart.

FATHER TIME

DEBUT *Seven Soldiers Frankenstein* #3 (Apr. 2006)
CURRENT VERSION *Frankenstein, Agent of S.H.A.D.E.* #1 (Nov. 2011)
BASE Ant Farm (mobile)
HEIGHT 4ft 1in **WEIGHT** 56 lbs
EYES Brown **HAIR** Black
POWERS/ABILITIES Natural leader; expert strategist and hand-to-hand combatant; powerful espionage connections.
ALLIES Creature Commandos, Ray Palmer

Every decade, the mysterious man known as Father Time generates a new body at random to act as his host. Currently housed in the body of a young Asian girl, Father Time is the active director of S.H.A.D.E., the Super Human Advanced Defense Executive, which is often at the forefront of metahuman conflicts. S.H.A.D.E. has a hand in many projects, including a strike force called the Creature Commandos, put together by Father Time and led by agent Frankenstein.

During Frankenstein's missions, Father Time often communicates with him via holographic projection, providing mission-critical information and instructions. Father Time's mobile headquarters is the Ant Farm, a three-inch indestructible globe that requires agents to deploy Ray Palmer's shrinking technology in order to enter it. An expert tactician and brilliant negotiator, the gruff Father Time often works with other top secret groups, such as Checkmate, to make sure S.H.A.D.E. runs smoothly. **MM**

TIME IS PRECIOUS
Despite appearances, Father Time is a seasoned leader. His innocent guises often lead his opponents to underestimate his abilities.

FATAL FIVE

DEBUT *Adventure Comics* (Vol. 1) #352 **(Jan. 1967)**
CURRENT VERSION *Legion of Super-Heroes* #17 **(Apr. 2013)**
MEMBERS/POWERS **Tharok:** Energy being with mind-control powers; **The Emerald Express:** Flight, force fields, energy projection, and other powers bestowed by the Emerald Eye of Ekron; **The Persuader:** Superhuman strength and endurance, atomic ax; **Validus:** Near-invulnerable juggernaut; **Mano:** Anti-matter touch; **Promethean Giant:** Colossal size and immense cosmic power.
ENEMIES Legion of Super-Heroes, Science Police, United Planets

When the United Planets were menaced by a cosmic threat known as the Sun-Eater, the Legion of Super-Heroes was ordered to collect five of the galaxy's most dangerous criminals to fight it: Tharok, Emerald Empress, Validus, Mano, and the Persuader. Once the Sun-Eater was vanquished—at the cost of the Legionnaire Ferro Lad's life—this criminal quintet remained together as the Fatal Five, though Mano missed out on their biggest battle.

After fighting the Legion of Super-Heroes for several years, Tharok plotted with the Emerald Empress, Validus, and the Persuader to destroy the Legion once and for all. The villains engineered the simultaneous shutdowns of planetary support systems across the United Planets, wreaking havoc on the homeworlds of multiple Legionnaires and disrupting their quark-relay communications. Emerald Empress then destroyed Weber's World and mortally wounded the legionnaire Mon-El, while Validus smashed his way through the Sorcerer's World.

In a final showdown with the battered Legion on Earth, Tharok unleashed the team's new "fifth member," one of the ancient Promethean Giants, long imprisoned by The Source. The Legion managed to free the giant from Tharok's control and eventually defeated the Fatal Five, but the United Planets was left devastated and the Legion of Super-Heroes was ordered to disband. **SW**

KEY
1 Validus
2 The Persuader
3 Emerald Empress
4 Tharok
5 Promethean Giant

ON THE RECORD

The original incarnation of the infamous Fatal Five was involved in several important cosmic events. In one notable encounter with the Legion of Super-Heroes, the Five recruited hundreds of their alternate-world counterparts to take on the Legion. For their part, the Legion had to join forces with their 20th-century counterparts the Teen Titans to battle the Fatal Five. During the Final Crisis event, the Five joined Superboy-Prime's Legion of Super-Villains to battle the Legion of Three Worlds.

A FORCE TO BE RECKONED WITH
The Fatal five proved to be one of the Legion's most formidable foes and even went head-to-head with Superman.

FAUST, FELIX

DEBUT *Justice League of America* (Vol. 1) #10 **(Mar. 1962)**
CURRENT VERSION *Justice League Dark* #9 **(Jul. 2012)**
REAL NAME Felix Faust
HEIGHT 5ft 11in **WEIGHT** 172 lbs.
EYES Gray **HAIR** Black
POWERS/ABILITIES Faust is a formidable sorcerer, drawing his mighty mystical power from a demonic bargain.
ALLIES Dr. Mist, Nick Necro, Demons Three, Crime Syndicate
ENEMIES Justice League Dark, A.R.G.U.S.

Felix Faust was once a third-rate sorcerer obsessed with finding the all-powerful Books of Magic. When he learned that the eternally damned sorcerer Nick Necro knew the location of the books, he pledged his soul to a demon to get Necro released from Hell. The pact gave Faust great power, but turned him into a withered and ghoulish figure. Necro and Faust found a box containing a map to the books but had no way to open it, so Faust tricked the Justice League Dark into capturing both him and the box.

When John Constantine used a mystic key to open it, Faust seized the map and escaped. Faust and Necro attempted to seize the books, but were outwitted by Constantine.

After the Crime Syndicate invaded Earth, Faust and Necro were enlisted to help with the construction of their Thaumaton weapon—powered by imprisoned occult beings including Black Orchid, Enchantress, Blue Devil, Sargon the Sorcerer, and Zatanna—to use against the entity that had destroyed their world. However, after a titanic battle in the mystical city of Nanda Parbat, Faust and Necro were defeated one again by Justice League Dark.

In the distant future, a time-traveling Justice League Dark encountered a monstrous future version of Faust. This being had achieved immortality, and he and his grotesque spawn were seemingly the last living beings. **SW**

ON THE RECORD

Felix Faust pledged his soul to the demon Neron, but was soon desperate to win it back. Faust posed as Doctor Fate and offered to bring Elongated Man Ralph Dibny's dead wife Sue back to life with a magic spell. In fact, the spell was intended to damn the hero; Faust hoped to trade Dibny's soul for his own and free himself from Neron's thrall. Dibny outwitted Faust and trapped him and Neron in the Tower of Fate. The deed cost Dibny his life, and he was reunited with Sue in the afterlife.

IN FAUST'S HANDS
Felix Faust was an early foe of the Justice League of America. The evil sorcerer used his command of magic to turn the JLA into his unwilling puppets.

FEARSOME FIVE

DEBUT *New Teen Titans* (Vol. 1) #3 (Jan. 1981)
CURRENT VERSION *Forever Evil* #1 (Nov. 2013)
MEMBERS/POWERS **Mammoth:** Strength and durability; **Gizmo:** Rebuilds technology to create weapons; **Jinx:** Casts magic spells if in contact with Earth; **Shimmer:** Transmutes materials; **Psimon:** Mind control, can kill with a thought.
ALLIES Crime Syndicate, Secret Society
ENEMIES Rogues, Metal Men

The Fearsome Five are a motley group of villains who combine impressive powers with an inability to work together. They were among the many super-villains broken out of prison by the Crime Syndicate, a group of invading super-villains from Earth-3. The Five eagerly accepted an invitation to join their Secret Society and help conquer the world.

The Fearsome Five and other villains were sent to punish the Rogues, a group of Flash's foes who had refused to cooperate with the Crime Syndicate. In the ensuing battle, the outnumbered Rogues fought valiantly and then forced the Five and their allies through one of Mirror Master's mirrors, which they then smashed. After this failure, Grid, the Crime Syndicate's artificial intelligence, teleported the Fearsome Five to assist in his battle against Cyborg and the Metal Men. However, the Five were outclassed again, being beaten and captured by Doc Magnus's metallic creations. **SW**

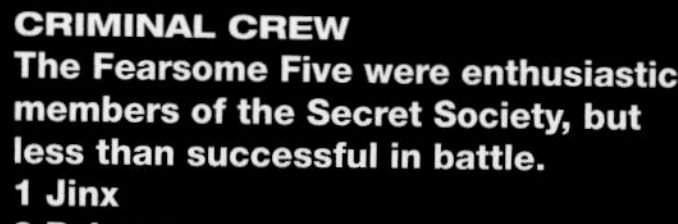
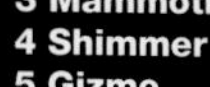

CRIMINAL CREW
The Fearsome Five were enthusiastic members of the Secret Society, but less than successful in battle.
1 Jinx
2 Psimon
3 Mammoth
4 Shimmer
5 Gizmo

FERRO LAD

DEBUT *Adventure Comics* (Vol. 1) #346 (Jul. 1966)
CURRENT VERSION *Legion of Super-Heroes* (Vol.7) #20 (Jul. 2013)
REAL NAME Andrew Nolan
EYES Green **HAIR** Brown
HEIGHT 5ft 7in **WEIGHT** 155 lbs
POWERS/ABILITIES Can transform his body into living iron, gaining great strength and durability.
ENEMIES Sun-Eater

Andrew Nolan of Earth was born in the 31st century. His ability to transform his body into living iron earned him a place in the Legion of Super-Heroes as Ferro Lad. When the galaxy was menaced by the Sun-Eater, Nolan sacrificed his own life to carry an Absorbatron Bomb into the core of this cosmic entity and end the Sun Eater's threat.

Years later, when the Legion and the United Planets were under attack from the Fatal Five, Legion members Polar Boy and the Invisible Kid took an unexpected detour while attempting to escape a Promethean Giant and ended up in a strange nether realm. There they encountered Ferro Lad and two of his deceased comrades, Earth-Man and the original Invisible Kid (Lyle Nor). Ferro Lad told the interlopers that they could return to the land of the living—but, if they were killed in battle, they would return to the afterlife permanently. With this warning in mind, Polar Boy and the Invisible Kid returned to Earth to fight the Fatal Five. **SW**

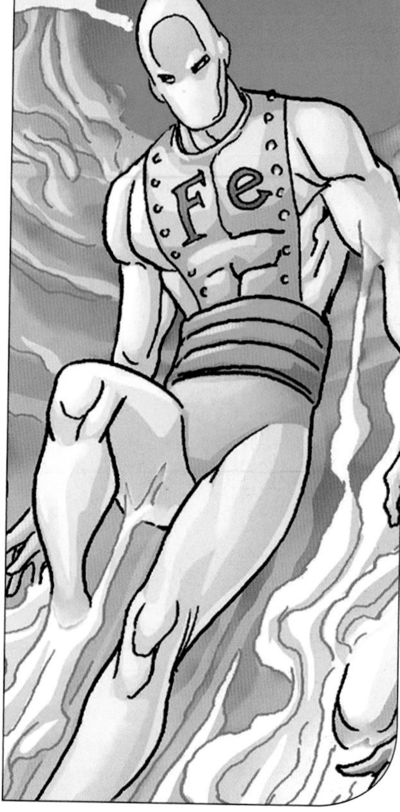

A HERO FROM THE PAST
The ghostly form of Ferro Lad gave Polar Boy and the Invisible Kid a somber warning when they visited the afterlife.

DARKSEID'S DEFENDERS
Big Barda returned to the forefront of the Furies to protect Darkseid from his own daughter, Grail... and brought backup.
1. Barda, 2. Mad Harriet, 3. Stompa, 4. Lashina, 5. Bernadeth, 6. Kanto, 7. Kalibak, 8. Steppenwolf

FEMALE FURIES

DEBUT *Mister Miracle* (Vol. 1) #6 (Jan.-Feb. 1972)
CURRENT VERSION *Earth 2 World's End* #1 (Dec. 2014)
BASE Apokolips
NOTABLE MEMBERS/POWERS **Big Barda:** Born leader armored with an Apokoliptian Aegis; **Mad Harriet:** Insane fighter with energy claws; **Stompa:** A Powerhouse with anti-matter boots; **Lashina:** Energy whip-armed warrior; **Bernadeth:** Team mentor who wields a deadly fahren-knife; **War:** Super-strong mind controller and formidable combatant; **Death:** Psychic with death touch and revival powers; **Famine:** Near-invulnerable killer who can devour life force; **Pestilence:** Rapid healer with disease immunity and ability to spread contagion.
ALLIES Darkseid, Steppenwolf, Desaad
ENEMIES Mister Miracle, Earth-2 World Army, Wonders of the World

The Female Furies are the elite warriors of Apokolips, trained from childhood in combat and indoctrinated to be utterly loyal to the planet's overlord, Darkseid. Among their ranks were battle-hardened leader Big Barda and Fury, who wielded energy whips. When Darkseid's forces attacked Earth-2, Barda seemingly defied her master and her fellow furies by escaping with Mister Miracle, a rebellious escapologist from New Genesis. However, she then betrayed Miracle to Darkseid, and was named Doyenne of the Furies.

Darkseid also recruited a cadre of new warriors from the Earth-2 universe and imbued them with terrifying powers, to create the Four Furies of Apokolips. Famine, Pestilence, War, and Death were his shock-troopers when Apokolips attacked Earth-2 once more. When Famine was seemingly killed in action, Helena Wayne (alias Huntress) was transformed into a new Famine to take her place. The Four Furies were ultimately betrayed by the former Famine and defeated.

Big Barda left Apokolips to reunite with her love, Mister Miracle, and the two fought side-by-side with the Justice League in the Darkseid War. After Darkseid fell, his deranged daughter, Grail, fused the League's stolen New Gods powers with Superwoman's baby to resurrect an even more powerful Darkseid, whom she sought to control. When all seemed lost, Barda turned up with reinforcements—the reformed Female Furies—to help turn the tide of battle. **SW**

ON THE RECORD

The Female Furies were trained by Granny Goodness to serve Darkseid. When Big Barda fled Apokolips to join her beloved Mister Miracle on Earth, the team was sent to attack the happy couple (and the planet's other Super Heroes) on numerous occasions. The Furies were presumed killed during the Death of the New Gods, but Mary Marvel then used the Anti-Life Equation to create new Furies from human females during the Final Crisis.

THE FIGHTING FURIES
On the trail of renegade Fury-turned-super-villain, Twilight, Supergirl had to confront the combined might of the Female Furies.

FIREBRAND

DEBUT *Police Comics* (Vol. 1) #1 (Aug. 1941) (as Rod Reilly); *Crisis Aftermath: Battle for Bludhaven* #1 (Jun. 2006) (as Andre Twist)
REAL NAME Andre Twist
BASE The Heartland
EYES Blue **HAIR** Blond
POWERS/ABILITIES Pyrokinesis.
ALLIES Teen Titans
ENEMIES Father Time, King Bullet, the Jester
AFFILIATIONS Freedom Fighters

Andre Twist was the fourth individual to assume the role of Firebrand. A courageous, opinionated, politically left-leaning resident of Blüdhaven, Twist gained extraordinary pyrokinetic superpowers when living weapon Chemo was dropped on his city.

Calling himself Firebrand, Twist began hearing voices in his head. They turned out to be Uncle Sam, urging him to be part of a new Freedom Fighters team. He was later captured and tortured by Father Time until freed by Uncle Sam.

Firebrand then joined the modern-day incarnation of the Freedom Fighters, Freedom Force, helping them stop various threats, including an alien invasion. He was crippled while fighting against King Bullet's armies, and was later killed by the Jester on his first mission back. **AC**

FIRE

DEBUT *Super Friends* #25 **(Oct. 1979)**
CURRENT VERSION *Justice League International* (Vol. 3) #1 **(Nov. 2011)**
REAL NAME Beatriz "Bea" Bonilla da Costa
HEIGHT 5ft 8in **WEIGHT** 140 lbs
EYES Green **HAIR** Green
POWERS/ABILITIES Can take on a fiery form at will, fly, and fire green energy blasts of flame.
ALLIES Ice
ENEMIES Peraxxus, Signal Men
AFFILIATIONS Justice League International

Beatriz "Bea" Bonilla da Costa was born in Brazil. Originally a spy for the Brazilian Secret Service, Bea was on a mission when she came into contact with a strange chemical mix called pyroplasm.

Her exposure to the substance gave her the metahuman ability to control a green flame which could cover her whole body and allow her to fly.

When Andre Briggs decided to create a Justice League International team that operated under the guidance of the United Nations, Bea was selected to be Brazil's representative. She fought alongside Ice, Guy Gardner, Rocket Red, Vixen, Godiva, and August General in Iron, under the leadership of Booster Gold. Bea helped the team defeat the alien Peraxxus, who was using Signal Men robots to try to destroy the world, after removing minerals and wealth from the planet to sell elsewhere in the universe. After defeating him, the JLI was about to meet the public when an explosion killed Rocket Red and left several members—including Bea—severely injured. **AC**

ON THE RECORD

Originally known as Green Fury, Bea made her debut fighting a brainwashed Superman in *Super Friends* #25 and later assisted the JLA on several cases.

Fire's original appearance was that of a more traditional costumed crime fighter. She was a member of the Global Guardians before joining the original Justice League International formed by Maxwell Lord. Her close friend, Ice, was also a member. Fire later joined the Checkmate organization and worked for Bruce Wayne.

JOINING FOR JUSTICE
Fire was one of 10 superpowered beings whose common goal was to champion justice and tolerance for humans and metahumans alike.

FIREFLY

DEBUT *Detective Comics* (Vol. 1) #184 **(Jun. 1952)**
CURRENT VERSION *Nightwing Annual* (Vol. 3) #1 **(Dec. 2013)**
REAL NAME Ted Carson
BASE Gotham City
EYES Blue **HAIR** Blond
POWERS/ABILITIES Pyromaniac with specialized armor that enables him to fly; expert in explosives and pyrotechnics.
ENEMIES Nightwing, Batgirl

When Ted Carson—the ex-boyfriend of movie star Cindy Cooke—was found dead in a burned-out building, it looked like he had been murdered. Around the same time an arsonist started to destroy anything in Gotham City linked to Cindy. The culprit turned out to be Firefly, a flying villain in a flaming metal suit.

When Nightwing and Barbara Gordon looked into the matter, it seemed that known-arsonist Garfield Lynns was Firefly. The heroes even found a clue in Lynns' empty apartment: a list of potential targets with only one location not yet destroyed. It turned out to be a false trail; Firefly had effectively maneuvered all the police into one place, which left Cindy unguarded. Realizing they had been duped, Nightwing raced to Cindy's penthouse, but arrived too late—Firefly attacked and seemingly killed the actress. However, the victim in the blaze turned out to be Cindy's agent.

Firefly was actually Ted Carson who had faked his own death and tried to fake Cindy's—he was desperate to give their relationship a fresh start. Nightwing and Barbara arrived in time to save Cindy from Ted, and bring him to justice. **AC**

ON THE RECORD

The original Firefly was special effects creator Garfield Lynns. This incarnation emitted intense lights from his belt, and his colorful appearance was in keeping with the lighter tone of Batman stories of the 1960s.

The second Firefly was Ted (Theodore) Carson who debuted in *Batman #126* (Sep. 1959). Again, he wasn't an arsonist so much as a winged villain who projected a deadly ray from a helmet lamp.

RAINBOW RIVAL
The original Firefly, known as 'The Man of 1,000 Lights,' projected his colorful light to distract and disorientate his victims.

FIRESTORM

DATA

DEBUT *Firestorm* (Vol. 1) #1 **(Mar. 1978)**
CURRENT VERSION *Fury of Firestorm: The Nuclear Men* #1 **(Nov. 2011)**
REAL NAME Ronald Roy "Ronnie" Raymond, Jason Rusch
BASE Walton Mills
EYES Blue (Ronnie); Brown (Jason)
HAIR Brown (Ronnie); Black (Jason)
POWERS/ABILITIES Ability to control and rearrange inorganic matter, fly, manipulate his own molecular structure, and emit energy blasts.
ENEMIES Helix, Deathstorm, Crime Syndicate
AFFILIATIONS Justice League

TAKE TWO FIRESTORMS... When they first gained their unique powers, football ace Ronnie and science student Jason both became Firestorms.

Ronnie Raymond and Jason Rusch were two High School students who had very little in common. When their molecular structures merged they became Firestorm the Nuclear Man. Despite their differences, the two teenagers have formed a strong bond—and helped make Firestorm one of the world's most powerful heroes.

Ronnie Raymond was the captain of the football team, and Jason Rusch a grade-A student devoted to science: The two had little to do with one another. When Rusch's friend and mentor Professor Stein conducted an experiment that found the "God Particle" (a particle that could alter the structure of the universe) he worried that it would fall into the wrong hands. So he sent samples in containers to four trusted friends—one of whom was Jason.

However, the Zither Corporation came into possession of this information and sold it worldwide, enabling nations to create nuclear-powered heroes. When the company sent mercenaries to Jason's high school to retrieve Stein's container, Jason opened it—bombarding himself, and the nearby Ronnie, with unstable particles that transformed them into Firestorms. Jason could transmute matter, while Ronnie was able to fire energy blasts. when they combined their bodies they became an unstable creature called Fury. Eventually, they learned to create a more stable version of the superpowered entity that came to be known as Firestorm. Ronnie controlled the body but shared the consciousness with Jason.

The new Super Hero defeated numerous threats including Helix, who worked for Zither Corporation. Firestorm also helped the Justice League stop an Atlantean invasion of Boston. After becoming involved in the Trinity War, Firestorm's connections with the Justice League resulted in tragedy when Deathstorm (an evil version of Firestorm from Earth-3) trapped the Justice League inside the Firestorm matrix, making it appear the heroes had died. The team was eventually freed and Ronnie and Jason were soon back in action as Firestorm. **AC**

NUCLEAR POWERED
Firestorm is a living nuclear reaction and one of the mightiest—and potentially deadliest—heroes in the world.

ON THE RECORD

Firestorm's appearance has hardly changed since his debut, despite various people being part of the Firestorm matrix.

Originally, the nuclear-powered hero was the result of student Ronnie Raymond and Professor Martin Stein being caught in an explosion at the Hudson nuclear facility. Ronnie and the Russian hero Pozhar later combined for another incarnation. Ronnie later died, passing the mantle to Detroit teenager Jason Rusch, with Martin Stein helping as part of the matrix. After Blackest Night, Ronnie came back, reprising his Firestorm role.

FIRESTORM AND FRIENDS
Firestorm has been part of several different line-ups of the Justice League.

FIREFIGHT
Candace Zither, boss of the mysterious ZitherTech, manipulates Ronnie and Jason into fighting one another.

CLASSIC STORIES

***Firestorm* (Vol. 1) #1 (Mar. 1978)**
Firestorm's origin is revealed, as Ronnie Raymond and Professor Martin Stein find themselves changed forever when they combine to become a nuclear-charged Super Hero.

***JLA* (Vol. 1) #69 (Oct. 2002)**
When the Justice League is trapped in Atlantis, Firestorm joins a new lineup of the team to rescue the original members.

***Firestorm: The Nuclear Man* (Vol. 3) #23-27 (May-Sep. 2006)**
One year after the *Final Crisis*, Jason Rusch merges with Lorraine Reilly (Firehawk) to create a new Firestorm and search for the missing Professor Stein.

THE FLASH

DATA

DEBUT *Showcase* #4 **(Sep.-Oct. 1956)**
CURRENT VERSION *The Flash* #1 **(Nov. 2011)**
REAL NAME Barry Allen
BASE Central City
HEIGHT 6ft **WEIGHT** 195 lbs **EYES** Blue **HAIR** Blond
POWERS/ABILITIES Super-speed, super-endurance, and accelerated healing; he can think quickly, mapping out the potential outcomes of a situation, and read books in an instant; can vibrate his molecular structure fast enough to pass through objects.
ALLIES Patty Spivot, Wally West, Green Lantern
ENEMIES The Rogues, Gorilla Grodd, Reverse-Flash, Professor Zoom
AFFILIATIONS Justice League

Barry Allen is the Flash, the fastest man alive. A living conduit for the Speed Force—a strange other-dimensional energy field that gives all speedsters their power—Barry is capable of amazing acceleration and uses his powers to fight crime in his hometown of Central City. The Flash is a founding member of the Justice League, joining with his fellow Super Heroes when Darkseid, ruler of Apokolips, and his demonic legions attacked Earth. He remains a key member of the team, and has formed lasting friendships with other members. The Flash not only runs at extraordinary speeds, he also has lightning quick wits!

AT A GLANCE...

Super-speed
As the self-professed fastest man alive, Barry Allen believes he can outrun Superman in a running race, even though Superman's ability to fly may give him the edge. The Flash's metahuman ability helps his body the friction caused by his high speeds and contain the damage it should ordinarily cause around him. He keeps his costume in a ring.

Rogues' gallery
A number of super-villains have become obsessed with the Flash. Chief among these are the Rogues—a group of criminals formed by Captain Cold. Operating out of Central City and Keystone City, the Rogues became "heroes" when they were tasked with hunting the Flash down after he briefly became a wanted man.

Speed Force
The Flash's speed comes from the Speed Force, which grants several speedster heroes and villains their powers. Barry Allen is one of those who have spent time living inside the Speed Force dimension.

Young Barry Allen's life changed forever when his mother was murdered and his father, Henry Allen, was blamed for the crime. But Barry never believed his father was guilty. Captain Darryl Frye, a close friend of Barry's parents, raised Barry as his own son and inspired Barry to join the police, where he worked in the Crime Scene Investigation department. One night, Barry was working late in his lab when lightning struck, showering the young investigator with a strange mix of chemicals. He woke in hospital, covered in bandages, but soon found the accident had given him amazing powers of speed. Determined to use these abilities for good, Barry became the Flash. He combined his role as a hero with his job at CSI, where he started dating Patty Spivot, who eventually learned Barry's secret identity. Eventually the hero gained a number of foes, including the Rogues—a bunch of blue-collar criminals who used weaponry to commit crimes while adhering to a strict code of not killing anyone.

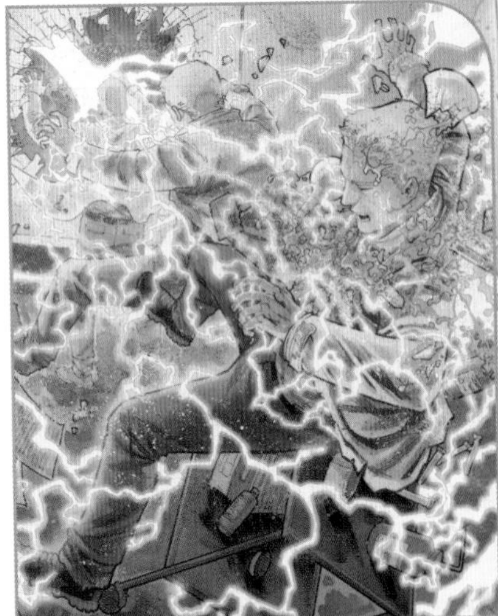

LIGHTNING FAST
Showered in laboratory chemicals and struck by lightning, Barry Allen ends up with astonishing powers.

Scientist Dr. Darwin Elias helped the Flash achieve a greater understanding of his powers, but warned him that the Speed Force was opening wormholes across Central City. the Flash eventually learned Elias was siphoning his Speed Force to use as an energy source. When the Flash, his friend Iris West, and some onlookers were pulled into the Speed Force during a fight with Captain Cold, Barry realized just how potent it was. The Speed Force had caused the extinction of the Mayans and speeded up the evolution of a tribe of gorillas in East Africa. While inside the Speed Force, the Flash met a fighter pilot called Turbine, who had been trapped within the energy field since World War II. It transpired that the wormholes were a result of Turbine's attempts to escape. The Flash managed to return home but couldn't find Iris and the others. He later returned to the Speed Force dimension during a fight with the superpowered simian, Gorilla Grodd. To keep innocent bystanders out

CLASSIC STORIES

***Showcase* #4 (Sep.-Oct. 1956)** Barry Allen makes his first appearance in this classic tale that heralded the start of comics' Silver Age. He also meets his first enemy, Turtle Man—the slowest man alive!

***The Flash* #123 (Sep. 1961)** Barry Allen meets the original Flash, Jay Garrick (of Earth-2), as he crosses over to Earth-2 for the first time and helps the retired Jay defeat three of his old enemies.

***Crisis on Infinite Earths* #8 (Nov. 1985)** Barry Allen's last stand, as the Flash sacrifices his life to save the universe from the Anti-Monitor's deadliest weapon.

***Flashpoint* Vol. 2 #1 (Jul. 2011)** The Flash wakes on an Earth not his own and must change reality itself to save the planet—even though doing so means the Flash must confront his darkest hour.

GORILLA WARFARE
When Gorilla Grodd led an invasion of Central City, the Flash joined forces with the Rogues to stand against the invading gorilla army. At first he seemed no match for Grodd and was only saved when a gorilla called Solivar sacrificed his own life to save Barry's. While Barry recovered, his "speed mind" tested every potential outcome of a rematch with Grodd. It led him to realize each confrontation in the city would end in disaster, so the Flash hauled him into the Speed Force, where he was more powerful and could easily defeat Grodd.

SPEED FORCE SHOWDOWN
The Flash takes on Gorilla Grodd, fighting the monstrous super ape in the heart of the mysterious Speed Force.

FLASH FACT
The world's greatest speedster can use the Speed Force to travel through time.

RACING DEATH
During the cataclysmic war against Darkseid, the Flash was forced to become the host for the cosmic grim reaper, the Black Racer, after killing the previous host. Granted divine powers, the Flash was now the God of Death.

"I'm Barry Allen. The Fastest Man Alive!"

THE FLASH

of harm's way, the Flash dragged Grodd into the Speed Force, where he defeated him and freed Iris and her friends.

Soon after, someone started killing people linked to the Speed Force. The killer—who called himself Reverse-Flash—turned out to be Iris West's younger brother, Daniel, who was trying to steal Speed Force energy to travel through time and alter his own past. The Flash managed to drain the Speed Force from Daniel and prevent changes in the timeline. Barry then learned that a time-traveling speedster called Professor Zoom (Eobard Thawne) was responsible for his mother's death—the Flash had acquired a deadly new foe. **AC**

REBIRTH

FAST AND FURIOUS

When Barry Allen rescued his original speedster protégé Wally West from other-dimensional oblivion, he sensed that some being or force had deliberately caused drastic changes in the universe over the course of the previous decade.

Now the Flash is determined to discover who is endangering the shape and history of reality. This is made no easier as he mentors hyper-fast assistant August Heart and hunts terrorists Black Hole, who have weaponized the Speed Force, creating a plague of citizen speedsters. With the serial-killer Godspeed haunting Central City, is the Fastest Man Alive quick enough to get to grips with the situation?

ON THE RECORD

Since the Flash's groundbreaking first appearance in 1940, several people have taken on the role, each adding something unique to the hero's mythos. Jay Garrick was the first Flash, making his debut in *Flash Comics* #1 (1940). He fought crime in New York City, although this was later changed to Keystone City.

A new era

Barry Allen made his first appearance as the Flash in *Showcase* #4 (Sep.–Oct. 1956). The story heralded a new style of Super Hero comics and marked the start of the Silver Age. This Flash also sported an all-new red costume. During his time as the Flash, Barry broke through the dimensional barrier between Earths to meet Jay Garrick.

Wally and Bart

Following Barry Allen's apparent demise during Crisis on Infinite Earths, Wally West took on the Flash identity. He uncovered the secret of the Speed Force and raced alongside other speedsters, such as Jay Garrick, Impulse, and Jesse Quick. It took a while for the new hero to feel worthy of his mentor's name, and when Wally disappeared, Bart Allen became the Flash until he was killed by the Rogues.

HEROIC DEMISE
The Flash prepares to make the ultimate sacrifice to stop the Anti-Monitor during Crisis on Infinite Earths.

Flash back

When Barry Allen escaped the Speed Force and returned to active duty, he had trouble adjusting to the world around him. But with the help of his old friend Green Lantern, he came to terms with the time he had missed when trapped. The change in reality brought about by Flashpoint left Barry younger and single—in the new reality he had never married Iris West.

SPEED FORCE HEROES
Flash (Wally West), Impulse (Bart Allen), Jay Garrick, and Johnny Quick—all inextricably linked by the Speed Force—race to save the day.

FIRST BORN

DEBUT *Wonder Woman* (Vol. 4) #12 (Oct. 2012)
BASE Olympus
HEIGHT 7ft 6in **WEIGHT** 375 lbs
EYES White **HAIR** Black
POWERS/ABILITIES Exceptional physical power and durability; gains strength from cannibalism; acquires knowledge by eating brains; wears impregnable dragon armor hide.
ALLIES Minotaur, Strife, Cassandra
ENEMIES Apollo, Zeus, Hades, Wonder Woman

The First Born was the first child of Zeus and Hera. When a witch foretold that the child would one day rule Olympus in Zeus' stead, the god had the baby taken to the African savanna, where he was left to die. However, the infant survived and was raised by hyenas and, in time, used his divine might to conquer an empire, seeking to make Zeus acknowledge him.

When Zeus remained silent, the First Born declared war on Olympus. The gods sent a wave to drown his army, while the warrior-king himself was swallowed up by the Earth. It took the First Born millennia to dig his way out. When he emerged in the 21st century, he set out to take the throne of Olympus, which he thought was rightfully his.

After clashing with Wonder Woman in London, he confronted the current ruler of Olympus, and killed him, devastating Olympus in the process. The First Born also conquered Hades, but was then hurled into the abyss by the new God of War: Wonder Woman. **SW**

UNGODLY RAGE
As the eldest son of Zeus, First Born traveled to Mount Olympus to claim the Olympian gods' throne.

FISHERMAN

DEBUT *Aquaman* (Vol. 1) #21 (May–Jun. 1965)
BASE Zandia
HEIGHT 6ft **WEIGHT** 196 lbs
EYES Blue **HAIR** Black
POWERS/ABILITIES Wields titanium rod and gas-bomb lures; hood boosts strength and allows breathing underwater.
ALLIES Shark, Kobra
ENEMIES Aquaman, Blue Devil, G'nort King Shark
AFFILIATIONS Terrible Trio

The Fisherman is an enigmatic maritime villain and longtime Aquaman foe. His signature weapon is a custom titanium-alloy fishing rod which he can use to entangle foes, slice them with a razor-sharp hook, or snag nearby objects. He also carries various fishing lures which function as gas bombs.

Fisherman's identity remains a mystery, but his standard modus operandi is to carry out daring seaborne thefts. During the Infinite Crisis he went on a murderous spree in Gotham City before being shot dead by police. Soon after, Aquaman encountered another Fisherman and made a terrifying discovery: the Fisherman's hood was an alien parasite which controlled its human host and gave them powers, such as breathing underwater. When the current host died, the parasite would find a new one. **SW**

FLAMEBIRD

DEBUT (As Bat-Girl) *Batman* #139 (Apr. 1961); (As Flamebird) *Secret Origins Annual* (Vol. 2) #3 (1989)
CURRENT VERSION *Batwoman* (Vol. 2) #1 (Nov. 2011)
REAL NAME Mary Elizabeth "Bette" Kane
BASE Gotham City
HEIGHT 5ft 6in **WEIGHT** 120 lbs
EYES Blue **HAIR** Blond
POWERS/ABILITIES Highly trained athlete and martial artist.
ENEMIES The Hook, Mister Freeze, Bane

Young Bette Kane took on the identity and costume of Flamebird when she joined the Teen Titans. She then moved to Gotham City to study, living with her cousin Kate Kane (Batwoman). Kate trained her in the ways of crime fighting, but made Bette wear nondescript clothing instead of her bright costume and codenamed her "Plebe."

However, when Kate decided she no longer wanted to put Bette at risk, Bette put on her Flamebird costume and recklessly attacked the serial killer Hook. She was severely injured and was found by agents of the Department of Extranormal Operations. They used her to uncover Batwoman's secret identity. After Bette recovered, her uncle Jake gave her additional training and a new suit equipped with a flamethrower. **SW**

FLAG JR., RICK

DEBUT *The Brave and the Bold* (Vol. 1) #25 (Aug.-Sep. 1959)
CURRENT VERSION *Suicide Squad: Rebirth* #1 (Aug. 2016)
REAL NAME Richard Rogers Flag, Jr.
BASE Belle Reve Penitentiary
HEIGHT 6ft 1in **WEIGHT** 189 lbs
EYES Blue **HAIR** Brown
POWERS/ABILITIES Military pilot and skilled tactician with extensive combat and special-operations training.
ALLIES Amanda Waller, Bronze Tiger, Nightshade
ENEMIES Rustam, Brimstone
AFFILIATIONS Suicide Squad

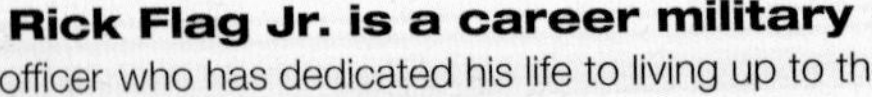

Rick Flag Jr. is a career military officer who has dedicated his life to living up to the legacy of his father, Richard Montgomery Flag. During World War II, Flag Sr. had been a combat pilot and commanding officer of a misfit unit nicknamed the Suicide Squadron, which he had turned into a highly effective combat unit. After the war, Flag Sr. joined the government's classified Task Force X and was killed the line of duty while fighting the War Wheel.

When Amanda Waller reactivated the Suicide Squad as a covert penal unit recruited largely from imprisoned super-villains, Richard Flag Jr. accepted the role of team leader, though he had objections to using known criminals as team members.

Despite Flag's misgivings, the Squadron's first mission (to defeat Brimstone at Mount Rushmore) was a success, and he led the team on a series of other high risk missions. He was declared missing in action when a prototype nuclear weapon exploded during a battle with Jihad forces in the nation of Qurac. Flag had actually survived and he spent years in a Quraci prison before being rescued by Bronze Tiger and rejoining the team. **SW**

COMMANDING PRESENCE
Flag is an expert tactician and leader, and has years of combat experience to back it up in a firefight!

FLAMINGO

DEBUT *Batman* (Vol. 1) #666 (Jul. 2007)
CURRENT VERSION *Batman* (Vol. 2) #1 (Nov. 2011)
REAL NAME Eduardo Flamingo
BASE Gotham City
EYES Blue **HAIR** White
POWERS/ABILITIES Skilled combatant.
ALLIES Mad Hatter, Scarecrow
ENEMIES Batman

After receiving radical brain surgery that turned him into an unpredictable killer, Eduardo Flamingo was a hitman for the Penitente Cartel before going solo. "The Flamingo" became notorious for his fashion choices (a pink jacket with gold epaulets), as well as his tendency to eat people's faces. Following a number of run-ins with Batman in Gotham City, he was imprisoned in Arkham Asylum. When the Crime Syndicate staged a prison break during its invasion of Earth, Flamingo joined the Secret Society of Super-Villains.

He sided with the Arkhamites in the war between Arkham Asylum and the prisoners of Blackgate Penitentiary, then served as a security guard when the Scarecrow took over Arkham during the Gothtopia incident. He escaped from Arkham, but was soon recaptured following an ill-advised attempt to play matador with the Batmobile. **SW**

FORAGER

DEBUT *New Gods* (Vol. 1) #9 (Jul. 1972)
BASE New Genesis
HEIGHT 5ft 10in **WEIGHT** 162 lbs
EYES Blue **HAIR** Black
POWERS/ABILITIES Super-speed and leaping; can climb walls with adheso-grips and fire acid from acid pod.
ALLIES Orion, Lightray, Batman
ENEMIES Darkseid, Mantis
AFFILIATIONS Bugs, the New Gods of New Genesis

Forager was a Bug, a species of micro-life introduced to New Genesis by the forces of Darkseid in the hopes that they would plunder the planet's food supplies.

The Bugs rapidly evolved a humanoid form, eking out a living in forgotten corners of the utopian planet. However, when Forager learned that Mantis of Apokolips was uniting the Bug colonies to invade Earth, he journeyed there via Boom Tube and helped Lightray and Orion fight Mantis' forces. Forager sacrificed himself to destroy a doomsday bomb and save the galaxy.

When Orion returned Forager's body to his people, they chose a female champion to continue his heroic legacy. She looked into the mysterious deaths of various New Gods, then ultimately left Earth to join the Challengers from Beyond. **SW**

FOREVER PEOPLE

DEBUT *Forever People* (Vol. 1) #1 (Feb.-Mar. 1971)
CURRENT VERSION *Infinity Man and the Forever People* #1 (Aug. 2014)
BASE Kirby (sentient communal reconstruction bio-engine), Venice Beach, California
CURRENT MEMBERS/POWERS **Dreamer Beautiful:** Creates illusions from others' minds; **Mark Moonrider:** Megaton touch—can fire blasts of pure force; **Big Bear:** Super-strength, can go into berserker rage; **Serafina Baldaur:** Bio-bursts dazzle or blind opponents; **Vykin Baldaur:** Can control his own density to absorb damage and deliver punishing blows.
ALLIES Infinity Man, Himon
ENEMIES Mantis, Aagog, Female Furies, Darkseid
AFFILIATIONS Academy of Higher Conscience

Straight-laced Vykin, spirited Serafina, rebellious Mark Moonrider, and the aptly named Dreamer Beautiful were an unlikely group of young New Gods who were thrown together on a field trip to Earth. They were met by the seasoned New God warrior Big Bear, who ran the local New Genesis headquarters (disguised as an apartment in Venice Beach, California). On a road trip to investigate problems at the Feast of Eden agricultural project in the Sudan, they were attacked by the Apokoliptian Mantis and his insectoid minions.

The team then discovered that when they all touched their Mother Box (an advanced sentient computer) and spoke the word "Taaru," they merged into a single mighty hero—Infinity Man—who defeated Mantis. They awoke in an alley, and Infinity Man appeared on nearby TV screens, telling them that they had been chosen to battle Darkseid of Apokolips and Highfather of New Genesis. They later fought the Red Lantern Guy Gardner, and Aagog of the Church of Yuga Khan and his Femmes Fatales. **SW**

ON THE RECORD

The original Forever People were Big Bear, Beautiful Dreamer, Mark Moonrider, Vykin, and young cowboy enthusiast, Serifan. When the powerful but enigmatic Infinity-Man was exiled to the inaccessible planet of Adon by Darkseid, the Forever People brought him back by switching places with him, leaving them exiled on that distant world. They were eventually able to return, but were slain by a mysterious killer in *Death of the New Gods*.

DRIVING FOREVER
The Forever People rode in a three-wheeled, all-terrain Super-cycle. Designed by the engineers of New Genesis, it could travel at supersonic speeds on the ground or in the air.

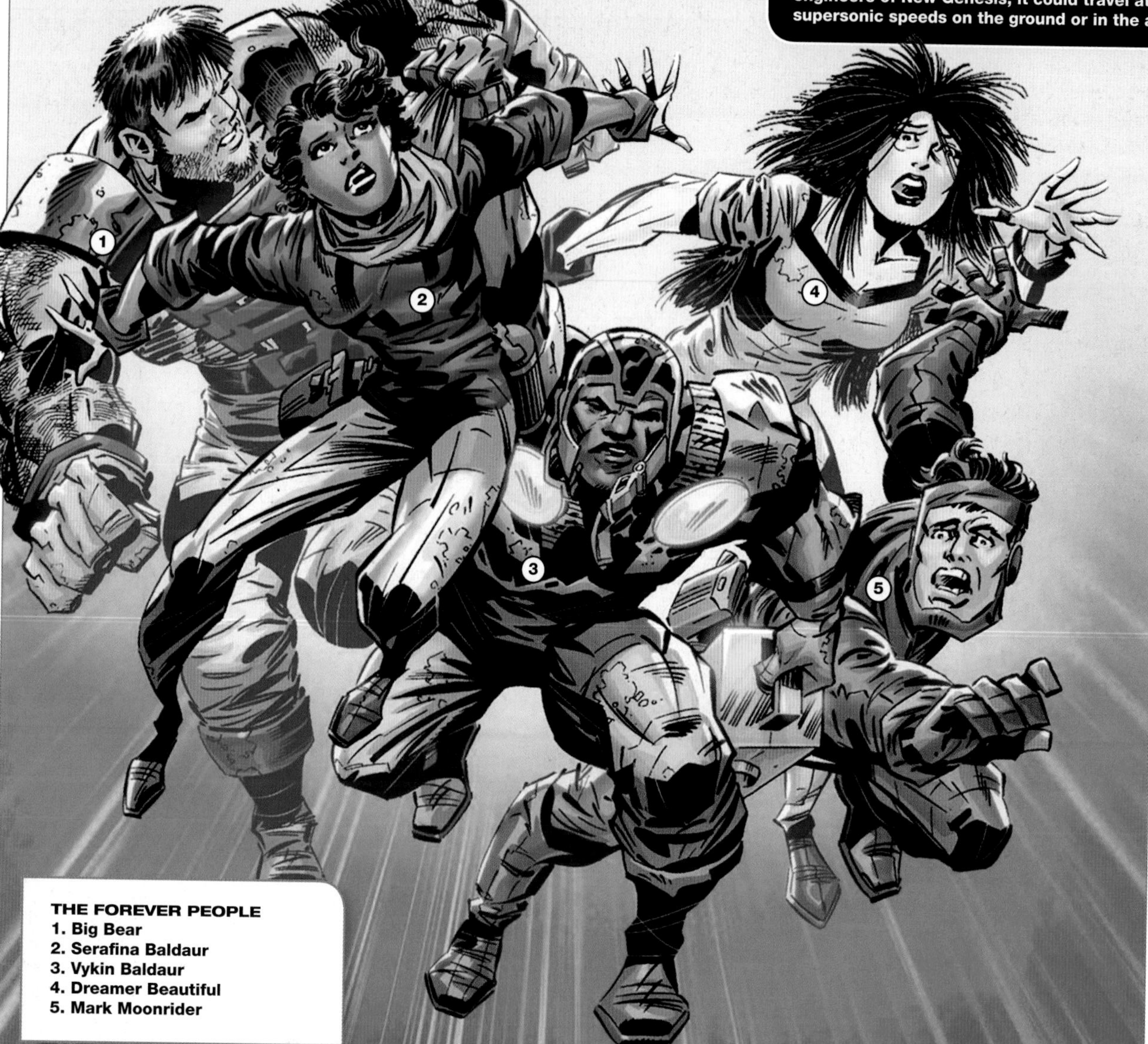

THE FOREVER PEOPLE
1. **Big Bear**
2. **Serafina Baldaur**
3. **Vykin Baldaur**
4. **Dreamer Beautiful**
5. **Mark Moonrider**

FORTUNE, AMOS

DEBUT *Justice League of America* (Vol. 1) #6 (Aug.–Sep. 1961)
BASE A paddle-wheel steamer on the Mississippi
HEIGHT 5ft 8in **WEIGHT** 233 lbs
EYES Black **HAIR** Black
POWERS/ABILITIES Advanced intellect and gambling ability makes him appear lucky; uses various tech as a member of the Royal Flush gang.
ENEMIES JLA, Roulette
AFFILIATIONS Royal Flush Gang

When Amos Fortune's father died, the only thing he left Amos was his lucky deck of cards. By age 16, Amos was making money through card tricks and hired four of his fellow students to be his lookouts.

They quickly became a gang and came to the attention of local gangster Jimmy the Gent. He employed them for several jobs, then sent them into a mobsters' card game. Amos won, but instead of giving the money to Jimmy, used it to arm his own group.

Inspired by the Royal Flush he'd had during the card game, Amos led the first "Royal Flush" gang, with members modeling themselves on playing cards. They fought the Justice League of America and later, Amos created a global network of Royal Flush gangs. Following another defeat at the hands of the JLA, Amos was shot by the wife of a deceased gang member. **AC**

FRANKENSTEIN

DEBUT *Detective Comics* #135 **(May 1948)**
CURRENT VERSION *Frankenstein: Agent of S.H.A.D.E.* #1 **(Nov. 2011)**
BASE Ant Farm **HAIR** Black **EYES** Brown
POWERS/ABILITIES Immortal zombie with no need to drink, eat, or breathe; skilled swordsman and marksman.
AFFILIATIONS S.H.A.D.E., Creature Commandos, Justice League Dark

Frankenstein is an agent of S.H.A.D.E. (Super Human Advanced Defense Executive) and occasional member of Justice League Dark. Created by Victor Frankenstein, the creature was born with a conscience and turned on his creator. After freeing prisoners about to be sacrificed for Victor's experiments, the creature left to explore the world. During his travels he was forced to come to terms with the nature of his origins and whether he was technically alive or dead. He took the name Frankenstein and was later given a purpose in life when he was recruited by S.H.A.D.E.'s commander, Father Time.

On some missions Frankenstein was also backed by the Creature Commandos, and he fought in both World Wars, as well as in the Korean conflict. He had a child with his wife, Lady Frankenstein (a S.H.A.D.E. agent known as The Bride), but she was forced to kill their son when he proved to be twisted and evil, and ultimately begged for his own death. After this tragedy, his wife left and Frankenstein continued working for S.H.A.D.E., saving the world numerous times from monstrous threats, including an alien consciousness trying to invade Earth. He also fought alongside Swamp Thing against the Rot and in the Trinity War as part of Justice League Dark. **AC**

ON THE RECORD

A creature named Ivan, referred to as Frankenstein's Monster, first appeared in *Detective Comics* in the 1940s. He was Dr. Victor Frankenstein's large and lumbering assistant who was returned to life following a huge electrical shock. Another version—more in keeping with the traditional origins of the creature—fought the Phantom Stranger. A more heroic variation met the Young All-Stars before emerging from the shadows in *Seven Soldiers: Frankenstein*, setting the stage for the latest incarnation.

MINDLESS MIGHT
A very different Frankenstein's Monster, nicknamed Ivan, once fought Batman and Robin in 19th-century Europe.

FOX, LUCIUS

DEBUT *Batman* #307 **(Jan. 1979)**
CURRENT VERSION *Detective Comics* (Vol. 2) #2 **(Dec. 2011)**
REAL NAME Lucius Fox
BASE Gotham City
HEIGHT 5ft 10in **WEIGHT** 170 lbs **EYES** Brown **HAIR** Black
POWERS/ABILITIES Exceptional business acumen coupled with excellent engineering and inventive skills.
ALLIES Bruce Wayne
AFFILIATIONS Wayne Enterprises

Lucius Fox is the CEO of megacorporation Wayne Enterprises and one of the most respected financial brains in the world. During his first stint at Wayne Enterprises, he was fired by Bruce Wayne's uncle, Philip Kane, when Kane tried to gain control of the business.

Fox briefly worked at the Gotham School of Engineering where he helped Bruce defeat "Doctor Death." He also helped Batman defeat the Riddler when the villain tried to create a "Zero Year" in Gotham City. Shortly after, Bruce rehired Lucius and made him the head of Wayne Enterprises. When Bruce went public with his support for Batman, Fox became more active, developing weaponry and technology systems for the Dark Knight. He created a new costume for Batwing, not realizing that his own son had secretly become the hero. Luke Fox's role as Batwing caused conflict with his father as Lucius was concerned his son was slacking when, in reality, he was fighting crime.

Fox is a married man with three children and, like all high-ranking members of Wayne Enterprises, has a tracking chip on him at all times. **AC**

EVERY MAN'S LAND
Lucius Fox had a career studded with many achievements. One of his greatest triumphs was in the aftermath of an earthquake that devastated Gotham City, when Fox's quick thinking stopped Lex Luthor's corporation from acquiring most of the city's real estate.

CORE CREW ASSEMBLED
1. Uncle Sam
2. Firebrand
3. The Ray
4. Black Condor
5. Phantom Lady
6. Human Bomb

FREEDOM FIGHTERS

FIRST APPEARANCE *Justice League of America* #107 (Sep.–Oct. 1973)
CURRENT VERSION *Human Bomb* #4 (May. 2013)
NOTABLE MEMBERS/POWERS **Uncle Sam:** The living embodiment of the American Dream; **The Ray:** Can absorb and control light; **Human Bomb:** Generates huge explosions; **Black Condor:** Super-strong and can fly at exceptional speeds; **Firebrand:** Pyrokinesis; **Phantom Lady:** Black light bands provide invisibility and intangibility; **Doll Man:** Can shrink down to a height of just six inches.
ALLIES Justice Society of America, Justice League of America
ENEMIES The Renegades, Father Time, Secret Society of Super-Villains

The Freedom Fighters are operatives of S.H.A.D.E., which protects America from alien and superhuman threats. They are led by Uncle Sam and have included a number of different heroes in their ranks. The most consistent line-up included the Ray, Black Condor, Firebrand, the Human Bomb, Phantom Girl, and Doll Man. Some members of the team were originally brought together by S.H.A.D.E.'s leader, Father Time, to track down a reborn Uncle Sam, but this was revealed as a ruse by Father Time to ensure the Freedom Fighters developed strong bonds and united against a common enemy. The team went on to combat both terrorists and aliens. Firebrand was killed in action when they faced the Jester.

Following Flashpoint, an updated group of heroes was assembled by a new embodiment of Uncle Sam. The team included new incarnations of the Human Bomb, the Ray, Phantom Lady, and Doll Man. **AC**

FIGHTERS REFRESHED
The new Uncle Sam introduced the Human Bomb to his teammates Phantom Lady, Doll Man, and the Ray.

ON THE RECORD

The original Freedom Fighters existed on Earth-X, an alternate version of Earth where the Nazis had won World War II. The Freedom Fighters were Super Heroes waging a war against them.

After ending the Nazi threat, the team sought further action and crossed over to Earth-1 where their allies—the Justice League of America—existed. While it took them a while to adjust to their new home, they continued their fight against evil.

FIGHTING SPIRIT OF LIBERTY
Uncle Sam and co. traveled to Earth, but their surprise appearance in Times Square saw them arrested for causing a public disturbance.

FUNKY FLASHMAN

DEBUT *Mister Miracle* #6 (Jan.–Feb. 1972)
HEIGHT 6ft 1in **WEIGHT** 170 lbs
EYES Blue **HAIR** Brown
POWERS/ABILITIES Charismatic master conman who can sell anything to anyone.
ALLIES Colonel Mockingbird (formerly)
ENEMIES Mister Miracle, Justice League
AFFILIATIONS Secret Society of Super-Villains

Funky Flashman is a charismatic and persuasive salesmen, who is more than a little dishonorable. He once lived off a monthly allowance granted him by Colonel Mockingbird, and after this stipend came to an end, attempted to convince Mister Miracle to act as his tour manager. While Mister Miracle's wife, Big Barda was suspicious of Flashman's motives, Mister Miracle accepted the offer. Barda's doubts were proved right when Flashman stole her husband's Mother Box. When Darkseid's Female Furies tracked the Mother Box to his abode, Flashman hurled his assistant, Houseroy, at them and made his escape.

Later, he used Mister Miracle's name to sell an intergalactic cleaning product and went on to lead the Society of Super-Villains, before being deposed by Gorilla Grodd. He was last seen selling hero-themed cars. **AC**

FURY

DEBUT *Wonder Woman* #300 (Feb. 1983)
CURRENT VERSION *Earth 2* (Vol. 1) #8 (Mar. 2013)
UNIVERSE Earth-2
EYES Blue **HAIR** Black
POWERS/ABILITIES Strength and speed of her mother, Wonder Woman; aggression and power of her father, Steppenwolf.
ALLIES Steppenwolf, Wonder Woman
ENEMIES Darkseid, Big Barda

Fury is the daughter of Earth-2's Wonder Woman and Steppenwolf. A ferocious fighter, she was trained by Big Barda and raised to believe in Steppenwolf's violent ways—even helping him wipe out her fellow Amazons. She eventually saw the error of her ways and helped Mister Miracle escape Darkseid's forces, joining Earth-2's heroes in their fight against the villain.

Fury survived Earth-2's destruction, and on the journey to a new planet her ship, the *TSS Aphrodite*, crashed and a radiation leak threatened the lives of all 77,000 people on board. In desperation, Fury merged their bodies with the souls of departed Amazonians that were stored in the Pandora Vessel—an ancient Themysciran artifact. These survivors established the secret kingdom of Amazonia on their new homeworld, where Fury began training a new generation of Amazons.

There have been other female warriors called Fury who have been inspired and empowered by the Amazons. The first of these, Helena Kosmatos, passed the mantle and name to her daughter, Lyta Trevor. **AC**

UNLEASHING FURY
Being half Amazon, Fury was gifted with wisdom, immortality, and super-strength. She was also a formidable warrior.

HELENA KOSMATOS
During World War II, Helena unwittingly unleashed the Furies—the Greek goddesses of vengeance—and became a vessel for their power. She channeled the spirit of the demonic Fury Tisiphone, the Blood Avenger.

LYTA TREVOR
Inheriting her mother Helena's powers, Lyta's life was marked by heroism and tragedy. After her husband, Hector Hall, vanished, her son Daniel was taken to become the lord of the Dreaming. Daniel finally reunited them all in his realm to protect them from the marauding Spectre.

G'NORT

DEBUT *Justice League International* (Vol. 1) #10 (Feb. 1988)
CURRENT VERSION *Green Lantern: New Guardians* #16 (Mar. 2013)
REAL NAME G'Nort Esplanade G'Neesmacher
HEIGHT 5ft 10in **WEIGHT** 195 lbs
EYES Black **HAIR** Reddish Brown
POWERS/ABILITIES Ability to overcome fear; power ring can create nearly anything its wearer imagines, permits flight and space travel.
ENEMIES Gods of the House of Tuath-Dan

Perhaps one of the oddest members of the Green Lantern Corps, the canine-like G'Nort is a proud ring bearer, despite only getting the job because his uncle called in a favor. After 17 years of Green Lantern training, G'Nort finally began his career as a Super Hero, although his assignment of a space sector was later revoked after he accidentally destroyed a planet.

While not often the most effective Green Lantern in a fight, G'Nort opposed Larfleeze on the planet Sorrow before teaming up with the so-called Agent Orange and discovering they were actually cousins. Together they took on the Gods of the House of Tuath-Dan, a horde of rampaging robots, and a sentient, inter-dimensional portal set on destroying Sorrow. After vanquishing their foes, G'Nort accepts a role as Larfleeze's sidekick. **MM**

GENERAL IMMORTUS

DEBUT *My Greatest Adventure* (Vol. 1) #80 (Jun. 1963)
HEIGHT 5ft 7in **WEIGHT** 132 lbs
EYES Blue **HAIR** Bald
POWERS/ABILITIES Brilliant criminal strategist with extremely high intellect; longevity.
ALLIES Professor Achilles Milo, Mr. Polka Dot, Sportsmaster, Condiment King
ENEMIES Doom Patrol, the Human Flame
AFFILIATIONS Brotherhood of Evil, Army of the Endangered

General Immortus is one of the original enemies of the Doom Patrol. No one knows how old he is, as he has extended his life for centuries with a mysterious elixir. After losing the formula to his potion, he hired the brilliant Dr. Niles Caulder, to recreate the formula. When Caulder learned of Immortus' identity and plan, he destroyed his work, and later, as The Chief, formed the Doom Patrol to thwart Immortus and his schemes.

After repeated clashes with the Doom Patrol, Immortus organized a new team of metahuman followers, featuring such minor criminals as Mr. Polka Dot and the Condiment King. He named this team the Army of the Endangered and had limited success until he crossed paths with another villain who would become his enemy: the Human Flame. **MM**

GARDNER, GUY

DEBUT *Green Lantern* (Vol. 1) #59 (Mar. 1968)
CURRENT VERSION *Green Lantern Corps* (Vol. 3) #1 (Nov. 2011)
REAL NAME Guy Gardner
HEIGHT 6ft **WEIGHT** 180 lbs **EYES** Blue **HAIR** Red
POWERS/ABILITIES Able to overcome great fear; weapons include Green Lantern ring, a device capable of creating nearly anything its wearer imagines, limited only by his or her will; the ring also allows for flight, force-fields, and space travel, and contains encyclopedic knowledge that it can impart to its wearer.
ALLIES Hal Jordan, John Stewart, Kilowog
ENEMIES Atrocitus, Sinestro
AFFILIATIONS Green Lantern Corps, Justice League International, Red Lantern Corps

BROTHERLY LOVE
Guy became his brother's personal punching bag in a self-sacrificing attempt to help Gerard deal with his issues.

Guy Gardner gained his attitude and famous chip on his shoulder at a young age. The product of a dysfunctional home, Guy had idolized his older brother, Gerard. Gerard was a football star in school, and when Guy's parents weren't doting on him, they were lavishing praise on Gloria, Guy's younger sister. However, when Guy's mother died, Gerard became abusive. Guy let his brother take his anger out on him, knowing his sibling needed to vent his rage. But when Gerard hit his sister, Guy lashed out with a baseball bat, causing his brother to be out of action for the football season. In turn, Guy's father, a decorated cop, violently lashed out towards Guy.

As an adult, Guy became a cop in the Baltimore Police Department as part of a long family tradition before getting kicked off the force after showing poor judgment. However, he later exhibited great courage saving his brother Gerard's life from a hail of bullets during a police shoot-out with a criminal gang. In that moment of unflinching bravery, a Green Lantern ring found Guy, and he began life as a fully-fledged hero, finding time to also serve briefly in the Justice League International. **MM**

ON THE RECORD

While he debuted in the late 1960s, Guy Gardner did not rise to real stardom until his placement in the Justice League International during the mid-1980s. Famous for losing a fight to Batman—it only lasted one punch—Gardner became a longtime member of the team and the love interest of fellow hero, Ice.

After a falling out with the Green Lantern Corps, Guy claimed a yellow power ring to continue fighting crime. He discovered his Vuldarian heritage and became a living weapon in the form of Warrior, using powers he would lose during Hal Jordan's return, when both reclaimed their Green Lantern status.

RESTAURANT OF CHOICE
Always one to stay in Super Hero circles, Guy Gardner opened his own heroically themed restaurant called Warriors.

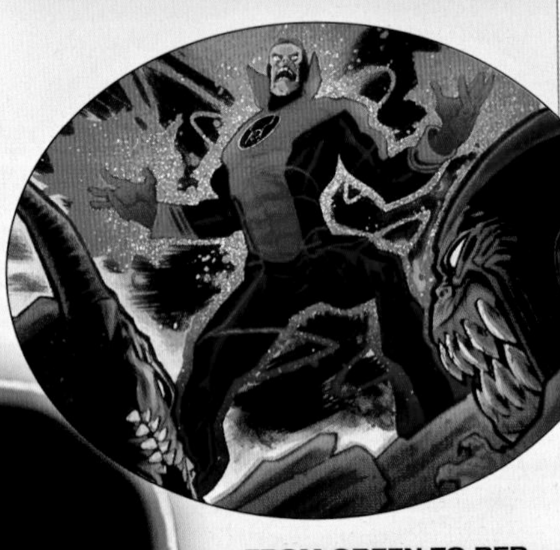

FROM GREEN TO RED
Guy took Atrocitus' Red Lantern Ring and joined a new corps, where he could channel his anger. He later returned to life as a Green Lantern.

G.C.P.D.

DATA

DEBUT *Detective Comics* (Vol. 1) #27 **(May 1939)**
CURRENT VERSION *Batman* (Vol. 2) #1 **(Nov. 2011)**
BASE Gotham City
NOTABLE MEMBERS COMMISSIONER JAMES GORDON; MAGGIE SAWYER; DETECTIVE HARVEY BULLOCK; DETECTIVE RENEE MONTOYA; DETECTIVE CARLOS ALVAREZ; DETECTIVE TRAVIS NIE; DETECTIVE TAMMY KEYES; DETECTIVE JIM CORRIGAN; OFFICER HENRY WALLACE; DETECTIVE MELODY MCKENNA; OFFICER NANCY STRODE; DETECTIVE NANCY YIP; COMMISSIONER JACK FORBES; COMMISSIONER JASON BARD; COMMISSIONER GILLIAN B. LOEB.
ALLIES The Batman Family, The Birds of Prey
ENEMIES Bane, Catwoman, Clayface, Joker, Mister Freeze, Penguin, Poison Ivy, Riddler, Scarecrow, Two-Face, Hugo Strange, to name a few.

AIR PATROL
Gotham City is known for the police blimps that dot the city's famous skyline—often making life tough for a certain rooftop-traveling vigilante.

The Gotham City Police Department has been marred by corruption almost since the founding of the city itself. It took the efforts of many good people to fight the corruption from the inside, rooting out the department's worst offenders. Now with shining stars like James Gordon, Harvey Bullock, Maggie Sawyer, and Renee Montoya, the G.C.P.D. is beginning to look like the honorable institution it always had the potential to be.

When James Gordon first reported to the G.C.P.D., transferring from Chicago, he was astounded to see how high the corruption reached. The incumbent Commissioner, Gillian B. Loeb, had his hands in a variety of criminal enterprises, and allowed many illegal actions to take place right under his nose. He even blatantly attended the outlawed dog fights that many of his officers organized.

Frustrated with his fellow officers, Gordon began to work with a few of the good apples among them—men like Harvey Bullock—and eventually rose in power thanks to his valiant efforts to save Gotham City during an attack by the Riddler during the so-called "Zero Year." Gordon became Commissioner, and began working side by side with another uniformed crusader in the form of the vigilante, Batman.

Following years of a success, James Gordon was framed for a crime he did not commit. He was jailed as the corrupt Jack Forbes stepped up to replace him, quickly replaced again by the equally unscrupulous Jason Bard. When Bard saw the error of his ways—thanks in part to the actions of Batman—he worked to free Gordon. While Gordon did not return to his position, the upstanding Maggie Sawyer was promoted to Commissioner, and Gordon moved to head the Batman Task Force, a special division of the G.C.P.D. that created its own Batman to patrol the city, while the real Dark Knight was MIA. Working with trusted partners like Bullock and Renee Montoya, Gordon continued to fight for his City while wearing a robotic Batman suit, proving that police work in Gotham City could be both dramatic and fantastic. **MM**

ON THE RECORD

Before the reality-altering events of Flashpoint, the Gotham City Police Department had been slowly developed since Commissioner Gordon's debut appearance alongside Batman in 1939's *Detective Comics* (Vol. 1) #27.

While characters such as Bullock, Montoya, Sawyer, and Gordon have appeared in the modern G.C.P.D., some officers have not yet been updated for the new continuity, including Crispus Allen, "Hardback" Bock, Josephine "Josie Mac" MacDonald, and the corrupt Jim Corrigan. Also notably absent is Detective Sarah Essen Gordon, James Gordon's second wife, who took over for him briefly as commissioner, and was part of a nascent G.C.P.D., played a signifcant role in the landmark *Batman: Year One* miniseries.

FLACK FOR FLASS
Arnold Flass was a notorious example of how corrupt the G.C.P.D. was early on. During *Batman: Year One*, Flass repeatedly clashed with the upright James Gordon, earning plenty of bruises for his efforts.

GOTHAM CITY'S FINEST?
1. Former Commissioner Jack Forbes
2. Former Commissioner Jason Bard
3. Detective Harvey Bullock
4. Former Commissioner Maggie Sawyer

G.C.P.D. BLUE
The G.C.P.D. is a brotherhood that has clashed with Batman nearly as many times as it has worked with him. In Gotham City, good cops are hard to come by.

BACK IN BLUE
James Gordon has recently returned to the role of police commissioner, much to the relief of many of Gotham City's citizens.

GENERAL ZOD

DATA

DEBUT *Adventure Comics* (Vol. 1) #283 **(Apr. 1961)**
CURRENT VERSION *Action Comics* (Vol. 2) #13 **(Dec. 2012)**
REAL NAME Dru-Zod
BASE Phantom Zone
HEIGHT 6ft 3in **WEIGHT** 215 lbs **EYES** Blue **HAIR** Black
POWERS/ABILITIES Under a yellow sun, all the solar-charged abilities of a Kryptonian—super-strength, speed, flight, invulnerability, and enhanced senses; possesses a keen strategic intellect; highly skilled in Kryptonian martial arts.
ALLIES Faora, Non
ENEMIES Superman, Supergirl, Justice League
AFFILIATIONS Phantom Zone Criminals, Military Academy of Krypton

CLASSIC STORIES

***Adventure Comics* (Vol. 1) #283 (Apr. 1961)** In a Superboy story flashback, General Zod debuts as an inmate of the Phantom Zone. Attempting to conquer Krypton with imperfect duplicates that look like Bizarros, Zod is eventually foiled by Jor-El.

***DC Comics Presents* (Vol. 1) #97 (Sep. 1986)** In the midst of *Crisis on Infinite Earths*, Zod and the rest of the Phantom Zone villains are destroyed, consumed by cosmic revenant Aethyr.

***Superman* (Vol. 2) #204–215 (Jun. 2004–May 2005)** An aging Zod kidnaps a million humans to take to an alternate Phantom Zone where they will be his subjects in his kingdom of Metropia.

DOMESTIC DISPUTES
Superman and Wonder Woman became targets for murder as soon as they freed Zod's wife Faora from the Phantom Zone.

I WILL ALWAYS BE YOUR MONSTER
Unrepentant, Zod and his comrades were banished to the Phantom Zone, convinced they would eventually return.

General Zod is a self-made man who remorselessly clawed his way to the top of Krypton's military. His dream was to add fresh triumphs to his planet's glorious annals of ancient conquest. A man born out of time, he made his own opportunities when modern pacifistic civilization provided none, and proved he was right when Krypton died while he lived on...

Dru-Zod was the child of emotionally distant parents who cared more for biological experiments than their son and thought nothing of taking him into Krypton's most remote and untamed regions. When they were attacked by swiftly proliferating monsters, his mother died instantly and the boy—without qualm or hesitation—maimed his father and threw him to the creatures to facilitate his own escape. He survived for a year until rescued by Jor-El and his brother Zor.

After years in the Military Academy, Zod won early fame when he and cadet Lara Lor-Van put down a military coup by their superior, Colonel Ekar. Zod executed the traitor himself. Despite his successes, Colonel Zod was discontent with modern society. Determined to reverse what he saw as Krypton's slide into pacifistic decadence, he faked evidence to incite a war with the neighboring Char, riding a wave of patriotic militarism which saw him promoted to General. His genocidal triumph ended when Jor-El uncovered his fraud and denounced him to the Science Council. Imprisoned in the Phantom Zone for decades, Zod's hatred festered until he and his fanatical subordinates Faora and Non found the means to escape and seek revenge. **WW**

ON THE RECORD

A minor villain since his 1961 debut, General Zod became a recurring threat in the years preceding the mid-1980s *Crisis on Infinite Earths*. In the 1986 *Superman* reboot, Zod and fellow Kryptonians Qwex-Ul and Zaora annihilated an alternate Earth, forcing Superman to end their lives.

However, Zod's demise was short lived and in subsequent years he returned in various incarnations. In 2010, following Brainiac's defeat and the establishment of New Krypton in Earth's solar system, Zod was released from the Phantom Zone to lead the Kryptonian military. However, the warmonger instigated a "100 Minute War" against Earth, resulting in New Krypton's destruction and his invariable return to the Zone.

UNFORGIVING
Whether addressing the last Son of El, inferior Earth-Men, or his own troops, Zod would never be content until he made all kneel before him.

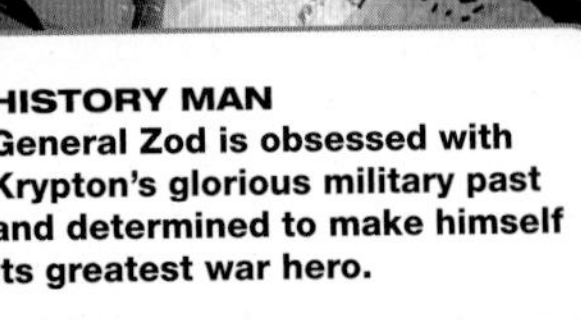

HISTORY MAN
General Zod is obsessed with Krypton's glorious military past and determined to make himself its greatest war hero.

GENERAL, THE

DEBUT *Captain Atom* (Vol. 2) #1 (Mar. 1987)
CURRENT VERSION *Captain Atom* (Vol. 3) #3 (Jan. 2012)
REAL NAME Wade Eiling
BASE Mobile
EYES Black **HAIR** Black
POWERS/ABILITIES Skilled tactician; highly trained in military combat; ruthless strategist.
ALLIES Dr. Heinrich Megala
ENEMIES Captain Atom, Firestorm, Superman
AFFILIATIONS US Army, Security Agencies

Professional soldier and ultra-patriot, Wade Eiling rose to the rank of General by always knowing where the next threat lay. In the days of alien incursions, masked supermen, and uncontrolled technological advancement, the highly decorated veteran was convinced that Super Heroes acting with public support—but no government control—were a menace to mankind.

The General toiled tirelessly and with no concern for ethics or human rights to ensure that quantum metahuman and former soldier Captain Atom remained a military asset. He called him "the super weapon that will keep America on top." Eiling later conspired to create Major Force as another secret weapon. He used him in attempts to press-gang Firestorm, the Nuclear Man, into being the latest asset in his stockpile. **WW**

GENTLEMAN GHOST

DEBUT *Flash Comics* (Vol. 1) #88 (Oct. 1947)
CURRENT VERSION *Savage Hawkman* (Vol. 1) #5 (Mar. 2012)
REAL NAME James Craddock
BASE Hell, Gotham City
HEIGHT Variable **WEIGHT** Variable
POWERS/ABILITIES Intangibility, invisibility, flight, teleportation, control of the dead.
ENEMIES Hawkman, Batman, Batwing, the Spectre
AFFILIATIONS Secret Society of Super-Villains

When 19th-century English highwayman James Craddock was executed for his many crimes, he went to Hell. Centuries later, he returned to Earth where, despite his ethereal powers, the spectral scoundrel desperately sought to regain physical form. He scoured the world for mystic artifacts that might provide a solution.

In New York City he came into conflict with Hawkman while procuring the arcane Mortis Orb, which could resurrect the dead. Yet that only gained Craddock an army of zombie slaves, not a new body. The Orb was later re-energized by contact with Hawkman's Nth metal, and Craddock again activated it, hoping to steal the life-force from the city's mortal inhabitants. Instead, the orb opened a portal to Hell and the ghost was forced back there. **WW**

GEO-FORCE

DEBUT *The Brave and the Bold* (Vol. 1) #200 (Jul. 1983)
CURRENT VERSION *Suicide Squad Most Wanted: Deadshot & Katana* #3 (May 2016)
REAL NAME Prince Brion Markov
BASE Markovia, US, Justice League Watchtower
HEIGHT 6ft **WEIGHT** 190 lbs
EYES Green **HAIR** Blond
POWERS/ABILITIES Super-strength and durability; lava blasts; Earth-moving.
ALLIES Batman, Superman
ENEMIES Baron Bedlam

Brion Markov was second-in-line to the throne of Markovia and volunteered to undergo scientific experimentation to become his nation's metahuman guardian. On gaining a variety of Earth-based abilities, he took the codename Geo-Force and quashed an invasion by usurper Baron Bedlam. The threat was ended with the aid of Batman and a number of other costumed heroes calling themselves the Outsiders.

Brion opted to remain with the new team, relocating to America where he was reunited with his half-sister, Tara Markov. Geo-Force eventually assumed command of the team when Batman left. The Outsiders proved a volatile group, and—after a brief time as Markovia's sovereign—Brion moved back to America to join the Justice League. **WW**

G.I. ZOMBIE

DEBUT *Star-Spangled War Stories Featuring G.I. Zombie* (Vol. 1) #1 (Sep. 2014)
REAL NAME Jared Kabe
EYES White **HAIR** Black
POWERS/ABILITIES Dead, but with full animation, regeneration, and consciousness; preternaturally heightened senses; extensive military combat experience.
ALLIES Carmen King, Gravedigger
ENEMIES Jeff Kennedy, Leo Conroy
AFFILIATIONS US Army, US Government

Jared Kabe has been a US Army top secret for decades, but exactly how many is strictly classified. He is the army's boots-on-the-ground weapon of last resort, handling the type of tricky missions no bombing raid, missile strike, or drone attack could accomplish. Jared has been dead for as long as he can remember: a soldier deployed by his commander, code name Gravedigger, to handle problems ranging from enemy armies to domestic terrorists with bio-weapons.

Kabe combines martial skills with a shrewd deductive mind and unnatural advantages such as regeneration from any injury, and freedom from fatigue and the need for sleep. However, he has a tendency to lose his faculties if he does not periodically eat human flesh. So when not in combat, Jared is given condemned criminals to feast on. **WW**

GIGANTA

DEBUT *Wonder Woman* (Vol. 1) #9 (Summer 1944)
CURRENT VERSION *Trinity of Sin: Pandora* #2 (Sep. 2013)
REAL NAME Doris Zuel
BASE Ivy Town
HEIGHT Variable **WEIGHT** Variable
EYES Green **HAIR** Red
POWERS/ABILITIES Super-strength and durability; limited invulnerability derived from the ability to increase her physical size and mass.
ALLIES Ryan Choi, Queen Clea
ENEMIES Wonder Woman, Green Lantern, Justice League
AFFILIATIONS Secret Society of Super-Villains, Secret Six, Injustice League, Villainy Incorporated

SHOCK TACTICS
Doctor Zuel was always ready for a fight and did not care what the human insects beneath her feet thought.

Doctor Doris Zuel was a brilliant scientist with a fatal blood disease. To save her own life, Doris Zuel attempted to place her consciousness into Wonder Woman's body, but instead ended up trapped in a gorilla named Giganta. Eventually escaping the beast's body, her mind and spirit lodged inside a comatose metahuman named Olga, and she gained her victim's mystical ability to alter size.

Doris became an adrenaline junkie, drunk on her newfound power. Apart from a brief period teaching at Ivy Town University—where she was romantically involved with Ryan Choi, the second Atom—she rejected science research to be a super-villain.

Confrontational and amoral, Giganta reveled in her shattering power and left scheming to more ambitious heads. She also preferred to work in a group, joining several mercenary or criminal organizations, but was equally happy to join semi-heroic teams such as the Secret Six or the government's Suicide Squad. The latter association proved particularly rewarding for Giganta as she was paid with the name of the man responsible for murdering her beloved Ryan and allowed to torture him to death. **WW**

ON THE RECORD

The original Giganta was a female gorilla subjected to evolutionary enhancement. She transformed into a powerful human woman who wanted Wonder Woman's boyfriend, Steve Trevor.

Giganta was far less comical on her introduction to the modern DC Universe: crushing jets, smashing buildings, and generally treating humans as if they were all bugs to be stepped on. Her lack of caution and consideration was revealed as a side-effect of her expansions: the bigger Giganta grew, the more her intellect diminished.

BRAWN OVER BRAINS
The post-Crisis Giganta, Doctor Zuel, learned that although rational reasoning had its benefits, brute force solved most problems more quickly.

GIZMO

DEBUT *New Teen Titans* (Vol. 1) #3 (Jan. 1981)
CURRENT VERSION *Forever Evil* #1 (Nov. 2013)
REAL NAME Mikron O'Jeneus
BASE Platinum Flats
EYES Green **HAIR** Bald
HEIGHT 4ft 2in **WEIGHT** 87 lbs
POWERS/ABILITIES Genius intellect, flight (jet pack), array of hi-tech weaponry and gadgets.
ENEMIES Teen Titans, Psimon, Birds of Prey, Dr. Sivana

A diminutive inventor with a gift for turning everyday objects into deadly devices, Mikron O'Jeneus sold hi-tech equipment to villains through his company Gizmo, Inc. As part of the Fearsome Five, he was defeated several times by the Teen Titans, before being shrunk down to microscopic size by teammate Psimon and later shot in the head by Dr. Sivana for failing to complete a mission.

Death did not spell the end of his career. He was resurrected by Macintech Research & Development in Platinum Flats, and joined the board of the Silicon Syndicate, a cabal of villains operating an extortion racket exploiting local hi-tech companies. This attracted the attention of the Birds of Prey, but Gizmo survived that encounter and still works with the Fearsome Five. **SW**

GLIDER

DEBUT *The Flash* (Vol. 1) #250 (Jun. 1977)
CURRENT VERSION *The Flash* (Vol. 4) #6 (Apr. 2012)
REAL NAME Lisa Snart
BASE Central City
EYES Blue **HAIR** Blond
HEIGHT 5ft 5in **WEIGHT** 117 lbs
POWERS/ABILITIES Projects an astral form that can fly and move through solid objects; trails razor-sharp tendrils.
ENEMIES Flash, Gorilla Grodd, Captain Cold

Lisa Snart is the sister of Leonard Snart—alias Rogues leader Captain Cold—and girlfriend of Sam Scudder, the Mirror Master. When Leonard forced the Rogues to use an experimental device designed to give them real powers, it exploded and put Lisa in a coma. She discovered that she could send out an astral form from her body, and set out to exact revenge on her brother, as the ethereal Glider.

Lisa took control of the Rogues and confronted Captain Cold and the Flash, but they joined forces when Central City was overrun by Gorilla Grodd and his ape army. Lisa then used her powers to pull Sam out of the Mirror World he was trapped in, destroying her astral form. She returned to save the Rogues when they were attacked by the Secret Society during the Crime Syndicate's invasion. **SW**

GLORIOUS GODFREY

DEBUT *Forever People* (Vol. 1) #3 (Jun.–Jul. 1971)
CURRENT VERSION *Batman and Robin* (Vol. 2) #32 (Aug. 2014)
REAL NAME Godfrey **BASE** Apokolips
EYES Amber **HAIR** Brown
HEIGHT 5ft 11in **WEIGHT** 195 lbs
POWERS/ABILITIES Immortal, with superhuman attributes; very persuasive voice.
ENEMIES New Genesis, Batman family

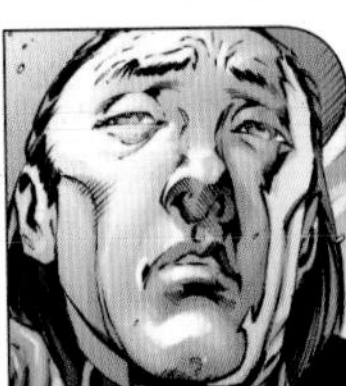

As arch-propagandist for Darkseid, Glorious Godfrey uses his great eloquence to persuade and deceive. He is often sent to other worlds to spread the influence of Apokolips through the mass media, usually taking on the role of a populist media personality.

When Darkseid was in stasis at Apokolips' core, Godfrey served his son, Kalibak, collecting the Chaos Sliver and the sarcophagus of Damian Wayne so that his master could power his Chaos Cannon. However, Batman was determined to get his son's body back, and followed him back to Apokolips. The Dark Knight tracked Godfrey down and defeated his elite Justifiers before forcing the villain to tell him where Damian was. Godfrey told him and even offered to take him there, but Batman did not trust the propagandist and silenced his compelling voice by slamming him to the ground. **SW**

GODIVA

DEBUT *New Teen Titans Annual* (Vol. 2) #3 (1987)
BASE Swiss Alps
EYES Red **HAIR** Black with gold streak
HEIGHT 5ft 9in **WEIGHT** 120 lbs
POWERS/ABILITIES Entrances and controls victims by shaking her hypnotic hair; resources include armed henchmen and robot dogs.
ALLIES Dr. Cornelius
ENEMIES Teen Titans

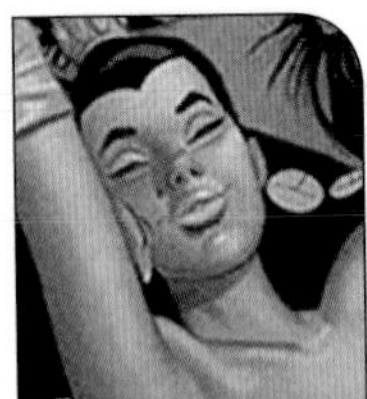

The mysterious mercenary Godiva claims to be the daughter of an African princess and a Chinese prince. She is very vain and capricious, insisting that she be filmed at all times, and killing employees for even the smallest infractions.

She kidnapped CIA agents John and Cherie Chase in Tokyo, but their son Danny escaped and received help from the Teen Titans, who saved them and foiled Godiva's plan to sell a hi-tech satellite to the highest bidder. Godiva freed herself and faced the Titans again when she was hired to kill a British spy. She eliminated her target and eluded the Titans, but failed to obtain the secret tape her client wanted. Godiva was also among the many villains who joined the sorceress Circe in a massive battle with Wonder Woman and her allies in Times Square. **SW**

GLOBAL GUARDIANS, THE

DEBUT *DC Comics Presents* #46 (Jun. 1982)
BASE The Dome
NOTABLE MEMBERS/POWERS **Crimson Fox III** (Vivian and Constance D'Aramis, France): Pheromone control; **Tasmanian Devil** (Hugh Dawkins, Australia): Transforms into giant marsupial; **Jet** (Celia Windward, Jamaica/Zamaron): Flight, electromagnetic powers; **Manticore** (real name unknown, Greece): Beast powers; **Gloss** (Xiang Po, China): Immortal, draws power from ley lines; **Freedom Beast** (Dominic Mndawe, South Africa): Mind control, super-strength, can merge animals; **Sandstorm** (real name unknown, Syria): Sand powers; **Tuatara** (Jeremy Wakefield, New Zealand): precognition; **Doctor Mist** (Nommo of Kor, Africa): Magic; **Little Mermaid** (Ulla Paske, Denmark): Aquatic being; **Rising Sun** (Isuma Yasunari, Japan): Absorbs and projects solar energy; **Seraph** (Chaim Levon, Israel): Various powers from ancient artifacts.

The Global Guardians' origins can be traced back to the early 1950s. With superhumans emerging around the world, the nations of the European Economic Community created the Dome, an organization to manage superhuman affairs and coordinate metahuman activity. The Dome eventually extended its membership to include almost every nation, and African sorcerer Dr. Mist oversaw the creation of the Dome's Super Hero team: the Global Guardians.

Despite its pan-national idealism, the team was not a success. On their first mission they were almost defeated by Injustice Unlimited, and only triumphed with timely help from Infinity, Inc. When the Global Guardians' funding was cut in favor of Justice League International, several Guardians accepted an invitation to relocate to a new Dome in the nation of Bialya. There, they fell prey to the mind-control powers of Bialya's Queen Bee, who used them against their allies in the JLI.

The Global Guardians later built another Dome in the Pacific and were deputized by the UN's covert Checkmate organization. Several members were subsequently murdered by the villain Prometheus. **SW**

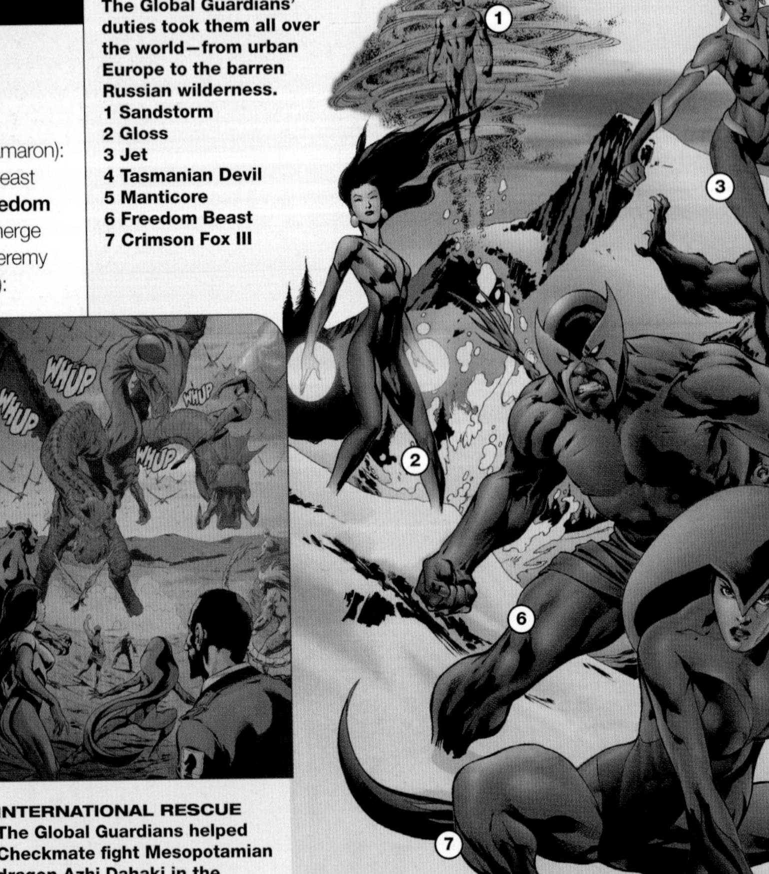

RAPID REACTION FORCE
The Global Guardians' duties took them all over the world—from urban Europe to the barren Russian wilderness.
1 Sandstorm
2 Gloss
3 Jet
4 Tasmanian Devil
5 Manticore
6 Freedom Beast
7 Crimson Fox III

INTERNATIONAL RESCUE
The Global Guardians helped Checkmate fight Mesopotamian dragon Azhi Dahaki in the Australian Outback.

GODIVA

DEBUT *Super Friends* (Vol. 1) #7 (Oct. 1977)
CURRENT VERSION *Justice League International* (Vol. 3) #1 (Nov. 2011)
REAL NAME Dora Leigh
EYES Blue **HAIR** Blond
POWERS/ABILITIES Can control her prehensile hair.
ALLIES Booster Gold
ENEMIES Peraxxus, O.M.A.C., the Burners
AFFILIATIONS Justice League International

When prehensile-haired British superhero Godiva (Dora Leigh) was offered a position in Justice League International, she was immediately attracted to the group's dashing leader, Booster Gold. However, she did think the team was lacking in power, and was proven right when they were forced to retreat by a giant robot controlled by alien asset-stripper Peraxxus. After Peraxxus captured Batman and the JLI, and placed them in cocoons, Godiva used her hair to remove a laser cutter from Batman's utility belt and free the team, allowing them to defeat the alien.

In clashes with OMAC and the super-terrorists the Burners, Godiva proved herself a valuable League member, and finally kissed Booster Gold. Things got awkward, however, when her old flame Olympian joined the team, just before the JLI disbanded. **SW**

GOG

DEBUT *Gog* #1 (Feb. 1998)
REAL NAME William Matthews
BASE Hidden jungle temple in the Democratic Republic of Congo
HEIGHT 6ft 3in **WEIGHT** 210 lbs
EYES Blue **HAIR** Brown
POWERS/ABILITIES Seemingly divine-level super-strength, teleportation, energy manipulation, healing, resurrection, and reality-altering powers.
ALLIES Gog (Third World god)
ENEMIES Infinity Man, Superman, Justice Society of America

DIVINE POWER Armed with the panoply and power staff of Gog, William Matthews became a match for the mightiest heroes.

In an ancient temple in the jungles of the Democratic Republic of Congo, American missionary William Matthews discovered the body of Gog, the last surviving god of the mythical Third World. Within the temple, William experienced terrifying visions that drove him insane; he became convinced that Gog would be resurrected and save the world. William took the god's name and staff, which bestowed upon him extraordinary powers. He then embarked on a mission to prepare for Gog's imminent resurrection by eliminating all "false gods."

His targets included Infinity Man, Hercules, and Superman, the latter whom he blamed for a nuclear disaster he had seen in a vision. When members of the Justice Society of America confronted him in his temple, Gog was absorbed into the face of the lost god, bringing the original Gog to life. The deity emerged from the earth and declared his peaceful intentions.

After seeing Gog perform miracles, some members of the JSA became his followers, but the team learned that Gog would soon bond with the Earth and potentially destroy it, and they turned on him. They cut off Gog's head, and the Superman of Earth-22 embedded it in the Source Wall. **SW**

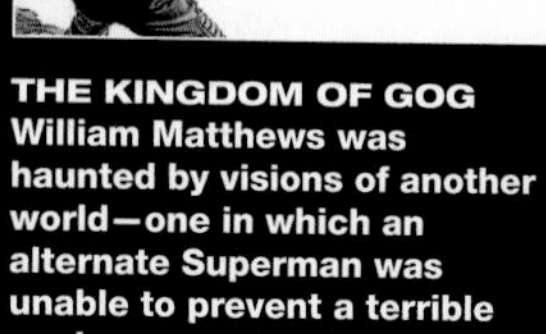

THE KINGDOM OF GOG William Matthews was haunted by visions of another world—one in which an alternate Superman was unable to prevent a terrible nuclear catastrophe.

GORDON JR., JAMES

DEBUT *Batman* (Vol. 1) #407 (May 1987)
CURRENT VERSION *Batgirl* (Vol. 4) #8 (Jun. 2012)
REAL NAME James Gordon, Jr.
BASE Gotham City
EYES Blue **HAIR** Red
POWERS/ABILITIES Skilled tactician and analyst; an expert with knives and explosives.
ALLIES Amanda Waller, Knightfall
ENEMIES Batgirl, Batman, Commissioner James Gordon
AFFILIATIONS Arkham Asylum inmates, Suicide Squad

James Gordon, Jr. is the son of Commissioner James Gordon and Eileen Gordon, and the younger brother of Barbara Gordon, alias Batgirl. As a child, James began displaying sociopathic tendencies, killing the family cat. When he grew up, he became a serial killer and was imprisoned in Arkham Asylum, where he helped protect Charise Carnes (the villain Knightfall).

James broke out of Arkham during a riot and began stalking his sister, even seducing her roommate, Alysia. However, when the Joker captured Barbara and was about to subject her to a twisted "wedding," James rescued her because he wanted to kill her himself. After engaging Barbara in a game of cat-and-mouse, he lured her to the Gotham Bay Aquarium. He struck her with a mallet, but Barbara threw a Batarang which impaled his eye and knocked him into the harbor.

James was presumed dead, but resurfaced as a member of Suicide Squad. Determined to prove himself—he was in love with his boss, Amanda Waller—he helped the team counter an attack by agents of the Crime Syndicate. **SW**

SIBLING RIVALRY James clashed with his sister Barbara in a life-and-death struggle that led to his disappearance.

ON THE RECORD

In the pre-Flashpoint universe, James' was Barbara Gordon's stepbrother. When he was just a baby, James Jr. was kidnapped by gangsters, and his father and Batman rescued him. James Jr. displayed murderous tendencies from a young age, possibly killing Barbara's friend, Bess Keller. He became a prolific serial killer and plotted to taint baby food with psychosis-triggering drugs, but was stabbed in the eye by Barbara during a battle. It slowed him down long enough for James' father to stop his son once and for all.

THERE'S SOMETHING ABOUT JIM, JR. Commissioner James Gordon was troubled by his own role in the dark path his son had taken.

GORDON, JAMES

DATA

DEBUT *Detective Comics* (Vol. 1) #27 **(May 1939)**
CURRENT VERSION *Detective Comics* (Vol. 2) #1 **(Nov. 2011)**
REAL NAME James W. Gordon
BASE Gotham City
HEIGHT 5ft 9in **WEIGHT** 168 lbs **EYES** Blue **HAIR** Red
POWERS/ABILITIES Natural leader with expertise in police procedure; highly trained fighter and former marine; long history of working with Batman and his allies; expert detective; weapons include police-issued firearm and robotic Batsuit armed with a variety of non-lethal, high-tech crime-fighting equipment.
ALLIES Batman, the Batman Family, Batgirl, Harvey Bullock
ENEMIES James Gordon, Jr., the Joker, Mr. Bloom
AFFILIATIONS G.C.P.D., Batman Task Force

BAT-COP
Gordon was invited to head up the Batman Task Force as the city's new Batman for a time. He got into shape, and became the best Batman he could be, piloting a giant mechanical suit.

ROUGH START
Gordon was suspicious of Bruce Wayne when the young man returned to Gotham City. By the same token, Bruce wrongly assumed that Gordon was a corrupt cop.

James Gordon is the law in Gotham City. Before his arrival from Chicago, Gotham City was mired in corruption, a seemingly impossible metropolis for the hero cop to bring to justice. Gordon worked his way up through the Gotham City Police Department to commissioner, setting the new standard for the force. He works hand-in-hand with the city's other protector, the vigilante known as the Batman.

Family man James Gordon transferred from the police force in Chicago to the Gotham City Police Department shortly before the death of Bruce Wayne's parents. Three weeks after his transfer, Gordon was still getting the lay of the land, realizing how corrupt his partner, Detective Dan Corrigan, truly was. Having had a rough time in Chicago, Gordon wanted the best for his young family, including his wife Barbara and his two kids, Barbara and James Jr.. When he discovered a police-run illegal dogfight—just the tip of the G.C.P.D.'s corruption that ran all the way up the ladder to Commissioner Loeb—Gordon stood up against his fellow officers, even after one of the dogs attacked him. A tough cop, he left, shook off his injuries, and walked his beat, only to discover the Waynes shot dead in a nearby alley.

From that day forward, Jim fought against the corruption of his city, working his way up to Lieutenant during Gotham City's "Zero Year," when Batman first appeared. At that time, Gordon paid several visits to the newly returned Bruce Wayne, perhaps suspicious that the resourceful young man may have ties to the city's newest vigilante. Despite Batman and Gordon remaining dubious of each other's intentions, the two began to work closely together, helping fight off the Riddler and saving the city from destruction. This act of valor earned Gordon a promotion to Commissioner, a position he kept until he was framed for a crime in recent years, and temporarily jailed. **MM**

ON THE RECORD

The Gordon bloodline has been the subject of constant revision in Batman's various comic book titles. In 1951, it was established that James Gordon had a son named Tony. However, Tony was soon overshadowed by Barbara Gordon, James' daughter and the heroine Batgirl.

After the events of *Crisis on Infinite Earths*, the Gordon family was reimagined in "Batman: Year One," which introduced his infant son James, and relegated Barbara to the role of adopted niece. The lineage became even more complex when *Batman: Gotham Knights #6* (August 2000) establish that Gordon had an affair with his brother's wife, making Barbara Gordon his true daughter by blood.

PARTNERS IN CRIME-BUSTING
Post-Crisis, Gordon's first wife left him just after his move to Gotham City from Chicago. Gordon remarried his colleague Detective Sarah Essen, who was later shot and killed by the Joker.

CLASSIC STORIES

***World's Finest Comics* (Vol. 1) #53 (Aug.-Sep. 1951)** Commissioner Gordon's private life is exposed as readers discover that he has a son named Tony.

***Batman* (Vol. 1) #404-407 (Feb.-May 1987)** Gordon arrives in Gotham City just as Batman first emerges, in this groundbreaking origin retelling that features a very human—and very tough—Jim Gordon.

***Batman: Gordon's Law* #1-4 (Dec. 1996-Mar. 1997)** Commissioner Gordon gets his first miniseries, which results in a sequel series *(Batman: Gordon of Gotham)* the following year.

GORILLA GRODD

DATA

DEBUT *The Flash* (Vol. 1) #106 **(Apr.–May 1959)**
CURRENT VERSION *The Flash* (Vol. 4) #7 **(May 2012)**
REAL NAME Grodd
BASE Gorilla City
HEIGHT 6ft 6in **WEIGHT** 600 lbs **EYES** Gray **HAIR** Black
POWERS/ABILITIES Violent and very strong; can control others with his mind; genius-level intellect; possesses psionic abilities to move objects remotely.
ALLIES Crime Syndicate
ENEMIES The Flash, Rogues, Solovar
AFFILIATIONS Gorilla City

FIRST CONTACT
During the Flash's first meeting with the inhabitants of Gorilla City, King Grodd hoped to gain Flash's speed force by consuming his enemy's brain.

GORILLA WARFARE
Grodd waged war against his fellow gorillas when they tried to make peace with the humans of Central City.

Gorilla Grodd is a violent and deadly super-villain. Since first meeting the Flash (Barry Allen) in Gorilla City, Grodd has had a deep hatred of the hero and believes if he can eat Flash's brains he will gain his powers. Grodd is not only fast and strong, but also has amazing psionic abilities following contact with the Speed Force.

When the Speed Force struck a tribe of gorillas deep in the jungles of Africa, it speeded up their intelligence and evolution. They then created their own kingdom, Gorilla City, and worshipped the "light"—their own name for the Speed Force. Grodd became their king moments before the Flash first arrived. Grodd had his own father killed and ate his brains, believing they would give him his father's power. The Flash escaped Gorilla City and defeated Grodd, who was buried under the rubble of an ancient temple during their fight. He was dug out by General Silverback and soon reclaimed his control over Gorilla City, leading the gorillas on an invasion of the Flash's home of Central City. Grodd nearly killed Flash, who was only saved when the gorilla known as Solovar risked his own life to rescue the hero.

The Flash later took Grodd into the Speed Force and defeated him in battle, leaving Grodd trapped there. Grodd was freed by the Crime Syndicate and found he now had increased psionic abilities. Arriving in Central City just as his fellow gorillas were making peace with the humans, Grodd took over, killing anyone—gorilla or human—who opposed him. With the Flash missing (seemingly killed by the Crime Syndicate), Gorilla Grodd renamed Central City "Gorilla City."

When the Rogues refused to join the Crime Syndicate's new order, the Syndicate sent Grodd and other super-villains to kill them. The Rogues won the day, however, with Mirror Master trapping Grodd and his fellow villains in a mirror dimension. **AC**

SUPER-CHARGED
When Gorilla Grodd escaped from the Speed Force, he was more powerful than ever.

ON THE RECORD

Gorilla Grodd has become ever more brutal and savage since his first appearance. His origins have also changed significantly. Originally Grodd and his fellow gorillas gained their amazing intellects thanks to a radioactive meteor falling on their land. This meteor was connected to the source of Green Lantern foe Hector Hammond's powers. At one point, Grodd and Hammond joined forces to fight the Flash and Green Lantern.

The source of Grodd's power was later altered to alien intervention. Grodd and his enemy Solovar both originally had telepathic abilities. The latter asked for the Flash's aid when Grodd tried to lead an invasion of Central City after he had used his strength and abilities to seize control of their kingdom.

APE ATTACK
The Flash (Wally West) tries to stop Grodd's rampage in Keystone City.

CLASSIC STORIES

***The Flash* #106 (May 1959)** In his debut, Grodd gains the secret of mind control from fellow gorilla Solovar and uses this power to seize control of Gorilla City.

***The Flash* (Vol. 2) #178 (Nov. 2001)** The Flash (Wally West) takes on Grodd, as the gorilla launches his most violent attack yet on Keystone City.

***Salvation Run* #4 (Apr. 2008)** When Gorilla Grodd is trapped on a prison planet with other super-villains, violence soon ensues as he brutally kills fellow gorilla Monsieur Mallah and the Brain.

GOTHAM ACADEMY

DEBUT *Gotham Academy* #1 **(Dec. 2014)**
BASE Gotham City
FACULTY **Headmaster Hammer:** Principal; **Professor MacPherson:** History; **Mr. Scarlett:** Librarian; **Professor Milo:** Chemistry; **Coach Humphreys:** Athletics; **Mr. Trent:** Drama; **Professor Hugo Strange:** Guidance Counselor; **Ms. Harriet:** Administrator
STUDENTS **Mia "Maps" Mizoguchi; Olive Silverlock; Kyle Mizoguchi; Pomeline Fritch; Colton Rivera; Heathcliff; Tristan Grey:** Exchange student; **Damian Wayne.**
ALLIES Batman
ENEMIES Clayface

Gotham Academy is a very old and exclusive private school with a sinister reputation. Bruce Wayne is its patron, providing funding as well as Wayne Foundation scholarships.

Freshman student Mia "Maps" Mizoguchi was thrilled to receive one of these scholarships. Having arrived at the Academy, she set about exploring its mysteries, dragging fellow student Olive Silverlock into her schemes. The pair had to be saved by Batman after falling from the school's ruined clock tower, and then explored the derelict North Hall, rumored to be haunted by the ghost of a former student, Millie Jane Cobblepot. Instead they found Killer Croc, who had escaped from Arkham Asylum through a system of tunnels leading to the school.

Mia and Olive, along with Mia's brother Kyle and fellow students Colton and Pomeline, formed a "Detective Club" to investigate other bizarre goings-on at the Academy. They discovered that the gym teacher was actually a werewolf, and foiled Clayface's attempt to ruin the school's performance of *Macbeth*. The group's most heartbreaking discovery was that Olive's mother Sybil had once been the villainess Calamity, who had been imprisoned in Arkham Asylum. **SW**

SCHOOL SLEUTHS
New pupil Mia Mizoguchi was determined to investigate Gotham Academy's mysteries, and recruited a motley gang to aid her investigations.
1 Pomeline Fritch 2 Colton Rivera
3 Kyle Mizoguchi 4 Olive Silverlock
5 Mia "Maps" Mizoguchi

GRAVEDIGGER

DEBUT *Men of War* **(Vol. 1) #1 (Aug. 1977)**
CURRENT VERSION *Men of War* **(Vol. 4) #4 (Feb. 2012)**
REAL NAME Ulysses Hazard
EYES Brown **HAIR** Bald
HEIGHT 6ft 2in **WEIGHT** 210 lbs
POWERS/ABILITIES Exceptional physical strength and endurance; skilled in multiple martial arts and the use of all weapons.
ENEMIES The Axis

Growing up in the American South in the early 20th century, Ulysses Hazard was a born fighter, battling both polio and racial prejudice. When the United States entered World War II, Hazard enlisted, but despite his evident skill and determination, he was assigned latrine and grave-digging duties because of his skin color. After proving his worth by single-handedly storming the Pentagon, he was used as a one-man strike force, gaining a cross-shaped facial scar and becoming a legend as Gravedigger. He survived the war, retiring a Colonel. Later, Tyson Sykes of Checkmate took the Gravedigger name.

Post-Flashpoint, Sgt. Joe Rock encountered an undead soldier calling himself Gravedigger and claiming to have fought in the American Civil War. His connection to Hazard is unknown. **SW**

GRACE

DEBUT *Outsiders* **(Vol. 3) #1 (Aug. 2003)**
REAL NAME Grace Choi
EYES Brown **HAIR** Red
HEIGHT 7ft **WEIGHT** 203 lbs
POWERS/ABILITIES Bana-Mighdall Amazon ancestry gives her superhuman strength, speed, and toughness, plus rapid healing ability.
ENEMIES Sabbac, Simon Hurt

As a child, Grace Choi ran away from a foster home, only to be captured by a child-slavery ring, and suffered terrible abuse for three years. When she was almost 12, her latent superpowers activated, and she used her newfound strength to free herself and the other kids. Grace eventually found work as a bouncer at metahuman nightclub Chaney's, where she was approached by Arsenal and recruited into the Outsiders. Though her brash and abrasive attitude caused some friction, she eventually settled into her role as the team's bruiser. She helped to disrupt the child-slavery ring that had abused her, and discovered that she was descended from the Bana-Mighdall Amazons.

When Batman took over the Outsiders, Grace invited her lover, Thunder, to tag along, but she quit when Thunder was rendered comatose by a booby trap. She later joined Black Lightning's Outsiders team, but it soon disbanded. **SW**

GRANNY GOODNESS

DEBUT *Mister Miracle* (Vol. 1) #2 **(May–Jun. 1971)**
CURRENT VERSION *Infinity Man and the Forever People* #8 **(May 2015)**
BASE Apokolips
HEIGHT 5ft 10in **WEIGHT** 256 lbs
EYES Blue **HAIR** White
POWERS/ABILITIES As a New God, Granny has superior strength, agility, stamina, and mental capabilities.
ENEMIES Mister Miracle, Big Barda
AFFILIATIONS Darkseid's Elite

Born and raised on Apokolips, the woman named Goodness was, like all denizens of that hellish world, taught that cruelty was a way of life, and that serving Darkseid, the planet's evil overlord, was all that mattered. As one of the "Lowlies"—Apokolips' oppressed peasant class—she was removed from her parents to train as one of Darkseid's elite warriors, the "Hounds." As part of her military indoctrination and to prove her absolute obedience, Darkseid forced Goodness to kill her beloved dog, Mercy, which earned the dark lord's admiration and her place as one of his Hounds.

In time, Goodness became commander of the elite Female Furies and mistress of Apokolips' orphanages. Taking the bitterly ironic title of Granny Goodness, she systematically crushed the spirits of her charges, turning them into obedient servants of Darkseid. However, the young man she dubbed "Scott Free" refused to be broken. He escaped to Earth, where he became the hero Mister Miracle—and to make matters worse, Big Barda, Granny Goodness's favorite Fury, left Apokolips to be with him.

Granny Goodness also caused utter chaos on Earth when she imprisoned the Olympian Gods, which triggered a war between the Amazons and the United States, with Granny posing as Athena to recruit human heroines to train as her new Furies. The plan ultimately failed. Later she was among the many victims of the Infinity-Man when he began killing the New Gods, but her spirit possessed the Alpha Lantern Kraken. In this form, she tried to take over the Green Lantern homeworld, Oa, but was captured by Hal Jordan. **SW**

GRAYVEN

DEBUT *Green Lantern* (Vol. 3) #71 (Feb. 1996)
REAL NAME Grayven
EYES Red **HAIR** Gray
HEIGHT 7ft 3in **WEIGHT** 665 lbs
POWERS/ABILITIES New God-level strength and endurance; can fire powerful energy blasts from his eyes.
ALLIES Brainiac 13
ENEMIES Green Lantern (Kyle Rayner), Darkstars, Superman, Imperiex

An illegitimate son of Darkseid, Grayven tried to prove he was a worthy successor to his sire by gathering a mighty fleet and cutting a destructive swath across the galaxy toward Apokolips. His advance was finally halted on the planet Rann, where he was defeated by Green Lantern (Kyle Rayner). Grayven was later banished for a time by Darkseid after plotting against his father with Brainiac 13.

Subsequently, when a mysterious figure began eliminating New Gods, Grayven built a Zeta-Beam to transport the killer to his father's throne room to fight Darkseid. However, the Martian Manhunter, disguised as harbinger of death, the Black Racer, told Grayven that he was not Darkseid's son. An unhinged Grayven teleported to Apokolips to seize the throne anyway, and was slain by the killer, revealed as Infinity-Man. **SW**

GREAT TEN, THE

DEBUT *52* #6 (Jun. 2006)
CURRENT VERSION *Batman/Superman* #32 (Jul. 2016)
BASE Great Wall Complex, China
MEMBERS/POWERS **Accomplished Perfect Physician** (Yao Fei): Heals or causes great damage with his voice; **August General in Iron** (Fang Zhifu): Armored skin, energy staff; **Celestial Archer** (Xu Tao): Fires energy arrows; **Ghost Fox Killer**: Death touch, controls ghosts of men she kills; **Immortal Man-in-Darkness** (Chen Nuo): Pilots advanced Dragonwing aircraft, built using Durlan technology; **Mother of Champions** (Wu Mei-Xing): Gives birth to 25 super-soldiers every three days; **Seven Deadly Brothers** (Yang Kei-Ying): Kung-fu master, splits into seven clones; **Shaolin Robot**: Ancient robot built for first emperor of China; **Socialist Red Guardsman** (Gu Lao): Radioactive; **Thundermind** (Zou Kang): Accesses the powers of the Buddhist Sidhis.

The Great Ten were created as a metahuman force to protect the People's Republic of China. The team assembled China's best heroes under Sun Tzu-quoting leader August General in Iron, and needed bureaucratic approval before going into battle.

They were first seen in action when Green Lanterns John Stewart and Hal Jordan entered Chinese airspace to capture Evil Star. Some time later, former Chinese ally Black Adam committed a massacre in Bialya and began a rampage across the world. The Great Ten attacked him when he entered China, but the villain quickly killed Immortal Man-in-Darkness and wrecked Shaolin Robot. Communications with Beijing were lost, so August General in Iron took the initiative and requested outside help to defeat Black Adam. A host of heroes from around the world descended on the villain, and Captain Marvel removed the villain's powers, ending his threat.

Following the war with Black Adam, the Great Ten focused their efforts on protecting China, intervening when Checkmate and the Outsiders attacked Chang Tzu's secret lab on Oolong Island. **SW**

PATRIOTIC POWER
The Great Ten are a formidable team, ready to lay down their lives in the service of China. 1 Socialist Red Guardsman; 2 Mother of Champions; 3 Celestial Archer; 4 Thundermind; 5 Seven Deadly Brothers; 6 Shaolin Robot; 7 Accomplished Perfect Physician; 8 Ghost Fox Killer; 9 August General in Iron

GRIFTER

DEBUT *WildC.A.T.s* (Vol. 1) #1 (Aug. 1992)
CURRENT VERSION *Grifter* #1 (Nov. 2011)
REAL NAME Cole Cash
BASE New Orleans, Louisiana
EYES Blue **HAIR** Blond
HEIGHT 6ft 3in **WEIGHT** 195 lbs
POWERS/ABILITIES Telekinesis; telepathy; can detect Daemonites; special forces veteran.
ENEMIES Daemonites, Helspont, Synge

Cole Cash, codename Grifter, was a member of the elite special ops unit Team 7, but left to make a living as a conman in New Orleans. After pulling off a particularly lucrative scam, he was kidnapped off the street by Daemonites, a spectral race of telepathic aliens intent on possessing human bodies and infiltrating society.

A Daemonite attempted to use Cole as a host, but he awoke and broke free before the transfer could be completed. He discovered that the disrupted process had given him psychic powers, as well as the ability to sense nearby Daemonites. On a plane out of town he fought and killed a Daemonite-possessed passenger, and found himself pursued by both the police and the aliens. Concealing his face with a red bandana, he began a one-man war against the invaders. **SW**

THE GUARDIAN

DEBUT *Star-Spangled Comics* #7 (Apr. 1942)
CURRENT VERSION *Superboy* (Vol. 6) #30 (Jun. 2014)
REAL NAME Michael (last name unknown)
BASE S.T.A.R. Labs Advanced Ideas Division, New York
EYES Brown **HAIR** Black
POWERS/ABILITIES Military training; equipped with a combination hoverboard/shield for protection and transport.
ALLIES Superboy
ENEMIES Parasite, Hammersmith, Leash, Rose Wilson, N.O.W.H.E.R.E.
AFFILIATIONS S.T.A.R. Labs

The man known only as "Michael" served in the United States Air Force before taking a job managing security for S.T.A.R. Labs' Advanced Ideas Division. There he was assigned the codename Guardian and provided with a blue-and-gold armored suit.

When a time-lost Superboy (Jon Lane Kent) ended up in New York, the Guardian took him back to Advanced Ideas Division for medical attention. The young hero saved the Guardian when the monstrous Parasite broke out of containment and wreaked havoc in the building.

The Guardian also took part in a mission to rescue Kon, a clone of Superboy, from a N.O.W.H.E.R.E. facility in Alaska. Kon merged with Jon, and the pair used their combined powers to temporarily boost the Guardian's strength. However, when they were attacked by a mob of hostile alternate-world Superboys, the Guardian was badly beaten. Ultimately, Jon and Kon managed to defeat their doppelgangers, send them back to their home realities, and get the Guardian to safety. **SW**

ON THE RECORD

The original Guardian was a police officer who took on the identity of the Guardian to fight crime in Suicide Slum, with the help of street kids the Newsboy Legion. Members of the Newsboy Legion grew up to work for genetics company Project Cadmus, and used Jim Harper's perfect DNA to clone a Guardian to work as chief of security. When the clones died, fled, or expired, more were created—and so Jim Harper's legacy continued.

FIGHTING THE GOOD FIGHT
During his career as the Guardian, Jim Harper battled a variety of foes, from Darkseid's fanatical Female Furies to Nazi agents!

GREEN ARROW

DATA

DEBUT *More Fun Comics* #73 **(Nov. 1941)**
CURRENT VERSION *Green Arrow* (Vol. 5) #1 **(Nov. 2011)**
REAL NAME Oliver Queen
BASE Seattle
HEIGHT 5ft 10in **WEIGHT** 176 lbs
EYES Green **HAIR** Blond
POWERS/ABILITIES Expert archer and highly trained martial artist. Excellent hunting skills.
ALLIES John Diggle, Emiko
ENEMIES Count Vertigo, Killer Moth, Red Dart, Richard Dragon, the Outsiders
AFFILIATIONS The Arrow Clan, Justice League of America, Justice League United

Oliver Queen is the Green Arrow, a hero who uses his skills as an expert archer to bring justice to the streets of Seattle. Son of billionaire industrialist Robert Queen, Oliver wasted his younger years as a playboy before a terrorist attack left him stranded on an island where he was forced to use his skills to survive. After three years, he returned home a changed man, determined to be something new, something better. Facing assassins and superpowered villains while dealing with secrets from his own family's past, the Green Arrow is determined to bring justice to the streets of his city, one arrow at a time.

AT A GLANCE...

Stranded
Oliver Queen rejected his father's attempts to make him take his heritage seriously and seemed destined to waste his life drifting from party to party. This changed dramatically when a terrorist explosion at his party on a Pacific oil rig killed everyone except Oliver and Tommy Merlyn. Stranded on a desert island, Oliver was forced to master the skills he'd once spurned, becoming an expert hunter and archer to survive.

Dangerous business
After returning to Seattle, Oliver used his role as head of Q-Core and the talents of his new ally, Jax, to create advanced armor and weaponry—including a number of special arrows, such as a grappling hook, electro, and anti-missile arrows. Oliver was also helped by ex-special forces soldier John Diggle and tech expert Naomi Singh.

Family secrets
After discovering his links to the Arrow Clan and meeting his half-sister, Emiko, Oliver returned to Seattle to continue his crusade against injustice, while also becoming Emiko's guardian. Both had trouble adjusting to their new roles but quickly developed a strong bond.

Oliver Queen was the heir to the Queen family fortune. He had everything, but seemed to turn his back on his birthright. His father, Robert Queen, owner of Queen Industries, tried and failed to instill some sense of commitment in his son—whether by creating positions for him in Queen Industries or by providing archery lessons—but Oliver preferred to party. He was eventually given a clerical job on an oil platform, but instead of working, Oliver threw a lavish party on the rig. When terrorists attacked, Oliver's guests were tied up and explosives planted around them. Oliver arrogantly thought he could save everyone, and shot the detonator out of the terrorist leader's hand, only for it to hit the side of the rig and set off the bombs. Only Oliver and his best friend, Tommy Merlyn, survived. Oliver was washed up on a desert island and, with the world thinking he was dead, was forced to use his skills to survive. By the time he left the island, Oliver was an expert archer and a changed man.

PARTY GUY
The young Oliver Queen would often show off his archery skills while drunk at parties. When he arranged a party on an oil rig, it changed his life forever.

On his return to Seattle, Oliver learned that his father had died and his close friend Walter Emerson had been placed in charge of Queen Industries. Oliver was given the subsidiary Q-Core to run, and soon began covertly using its resources, along with his own wealth, to fuel his vigilante activities. In time, two employees—Naomi Singh and Jax—joined him, respectively providing tech and weapons support.

Oliver briefly fought alongside the Justice League, but was refused membership. He later joined rival team the Justice League of America. However, his crime-fighting caused problems in his personal life, with Emerson believing Oliver was wasting his time partying again. When Emerson confronted Oliver, he was about to reveal a secret about Oliver's past when he was assassinated by Komodo (who was later revealed to be Simon Lacroix, Robert Queen's ex-protégé). Oliver was framed for Emerson's murder and forced to go on the run.

Thanks to a blind sensei called Magus, Oliver learned that his father had been obsessed with the legend of a Green Arrow —a fabled totem. Whoever possessed it would become leader of the clandestine Arrow Clan,

CLASSIC STORIES

***Green Lantern* (Vol. 2) #85 (Aug.-Sept. 1971)** When Green Arrow learns his sidekick, Roy Harper, has gone down a dark path and become a drug addict, Green Arrow and Green Lantern try to help him and find the dealer responsible.

***Green Arrow: The Longbow Hunters* #1-3 (Aug.-Oct. 1987)** Oliver Queen and Dinah Lance (Black Canary) grow closer as he moves from Star City to her home of Seattle, but when he crosses paths with the assassin called Shado, and Black Canary is viciously attacked, Oliver's life changes forever.

***Green Arrow* #17-24 (Feb.-Sep. 2013)** Oliver Queen is attacked by a deadly new foe—the assassin Komodo—and learns shocking secrets about his past. Oliver's life and his adventures as the Green Arrow take a new direction, with some close to Oliver paying the ultimate price.

THE MIDAS TOUCH
Blood Rose, a spurned lover of Oliver Queen, sought revenge on the millionaire, helped by her lover, Midas. Midas had once been a scientist working on a bacterial method of cleaning toxic waste, but became a monster after getting caught in an explosion caused by ecoterrorists. Green Arrow barely survived their first encounter, Blood Rose nearly killing him.

Oliver's allies performed scans that revealed Blood Rose was actually a robot. Blood Rose and Midas were seemingly destroyed in an explosion during their final confrontation with Green Arrow. However, the pair survived, Midas starting to rebuild Blood Rose as they traveled to Metropolis.

TOXIC TROUBLE
The monstrous Midas—whose touch could kill—and his robotic lover, Blood Rose, tried to take down Green Arrow.

REBIRTH

OPPOSITES ATTRACT

When social activist and spoiled rich kid Oliver Queen meets hard-headed realist Dinah Lance, their beliefs affect the way they crush crime. If they want justice for the innocent and downtrodden, why are they fighting each other rather than the slavers harvesting Seattle's homeless? Also, who has corrupted Queen Industries from within? And how did they turn Oliver's sister Emi and her mother Shado into assassins hungry for Green Arrow's blood?

SHADO
Oliver encountered the deadly assassin Shado, his father's old lover and the mother of Emiko, his half-sister.

one of several clans linked to ancient weaponry. Emerson and Robert had arranged for Oliver to be stranded on the island, hoping it would toughen him up for what lay ahead—conflict with a secret group called the Outsiders.

While searching for the arrow, Oliver discovered that his father was still alive and had once had an affair with the assassin Shado, with whom he had a daughter, Emiko. Komodo, in league with the Outsiders, had kidnapped Emiko and raised the child as his own daughter, telling her Shado was dead and Oliver Queen was her enemy. When Komodo and the Outsiders embarked on a mission of mass destruction, Oliver, Robert, and Shado, who had joined forces with them, intervened. Along the way Emiko learned the truth about her parentage and that Komodo had lied to her. Robert died saving Emiko's life and in revenge she killed Komodo. For his part, rather than assume his role as leader of the Arrow Clan, Oliver returned to Seattle to continue his war on crime. **AC**

ON THE RECORD

Green Arrow has undergone many changes since his first appearance in 1941. On his debut, Green Arrow, aka Oliver Queen, was part of a crime-fighting duo with teen sidekick Speedy (Roy Harper). He not only used trick arrows to combat criminals, but also drove an arrow-shaped car and operated from the Arrow Cave. His physical appearance was more like the traditional Hollywood image of Robin Hood.

Road trip

In the late 1960s, Oliver Queen lost his fortune but gained newfound empathy for the common man and shifted left in his political views. He teamed up with the second Green Lantern (Hal Jordan) to see what was really happening in America. The two went on a road trip across the USA, helping the less fortunate along the way. Oliver also tried to help Roy Harper overcome his drug addiction.

Hunters

While the Crisis on Infinite Earths left Oliver's past relatively unchanged, he began to feel disconnected from his life as a hero, and went back to basics. After spending several years in Seattle with Black Canary, he separated from his longtime lover and later had a chance reunion with his adult son, Connor Hawke.

Back from the dead

Oliver Queen eventually gave his life saving people from a terrorist bomb blast. When his friend Hal Jordan became the villain Parallax, he used his cosmic abilities to return Oliver from the dead. The resurrected Oliver then had to reclaim his soul, with the help of his friends. He made a fresh start with a new Speedy, the ex-drug addict Mia Dearden. Oliver later became mayor of Star City, marrying his old flame, Black Canary.

ANOTHER LIFE
After a long and often troubled relationship, Green Arrow proposed to Black Canary. The two were later married.

SHARP SHOOTER
While lacking in superpowers, the Green Arrow's skills as an archer make him a deadly hero, intent on bringing justice to the crime-ridden streets of Seattle.

"My name is Oliver Queen... the Green Arrow. And I'm just getting started."

OLIVER QUEEN

GREEN LANTERN

DATA

DEBUT *Showcase* (Vol. 1) #22 **(Oct. 1959)**
CURRENT VERSION *Justice League* (Vol. 2) #1 **(Oct. 2011)**
REAL NAME Harold "Hal" Jordan
BASE Coast City, California
HEIGHT 6ft 2in **WEIGHT** 200 lbs
EYES Brown **HAIR** Brown
POWERS/ABILITIES Indomitable willpower commanding a power ring that is able to materialize hard-light constructs, translate languages, facilitate in-planet and intergalactic flight, and protect against hostile environments and enemy attack.
ALLIES Flash (Barry Allen), John Stewart
ENEMIES Sinestro, Black Hand
AFFILIATIONS Green Lantern Corps, Justice League

Hal Jordan was Earth's first Green Lantern. Valiant, honest, and able to conquer great fear, he battled threats alien and terrestrial, implementing unyielding willpower through a ring able to create constructs of anything he could imagine. Part of a 72,000-strong intergalactic police force, he patrolled space sector 2814, tasked with protecting all life, yet found it increasingly difficult to blindly follow the directives of his Oan masters, the Guardians of the Universe. While colleagues ignored their own misgivings, Hal continually spoke out, even as his triumphant exploits won him a reputation as the foremost Green Lantern in history.

AT A GLANCE...

High flyer
After witnessing his father's death, Hal grew up a troubled, attention-seeking risk taker. On his 18th birthday he enlisted in the Air Force, resolved to be a hotshot pilot like his dad, but his bad attitude ended that dream too.

Battle of wills
Hal's apparently infinite power and antipathy to authority made him dangerously reckless and overconfident. When Apokolips invaded Earth, Hal trampled over Batman's jurisdiction, deriding his merely human capabilities. This earned him the Dark Knight's eternal distrust and disdain.

Fear my power
The Green Lanterns' power rings operate on intense concentration, allowing users to shape green light into solid objects. The rings can perform any task imaginable, fueled by the green energy of willpower generated by all lifeforms.

Love conquers all
Hal's unattainable off-and-on girlfriend Carol Ferris was beguiled into joining the rival Star Sapphire Corps: warrior women whose rings are powered by the violet light of love.

CLASSIC STORIES

***Green Lantern* Vol. 2 #40 (Oct. 1965)** The origin of the Guardians of the Universe and the introduction of obsessed Oan researcher Krona lay the groundwork for decades of cosmic storylines.

***Green Lantern* Vol. 2 #76 (Apr. 1970)** Green Lantern accepts reduced duties and powers in order to investigate the nature of good and evil, with social reformer Green Arrow as his guide.

***Green Lantern* Vol. 4 #25 (Jan. 2008)** The Sinestro Corps War climaxes with the renegade Green Lantern's utter defeat, heralding a cataclysmic War of Light and a universal uprising of the corrupted dead.

Young Hal lost all sense of fear after watching his dad, a pilot, die in a plane crash. Years later, while stubbornly following in his father's footsteps, he was abducted by a dying alien, Abin Sur. Sur wanted Hal to replace him in the Green Lantern Corps, an intergalactic police force that had safeguarded the universe for billions of years.

Hal accepted and was summoned for basic training to the Corps headquarters on the planet Oa. On completion, he was assigned to Thaal Sinestro of Korugar, who was considered the "Greatest Green Lantern" for his unparalleled ability to keep order in his space sector. Sinestro befriended the idealistic, hot-headed human, mentoring his transition from rookie to fully qualified officer, but their relationship soured when Hal discovered why Sector 1417 was so peaceful. Sinestro had conquered the sector and was governing it as an absolute dictator.

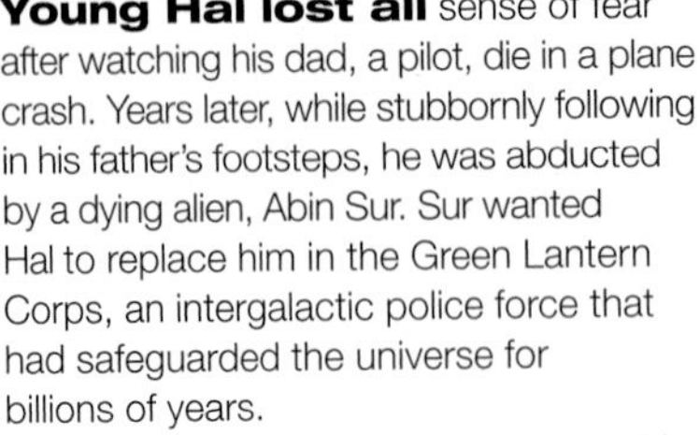

FEAR NO EVIL
Kicked out of the Air Force, shunned by his family, and about to lose his menial mechanic's job, Hal was summoned to dying Abin Sur's side and offered the universe on a plate.

Following a tremendous struggle, Hal liberated Korugar. The Guardians banished Sinestro to the anti-matter universe, where the renegade worked with the Weaponers of Qward to develop yellow power rings. Armed with these, Sinestro eventually formed his own Corps to terrorize the positive-matter universe.

For years Jordan excelled, defeating innumerable menaces, but invariably at great cost to his private life. Personal and romantic relationships foundered and he started to seriously question his masters' edicts, resulting in him taking numerous leaves of absence, which he spent roaming the United States in search of personal fulfillment and renewed perspective.

The call of duty and the stars brought Hal back to the Corps, but when Coast City was destroyed, he snapped. Grief led to possession by the yellow-hued fear parasite Parallax, who induced Jordan to eradicate the Corps and restore Coast City by reordering time. Only the dogged resistance of Earth's heroes prevented multiversal armageddon.

MASTER AND SERVANT
Inexplicably restored to Green Lantern status over his own strenuous objections, the former fugitive Sinestro sought to make amends by removing the remnants of his Sinestro Corps from Korugar. To keep the project secret from the Guardians, he compelled Hal to assist him, armed with a lesser power ring created by his own green energies. When his homeworld was freed, he gloatingly returned Hal to Earth, with no way to recharge the illicit ring.

RINGING ENDORSEMENT
Though he never missed an opportunity to belittle his former rookie's capabilities, Sinestro knew that no ring wielder of any color on the Emotional Scale could match Hal Jordan.

"Beware my Power... Green Lantern's Light."

HAL JORDAN

His plan thwarted, Hal slowly regained his sanity, sacrificing his life to reignite the Earth's sun after a cosmic force had consumed it. A time of penance followed, with Hal's soul becoming the moderating conscience of the Spectre, before he was redeemed, purged of Parallax, and resurrected, enabling him to join a renewed Green Lantern Corps.

The need for his skills and leadership in the Corps was never greater. The universe was in turmoil with the Guardians embroiled in a War of Light, a monumental struggle against the risen dead of Nekron's Black Lantern Corps and attacks from the rogue Oan, Krona. During the battle, Hal killed Krona, and was summarily expelled and exiled to Earth. Soon after, Sinestro—forced against his will to rejoin the Green Lanterns—offered Hal an unsanctioned power ring in return for his assistance on secret tasks. That unhappy alliance saw Hal transcend life itself: confronting Nekron as a Black Lantern and battling apocalyptic First Lantern Volthoom and Sinestro himself (who showed his true colors by murdering the Guardians). In the aftermath, Hal Jordan reorganized the Corps and became its first commander: hailed the Greatest Green Lantern of All. **WW**

REBIRTH

GREEN LANTERN CORPS
With the Guardians of the Universe disgraced and the Green Lantern Corps seemingly disappeared, veteran Emerald Gladiator Hal Jordan must recruit and run a rookie Corps. The team comprises fallible, fragile mortals struggling to hold the tide against the new universal order brutally imposed by the Sinestro Corps.

Armed with unswerving determination and a unique new power ring he has constructed, Hal sets out on a mission make his universe a safer place. Sinestro, however, has other ideas, having set his sights on annihilating his longtime nemesis.

GREEN FOR FREEDOM
When the Guardians sought to eradicate free will and replace the Green Lanterns with a Third Army, Hal Jordan and Sinestro's power ring searched out criminal Simon Baz. The ring warned Baz to stay away from Oa, but the Third Army soon came hunting for him.

ON THE RECORD

On first joining the cosmos-spanning Green Lantern Corps, Hal Jordan was a loyal, obedient servant, doing whatever the Guardians dictated without question or quibble. However, as the years passed, he increasingly began to feel their edicts were far from omniscient.

Mosaic World
An early sign of the Guardians' fallibility came when Appa Ali Apsa went mad. Abducting communities from worlds he had visited, the "Old Timer" transplanted them to a distant planet, pitting the terrified townships against each other in bizarre social experiments. It took the united will of Hal and fellow Earthian Green Lanterns John Stewart and Guy Gardner to stop him. The combined efforts of the Green Lantern Corps and Justice League were then able to restore the victims to their proper places in the universe.

Emerald Twilight
After years of faithful service, Hal rebelled against the Guardians when they refused to let him change history and restore Coast City after Mongol destroyed it. Unbeknownst to anyone, Jordan was infected by the fear parasite Parallax, which had been imprisoned for eons in the Central Power Battery on Oa. It drove Hal to attack hundreds of his comrades, stealing their power rings as he stormed across the universe to a titanic confrontation with the Guardians' last hope—a freed and restored Sinestro.

Even the arch-renegade could not stop Hal from destroying the Battery and ending billions of years of Green Lantern-enforced peace and order. However, when the Earth's sun was destroyed, Hal expended all his energy to revive the dying star and save the planet.

REDEMPTION
After eradicating the Green Lantern Corps, the deranged, Parallax-possessed Hal Jordan became a despised pariah. It took the threat of Earth's extermination to bring him to his senses.

TO SERVE AND PROTECT THE UNIVERSE
Years of confronting evil and saving billions of lives have taught Hal that Power and Will are worthless without empathy and a sense of purpose.

GREEN LANTERN CORPS

DATA

DEBUT *Green Lantern* (Vol. 2) #9 **(Nov.-Dec. 1961)**
CURRENT VERSION *Green Lantern Corps* (Vol. 3) #1 **(Nov. 2011)**
BASE Oa, Mogo
NOTABLE MEMBERS/POWERS 72,000 active agents plus ancillaries, drawn from across the multiverse; use willpower to operate power rings able to materialize hard-light constructs.
HAL JORDAN (Corps Leader); **MOGO** (Living planet and base); **GUY GARDNER** (Seconded to Red and later Blue Lantern Corps); **KILOWOG** (Protocol Officer); **SORANIK NATU** (Medical Officer) **VOZ** (Sciencell Warden); **JOHN STEWART**; **KYLE RAYNER**; **ABIN SUR**; **SIMON BAZ**; **JESSICA CRUZ**; **TWO-SIX**; **SALAAK**; **LOK NEBOORA**; **GORIN-SUNN**; **ARISIA RRAB**; **SODAM YAT**
ALLIES New Gods, Red Lantern Corps, Blue Lantern Corps
ENEMIES Manhunters, Nekron, Sinestro Corps, Qwardians, Relic, Volthoom, Larfleeze, Black Hand, Third Army, Superboy-Prime
AFFILIATIONS Darkstars, Zamarons, Indigo Tribe, Star Sapphire Corps, Justice League

The Green Lantern Corps is a peacekeeping force created over three billion years ago by the self-appointed Guardians of the Universe. The immortals sought to maintain order and foster the rise of civilization amongst lesser beings throughout the cosmos. Methodically dividing all of space into 3,600 sectors, they personally selected the organization's peace-keeping officers from all over creation. Over eons the Guardians developed automated systems and now the power rings all Green Lanterns employ automatically seek out honest beings capable of overcoming great fear whenever a wielder dies in the line of duty.

AT A GLANCE...

Central Power Battery
The colossal, lantern-like engine on Oa condenses the willpower of all sentient life in the universe and redistributes it as green light to each Green Lantern officer's personal power battery. The finite energy-charge in each officer's ring is replenished by touching it to their personal battery long enough for them to utter the sacred oath.
In Brightest Day, In Blackest Night;
No evil shall escape my sight.
Let those who worship evil's might,
Beware my power... Green Lantern's light!

FULL MENTAL JACKET
Courage, good intentions and the mightiest personal weapon in the universe are not enough. The Corps' physically and mentally punishing basic training teaches recruits to fight under extreme pressure against multiple foes and that clear thinking will always win the day.

Enhanced security
After three billion years, the Guardians abruptly altered how their Green Lanterns operated. Without disclosing that they now considered lone agents untrustworthy, the Oans doubled the ranks, with officers native to each sector patrolling in pairs. This caused friction as the traditionally independent Lanterns often could not collaborate or cooperate.

CLASSIC STORIES

***Tales of the Green Lantern Corps* (Vol. 1) #1-3 (May-July 1981)** The entire Corps is mustered when Krona attempts to return the universe to its primal state, allowing death-personification Nekron access to the realm of the living.

***Tales of the Green Lantern Corps Annual* (Vol. 1) #2 (1986)** The Guardians' fallibility is exposed in "Tygers" when Abin Sur visits proscribed planetary prison Ysmault and is infected with fear by the prophecies of the Five Inversions.

***Green Lantern Corps* (Vol. 2) #20-26 (March-Sept 2008)** A contingent of Green Lanterns dispatched on a "Ring Quest" to confiscate deadly yellow power rings clashes with cosmic terrorist Mongul who has revived the Sinestro Corps under his own leadership.

From the earliest eons of existence, the immortals of Oa sought to impose order on universal chaos which they saw manifested as acts of evil perpetrated by deviant or antisocial beings.

Their first solution was a vast army of robotic Manhunters who policed a scrupulously demarcated cosmos; reacting to crises, suppressing violence and preventing disorder from spreading.

When the Manhunters malfunctioned, exterminating all but five organisms in Sector 666, the appalled Guardians of the Universe sealed the entire region, suppressed all knowledge of the event, and mothballed their mechanical agents. Some of the mechanoids, however, refused to abort their programmed mission, vanishing into the dark corners of the universe to plot revenge.

The Guardians replaced their artificial intermediaries with sentient beings recruited from the 3,600 sectors into which they had divided the universe: individuals capable of swift assessment and certain judgment. They would also be fearless, honest, and dedicated to preserving life, maintaining order, and furthering progress.

Originally, one Green Lantern was stationed per sector, operating with complete autonomy within their territory. However, following a series of cataclysmic universal conflicts long-anticipated by the Guardians— prophesied as the War of Light and Darkest Night—the Oans rewrote their sacred code of conduct.

The most important change was the removal of an ancient prohibition against taking life, but they also doubled the number of Green Lanterns: utilizing teams of two per sector operating from a deep-space precinct house. The Guardians, obviously unsettled by unfolding events, also created cyborg Alpha Lanterns to enforce their edicts and formally police the actions of their regulation agents.

INFERNAL AFFAIRS
Designed to ensure wilful individuals toed the Guardians' line, the Alpha Lanterns found it hard to break the bonds of camaraderie when ordered to destroy the Green Lantern Corps.

FEARSOME
For millennia the Guardians used Urak to store power batteries, and the energies made the resource-poor world flourish. When they changed policy and withdrew them, Urak's ecology crashed. Now, with an uncanny capacity to overwhelm willpower, the Keepers erupt upon the universe, slaughtering at will and especially targeting Green Lanterns. When John Stewart's squad are overcome he has to kill one of his team to preserve Oa's security and Guy Gardner's only viable rescue plan involved resurrecting the Mean Machine—the meanest, most ornery officers in the Corps.

WILLPOWER WIPEOUT
The Keepers wanted other worlds' resources to rebuild Urak, but also relished the chance to slaughter the Guardians' 'pets' in the Green Lantern Corps.

OLD HANDS, NEW BLOOD
New recruits ensure continuity of service, learning from Corps veterans. Among the best are:
1 Kilowog
2 Simon Baz
3 Arisia Rrab
4 Gorin-Sunn
5 John Stewart
6 Guy Gardner
7 2-6-8-1-7-9-5 of Numericon. Known as "Two-Six"
8 Salaak
9 Lok Neboora

REBIRTH

GIVEN THE GREEN LIGHT
Simon Baz and Jessica Cruz are the Green Lantern Corps' latest recruits and, despite disliking one another, they have been ordered to work together as Earth's Green Lanterns by their boss, Hal Jordan.

The world doesn't want them and they don't trust each other, but the rookies will have to shape up soon as they investigate an alien killer loose on Earth. And waiting in the wings are Red Lanterns Atrocitus, Dex-Starr, and Bleez, who have targeted Baz and Cruz for eradication as the first step in unleashing a Red Dawn of Rage amongst the humans.

Now organized along more military lines, the Corps administrative offices were based on Oa, which housed the immense Central Power Battery; Sciencells containing the universe's greatest felons and menaces; the Crypt of Fallen Lanterns; and an off-duty bar and hostelry. The Oans eventually betrayed their faithful servants and were destroyed by Sinestro and Relic. Survivors of Green Lantern Corps relocated to Mogo, resolved to rebuild their ranks and reputation under mortal commander Hal Jordan and the newly returned Templar Guardians. **WW**

ON THE RECORD

Originally the Green Lantern Corps were depicted as running their own affairs within their personal interstellar beat, separate from the Guardians and seldom impinging upon each others' jurisdictions.

Emerald Army
During the 1960s the Corps' ranks expanded and were cautiously explored. A huge variety of valiant alien Green Lanterns were introduced, but though many become eagerly anticipated guest-stars, none were quite as effective as Earth's Hal Jordan. He frequently won the day with solutions beyond his peers' comprehension, and even managed to come back from the dead.

Green Lantern Citadel
Following the multiverse-altering Crisis on Infinite Earths, the Corps was relieved of strict assignments to specific sectors, and both the Guardians and the female Oans who had evolved into the Zamarons retired from the universe for a period of reflection and contemplation. Advised that Earth would play a crucial role during the next millennium, several Green Lanterns—Katma Tui, Salakk, Ch'p, Kilowog, and Arisia—relocated to that world with Hal Jordan, John Stewart, and maverick Guy Gardner and were on hand to witness the transformation of so-called "New Guardians."

Sinestro Corps War
The Corps faced their greatest challenge when the renegade Sinestro launched an all-out attack on the cosmos. Although Sinestro was defeated, the Guardians' heavy-handed response to the attack ultimately led to their demise, and a fully independent Green Lantern Corps.

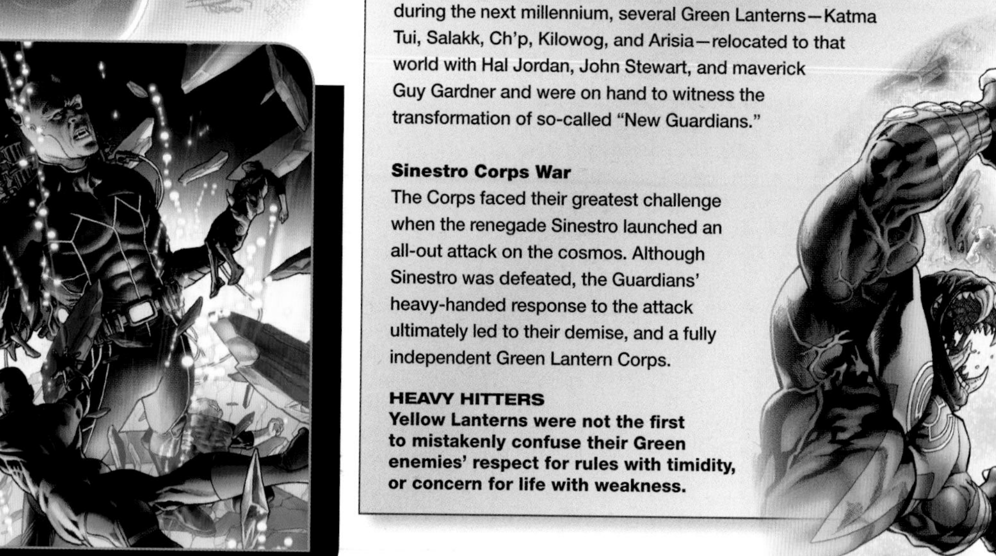

HEAVY HITTERS
Yellow Lanterns were not the first to mistakenly confuse their Green enemies' respect for rules with timidity, or concern for life with weakness.

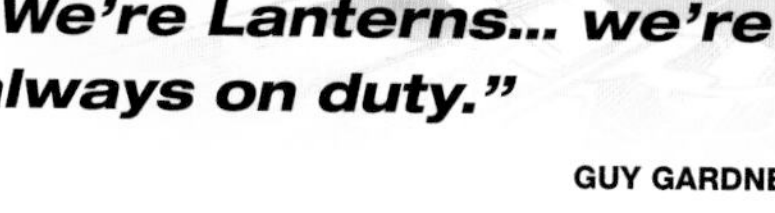

"We're Lanterns... we're always on duty."

GUY GARDNER

LIGHTS OUT
Relic, a survivor from the universe before the Big Bang, claimed the Green Lanterns of his universe—"the Lightsmiths"—were responsible for its destruction. Believing that the Green Lantern Corps posed a similar threat to this universe he decided to take action.

Destroying Oa and the Blue Lantern planet Odym, he embroiled the Corps in a war against the New Gods and sought sole control of the vast reservoir of Spectrum power, forcing the Lanterns to ally with archenemy Black Hand.

THE POWER OF RELIC
Beaten back by Relic's force field, the Corps could not prevent the massive, remorseless being from draining the Central Power Battery and destroying Oa.

GUARDIANS OF THE UNIVERSE

DEBUT *Green Lantern* (Vol. 2) #1 **(Jul.-Aug. 1960)**
CURRENT VERSION *Green Lantern* (Vol. 5) #1 **(Nov. 2011)**
BASE Oa
POWERS/ABILITIES Immortality; supreme intellects; psionic powers including telepathy and telekinesis.
ALLIES Templar Guardians, Manhunters (formerly), Green Lantern Corps (formerly), Third Army
ENEMIES Sinestro, Atrocitus, Weaponers of Qward, Manhunters, Empire of Tears, Parallax, Volthoom, Larfleeze, Spider Guild, the Reach, Mad God of Sector 3600, the Red, Blue, and Green Lantern Corps
AFFILIATIONS Zamarons, Psions, Controllers, Darkstars

Creation's oldest civilization developed on the planet Maltus where some inhabitants evolved into intellectual super-beings: scientist-philosophers with an unquenchable thirst for knowledge. Experiments by one of their number, called Krona, who wanted to discover the very origins of creation, critically damaged the universe, and his comrades resolved to become its Guardians. Relocating to the planet Oa, the Guardians dedicated their mighty brains to eradicating chaos. Eons passed and their bodies atrophied—decreasing in size as their mental powers grew. Ideological schisms developed and factions left to form Controllers and Zamarons, among others.

The Oans tapped the Emotional Electromagnetic Spectrum, concentrating the universal pool of willpower in a Central Battery while suppressing other colors. Green was used to fuel a succession of peacekeeping militias, beginning with robotic Manhunters. These malfunctioned, slaughtering an entire space sector, and were replaced by living recruits—Hallas—who in turn were supplanted by the Green Lantern Corps.

After billions of years struggling against unceasing evil, the Guardians' altruistic atonement soured. They began to impose their own logical thought processes upon unruly life, seeking to obliterate free will through their bio-manufactured Third Army. Ultimately, most of the Guardians were killed by their renegade agent, Sinestro. **WW**

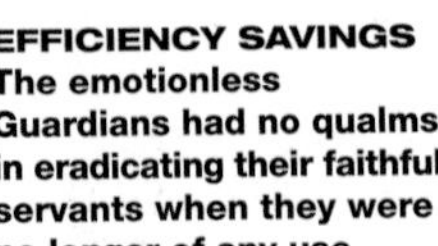

EFFICIENCY SAVINGS
The emotionless Guardians had no qualms in eradicating their faithful servants when they were no longer of any use.

ON THE RECORD

The Guardians began as patriarchal advisers, but over time, their omniscient benevolence was seen as dictatorial manipulation and their seeming solidarity was questioned by many—including one of their own.

During the 1970s, Appa Ali Apsa, also known as the "Old Timer," abandoned emotionless immortality to travel with Hal Jordan and Oliver Queen. A sensitive companion, he strove to understand the lesser creatures in his care, but eventually descended into lethal insanity.

ISOLATED INCIDENT
Appa Ali Apsa's separation from his immortal brethren taught him the value of emotions, but eventually drove him to madness and murder.

BLAST FROM THE PAST
The Oans' plans to eradicate free will were resisted by their distant and still-compassionate cousins of the Templar Guardian Sect.

GUNNER AND SARGE

DEBUT *All-American Men of War* #67 (Mar. 1959)
REAL NAME "Gunner" MacKay, Sarge Clay
POWERS/ABILITIES Fully trained US Marines in peak physical condition; exceptional reactions and marksmanship.
ALLIES Pooch, Captain Storm, Johnny Cloud, Mademoiselle Marie, Haunted Tank crew
ENEMIES Nazi Germany, Japanese Empire
AFFILIATIONS US Marine Corps, the Losers

"Gunner" McKay and his military mentor "Sarge" Clay had a unique tactic for fighting the Japanese on a succession of Pacific Islands during World War II. The young private was an astonishingly fast and accurate shot with any weapon and would hang back or conceal himself while Sarge would deliberately make himself a target for enemy fire. The veteran trusted that his own years of experience would allow him to anticipate or evade the inevitable attack long enough for his infallible comrade to finish off the shooters.

They were assisted by a highly intelligent battle dog named Pooch, who accompanied them when—with Naval Captain Storm and pilot Johnny Cloud—they became part of a Special Operations squad nicknamed "the Losers" because of their bad luck.

The Losers were eventually killed in combat, but Gunner was soon recovered and resurrected as a cyborg-zombie, becoming part of the covert military unit dubbed the Creature Commandos. **WW**

BROTHERS IN ARMS
Before joining the Losers, Gunner and Sarge fought as an effective team in many brutal battles against the Imperial Japanese Army.

GUNFIRE

DEBUT *Deathstroke the Terminator Annual* (Vol. 1) #2 (Oct. 1993)
REAL NAME Andrew Van Horn
BASE New York City
HEIGHT 6ft 1in **WEIGHT** 190 lbs
EYES Green **HAIR** Red
POWERS/ABILITIES Can agitate molecules in matter, causing them to create blasts; wears customized hi-tech armor.
ALLIES Argus, Anima, Ballistic, Geist, Hook
ENEMIES Venev, Ragnarok, Mirror Master

Young businessman Andrew Van Horn's metagene was triggered when, as part of a concerted invasion of Earth, he was attacked and left for dead by a spinal-fluid-consuming alien. In the aftermath, the stunned survivor developed the power to ferociously agitate molecules and redirect them as blasts of concussive force, initially using any object he could hold in his hands.

Equipped with a prototype suit of polymer armor built by his munitions company, Andrew hunted the creature that had "killed" him and thereafter became the globe-trotting Super Hero Gunfire. The same attack that transformed Andrew also killed and mutated his father Gunther, who became his deranged arch-enemy, Ragnarok.

After finally defeating his father, Gunfire attempted to monetize his gifts by joining other metahuman survivors of the alien attack in a corporately funded team called the Blood Pack. Gunfire retired after his hands were cut off by the super-villain Prometheus. **WW**

HAND WEAPON
Gunfire's ability to transform any object's mass into blasts of concussive energy effectively turned anything he held into a firearm.

GYPSY

DEBUT *Justice League of America Annual* (Vol. 1) #2 **(Oct. 1984)**
CURRENT VERSION *Justice League of America's Vibe* (Vol. 1) #1 **(Apr. 2013)**
REAL NAME Cynnthia Mordeth
HEIGHT 5ft 6in **WEIGHT** 110 lbs **EYES** Brown **HAIR** Black
POWERS/ABILITIES Mystically generated illusion casting; light-bending; sound projection and distortion; advanced unarmed combat techniques.
ALLIES Vibe, Breacher
ENEMIES Mistress Mordeth, Amanda Waller, Rupture
AFFILIATIONS Traders of Piradell

GYPSY MAGIC
Vibe's every instinct said to trust the captivating Circus detainee, even though his A.R.G.U.S. bosses said Gypsy was a threat to the entire planet.

Unearthly refugee Cynnthia Mordeth always led a fairytale life. Her trans-dimensional trader father entered into a dynastic marriage with a rival tribe's queen and was reduced to a monstrous man-shaped packet of sentient energy. Her mother also transformed, becoming a planet-ravaging predator. Gypsy fled across myriad dimensions, unaware that she was the key to her mother's invasion plan for other realms.

On Earth, Cynnthia was imprisoned by the US government agency A.R.G.U.S., never realizing it was all part of a bargain between her father and agent Amanda Waller. Cynnthia was caged in the Circus—a clandestine containment facility built to hold metahumans from other universes—and used to trick Cisco "Vibe" Ramon into becoming Waller's inter-dimensional alarm system and watchdog.

When Gypsy escaped, she befriended Cisco and slowly won him over to her cause. Together they traversed several multiversal breaches, eventually arriving on Cynnthia's homeworld Piradell. Here they destroyed the evil Mistress Mordeth after liberating Cisco's older brother Armando from murderous servitude to her.

On returning to Earth, Gypsy helped Vibe renegotiate the terms of his employment with Waller and A.R.G.U.S., before vanishing from public view. **WW**

ON THE RECORD

The original Gypsy was teenager Cindy Reynolds, who fled suburbia when her metahuman abilities abruptly manifested themselves. Living on the streets of Detroit, she survived using her chameleon-camouflage and illusion-casting powers.

Gypsy joined a reconfigured Justice League that included Vibe, Dale Gunn, and the Martian Manhunter. She later became a valued, covert operative of special ps organization Justice League Task Force, and then joined Barbara Gordon's Birds of Prey team.

HIDE AND SEEK
Gypsy's guileful intelligence-gathering and undetectable groundwork usually led to a punishing follow-up from her mighty, but not-so-subtle, associates.

HIGHER PLANES DRIFTER
After years of traversing dimensions and fleeing from every conceivable danger, Gypsy finally realized safety lay in confronting her pursuers.

HARLEY QUINN

DATA

DEBUT *The Batman Adventures* (Vol. 1) #12 **(Sep. 1993)**
CURRENT VERSION *Suicide Squad* (Vol. 4) #1 **(Nov. 2011)**
REAL NAME Harleen Frances Quinzel
BASE Coney Island, Brooklyn, New York
HEIGHT 5ft 7in **WEIGHT** 115 lbs
EYES Blue **HAIR** Red/Black
POWERS/ABILITIES Unpredictable due to insanity; extremely agile and a capable fighter; highly intelligent with a great deal of knowledge in psychiatry; adept at manipulating others; weapons include a giant mallet and a variety of clown-themed items.
ALLIES Poison Ivy, the Joker, Scarecrow, Power Girl
ENEMIES Batman, the Batman Family
AFFILIATIONS Suicide Squad

To say Harley Quinn is a little bit disturbed is putting it mildly. Dangerously psychotic with an ever-changing focus in life, Harley has been a psychiatrist, the Joker's lethal sidekick, a key member of a secret government-sponsored strike force, a Brooklyn landlady, a roller derby champion, a burlesque dancer, a nurse, and even a wannabe Super Hero for a brief time. With little regard for human life, and yet a strict moral code that often sees her fighting for the underdog, Harley Quinn has left a bloody trail of violence and chaos in her wake from Gotham City all the way to the Big Apple.

AT A GLANCE...

Who's that girl?
Much like the Joker, Harley's mental instability has led to a conflicting origin story. Most versions agree that she was a former Arkham Asylum psychiatrist who fell in love with her main subject, the Joker, and quickly dropped everything for a chance to impress him as the villain Harley Quinn.

Boy trouble
Harley tried to play the role of the doting girlfriend to the insane Joker, despite him tossing her into a vat of chemicals. She acted ditzier than usual to attract him, but soon found that the Clown Prince of Crime tired of her, eventually discarding her like yesterday's whoopee cushion.

Wardrobe changes
Harley Quinn has adopted several looks over the years, from the caped costume she sported as a member of the Suicide Squad, to the roller skating costume she would wear when participating in the occasional—and often bloody—sport of roller derby.

CLASSIC STORIES

***The Batman Adventures: Mad Love* #1 (Feb. 1994)** Harley Quinn's obsession with the Clown Prince of Crime is examined in this comic that shines a light on Harley's origin, as well as the couple's abusive relationship.

***Batman: Harley Quinn* #1 (Oct. 1999)** Harley navigates her way into the DC Universe during this special prestige-format tie-in with the epic "Batman: No Man's Land" crossover.

***Gotham City Sirens* #1 (Aug. 2009)** Catwoman, Poison Ivy, and Harley all share the spotlight in this ongoing series featuring Gotham City's most infamous femme fatales.

***Harley Quinn* (Vol. 2) Annual #1 (Dec. 2014)** Readers are treated to a comic as zany as Harley herself in this special scratch-and-sniff issue that featured a disclaimer from DC due to some of its more controversial scents.

Dr. Harleen Quinzel's dramatic transformation into the super-villain Harley Quinn is a tale that has changed over the years due to Harley's own retellings and her penchant for exaggeration. According to Harley's latest version, she grew up in a fairly quiet neighborhood in Brooklyn, New York. Harleen had several brothers, and a bit of a delinquent streak. She soon met a like-minded boy named Bernie Bash, who proved even more dangerously unstable than Harleen. To win her affections, Bernie threw their classmate Bonnie Harper out of his car into the path of an oncoming truck. Bonnie had picked on Harleen in school, and Quinzel was moved by Bernie's "romantic" gesture. When he was arrested, Harleen broke into Bernie's parents' place and stole a stuffed beaver to remember him by, a beaver she would later talk to as if it were a real person. Harleen experienced her first heartbreak at Bernie's arrest, one worsened when he was killed while in juvenile detention.

After concentrating on her studies, Harleen won several scholarships to Gotham University. She graduated at the top of her class and found work as a psychiatrist at a prominent hospital in Gotham City. Fascinated by the criminal mind, Harleen transferred to Arkham Asylum. And that's where her various stories begin to diverge.

Originally, Harleen claimed that she fell in love with one of Arkham's most dangerous inmates, the Joker, and after being scolded by her superior, stabbed her before fleeing with the Joker. He took Harleen to the A.C.E. Chemical Plant and dropped her in a vat of chemicals that bleached her skin white, and colored her hair red and black. She went insane, called herself Harley Quinn, and embarked on a romance with the Joker.

YOUNG SCHOLAR
From an early age, Harleen had a keen interest in psychiatry. Amadeus Arkham's *Studying the Criminal Mind* gave her an insight into how to manipulate people.

FALLING FOR IT
Harleen was betrayed by the Joker when he threw her into a vat of chemicals.

SQUAD LIFE
When government agent Amanda Waller decided to set up Task Force X, a covert strike force made up entirely of super-villains, Harley Quinn was one of her first recruits. Knowing that Harley was sharper than she often let on, and fully capable of holding her own in a fight, Waller had Quinn kidnapped and tortured alongside several other villains, including Batman's foes Black Spider and Deadshot. Refusing to buckle under pressure, Harley passed the cruel test, and was officially recruited into the so-called Suicide Squad, a team she has stayed with over time. Harley even had a brief romantic fling with fellow member Deadshot.

THE JOKER'S GIRLS
Sparks flew when Harley was placed on the same incarnation of the Suicide Squad as her rival, the so-called Joker's Daughter. Harley nearly killed her.

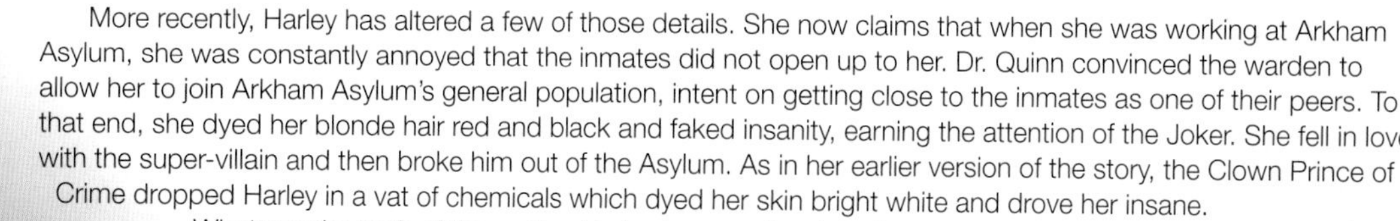

More recently, Harley has altered a few of those details. She now claims that when she was working at Arkham Asylum, she was constantly annoyed that the inmates did not open up to her. Dr. Quinn convinced the warden to allow her to join Arkham Asylum's general population, intent on getting close to the inmates as one of their peers. To that end, she dyed her blonde hair red and black and faked insanity, earning the attention of the Joker. She fell in love with the super-villain and then broke him out of the Asylum. As in her earlier version of the story, the Clown Prince of Crime dropped Harley in a vat of chemicals which dyed her skin bright white and drove her insane.

Whatever the truth of the matter, Harley became the Joker's number one accomplice for a short time, acting even crazier than usual to keep his attention, but he soon broke off their relationship. Harley went from one job to the next, working for the government as part of the Suicide Squad, and then becoming a landlady in Coney Island, Brooklyn. Be warned, however, Harley is still more than up for causing plenty of mayhem from time to time. **MM**

"How cool would it be to have my own comic book?"

HARLEY QUINN

REBIRTH

MAD SKILLS

Harley Quinn has so many conflicted aspects to her personality that you never know what to expect.

However, now she is surprising even herself by assuming the most unexpected and rarefied of roles. As the newly installed protector and champion of the underdogs in her neighbourhood, she is determined to save the poor beleaguered slobs of Coney Island from a zombie apocalypse.

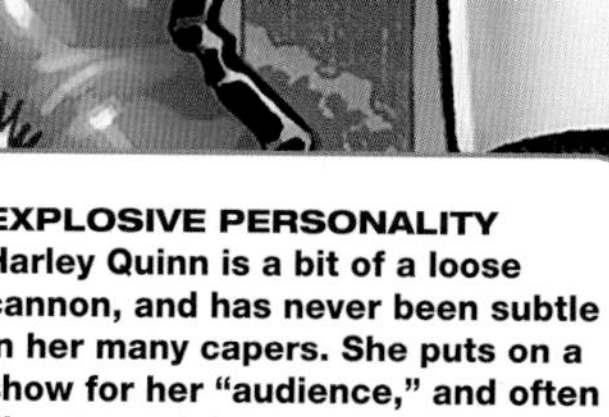

EXPLOSIVE PERSONALITY
Harley Quinn is a bit of a loose cannon, and has never been subtle in her many capers. She puts on a show for her "audience," and often likes to end things with a bang.

PLAYING WITH POWER

The Earth-2 heroine Power Girl found herself in one compromising position after another when Harley found the otherworldly supergirl having crash-landed near her Brooklyn home. She decided to convince the amnesiac Power Girl that they were Super Hero partners, and even began fighting crime as Power Girl's sidekick, just for the sheer enjoyment of it. However, when this dysfunctional duo crossed paths with super-villains Clock King and the Sportsmaster, they found themselves on several adventures through the far reaches of space. Eventually, they fought their way home, only for Power Girl to regain her memories and quickly quit her partnership with Harley.

GIRL TROUBLE
When Power Girl finally found out the truth about her "Super Hero" partner Harley Quinn, it took all her heroic restraint not to totally pummel her former "sidekick."

ON THE RECORD

Harley Quinn now stars in two monthly comic book titles. However, this popular *Batman* character's fame doesn't originally stem from the comics themselves, but rather from her original appearances on the award-winning cartoon, *Batman: The Animated Series.*

Super Harley

Harley Quinn first appeared on *Batman: The Animated Series* as the Joker's moll, and soon found her way into the tie-in comic book series *The Batman Adventures* in 1993. It was six more years before she drifted into the mainstream DC Universe, introduced in her own one-shot special during the epic "Batman: No Man's Land" crossover between all the *Batman* titles. In this version of her origin, Harley wasn't actually a doctor of psychiatry, but simply an intern. She fell in love with the Joker, broke him out of prison, and adopted a clown look complete with a red-and-black jester cowl to get his attention.

Toxic friendship

After the Joker first attempted to kill Harley, she befriended Poison Ivy. The eco-terrorist took a liking to Harley's zany antics and gifted her with a formula that made Harley mostly immune to toxins and poisons, and gave the kooky clown-in-training enhanced agility and strength. Now ready to go toe-to-toe with the Batman himself, Harley truly began her career of crime.

TRICKY TRIO
Harley not only became fast friends with Poison Ivy, but also with Catwoman, who later began living with the pair despite their many obvious differences and approaches to crime.

H'EL

DEBUT *Supergirl* (Vol. 6) #13 (Dec. 2012)
EYES White **HAIR** Black
POWERS/ABILITIES All the physical enhancements of a Kryptonian under a yellow sun, plus telepathy, telekinesis, teleportation, force field projection, limited mind control, size alteration, astral projection, and time manipulation.
ALLIES Supergirl
ENEMIES Superman, Superboy, Supergirl, Justice League, Teen Titans

H'El attacked Earth believing he was acting for the House of El. He had spent decades exploring the universe, preserving Krypton's history. Finding cousins on Earth, H'El resolved to turn back time. When he tried to avert Krypton's destruction using Earth's sun as fuel, he was defeated by Earth's defenders and fell through a time rift.

Arriving on Krypton when Jor-El was a student, H'El learned he was a clone-hybrid spontaneously generated from millions of Kryptonian cell-samples. A freak accident had created him within a star-spanning time-capsule; his aberrant mind forming from the historical records archived on the vessel.

Enraged, H'El staged a multi-chronal assault which simultaneously besieged Krypton in three different eras. He was again defeated by Superman, Superboy, and Supergirl and left trapped in a time loop. **WW**

H.I.V.E.

DEBUT *New Teen Titans* (Vol. 1) #1 (Nov. 1980)
CURRENT VERSION *Superboy* (Vol. 6) #20 (Jul. 2013)
BASE Metropolis
REAL NAME Holistic Integration for Viral Equality
ENEMIES Superman, Hector Hammond, Superboy, Psycho Pirate, Killer Frost
AFFILIATIONS N.O.W.H.E.R.E., Psiphon, Dr. Psycho

The clandestine organization known as H.I.V.E. was created by persons unknown for ostensibly altruistic reasons. Its avowed purpose—as defined by the ruling H.I.V.E. Queen—is to release the world from the bondage of individual freedoms and create global parity for every living creature on Earth. To these ends, they have abducted children, murdered thousands of innocents, and consorted with criminals, all while making a tidy profit. Casualties have included scientist Dr. Caitlin Snow, who was transformed into Killer Frost after H.I.V.E. sabotaged her invention to protect its own financial interests in the energy industry.

But H.I.V.E.'s major area of endeavor is psionics. For years it has stolen humans with telepathic potential, turning them into warriors, research subjects, or drones. **WW**

HADES

DEBUT *Wonder Woman* (Vol. 1) #329 (Feb. 1986)
CURRENT VERSION *Wonder Woman* (Vol. 4) #5 (Mar. 2012)
BASE Hell, Sphere of the Gods
POWERS/ABILITIES Immortality; telepathy; metamorphosis; illusions; control of the dead.
ALLIES Persephone, Poseidon
ENEMIES First Born, Hephaestus
AFFILIATIONS Gods of Olympus

Hades is one of the most powerful of the Olympian gods. When he and his brothers Zeus and Poseidon slew their father Chronos, his brothers claimed dominion of the skies and seas respectively, and Hades was left with the underworld, the realm of spirits. His kingdom is built from all the souls that have entered his realm, which Hades reshapes into settings to suit his mood.

When Zeus died, his queen Hera took on his role, sparking a civil war that embroiled the Olympians and their offspring in a catastrophic conflict. Devious, bored, mistrusting, and incapable of love, Hades agreed to Wonder Woman's peace plan for him to wed Hera. When this failed, he tried to forcibly marry Diana instead, but was foiled by Hephaestus. As the war raged, Hades was seemingly killed by First Born. **WW**

HAMMER AND SICKLE

DEBUT *Outsiders* (Vol. 1) #10 (Aug. 1986)
REAL NAMES Boris and Natasha Ulyanov
BASE Russia **EYES** Blue **HAIR** Blonde
POWERS/ABILITIES
Hammer Enhanced strength; durability; wields a large war hammer; **Sickle** Enhanced speed; agility; wields a razor-sharp sickle.
ENEMIES Outsiders, Suicide Squad, Catwoman, New Teen Titans, Red Star
AFFILIATIONS People's Heroes, Red Shadows, the Society

Russian Boris Ulyanov was dedicated to the Soviet Union in its dying years. With his wife Natasha, he was augmented by state scientists to counter American patriotic groups such as the Force of July.

Boris—wielding a bone-crushing hammer with mutant super-strength and vitality—became field leader of the People's Heroes. His squad handled both internal threats and covert missions beyond Russia's borders. Natasha used a sickle with her enhanced speed and agility, serving beside Boris in the team (and its successor Red Shadows) as they repeatedly clashed with the Outsiders and the Suicide Squad.

Eventually the Ulyanovs began operating as a duo, battling the Teen Titans over Russian fugitive Red Star. When the Berlin Wall fell, Hammer and Sickle fell out of favor in the new Russia. They left to become superpowered mercenaries and assassins in the West, joining super-villain coalition the Society and clashing with Catwoman. **WW**

FROM RUSSIA WITH HATE
Boris and Natasha readily adapted their lethal skills to the unique demands and rewards of the American underworld's capitalist economy.

HALO

DEBUT *The Brave and the Bold* (Vol. 1) #200 (Jul. 1983)
REAL NAMES Gabrielle Doe, Violet Harper, Marissa Barron
BASE Gotham City
HEIGHT 5ft 7in **WEIGHT** 120 lbs **EYES** Blue **HAIR** Blonde
POWERS/ABILITIES Resurrection; spectrum of light-based effects, generated as bodily auras or haloes (Red: heat; Orange: concussive force; Yellow: blinding light; Green: stasis effect; Blue: holographic distortion; Indigo: tractor beam); used in combination the light effects afford physical protection and flight; using the Violet power suppresses Halo's personality, allowing the deceased Violet Harper to take control of the body.
ALLIES Batman, Katana, Sebastian Faust, Alfred Pennyworth
ENEMIES Violet Harper, Marissa Barron, Masters of Disaster

Halo was born when teenage sociopath Violet Harper was murdered by the costumed assassin Synoide. The crime was invisibly observed by an ancient light entity—one of the Aurakles—which accidentally became trapped in the corpse, reanimating it while also bestowing a range of abilities. Violet's personality was suppressed, leaving an innocent amnesiac who took the name Gabrielle Doe. Her light-based superpowers brought her to the attention of Batman, who recruited and trained her as part of his undercover team the Outsiders.

After many adventures, the still largely naïve and innocent Gaby was murdered on the orders of criminal mastermind Marissa Barron, who also died in the attack. The Aurakle then transferred itself into Barron's body, which promptly resurrected with Gaby's personality and powers. Resuming her career on the fringes of the Super Hero community, Halo withdrew further from the spotlight. During a mission for Red Robin and Batman Incorporated she was lost and declared dead. She now operates completely off the grid as part of the Dead Heroes Club, taking on covert missions for Batman. **WW**

BEACON OF HOPE
Halo's immense powers were balanced by a childlike nature and desire to please. However, she developed a hard-won maturity during the Blackest Night. She was especially effective against Black Lanterns, mercilessly eradicating Katana's resurrected children and Geo-Force's sister Terra.

THINKING MAN'S VILLAIN
Anyone who mistook Hector Hammond's paralysis for helplessness learned to their cost that vengeance and agony are all in the mind.

HAMMOND, HECTOR

DEBUT *Green Lantern* (Vol. 2) #5 **(Apr. 1961)**
CURRENT VERSION *Superman* (Vol. 3) #18 **(May 2013)**
BASE Metropolis; Coast City, California
HEIGHT 5ft 1in **WEIGHT** 156 lbs
EYES Brown **HAIR** Brown
POWERS/ABILITIES Hyper-advanced intellect and numerous psionic abilities, including telepathy, telekinesis, mind control, mental blasts, and illusion creation.
ENEMIES Green Lantern, Superman, Orion, Sinestro
AFFILIATIONS H.I.V.E., Secret Society of Super-Villains

Arrogant astrophysics and aeronautics consultant Hector Hammond retrieved a xenomineral from a crashed spaceship. The vessel belonged to the extraterrestrial Abin Sur, who died, passing on his Green Lantern power ring and mission to Hal Jordan. Exposed to the alien rock, Hammond's mind began expanding exponentially, and he quickly became a menace to everyone around him. His burgeoning psionic powers proved too much for rookie ring-bearer Jordan, but Hammond was easily overwhelmed by seasoned Green Lantern Sinestro, Hal's mentor. Imprisoned in isolation and studied by a succession of doctors and scientists, Hammond's powers continued to expand—as did his skull.

When he overcame the drugs sedating him, Hammond was incapable of physical movement, but he possessed a host of deadly psionic weapons. He could feed parasitically on the minds of others and he hungered for dominance. His psychic range spanned galaxies and his cruelly playful predations have caused chaos for the Guardians on Oa and on the homeworld of the New Gods. **WW**

QUEEN FOR A DAY
H.I.V.E.'s psionic empress was no match for the decrepit-seeming Hammond.

ON THE RECORD

The original Hector Hammond was a petty crook who found a meteor that could evolve organic life. He used it on kidnapped scientists, enriching himself through their discoveries—until Green Lantern intervened. Hammond evolved himself too, but the high cost of increased mental powers was total loss of physical mobility.

From his cell, Hammond plagued many heroes, including Flash, the Justice League, and Superman, but always reserved his greatest hatred for Hal Jordan.

BODY OF EXPERIENCE
Forced to live life vicariously, Hammond was determined the lives he plundered would be full of adventure, glamor, triumph, and tragedy.

HANGMEN

DEBUT *Titans* (Vol. 1) #21 (Nov. 2000)
NOTABLE MEMBERS Breathtaker, Provoke, Shock Trauma, Stranglehold, Killshot
ALLIES Dr. Psycho
ENEMIES Titans, Batman II (Dick Grayson) and Robin
AFFILIATIONS the Society, Secret Society of Super-Villains

The Hangmen were mercenaries hired to assassinate the terrorist Cheshire by Quraci nationalists, which brought them into repeated conflict with the Titans. The asphyxiation-themed team joined the Battle of Metropolis as part of the Secret Society of Super-Villains, but preferred looting to fighting. For dereliction of duty they were supposedly killed by Doctor Psycho, but he had faked their deaths in return for a huge bribe.

In fact, the Hangmen were executed months later by the Spectre, after they tried to ally themselves with Libra's new incarnation of the Secret Society of Super-Villains during the Infinite Crisis. Their costumed identities and murder methods were then appropriated by a new group of anonymous felons based in Gotham City, who clashed with Dick Grayson and Damian Wayne, the second Batman and Robin team. **WW**

HARBINGER

DEBUT *New Teen Titans Annual* (Vol. 1) #2 (1983) (as Lyla); *Crisis on Infinite Earths* #1 (Apr. 1985) (as Harbinger)
CURRENT VERSION *The Multiversity* #1 (Oct. 2014)
BASE House of Heroes
EYES Orange **HAIR** Blonde
POWERS/ABILITIES Multiversal omniscience; Transmatter Cubes summon agents.
ALLIES All heroes in the known multiverse
ENEMIES Gentry, He Whose Hand is Empty

Harbinger is the hyper-evolved artificial intelligence that administers the 52 universes known as the Orrery of Worlds, within the greater multiverse. Her face and personality are based on Lyla Michaels, who faithfully served yet ultimately murdered the original Monitor during the Crisis on Infinite Earths. These multiversal realignments occur from time to time and are referred to as "Crises" by the mortals who endure them.

The Harbinger AI eventually gained full autonomy and inherited the Monitor's mission to safeguard the multiverse after Nix Uotan was captured by the "Gentry," invaders from beyond. She sought out an army of Super Heroes, transported them to the transdimensional House of Heroes and supervised their battle to save the Monitor and all realities. **WW**

HARVEST

DEBUT *Teen Titans* (Vol. 4) #7 (May 2012)
BASE The Colony
POWERS/ABILITIES Advanced military training; chronokinesis; centuries of stolen futuristic weapons and technologies.
ALLIES Jon Lane Kent
ENEMIES Teen Titans, Superboy
AFFILIATIONS N.O.W.H.E.R.E., Ravagers

Harvest was a colonel in the militia of Earth's 31st century and spent his life battling metahumans as they attempted to eradicate the human populace. When his son was killed, he finally resolved to rewrite history. He began traveling incrementally backward in time, and with each stop gathered more technology and power, gradually transforming himself into a lethal and inhuman monster. To aid him in his misguided mission to save mankind, Harvest kidnapped and indoctrinated Jon Lane Kent, the son of Superman and Lois Lane from a possible future reality.

Arriving in the 21st century, he created N.O.W.H.E.R.E., gathering young metahumans and forcing them to kill each other in a periodic Culling. The survivors would form the basis of Harvest's army of Ravagers. His obsessive campaigns brought him repeatedly into conflict with Superboy and the Teen Titans, and he was killed after attempting to combine a mass of metahuman DNA into an ultimate weapon. **WW**

MILLENNIUM MAN
Nothing he'd seen over a thousand years of history convinced Harvest to abandon his dream of a world without metahumans.

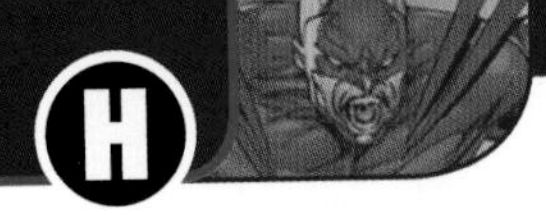

HAUNTED TANK

DEBUT *G. I. Combat* #87 (May 1961)
CURRENT VERSION *G. I. Combat* (Vol. 2) #5 (Dec. 2012)
BASE Mobile
POWERS/ABILITIES Haunted by the ghost of General James Ewell Brown Stuart and members of the crew connected to the tank; provides protection against magical attack and can also teleport.
ENEMIES Nazis

In World War II, the Haunted Tank was commanded by Jeb Stuart and watched over by the ghost of one of his ancestors—a confederate general named James Ewell Brown Stuart. In 1942, Jeb was ordered to locate a stash of mystical artifacts collected by Hitler, and ended up using the Tank to fight several strange threats along the way.

Years later, when Jeb was 98, the Tank materialized outside his house after his grandson, Sergeant Scott Stuart, was captured in Afghanistan. Old Jeb and the tank vanished in front of A.R.G.U.S. agents who had traced the tank after it had gone missing from a vault. They reappeared in Afghanistan, where Jeb saved his grandson. The tank then teleported to the North Pole, where they stopped descendants of World War II Nazis unleashing a deadly "Warwheel," piloted by a Nazi Ghost.

Jeb died in action, but his ghost seemingly lived on in the vehicle, talking to his grandson who had inherited the family connection to the Haunted Tank. **AC**

GUARDIAN GHOST
The Light Tank M3 Stuart was possessed by the ghost of Jeb Stuart's ancestor. Jeb could see and hear the ghost, who offered guidance in combat.

HAWK, SON OF TOMAHAWK

DEBUT *Tomahawk* #131 (Dec. 1970)
BASE Echo Valley, Mid-West America
HEIGHT 5ft 10in **WEIGHT** 166 lbs
EYES Blue **HAIR** Brown with blond streak
POWERS/ABILITIES Expert horseman, tracker, and hunter.
ALLIES Firehair, Jonah Hex, Swamp Thing
ENEMIES Black Bison, Wise Owl

Hawk was a western hero born in 1800. He was the son of Tomahawk (Tom Hawk), a famous revolutionary hero, and a Native American woman called Moon Fawn. Hawk was raised in Echo Valley and learned the ways of the Wild West from his father, and the secrets of Native American culture from his mother. He became an expert tracker, hunter, and fighter. He had one brother, Small Eagle.

Hawk was soon helping others and formed a close friendship with the heroic Firehair. Later, he joined forces with other Old West heroes to fight the mystical villain Black Bison. Hawk helped Swamp Thing when he time-traveled to the 1870s. Bison gave Swamp Thing a magic talisman, the Claw of Aelkhünd, to help him return to his own time. Just before he died, Hawk published his autobiography. **AC**

HAWKFIRE

DEBUT *Batwoman* (Vol. 2) #16 (Mar. 2013)
REAL NAME Mary Elizabeth Kane
BASE Gotham City
HEIGHT 5ft 6in **WEIGHT** 120 lbs
EYES Blue **HAIR** Blonde
POWERS/ABILITIES Olympic-level gymnast and swimmer; highly trained fighter.
ALLIES Batwoman
ENEMIES The Hook

Mary Elizabeth "Bette" Kane enjoyed a highly privileged upbringing as part of Gotham City's rich Kane family. She was a successful tennis player and skilled in martial arts and gymnastics. When she discovered Dick Grayson was Robin, she decided to become a hero, too. Bette called herself Flamebird and joined the Teen Titans.

Bette moved to Gotham City and learned that her cousin, Kate Kane, was secretly Batwoman. Batwoman proved a strict teacher, burning Bette's old costumes and renaming her "Plebe." A battle with the monstrous Hook left Bette in a coma, but she recovered and returned to crime fighting when Medusa attacked her cousin and Wonder Woman. Wearing a new costume and calling herself Hawkfire, Bette battled Hook once more and this time tore his signature weapon from his arm. She continued to fight crime in Gotham City alongside Batwoman. **AC**

HAWK AND DOVE

DEBUT *Showcase* #75 (Jun. 1968)
CURRENT VERSION *Hawk & Dove* (Vol. 5) #1 (Nov. 2011)
REAL NAMES Hank Hall (Hawk) and Dawn Granger (Dove)
BASE Washington, D.C.
HEIGHT 6ft 1in (Hawk); 5ft 9in (Dove)
WEIGHT 197 lbs (Hawk); 120 lbs (Dove)
EYES Brown (Hawk); Blue (Dove)
HAIR Brown (Hawk); White (Dove)
POWERS/ABILITIES **Hawk**: Enhanced agility, strength, body density and vision, healing factor; **Dove**: Enhanced strength, intelligence, and empathy, flight, danger sense.
ALLIES District of Columbia Police Department, Deadman, Batman
ENEMIES Alexander Quirk, Condor, Swan, the D'yak, Blockbuster, The Hunter

When brothers Hank and Don Hall discovered that criminals were planning to murder their father, Don wished that they had the power to save him—and the Gods of War and Peace answered. Brash and aggressive Hank was transformed into Hawk, the Avatar of War, while calm and rational Don became Dove, Avatar of Peace. They saved their father and then used their powers to become a Super Hero duo, but Don later died in action during a reality-altering crisis. The bereft Hawk only became more enraged without the stabilizing influence of his brother. He joined the New Titans, but his volatile temperament proved too much for his teammates.

Balance of a sort returned for Hank in the shape of Dawn Granger, whom the gods chose to be the new Dove, and the two heroes reluctantly formed a new partnership. Mirroring Hank's relationship with his brother, the duo clashed over ethical questions, with Hank favoring force and Dawn preferring pacifism and reason; but they united to face fellow avatars Condor and Swan, as well as the mysterious D'yak. Hawk and Dove also encountered the Teen Titans when the young heroes investigated a sinister mystery in the small town of Hatton Corners in the east of the United States. **SW**

ON THE RECORD

The pre-Flashpoint Don and Hank Hall received their powers from the Lords of Chaos and Order, and joined the Teen Titans. When Don died during the Crisis on Infinite Earths, Dawn Granger took his place as Dove.

Their partnership ended when Dawn was seemingly slain by Monarch, an evil future version of Hank. Hank then became the time-warping villain Extant and was later killed, only to be reborn as a zombie in Blackest Night where he fought the new Hawk and Dove—Holly and Dawn Granger—and was brought back to life by the power of the white light.

OPPOSITES ATTRACT?
Hawk and Dove's relationship was marked by tension, but when combined, they could be an unstoppable force for good.

HAWKMAN

DATA

DEBUT *Flash Comics* #1 **(Jan. 1940)**
CURRENT VERSION *Savage Hawkman* #1 **(Nov. 2011)**
REAL NAME Katar Hol
BASE Manhattan
HEIGHT 6ft 1in **WEIGHT** 195 lbs
EYES Brown **HAIR** Brown
POWERS/ABILITIES Thanagarian Nth metal creates wings and weaponry; extensive battle training.
ALLIES Shayera Thal (formerly)
ENEMIES Morphicius, Corsar
AFFILIATIONS Justice League of America

Katar Hol is Hawkman, a hero born on the alien world of Thanagar, but forced to flee for a crime he did not commit. Hated by many of his own race and hunted by the woman he once loved, Hol now lives on Earth as archaeologist Carter Hall. He uses the powerful Nth metal to become the high-flying vigilante known as Hawkman.

DEADLY ENEMY
When the precious Nth metal bonded with Katar Hol, the crazed Emperor Corsar attacked him. Their fight concluded with Corsar seemingly dead.

Katar Hol hails from the distant world of Thanagar. After upsetting one of the ruling elite, he was sentenced to fight in the arena. However, Katar emerged a champion, his success catching the eye of the aging Emperor Provis, who granted him his freedom. Katar and Emperor Provis' daughter, Shayera Thal, fell in love and Katar was accepted into the royal family. He even befriended Shayera's arrogant and conniving brother, Corsar.

When alien Daemonites unleashed a plague on Thanagar, the native inhabitants lost their wings. Many—including the Emperor—died. Corsar Thal succeeded his father and went to war. He wanted to use Nth metal to make his people strong again, but the piece they mined bonded to Katar Hol—rebuilding his wings. Corsar attacked Katar, but was killed in an accident. Despite his innocence, Shayera blamed Katar for her brother's death and felt she could never forgive him.

Forced to flee his homeworld, Katar ended up on Earth, crash-landing in the ocean with no memory of his past apart from his name—which rescuers misheard as Carter Hall. He made a new life for himself, becoming the hero Hawkman. In time, Thanagarians tracked him down and Corsar was revealed to still be alive. Shayera realized she had been wrong about Katar and sacrificed her life to prevent her brother destroying Earth. Katar later joined the JLA and fought beside them during the Trinity War. **AC**

NTH METAL
Hawkman's weaponry and wings were created by the mysterious substance known as Nth metal, mined on the planet Thanagar.

TEAMWORK
Hawkman was recruited to be a part of the JLA by Amanda Waller.

ON THE RECORD

Originally a reincarnation of the Egyptian Prince Khufu, Hawkman's physical appearance has changed little since his debut. Reborn as archaeologist Carter Hall, he adopted the hawk emblem of the Egyptian God Horus for his role as the hero Hawkman. He also began searching for his lost love, Princess Chay-Ara, who had been reincarnated as Shiera Sanders and after they met became Hawkgirl. Hawkman was chairman of the JSA and owned a hawk, Big Red.

When the hero was revived in the 1960s, his backstory was changed. He became a Thanagarian law enforcer who had traveled to Earth in pursuit of a criminal and decided to remain there to fight crime.

GOLDEN AGE
Hawkman's look has remained largely the same: enormous wings, a winged mask, and, since he was an archaeologist, weapons borrowed from the museum he curated.

CLASSIC STORIES

***Hawkworld* #1–3 (Aug.–Oct. 1989)** Katar Hol lives on Hawkworld, working as one of the Wingmen militia. When he uncovers a conspiracy, it almost destroys him.

***JSA: The Return of Hawkman* #22–25 (May–Aug. 2001)** The JSA and Hawkgirl travel to Thanagar, where she learns the truth about Hawkman's past and helps bring him back to life.

***Hawkman* (Vol. 4) #1–6 (May–Oct. 2002)** Hawkman meets his true love, Hawkgirl, once more. However, Kendra Saunders—the new Hawkgirl—has no memory of her past lives.

STORM OVER MANHATTAN
When Hawkman was briefly a wanted man, he found himself facing off against Deathstroke the Terminator.

HAWKGIRL

DATA

DEBUT (As Shiera Sanders) *Flash Comics* #1 (Jan. 1940); (As Hawkgirl) *All-Star Comics* (Vol. 1) #5 **(Jun.–Jul. 1941)**
CURRENT VERSION *Earth 2* #2 **(Aug. 2012)**
REAL NAME Kendra Munoz-Saunders
BASE Earth-2
HEIGHT 5ft 9in **WEIGHT** 135 lbs **EYES** Hazel **HAIR** Brown
POWERS/ABILITIES Trained archaeologist; wings bonded to her body enable her to fly; highly skilled with a crossbow.
ALLIES The Flash (Jason Garrick), Green Lantern (Alan Scott)
ENEMIES Darkseid, Solomon Grundy
AFFILIATIONS The Wonders of the World

FRIENDLY FIRE
Having traced Green Lantern (Alan Scott) to his Manhattan penthouse, Hawkgirl tried to convince him to join the Wonders of the World.

On the world known as Earth-2, Kendra Munoz-Saunders was Hawkgirl, a winged hero who gained powers after investigating an ancient Egyptian tomb. Unsure how her powers came to be, Kendra nonetheless promised to use them for the greater good—no matter how dangerous the threats she faced. As a survivor of that world's destruction, Hawkgirl now lives on a new world, protecting fellow survivors from the unknown.

Kendra Munoz-Saunders was an archaeologist and treasure hunter who lived on Earth-2, a world that had lost Superman, Batman, and Wonder Woman during a war against Darkseid's evil forces. She was hired by the World Army to investigate the tomb of Nabu in Egypt, accompanied by Egyptian scholar Khalid Ben-Hassin. Searching the tomb, Kendra was mysteriously transformed into a winged warrior, while at the same time in another part of the tomb, Khalid found the helmet of Nabu and became the mystic warrior Doctor Fate. Kendra soon gained the name Hawkgirl and not long after quit the World Army.

Doctor Fate guided her to meet the Earth-2 Flash in Poland, where the pair were joined by the Green Lantern. The heroes left for the US to battle Solomon Grundy—a monstrous avatar of the Rot—in Washington, DC. Here the hero Atom came to their aid, although he had originally been sent by the World Army to bring Kendra back into their service. After defeating Grundy, Atom once more tried to capture Hawkgirl—only for the Flash to aid her escape. All five heroes eventually became good friends and joined forces to form the Wonders of the World team.

Their services were no more desperately needed than when Darkseid and his army returned with overwhelming force to lay waste to their planet. When the heroes realized their world was doomed, Hawkgirl fought a rearguard action to give as many people as much time as possible to escape the planet on city-sized spaceships. Once these survivors arrived on their new homeworld, Hawkgirl set off to scout the terrain for them. **AC**

ON THE RECORD

The original Hawkgirl was Shiera Sanders Hall, who first appeared in *Flash Comics* #1 (Jan. 1940) as the girlfriend of Hawkman. In *All-Star Comics* #5 (Jun.–Jul. 1941), Shiera used Hawkman's costume to defeat some villains and decided to fight alongside him as Hawkgirl. In her 1960s incarnation, Shiera was a law enforcement official who traveled to Earth with her lover, Hawkman. After several continuity changes, Hawkgirl was reintroduced as a member of the JSA in 1999. This version's alter ego was Kendra Saunders, a distant cousin of the very first Hawkgirl.

IMMORTAL LOVE
Hawkman and Hawkgirl's love has survived countless reincarnations over thousands of years.

WINGED WARRIOR
On Earth-2, Hawkgirl was one of the main heroes fighting against Darkseid's malevolent forces.

LONDON FALLING
Hawkgirl and Doctor Fate discovered that London was under attack from one of Apokolips' invaders.

CLASSIC STORIES

***Hawkgirl* (Vol. 1) #50 (May 2006)** As part of the "One Year Later" event, Hawkgirl starts a new life in St. Roch, but soon finds herself troubled by nightmares of Hawkman.

***Blackest Night* #1–8 (Jun. 2009–Mar. 2010)** Hawkman and Hawkgirl are murdered only to return as Black Lanterns. Hawkgirl is reborn at the end of the series, but with a new set of memories.

***Earth 2: Society* #8 (Mar. 2016)** While searching their new world, Kendra learns that Fury is training a new generation of Amazons.

HAWKWOMAN

DEBUT *The Brave and the Bold* **#34 (Feb.–Mar. 1961)**
CURRENT VERSION *The Savage Hawkman* **#9 (Jul. 2012)**
REAL NAME Shayera Hol
BASE Thanagar
HEIGHT 5ft 7in **WEIGHT** 145 lbs
EYES Blue **HAIR** Red/Blonde
POWERS/ABILITIES With the use of Nth metal, Thayera has the ability to fly.

Shayera Hol came to Earth with her husband, Katar Hol (a pre-Flashpoint Hawkman) in pursuit of a criminal from their homeworld of Thanagar. The pair remained on Earth to fight crime and joined the Justice League of America. Shayera later separated from Katar and tried to become a policewoman in Detroit. But it wasn't long before she put on her armor once more to fight the shape-shifting criminal Byth.

By the time of the Rann-Thanagar War, Shayera had left Earth to fight with the Thanagarian army. She was killed in battle by Queen Komand'r of Tamaran, aka Blackfire.

Post-Flashpoint, Shayera Hol was the daughter of Thanagar Emperor Provis. She mistakenly thought her lover, Katar Hol, had killed her brother Corsar. A vengeful Shayera tracked Katar to Earth, only to find Corsar was alive, but insane. She died saving Earth. **AC**

HAZARD

DEBUT *Infinity, Inc.* **#34 (Jan. 1987)**
REAL NAME Rebecca "Becky" Sharpe
HEIGHT 5ft 6in **WEIGHT** 112 lbs
EYES Green **HAIR** Red
POWERS/ABILITIES Psionic powers and mystic dice give her the ability to bring good or bad luck to others.
ENEMIES Infinity, Inc., Global Guardians
AFFILIATIONS Injustice Unlimited

Becky Sharpe was the granddaughter of Steven Sharpe, an infamous hustler known as the Gambler, and member of the original Injustice Society. Despite his skills, Steven lost all his money gambling at the Taj Mahal casino in Las Vegas, which had rigged the games in their favor. Haunted by the loss, he killed himself shortly after.

When Becky learned of this, she swore to avenge her grandfather. She gained psionic powers and a set of mystical dice that enabled her to give good or bad luck to others. Calling herself Hazard, she joined the Wizard's Injustice Unlimited group after being told the group would not kill, and coerced Wildcat II and Tasmanian Devil into helping her bankrupt the casino that had caused her grandfather's death. As a member of Injustice Unlimited, she fought Infinity, Inc. and the Global Guardians. She left the group when she realized her teammates were willing to kill after all. **AC**

HEAT WAVE

DEBUT *The Flash* (Vol. 1) #140 **(Nov. 1963)**
CURRENT VERSION *The Flash* (Vol. 4) #11 **(Sep. 2012)**
REAL NAME Mick Rory
BASE Central City
HEIGHT 5ft 11in **WEIGHT** 179 lbs
EYES Blue **HAIR** Bald
POWERS/ABILITIES Creates flame with his body and fires it from his chest; possesses Heat Gun.
ALLIES Captain Cold
ENEMIES The Flash, Crime Syndicate
AFFILIATIONS The Rogues

Mick Rory was obsessed with fire from an early age. Raised on a farm, he set fire to his home when he was bored and was mesmerized by the flames as they burned the house down. After several similar incidents, Rory—by then a pyromaniac—ended up in Central City and decided to use his obsession to become a super-villain. Calling himself Heat Wave, he created a protective costume for himself and used a small flamethrower to cause panic in his victims. He was defeated by the Flash, and eventually joined a group of villains called the Rogues.

When Captain Cold tried to give himself and his fellow Rogues metahuman powers using a genome recorder, a horrific accident left Heat Wave covered in burns, but with the ability to emit flames from his chest. Heat Wave remained a key member of the Rogues, fighting alongside his allies when they opposed the rule of the Crime Syndicate and when they became mercenaries hired to hunt down and eliminate the Flash. **AC**

ON THE RECORD

Heat Wave originally made a costume of asbestos (before the dangers of asbestos were known) to protect himself from his flamethrower and the fire it created. During his first appearance he teamed up with Captain Cold to attack the Flash, but the two villains fell out when they realized they were both attracted to a local television personality named Dream Girl.

He also temporarily went straight and helped the Flash catch a corrupt parole officer using his Heat Wave costume and weaponry. Though, it wasn't long before he was back to his villainous fiery ways.

FIREARMED AND DANGEROUS
Heat Wave wore a flame-retardant suit and used a Heat Gun—a re-purposed flamethrower—with which he could create firestorms and raise the ambient temperature of his surroundings.

AN INCENDIARY TEMPER
When Heat Wave gets angry, he can engulf buildings in flames. In this instance, drinkers at the Keystone Saloon were rescued just in time by the Flash (Barry Allen).

FAN OF FLAMES
As a pyrokinetic, Heat Wave generates flames from an opening in his chest. He wears protective goggles and armor.

HELIX

DEBUT *The Fury of Firestorm* #3 (Jan. 2012)
BASE Zither-Tec
HEIGHT 9ft 8in **WEIGHT** 550 lbs
HAIR None **EYES** Orange
POWERS/ABILITIES Can unleash nuclear powered blasts of heat and energy; enhanced strength; teleportation.
ALLIES Candace Zither
ENEMIES Firestorm

Zither-Tec director Candace Zither transformed her husband Roger into the nuclear-powered being Helix during secret experiments that also led to the creation of Firestorm. Deranged by the experience, Helix was unleashed to battle the two men who together created Firestorm—Jason Rusch and Ronnie Raymond. They unexpectedly merged into a ferocious new being known as Fury, who decapitated Helix. He survived to attack Firestorm again, and was again defeated, this time by being taken in to space where his energies were expected to dissipate—but his ultimate fate remains unknown.

A previous organization known as Helix was a team of genetically engineered humans who fought Infinity, Inc. and other Super Heroes, until Mr. Bones brought them under the wing of the Department of Extranormal Operations. **AI**

HELLGRAMMITE

DEBUT *Brave and the Bold* #80 (Oct.-Nov. 1968)
BASE Metropolis
REAL NAME Roderick Rose
HEIGHT 6ft 1in **WEIGHT** 325 lbs
HAIR None **EYES** Red
POWERS/ABILITIES Enhanced strength and speed; spins super-tough webs; can transform enemies into larvae.
ALLIES Neron, Bloodsport
ENEMIES Superman, Batman, Green Arrow

Roderick Rose, an expert entomologist, became a superhuman after exposure to a mutating agent gave him a thick exoskeleton, super-human strength and the ability to leap like a grasshopper. Calling himself Hellgrammite, after a type of fly larva, Rose fought Super Heroes including Batman and Green Arrow, and discovered that he could transform other humans into subservient, larval versions of himself.

A deal with the demon Neron gave Hellgrammite enhanced powers and he became fixated on the most powerful Super Hero of all: Superman. He joined Bloodsport, Riot, and other villains to gang up on the Man of Steel when he reappeared after the Infinite Crisis, but they failed in their mission. Hellgrammite was subsequently defeated by Donna Troy, following the destruction of Star City at the hands of his ally, Prometheus. **AI**

HERALD (VOX)

DEBUT *Teen Titans* (Vol. 1) #26 (Mar.–Apr. 1970)
CURRENT VERSION *Titans Hunt* #1 (Dec. 2015)
BASE San Francisco
REAL NAME Malcolm Duncan
HEIGHT 6ft 1in **WEIGHT** 210 lbs
HAIR Black **EYES** Brown
POWERS/ABILITIES Gabriel's Horn opens space-time warps; expert boxer.
ENEMIES Doctor Light

Malcolm "Mal" Duncan was raised in Harlem, New York, with his sister Cindy. When Cindy was harassed by a racist street gang, Mal attacked them. He was soon helped by the Teen Titans, who had given up their costumed identities and happened to be nearby. Joining the Titans, but possessing no superpowers, Mal felt like an ineffectual outsider, until Karen Beecher, the Bumblebee, helped him create the Gabriel's Horn, a weapon with teleporting powers. Becoming the Herald, Mal helped the Titans defeat the first Doctor Light. However, unknown to Mal, his Horn had been corrupted by the villainous Gargoyle, who hoped to tear a hole in the dimensional fabric to release his master, the Antithesis. After the Titans defeated these villains, Mal destroyed the Horn.

During the Infinite Crisis, Mal Duncan suffered an accident in space that left him unable to speak. After accepting a cybernetic voice box similar to the Gabriel's Horn, he joined Doom Patrol as Vox. **AI**

HERALDING A CHANGE
Formerly known as Herald, because he appeared first when teleporting groups using Gabriel's Horn, Duncan became Vox after losing and regaining his voice.

HELSPONT, LORD

DEBUT WildC.A.T.s #1 (Aug. 1992)
CURRENT VERSION *Superman* (Vol. 3) #7 (May 2012)
HEIGHT 6ft 9in **WEIGHT** 375 lbs
POWERS/ABILITIES Healing factor, chronokinesis, shapeshifting, phasing, can possess others' bodies.
ENEMIES Superman
AFFILIATIONS Daemonites

A legendary Daemonite conqueror and warrior, Lord Helspont ruthlessly expanded the Daemonite hegemony over countless planets and peoples. His growing list of exploits gradually provoked jealous Daemonite rivals to plot against him and betray him.

Helspont was defeated and imprisoned within the Eye, a giant starship that would later become the headquarters of the covert planetary defense squad Stormwatch. Harry Tanner, Stormwatch's Eminence of Blades, inadvertently destroyed the Eye, causing wreckage to rain down upon Earth's surface—including Helspont's cell, which crashed down in the Himalayas. The Daemonite lord freed himself and established a new base from where he could recreate his former dominance. His activities drew the attention of Superman, who engaged Helspont in a fierce battle. Initially, Helspont overpowered the Man of Steel and then tried to win him over as an ally, claiming that they were both too good for the people they had tried to help—and that Superman would eventually be betrayed just as he had been.

Helspont offered to steer clear of Earth if the Man of Steel would assist him exact his revenge on the treacherous Daemonites. Superman, of course, refused this offer, sparking an inconclusive battle that raged across the mountains and only ended when Helspont teleported away, doubtless to pursue his vengeful ambitions by other means. **AI**

ON THE RECORD

Helspont first appeared as an enemy of the WildC.A.T.s, a team of human-alien hybrids formed by the alien Kheran Lord Emp to counter the Daemonite infiltration of Earth. He and the militant hero Mr. Majestic had a particularly vicious hatred for each other, and it was Mr. Majestic who thought he had destroyed Helspont once and for all in a battle over the doomsday machine called the Planet Shaper.

C.A.T. FIGHT
Helspont and Mr. Majestic squared off after the WildC.A.T.s discovered his plans to unleash the world-destroying Planet Shaper.

HERCULES

DEBUT *All-Star Comics* #8 (Dec. 1941)
CURRENT VERSION *Aquaman* (Vol. 7) #29 (May 2014)
BASE Olympus
HEIGHT 6ft 5in **WEIGHT** 327 lbs
HAIR Black **EYES** Blue
POWERS/ABILITIES Immortality; super-strength.
ALLIES Wonder Woman
ENEMIES Giant-Born
AFFILIATIONS Olympian Gods

RUNNING AMOK
Hercules, out to avenge his ancient betrayal by the king of Atlantis, vents his rage on Aquaman.

Hercules (or Heracles) is the champion of Greek myth and son of Zeus, king of the Olympian Gods. After performing legendary labors during the era of antiquity and clashing with the ancient Amazons, Hercules vanished from history for centuries. He was not even seen during the fearsome battle for the throne of Olympus after Zeus disappeared. It was revealed much later that Hercules had helped Atlan, the ancient king of Atlantis, battle and imprison the monstrous beings known as the Giant-Born. His efforts saved Atlantis, but he was betrayed by Atlan and imprisoned with the Giant-Born in Hell.

The Giant-Born eventually warped Hercules' mind and transformed him into a weapon at their disposal. When they were released from Hell to attack Atlantis once again, Hercules was an instrument of their vengeance. He fought Aquaman and Mera before Aquaman called in Wonder Woman to save Atlantis once more and restore Hercules to his senses. **AI**

HERETIC, THE

DEBUT *Batman and Robin* #12 (Jul. 2010)
CURRENT VERSION *Batman Incorporated* #1 (Jul. 2012)
HEIGHT 6ft 2in **WEIGHT:** 200 lbs
HAIR Black **EYES** Blue
POWERS/ABILITIES Superhuman strength.
ALLIES Talia al Ghūl
ENEMIES Batman, Robin, Nightwing
AFFILIATIONS Leviathan

BORN OF VENGEANCE
Talia al Ghūl created a new son to do her bidding after the original Damian Wayne chose to follow his father's path instead of hers.

Talia al Ghūl's vision of a ruling family composed of her, Batman, and the child they would bear together broke down when Batman refused her advances and their son Damian would not go along with her subsequent plan to undermine the Dark Knight. In anger, Talia disowned Damian and created a clone of him; gestated in the body of a whale and given metahuman powers through experimental surgeries.

Known as the Heretic, the clone became Talia al Ghūl's chief bodyguard when she appeared as leader of Leviathan. Heretic also hunted down several of the international members of Batman Incorporated before killing the original Damian Wayne during a savage fight at Wayne Tower. Having developed free will, the Heretic went against his mother's wishes, declaring himself Batman and the new ruler of Gotham City. The real Batman fought back and the Heretic died at Talia al Ghūl's hand, decapitated before his body was blown up in a massive explosion that also destroyed Wayne Tower. **AI**

GUNS BLAZING
Jonah Hex doesn't usually go for subtlety. He fires his six-guns until there's no one left to fire back.

HEX, JONAH

DEBUT *All-Star Western* (Vol. 1) #10 **(Feb.-Mar. 1972)**
CURRENT VERSION *All-Star Western* (Vol. 3) #1 **(Nov. 2011)**
BASE American Old West frontier
REAL NAME Jonah Woodson Hex
HEIGHT 5ft 11in **WEIGHT** 189 lbs **HAIR** Red **EYES** Blue
POWERS/ABILITIES Uncanny marksman, skilled with a tomahawk; indomitable courage, and fierce strength of conviction.
ALLIES Amadeus Arkham
ENEMIES Court of Owls

WET WORK
Jonah Hex and Amadeus Arkham took a shortcut through a strangely familiar cave when they investigated the deadly Court of Owls.

As if cursed by his name, Jonah Hex's life was blighted by bad luck. Born in 1839, he was the son of a brutal drunk and his meek wife. Abandoned by his mother, Hex was sold by his father to an Apache tribe. He was raised as an Apache until a jealous rival, Noh-Tante, betrayed him.

Although against slavery, Hex fought with the Confederacy in the Civil War. After the war, in a fight over his beloved, White Fawn, he killed Noh-Tante and was scarred with a burning tomahawk. Later, Amadeus Arkham asked Hex to help hunt down the serial killer the Gotham Butcher. This uncovered two secret societies: the followers of the Crime Bible and the Court of Owls. Capitalizing on the rivalry between the two groups, Hex and Arkham defeated the followers of the Crime Bible and forged a friendship with Alan Wayne, who funded the building of Arkham Asylum.

Over a century later, an adventure with a time-traveling Booster Gold went awry and Jonah appeared in the 21st Century, encountering Superman and the Swamp Thing, before having his face reconstructed after a motorcycle accident. Gold was able to return Hex to his home century, where he killed a man impersonating his scarred self and began a new life at sea with Tallulah Black by his side. **AI**

ON THE RECORD

In his previous incarnation, Jonah Hex became a feared bounty hunter and fathered a child with a woman named Mei Ling. She left him after he broke a promise to give up his violent ways.

His most outlandish adventure was a time-traveling odyssey in which he teamed up with a future Batman to battle the crime syndicate known as the Combine.

Hex was finally killed by a bank robber and his taxidermied body was displayed in a New York City amusement park. He was later reanimated as part of the Black Lantern Corps, but returned to death following Hal Jordan's triumph over Nekron.

DEAD OR ALIVE
Jonah Hex, bounty hunter, has often had a hefty reward placed on his own head.

HIGHFATHER

DEBUT *New Gods* (Vol. 1) #1 **(Feb.–Mar. 1971)**
CURRENT VERSION *Wonder Woman* (Vol. 4) #14 **(Jan. 2013)**
REAL NAME Izaya **BASE** New Genesis
HEIGHT 6ft 4in **WEIGHT** 277 lbs **EYES** Blue **HAIR** Black
POWERS/ABILITIES As a New God, Highfather is immortal and has superhuman mental and physical abilities; finely attuned to disturbances in the cosmic Source.
ALLIES Metron, Himon, Orion, Divine Guards, Council of Eight
ENEMIES Darkseid, all Lantern Corps
AFFILIATIONS New Gods of New Genesis

Izaya was born millennia ago on the planet Genesis. He was the son of Yuga Khan, one of the merciless Old Gods who ruled that world. While Izaya was a peaceful man, his younger brother Uxas despised the Old Gods and began a war against them. The Old Gods were defeated, and Uxas stole their power to become the New God Darkseid, while a dying Old God bequeathed the remains of his power to Izaya, also transforming him into a New God. When Izaya tried to persuade Darkseid that they should unite to create a peaceful world, his brother destroyed Genesis and the two went their separate ways.

Izaya built the floating city of New Genesis for his people, but it was constantly besieged by his brother's forces. Izaya consulted the Source Shard, which told him that, to secure peace, he must exchange his son, Scot, for Darkseid's scion, Orion. Izaya was torn between emotion and duty, and when he chose duty, his conscience departed, in the form of Infinity-Man. In that moment, the compassionate Izaya turned into the authoritarian Highfather. Obsessed with defeating Darkseid, he declared war on the Green Lanterns in the hope of taking their power. The war left New Genesis in ruins, and Highfather realized the folly of his deeds, rediscovering his compassion. **SW**

ON THE RECORD

In pre-Flashpoint reality, Izaya was not Uxas' brother, but a warlord from the planet of New Genesis. Darkseid had Izaya's wife Avia killed, provoking New Genesis into attacking Apokolips.

Disillusioned by the bloody conflict, Izaya discovered the mysterious secret of the Source and became the peaceful, benevolent Highfather, securing a treaty with Apokolips. Highfather was slain by the war-god Ares, and the human, Takion, took his place as leader of New Genesis.

WAR AND PEACE
Highfather's commitment to peace transformed New Genesis society and inspired Super Heroes across the universe.

HIMON

DEBUT ***Mister Miracle* (Vol. 1) #9 (Jul.–Aug. 1972)**
CURRENT VERSION ***Infinity Man and the Forever People* #1 (Aug. 2014)**
REAL NAME Himon
BASE Academy of Higher Conscience
EYES Blue **HAIR** Gray
HEIGHT 5ft 8in **WEIGHT** 163 lbs
POWERS/ABILITIES A New God, Himon is immortal, and physically and mentally superior to a human; a master of New Genesis technology.

Himon was the headmaster at the Academy of Higher consciousness on New Genesis. He educated young minds, and indoctrinated them with the philosophies of Highfather, New Genesis' ruler. His by-the-book approach did not sit well with his more laid-back subordinates, including Big Bear. Himon tried to stop the Forever People from going to Earth to join Big Bear by giving them a faulty Mother Box, but Vykin made it work.

On Earth, the team encountered Infinity Man, an opponent of Highfather's benevolent autocracy. Himon sent Vykin's girlfriend Serafina to retrieve the Forever People and lied to Highfather about what had happened, knowing that news of the Infinity Man would disturb him. The Infinity Man then appeared out of a Boom Tube and warned Himon off interfering with in his plans. **SW**

HIPPOLYTA

DEBUT *All-Star Comics* #8 **(Dec. 1941–Jan. 1942)**
CURRENT VERSION *Wonder Woman* (Vol. 4) #2 **(Dec. 2011)**
REAL NAME Hippolyta **BASE** Paradise Island
HEIGHT 5ft 9in **WEIGHT** 150 lbs
EYES Blue **HAIR** Blonde
POWERS/ABILITIES As an Amazon of Themyscira, has received divine blessings that bestow enhanced physical and mental capabilities.
ALLIES Wonder Woman, Zeus, Demon Knights
ENEMIES Hera, Cain, Strife
AFFILIATIONS Amazons of Themyscira

Queen Hippolyta ruled the Amazons of Paradise Island for many centuries. One night, Hippolyta encountered the god Zeus in the form of a spear-wielding warrior. They dueled, and the god seduced her with his martial skills. Hippolyta later gave birth to Princess Diana (Wonder Woman), but fearing the wrath of Zeus' wife Hera, claimed that she had shaped Diana from clay, which was then brought to life by divine means.

When Diana was fully grown she ventured into the world beyond Themyscira and returned with a woman named Zola, who was pregnant with another of Zeus' children. This drew Hera to Paradise Island and Hippolyta apologized for sleeping with her husband, offering her life as recompense. Hera refused Hippolyta's offer; instead, she transformed the queen into a clay statue and the Amazons into snakes. Although her subjects were soon restored, Hippolyta herself was dissolved in a storm and she became one with the island.

ON THE RECORD

Before Flashpoint, the Amazons were created when the Olympian goddesses fashioned new living bodies from seabed clay for the souls of women who had been slain by men. Hippolyta was the first to swim to the surface, so she became queen. Hippolyta was fiercely protective of her daughter Diana (Wonder Woman), but could not prevent her being killed by Neron. Hippolyta then took on the role of Wonder Woman herself, becoming a member of the Justice Society of America. She died battling the alien Imperiex.

AMAZON QUEEN
Hippolyta ruled Themyscira for many centuries, dealing both with mythical threats and the encroachment of modernity.

HITMAN

DEBUT ***Demon Annual* (Vol. 3) #2 (1993)**
REAL NAME Tommy Monaghan
BASE Noonan's Bar, Gotham City
EYES Black **HAIR** Black
HEIGHT 6ft **WEIGHT** 185 lbs
POWERS/ABILITIES Telepathy; night vision; expert marksman and street fighter.
ENEMIES Dubelz crime family, Glonth, the Mawzir, the Arkanonne, Mr. Truman

Irish-American Tommy Monaghan was raised in an orphanage and served with honor in the Marine Corps during Operation Desert Storm. He then became Hitman, though he would never kill targets unless they "deserved it." While Hitman was stalking mobster Robert Dubelz, he was infected by the alien parasite Glonth.

The alien's attack gave Hitman useful combat powers of telepathy and night vision that attracted the attention of the Arkannone, Hell's Lords of the Gun. When Hitman refused to join up with them, they attacked him, but he gunned them down with help from the demon Etrigan.

Tommy repeatedly came into conflict with CIA agent Mr. Truman, and when Truman launched an all-out attack on him at Noonan's Bar, Tommy went down in a blaze of glory, taking Truman with him. **SW**

HOURMAN

DEBUT *Adventure Comics* #48 **(Mar. 1940)**
CURRENT VERSION *Earth 2: Society* #6 **(Jan. 2016)**
REAL NAME: Richard "Rick" Tyler
BASE New Gotham City
EYES Brown **HAIR** Brown
POWERS/ABILITIES Miraclo pill gives incredible strength, speed and durability for an hour, but some formulations of Miraclo can incapacitate or mind-control him.
ALLIES Doctor Impossible, Johnny Sorrow, Anarky
ENEMIES Batman (Thomas Wayne), Kyle Nimbus
AFFILIATIONS Wonders of the World

BLINDED BY RAGE
Consumed by his desire for revenge, Rick Tyler slid into villainy—before Batman showed him the error of his ways.

POWER BOOST
Miraclo gave Rick Tyler the might to take on Earth-2's Superman (Val-Zod).

The Rick Tyler of Earth-2 reality was the son of Rex Tyler, boss of TylerCo and inventor of the Miraclo serum, which was stolen by Thomas Wayne (Earth-2's former Batman). When Rick's father was killed in a war with Apokolips, Rick was determined to reclaim his birthright. As Hourman, he managed to acquire Miraclo with Jimmy Olsen, who had gained superpowers via New Gods' technology and become the villainous Doctor Impossible. Hourman joined Impossible, Johnny Sorrow, and Anarky when they clashed with Earth-2's Batman, Flash, and Superman.

When Hourman was stripped of his Miraclo by the Flash, evil entrepreneur Kyle Nimbus supplied him with a version laced with a mind-control chemical. Under its influence, Hourman attacked Batman (Dick Grayson). However, Batman incapacitated him with a dose of reformulated Miraclo and persuaded him to join the Wonders of the World Super Hero team. Rick embraced the opportunity to fight for a worthy cause, and Batman provided him with a supply of pure Miraclo. **SW**

ON THE RECORD

Several characters have taken the codename Hourman. The first was brilliant chemist Rex Tyler, who invented a vitamin he called Miraclo. This gave Rex superpowers—but only for one hour. Donning a distinctive caped and hooded costume, he became the hero Hourman, a founding member of the Justice Society of America. Unfortunately, Rex became addicted to Miraclo and, despite his best efforts, he was unable to develop a non-addictive version. Rex was almost killed by the time-warping villain Extant during Zero Hour, but Hourman III (Matthew Tyler) switched places to save him.

Rex's son, Rick, didn't want to follow in his father's footsteps, as a chemist or a hero, but, during the *Crisis on Infinite Earths*, he finally put on the Hourman costume and took Miraclo to continue his father's legacy. Rex became one of many second-generation heroes in a new JSA but, like his father, he suffered from Miraclo addiction.

The third Hourman was a robot created in the 853rd century using software derived from Rex Tyler's DNA. This Hourman used New Gods technology to travel back in time to meet his predecessors and sacrificed himself so that Rex Tyler could live again.

THE TIMES THEY ARE A-CHANGIN'
Like the march of time itself, the Hourman legacy has continued through the centuries.
1 Hourman I (Rex Tyler)
2 Hourman II (Rick Tyler)
3 Hourman III (Matthew Tyler)

HUMAN DEFENSE CORPS

DEBUT *Human Defense Corps* #1 **(Jul. 2003)**
BASE Area 53 (underwater), Fort Olympus (satellite)
NOTABLE MEMBERS **Sgt. Montgomery Kelly**; **Pt. Chad Kiyahani**; **Colin Mitchell** (specialist); **Charlie Graham** (chaplain); **Pt. Eric Stewart**; **Pt. David Page**; **Col. Reno Rosetti**; **Dr. Zaius** (ape biology researcher); **Calcabrina** ("pet" demon).
ALLIES US military, Gen. Sam Lane
ENEMIES Neron, Calcabrina, Durlans, Khund

During his brief term in office, President Luthor created the Human Defense Corps task force to counter alien threats, believing that the Justice League could not be relied on. The elite 10,000-man unit was equipped with cutting-edge gear, including advanced firearms, powered exoskeletons, amphibious assault aircraft, and S.A.R.G.E. remote-controlled scout vehicles.

In Bulgaria, the troops faced vampire forces and drove them off with "holy napalm" strikes. They followed up with an amphibious strike across the river Styx into Hell itself, where Sgt. Montgomery Kelly (who had demon ancestry) became a ruler. The Corps was later integrated into Project 7734, an anti-alien task force run by General Sam Lane. It conducted actions against Kryptonians when the city of Kandor and its population arrived on Earth. **SW**

HUMAN TARGET

DEBUT *Action Comics* **(Vol. 1) #419 (Dec. 1972)**
REAL NAME Christopher Chance
BASE Boston, Massachusetts
EYES Blue **HAIR** Black
HEIGHT 6ft **WEIGHT** 180 lbs
POWERS/ABILITIES Master of disguise; actor; expert martial artist; superb athlete.
ALLIES Batman, Angel O'Day, Harvey Bullock, Jonny Double
ENEMIES Deadshot

When Christopher Chance was just a boy, a loan-shark sent a hitman to murder his father over a bad debt. The lad tried to stand in the killer's way, but could not save his father. When Chance grew up, he became a bodyguard, the Human Target, who specialized in impersonating clients who had been marked for death. In his time, he has masqueraded as a rodeo rider, an elderly oil magnate, and a tightrope walker. Chance was even hired to impersonate Bruce Wayne while Batman was recovering from a vampire bite. The assassin Deadshot soon had the fake Wayne in his sights, and the Dark Knight had to go into action to save the Human Target's life.

There is a big drawback to Chance's line of work: he has become so adept at imitating others that he has begun to lose his own identity. **SW**

HUNTER, RIP

DATA

DEBUT *Showcase* #20 **(May–Jun. 1959)**
CURRENT VERSION *Convergence: Booster Gold* (Vol. 1) #1 **(Jun. 2015)**
REAL NAME Classified (possibly Richard or Ripley Carter)
BASE Vanishing Point
EYES Blue **HAIR** Blond
POWERS/ABILITIES Genius-level intellect, adept in physics, engineering, spatio-temporal mechanics and theory; skilled tactician and strategist; proficient in many martial arts and the use of ancient and future weaponry.
ALLIES Booster Gold, Michelle Carter, Skeets, Supernova, Waverider
ENEMIES The Time Stealers, Per Degaton, Mr. Mind, Ultra-Humanite
AFFILIATIONS Time Masters, Linear Men, Forgotten Heroes

IT'S ALL IN THE TIMING
When Rip finally found his long-missing father, it was only to lose him forever by transforming him into cosmic chrononaut Waverider.

MAN OF ACTION
Rip Hunter is a genius and master of temporal theory, but he is also a rough-and-tumble adventurer who has survived in dozens of dangerous epochs.

NEW WORLDS
Rip Hunter and Booster Gold used a Time Sphere to travel among the 52 Earths of a newly birthed multiverse.

The man calling himself Rip Hunter learned how to navigate the time-barrier before building his Time Spheres to travel through history. He resolved to safeguard the timeline from all who would twist it to their own ends. Possessing an unparalleled understanding of causality and the timestream, Rip obscured his origins and identity to deter attacks by time-traveling assassins who could go back in time to when he was a child and erase him from history.

Chronicling the history of a time-traveler is invariably tricky. Rip Hunter may be the same hero who served with temporal enforcers the Linear Men, helping unify parallel timelines during the *Crisis on Infinite Earths*. He could be an alternate incarnation from a parallel Earth or timeline that no longer exists. Whatever his origins, he certainly knows how to cover his tracks. The Rip Hunter who consistently interacts with Earth's modern Super Heroes also protects their history from manipulation by time-traveling villains.

Following the reality-shredding Infinite Crisis—which resulted in the creation of a new cosmology of 52 parallel realities—Hunter recruited 25th-century hero Booster Gold to save all of existence from the cosmic devourer Mr. Mind and bring stability to the new multiverse. He and Booster later formed the core of a fluctuating team that countered plots by Despero, Per Degaton, Ultra-Humanite, Black Beetle, and others to rewrite history and warp reality. Even Booster was not immune to temptation: he tried to change history by preventing the murder of his friend Ted Kord. Eventually, though, Booster realized the scale of his selfish crime and reordered reality, proving himself worthy of the rank of Time Master. Rip later admitted that Booster would one day become his father.

Rip Hunter emerged largely unchanged from the reality-altering Flashpoint event. In the aftermath he sought out his father and met a different Booster Gold instead. They located Rip's future dad just as another chronal crisis began: a lethal Convergence in which past, present, and previously erased realities were thrown into conflict, involving every Super Hero from every possible point of existence. **SW**

ON THE RECORD

The original Rip Hunter, was a clean-cut scientist/adventurer who built his Time Spheres to uncover the secrets of history. With mechanic Jeff Smith, girlfriend Bonnie Baxter, and her little brother Corky, Rip traveled across Earth's past and future, encountering infamous individuals like Cleopatra, Kublai Khan, and Adolf Hitler along the way. They also encountered an extraordinary number of alien races who had visited our world but who had been lost to history.

HISTORY LESSONS
Rip and his fellow Time Hunters soon learned to expect the unexpected when the ventured into a new era.

CLASSIC STORIES

***Showcase* #20 (May–Jun. 1959)**
In their very first adventure, the original Rip Hunter and the first Time Masters team take a trip back into prehistory, where they battle dinosaurs and criminals.

***Time Masters* #1–8 (Feb.–Sep. 1990)**
Rip Hunter's time-travel research makes him a target for Vandal Savage and the Illuminati. He and his fellow Time Masters uncover their conspiracy and battle them at key moments in history.

***Time Masters: Vanishing Point* #1–5 (Sep. 2010–Feb. 2011)**
Rip, Booster Gold, Green Lantern, and Superman team up with Batman, who has been cast adrift in time after battling Darkseid during the Final Crisis.

HUNTER, TIM

DEBUT *The Books of Magic* (Vol. 1) #1 (Jan. 1990)
CURRENT VERSION *Justice League Dark* (Vol. 1) #11 (Sep. 2012)
BASE The Wild Area
EYES Brown **HAIR** Brown
POWERS/ABILITIES A magician of huge potential, prophesied to be the only person who can safely wield the Books of Magic.
ALLIES Justice League Dark
ENEMIES Felix Faust, Nick Necro, Dr. Mist

Timothy Hunter is a teenage boy said to be the only person who could use the mighty Books of Magic without being corrupted. Zatanna and John Constantine sought him out in London to teach him magic, but he was overwhelmed by the experience and chose to return to his mundane life.

However, when Justice League Dark tried to claim the books to stop them falling into the hands of the evil Felix Faust, Tim helped to recover the arcane volumes. When he opened one of the books he was teleported to a dimension called the Wild Area. Its magical denizens told him that he was Hunter, the descendant of their long-lost mage-king, and that they had been conquered by the technology-wielding humans of Epoch. With assistance from his father, Tim helped to free the magic land and decided to remain there. **SW**

HUNTRESS

DEBUT *All-Star Comics* #69 (Nov.-Dec. 1977)
CURRENT VERSION *The Huntress* (Vol. 3) #1 (Dec. 2011)
REAL NAME Helena Wayne
HEIGHT 5ft 11in **WEIGHT** 130 lbs **EYES** Blue **HAIR** Black
POWERS/ABILITIES Extensive training in acrobatics, stealth, and martial arts; expert shot with a crossbow.
ALLIES Power Girl, Wonders of the World **ENEMIES** Steppenwolf, Desaad

Helena Wayne is the daughter of Earth-2's Bruce Wayne and Selina Kyle (Batman and Catwoman), and served as Robin. When the forces of Apokolips attacked Earth-2 her parents were killed, and Helena and her friend Kara Zor-El (Earth-2's Supergirl) went into a Boom Tube and ended up on Earth-1. They took new identities (with Helena becoming Helena Bertinelli/Huntress and Kara becoming Karen Starr/Power Girl), and Helena established herself as a crossbow-wielding protector of abused women.

Helena and Kara were attacked several times by the Apokoliptian villain Desaad, who had also been exiled to that reality. They finally found a portal back to Earth-2, which was under attack by Darkseid and Apokolips, but Helena was captured by Desaad and transformed into the grotesque Famine, one of Darkseid's Four Furies. However, her friends returned her to human form and she left Earth-2 with other survivors before it was destroyed. **SW**

ON THE RECORD

Helena Bertinelli, in her pre-Flashpoint incarnation, was the daughter of one of Gotham City's Mafia bosses. After she saw her family massacred, she trained to become the Huntress and declared her own personal war on organized crime. Batman did not approve of her violent methods, but she befriended other members of the Batman Family and eventually found a home in Oracle's all-female Birds of Prey team, becoming a long-term member.

CODE OF VENGEANCE
After her family was slaughtered, Helena turned herself into a ruthless anti-Mob vigilante.

HUSH

DEBUT *Batman* (Vol. 1) #609 (Jan. 2003)
CURRENT VERSION *Batman Eternal* #21 (Oct. 2014)
REAL NAME Thomas Elliot
BASE Gotham City
HEIGHT 6ft 3in **WEIGHT** 220 lbs **EYES** Blue **HAIR** Red
POWERS/ABILITIES Tactical genius; expert surgeon; skilled marksman with a pistol; uses holograms to create decoys.
ALLIES Jason Bard, the Architect
ENEMIES Batman, Batman Family, Spoiler

When Tommy Elliot was a child, he idolized his best friend Bruce Wayne. He even went so far as to kill his own parents so he would be an orphan just like Bruce. However, Bruce finally rejected Tommy when his friend began to impersonate him, and Tommy became obsessed with destroying his former idol. Swathing his head in bandages, he became a sworn nemesis to both Bruce Wayne and Batman as the obsessive surgeon and master criminal Hush.

After launching a series of bloody attacks on Batman and his loved ones, Hush vanished for a time, but later resurfaced with a new plan to rip Batman's life apart. He framed Commissioner Jim Gordon for murder, injected Alfred with fear toxin, and triggered riots and terrorist attacks all over Gotham City. His masterstroke was destroying Arkham Asylum, leading to a mass breakout by its inmates.

Hush then blew up Batman's secret weapons caches underneath the city, which led to Wayne Enterprises' assets being seized by the authorities. Batman finally captured and imprisoned Hush, but when an alliance of villains attacked Gotham City, Hush escaped and used the Batcave's array of technological resources against the Batman Family before being knocked out by Alfred. **SW**

BURNING RAGE
Hush's ultimate objective is to destroy Batman and everything he holds dear—including Gotham City.

ON THE RECORD

The pre-Flashpoint Hush was traumatized by an abusive childhood and plotted to kill his parents to get their money. He harbored a grudge against his childhood friend Bruce Wayne because of Bruce's wealth and status. As Hush, he plotted with the Riddler to destroy Batman through a series of attacks intended to break his body and spirit. In "Heart of Hush" he intensified his campaign of terror by literally stealing the heart of Batman's beloved Catwoman.

EQUAL AND OPPOSITE
Tommy Elliot would stop at nothing to assume every aspect of Bruce Wayne's life, including replacing him as Batman.

IBAC

DEBUT *Captain Marvel Adventures* #8 (Mar. 1942)
CURRENT VERSION *Justice League of America* (Vol. 3) #7.4 (Nov. 2013)
BASE Kahndaq
EYES Black **HAIR** Brown
POWERS/ABILITIES Skilled and ruthless as both a general and a warrior.
ENEMIES Black Adam

Almost 4,000 years ago, a barbarian warlord known only as "Ibac the First" invaded the country of Kahndaq and enslaved its people. He forced them to build a mighty capital and erect temples to his gods. The people of Kahndaq rose up against him, but their rebellion was brutally put down by Ibac's hordes. Among the victims were the wife, children, and nephews of a man called Adam. The gods of Kahndaq gave Adam their power so that he could free his nation; he struck down Ibac's soldiers with lightning before turning the tyrant's body to stone.

The story of Ibac and Black Adam has become legend, but the statue of Ibac contorted in his death throes still stands in the capital as a warning to tyrants. Ironically, a dictatorial president, also named Ibac, now rules Kahndaq. **SW**

ICEMAIDEN

DEBUT *Super Friends* (Vol. 1) #9 (Dec. 1977)
REAL NAME Sigrid Nansen
EYES Blue **HAIR** White
POWERS/ABILITIES Cryokinesis—can control cold and ice, and create icy armor.
ENEMIES Delores Winters, Mist
AFFILIATIONS Global Guardians, Justice League, Justice League International

Sigrid Nansen's dedicated scientist mother forced her to take part in a series of experiments by the Norwegian government to replicate the powers of a mythical tribe of ice-people. The tests succeeded, giving Sigrid cryogenetic powers, but also turning her skin blue. Sigrid was selected to join Dr. Mist's international Global Guardians team.

When Tora Olafsdotter (a genuine member of Norway's ice-people tribe) joined the Global Guardians as Ice, Sigrid felt outclassed and left. After Ice was killed by Overmaster, Icemaiden agreed to take her place in Justice League International. She was tricked into deserting the team by the villain Mist, who took her form to attack the JLI from within, killing Amazing Man, Blue Devil, and Crimson Fox. Sigrid was later captured by an organ-stealing operation run by Delores Winters, who grafted Icemaiden's skin onto herself, gaining her powers. **SW**

ICE

DEBUT *Justice League International* (Vol. 1) #12 (Apr. 1988)
CURRENT VERSION *Justice League International* (Vol. 3) #1 (Nov. 2011)
REAL NAME Tora Olafsdotter
HEIGHT 5ft 7in **WEIGHT** 163 lbs
EYES Blue **HAIR** White
POWERS/ABILITIES Uses cryokinesis to hurl freezing blasts, create ice constructs, and fly by levitating a platform of ice.
ALLIES Fire (Beatriz Bonilla Da Costanza), Green Lantern (Guy Gardner)
ENEMIES Peraxxus
AFFILIATIONS Justice League International

Born with cryogenic powers, Norwegian Tora Olafsdotter decided to leave her native country to pursue a Super Hero career as Ice. She soon formed a close friendship with fellow heroine Fire, and dated the temperamental Green Lantern Guy Gardner.

Ice was selected as the Scandinavian member for the UN-sponsored Justice League International team. On their first mission to Peru, she was caught in a thermal blast from a giant alien robot, forcing the team to retreat. The JLI subsequently confronted the robot's master, the alien resource-plunderer Peraxxus, and drove him away. Later, while the JLI were onstage at a publicity event, a bomb exploded. Team member Rocket Red was killed and Ice was seriously injured, requiring emergency surgery.

After recovering, Ice did not rejoin Justice League International, and later, when she and Guy broke up after an argument, she left to spend time alone in the mountains. Guy turned up at her cabin as a Red Lantern and tried to reconcile with her. Ice had her doubts, but once he proved that he really did have his inner rage under control, she agreed to accompany him on a seaside vacation to Dubai. **SW**

OPPOSITES ATTRACT
Ice's fiery romance with hot-headed Red Lantern Guy Gardner was a constant cycle of break-up and make-up.

CHILLING OUT
Ice's cryogenic powers gave her many options in combat, allowing her to freeze enemies, generate ice barriers, or create slides for rapid action.

ON THE RECORD

Pre-Flashpoint, Ice was princess of an isolated tribe of ice-people who possessed cold-based powers. She left her people to join the Global Guardians and then Justice League International.

Ice was seemingly killed by the villain Overmaster, but her cryogenically preserved body was found by the Birds of Prey. She recovered, but was traumatized by the experience and unleashed a mighty ice storm endangering everyone. Finally coming to her senses—after a firm slap from the Huntress—she left with the Birds of Prey for a new life.

CHILD OF THE NORTH
Ice originally served as a representative of Norway in the Global Guardians, but soon found her own identity as a hero.

ICICLE

DEBUT *Infinity Inc.* (Vol. 1) #34 **(Jan. 1987)**
CURRENT VERSION *Green Team: Teen Trillionaires* #5 **(Dec. 2013)**
REAL NAME Cameron Mahkent
HEIGHT 5ft 11in **WEIGHT** 175 lbs
EYES White **HAIR** None
POWERS/ABILITIES Ice-control and ice-generation powers. His body appears to be made of living ice and can alter shape as required.
ALLIES Bellachek Temple
ENEMIES Green Team, Nightwing

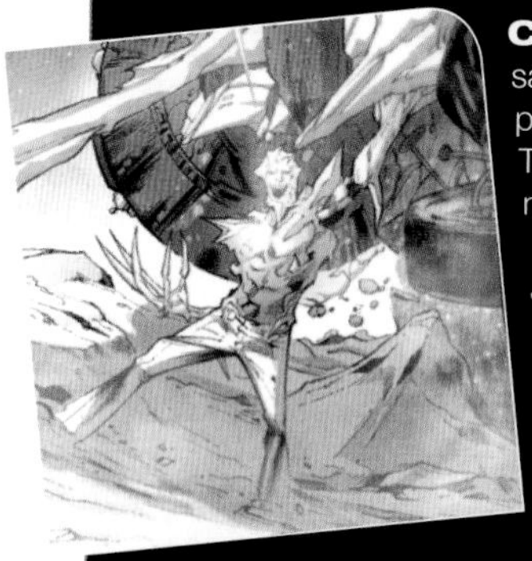

FROZEN SOLID
Icicle used his power to down the Green Team's spacecraft on Bellachek Temple's asteroid.

Cameron Mahkent was a ruthless and sadistic career criminal who was given ice-generation powers by the mysterious and mega-wealthy Bellachek Temple. Thrilled by this upgrade, Mahkent adopted the name Icicle and trained in the use of his powers.

Bellachek gave Icicle a special assignment: to guard a meteor while it was being stripped of minerals by nanobots, and then crash it into Southern California. This act would potentially kill millions of innocent people, but Icicle did not care so long as he was well paid. When the rich-kid Super Heroes of the Green Team arrived on the meteor to investigate, Icicle iced up their craft and caused it to crash-land. He then used his cold-based powers to freeze up the nano-armor of team leader Commodore Murphy, before rupturing their ship with expanding ice.

The Green Team battled Icicle, but it seemed that the villain had them outmatched, creating an array of ice-weapons with which to attack them. In the end, the Green Team caused an explosion that tore the meteor in half, leaving Icicle marooned in space. His fate remains unknown. **SW**

ON THE RECORD

Pre-Flashpoint, Cameron Mahkent was the son of the original villainous Icicle, Joar Mahkent, who debuted in *All-American Comics* (Vol. 1) #90 (Oct. 1947). Cameron's powers were innate, as his DNA had been altered by exposure to his father's cold-projector.

He served in the Injustice Society, first under the Wizard and then under Johnny Sorrow, and joined the Secret Society of Super-Villains during Infinite Crisis. While in the Injustice Society, he met Tigress, and they later had a daughter.

COLD-BLOODED
Cameron Mahkent inherited his powers (and morality) from his father, and carried on the family tradition by becoming a super-villain.

CHILLS AND THRILLS
Icicle displayed a sadistic glee when he got the chance to use his icy abilities against the Green Team.

IGNITION

DEBUT *Adventures of Superman* **(Vol. 1) #582 (Sep. 2000)**
HEIGHT 7ft 5in **WEIGHT** 568 lbs
POWERS/ABILITIES Suit provides heavy armor protection, immense strength, flight, and energy projection powers.
ALLIES Emperor Joker
ENEMIES Superman
AFFILIATIONS Joker's League of Anarchy, Zod Squad

Superman first encountered Ignition on a bizarre version of Earth that the Joker created after stealing Mr. Mxyzptlk's reality-warping powers.

A hulking juggernaut, Ignition was a member of the Joker's League of Anarchy in the city of Meflopolis. However, the Joker later denied creating him, hinting that Ignition may have actually come from the real universe.

Superman assumed that Ignition vanished when the Joker's mad realm did. He was shocked when the armored villain reappeared as part of Zod's conquering army in the former Soviet nation of Pokolistan. Ignition was assigned to protect the solar converter arrays Zod was using to change the Sun's color from yellow to red. Metallo attacked the arrays, overwhelming Ignition and wiping out the converters. After the Man of Steel defeated Zod, Ignition disappeared. **SW**

IMMORTAL MAN

DEBUT *Strange Adventures* **(Vol. 1) #177 (Jun. 1965)**
CURRENT VERSION ***The Multiversity: The Society of Super-Heroes: Conquerors of the World* #1 (Nov. 2014)**
REAL NAME Klarn Arg
POWERS/ABILITIES Powers of reincarnation; telekinesis, flight, can fire flaming eye blasts.

In prehistoric times, Klarn Arg was the defender of his tribe and a fierce opponent of the vicious Vandar Adg. One day, as they faced each other, a meteor exploded above them. Its radiation bathed Vandar, making him immortal, while Klarn found a jewel from the meteor that reincarnated him upon death. Vandar took the name Vandal Savage, while Klarn became the Immortal Man and perished many times battling his sworn and ancient enemy.

In the 20th century, the Immortal Man recruited a team of Forgotten Heroes to help fight Savage. He gave his life during the *Crisis on Infinite Earths*, and soon after was captured by Savage and cryogenically frozen. Klarn seemingly suffered a final death when Savage released him to battle the Warp Child and wipe the entity from creation. However, he appeared during the Multiversity event to turn the tables on Vandal, unleashing a far bigger threat in the process. **SW**

IMPERIEX

DEBUT *Superman* (Vol. 2) #153 (Feb. 2000)
HEIGHT 6ft 7in **WEIGHT** 986 lbs
EYES Red **HAIR** None
POWERS/ABILITIES Manipulates entropy; incomprehensible strength and durability; black hole generation; universe destruction.
ENEMIES Superman, President Lex Luthor, Mongul, Brainiac 13, Darkseid
AFFILIATIONS Hollowers, Warworld

Imperiex is a conceptual entity: the sentient embodiment of entropy. Composed of pure energy, the "Destroyer of Galaxies" is the agent of irresistible decline and obliteration, existing since time began and preceding the birth of the first universe. Generally clad in robotic armor, its function is to eradicate each old, flawed universe, one by one, and create—via a Big Bang—a new one, in the quest to produce a perfect universe.

Discerning Earth was the focal point of current existence, Imperiex targeted the world with drones as it drew closer, casually destroying all planets in its path. It was impeded by an unlikely coalition of heroes from Earth and other worlds, and lesser world ravagers such as Doomsday and Darkseid. These resisters trapped Imperiex's consciousness inside Warworld and propelled it through a temporal Boom Tube to the beginning of time. Here it triggered its inevitable Big Bang and paradoxically began the present universe. **WW**

FACE OF DOOM
A primal force on a cosmic scale, Imperiex Prime could concentrate its consciousness and interact with combatants on a personal level.

INDIGO TRIBE

DEBUT *Green Lantern* (Vol. 4) #25 (Jan. 2008)
CURRENT VERSION *Green Lantern: New Guardians* (Vol. 1) #1 (Nov. 2011)
BASE Nok
POWERS/ABILITIES Flight; teleportation; protective force-fields; aura projection; energy-casting; light construct creation; close-range channeling of other colors of the Emotional Spectrum (all manipulated through power staffs augmented by their rings).
ALLIES Green Lantern Corps, Blue Lantern Corps
ENEMIES Sinestro, Black Hand, Third Army, Guardians of the Universe
AFFILIATIONS Natromo, New Guardians

The nomadic Indigo Tribe utilize the Emotional Spectrum's light of compassion, drawn from every living being in creation. The light is embodied by patron entity Proselyte, who personifies the mantra "Rage grows from murder. Hope from Prayer. And at last, Compassion is offered to us all."

Indigo Lanterns are all former criminals—killers, or worse. But compassion's radiance suppressed their other emotions and compelled them to change. They are constantly re-examining their awful pasts, while acting in a benevolent, life-affirming manner. Their actions are unpredictable. The Tribe generally refrain from assertive action, preferring to intervene only as a last resort.

The arcane monk Natromo originally harnessed the light for Green Lantern Abin Sur. He foresaw that the Guardians of the Universe would eventually betray the Corps, becoming a threat to the whole of creation. Needing a force to counter the Guardians emotionless might, Sur believed success would come not through conflict but through rehabilitation.

The Indigo Tribe speak a language that is untranslatable by other beings or by green power rings. Their oath is:

Tor lorek san, bor nakka mur,
Natromo faan tornek wot ur.
Ter Lantern ker lo Abin Sur,
Taan lek lek nok—Formorrow Sur! **WW**

LAST RESORT
The aloof and enigmatic Indigo Tribe only appear to intervene when life itself is in the direst need and all other agencies have failed.

ON THE RECORD

The Indigo Tribe are the least understood of the various Lantern Corps. Though not pacifistic, they seem strictly reactive, preferring to distance themselves from conflict and advance their own agenda unless the universe itself is imperiled. Their staffs and rings negate the other colors of the Emotional Spectrum, even Black Lantern energies, which made them the deciding factor in overcoming the risen dead during the War of Light's Blackest Night.

RAINBOW WARRIORS
The rapacious, reawakened dead would have ultimately consumed all life had not the Indigo nomads finally joined and completed the universe's spectrum of champions.

INDIGO 1

DEBUT *Green Lantern* (Vol. 4) #25 **(Jan. 2008)**
CURRENT VERSION *Green Lantern* (Vol. 5) #6 **(Apr. 2012)**
REAL NAME Iroque
BASE Nok
EYES Indigo **HAIR** Purple
POWERS/ABILITIES Leadership and fierce compassion; flight; teleportation; protective force-fields; aura projection; energy-casting; light-construct creation; channeling of other colors on the Emotional Spectrum (all manipulated through her power staff or ring).
ALLIES Hal Jordan, Kyle Rayner
ENEMIES Sinestro, Black Hand, Guardians of the Universe
AFFILIATIONS Indigo Tribe, Natromo, New Guardians

Iroque was a lethal villain who battled Green Lantern Abin Sur and considered her greatest triumph to be eliminating his daughter. Abin later brought Iroque to the former prison-planet Nok, where he had conspired with the aged cleric, Natromo, to construct a power battery that would utilize the rarest light of the Emotional Spectrum, indigo.

Iroque was forced to wear an indigo ring, and was instantly overwhelmed by the horrific consequences of her past actions. She became driven to make amends, and tirelessly began the slow process of recruiting others to the Indigo Tribe's cause. No one wears an indigo ring voluntarily, and so Iroque had to ruthlessly coerce her disciples—drawn from the worst malefactors in existence—to become members of the growing Tribe. They patiently awaited the time foreseen by Abin Sur, when the Guardians would betray the universe, and they would be called to defend it.

Indigo 1's greatest achievement came after Nok's Central Power Battery was destroyed. Deprived of their rings' constant compassion, the rest of the tribe all reverted to the monsters they had once been. Iroque, however, had permanently changed, experiencing genuine remorse, which enabled Natromo to reconstruct the Battery and continue the crusade. **WW**

ON THE RECORD

Indigo 1 always pursued undisclosed aims, dictated solely by her innate compassion. After Sinestro was forcibly returned to the ranks of the Green Lanterns, he was abducted to Nok and forced to wear an indigo power ring.

His spiritual redemption took immediate effect and was only halted by the sudden destruction of the Indigo Tribe's Central Power Battery. If not for this, Iroque might have been able to rehabilitate one of the universe's greatest threats.

FALLEN HERO
Iroque's determined persuasions dug deep into Sinestro's black soul and reached the noble champion he used to be.

INFERIOR FIVE

DEBUT *Showcase* #62 **(May–Jun. 1966)**
CURRENT VERSION *Bat-Mite* #5 **(Dec. 2015)**
UNIVERSE Earth-12
BASE Megalopolis
MEMBERS/POWERS **Merryman**: Smart but puny; **White Feather**: Omniphobic archer; **Dumb Bunny**: Super-strong and hyper dense; **Awkward Man**: Super-strong, invulnerable, but super-clumsy; **The Blimp**: Floats in air, but lacks propulsive force.
ALLIES Police Chief Geronimo
ENEMIES Man-Mountain, Masked Swastika, Sparrow, Speed Demon, Silver Sorceress
AFFILIATIONS Freedom Brigade, Captain Carrot and the Zoo Crew

The Inferior Five are the saddest legacy heroes in creation. Children of World War II's legendary Freedom Brigade, they were each pressured by their doting parents into forming a new anti-evil alliance, despite an utter lack of dedication or even interest in crime-busting.

Though their combined skills and super-abilities are impressive—especially Leander Brent/Awkward Man's capacity for accident-induced collateral damage—their motivations for taking up costumed crusading are simply nonexistent. Comic book artist Myron Victor would far rather draw super-villains than fight one as Merryman, while Herman (Blimp) Cramer only wants to create meals in his little diner. Photographer William (White Feather) King is even afraid of the models he photographs, except for sweet and very, very simple Athena (Dumb Bunny), but is even more scared of admitting it to his dad.

Against all odds, the quivering quintet have beaten a remarkable number of sinister adversaries—usually by sheer luck, as much as concerted effort—and have made their families proud. However, they still regard any day in which they keep their civilian clothes on and their dignity intact as a major victory. **WW**

ON THE RECORD

As a satire on Super Hero comics and popular culture, the Inferior Five clashed with many extremely familiar-looking enemies, such as a team of hip and kooky young mutants, Norse gods, jungle men, and a nerdy guy who got big and green when he was angry.

However their greatest challenge came when all their DC stablemates and even the company's creative staff rose in revolt at their embarrassing antics.

POLITENESS COUNTS
Crime and injustice had little to fear when the Inferior Five suited up for action.

LUTHOR'S LEAGUE
1 Vaporlock
2 Vanilla
3 Amazing Woman
4/5 Nuklon

INFINITY, INC.

DEBUT *All-Star Squadron* (Vol. 1) #25 **(Sep. 1983)**
CURRENT VERSION *52* (Vol. 1) #9 **(Jul. 2006)**
NOTABLE MEMBERS/POWERS (ORIGINAL TEAM) Star-Spangled Kid (Sylvester Pemberton): Cosmic converter belt; **Fury** (Lyta Trevor): Super-strong, immune to magic; **Jade** (Jennifer-Lynn Hayden): Green Lantern; **Nuklon** (Albert Rothstein): Density control; **Power Girl** (Kara Zor-L): Kryptonian; **Brainwave, Jr.** (Hank King, Jr.): Psychic powers; **Northwind** (Norda Cantrell): Flight, magic; **Mr. Bones**: Cyanide touch; **Silver Scarab** (Hector Hall): Flight; **Wildcat** (Yolanda Montez): Superb agility and claws.
NOTABLE MEMBERS/POWERS (LUTHOR'S TEAM) Steel (John Henry Irons): Powered armor, kinetic hammer; **Vaporlock** (Natasha Irons): Flight, magic; **Amazing Woman** (Erik Storn): Gender transformation; **Vanilla** (Mercy Graves): Weapons expert, superb fighter; **Nuklon** (Gerome McKenna): Self-duplication.
ENEMIES Ultra-Humanite, Solomon Grundy, Dr. Benjamin Love

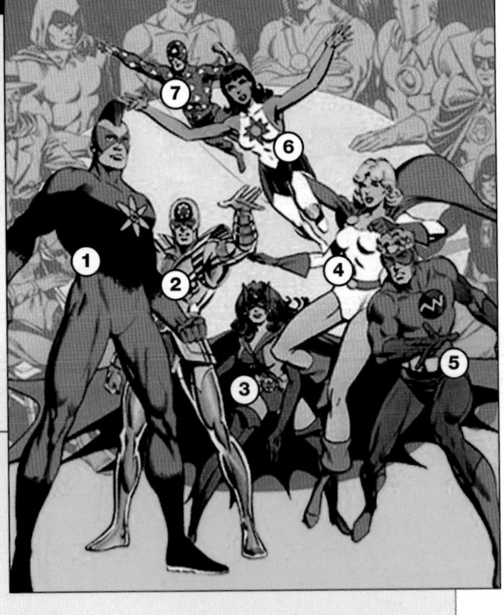

NEXT GENERATION HEROES—THE FIRST INFINITY, INC.
1 Nuklon
2 Silver Scarab
3 Huntress
4 Power Girl
5 Brainwave, Jr.
6 Jade
7 Star-Spangled Kid

Infinity, Inc. started as a junior counterpart to the Justice Society of America. When four young heroes were denied membership in the JSA, the Star-Spangled Kid (Sylvester Pemberton) proposed that they start their own team, and Infinity, Inc. was born. The teens were transported back to World War II and manipulated into turning against the Justice Society. It was an inauspicious beginning, but the team went on to have a series of more successful adventures, and quickly earned the respect of their seniors.

When Infinity, Inc. clashed with mad scientist Dr. Benjamin Love, they also recruited two of his test subjects, Mr. Bones and Wildcat (Yolanda Montez). However, this would ultimately lead to tragedy. While fighting Solomon Grundy, Mr. Bones was hurled into Skyman (as the Star-Spangled Kid now called himself) and accidentally killed him with his cyanide touch. Devastated by the loss of their leader, the team broke up.

The Infinity, Inc. name was later used by heroes who had largely acquired their powers from Lex Luthor's Everyman Project. Dubbed "Luthor's Own Justice League" by the media, the new Infinity Inc. were a publicity coup for LexCorp and a defense against rogue metahumans created by it. The team was led by Steel and included Vaporlock, Amazing Woman, Nuklon, Everyman, Vanilla, and the new Skyman. **SW**

INFINITY MAN

DEBUT *Forever People* (Vol. 1) #1 (Feb.–Mar. 1971)
CURRENT VERSION *Infinity Man and the Forever People* #2 (Sep. 2014)
BASE New Genesis
HEIGHT 6ft 4in **WEIGHT** 247 lbs
POWERS/ABILITIES Flight, energy bursts, incredible strength, and durability.
ENEMIES Mantis, Himon

Infinity Man is the physical manifestation of all that was compassionate within Izaya, Lord of New Genesis. Infinity Man split away from him, and Izaya became Highfather, who was committed to preserving peace and order rather than freedom. On a quest to redeem Highfather, Infinity Man chose as his agents five young New Gods—the Forever People.

When the Forever People were attacked on Earth by the villain Mantis, their sentient Mother Box began to glow. They touched the Box and disappeared in a flash of light. They were replaced by the imposing Infinity Man, who drove off Mantis. After the Forever People awoke in an alley, Infinity Man appeared on nearby TV monitors. He told them that together they would fight for freedom from both the benevolent despotism of Highfather and the cruel oppression of his evil brother, Darkseid. **SW**

INJUSTICE GANG

DEBUT *Justice League of America* (Vol. 1) #111 **(May-Jun. 1974)** (Libra team); *JLA* (Vol. 1) #9 **(Sep. 1977)** (Luthor team)
MEMBERS/POWERS (LIBRA TEAM) Libra (Justin Ballantine): Superpower absorption; **Chronos** (David Clinton): Time manipulation; **Mirror Master** (Sam Scudder): Laser blasts; **Scarecrow** (Dr. Jonathan Crane): Fear toxins; **Poison Ivy** (Pamela Isley): Plant control, poisons; **Shadow-Thief** (Carl Sands): Shifts into shadow state; **Tattooed Man** (Abel Tarrant): Living tattoos.
MEMBERS/POWERS (LUTHOR TEAM) Joker: Joker venom, deadly gadgets; **Doctor Light** (Arthur Light): Light powers; **Mirror Master** (Evan McCulloch): Mirror dimensional travel powers; **Ocean Master** (Orm Marius): Strength, underwater adaptation, controls sea life; **Jemm**: Flight, super-strength, psychic powers; **Circe**: Sorcery; **Queen Bee** (Zazzala): Stingers, mind-fogging pollen; **The General** (Wade Eiling): Super-strength and durability; **Prometheus**: Cybernetic enhancement.

The first Injustice Gang was made up of six villains recruited by the enigmatic Libra, ostensibly to balance out the Justice League. The Injustice Gang even operated from a satellite that orbited Earth on the opposite side from the JLA's. The Injustice Gang went off to battle the JLA, but they had been tricked; Libra had used them to lure the JLA out so he could steal half the heroes' powers with his Energy Transmortifier. Having taken their power into himself, Libra began to expand in size and was absorbed into the cosmos. The Injustice Gang then briefly worked for the Construct and Abra Kadabra before disbanding.

When Superman became leader of the JLA, Lex Luthor created a new Injustice Gang to oppose what he saw as an escalation in the conflict between himself and the Man of Steel. He tried to sow dissent within the JLA and force it to break up, but was unsuccessful. Lex's revamped Injustice Gang was also a failure, falling under the control of the alien weapon Mageddon before being defeated. **SW**

INJUSTICE LEAGUE

DEBUT *Justice League International* (Vol. 1) #23 **(Jan. 1989)**
CURRENT VERSION *Forever Evil* #3 **(Jan. 2014)**
MEMBERS/POWERS **Lex Luthor:** Amoral genius; **Black Manta:** Optic blasts; **Black Adam** (Teth-Adam): Godlike power; **Subject B-0:** Unfinished Superman clone; **Captain Cold** (Leonard Snart): Cryogenic powers.
ALLIES Batman, Catwoman, Justice League
ENEMIES Crime Syndicate, Secret Society
AFFILIATIONS Justice League

When the Crime Syndicate (an evil version of the Justice League from Earth-3) invaded and took the Justice League teams out of action, many of the world's super-villains chose to serve the conquerors and became part of their so-called Secret Society. Not so Lex Luthor. He decided that if the Justice League couldn't free the world, it was up to him to do it.

After retrieving a suit of powered armor from LexCorp, he recruited fellow refuseniks Black Adam, Black Manta, and Captain Cold into his own Injustice League, along with half-finished Superman clone B-0. After linking up with Batman, Catwoman, Sinestro, and Deathstroke, the Injustice League confronted the Crime Syndicate. B-0 was killed, but Lex defeated Ultraman and Mazahs (an alternate-world Lex Luthor with Shazam's powers), and Captain Cold killed Johnny Quick. This gave Batman the chance to release the Justice League from their prison within the Firestorm Matrix.

With the Crime Syndicate beaten, the Justice League agreed to wipe the records of the Injustice Society members. Without the threat of the Crime Syndicate to unite them, the Injustice Society disbanded—although Captain Cold and Lex Luthor decided to join the Justice League. **SW**

ON THE RECORD

The first pre-Flashpoint Injustice League was an incompetent team of Justice League International foes who were hired as "Justice League Antarctica" by Maxwell Lord. However, *Silver Age: Showcase* #1 chronicles the adventures of an even earlier Injustice League, which included Lex Luthor. Luthor also founded Injustice League Unlimited, a large team that enjoyed some success against the JLA, but which is most famous for crashing Green Arrow and Black Canary's wedding.

THE TABLES TURNED
The Injustice League had their heroic opposite numbers on the ropes on numerous occasions, as when they tortured the Justice League to enrage Superman.

INJUSTICE SOCIETY

DEBUT *All-Star Comics* #37 **(Oct.–Nov. 1947)**
NOTABLE MEMBERS/POWERS (FIRST TEAM) **Wizard** (William Zard): Magician, illusionist; **Brain Wave** (Henry King, Sr.): Psychic powers; **Gambler** (Steven Sharpe III): Master of disguise; **Per Degaton**: Precognition, time travel; **Thinker** (Clifford DeVoe): Mind control, telekinesis; **Vandal Savage**: Immortality, vast mental and physical abilities; **Fiddler** (Isaac Bowin): Musical hypnosis; **Harlequin** (Molly Mayne): Hypnotic glasses; **Shade** (Richard Swift): Shadow powers; **Solomon Grundy** (Cyrus Gold): Super-strength.
NOTABLE MEMBERS/POWERS (LATER TEAM) **Johnny Sorrow**: Psychic, deadly gaze; **Tigress** (Artemis Crock): Athlete; **Geomancer**: Elemental control of earth; **Icicle** (Cameron Mahkent): Cryogenic powers; **Killer Wasp**: Flight, electrical blasts.

The Injustice Society was founded by the Wizard with the objectives of defeating the Justice Society and taking over America. The Society used various ploys to trap the JSA team members, before putting them on trial. However, Green Lantern was able to infiltrate the proceedings and free his comrades, leading to defeat for the villains. The Wizard went on to convene at least two more Injustice Societies, who also met with limited success.

Some decades later, Johnny Sorrow formed another Injustice Society. This team attacked the JSA headquarters, but they were beaten single-handedly by grizzled boxer Wildcat—who was nursing an injured arm at the time! Sorrow then used the Injustice Society as pawns to summon the reality-devouring King of Tears, but both were vanquished thanks to the Flash, who cast the King of Tears to another dimension.

Subsequently, the Wizard founded yet another Injustice Society, which Johnny Sorrow quickly took over. He used the Injustice Society's members as sacrifices to bring back the King of Tears, and kidnapped young JSA All-Stars member Stargirl for a ritual intended to restore him to human form. Once again, he was defeated. **SW**

ANTISOCIAL SOCIETY
1 Wizard
2 Rag Doll
3 Solomon Grundy
4 Gentleman Ghost
5 Tigress
6 Icicle

VILLAINS UNITED
The Injustice Society's very first attempt to bring down the Justice Society almost succeeded. The heroes were at the villains' mercy—until Green Lantern outwitted the bad guys.

INQUE

DEBUT *Batman Beyond* (Vol. 1) #6 (Aug. 1999)
CURRENT VERSION *Batman Beyond* (Vol. 5) #2 (Sep. 2015)
EYES Gray **HAIR** Black
POWERS/ABILITIES Liquidized shapeshifting—can alter form at will to create tendrils, spikes, or waves, but body can be temporarily disrupted by a hard enough blow.
ENEMIES Brother Eye, Batman (Terry McGinnis)

In a near-future, Brother Eye (an artificial intelligence created by Batman and Mister Terrific) launched a campaign to gain control of humanity by using a techno-organic virus to transform people into cyborg slaves. Inque was a corporate saboteur, turned into a liquidized shapeshifter by mutagenic experiments, who frequently clashed with the second Batman (Terry McGinnis). She was blackmailed into working for Brother Eye after it kidnapped her daughter Deana and held her hostage on the Moon.

Brother Eye ordered Inque to capture the third Batman (Tim Drake) and Commissioner Barbara Gordon. After an intense battle, Inque snared the pair with her viscous form and took them back to Brother Eye for "conversion." However, Batman managed to escape with Gordon and pledged to help Inque get Deana back. Inque joined Batman's fight against Brother Eye and sacrificed her own life to destroy the malignant artificial intelligence. **SW**

GO WITH THE FLOW
Inque's liquid form made it possible for her to flow around opponents' attacks and then form weapons to deliver devastating strikes.

INTERGANG

DEBUT *Superman's Pal, Jimmy Olsen* (Vol. 1) #133 (Oct. 1970)
CURRENT VERSION *Superman: Lois & Clark* #1 (Dec. 2015)
BASE Metropolis
CURRENT MEMBERS/POWERS **Whisper A'Daire**: Poison spit; **Johnny Stitches**: Gang boss whose face is stitched togther with animal and human skin.
FORMER MEMBERS/POWERS **"Moxie" Mannheim**: Intergang's shrewd first boss; **Bruno "Ugly" Mannheim**: Massive size and strength, ruthless disposition; **Morgan Edge**: Consummate wheeler dealer
ENEMIES Superman, Batman Family, Jimmy Olsen, the Question

Intergang is a criminal organization, run like a business corporation by media mogul Morgan Edge, with extensive resources and an international reach. It has had secret investors, including Desaad of Apokolips and his master Darkseid, who wished to spread chaos and evil on Earth. Intergang was supplied with advanced Apokoliptian weaponry, which helped it to become a force to be reckoned with in the criminal underworld.

When Edge was hospitalized with a heart attack, Intergang underwent a series of leadership changes. First the gangster "Ugly" Mannheim took charge. After he was seemingly killed in a Boom Tube accident, his father Moxie Mannheim took over. Lex Luthor then conspired to take control of Intergang from behind the scenes, with Moxie serving as a figurehead for the organization until he was murdered by Superboy-Prime.

"Ugly" Mannheim then unexpectedly resurfaced, claiming to have been "reborn" as a devotee of the Religion of Crime. He used Intergang to spread its commandments. Cultists worshiped the Biblical character of Cain—whom they regarded as the first-ever murderer—and practiced human sacrifice and cannibalism. Intergang's influence grew as it expanded operations into Africa and Gotham City, and effectively took control of the Metropolis underworld. **SW**

ALIEN ARSENAL
Bruno Mannheim's Intergang was supplied with Apokoliptian weapons, giving its Gassers, Wall-Crawlers, and Shock Troops an edge in gang warfare in Gotham City, Metropolis, and beyond.

UNHOLY HUNGER
When he returned from the dead, Bruno Mannheim was a fanatical devotee of the Religion of Crime. He set about taking control of the Metropolis underworld by killing (and eating) his rivals.

PATCHWORK MAN
After Johnny Denetto was horribly mutilated and left for dead, Bruno Mannheim stitched him back together and recruited him into Intergang. As Johnny Stitches, Denetto took control of Intergang's operations in Gotham City.

INTERNATIONAL ULTRAMARINE CORPS

DEBUT *DC One Million* #2 (Nov. 1998)
BASE Superbia
MEMBERS **Warmaker One** (Lt. Scott Sawyer); **4D** (Capt. Lea Corbin); **Flow/Glob** (Maj. Dan Stone); **Pulse 8** (Capt. John Wether); **Knight** (Cyril Sheldrake); **Squire** (Beryl Hutchinson); **Goraiko**; **Vixen** (Mari McCabe); **Jack O'Lantern** (Liam McHugh); **Kid Impala**; **Olympian** (Aristides Demetrios); **Tasmanian Devil** (Hugh Dawkins); **Fleur-de-Lis** (Noelle Avril).
ENEMIES Gen. Wade Eiling/Shaggy Man, Gorilla Grodd, Sheeda

With global threats escalating, Gen. Wade Eiling decided the US needed a national hero team. Four soldiers were genetically engineered into superhumans: Warmaker One, 4D, Flow, and Pulse 8 became the International Ultramarine Corps. As a test, Eiling had them attack the JLA. However, when they learned Eiling had gone insane and transplanted his personality into the unstoppable Shaggy Man, they joined forces with the JLA and exiled Eiling to an asteroid.

The Corps then used their powers to create the floating city of Superbia above the ruins of Montevideo and declared that they would accept heroes of all nations into the International Ultramarine Corps. However, they suffered a setback when Gorilla Grodd took control of Superbia and the parasitic Sheeda took control of the team. After the JLA defeated the mind-controlled Ultramarines, they sent the team to serve as heroes in the young universe of Qwewq. **SW**

LEAGUE OF NATIONS
Although the International Ultramarine Corps was founded on high ideals, it proved to be far less than effective in practice.

IRONS, NATASHA

DEBUT *Steel* (Vol. 2) #1 (Feb. 1994)
CURRENT VERSION *Action Comics* (Vol. 2) #7 (May 2012)
EYES Brown **HAIR** Black
HEIGHT 5ft 6in **WEIGHT** 106 lbs
POWERS/ABILITIES **As Steel**: armor gives protection, rocket boots, magnetic hammer; **as Starlight**: superhuman strength and endurance, flight; **as Vaporlock**: can turn into gas.
ALLIES Steel, Superman, Batman
ENEMIES Desaad, Plasma, Black Adam

Natasha Irons shared a gift for technology with her engineer uncle John Henry Irons. The teen quickly became involved in his adventures as the armored Super Hero Steel, and when Henry retired he built her a suit of her own so she could become the new Steel. However, he was furious when she ditched city-cleanup duties to try out for the Teen Titans, and he took her armor apart to teach her a lesson.

After failing to reassemble it, Natasha volunteered for Lex Luthor's Everyman Program, angering Henry further. Luthor's genetic enhancement procedure gave her flight and other powers, and she joined Infinity, Inc. as Starlight. When she developed the ability to turn to gas, she changed her codename to Vaporlock. She and Infinity Inc. were forced to fight in the Dark Side Club's gladiatorial games, but were rescued by the Titans. **SW**

A STAR IS BORN?
The Everyman Project gave Natasha extraordinary powers, and she joined Infinity, Inc. as Starlight. However, she soon learned her newfound abilities were not permanent.

INVISIBLE KID

DEBUT *Legion of Super Heroes Annual* (Vol. 2) #1 (1982)
CURRENT VERSION *Legion of Super-Heroes* (Vol. 7) #1 (Nov. 2011)
REAL NAME Jacques Foccart
BASE Legion headquarters, 31st century
EYES Brown **HAIR** Brown with white streak
HEIGHT 5ft 9in **WEIGHT** 170 lbs
POWERS/ABILITIES Invisibility; teleportation into the afterlife; Legion flight ring gives flight and life-support in space.

When the Legion of Super-Heroes suffered heavy losses in action, one of the victim was Lyle Norg, the first Invisible Kid. Legion Academy member Jacques Foccart took the formula that Norg had used to give himself invisibility powers and became the new Invisible Kid.

The Legion and the United Planets were then attacked by the Fatal Five, who caused chaos on many worlds. When the Invisible Kid was on a cruiser that crashed into one of the massive Stone Promethean Giants, he used his powers to save himself and fellow Legionnaire Polar Boy by instinctively teleporting himself to what appeared to be the afterlife. Here he met the spirit of Lyle Norg. The Invisible Kid then teleported himself and Polar Boy back to Earth, where they helped defeat the Fatal Five. **SW**

ION

DEBUT *Green Lantern Sinestro Corps Special* #1 (Aug. 2007)
EYES Green **HAIR** None
POWERS/ABILITIES Interstellar flight; space/time manipulation; creates manifest green energy constructs.
ALLIES Green Lantern Corps
ENEMIES Relic, Anti-Monitor, Sinestro
AFFILIATIONS Emotional energy entities

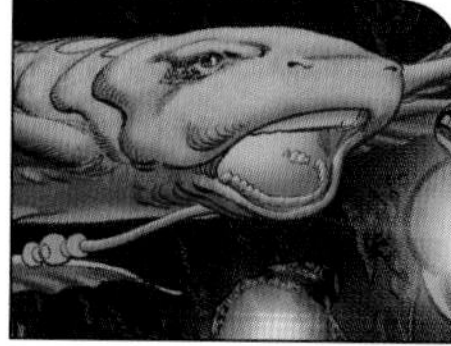

Ion is the living embodiment of willpower, represented by the color green on the Emotional Spectrum. It was long contained within the Central Power Battery on Oa, where it provided energy for the power rings of the Green Lantern Corps. When the Battery was destroyed, the entity took Kyle Rayner as its host and transformed him into the hero known as Ion.

During the Sinestro Corps War, Sinestro physically drew the Ion entity from Rayner and imprisoned it at Qward, but it was retrieved by the Lanterns and bonded with Sodam Yat. When the power of all the Lantern Corps began to ebb, a being called Relic destroyed the Green Lantern Battery and warned that the energies of the Emotional Spectrum were running out. Ion and the other entities sacrificed themselves to replenish the energies of the Emotional Spectrum and save reality. **SW**

ISIS

DEBUT *52* #3 (May 2006)
CURRENT VERSION *Justice League of America* (Vol. 3) #7.4 (Nov. 2013)
REAL NAME Adrianna Tomaz
BASE Shiruta, Kahndaq
HEIGHT 6ft 1in **WEIGHT** 135 lbs
POWERS/ABILITIES Super-strength; flight; mastery of the elements; healing.
ENEMIES Intergang, Death, Felix Faust

Egyptian Adrianna Tomaz was enslaved by Intergang and gifted to Black Adam, the superpowered ruler of Kahndaq. Adam killed the criminals and set Adrianna free. Captivated by her courage, honesty, and desire for justice, Adam took her as his consort and gave her a mystic amulet that transformed her into the divinely empowered Isis.

Adrianna freed her brother Amon (Osiris) from slavery, but both were killed by a vengeful Intergang. Adam tried to raise Isis from the dead but was tricked by the evil sorcerer Felix Faust, who returned Isis to life, but as his unwilling slave. Isis broke free and exacted a gruesome revenge on Faust. She had become embittered and ruthless, and set herself up as absolute ruler of Kahndaq.

After Flashpoint, Adrianna was a young Kahndaqi who summoned Black Adam to free her nation when her brother was killed by the country's cruel dictator. **SW**

DIVINE RIGHT
The Amulet of Isis that empowered Adrianna belonged to Queen Pharoah Hatshepsut of the 15th Dynasty, who used it to bring peace to her kingdom.

CHANGE OF HEART
Devastated after her brother was shot by security forces, Adrianna joined the fight to overthrow Kahndaq's corrupt dictatorship.

JACK O'LANTERN

DEBUT *Super Friends* (Vol. 1) #8 (Nov. 1977) (Daniel Cormac); *Justice League Quarterly* #14 (Mar. 1994) (Liam McHugh)
REAL NAME Liam McHugh
EYES Blue **HAIR** Blond
HEIGHT 5ft 11in **WEIGHT** 188 lbs
POWERS/ABILITIES Lantern provides flight, teleportation, increased strength, and fog summoning.
AFFILIATIONS: Leymen (Primal Force), International Ultramarine Corps

The first Jack O'Lantern, named Daniel Cormac, was given a magic lantern by the fairy queen Maeve. He fell foul of a power struggle in Bialya between would-be dictator Colonel Harjarvti and the country's ruler, Queen Bee. She gave the lantern to native Bialyan Marvin Noronsa, who was killed in a bombing incident.

The lantern then passed to Cormac's cousin, Liam McHugh. He managed to absorb the lantern's powers, so no longer needed to carry it. McHugh served with Dr. Mist's Leymen and the International Ultramarine Corps. He was later taken over by an alien Sheeda spine-rider and made to join Gorilla Grodd's latest bid to destroy humanity. McHugh escaped and went on to safeguard the sentient, time-traveling universe Qwewq (Neh-Buh-Loh). **SW**

JADE

DEBUT *All-Star Squadron* #25 (Sep. 1983)
REAL NAME Jennifer-Lynn Hayden
EYES Green **HAIR** Dark green
HEIGHT 5ft 3in **WEIGHT:** 110 lbs
POWERS/ABILITIES Starheart creates energy constructs; controls plants and can photosynthesize; wields Green Lantern Power Ring.
ALLIES: Kyle Rayner, Alan Scott, Todd Rice
ENEMIES: Alexander Luthor, Jr.
AFFILIATIONS: Green Lantern Corps

Jennifer-Lynn Hayden and her brother Todd Rice (Obsidian) are the children of Green Lantern Alan Scott and the villainess Thorn. They were given up for adoption and raised separately. Jennifer-Lynn discovered her ability to wield the Starheart when she was attacked as a teen; the use of her powers turned her hair and skin green. She reconnected with her brother and they signed up with Infinity, Inc. Jade had a relationship with Green Lantern Kyle Rayner, who gave her a power ring after she lost her Starheart powers. She joined the Outsiders and was killed during Infinite Crisis.

Jade came back as a Black Lantern to haunt Kyle during Blackest Night, but was returned to life by the power of the White Lantern and helped to combat the power of the Starheart-controlled Obsidian. **SW**

JEMM, SON OF SATURN

DEBUT *Jemm, Son of Saturn* #1 (Sep. 1984)
REAL NAME Jemm **BASE** Saturn
EYES Yellow **HAIR** None
HEIGHT 6ft 6in **WEIGHT** 340 lbs
POWERS/ABILITIES Flight and superhuman strength; forehead gem senses others' emotions and emits force beams.
ALLIES J'onn J'onzz
ENEMIES: Claudius Tull, Jogarr, Synn
AFFILIATIONS: Red Saturnians, formerly Injustice Gang

Jemm is the prince of the Red Saturnians, a race created by the Green Martians. His people were at war with the rival White Saturnians, but Jemm was born with a gem in his forehead, a sign that he was destined to bring peace to Saturn. After the White Saturnians killed his family, Jemm fled to Earth, where Lex Luthor used the mind-controlling Worlogog to make him join his Injustice Gang as a rival to J'onn J'onzz, the Martian Manhunter. He was freed from Luthor's control by the JLA, and the Martian Manhunter helped him to recover.

Jenn then married the White Saturnian Cha'rissa, bringing peace to the races of Saturn. He sided with the Rannians in the Rann-Thanagar War, and represented his people's interests when new Krypton was created in the solar system. **SW**

JINX

DEBUT *Tales of the Teen Titans* #56 (Aug. 1985)
CURRENT VERSION *Forever Evil* #1 (Nov. 2013)
EYES Brown **HAIR** None
HEIGHT 5ft 9in **WEIGHT** 136 lbs
POWERS/ABILITIES Sorcery
ALLIES Dr. Sivana, Calculator
ENEMIES: Teen Titans, Superman, Wonder Woman
AFFILIATIONS Fearsome Five

Jinx studied magic in her native India, but after she murdered her fellow students and teachers she was confined at S.T.A.R. Labs. She was broken out by the Fearsome Five, who recruited her, and she clashed with their enemies the Teen Titans.

The team broke up following a battle with Superman, and Jinx was locked up in Alcatraz with other group members. She and the rest of the Five were freed by Dr. Sivana. He ordered them to attack LexCorp facilities, but they were stopped by the Outsiders. Jinx joined the Injustice League and was briefly exiled to the planet Salvation, before rejoining the Five for a rematch with the Titans.

A post-Flashpoint incarnation of Jinx appeared alongside the rest of the Fearsome Five as part of The Outsider's Secret Society of Super-Villains. **SW**

JERICHO

DEBUT *Tales of the Teen Titans* #42 (May 1984)
CURRENT VERSION *Deathstroke* (Vol. 2) #0 (Nov. 2012)
REAL NAME Joseph Wilson
HEIGHT 6ft **WEIGHT** 195 lbs
EYES Blue **HAIR** Green
POWERS/ABILITIES Can control the minds of others, or tear their bodies apart with his psychic powers.
ALLIES Adeline Wilson, Rose Wilson (Ravager), Slade Wilson (Deathstroke), Grant Wilson
ENEMIES Odysseus, Lynch

Joseph Wilson is the second son of Slade Wilson, better known as the legendary mercenary Deathstroke. He was believed to have been killed along with his mother Adeline when Slade's enemies attacked their home. However, mother and son secretly survived, and Adeline raised Joseph to hate his father for what had happened to their family.

Using the codename Jericho, Joseph worked for the mysterious Lynch, who wanted to use Joseph's mind-control powers to control a powerful superhuman called Majestic. However, Joseph had other ideas: he took control of Majestic, Adeline, and his older brother Grant, to launch a blistering attack on his father. After a bloody battle, Jericho tried to fend off his father by holding Grant hostage, but Deathstroke seemingly killed both his sons with a single sword thrust.

Jericho somehow survived and was captured by his grandfather Odysseus, who experimented on him and siphoned off his psychic power to augment his own. Deathstroke rescued Jericho, who then went to Gotham City to get help from his sister Rose (Ravager). They were betrayed to Odysseus, and Jericho and Rose were only saved when Deathstroke stormed in and killed his father Odysseus to save his own children. **SW**

ON THE RECORD

The original Jericho possessed formidable psychic powers and joined the Teen Titans team, despite the fact that they were bitter foes of his father, Deathstroke. However, he was then possessed by the warped souls of Azarath, who turned him against the Titans. Deathstroke was forced to kill Jericho to release him from their possession. Jericho's soul survived but was driven insane, and it went on to wreak havoc in a succession of unwilling host bodies.

THE CURSE OF AZARATH
In a tragic twist of fate, the Souls of Azarath drove Jericho mad, transforming him into a vicious, violent monster.

JOKER KING

DEBUT *Batman Beyond* (Vol. 4) #5 (Jul. 2011)
REAL NAME Doug Tan
BASE Gotham City
EYES One black, one white
HAIR Green tufts
POWERS/ABILITIES Leadership; highly intelligent but totally amoral; great stamina.
ALLIES Pally Otchee
ENEMIES Batman (Terry McGinnis), Bruce Wayne
AFFILIATIONS Jokerz

Growing up in the near future, Doug Tan was a troubled young man who became obsessed with the Joker and the "Jokerz" youth subculture that imitated him. Most Jokerz simply used the Joker's nihilistic philosophy as an excuse to cause mayhem, but Tan wanted to reveal the Joker's real message to the world: life is meaningless, and the joke is on you.

As the Joker King, he used mind-controlling drugs to convince the Jokerz to don suicide vests and cause total carnage in Gotham City. He then set off for Gotham Mercy hospital to kill his sister, Dana. In the hospital, he clashed with an elderly Bruce Wayne, who managed to send a warning to Terry McGinnis, Dana's boyfriend and that era's Batman. Now aware of the nature of the threat, McGinnis swooped in to save Dana and, following a fierce battle with Batman and Wayne, the Joker King died after he fell off a ledge and slammed head-first into a wall. **SW**

BEYOND PARODY
Frustrated by the Jokerz' petty crimes and lack of ambition, Tan decided to take over and make them truly worthy of their namesake.

JOKERZ

DEBUT *Batman Beyond* (Vol. 1) #1 (Mar. 1999)
BASE Gotham City
KEY MEMBER Impostor Joker (Winslow Heath): Leader of innumerable faceless goons
ENEMIES Batman, G.C.P.D., Batman vigilantes

Following the apparent death of the Joker, Gotham City was plagued by mobs of Jokerz. These costumed Joker fans were hooked on a street drug called Joker Juice and took part in flash mobs to cause the maximum amount of non-lethal mayhem, with looting, vandalism, and the like. The Joker imitator who started the craze and supplied the Joker Juice upped the stakes by shooting a police officer, which led to the shooting of a Jokerz member. Soon after, an impostor Batman appeared on TV, urging citizens to fight the Jokerz, and violence escalated across the city.

Batman discovered that the leader of the Jokerz was a man named Winslow Heath, who had been poisoned by Joker Venom many years ago and wanted revenge on Batman for not ending the threat of the Joker permanently. After a climactic battle in a Hall of Mirrors, Batman defeated the Batman imitator: it was none other than Winslow Heath, who had instigated the "Impostor War" from both sides.

Many years in the future, a similar gang also using the Jokerz name would emerge, led by a ruthless individual going by the name of the Joker King. **SW**

DOWN WITH THE CLOWN
The Jokerz started out just wanting to have some crazy fun—but things soon got out of control, forcing Batman to enter the fray.

JOKER'S DAUGHTER

DEBUT *Batman Family* #6 (Jul.–Aug. 1976)
CURRENT VERSION *Catwoman* (Vol. 4) #23 (Oct. 2013)
REAL NAME Duela Dent
BASE The Nethers, Gotham City
EYES: Blue (left), Green (right) **HAIR:** Pink
POWERS/ABILITIES Insanity and viciousness give her an edge in combat.
ALLIES Dollmaker, Red Hood, Arsenal
ENEMIES Batman, Catwoman, Harley Quinn, Charon

Duela Dent, the girl who calls herself the Joker's Daughter, had a conventional upbringing in Gotham City's suburbs. She developed a morbid fascination with the twisted and ugly, going so far as to scar her own face. In her teens she ran away from home and found her way to the subterranean Nethers where Gotham City's homeless eked out a living.

She found the Joker's flayed face floating in the water and at first mistook it for her own reflection. She placed the Joker's visage over her own and immediately felt that it gave her power. Calling herself the Joker's Daughter, she became obsessed with the Clown Prince of Crime and tried to attract his attention by committing acts of mayhem. She even had the Dollmaker stitch the Joker's face to her own. After taking part in a plot to summon Deacon Blackfire, she joined the Suicide Squad, but left after clashing with Harley Quinn. **SW**

UGLY IS THE NEW BEAUTIFUL
Wearing the Joker's face, the Joker's Daughter has launched her own psychotic war on society's ideas of beauty.

JUDOMASTER

DEBUT *Special War Series* #4 (Nov. 1965) (Rip Jagger); *Birds of Prey* (Vol. 1) #100 (Jan. 2007) (Sonia Sato)
CURRENT VERSION (Sonia Sato) *Earth 2* #9 (Apr. 2013)
REAL NAME Sonia Sato
EYES Brown **HAIR** Black
POWERS/ABILITIES Martial arts expert; aversion field makes it impossible for attacks aimed at her to hit (though field does not work against random or area-effect attacks).

The first Judomaster was Sgt. Hadley "Rip" Jagger, who used his judo skills to fight Japanese soldiers during World War II. After he was killed during the Infinite Crisis, the name was briefly used by an unnamed hero before it was taken by Sonia Sato, the daughter of Yakuza hitman Yoshio Sato. When Sonia was born, he tried to quit the Yakuza, but was killed. Sonia mastered martial arts to avenge her father. She was recruited by Oracle of the Birds of Prey to help break an innocent girl out of prison and served with the team on subsequent missions.

In New York, she was attacked by the Blood Soldiers, a superpowered squad of Yakuza hitmen. The Justice Society stepped in to help her and she eventually joined up, siding with Gog when he caused a schism in the team. Sonia fell in love with team member Damage, and was distraught when he was killed during the Blackest Night. **SW**

HARD TARGET
Sonia's metahuman aversion-field power came in very handy when facing gun-wielding enemies of the Birds of Prey.

THE JOKER

DATA

DEBUT *Batman* (Vol. 1) #1 **(Spring 1940)**
CURRENT VERSION *Detective Comics* (Vol. 2) #1 **(Nov. 2011)**
REAL NAME Unknown **BASE** Gotham City
HEIGHT 6ft 5in **WEIGHT** 192 lbs **EYES** Green **HAIR** Green
POWERS/ABILITIES Unpredictable actions and fighting techniques due to extreme insanity; natural, charismatic leader and brilliant strategist; agile and relentless fighter; twisted genius; adept in chemistry; has used chemical compound Dionesium to heal wounds; weapons include a variety of clown- and joke-themed deadly devices, as well as the deadly toxin known as Joker Venom.
ALLIES Harley Quinn, Jackanapes, The Joker's Daughter
ENEMIES Batman, the Batman Family, Commissioner James Gordon
AFFILIATIONS Arkham Asylum inmates, Red Hood Gang

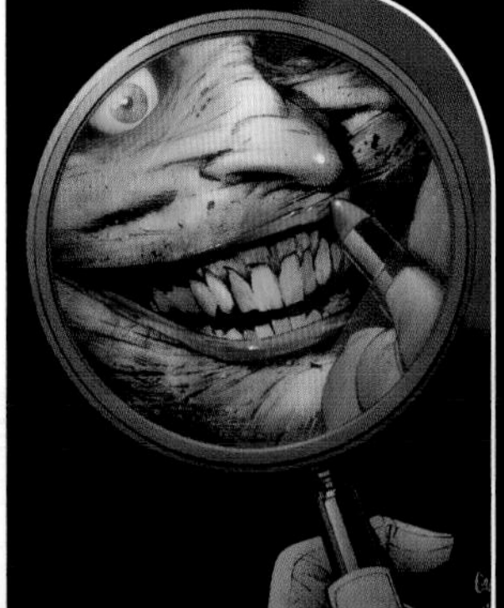

The Joker possesses what must arguably be the most dangerous criminal mind on the planet. With no moral compass to speak of, and a sick sense of humor that derives joy from witnessing the pain of others, the notorious Clown Prince of Crime is the smiling foil to the Batman's grim and serious demeanor. With a reputation as infamous as that of the Dark Knight, the Joker has become a one-man movement in the city of Gotham City, attracting a sea of followers as he proceeds to indulge in unthinkable crimes that would give even the cruelest career criminal pause.

AT A GLANCE...

Mystery man
The Joker's past remains a mystery, but Batman believes his nemesis was once the brilliant leader of the Red Hood Gang, a criminal outfit that plagued Gotham City during the first year of Batman's career. After a fall into a vat of chemicals stained his skin white and his hair green, Red Hood One opted for a career as the Joker, giving in to his every insane impulse.

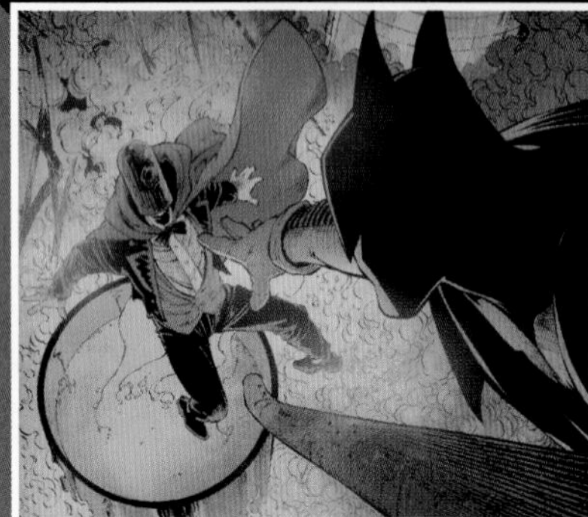

Tools of the trade
The Joker employs a variety of clown- and circus-themed weaponry, ranging from razor-sharp playing cards to acid-squirting lapel flowers. He often sets up shop in deserted card factories or on dilapidated former circus grounds, keeping to his favorite themes.

Insane inspiration
The Joker has inspired many criminals to follow in his footsteps, most notably his on again/off again romantic interest, Harley Quinn. But Harley isn't alone in her obsession with the so-called Clown Prince of Crime. The underground villain called Joker's Daughter also strives to imitate Gotham City's most notorious and feared criminal.

CLASSIC STORIES

***Detective Comics* (Vol. 1) #168 (Feb. 1951)** The Joker's origin is explored for the first time, introducing the concept of the Red Hood, and the incident that birthed Batman's greatest foe.

***Batman: The Killing Joke* #1 (Mar. 1988)** The Joker's origin is given a modern twist as the villain indulges in his latest criminal campaign: an attempt to drive Commissioner Gordon as crazy as the Joker is himself.

***Batman* (Vol. 1) #426-429 (Dec. 1988-Jan. 1989)** In "A Death in the Family," Batman faces real tragedy once again when the Joker successfully kills the second Robin, Jason Todd.

***Arkham Asylum* #1 (Oct. 1989)** The madmen are running the asylum when the Clown Prince of Crime takes over Arkham, aided and abetted by some of Gotham City's most dangerous psychopaths.

Little is known about the true past of the Joker. The madman has created a vast number of legends surrounding his crazed persona, some insisting that he is an ancient trickster being, as old as Gotham City itself. The only version of his past known to the world consists of conflicting stories that the Joker himself tells, often to manipulate those within earshot to one of his twisted causes or schemes.

According to the Joker, he lived a rough childhood, raised in part by his Aunt Eunice. She was mentally unstable herself, and scrubbed her young nephew with bleach in order to get him clean. When the young Joker returned from school after being beat up by a female classmate, he was again beaten by his enraged aunt. The young boy grew up in squalor with very little to eat and was ridiculed by his classmates on a regular basis. His only comfort during that time was a stuffed toy monkey he called Gaggy.

GOING JACKANAPES
The boy destined to become the Joker loved his toy monkey Gaggy. So much so that when the adult Joker discovered a gorilla at Gotham City Zoo, he kidnapped it and made it his "henchman," Jackanapes.

While much of the rest of the Joker's past remains shrouded in mystery, Batman believes that there is a strong possibility that the deranged criminal led the notorious Red Hood Gang when he reached adulthood. A ruthless organization bent on taking over Gotham City's underworld, the Red Hood Gang had risen to power during the time when Batman first emerged on the crime-fighting scene.

Though still working out the kinks of combating crime, Batman managed to take down the Red Hood Gang during a confrontation in a processing plant known as A.C.E. Chemical. It was here he fought the gang's leader, Red Hood One, in a ferocious conflict that saw the villain opt to fall into a vat of chemicals rather than be saved by Batman. After the event, Batman tried to research Red Hood One's identity, only to find more questions at every turn. It seemed that the original leader, Liam Distal, had been killed at an amusement park, and had been replaced by whomever Batman had battled at A.C.E. Chemical.

Soon after the Dark Knight successfully dismantled the Red Hood Gang, the Joker—who had taken to calling himself the Clown Prince of Crime—emerged in Gotham City.

MASKING HIS EVIL
The Joker wore the skin from his face as a macabre mask, held on by a strap he wrapped around his head. The villain later lost this mask, and it was found by a girl living in Gotham City's underground society. She went on to adopt the name of Joker's Daughter.

DEATH OF THE FAMILY
After enduring a bizarre ritual performed by the Dollmaker of having his face literally cut from his head, the Joker returned to Batman's life, kidnapping those close to Batman and Bruce Wayne. Holed up in Arkham Asylum with a few fellow criminals including Two-Face and Penguin, the Joker then tricked the Batman Family into believing that he had cut off their faces as well. While Batman managed to save his partners, a rift formed between the family, one caused by secrets the Dark Knight had kept from those closest to him.

JOKER'S GARAGE
When the Joker set his sights on the Batman Family, he dressed as a mechanic with a dangerous tool belt.

The Joker had bleached white skin, green hair, and a perverted sense of humor that could only result from extreme insanity. As he committed crime after crime, he revealed not only an obsession with clown-related imagery, but also with Batman himself. The Joker seemed to feel it was his job to better the Batman by challenging him at every opportunity. He even decided to maneuver a young man named Jason Todd into a position to become the second Robin, just to kill the youth and hurt Batman by association. With an ever mounting body count, the Joker became known as Batman's arch-enemy, one he seemed fated to battle time and time again.

That endless fight would reach a seeming conclusion when the Joker unleashed a virus on Gotham, turning its citizens into grinning, violent, zombie-like pawns. Batman was able to cure the virus, but fought the Joker in a battle that nearly cost the pair their lives. The Joker has recently resurfaced in Gotham City, proving that his role as the deadly thorn in Batman's side is far from over. **MM**

ENDGAME

The Joker turned almost the entire Justice League against Batman using his Joker virus, forcing the Dark Knight to adopt a protective battle suit dubbed the Justice Buster to confront them. Barely escaping with his life, Batman realized that this time, the Joker had raised the stakes and seemed to be playing for keeps. The Dark Knight tracked down a cure for the virus despite a wealth of misinformation spread through various sources. He discovered that the Joker was indeed a mortal man, despite what the legends would have the citizens of Gotham City believe.

SUPER JOKER
A Jokerized Superman with no moral scruples was easily the biggest threat Batman had to face during his battle with the Justice League—who were all under the influence of the Joker's toxin.

"I'm the one who laughs... at the great joke... that any of it matters."
THE JOKER

THE ETERNAL JOKE
The Joker is obsessed with Batman, a relationship the Dark Knight is often forced to return in kind to save innocents from the Joker's disturbed schemes.

ON THE RECORD

The Joker has been a part of the Batman mythos almost from the beginning. When he first appeared, he was portrayed as a murdering clown, but like Batman, his image softened over the course of the 1950s and 1960s. When the 1970s rolled around, the Joker was once again returned to his dark, menacing roots, becoming the maniacal threat he was destined to be.

The man who laughs

The earliest incarnation of the Joker was a cutthroat killer, who planned to murder the city's most notable officials at midnight on each occasion. He was brought to justice by Batman, but would return in later in that same issue.

THE JOKER'S FIVE-WAY REVENGE
Back to his murderous self in the 1970s, the Joker killed four former associates in bizarre ways as Batman desperately sought to stop the death of the fifth. Their tumultuous battle came to a head in an aquarium near Gotham City's docks.

Playing his cards right

The Joker's dangerous persona was only amplified in the wake of the continuity-altering event *Crisis on Infinite Earths*. His sick crimes would become even more twisted as he shot and paralyzed Barbara Gordon, and then photographed her wounded body in an attempt to drive her father, Commissioner James Gordon, insane. Gordon proved a stronger man than the Joker, however, and Batman soon returned the villain to captivity.

Pushed to the edge

But the Joker was not done with the Batman Family. He went on to kidnap the second Robin, Jason Todd, and savagely beat the young man before killing him outright in an explosion. This murder nearly drove Batman over the edge, but he maintained his moral code, and never stooped to the insane villain's level.

THE JOKER'S DEATHS
Following Jason Todd's death at the hands of the Joker, Batman believed the villain had perished in a helicopter crash. However, the Clown Prince of Crime would not be so easily killed.

THE JUSTICE LEAGUE

DATA

DEBUT *The Brave and the Bold* #28 **(Feb.-Mar. 1960)**
CURRENT VERSION *Justice League* (Vol. 2) #6 **(Jul. 2012)**
BASE Watchtower
CURRENT MEMBERS/POWERS AND ABILITIES
SUPERMAN (JOR-EL/CLARK KENT) Kryptonian superpowers; **WONDER WOMAN (DIANA)** Strength, flight, Lasso of Truth; **BATMAN (BRUCE WAYNE)** Intellect, combat, and investigative training; **FLASH (BARRY ALLEN)** Speed Force-derived super-speed; **AQUAMAN (ARTHUR CURRY)** Strength, marine telepathy, Trident of Poseidon; **SHAZAM (WILLIAM BATSON)** Magic, powers over Living Lightning; **CYBORG (VIC STONE)** Cybernetic enhancements; **LEX LUTHOR** Genius intellect, powered battle suit; **GREEN LANTERNS (JESSICA CRUZ/ SIMON BAZ)** Energy projection and constructs
FORMER MEMBERS/POWERS AND ABILITIES
MARTIAN MANHUNTER (J'ONN J'ONZZ) Martian superpowers; **GREEN LANTERN (HAL JORDAN)** Power ring manifests user's willpower; **ATOM (RHONDA PINEDA)** Ability to shrink down to sub-atomic levels; **ELEMENT WOMAN (EMILY SUNG)** Molecular metamorphosis; **FIRESTORM (RONNIE RAYMOND/JASON RUSCH)** Nuclear generated Firestorm Matrix provides ability to control and manipulate matter.
ENEMIES Secret Society of Super-Villains, Crime Syndicate of America, Darkseid

The Justice League is the foremost Super Hero team in the known worlds. Governments seek their aid. Other heroes want to join them. Every villain out to make a reputation takes them on, and every would-be conqueror of Earth knows they are the planet's first line of defense. This prominence has not come without cost, however, with the stress sometimes threatening to break the team apart. Whatever their passing disagreements with each other, they remain united against external threats.

The core members of the Justice League—Superman, Batman, Wonder Woman, Flash, Green Lantern, and Aquaman—first came together as each of them hunted the source of strange occurrences in their respective cities that prefigured an attack by Darkseid. Teenager Vic Stone, critically injured in the attack, became Cyborg when his father implanted experimental cybernetics in his dying body. This occurred just in time for him to take part in the counterattack against Darkseid and his Parademons, during which Batman rescued the kidnapped Superman from Apokolips. The team then welcomed Cyborg as a member. Sometime later, writer David Graves named the team the Justice League in a book about the events; they preferred this to the Flash's off-the-cuff suggestion of "Super Seven."

Conflict erupted between the Justice League, the similarly titled Justice League of America, and the occult-oriented Justice League Dark after Shazam took the remains of Black Adam to Kahndaq for burial. His actions created an international incident by breaching Kahndaq's borders. In one of the team's first encounters, Superman lost control of his powers and killed Doctor Light. The three groups then clashed again over the powerful artifact Pandora's Box. During the battle, Firestorm and Element Woman found the source of Superman's problems: a sliver of Kryptonite in his brain. Around this time, the demon Despero launched an attack on the JL's orbiting HQ, Watchtower, causing it to crash in Rhode Island.

LEAGUES IN CONFLICT
As an international incident brewed in Kahndaq, the Justice League and the Justice League of America faced off over Pandora's Box.

The mysterious Outsider appeared seemingly from nowhere and took control of Pandora's Box, using it to open a portal to Earth-3, from which emerged the Crime Syndicate—the villainous Earth-3 version of the Justice League. Cyborg's cybernetics tore themselves free of his body and rearranged themselves into the sentient Grid, allied with the Crime Syndicate—nearly killing Cyborg in the process. A number of key JLA and JL heroes were trapped within a matrix created from the two parts of Firestorm after Ultraman altered the Moon's orbit, which deprived Superman of his Kryptonian strength and destabilized Firestorm. Atom revealed that she had placed the Kryptonite in Superman's brain and that she was in fact Atomica of the Crime Syndicate, a mole within the Justice League. After this revelation, the Crime Syndicate attacked, bolstered by the Secret Society of Super-Villains.

AT A GLANCE...

The world's greatest
The Justice League of America is the first great Super Hero team, and still the standard by which all others are judged. Brought together to face a menace that no hero could confront alone, the Justice League has consistently taken a stand against the most dangerous threats the universe can throw at them, and come out on top.

Watchtower
The orbiting Watchtower was the Justice League's HQ, containing research and training facilities, as well as living spaces for League members and their guests. It was destroyed by Despero and later rebuilt in orbit with the financial backing of Lex Luthor.

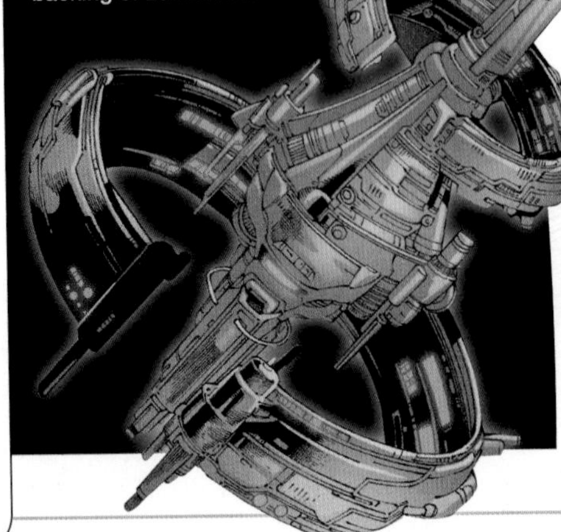

CLASSIC STORIES

***Justice League of America* (Vol. 1) #21-22 (Aug.-Sep. 1963)** The JLA and Justice Society of America team up for the first time, in "Crisis on Earth-One!" and "Crisis on Earth-Two!", before the introduction of Earth-3's Crime Syndicate of America the next year.

***Justice League of America Annual* (Vol. 1) #2 (Oct. 1984)** The original JLA's failure to handle a Martian invasion results in Aquaman dissolving the team. He starts anew with a headquarters in Detroit, admitting only heroes willing to commit full-time to the task of representing the JLA. The new roster consists of Aquaman, Zatanna, Martian Manhunter, Elongated Man, the Vixen, and three younger recruits: Gypsy, Steel, and Vibe.

***Final Crisis* #1-7 (Jul. 2008-Mar. 2009)** The deaths of Martian Manhunter and Batman, together with the resignations of Wonder Woman and Superman, leave the remaining members of the JLA scrambling to fight the New Gods and the spirit of a fallen Darkseid.

ROCKY BEGINNING
The heroes who came together to form the Justice League at first responded individually to signs of Darkseid's attempt to breach the dimensional barrier and conquer Earth-1 to use as a Parademon breeding ground. As they met each other, their first reaction was often suspicion; but when they were forced to band together, they learned how powerful they could be—and how powerful they would need to be against godlike adversaries like Darkseid.

FIRST IMPRESSIONS
The soon-to-be Justice League first met under trying circumstances.

Seeing the threat escalate, a number of villains—including Lex Luthor, Black Manta, and the resurrected Black Adam—defected from the Society, joining forces with the heroes in their counterattack against the Crime Syndicate, which had based itself in the Watchtower ruins. The combined team left a trail of bodies, including the Outsider, but inadvertently released Alexander Luthor, Lex's Earth-3 counterpart. Possessing that world's version of the powers of Shazam, he ran amok, killing Johnny Quick and others before being dispatched by Lex Luthor. Black Adam and Sinestro returned the Moon to its natural orbit, ending the eclipse that made Firestorm a prison and freeing the remaining heroes. The Crime Syndicate were brutally finished off, save for the captured Ultraman and Superwoman (pregnant with Alexander Luthor's child) and the missing Owlman. Lex Luthor removed the Kryptonite from Superman and—despite Superman's objections—was admitted to the League, with Shazam, Captain Cold, and Power Ring, who had all proved themselves.

The group claimed the Justice League of America name and focused on the resurgent threat of Darkseid, who was still enraged that the League had stopped his earlier attempt to use Earth as a Parademon factory. The New God Metron intervened, taking the heroes to the Rock of Eternity, where Batman sat in the Mobius Chair, channeling the power of the New Gods. The Justice League returned to Earth as Mobius destroyed Darkseid in a final battle involving the Flash. **AI**

"It's time to be the team they thought we were, instead of the team we've been this past five years."

AQUAMAN

JLA ASSEMBLED
Familiar faces are joined by more recent additions—including Superman's long-time arch-enemy.
1 Superman
2 Wonder Woman
3 Lex Luthor
4 Power Ring
5 Batman
6 The Flash
7 Shazam
8 Cyborg
9 Aquaman

ON THE RECORD

The JLA came into being as a reboot of the Justice Society of America, which flourished in the 1940s, but was later shelved during the 1950s as Super Hero comics had to share the stage with new genres. Some JSA members became part of the JLA's origins in 1960, when the League's founding members first came together to fight the alien menace Starro.

New beginnings

A flagship title for decades, the Justice League of America in its various incarnations has had nearly as many origin stories as members. The first of these related the story of an invasion by the alien Appellaxians, which none of the solo heroes could successfully repel. Only by banding together could they save the Earth—and the JLA was born. This origin story has been modified numerous times over the years and has involved a varying roster of founding members.

GOING SMALL
A JLA including Hawkman, Black Canary, and Red Tornado hunted for the Atom in the Microcosmos.

What's in a name?

The original Justice League of America is informally known as the Justice League or by its initials JLA. But there have also been different iterations of the group under various names over the years: Justice League Detroit, Justice League International, Justice League Europe, Justice League United... What they all have in common is some of the original Justice League's members, and a version of the original Justice League's mandate: to protect and defend the people of Earth against the forces of evil.

STEALING A LOOK
No sooner had the new 1990s JLA team formed than their likenesses—including the new blue Superman—were assumed by evil hard light constructs created and controlled by the Injustice Gang.

REBIRTH

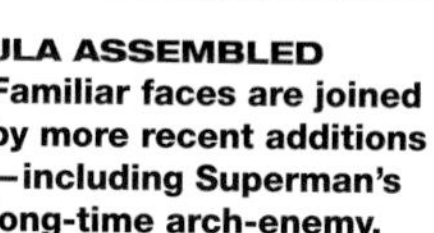

REUNITED FOR THE FIRST TIME

After defeating Darkseid and surviving the temporary god-like powers bestowed on them by the Anti-Life Equation, the Justice League reunites to protect the Earth from a new wave of almighty menaces.

However, can a team carrying raw recruits like rookie Green Lanterns Jessica Cruz and Simon Baz—not to mention an alternate-Earth Superman nobody knows—even tell if the threats are coming from outside the group or within it?

JUSTICE LEAGUE DARK

DEBUT *Justice League Dark* #1 (Nov. 2011)
BASE House of Mystery
MEMBERS/POWERS **Madame Xanadu**: Wide array of magical powers; **Constantine**: Magical and occult knowledge; **Deadman**: Possession of human hosts, telepathy; **Zatanna**: Magical effects; **Andrew Bennett**: Mind control, shapeshifting; **Black Orchid**: Elemental force powers; **Swamp Thing**: Shapeshifting, control over plants; **Nightmare Nurse**: Magical abilities including hard energy constructs.

Madame Xanadu brought together the team later known as Justice League Dark after suffering a vision of a horrific future only they could prevent. She separated the Enchantress from her mortal host June Moone and the witch became unstable, setting out on a lethal rampage as she attempted to find and rejoin June Moone. To protect her, Madame Xanadu gathered a group of magic-wielding heroes, and John Constantine merged the Enchantress and June into a single, more stable being.

Madame Xanadu's vision then came to pass as the death of vampire Andrew Bennett unleashed Cain, sire of all vampires. A returned Bennett destroyed Cain and pacified his army. After this success, Steve Trevor enlisted the group to help A.R.G.U.S. protect its store of mystical artifacts from the wizard Felix Faust, and officially named them Justice League Dark, recognizing the need for a specialized force to handle occult and magical threats. **AI**

DARKNESS WITHIN AND WITHOUT
They have their share of internal rivalries and discord, but when they stand together, the Justice League Dark can overcome any occult threat.

JUSTICE LEAGUE OF AMERICA

CURRENT VERSION *Justice League of America* (Vol. 3) #1 (Apr. 2013)
BASE A.R.G.U.S. Headquarters
MEMBERS/POWERS **Steve Trevor**: Tactics, firearms; **Hawkman**: Super-strength, flight; **Martian Manhunter**: Mind control, shapeshifting; **Katana**: Martial arts; **Catwoman**: Acrobatics, unarmed combat; **Vibe**: Emits energy; **Stargirl**: Powers from belt and staff; **Green Lantern**: Ring produces energy constructs; **Green Arrow**: Archery, acrobatics, unarmed combat.

A.R.G.U.S. director Amanda Waller enlisted Steve Trevor to create the Justice League of America as a failsafe should the original Justice League ever go rogue, leveraging concerns about a budding romance between Superman and Wonder Woman.

The JLA saw its first action in Kahndaq, when it followed the Justice League there to try to mitigate the effects of the diplomatic incident caused by Shazam entering the territory to repatriate the remains of Black Adam. A battle broke out between the teams, fueled by the presence of Pandora's Box.

The JLA was dissolved after the Crime Syndicate of America's attack, during which Vibe disappeared and Green Arrow was badly wounded; its members found their way into other teams, including the Canada-based Justice League United. Following the dissolution of the JLA, the original Justice League assumed its title in full. **AI**

DEFENDING EARTH
The Justice League of America was chartered to stand against all enemies foreign and domestic... and, as it turned out, from other Earths as well.

JUSTICE LEAGUE INTERNATIONAL

DEBUT *Justice League International* (Vol. 1) #7 (Nov. 1987)
CURRENT VERSION *Justice League International* Vol. 3 #1 (Sep. 2011)
BASE Washington, DC
MEMBERS/POWERS **Booster Gold**: Legion flight ring, power suit; **Fire**: Thermal energy blasts; **Godiva**: Prehensile hair; **Green Lantern**: Power Ring; **Ice**: Ice creation and control; **Firehawk**: Flight, light energy control; **Vixen**: Totem powers; **Batwing**: Military training, computers; **O.M.A.C.**: Biotech weapon; **Blue Beetle**: Alien scarab powers; **August General in Iron**: Armored, energy manipulation.

The Justice League International was the brainchild of UN director Andre Briggs, who believed a global team of Super Heroes would be a useful counterweight to the US-centric Justice League. Based at the Hall of Justice, Washington, D.C., the JLI was led by Booster Gold, and only admitted members with public identities. Batman was refused admission for this reason, but he provided the group with assistance in its battles against Peraxxus and the Signal Men.

An attack by the Breakdown-led group of villains known as the Burners killed Rocket Red and left Vixen, Ice, and Fire with disabling injuries. This led Booster Gold to recruit O.M.A.C., Batwing, and Firehawk as replacements. Not long afterward, the JLI was disbanded following a dispute between Green Lantern (Guy Gardner) and Booster Gold, and a devastating attack by the rogue AI satellite Brother Eye. **AI**

NO SECRETS
Building on the legacy of the JLA, but with a consciously global perspective, the Justice League International fractured after losing several of its members in early missions.

JUSTICE LEAGUE UNITED

DEBUT *Justice League United* #0 (Jun. 2014)
BASE Canada
MEMBERS/POWERS **Martian Manhunter**: Super-strength, mind control, shapeshifting; **Stargirl**: Cosmic converter belt and staff powers; **Green Arrow**: Archery, acrobatics, unarmed combat; **Adam Strange**: Advanced Rannian tech and weapons; **Animal Man**: Shapeshifting, animal control, and telepathy; **Supergirl**: Super-strength, flight, invulnerability; **Equinox**: Powers of Cree Midayo.

Martian Manhunter, Stargirl, and Green Arrow formed the Justice League United after the dissolution of the A.R.G.U.S.-sanctioned Justice League of America. Basing themselves in Canada, they recruited a number of other unaffiliated heroes, including a new member, the Cree girl known as Equinox.

The team's major battle was against the scheming Lord Byth, who sought to synthesize a number of alien genomes into a being he called Ultra the Multi-Alien. Byth corrupted a project begun by the people of Rann—who envisioned Ultra as a sign of the interconnectedness of all sentient beings—instead planning to create the Slayer of Worlds. The JLU fought to prevent Byth realizing his apocalyptic goal. Members of the team then split into several different groups to battle the Breakers, a mysterious force causing disruptions in space-time, and ultimately journeyed to the House of Secrets for answers. **AI**

SPLINTER CELL
The Martian Manhunter oversees a group which is beyond the grasp of A.R.G.U.S. and outside the currents of US politics.

JUSTICE SOCIETY OF AMERICA

DATA

DEBUT *All-Star Comics* #3 **(Dec. 1940)**
CURRENT VERSION *Wonders of the World Earth-2* #1 **(Jul. 2012)**
UNIVERSE Earth-2
MEMBERS/POWERS/ABILITIES **DOCTOR FATE (KHALID BEN-HASSIN)** Helmet of Nabu conveys various magical powers; **FLASH (JAY GARRICK)** Super-speed; **GREEN LANTERN (ALAN SCOTT)** Lantern Corps ring conveys various powers including flight and the creation of energy constructs; **HAWKGIRL (KENDRA MUNOZ-SAUNDERS)** Strength, flight and regeneration; **HUNTRESS (HELENA WAYNE)** Martial arts, stealth, archery and marksmanship; **POWER GIRL (KARA ZOR-EL)** Kryptonian strength, invulnerability, flight, heat- and x-ray vision; **SUPERMAN (VAL-ZOD)** Kryptonian strength, invulnerability, flight, heat- and x-ray-vision; **RED TORNADO (LOIS LANE'S CONSCIOUSNESS)** Flight, strength, android body with aerokinetic abilities; **BATMAN (DICK GRAYSON)** Hand-to-hand combat, hi-tech devices, investigative acumen.
ALLIES Mister Miracle, Aquawoman
ENEMIES Steppenwolf, Hunger Dogs
AFFILIATIONS World Army

VALIANT SACRIFICE
The Ternion battled against an endless Apokoliptian horde of Parademons.

The original Wonders of Earth-2, where superpowered beings were very rare, were led by the Ternion—Superman, Wonder Woman, and Batman. After their heroic deaths defending their world against the forces of Apokolips, the legacy was taken up by a new generation of Wonders, determined to live up to the Ternion's example and protect Earth-2 from any threat.

Five years after the legendary stand of the original Wonders of the World against Steppenwolf and the Parademons, new Wonders began to appear. Flash, the Green Lantern, and Hawkgirl banded together to defeat the Man of Grey, Solomon Grundy, before he could corrupt the lifeforce of Earth-2. Doctor Fate joined soon after, and the Wonders confronted the resurgent threat of Steppenwolf and his trio of Hunger Dogs. Their first battle with Apokoliptian villains ended in defeat and the death of Green Lantern Alan Scott, but one of the Hunger Dogs—Brutaal—then turned on Steppenwolf, killing him before revealing that he was seemingly Superman. A new Batman freed imprisoned Wonders from Arkham Base, adding Aquawoman, Accountable (James Olsen), and Red Tornado to the team, as well as the Kryptonian Val-Zod. The would-be Superman took control of the Parademons and tried to transport Earth-2 into Apokolips space using the genius of Terry Sloan, Mister Miracle, and Mister Terrific.

The plan was only thwarted when Red Tornado, who carried the memories of Lois Lane, forced the prospective Superman to realize he was a clone. His body—and the scheme—then crumbled. The Wonders' troubles weren't over, however. Darkseid attempted another invasion, and it was revealed that he had made a deal with Highfather under which the New Gods would not interfere with Darkseid's plan, as long as Darkseid consented to focus only on one Earth. Unfortunately for the Wonders, Darkseid chose to target Earth-2, precipitating a battle not just for their lives but for the existence of the planet itself. **AI**

WONDERS OF THE WORLD
The core Wonders, standing at the head of the World Army against any and all threats to Earth-2.
1 Huntress
2 Power Girl
3 Batman
4 Superman
5 Red Tornado
6 Doctor Fate
7 Flash
8 Green Lantern
9 Hawkgirl

ON THE RECORD

The Justice Society of America is the first Super Hero team in the history of comic books, and has existed in one form or another since 1940. A number of characters made their debuts during this time, most notably Wonder Woman (as the team's secretary!) in 1942. Headliners like the Flash and Green Lantern mingled with lesser-known players such as the Atom and Dr. Mid-Nite for a decade before going on hiatus.

The JSA returned in 1963, soon beginning a series of memorable team-ups with Earth-1's Justice League. A revived Justice Society feature in the 1970s even revealed the secret of the team's formation and the confrontation with Congress that caused the heroes to retire.

WHERE IT ALL BEGAN
The first meeting of the Justice Society of America. In attendance: the Atom, Sandman, the Spectre, Flash, Hawkman, Dr. Fate, Green Lantern, and Hourman.

WILL WONDERS CEASE?
Things looked grim for the Wonders of the World and for Earth-2, as an Apokoliptian drill bore down on the planet. But the Wonders never quit, and Apokolips hasn't yet seen the last of Doctor Fate.

CLASSIC STORIES

***All-Star Comics* #11 (Jun.-Jul. 1942)** In a surge of patriotism following the attack on Pearl Harbor, the JSA members disbanded to enlist in the armed forces. The well-intentioned heroes proved such a disruptive influence that the government asked them to resume their costumed activities as the Justice Battalion.

***Justice League of America* (Vol. 1) #21-22 (Aug.-Sep. 1963)** The first meeting of the JSA and JLA, kicking off a decades-long series of collaborative adventures spanning Earth-1 and Earth-2.

***JSA* (Vol. 1) #16-21 (Nov. 2000-Apr. 2001)** A reconstituted JSA faces a new Injustice Society headed up by Black Adam, who would later assist the JSA in bringing Hawkman back to life.

KALMAKU, TOM

DEBUT *Green Lantern* (Vol. 2) #2 (Sep.–Oct. 1960)
CURRENT VERSION *Green Lantern* (Vol. 5) #3 (Jan. 2012)
REAL NAME Thomas Kalmaku
BASE Ferris Aircraft, Coast City
EYES Brown **HAIR** Black
HEIGHT 5ft 7in **WEIGHT** 155 lbs
POWERS/ABILITIES Skilled mechanic and engineer
ALLIES Green Lantern (Hal Jordan)

Tom Kalmaku is an Inuit from Alaska who traveled to California and landed a job at Ferris Aircraft as a mechanic and engineer. His keen intelligence and work ethic made him a vital part of the team. He became good friends with test pilot Hal Jordan and a huge fan of Coast City's new Super Hero, Green Lantern.

Tom soon worked out that Hal was Green Lantern but kept quiet about it, and Hal trusted him with his secret. Tom was also rumored to keep a secret journal of Hal's adventures under lock and key. It was Tom who alerted Carol Ferris when Hal teamed up with his old enemy Sinestro. After Hal went missing, Tom and Carol opened Hal's locker to look for clues to his whereabouts. To their embarrassment, they discovered a wedding ring that Hal had bought for Carol. **SW**

KAMANDI

DEBUT *Kamandi, the Last Boy on Earth* #1 (Oct.–Nov. 1972)
REAL NAME Kamandi
EYES Blue **HAIR** Blond
HEIGHT 5ft 8in **WEIGHT** 159 lbs
POWERS/ABILITIES Resourceful survivor and warrior; skilled with firearms.
ALLIES Ben Boxer, Steve, Renzi, Doctor Canus, Prince Tuftan, Pyra, Spirit, Mylock Bloodstalker
ENEMIES Great Caesar, Tiger-Empire, Rat Society, United States of Lions, Czar Simian

The boy named Kamandi was born in the aftermath of a disaster that destroyed human civilization. Kamandi was raised by his grandfather in bunker Command D, from which he got his name. When Kamandi ventured outside the safety of the bunker, he discovered that the humans he encountered behaved like dumb beasts, and that animals, mutated into humanoid form by the mutagen Cortexin, were now the dominant life forms on the planet. Meanwhile, the bunker was raided by humanoid wolves, which killed his grandfather.

"The Last Boy on Earth" was captured by the Tiger Empire, but broke free with canine scientist Doctor Canus and radioactive mutant Ben Boxer, setting off in search of a way to restore human civilization. Kamandi briefly traveled back in time to 20th-century Metropolis and met Superman. Later, a group of alternate-Earth heroes visited his epoch during the *Crisis on Infinite Earths*. **SW**

STRANGE NEW WORLD
After years underground, Kamandi found himself confronted by a bizarre new Earth that had been changed almost beyond recognition.

KANTO

DEBUT: *Mister Miracle* (Vol. 1) #7 (Mar.–Apr. 1972)
CURRENT VERSION *Justice League* (Vol. 2) #41 (Aug. 2015)
REAL NAME Iluthin **BASE** Apokolips
EYES Blue **HAIR** Brown
HEIGHT 5ft 11½in **WEIGHT** 170 lbs
POWERS/ABILITIES Immortality; tracks prey with Mother Box.
ALLIES Darkseid, Lashina, Desaad
ENEMIES Mister Miracle, Justice League

Darkseid's favorite assassin, Kanto, is a relentless and sadistic killer. Armed with a dagger-shaped Mother Box, he can track targets across space and time. Only Mister Miracle has ever escaped Kanto, and he was determined to rectify that situation.

Darkseid sent Kanto and Lashina to Earth to hunt down Myrina Black, the Amazon mother of Darkseid's daughter, Grail. When Darkseid invaded Earth, however, he was killed by the Anti-Monitor and the Black Racer, leaving Kanto and Darkseid's other minions to face Mister Miracle and the Justice League. In the battle, Kanto hurled his blade into Mister Miracle's side, but the New God was saved when his wife, Big Barda, charged into battle via Boom Tube and teleported Kanto to parts unknown with her Mega-Rod. **SW**

KALIBAK

DEBUT *New Gods* (Vol. 1) #1 (Feb.-Mar. 1971)
CURRENT VERSION *Batman and Robin* (Vol. 2) #33 (Sep. 2014)
REAL NAME Kalibak **BASE** Apokolips
HEIGHT 6ft 9in **WEIGHT** 469 lbs **EYES** Red **HAIR** Black
POWERS/ABILITIES As a New God, he is immortal and has superhuman physical strength and toughness; wields powerful Apokoliptian weaponry.
ALLIES Darkseid, Glorious Godfrey, Desaad
ENEMIES Batman, Batman Family, New Genesis, Earth-2's World Army, James Olsen, Big Barda
AFFILIATIONS Apokolips

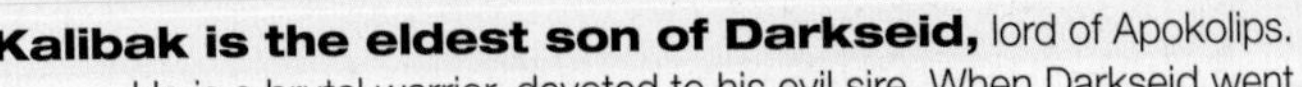

Kalibak is the eldest son of Darkseid, lord of Apokolips. He is a brutal warrior, devoted to his evil sire. When Darkseid went into stasis following his defeat on Earth, Kalibak took command and prepared to use the Chaos Cannon (powered by a Chaos Shard and the body of Batman's son Damian) to destroy inhabited planets and channel their energies back to Apokolips. Batman and his associates foiled the plan by snatching Damian's body and taking it back to Earth. Kalibak pursued them, but after a fierce battle in the Batcave he was knocked back through the portal to Apokolips.

When Darkseid's forces attacked Earth-2, Kalibak led Parademon troopers and took down James Olsen, who had gained New God powers. Darkseid's forces conquered Earth-2 and Apokolips destroyed the planet, though many inhabitants escaped via spacecraft.

Kalibak fought alongside Darkseid when he attacked Earth-0, but was blinded by his half-sister Grail. Despite his wound (and his father being killed by the Anti-Monitor) Kalibak kept fighting until he was finally taken down by Big Barda. **SW**

ON THE RECORD

The original Kalibak was a fierce adversary of Orion, his half-brother who had pledged allegiance to New Genesis, and they clashed on many occasions. Though Kalibak constantly sought his father's approval, he was punished when he slew Darkseid's interrogator, Desaad. The ruler of Apokolips killed him with his Omega Beams, but later brought resurrected him.

Kalibak was again destroyed by Infinity-Man during the Death of the New Gods event, but was reborn on Earth in a tigerlike form.

EARTH-SHAKING ENCOUNTER
On Earth, Kalibak caused widespread destruction when he clashed with his half-brother Orion.

KARATE KID

DEBUT *Adventure Comics* (Vol. 1) #346 (Jul. 1966)
CURRENT VERSION *Legion of Super-Heroes* (Vol. 7) #22 (Sep. 2013)
REAL NAME Val Armorr
HEIGHT 6ft **WEIGHT** 185 lbs
POWERS/ABILITIES Master of all martial arts disciplines; can fly with Legion flight ring.
ALLIES Princess Projectra, Diamondeth
ENEMIES Nemesis Kid, Legion of Super-Villains, Major Disaster, Fatal Five

Born on 31st-century Earth to a Japanese crime lord and an American secret agent, Val was raised by martial arts mater Sensei Toshiaki (White Crane) and trained to be a living weapon. He joined the Legion of Super-Heroes and proved his bravery in combat against many villains, although his martial arts were not always a match for superpowers. He briefly served as leader of the Legion before marrying Princess Projectra of Orando.

Val was seen to be killed while fighting to protect Orando from Nemesis Kid and the Legion of Super-Villains. However, he later returned to life through some unknown means. Reunited with Projectra (now known as Sensor Girl), he helped free a Promethean Giant from Tharok's control before joining his wife on Orando. **SW**

KATANA

DEBUT *Brave and the Bold* (Vol. 1) #200 **(Jul. 1983)** (as Tatsu Yamashiro)
CURRENT VERSION *Birds of Prey* (Vol. 3) #1 **(Nov. 2011)**
REAL NAME Tatsu Toro
EYES Brown **HAIR** Black
POWERS/ABILITIES Expert acrobat, martial artist, and swordswoman.
ALLIES Green Arrow, Sickle
ENEMIES Mona Shard, the Cleaners, Onyx, Dagger Clan, Poison Ivy, Killer Croc
AFFILIATIONS Birds of Prey, Outsiders, Sword Clan

When Tatsu was a child her best friends were brothers Takeo and Maseo. Both fell in love with her, but she ultimately married Maseo. The brothers were members of the Sword Clan, one of several groups that made up the Outsiders, a secret organization devoted to preserving the balance of the world by eliminating evil and corruption. When Tatsu saw Takeo and Maseo arguing about her, she intervened and accidentally killed her husband with his sacred sword, Soultaker, which had absorbed his spirit. Overwhelmed by grief, she took up Soultaker as a way of staying close to her beloved husband and went out to seek redemption as the heroine Katana.

On the advice of her husband, whose spirit would speak to her through Soultaker, she briefly joined the Birds of Prey team and helped them battle the terrorists, the Cleaners, and Poison Ivy. After coming into conflict with the mysterious Dagger Clan in Japan, Katana left the team to find out more about the Soultaker and the Sword Clan.

When Killer Croc broke the sword and released Maseo's spirit, her late husband told Katana that she had to let go of him and dedicate herself to redeeming the warring Outsiders. After Soultaker was reforged, she became head of the Sword Clan and helped Green Arrow to defeat the Fist, Spear, Shield, and Axe clans when they planned a large-scale terror attack on Prague. **SW**

ON THE RECORD

The original Katana was Tatsu Yamashiro, whose husband, Maseo was slain with the magical sword Soultaker, wielded by his jealous gangster brother Takeo. Tatsu took up the Soultaker, trained as a samurai and, as Katana, joined Batman's Outsiders. Takeo later tracked Katana to Gotham City and released all the souls in the Soultaker sword to attack her. After a long battle, Katana killed Takeo.

During Blackest Night, Katana battled her undead husband, who had been raised from the grave by the Black Lanterns.

BETTER THAN THE MOVIES
While serving with Halo and Looker in the Outsiders, Katana clashed with Tengu spirits and Japanese gangsters in Hollywood!

KELLEY, CARRIE

DEBUT *Batman: The Dark Knight* #1 (1986)
CURRENT VERSION *Batman and Robin* (Vol. 2) #19 (Jun. 2013)
BASE Gotham City
EYES Red **HAIR** Green
POWERS/ABILITIES Skilled actor; encyclopedic knowledge of Shakespeare.
ALLIES Damian Wayne, Alfred, Titus
AFFILIATIONS Batman household

Drama student Carrie Kelley was hired by Bruce Wayne's son Damian (Robin) to give him acting lessons so he could experience what it was like to be someone else. When Damian didn't show up for his lessons, she left her bill and a note for him at Wayne Manor. Bruce gave her a hefty check, but did not reveal the truth: his son had been brutally killed battling the Heretic. Carrie sensed that Bruce was hiding something, so she visited the Manor once more, demanding to see Damian. Bruce gruffly informed her that Damian was studying overseas and told Alfred to show her out. Before she left, however, the butler hired her to take care of the Manor's Great Dane, Titus. Bruce was less than pleased when he found out, but he allowed Carrie to become part of the household.

Pre-Flashpoint in a future Gotham City, Carrie Kelley was a 13-year-old Batman fangirl who became the new Robin after saving the out-of-retirement and out-of-condition Dark Knight from the Mutant gang leader. She then helped track down and defeat the Joker, and later took on the mantle of Catgirl. **SW**

ACTING ON INSTINCT
Smart and sassy actor Carrie Kelley knew Bruce Wayne was concealing something when she turned up at Wayne Manor to see his son Damian.

KGBEAST

DEBUT *Batman* (Vol. 1) #417 (Mar. 1988)
CURRENT VERSION *New Suicide Squad* #2 (Oct. 2014)
REAL NAME Anatoli Knyazev
BASE Research Station Gagarin, the moon
EYES Blue **HAIR** Blond
HEIGHT 6ft 3in **WEIGHT** 231 lbs
POWERS/ABILITIES Espionage and combat training; cybernetically enhanced body; cannon replaces missing arm.
ENEMIES The Operative, the Others

Anatoli Knyazev was an old-school Cold War warrior. He served heroically in the KGB, earning the codename KGBeast, and even cut off his own arm to escape an American agent. When the Soviet Union fell, he became the commander of a Russian counter-terrorist unit. KGBeast was critically injured in a shoot-out with the Suicide Squad in the Moscow subway, but Mars Systems literally rebuilt him for combat.

He then joined Soviet veteran NKVDemon in the lethal super-villain team Mayhem. The group plotted to bring back the glory days of the Soviet Union by holding the world to ransom with an aging nuclear-armed satellite. This brought him into conflict with the Others, a Super Hero squad that included an old foe from his Cold War days: the Operative. In a hard-fought struggle, Mayhem's plan was foiled by the Others, and the Operative destroyed KGBeast's arm cannon before finishing him off in hand-to-hand combat. **SW**

BLAST FROM THE PAST
The Soviet Union may have collapsed, but for KGBeast, the Cold War never ended. He plotted to use nuclear terror to restore Russia's prestige.

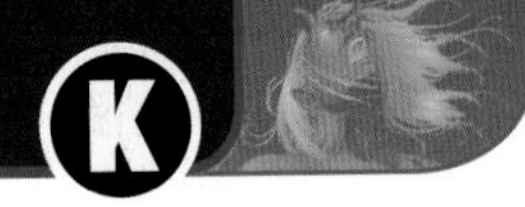

KENTS, THE

DEBUT *Superman* (Vol. 1) #1 **(Jun. 1939)**
CURRENT VERSION *Action Comics* (Vol. 2) #5 **(Mar. 2012)**
BASE Smallville, Kansas
POWERS/ABILITIES Ordinary pioneering humans, with strong ideals and clearly defined principles and ethics.
ALLIES The Ross Family, the Lang Family
ENEMIES John Wesley Hardin, Jesse James gang, Charley Quantrill
AFFILIATIONS Jonah Hex, Scalphunter, Bill Hickock, George Armstrong Custer

MEN OF IRON
The Kents had always worked hard and put their lives on the line to protect their family, friends, and most cherished beliefs.

The patrilineal side of the Kent family traces its history back to 6th-century England, where Sir Brian Kent battled tyranny as the Silent Knight. A thousand years later, the family had fallen from the aristocracy and at least one branch sought a better life in the New World.

In 1854, patriarch and abolitionist Silas Kent was active in the anti-slavery movement. A printer and pamphleteer, he migrated west, settling in Lawrence, Kansas, with his oldest sons Nathaniel and Jebediah. His wife Abigail had remained in Boston to raise their remaining seven children. When she died three years later, the children remained in Massachusetts.

After the Civil War and Reconstruction, the Kansas Kents generally stuck to their lands as farmers, although a succession of Kent men proudly served in America's overseas wars.

The line looked likely to end in the 20th century with Jonathan and Martha Kent, until the childless couple found a son who fell to Earth in a rocketship. They subsequently raised him in the traditions and morals which had shaped generations of Kents. The child was called Clark and would grow up to be the world's foremost Super Hero, an indomitable defender of truth and justice—Superman. **WW**

FAMILY HONOR
Jonathan and Martha's foundling son was destined to become the most famous Kent in the family's long and valiant history—at least to those who knew his secret identity.

ON THE RECORD

When baby Kal-El crashed to Earth he was adopted by a couple desperate for a child of their own. In the years that followed, while their status remained constant, the Kents' ages varied to suit the times.

In Superman #1 (1939), they were elderly and died before their son began his heroic career. In the 1960s, they were rejuvenated by alien science to become spry 40-year olds. However, the biggest change came in the 1986 reboot, where Mr. and Mrs. Kent again became an older couple, but never died; instead offering parental love and guidance to the Man of Steel.

HEAVEN SENT
The infant found by aging Jonathan and Martha was not just the answer to their prayers, but would become the savior of the world.

KHUNDS, THE

DEBUT *Adventure Comics* (Vol. 1) #346 (Jul. 1966)
CURRENT VERSION *Deathstroke* (Vol. 2) #10 (Aug. 2012)
BASE Khundia, Khundish Empire **HAIR** Black
POWERS/ABILITIES Aggressive and militaristic; urgent drive for status and territory.
ALLIES Dark Circle
ENEMIES United Planets, Thanagarians, Legion of Super-Heroes
AFFILIATIONS Alien Alliance, Dominators

Khunds are an extremely aggressive, territorial warrior-race who began carving out an intergalactic empire as soon as they freed themselves from the bounds of their heavy-gravity homeworld.

Their culture is based on confrontation and dominance. Khunds consider all other species as inferior and every contact with a new culture is an opportunity for conquest and expansion. The Empire is a constantly shifting hierarchy of competing warlords with the mightiest fighter ruling only for as long as he can defeat all challengers.

The most arrogant and belligerent members of the species take enormous pride in having their bodies cybernetically augmented: recreating themselves as living weapons. To a Khund, victory is everything and must be won at any price. **WW**

KID DEVIL

DEBUT *The Fury of Firestorm* #24 (Jun. 1984) (as Eddie); *Blue Devil* #14 (Jul. 1985) (as Kid Devil)
CURRENT VERSION (As Eddie) *DC Universe Presents* #15 (Jan. 2013)
REAL NAME Edward Alan Bloomberg
BASE Titans Tower III, San Francisco, California
EYES Yellow **HAIR** Gray
POWERS/ABILITIES Demonic power; flame breath; superhuman strength; burning skin.
ALLIES Blue Devil, Rose Wilson, Zachary Zatara
ENEMIES Niles Caulder, Kid Crusader
AFFILIATIONS Teen Titans, Young Justice

Until he met Daniel Cassidy, Eddie Bloomberg—a gopher in his Aunt Marla Bloom's film production company—dreamed of being a famous actor like his aunt. Once he saw Cassidy's Blue Devil in action, however, Eddie would settle for nothing less than being a hero too. At first, he used Cassidy's special effects to operate as Kid Devil, even joining Blue Devil for a time as his sidekick—but with little success or approval. When the demon Neron offered Eddie true power in exchange for his soul, he jumped at the chance and learned to regret his decision.

After losing his powers, Eddie returned to Hell and discovered that Neron had only activated his metagene and never truly gave him demonic abilities. However, even without his powers, Eddie continued to assist his Teen Titans comrades as best he could, ultimately sacrificing his life to save theirs. **WW**

DEVIL IN THE DETAIL
Eddie's breath is hotter than flame, his skin itself can sear flesh, he has a prehensile tail and retractable wings, and he can teleport.

KID ETERNITY

DEBUT *Hit Comics* (Vol. 1) #25 (Dec. 1942)
CURRENT VERSION *National Comics: Eternity* (Vol. 1) #1 (Sep. 2012)
REAL NAME Christopher "Kit" Freeman
BASE New York City
HEIGHT 5ft 10in **WEIGHT** 164 lbs
EYES Blue **HAIR** Black
POWERS/ABILITIES Able to communicate with the newly dead for up to 24 hours.
ALLIES Mr. Keeper

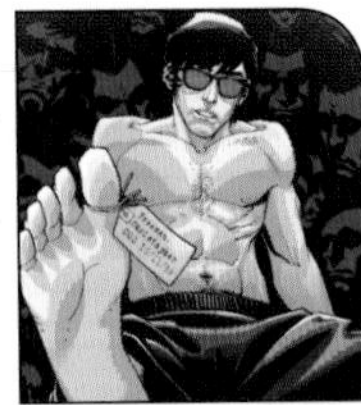

Chris Freeman was arguing with his N.Y.P.D. detective dad when they were both shot. He remembered dying and arriving in a grotesque waiting area with the rest of the newly deceased. His dad grabbed him, begging Chris not to leave him there. What Chris did not know was why or how he had returned to life, or how his dad's corpse could say "you should be here, not me…"

Working at the Police Morgue, Chris soon discovered a strange new ability: he could bring back dead people—"Fresh Ones"—and help them settle any unfinished business. When Darby Quinn was killed, Chris helped his ghost catch the murderer, only to find Quinn was a violent aggressor and had been shot in self defense. It also brought Freeman into conflict with the spectral Mr. Keeper, who warned him there were rules he needed to follow. **WW**

K

KID FLASH

DEBUT *The Flash* (Vol. 1) #110 **(Dec. 1959–Jan. 1960)**
CURRENT VERSION *The Flash* (Vol. 4) #30 **(Jun. 2014)**
REAL NAME Wallace Rudolph West **BASE** Central City
EYES Brown **HAIR** Black
POWERS/ABILITIES Super-speed; rapid healing; ability to absorb Speed Force energy; time-travel.
ALLIES Teen Titans, Barry Allen
ENEMIES Professor Zoom, Future Flash
AFFILIATIONS Iris West, Daniel West/the Reverse-Flash

Wally West's father Rudy walked out on his family when the boy was still young. When his mother vanished in the Crime Syndicate's attack on Central City, 12-year-old Wally ended up with his aunt Iris. Soon after, Wally was arrested by Barry Allen for vandalism, but despite the shaky start, and thanks to Iris' persistence, they became firm friends.

Twenty years in the future, a grief-maddened Barry Allen had seen his friends suffer and die while the Speed Force ruptured from being over-used for time-travel by numerous speedsters. As the Future Flash, Barry then raced back over his decades-long career, rectifying every failure, and intending to murder his younger self and use the liberated energies to "correct" history—and seal the temporal breach his actions had caused.

The future Barry was thwarted by an older Wally who was also a speedster. Allowing both Flashes' energies to pass through him, Wally sacrificed his life to reset history. He returned to his juvenile self, unaware of what had happened or that the trans-dimensional Speed Force had altered him and would soon make him a super-fast Super Hero too. **WW**

ON THE RECORD

Kid Flash was the first original sidekick of DC Comics' Silver Age; offering a youngster's perspective to the adventures of the Fastest Man Alive. Wally West shared cases with his mentor and joined fellow super-kids in the Teen Titans before inheriting the mantle and responsibilities of the Flash after Barry Allen gave his life during the *Crisis on Infinite Earths*.

Wally's sometime-sidekick and eventual successor was Bart Allen—aka Impulse—who inherited his grandfather's powers and costumed identity before being killed by Flash's Rogues.

Both champions were revealed to have a connection to the extra-dimensional Speed-Force, unlike Bar Torr, whose hyper-velocity remains an unexplained accident. He was a terrorist insurgent in his own time, but later learned how to be a hero, battling beside the young metahumans of the 21st century as Kid Flash. After serving time for his crimes he returned to our era and rejoined a new Teen Titans.

WALLY WEST
Flash's little helper rapidly evolved into a vibrant hero succeeding on his on terms.

BART ALLEN
Barry Allen's grandson came back in time to master the velocity that was hyper-aging him to an early death.

BAR TORR
The amnesiac speedster from the 30th century learned how to run fast enough to escape the shame of his evil past.

KILOWOG

DEBUT *Green Lantern Corps* (Vol. 1) #201 **(Jun. 1986)**
CURRENT VERSION *Green Lantern Corps* (Vol. 3) #1 **(Nov. 2011)**
BASE Oa, Mogo
HEIGHT 8ft 3in **WEIGHT** 720 lbs
EYES Red **HAIR** None
POWERS/ABILITIES Inspirational trainer, brilliant geneticist and technologist, skilled engineer, ferocious hand-to-hand fighter employing vast bulk and strength; experienced and imaginative wielder of the light of Willpower, channeled through a standard Green Lantern power ring.
ALLIES Guy Gardner, John Stewart, Salaak, Hal Jordan
ENEMIES Sinestro
AFFILIATIONS Green Lantern Corps, Rocket Red Brigade

Kilowog was a brilliant geneticist on bustling, over-crowded Bolovax Vik. After selection as Sector 674's Green Lantern, the psychic wrench of abandoning his species was tremendous, but Kilowog was also proud to serve the greater universe in his new role.

When his homeworld was destroyed during the *Crisis on Infinite Earths*, the towering Green Lantern was able to save all 16 billion Bolovaxians by converting them to energy and storing them in his power ring. Unfortunately for him, Kilowog was not around to repeat the feat when Sinestro eradicated the race after they were resettled on a new planet. With his race twice-lost, Kilowog dedicated his life to the Green Lantern Corps. His entire nature is centered on being part of a greater whole and he found purpose in training new recruits, giving them all the tools and experience necessary to survive the most dangerous job in creation.

The greatest treachery in his life came when he discovered that the Guardians of the Universe had betrayed their own principles, turning upon the peacekeepers they had created and attempting to eradicate Free Will with their abhorrent Third Army. Following the Guardians defeat and destruction at the hands of Sinestro, Kilowog stepped down as the Corps' Chief Drill Instructor, reluctantly assuming the critical role of Protocol Officer and Chief Administrator for the now autonomously run Green Lantern Corps. **WW**

FATHER FIGURE
Having lost his family and world twice, Kilowog was deeply invested in making sure his rookies were ready for anything.

ON THE RECORD

A lonely alien craving the tight communal affinity of Bolovaxians, Kilowog was drawn to his lost culture's closest equivalent: Communism. He began to associate with the leaders of the Soviet Union and used his alien science to complete their Rocket Red armored super-soldier program.

His disappointment in discovering that everyday practice did not live up to philosophical principles quickly drove Kilowog back to his only true comrades: the Green Lantern Corps.

THE GREATER GOOD
Kilowog could not grasp why his human Green Lantern friends thought his political associations would lead to trouble.

KILLER CROC

DATA

DEBUT *Detective Comics* (Vol. 1) #523 **(Feb. 1983)**
UPDATE *Batman* (Vol. 2) #1 **(Nov. 2011)**
REAL NAME Waylon Jones
BASE Gotham City
HEIGHT 6ft 5in **WEIGHT** 268 lbs
EYES Red **HAIR** None
POWERS/ABILITIES Rare skin condition allows for enhanced durability; enhanced strength and endurance; excellent fighter with history of wrestling alligators; sharp teeth and claws.
ALLIES Arsenal, Catwoman
ENEMIES Batman, The Batman Family, Bane
AFFILIATIONS Arkham Asylum inmates

Killer Croc may not be the sharpest knife in the drawer, but his razor-like claws and teeth certainly make up for it. Almost more animal than man, this ferocious super-villain has challenged Batman to many fights—ones that the Dark Knight has been lucky to walk away from in one piece. Killer Croc is truly a force to be feared and remains one of the most dangerous inmates ever to be housed in Arkham Asylum.

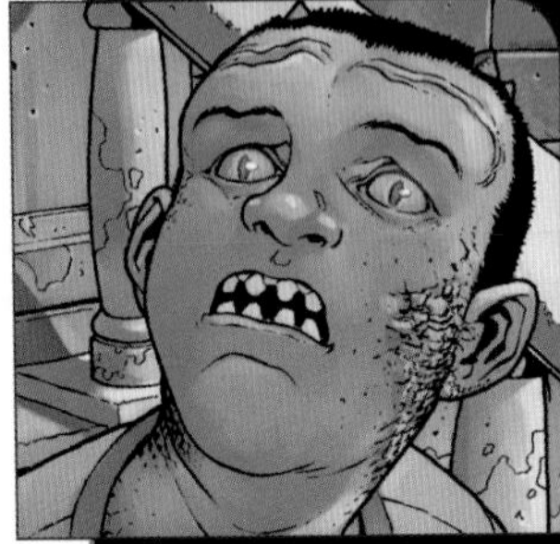

MOCK THE CROC
As a boy, Waylon Jones's skin condition caused him to be mocked by his peers, leading to the nickname Croc, which he would later embrace.

Waylon Jones had always been different. Growing up in a poor neighborhood in Gotham City, he lived a lonely life with his Aunt Flowers. With no parents of his own, Waylon had only his aunt to look up to, but she despised her nephew because of the way he looked. Born with a rare medical condition that caused scales to form on his body and bumpy horn-like protrusions to grow on his head, as well as giving him jagged teeth and claws, Waylon was cruelly nicknamed "Croc" by the local kids. His aunt attempted to scrub off Waylon's scales when they first emerged, but had no luck making her nephew appear as normal as the boys and girls that mocked him.

Years later, Waylon made his way to Jacksonville, Florida and became a sideshow act wrestling alligators in the Eddie Geisel Circus Sideshow. Now completely covered in hard green scales, Waylon was dubbed Killer Croc. Waylon eventually became frustrated with his low income from Geisel, and literally bit the hand that fed him, quitting the act and returning to Gotham City to become a thief. He soon crossed paths with Batman and the original Robin during a jewelry heist. The two heroes brought him to justice, but would go on to see the fierce villain escape incarceration at Arkham Asylum time and again. On one occasion, he even chomped off the hand of one of the Asylum's toughest guards, Aaron Cash.

With his own skewed moral code, Killer Croc has befriended heroes like Arsenal, and worked for other criminals, including Catwoman. He has also been known to become a protector for those who live in Gotham City's sewers, but in his heart remains an anger that seemingly cannot be quenched. **MM**

ON THE RECORD

First appearing shortly before the epic maxiseries *Crisis on Infinite Earths*, the original incarnation of Killer Croc was far smarter than his savage post-Flashpoint successor.

Depicted as a criminal mastermind slowly taking over Gotham City's underworld, Killer Croc—also called King Croc—murdered the Flying Todds, Gotham City's newest trapeze act sensation. The Todds' son, Jason, survived, and would go on to become the second Robin. Some years later, Jason's story was rewritten with the future Robin now being depicted as an orphaned street kid with little historical connection to Killer Croc.

KILLER OR KING?
In his later appearances, Killer Croc had become simply muscle-for-hire, a far cry from the gang boss that earned a feared reputation as King Croc.

WHAT LIES BENEATH
Killer Croc can often be found in the sewers, with the old tunnels providing him with the perfect hideaway. Croc often takes charge of some of the other forgotten souls who dwell there.

CLASSIC STORIES

***Detective Comics* (Vol. 1) #525 (Apr. 1983)** Batman tangles with Killer Croc in the Gotham City sewers, realizing how ferocious his new opponent truly is.

***Batman* (Vol. 1) #359 (May 1983)** Killer Croc's origin is told for the first time as he declares himself "King Croc," and takes his place as one of Gotham City's major criminals.

***Batman* (Vol. 1) #489 (Feb. 1993)** Croc is given the spotlight as he takes on Robin, Azrael, and the threat of a formidable new villain, Bane.

***Batman* (Vol. 1) #608 (Dec. 2002)** Killer Croc is mutated into a more animalistic state thanks to the meddling of new Batman foe, Hush.

BATTLE OF THE BRAWN
The powerful villain Bane challenged Killer Croc for territory while clad in a makeshift Batsuit. Bane came out on top, besting the scaly beast in fierce combat.

K

KILLER FROST

DEBUT *Firestorm* (Vol. 1) #3 (Jun. 1978)
CURRENT VERSION *The Fury of Firestorm: The Nuclear Man* #19 (Jun. 2013)
REAL NAME Dr. Caitlin Snow
HEIGHT 5ft 4in **WEIGHT** 123 lbs
EYES Blue **HAIR** White
POWERS/ABILITIES Can project ice and snow from her fingertips; feeds off others' heat.
ALLIES Steve Trevor
ENEMIES Firestorm
AFFILIATIONS S.T.A.R. Labs

Dr. Caitlin Snow was a brilliant employee of the Science and Technology Advanced Research Laboratories (S.T.A.R. Labs) who was assigned to their Arctic base. Here she found that her fellow scientists had been stymied in their work on a thermodynamic ultraconductor engine. Not knowing that her peers were associated with the terrorist group H.I.V.E., Snow was blindsided by her fellow doctors and locked in with the experimental machine. While trying to save herself by pulling out the machine's coolant wires, Caitlin was fused with ice and she was transformed into Killer Frost.

Killer Frost soon discovered she needed to "feed" on heat from living things, and that the energy created by Firestorm was the only thing that sated her hunger, prompting many clashes with the hero. **MM**

KILLER MOTH

DEBUT *Green Arrow* (Vol. 5) #25 (Jan. 2014)
EYES Black **HAIR** Black
POWERS/ABILITIES Uses super-powerful compressed-air gun to create concussive force blasts and defensive screens.
ALLIES Richard Dragon, Brick, Red, Count Vertigo
ENEMIES Green Arrow, Batman, Emiko Queen
AFFILIATIONS Longbow Hunters

The anonymous sociopath known as Killer Moth first appeared during the catastrophic superstorm that ravaged Gotham City in Year Zero. Obsessed with moths and money, he tried to kidnap billionaire Moira Queen, who was leading relief efforts during the crisis. His homemade high-impact air gun made short work of her security detail, but was no defense against the then relatively unknown vigilantes Batman and Green Arrow.

He reappeared six years later in Seattle. Using an upgraded air-blast rig he joined the Longbow Hunters: a squad of costumed mercenaries paid $30 million to destroy everything that Green Arrow cherished. However, despite his murderous ways and the power of his invention, Killer Moth was a physical coward and easily subdued. He was humiliatingly outsmarted and beaten by Oliver Queen's assistant Naomi Singh and her little sister Emiko. **MM**

KING SHARK

DEBUT *Superboy* (Vol. 4) #0 (Oct. 1994)
CURRENT VERSION *Suicide Squad* (Vol. 4) #1 (Nov. 2011)
REAL NAME Nanaue **BASE** Mobile
HEIGHT 7ft 2in **WEIGHT** 380 lbs
EYES Red **HAIR** None
POWERS/ABILITIES Giant shark-like humanoid possessing incredible strength.
ALLIES Mera, Aqualad
ENEMIES Aquaman, Superboy
AFFILIATIONS Suicide Squad, the Society

The super-villain known as King Shark is the son of Kamo, a being convinced that he was an ancient Hawaiian deity. When government agent Amanda Waller took Kamo into custody, she also kidnapped his son, King Shark. Considered the "first child of Belle Reve," King Shark was raised in the high security prison. As an adult, King Shark was tortured by Amanda Waller as part of the loyalty test during her vetting process for Task Force X —a clandestine government strike force more commonly called the Suicide Squad.

King Shark joined the Suicide Squad and while he has on occasion eaten a team member, he proved to be an effective operative before disappearing during a mission. He later resurfaced as a loyal servant of the amphibious Queen Mera. **MM**

KLARION

DEBUT *The Demon* (Vol. 1) #7 (Mar. 1973)
CURRENT VERSION *Klarion* #1 (Dec. 2014)
REAL NAME Klarion Bleak
BASE New York City
HEIGHT 5ft 11in **WEIGHT** 113 lbs
EYES Black **HAIR** Black
POWERS/ABILITIES Flight; teleportation; energy projection; changes skin color to beige.
ALLIES Teekl, Beelzebub, Piper, Oblivion, Rasp
ENEMIES The Necropolitan Club, Teen Titans
AFFILIATIONS The Elite

Hailing from a magical dimension, Klarion was a student of the dark mystical arts. When he lashed out at his teacher using magic, he realized that he couldn't return home again, and set off for another dimension entirely, and made his new home on Earth, in New York City. There he began to work and train at the Moody Museum under a mysterious woman named Piper, meeting several new magical allies.

Klarion was soon recruited into Manchester Black's organization, the Elite, and fought against the Teen Titans when the heroes refused to hand over Superboy, a fugitive from the law at the time. Klarion recently came into conflict with the Secret Six when their teen member Black Alice began disrupting the magical community with her uncontrollable hex powers. **MM**

KILLER SHARK III

DEBUT *Blackhawk* (Vol. 1) #50 (Mar. 1952) (Killer Shark I); *Birds of Prey* (Vol. 1) #114 (Mar. 2008) (Killer Shark III)
BASE Series of hidden bases
HEIGHT 5ft 11in **WEIGHT** 214 lbs
EYES Blue **HAIR** Black
POWERS/ABILITIES Self-made millionaire; superb athlete; sharp teeth; customized weaponry.
ALLIES Queen Killer Shark, Killer Shark I
ENEMIES Lady Blackhawk, Birds of Prey

The man calling himself Killer Shark is the grandson of the original Killer Shark, a pirate of the Pacific Ocean. The elder Killer Shark raided ships using a variety of high tech devices to make off with his stolen loot. He was also a sworn enemy of the famous pilots called the Blackhawks, and even invented a serum that could make others do his bidding.

When his grandson inherited his mantle and arsenal, a new Killer Shark was born. He quickly tracked down and kidnapped the time-displaced Lady Blackhawk, using his grandfather's serum to change her into Lady Killer Shark. He was infatuated with his new "partner," but when Lady Blackhawk's Birds of Prey teammate Huntress came her rescue, Killer Shark attempted to force her to become his slave as well, leading to his ultimate defeat. **MM**

KING SNAKE

DEBUT *Robin* (Vol. 1) #2 (Feb. 1991)
REAL NAME Sir Edmund Dorrance
BASE Gotham City
HEIGHT 6ft 2in **WEIGHT** 220 lbs
EYES White (Blind) **HAIR** Blond
POWERS/ABILITIES Expert martial artist; ties to the criminal underworld.
ALLIES Lynx, Bane
ENEMIES Batman, Red Robin, the Batman Family
AFFILIATIONS Kobra, Black Lantern Corps

A mercenary who traveled to the island nation of Santa Prisca, Sir Edmund Dorrance lost his eyesight during a covert government commando raid on his forces. Dorrance escaped, leaving behind his son, whom he'd fathered with a local rebel. While the child would go on to become the super-villain Bane, Edmund himself became better known as King Snake when he rose up the criminal ladder to become a gang lord.

After repeated clashes with the hero Robin (Tim Drake), and an attempt to take over the international terrorist cult, Kobra, King Snake fell to his death during a conflict with Batman and Bane. However, Dorrance would temporarily return to terrorize Gotham City during the *Blackest Night* event as a member of the undead Black Lantern Corps. **MM**

KINETIX

DEBUT *Legion of Super-Heroes* (Vol. 4) #66 (Mar. 1995)
REAL NAME Zoe Saugin
BASE Metropolis, 31st Century, Earth-247
HEIGHT 5ft 4in **WEIGHT** 118 lbs
EYES Green **HAIR** Auburn
POWERS/ABILITIES Can animate and transform objects; possesses Legion flight ring.
ALLIES Shrinking Violet, XS, Leviathan
ENEMIES Emerald Eye, Superboy-Prime

Zoe Saugin hailed from her homeworld of Aleph, located in the universe of Earth-247. She once saved her mother's life with a magical artifact, prompting her to embark on a quest for other forms of mystical energy, until she had gained significant superpowers. Presented to the Legion of Super-Heroes as a recruit by her home planet, Zoe adopted the name Kinetix and was accepted as a Legionnaire.

After years of service with the team, Kinetix was altered by the entity known as Terrorforms, and evolved into a new form. Later, she fell in battle alongside her fellow Legionnaires against the powerhouse villain Superboy-Prime during the Final Crisis event. A statue of Kinetix was sculpted to remember her time on the team and unveiled at a solemn ceremony led by her fellow Legionnaires Dawnstar and Wildfire. **MM**

KNIGHTFALL

DEBUT *Batgirl* (Vol. 4) #10 (Aug. 2012)
REAL NAME Charise Carnes
BASE Gotham City
HEIGHT 5ft 11in **WEIGHT** 141 lbs
EYES Green **HAIR** Blond
POWERS/ABILITIES Wealthy manipulator and actor; adept martial artist; well-connected.
ALLIES Mirror, Grotesque, Gretel, James Gordon, Jr.
ENEMIES Batgirl, Birds of Prey, Batwoman
AFFILIATIONS The Disgraced

When she was younger, Charise Carnes had a hard time finding a boy to love her for who she was. The daughter of a wealthy real estate baron, young Charise constantly met people who just liked her for her money. But when she met a boy named Trevor, she thought he was truly different.

Unfortunately, Charis was wrong: Trevor killed her family in front of her eyes. Instead of reporting the murderer, however, Charise kept quiet, plotting her revenge. Sentenced for the crimes, she reemerged from her time at Arkham Asylum as Knightfall, kidnapping and torturing Trevor and clashing with Batgirl several times. All the while, Charise managed to use her past to help position herself as a well respected member of society until her ultimate defeat at the hands of Batgirl and her allies. **MM**

KNIGHT AND SQUIRE

DEBUT Knight and Squire (Cyril): *Batman* (Vol. 1) #62 (Dec. 1950–Jan. 1951); Squire (Beryl): *JLA* (Vol. 1) #26 (Feb. 1999)
CURRENT VERSION *Batman Incorporated* (Vol. 2) #0 (Nov. 2012)
REAL NAMES Sir Cyril Sheldrake (Knight); Beryl Hutchinson (Squire, then, later, Knight)
HEIGHT 5ft 11in (Knight); 5ft 6in (Squire)
WEIGHT 175 lbs (Knight); 131 lbs (Squire)
EYES Brown (Knight); Blue (Squire)
HAIR Brown (Knight); Red (Squire)
POWERS/ABILITIES **Knight**: Talented detective, trained acrobat, proficient in unarmed combat; **Squire**: Trained acrobat, martial artist, multilingual, genius-level problem-solver.

British crime fighters Knight and Squire are a generational hero-team with their origins in World War II, when Percy Sheldrake—a boy of noble birth—became sidekick to the mystic warrior Shining Knight.

As an adult, Percy trained his son Cyril to be his ally, and together they tackled injustice as Knight and Squire until Percy was killed by their arch-enemy Springheeled Jack.

Cyril sank into depression until local lass Beryl Hutchinson helped him. He revived the family tradition with Beryl as his new Squire.

When Cyril was killed fighting a giant monster clone of Damian Wayne, Beryl took over the Knight's mantle. **WW**

KNOCKOUT

DEBUT *Superboy* (Vol. 4) #1 (Feb. 1994)
CURRENT VERSION *Secret Six* (Vol. 4) #12 (May 2016)
HEIGHT 6ft 1in **WEIGHT** 200 lbs
EYES Blue **HAIR** Red
POWERS/ABILITIES Superhuman strength and durability; regeneration.
ALLIES Scandal Savage, Rag Doll, Dubbilex
ENEMIES Female Furies, Granny Goodness, Silicon Dragons, Vandal Savage
AFFILIATIONS Female Furies, Secret Six

Knockout rejected the brutal warrior's life in Darkseid's Female Furies and fled to Earth to have fun. Working as an exotic dancer in Hawaii, she clashed repeatedly with Superboy before being recruited into the Suicide Squad. Knockout always walked a fine line between hero and villain; often pushing the heroes and villains she hung out with into less and less ethical actions.

She later joined metahuman mercenaries the Secret Six where, at the request of its leader—and her latest love—Scandal Savage, Knockout, aka "Kayo," infiltrated Lex Luthor's super-villain group, the Society.

After a period of thrilling capers on the run with Scandal, Knockout was killed by Infinity-Man. Her soul went to Hell, but was rescued by Secret Six comrade Rag Doll, who voluntarily took her place there. **WW**

KOBRA

DEBUT *Kobra* (Vol. 1) #1 (Feb.–Mar. 1976)
CURRENT VERSION *Convergence Titans* #2 (July 2015)
REAL NAME Jeffrey Franklin Burr
BASE Tibet
HEIGHT 6ft 2in **WEIGHT** 200 lbs
EYES Black **HAIR** Bald
POWERS/ABILITIES Charismatic leader; genius-level intellect; expert in unarmed combat.
ENEMIES Checkmate, Suicide Squad, Jason Burr, Superman, Batman, Wonder Woman

Jeffrey Burr was stolen moments after his birth by acolytes of the ancient Kobra Cult and raised in the murderous ways of the snake-worshipers. As "Naga-Naga," his education was extensive, as befitted one who was destined to rule the world.

Jeffrey's twin brother Jason had a regular upbringing, until government agents revealed to him that he was psychically linked to a brother he knew nothing about. The lawmen wanted to use that connection to control his brother, now called Kobra. Despite the efforts of several Super Heroes, Kobra circumvented this link and had Jason killed before expanding his terrorist depredations around the globe. Some time later, Black Adam killed Jeffrey, and the role of Kobra went to his arch-nemesis and resurrected brother, Jason. **WW**

KOMODO

DEBUT *Green Arrow* (Vol. 5) #17 (Apr. 2013)
REAL NAME Simon Lacroix
HEIGHT 5ft 10in **WEIGHT** 176 lbs
EYES Black **HAIR** Black
POWERS/ABILITIES Highly intelligent; martial artist; highly skilled in Kyudo archery.
ALLIES Mr. Kryp
ENEMIES Green Arrow, Shado, the Bear
AFFILIATIONS Outsiders, Arrow Clan, Magus

Born into abject poverty, Simon Lacroix amassed a huge personal fortune over time through sheer grit and his own innate brilliance. Working under Robert Queen, Simon shared his boss' obsession with the obscure martial cult, the Arrow Clan. He was the son Robert had always wanted, rather than the wastrel Oliver, who was an embarrassment to the Queens.

A man of overweening ambition, Lacroix then murdered Robert, adopted his illicit daughter Emiko, and trained with the bow until he became one of the world's most lethal archers. Stealing the Queen fortune through his own company, Stellmore International, Lacroix adopted the masked identity of Komodo and framed Green Arrow for murder. A confrontation ensued, and after a battle with Green Arrow, Komodo lost an eye. He was later killed by Emiko when she learned of her true parentage. **WW**

KRONA

DEBUT *Green Lantern* (Vol. 2) #40 (Oct. 1965)
CURRENT VERSION *Red Lanterns* #1 (Nov. 2011)
BASE Maltus
HEIGHT 3ft 5in **WEIGHT** 62 lbs **EYES** Green **HAIR** Black
POWERS/ABILITIES Immortality; full range of psionic abilities possessed by hyper-evolved Maltusians; flight; energy manipulation and projection; mind-control; overwhelming intellect and advanced technical genius.
ALLIES Nekron
ENEMIES Guardians of the Universe, Green Lantern Corps
AFFILIATIONS Guardians of the Universe, Black Lantern Corps

Krona was the most exalted of the scientific super-beings who developed on Maltus when the universe was young. Obsessed with discovering how creation began, he ignored all warnings and built a machine that took him back to the dawn of time. The moment he glimpsed the birth of everything, his machine exploded, fracturing reality into a multiverse, and shortening the lifespan of all existence. This mishap also created the anti-matter universe, unleashing evil upon all life. In response, his colleagues declared themselves Guardians of the Universe, eschewing all emotion and developing chaos-suppressing organizations to mitigate the damage Krona had caused. Krona was converted into energy and set to eternally orbit the cosmos he had despoiled. The super-Maltusians subsequently divided into squabbling factions: Zamarons, Controllers, and Guardians.

Billions of years later, Krona repeated his experiment, but was foiled by Green Lantern Hal Jordan. Returned to his energy state, the renegade then penetrated the Death Dimension and allied with Nekron, leading to the rise of Black Lanterns and the Blackest Night. After attempting to seize the Emotional Spectrum's Light Entities in his obsession to learn the origins of creation, Krona was executed by Jordan. His body was given to Atrocitus by Guardian Ganthet, but was stolen by the Red Lantern's son, Abysmus. The latter desecrated and consumed Krona's body to acquire the power remaining within. **WW**

KNOWLEDGE IS POWER
Krona was enslaved by his need for answers and was oblivious to the untold suffering caused by his curiosity.

KRYPTONITE MAN

DEBUT *Action Comics* (Vol. 1) #249 (Feb. 1959)
CURRENT VERSION *Action Comics* (Vol. 2) #5 (Mar. 2012)
REAL NAME Clay Ramsay
BASE Metropolis
EYES Blue **HAIR** Brown
POWERS/ABILITIES Radiation absorption and generation, superhuman strength, and flight.
ALLIES Dr. Abernathy, General Sam Lane
ENEMIES Superman, Steel
AFFILIATIONS Anti-Superman Army, K-Men

Bully and wife-beater Clay Ramsay was an early recipient of Superman's justice after the caped hero debuted in Metropolis. Tossed into Hob's Bay, the psychopath transferred all his rage onto the Man of Steel. Increasingly unstable, Ramsay tried suing Superman after his wife left him, then volunteered for Lex Luthor's Project K-Man.

Luthor needed a Superman deterrent and intended to use stolen Kryptonite to create a countermeasure. Clay's hatred for "the alien" made him the perfect subject.

During the first treatment, Ramsay was accidentally given excess energy. Super-strong and radioactive, he escaped and attacked Superman, but was defeated and arrested. In custody, Clay was conscripted by General Sam Lane to be his secret anti-Superman weapon. **WW**

KRYPTO

DEBUT *Adventure Comics* (Vol. 1) #210 **(Mar. 1955)**
CURRENT VERSION *Action Comics* (Vol. 2) #3 **(Jan. 2012)**
REAL NAME Krypto
BASE Phantom Zone, Earth
EYES Blue **HAIR** White
POWERS/ABILITIES Brave, loyal, determined; relatively advanced intelligence; flight, super-strength, speed, endurance; all the sensory and solar-fueled enhancements of Kryptonian physiology.
ALLIES Superman, Superboy, Phantom Stranger
ENEMIES Kryptonite Man, Xa-Du, the Phantom King
AFFILIATIONS Supergirl, Wonder Woman

A BOY AND HIS DOG
Krypto and Superboy share a common bond: both are outcasts, science-enhanced instinctive warriors, and fiercely protective of their friends and family.

TRUE LOVE
Despite all the tragedies that stemmed from Krypton's destruction, Superman's joy was boundless after finding his oldest childhood friend was still alive.

With Krypton crumbling to pieces around him, a desperate Jor-El sought refuge for his family in the Phantom Zone. When the prisoners exiled there threatened baby Kal-El, the El family's faithful guard dog Krypto savagely drove off the attackers, but was dragged into the timeless dimension with them. Deprived of all other options, Jor-El entrusted the life of his son to an experimental rocketship that he directed toward the planet Earth, and died with his wife and race.

As Krypton exploded, the valiant hound—reduced to an intangible, timeless ghost—stayed close to his young charge. Despite being trapped behind imperceptible dimensional walls, Krypto loyally continued watching over Kal-El as he grew up on Earth.

Decades later, when Phantom King Xa-Du trapped Superman in the Zone, Krypto was ready. Working alongside the mystic wanderer Phantom Stranger, Krypto saved the Man of Steel and was rewarded with freedom when his master physically dragged him back into the material world.

Super-charged by yellow solar radiation, Krypto quickly adapted to his new solid-state existence. He mixes exploratory wanderings around the world with the sacred duty of protecting his new two-legged family, which included the youthful El clone Superboy. **WW**

ON THE RECORD

Superman's best friend has always been his dog. A test-subject in Jor-El's rocketry experiments, canine Krypto was trapped in suspended animation n space for years, first coming to Earth when Clark Kent was still a Superboy.

For decades, the Hound of Steel split his time between Earthly adventures and roaming across time and space. Faithful unto death, the Silver Age Krypto perished saving his beloved master from Kryptonite-Man.

FRISKY BUSINESS
Superboy's elation with Krypto's reemergence in his life was always tempered by the problems the Dog of Steel's playful antics could cause.

KRYPTONIANS

DEBUT *Action Comics* (Vol. 1) #1 **(Jun. 1938)**
CURRENT VERSION *Supergirl* (Vol. 6) #2 **(Dec. 2011)**
POWERS/ABILITIES On Krypton: high intelligence, dense molecular structure, cells capable of absorbing and storing certain frequencies of radiation. Under a yellow sun: super-strength, speed, flight, invulnerability, enhanced senses—all fueled by exposure to solar energy.
ENEMIES The Char, Brainiac, the Multitude

SOLAR SUPERPOWER
All Krypton's lifeforms possess a cellular structure that hyper-efficiently processes yellow solar radiation. They gain superpowers after prolonged exposure.

Krypton was a super-dense world circling the red sun Rao. Despite its immense gravity, a passionate, adventurous, and intelligent humanoid race flourished there. Over millennia—filled with periodic outbreaks of destructive warfare—Kryptonians reached an impressive level of technological advancement. Much of their later civilization was based on a multi-purpose crystal mineral: Sunstone.

For a time, Kryptonians were starfaring, but as a result of increasing planetary conflicts, they eventually lost the secret of escaping the planet's potent gravity-well. They also developed cloning to a high degree, but when the mass-produced duplicates became entrenched as a slave species, the clones rose up in bloody revolt. The atrocities that followed led to cloning being outlawed and, over time, utterly detested.

Ultimately, Kryptonian culture was ended through ignorance and arrogance. The ruling Council refused to acknowledge the findings of leading scientist Jor-El when he discovered the planet's core was highly unstable and heading toward an annihilating atomic detonation. **WW**

ON THE RECORD

An iteration of Krypton seems to exist in each of the 52 universes of the multiverse. Krypton-23's last survivor became his adopted Earth's American President Calvin Ellis, while on Earth-10 the stellar foundling crash-landed in Nazi Germany and his presence resulted in that world's surrender to global fascism.

The most radical alternate was Earth-3's evil paragon Ultraman, who gained power by consuming Kryptonite and lost strength under a yellow sun.

ACME OF CIVILIZATION
Every incarnation of Krypton had used science to create a virtual paradise; but none could modify the all-too-human failings of its citizens.

LADY SHIVA

DATA

DEBUT *Richard Dragon, Kung-Fu Fighter* (Vol. 1) #5 **(Dec. 1975–Jan. 1976)**
CURRENT VERSION *Nightwing* (Vol. 3) #0 **(Nov. 2012)**
BASE Mobile
REAL NAME Sandra Wu-San
HEIGHT 5ft 8in **WEIGHT** 141 lbs
HAIR Brown **EYES** Green
POWERS/ABILITIES Universal mastery of martial arts, including unarmed combat and a wide array of weapons.
ALLIES Richard Dragon, Batman
ENEMIES Batgirl
AFFILIATIONS League of Assassins, Birds of Prey

MORTAL COMBAT
Lady Shiva returned to Gotham City where she fought Nightwing (Dick Grayson) and noted how his skills had improved since their last bout.

DEATH OF DEATHSTROKE?
Lady Shiva urged fellow martial artist Bronze Tiger to trace his old friend and drinking partner, Deathstroke—and kill him.

Mastering a number of different martial arts and weapons skills in her childhood, Lady Shiva was an expert assassin by the time she was a teenager. No less an authority than Batman has said she is without peer as a hand-to-hand combatant, and her skill with blades is equally superb.

A childhood filled with trauma—much of which remains a mystery—drove Sandra Wu-San to strike back at those who had wronged her. She trained hard to become an exceptional martial artist and, later, an assassin for hire. Wu-San joined the League of Assassins and became known as Lady Shiva, after the Hindu god of destruction.

Neither a conventional hero or villain, she has both fought and allied with a number of different heroes over the years, including Batman, Robin, Red Hood, and Nightwing. As an adult, she fought Dick Grayson the first time he went into the field as Robin to save Batman, defeating him easily and then advising him to get out of Batman's shadow and forge his own identity. Several years later, she battled Nightwing and realized Grayson had taken her advice. As a trainer for the League of Assassins, she taught Red Hood, Bronze Tiger, and others, and allied with the League to fight off an Untitled infiltration of their hidden base.

The only time she has met a decisive defeat in combat, it was her overconfidence that was her downfall, as Red Hood disabled her with a move she herself had taught him years before. She is often thought to have red hair because the hood of her costume features a long red braid interwoven with blades, but this is a misdirection, used to help her keep her true identity a secret. **AI**

ON THE RECORD

Lady Shiva was said to be the mother of Cassandra Cain, and challenged her daughter to a series of battles when the young woman first became Batgirl. With each duel, she taught Cassandra a little more, freeing the hero of her death wish. Eventually, Batgirl turned the tables on her mother and defeated Lady Shiva by forcing her to confront her own desire for death.

Shiva has also demonstrated surprising loyalty to former teammates who have also been enemies. When Spy Smasher seized control of the Birds of Prey, Lady Shiva came to Oracle's defense.

JADE WARRIOR
Lady Shiva was briefly a member of the Birds of Prey, adopting the name Jade Canary.

CLASSIC STORIES

***Batman* (Vol. 1) #509 (Jul. 1994)**
After the Batman is paralyzed by Bane, Lady Shiva works with him to regain not just the use of his legs, but his fighting spirit.

***Batgirl* (Vol. 1) #73 (Apr. 2006)**
Lady Shiva apparently dies in a battle to the death with Cassandra Cain, who is unaware that she has been fighting her own mother.

L.E.G.I.O.N.

DEBUT *L.E.G.I.O.N.* #1 (Feb. 1989)
CURRENT VERSION *Threshold* (Vol. 1) #3 (May 2013)
MEMBERS/POWERS **Vril Dox II** (leader): 12th-level intellect; **Captain Comet:** Telekinetic; **Davroth Catto:** Flight; **Darkstar** (Lydea Mallor): Projects negative energy; **Marij'n** and **Garryn Bek**: No superhuman abilities; **Amon Hakk**: Khund strength; **Lobo**: Regenerative abilities; **Zena Moonstruk**: Light control; **Stealth**: Soundwave control; **Strata**: Super-strength; **Garv**: Telepath.
ALLIES Green Lantern Corps, JLA, Omega Man

Formed after an alien invasion of Earth, the Licensed Extra-Governmental Interstellar Operatives Network (L.E.G.I.O.N.) is a heroic peacekeeping force that protects planets that subscribe to its service. The brilliant Coluan, Vril Dox II (son of Brainiac), founded L.E.G.I.O.N. after he and its original core members escaped from a Dominator-run "Starlag" prison camp.

On their first mission, Vril Dox and his compatriots liberated Dox's homeworld of Colu from the domineering grip of the ruling computer tyrants. They then cleaned out the riffraff from the vile planet of Cairn—the galaxy's "drug world"—and made it their headquarters, though they established satellite command centers on every planet where they mounted sustained operations.

L.E.G.I.O.N.'s rapid run of triumphs lured several high-paying clients and attracted new members, which led to the membership roster remaining in constant flux. L.E.G.I.O.N. continued its success until Dox's super-smart, malevolent son, Lyrl, usurped control and led the group down a very different path. In response, several members formed a rival team, R.E.B.E.L.S., to restore L.E.G.I.O.N.'s good name. Vril Dox eventually returned as the L.E.G.I.O.N.'s leader, just in time for the Rann-Thanagar War, and the team has since appeared battling alongside various Lantern Corps. **AI**

LICENSED TO PROTECT
If you have an interplanetary crisis on your hands, L.E.G.I.O.N. will solve it... once they resolve their own issues.

LADY BLACKHAWK

DEBUT *Blackhawk* #133 (Feb. 1959)
CURRENT VERSION *Blackhawks* #1 (Nov. 2011)
BASE Aerie
HEIGHT 5ft 7in **WEIGHT** 117 lbs
HAIR Black **EYES** Brown
ABILITIES Expert pilot, markswoman, and unarmed combatant.
ALLIES Oracle
ENEMIES Court of Owls, Secret Six
AFFILIATIONS Blackhawks, Birds of Prey

The first Lady Blackhawk, Zinda Blake, became an expert pilot during World War II with the intention of becoming the first female member of the legendary Blackhawks. Soon accepted among their number, Blake joined their wartime exploits and fought Killer Shark.

After the reality-warping event Zero Hour, Lady Blackhawk joined the Birds of Prey as a pilot, her loyalty contingent on Oracle's role as team leader. Another Lady Blackhawk—Natalie Reed—served with the team from World War II into the Cold War years.

A third, as yet unnamed Lady Blackhawk, wearing an eye patch, has appeared as part of a Blackhawks covert-ops team. The group shut down the mysterious Mother Machine, averting the threat of a cyber-attack and a global release of dangerous nanotechnology. **AI**

TRIGGER-HAPPY
With the Birds of Prey or on her own, Lady Blackhawk can't wait for the shooting to start.

NEW BLACKHAWK
Little is known about the most recent Lady Blackhawk, but she follows in the footsteps of her pilot predecessors.

LANG, LANA

DEBUT *Superboy* (Vol. 1) #10 **(Sep.–Oct. 1950)**
CURRENT VERSION *Action Comics* (Vol. 2) #6 **(Apr. 2012)**
BASE Metropolis, Smallville
HEIGHT 5ft 7in **WEIGHT** 127 lbs **HAIR** Red **EYES** Blue
POWERS/ABILITIES No superpowers, but a fiercely loyal friend with an unbreakable will; a skilled engineer.
ALLIES Superman
ENEMIES Lex Luthor

Lana Lang was a close childhood friend of Clark Kent's and one of the first people on Earth to learn of his extraordinary abilities. As teenagers, they started to get romantic, and they were at a dance together when Clark received the news that his parents had died in a car accident.

Lana supported Clark's dream of becoming a reporter, and left Smallville herself, eventually establishing a career as an electrical engineer. Not one to hide from danger, she managed to get a tanker's engines going in time to avert a deadly collision (with a little help from Superman), and later she was glad to see him again when a drilling project released a monster from deep underground—leading to an adventure in Imperial Subterranea.

Back in Smallville, Lana helped Wonder Woman work out how Superman was affected by his battle with Doomsday. She also uncovered Brainiac's plot to use the brains of comatose humans—including her parents'—to create a super network.

After the Man of Steel gave his life to save his adopted planet, Lana Lang turned up at his memorial in Metropolis to keep a promise to Clark: to bury him with his parents in Smallville. She was interrupted by the recently revealed alternate Earth Clark Kent, who had a plan to resurrect Superman. When that failed, he helped Lana re-bury her friend's remains. **AI**

LASTING LEGACY
Lana guided the alternate Earth Clark Kent to Superman's Fortress of Solitude hoping he could find a Regeneration Matrix to revive the Man of Steel. Sadly, the artifact didn't exist in this Earth's Fortress.

ON THE RECORD

An earlier story about Lana Lang had her marrying Pete Ross, who became Vice President in Lex Luthor's White House (and later President when Luthor was forced from office). Feeling stifled in her role as First Lady—and also still bearing conflicted feelings about Clark—she divorced Pete and restarted her career. Later, Lana became the uncompromising CEO of LexCorp, and survived an alien attempt to turn her into a new Insect Queen, a nod to her insectoid transformations in both her Silver and Bronze Age incarnations (pictured right).

LL + KAL-EL
Superman was often the subject of intense professional and personal rivalry between Lana Lang and the equally ambitious Lois Lane.

LANE, LOIS

DATA

DEBUT *Action Comics* (Vol. 1) #1 **(Jun. 1938)**
CURRENT VERSION *Action Comics* (Vol. 2) #1 **(Nov. 2011)**
BASE Metropolis
HEIGHT 5ft 7in **WEIGHT** 120 lbs **EYES** Blue **HAIR** Black
POWERS/ABILITIES Insatiable curiosity, excellent deductive reasoning, militarily trained in unarmed combat, briefly obtained and used telepathic powers while one of The Twenty.
ALLIES Jimmy Olsen, Perry White, Clark Kent, Jonathan Carroll
ENEMIES Brainiac, The Twenty, Lex Luthor, the Cartel, Scarecrow, Xa-Du the Phantom King, Lord Vyndktvx, Nimrod the Hunter, the Agent, Dr. Osterman
AFFILIATIONS The *Daily Planet* newspaper, Galaxy Broadcasting System/the Planet Global Network

Fiercely independent, relentlessly inquisitive, and possessing an unflinching sense of right and wrong, Lois Lane is one of the world's most successful and influential investigative reporters. As she perfected her craft under legendary editor-in-chief Perry White at Metropolis' prestigious *Daily Planet*, Lois wrote innumerable high-profile stories, winning the envy and respect of her coworkers. Already a star reporter, her journalistic immortality was assured when—together with photographer Jimmy Olsen—Lois secured the first interviews with and official pictures of the mystery news sensation known as Superman.

AT A GLANCE...

Boss lady
Despite having many misgivings, Lois' keen ambition drove her to accept a high-paying management job with media baron Morgan Edge. Quickly disgusted with having to massage news for ratings, Lois returned to the *Daily Planet*, where journalistic integrity was paramount. With Perry White in charge, Lois soon regained her formidable reputation.

Heart of the matter
Lois' relationship with the celebrated war correspondent Jonathan Carroll was undeniably hard on Clark. However, he could not deny that his dashing rival truly loved Lois, and wanted what was best for her.

Oh, little sister
Lois' sister withered rather than blossomed under Sam Lane's parentage. A wild, rebellious kid, she grew up troubled and aimless. However, no matter how bad things were, Lucy always knew Lois would be there to pick up the pieces and clean up her messes.

Lois Lane was raised on US military bases around the world; an army brat constantly on the move as her soldier father, Sam Lane, rapidly advanced to the position of General. She is extremely protective of her younger sister Lucy, having become the Lane family's de facto mother in her teens, following Ella Lane's death from a mystery ailment.

As Sam grieved, he compensated by pushing Lois to excel in physical activities. He trained her in unarmed combat, small-arms techniques, and ensured she became a qualified pilot. Consequently, Lois grew up with a potent sense of self-reliance and was always hungry to know all the answers: something which grew increasingly difficult as her father was regularly promoted into ever-higher-security positions.

At work, Lois liked her self-effacing, bumbling *Daily Planet* colleague Clark Kent, admiring his genuine warmth and fellow feeling for the weak and the downtrodden. Lois respected Clark's incisive mind and his hunger for the truth, but she often had a feeling that there was something he was keeping from her.

As a journalist, her tenacious, razor-sharp instincts quickly took Lois to the top, prompting communications tycoon Morgan Edge to appoint her head of the Media Division when his Galaxy Broadcasting System acquired the *Daily Planet*. Lois was moved into television and a management role, becoming executive producer of the nightly news and "Vice President of New Media" for Edge's Planet Global Network. Before long however, the prioritizing of celebrities over real news—and sales over ethics—became too much for Lois, and she returned to the *Daily Planet* and honest journalism.

Lois' nose for news has often endangered her life, and even humanity itself. When a five-year search for missing persons dubbed "The Twenty" led Lois Lane to Senator Hume, she uncovered a cadre of mortals granted psionic powers by alien scientist Brainiac—who was preparing to invade Earth. Lois herself was then cursed with these abilities. At first, they enabled her to aid Superman, but eventually made her the Collector of Worlds' slave. While battling the psionically-charged Lois, Superman was able to give her the final impetus needed to resist Brainiac's programming.

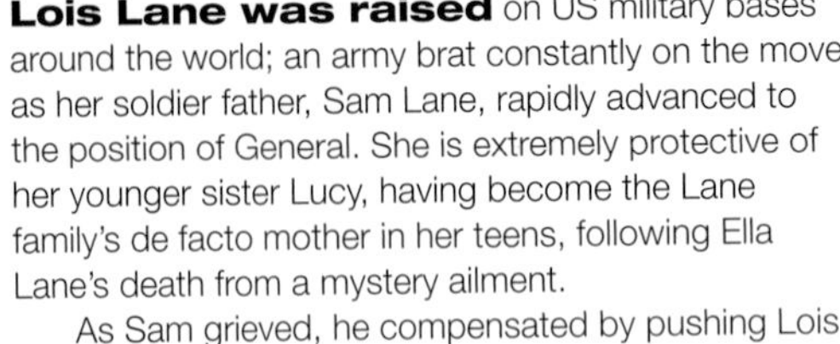

FACE THE PRESS
Lois could be deceptive, insistent, sympathetic, and incisive: in order to extract the truth from the most reticent interviewee.

CLASSIC STORIES

***Superman's Girlfriend Lois Lane* (Vol. 1) #15 (Feb. 1960)** All Lois' dreams seemingly came true when Kryptonian wed Earthling in "The Super-Family of Steel!" However, the happy ending was actually for doppelgängers Sylvia DeWitt and Van-Zee of Kandor.

***Superman's Girlfriend Lois Lane* (Vol. 1) #70 (Nov. 1966)** In a clever, fun story, Lois is mesmerized into becoming Catwoman while the real villainess magically transforms Superman into her cat.

***Superman's Girlfriend Lois Lane* (Vol. 1) #93 (Jul. 1969)** Superman's camaraderie with Wonder Woman—now a mortal adventurer—triggers insecurities that Lois must overcome to save the heroine's life.

***Superman's Girlfriend Lois Lane* (Vol. 1) #111 (Jul. 1971)** Lois first encountered Darkseid's secret invasion of Earth after being attacked by a tiny Justice League from the villain's "Evil Factory."

FAMILY FAVORITES
The most consistent problem in Lois' life has been her strained relationship with her father. Not only does she hate General Sam Lane's smug self-assurance and lifelong habit of keeping secrets—from the general public and especially from her—but their diametrically opposed attitudes to Superman frequently set them at odds. On more than one occasion, Lois' persistent prying has uncovered things the military wanted to keep hidden, and only Sam Lane's influence has kept her out of jail.

LOVE AND WAR
Sam Lane adores his troublesome daughter, but does not trust her with any of the secrets he is duty-bound to keep.

SUPERMAN UNCHAINED

When anti-technology sect Ascension started sabotaging satellites, Superman discovered the US Army had been deploying a superpowered alien as their secret weapon since 1938. The living weapon Wraith was more powerful than Superman, but could not defeat or subvert his undisciplined rival, and Lois became embroiled in the cover-up orchestrated by her father.

The entire affair escalated when General Lane tried to kill Superman and confiscate the alien technology in his Fortress of Solitude, even as the race that spawned Wraith made its move to conquer Earth.

HELPING HANDS
With Superman out-powered by Wraith, only Lois' use of the miraculous Earthstone could save the world from certain armageddon.

On another occasion, Lois' investigations into the secret of the Blake Farm Ghost resulted in her sustaining life-threatening injuries when she was hit by a fire engine. After being informed by hospital staff that doctors could not save her, Superman spent mere seconds reading up on surgical techniques, and then operated on Lois himself using his X-ray vision and super-speed, thereby saving her life.

Officially credited with naming Metropolis' notorious vigilante "Superman," Lois Lane shows little or no journalistic neutrality when it comes to the Man of Steel. She sees him as a savior and beacon of hope for ordinary people in a very hostile world. **WW**

REBIRTH

IT'S A BIRD, IT'S A PLANE...

With Superman deceased and many fraudsters and impostors battling to steal his name and reputation, Lois Lane swears to carry on his true legacy. For years she has fought for truth and exposed injustice as an acclaimed journalist, but now, as Superwoman, she can personally take action against the criminals, madmen, and monsters who prey on the defenseless. Even if her new super-powers are killing her.

"This is why I was a prize-winning reporter while you were still baling hay."

LOIS LANE

UNCOVERING THE TRUTH
Painfully aware that ordinary people suffer when the rich and powerful hide dirty secrets, Lois Lane tries to balance the scales while exposing the truth.

ALIEN AGENDA
Though not one of Brainiac's original Twenty, Lois proved the most effective. Her psionic powers briefly made her a match for Superman, until her resolutely independent streak rejected the transformation.

ON THE RECORD

Lois Lane was the first female character of the DC Universe, debuting in 1938 in the original Superman story in *Action Comics* #1. An ambitious, glamorous, scoop-hungry reporter, Lois was prepared to ditch Clark in the middle of a hard-earned date just to infiltrate a mobster's operation and get her story. She went too far, however, and Superman had to step in for the first of many saves.

Hold the front page

After months being the Man of Steel's foil and romantic interest, Lois won her own solo series in *Superman #28* (May 1944). Light-hearted, action-packed and comedic, the short tales usually depicted her getting into and out of scrapes without any superpowered back-up. Following the *Crisis on Infinite Earths* storyline, Lois took that independence a step further. Sophisticated, globally renowned and seemingly infallible, she consorted with kings, presidents, and billionaires who were generally terrified that she would ferret out their darkest secrets.

SOUL-SISTER
When comics started to become more socially relevant, the new go-getting Lois would do anything to get to the heart of a story. However, no journalist ever went as deeply undercover as Lois, when, with a little help from Superman's Plastimold machine, she transformed herself into an African-American woman to fully investigate racial prejudice in her city.

Love triangle

For more than 60 years, the Last Son of Krypton loved only one woman, but was his own rival for her affections. Lois Lane only had eyes for Superman, spurning every advance from her timid coworker Clark Kent. That painful quandary finally ended when Clark revealed his identity to Lois and they married. The new status quo benefited their journalistic partnership. Lois' competition with Clark for headlines became keener than ever, but now they both knew when to bolster the power of the press with a helping hand from Superman.

PAGING MRS. SUPERMAN
Lois and Clark's wedding was not the end of their love story, only the beginning...

LARFLEEZE

DEBUT *DC Universe* (Vol. 1) #0 **(Jun. 2008)**
CURRENT VERSION *Green Lantern: New Guardians* (Vol. 1) #3 **(Jan. 2012)**
BASE Larfleezia, Okaara
EYES White **HAIR** Orange
POWERS/ABILITIES Sole wielder of the Emotional Spectrum's orange light of Avarice, which offers immortality, flight, force-field protection, light constructs and animation; magic absorption; "hears" objects and people begging to be owned, then steals the personalities of those he kills and resurrects them as light-construct entities.
ENEMIES Guardians of the Universe, Green Lantern Corps, Invictus, Sena the Wanderer
AFFILIATIONS Orange Lantern Corps, New Guardians, Pulsar Stargrave, G'Nort

LIGHT'S OUT
For billions of years, Larfleeze obsessively ensured that nothing threatened his right to take whatever he wanted whenever he saw it.

Larfleeze, also known as Agent Orange, is the sole wielder of the orange light of Avarice. The most self-destructive color of the universe's Emotional Spectrum, it precludes sharing and those it illuminates will fight for what they want until only one remains. Its power infects the mind and effectively owns its possessor.

The embodiment of Avarice is Ophidian, who lives inside the battery and causes Larfleeze to hunger voraciously for everything he sees. Over billions of years, Agent Orange has indiscriminately turned his homeworld into a vast planetary hoard of junk, treasure, and corpses. He is the only Orange Lantern in the universe, but this incalculable, unshared power allows him to store the souls of every creature he has killed and resurrect them as semi-sentient light-constructs. To protect his most prized possession, the immensely long-lived Larfleeze has absorbed his Orange Lantern, becoming a living power battery. His unique oath reflects his philosophy:

What's mine is mine
and mine and mine,
And mine, and mine, and mine!
Not yours! **WW**

ON THE RECORD

Billions of years ago, thieves stole the fear entity Parallax from the planet Maltus. Fleeing the Guardians' robotic Manhunters, the bandits followed a map created by renegade Krona to the planet Okaara in the Vega system, where they found the orange power battery of Avarice. They squabbled over it until only Larfleeze remained.

Unable to defeat Larfleeze, the Guardians bargained with him, promising him immunity and total autonomy of the Vega system in return for Parallax.

COLLECTOR MANIA
The things Larfleeze craves most are the rings and batteries belonging to the other Lanterns Corps.

LASHINA

DEBUT *Mister Miracle* (Vol. 1) #6 **(Jan.-Feb. 1972)**
CURRENT VERSION *Infinity Man and the Forever People* #8 **(Apr. 2015)**
BASE Apokolips
HEIGHT 6ft 6in **WEIGHT** 225 lbs
EYES Blue **HAIR** Black
POWERS/ABILITIES Superhuman strength and durability; devastating skill with razor-sharp, flexible steel bands and straps; hands-on familiarity with all forms of weapons.
ALLIES Amanda Waller, Big Barda
ENEMIES Granny Goodness, Bernadeth
AFFILIATIONS Female Furies, Suicide Squad, Dark Side Club

WARRIOR WOMAN
As one of Granny Goodness's most gifted Female Furies, Lashina knew the value of trusted comrades *and* when to sacrifice them.

Lashina was one of the deadliest warriors to graduate from Granny Goodness's hellish Apokolips orphanage. Her incalculable military value was proven by the number of times Darkseid resurrected her.

Fast, strong, and calculating, she served as Big Barda's second-in-command in superpowered shock trooper unit the Female Furies. When Barda defected to Earth with Mister Miracle, Lashina led the team ordered to return the traitor to Apokolips. Instead, the Furies stayed on Earth for months, reveling in the freedoms of the primitive world. Before long, however, the Furies grew bored and returned to base, prepared to face their punishment for going AWOL.

Eventually Lashina was appointed team leader—to the dismay of rival Fury, Bernadeth—and dispatched to Earth to retrieve captured Apokoliptian demagogue Glorious Godfrey. Seizing her moment, Bernadeth struck, wounding Lashina and leaving her for dead. The plotter died for her betrayal when Lashina returned as Duchess, leading the ferocious metahumans of the Suicide Squad in a counterattack on Apokolips. **WW**

LEAGUE OF ASSASSINS

DEBUT *Strange Adventures* (Vol. 1) #215 **(Dec. 1968)**
CURRENT VERSION *Batman Incorporated* (Vol. 2) #2 **(Aug. 2012)**
BASE 'Eth Alth'eban
POWERS/ABILITIES Trained in multifarious aspects of murder and assassination, from hand-to-hand combat to expertise in all manner of exotic weaponry.
ALLIES Leviathan
ENEMIES Batman, Red Robin, Nightwing, Batman Incorporated
AFFILIATIONS Rā's al Ghūl, Doctor Darrk, the Sensei, the Demon's Head, Demon Fang

The League of Assassins—also known as the League or Society of Shadows—is an ancient secret organization created by the immortal Rā's al Ghūl to further his plans to destroy decadent civilizations and create an ordered world under his rule.

For centuries, the League has sold its services—singly, through teams of agents, or as a whole—to the great and powerful of many nations. This allowed it to fund its own agenda and to gain clandestine political advantage. It is also the greatest teacher of the combat arts in history. Responsible for the training of numerous warriors and villains, its students also include heroes such as Damian Wayne, Red Robin, Red Hood, and Batgirl/Black Bat.

In recent decades, the Society has suffered from continual internecine conflict, as deputies appointed by Rā's al Ghūl overstepped their bounds or sought to seize complete control. This resulted in a number of splinter groups of assassins becoming competition and hindrances to the League. Another major stumbling block has been the loss of their cloak of anonymity, as the efforts of an increasing number of Super Heroes have successfully brought the Society's hidden efforts out of the shadows. **WW**

KILLER ELITE
Whether through blade, bullet, missile, toxin, empty hand, or magic, for centuries the aim of the League of Assassins never faltered or failed.

ON THE RECORD

The League was revealed as a family business after Rā's al Ghūl died. His daughters Talia and Nyssa inherited control, but a schism saw one faction trying to resurrect their master: seeking to implant Rā's' spirit in Talia and Batman's son Damian. Another group pledged allegiance to the Sensei; the assassin-teacher who had coordinated the global murder enterprise for centuries. Revealed as Rā's' father, he ruthlessly cemented his control in a campaign the Dark Knight only barely thwarted.

THE ART OF DEATH
With Rā's gone, the Sensei believed nothing could hinder his ambitions, but found Batman to be even more relentless and formidable than his diabolical offspring.

LEGION OF SUBSTITUTE HEROES

DEBUT *Adventure Comics* (Vol. 1) #306 (Mar. 1963)
BASE 31st-century Metropolis
KEY MEMBERS Antennae Boy, Chlorophyll Kid, Color Kid, Double Header, Dream Girl, Fire Lad, Infectious Lass, Night Girl, Polar Boy, Porcupine Pete, Rainbow Girl, Star Boy, Stone Boy
ENEMIES Ambush Bug, Plant Men, Captain Freeze
AFFILIATIONS Legion of Super-Heroes, Science Police

Not every applicant is deemed suitable for membership in the Legion of Super-Heroes—even if they have superpowers and the best intentions. The Substitutes were all originally rejected because they were considered a liability to others or a danger to themselves, but came together in a support group under Polar Boy and Night Girl to prove the Legionnaires wrong.

Always working outside the spotlight, the Substitutes performed many valiant deeds, slowly gaining the real Legion's respect, and took in former Legionnaires Dream Girl and Star Boy when they lost their place on the lead team. Their egalitarian attitude meant that eventually the squad was heavy with real no-hopers such as Antennae Boy or Double Header, and became something of a joke.

However, Polar Boy and Night Girl's inclusivity won out, and even after they were promoted to the big leagues, "the Subs" continued to thrive, nurturing lesser lights and encouraging them to shine. **WW**

AGAINST ALL ODDS
Whenever all hope seemed lost, the Substitute Legion always proved that ingenuity, guts, and determination were superior to any superpower.

LEGION OF SUPER-PETS

DEBUT *Adventure Comics* (Vol. 1) #293 (Feb. 1962)
BASE 30th-century Metropolis
MEMBERS Krypto, Beppo, Streaky, Comet, Proty II
ALLIES Superman, Superboy, Supergirl, Jimmy Olsen, Chameleon Boy, Saturn Girl
ENEMIES Brain-Globes of Rambat, Rikkor Rost, the people of Than
AFFILIATIONS Legion of Super-Heroes, Legion of Substitute Heroes.

The Legion of Super-Pets was formed out of desperate necessity. When planetary plunderers the Brain-Globes of Rambat attempted to steal Earth, neither Superboy nor the Legion of Super-Heroes could withstand their psionic mental domination. But this was not the case for the valiant animal companions of the Boy of Steel or his cousin Supergirl. Using a time-bubble, the Legionnaires gathered Kryptonian survivors Krypto the Superdog and Beppo the Super-Monkey, plus Earthborn pets Streaky the Super-Cat and Comet the Super-Horse, to drive the marauders away. Later, the Super-Pets inducted Chameleon Boy's telepathic Protean pet Proty II into their ranks.

The time-traveling pets were formally invested as the Animal Branch of the Legion of Super-Heroes. Although convening sporadically, they were always ready to lend a paw or hoof to save the world and protect those weaker than themselves. **WW**

UNCONDITIONAL LOVE
Though devoted to their human comrades, the Super-Pets would never stand for being bullied or treated like lesser beings.

LEGION OF SUPER-HEROES

DATA

DEBUT *Adventure Comics* (Vol. 1) #247 **(Apr. 1958)**
CURRENT VERSION *Legion of Super-Heroes* (Vol. 7) #1 **(Nov. 2011)**
BASE 31st Century Metropolis
NOTABLE MEMBERS/POWERS
BLACK WITCH (MYSA NAL) Arsenal of magic spells;
BLOK Silicon-based living mineral, super-strength, durability;
BOUNCING BOY (CHUCK TAINE) Ability to inflate and bounce;
BRAINIAC 5 (QUERL DOX) 12th-level super-intellect;
CHAMELEON BOY (REEP DAGGLE) Shapeshifting;
CHEMICAL KID (HADRU JAMIK) Ability to alter chemical reactions;
COMET QUEEN (GRAVA) Space flight, comet gas extrusion;
COSMIC BOY (ROKK KRINN) Generation of magnetic fields;
DRAGONWING (MARYA PAI) Fire breath, exhalation of acid;
DREAM GIRL (NURA NAL) Dream interpretation to foretell the future;
ELEMENT LAD (JAN ARRAH) Transmutation of elements;
GLORITH Time-based magic manipulation;
HARMONIA (HARMONIA LI) Immortal, control of elemental forces;
INVISIBLE KID (JACQUES FOCART) Bends light to go unseen;
TRIPLICATE GIRL (LUORNU DURGO) Can split into multiple bodies;
LIGHTNING LAD (GARTH RANZZ) Generation of electricity;
LIGHTNING LASS (AYLA RANZZ) Generation of electricity;
MON-EL (LAR GAND) Super-strength, flight, invulnerability;
PHANTOM GIRL (TINYA WAZZO) Ability to phase through solids;
POLAR BOY (BREK BANNIN) Generation of cold, ice, and snow;
SATURN GIRL (IMRA ARDEEN) Extremely powerful telepath;
SHADOW LASS (TASMIA MALLOR) Generation of darkness;
SHRINKING VIOLET (SALU DIGBY) Size reduction;
STARMAN (THOM KALLOR) Can increase objects' weight/mass;
SUN BOY (DIRK MORGNA) Electromagnetic radiation;
ULTRA BOY (JO NAH) Superhuman strength, flight, super-speed.
ALLIES Wanderers, Heroes of Lallor
ENEMIES Dominators, Dark Circle, Mordru
AFFILIATIONS United Planets, Science Police

Once upon a future time, three teens who were inspired by legends of the greatest hero of all, Superman, decided to emulate their idol and do good deeds using their own special powers and abilities. With financial backing from multi-billionaire R.J. Brande, they formed a team and encouraged similar youngsters from across the universe to join them. Cosmic Boy Rokk Krinn, Lightning Lad Garth Ranzz, and Saturn Girl Imra Ardeen envisioned a great Legion of Super-Heroes.

When the Legion of Super-Heroes began auditioning applicants in 31st-century Metropolis, their only stipulations were that prospective members must be below the legal voting age and possess at least one natural and individual superpower. Predictably, there was no shortage of capable volunteers, but for every successful candidate there were many cheats, celebrity seekers, and even opportunistic criminals—all trying to take advantage of the new team's growing notoriety.

Some of the rejected hopefuls formed their own clandestine club: a publicity-shy Legion of Substitute Heroes that would handle minor tasks that the official team was too busy to tackle. For other, less well-intentioned rejects however, failure simply led to them stealing the idea and banding together as the murderous, self-serving Legion of Super-Villains.

As time passed, the Legion grew in numbers and strength. Its numerous humanitarian relief efforts and unfailing successes against bandits, raiders, invaders, mad scientists, and worse eventually prompted the leaders of the federation of civilizations, collectively known as the United Planets (UP), to incorporate the ever-changing band of young champions into its own official governmental security structure.

The Legion became a key component in UP defense protocols, leading to the creation of a top security Legion Academy (later renamed the United Planets Militia Academy). Its primary function is to fully train successful applicants for the demanding and hazardous life they have chosen. The facility is located at Montauk Point, with former Legionnaires Bouncing Boy and Triplicate Girl heading the teaching faculty. Even the unsuccessful candidates are considered to be highly valuable assets, and they generally find work in the Science Police or in the military of many worlds.

LEGION LOST
The Legion fought for its autonomy and existence when a time-bubble accident seemingly killed seven members. The explosion actually marooned them in the early 21st century, to which they had to adapt while finding a way home.

AT A GLANCE...

Flight ring
The flight ring is the symbol of membership in the Legion of Super-Heroes and enables the wearer to fly in any environment. Made from the artificial element Valorium, which has anti-gravity properties, the ring is thought-activated and engraved with a signature "L."

CLASSIC STORIES

***Adventure Comics* (Vol. 1) #352-353 (Jan.-Feb. 1967)** A short-handed Legion recruits five of the universe's greatest villains to help save Earth from a Sun-Eater. The plan succeeds at the cost of Ferro Lad's life, but results in the villainous quintet forming the Fatal Five.

***Legion of Super-Heroes* (Vol. 2) #287, 290-294 (May, Aug.-Dec. 1982)** Entire worlds are devastated by shadowy agents of a Great Darkness as the Legion battles ancient heroes and villains who are gathering artifacts to restore the ultimate evil: Darkseid.

***Final Crisis: Legion of 3 Worlds* (Vol. 1) #1-5 (Oct. 2008-Sep. 2009)** Reality is ripped apart and rewritten as three iterations from separate reboots are amalgamated and incorporated into the Legion of Prime Earth.

HOSTILE WORLD
Chameleon Boy led a Legion Espionage Squad unit comprising veterans and raw recruits to a United Planets Border Watchworld to investigate several security breaches. The incursions turned out to be the work of aggressively colonial Dominators, who were attempting to crossbreed their warrior castes with metahumans. With war imminent and the UP refusing to act, Mon-El led the Legion into action without approval. He discovered the invaders had co-opted and weaponized a fellow Daxamite, providing him with more raw power than even a 31st-century Superman could handle.

DOMINATION AND SUBMISSION
Dominator-augmented and controlled Res-Vir was more than a match for any number of Legionnaires, but his power could not compete with their wits.

RETURN OF THE FATAL FIVE
A resurgent Fatal Five attacked different worlds of the UP, utilizing the stolen power of a godlike Promethean Giant to disrupt the ubiquitous Quark technology which ran the entire UP. Hard-pressed on every front, and with Sun Boy, one of its longest-serving comrades killed, the depleted—but nonetheless undaunted—Legion scored its greatest and most important victory, only to be forcibly disbanded by the United Planets Council.

FIGHT TO THE FINISH
The universe's most vicious killers believed they had finally found the formula for ultimate conquest, but had not reckoned on the Legion's indomitable dedication.

ON THE RECORD

The Legion is probably the most rebooted Super Hero team of all time, although initially not the most serious. On their debut, Saturn Girl, Cosmic Boy, and Lightning Lad traveled into the past and invited Superboy to join, only to reject him as part of a prank. His stoic acceptance of their judgment won him a place on the team.

Unstoppable
After several guest appearances, the Legion became the lead feature in *Adventure Comics* in 1958, beginning a series of quirky futuristic adventures with Superboy as a regular guest star and amazed observer of life in the future. The team was so ahead of the times that its members elected a female—Saturn Girl—as their new leader in 1962!

Having saved the United Planets from the Fatal Five, the members of the Legion were rewarded for their valor with a hugely impressive new headquarters complex. It was payment from the grateful governments of many worlds and confirmed the Legion's vital role in intergalactic peacekeeping. However, during construction, a hidden coalition of belligerent races attacked Earth in overwhelming numbers. They were only defeated by use of a reality-warping Miracle Machine the Legion had been given by the Oan splinter group known as the Controllers.

MIRACLE CITADEL
After constructing the new Legion Plaza, the Miracle Machine was sealed away.

Future tense
After numerous reboots excised Superman from Legion continuity, Kal-El eventually returned to share adventures with the future teenagers. But when he visited them as Superman, Kal-El found his boyhood companions were pariahs and his historical reputation had been twisted by extreme xenophobia—resulting in the abuse of Earth's alien population. Moreover, the planet now basked under the rays of a red sun. It took everything he and the Legion could do to set the sky straight and save the world's captive aliens.

TIME AFTER TIME
With Superman's help, the Legion foiled a supremacist plan to rewrite history: eventually re-establishing a tolerant, civilised future for Earth.

"There's a lot of different kinds of power in the universe."
ULTRA BOY

ASSEMBLED AND CORRECT
1 Mon-El
2 Invisible Kid
3 Lightning Lass
4 Shrinking Violet
5 Cosmic Boy
6 Shadow Lass
7 Polar Boy
8 Element Lad
9 Sun Boy
10 Comet Queen
11 Dream Girl
12 Glorith
13 Harmonia
14 Starman
15 Brainiac 5

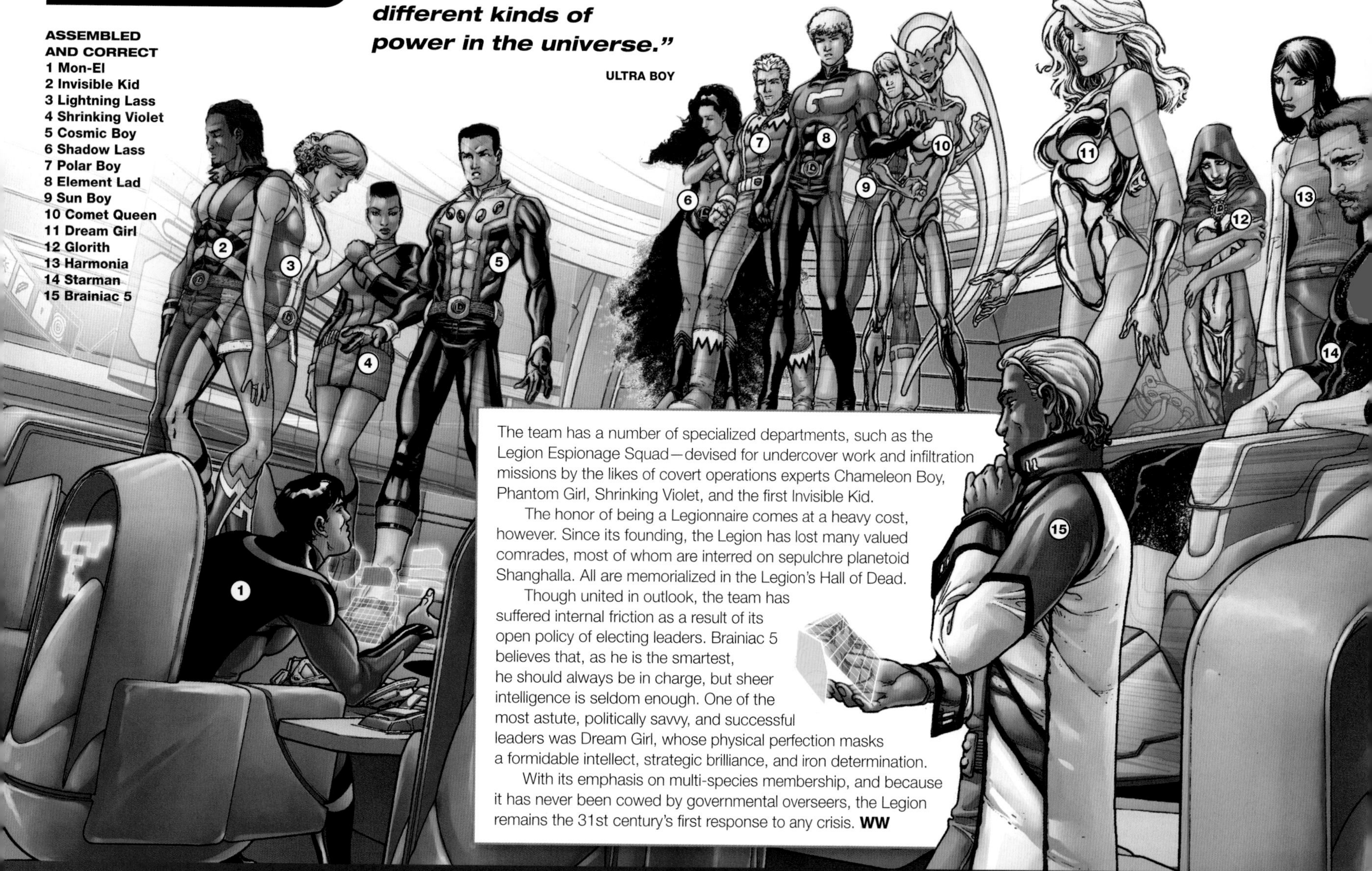

The team has a number of specialized departments, such as the Legion Espionage Squad—devised for undercover work and infiltration missions by the likes of covert operations experts Chameleon Boy, Phantom Girl, Shrinking Violet, and the first Invisible Kid.

The honor of being a Legionnaire comes at a heavy cost, however. Since its founding, the Legion has lost many valued comrades, most of whom are interred on sepulchre planetoid Shanghalla. All are memorialized in the Legion's Hall of Dead.

Though united in outlook, the team has suffered internal friction as a result of its open policy of electing leaders. Brainiac 5 believes that, as he is the smartest, he should always be in charge, but sheer intelligence is seldom enough. One of the most astute, politically savvy, and successful leaders was Dream Girl, whose physical perfection masks a formidable intellect, strategic brilliance, and iron determination.

With its emphasis on multi-species membership, and because it has never been cowed by governmental overseers, the Legion remains the 31st century's first response to any crisis. **WW**

LEMARIS, LORI

DEBUT *Superman* (Vol. 1) #129 (May 1959)
REAL NAME Lori Lemaris
BASE Atlantis
EYES Blue **HAIR** Brown
HEIGHT 5ft 9in **WEIGHT** 145 lbs
POWERS/ABILITIES: Telepathic communication; can survive on land or above water; tail transforms into legs on land.
ALLIES Superman
ENEMIES Advance Man, Ronal

Lori Lemaris dated Clark Kent when they were at college together, before he had adopted his Superman alter ego. She was confined to a wheelchair and revealed to Clark the reason why: She was a mermaid from the sub-aquatic city of Tritonis and the chair allowed her to hide her tail.

Superman returned her to Tritonis after she was injured. A dashing researcher named Ronal healed her with the magical Black Staff, which enabled him to reshape flesh. Lori and Ronal married, but her husband was corrupted by the Staff. He attacked Lori and was turned to stone after Superman shattered the Staff's gem.

Despite some tensions with Lois Lane, Lori was bridesmaid at Lois and Clark's wedding. She also had a brief career as a hero, taking on the villainous cosmic herald, the Advance Man. **SW**

LEVIATHAN

DEBUT *Batman: the Return* #1 (Jan. 2011)
CURRENT VERSION *Batman Incorporated* (Vol. 2) #1 (Jul. 2012)
BASE Crime Alley
MEMBERS/POWERS Talia al Ghūl: Trained assassin; **The Heretic:** Monstrous Damian Wayne clone, trained in combat; **Goatboy:** Rocket rifle; **Doctor Daedalus** (Otto Netz): Master tactician.
ALLIES Mutants gang, League of Assassins
ENEMIES Batman, Inc., Batmen of All Nations

Leviathan was a mysterious criminal organization that infiltrated and corrupted Gotham City. Led by a slender figure in a mask and her monstrous bodyguard, Leviathan's gangs of animal-masked goons eliminated rival gangsters and spread terror. Batman, Robin (Damian Wayne), and the other members of Batman Incorporated investigated Leviathan's activities and fought their man-bats, gangsters, and armies of crazed children.

The leader of Leviathan was finally revealed to be Bruce Wayne's former lover, Talia al Ghūl. When their son, Damian, had left her to be with his father, Talia created Leviathan to punish Batman. Damian was slain by Talia's bodyguard, the Heretic; Talia herself was killed by Kathy Kane of Spyral, ending Leviathan's threat. **SW**

LILITH

DEBUT *Teen Titans* (Vol. 1) #25 (Jan.–Feb. 1970)
CURRENT VERSION *Titans Hunt* #1 (Dec. 2015)
REAL NAME Lilith Clay
EYES Green **HAIR** Red
HEIGHT 5ft 6in **WEIGHT** 104 lbs
POWERS/ABILITIES Alpha-class psionic with telepathic powers; can blank minds and create psychic projections.
ENEMIES Mr. Twister
AFFILIATIONS: Teen Titans

A member of the original Teen Titans, Lilith was with the team when they investigated rumors of a monstrous being lurking in the woods near the town of Hatton Corners. There the team encountered a powerful demonic entity named Mr. Twister, who forced them to perform a ritual that would allow him to fully enter our world. Team member Herald could only stop this by using her powers to blank the Titans' memories, making them forget that they had ever met each other.

While some ex-Titans continued to serve as heroes, Lilith worked as an addiction counselor. However, Mr. Twister began whispering in her head, gradually reawakening her memories as he plotted to draw her and her teammates back to Hatton Corners to complete the ritual. **SW**

LINEAR MAN

DEBUT: *Adventures of Superman* (Vol. 1) #476 (Mar. 1991)
REAL NAME Travis O'Connell
BASE Vanishing Point
EYES Blue **HAIR** Black
POWERS/ABILITIES Futuristic weaponry; uses wrist device to open time vortices.
ALLIES Superman
ENEMIES Booster Gold
AFFILIATIONS Linear Men

Travis O'Connell is a member of time-travel regulation team the Linear Men. He went rogue to hunt down Booster Gold for unauthorized use of time-travel technology and transport him back to the 25th century. However, when O'Connell tried to apprehend Booster, Superman intervened, and was sucked into a time vortex.

To correct his error, O'Connell tried to bring the hero back to the 20th century using a series of time jumps. During his temporal travels, Superman helped to prevent the madman Dev-Em from destroying the moon, which resulted in massive changes to the time stream. O'Connell realized that his brash attempt to capture Booster Gold had led to a cascade of events that had altered history. He bravely sacrificed himself by destroying the moon, flinging Superman back to the present. **SW**

LIGHTRAY

DEBUT *New Gods* (Vol. 1) #1 (Feb.-Mar. 1971)
CURRENT VERSION *Green Lantern/New Gods: Godhead* #1 (Dec. 2014)
BASE New Genesis
HEIGHT 6ft **WEIGHT** 181 lbs **EYES** Blue **HAIR** Strawberry blond
POWERS/ABILITIES As a New God, Lightray is immortal and has physical capabilities beyond those of an ordinary human; he can also fly and fire blasts of energy from his hands.
ALLIES Orion
ENEMIES Darkseid, every Lantern Corps
AFFILIATIONS New Gods, the Council of Eight

Lightray is a New God and a general of New Genesis. His positivity, charm, and enthusiasm contrast sharply with the temperamental attitude of Orion—foster son of New Genesis' leader, Highfather—but the two are nevertheless close friends.

Hoping to find a clue to unlocking the powerful Life Equation, Highfather dispatched Lightray and the other members of the trusted Council of Eight to acquire power rings from the various Lantern Corps. The theft of power rings by the Council of Eight provoked the Lantern Corps to unite and take action. Black Hand of the Black Lantern Corps used his powers to raise undead leviathans from within the Source Wall itself. The Lanterns then used a redirected Boom Tube to transport the rampaging undead monstrosities directly to New Genesis. Lightray flew into battle, but was snatched up by one of the monsters, and was only saved when Orion blew up the creature's head (ruining his friend's uniform).

As Highfather watched his city being destroyed, he realized the folly of his arrogance, and a truce was brokered. Lightray and his people then faced the task of rebuilding their ruined utopia. **SW**

ON THE RECORD

In his pre-Flashpoint incarnation, Lightray (or Sollis, his proper name) was a close companion of Orion's, and even joined him in the Justice League while they were on Earth. It was while on Earth that Lightray died. He was struck by a freak shower of meteors and perished in front of a shocked Jimmy Olsen—a prosaic end for a New God.

THE LIGHTBRINGER
When Lightray journeyed to Earth and tried to raise a human woman from the dead, he discovered that power sometimes comes at a terrible cost.

LIGHTNING LAD

DATA

DEBUT *Adventure Comics* (Vol. 1) #247 **(Apr. 1958)**
CURRENT VERSION *Legion: Secret Origin* #1 **(Dec. 2011)**
REAL NAME Garth Ranzz
BASE Legion of Super-Heroes HQ, 31st century Metropolis
HEIGHT 5ft 10ins **WEIGHT** 145 lbs
EYES Blue **HAIR** Red
POWERS/ABILITIES Generation and manipulation of electricity.
ALLIES Superman, Imra Ardeen, Rokk Krinn,
ENEMIES Time Trapper, Legion of Super-Villains, Fatal Five, Dark Circle
AFFILIATIONS Legion of Super-Heroes

LEADERSHIP POTENTIAL
Despite his youth and impetuous nature, Lightning Lad feels an intense responsibility for the young Legionnaires under his direct command.

POWER TRIO
The Legion of Super-Heroes came into being when Lightning Lad, Cosmic Boy, and Saturn Girl teamed up to save businessman R.J. Brande from an assassination attempt.

Lightning Lad is a founder member of the Legion of Super-Heroes. Tempestuous and headstrong, he frequently lashes out before he thinks, but with the vast electrical power he wields, usually carries the day. He shares his abilities with his twin sister, Lightning Lass—who has also served as a Legionnaire—and their older brother Mekt, who, as Lightning Lord, is an original member of the Legion of Super-Villains.

When twin Winathians Garth and Ayla Ranzz crash-landed on the storm-wracked planet Korbal with their older brother Mekt, they tried to utilize the indigenous Lightning Monsters' bioelectricity to recharge their ship's depleted batteries. Instead, the beasts turned their fearsome voltage on the teenagers, permanently energizing their bodies. Realizing that they could now generate megawatts of power and project electrical blasts, the three youngsters used their new gifts to fix their ship and escape.

Though twins are the norm on Winath, Mekt was a singular child who grew up emotionally disturbed. He vanished after the Korbal incident, and Garth began searching the galaxy for him. The quest led to an Earth-bound ship, where he met Braalian Rokk Krinn and Titanian Imra Ardeen (the future Cosmic Boy and Saturn Girl). When Imra's telepathy uncovered a murder plot, the group managed to foil the attempt. The grateful near victim, billionaire R.J. Brande, offered to set them up in their own official peacekeeping team. Strongly attracted to Imra and keenly aware that Brande's resources could help him find Mekt, adventure-loving Garth agreed, and the Legion of Super-Heroes was born.

Rash and reckless, Garth was a shining example of unflagging heroism, enduring injury and even death in the line of duty. After years of service, he eventually married Imra, and they retired to raise their children, though they always answered the call whenever their friends needed their help. **WW**

ON THE RECORD

Lightning Lad is either the unluckiest hero in the universe, or the most fortunate. He gained superpowers from an animal attack that should have killed him, died in battle, and was resurrected. He lost an arm to a monstrous space creature and grew it back—thanks to the scientific genius of Dr. Zan Orbal, who worked for the super-villain Prince Evillo—and after a life of amazing adventure, married his sweetheart and settled down.

Then the Time Trapper tried to alter the events that created the Legion. He kidnapped Garth's baby to control the hero, but was unprepared for Garth's mature response, when the distraught dad called in Rokk and Imra to help get the child back.

SHOCK TACTICS
Always considered impetuous and hot-tempered, Lightning Lad surprised friends and foes alike when his son was abducted by the Time Trapper.

FATAL CONFLICT
When the Fatal Five declared war on the Legion, Lightning Lad faced the mighty Persuader in a climactic battle on Earth.

CLASSIC STORIES

***Adventure Comics* (Vol. 1) #305 (Jan. 1963)** Garth is the first Legionnaire to die in action, saving Saturn Girl from space marauder Zaryan the Conqueror.

***Adventure Comics* (Vol. 1) #332 (May 1965)** When Garth loses an arm battling the Super-Moby Dick of Space, the shock deranges him. His obsessive hunt for the beast almost costs him his sanity and place in the Legion.

***Legion of Super-Heroes* (Vol. 2) #302 (Aug. 1983)** Garth cataclysmically and definitively clashes with his brother Mekt for the love and allegiance of their sister Ayla following her resignation from the Legion.

LIVEWIRE

DEBUT *Superman Adventures* #5 (Mar. 1997)
CURRENT VERSION *Justice League* (Vol. 2) #30 (Jul. 2014)
REAL NAME Leslie Willis
BASE Stryker's Island penitentiary
EYES Blue **HAIR** Pale blue
POWERS/ABILITIES Electricity absorption and projection; flight using electromagnetic fields.
ALLIES Killer Frost, Atomic Skull, Killer Croc, Shockwave
ENEMIES Batman (James Gordon), Superman
AFFILIATIONS Secret Society of Villains

Leslie Willis was a notorious vlogger famous for pulling off outrageous stunts. She was transformed into a being of pure electricity when a high-voltage prank went wrong. Leslie joined the Secret Society of Super-Villains and clashed with Superman in Metropolis. She was then caught in an energy trap by Batman and imprisoned in Stryker's Island penitentiary.

The Hooq Cult set Livewire free and she went on a rampage, using the Burnside electricity plant to charge up her powers. Defeated by Batgirl and new Batman James Gordon, she was imprisoned once again. This time, Livewire was freed by mysterious beings with energy powers. She joined forces with other villains in Metropolis, but they were defeated by Superman. **SW**

LOOKER

DEBUT *Batman and the Outsiders* (Vol. 1) #25 (Sep. 1985) (as Emily); *Batman and the Outsiders* (Vol. 1) #31 (Mar. 1986) (as Looker)
CURRENT VERSION *Batman, Inc.* (Vol. 2) #1 (Jul. 2012)
REAL NAME Emily 'Lia' Briggs
BASE Gotham City
HEIGHT 5ft 10in **WEIGHT** 115 lbs
EYES Blue **HAIR** Red
POWERS/ABILITIES Telepathy; telekinesis; levitation; mind control; vampiric powers.
ENEMIES Leviathan

Meek librarian Emily Briggs was kidnapped by inhabitants of the underground realm of Abyssia and exposed to light from Halley's Comet. She received incredible psionic superpowers and striking looks. Emily was rescued by Batman and the Outsiders, and began working as a supermodel. Emily (or 'Lia', as she preferred to be known) later joined the Outsiders under the codename Looker, and became a vampire after being bitten by a bloodsucker in the East European nation of Markovia.

The Outsiders were seemingly killed when Talia al Ghūl blew up a satellite with them onboard, but they later resurfaced in Gotham City and secretly helped Batman fight Talia's Leviathan conspiracy. They managed to locate one of Leviathan's secret bases, but it was booby-trapped and exploded. Looker used her force-field-generating power to save her comrades' lives, but they were all badly injured by the explosion. **SW**

KILLER LOOKS
Lia Briggs' newfound powers and appearance caused some rivalry among the Outsiders, but that didn't stop the psychic vampire trying to save their lives.

LORD HAVOK

DEBUT *Justice League Quarterly* #3 (Summer 1991)
CURRENT VERSION *The Multiversity* #1 (Oct. 2014)
BASE Earth-8
REAL NAME Damon (last name unknown)
EYES Brown **HAIR** Unknown
POWERS/ABILITIES Wields the Lightning-Axe of Wundajin and the Omni-Gauntlets.
ENEMIES the Retaliators, the Future Family, the G-Men

An inhabitant of Earth-8, the man who used to be known simply as Damon was transformed by an experiment performed by Frank Future—the flexible-limbed genius of the Future Family Super Hero team. Traumatized and physically scarred by this event, Damon hid his face behind a forbidding skull mask and turned himself into the super-villain Lord Havok.

He stole three magical artifacts—the Omni-Gauntlets, the Lightning-Axe of Wundajin, and finally the Genesis Egg, which he believed would allow him to tap into the Power Eternal. When he tried to hatch the egg, however, he was confronted by Frank Future, the Retaliators super-team, and a group of multi-dimensional heroes. Frank begged him not to allow the egg to hatch, but Havok refused and demanded that Future kneel before him. When the egg hatched, Havok was driven insane by a vision of the entities within it, and was killed by one of the Retaliators. **SW**

LOCK-UP

DEBUT *Robin* (Vol. 4) #24 (Jan. 1996)
CURRENT VERSION *Batman Eternal* (Vol. 1) #3 (Jun. 2014)
REAL NAME Lyle Bolton
EYES Blue **HAIR** Blond
POWERS/ABILITIES Escapologist; expert hand-to-hand combatant; wields a cattle prod and steel chain.
ENEMIES Batman, Robin, Nightwing
AFFILIATIONS Secret Society of Super-Villains, Cluemaster's unnamed gang

Lyle Bolton was obsessed with becoming a law enforcer, but was expelled from the Police Academy and then kicked out of various security jobs for his brutality. Adopting the codename "Lock-Up," Bolton began capturing felons as a vigilante and taking out any police who got in his way. Lock-Up's captives, including Two-Face and Killer Moth, were incarcerated in his private prison and subjected to savage treatment. When his facility was discovered, Lock-Up tried to drown his inmates, but was stopped by Batman, Robin, and Nightwing.

When Gotham City descended into anarchy, Lock-Up took over Blackgate Penitentiary on Batman's instruction. Later, he was one of the criminals sent into exile on the planet Salvation. After his return, he joined a super-villain group led by Cluemaster. **SW**

LORD CHAOS

DEBUT *The New Titans Annual* (Vol. 1) #7 (1991)
REAL NAME Robert Long
BASE An alternate-future Earth
HEIGHT 6ft 2in **WEIGHT** 196 lbs
EYES Black **HAIR** Gold
POWERS/ABILITIES Possesses powers of Titan gods including super-strength, light-blasts, and flight; ability to command the earth and sea.
ENEMIES Team Titans, Teen Titans, Titans of Myth

In an alternate future, Troia (Donna Troy) and her husband Terry Long had a son named Robert, who had inherited Troia's godlike powers. Possessing such power from birth drove Robert mad; he killed his mother and conquered the world as Lord Chaos.

A group of superpowered rebels calling themselves the Team Titans traveled to the past to kill Donna and prevent Lord Chaos from being born. However, learning of their plan, Lord Chaos traveled back in time to stop the Team Titans, and summoned his soldiers from the future to conquer the world.

Donna Troy battled her son and called on the Titans of Myth to remove the godlike powers from them both. The Titans of Myth agreed, taking the insane entity to their realm, but leaving the infant Robert Long in his mother's arms.

Robert was later killed in a car accident. However, Lord Chaos returned in undead form to attack Donna during the events of Blackest Night. **SW**

POWER AND GLORY
Possessing the might of the Titanic gods from birth proved too much for young Robert Long—and he was quickly driven to madness.

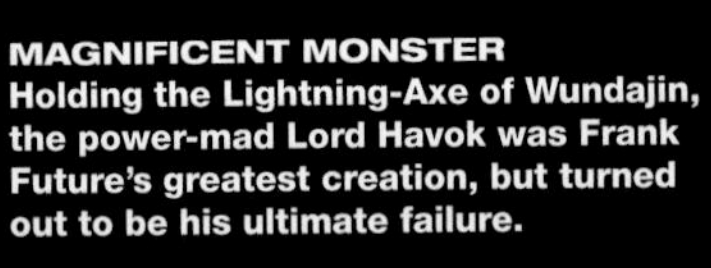

MAGNIFICENT MONSTER
Holding the Lightning-Axe of Wundajin, the power-mad Lord Havok was Frank Future's greatest creation, but turned out to be his ultimate failure.

LOBO

DATA

DEBUT *Omega Men* (Vol. 1) #3 **(Jun. 1983)**
CURRENT VERSION *Justice League* (Vol. 2) #23.2 **(Nov. 2013)**
HEIGHT 5ft 11in **WEIGHT** 227 lbs
EYES Red **HAIR** Black with glowing-blue highlights
POWERS/ABILITIES Regenerative healing; can withstand exposure to space vacuum; super-strength, stamina and enhanced durability, super-senses; genius-level intellect; large arsenal of advanced weapons; custom-built spacecraft and heavily armored monowheel for ground transportation.
ALLIES Superman, Sinestro, Emily, Luna, Rave
ENEMIES Supergirl, unnamed Lobo pretender, unnamed Xrexian assassin
AFFILIATIONS Czarnian royal bodyguard (formerly)

THE MAIN MAN
Lobo decapitated the thug who had claimed his name—a being who bore a striking resemblance to the pre-Flashpoint Lobo.

Lobo is the last survivor of the alien Czarnian race, a hired killer whose combination of ruthlessness, razor-sharp intelligence, and superlative combat skills make him the most feared assassin in the universe. However, despite his callous nature, this stone-cold killer is haunted by his role in the destruction of his home planet.

The being who would become Lobo was an officer of the Emperor of Czarnia and the lover of the emperor's daughter. The life-forces of the emperor and the planet Czarnia itself were linked, but the emperor had gone mad, causing tectonic upheavals across the planet. When the officer confronted the emperor about his insanity, the princess intervened and he accidentally stabbed her. Overwhelmed by grief, the officer killed the emperor—leading to Czarnia itself imploding.

The officer was the only one to escape, and realized that he had become the being told of in prophecy: Lobo, the destroyer of Czarnia.

Lobo then embarked on a career as an intergalactic hitman, and his fierce professionalism and commitment to carrying out his contracts at any cost earned him a reputation as the deadliest assassin in the universe. However, he remained anguished by the past and even cauterized his brainstem to stop the recurring nightmares he had of the death of Czarnia.

When Lobo heard that another killer was using his name, he tracked down and dispatched the impostor in brutal fashion, making it clear that he was the real Lobo. The Czarnian was then hired to kill eight assassins who were being paid to destroy Earth. While on this special mission, he clashed with an assassin from Czarnia's sister planet of Xrexia, who claimed that she caused the emperor's madness. Lobo killed her and went after her employer. **SW**

ON THE RECORD

The pre-Flashpoint Lobo was simply born to be bad. When he was a teenager, he created a plague of bugs that killed all five billion inhabitants on his homeworld of Czarnia—because he hated them all and wanted to be unique. (The only other Czarnian to survive was his fourth-grade teacher, Miss Tribb.)

Lobo set off on his SpazFrag666 spacehog to prove that he was the meanest "bastich" in the universe. While working as a bounty hunter, he tangled with the Omega Men, the Teen Titans, and the legions of Hell itself. He did have a softer side, which was later revealed.

BAD TO THE BONE?
Unlike his deadly-serious successor, the original Lobo was just a violent party animal (with a soft spot for Space Dolphins).

UP CLOSE AND PERSONAL
Lobo has mastered a vast arsenal of weapons, including the latest in hi-tech killing devices. However, he prefers to eliminate his opponents the old-fashioned way: with razor-sharp blades.

LANTERN HUNT
After testing the hitman's abilities, Sinestro of the Yellow Lantern Corps hired Lobo to take the rings of the other Lantern Corps.

CLASSIC STORIES

***Lobo Paramilitary Christmas Special* #1 (Dec. 1991)** The Easter Bunny hires Lobo to kill Santa Claus himself–but jolly old Saint Nick is not going down without a fight.

***Lobo's Back* #1-4 (May-Nov. 1992)** Lobo is killed by two of his rivals, but after wreaking havoc in Heaven and Hell he comes back from the dead to enact his revenge.

***Lobo Annual* (Vol. 3) #1 (Sep. 2015)** Lobo accepts perhaps the most dangerous assignment of his entire career: to kill Sinestro, leader of the infamous and deadly Yellow Lantern Corps!

LORD OF TIME

DEBUT *Justice League of America* (Vol. 1) #10 (Mar. 1962)
BASE Palace of Eternity; Timepoint
HEIGHT 5ft 9in **WEIGHT** 159 lbs
EYES Blue **HAIR** Black
POWERS/ABILITIES Technology-assisted time travel and weaponry.

An immensely powerful individual from the year 3786, the Lord of Time attacked the 20th century Justice League of America using his miraculous chrono-cube to peel back the fourth-dimensional veil of time. After his initial defeat by the JLA, this sinister fugitive from the future learned to move laterally and diagonally through history, accessing armies and armaments spanning millions of years. He also built an artificial intelligence, the Eternity Brain, which tracked and displaced people in time. His ultimate goal was nothing less than conquering all space and time, and plotted to rid himself of the JLA, by traveling back in time to eliminate their ancestors.

At some point, the Lord of Time created a frozen moment in history called Timepoint, evolving into a being known as Epoch who was determined to master the timestream, changing events to grant him power. **AI/RG**

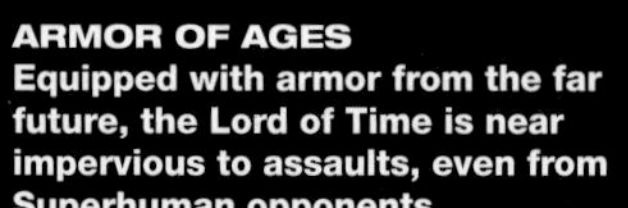

ARMOR OF AGES
Equipped with armor from the far future, the Lord of Time is near impervious to assaults, even from Superhuman opponents.

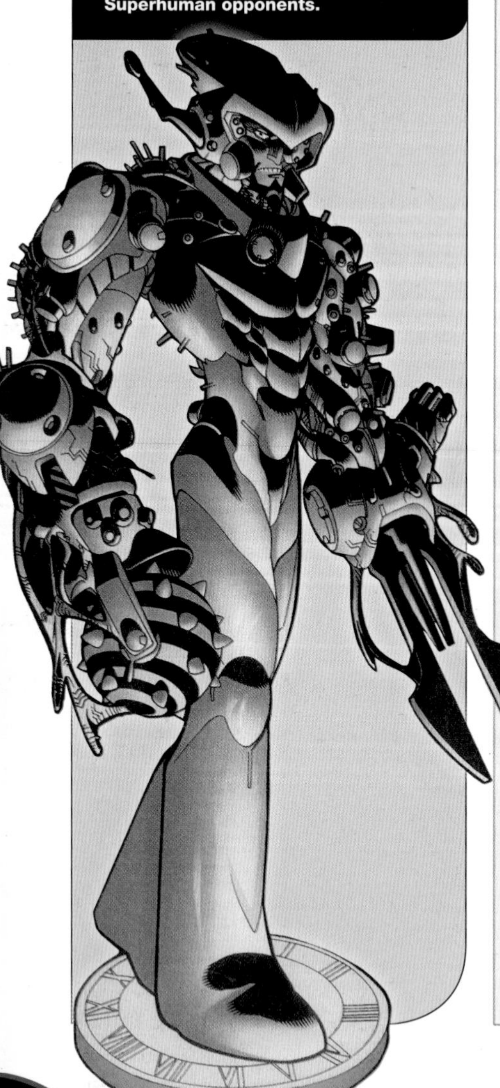

LORD, MAXWELL

DEBUT *Justice League* (Vol. 1) #1 **(May 1987)**
CURRENT VERSION *O.M.A.C.* (Vol. 4) #2 **(Dec. 2011)**
REAL NAME Maxwell Lord IV
BASE Mount Rushmore
HEIGHT 6ft 2in **WEIGHT** 185 lbs **EYES** Brown **HAIR** Brown
POWERS/ABILITIES Telepathic mind control, brilliant strategist.
ALLIES Mokkari, Sarge Steel
ENEMIES Brother Eye
AFFILIATIONS Checkmate, S.H.A.D.E.

OUTSIDE THE LAW
Although Lord's Checkmate organization was the world's premier spy agency, its allegiances remained unclear.

The unquestioned leader of Checkmate, a Task Force X division now referred to as a Global Peace Agency, Maxwell Lord oversaw the group's covert operations from a headquarters bunker within Mount Rushmore. The organization's endeavors were centered around a sophisticated surveillance network that used advanced hologram and hard-light technologies. Lord kept tabs on Checkmate's Cadmus Project—a government project designed to take precautions in case the Justice League ever took the law into their own hands. He also put elite Checkmate agents in the field when the sentient satellite Brother Eye went rogue and created O.M.A.C. (One-Machine Attack Construct) from the scientist Kevin Kho. When successive teams led by Sarge Steel and later Mokkari fail, Lord calls S.H.A.D.E. in to help deal with the threat, and their top operative Frankenstein nearly kills O.M.A.C..

While dispatching his units to hunt down O.M.A.C., Lord himself had to fend off an assassination attempt by a soldier that Brother Eye had subverted. Using his mind-control powers, Lord forced the would-be assassin to turn the gun on himself. He then outsmarted Brother Eye by magnetizing the satellite's hull, which caused a number of passing asteroids to coalesce and trap Brother Eye inside, presumably to burn up on re-entry into Earth's atmosphere. Lord would have continued the pursuit of O.M.A.C., but Brother Eye's last act was to give Kho control over his O.M.A.C. body, and Lord called off the operation, believing the bio-tech warrior was no longer an immediate threat. **AI**

ON THE RECORD

Pre-Flashpoint, Maxwell Lord caused a terrible crisis of conscience for Wonder Woman after he used his mind-control powers to turn Superman into a weapon. This was part of his plot to exterminate the world's metahumans using Brother Eye and O.M.A.C. Faced with the choice between saving millions of lives and keeping her oath never to kill, Wonder Woman killed Lord, and has lived with the consequences ever since.

CHAIN OF DEATH
Blue Beetle attacked Lord when he discovered his plot to wipe out the world's metahumans. Lord ended the fight by shooting Beetle in the head, only to have his own life taken by Wonder Woman, ending his schemes once and for all.

LORING, JEAN

DEBUT *Showcase* #34 (Sep.–Oct. 1961)
HEIGHT 5ft 8in **WEIGHT** 130 lbs
EYES Green **HAIR** Black
POWERS/ABILITIES As Eclipso, Jean possesses vast magical powers, as well as flight and invulnerability.
ENEMIES Spectre, Shadowpact, Elongated Man, Mary Marvel

Jean Loring was once a notable attorney and the wife of Ray Palmer, the Atom. After Ray's demanding double life came between the two of them, they divorced and Loring continued her law career in Ivy Town until suffering a complete mental collapse. She became convinced that she could restore her marriage to Ray by threatening or killing the loved ones of the Justice League of America. To that end, she shrunk herself using one of Ray's old costumes, and murdered Elongated Man's wife, Sue Dibny, by giving her a stroke. When her crime was discovered, Loring served a term in Arkham Asylum until she was infected by the sinister spirit of Eclipso and became his human host.

As Eclipso, she seduced the Spectre into killing hundreds of Earth's magic-users to bring about an end to the Ninth Age of Magic. The Shadowpact fought the Spectre and banished Loring into orbit around the Sun, but she returned, still bearing Eclipso's powers, and tried without success to corrupt the spirit of Mary Marvel. **AI**

HEART OF DARKNESS
While confined in Arkham, Loring came across one of the black diamond shards of Eclipso's Heart of Darkness, and was instantly possessed by it.

WORD OF POWER
When Alexander Luthor shouted the word "Mazahs!" he unleashed the power of the dark lightning. In moments, he killed both Johnny Quick and Bizarro.

LUTHOR, ALEXANDER

DEBUT *DC Comics Present Annual* #1 (1982)
CURRENT VERSION *Justice League* (Vol. 2) #23 (Oct. 2013)
BASE Earth-3
HEIGHT 6ft 3in **WEIGHT** 210 lbs
EYES Blue **HAIR** Red
POWERS/ABILITIES Analogous to those of Shazam; additionally absorbs the powers of anyone he kills.
ALLIES Superwoman
ENEMIES Crime Syndicate, Justice League

Alexander Luthor is the Shazam of Earth-3, known as Mazahs. His version of Shazam's powers included the ability to absorb and retain the powers of any metahuman he killed. A mortal enemy of the Crime Syndicate of America and one of the few Earth-3 heroes to survive opposing them, he was brought to Earth-1 as a prisoner and held in the Justice League's Watchtower.

Released in the chaos of the battle between the combined Justice Leagues and the Crime Syndicate, he used his word of power to join the fray and declared he would kill everyone present, hero and villain alike. His rampage was only stopped when Lex Luthor realized that he had the same voice, and depowered Alexander with his own word of power. Lex then killed Alexander to avenge the fallen Bizarro—and of course save his own life. After his death, it was revealed that the Crime Syndicate's Superwoman was carrying Alexander Luthor's child. **AI**

LOSERS, THE

DEBUT *G.I. Combat* (Vol. 1) #138 (Nov. 1969)
BASE Europe and Asia during World War II
MEMBERS/ABILITIES **Captain Storm:** Indomitable will, a natural leader; **Gunner:** Commando skills, expert marksman; **Johnny Cloud:** One of the greatest fighter pilots of World War II; **Ona Tornsen:** Expert markswoman; **Pooch:** Specially trained military dog; **Sarge:** Commando skills; expert marksman.
ALLIES Haunted Tank, Sergeant Rock, Easy Company
ENEMIES Nazi Germany, Empire of Japan
AFFILIATIONS U.S. Army, Navy, and Air Force

The Losers were Allied servicemen during World War II, each of whom had suffered serious failures during their military careers. The crew of Captain Storm's first command, PT-47, had been massacred by a Japanese submarine; a rookie pilot flying alongside Johnny Cloud had been killed in combat; and a band of raw recruits led by Gunner and Sarge had been wiped out during their first patrol. After Sgt. Jeb Stuart, commander of the Haunted Tank, persuaded the soldiers to help him destroy a Nazi radar tower, the four men stayed together, united by the Military High Command as a special task force.

Briefly recruiting a fifth member, a Norwegian resistance fighter named Ona, the unit fought Axis tyranny across Europe and Asia, never quite shaking their self-imposed status as "Losers."

Tragically, all four men and their canine sidekick, Pooch, died in action during the final days of World War II. Decades later Gunner was resurrected by Project M and recruited for the new Creature Commandos unit. **AI/PJ**

SUICIDE MISSIONS
Despite their seemingly terrible luck, the Losers had a knack of surviving against impossible odds.

THE LOSERS
1 Gunner
2 Johnny Cloud
3 Captain Storm
4 Ona
5 Sarge
6 Pooch

LUTHOR, LEX

DATA

DEBUT *Action Comics* (Vol. 1) #23 **(Apr. 1940)** (as red-headed, thin mad scientist); *Superman* (Vol. 1) #10 **(May–Jun. 1941)** (as bald, heavyset mad scientist)
CURRENT VERSION *Action Comics* (Vol. 2) #1 **(Nov. 2011)**
REAL NAME Alexander Joseph "Lex" Luthor
BASE Metropolis
HEIGHT 6ft 2in **WEIGHT** 210 lbs
EYES Green **HAIR** None
POWERS/ABILITIES Genius-level intellect and a technologically advanced warsuit.
ALLIES Captain Cold, Brainiac, Bizarro
ENEMIES Superman, Batman, Sinestro, Black Hand
AFFILIATIONS LexCorp, Justice League, Injustice League

Alexander Luthor is a very complex man. He is an intellectual genius, a flamboyant scientist, and a billionaire entrepreneur. However, he is also an utterly amoral, sociopathic super-villain, as well as an adulation-hungry would-be hero. Lex's innate intellectual brilliance in a wide number of scientific disciplines is coupled with an obsessive need to be the undisputed best at whatever endeavor he attempts. Moreover, despite his vast organization of go-betweens and employees, Lex will get his own hands dirty when required. Unhindered by any scruple or ethical compass, Lex gets what Lex wants, and woe betide anybody who gets in his way.

AT A GLANCE...

Absolute self belief
Luthor believed no human was his equal and—after capturing Superman—set out to prove no alien was either. Lex had supreme confidence in his own intellect and scientific knowledge and was prepared to use any means necessary to get what he wanted.

Business matters
Global conglomerate LexCorp is built upon Luthor's inventions and provides employment for most of Metropolis. As a generous, philanthropic owner, Lex basks in the adoration of the masses while his cutting-edge research facilities secretly develop the weapons he needs to combat Superman. LexCorp gives him two powers his enemy lacks: unlimited funds and the trust of international governments.

War footing
Though his most powerful weapon is his own intellect, Luthor has spent billions creating an armored outfit that will make him the superior of any alien or metahuman.

Luthor came to Metropolis from Kansas, where he had left his sickly sister, Lena. She suffered from a mystery illness that Lex—as a scientist—might have cured, but since he was uncertain of the outcome, he chose not to try in case he was seen to fail.

Lex was a military scientific advisor to Lois Lane's father, General Sam Lane, when Superman first appeared; however, Lex was already making plans for his own future. He was covertly feeding information to journalist Clark Kent about the publicly lauded business king—and secret crime overlord—Glen Glenmorgan, whose crown he was intent on claiming. He also established a trade agreement with an alien entity, the Brain InterActive Construct known as Brainiac, or the Collector of Worlds, who gave Lex advanced scientific knowledge in exchange for strategic data about Earth.

This double-dealing caused Luthor's fall from grace and wrecked his reputation, once the Collector of Worlds miniaturized and bottled the city of Metropolis. Though Superman saved the city, journalist Lois Lane exposed to the world the duplicity of her father's science advisor. Consequently, Luthor's contract was terminated by Sam Lane. But before being kicked off base, Lex stole samples of Superman's blood and fragments of the radioactive xenomineral that had powered the Kryptonian's rocket ship.

The science genius thrived in the private sector, becoming a hugely successful businessman and industrial technologist. His lab work was not restricted to commerce, however. From Superman's blood, Lex created prototype cloned servants, such as Bizarro. Meanwhile, the green mineral was used against Metropolis' favorite hero after Lex created Project K-Man, transforming wife-beater Clay Ramsay into an anti-Superman weapon.

Luthor has made contingency planning into an art form. He deduced Batman's secret identity and later used that knowledge to blackmail his way into Earth's team of Super Heroes, the Justice League. He designed an inescapable Hypermax Prison in Utah and then became its only inmate. Before his lawyers eventually freed him, Lex was often visited by Superman, who would pick his brains in times of crisis, such as when the rogue Kryptonian named H'El attempted to restore his extinct planet by sacrificing Earth.

ETERNAL ENEMIES
As soon as Superman dared to manhandle him, Luthor knew he could never rest until the alien was humbled and destroyed.

CLASSIC STORIES

***Superman* (Vol. 1) #38 (Jan.-Feb. 1946)** Luthor uses an atomic bomb on Superman. Scheduled to appear in 1944, the story was embargoed by the Defense Department until World War II ended.

***The Joker* (Vol. 1) #7 (May-Jun. 1976)** Luthor switches personalities with the Joker, and a coldly rational Clown Prince of Crime hunts a literally mad scientist who would rather die than surrender the freedom of insanity.

***Action Comics* (Vol. 1) #660 (Dec. 1990)** Fatally irradiated by Kryptonite, Luthor fakes his own death. His brain is transplanted into a healthy young clone with red hair and paperwork to prove he is Luthor's son.

FOREVER EVIL
When the Crime Syndicate from Earth-3 invaded Earth, they recruited a host of super-villains to act as their vanguard and overwhelmed the world's heroic defenders. Lex Luthor refused to be subservient to another's will and organized like-minded metahuman criminals in an Injustice League. His nefarious team defeated the extra-dimensional conquerors, liberated Earth's captive heroes, and thus saved humanity. In the aftermath, this most improbable hero even connived his way into the ranks of the Justice League.

CORPORATE RAIDER
Lex Luthor was never going to be a team player, unless he was in complete control of the team and giving the orders.

SUPERMAN UNCHAINED
With Superman distracted by battling the anti-technology atrocities of the terrorist group known as Ascension, and enduring increased attacks from a super-powered extraterrestrial named Wraith, Lex Luthor broke out of the Metropolis Armory Ward High Security prison.

After capturing and torturing Jimmy Olsen as part of his scheme to kill Superman, Luthor planned to save Earth from an alien invasion and become the world's most popular hero. Luthor knew the U.S. military had been covertly deploying Wraith since World War II. However, he never expected the alien to sacrifice its own life to stop the invasion and save both Superman and Earth.

EXO-SKELETON EXIT
With just the meager materials at hand in his cell, Lex built an armored and automated jail escape outfit.

"It's time to stop being selfish. The world needs Lex Luthor."

Lex Luthor

Luthor always smugly complied with prison rules, but hid the fact that he could easily free himself and was controlling his own affairs from his prison cell. He passed much of his time devising ways to break into Superman's Fortress of Solitude.

The only time Lex ever displayed regret, remorse, or fellow feeling was when his super-clone, Bizarro, died saving him. He has never lost his xenophobic conviction that aliens and metahumans will destroy civilization, or subjugate humanity, and genuinely believes everything he does is for the good of mankind. His only weakness appears to be an abiding need for the adulation of the masses he despises and his desire to see Superman destroyed. **WW**

REBIRTH

METROPOLIS MARVEL
After years of struggling against Superman, Luthor realized that he should simply become the hero he despised. With the Man of Steel dead, mimicking the power-set was easy. The real test was not slipping too far into the role of altruistic, self-sacrificing do-gooder.

However, Lex did not anticipate another Kryptonian claiming the title, nor Doomsday returning to attack them both.

ON THE RECORD

When he debuted, Luthor was the quintessential mad scientist. He was first depicted as a red-headed savant, but, following confusion among the artists drawing Superman's stories at the time, he was accidentally switched with his own bald, burly henchman. The change stuck, and so the iconic, bald-headed evildoer has remained.

War of the worlds
After years of robbing banks and bedeviling the Man of Tomorrow with super-science gadgets—and barely a shred of success—Luthor was drastically overhauled in the early 1980s. After another humiliating and inconclusive clash, Luthor retired to the planet Lexor where he had long been considered a global hero and settled down with his wife Ardora. Sadly, due to a tragic misunderstanding, she and her entire world were obliterated. Blaming Superman, Lex rededicated his life to destroying his archenemy.

RING OF DEATH
Luthor believed his stolen Kryptonite ring protected him from attack by Superman, unaware that its alien radioactivity was slowly killing him.

Captain of industry
Following the events of the Infinite Crisis storyline, Luthor began a supposedly philanthropic campaign to give ordinary people superpowers. His attention-seeking Everyman Project started well, with the first recipients becoming the latest incarnation of Infinity Incorporated, but the intention was actually to give the billionaire unbeatable metahuman abilities and ended up costing the lives of most of his test subjects.

President Lex
The maligned magnate achieved his greatest triumph when his money, technology, and publicity machine gained him the presidency of the United States. He even won acclaim for spearheading Earth's defense against a colossal alien incursion by the cosmic force of destruction, Imperiex. His vindictiveness and chicanery eventually proved his downfall, and Luther was exposed for conspiring with the enemy Darkseid during Our World at War, and removed by Batman and Superman.

HAIL TO THE CHIEF
Though he knew Luthor could not have won the election fairly, Superman had no proof and had to wait for his gloating enemy to make a mistake.

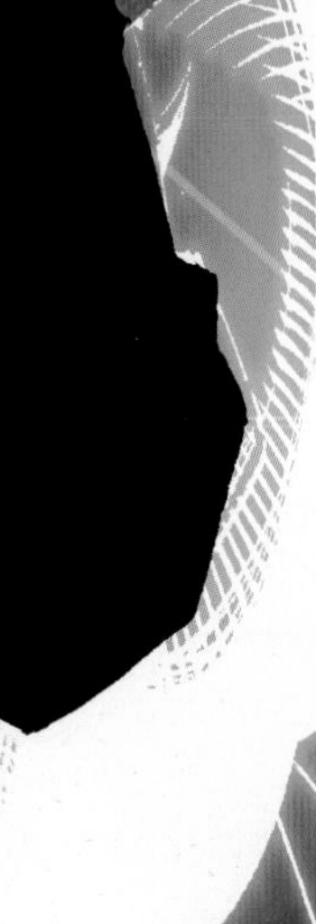

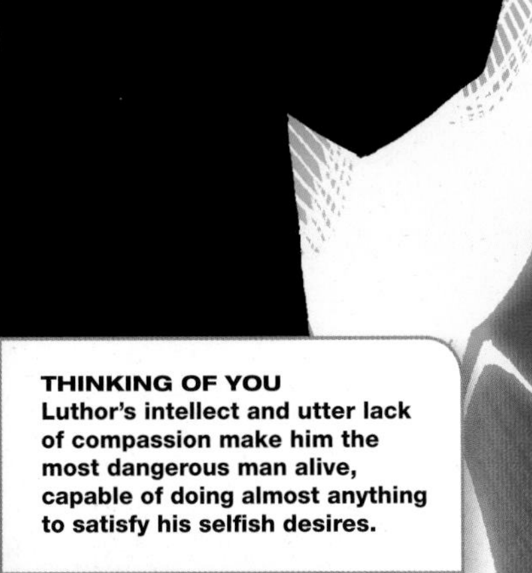

THINKING OF YOU
Luthor's intellect and utter lack of compassion make him the most dangerous man alive, capable of doing almost anything to satisfy his selfish desires.

MAD HARRIET

DEBUT *Mr. Miracle* (Vol.1) #6 **(Feb. 1972)**
CURRENT VERSION *Justice League* #50 **(Jul. 2016)**
BASE Apokolips
HEIGHT 5ft 10in **WEIGHT** 146 lbs
EYES Black **HAIR** Green
POWERS/ABILITIES Fierce and ruthless warrior, trained by Granny Goodness; weapons include energy claws; superhuman agility, strength, durability, and endurance; extremely unpredictable.
ALLIES Granny Goodness, Lashina, Stompa, Bernadeth
ENEMIES Big Barda, Mr. Miracle
AFFILIATIONS Female Furies

The planet Apokolips has given rise to some of the most lethal and frightening villains in the universe. But perhaps the most insane is Mad Harriet, a member of Darkseid's infamous Female Furies. The twisted result of a life raised in Granny Goodness' corrupt orphanage, Mad Harriet revels in torture and pain. Taking orders from Bernadeth, the sister of Darkseid's premier lackey and torturer, Desaad, Mad Harriet has a reputation of being a so-called "psychopathic harpy," quick to use the slashing power spikes on her armed gauntlets.

Mad Harriet's first commander was Big Barda, who led the Female Furies. However, when Barda defected, fleeing Apokolips for a life with her true love, Mr. Miracle, the Female Furies pursued her to Earth. Barda briefly convinced them to abandon Darkseid and work with her and Mr. Miracle, but their true loyalties soon reemerged, and the team resumed their roles as Darkseid's killer elite. Mad Harriet was most recently seen joining forces with Big Barda and the Furies to fight Darkseid's daughter, Grail, who had enslaved a newly resurrected Darkseid. **MM**

ON THE RECORD

One of Mad Harriet's fiercest battles was with the Suicide Squad over the fate of Glorious Godfrey. During the fight, she was nearly killed when her energy claws backfired as she slashed at Bronze Tiger. She was far less fortunate in Countdown to Final Crisis, when she was accidentally incinerated by Apokolips' Dog Soldiers during a confrontation with Mary Marvel, Harley Quinn, and Catwoman.

MAD, BAD, AND FUN TO KNOW Harriet and Harley turned a slug-fest into a hug-fest when they realized how much they have in common, especially their dubious sanity.

THE MAD HATTER

DEBUT *Batman* (Vol. 1) #49 **(Oct./Nov. 1948)**
CURRENT VERSION *Batman: The Dark Knight* (Vol. 2) #8 **(Jun. 2012)**
REAL NAME Jervis Tetch
BASE Gotham City
HEIGHT 4ft 8in **WEIGHT** 149 lbs **EYES** Blue **HAIR** Red
POWERS/ABILITIES Extremely intelligent inventor and technician; uses drugged tea to enhance his own physical abilities; technological innovations let him control the minds of others.
ALLIES Tweedledee, Tweedledum
ENEMIES Batman, Red Robin, Bluebird, Black Mask, Anarky
AFFILIATIONS Secret Society

Jervis Tetch lived a tortured life, mostly due to his appearance. As a young boy, he became obsessed with Lewis Carroll's *Alice in Wonderland* stories. This, combined with his father's haberdashery shop, would influence the later super-villain identity he would adopt for himself.

As a boy, Jervis fell in love with a girl named Alice. While he was often undermined and bullied by his classmates, Jervis worked up the nerve to ask Alice on a date, and she accepted, accompanying him to a theme park called Wonderland. That day was the best day of his life, and Tetch became obsessed with it, even though Alice rejected him at a dance soon afterward. Highly sensitive about his short stature, Jervis began experimental testosterone therapy that altered his mind and slowly drove him insane.

Years later, Jervis adopted the identity of the Mad Hatter and began hunting for his "Alice" over and over again, even killing the real Alice when he discovered that she was no longer the radiant beauty he remembered from his "perfect day." With his inventive genius, the Mad Hatter developed mind-control devices designed to make future "Alices" more receptive to his every command. **MM**

ALICE DOESN'T LIVE HERE ANYMORE One of the many "Alices" the Mad Hatter was obsessed with and eventually killed was the sister of the future villain Anarky, who sought revenge for Tetch's crime.

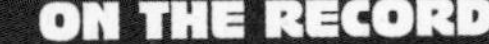

ON THE RECORD

The Mad Hatter first appeared in 1948, in the same issue of *Batman* that featured another new addition to the Dark Knight's supporting cast—love interest Vicki Vale. His appearance was short-lived as Batman foiled his plan and he was locked away in Gotham Pen. While incarcerated, an impostor turned up on the scene in 1956 taking his name and MO, but sporting a handlebar mustache and a sane mind. The two Mad Hatters took turns matching wits with Batman over the years, but the later villain changed his name to Hatman in 2010.

The Hatter later joined the Secret Six, helping them escape from the Doom Patrol, and Ragdoll rewarded him by pushing him off a bridge. He survived and sought revenge, only to find himself once more falling from a bridge to his apparent death after Ragdoll tossed his precious hat over the edge.

A HATTER FOR ALL OCCASIONS Hatman made a reappearance in *Batman* #700 (Aug. 2010), attempting (and failing) to brainwash Robin, Batman, and Batgirl—and establishing his own credentials as a top-hatted trickster.

MADAME ROUGE

DEBUT *Doom Patrol* (Vol. 1) #86 (Mar. 1964)
CURRENT VERSION (Maddy Rouge) *My Greatest Adventure* (Vol. 2) #1 (Dec. 2011)
REAL NAME Laura DeMille
HEIGHT 5ft 6in **WEIGHT** 118 lbs
EYES Blue **HAIR** Black
POWERS/ABILITIES Stretching her body to incredible lengths; reshaping facial features.
ENEMIES Doom Patrol, Teen Titans

The first female member of the super-villain group the Brotherhood of Evil, Madame Rouge was originally a French film actress named Laura DeMille, who suffered from schizophrenia following a car accident. Mr. Brain and Monsieur Mallah used a ray treatment to suppress her kind side and help her along the road to villainy.

DeMille adopted the name Madame Rouge, and was given powers by the brilliant Brain. Despite being attracted to the Doom Patrol's chief, Dr. Niles Caulder, Madame Rouge fought his team many times, until the Doom Patrol seemingly sacrificed their lives to save a small New England fishing town from the Brotherhood of Evil. Years later, during a conflict with the Teen Titans, Madame Rouge was knocked into machinery that restored her original personality, but ultimately killed her. She later returned briefly in undead form as a member of the Black Lantern Corps. **MM**

MAELSTROM

DEBUT *Superman/Supergirl: Maelstrom* #1 (Jan. 2009)
REAL NAME Maelstrom
BASE Apokolips
HEIGHT 6ft 2in **WEIGHT** 345 lbs
EYES Blue **HAIR** Black
POWERS/ABILITIES Superhuman strength, endurance, and durability; expert combatant; uses buzz-saw-like blade and Apokolips armor.
ENEMIES Superman, Supergirl

On the hellish planet Apokolips, Darkseid lords over millions of lowlies. But one of his laborers, a woman named Maelstrom, loved him and longed to be his next bride. To catch Darkseid's eye, she decided to give him a very special gift: Superman's corpse.

She convinced her accomplice Hadrok to steal a boom-tube device for her, killed him, and then traveled to Earth to locate Superman. She encountered and defeated Supergirl, but lost her fight with Superman, who destroyed her Boom-Tube generator while hurling her back to Apokolips. There she was relegated to the Terrorium arena and later the slave pits by Granny Goodness, but was eventually allowed to resume her war on Superman by Darkseid himself. She failed again in her goal when Supergirl and Superman teamed up to stop her and her new allies, the Female Furies. **MM**

MAGENTA

DEBUT *New Teen Titans* (Vol. 1) #17 (Mar. 1982)
REAL NAME Francis (Frances) Kane
BASE Keystone City
HEIGHT 5ft 7in **WEIGHT** 134 lbs
EYES Blue **HAIR** Purple
POWERS/ABILITIES Able to manipulate magnetic waves to move metal objects.
ALLIES Flash (Wally West), Cicada
ENEMIES Flash (Wally West), Dr. Polaris
AFFILIATIONS Teen Titans, Rogues

A longtime friend of Wally West's and a fellow former Blue Valley resident, Francis Kane had formed an early bond with Wally that wasn't easily broken. One day, when the two were attending Blue Valley College, Wally walked Francis home, only to find her mom attempting to speak to her dead brother and father through a séance. Francis seemed to disappear in a vortex of spiraling energy, and reemerged with magnetic superpowers.

Told that she was damned by her mother, Francis' powers went haywire, and it seemed a magnetic demon was possessing her, one the Teen Titans had to fight into submission. In truth, Francis had excessive magnetic waves in her brain, and Dr. Polaris tried to use them to travel back to Earth from the dimension to which Green Lantern had banished him. Later, tricked into becoming a sleeper agent by Dr. Alysia Damalis at S.T.A.R. Labs, Francis developed an alter ego named Magenta, and frequently clashed with the Flash. **MM**

MADAME XANADU

DEBUT *Doorway to Nightmare* #1 (Jan.-Feb. 1978)
CURRENT VERSION *Justice League Dark* #1 (Nov. 2011)
REAL NAME Nimue Inwudu
BASE Mobile
HEIGHT 5ft 9in **WEIGHT** 125 lbs **EYES** Green **HAIR** Black
POWERS/ABILITIES Sorceress well versed in the use of the mystic arts; able to predict the future to a degree, normally using Tarot cards; seemingly immortal and doesn't age.
ALLIES John Constantine, Shade the Changing Man, Zatanna, Etrigan the Demon
ENEMIES Felix Faust, the Blight, Mordru, Dr. Destiny
AFFILIATIONS Demon Knights, Justice League Dark

A LONELY ROAD Madame Xanadu's romances have ranged from Etrigan to Jason Blood. She steered clear of Deadman, however, realizing that she had to walk a lonely path.

In the time of King Arthur, after the fall of Camelot, Jason Blood was cursed with the demon Etrigan, who was bonded to his form as a result of the machinations of the famous sorcerer Merlyn. Alongside his young love, Nimue Inwudu, who changed her name to Madame Xanadu to hide her identity, the two met the Shining Knight, Al Jabr, Exoristos, Vandal Savage, and the Horsewoman, and teamed up to form the Demon Knights, opponents to the malevolent mage Mordru.

Centuries later, Madame Xanadu began to realize that the world was entering a time of great danger. She started assembling a team to deal with the coming threat, including Shade the Changing Man, Deadman, Zatanna, John Constantine, and Mindwarp. But in order to unite those magical beings, who were strangers to each other, she had to escalate the conflict by helping the Enchantress fight her new champions. While the team stopped Enchantress, they also discovered Xanadu's treachery at the same time. Yet, when needed to tackle magical and supernatural threats, they returned to the thick of the action as the Justice League Dark. The team gained new members, and Xanadu continued to work with them. But the group disbanded after several missions together. **MM**

ON THE RECORD

Madame Xanadu was created in the late 1970s for the short-lived *Doorway to Nightmare* series. Three years later, she appeared in a self-titled one-shot comic and did not feature in an ongoing series until 2008, when her origins and her connection to the wizard Merlin, Etrigan the Demon, and King Arthur were fully explored.

Madame Xanadu's cruelest encounter came during the Day of Vengeance, when a deranged Spectre began eradicating magic and removed her tarot-reading powers of foresight, by taking her eyes. Despite helping defeat the Spectre, she remained blind for the rest of her pre-Flashpoint career.

TEAM PLAYER Often joining forces with other magical characters, Madame Xanadu formed the Sentinels of Magic with heroes such as Doctor Fate, Faust and Ragman.

MAGOG

DEBUT *Kingdom Come* #1 (May 1996)
CURRENT VERSION *Superman/Wonder Woman* #13 (Jan. 2015)
REAL NAME David Reid
HEIGHT 6ft 4in **WEIGHT** 336 lbs **EYES** One blue, one white **HAIR** Blond
POWERS/ABILITIES Empowered by the Fusion Stone composed of a transmutational element; superhuman strength, endurance, and durability; trident capable of firing powerful energy blasts.
ALLIES Circe
ENEMIES Superman, Wonder Woman, Atomic Skull, Major Disaster

When Darkseid's Parademon army invaded Earth, a boy named David Reid lost both his parents in the chaos. Although the Justice League rose up and harried Darkseid back to his home planet of Apokolips, Reid held nothing but hatred in his heart for the Super Heroes who had failed to save his family. Years later, he was living on the street when he was paid a visit by the sorceress Circe, who wanted to test a "Fusion Stone" on a willing subject. The stone granted Reid superhuman powers, but, as Circe willed, he forgot his past for a time.

Armed with a powerful energy lance and calling himself Wonderstar, Reid fought the villains Atomic Skull and Major Disaster and defeated them. He then faced Superman and Wonder Woman and, as his memories returned, revealed himself to be Magog. He and Circe did their best to defeat the Man of Steel and Wonder Woman, but failed. Superman showed Magog what it meant to be a true Super Hero; unfortunately, the villain was too set in his ways to heed the Man of Steel's lesson. **MM**

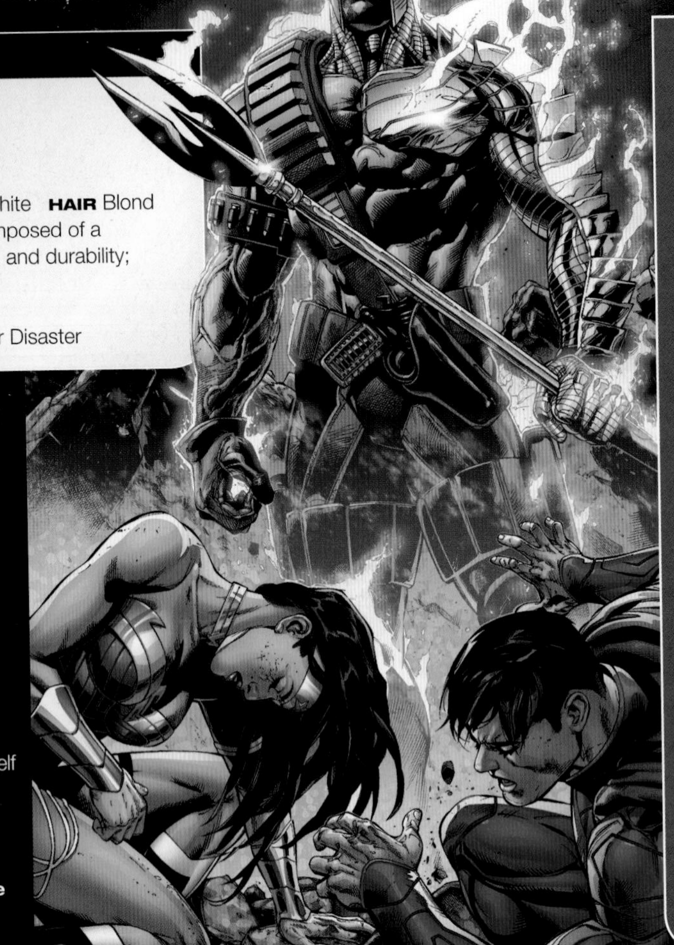

BEATING THE BEST
Obsessed with ridding the world of Super Heroes, Magog proved a very formidable force.

ON THE RECORD

Magog first appeared in the *Kingdom Come* miniseries in 1996. In this Earth-22 reality, Magog was one of the upstarts whose violence inspired genuine Super Heroes, led by Superman, to teach a younger generation what it meant to be a hero. Magog was later introduced in 2008 in *Justice Society of America*. This Magog was a descendant of F.D. Roosevelt named David Reid, a former marine who became a member of the JSA. Later, during the events of Brightest Day, Reid was deceived and forced to kill himself by Maxwell Lord.

GOG-SMACKED
A source of friction inside the JSA, Magog was given his own series in 2009, during which he is depicted being controlled by the Cult of Gog, and sacrificing himself to defeat them.

MAJOR DISASTER

DEBUT *Green Lantern* (Vol. 2) #43 (Mar. 1966)
CURRENT VERSION *Superman/Wonder Woman* (Vol. 2) #13 (Jan. 2015)
REAL NAME Paul Booker
HEIGHT 5ft 11in **WEIGHT** 195 lbs
EYES Blue **HAIR** Black
POWERS/ABILITIES Able to create massive disasters such as earthquakes, hurricanes, and storms by tthe power of thought alone.
ALLIES Atomic Skull
ENEMIES Superman, Wonder Woman, Magog

Major Disaster was a Green Lantern foe who fabricated disasters for his own evil ends. Not quite as successful as he'd hoped, Major Disaster later became a member of the little-respected team Justice League Antarctica. After a major power upgrade from the demon Neron, he joined Justice League America, giving the Super Hero life a real try.

Little is known of Major Disaster's history after the Flashpoint event, however, he has been observed returning to his criminal ways. Teaming up with the Superman villain Atomic Skull, Major Disaster interrupted a date between Superman and Wonder Woman by attacking the Indian Point Nuclear Power Plant for a mysterious client. He created a hurricane, then aimed a hailstorm at Wonder Woman, followed by a ruptured gas line and a lightning attack. He was subsequently bested by the villain Magog in disguise as a hero going by the name of Wonderstar. **MM**

FORCE OF NATURE
Major Disaster was able to call down lightning to attack Superman and Wonder Woman.

MAJOR FORCE

DEBUT *Captain Atom* (Vol. 1) #12 (Feb. 1988)
CURRENT VERSION *Voodoo* (Vol. 2) #2 (Jun. 2013)
HEIGHT 6ft 5in **WEIGHT** 280 lbs
EYES White **HAIR** White
POWERS/ABILITIES Able to project energy; superhuman strength, endurance, and durability.
ALLIES General Eiling
ENEMIES Firestorm, Superman, Hyena, Killer Frost

Major Force is a US government operative answerable to General Eiling. It is believed that he formerly operated as Black Jack for a clandestine group called the Black Razors. Black Jack was allegedly decapitated early in his career, yet he seems to have somehow survived the encounter (or been replaced by an as yet unknown new player). He then reemerged as the government agent Major Force in order to rescue Firestorm.

Major Force later helped Firestorm fight off attacks by the Hyena, Killer Frost, Multiplex, Typhoon, Plastique, and Black Bison, with the intention of getting Firestorm to work for the US government. After these super-villains were defeated, Major Force used a special camera flash to render Firestorm unconscious and take him back to General Eiling's base. Unfortunately for Eiling, Superman was alerted to their underhand scheme and crashed into the secure facility, easily taking down Major Force and freeing Firestorm in the process. **MM**

TOUGH AS NAILS
Major Force is covered in a metallic alloy of sorts that grants him enhanced endurance, much like the Super Hero Captain Atom.

MAMMOTH

DEBUT *The New Teen Titans* (Vol. 1) #3 (Jan. 1981)
CURRENT VERSION *Forever Evil* #1 (Nov. 2013)
REAL NAME Baran Flinders
HEIGHT 6ft 5in **WEIGHT** 300 lbs
EYES Blue **HAIR** Red
POWERS/ABILITIES Superhuman strength, endurance, and durability; prone to fits of rage due to state of emotional underdevelopment.
ALLIES Shimmer, Mr. Whisper
ENEMIES Superman, Wonder Woman

Baran Flinders and his sister Selinda were born in Australia. As children they were bullied at school when their metahuman powers manifested themselves. They were subsequently taken to the renowned Dr. Helga Jace who augmented, and taught them how to control, their natural abilities. They later became criminals and enemies of the Teen Titans and Superman, taking the names Mammoth (Baran) and Shimmer (Selinda).

Post-Flashpoint, Mammoth has only made a few appearances, associating with the Secret Society and fighting alongside his Fearsome Five allies when they attacked Cyborg and the Metal Men. He has also battled Superman and Wonder Woman, and most recently, served as a lackey for the mysterious Mr. Whisper. **MM**

BRUTE FORCE
Mammoth showed very few signs of humanity when he viciously attacked the Titans. It was as if Mr. Whisper's influence was driving the brute insane.

MAN-BAT

DEBUT *Detective Comics* (Vol. 1) #400 (Jun. 1970)
CURRENT VERSION *Detective Comics* (Vol. 2) #19 (Jun. 2013)
REAL NAME Dr. Kirk Langstrom
BASE Gotham City
HEIGHT 6ft 1in **WEIGHT** 201 lbs **EYES** Brown/red **HAIR** Brown
POWERS/ABILITIES Serum grants superhuman strength, endurance, speed, agility, reflexes, and durability; flight; genius-level intellect with a keen interest in the sciences; government connections.
ALLIES The Outlaws, Batman
ENEMIES Batman, the Batman Family, Bat-Queen
AFFILIATIONS S.H.A.D.E., Gotham Academy

Dr. Kirk Langstrom was a dedicated and noble scientist who wanted to use his specialist knowledge to find a cure for the deaf. To that end, he developed the Langstrom Atavistic Gene Recall Serum, only to see his test subjects transformed into hideous, bat-like creatures. Matters went from bad to worse, when a sample of Kirk's serum was stolen, and the serum was released on the 900 block of Gotham City.

With the city plagued by a huge Man-Bat infestation, Langstrom swiftly developed an anti-virus to fight this outbreak and, to avoid any further disasters, tested it on himself. Ultimately, Langstrom's antidote cured those already infected with his original serum, but unfortunately changed Kirk into the sole remaining Man-Bat.

Langstrom subsequently managed to gain control over his transformations into Man-Bat—at least for a time. This enabled him to find work at Gotham Academy, as its resident science teacher, and at the clandestine counter-terrorism organization S.H.A.D.E.

Kirk was not the only member of his family to stalk the night as a bat-like creature. His wife, Francine, also developed a serum of sorts and turned into the terrifying Bat-Queen, while Kirk's father, Abraham, transformed himself into a villainous Man-Bat. **MM**

ON THE RECORD

Dr. Kirk Langstrom was first introduced in *Detective Comics* #400 (Jun. 1970), as a bat expert seeking to harness the sonar-like abilities of bats. His bat-serum transformed him into a giant bat, and later did the same to his girlfriend, Francine Lee (later Langstrom). Later, Man-Bat learned how to control his abilities with a pill, and fought injustice, sometimes alongside private-eye Jason Bard. His heroics were spotlighted in his own 1975 mini-series, in which he took on the Batman villain, Ten-Eyed Man.

BATMAN V. MAN-BAT
Batman had battled many bizarre foes, but even he wasn't prepared for a bestial version of himself: Man-Bat.

MAN OF SCIENCE
Dr. Langstrom had only the best intentions when developing the serum that would become known as the Man-Bat formula.

M

MANHUNTER

DATA

DEBUT *Manhunter* (Vol. 3) #1 **(Oct. 2004)**
CURRENT VERSION *Gotham by Midnight* #6 **(Aug. 2015)**
REAL NAME Kate Spencer
BASE Los Angeles, California; mobile
EYES Blue **HAIR** Black
POWERS/ABILITIES Incisive intellect, dogged determination and peak physical constitution; trained in martial arts; extraterrestrial Darkstar Exo-Mantle affords superhuman strength; clawed gauntlets, power staff.
ALLIES Dylan Battles, Mr. Bones, Cameron Chase, Wonder Woman, Ragman, Blue Beetle
ENEMIES Copperhead, Shadow-Thief, Hugo Strange, the Society, Dumas, Walter Pratt, Sweeney Todd
AFFILIATIONS Department of Extranormal Operations, Suicide Squad, Birds of Prey

HELP AT HAND
Manhunter's crime-crushing crusade relied on her courage, and reformed henchman Dylan Battles' gift for customizing weaponry.

With the US justice system increasingly unable to deal with metahuman criminality or the ruthless tactics of modern human predators, legal advocate Kate Spencer decided to take the law into her own hands. Armed with lethal alien weaponry and wearing armor, Kate adopted a codename taken from the villains and monsters she despised. She now stalks the night as Manhunter, bringing swift and certain retribution to the guilty, and salvation to the oppressed.

NEVER SURRENDER
Whatever the odds, and despite possessing none of the powers other family members were blessed with, Kate Spencer could never accept defeat.

Though initially unaware of the fact, Kate Spencer comes from a long line of heroes and villains. The truth only emerged after she lost faith in her job as a Federal prosecutor. Despite her best legal efforts, the reptilian Copperhead—who had murdered and eaten many victims—evaded the death penalty and killed again. Enraged and frustrated, Kate stole impounded technology from an evidence room and used it to hunt down and execute the cannibal. Deciding to continue her clandestine activities, she sought out underworld armorer Dylan Battles and blackmailed him into maintaining and improving her purloined gadgetry, undertaking a perilous campaign to punish those she judged guilty.

Her actions brought her into conflict with heroes and villains, including Mark Shaw—the previous masked adventurer to employ the title Manhunter—and she eventually learned that she had descended from a line of mighty metahumans. Kate's great-grandfather was legendary World War I super-warrior Hugo Danner, her grandparents were WWII heroes Iron Munro and Phantom Lady, and her own father Walter Pratt was one of the super-villains Kate regularly battled. Even Kate's young son Ramsey appeared to be developing astonishing powers.

Despite lacking metahuman advantages herself, gutsy Kate stopped some of the worst monsters threatening mankind. She eventually became a valuable asset of the Federal Government Department of Extranormal Operations, while also freelancing with the Birds of Prey and the Batman Family. **WW**

SNAKEBITE
Despite her inexperience, Manhunter applied the oldest of all human laws to Copperhead: "a life for a life."

CLASSIC STORIES

***Manhunter* (Vol. 3) #20 (May 2006)** Kate is forced to defend the vile Dr. Psycho in court, but is distracted by her son Ramsey who deduces that she is secretly Manhunter.

***Manhunter* (Vol. 3) #37–38 (Feb.–Mar. 2009)** Offering a tantalizing glimpse of things to come, Manhunter Kate Spencer gives Ramsey a costume of his own so he can continue in the family's masked hero traditions.

***Batman: Battle for the Cowl* (Vol. 1) #1–3 (May–Jul. 2009)** With Batman declared dead, Manhunter relocates to Gotham City and joins the Batman Family during the struggle to appoint the Dark Knight's successor.

ON THE RECORD

In 1942, Dan Richards and Paul Kirk simultaneously, but independently, took the name Manhunter. Kirk was killed in action, but was resurrected decades later by a cabal of scientists. He was their biologically augmented enforcer, but rebelled and died while eliminating them. His clone later led the Secret Society of Super-Villains, but perished battling Darkseid.

As part of their war against the Guardians of Oa, the robotic Manhunters set up the Shan cult on many planets. On Earth they recruited Dan Richards and later Mark Shaw. When Shaw met the Justice League, the Manhunters were exposed as the interstellar monsters they were. Shaw surrendered the name to mystic hunter Chase Lawler before clone Kirk DePaul took it. Both were later murdered by Shaw, who became the serial killer Dumas.

DARK KNIGHT DÉJÀ VU
Batman had worked with the first Manhunter, Paul Kirk, and later met his masked clone, Kirk DePaul.

MANCHESTER BLACK

DEBUT *Action Comics* (Vol. 1) #775 (Mar. 2001)
CURRENT VERSION *Teen Titans* (Vol. 5) #1 (Sep. 2014)
BASE New York City
HEIGHT 6ft **WEIGHT** 210 lbs
EYES Brown **HAIR** Purple
POWERS/ABILITIES Charismatic scientific genius; telekinetic ability; skilled manipulator.
ALLIES Josiah Power, Teen Titans, Algorithm
ENEMIES Algorithm, Teen Titans
AFFILIATIONS S.T.A.R. Labs, the Elite

As chief of S.T.A.R. Labs' Advanced Ideas Division, British scientist Manchester Black prided himself on being one step ahead. His job was keeping the company at the cutting edge, and his scientific brilliance was complemented by his utter amorality and deftness in "managing" people.

To trick the Teen Titans into working with S.T.A.R. Labs and for him, Black orchestrated deadly attacks upon himself and New York City by Algorithm—a killer AI that he had secretly created. Black was unaware Red Robin had become suspicious of his motives and had assigned Beast Boy to shadow the technologist.

However, Black began altering the team members' abilities, conning them into dealing with crises of which he had prior knowledge. His ultimate aims remain undisclosed. **WW**

MANITOU RAVEN

DEBUT *JLA* (Vol. 1) #66 (Jul. 2002)
BASE The Factory, New Jersey; Justice League Watchtower, the moon
HEIGHT 5ft 9ins **WEIGHT** 159 lbs
EYES White **HAIR** Black
POWERS/ABILITIES Magical adept utilizing Native American occultism; time travel.
ALLIES Manitou Dawn, Naif al-Sheikh, Vera Black, J'onn J'onzz, Major Disaster
ENEMIES Gamemnae, Manchester Black
AFFILIATIONS League of Ancients, Justice League of America, Justice League Elite

Manitou Raven was a mystic master of the Obsidian Age people who became the Apache tribe. With his sorceress wife Manitou Dawn, he joined a coalition of super-powered champions, the League of Ancients.

Three thousand years ago, Raven and Dawn were tricked by Gamemnae of Atlantis into attacking the 21st-century Justice League. After realizing they were duped, the Manitous helped defeat Gamemnae, and then moved to the future to join the JL, where their magical abilities made them invaluable.

A hard-liner, Raven joined the black ops Justice League Elite. He died saving the team from a bomb, but this did not end his service. His mantle of power passed to his wife, and his spirit often appears to her, offering her sage advice. **WW**

MANNHEIM, BRUNO

DEBUT *Superman's Pal, Jimmy Olsen* (Vol. 1) #139 (Jul. 1971)
CURRENT VERSION *Superman: Lois & Clark* #3 (Feb. 2016)
BASE Metropolis
EYES Black **HAIR** Black
POWERS/ABILITIES Devious and ruthless; immense physical strength; religious fanaticism.
ENEMIES Superman, Jimmy Olsen, the Guardian, Renée Montoya, Nightwing, Batwoman

Bruno "Ugly" Mannheim came from a long line of thugs and career criminals. Following in the footsteps of his mobster father—known as "Boss Moxie"—Bruno strong-armed his way out of Metropolis' Suicide Slum and climbed the ladder of corruption until he was chief of underworld super-syndicate Intergang.

Under Darkseid, he was "reborn" as a devout believer in the Religion of Crime as espoused in the vile Crime Bible. His savage tendencies magnified by the dark faith, Mannheim began recruiting super-villains, turning Intergang into a legion of monsters. Those who did not convert, he killed and ate.

Physically mutating, he attempted to turn Gotham City into Little Apokolips, but was foiled and killed by Nightwing, Batwoman, and the Question. **WW**

MANTIS

DEBUT *Forever People* (Vol. 1) #2 (Apr.–May 1971)
CURRENT VERSION *Infinity Man and the Forever People* (Vol. 1) #1 (Aug. 2014)
REAL NAME Omar Bashir
BASE Feast of Eden, Sudan
HEIGHT 6ft 4in **WEIGHT** 225 lbs
EYES Orange **HAIR** Bald
POWERS/ABILITIES Superhuman strength and speed; limited flight, energy absorption.
ENEMIES Forever People, Infinity-Man
AFFILIATIONS The Swarm, Darkseid

Mantis is a ruthlessly destructive being, born from a freak combination of human agriculture, New Gods technology, and good intentions. A New Genesis faction had been secretly working with human scientists to try to solve world hunger. They planned to replace Earth's deserts with topsoil from different dimensions and use insects to cross-pollinate the resulting crops. Their efforts went horribly awry when Apokolips intervened, with human project-leader Omar Bashir mutating into Mantis, an insectoid berserker.

Aggressive and driven by a need to defend his swarm's territory, Mantis is the only known sentient member of the new species. Determined to become Earth's dominant life-form, his insectoids breed by mutating their victims into drones. **WW**

MANHUNTERS

DEBUT *1st Issue Special* (Vol. 1) #5 (Aug. 1975)
CURRENT VERSION *Red Lanterns* #1 (Nov. 2011)
BASE Warworld, Orinda, Biot, Oa
POWERS/ABILITIES Virtually indestructible; adept at deception and strategic planning; possess advanced science and weaponry.
ALLIES Sinestro Corps
ENEMIES Guardians of the Universe, Green Lantern Corps, Darkstars, JLA, JSA
AFFILIATIONS Guardians of the Universe, Manhunter agents

The Manhunters were constructed by the Guardians of Oa billions of years ago as their first attempt to police the Universe. When the robots' programming was corrupted by the renegade Oan, Krona, the units developed emotions—especially pride and arrogance—and mutinied. After they eradicated life in Sector 666, most Manhunters were scrapped, but many escaped and went into hiding.

However, their core directive remained: they were designed to stalk prey and enact justice, but now their leader would dictate what that meant. Executing their pledge "No man escapes the Manhunters," they infiltrated countless worlds, planting undercover agents throughout secret societies and Super Hero groups, and offering power and justice to the helpless. Their ultimate aim, though, was vengeance against the Guardians.

On Earth, the Manhunters formed the Shan sect, which, for centuries, did worthwhile work from the shadows. The Shan's last recruit was frustrated public defender Mark Shaw, whose good intentions were subverted to the Prime Manhunter's scheme to forever discredit the Guardians.

The Manhunters' greatest strike came when the Guardians reunited with their Oan females, the Zamarons, to facilitate the next stage in universal evolution. The genders had separated billions of years earlier, unable to agree on how to handle Krona. To crush the Guardians' plans, every Earthly Manhunter asset was activated to counter the heroes safeguarding the "New Guardians" birth. The scale and foresight of the robots' planning and attacks was staggering, but a coalition of champions comprising the Justice League, Suicide Squad, Outsiders, Teen Titans, Infinity, Inc., Legion of Super-Heroes, and more prevailed—but not without great loss.

Regularly discovered and destroyed, the Manhunters seem eternal: perpetually rebuilding in secret before remorselessly striking again. **WW**

LETHAL WEAPONS Not every valiant defender survived the concerted assault of the manhunting mechanical monsters.

MARCH, LINCOLN

DEBUT *Batman* (Vol. 2) #1 (Nov. 2011)
REAL NAME Claims to be Thomas Wayne, Jr.
BASE Gotham City
EYES Blue **HAIR** Black
POWERS/ABILITIES Superhuman powers; Talon Suit affords flight, protection, weaponry.
ALLIES Cluemaster
ENEMIES Batman, Court of Owls
AFFILIATIONS March Venture, Court of Owls, Willowwood Home for Children

Lincoln March had a hidden agenda when he first met Bruce Wayne. He believed himself to be Bruce's long-lost younger brother Thomas Jr., reared in secret as protection from insidious power-brokers the Court of Owls. March felt cheated of his destiny, since the Court found him anyway and trained him as their pawn. He was meant to run Wayne's financial empire for them, but failed in that task and was reinvented as a financier and Gotham City mayoral candidate.

After joining the Court's top tier—and murdering most of them—March donned prototype hi-tech Talon armor to fight Batman. Soundly beaten, he seemingly died but actually retreated into the shadows, attacking Batman's family via proxy villain Cluemaster. This also failed, and the Court of Owls put him in suspended animation. **WW**

MARTIAN MANHUNTER

DATA

DEBUT *Detective Comics* #225 **(Nov. 1955)**
CURRENT VERSION *Stormwatch* (Vol. 3) #1 **(Nov. 2011)**
REAL NAME J'onn J'onzz **BASE** Earth
HEIGHT 6ft 7in **WEIGHT** 300 lbs **EYES** Red **HAIR** None
POWERS/ABILITIES Physical near-invulnerability, regenerative abilities, and superhuman strength; flight; telepathy; telekinesis; shape-shifting; phase-shifting; regeneration; Martian vision can see through solid objects and project various forms of energy; genius-level intellect and strong leadership skills.
ALLIES Superman, Stargirl
ENEMIES Ma'alefa'ak, White Martians
AFFILIATIONS Justice League, Stormwatch, Justice League United, Justice League of America

The Martian Manhunter is—according to Superman—the most powerful being on Earth. But even more than his powers, it is his idealism and resolute pursuit of justice that set him apart. He becomes the moral compass of any group he joins, the memory of his lost family driving him to save others from suffering the grief he continues to feel. With immense powers, including shape-shifting and mind control, J'onn J'onzz can do almost anything—and knows that such power must be guided by a true belief in what's right. Though not human, he is perhaps the most empathetic of heroes, an irony not lost on J'onn himself.

AT A GLANCE...

Many faces
His ability to shape-shift has always been key to Martian Manhunter's success. He usually assumes other human-sized forms—notably taking Catwoman's shape to infiltrate the Secret Society of Super-Villains—but is capable of more incredible transformations as well.

Mars attacks
For many years it was thought that the Martian Manhunter was the last of his kind. However, this was not the case, and the Living Mars of J'onn's distant memories had just been waiting to be reborn. Unfortunately, its rebirth can only come at the cost of Earth becoming as barren and lifeless as Mars.

Pyrophobia
The Martian Manhunter has a strong aversion to fire, long thought to be a physical vulnerability. But it stems from the trauma of seeing so many other Martians die of H'ronmeer's Curse, a telepathic plague that killed victims with psychic fire.

A million years ago, J'onn J'onzz was expelled from Mars by the planet's living spirit, after his brother Ma'alefa'ak remade him into a living weapon that the spirit considered an abomination. His memories obscured, J'onn wandered Earth, taking on different shapes, creating secret identities, and resolving to combat his loneliness by doing what he could to bring justice to this world of people who feared him.

Having found like-minded heroes and even friends in the Justice League, a serious disagreement saw J'onn leave and briefly ally himself with Stormwatch, an ancient secret organization tasked with defending Earth from alien threats. After he negotiated his exit from Stormwatch with the team's overseers, the Shadow Cabinet, he used his telepathic powers to mind-wipe the other members so they had no recollection of his membership. Recruited to the new Justice League of America (JLA) created by A.R.G.U.S.'s Steve Trevor and Amanda Waller, J'onn was trained to be that group's designated counterpoint to Superman, should the original Justice League ever turn against humanity. This goverment-sponsored JLA disbanded shortly thereafter, and J'onn joined with other former members to establish the Justice League United (JLU).

With the Crime Syndicate poised to invade Earth-1, the Secret Society of Super-Villains trapped J'onn and several other heroes within a matrix created by the splitting of Firestorm's dual identity. He broke free by working in tandem with Stargirl, who became an important partner, following J'onn to the Justice League United team when the JLA was disbanded. With the Canada-based JLU, J'onn faced the cosmic threat of Lord Byth Rokk, who had used the DNA of various alien races to create a fast-growing hybrid infant known as Ultra the Multi-Alien. Byth planned to cultivate Ultra into a universe-destroying being called Infinitus. To slow the JLU's response, he created a dimensional rift that unleashed a plague of Infinity Wraiths—and also accelerated the growth of Infinitus. J'onn tried to convince Ultra to resist Byth's plans, but ultimately had to take the drastic action of reaching into its mind and forcibly extracting the portion that would become Infinitus. With the closing of the dimensional rift, this thwarted Byth's plan, but he evaded justice by fleeing into the distant past of Thanagar, his home planet.

BREAKUP
A falling-out with other team members led to Martian Manhunter's exit from the Justice League and his temporary membership in the new A.R.G.U.S.-led Justice League of America... or did it?

DESPERATE MEASURES
With the Crime Syndicate on the rampage, the Martian Manhunter teamed up with Stargirl to fight Despero after she had freed the two them from the Firestorm Matrix. Meanwhile, the clock ticked down toward Firestorm's catastrophic nuclear detonation, which would kill every member of the Justice League still trapped within the Matrix's mind-manipulating prison.

NO DESPAIR
To buy Stargirl time to work out how to defeat Despero and save the JL from Firestorm, the Martian Manhunter allowed Despero to beat him nearly to death.

CLASSIC STORIES

***JLA: Year One* #1-12 (Jan.-Dec. 1998)** This origin story of the Justice League of America demonstrates that the Martian Manhunter was the heart and soul of the team from its inception.

***Martian Manhunter: American Secrets* #1-3 (Aug.-Oct. 1992)** J'onn J'onzz is on his own in this claustrophobic thriller, investigating a vast conspiracy touching on the signature elements of 1950s America: game shows, the birth of rock'n'roll and suburbia, and Cold War paranoia.

***Final Crisis: Requiem* (Jul. 2008)** The JLA and dozens of other heroes gather at J'onn's funeral, reflecting on his life through a cascading series of flashbacks.

CRUMBS AND RAISINS, RAISINS AND CRUMBS
One of the separate embodied fragments of the Martian Manhunter's personality is Mr. Biscuits, his subconscious come to life.

J'onn J'onzz's story took a shocking turn when he discovered that his entire life had been an implanted memory, created by his evil twin brother Ma'alefa'ak to obscure the fact that he was in fact a living weapon sent to Earth by the last surviving Martians. Their goal was to use him to recreate the lost Living Mars, which involved draining Earth of its living essence. As terrorist attacks by other Martian sleeper agents erupted all over the world, J'onn fought Ma'alefa'ak's plan by destroying himself and distributing his consciousness among several other beings—Mr. Biscuits, Pearl, Mould, and Daryl Wessel. Martian agents hunted them, while J'onn's split personalities argued about whether they should preserve Earth or restore Mars. Spurred by Mould's choice of Mars, the different personae came together again at the moment Living Mars was created. Ma'alefa'ak's plan had not entirely worked, however; both Earth and Mars were now alive, but in such close proximity that they could not both survive.

Meanwhile, the rest of the original Justice League members learned their memories of J'onn fighting his way out of the group were also implanted. The reality of the situation remains to be seen. **AI**

RED RISING
Ma'alefa'ak's plan to recreate the Living Mars forced the Martian Manhunter to choose between the planet he had left behind and the world he'd made his home. After Ma'alefa'ak's blood magic destabilized reality and time on both Earth and Mars, disconnected aspects of the Martian Manhunter fought on Mars to save Earth. With Earth and Mars on a collision course and billions of lives hanging in the balance, J'onn J'onzz had to settle the ancient family feud that threatened to engulf both planets. J'onn may have been created as a weapon, but he would decide who that weapon would be used against.

FRATRICIDAL WEAPON
Ma'alefa'ak's ultimate bioweapon, the Martian Man-Eater comprised multiple White Martians, the Red Planet's warrior caste.

ON THE RECORD

The Martian Manhunter's earliest adventures were a classic blend of science fiction and noir. Brought to Earth by Dr. Mark Erdel's teleportation experiment, then stranded by Erdel's death, he chose to use his powers to fight crime as Detective John Johns, until Earth's technology had advanced sufficiently for him to return home.

Ma'aleca'andra
In his first solo series, the Martian Manhunter's origins were revised. He was said to assume a hybrid Martian-Earthling appearance, masking his true form. Dr. Erdel's teleportation experiment was also revealed to have catapulted J'onn not just through space but time, leaving him thousands of years distant from the planet (Ma'aleca'andra, in the Martian tongue) he once knew.

Playing with fire
J'onn J'onzz's vulnerability to fire and his fear of it soon became common knowledge among the JLA's enemies, causing him problems and also endangering the team on a number of occasions. Grappling with his fear, he tried to confront it by making a deal with the fiery villainness Scorch, and as a result he was briefly transformed into Fernus, the Burning Martian, before the other members of the JLA helped him regain control.

Showing his true face
In "The Others Among Us," J'onn discovered a secret project subjecting captive Martians to brutal experiments designed to uncover their powers and control the power of H'ronmeer's Curse. During the course of this story, J'onn became stuck in his true form due to psychic battles against other disguised White and Green Martians.

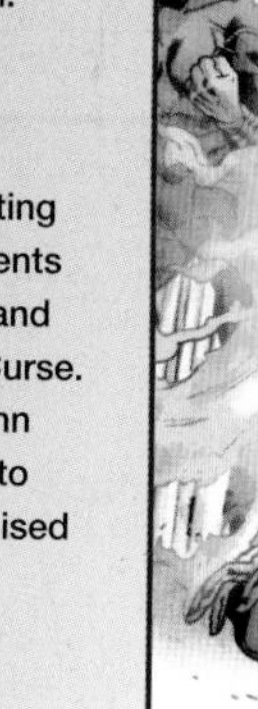

WORST NIGHTMARE
Recalling the lethal fire of H'ronmeer's Curse, the Martian Manhunter died in flames at the start of Final Crisis.

"There isn't much justice in this world. Perhaps that's why it is so satisfying to occasionally make some."

MARTIAN MANHUNTER

NATIVE FORM
Now his identity is more widely known, J'onn no longer feels the need to maintain a human appearance, and assumes his native Martian form by default.

MARONI, SALVATORE

DEBUT *Detective Comics* (Vol. 1) #66 (Aug. 1942)
CURRENT VERSION *Nightwing* (Vol. 2) #25 (Jan. 2014)
BASE Gotham City
HEIGHT 5ft 11in **WEIGHT** 227 lbs
EYES Brown **HAIR** Black
POWERS/ABILITIES Smart mob boss with many connections in the underworld.
ALLIES C.J. Maroni, C.C. Haly
ENEMIES Two-Face, Batman, Batman Family
AFFILIATIONS Maroni Crime Family

Salvatore "Boss" Maroni was one of Gotham City's most notorious gangsters and the sometime rival/sometime ally of the Falcone crime family. Before the reality-changing Flashpoint event, Maroni was responsible for creating the super-villain Two-Face when he hurled a vial of acid at DA Harvey Dent, scarring Dent's face.

In modern continuity, that dubious honor falls to the criminal Erin McKillen, though Maroni is still a mob boss and owner of a movie theater. When a young Dick Grayson was watching a film at Maroni's movie house, Gotham City lost power as part of the event later dubbed Zero Year. Grayson teamed up with Salvatore's son, C.J., and the two managed to escape an encounter with the villain Amygdala, the Grayson family earning Maroni's gratitude in the process. **AI**

MARY, QUEEN OF BLOOD

DEBUT *House of Mystery* #290 (Mar. 1979)
CURRENT VERSION *I, Vampire* #1 (Nov. 2011)
REAL NAME Mary Seward
EYES Red **HAIR** Red
POWERS/ABILITIES Vampiric hypnosis and strength; shape-changing; regeneration and immortality, but vulnerability to sunlight.
ENEMIES Andrew Bennett, Van Helsing

Created by vampire Andrew Bennett, Mary Seward spent centuries as his companion. Their disagreement over how vampires should interact with humans sharpened into open conflict when Mary gathered the Cult of the Blood Red Moon and embarked on a war against the guardians of humanity. Bennett tried to kill her, but was stopped by Batman, before teenage vampire hunter Tig Rafelson killed Bennett.

When John Constantine brought Bennett back to life, Andrew and Mary joined together at the head of all vampires after the death of the primordial vampire Cain. She fought Bennet for control before a climactic battle between vampires and the Van Helsing-led vampire hunters culminated in Bennett absorbing the vampiric powers of every living vampire—and assuming Cain's evil role. Mary was then pitted against Bennett once more, despite remembering their history as lovers. **AI**

MARY MARVEL

DEBUT *Captain Marvel Adventures* #18 (Dec. 1942)
CURRENT VERSION *Justice League* (Vol. 2) #8 (Jun. 2012)
REAL NAME Mary Bromfield
BASE Philadelphia
HEIGHT 5ft 6in **WEIGHT** 139 lbs **EYES** Blue **HAIR** Auburn
POWERS/ABILITIES Access to the powers of Shazam, including enhanced strength and durability, the Living Lightning, and other magical abilities.
ALLIES Shazam
ENEMIES Black Adam
AFFILIATIONS The Shazam Family

CONFIDANT
When Billy Batson became aware of what it meant to have the powers of Shazam, he knew he could share his misgivings with Mary Bromfield.

Mary Bromfield is one of Mr. and Mrs. Vasquez's foster children, along with Billy Batson and the others who become the Shazam Family—Pedro Pena, Eugene Choi, and Darla Dudley. She has been in the Vasquez house longer than the other foster children, and as a result becomes something of a mother figure to the younger kids. They all look to her for advice and guidance, putting her in a position of responsibility when situations arise that they cannot discuss with the Vasquezes.

When Black Adam confronted Shazam, the hero shared his powers with the entire group, and Mary became Lady Shazam, granted the same super-strength and powers over the Living Lightning that were bestowed on Shazam. After defeating Black Adam, all of the children were bound together by their experience and knowledge of Billy Batson's secret. Mary assumed a leadership role in the team, and also helped Billy come to terms with the powers of Shazam—as well as his knowledge that he was far from the Wizard's first choice. **AI**

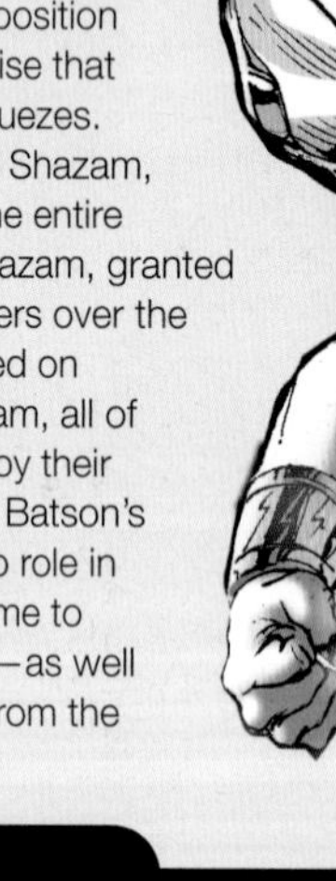

ON THE RECORD

In previous incarnations of the character, Mary drew her powers from a different set of gods making up the word Shazam: Selena, Hippolyta, Ariadne, Zephyrus, Aurora, and Minerva. Mary and the other members of the Shazam family have been in and out of the Justice League over the years, and she was also a core member of the Super Buddies, when she survived a literal trip to Hell and back.

During Final Crisis, Mary was one of a number of heroes corrupted and turned into Darkseid's thralls until Freddy Freeman managed to overcome Desaad's influence by catching hold of Mary and shouting "Shazam!" to transform her back to her normal self.

POWERED BY MIGHTY WOMEN
Mary discovered that being part of the Shazam family was more fun than she'd expected.

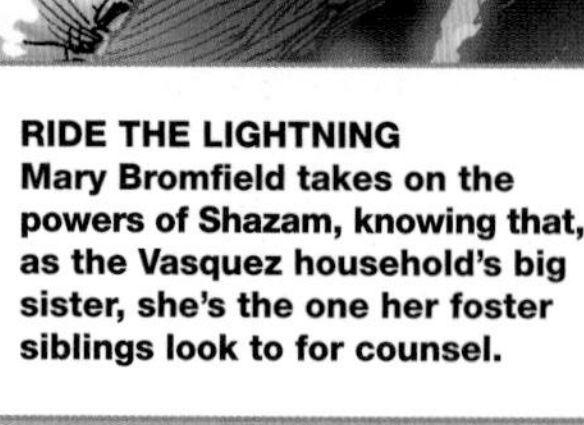

RIDE THE LIGHTNING
Mary Bromfield takes on the powers of Shazam, knowing that, as the Vasquez household's big sister, she's the one her foster siblings look to for counsel.

MATTER-EATER LAD

DEBUT *Adventure Comics* #303 (Dec. 1963)
REAL NAME Tenzil Kem
BASE Bismoll
HEIGHT 5ft 10in **WEIGHT** 150 lbs
EYES Blue **HAIR** Black
POWERS/ABILITIES Able to ingest and break down any form of matter.
ALLIES Mon-El, Saturn Queen
ENEMIES Dominators, Superboy-Prime
AFFILIATIONS Legion of Super-Heroes

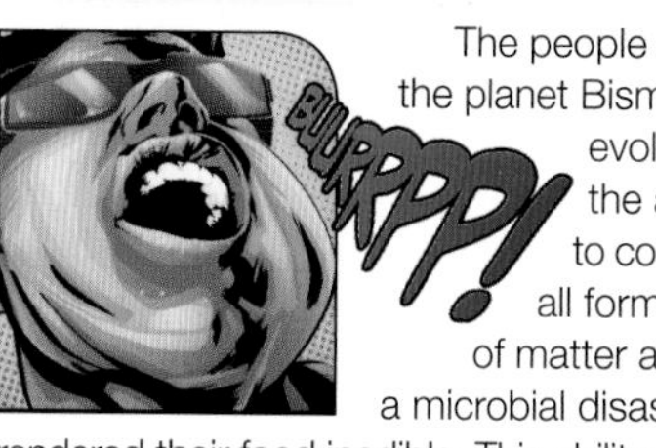

The people of the planet Bismoll evolved the ability to consume all forms of matter after a microbial disaster rendered their food inedible. This ability made Tenzil Kem an indispensable member of the Legion of Super-Heroes. With Matter-Eater Lad on their team, the Legion could escape any confinement—and destroy any weapon.

His Legion membership made him a celebrity on Bismoll, and he took on a political role there. Even serving as a full-time senator, Kem was always ready to rejoin the Legion during times of need. At times, his eating power had unpleasant side effects, as when he was driven temporarily insane by eating the Miracle Machine, before being cured by Brainiac 5. He also traveled back to the 21st century with the Legion to help Mon-El retrieve bottled cities stolen by Brainiac. **AI**

MEANSTREAK

DEBUT *Justice League America* (Vol. 2) #78 (Aug. 1993)
CURRENT VERSION *Convergence: Batman and Robin* #1 (June 2015)
HEIGHT 5ft 8in **WEIGHT** 144 lbs
EYES Blue **HAIR** Blond
POWERS/ABILITIES Creation of blades and projectiles made of flaming energy.
ENEMIES Justice League of America
AFFILIATIONS New Extremists

The sadistic, chaos-loving Meanstreak became part of a mercenary group the New Extremists at the invitation of the extra-dimensional being, Dreamslayer, who sought to destroy the JLA. The plot failed, but Dreamslayer tried again, using a cult called the Flock of the Machine, which possessed a dangerous device granted to them by the Overmaster, whom they worshiped. When this also failed, the Overmaster took direct control of the New Extremists from Dreamslayer, who had been his pawn from the beginning.

The New Extremists became part of the super-villain army, the Cadre, fighting the JLA again as part of the Overmaster's test of humanity's worth. After the collapse of the Cadre, the Overmaster turned Meanstreak and her fellow New Extremists loose. They were later exiled to the planet Salvation, but are thought to still be active. **AI**

MENAGERIE

DEBUT *Forever Evil: A.R.G.U.S.* #5 (Apr. 2014)
MEMBERS/POWERS Cheetah, Weasel, Lion-Mane, Hellhound, Elephant Man, Primape, Zebra-Man, Mauschen (formely).
BASE Central Park, New York
ENEMIES A.R.G.U.S.
AFFILIATIONS Crime Syndicate of America

The Menagerie were an animal-themed group assembled by the Cheetah with the help of Wonder Woman's stolen Lasso of Truth. Operating from a secret location inside Central Park, the team allied themselves with the Crime Syndicate of America.

The Menagerie attacked and kidnapped Steve Trevor and Killer Frost, who were searching for Firestorm to help free the Justice League members trapped within his matrix. Holding Trevor and Killer Frost in a cage in Central Park Zoo, Cheetah tried to use the Lasso of Truth to seduce Trevor into joining her and unleash his primal desires, but he resisted, seizing control of the Lasso. For her part, Killer Frost needed to siphon energy to keep herself alive, and drained the mouse-like Mauschen's life force, which she used to freeze the rest of the Menagerie in place. **AI**

MENTO

DEBUT *Doom Patrol* (Vol. 1) #91 (Nov. 1964)
CURRENT VERSION *Justice League Dark* #12 (Aug. 2012)
REAL NAME Steve Dayton
HEIGHT 5ft 10in **WEIGHT** 178 lbs
EYES Blue **HAIR** Brown
POWERS/ABILITIES Granted numerous psychokinetic powers by the Mento Helmet.
ALLIES Elasti-Girl, Beast Boy
AFFILIATIONS Justice League Dark, Doom Patrol

Wealthy businessman Steve Dayton created the Mento Helmet to enhance his mental powers and catch the eye of the Doom Patrol's Elasti-Girl. This led to a long-standing affiliation with the Doom Patrol, despite tensions within the group, some of whom didn't trust the self-styled hero.

Mento's reckless perfecting of his powers came at a cost to his psyche, at least twice making him mentally unbalanced. The first time, Raven cured him, but during his second period of insanity, he acted as the Crimelord for some time until the Teen Titans finally stopped him. Later, Mento appeared with the Justice League Dark during their pursuit of the Books of Magic, lending his psychic powers to their collective search for the Books and also helping Constantine stay one step ahead of Steve Trevor and A.R.G.U.S. **AI**

MAXIMA

DEBUT *Action Comics* #645 (Nov. 1989)
CURRENT VERSION *Supergirl* (Vol. 6) #36 (Jan 2015)
HEIGHT 6ft 2in **WEIGHT** 164 lbs
EYES Green **HAIR** Red
POWERS/ABILITIES Flight; super-strength; psychokinetic manipulation of matter.
ALLIES Supergirl
ENEMIES H'el, Roho
AFFILIATIONS Crucible Academy

Hailing from the planet Almeracia, the young Maxima joined the Crucible Academy, where the champions of each race were trained and molded into protectors of their people. Headstrong and sharp-tongued, Maxima had trouble with authority, which led to conflicts with other Academy students—including Supergirl at first. The two later formed a bond and fought together against enemies who sought to subvert and overthrow the Academy. Becoming attracted to Supergirl, Maxima helped her protect Superboy from H'El and other malign members of the Academy. In the process, Maxima also helped Supergirl overcome her Kryptonian prejudice against clones.

Maxima then put her leadership qualities to good use, accepting an ongoing position with the Academy. It is now her responsibility to train the next generation of students. **AI**

MEN FROM N.O.W.H.E.R.E.

DEBUT *Doom Patrol* (Vol. 2) #35 (Aug. 1990)
POWERS/ABILITIES Use invisible guns; able to transform children's toys into weapons; teleportation via tears in their coats.
ALLIES Darren Jones
ENEMIES Doom Patrol

The Men from N.O.W.H.E.R.E. were created during World War II by a shadowy group known only as the Agency, who were on a mission to eliminate anything different or eccentric from the world. The agency used a being known as the Telephone Avatar to extract the soul husks from humans. These husks had a variety of strange and terrifying powers, enhanced when they captured Doom Patrol's Flex Mentallo and forced him to create their weapons. The weapons were unleashed on the Doom Patrol when the Men from N.O.W.H.E.R.E. tried to force one of their members, Dorothy Spinner, to free the Telephone Avatar. However, the Avatar was accidentally destroyed, along with the Men from N.O.W.H.E.R.E.

After their deaths, a false version of the Men from N.O.W.H.E.R.E. appeared, brought into existence by a strange device known as the Delirium Box. Even more bizarre than the originals, these men spoke only in phrases using words whose first letters spelled out NOWHERE. Their leader, the insane Pentagon operative Darren Jones, sent them to kill Danny the Street, but the entire Doom Patrol banded together to defeat them once and for all. **AI**

ACROSTIC ANTAGONISTS
Never Open William's Head, Evil Reptiles Emerge. Now Oblivion Waits, Hideous Evil Requires Elimination

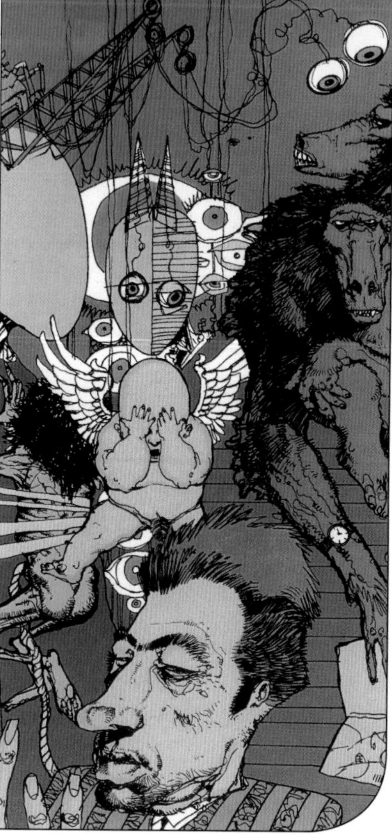

MERCURY, MAX

DEBUT *National Comics* #5 (Nov. 1940)
BASE Manchester, Alabama
HEIGHT 6ft 1in **WEIGHT** 188 lbs
EYES Blue **HAIR** Gray
POWERS/ABILITIES Super-speed; vibrational frequency shifting permits his body to pass through solid matter.
ALLIES Flash
ENEMIES Professor Zoom
AFFILIATIONS Freedom Fighters

Max Mercury was imbued with the power of the Speed Force as a member of the US Cavalry in the 19th century, following a massacre of Native Americans. A dying shaman enchanted Max, granting him unlimited super-speed and the ability to shift his molecules and pass through solid objects.

Known over the years as Quicksilver, Windrunner, Whip Whirlwind, and the Zen Master of Speed, Max tried to penetrate the mysteries of the Speed Force many times. Each time he found himself skipping forward in time, with the result that he now finds himself in the 21st century.

Over the years, he has served as a mentor to Barry Allen, Wally West, Johnny Quick, and Bart Allen, lending his experience and knowledge of the Speed Force to their battles against Professor Zoom, Superboy-Prime, and the Rival. **AI**

MERA

DATA

DEBUT *Aquaman* (Vol. 1) #11 **(Sep.-Oct. 1963)**
CURRENT VERSION *Aquaman* (Vol. 7) #1 **(Nov. 2011)**
BASE Atlantis
HEIGHT 5ft 9in **WEIGHT** 160 lbs
EYES Blue **HAIR** Red
POWERS/ABILITIES Water breathing; telekinetic creation of solid water shapes; enhanced strength.
ALLIES Aquaman
ENEMIES Ocean Master, Dead King
AFFILIATIONS Justice League

A LOVE SUPREME
After everything they've been through, Aquaman and Mera stand firmly together. Coming from Xebel, Mera also helps to extend Aquaman's influence over the subsea realms beyond the city of Atlantis.

TROUBLED HERITAGE
Mera has spent her life reconciling Xebelian hatred for Atlantis with her own personal love for Aquaman.

Aquaman's lover and later Queen of Atlantis, Mera is a highly trained assassin from the Atlantean nation of Xebel and a powerful telekinetic. She gave it all up to find a new life with Arthur Curry on land, only to be dragged back into the ancient rivalries of her home kingdom.

A native of the aquatic kingdom of Xebel, an ancient penal colony for rebellious Atlanteans, Mera was trained as an assassin and grew up with a deep suspicion of Atlantis. Despite this, she met and fell in love with Aquaman, and they were married. When he left Atlantis to make a life in the surface world, she went with him, but had difficulty adjusting.

She got a welcome chance to return to adventuring during Aquaman and the Others' quest to fight Black Manta and retrieve stolen Atlantean artifacts. However, this was only brief respite from the alienation and hostility she experienced on land. She returned to the oceans to fight against the Dead King when he unleashed freezing attacks against the East Coast. He captured her and forced her to reveal the location of Xebel, but she freed herself and arrived just ahead of him, enlisting the aid of Nereus, the king of Xebel, to whom she was unknowingly betrothed.

Throughout her trials, Mera grappled with anger, even as it sometimes proved to be an asset. She grew into a powerful ally for Aquaman as she mastered her childhood hatred for all things Atlantean, and began to learn how to channel her ferocious temper in more productive directions. Her Xebelian heritage continued to cause conflicts in her relationship with Aquaman, but they surmounted these obstacles to become King and Queen of Atlantis, rebuilding the kingdom after the Ocean Master's disastrous attack on the surface world and damage suffered during the Dead King's return. **AI**

ELEMENTAL RAGE
Not even Black Manta can withstand Mera's powers when she really gives in to her emotions.

ON THE RECORD

Originally the free-spirited queen of an other-dimensional realm, Mera left it all to marry Aquaman. The murder of their son by Black Manta compounded emotional instability she was experiencing due to unknown factors in the Earthly environment. She and her husband experienced long separations in the years that followed.

During Blackest Night, Mera was able to fight off the Black Lanterns while she kept her emotions in check, but when her anger spiraled out of control, she was brought into the Red Lantern Corps, and nearly died in battle.

ROYAL FURY
Mera has a reputation as the emotional one, but when she is hurt or endangered, Aquaman flashes a temper of his own.

CLASSIC STORIES

***Aquaman: Sword of Atlantis* #40–45 (Apr.-Sep. 2006)** Mera leads a band of survivors after the destruction of Atlantis by the Spectre. She holds out against growing chaos under the oceans before reuniting with Aquaman against the threat of the Ocean Master.

***Aquaman* (Vol. 1) #58–60 (Oct.-Nov. 1977; Feb.-Mar. 1978)** Black Manta kidnaps Mera's child Aquababy and traps him in a tank designed to suffocate him. Mera embarks on a quest to Xebel to find the device to free him. She succeeds, but returns too late to save her baby.

MERLYN

DEBUT *Justice League of America* (Vol. 1) #94 **(Nov. 1971)**
CURRENT VERSION *Green Arrow* (Vol. 5) #0 **(Nov. 2012)**
REAL NAME Thomas Merlyn
HEIGHT 6ft 3in **WEIGHT** 185 lbs
EYES Blue **HAIR** Black
POWERS/ABILITIES Expert archer and hand-to-hand combatant.
ALLIES The King
ENEMIES Green Arrow

Tommy Merlyn was best friends with a young Oliver Queen, who never missed an opportunity to live up to his playboy lifestyle. At a party on an oil rig in the Pacific Ocean, waiting for a rock band to arrive, Oliver was showing off his archery skills when terrorists attacked. The assailants had rigged the platform—and several of the people aboard—to explode, while they siphoned off the oil. Escaping with Tommy but desperate to save his girlfriend Leena, Oliver shot the detonator out of the lead terrorist's hand, but it hit the rig's frame. Tommy saved Oliver's life from the ensuing explosion, but was badly burned himself. With a last warning to Oliver that his recklessness would keep putting others' lives in danger, he slipped into a coma. He was slowly nursed back to health by monks in a remote monastery.

Years later, Tommy resurfaced, having become a mercenary—and expert archer—going by the name of Merlyn. In the employ of the notorious crime lord known as The King, Merlyn crossed paths with his old friend Oliver Queen, proving himself just as skilled an archer and fighter as the Green Arrow. However, when he finally recognized Oliver during close combat, Merlyn didn't have the heart to kill him. Instead he vanished, leaving Green Arrow wondering why. **AI**

PRESCIENT WARNING
Tommy Merlyn argued with Oliver Queen over how to deal with the terrorists who had crashed their party. This would be the last time they saw each other as friends.

ON THE RECORD

Previous versions of Merlyn's origin story begin with an archery duel between him and Green Arrow—which Merlyn wins. Their rivalry thus established, they battled numerous times over the years, notably at Green Arrow's wedding to Black Canary. Merlyn's less than savory alliances have included a deal with the demon Neron, and with the League of Assassins, witnessing the resurrection of Rā's al Ghūl.

BLACK OPS
As a mercenary, Merlyn has always had a reputation for peerless archery skills, and the ability to surprise any target—even getting the drop on the Flash.

METAL MEN

DEBUT *Showcase* #37 **(Mar.-Apr. 1962)**
CURRENT VERSION *Justice League* (Vol. 2) #28 **(Apr. 2014)**
BASE Metropolis
MEMBERS/POWERS Gold: Analytical intelligence, malleable form; **Lead**: Strength, radiation and energy shielding; **Iron**: Strength, durability, malleable form; **Mercury**: Liquid metal form; **Platinum**: Malleable form.
ALLIES Doctor Magnus, Cyborg
ENEMIES Grid, Crime Syndicate of America
AFFILIATIONS Justice League

Doctor Will Magnus created the Metal Men as part of a military project, supposedly designing a team of autonomous robots capable of operating in hazardous environments. To this end, the robotics genius developed a revolutionary piece of technology—a responsometer—which created a coherent form and personality from the innate intelligence and properties of any material.

After Doctor Magnus discovered the Metal Men were intended to be assassins, they rebelled, seeking refuge in his home. Another one of his responsometers, stolen by a thief and dropped into a vat of chemicals, created the toxic monster Chemo. When the creature attacked them, the Metal Men sacrificed themselves to destroy it.

However, Doctor Magnus was able to recreate the team at Cyborg's request to battle Grid and the Crime Syndicate of America. They succeeded in shutting Grid down, after which Platinum was considered for membership in the Justice League. This plan was put on hold when she malfunctioned during their initial meeting, but the Metal Men remain a valuable asset due to their strength, loyalty, and potential to combine into different alloys. **AI**

HEAVY METAL
The Metal Men allied (and alloyed) against all threats.

ON THE RECORD

Over the years, responsometers have been used to create dangerous alternate Metal Men. Magnus' brother David once used a device stolen from T.O. Morrow to transform them into the Death Metal Men: Uranium, Strontium, Thorium, Radium, Lithium, Polonium, and Fermium. Once, Chang Tzu tried to force Magnus to build a Plutonium Man, but Magnus outwitted him and rebuilt the originals.

ROGUE ELEMENTS
When responsometers fell into the wrong hands, the variant Metal Men thus created have been deadly opponents to the original team, as well as to Doctor Magnus.

METALLO

DATA

DEBUT *Action Comics* (Vol. 1) #252 **(May 1959)**
CURRENT VERSION *Action Comics* (Vol. 2) #1 **(Nov. 2011)**
REAL NAME John Wayne Corben
EYES Green **HAIR** Brown
POWERS/ABILITIES Massively powerful armored body equipped with life-support systems and an arsenal of rockets and guns; can emit Kryptonite radiation from chest cavity.
ALLIES Lois Lane, General Lane
ENEMIES Superman, Metal-2.0, Ultraman, Brainiac
AFFILIATIONS United States Army, Secret Society

SACRIFICE
When Metallo attacked General Lane's base, Lane's newest cyborg—Metal-2.0—self-destructed in a vain attempt to destroy his predecessor.

OUT OF CONTROL
As soon as Metallo was activated, he was taken over by Brainiac.

Metallo is made up of two vital components—an advanced suit of battle armor and a human soldier called John Corben—linked together by a cybernetic interface and powered by Kryptonite. Metallo was taken over by the alien intelligence known as Brainiac and then used as a living weapon against Superman by General Lane of the US military, but Corben was in a constant battle to regain control of his destiny.

John Corben was a career soldier working under General Lane on "Project Steel Soldier." This involved the development of a suit of exo-armor that connected directly to the nervous system of the wearer via Dr. Henry Irons' experimental Metal-Zero interface. Corben volunteered to put on the experimental Steel Soldier armor, but when the suit connected to his nervous system both he and the suit were immediately taken over by the alien intelligence Brainiac. The self-professed Collector of Worlds proceeded to use Metallo as a weapon when he launched his first attack on Earth, but was defeated by Superman.

General Lane later reactivated Metallo by using Kryptonite as a power source and sent him into action in the Middle East. When Metallo massacred civilians, Lane attempted to have him destroyed. Metallo was reactivated once more by minions of the Crime Syndicate and agreed to join their Secret Society, but was deactivated when Ultraman brutally removed Metallo's core to feed his own Kryptonite addiction.

Metallo was impounded by Lane, until a Doomsday-infected Superman threatened the world. General Lane's daughter Lois—the woman Corben long had been in love with—asked him to help defend the planet, so Corben sacrificed himself to drive the Kryptonian away.

When Brainiac returned to invade Earth, he used nanites to take control of Lois and give her incredible superpowers. However, Lois escaped his control and used her powers to recreate Metallo, who helped her to fight off Brainiac's threat. In the aftermath of the conflict with Brainiac, Superman and Lois entrusted Metallo with the duty of protecting Metropolis. Finally at peace, John Corben took on the role of hero and protector. **SW**

ON THE RECORD

Pre-Flashpoint, there were different iterations of both Corben and Metallo. The original Silver-Age Corben was an unscrupulous journalist with a grudge against Superman. His brain was placed in a Kryptonite-powered body after an accident. However, when he confronted the Man of Steel, Corben discovered the Kryptonite was fake and, unable to recharge himself, died of a heart attack.

A reimagined account in the late 1980s depicted Corben as a conman whose brain was transplanted into a metal body following a traffic accident. This Corben made a deal with the demon Neron and was turned into a demonic metal juggernaut.

RADIOACTIVE HEART
In all versions, Kryptonite is the source of Metallo's power and Superman's greatest weakness.

METALLO RETURNS
Lois Lane used her Brainiac-given powers to revive John Corben/Metallo, to help defend their city, Metropolis.

CLASSIC STORIES

***Action Comics* (Vol. 1) #252 (May 1959)** In his very first appearance, John Corben becomes Metallo and traps Superman—but dies after mistaking a model of Kryptonite for the real thing.

***Superman: Secret Origin* #1-6 (Nov. 2009-Oct. 2010)** In this gripping new Superman origin story, Lex Luthor turns soldier John Corben into a living weapon to use against the Kryptonian.

***Action Comics* (Vol. 2) #23.4 (Nov. 2013)** After General Lane tries to eliminate Metallo, the juggernaut seeks revenge and has an epic battle with a former friend, transformed into Metal-2.0.

METAMORPHO

DEBUT *The Brave and the Bold* #57 **(Dec. 1964–Jan. 1965)**
CURRENT VERSION *Legends of Tomorrow Anthology* #1 **(May 2016)**
REAL NAME Rex Mason
HEIGHT 6ft 1in **WEIGHT** 200 lbs
EYES Black **HAIR** None
POWERS/ABILITIES Can transform his body (or parts of it) into any element contained in the human body, potentially giving him incredible strength, flexibility, and durability.
ALLIES Batman, Metal Men, Sapphire Stagg, Java, Algon
ENEMIES Simon Stagg, Manhunters, Hyperclan, Masters of Disaster, O.M.A.C.
AFFILIATIONS Outsiders, Justice League Europe

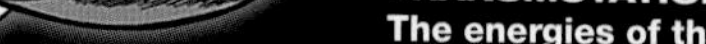

TRANSMUTATION
The energies of the mysterious meteor changed Rex Mason into a bizarre being with powers of elemental-control.

Rex Mason was a rugged adventurer who made the near-fatal mistake of falling in love with his employer's daughter. Simon Stagg did not want his beloved Sapphire involved with a mercenary, so he plotted Mason's demise. Stagg sent him to explore the pyramid of Akh-Ton in search of the Orb of Ra, and then arranged for one of his henchmen to steal the Orb and leave Rex in the pyramid to die.

Rex was trapped in a chamber and exposed to radiation from a meteor that had been kept there for years. The radiation radically altered his physiology, turning him into Metamorpho, the Element Man, a being who could change shape or transform into any element found in human physiology.

Rex escaped the chamber and set off in search of a cure for his condition. In Markovia, he rescued Bruce Wayne's employee, Lucius Fox, and an impressed Batman made him a founding member of his Outsiders team. As Metamorpho, Rex would remain a core member of the group for decades; he would also serve in the Justice League and Justice League Europe. Metamorpho sacrificed his life to save his teammates when they were attacked by the Hyperclan, but was resurrected thanks to the intervention of Sapphire. **SW**

HANDYMAN
Rex Mason's flexible physiology enabled him to come up with the right tool to sort out almost any problem.

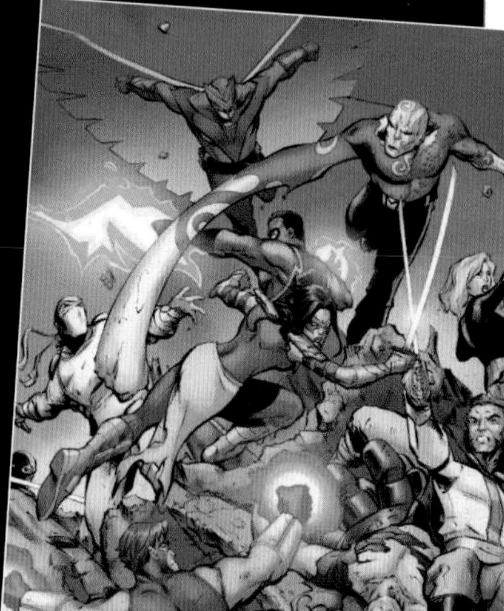

TEAM PLAYER
In the Outsiders, Rex Mason found a team that valued his powers and accepted his bizarre appearance. He served in various incarnations of the group.

METRON

DEBUT *New Gods* (Vol. 1) #1 **(Feb.–Mar. 1971)**
CURRENT VERSION *Green Lantern/New Gods: Godhead* #1 **(Dec. 2014)**
HEIGHT 6ft 1in **WEIGHT** 190 lbs **EYES** Blue **HAIR** Black
POWERS/ABILITIES His personal powers are unknown, though he has a talent for escapology; Mobius Chair provides pan-dimensional travel, the ability to access any knowledge in the universe, and force-field protection.
ALLIES Highfather, Orion
ENEMIES Justice League, Anti-Monitor

The origins and identity of Metron are a mystery, but at some point in the past he received an amazing chair from an enigmatic figure calling himself Mobius. The Mobius Chair allowed Metron to traverse time, space, and dimensions and provided him with all the knowledge in the universe—except for the identity of his mysterious benefactor. On his journeys across dimensions, Metron witnessed multiple crises that destroyed and remade reality, causing damage to the very fabric of existence.

Metron feared that a clash between Darkseid and the Anti-Monitor would lead to universal annihilation. Determined to avert this, he became the advisor to Darkseid's enemy, the New God Highfather of New Genesis, and attempted to manipulate events to eliminate Darkseid before his confrontation with the Anti-Monitor. Metron went so far as to engineer a conflict between New Genesis and the Lantern Corps in the hope that the power of the Lanterns' rings could be harnessed to defeat the evil overlord. Metron attempted to dissuade the Justice League from battling the Anti-Monitor on Earth, but was pulled from the Mobius Chair by Wonder Woman's lasso, and Batman briefly commandeered it. Metron, along with the Chair's new occupant, the Owlman, was then destroyed by an unimaginably powerful entity, Dr. Manhattan. **SW**

ON THE RECORD

The original Metron was also a cool and detached seeker after knowledge, but he occasionally served as a teacher and mentor to Orion and Lightray, as well as advising young Scott Free. When the Source began eliminating the New Gods, Metron looked on impartially—until his former student Mister Miracle was slain. At that point, Metron demanded to be destroyed as well, and the Source slew him.

POWER BEHIND THE THRONE
Metron initially served as an advisor to Highfather, sharing his cosmic knowledge with the New Gods of New Genesis.

MIDNIGHTER

DATA

DEBUT *Stormwatch* (Vol. 2) #4 **(Feb. 1998)**
CURRENT VERSION *Flashpoint* (Vol. 2) #5 **(Oct. 2011)**
BASE Skywatch
HEIGHT 6ft 5in **WEIGHT** 285 lbs **EYES** Brown **HAIR** Brown
POWERS/ABILITIES Extensive cybernetic components grant Midnighter enhanced speed, strength, and durability; a Neural-Inductive Combat Simulator in his brain allows him to anticipate any opponent's moves.
ALLIES Apollo, Zealot, Dick Grayson, the Gardener, Batman Family
ENEMIES Scourge of Worlds, Gravity Miners, Hidden People, Grifter, the Kollective, Extremax, Spyral
AFFILIATIONS Stormwatch, the God Garden

CLASSIC STORIES

***Stormwatch* (Vol. 3) #15–16 (Feb.–Mar. 2013)** Accused of betraying Stormwatch, Midnighter is forced to go on the run in Antarctica—pursued by his enraged lover, Apollo!

***Stormwatch* (Vol. 3) #23–24 (Oct.–Nov. 2013)** Midnighter suffers a series of traumatic flashbacks to the alien experiments he was subjected to as a child, giving an insight into the events that helped create this tormented hero.

***Midnighter* (Vol. 2) #1 (Aug. 2015)** In a shocking turn of events, Midnighter leaves Stormwatch and Apollo behind to go and work for the Gardener, proprietress of the orbital God Garden.

THE MAKING OF MIDNIGHTER
Years of agonizing cybernetic surgery transformed a farm boy into something both more and less than human.

POWER OF PRECOGNITION
Midnighter's uncanny ability to predict an opponent's moves in advance gives him a deadly edge in combat.

Midnighter is a dark hero who uses his violent impulses to fight for justice. After receiving cybernetic enhancements from unknown beings, he began his career as a vigilante, before being recruited into Stormwatch, a team dedicated to protecting Earth from alien incursions. He formed a close partnership with fellow Stormwatch member Apollo, and they became lovers as well as teammates.

The boy who would become Midnighter was kidnapped when he was 14 and subjected to years of painful cybernetic augmentation that boosted his strength, speed, and senses. After escaping, he used his powers to become a mercenary and vigilante, venting his psychopathic tendencies on victims who deserved it. He also tracked down another escapee from the aliens' tests, who was fighting crime using his solar-based powers as the Super Hero Apollo.

Midnighter and Apollo were then approached by Stormwatch, a centuries-old organization devoted to defending the Earth. The duo were initially reluctant to join, but after fighting alongside the heroes, Midnighter realized that joining Stormwatch would keep him from becoming evil, and persuaded Apollo to sign up too. The pair also found that they were attracted to each other, and eventually became partners, fighting side by side against threats including the Gravity Miners and Etrigan the Demon (a former member of Stormwatch precursors, the Demon Knights).

When Harry Tanner attempted to take control of Stormwatch, he framed Midnighter as a traitor, and the antihero was forced to go on the run in Antarctica, pursued by his furious lover. Jenny Quantum discovered Tanner's deception, and Apollo and Midnighter reconciled. The pair were included in a revamped Stormwatch team that defended Earth from the timeline-altering Kollective and the powerful Extremax. Midnighter then broke up with Apollo, believing the hero deserved better, and was seconded to work as an agent for the mysterious Gardener. **SW**

VIOLENT TENDENCIES
Midnighter is a self-confessed psychopath, but chooses to use his gift for violence against the guilty rather than the innocent.

PARTNERS IN CRIME FIGHTING
In Stormwatch, Midnighter and Apollo became teammates and eventually lovers.

ON THE RECORD

Midnighter was originally a covert black ops Stormwatch agent. When the team was destroyed, he was recruited into the Authority, a group that fought relentlessly for the greater good—even if it brought them into conflict with multinational corporations and the United States Government.

In this incarnation, Midnighter and his teammate Apollo also married and adopted fellow Authority member Jenny Sparks. Following the terrible devastation of Earth during the *Number of the Beast* event, Midnighter and the reconvened Authority set out to restore order to the planet.

A FORCE FOR GOOD?
Midnighter embodied the ruthless zeal of the Authority team. He and his comrades proved willing to defy the world in their pursuit of justice.

MIDNIGHT

DEBUT *Smash Comics* #18 (Jan. 1941)
REAL NAME Dave Clark
BASE New York City
HEIGHT 6ft **WEIGHT** 190 lbs
EYES Blue **HAIR** Black
POWERS/ABILITIES Expert detective and martial artist; uses a vacuum gun to fire a cable for scaling buildings.
ALLIES Doc Wackey, Gabby, Sniffer Snoop
ENEMIES Morris Carleton
AFFILIATIONS All-Star Squadron

Dave Clark was a popular newsreader for New York's UXAM radio station. When an apartment building collapsed, he helped drag people from the rubble and discovered that the block had been built by the corrupt Carleton Construction Company. Inspired by the hero of the radio serial *The Man Called Midnight*, he put on a mask and assumed the code name Midnight. He intimidated Carleton's owner into donating funds to those injured in the disaster, and got word out about the shoddy construction of a Carleton dam before it collapsed, saving many lives. When the clock struck 12 that evening, Midnight confronted Carleton and forced him to confess his crimes.

Midnight continued to fight for justice, battling Nazis as part of the All-Star Squadron and the Freedom Fighters. **SW**

MINDWARP

DEBUT *Flashpoint: Secret Seven* #2 (Sep. 2011)
CURRENT VERSION *Justice League Dark* #3 (Jan. 2012)
REAL NAME Jay Young
BASE Los Angeles, California
EYES Blue **HAIR** Blond
POWERS/ABILITIES Can release a powerful "seizure soul" from his body—and can sometimes even control it.
ALLIES Justice League Dark
ENEMIES Enchantress

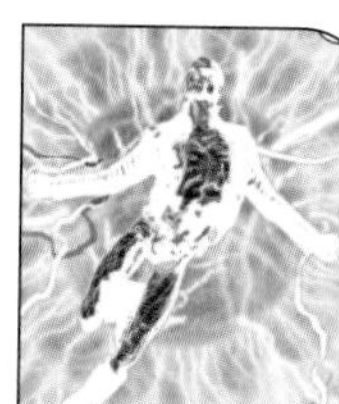

Jay Young, alias Mindwarp, was a gleefully psychotic nihilist with the ability to release an astral "seizure soul" from his body. Madame Xanadu asked Shade the Changing Man to recruit Jay into Justice League Dark to help fight the Enchantress, but Mindwarp rejected Shade's offer. However, when the League did face the Enchantress, Jay turned up to help, claiming that her magical influence had made his seizure soul unstable. Mindwarp's power helped to unite the Enchantress with her human host, June Moone, ending her threat.

Mindwarp was subsequently captured by forces loyal to the Crime Syndicate. He was subjected to agonizing mystical experimentation, and then destroyed while being used to power a test-firing of the Syndicate's Thaumaton device. **SW**

MISFIT

DEBUT *Birds of Prey* (Vol. 1) #96 (Sep. 2006)
CURRENT VERSION *Batgirl* (Vol. 4) #34 (Oct. 2014)
REAL NAME Charlotte Gage-Radcliffe
EYES Blue **HAIR** Red
POWERS/ABILITIES Possesses the ability to "bounce" (teleport) from place to place.
ENEMIES Black Alice

Growing up, young Charlotte Gage-Radcliffe idolized Super Heroes, especially Batgirl. Charlotte even possessed a superpower—the ability to "bounce" (or teleport). When her family perished in a fire, the orphaned Charlotte decided to become the "new Batgirl" by donning a homemade costume and fighting street crime. Barbara Gordon, alias the Birds of Prey's Oracle, tried to convince her to give up her new career, but Charlotte instead adopted a new identity as Misfit. She began tagging along on missions with the Birds of Prey and was gradually accepted by the team, though her impulsive nature caused problems.

Misfit later applied to join the Teen Titans, but was rejected. After Bruce Wayne was killed, she helped keep order in Gotham City working as part of Oracle's crime fighting Network, but subsequently went to live with a foster family. **SW**

MISS AMERICA

DEBUT *Military Comics* #1 (Aug. 1941)
REAL NAME Joan Dale
BASE The Heartland
HEIGHT 5ft 7in **WEIGHT** 133 lbs
EYES Blue **HAIR** Brown
POWERS/ABILITIES Matter transmutation.
ENEMIES Red Bee, android Miss America
AFFILIATIONS All-Star Squadron, Freedom Fighters, Justice Society of America

During World War II, reporter Joan Dale was knocked unconscious while visiting the Statue of Liberty and taken to the top-secret Project M facility. Here, under the direction of Professor Mazursky, she was subjected to a process that granted her matter-transmutation powers. Unaware of what had been done to her, Joan experienced a vision in which the Statue of Liberty told her that she had been given special powers to use in the defense of her nation. On the ferry back to New York, she turned a pair of pro-Nazi thugs into birds. Adopting the code name Miss America, Joan joined the wartime Freedom Fighters team.

Joan later retired and married Admiral Derek Trevor, but after he died she resumed her heroic career, joining Uncle Sam's new Freedom Fighters. She was presumed killed after exploding in space, but was reborn in a younger body as Miss Cosmos. **SW**

MIRROR MASTER

DEBUT *The Flash* (Vol. 1) #105 (Feb.–Mar. 1959)
CURRENT VERSION *The Flash* (Vol. 4) #12 (Oct. 2012)
REAL NAME Samuel Joseph "Sam" Scudder
BASE Central City
HEIGHT 5ft 10in **WEIGHT** 175 lbs **EYES** Brown **HAIR** Brown
POWERS/ABILITIES Trapped in the Mirror World, a realm that lies within all reflective surfaces, he can see out of any mirror and take people into this realm, where he has complete control.
ALLIES Dr. Darwin Elias
ENEMIES Flash, Gorilla Grodd, Crime Syndicate, Secret Society
AFFILIATIONS The Rogues

TIME FOR REFLECTION
Mirror Master can emerge from any reflective surface and drag victims back to the Mirror World.

Sam Scudder was a criminal who used the code name Mirror Master and wielded a gun that gave him power over reflective surfaces. He was a member of the Rogues, a team of villains who used themed hi-tech weapons in their crimes. The group was led by Captain Cold, whose sister, Lisa, became Sam's girlfriend.

Despite their hi-tech gadgetry, the Rogues' heists were often stopped by the Flash, who could literally run rings around them. However, Dr. Darwin Elias offered Captain Cold access to a Genome Recoder that could write the powers of the Rogues' weapons into their DNA, allowing them to combat the Flash on equal terms. Unfortunately, while they were using the device, it exploded. The Rogues received their powers, but Lisa was rendered comatose by the blast, gaining the ability to project an astral form, while Mirror Master was trapped in the Mirror World, a dimension that lay behind all reflective surfaces. Lisa used her astral-projection powers to give Sam the ability to emerge from the Mirror World, but this caused her to lose her own astral form. **SW**

ON THE RECORD

The original Sam Scudder discovered how to exploit the amazing properties of mirrors while in prison. Taking the name Mirror Master, he escaped and went on to become a member of the Rogues and the Secret Society of Super-Villains.

Scudder was killed during *Crisis on Infinite Earths*, but the Mirror Master name was subsequently "borrowed" by Captain Boomerang and then Evan McCulloch. Scudder later returned in undead form during *Blackest Night*.

MIRROR IMAGE
Sam Scudder trapped Barry Allen within reflective prisons, but when Wally West leapt into action as Kid Flash, the Mirror Master thought he was seeing double!

M

MISS MARTIAN

DEBUT *Teen Titans* (Vol. 3) #37 (Aug. 2006)
CURRENT VERSION *Teen Titans* (Vol. 4) #1 (Nov. 2011)
REAL NAME M'gann M'orzz
HEIGHT 5ft 10in **WEIGHT** 135 lbs
EYES Red **HAIR** Red (in disguise)
POWERS/ABILITIES Superhuman strength endurance, and durability; flight; shapeshifting; telepathy; enhanced senses; Martian vision.
ALLIES Red Devil, Aquagirl, Martian Manhunter
ENEMIES Terror Titans, Clock King

While she has only appeared post-Flashpoint in a picture on Red Robin's computer files, prior to that, Miss Martian was a trusted member of the Teen Titans. Full of energy and perhaps a little naïve, Miss Martian was quick to make friends and even established a human identity for herself in the form of Megan Morse.

However, beneath her green-skinned exterior, Miss Martian hid a dark secret. Instead of being from the same benevolent race as the Super Hero known as the Martian Manhunter, Miss Martian was actually from the race of cruel White Martians known for their violence and an infamous attack on the JLA. The Teen Titans accepted M'gann despite her people's reputation, allowing Miss Martian to show her true heroic nature time and time again. **MM**

GREEN GUISE
In her true White Martian form, M'gann has a chalky-white body covered with spines, a long tail, and glowing red eyes.

MR. MXYZPTLK

DEBUT *Superman* (Vol. 1) #30 **(Sep.-Oct. 1944)**
CURRENT VERSION *Action Comics* (Vol. 2) #0 **(Nov. 2012)**
REAL NAME Mxyzptlk
BASE 5th Dimension
HEIGHT Variable **WEIGHT** Variable **EYES** Variable **HAIR** Variable
POWERS/ABILITIES Able to bend reality itself in ways only understandable to inhabitants of the 5th Dimension, including moving through time and space unencumbered, animating inanimate objects, and creating matter from nothingness.
ALLIES Gsptlnz (Mrs. Nyxly)
ENEMIES Lord Vyndktvx, Superman

Mr. Mxyzptlk hailed from the so-called 5th dimension. Superman first learned of this otherworldly imp when he moved into his own Metropolis apartment after finding work at *The Daily Star* as Clark Kent. However, when Clark's landlady, Mrs. Nyxly, first mentioned her husband, she referred to him as a stage conjurer who went by the handle "Mystic Mr. Triple X". She told Clark that a rival magician messed with one of his tricks and that he was suffering in a coma for the last seven years. However, Nyxly's story only scratched the surface of the truth.

In reality, Mrs. Nyxly was a princess from the 5th Dimension named Gsptlnz. Mr. Mxyzptlk had become her father's royal sorcerer, edging out the former court magician, Lord Vyndktvx. An enraged Vyndktvx swore revenge, but killed Gsptlnz's father by mistake. Fearing for her own life, Gsptlnz fled to Earth, leaving her beloved Mr. Mxyzptlk behind in the 5th Dimension. **MM**

ON THE RECORD

Mr. Mxyzptlk has plagued Superman as far back as the Golden Age of Comics, though his name was originally spelled Mxyztplk. A classic member of Superman's Rogues Gallery, Mxy originally faced Superman as a cartoony bald man in a purple suit who would return to harass the Man of Steel every 90 days, only leaving Superman's reality when he was tricked into saying his own name backwards.

By *Superman* (Vol. 1) #131 (Aug. 1959), the mischievous Mr. Mxyzptlk's name gained its modern spelling, and he was sporting his trademark orange suit and white hair.

MEAN MXY
In a story set before the reality-altering *Crisis on Infinite Earths*, Mxy showed his true colors when he transformed from prankster to murderous villain in a possible future for Superman.

MISTER E

DEBUT *Secrets of Haunted House* #31 (Dec. 1980)
CURRENT VERSION *Constantine* (Vol. 1) #1 (May 2013)
BASE The Bernese Alps, Switzerland
HEIGHT 6ft 3in **WEIGHT** 190 lbs
EYES White **HAIR** White
POWERS/ABILITIES Very powerful magician, able to teleport and rip a person's soul from their body; cane channels dark magic.
ENEMIES John Constantine

An enemy of Justice League Dark member John Constantine, the man known as Mister E was a good magician corrupted by the temptations of magic. A member of the Cult of the Cold Flame—a group of sorcerers that included the deceased Zatara and Sargon, as well as the evil Tannarak—Mister E was originally regarded as a hero.

While his past is shrouded in mystery, it is commonly believed that Mister E went insane after he cast a magic spell that liquefied his eyeballs. He became instantly blind, and much more susceptible to the darker side of the magic world. As a part of the Cold Flame, he united with other mystics and began to eliminate those magicians not loyal to their cause. This forced him into a confrontation with Constantine, who ran him through with the mystical Moonblade. **MM**

MISTER MIND

DEBUT *Captain Marvel Adventures* #22 (Mar. 1943)
CURRENT VERSION *Justice League* (Vol. 2) #21 (Aug. 2013)
HEIGHT 3in **WEIGHT** 5 oz
EYES Black **HAIR** None
POWERS/ABILITIES Extremely intelligent Venusian worm possessing knowledge of Earth; telepathic; telekinetic; able to alter the fabric of time and space during metamorphosis.
ENEMIES Shazam

One of Shazam's most dangerous and notorious enemies, the alien worm named Mister Mind has only recently reared his ugly head in the new reality established after the Flashpoint event. When the villain Dr. Sivana was in New York's subway tunnels, looking for an entrance to the mythical Rock of Eternity in hopes of gaining superpowers, he discovered a small glass bell jar. Inside, resting on a cushion, was a sealed glass bottle, containing a talking alien worm.

Introducing himself as Mister Mind, the worm said he had been watching Sivana, and the magic that had infected him. He claimed the magic had eaten away at Sivana's body, but not his mind, and he wished to speak to the doctor now that they had a moment alone. Together, they began to plot against Shazam and his allies. **MM**

MISTER NOBODY

DEBUT *Doom Patrol* (Vol. 1) #86 (Mar. 1964) (as Morden)
REAL NAME Eric Morden
HEIGHT 5ft 8in **EYES** Red **HAIR** None
POWERS/ABILITIES Exists in a pseudo-dimensional state; possesses an abstract body; can psychically induce state of anarchy/insanity in other human beings.
ALLIES Dr. Bruckner, Sleepwalk, Frenzy, the Fog
ENEMIES Doom Patrol, Brotherhood of Evil
AFFILIATIONS Brotherhood of Dada

When Eric Morden opted to join the Brotherhood of Evil, his dream of life as a super-villain soon went awry, forcing him to flee to Paraguay to escape his new "allies" in the Brotherhood. After meeting a former Nazi war criminal named Dr. Bruckner, Morden agreed to visit the doctor's "white room," where he could be born anew.

Locked in a sensory deprivation chamber for what seemed like centuries, Morden was driven insane, and with the help of Bruckner's mysterious serums, was transformed into the abstract villain Mister Nobody. Now as powerful as he had ever hoped to be, Mister Nobody united several other super-powered outcasts, forming the Brotherhood of Dada. They confronted the heroes of the Doom Patrol in Paris, but were ultimately defeated. **MM**

MR. FREEZE

DATA

DEBUT *Batman* (Vol. 1) #121 **(Feb. 1959)**
CURRENT VERSION *Batman* (Vol. 2) #1 **(Nov. 2011)**
REAL NAME Dr. Victor Fries
BASE Gotham City
HEIGHT 6ft **WEIGHT** 190 lbs **EYES** Blue **HAIR** None
POWERS/ABILITIES Genius-level intellect with a keen scientific mind; claims to not feel emotions; sophisticated refrigeration suit sustains low temperature and grants superhuman strength, durability, and endurance; developed quick-freeze technology that he utilizes in the form of freeze guns and grenades.
ALLIES Starling, Scarecrow, Harley Quinn, Merry-Maker, Professor Pyg
ENEMIES Batman, the Batman Family, Birds of Prey, Court of Owls
AFFILIATIONS Wayne Enterprises (formerly)

FROZEN FEELINGS
Fries had written his doctorate on Nora Fields, the first woman to ever undergo cryogenic stasis. He became completely obsessed with her, convincing himself that they were married.

At first glance, Mr. Freeze seems like a sympathetic criminal. After all, he has devoted his life to looking for a cure for his beloved Nora so that she may be thawed from her cryogenic state and reunited with him. In fact, Victor Fries is a dangerous sociopath whose refusal to accept reality has transformed him into a super-villain.

Victor Fries watched his father walk out on his family when he was only a young boy, abandoning both his mother and himself to a lonely life in Gotham City. Later relocating to Lowell, Nebraska, Victor's mother slowly lost her grip on reality, ending up sick and wheelchair-bound. While still a boy, Victor pushed her out onto a frozen lake, shoving her wheelchair into a hole in the ice. When his mother tried to climb out, Victor pushed her under the water again, preferring her to be frozen and "cured" of all her ills, than to go on suffering. She would not be discovered until the following spring.

As he matured, Victor carried with him his obsession for cold. He became a doctor in the field of cryogenics, and found work at Wayne Tower Laboratories. Meeting Bruce Wayne when Wayne returned from his travels abroad (during his training to become Batman), Fries immediately took a dislike to the young billionaire. Bruce wasn't comfortable with Victor's research into reanimating frozen bodies, and soon shut the project down. Infatuated with Nora Fields, a woman who had died in the 1960s, Fries began referring to her as his wife, and refused to let Wayne take away his prized subject. Victor threw a chair at Bruce when confronted, causing a lab accident that required Fries to wear a refrigerated suit, his body no longer able to function in normal temperatures. Armed with freezing technology and a vendetta against Bruce Wayne, Victor adopted the name Mr. Freeze and began a murderous campaign against Gotham City. **MM**

MELTING THE ICE
When Mr. Freeze joined a mass breakout of Arkham Asylum's most dangerous inmates, Batman used thermal gloves to make short work of the cold-blooded criminal.

ON THE RECORD

When he debuted in 1959, Mr. Freeze was a renegade scientist-turned-criminal named Mr. Zero. Intended as a one-off villain, he returned in the late 1960s bearing his current moniker, Mr. Freeze.

Over the years, Mr. Freeze was a minor Batman rogue, making a few guest appearances until the 1980s, which featured a number of costume changes. It wasn't until after *Crisis on Infinite Earths* and thanks in part to *Batman: The Animated Series*, that Victor Fries was given his origin story. The tragic tale helped elevate him to the status of one of Batman's greatest foes.

ZERO TOLERANCE
In his first appearance Mr. Freeze was Mr. Zero, a scientist whose ice gun backfired, spilling a freezing solution over him. It meant he could now only survive in sub-zero temperatures.

CLASSIC STORIES

***Batman* (Vol. 1) #121 (Feb. 1959)** Called Mr. Zero in this first appearance, Mr. Freeze begins a series of robberies using a gun capable of projecting both cold and heat.

***Detective Comics* (Vol. 1) #373 (Mar. 1968)** Mr. Zero returns to plague Batman in a new costume and with a new name: Mr. Freeze.

***Batman: Mr. Freeze* #1 (May 1997)** Mr. Freeze is provided a fitting modern origin story, inspired in part by the acclaimed *Batman: The Animated Series.*

***Batman Annual* (Vol. 1) #1 (Jul. 2012)** Post-Flashpoint, Mr. Freeze's origin is updated, revealing that Victor's "wife" Nora was never his wife at all.

MISTER MIRACLE

DATA

DEBUT *Mister Miracle* (Vol. 1) #1 **(Mar.-Apr. 1971)**
CURRENT VERSION *Earth 2* #11 **(Jun. 2013)**
REAL NAME Scott
BASE New Genesis
HEIGHT 6ft **WEIGHT** 185 lbs **EYES** Brown **HAIR** Brown
POWERS/ABILITIES Superhuman mental and physical attributes of the New Gods; master escapologist; access to advanced New God technology, including Aero-Discs (enable flight and can be used as weapons) and a sentient Mother Box (provides healing, data, and generates Boom Tubes for transportation).
ALLIES Shilo Norman, Big Barda, Fury, Mister Terrific, the Justice League
ENEMIES Darkseid, Bedlam, Steppenwolf, Kanto, Granny Goodness
AFFILIATIONS New Gods of New Genesis

ESCAPING GRAVITY
His Aero-Discs allow Scott to take to the skies, providing essential mobility for this freedom fighter.

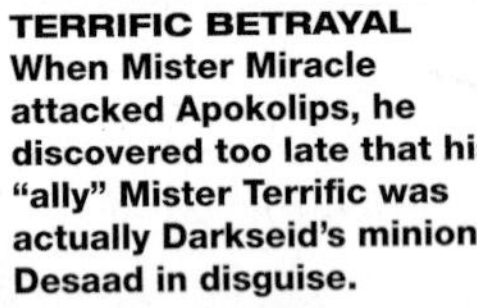

TERRIFIC BETRAYAL
When Mister Miracle attacked Apokolips, he discovered too late that his "ally" Mister Terrific was actually Darkseid's minion Desaad in disguise.

ON THE RUN
He may have escaped from Apokolips, but Mister Miracle soon discovered that Darkseid and his evil minions would stop at nothing to get him back.

Born a New God in utopian New Genesis, Scott was raised as a slave on the grim planet of Apokolips. However, he refused to let his spirit be broken, escaping to become Mister Miracle—a symbol of freedom and sworn enemy of Apokolips's evil ruler, Darkseid.

Scott was born the son of Highfather, ruler of the New God city of New Genesis. When Scott was seven years old, Highfather and the tyrannical Darkseid of Apokolips exchanged heirs as part of a peace agreement, and Scott was imprisoned in the Apokolips slave pits. He eventually escaped and joined the anti-Darkseid underground, falling in love with Big Barda, a renegade member of Darkseid's Female Furies. Scott and Barda fled to Earth-2, where Scott met retired escapologist Shilo Norman. He gave Scott his old stage name of "Mister Miracle" along with a garish costume, which Scott upgraded using New God technology.

When Apokolips attacked Earth-2, Mister Miracle and Big Barda launched a stealth assault on the Mobius chamber at the core of Apokolips, where Darkseid was trapped in stasis. Following Big Barda's advice to use Boom Spheres to defeat Darkseid, Scott merely released the villain, and was easily defeated. Big Barda had betrayed him. Mister Miracle was imprisoned and tormented in the Pits of Apokolips, but later freed by Darkseid's former soldier, Fury. Darkseid conquered Earth-2, but the heroism of Mister Miracle and his allies helped many inhabitants escape. Mister Miracle then intervened when Earth-0 was attacked by Darkseid. The overlord was slain in the conflict, and in the aftermath Scott was reunited and reconciled with his beloved Big Barda. **SW**

ON THE RECORD

The first Mister Miracle series introduced Scott Free and his wife Big Barda, showing his meeting with Thaddeus Brown, who gave him the Mister Miracle identity. Scott helped protect Earth as a solo hero and with the Justice League International, and on retiring gave his name and costume to his protégé Shilo Norman.

Scott became the vessel for the Anti-Life Equation, a power desired by Darkseid, and when Big Barda was murdered, he used it to hunt down the killer. Scott perished in the Death of the New Gods, but he and Barda returned after the Final Crisis.

BREAK A LEG
On Earth, Mister Miracle went into showbiz, wowing the crowds with terrifying acts of escape-artistry.

CLASSIC STORIES

***Mister Miracle* (Vol. 1) #9 (Jul.-Aug. 1972)** Tells the thrilling story of how Scott Free meets Himon of New Genesis—and escapes from Apokolips and Darkseid.

***Seven Soldiers: Mister Miracle* #1-4 (Nov. 2005-May 2006)** Shilo Norman escapes death after taking on the identity of Mister Miracle from Scott Free.

***Earth 2: World's End* #9-11 (Feb. 2015)** Mister Miracle faces betrayal and defeat when he ventures into the heart of Apokolips to confront Darkseid.

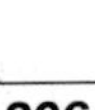

MISTER TERRIFIC

DEBUT *Sensation Comics* (Vol. 1) #1 **(Jan. 1942)** (as Terry Sloane); *Spectre* (Vol. 3) #54 **(Jun. 1997)** (as Michael Holt)
CURRENT VERSION *Mister Terrific* #1 **(Nov. 2011)**
REAL NAME Michael Holt
BASE Holt Industries, Los Angeles
HEIGHT 6ft 2in **WEIGHT** 215 lbs **EYES** Brown **HAIR** Black
POWERS/ABILITIES Olympic gold medalist decathlete; genius and inventor; hovering T-Spheres can detonate, project holograms, gather data, and allow flight; T-Suit provides protection; T-Mask guards against electronic detection.
ALLIES Power Girl
ENEMIES Brainstorm, the Kryl, the Tomorrow Thief, Digitus

Michael Holt is one of the most intelligent people in the world, with multiple doctorates to his name, his own company (Holt Industries), and a half-billion-dollar fortune. However, his life was changed forever when his beloved wife Paula died in a traffic accident. Michael was devastated and considering suicide when a mysterious figure claiming to be his son from an alternate reality emerged from a dimensional rift and told him that he had a duty to change the world.

To this end, Michael set up a non-profit organization dedicated to advancing science, and began his Super Hero career as Mister Terrific. Operating out of his ninth-dimensional T-Sanctuary and wielding his multifunction T-Spheres, he fought a number of high-tech villains. However, while investigating a quantum tunneling experiment, he was sucked into a quantum portal and ended up in the alternate reality of Earth-2. After being captured briefly by mastermind Terry Sloan, Mister Terrific joined a new super-team: the Justice Society. When Earth-2 was subsequently destroyed by the overwhelming forces of Apokolips, Michael escaped, but back on his world, Darkseid's minion Desaad had assumed Michael Holt's identity for his own nefarious purposes. **SW**

ON THE RECORD

The pre-Flashpoint Michael Holt lost his wife in an accident and was visited by the Spectre, who told him about the Golden Age Mister Terrific (Terry Sloane). This inspired Holt to become a Super Hero and continue the Mister Terrific legacy. He became the chairman of the Justice Society of America and developed a friendly rivalry with Batman. In an ironic twist, the post-Flashpoint Michael Holt was captured by Earth-2's Mister Terrific, Terry Sloan, when he was stranded in that reality.

OLD SCHOOL
The original Mister Terrific, Terry Sloane, demonstrated how crime fighting was done back in the Golden Age.

MISTER ZSASZ

DEBUT *Shadow of the Bat* #1 **(Jun. 1992)**
CURRENT VERSION *Batman* (Vol. 2) #1 **(Nov. 2011)**
NAME Victor Zsasz
BASE Gotham City
HEIGHT 5ft 8in **WEIGHT** 150 lbs **EYES** Brown **HAIR** Brown
POWERS/ABILITIES High intelligence; great physical strength and resilience; psychotically vicious and unpredictable, making him a deadly opponent in hand-to-hand combat.
ALLIES Emperor Penguin
ENEMIES Batman, the Penguin, the Batman Family, the Joker
AFFILIATIONS Arkham Asylum

Mister Zsasz is one of Gotham City's most ruthless serial killers. Zsasz's descent into madness began after his parents died—he gambled away their fortune at the Penguin's Iceberg Casino, and when the money ran out, the Penguin suggested he should go and kill himself. As Zsasz was about to do just that, he was attacked by a knife-wielding madman. Zsasz dispatched his assailant and experienced an epiphany: life was meaningless, but killing made everything make sense. He then embarked on a murder spree, slaying hundreds of victims and making a record of each kill with another cut on his body.

Zsasz was captured by Batman and imprisoned in Arkham Asylum, but escaped several times. He was dosed with a fear-inhibiting drug by Two-Face and battled Batgirl in the Narrows, and during the Time of the Joker he was briefly transformed into a Man-Bat by Emperor Penguin. When the Arkham War broke out, Zsasz joined the asylum inmates in their battle against Blackgate Penitentiary. Zsasz was suspected of carrying out a series of gruesome murders at the new Arkham Manor asylum, but he had actually been imprisoned and tortured by the real perpetrator: the Joker. **SW**

ON THE RECORD

In his pre-Flashpoint debut, Zsasz was a patient at Arkham Asylum who used a secret passage to escape by night and continue his murder spree. This forced Batman to enter the asylum undercover as an inmate in order to track him down. Zsasz was a member of the Secret Society of Super-Villains, and later joined the Black Mask's gang, setting up a horrific underground fighting club where children were forced to fight to the death.

DEADLY OBSESSION
When Alfred survived an attack by Zsasz, the serial killer became obsessed with finishing off Bruce Wayne's manservant, until he was ultimately defeated by Batman.

M

MIZOGUCHI, MAPS

DEBUT *Gotham Academy* (Vol. 1) #1 (Oct. 2014)
REAL NAME Mia Mizoguchi
BASE Gotham City
HEIGHT 4ft 6in
EYES Brown **HAIR** Brown
POWERS/ABILITIES Brilliant intellect and problem-solving ability; obsessive compulsion with ferreting out secrets; accomplished artist, skilled designer, and cartographer.
ENEMIES Headmaster Hammer, Eric Jorgensen, Heathcliff, Lucy

Mia "Maps" Mizoguchi loves solving puzzles. On starting at prestigious, spooky-looking Gotham Academy, she soon stumbled upon a genuine mystery featuring ghost sightings and strange symbols. There was even a black-magic cult and a vampire-like young man-bat hanging around the school.

Another tantalizing enigma was her new best friend—and her brother's ex-girlfriend—Olive Silverlock. She shared Maps' hunger for answers and didn't mock her habit of drawing maps to help sort out problems.

With mean-girl Pomeline Fritch, Maps and Olive rooted out a monster with hidden links to Arkham Asylum. They haven't yet determined Batman's connection to the school but it's high on the agenda of their new Gotham Detective Club. **WW**

MOCKINGBIRD

DEBUT *Secret Six* (Vol. 1) #1 (Apr.–May 1968)
CURRENT VERSION *Secret Six* (Vol. 4) #1 (Feb. 2015)
REAL NAMES Edward Nygma, Lex Luthor, Amanda Waller, Carlo di Rienzi, August Durant
POWERS/ABILITIES Fierce intellect; extreme duplicity; ruthless drive.
AFFILIATIONS Secret Six, Project Mockingbird

Mockingbird is the designation used by a series of master manipulators. Each of these has at various times controlled—through blackmail and subterfuge—teams of operatives codenamed the Secret Six. The first Mockingbird was August Durant. He covertly provided information and equipment necessary for the Secret Six to remove many global threats and "untouchable" criminals.

The latest Mockingbird was Edward Nygma, the infamous Riddler. For a year, he held captive and tortured six superhuman outcasts before allowing them to escape. He believed that one of them had purloined a gem he keenly wanted to woo another man's wife. None of his dupes knew their tormentor's identity or that their liberty and new undercover lives were facets of his elaborate scheme to find the culprit and retrieve his prize. **WW**

MONARCH

DEBUT *Armageddon 2001* (Vol. 1) #1 (May 1991)
REAL NAME Hank Hall
BASE Mobile
HEIGHT 6ft 1in **WEIGHT** 197 lbs
EYES Red **HAIR** Brown
POWERS/ABILITIES Advanced technologies and sophisticated warsuit provide superhuman strength and durability, energy-projection, teleportation, time-stream manipulation, and travel between parallel universes.
ENEMIES Waverider, Linear Men, Captain Atom

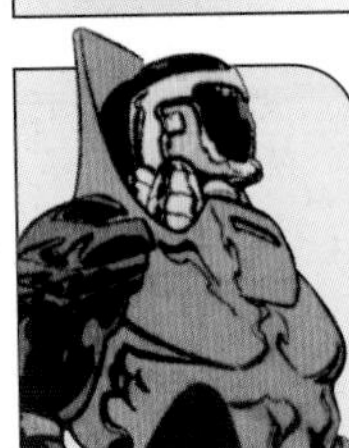

Monarch is a living paradox, created by the unchecked use of time travel. An alternate Earth's ultimate tyrant, he was originally Hank Hall, the hero Hawk, driven mad by the death of his partner Dove. With stolen technology, Hall carved out an empire as Monarch. His rule was threatened by time-traveling rebel Waverider, who visited the time of Monarch's creation to end his domination before it began. The attempt left Hall/Monarch lost in time: locked in combat with Captain Atom. During the battle, Hall emerged as the chronal chaos-bringer Extant, while Atom became locked inside Hall's warsuit as an even more diabolical Monarch.

Even after Atom escaped the suit, he was unsure whether another Monarch might be lurking in some fold of time/space to begin anew his campaign of terror. **WW**

MONSIEUR MALLAH

DEBUT *Doom Patrol* (Vol. 1) #86 (Mar. 1964)
CURRENT VERSION *Teen Titans* (Vol. 5) #20 (Jul. 2016)
HEIGHT 6ft 3in **WEIGHT** 345 lbs
EYES Brown **HAIR** Brown
POWERS/ABILITIES Super-genius intellect; enhanced strength, speed, and reflexes; altered vocal cords enable speech; skilled engineer.
ALLIES The Brain
ENEMIES Doom Patrol, Teen Titans, Gorilla Grodd
AFFILIATIONS Brotherhood of Evil

Monsieur Mallah is an African gorilla whose intelligence and physical attributes have been boosted by radical medical treatments. These procedures were carried out by an unknown French scientist who was later murdered. The artificially evolved great ape saved his creator by surgically transplanting the scientist's brain into a life-support system named the Brain.

Mallah acted as the Brain's hands, enhancing its cerebral support unit and creating a true Master of Evil. Together they built an international crime organization that terrorized the world, clashing with numerous Super Hero groups, most especially Niles Caulder's Doom Patrol

Educated, erudite and urbane, Mallah adores his creator with a passion matched only by his ferocity when angered. **WW**

MON-EL

DEBUT *Superboy* (Vol. 1) #89 (Jun. 1961)
CURRENT VERSION *Legion of Super-Heroes* (Vol. 7) #1 (Nov. 2011)
REAL NAME Lar Gand
BASE 31st-century Metropolis
HEIGHT 6ft 2in **WEIGHT** 200 lbs **EYES** Blue **HAIR** Black
POWERS/ABILITIES Highly skilled tactician; brilliant scientist and historian; passionate explorer; super-strength, speed, flight, invulnerability and enhanced senses, fueled by exposure to solar radiation from a yellow sun.
ALLIES Superman, Supergirl, Krypto, Brainiac 5, Shadow Lass
ENEMIES Dominators, Dark Circle, Time Trapper
AFFILIATIONS Legion of Super-Heroes, Science Police, United Planets Council, Wanderers, Green Lantern Corps, Justice League of America

Lar Gand fled his fanatically insular and xenophobic birthworld Daxam to become a wanderer and child of the cosmos. Arriving on Earth—on a Monday—he was befriended by Superman, who mistakenly assumed Lar to be a member of his own family and dubbed him Mon-El. Though possessing all the extraordinary powers of a Kryptonian under Earth's yellow sun, Daxamites are lethally sensitive to the element lead. Following a brief but intense period of heroic endeavor, Mon-El finally succumbed to incurable toxic shock from long exposure to the ubiquitous mineral.

Superman saved Mon-El's life by projecting him into the Phantom Zone. There he stayed, an intangible, invisible observer of the material world. A thousand years later, Mon-El was saved when Saturn Girl and Brainiac 5 perfected a serum that cured his lead poisoning, enabling him to emerge once more into the physical world. Mon-El became one of the most effective leaders of the Legion of Super-Heroes, combining 10 centuries of keenly-observed experience with immense drive. His years of helplessness only strengthened his resolve to defeat tyrants and monsters. **WW**

ON THE RECORD

Lar Gand received a major makeover in the 1990s. With Superman's continuity drastically revised, Mon-El became Valor, a Daxamite atoning for his father's role in a Dominator-led invasion of Earth. Rescuing thousands of humans transformed by metagene experiments, Valor transported them to uninhabited planets: homeworlds for the empowered races that would comprise the United Planets a millennium later. Valor later inspired the formation of the Legion of Super-Heroes.

MESSIAH MOMENT
Valor was a cosmic legend: a super-savior seeding a string of barrier worlds between Earth and the aggressive Dominion empire with super-powered metahumans.

MONSTER SOCIETY OF EVIL

DEBUT *Captain Marvel Adventures* (Vol. 1) #22 (Mar. 1943)
CURRENT VERSION *The Multiversity: Thunderworld Adventures* (Vol. 1) #1 (Feb. 2015)
UNIVERSE Earth-5
KEY MEMBERS/POWERS **Mister Mind** (Venusian worm); **Dr. Sivana** (criminal genius); **Captain Nazi** (fascist superman); **Crocodile Man** (humanoid crocodile); **I.B.A.C.** (mystic composite of famous tyrants' powers); **Evil Eye** (giant with hypnotic gaze); **Mister Atom** (giant nuclear robot).

The Monster Society of Evil was created by hyper-intelligent Venusian worm Mister Mind during World War II to fuel global conquest, a goal opposed by the heroic Captain Marvel. The Society was composed of spies from the Axis powers, metahuman or mystical villains, and malevolent monsters.

The Monster Society's greatest folly was never attacking as a group but always opting to tackle opponents individually. Even in later years when mad scientist Dr. Sivana took charge, it proved impossible to get the monsters to cooperate with one other.

Although the membership has fluctuated over the years, the aims of the Monster Society have remained constant: to crush the Marvel Family, terrorize decent folk, and cause as much carnage and wanton destruction as possible. **WW**

MONGUL

DEBUT *DC Comics Presents* (Vol. 1) #27 **(Nov. 1980)**
CURRENT VERSION *Green Lantern* (Vol. 5) #23.2 **(Nov. 2013)**
BASE Warworld, mobile
HEIGHT 8ft **WEIGHT** 1,125 lbs **EYES** Red **HAIR** Bald
POWERS/ABILITIES Super-strength, speed, stamina and invulnerability, fire vision, ruthless pragmatism, strategic genius; able to instill great fear and wield multiple Yellow Lantern Corps power rings.
ALLIES Toymaster, Cyborg-Superman
ENEMIES Superman, Batman, Wonder Woman, Green Lantern Corps, Arkillo
AFFILIATIONS Warworld, Jochi, Sinestro Corps

One of the universe's most feared tyrants, Mongul is a violent alien brute with an insatiable hunger for battle and domination. Descended from a line of killer kings, Mongul revels in death and destruction, and appears never happier than when completely crushing an opponent. A remorseless, terrifying foe, he once usurped control of the Sinestro Corps before being defeated by a coalition of Green and Yellow Lanterns.

However, belying his bestial appearance and monstrous deeds, Mongul also possesses a shrewd and calculating mind. He knows that true power comes from governance and control, not threats and bloodletting. Whether through his monumental intergalactic engine of death, Warworld, or subtler machinations, such as enslaving Earth's population through computer games, Mongul craves subjects to rule over.

Mongul is the ultimate battle-hardened pragmatist and utterly ruthless. He is perfectly willing to switch sides in the middle of a conflict and sacrifice his allies if he thinks that doing so will save his life or secure some temporary tactical advantage. After his first defeat by Superman, his son Jochi restored the shattered Warworld to full destructive functionality and began a new reign of terror. However, when Jochi displayed mercy to his subjects, Mongul killed him without hesitation. Self preservation was the key to Mongul making a deal with Wonder Woman and Superman to utilize his Warworld to defeat another world conqueror, Brainiac. **WW**

ON THE RECORD

The original Mongul looked like an unreasoning brute but schemed like a Machiavelli. His most insidious assault involved giving Superman everything the Man of Steel could ever want.

Utilizing a parasitic plant which paralyzed its victims while feeding them dreams of their deepest desires come true, Mongul attempted to plunder the Fortress of Solitude. However, he had not bargained on for the spirited resistance of Superman's friends and allies.

IMPLANTING UTOPIA
Once Mongul's Black Mercy plant had overwhelmed Superman, the villain was free to employ savage force against Batman, Robin, and Wonder Woman.

MONITOR

DEBUT *New Teen Titans* (Vol. 1) #21 **(Jul. 1982)** (the Monitor); *Countdown to Final Crisis* #21 **(Oct. 6, 2007)** (Nix Uotan)
CURRENT VERSION *The Multiversity* (Vol. 1) #1 **(Oct. 2014)**
UNIVERSE All of them **REAL NAME** Nix Uotan
BASE Hall of Heroes in the Orrery of Worlds
HEIGHT Variable **WEIGHT** Variable **EYES** White **HAIR** Black
POWERS/ABILITIES Immortality; genius-level intellect; cosmic awareness; dimensional manipulation; energy projection; transformation and size alteration; psionics; teleportation; matter manipulation; superhuman strength, speed, durability, and flight.
ALLIES Mr. Stubbs, Harbinger, Operation Justice Battalion
ENEMIES The Gentry, the Empty Hand
AFFILIATIONS All heroes in every universe of the known multiverse

When Maltusian renegade Krona meddled with creation, existence, and time, cleaving reality into a multiverse, two beings spontaneously formed. The Monitor oversaw all positive-matter realities, while his opposite, an Anti-Monitor inimical to all life, schemed from an antimatter universe. After billions of years, a sequence of cosmic crises reconfigured reality once more, eventually resulting in 52 separate universes, with Earth at the heart of every one and a single Monitor overseeing each. When war broke out between the Monitors, existence was once again overwritten. In the end only one Monitor was left standing to safeguard all the realities that remained.

At the heart of the region between universes resides Nix Uotan, safeguarding the integrity of those dimensions that comprise the Orrery of Worlds. His duty is to protect life in each universe from dangers beyond the interdimensional border-region, the Bleed, or creatures from any reality who might escape their proper place to threaten other planes of existence. When not living as a normal teenager, Nix Uotan the Superjudge ventures forth to stop incursions from the unknown and repair damage to fragile realities. **WW**

ON THE RECORD

The Monitor first appeared as an enigmatic, technologically advanced power-broker, providing weaponry and super-villains to criminals needing specific Super Hero countermeasures. From his hidden satellite he watched and appraised the world's metahumans, and not until landmark series *Crisis on Infinite Earths* did his real motivations emerge. This almighty immortal was gathering soldiers to help battle a mysterious enemy eradicating all time, space, and alternate dimensions with an irresistible wave of antimatter.

WATCH AND LEARN
In his war to save all life, the Monitor chose his tools carefully for power, intelligence, courage, and, especially, determination.

M

MONTOYA, RENEE

DATA

DEBUT *Batman* (Vol. 1) #475 **(Mar. 1992)**
CURRENT VERSION *Convergence Justice League* #2 **(Jul. 2015)**
BASE Gotham City
HEIGHT 5ft 8in **WEIGHT** 144 lbs **EYES** Brown **HAIR** Black
POWERS/ABILITIES Very intelligent with strong set of ethics; natural team player; expertise in police procedure and knowledge of the law; skilled detective; excellent physical condition; natural fighter trained by the G.C.P.D. and Harvey Bullock.
ALLIES Harvey Dent, James Gordon, Batman, Batwoman
ENEMIES Detective Nancy Yip, Joker's Daughter
AFFILIATIONS Gotham City Police Department

ONE GOOD COP
Montoya is a no-nonsense cop and one of the few people on the G.C.P.D. that can put the opinionated Harvey Bullock in his place.

A KEEN EYE
Montoya is a natural detective and not afraid of a fight. These traits make her very well suited to the rough-and-tumble policing of Gotham City.

Renee Montoya is a good and honorable cop, an invaluable asset to the Gotham City Police Department. By nature a very private person, she only reveals her true feelings and emotions to her closest friends and confidants, which usually means her partner on the police force. Lately, that partner has been the boisterous Harvey Bullock, the perfect slovenly foil to Renee's organized and procedural personality.

A shining star during her training to become an officer in the Gotham City Police Department (G.C.P.D.), Renee Montoya was given Harvey Bullock as her superior and drill instructor. Renee's tenacity, quick wits, and drive soon earned her high marks, and her willingness to get involved in a brawl or two—as well as her extremely low tolerance for nonsense—put her in the good graces of Harvey Bullock. This jaded cop on the G.C.P.D. had become one of the few good apples in a rotten bunch of police officers. The G.C.P.D. was known for its corruption, but officers like Bullock and James Gordon—another rising star—were starting to turn the department around and make it a force for good in a city of shadows. Renee Montoya wanted nothing more than to be as honorable as the men she looked up to, but she wouldn't get the chance for several years.

After graduating, Renee opted not to stay in Gotham City. She moved to Blüdhaven, another city known for its high crime rate, and stayed there for a few years before heading back to Gotham City and reuniting with her old mentor. She and Harvey picked up right where they left off, but this time as peers, and she has once again become a valuable asset to the G.C.P.D., despite her short tenure with the department. She helped fight against the Joker's Daughter as part of the Batman Task Force that supported Jim Gordon's tenure as Batman, and she also aided the department in rooting out Bullock's corrupt fellow officer and then girlfriend, Nancy Yip. **MM**

CLASSIC STORIES

***Gotham Central* #6–10 (Jun.–Oct. 2003)** Renee is revealed to be gay, while struggling to fight off the attentions of the obsessed Two-Face.

***Gotham Central* #38–40 (Feb.–Apr. 2006)** Montoya quits the Gotham City Police force after nearly killing a corrupt police officer, Jimmy Corrigan.

***52* #1–52 (May 2006–May 2007)** Montoya goes from life as an alcoholic to one as a Super Hero, stepping up to the plate as the new Question.

***Detective Comics* (Vol. 2) #41–44 (Aug.–Nov. 2015)** Montoya returns to the G.C.P.D. to join the Batman Task Force after years of serving on the Blüdhaven police force.

ON THE RECORD

Before the Flashpoint miniseries, Montoya began her career as an assistant to Commissioner James Gordon. The role came in advance of her part as a cop cast member in *Batman: The Animated Series* and Renee soon became a G.C.P.D. regular in the comics as Harvey Bullock's long-suffering partner.

She became a Super Hero in her own right during the maxiseries *52*, when her relationship with Batwoman Kate Kane was showcased, as was her protégé relationship with Vic Sage, the original Question. When the Question died, Renee adopted his mantle, becoming the first female incarnation of that hero.

ANOTHER QUESTION
As the new Question, Renee Montoya adopted Vic Sage's signature blank face mask, which adhered to the skin when exposed to a chemical gas.

MONSTRESS

DEBUT *Legion of Super-Heroes* (Vol. 4) #82 (Jul. 1996)
CURRENT VERSION *Justice League United* #8 (Mar. 2015)
REAL NAME Candi Pyponte-LeParc III
BASE U.P. Space, 31st century
HEIGHT 6ft 4in **WEIGHT** 265 lbs
EYES Orange **HAIR** Orange
POWERS/ABILITIES Superhuman strength, endurance, durability; wears Legion flight ring.
ALLIES Star Boy, Atom'X, Insect Queen
ENEMIES Element Lad, the Blight

Monstress is not only a powerhouse member of the Legion of Super-Heroes, she is also a fashionista and a caring, gentle soul. While she has recently reemerged in post-Flashpoint continuity, Monstress is most associated with Earth-247, where she hailed from the planet Xanthu.

Monstress originally served on the Uncanny Amazers, sporting a green color. During that time, she worked with another future Legionnaire, Star Boy, as well as heroes Atom'X and the Insect Queen. She later turned orange. As a member of the Legion who joined during a recruitment drive, Monstress served her team well until she was killed by Element Lad during a time when she became lost in space with several Legionnaire teammates. **MM**

MORDRU

DEBUT *Adventure Comics* (Vol. 1) #369 (Jun. 1968)
CURRENT VERSION *Demon Knights* #1 (Nov. 2011)
BASE Zerox, the Sorcerer's World
HEIGHT 7ft 6in **WEIGHT** 300 lbs
EYES Hazel **HAIR** Auburn
POWERS/ABILITIES Ultimate-level magic-wielder; superhuman strength; immortal.
ENEMIES Nabu, Doctor Fate, JSA, the Spectre

Mordru is the most powerful mage in creation: an immortal energy being who inhabits a material host to remain in the physical world. As a Lord of Chaos, he shaped the beliefs of lesser life-forms in eons past before pursuing his goal: the sole domination of all existence. To this end, he seeks sorcerous artifacts, such as the Amulet of Fate, to add to his arcane arsenal.

Mordru's only weakness is a paralyzing fear of entombment. Many battles have been lost because opponents buried him alive or trapped him in confined spaces. Thus he has preferred to dominate through physical force: employing his Sons of Anubis cult in the 21st century and interstellar armies in the 31st. Overconfidence has proved to be his undoing, whether fighting Nabu, Lord of Order, or mortal foes like the JSA and Legion of Super-Heroes. **WW**

MORGAN, JENNIFER

DEBUT *Warlord* (Vol. 1) #38 (Oct. 1980)
BASE Skartaris
HEIGHT 5ft 6in **WEIGHT** 122 lbs
EYES Blue **HAIR** White
POWERS/ABILITIES Powerful sorceress; can create magic bolts of energy, generate force-fields, teleport, and conjure images of past events.
ALLIES Warlord, Joshua Morgan
ENEMIES Ashiya, Deimos

The daughter of Lt. Col. Travis Morgan, aka Warlord—the hero of the underground world of Skartaris—Jennifer Morgan eventually followed in her father's footsteps, winding up in the otherworldly reality that he had stumbled on many years previously.

Believing her father had died in a plane crash when she was 10 years old, Jennifer was later reunited with Travis after learning about Skartaris and searching it out. There she was taught the ways of sorcery by a witch named Ashiya, before learning of the sorceress's ill intentions. She battled Ashiya and eventually defeated her with the use of her newly developed magical skills. As a result, she became known as Lady Jennifer, the supreme sorceress of Skartaris. Despite being close to her, Warlord felt uncomfortable with his daughter's magic up until he died. **MM**

MULTIPLEX

DEBUT *Firestorm* (Vol. 1) #1 (Mar. 1978)
CURRENT VERSION *Justice League* (Vol. 2) #13 (Dec. 2012)
REAL NAME Dalton Black
HEIGHT 6ft **WEIGHT** 188 lbs
EYES Blue **HAIR** Black
POWERS/ABILITIES Capable hand-to-hand combatant; able to duplicate his form.
ALLIES Killer Frost, Plastique, Hyena, Typhoon
ENEMIES Firestorm, Green Arrow, Midnighter
AFFILIATIONS The Secret Society

Dalton Black was the assistant of Professor Martin Stein, the scientist who created Firestorm. Before Stein could fire Black for trying to sell his secrets, Black used Stein's machinery, unwittingly unleashing a surge of energy that left him with the ability to multiply his form. Dalton became the criminal Multiplex and tried to hijack a shipment of high-end electronics in Seattle. Green Arrow took out his duplicates, but Multiplex himself escaped.

After teaming up with other villains to fight Firestorm, Multiplex served as hired muscle for a criminal named Mr. Rohmer. When the Super Hero Midnighter interrogated Rohmer to locate technology stolen from the God Garden satellite, Rohmer ordered Black to fight the violent vigilante—a battle that Multiplex didn't walk away from. **MM**

MOONRIDER

DEBUT *Forever People* #1 (Feb.–Mar. 1971)
CURRENT VERSION *Infinity Man and the Forever People* #1 (Aug. 2014)
REAL NAME Mark Moonrider
BASE New Genesis; Venice Beach, California
HEIGHT 5ft 11in **WEIGHT** 169 lbs
EYES Blue **HAIR** Black
POWERS/ABILITIES "Megaton touch" can cause explosions; skilled combatant.
ALLIES Infinity Man
ENEMIES Darkseid, Mantis, Femmes Fatales

Mark Moonrider was a resident of the planet New Genesis when he first traveled to Earth. There he was partnered with his friend Dreamer Beautiful, who wished to complete an assignment to help advance mankind. The pair was joined by fellow New Genesis natives Vykin Baldaur and Vykin's sister Serafina. On Earth, the group met up with another New God, Big Bear, and set up camp in Venice Beach, California, with the help of Big Bear's communal reconstruction bio engine.

Moonrider soon joined the Super Hero team the Forever People, facing villains from New Genesis' rival planet Apokolips, including Mantis and the Femmes Fatales. The Forever People discovered they could also switch places with an entity called the Infinity Man, a mysterious and powerful being whose true motives remain unknown. **MM**

MORGAINE LE FEY

DEBUT *Batman* #36 (Aug.–Sep. 1946)
CURRENT VERSION *Demon Knights* #11 (Sep. 2012)
REAL NAME Also known as Morgan le Fay
HEIGHT 5ft 10in **WEIGHT** 148 lbs
EYES Blue **HAIR** Black
POWERS/ABILITIES Sorceress; can fly, create illusions, and generate force blasts.
ALLIES Nocturna, Man O'War, Absinthe, Scatter
ENEMIES The Demon, the Unknowns, Aquaman, the Others

A sorceress hailing from the time of Camelot and King Arthur, Morgaine le Fey presented a dire threat to mankind, and was opposed by The Demon (aka Etrigan). In the modern era, Morgaine was incensed that humans were slowly destroying their own planet. She tried to steal the Atlantean helmet of the hero Vostok-X to escape Earth, only to have the item reject her. With Aquaman and the Super Hero team the Others on her trail to retrieve the helmet, Morgaine revealed herself in a battle that ended abruptly with her vanishing in a flash of light.

Morgaine resurfaced with a new scheme to alter the very fabric of reality. She was defeated by the Unknowns, a new group of vigilantes led by Batwoman and including Morgaine's old foe, Etrigan. **MM**

MOVEMENT, THE

DEBUT *The Movement* #1 (Jul. 2013)
BASE Coral City
MEMBERS/POWERS **Virtue** Team leader, can "ride" and manipulate emotions; **Katharsis** Artificial wings to enable flight, and combat skills; **Mouse** Empathy and communication with rats; **Tremor** Can generate vibrations strong enough to create earthquakes; **Vengeance Moth** Becomes a glowing green moth to enable flight and energy projection; **Burden** Metamorphosis and levitation.
ENEMIES James Cannon, Coral City Police Department, the Graveyard Faction

In the troubled town of Coral City, a group of renegade teenagers decided to make a positive change in the world and started the Movement. Setting up camp in a former sweatshop, the Movement's mission included rescuing misunderstood youth—such as troubled teenager Burden—from the police, as well as exposing corrupt police officers.

Finding an enemy in James Cannon, who ran Coral City through various corrupt enterprises, team member Katharsis confronted him while on the trail of a serial killer—who turned out to be Cannon's own son, Terry. As the Movement gained greater influence in other cities, including Metropolis, the team battled the Graveyard Faction. They then tracked down Terry and helped to end his reign of terror. **MM**

MURMUR

DEBUT *The Flash: Iron Heights* #1 (Aug. 2001)
REAL NAME Dr. Michael Christian Amar
BASE Keystone City; Central City
HEIGHT 5ft 8in **WEIGHT** 155 lbs
EYES Brown **HAIR** Black
POWERS/ABILITIES Skilled surgeon with an impressive knowledge of medical science; unpredictable and unstable killer.
ALLIES Girder, Magenta, Mirror Master
ENEMIES Flash (Wally West)

Formerly a highly respected surgeon, Dr. Michael Christian Amar was well known in both Central City and Keystone City. However, in his spare time, he also stalked the streets as the costumed serial killer called Murmur, nicknamed by the local papers due to his uncontrollable tendency to mutter. Murmur was finally caught by the Keystone police, identified by his speech impediment.

Not one to make the same mistake twice, Murmur cut out his own tongue and stitched his lips together in a sick display of his mental instability. He then gained even more notoriety when he instigated a massive breakout in the infamous Iron Heights penitentiary, and later went on to join the ranks of Flash's Rogues. Murmur has also fought the Secret Six, though he hasn't been seen in recent years. **MM**

N.O.W.H.E.R.E.

DEBUT *Superboy* (Vol. 6) #1 (Nov. 2011)
NOTABLE MEMBERS/POWERS Harvest (leader): Futuristic weapons, flight; **Centerhall**: Body of psionic energy; **Director Templar**: Body contains vicious parasites; **Omen**: Precognitive telepath; **Leash**: Energy whips, psionic powers; **Grunge**: Acquires properties of matter; **Misbelief**: Illusionist; **Psykill**: Cyborg; **Warblade**: Creates blades from body; **Ridge**: Superhuman; **Crush**: Shapeshifter; **Fuji**: Body of cosmic energy.
ENEMIES Superboy, Teen Titans, Legion Lost

N.O.W.H.E.R.E. was a secret organization created by Harvest, a mysterious figure with access to 31st-century technology. Its objective was to control the next generation of metahumans, and its underground base was called the Colony.

Metahuman test subjects were forced to battle to the death in a process called the Culling. The winners were inducted into the Ravagers, N.O.W.H.E.R.E.'s elite strike force. One of N.O.W.H.E.R.E.'s most ambitious projects was the creation of Superboy (Kon-El), a half-Kryptonian, half-human clone. He escaped and allied with the Teen Titans to destroy the Colony. Harvest built a new Colony in Africa but he was killed and his facility destroyed in a battle with the Teen Titans, possibly spelling the end of N.O.W.H.E.R.E. **SW**

NABU

DEBUT *More Fun Comics* #67 (May 1941)
CURRENT VERSION *Doctor Fate* (Vol. 4) #1 (Aug. 2015)
BASE The Helmet of Fate
EYES Brown **HAIR** Bald
POWERS/ABILITIES Through Helmet of Fate, can communicate with Khalid Nassour and show him visions; can also make the Helmet fly and access computers.
ALLIES Thoth, Khalid Nassour (Doctor fate)
ENEMIES Anubis

Born in Egypt two thousand years ago, Nabu was a priest of Thoth the Wise. When Nabu died, his spirit was chosen to inhabit Thoth's golden helmet, to guide those who would wear it and take on the role of Doctor Fate.

In the 21st century, the goddess Bastet chose Egyptian-American med student Khalid Nassour to wear the helmet, and Nabu persuaded the skeptical young man to become Doctor Fate and serve the will of Thoth by healing the world. Nabu provided guidance as Khalid learned to use the elemental powers of Fate to battle Anubis, God of the Dead. Yet Nabu knew that Khalid had to find his own path to wisdom. He was called away from the helmet, though Khalid later bumped into his spirit guide at the Mont Saint-Michel abbey in Normandy. **SW**

NECRO, NICK

DEBUT *Justice League Dark* #12 (Oct. 2012)
REAL NAME Nicholas Edgar Nolan
BASE Hell
EYES Blue **HAIR** Black
POWERS/ABILITIES Master sorcerer with vast occult knowledge and great power.
ENEMIES Cult of the Cold Flame, Justice League Dark

Nick Necro was one of New York's most successful sorcerers, and was dating the glamorous young magician Zatanna Zatara when he was approached by John Constantine, who begged him for instruction. Necro refused, but when Constantine saved him from a Cult of the Cold Flame assassin, he relented. Necro taught Zatanna and Constantine magic, and together they formed a formidable coven to battle the Cult.

While Nick became obsessed with finding the all-powerful Books of Magic, Zatanna cheated on him with John. Nick lured the pair into a trap, but was dragged to Hell when a ritual went wrong. Necro was summoned from Hell by Felix Faust to help him find the Books of Magic and he again clashed with Zatanna and Constantine, now a part of Justice League Dark. When the Crime Syndicate invaded Earth-0, Necro helped run their occult Thaumaton Project, but he was killed by John Constantine. **SW**

NEGATIVE MAN

DEBUT *My Greatest Adventure* #80 (Jun. 1963)
CURRENT VERSION *Justice League* (Vol. 2) #30 (Jul. 2014)
REAL NAME Larry Trainor
HEIGHT 5ft 10in **WEIGHT** 180 lbs
POWERS/ABILITIES Releases a powerful negative-energy being from his body, but will die if it does not return within 60 seconds.
ENEMIES Justice League

Airline pilot Larry Trainor's life changed when his plane crashed. Larry had no memory of what happened, but Dr. Niles Caulder, aka the Chief, told him that he had been exposed to a toxin that made him so radioactive that the doctors treating him had died of cancer. The Chief claimed to have swathed his body in lead-lined bandages to contain the radiation. He also told Trainor that he was now host to a negative-energy being that endowed him with superpowers.

Feeling that he owed the Chief his life, Trainor joined his Doom Patrol as Negative Man. The Chief sent his team to apprehend Jessica Cruz and acquire her Green Lantern power ring but, during a faceoff with the Justice League, Larry and the Doom Patrol helped endangered civilians instead of grabbing Cruz, proving that they were not totally under the Chief's thumb. **SW**

NATU, SORANIK

DEBUT *Green Lantern Corps: Recharge* #1 (Nov. 2005)
CURRENT VERSION *Green Lantern Corps Annual* (Vol. 3) #1 (Mar. 2013)
BASE Korugar
EYES Purple (yellow when Yellow Lantern) **HAIR** Black
POWERS/ABILITIES Expert neurosurgeon; as a Yellow Lantern can create constructs of yellow energy by tapping into the emotion of fear.
ALLIES Sinestro, Kyle Rayner
ENEMIES Spider Guild
AFFILIATIONS Sinestro Corps; formerly Green Lantern Corps

FATHER KNOWS BEST
Sinestro used threats and blackmail to make Natu accept a Yellow Lantern power ring.

Soranik Natu was a neurosurgeon from the planet Korugar in Sector 1417. The Korugarians despised the Green Lantern Corps because Sinestro, the first Korugarian to join the Corps, had set himself up as absolute ruler of the planet. However, when a Green Lantern power ring chose Natu as its next bearer, she reluctantly accepted and worked alongside other Lanterns to fight the threat of the star-extinguishing Spider Guild. She later returned to Korugar, becoming a unifying force on the planet after seemingly defeating Sinestro.

When Sinestro returned as the head of the fear-wielding Sinestro Corps, Natu joined the Green Lanterns to fight him and began a relationship with Green Lantern Kyle Rayner. In the aftermath of the war, Sinestro revealed that he was Natu's father, and that he was proud of her for uniting the planet.

During the Blackest Night event, Natu saw Kyle sacrifice himself to defend his fellow Green Lanterns, but their ally Star Sapphire (Miri Raim) tapped into Natu's love for Kyle to bring him back to life. Sinestro was determined to have Natu by his side, and when the Korigarians were almost wiped out by the First Lantern Volthoom, Sinestro promised to save the survivors—providing Natu joined him and became a member of the Sinestro Corps. **SW**

NEGATIVE WOMAN

DEBUT *Showcase* #94 (Aug.–Sep. 1977)
CURRENT VERSION *Justice League* (Vol. 2) #24 (Dec. 2013)
REAL NAME Valentina Vostok
EYES Blue **HAIR** Blonde
POWERS/ABILITIES Can release a negative-energy being from her body.

Soviet pilot Lt. Col. Valentina Vostok defected to the US in an experimental long-range fighter but crashed into the sea near Codsville, Maine, where the Doom Patrol had seemingly been wiped out. The energy-being that had inhabited the former Negative Man (Larry Trainor) entered her body and transformed her into a powerful negative-energy form. She joined a new Doom Patrol led by Celsius and had a relationship with fellow member Tempest, but when her power turned her radioactive, they had to break up. Larry Trainor returned from the dead and the negative-energy returned to him.

Valentina left to work in the espionage community and was promoted to the role of White Queen in Checkmate. She died during the Final Crisis, but returned in undead form during Blackest Night to attack Negative Man. Post-Flashpoint, Valentina was a member of the Doom Patrol, but was killed by Atomica and Johnny Quick, when the Crime Syndicate invaded Earth-0. **SW**

NEKRON

DEBUT *Tales of the Green Lantern Corps* #2 **(Jun. 1981)**
BASE The Land of the Unliving
EYES Black **HAIR** None
POWERS/ABILITIES Immensely powerful avatar of death; can kill with a touch, reanimate the dead as Black Lanterns, fire blasts of dark lightning, and warp reality; draws strength from death.
ALLIES Black Hand
ENEMIES The Guardians of Oa, heroes of Earth, the Lantern Corps
AFFILIATIONS Black Lantern Corps

Nekron is an ancient embodiment of darkness, created by the universe itself to oppose life. He is the ruler of the limbo-like Dead Zone that holds souls awaiting judgment, though he, too, is trapped there. When the Guardians of Oa banished the renegade Oan, Krona, he ended up in Nekron's realm, and his presence there created a rift leading to the mortal universe. Nekron was then able to see into Earth's reality and became completely obsessed with destroying it.

During the Blackest Night, he released Black Lantern power rings into the universe. These sought out heroes and villains who were dead or had returned from death and transformed them into gruesome Black Lanterns. Heroes suddenly found themselves battling friends, enemies, and lovers, who had returned from the grave to make war on the living. Using the dark energies released by the Black Lanterns' slaughter, Nekron's henchman, Black Hand, summoned his master into Earth's universe. Nekron then tried to destroy the Entity, the embodiment of all life, but was defeated when Hal Jordan bonded with the Entity to become a White Lantern.

Nekron briefly possessed Swamp Thing during the Brightest Day, and Hal Jordan summoned him to defeat the threat of Volthoom, the First Lantern. **SW**

NEMESIS

DEBUT *The Brave and the Bold* (Vol. 1) #166 (Sep. 1980)
CURRENT VERSION *Grayson* #9 (Aug. 2015)
REAL NAME Thomas Andrew Tresser
BASE Dept. Metahuman Affairs, Washington, DC
HEIGHT 5ft 10in **WEIGHT** 170 lbs
EYES Blue **HAIR** Blond
ABILITIES Master of disguise; espionage expert; gadgets include bugs, concussion gun, and paralysis pistol.
ENEMIES The Council, Jihad

Tom Tresser and his brother Chris were operatives in a secret government agency. When his brother was brainwashed by the Council, Tom took the codename Nemesis and set out to bring down the Council using his spying skills. After seemingly dying in a helicopter crash, he secretly joined the Suicide Squad before being seconded to the Shadow Fighters to battle the dark being Eclipso. Nemesis then joined the Department of Metahuman Affairs. During the war between the Amazons and the US he went renegade to help Wonder Woman and was honored with Amazon citizenship.

After the Final Crisis event, Tom was forcibly recruited into the Global Peace Agency, and ended up questioning his own sanity after being sent on a series of mind-bending missions. **SW**

NERON

DEBUT *Underworld Unleashed* #1 **(Nov. 1995)**
CURRENT VERSION *Green Lantern* (Vol. 5) #20 **(Jul. 2013)**
BASE Club Midnight
HEIGHT 7ft 2in **WEIGHT** 285 lbs **EYES** Blue **HAIR** Blond
POWERS/ABILITIES Master of sorcery, with superhumanly powerful demonic physiology; can breathe flesh-melting flames.
ALLIES Mister Rumor
ENEMIES John Constantine, Papa Midnite
AFFILIATIONS The demons of Hell

The minor demon Neron capitalized on strife in Hell to become the ruler of its largest arch-dukedom. He specialized in making Faustian pacts with mortals to gain their souls, the damned currency of Hell. He frequently appeared on Earth to make deals, and took control of Papa Midnite's occult nightclub in New York City. With help from his business partner Mister Rumor, he also began buying up New York real estate.

Neron's plan was to turn New York City into a massive mystic bazaar where humans could purchase magic in return for their souls. Papa Midnite enlisted John Constantine in an attempt to get the Midnight Club back, but they were discovered and imprisoned in Hell. Neron then led his demonic host to take over New York, but John Constantine escaped from Hell to oppose him. **SW**

ON THE RECORD

Neron first appeared during *Underworld Unleashed* as the demon who offered heroes and villains great power in return for their souls. Dozens of villains accepted and raised merry Hell before they were damned. When Neron was tricked and trapped in the Tower of Fate by the Elongated Man, a war broke out in the infernal regions, with Blaze and Satanus attempting to take over. When Neron broke free and returned to Hell, he was beheaded by Satanus.

DECAPITATED DEMON
After being trapped in the Tower of Fate, Neron paid the gruesome price for losing a civil war in Hell.

NEUTRON

DEBUT *Action Comics* (Vol. 1) #525 (Nov. 1981)
CURRENT VERSION *Justice League* (Vol. 2) #35 (Dec. 2014)
REAL NAME Nathaniel Tryon
POWERS/ABILITIES Can project blasts of radiation from hands.
ENEMIES Lex Luthor, Justice League

Nathaniel Tryon was a security guard at the Metropolis Power Plant, but a meltdown transformed his body into living nuclear energy, requiring him to wear a containment suit. As Neutron, he used his new radiation-blast power to kill those responsible for the accident. He then became a mercenary, accepting a contract to kill Lex Luthor.

Neutron was defeated by Aquaman, but one of his blasts ruptured the unit holding Luthor's experimental Amazo virus. The virus spread across the city, and also infected Neutron, reacting with his radioactive form to create virulent cancers. He was also briefly possessed by the virus' collective consciousness before Luthor deployed a vaccine. Neutron was left powerless and cancer-ridden, but Luthor would not let him die—after all, he knew the identity of the person who wanted Luthor dead.

Pre-Flashpoint, Neutron was a petty thug turned radioactive super-villain, who held a particular grudge against Superman. **SW**

NEW GODS, THE

DATA

DEBUT *The New Gods* (Vol. 1) #1 **(Feb.-Mar. 1971)**
CURRENT VERSION *Justice League* (Vol. 2) #3 **(Jan. 2012)**
BASE New Genesis/Apokolips
MEMBERS/POWERS
New Genesis:
HIGHFATHER Charisma, link to Source, can inhibit others' powers; **ORION** Warrior, A4 platform allows flight, teleportation, energy blasts; **MISTER MIRACLE** Escape artist, access to teleportation, flight; **HIMON** Genius, expert in New Genesis science and culture; **LIGHTRAY** Flight, absorbs solar energies that he emits as energy blasts; **BEKKA** Commands absolute adoration and loyalty from others; **HYALT** Burns with cosmic fire, armor serves as mobile forge; **METRON** Mobius Chair generates force-fields, allows space and time travel, and provides instant knowledge; **MALHEDRON** Wields powerful energy hammer; **THE FOREVER PEOPLE** Together they summon the mighty Infinity Man; **INFINITY MAN** Flight, teleportation, telepathy, energy blasts, healing.
Apokolips:
DARKSEID Omega Effect energies, including deadly Omega Beams; **DESAAD** Expert torturer, illusionist, turns beings into Parademons; **KALIBAK** Strong, tough, keen sense of smell; **BEDLAM** Psychic energy being, can control multiple android bodies; **BIG BARDA** Warrior and leader, wears Apokoliptian Aegis armor; **LOWEST** Ruthless overseer and disciplinarian; **RECTIFIER** Robotic engineer with control over Apokolips' systems.

The New Gods are an ancient race who possess prodigious power and superior technology. Each god is equal in might to one of Earth's Super Heroes. They are also a race locked in perpetual war. The New Gods of New Genesis, ruled by Highfather, are devoted to peace and order, and are in costant bitter conflict with their warlike brethren on hellish Apokolips, ruled over by the mighty tyrant Darkseid.

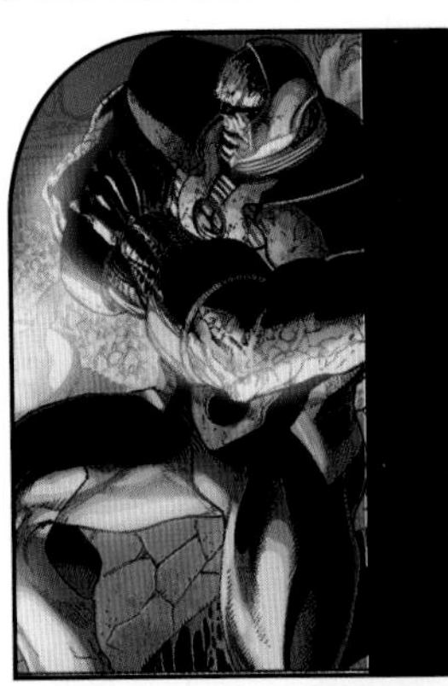

The story of the New Gods begins in the distant past, on an untouchable, unreachable plane separate from the rest of the universe. The primordial planet of Genesis was ruled over by the wild and capricious Old Gods, who reveled in chaos, while the lesser beings that would become known as the New Gods scrabbled out a living amid that chaos. One of these lesser beings, named Uxas, bore a burning hatred against the Old Gods and led a war against them. The Old Gods were slain, but then another war broke out between the evil Uxas, who would later become known as Darkseid, and his good brother Izaya, who would become Highfather. After a long war that devastated Genesis, Izaya finally triumphed. His people built the Utopian city of New Genesis that floats above their planet, while Darkseid and his minions created the hellish world of Apokolips. The latter then set out across the universe in search of new worlds to conquer. Peace was established between the two when Highfather and Darkseid exchanged sons: Orion was raised on New Genesis, while Scot (who would become Mister Miracle) was imprisoned in the Slave Pits of Apokolips.

GENESIS WAR
Uxas and Izaya led the New Gods in a war of annihilation against the chaotic Old Gods. The conflict ended when Uxas slew his own father, Yuga Khan.

Cruelty and oppression are a way of life on Apokolips. At the bottom of the hierarchy are the Lowlies and Plague Dogs, who work in the Slave Camps or are fed into the Fire Pits that fuel Apokolips' forges and munitions factories. Above them are the dreaded Parademons, genetically engineered monsters bred only for war, and above the Parademons are the various minions of Darkseid, who compete for the favor of their master. Among them are the general Steppenwolf, the interrogator Desaad, and Darkseid's warrior son, Kalibak.

Apokolips travels through space, conquering and consuming worlds—Earth-2 was one world that suffered this fate. The heroes of Earth-2 repulsed one attack by the forces of Apokolips, led by Steppenwolf, but five years later, Darkseid himself commanded his hordes as he sought to destroy the planet and plunder its energies. Despite fierce resistance from Super Hero team the Wonders of the World and the World Army, the defenders were ultimately overwhelmed by Darkseid's forces and their world was consumed by Apokolips. Several of the inhabitants escaped, however, and set out to establish new lives elsewhere in the multiverse. Later, when Darkseid led an attack on Earth-0, he was killed by the Anti-Monitor and the Black Racer, leading to a power vacuum on Apokolips.

AT A GLANCE...

Smart technology
New Gods technology is so advanced that many of its devices are actually sentient—from Orion's A4 transport harness to Kirby, the living house belonging to the Forever People. But perhaps the most incredible device of all is the Mother Box. This bonds to its owner and serves as a multifunction tool, a data source, and medical kit, evolving to suit its user's needs.

Boom Tubes
Boom Tubes are the preferred method of transportation for the New Gods. These interdimensional tunnels can be generated by Mother Boxes or other devices, and allow their users to cross between planets and even realities with ease. The name comes from the distinctive sound they make when activated.

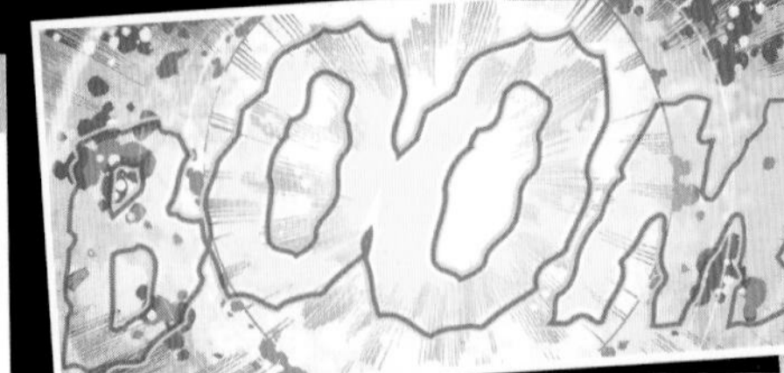

CLASSIC STORIES

***The Forever People* (Vol. 1) #1-11 (Feb.-Mar. 1971-Oct.-Nov. 1972)**
This gleefully psychedelic story introduced the freewheeling adventures of New God youngsters the Forever People, chronicling their journey to Earth and beyond

***Mister Miracle* (Vol. 1) #1-18 (Mar.-Apr. 1971-Feb.-Mar. 1974)**
This series tells the story of perhaps the most famous New Gods hero, the escape artist Mister Miracle, and his formidable warrior wife, Big Barda.

***DC Graphic Novel* #4 (Mar. 1985)**
"The Hunger Dogs" relates the story of the oppressed underclass of Apokolips, who rise up and overthrow their evil master, Darkseid.

NEW GOD VS. NEW GOD
While the forces of Apokolips launched their attack on Earth-2, a conflict between New Gods was breaking out within Apokolips itself. Mister Miracle and the renegade warrior women Fury and Big Barda attacked the Court of Apokolips, and Miracle journeyed to the Mobius Chamber at the core of the planet to confront his adoptive "father," Darkseid. In this conflict, the evil overlord emerged triumphant, though Mister Miracle escaped to continue his struggle against Apokolips.

FATHER VS. SON
Mister Miracle battles Darkseid, who once condemned him to the slave camps of Apokolips.

NOW AND FOREVER PEOPLE
When young New Genesis citizens Serafina, Vykin, Mark Moonrider, and Dreamer Beautiful went on a field trip to the primitive planet of Earth, they encountered a mysterious being—the Infinity Man. Under his guidance, they realized they had to rebel against both the benign authority of Highfather and the oppression of Darkseid to bring freedom to the multiverse.

The New Gods of New Genesis are more peaceful in their interactions with other worlds, believing that their purpose is to help guide lesser races away from darkness and to spread peace and harmony. Its heroes journey out to fight evil on other worlds, and it has set up research projects on other worlds to extend the benefits of its advanced science. However, the inhabitants of New Genesis are not immune to pride and arrogance: while searching for the secret of the fabled Life Equation, Highfather inadvertently triggered a devastating war with the various Lantern Corps that left his city in ruins. **SW**

"Do not dare to question my motives, human. We New Gods have worked for ages beyond your imagination to protect the multiverse."

HIGHFATHER

GODHEAD
Highfather of New Genesis was obsessed with unlocking the power of the legendary Life Equation, which he believed would allow him to permanently defeat Darkseid. His advisor Metron told him the secret might lie in the power rings of the Lantern Corps. Highfather dispatched warriors to steal the rings, plotting to use their energies to transform the universe's mortal races into powerful, obedient warriors able to withstand Darkseid. But he underestimated the might of the unified Lantern Corps, who proved that mortals could be a match for the New Gods.

GODS VS. MORTALS
Highfather tried to claim the power of the Lantern Corps, provoking a war that shook New Genesis to its foundations.

GODS ABOVE
The New Gods have undergone many deaths, rebirths, and transformations over the millennia. Although Highfather, Darkseid, Orion, and Mister Miracle have remained much the same, Desaad and Kanto have changed appearance radically, the boyish Serafin has become Vykin's sister Serafina, and some—including Takion and Virman Vundabar—appear to no longer exist.

ON THE RECORD

In the pre-Flashpoint universe, Apokolips and New Genesis were planets created when the primal world of Genesis was split. In this reality, Uxas was not related to Izaya, but was an heir to the throne of Apokolips. He provoked a war with New Genesis by having Izaya's wife killed.

Genesis of the New Gods
The first New Gods series laid the cornerstone for an entire cosmic mythology. The main plotline involved Orion battling Darkseid's insidious plots to take over Earth. The series set up the long-running conflict between the hero and his estranged father and introduced other significant characters, notably Orion's comrade Lightray and the Black Racer, the New Gods' incarnation of death. However, the epic story also provided background for the entire New Gods saga, chronicling the creation of Apokolips and New Genesis, the war that broke out between them following the death of Izaya's wife Avia, and the spiritual journey that Izaya underwent to make contact with the Source and become the peaceful Highfather.

Death of the New Gods
This story saw the era of Apokolips and New Genesis come to an end. When the New Gods were hunted down by an unknown killer, Superman went on a quest to find out why, and made a disturbing discovery: the killer was the Source itself, the primal life force of the universe. The Source was eliminating the New Gods to end the conflict between New Genesis and Apokolips so that they could be joined to create a new, perfect Fifth World.

COSMIC TRAGEDY
The Man of Steel was devastated by the destruction of an entire race—including many of his friends and allies.

Final Crisis
The fallout from the Death of the New Gods led directly to the reality-threatening Final Crisis. Though the New Gods were slain, their spirits found new homes on Earth in human or other hosts. Darkseid (in the guise of human gangster Boss Dark Side) and his minions plotted to eliminate the world's heroes and conquer Earth with the power of the Anti-Life Equation, sending the entire multiverse spiraling toward destruction. Darkseid seemingly killed Batman in an epic confrontation, but Superman destroyed Darkseid's essence by singing a single note.

EVIL INFLUENCE
During Final Crisis, the Anti-Life Equation transformed Wonder Woman and other Earth heroines into Female Furies serving Darkseid.

NEW GUARDIANS

DEBUT *Green Lanterns: New Guardians* #1 **(Nov. 2011)**
CURRENT MEMBERS Kyle Rayner (Green Lantern); **Munk** (Indigo Tribe); **Saint Walker** (Blue Lantern Corps); **Atrocitus** (Red Lantern Corps); **Larfleeze** (Orange Lantern Corps); **Arkillo** (Sinestro Corps); **Carol Ferris** (Star Sapphire Corps)
ENEMIES Invictus

The New Guardians came into being when Green Lantern Kyle Rayner found himself in possession of rings from other Corps, which had left their previous owners for him. Not knowing why, Rayner became the subject of a galactic manhunt as various Corps tried to retrieve their rings. When the Guardians attacked Rayner, assuming he had stolen the rings, he was helped by Saint Walker and Larfleeze, and even his pursuers, who united to defend him. Later, Larfleeze revealed that the Archangel Invictus caused the rings' migration, and they, as the New Guardians, had to defeat him before he destroyed the entire Vega System.

The team fought and defeated Invictus, after which they discovered that the exiled Guardian Sayd was really responsible for the ring incident, because she believed Rayner was the only Lantern who could harness all seven aspects of the Emotional Spectrum—and only by doing so could they beat Invictus.

An earlier team of New Guardians was chosen from several nations as representatives of the human race and enhanced to be the next stage in humankind's evolution. **AI**

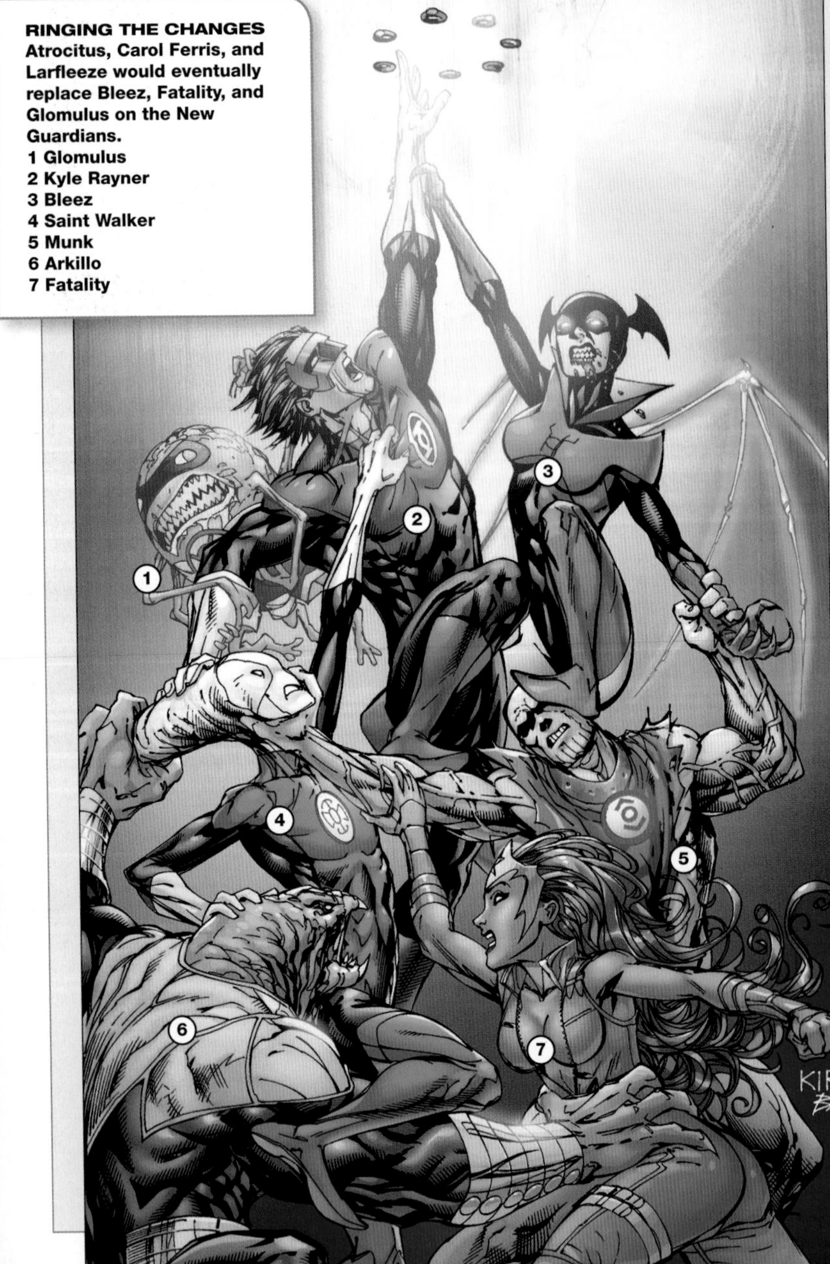

RINGING THE CHANGES
Atrocitus, Carol Ferris, and Larfleeze would eventually replace Bleez, Fatality, and Glomulus on the New Guardians.
1 Glomulus
2 Kyle Rayner
3 Bleez
4 Saint Walker
5 Munk
6 Arkillo
7 Fatality

NEWSBOY LEGION

DEBUT *Star Spangled Comics* #7 (Apr. 1942)
BASE Metropolis
MEMBERS Big Words, Gabby, Scrapper, Tommy Tompkins, Walter Johnson, Famous Bobby
ALLIES Guardian, Superboy
ENEMIES Lex Luthor

The Newsboy Legion was a team of reformed juvenile delinquents. They roamed the streets of Metropolis under the watchful eye of the costumed Guardian—police officer Jim Harper—who wanted to protect the orphans from the hard life of the streets. Growing up during World War II, the Legion later formed Project Cadmus, a pioneering genetic research facility.

An early Cadmus endeavor was the cloning of Jim Harper, which granted the Guardian new life. The Cadmus facility was subsequently attacked by the Apokoliptian creature Sleez and, during Sleez's brief takeover, teenage clones of the now-adult Legion appeared, effectively recreating the original Legion and setting it up for new adventures. These included the admission of the first female Newsboy Legionnaire, Famous Bobby. **AI**

WHIZZING AROUND
The Newsboy Legion got themselves into a lot of scrapes over the years, and got out of more than a few thanks to Cadmus tech like the Whizz Wagon.

1 Guardian
2 Gabby
3 Walter "Flip" Johnson
4 Tommy Tompkins
5 Big Words
6 Scrapper

NIGHT FORCE

DEBUT *New Teen Titans* (Vol. 1) #21 (Jul. 1982)
CURRENT VERSION *Night Force* (Vol. 3) #1 (May 2012)
MEMBERS Jim Duffy, Zoe Davis, Brian Greene
BASE Washington, DC
ALLIES Baron Winter
ENEMIES Kassandra Fey

Baron Winters gathered the Night Force to fight evils he could not, due to his inability to leave Wintersgate Manor, except by traveling to other time periods. Guided by the Book of Night, he brought together police officer Jim Duffy, Zoe Davis, and Senator Brian Greene to fight the Gatherers, a shadowy group led by the seemingly ageless mystic Kassandra Fey.

The Gatherers had spent centuries breeding psychic demons, and were close to perfecting the creatures. All the while Kassandra had been siphoning Baron Winters' powers, using the peculiar nature of Wintersgate, which exists at a nexus of different times. She used Zoe Davis as a vessel, and Brian Greene as the unknowing parent of successive generations of the demonic creatures. Realizing Kassandra was manipulating them, the team fought back, and Jim Duffy killed Kassandra. Thus established, the swiftly assembled team now takes on cases for Baron Winters as his specialist occult investigation team—Night Force. **AI**

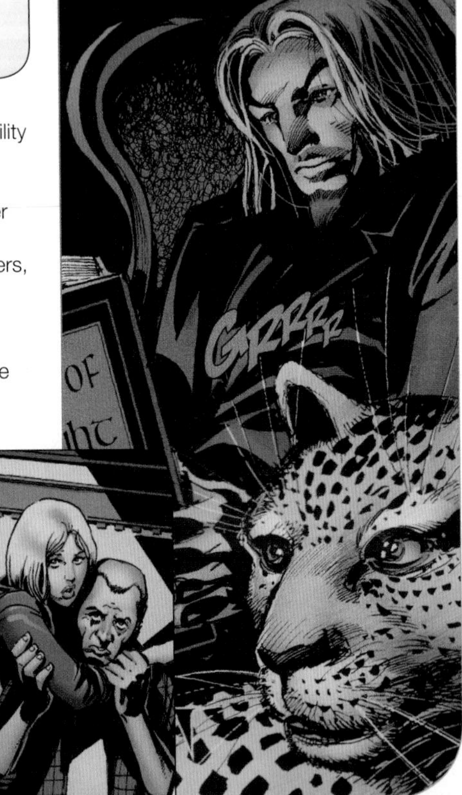

MASTERMIND
Baron Winters schemes from his chair with his pet leopard Merlin... while Jim Duffy and Zoe Davis get a crash course in the occult.

NIGHTMASTER

DEBUT *Showcase* **#82 (May 1969)**
REAL NAME James Rook
BASE New York City
HEIGHT 6ft 1in **WEIGHT** 183 lbs
EYES Blue **HAIR** Gray
POWERS/ABILITIES The sword of night detects danger, deflects energy, and compels enemies to speak the truth.
ENEMIES Pentacle, Lord Meh
AFFILIATIONS Shadowpact

Rock musician Jim Rook and his girlfriend Janet Jones were transported from a decrepit shop called Oblivion Inc. to the other-dimensional realm of Myrra. There Rook discovered he was heir to the Myrran hero Nightshade and was granted his ancestor's Sword of Night. After liberating Myrra from the tyranny of evil warlocks, Rook and Janet returned to Earth, and Nightmaster joined Shadowpact to combat mystical threats, eventually becoming the group's reluctant leader.

Later, on a devastated Myrra, Rook cured the magically afflicted Unbound, using a spell created by the Enchantress that harnessed his innate goodness. He remained to help rebuild and protect Myrra after the rest of Shadowpact departed for Earth, then returned to New York—just in time to battle Lord Meh and free the captured team. **AI**

NIGHTSHADE

DEBUT *Captain Atom* **(Vol. 1) #82 (Sep. 1966)**
REAL NAME Eve Eden
BASE Washington, DC
HEIGHT 5ft 8in **WEIGHT** 139 lbs
EYES Blue **HAIR** Black
POWERS/ABILITIES Dimensional travel via the Land of Nightshades; creation and manipulation of tangible shadows; shadow form.
ALLIES Nemesis, Enchantress
ENEMIES Gorilla Grodd, Spectre

Eve Eden's mother Maureen was Queen of the Land of the Nightshades, a mystic dimension. Maureen took Eve and her brother Larry to the Nightshade world, where Maureen was attacked by the Incubus, which abducted Larry. Eve promised her dying mother that she would rescue Larry.

She became government agent Nightshade and joined the Suicide Squad when its chief, Amanda Waller, promised that the team would help her find Larry. The Squad discovered that Larry was possessed by the Incubus, and Deadshot was forced to kill him to destroy the vile being. Nightshade then joined a group of magic-wielding heroes to fight the Spectre. Some of those heroes, including Nightshade, continued to combat mystic threats as the supernatural team Shadowpact. **AI**

NKVDEMON

DEBUT *Batman* **#445 (Mar. 1990)**
CURRENT VERSION *Aquaman and the Others* **#7 (Jan. 2015)**
REAL NAME Gregor Dosynski
HEIGHT 6ft 4in **WEIGHT** 240 lbs
EYES Red **HAIR** None
POWERS/ABILITIES Experimentally enhanced strength, stamina, and pain resistance; proficiency with firearms and hand-to-hand combat.
ENEMIES Aquaman, the Others

A protégé of the KGBeast, Gregor Dosynski was trained and enhanced as part of a secret Russian biotech project. This left him with superhuman mental toughness and pain resistance, as well as red skin and a demonic appearance—hence his codename: NKVDemon. NKVDemon became part of the villainous team Mayhem, alongside Cheshire, Maelstrom, Stranglehold, and his mentor KGBeast.

The group battled Aquaman and the Others while trying to reactivate a Soviet-era satellite and launch its nuclear missiles at targets on Earth. Facing off against Prisoner of War, NKVDemon ended up on the losing side of the battle. The Others were able to divert the missile—with the help of Vostok-X, one of the KGBeast's former associates now aligned with the Others. Vostok-X redirected it toward his Moon base and apparently died in the blast. The NKVDemon presumably escaped, perhaps to write the next chapter in his violent history with Aquaman. **MM**

FACE OF EVIL
The use of various experimental steroids turned NKVDemon into a powerful combatant, but also gave him a truly terrifying appearance.

NIGHTMARE NURSE

DEBUT *Phantom Stranger* **(Vol. 4) #8 (Jul. 2013)**
REAL NAME Asa
HEIGHT 5ft 9in **WEIGHT** 130 lbs
EYES Red **HAIR** Red
POWERS/ABILITIES Unsurpassed spiritual healing abilities, especially for serious supernatural ailments; known to create energy constructs.
ALLIES: Deadman, John Constantine
ENEMIES Blight, Crime Syndicate of America

Even among her decidedly strange colleagues in the Justice League Dark, Nightmare Nurse stood out as a real mystery. Zatanna summoned her after the Question stabbed the Phantom Stranger, knowing only her powers could heal this supernatural wound. Nightmare Nurse, irritated at the summons, was nevertheless bound to help because the gods Apollo and Panacea themselves had once made her swear the Hippocratic Oath.

After helping the Stranger by retrieving his soul from the land of Non, Nightmare Nurse stayed with Justice League Dark through the Trinity War and the team's battle against the alien Blight. She and John Constantine have a romantic past that did not end happily for either of them. In addition to her healing prowess, Nightmare Nurse was able to create a clone of the Swamp Thing, though it only survived for a short time. **AI**

NIMROD

DEBUT *Shadow of the Bat* **#7 (Dec. 1992)**
REAL NAME Dean Hunter
BASE Gotham City
HEIGHT 6ft 2in **WEIGHT** 195 lbs
EYES Blue **HAIR** Blond
POWERS/ABILITIES Military camouflage suit can turn invisible; infrared targeting goggles; gauntlet-mounted mini gun.
ENEMIES Batman, Robin

Photographer Dean Hunter got into a fight with the villain Chancer in Texas, during which Hunter's girlfriend was killed. Chancer escaped and Hunter was accused of murder. He escaped from prison and stole an experimental military suit, vowing to hunt Chancer down. The chase led him to Gotham City, where, as Nimrod, he initially interfered with Batman's pursuit of Chancer, who had joined the Misfits gang.

Nimrod later redeemed himself by helping Robin figure out where the Misfits were holding Batman, Commissioner Gordon, and Mayor Krol, saving their lives. Nimrod attacked the Misfits, determined to capture Chancer and get the truth out about what had happened in Texas. Batman arrived in time to help take down the gang, and both Chancer and Dean Hunter were taken to prison—but Hunter still believes he will be exonerated. **AI**

NOBODY

DEBUT *Batman and Robin* **(Vol. 2) #1 (Nov. 2011)**
REAL NAME Morgan Ducard; Maya Ducard
BASE Gotham City
HEIGHT 6ft 1in **WEIGHT** 195 lbs
EYES Brown **HAIR** None
POWERS/ABILITIES Skilled marksman and hand-to-hand combatant, expert torturer.
ENEMIES Batman, Damian Wayne

Son of the assassin Henri Ducard and the spy Felicity Strode, Morgan Ducard killed his mother when he thought she might betray Henri, and was then instructed in the family business—killing. Bruce Wayne also trained alongside Morgan under Henri Ducard's tutelage, kicking off a lifelong rivalry. Henri ordered Morgan to kill Bruce, but instead Bruce defeated Morgan, disgracing him in his father's eyes.

Vowing revenge and adopting the persona NoBody, Morgan embarked on a killing spree in Gotham City and also tried to corrupt Batman's son Damian. NoBody taunted Damian until Damian lost control and killed him. Morgan's daughter Maya, also raised to be an assassin, assumed her father's legacy as NoBody and sought revenge on Damian—but ultimately reached a wary reconciliation with him. **AI**

NORTHWIND

DEBUT *All-Star Squadron* **#25 (Sep. 1983)**
REAL NAME Norda Cantrell
HEIGHT 6ft **WEIGHT** 195 lbs
EYES Brown **HAIR** None
POWERS/ABILITIES Flight, enhanced strength and stamina, communication with birds.
ALLIES Black Adam, Atom Smasher
ENEMIES Hawkman
AFFILIATIONS Infinity, Inc.

Hybrid child of human anthropologist Fred Cantrell and a Feitherian mother, Norda Cantrell grew up in the hidden city of Feather in northern Greenland. As the godson of Hawkman Carter Hall, Norda formed a rivalry with Hawkman's son Hector, (later Doctor Fate). As an adult, Norda joined Infinity, Inc. as Northwind. After Hector Hall's death, he helped the Feitherians rebuild their home into New Feithera.

Initially possessing an avian-human hybrid form, Northwind transformed into a fully birdlike creature. Now unable to speak, he continued as a vigilante, joining with Black Adam and others in executing villains. Hawkman tore off Northwind's wings, hoping to stop him killing, but the wings grew back and Northwind helped Black Adam to take control of Kahndaq, his home country. **AI**

NIGHTWING

DATA

DEBUT *Detective Comics* (Vol. 1) # 38 **(Apr. 1940)**
CURRENT VERSION *Nightwing* (Vol. 3) # 1 **(Nov. 2011)**
REAL NAME Richard Grayson
BASE Gotham City, New York City (with Titans)
HEIGHT 5ft 10in **WEIGHT** 175 lbs **EYES** Blue **HAIR** Black
POWERS/ABILITIES Highly skilled martial artist, trained personally by Batman; expert acrobat, gymnast, and escape artist; extremely athletic and agile; highly intelligent with advanced knowledge of a variety of technologies; natural leader and strategist; weapons include Escrima sticks and has access to Batcave technology and gadgets.
ALLIES Batman, The Batman Family, Helena Bertinelli, Tim Drake
ENEMIES Prankster, Paragon, Tony Zucco
AFFILIATIONS Titans, Spyral, Batman, Inc., Teen Titans

Dick Grayson has made a name for himself over the years, and on more than one occasion. The original Robin to Bruce Wayne's Batman, Grayson later graduated to the role of Nightwing. After his identity was publicly exposed, he traded in his costume to become a superspy for the covert organization Spyral. Throughout his valiant life, Grayson has proven himself to be one of the most resilient and brilliant crime fighters in the world and a natural leader. His charisma is as potent as his combat skills, acrobatic flair, and deductive gifts. He is a hero's hero who maintains an infectiously positive outlook despite facing much tragedy in his life.

AT A GLANCE...

Running away from the Circus
A popular acrobat and the young star of Haly's Circus' the Flying Graysons, Dick Grayson's life was turned upside down when his parents were murdered during a trapeze performance while visiting Gotham City. Dick was soon taken in by the wealthy Bruce Wayne, becoming his ward.

The first Robin
After Grayson learned that Batman and Bruce Wayne were one and the same, he began to train with the hero and then adopted the identity of the crime fighter Robin. As the youthful counterpart to the Dark Knight, Grayson set the tone for the other Robins who would later follow in his footsteps.

Enter... Nightwing
After leaving Gotham City to team up with other young heroes, Dick Grayson became Nightwing, determined to step out of Batman's shadow. His career later saw him set up camp temporarily in the city of Chicago, where he quickly discovered that vigilantes were quite unwelcome.

I Spy
After his secret identity was outed by the invading Crime Syndicate, Grayson was nearly killed by the powerful villains. He took the opportunity to fake his own death and join the spy organization Spyral.

As the juvenile star of popular circus attraction The Flying Graysons, Dick already knew the thrill of defying death at an early age. The only son of John and Mary Grayson—the senior performers in his family's high-wire act for Haly's Circus—Dick was doted on by his parents, and strived to be the best son he could be.

Tragically, Dick was destined to live a life with highs and lows comparable to the rollercoasters on Gotham City's famous Amusement Mile. Nothing struck the boy as deeply as the night when he watched his parents plummet to the ground during their renowned trapeze act. Their equipment had been sabotaged by a low-level mob enforcer named Anthony Zucco, and two of the three Flying Graysons fell to their deaths in front of a packed Gotham City crowd that included billionaire playboy Bruce Wayne.

Bruce saw something of himself in Dick, and decided to make him his ward. Driven by a thirst for justice to punish the criminals responsible for his parents' death, Dick proved every bit as bright and capable as Bruce believed him to be. To help Dick work through his pain, Bruce revealed his Batman identity to the boy, and gave him access to the Batcave beneath Wayne Manor. Dick had witnessed Zucco threatening the owner of Haly's Circus shortly before his parents' murder and, with Batman's training, soon became the young crime-busting hero Robin, taking the fight directly to crooks like Zucco.

After spending several successful years fighting crime with Batman in the field, Grayson felt the need to spread his wings for a change, working with other young heroes and eventually co-founding the original Teen Titans. Soon after, Dick set out on his own as Nightwing, adopting first a blue-and-yellow costume, and later a red-and-black uniform armored in a similar fashion to the Batsuit worn by Batman. This outfit employed similar devices to the Dark Knight's Utility Belt, including a grappling hook, plus Nightwing's personal touches, such as his weapon of choice, Escrima sticks.

LEARNING CURVE
Dick had been coached as a circus acrobat since infancy and his dogged determination to avenge his parents made him an ideal candidate for Batman's brutal training regimen.

FOREVER EVIL
Hailing from Earth-3, the Crime Syndicate—the corrupt equivalent of Earth-0's Justice League—invaded Nightwing's world with the hopes of global conquest. Nearly achieving that goal, the Syndicate kidnapped and brutalized Nightwing, revealing his secret identity to everyone. The Syndicate then hooked up Grayson to a bomb that would be triggered if he was removed from the device. Lex Luthor had to temporarily kill Dick to enable him to disarm the bomb, resuscitating Grayson with adrenaline immediately afterwards.

Presumed dead by the Super Hero community at large, Grayson opted to use that to his advantage and work deep undercover for Batman at Spyral.

EXPOSED
Nightwing's alter ego of Dick Grayson was exposed on camera by Superwoman of the Crime Syndicate, effectively ending the hero's career as Nightwing, for a time.

CLASSIC STORIES

***Star Spangled Comics* #65 (Feb. 1947)** As Robin, Dick Grayson is awarded his own solo feature, even nabbing the coveted cover spot in his debut.

***Tales of the Teen Titans* #44 (Jul. 1984)** Dick graduates from his position as Robin to become the hero Nightwing during the dramatic storyline "The Judas Contract."

***Nightwing* (Vol. 2) #1 (Oct. 1996)** Grayson sets up shop in the new town of Blüdhaven, earning his own Rogues Gallery in his first ever ongoing series.

***Robin: Year One* #s 1–4 (Dec. 2000–Mar. 2001)** Dick's past is delved into, documenting his early years as Robin and pitting him against the likes of Mad Hatter and Two-Face.

RETURN FROM THE DEAD

After Spyral's regime change, and Bruce Wayne's near death at the hands of the Joker, Dick Grayson returned to Gotham City to reveal to the Batman Family that he was indeed alive and well. While Spyral's Agent Zero believed that Grayson was indeed saying his goodbyes to his friends, Dick was secretly delivering a code to his allies, continuing to work against the agency he appeared to serve.

HIT LIST
When Grayson revealed to his friends that he was alive, most took the news well—aside from Red Hood, who was less than happy about being tricked.

When Grayson discovered that Zucco was alive and had made a new life for himself as Billy Lester—an aide to Chicago's mayor—Nightwing moved to Chicago for a time, determined to bring Zucco to justice. As fate would have it, Nightwing then had to join forces with his enemy, to battle the greater threat posed by the maniacal villain known as the Prankster. Once they had defeated the costumed criminal, Nightwing was finally able to put Zucco behind bars.

After being kidnapped by the Earth-3 villains the Crime Syndicate, Nightwing's secret identity was exposed to the entire world. His response was to fake his own death, and use the opportunity to join Spyral; a secret organization which kept tabs on the world's superhumans. Unbeknownst to his new employers, Grayson—now called Agent 37—was actually working as a mole for Batman, helping him end Spyral's corrupt regime and ushering in a new era for the agency. With that achieved, Grayson chose to stay on, forming an alliance with Spyral's new operational head, Helena Bertinelli. However, he still secretly harbored plans to dismantle the organization from the inside.

Recently, convinced he could more good as a Super Hero, Grayson resumed his Nightwing persona and returned to his embattled home town Gotham City, resolved to carve his own path while helping those he loved most in the world. **MM**

REBIRTH

TITANS TOGETHER!

With the explosive return of original junior speedster Wally West to a reformed and fragile new reality, the original Teen Titans are back! These greatest of friends and comrades are reunited and resolved to continue their original mission to make the world a better place for all. This time, however, will Titans Kid Flash, Donna Troy, Roy Harper, Garth of Atlantis, and Lilith be as willing to unquestioningly follow the orders of their conflicted, confidence-shakened field-leader Nightwing?

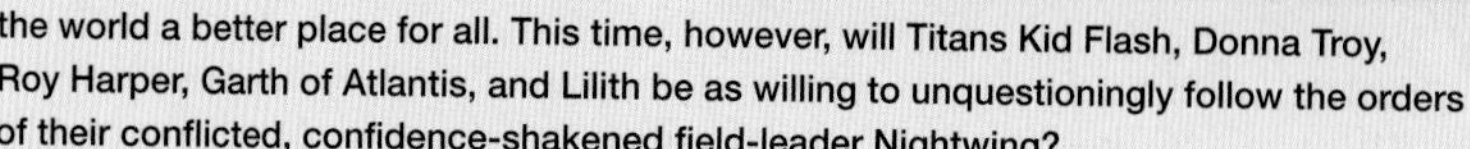

ON THE RECORD

One of the oldest and most popular characters in DC Comics' pantheon, Dick Grayson was originally introduced into Batman comics to brighten up the Dark Knight's grim world. Aging over the years along with his audience, Dick continues to uphold that upbeat and uplifting tradition, no matter what his incarnation.

Stalwart sidekick

Debuting only 11 issues after Batman, Robin quickly earned his place as an invaluable ally by proving himself in fight after fight. Unlike many characters that debuted in the Golden Age of Comics in the 1930s and 1940s, Robin's tragic backstory has changed little in the years since, despite continuity-altering events such as *Crisis on Infinite Earths*. Throughout all his incarnations, Dick Grayson was the son of circus aerialists, who was adopted by Bruce Wayne (aka Batman) after his parents were killed by gangster Anthony Zucco. After years of fighting by Batman's side, Robin eventually left the Batcave to attend college at Hudson University.

TEEN TITANS
A youthful version of the JLA, the Teen Titans featured Robin as the team's leader from the outset. In the 1980s, when the title was relaunched with new characters, Robin grew more independent than ever, living in Titan's Tower and later changing his codename to Nightwing.

Return to Gotham City

As Batman gained a new Robin in the form of young hero Jason Todd, Dick Grayson graduated to the title Nightwing, and continued his tenure with the Teen Titans, only rarely making appearances in Gotham City. Finally leaving the Titans, Nightwing headed back home to Gotham for a while, before once again setting out for new territory, becoming the protector of Gotham City's crime-ridden neighboring town of Blüdhaven. But no matter what Dick accomplished on his own, he would always return to the Batcave. In fact, when Batman was lost in time due to the machinations of the villain Darkseid, Dick valiantly stepped into his mentor's boots as the new Dark Knight, teaming up with the newest Robin, Damian Wayne.

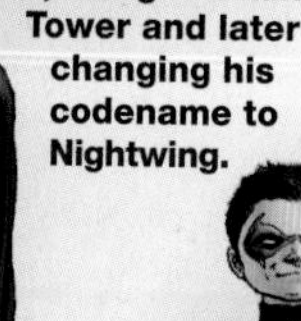

DARK AND LIGHT
Always an optimist and one to make light of nearly any situation, when Dick Grayson stepped into the role of Batman, he made quite the contrast to Damian Wayne, a brooding and troubled young Robin.

"I was Robin. I was the first."

DICK GRAYSON

NIGHT HAWK
In every widely differing aspect of his crime-fighting career, Nightwing has hunted villains and criminals like an implacable agent of justice.

OBLIVION

DEBUT *Green Lantern: New Guardians Annual* (Vol. 1) #2 (Jun. 2014)
REAL NAME Kyle Rayner (evil doppelganger)
HEIGHT Variable **WEIGHT** Variable
EYES Red **HAIR** Black
POWERS/ABILITIES Superhuman strength, shape-shifting, telepathy, illusion casting, energy projection, and construct manipulation.
ALLIES Carol Ferris
ENEMIES Kyle Rayner

Formed after Kyle Rayner broke through the Source Wall surrounding the universe, Oblivion is a dark doppelganger of Kyle created from the fear, greed, and rage inside the former Green Lantern.

Possessing his progenitor's memories, Oblivion headed for Earth and, believing himself the original, tried living Kyle's life. His twisted sensibilities soon came to the fore, and he terrorized an entire town with illusions, mutating the populace into monsters. The real Kyle Rayner found that he could not defeat his mirror image and the stalemate was only broken when Kyle's father intervened. Oblivion recovered and struck again, but realizing its origins, Kyle merged with Oblivion, reabsorbing his own base instincts. He then returned to the edge of the universe and dragged them both back beyond the Source Wall. **WW**

OBSIDIAN

DEBUT *All-Star Squadron* (Vol. 1) #25 (Sep. 1983)
CURRENT VERSION *Earth 2: World's End* (Vol. 1) #8 (Jan. 2015)
REAL NAME Todd James Rice
HEIGHT 5ft 11in **WEIGHT** 193 lbs
EYES Brown **HAIR** Brown
POWERS/ABILITIES Transformation into a shadow form, superhuman strength, flight, size alteration, shadow construct manipulation.
ALLIES Jade, Alan Scott, Damon Matthews
ENEMIES Ian Karkull, Mordru, Eclipso

Todd Rice was raised in an abusive foster home. As a teenager, he found his twin sister, Jennie-Lynn Hayden. As Jade and Obsidian, they joined with other second-generation metahumans to form Infinity Incorporated. The siblings later learned that their real father was the Emerald Crusader Alan Scott, and their mother was Rose Canton, aka the insane plant marauder Thorn.

Todd's shadowy powers stemmed from a connection to a mystical realm of darkness. He was diagnosed as schizophrenic after his mood swings saw him become both a valued member of the JSA and, briefly, one of its greatest enemies. When Jade died, his powers vanished and he retired. They eventually returned and Obsidian rejoined the JSA and later the Justice League. **WW**

ODYSSEUS

DEBUT *Deathstroke* (Vol. 2) #8 (Jun. 2012)
CURRENT VERSION *Deathstroke* (Vol. 3) #3 (Feb. 2015)
REAL NAME Charles Wilson
EYES (One) Green **HAIR** White
POWERS/ABILITIES Hypnosis, possession, and mind control; highly skilled in unarmed combat and swordsmanship.
ALLIES Lady Shiva, Bronze Tiger
ENEMIES Deathstroke the Terminator, Red Fury, I Ching, Rose Wilson, Interpol

Charles Wilson was a devious monster when he worked for the CIA. He schooled his son Slade in soldiering, making his childhood a living hell, but providing the grounding Slade required to become Deathstroke the Terminator. When Charles died, the world became a better place. Then his grandson, Jericho, was forced to resurrect him, and Charles—now known as Odysseus—used his powers and charisma to rise to the forefront of the League of Assassins. He employed his mind-control abilities to drive entire nations into bloody conflict.

Odysseus abducted his grandchildren, Jericho and Rose, needing their metahuman gifts to bolster his psionic grip and murderous army. His terror campaign was opposed by Deathstroke and his allies, resulting in Charles Wilson's second death. **WW**

OLYMPIAN

DEBUT *Super Friends* (Vol. 1) #9 (Dec. 1977)
CURRENT VERSION *Justice League International Annual* (Vol. 3) #1 (Oct. 2012)
REAL NAME Aristides Demetrios
BASE Greece
EYES Brown **HAIR** Black
POWERS/ABILITIES Superhuman strength of Herakles, flight of Zetes and Kalai, X-ray vision of Lynkeus, super-speed of Atalanta, and more.
ENEMIES Echidne, Queen Bee, Fain Y'onia, Brother Eye

Aristides Demetrios is a modern hero from an ancient culture. Wearing the legendary Golden Fleece, the Olympian can access the superhuman powers, skills, and gifts of every member of the fabled Argonauts, the army of great warriors and demi-gods who accompanied Jason on his legendary quest. Over time, the different personalities of the Fleece's power donors have sought to assert themselves, making the Olympian an unpredictable and fractious ally.

Demetrios was recruited as Greece's representative in the international Super Hero team the Global Guardians, and later served with distinction in the Ultramarine Corps. Because of his divine armaments, the Olympian has become an occasional agent of the Greek Gods—notably Zeus—and has even claimed to be one of them. **WW**

OCEAN MASTER

DEBUT *Aquaman* (Vol. 1) #29 (Sep.-Oct. 1966)
CURRENT VERSION *Aquaman* (Vol. 7) #0 (Nov. 2012)
REAL NAME Orm the First
BASE Atlantis
HEIGHT 5ft 11ins **WEIGHT** 200 lbs
EYES Black **HAIR** Black
POWERS/ABILITIES Superhuman strength, speed, endurance, and durability; water-breathing and possession of mystic artifacts that bestow control of weather patterns and massive volumes of water.
ALLIES General Rodunn
ENEMIES Aquaman, Mera, Justice League, Vulko
AFFILIATIONS Throne of Atlantis, the Trench, Belle Reve Penitentiary

Orm has no love for air-breathing humanity, but is a dutiful Atlantean warrior ruled by an adamantine code of conduct. When his half-brother, Arthur Curry, abdicated Atlantis's throne to live in the sun as Aquaman, Orm assumed the position of ruler, making every decision for the benefit of his people, despite his passionate inclinations to attack the surface-dwellers.

Thus, when hidden plotter Vulko subtly orchestrated a war between Atlantis and America, Ocean Master delighted in carrying out a punitive action against the callous, air-breathing creatures who had polluted his seas for hundreds of years. Enacting Aquaman's cautiously-prepared Atlantean War Plans, Orm launched a devastating attack on America's Eastern Seaboard, inundating Gotham City, Metropolis, and Boston. Thousands of humans drowned before Aquaman, Mera, and the Justice League finally turned back the tides.

The war ended when Orm yielded the throne to Arthur Curry, glad that the true king would sit upon the throne once again. Orm was shocked when his brother betrayed him, handing him over to the surface-dwellers to be caged like a common malefactor. Orm quickly and easily escaped Belle Reve Penitentiary, and remains vengefully at large. **WW**

ROYAL AGENDA
Orm didn't hate the sea-befouling surface-dwellers; he simply preferred not to share the planet with them.

ON THE RECORD

Originally, Ocean Master was a sub-sea plunderer who continually harassed Aquaman for reasons even he could not fathom. It took an alien invasion and the unseen intervention of Deadman to break long-standing mental blocks inside Orm's mind and reveal to the villain that he was in fact the Sea King's half-brother. Their rivalry intensified after that revelation. In every Aquaman retcon since, Ocean Master has been Arthur Curry's ultimate and signature archenemy.

BROTHERS AT ARMS
Even bonds of blood could not prevent Aquaman and Ocean Master continually battling for supremacy and survival.

OLYMPIAN GODS

DEBUT *All-Star Comics* (Vol. 1) #8 **(Dec. 1941)**
CURRENT VERSION *Wonder Woman* #1 **(Nov. 2011)**
BASE Mount Olympus
MEMBERS/ROLE Zeus: Sky-God—ruler of the Gods of Olympus; **Hera:** Goddess of Women and Marriage; **Poseidon:** God of the Seas; **Hades:** God of the Underworld; **Demeter:** Goddess of Harvest and Abundance; **Hestia:** Goddess of Home; **Aphrodite:** Goddess of Love, Beauty, Pleasure, and Procreation; **Dionysus:** God of Wine and Revelry; **Hermes:** Messenger God—patron of Thieves, Healers, and Travelers; **Apollo:** God of Light, Poetry, Music, and Herdsmen; **Ares:** God of War; **Artemis:** Goddess of the Hunt; **Athena:** Goddess of Wisdom, Warfare, Inspiration, Justice, Civilization, and Law.
ENEMIES First Born
AFFILIATIONS The Amazons, Atlanteans

The immortal Gods of Olympus are a race of powerful and capricious extra-dimensional entities who achieved fame and notoriety in mankind's distant prehistory. Attaching themselves to the tribes of what is now Greece, they began feeding off the worship of mortals.

Their exploits shaped culture and progress as the Gods championed human heroes, propagated monsters, and bred with the lesser creatures who feared and adored them. The result of centuries of dalliance was a race of powerful demi-gods, including Deimos, Enyo, Phobos, Dionysus, Eris, Hecate, Harmonia, Morpheus, Persephone, Triton, Hercules (Heracles), and Diana, the champion known as Wonder Woman.

The Gods constantly squabbled among themselves before growing bored and retreating from the forefront of human affairs. Now they interact with mortals only in secret, when their offspring threaten to cause mischief, or if some cosmic crisis forces them to act in defense of their own lives or interests. **WW**

OLYMPIAN IMMORTALS
1 Poseidon
2 Zeus
3 Hades
4 Demeter
5 Hera
6 Apollo
7 Dionysus
8 Hermes
9 Aphrodite
10 Artemis
11 Athena
12 Hestia
13 Hercules

ON THE RECORD

Olympians were most commonly seen causing problems for Wonder Woman and the Amazons of Paradise Island. In her first incarnation, Olympian goddesses sponsored the Amazon Princess' battles for America and democracy, but were repeatedly obstructed by the War God and other patriarchal troublemakers. In her 1980s incarnation, Diana's devotion to the Olympian Gods was emphasized, but they still gave her plenty of grief and torment. Her tenacity and nobility, however, led to her joining their pantheon as the Goddess of Truth.

MARS ON THE WARPATH
Wonder Woman and Aquaman tried to stop the God of War—confusingly named Mars, not Ares—from inciting conflict between the Amazons and Atlanteans.

OLSEN, JIMMY

DEBUT *Superman* (Vol. 1) #13 **(Nov.-Dec. 1941)**
CURRENT VERSION *Action Comics* (Vol. 3) #1 **(Nov. 2011)**
REAL NAME James Bartholomew Olsen
BASE Metropolis
HEIGHT 5ft 7ins **WEIGHT** 150 lbs
EYES Green **HAIR** Red
POWERS/ABILITIES Fearless and loyal; skilled photographer with keen deductive instincts and journalistic smarts; possesses a signal watch that only Superman and other metahumans can hear.
ALLIES Clark Kent, Lois Lane, Perry White, Bizarro, Ron Troupe, Steve Lombard
ENEMIES Lex Luthor, Morgan Edge, Regis Tuttle
AFFILIATIONS *Daily Planet* staff, Senator Sam Lane

James Bartholomew Olsen was one of the richest kids in America, but never wanted a single penny of his unscrupulous parents' money. He was ashamed of how his family made their fortune and, when he inherited it, promptly gave all the cash to charity.

Jimmy needed to prove his own worth to the world, and that began when he took the first official photographs of Superman, sharing this global scoop with his friend and journalistic mentor Lois Lane. The photojournalist cub-reporter quickly struck up a friendship with new *Daily Planet* reporter Clark Kent, who shared his love of computer games and cheesy B-movie science fiction films. Despite often getting on each other's nerves, they frequently shared an apartment.

Thanks to his close friendship with Clark—and, independently, with Clark's alter ego, Superman—Jimmy has witnessed and documented some of the most catastrophic events in Metropolis' and the world's history, earning the somewhat condescending nickname of "Superman's Pal." The relationship has also made him a target for the Man of Steel's enemies, such as Lex Luthor, who once kidnapped and tortured Jimmy just to get Superman's attention. After years of secrecy, Clark finally shared his true identity with Jimmy. **WW**

A FRIEND IN NEED
Jimmy Olsen is always prepared to put his life on the line for his friends, such as acting as a human shield when Superman lost his powers.

ON THE RECORD

Jimmy graduated from sidekick to comedy foil in his own title in 1954. As frequently as he proved his journalistic talents, he was often transformed in bizarre ways that made him a menace to society. Everything changed in 1970 when Jimmy emerged as a determined, two-fisted investigator, exposing secret cloning projects, New Gods, and re-imagined monsters beside a revived Newsboy Legion. Jimmy had become the *Daily Planet*'s crusading Mister Action.

TROUBLE MAGNET
In the 1960s, Jimmy's curiosity often led him into weird situations. On one occasion he became a rampaging Giant Turtle Man after testing an enlarging ray gun. As always, Superman was on hand to save the day.

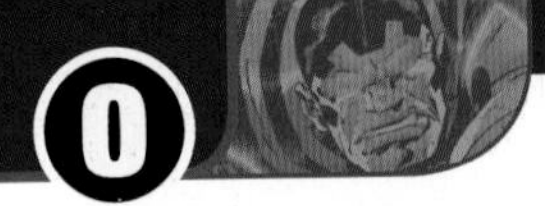

O.M.A.C.

DEBUT *O.M.A.C.* #1 (Sep.–Oct. 1974)
CURRENT VERSION *O.M.A.C.* (Vol. 4) #1 (Nov. 2011)
REAL NAME Kevin Kho
HEIGHT Variable **WEIGHT** Variable
EYES Yellow **HAIR** Blue
POWERS/ABILITIES Energy-projection; super-strong; can be teleported by Brother Eye.
ALLIES Jody Robbins, Brother Eye
ENEMIES Cadmus Industries, Checkmate, Amazing Man, Psi-Fi Man, Suicide Squad

Born in Cambodia, Kevin Kho was orphaned when his family was killed by warlords. Emigrating to the US, he studied genetics and obtained a job with Cadmus Industries. The Artificial Intelligence, Brother Eye, transformed Kho into a superpowered, techno-organic juggernaut called One-Machine Attack Construct (O.M.A.C.) and used him to plunder Cadmus' data.

Kho eventually regained control from Brother Eye while in O.M.A.C. form, but became trapped in that body. O.M.A.C. joined Justice League International, but Brother Eye took control again and betrayed the team. The Crime Syndicate then used O.M.A.C. against the Suicide Squad, until he was knocked through a portal to another dimension, where he helped Justice League United battle Nazis. **SW**

TRANSFORMED MAN
The life of conflict-scarred, OCD sufferer Kevin Kho was changed forever when Brother Eye turned him into O.M.A.C.

WORD OF POWER
By uttering the word "Omactivate," Kevin Kho becomes the virtually unstoppable O.M.A.C.

ORANGE LANTERN CORPS

DEBUT *Green Lantern* (Vol. 4) #25 (Jan. 2008)
CURRENT VERSION *Green Lantern: New Guardians* #3 (Jan. 2012)
BASE Larfleezia
MEMBERS **Larfleeze**; **Glomulus**; **Grubber**; **Gretti**; **Ceebiss**; **Clypta**; **Nat Nat**; **Blume**; **Sound Dancer**; **Warp Wrap**.
ALLIES New Guardians, Lantern Corps
ENEMIES Guardians of the Universe, Green Lanterns, Invictus, Sena the Wanderer, Third Army

Larfleeze is the bearer of the Orange Lantern Ring, which is powered by his bottomless greed—and he does not like to share. While all the other Lantern Corps are made up of multiple members, Larfleeze uses his ring to create his very own Orange Lantern Corps. The ring absorbs his defeated foes and he can summon them forth as Orange energy constructs. These helped Larfleeze to kill the angelic inhabitants of the Orrery (though he was unable to absorb one of them with his ring) and his subsequent conflict with the sole survivor, Invictus.

However, the constructs were not always obedient, and they went out of control after Larfleeze's "pet" Guardian, Sayd, tampered with his ring. Cosmic entity Sena the Wanderer then transformed seven constructs into living beings again, and they turned against Larfleeze as fully-fledged Orange Lanterns. He was briefly enslaved by them, before stripping them of their power and marooning them on a distant planet. **SW**

AGENT ORANGE
The larcenous Larfleeze would absorb his enemies' personality imprints into his power ring, then summon them as members of his Orange Lantern Corps.

OMEGA MEN

DEBUT *Green Lantern* (Vol. 2) #141 (Jun. 1981)
CURRENT VERSION *Deathstroke* (Vol. 2) #9 (Jul. 2012)
BASE Vega
KEY MEMBERS **Tigorr**: Takes beast form; **Primus**: Mastermind; **Broot**: Enhanced strength, damage-resistant hide; **Scrapps**: Proficient gunslinger; **DOC**: Reformed war robot; **Kalista**: Swordswoman; **Kyle Rayner**: White Lantern ring.
ENEMIES The Citadel, Pontifex of Changralyn

The Omega Men are fierce rebels who fought to free the planets of the Vega system from the rule of the oppressive Citadel. The motley crew included idealistic leader Primus, armor-skinned Broot, reformed war robot DOC, and Scrapps, the last survivor of the planet Voorl. When human White Lantern Kyle Rayner visited Vega, the Omega Men captured him and seemingly executed him live on film. In reality, they forced him to join their ranks.

Subsequently, they stole the Citadel Viceroy's spacecraft, "kidnapped" Kalista, Princess of the Bramins of Euphorix, (who was the group's mastermind), and stole a sacred artifact belonging to the pacifist aliens, the Changralyn. The Omega Men also revealed that the Citadel had committed genocide on Voorl to plunder its reserves of the rare mineral Stellarium. **SW**

ONOMATOPOEIA

DEBUT *Green Arrow* (Vol. 3) #12 (Mar. 2002)
BASE Gotham City
HEIGHT 5ft 11in **WEIGHT** 180 lbs
POWERS/ABILITIES Stealth; brutally effective killer with a variety of sound-based weapons.
ALLIES The Joker
ENEMIES Green Arrow, Batman, Connor Hawke
AFFILIATIONS Secret Society of Super-Villains

Onomatopoeia is a mysterious, armed, and dangerous serial killer with the strange ability to imitate the sounds around him; the last thing his victim is likely to hear is the word "BANG!" His first high-profile target was Connor Hawke (the second Green Arrow). After Connor barely survived Onomatopoeia's attack, the villain tried to kill him in his hospital bed—but was stopped by Connor's father Oliver Queen (the first Green Arrow) and Black Canary.

Onomatopoeia later joined the Secret Society of Super-Villains during the Infinite Crisis and was considered for membership of the Suicide Squad, but was rejected. He shot and almost killed Deadshot and then freed the Joker from Arkham Asylum to distract Batman, his most prized target. When that plan failed, Onomatopoeia masqueraded as the vigilante Baphomet, gaining Batman's trust before killing Bruce Wayne's lover, Silver St. Cloud. **SW**

ONYX

DEBUT *Detective Comics* (Vol. 1) #546 (Jan. 1985)
CURRENT VERSION *Green Arrow* (Vol. 5) #28 (Apr. 2014)
HEIGHT 5ft 9in **WEIGHT** 120 lbs
EYES Brown **HAIR** Black with white streak
POWERS/ABILITIES Unarmed combat.
ALLIES Komodo
ENEMIES Green Arrow, Katana, Mask Clan, Shield Clan, Spear Clan

Onyx is the leader of the Fist Clan, a sub-group of the Outsiders organization and one of four "pure" martial clans that facilitated Komodo's plot to conquer Europe. When Shado, Robert Queen, and Green Arrow attacked the Outsiders' base in Prague to disrupt their plans, Onyx ordered the Fist Clan to kill the intruders, but Katana and the Sword and Axe clans helped the archers.

During the battle, Onyx went to launch a freighter holding a payload that could devastate Seattle. Katana gave chase and they fought a savage duel on the vessel. Onyx offered mercy if Katana relinquished her sword and joined the Fist Clan. Katana replied with a lightning slash that severed Onyx's left arm at the elbow—forcing her to surrender.

Pre-Flashpoint, Onyx Adams was a League of Assassins killer, who turned her back on the League to join forces with Green Arrow, Batman, and the Birds of Prey. **SW**

ORDER OF ST. DUMAS

DEBUT *Batman: Sword of Azrael* #1 (Oct. 1992)
CURRENT VERSION *Batman and Robin Eternal* #9 (Feb. 2016)
MEMBERS/POWERS **Saint Dumas**: Leader, directly linked to Gnosis' data systems; **Azrael**: (Jean-Paul Valley) Flaming sword, incapacitates foes with a touch by uploading the Icthys algorithm into their brains.
ALLIES Mother
ENEMIES Red Robin, Red Hood, Bane

The Order of St. Dumas is a quasi-religious group dedicated to finding the truth of the universe through scientific knowledge. When Red Robin and Red Hood infiltrated the Order's church in Santa Prisca, they found that it was actually a hi-tech facility patrolled by cybernetic monks. They uncovered evidence that the Order had links to a mysterious underworld figure called Mother. The heroes were then driven off by Azrael, a dangerous fanatic with a lethal touch who believed he was the Order's chosen warrior-angel.

They later visited the Order's HQ, the ancient hidden city of Gnosis, and met "Saint" Dumas. He admitted that Azrael was the product of neural programming, and wanted Red Robin to replace him. Red Robin disabled Gnosis' systems and Dumas fled when Azrael turned against him. **SW**

ORION

DATA

DEBUT *New Gods* (Vol. 1) #1 **(Feb.-Mar. 1967)**
CURRENT VERSION *Wonder Woman* (Vol. 4) #12 **(Oct. 2012)**
BASE New Genesis
HEIGHT 6ft 1in **WEIGHT** 195 lbs
EYES Red **HAIR** Red-blond
POWERS/ABILITIES As a New God, Orion is immortal with superhuman physical and mental attributes; his sentient transport platform, called A4, can fly, create teleporting Boom Tubes, locate targets, and fire energy beams; A4's harness can also communicate directly with Orion; his Mother Box creates telepathic links with others' minds, and can block psychic influences.
ALLIES Milan, Highfather
ENEMIES First Born, Darkseid, Hector Hammond, all Lantern Corps
AFFILIATIONS New Genesis, Council of Eight, Divine Guard

GOD VS. GOD
In London, Orion found an opponent worthy of his mettle when he took on the First Born, the savage first son of Zeus, King of the Olympian gods.

SYMBIOTIC RIDE
A4, Orion's sentient transport platform, is more than just a combination vehicle, weapons system, and sensor suite—Orion sees it as a technological extension of himself.

Orion is the son of Darkseid, evil lord of Apokolips, but he was raised by the benevolent Highfather, ruler of the utopian world of New Genesis. The heroic warrior has battled many foes across the cosmos, but the greatest struggle he faces is within himself. While attempting to uphold the peaceful ideals of his adopted home, he must also contain the seething rage that is his legacy as the son of Darkseid.

FACE OF FURY
Orion tries to present a calm face to the world, but when he loses his temper, his warlike, violent Apokoliptian side surfaces.

When Orion was a child, he was sent to live on New Genesis as part of a short-lived peace treaty between Darkseid—his father—and Highfather, New Genesis' ruler. Orion tried to embrace the unfamiliar, placid ways of his new home, but his quick temper and impulsive nature frequently got him into trouble.

On one of his first missions, Orion was dispatched by Highfather to Earth to deal with a potentially apocalyptic menace to the universe. However, when Orion discovered that the "menace" was in reality a baby called Zeke (the reborn Olympian god Zeus), he teamed up with Wonder Woman to protect the child from the evil First Born instead. A less than repentant Orion thus earned himself a strong rebuke from his foster-father.

When the New God's Prophecy Wall showed Orion an image of Superman and claimed he was a threat to all existence, Orion attacked the Man of Steel. However, he quickly determined that the issue was not Superman himself, but the psyche of the villain Hector Hammond, who had hitched a ride in Superman's mind. Orion quickly extracted the villain with his Mother Box.

Later, Highfather hatched a plan to use the power of the Lantern Corps to fight Darkseid, and sent Orion and the other members of the Council of Eight to acquire power rings from the various Corps. Orion took the Green Lantern power ring belonging to the sentient planet Mogo. This triggered a needless and crippling war between the Lanterns and New Genesis, in which Orion commanded Highfather's Divine Guard. **SW**

ON THE RECORD

The original Orion shares the same background as his post-Flashpoint incarnation, but his life is defined by his anger at his evil father, Darkseid. After gaining control of the Anti-Life Equation, Orion managed to seize his birthright as ruler of Apokolips for a time.

Orion then joined fellow renegade Apokoliptian Big Barda in the Justice League of America, helping them defeat the war-mongering entity Mageddon. He killed Darkseid in a dramatic battle prior to the Infinite Crisis. However, his father returned and fired a special bullet backward in time to dispatch his son.

SIBLING RIVALRY
In a battle of Titanic proportions, Orion fought his brother Kalibak, the eldest son of Darkseid.

FIGHTING MAD
Orion relishes a battle with a worthy foe—and he faced the challenge of a lifetime when he clashed with Superman himself, who had been possessed by Hector Hammond.

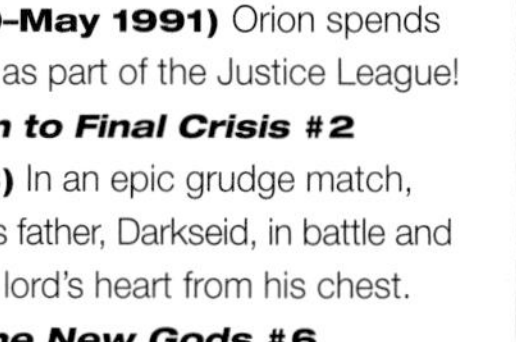

CLASSIC STORIES

***New Gods* (Vol. 3) #2 (Mar. 1989)** In a dramatic story, Orion confronts his own prejudices as he returns the body of the hero Forager to his people.

***Justice League America* #42–50 (Sep. 1990–May 1991)** Orion spends time on Earth as part of the Justice League!

***Countdown to Final Crisis* #2 (Apr. 2008)** In an epic grudge match, Orion faces his father, Darkseid, in battle and pulls the dark lord's heart from his chest.

***Death of the New Gods* #6 (Apr. 2008)** Orion bravely sacrifices himself in an attempt to slay the being that is killing the New Gods.

ORPHAN

DEBUT *Batman* (Vol. 1) #567 **(Jul. 1999)** (as Cassandra Cain); *Batman Incorporated* (Vol. 1) #6 **(Jun. 2011)** (as Black Bat)
CURRENT VERSION *Batman and Robin Eternal* (Vol. 1) #1 **(Dec. 2015)**
REAL NAME Cassandra Cain
BASE Hong Kong
HEIGHT 5ft 5ins **WEIGHT** 110 lbs **EYES** Blue **HAIR** Black
POWERS/ABILITIES Supreme martial artist, augmented by Batman's training, able to read body language and anticipate opponents' attacks.
ALLIES Red Robin, Dick Grayson, Batman
ENEMIES Mother, David Cain
AFFILIATIONS Batman Incorporated, League of Assassins, the Nursery

Cassandra Cain is the daughter of master assassin David Cain, who worked as the Orphan for the manipulative mastermind, Mother. Cassandra was raised in complete isolation, denied human warmth and contact, and subjected to long periods of sensory deprivation interspersed with constant and brutal martial arts training. Her language skills were deliberately impeded to develop an instinctive sense of body-language, enabling her to predict her target's every movement.

This tough, unorthox training regime contravened Mother's own methods of indoctrinating the children she stole. David Cain had intended Cassandra to be a gift for Mother, but he was reprimanded for bringing up his daughter in such an inefficient manner. Cassandra was banished from the Nursery run by Mother, but she continued to train in secret.

Appalled by what she was forced to do, Cassandra eventually escaped. Freed from Cain's influence, she resurfaced in Hong Kong and met Batman who recruited her as his secret agent, despite her experiences rendering her almost mute. After years working in the shadows, she recently emerged as a member of the Dark Knight's team, adopting the name Orphan. **WW**

ON THE RECORD

Cassandra Cain debuted during the "No Man's Land" saga. She stalked the earthquake-shattered Gotham City like a solitary, silent ghost, enforcing Batman's law as the fourth Batgirl.

Upon officially joining the Batman family, her training was in reading, writing, and social interaction, not combat. When she learned that the world's greatest killer, Lady Shiva, was her mother, Cassandra briefly led the League of Assassins, before being legally adopted by Bruce Wayne.

SILENT PARTNER
Despite never having learned to speak, Black Bat had developed painfully clear and memorable ways of getting her message across.

OUTLAWS, THE

DEBUT *Red Hood and the Outlaws* #1 (Nov. 2011)
CURRENT VERSION *Red Hood and the Outlaws* #1 (Aug. 2016)
NOTABLE MEMBERS/POWERS
Red Hood: Martial arts, marksman, detective;
Arsenal: Archery, acrobatics, brilliant mind;
Starfire: Super-strength; flight; energy projection;
Bizarro: imperfect copy of Superman's powers;
Artemis: Amazonian powers and abilities.
ENEMIES League of Assassins, Midas

When the vigilante Red Hood saw that fellow former sidekick Arsenal was imprisoned in a corrupt penitentiary in the eastern nation of Qurac, he donned a sophisticated disguise and broke Arsenal out of jail with the help of his secret weapon, the Tamaranean powerhouse called Starfire. The trio soon found that they had more in common than they at first realized, and set up a headquarters on an uncharted island, where Starfire's spacecraft had originally crashed.

Becoming the Outlaws, they embarked on a variety of missions, including teaming up with the Teen Titans to stop a riot caused by the Joker, and helping Starfire return to her homeworld Tamaran and reconcile, for a time, with her sister, Blackfire. Starfire and Arsenal began a romance, but they both left the group to pursue their own separate destinies.

The team's mainstay, Red Hood, was recently joined by the Amazonian warrior Artemis and the flawed Kryptonian clone Bizarro. The Outlaws now hire themselves out as mercenaries. **MM**

OSIRIS

DEBUT *Teen Titans* (Vol. 3) #38 (Sep. 2006)
CURRENT VERSION *Justice League of America* (Vol. 3) #7.4 (Nov. 2013)
REAL NAME Amon Tomaz **BASE** Kahndaq
HEIGHT 5ft 10in **WEIGHT** 164 lbs
EYES Brown **HAIR** Black
POWERS/ABILITIES Super-strength, flight, superspeed, invulnerability, enhanced stamina.
ENEMIES Famine, Ibac

Amon Tomaz was beaten to near death by Intergang but he was rescued by his sister and Black Adam, the latter sharing his powers with the crippled teenager. Amon became Osiris and a member of the Black Marvel Family. Traveling to the US with his crocodile Sobek, Osiris briefly joined the Teen Titans, but killed the Persuader after he threatened his sister. Wracked with guilt, Osiris was convinced by Sobek to revert to his Amon form. Sobek then revealed himself as Famine, one of the Four Horsemen of Apokolips, and devoured the powerless Amon.

After Flashpoint, Amon was a Kahndaqi teenager without superpowers. A freedom fighter with the Sons of Adam, he translated an ancient spell that resurrected Black Adam, but was killed by Kahndaq soldiers. Adam made short work of the killers and Kahndaq's ruler, installing himself as the country's true protector. **MM**

OTHERS, THE

DEBUT *Aquaman* (Vol. 7) #7 (May 2012)
NOTABLE MEMBERS
Aquaman: Amphibious Super Hero; **Operative:** Super spy; **Prisoner of War:** Force field generation; communication with comrades' ghosts; **Ya'Wara:** Jaguar goddess of Amazon; **Sky Alchesay:** Necromancy, teleporting; **Vostok-X:** Magical Atlantean Helmet.
ENEMIES Black Manta, Mayhem

Six years ago, Arthur Curry abandoned life on the land to live in the oceans. Before he officially adopted the name Aquaman, he fought with the Others, a diverse group of humans and superhumans who banded together to reclaim the dead sea king Atlan's ancient Atlantean artifacts. Aquaman also used the artifacts as bait in his hunt for Black Manta, the man he thought responsible for the death of his father, Atlan.

Joining him on the hunt was the fierce Brazilian fighter Ya'Wara, the precognitive Kahina the Seer, Russian Super Hero Vostok-X, the possessed Prisoner of War, and aging super-spy Operative. Years later, Black Manta killed several of the Others including the Seer and Vostok-X, before Aquaman brought him to justice.

The Others continued their fight, however, and were later joined by Sky Alchesay, a Native American mystically linked with the Ghost Lands, Kahina's sister Sayeh as the new Seer, and another Vostok-X. This team triumphed over several threats, including the terrorist group Mayhem. **MM**

FIGHTING WELL WITH OTHERS
The Others came from very different backgrounds, but found their diverse experiences useful in any given battle.
1 Aquaman
2 Operative
3 Prisoner of War
4 Ya'Wara
5 Sky Alchesay

OUTLAWS REBORN
Red Hood recently returned to his old stomping ground Gotham City, where he was joined by two new Outlaws.
1 Red Hood
2 Bizarro
3 Artemis

OUTSIDERS, THE

DEBUT *The Brave and the Bold* (Vol. 1) #200 **(Jul. 1983)**
BASE Gotham City, Los Angeles, Brooklyn
NOTABLE MEMBERS/POWERS **Batman**: genius detective; **Black Lightning**: Electokinesis, electric blasts; **Geo-Force**: Geokinesis; **Metamorpho**: Shape-shifting, invulnerablity; **Halo**: Light-spectrum-related powers; **Katana**: Wields magical Soultaker sword; **Looker**: Psionic powers; **Windfall**: Control of winds; **Atomic Knight**: Atomic-powered armor, precognition; **Technocrat**: Hi-tech battlesuit; **Wylde**: Half man, half bear; **Faust**: Sorcerous powers; **Eradicator**: Energy manipulation; **Owlman**: Brilliant detective; **Creeper**: Super-strong Japanese demon, with mind control powers; **Freight Train**: Absorbs kinetic energy; **Grace**: Amazonian heritage; **Thunder**: Energy projection.
ENEMIES Kobra Cult, Fearsome Five, Baron Bedlam, Church of Blood

OUTSIDE JUSTICE
When the Justice League of America refused to join Batman's mission to Markovia, the Dark Knight quit their ranks in dramatic fashion. This freed him to form his own team of Super Heroes, the Outsiders.

The first Outsiders were a ragtag group of heroic misfits brought together by fate and a determined Dark Knight during a mission that took them to the European nation of Markovia. Helping to foil a revolutionary coup led by the super-villain Baron Bedlam, the Outsiders decided to stay together.

They returned to Gotham City and established a headquarters of sorts in the seldom-used Batcave beneath the Wayne Foundation building. Batman grew to trust the team, even revealing his secret identity to them before they branched out on their own with new member Looker and set up shop on the West Coast.

After the Millennium event rocked their roster, depowering Looker and causing Halo to fall into a coma, the team disbanded. They reformed years later when another crisis hit Geo-Force's home country of Markovia.

Years afterwards, Nightwing and Arsenal became members in a new version of the Outsiders with little connection to the first team. In their latest incarnation, Alfred Pennyworth recruited the original members, and a few new players, to re-form the Outsiders when Bruce Wayne was seemingly eliminated by Darkseid. **MM**

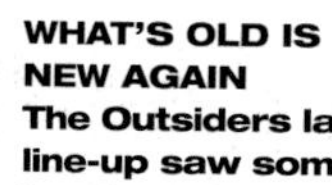

WHAT'S OLD IS NEW AGAIN
The Outsiders latest line-up saw some old hands and new faces.
1 Black Lightning
2 Katana
3 Geo-Force
4 Metamorpho
5 Creeper
6 Owlman

TEAMS FOR THE TIMES
The Outsiders' roster has changed often over the years, including a new team in the 1990s and an incarnation in the early 2000s with most of the key former members absent.

ORPHEUS

DEBUT *Batman: Orpheus Rising* #1 (Oct. 2001)
REAL NAME Gavin King
BASE Gotham City
HEIGHT 6ft 2in **WEIGHT** 195 lbs
EYES Brown **HAIR** Black
POWERS/ABILITIES Expert martial artist and gymnast; costume loaded with hi-tech gadgets and weapons including a sonic spike, smoke bombs, and a helmet with advanced vision capabilities.
ENEMIES Black Mask

Young Gavin King dreamed of becoming a professional singer and dancer and was bullied as a result. He studied martial arts to defend himself and proved to be a natural. After graduating from college, Gavin joined a touring dance troupe, witnessing the horrors and injustices of some of the worst parts of the world firsthand.

He was soon recruited into a secret organization set up to fight society's ills, and given financial help and training, as well as a costume and weaponry. He became Orpheus and fought crime in Gotham City while, by day, working as a record and video producer. He found a reluctant ally in Batman, and also worked with another well-traveled hero, Onyx. All his training and technology proved in vain: Black Mask killed him during a gang war and, to add insult to injury, briefly took his place as Orpheus. **MM**

OUTSIDER, THE

DEBUT *Detective Comics* (Vol. 1) #334 (Dec. 1964)
CURRENT VERSION *Justice League* #6 (Apr. 2012)
REAL NAME Alfred Pennyworth
HEIGHT 6ft **WEIGHT** 160 lbs
EYES Brown **HAIR** Black
POWERS/ABILITIES Master strategist; access to Wayne family fortune; well connected in the underworld of both Earth-3 and Earth-0.
ENEMIES Justice League, Batman

On Earth-3, a parallel world to the Justice League's Earth-0, evil counterparts of famous Super Heroes ruled as the Crime Syndicate. One of the its most devious leaders was Owlman, aka Thomas Wayne, Jr., Bruce Wayne's older brother. Thomas had his butler Alfred Pennyworth shoot and kill his parents as well as Bruce.

Later, trying to defend his master from his archenemy, the Joker, Alfred was infected by an Earth-3 version of the Joker venom, and developed deathly pale skin and a compulsive laugh as a result. He took advantage of Darkseid's attack on Earth-0 to make his way there and set up a Secret Society of that world's worst super-villains. He then used Pandora's Box to allow the Crime Syndicate to travel to Earth-0 and nearly conquer it. He was subsequently stabbed to death by Black Manta. **MM**

OVERMASTER

DEBUT *Justice League of America* (Vol. 1) #233 (Dec. 1984)
CURRENT VERSION *Justice League United Annual* #1 (Dec. 2014)
HEIGHT 8ft **WEIGHT** 350 lbs
EYES Yellow **HAIR** None
POWERS/ABILITIES Superhuman strength and endurance; possesses advanced weaponry.
ENEMIES Legion of Super-Heroes, JLU

The Overmaster was one of the Justice League's deadliest foes. A self-styled celestial judge, he destroyed worlds he considered unworthy. When he came to Earth, he created a team of super-villains, the Cadre, to test mankind's Super Heroes, and the JLA met the challenge.

Post-Flashpoint, Overmaster became part of a new Cadre, now a mercenary group hired by the super-villain Byth to capture Ultra the Multi-Alien, who was destined to become Infinitus, a cosmic entity that could destroy galaxies. To avert this threat, the 31st-century Legion of Super-Heroes traveled back in time and joined forces with Justice League United to battle the Cadre. Despite Overmaster's vast strength, he was no match for Mon-El and Saturn Girl. Reeling from Saturn Girl's mind attack, he was knocked almost unconscious by Mon-El, but Byth escaped with the captured Ultra. **MM**

OWLWOMAN

DEBUT *Super Friends* (Vol. 1) #7 (Oct. 1977)
REAL NAME Wenonah Littlebird
BASE The New Dome
HEIGHT 5ft 5in **WEIGHT** 125 lbs
EYES Brown **HAIR** Black
POWERS/ABILITIES Flight; superhuman strength; night vision; superhuman tracking abilities; manufactured, self-growing claws.
ALLIES Jack O'Lantern, Dr. Mist
ENEMIES O.M.A.C., Justice League Europe

Wenonah Littlebird was bestowed with superhuman powers by the spirit of her Native American tribe. Opting to use her new abilities to help not just her people, but the whole world, Wenonah joined the Global Guardians as Owlwoman. She was later brainwashed by Queen Bee, the corrupt ruler of the nation of Bialya, who operated on Littlebird, giving her artificial claws that grow when needed. With the help of Dr. Mist, Owlwoman and the Guardians escaped Queen Bee, establishing their headquarters in the New Dome, in the Pacific Ocean.

Owlwoman helped Wonder Woman defeat the sorceress Circe after she had transformed male Super Heroes into rampaging half-man/half-beast creatures. Owlwoman was also glimpsed during Infinite Crisis, battling the O.M.A.C. androids alongside Black Condor. **MM**

PANDORA

DEBUT *Flashpoint* (Vol. 2) #5 **(Oct. 2011)**
BASE Mobile
EYES Blue **HAIR** Purple
POWERS/ABILITIES Immortality, super-strength, speed and durability; magic focused through her pistols; highly advanced martial arts skills, especially in conjunction with throwing knives and Kusurigama chain-sickle; manifests mystical Light Armor.
ALLIES Flash, Phantom Stranger, John Constantine, Vandal Savage
ENEMIES Seven Deadly Sins, The Outsider, Crime Syndicate, The Blight, Nick Necro, Felix Faust
AFFILIATIONS Trinity of Sin, Circle of Eternity, Justice League Dark

Ten millennia ago in Macedonia, Pandora was tricked into opening a strange mystic receptacle and released the Seven Deadly Sins into the world. The spirits possessed her tribe and kin, making them kill each other in a terrifying display of malign corruption. For her "transgression," Pandora was condemned to immortality by the divinities of the Council of Eternity. She was doomed to forever wander the planet, experiencing the horrors her act unleashed upon humanity.

Every effort of the woman the Council called the "mother of monsters" to counter the Sins' depredations resulted in greater torment for their mortal prey. Eventually, Pandora decided to put her curse to good use, resolving to battle the Sins directly. Thanks to the curse, she already possessed unnatural physical advantages of enhanced strength, speed, and invulnerability. She further boosted her power by studying martial arts and magic, and by upgrading the weaponry she carried.

Recently, the Wizard of Shazam—the last survivor of the Circle of Eternity—came to her and apologized for the injustice they had inflicted upon her. He also hinted that an alliance with some of humanity's Super Heroes could hold the key to defeating the Sins and gaining her some peace of mind. She was last seen battling the Phantom Stranger, who demanded she return the mystical box, as she could not be trusted with it. She refused and upon defeating the Stranger in a fierce display of power, continued her mission to destroy the Seven Deadly Sins. **WW**

STEPS TO HEAVEN Pandora, the Phantom Stranger, and the Question had been judged as humanity's greatest sinners before their individual paths of atonement reunited them in a perpetual battle to protect humanity from supernatural horror.

PANTHA

DEBUT *New Titans* (Vol. 1) #73 (Feb. 1991)
REAL NAME Rosabelle Mendez
BASE Metropolis
HEIGHT 6ft 8in **WEIGHT** 125 lbs
EYES Red **HAIR** Auburn
POWERS/ABILITIES Superhuman speed, strength, reflexes, agility, leaping; accelerated healing, fangs, and retractable claws.
ENEMIES Wildebeest Society, Jericho, Catwoman, Orion, Superboy-Prime

Rosabelle Mendez was abducted by the insidious Wildebeest Society, becoming part of their program to create metahuman soldiers. After enduring agonizing experiments, she escaped, permanently transformed into a ferocious were-creature. She possessed no memory of her past life and was not sure if she was more cat than human. Pantha found refuge with the Teen Titans, becoming a powerful but outspoken member of the team, antagonizing many of her female teammates, such as Starfire and Flamebird. If no villains were handy she was happy to scrap with her new friends.

Pantha grudgingly became foster-mum to another of Wildebeest's bizarre genetic experiments—super-strong toddler Baby Wildebeest—and gradually retired from the Super Hero scene. **WW**

PARALLAX

DEBUT *Green Lantern* (Vol. 3) #50 **(Mar. 1994)**
CURRENT VERSION *Green Lantern* (Vol. 5) #20 **(Jul. 2013)**
REAL NAME Parallax **BASE** Qward, Anti Matter Universe
HEIGHT Variable **WEIGHT** Variable **EYES** Yellow **HAIR** None
POWERS/ABILITIES Immortality, possession, mind-control, energy-generation, time-manipulation; projection of fear, from anxiety to insane terror.
ENEMIES All other embodiments of the Emotional Spectrum, Green Lantern Corps, Krona, Sinestro
AFFILIATIONS Emotional Spectrum, the Anti-Monitor

The Emotional Spectrum formed at the earliest moments of creation, each hue manifesting the living embodiment of an emotion. Parallax arose from the fears of every living creature. Roaming the cosmos, it spitefully eradicated entire civilizations through their own terrors. The Guardians of the Universe captured Parallax and locked it within their Central Power Battery on Oa. Here it served to limit the power of the Guardians' Green Lantern Corps by rendering their rings useless against anything colored yellow.

Millennia later, with the aid of arch-renegade Sinestro, Parallax escaped by possessing Hal Jordan and eroding his will. Free to create chaos, Parallax went on to possess a number of heroic hosts, such as Kyle Rayner, Barry Allen and the Oan Ganthet, but met its match attempting to bind Sinestro. His will proved too much for Parallax, which became a power-source for the true Lord of Fear. **WW**

YELLOW FEVER Parallax's presence bestowed enormous power, but caused paranoia and insanity.

ON THE RECORD

Hal Jordan lapsed into despondency when his loved ones died in the destruction of Coast City. This finally allowed Parallax to take possession of him. It had entered his mind years previously when Hal entered the Central Power Battery on Oa, but it had been unable to overcome the human's iron willpower until tragedy derailed his thought processes. The composite Parallax creature quickly destroyed the Green Lantern Corps, and almost ended all creation.

LITTLE WHITE LIE Every being possessed by Parallax experiences a huge power gain and commensurate mania, and grows a telltale white streak in their hair.

PARASITE

DEBUT *Action Comics* (Vol. 1) #340 **(Aug. 1966)**
CURRENT VERSION *Forever Evil* #1 **(Nov. 2013)**
REAL NAME Joshua Michael Allen
BASE Suicide Slum, Metropolis
HEIGHT Variable **WEIGHT** Variable **EYES** Green **HAIR** None
POWERS/ABILITIES Life-energy absorption; temporary metahuman-power absorption; size alteration.
ENEMIES Superman, Superboy (Jon Lane Kent), Justice League of America, Lois Lane
AFFILIATIONS Suicide Squad, Secret Society of Super-Villains

Joshua Allen was one of the fastest, rudest, and most obnoxious bike messengers to ever ride the streets of Metropolis. He also frequently helped himself to the items he was supposed to be delivering for clients. Joshua's life changed irrevocably after he crashed into a protoplasmic monstrosity in the street. Blinded by road-rage, he attacked the slimy green blob and suffered a huge electric shock from downed power-lines... and then lost consciousness.

He awoke in hospital with a broken leg, diagnosed as suffering from alien flu. Unable to work, his life spiraled out of control. When he was called into S.T.A.R. Labs for a check on the virus, their machinery triggered a ghastly mutation. In one explosive instant Joshua accidentally killed the doctors by sucking out all their life-energy.

Draining homeless people, the aged, and even rats for a few hours of life, he hit bottom and decided to kill himself. He was saved by Superman and that euphoric momentary contact also released his inner monster. Temporarily satiated by the Man of Steel's incredible powers, the Parasite became obsessed with leeching metahuman might: a deadly predator casually consuming mere mortal morsels while planning his next attack on the Man of Tomorrow. **WW**

THE BLOB Josh had seen some incredible things on the streets of Metropolis, but the escaped alien snot-monster was something else.

ON THE RECORD

The Parasite has changed many times since his Silver Age debut. Originally, Raymond Jensen was exposed to radioactive waste and became a walking sponge who absorbed Superman's powers until they were roughly equals. However, as decades passed, the character became a far darker, deadlier, and more primal menace.

Memories and life-force became the favorite fodder for the monstrous creature who could become Superman's physical equal but never his mental match.

CONSPICUOUS CONSUMPTION No iteration of the Parasite has ever listened to the wise old adage about not playing with your food.

FEEDING FRENZY Superman's superpowers were a nice appetizer, but the Parasite wanted to eat the Man of Steel.

PARIAH

DEBUT *Crisis on Infinite Earths* (Vol. 1) #1 (Apr. 1985)
CURRENT VERSION *Justice League of America's Vibe* (Vol. 1) #1 (Apr. 2013)
REAL NAME Kell Mossa **BASE** Metropolis
HEIGHT 5ft 11in **WEIGHT** 165 lbs
EYES Black **HAIR** Purple
POWERS/ABILITIES Immortality, invulnerability, teleportation, flight; vast technological and medical knowledge.
ENEMIES Anti-Monitor, Alexander Luthor

Kell Mossa was the greatest scientist of New Earth, but he was cursed with an insatiable hunger for knowledge. Using antimatter as a power-source, he arrogantly tried to discover the origins of the universe. His actions roused the Anti-Monitor, causing the monster to begin its eradication of the infinite Earths of the multiverse. As a result, Mossa became a cosmic Pariah, fated to arrive in a universe just before its destruction. He tumbled from one dimension to another, warning each Earth's heroes to unite or die.

With the Crisis averted and the Anti-Monitor defeated, Mossa retired, assuming his penance was over. However, another Infinite Crisis began and Pariah was murdered by his supposed ally, Alexander Luthor of Earth-3. **WW**

PARK, LINDA

DEBUT *The Flash* (Vol. 2) #28 (Jul. 1989)
REAL NAME Linda Jasmine Park-West
BASE Keystone City
HEIGHT 5ft 6in **WEIGHT** 120 lbs
EYES Brown **HAIR** Black
POWERS/ABILITIES Keen deductive skills and journalistic training.
ENEMIES Frances Kane, Zoom (Hunter Zoloman), Kobra Cult, Mirror Master

Linda Park was a television reporter fed up with fronting puff-pieces. She changed tack and quickly carved out a reputation as a gifted investigative journalist. One of her earliest scoops was interviewing Wally West, who had gone public as the latest speedster to call himself the Flash. They were soon a couple, but, despite the dangers of dating a Super Hero, Linda refused to allow herself to be a sidekick or shadow and continued exposing corruption.

Her diligent research brought her up against criminal maniacs such as Kobra and Mirror Master, as well as monsters like Gorilla Grodd. However, her greatest trial came after she married Wally: time-warping psychopath Zoom wanted to kill Linda to make Wally a better—tragedy-honed—hero. He did not reckon on the power of Wally and Linda's love. **WW**

PARLIAMENT OF TREES, THE

DEBUT *Swamp Thing* (Vol. 2) #47 **(Apr. 1986)**
CURRENT VERSION *Swamp Thing* (Vol. 5) #1 **(Nov. 2011)**
BASE The Grove
NOTABLE MEMBERS/POWERS All members of the Parliament possess plant-based physiology and powers, and can control all forms of plant life. **Swamp Thing** (Alec Holland); **Yggdrasil:** First elemental; **Tuuru:** Second elemental; **Eyam:** Third elemental; **Bog Venus**; **Ghost Hiding in the Rushes**; **Kettle Hole Devil**; **Saint Columba**; **Albert Hollerer, Great Url**; **Jack in the Green**; **Lady Jane**
ALLIES Parliament of Limbs
ENEMIES Parliament of Decay

Swamp Thing is an elemental, an avatar for the Green, the mystical force that unites all plant life across the globe and beyond. While Alec Holland is the most recent avatar, there have been many before him that have since moved on. Some of these former avatars make up the Parliament of Trees, a linked collective capable of great wisdom, which can even, on occasion, bestow power upon the current avatar.

The Parliament of Trees considers itself the congress of all Swamp Things past, and has been around far longer than mankind. One member was even formerly a trilobite.

When Alec Holland was murdered by Anton Arcane, his body rotted in the swamp before he could take up his destined role as the current avatar of the Green. The Parliament had to be patient and careful, waiting five long years before Alec was resurrected. It was longer still before Alec came to accept his destiny. In fact, it took a rare visit from former Swamp Thing and Parliament member A.H. Rodgers—as well as being made to see the danger of a world without an avatar—before Alec finally agreed to become the Swamp Thing.

Holland later abolished the Parliament after they punished him for refusing to murder the villain known as the Seeder. **MM**

GREEN ARMY
To combat the forces of the Metal and their leader, Lady Weeds, Swamp Thing led a troop of former avatars of the Green onto the battlefield.

ON THE RECORD

The Parliament of Trees was first introduced in the 1980s when they met an earlier version of Swamp Thing, who, for a time, believed he was actually Alec Holland. Some of these members included: Yggdrasil, an elemental based on the DNA helix; Eyam, a former trilobite; and Tuuru.

The Parliament was responsible for the birth of the Swamp Thing that predated the true Alec Holland version, as well as the source of his daughter Tefé's powers. It was also notable for fighting a battle with another collective consciousness, this one known as the Grey.

THE PARLIAMENT IN ACTION
Tefé was the daughter of the Swamp Thing that once believed he was Alec Holland and his love, Abigail Holland. Abigail had been implanted with a new plant elemental called the Sprout, created by the Parliament.

PATCHWORK MAN

DEBUT *Swamp Thing* (Vol. 1) #2 **(Dec. 1972–Jan. 1973)** (Gregori Arcane); *Weird War Tales* (Vol. 1) #93 **(Nov. 1980)** (Elliott Taylor)
REAL NAME Gregori Arcane
HEIGHT 6ft 8in **WEIGHT** 330 lbs **EYES** Blue **HAIR** Gray-black
POWERS/ABILITIES Superhuman strength, ability to stay alive despite much deterioration, resistant to effects of injuries.
ALLIES Abigail Arcane
ENEMIES Anton Arcane, Swamp Thing

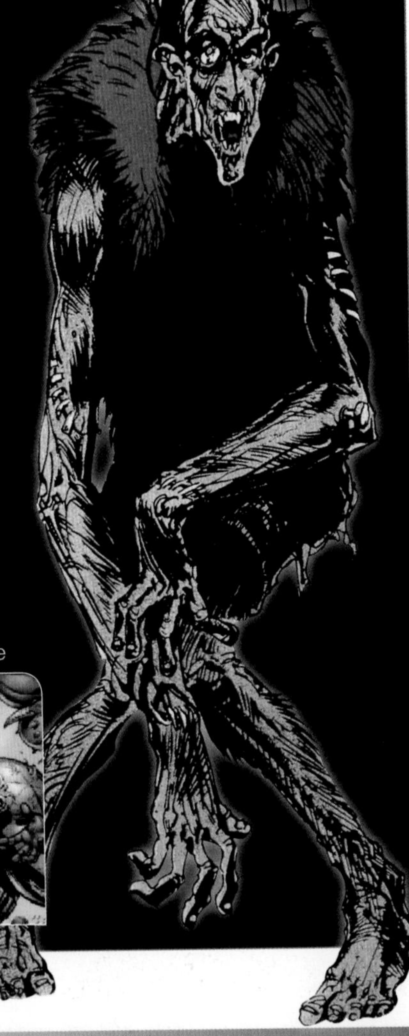

Gregori Arcane lived a tormented life, virtually from birth. The youngest of three Arcane children, Gregori was often physically abused by his other brother, Anton. When Anton was apparently fatally wounded during World War II, Gregori was finally able to get on with his life, pursuing a promising career as a businessman in Europe. However, Gregori's tragic life continued to spiral downward. He lost his wife when she died giving birth to their daughter, Abigail. Years later, in danger of losing custody of his daughter, he returned from a business trip and discovered that Abigail was missing. Gregori searched for her, but stumbled onto a minefield and was killed.

Gregori's body was found by his brother Anton, who had in fact survived the war and used magic and science to reanimate his brother. Now the misshapen Patchwork Man, Gregori sought vengeance against his brother, but was imprisoned in Anton's dungeon. Swamp Thing accidentally freed him and Gregori then went searching for his now-adult daughter, Abigail. After several encounters and clashes with Swamp Thing and Abigail, the Patchwork Man sacrificed himself to save Abigail's life.

Gregori had a successor in the form of Elliot "Lucky" Taylor, a member of the Creature Commandos. Serving alongside a vampire and a werewolf, among other oddities, this Patchwork Man had been stitched back together after stepping on a mine. Incredibly strong and practically invulnerable, he was the Commandos' resident powerhouse. **MM**

STITCHED UP
The second Patchwork Man was a product of the US government's covert Project M, creating soldiers that would instill fear in their opponents.

PEACEMAKER

DEBUT *The Fightin' 5* #40 **(Nov. 1966)**
REAL NAME Christopher Smith (born Schmidt)
BASE Geneva, Switzerland
HEIGHT 6ft 2in **WEIGHT** 205 lbs
EYES Blue **HAIR** Black
POWERS/ABILITIES Expert hand-to-hand combatant; proficient marksman; adept pilot.
ENEMIES Eclipso, the Reach

At the tender age of five, Christopher Schmidt witnessed the death of his father, an Austrian Nazi Party member who committed suicide rather than face trial for his war crimes. Christopher's mother took her son to America and changed their last name to Smith. As an adult, Christopher enlisted in the US Army and led a unit that massacred an entire Vietnamese village. Convicted of wrongdoing, he was offered an early release if he participated in the government program Project: Peacemaker.

While Christopher showed great promise as an elite soldier in training, the project was defunded, and Christopher returned to Austria. He established the Pax Institute in Geneva, Switzerland, and started his own version of Project: Peacemaker, fighting for justice to atone for his family's past sins. He was later apparently killed by Eclipso, before mysteriously returning to aid the Blue Beetle (Jaime Reyes). **MM**

THE PENGUIN

DATA

DEBUT *Detective Comics* (Vol. 1) #58 **(Dec. 1941)**
CURRENT VERSION *Penguin: Pain and Prejudice* #1 **(Dec. 2011)**
REAL NAME Oswald Chesterfield Cobblepot
BASE Gotham City
HEIGHT 5ft 2in **WEIGHT** 175 lbs **EYES** Blue **HAIR** Black
POWERS/ABILITIES Brilliant and ruthless strategist; has connections in nearly every faction of the Gotham City criminal underworld; weapons include deadly penguin-themed inventions and a variety of trick umbrellas.
ALLIES Lark, Catwoman, Mr. Toxic, Hypnotic, Mr. Combustible
ENEMIES: Batman, Batman Family, Black Canary, Emperor Blackgate

FENCING LESSONS
Though much more comfortable dealing in stolen goods from behind a desk, the Penguin is not afraid to use his lethal trick umbrellas in a fight.

BAD EDUCATION
At boarding school, Oswald was defended from bullies by family friend Carter Winston, who would grow up to become Governor—and a thorn in Penguin's side.

Oswald Cobblepot has been known as "the Penguin" for most of his life. First teased with the name as a child, he later embraced it, turning the mocking insult into a moniker fearfully whispered in the darkest corners of Gotham City. Hailing from a rich family with a history of corruption, the Penguin lived up to his legacy. He became a crime boss who is only kept in check by another feared Gotham City figure—Batman.

The Cobblepot family is a renowned institution in Gotham City, as old as the Waynes, yet tarred by decades of corruption. Oswald Chesterfield Cobblepot was born into this life of luxury, albeit with a pointy nose and other features that reminded his classmates of a penguin. While ridiculed by his peers, brothers, and even his cruel father, Oswald was doted on by his mother, who called him her "beautiful boy."

With only pet birds to keep him company, and a brilliant mind for technology and strategy, Oswald began plotting against those who had wronged him. He was soon responsible for not only the deaths of his three brothers, but also his father, who died of pneumonia. While appearing innocent in the eyes of the law and his mother, Oswald had a hand in all these deaths. However, after his father's passing, Oswald was forced to carry an umbrella with him at all times by his mother, who was terrified of losing her last son to the same fate that had claimed her husband.

With the Cobblepot name not as esteemed as it once was, Oswald embarked on a criminal career. He used whatever authority remained in his family legacy and positioned himself at the head of the Gotham City underworld. He soon had his hands in everything from jewelry theft to illegal weapons trafficking. He also opened the Iceberg Casino, a floating ice-themed nightspot as his legitimate cover. Now he was able to rub elbows with criminals and Gotham City's elite, adding more infamy to the Cobblepot name. **MM**

ON THE RECORD

While mostly glossed over in modern retellings of the Penguin and his origins, the original version of the so-called Foul Fiend, who debuted in the 1940s, had very different methods to the modern day incarnation. While both show a penchant for umbrella weaponry and Penguin-inspired technology, the original Penguin was much more hands-on when it came to taking on the Batman. He'd often physically challenge the Dark Knight during his many robbery attempts, besting the hero on several occasions with his trick weaponry.

It wasn't until the 1990s, that the Penguin evolved into the now familiar Machiavellian crime boss, gaining much power and prestige during the No Man's Land event.

KING PENGUIN
In one audacious scheme, the Penguin kidnapped the young Peeble IV, ruler of the nation of Swawak, to gain control of the boy's kingdom.

CLASSIC STORIES

***Batman* (Vol. 1) #25 (Oct./Nov. 1944)**
The Dark Knight's two greatest foes, the Penguin and the Joker, team up for the first time to take on Batman and Robin.

***Batman* (Vol. 1) #155 (May 1963)**
The Penguin is reintroduced for the Silver Age of comics, complete with giant animatronic birds and his Penguin-Blimp.

***The Best of DC* #10 (Mar. 1981)**
After decades of facing the Dynamic Duo, the Penguin is finally given an origin, introducing his overbearing mother.

***"The Penguin Affair," Batman* (Vol. 1) #448–449, *Detective Comics* (Vol. 1) #615 (Jun. 1990)**
Batman and the Penguin battle in a game of wits (and chess) in this three-part tale, which introduces the brilliant Harold Allnut and Penguin's moll, Lark.

PENNYWORTH, ALFRED

DATA

DEBUT *Batman* (Vol. 1) #16 **(Apr./May 1943)**
CURRENT VERSION *Batman* (Vol. 2) #1 **(Nov. 2011)**
REAL NAME Alfred Pennyworth
ALSO KNOWN AS Penny One
BASE Gotham City
HEIGHT 6ft **WEIGHT** 160 lbs
EYES Blue **HAIR** Black
POWERS/ABILITIES Expert with the Batcomputer; highly intelligent and brilliant strategist; capable detective; accomplished actor with skills in makeup and wardrobe; skilled surgeon with military training.
ALLIES Batman, the Batman Family, Julia Pennyworth
ENEMIES Arkham Asylum Inmates, Hush
AFFILIATIONS The Robin movement

FATHER FIGURE
Bruce had no interest in replacing his father after Thomas Wayne's death. But the solitary orphan found a loving surrogate father figure in Alfred.

Every hero needs a right-hand man, and Alfred Pennyworth is precisely that for the Dark Knight of Gotham City. Formerly Thomas and Martha Wayne's butler, Alfred stayed on at Wayne Manor after they were murdered during a mugging, serving as a guardian for their young son Bruce. Alfred remains Batman's most loyal confidant, not only keeping Bruce's daily life on track, but also aiding the Dark Knight on his crime-busting missions from the safety of the Batcave.

Alfred was an actor with a military background whose life changed dramatically when he took over his father's duties at Wayne Manor. Jarvis Pennyworth had been the primary butler to Thomas and Martha Wayne and had doted on their young son Bruce. Jarvis' fate was sealed when he ignored a message from corrupt secret society the Court of Owls to drive Martha Wayne to a location where she would be dealt with. Angry that the butler had refused to carry out their orders, the Court sent one of their Talon assassins to murder him. Alfred never received a warning letter that Jarvis had penned to him and took over his father's position in the Wayne household. As the Waynes' butler, Alfred took his responsibilities very seriously. When Thomas and Martha were murdered by small-time criminal Joe Chill, Alfred tried his best to raise young Bruce in a secure environment. However, as Bruce grew older, Alfred became concerned at his charge's determination to make a positive difference in Gotham City.

Bruce traveled abroad to gain the requisite knowledge and training for his vigilante mission. When he returned home, Alfred was there for him. While Alfred didn't always approve of Bruce's methods as he embarked on life as a Super Hero crime fighter, Alfred assisted his master with his medical expertise and good sense. He also operated the sophisticated Batcomputer in the Batcave beneath Wayne Manor. Alfred's loyalty to Batman and his mission remained steadfast. When Batman's ally, James Gordon, took over Bruce Wayne's Batman role, Alfred even took it upon himself to organize the Robin vigilante movement in Gotham City. **MM**

GENTLEMAN'S GENTLEMAN
Alfred Pennyworth is privy to the greatest secret in Gotham City, the identity of Batman. Alfred treats the driven Bruce Wayne like the son he never had, and only wishes to see his master happy and healthy.

ON THE RECORD

When Alfred debuted in 1943, he looked little like his modern-day counterpart. He was a rather a large man, clumsy and bumbling, whose last name was Beagle, as revealed in a 1945 issue of *Detective Comics*.

Alfred slimmed down during the latter part of the 1940s and, by 1969, he had gained a new last name—Pennyworth—and was well on his way to being the butler known by readers everywhere.

Years later, in 2005, it was revealed that Alfred had indeed been named Alfred Beagle, but had changed his name while working as an agent for Her Majesty's Secret Service, MI6. There was clearly more to Alfred than met the eye.

SUBSTITUTE PARENTS
The two people who primarily raised young Bruce, Alfred and the Wayne family doctor Leslie Thompkins, had a romance. Their relationship was explored in post-Crisis stories.

BEWARE OF THE BUTLER
With his military background, Alfred doesn't quite share Batman's anti-gun stance. However, he respects Bruce's beliefs on weapons, and never questions them.

CLASSIC STORIES

***Batman* (Vol. 1) #22 (Apr./May 1944)** Only a year after his debut, Alfred gets his own backup story, complete with a spot front and center on this issue's cover.

***Detective Comics* (Vol. 1) #328 (Jun. 1964)** Alfred is killed (albeit temporarily) in this issue, which saw Batman create the Alfred Foundation in memory of his fallen butler.

***Detective Comics* (Vol. 1) #501 (Apr. 1981)** Alfred's past as a soldier is delved into as fans are introduced to Julia Pennyworth, his daughter with war hero Mlle. Marie.

***Nightwing: Alfred's Return* #1 (Jul. 1995)** Having left the Dark Knight's service and traveled to London, Alfred is convinced to return home to Gotham City by Nightwing.

PENNYWORTH, JULIA

DEBUT *Detective Comics* (Vol. 1) #501 (Apr. 1981)
CURRENT VERSION *Batman Eternal* #8 (Jul. 2014)
REAL NAME Julia Pennyworth
ALSO KNOWN AS Penny Two
BASE Gotham City
HEIGHT 5ft 8in **WEIGHT** 129 lbs
EYES Brown **HAIR** Black
POWERS/ABILITIES Highly trained special agent and marksman; efficient strategist.

On an investigation in Hong Kong into the activities of crime boss Carmine Falcone, Batman crossed paths with an agent for the British Special Reconnaissance Regiment (SRR). She was stabbed, and almost killed, by one of Falcone's criminal rivals, Shen Fang. Batman discovered that this agent was none other than Julia Pennyworth, the estranged daughter of his faithful butler, Alfred. He took Julia back with him to Wayne Manor to recover, and there she reconciled with her father and eventually learned Batman's secret identity. She adopted the codename Penny-Two and helped Batman from the relative safety of the Batcave while he was "in the field."

When Batman was believed killed after an encounter with the Joker, Julia worked with the G.C.P.D'.s Batman Task Force as Julia Perry. She aided Police Commissioner Jim Gordon during his tenure as Batman, providing him with tactical advice, much as she had done for Bruce Wayne. **MM**

LIKE FATHER, LIKE DAUGHTER
Julia saw the importance of Batman's mission, just like her father. While's she's good with her fists, she's just as happy working behind-the-scenes.

PHANTOM LADY

DEBUT *Police Comics* #1 (Aug. 1941)
CURRENT VERSION *Phantom Lady and Doll Man* #1 (Oct. 2012)
REAL NAME Jennifer Knight
BASE Metropolis
HEIGHT 5ft 6in **WEIGHT** 128 lbs
EYES Green **HAIR** Black
POWERS/ABILITIES Adept combatant; can pass through solid objects; black light gloves project black fog or hard light weapons.
ENEMIES The Bender Family, Funerella

Jennifer Knight's father was a reporter for the *Daily Planet* until he and his family were murdered on Christmas Eve by crime boss Robert Bender. This brutal act was witnessed by Jennifer when she was only six years old. When she grew up, Jennifer became a journalist like her father, and managed to get close to Cyrus Bender, the son of the now-deceased Robert.

Jennifer eventually stole Cyrus' cellphone and discovered a video on it showing Cyrus killing his own father. Determined to bring Cyrus to justice, she teamed up with her old friend, genius inventor Dane Maxwell, but the pair were captured by Bender's goons. Dane was shrunk to the size of a doll with his own experimental technology, but rescued Jennifer by utilizing some of his other inventive weaponry. Outfitting both Jennifer and himself in hi-tech Super Hero gear, the two became Phantom Lady and Doll Man, and finally took Cyrus Bender down. **MM**

ODD COUPLE
With their different personalities and size, Phantom Lady and Doll Man make an interesting pair. Yet they are strongly attracted to each other.

PEOPLE'S HEROES, THE

DEBUT *The Outsiders* (Vol. 1) # 10 (Aug. 1986)
BASE Russia
NOTABLE MEMBERS Hammer; Sickle; Pravda; Molotov; Bolshoi; Stalnoivolk.
ALLIES Red Shadows
ENEMIES Outsiders, Fusion, Suicide Squad

The superhuman force known as the People's Heroes first debuted when the Outsiders Super Hero team headed to Mozambia, Africa, to rescue Black Lightning's ex-wife from the tyrant Edward Bentama. As a result of Bentama's ties to the Soviet Union, the People's Heroes arrived in Africa to tackle the Outsiders. This team included the super-strong Hammer, the blades expert Sickle, the psionically powered Pravda, the explosive Molotov, and the super-speedster Bolshoi.

The People's Heroes defeated the Outsiders and saw most of the team taken to a prison camp. However, the Outsiders soon escaped the camp and overcame the People's Heroes. The Soviet team later found themselves the unlikely partners of the Outsiders and the Force of July, a patriotic team of American super-soldiers, when facing the even greater threat of an insane former associate, the villain Fusion.

In later years, Hammer and Sickle left the group, facing enemies like Catwoman in Gotham City, while the remaining members fought the Suicide Squad alongside their new powerhouse member Stalnoivolk. **MM**

PERESTROIKA STRIKE FORCE
Reporting directly to Premier Mikhail Gorbachev, the People's Heroes struck a hammer and sickle blow for national Soviet pride, but were villains at heart.

THE ORIGINAL PEOPLE'S HEROES
1 Bolshoi
2 Sickle
3 Hammer
4 Molotov
5 Pravda

PHOBIA

DEBUT *The New Teen Titans* (Vol. 1) #14 (Dec. 1981)
CURRENT VERSION *Blue Beetle* (Vol. 3) #1 (Nov. 2011)
REAL NAME Angela Hawkins III
HEIGHT 5ft 11in **WEIGHT** 138 lbs
EYES Green **HAIR** Black
POWERS/ABILITIES Able to discover an enemy's worst fear and manifest it inside his or her mind; capable hand-to-hand combatant.
ENEMIES Blue Beetle, Brutale, La Dama

Before the Flashpoint event, Phobia was a recurring enemy of the Teen Titans.

She later reappeared, her past shrouded in mystery, to fight a new foe: Blue Beetle Jaime Reyes. A super-villain for hire, Phobia first encountered Reyes when she and several other members of the Brotherhood of Evil were seeking an ancient artifact called the Blue Beetle. Said to have been originally discovered in a Mayan Pyramid, the Blue Beetle was prized by Phobia's employers, the Brain and Monsieur Mallah. During her efforts to obtain the item, Phobia was attacked by rival super-villains hired by the crime boss La Dama. In the ensuing chaos, the Blue Beetle fell into the hands of Jaime Reyes, who was transformed by the artifact into the Super Hero of the same name. **MM**

PHOBOS

DEBUT *Wonder Woman* (Vol. 1) # 183 (Jul.–Aug. 1969)
REAL NAME Phobos
BASE The Netherworld
HEIGHT 7ft 7in **WEIGHT** 459 lbs
EYES Red **HAIR** Flaming red
POWERS/ABILITIES Olympian god able to physically manifest an enemy's greatest fear; essentially invulnerable.
ALLIES Eris, Deimos, Circe
ENEMIES Wonder Woman, Batman
AFFILIATIONS Olympian Gods

Phobos is the God of Fear, thought to be the stuff of Greek legend. However, to Wonder Woman, he was as real as any other super-villain she faced. The son of Ares, Phobos became infamous when he attempted to help the God of War ignite World War III and destroy the Earth in the process, but was stopped by Wonder Woman.

Phobos' most memorable clash with the Amazing Amazon occurred when he merged with the Batman villain Scarecrow before combining his body with the Dark Knight himself. Meanwhile, Phobos' sister Eris joined her form with Poison Ivy, and their brother Deimos merged with the Joker. It took the combined efforts of Wonder Woman and Batman to defeat the immortal siblings' threat to Gotham City. **MM**

PIED PIPER

DEBUT *The Flash* (Vol. 1) #106 (Apr.–May 1959)
CURRENT VERSION *The Flash* (Vol. 4) #8 (Jun. 2012)
REAL NAME Hartley Rathaway
BASE Central City
HEIGHT 5ft 10in **WEIGHT** 158 lbs
EYES Blue **HAIR** Red
POWERS/ABILITIES Brilliant engineer with augmented hearing; electronic flute induces mind-control, force fields and destructive vibrations.
ENEMIES Gorilla Grodd

Hartley Rathaway was born deaf and his rich parents shunned him even after doctors fixed his hearing. Hartley, however, had become obsessed with music and the wonders of acoustic science. He created incredible inventions and—conflicted by years of filial neglect and realizing he was gay—became the attention-seeking super-criminal Pied Piper. Hartley battled the Flash and joined the infamous Rogues, but, not needing money and graced with a social conscience, he reformed and turned to writing music.

Hartley occasionally reactivated his Pied Piper identity to battle threats to Central City such as an invasion by Grodd's super gorillas, even though those forays threatened his relationship with police crime-lab director David Singh. **WW**

PLANETEERS, THE

DEBUT *Real Fact Comics* #16 (Sep.–Oct. 1948)
BASE Late 21st-century Gotham City
NOTABLE MEMBERS General Vurian of Venus; Squadron Commander Hega; Colonel Tommy Tomorrow; Captain Brent Wood; Captain Lenk; Cadet Hjaro; Cadet Lo-Duey of Mars
ALLIES Interplanetary Zoo, Operation Noah's Ark
ENEMIES Chardu of Mercury, Dr. Klik, Nkolo, Prime Minister Bsorbo of Roukar, Dr. Suvu of Jupiter

The Planeteers is a multispecies organization created on Earth for space exploration and research. As links between the various interplanetary civilizations of the solar system grew during the mid-21st century, the star-roving project evolved into a galactic militia that was wholly dedicated to fostering peaceful interaction between intergalactic species.

In essence a space navy, the Planeteers patrol the space lanes, facilitating trade, exploring uncharted regions, and undertaking rescue missions. They also remain vigilant to root out space pirates that threaten the stability of the Federation of Worlds.

Planeteers are trained in scientific research, detective work, and military tactics. They graduate from prestigious Planeteer Academy—dubbed "Spaceport West Point"—and serve in ships of the line before deciding upon a career specialization. **WW**

PLASMUS

DEBUT *New Teen Titans* (Vol. 1) #14 (Dec. 1981)
CURRENT VERSION *Blue Beetle* (Vol. 9) #1 (Nov. 2011)
REAL NAME Otto von Furth
BASE Paris, France
HEIGHT 6ft 4in **WEIGHT** Variable
EYES Yellow **HAIR** None
POWERS/ABILITIES Malleable body; radioactive; acidic death-touch.
ALLIES Warp, Phobia, Society of Super-Villains
ENEMIES Teen Titans, Blue Beetle

German miner Otto von Furth was trapped in a cave-in and spent several days exposed to unknown radiations before being rescued. As he lay dying, he was abducted from hospital by Nazi war criminal General Zahl, who saved him by further mutating him, until his body stabilized as an amorphous mass of acidic, super-heated protoplasm. Now a living terror weapon, Otto called himself Plasmus and joined Zahl in the Brotherhood of Evil, staying on with the group when his re-creator perished in battle.

Plasmus joined his occasional allies Warp and Phobia in the Secret Society of Super-Villains. He also robbed banks and corporations, claiming to be amassing loot from the kinds of institutions he held responsible for his monstrous state. **WW**

PLASTIQUE

DEBUT *The Fury of Firestorm* #7 (Dec. 1982)
CURRENT VERSION *The Fury of Firestorm* #18 (May 2013)
REAL NAME Bette Sans Souci
HEIGHT 5ft 6in **WEIGHT** 123 lbs
EYES Blue **HAIR** Red
POWERS/ABILITIES Explosives and munitions expert who can turn objects into bombs; able to project concussive blasts from her hands.
ENEMIES Firestorm, the Nuclear Men, the Rogues, A.R.G.U.S., Checkmate

Canadian Bette San Souci was a terrorist armorer, expert in making explosive ordnance for others. Eventually, she went public as Plastique, a walking bomb wearing a costume covered with different incendiary charges. She later acquired the ability to project concussive blasts and turn found objects into bombs.

As her abilities developed, her radical ideology waned. After serving with the Suicide Squad, Plastique became a thief and metahuman mercenary. She was part of a coalition targeting Firestorm before joining the Secret Society run by the Outsider.

In advance of the Crime Syndicate's invasion of Earth, she attempted to murder Madame Xanadu, infiltrated A.R.G.U.S., and sought to win the bounty on the heads of Central City's notorious Rogues. **WW**

PLASTIC MAN

DEBUT *Police Comics* #1 (Aug. 1941)
CURRENT VERSION *Justice League International* (Vol. 3) #1 (Nov. 2011)
REAL NAME Patrick Edward "Eel" O'Brian **BASE** Mammoth City
HEIGHT 6ft 1in/variable **WEIGHT** 178 lbs **EYES** Blue **HAIR** Black
POWERS/ABILITIES Completely malleable body; flexible skeleton; movable internal organs; extreme contortionism; shape-changing.
ALLIES Woozy Winks, Batman, Chief Branner, Agent Nancy Morgan
ENEMIES Dr. Dratt, the Red Herring, Granite Lady, Lex Luthor

RUBBER BAND MAN Plastic Man bends over backwards, sideways, and any old way to uphold the law.

Plastic Man has fought crime since the 1940s, using his astoundingly pliable form, deductive mind, and knowledge of the underworld to bring to justice some of the world's strangest villains. "Plas" worked as a private eye with his dim but loyal assistant Woozy Winks. He was also FBI liaison to the All-Star Squadron and Freedom Fighters during World War II and, decades later, served with the Justice League of America.

Plastic Man knew how criminals thought because he was one. Sharp shyster Patrick "Eel" O'Brian always outwitted the cops, but was betrayed by his own crew during a chemical factory heist. Shot, doused in strange acid, and left for dead, Eel was saved by monks who nursed him back to health. While recuperating, he realized the ordeal had changed his body. He could now infinitely change his shape and appearance and resolved to follow the example of the good clerics who saved him to protect decent people from the kind of rat he once was.

PLASTIC FANTASTIC Ambitious mobster Eel O'Brian never imagined any of this metahuman nonsense could affect an ordinary guy like him.

As Plastic Man, O'Brian worked for the police and FBI, never revealing he was still a wanted criminal. He even maintained his original persona, allowing him to cozy up to the mobsters he was hunting. Plas fostered a reputation for silliness, with a nervous habit of shapeshifting into common objects to surprise friends and foes alike.

Post-Flashpoint, "Eel" O'Brian remained an unrepentant thief who saw the time for minor criminals like him was over when Earth-3's Crime Syndicate invaded. With the heroes gone and super-crooks forming an army, he knew he was next, but fate played a vicious trick after Owlman attacked him. Shot and doused in weird chemicals, Eel's body began to inexplicably and agonizingly change. **WW**

PHANTOM STRANGER

DATA

DEBUT *Phantom Stranger* (Vol. 1) #1 **(Aug.-Sep. 1952)**
CURRENT VERSION *Justice League* (Vol. 2) #6 **(Apr. 2012)**
REAL NAME Judas Iscariot
HEIGHT 6ft 2in **WEIGHT** 185 lbs
EYES White **HAIR** Grey/White
POWERS/ABILITIES Immortality; skilled magic-user capable of flight, teleportation, energy-projection, invisibility, transformation, size-alteration, and the ability to stop time.
ALLIES Pandora, the Question, Chris Esperanza, John Constantine, Jim Corrigan, Doctor Terrence Thirteen
ENEMIES The Spectre, Haunted Highwayman, Sin Eater, Sons of Trigon
AFFILIATIONS Trinity of Sin, Council of Wizards, Justice League Dark

ROAD TO NOWHERE
Humanity's most reviled traitor learned over restless centuries that the only way to pay for his sin was saving the innocent and challenging the guilty.

AN UNWELCOME REUNION
As the centuries unfolded, it was inevitable that the restless Trinity of Sin would meet again: sometimes as allies but more often in acrimony, as when the Phantom Stranger encountered Pandora.

The Phantom Stranger is eternally atoning for committing the greatest sin in human history: betraying Jesus the Messiah for 30 pieces of silver to the religious authorities. In despair at his treachery, Jesus' former disciple, Judas Iscariot, tried to kill himself, but was brought before a Council of Wizards. He was deemed to be part of a Trinity of Sin—along with Pandora and the Question—and given a harsh punishment.

IN MYSTERIOUS WAYS
His noble intentions led to death and disaster, but Phantom's Stranger's failure was preordained to revive the Spirit of Vengeance when Earth needed him most.

Judas was compelled to walk amongst mankind on Earth forever and doomed to wear the blood-money for his betrayal around his neck. Returned to the scene of his appalling crime, a Great Voice ordered him to don the transformative robe of the One he had betrayed and begin his eternal penance. As the Phantom Stranger, Judas wandered the Earth for centuries, constantly seeking to atone for his crime, but unable to pause for long in any one place or enjoy human company—a stranger to all. As he wearily roamed, he waited for the Voice to command him again.

In recent times, the Voice told the Phantom Stranger to help ex-Gotham City police detective Jim Corrigan save his kidnapped fiancée, Gwen. The Stranger located Gwen, but unknowingly led the detective into a trap, and both Corrigan and Gwen were killed. The Voice imbued Corrigan's soul with the Spirit of Vengeance and he became the Spectre. The Spectre accused the Phantom Stranger of betrayal and would have destroyed him, had the Voice not intervened. The curse of treachery still lay heavy upon the Phantom Stranger, but at least his shameful, burdensome necklace now held one less coin.

The Phantom Stranger knows that his terrible curse remains—he is doomed to betray anyone that he tries to help on his long and tortured path toward eventual forgiveness. **WW**

ON THE RECORD

The Phantom Stranger of the 1950s was a complete mystery: a trenchcoated wanderer debunking charlatans, battling science-based threats, and defeating aliens from outer space.

As the 1960s closed, he returned as an enigmatic, mystic champion. In this incarnation, he confronted a legion of arcane enemies and eventually joined the Justice League of America. Such was his pervasive aura of mystery that, when his origins were finally revealed in *Secret Origins* #10 (Jan. 1987), readers were presented with four possible stories from which to choose.

MAN OF MYSTERY
The inscrutable Phantom Stranger instinctively seemed to know where and when someone needed his unique brand of problem-solving.

CLASSIC STORIES

***Phantom Stranger* (Vol. 2) #4 (Dec. 1969)** Dr. Thirteen inadvertently liberates Tala, the demonic Queen of Evil; the Phantom Stranger defeats her, but gains an implacable enemy.

***Phantom Stranger* (Vol. 3) #1-4 (Oct. 1987-Jan. 1988)** Reduced to a mere mortal, the Stranger battles Eclipso, Spirit of Wrath, before the villain transforms Earth into a realm of ultimate darkness.

***Legends* (Vol. 1) #1-6 (Nov. 1986-Apr. 1987)** The Phantom Stranger foils Darkseid's attempts to destroy Earth's concept of heroism.

POISON IVY

DATA

DEBUT *Batman* (Vol. 1) # 181 **(Jun. 1966)**
CURRENT VERSION *Birds of Prey* (Vol. 3) # 1 **(Nov. 2011)**
REAL NAME Pamela Lillian Isley
BASE Gotham City
HEIGHT 5ft 8in **WEIGHT** 115 lbs
EYES Green **HAIR** Red
POWERS/ABILITIES Controls and manipulates all plant life; immune to poisons and toxins; can transmit toxins and poisons via a kiss; wields plant-based pheromones that can cause people to fall under her hypnotic spell; highly intelligent and adept at botany and chemistry.
ALLIES Harley Quinn, Clayface
ENEMIES Batman, the Batman Family
AFFILIATIONS Birds of Prey, Justice League United

A TOUCH OF POISON
All plant life is ripe for Poison Ivy's control. She can grow a vine with a thought, or turn a harmless Venus fly trap into a deadly attack dog.

BUDDING GENIUS
Although sunlight damaged her delicate pale skin, little Pamela's only escape from a life of domestic terror was beside her mother in their lush and well-tended garden.

Poison Ivy is more than a simple super-villain. She's a complex creature, often appearing more plant than human. Ivy is an eco-terrorist with only the lives of plants the world over her concern. And while her objective of saving the planet from mankind's pollutants and deforestation is a noble one, the means by which she works towards that goal are borderline insane, making her another formidable figure in Batman's Rogues Gallery.

Pamela Isley grew up in an abusive home. Her mother was a kindly woman who enjoyed growing plants in her garden, an activity Pamela became very fond of. However, Pamela's father was a cruel man, who would routinely beat her mother. He'd buy her mother flowers for her garden as an apology, and she would take him back, despite her better instincts. This domestic violence escalated until the day Pamela's father killed her mother, burying her out back in that same garden. He was later taken into police custody, leaving Pamela alone in the world.

In college, Pamela's interest in chemistry grew. She developed pheromone pills by illegal means, landing her on academic probation. Using her pills and her natural charms, Isley seduced the dean into dropping all charges. Her next target was her father, whom Pamela went to visit in jail. Before leaving, she kissed him on the lips while wearing a toxic lipstick. Her father died in the jail, with no one wise to her.

Pamela went on to intern for Wayne Enterprises, working in their Bio-Chem division. She began to perfect her pheromone technology, but was fired when she tried to sell Bruce Wayne on the amoral concept. During a struggle in the lab, she was splashed with chemicals, which would grant her the plant-controlling abilities of Poison Ivy. She soon embarked on a criminal career, feeling a connection with the Green, the mystical web that connects all plant life. Mentally unhinged, she feels it's her destiny to create a plant-based utopia, while also destroying the world of man. **MM**

ON THE RECORD

In her original incarnation, Poison Ivy hadn't evolved into the physical threat she'd represent in her later appearances. Before the Crisis on Infinite Earths, Ivy was merely an attractive criminal with a gimmick, and a crush on the Dark Knight Detective.

After Crisis, she fully displayed her plant powers, joining the Suicide Squad briefly before signing up with a more informal team, the Gotham City Sirens, in the 2000s. This post-Crisis version of Ivy also had a hand in the origin of another femme fatale, Harley Quinn, when she served her a concoction that gave Harley enhanced reflexes and strength.

KNIGHT MOVES
Poison Ivy proved her stature as one of Batman's main foes during "Knightfall," when she massed a squad of enthralled warriors to take on the Dark Knight.

IN THE GARDEN OF EVIL
Poison Ivy was a dedicated and valiant member of the Birds of Prey, but only until she no longer had any use for them.

CLASSIC STORIES

***Batman* (Vol. 1) #181 (Jun. 1966)**
Poison Ivy debuts in Gotham City, proclaiming herself public enemy number one and catching the eye of the Dark Knight.

***Batman* (Vol. 1) #344 (Feb. 1982)**
Poison Ivy truly develops her plant-based powers as she attempts to destroy the Wayne Foundation.

***Batman: Poison Ivy* #1 (May 1997)**
In this one-shot, Poison Ivy's origin is retold for a modern audience, placing her first appearance much earlier in Batman's career.

***Batman: Shadow of the Bat* #88, *Batman* (Vol. 1) #568, *Detective Comics* (Vol. 1) #735 (Aug. 1999)**
Poison Ivy gains a green skin tone as she takes over Robinson Park during this chapter of the "No Man's Land" epic.

POWER GIRL (KARA ZOR-EL)

DEBUT *All-Star Comics* (Vol. 1) #58 **(Jan.–Feb. 1976)**
CURRENT VERSION *Mister Terrific* (Vol. 1) #1 **(Nov. 2011)**
REAL NAME Kara Zor-El, Karen Starr
BASE Starr Island on Earth-2, Micronesia on Earth-1
HEIGHT 5ft 11in **WEIGHT** 180 lbs
EYES Blue **HAIR** Blonde
POWERS/ABILITIES Genius-level intellect; super-strength; super-speed; flight; invulnerability; enhanced senses all fuelled by solar energy from a yellow sun.
ALLIES Huntress, Lois Lane, Tanya Spear, Dr. Gerhard, Val-Zod
ENEMIES Desaad, Kaizen Gamorra, Brutaal, Darkseid
AFFILIATIONS Eight Wonders of the World, Michael Holt

Kara Zor-El escaped Krypton and gained astounding abilities under Earth-2's yellow sun. Adopted by Clark Kent and his wife Lois Lane, she was coached by Superman (her cousin, Kal-El) to be his secret weapon and eventual partner. Kara yearned to publicly join the world's heroes, but invasion from Apokolips ended the dream forever.

When Superman, Batman, and Wonder Woman were killed, Kara and her friend Robin were catapulted out of their universe and into another. On Earth-1, Kara recreated herself as technology entrepreneur Karen Starr, building a company dedicated to bridging dimensions, to help her find her way back to Earth-2. As Power Girl she covertly secured funds and confiscated useful technologies to realize that wish. Only Robin—now calling herself Huntress—along with trusted assistant Somya Spears, and chief scientist Dr. Gerhard knew Karen's true nature and goals.

Despite occasional forays into super-heroics and clashes with Earth-2 nemesis Desaad, Karen's quest eventually bore fruit. Power Girl and Huntress returned home, to join Earth-2's surviving heroes in their fight against Darkseid. **MM**

ON THE RECORD

LOOKS LIKE TEEN SPIRIT
One of DC Comics' first legacy heroes, Power Girl debuted in 1976 as a youthful rebel within the company's oldest super team, the Justice Society of America.

Power Girl was created to add elements of youthful rebellion to the newly-revived Justice Society of America. Bored being cousin Superman's secret weapon, the impatient teenager ignored his orders to stay hidden and exploded into very public action alongside to save the aging heroes from the menace of Brainwave. She gradually evolved from obnoxious brat into the backbone of the team and eventually its leader.

Kara served with distinction in both Justice League America and Justice League International and became a stellar solo star, surviving numerous reality-altering events virtually unchanged, aside from her constantly overwritten origin story. She was also one of the few heroes equally at home in humorous and action-adventure tales. She developed aggressive mood-swings after bingeing on a diet soda to which she was allergic, leading to her being possessed by the Spirit of Wrath, Eclipso.

In all situations, whether smashing subterranean invasions, repelling mystical incursions, or simply accompanying alien princesses to Earth nightclubs, Power Girl always proved her take-charge, no-nonsense attitude was the quickest way to get the job done.

POWER GIRL (TANYA SPEARS)

DEBUT *Worlds' Finest* #23 **(Jul. 2014)**
BASE New York City
REAL NAME Tanya Spears
HEIGHT 5ft 3in **WEIGHT** 120 lbs **EYES** Brown **HAIR** Black
POWERS/ABILITIES Genius intellect; superhuman strength; the ability to alter her size at will.
ALLIES Karen Starr, Huntress
ENEMIES Desaad, Manchester Black
AFFILIATIONS Teen Titans

HEAVY LIFTER
Tanya shows off her prodigious strength, impressing even the usually blasé Wonder Girl.

Tanya Spears inherited the role of Power Girl, after her predecessor—Karen Starr—returned to Earth-2, leaving her company, her fortune, and her Super Hero name to the daughter of her greatest friend, Somya Spears. Somya had run Starr Industries for Karen, allowing the displaced Kryptonian to fight injustice and find a way back home.

Somya's daughter Tanya was a scientific prodigy. By the age of 17, she had earned a postdoctoral fellowship at the Massachusetts Institute of Technology. Later, while working at Starr Industries, Tanya was taken hostage by a terrorist determined to steal nuclear isotopes produced by the company. She was rescued by Karen Starr's Earth-2 partner Huntress, who captured the terrorist; during the incident Tanya was accidentally exposed to isotope radiation.

As Huntress and Karen prepared for their return to Earth-2, Tanya was attacked by the exiled Apokoliptian Desaad, who realized he could use her newfound power to follow the heroes to their homeworld and rejoin his master, Darkseid. In the ensuing assault, Starr Industries' lab was completely destroyed. However, when rescue workers started digging her out of the rubble, Tanya discovered she had acquired some of Power Girl's metahuman abilities. She later learned from Karen Starr's lawyers that those powers were a parting gift from a grateful friend. Karen had also legally transferred her codename Power Girl to Tanya as well as all her money and properties. Seeking help to understand her new, extraordinary abilities and her new, heroic direction in life, Tanya left Boston for New York, hoping to join the Teen Titans. After an initial misunderstanding that allied her with Manchester Black's new Elite team, she achieved her goal and became a mainstay of the Teen Titans. **AI**

SUPER-SIZE ME
She may be a superpowered genius, but Tanya Spears is also a teenager coming to terms with her new powers—as the manipulative Manchester Black quickly learned to his cost.

POWER COMPANY

DEBUT *JLA* (Vol. 1) #61 **(Feb. 2002)**
CURRENT VERSION *Teen Titans* (Vol. 5) #1 **(Sep. 2014)** (Josiah Power only)
BASE San Francisco, California
MEMBERS AND POWERS **Josiah Power**: Very powerful metahuman; **Manhunter**: Enhanced speed, rapid healing, martial arts; **Skyrocket**: Energy-manipulating harness; **Witchfire**: Magic-wielder; **Bork**: Super-strength, invulnerability; **Sapphire**: Telekinesis; **Striker Z**: Super-strength; capable of energy absorption and release; **Firestorm**: Flight, nuclear transmutation.
ALLIES Superman, Green Arrow, Wonder Woman, Nightwing
ENEMIES Black Dragon Society, Doctor Cyber, Cadre, Dragoneer, Strike Force, Jack Spheer, Crime Syndicate of America
AFFILIATIONS Conglomerate, Blood Pack, Hero Hotline, S.T.A.R. Corps, Captains of Industry, S.T.A.R. Labs

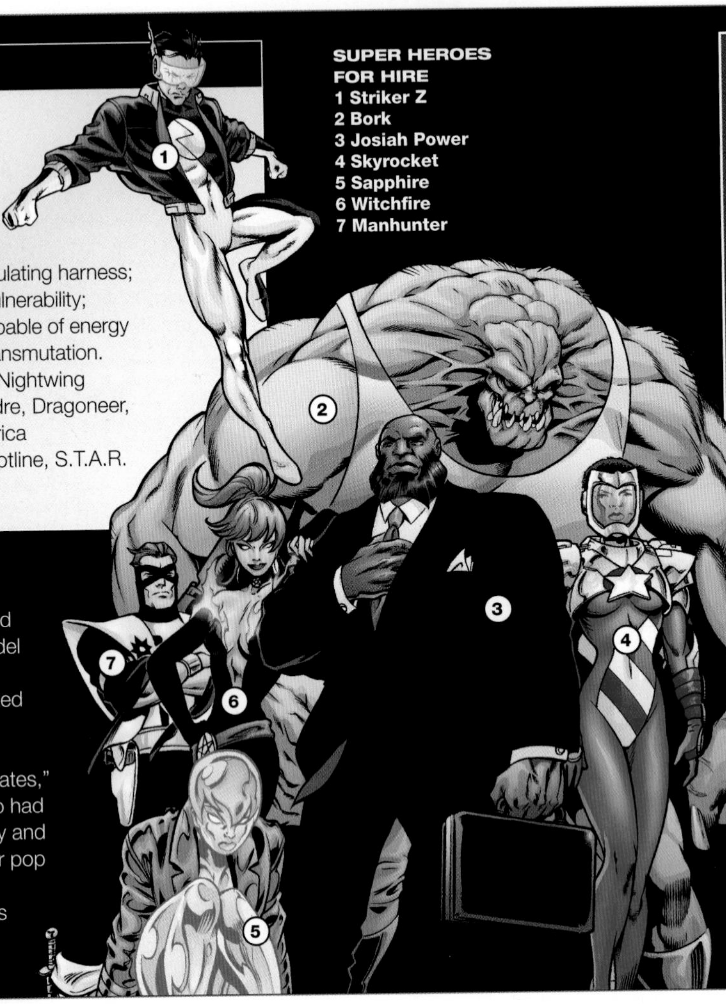

SUPER HEROES FOR HIRE
1 Striker Z
2 Bork
3 Josiah Power
4 Skyrocket
5 Sapphire
6 Witchfire
7 Manhunter

The Power Company was a Super Hero team created by attorney Josiah Power. When his metagene triggered in the middle of a trial, he was fired from his law firm. Power then devised a business model providing Super Hero services to paying clients. He recruited some minor champions and supplemented them with established characters, such as Firestorm.

Set up along the lines of a law firm, the front line Super Heroes were divided into "Partners" or "Associates," supported by specialists and administrative staff, who had extensive experience with the metahuman community and weird science. Power's personal assistant was former pop star Silver Shannon (of The Maniaks) and the Power Company boasted high profile contracts with the likes of S.T.A.R. Labs and St. Claire Industries. After initial success, the business is now "on hiatus." **WW**

ON THE RECORD

The Power Company was composed of established characters and newcomers, but the most controversial recruit was undoubtedly Carl Bork. The hulking, constantly-mutating behemoth was originally a brutal petty criminal who strong-armed his way to top of the gangs running Gotham City's Docks. Bork's invulnerability stemmed from a mystic idol carved in his likeness by a witch doctor, and only ended after the Flash hurled the devilish totem into the sun.

HEAVY HITTER
Bork was slow and stupid, but painfully epitomized the concept that whatever can't be hurt can't be stopped.

POLAR BOY

DEBUT *Adventure Comics* (Vol. 1) #306 (Mar. 1963)
CURRENT VERSION *Legion of Super-Heroes* Vol. 7 #1 (Nov. 2011)
REAL NAME Brek Bannin
BASE Legion HQ, 31st-century Metropolis
HEIGHT 5ft 5in **WEIGHT** 140 lbs
EYES Blue **HAIR** Blond
POWERS/ABILITIES Generation of extreme cold, ice and snow; exceptional strategist.
ENEMIES Ambush Bug, Plant Men, Captain Freeze

STAY COOL
Polar Boy never allowed any setback or mishap to divert him from his ultimate goal of being a Legionnaire.

Hailing from the super-hot planet Tharr, Brek Bannin came to Earth to be a hero. He was the youngest candidate ever to audition for the Legion of Super-Heroes and this, in part, was the reason for his rejection. The other was that in his eagerness to please, he lost control of his ability to project waves of intense cold. Undeterred, Brek met with other unsuccessful applicants to create a replacement team. His aim was to aid the Legion in secret and prove them wrong for rejecting himself and his comrades.

He proved an able leader and over the years forged the Legion of Substitute Heroes into a top-rate fighting unit. Polar Boy was eventually rewarded by finally being inducted into the Legion of Super-Heroes. Before long his efficiency under increasingly dangerous circumstances saw Brek elected leader of his new team, too. **WW**

PRAXIS

DEBUT *The Spectre* (Vol. 2) #24 (Feb. 1989)
REAL NAME Jason Praxis
BASE Portland, Oregon
HEIGHT 6ft 7in **WEIGHT** 168 lbs
EYES Blue **HAIR** Blond
POWERS/ABILITIES Psionic powers including telepathy, telekinesis, mind-reading and mind-control, psionic shields, mind-blasts, illusion-casting, and camouflage; good detective.
ENEMIES Richard Redditch, Ghast, Dexter Defarge

HAUNTED BY EVIL
Praxis was continually conflicted—feeling degraded whenever he used his abominable abilities to help victims of horrific crimes.

Jason Praxis never liked using his vast array of psionic gifts to solve crimes, even though they inevitably drew him into the weirdest and most uncanny cases. This was because he gained most of them from a serial killer. Praxis had been hunting metahuman maniac Richard Redditch, but when he—and the Spectre—cornered the killer, Redditch possessed him. Redditch died in Jason's body, leaving behind his murderous proclivities like a dark stain.

Eventually, the lawman realized he could do good with Redditch's powers and began a Super Hero career with Booster Gold's team the Conglomerate. When that didn't pan out, he went back to detective work, but supernatural menaces still seemed drawn to him. Relocated to Oregon, Praxis joined FBI agent Deanna Walker to stop magician Dexter Defarge resurrecting the antediluvian demon Ghast. Praxis was helped out by the Justice League and then went into semi-retirement. **WW**

PRIMAL FORCE

DEBUT *Primal Force* (Vol. 1) #0 (Oct. 1994)
BASE Manhattan, New York City
MEMBERS AND POWERS **Doctor Mist**: Immortal magician and sage; **Claw**: Demonic right hand gives superpowers; **Nightmaster**: Magic sword; **Golem**: Super-strength; **Jack O'Lantern**: Magic lantern bestows superpowers; **Meridian Mychaels**: Teleportation martial artist; **Red Tornado**: Creates air vortexes; **Black Condor**: Flight, telekinesis; **Willpower**: Electromagnetism.
ALLIES Superman, the Water Woman, Zatanna
ENEMIES Cataclysm, Satannus, Cult of August, Master Chu, Prince Inferno

For 2,000 years mystic warriors the Leymen secretly protected humanity from magical threats. They were originally gathered by immortal mage Nommo—known today as Doctor Mist—and, armed with mystic Ley Pendulums, they patrolled the Earth via its network of Ley Lines.

When the modern cabal was eradicated during Zero Hour, Mist's sorcerous protocols came into play and a new squad was hastily gathered by Mist's agent, the Water Woman. This ill-prepared band was equipped with its own Ley Pendulums and began battling ancient and modern sorcerers and sects. Calling themselves Primal Force, they were drawn to many supernatural and magical crises, but eventually fell battling the monstrous Cataclysm. The survivors joined groups such as Shadowpact, and awaited the Water Woman's next call to arms. **WW**

THE LAST HURRAH
Despite their desperate determination and dedication, the last gathering of Leymen was a force destined to fail.
1 Golem
2 Black Condor
3 Will Power
4 Meridian Mychaels
5 Jack O'Lantern
6 Red Tornado
7 Claw

PREZ

DEBUT *Prez* (Vol. 1) #1 **(Aug.-Sep. 1973)**
CURRENT VERSION *Convergence: Batgirl* (Vol. 1) #2 **(Jul. 2015)**
REAL NAME Beth Ross
BASE Eugene, Oregon; Washington, DC, 2036
EYES Green **HAIR** Bleach blonde
POWERS/ABILITIES Honesty, common sense, compassion, straight talking, hatred of hypocrites.
ALLIES Vice President Preston Rickard, Amber Waves, Joni Andersen
ENEMIES Senator Jay Thorn, Senator Tom Downey, Boss Smiley, Grizzly Tobacco, Pharmaduke
AFFILIATIONS Li'l Doggies House of Corndogs, Anonymous

Working in a fast-food franchise, 19-year-old Beth Ross accidentally battered and deep-fried her own hair. When friends posted a video of the incident online, "Corndog Girl" went viral. In election year 2036, owing to public apathy and the venality of politicians, an amendment was passed allowing voting by email and social media. With Beth trending stratospherically, hacker collective Anonymous launched a campaign and, despite political chicanery, good-hearted Beth became President. Her first order of duty was to overturn centuries of institutional corruption. She filled her cabinet with "actual smart people" and made the most hated politician in America—Preston Rickard—her Vice President. As he himself pointed out, no one would try to assassinate her if he was next in line for the top job. **WW**

SOCIALLY AWARE
Beth had no interest in politics, but was determined that people like her dad shouldn't have to die because they were poor.

ON THE RECORD

Teenage US President Prez Rickard debuted in 1973, working tirelessly to make America a cooler, hipper, and more surreal place. His idealistic vision for the Land of the Free was bitterly contested by vested corporate interests—exemplified by Boss Smiley—and his tenure was plagued by various bizarre attacks. He was even saved from a marauding witch by Supergirl. His legacy in the modern, post-Flashpoint re-imagining can be seen in the person of Vice-President Preston Rickard.

DEMOCRACY IN ACTION
Prez was elected after the voting age was lowered to include teenagers, and he stormed in on a "Youth Protest" landslide.

PROFESSOR IVO

DEBUT *Brave and the Bold* (Vol. 1) #30 **(Jun.-Jul. 1960)**
CURRENT VERSION *Justice League* (Vol. 2) #3 **(Jan. 2012)**
REAL NAME Anthony Ivo
EYES Black **HAIR** None
POWERS/ABILITIES Genius intellect, advanced knowledge of engineering, computer science, chemistry and biology; indefinitely extended lifespan; mutated form, which is bullet- and energy-blast-proof and toxin-resistant.
ALLIES The Outsider, T.O. Morrow, Amazo
ENEMIES Justice League, Justice League of America, Green Arrow
AFFILIATIONS Silas Stone, S.T.A.R. Labs, A.R.G.U.S., Secret Society of Super-Villains, Ivy University

Anthony Ivo is a true mad scientist, obsessed with results and careless of the harm his work causes. He was head of the Cellular and Structural Biology Department at Ivy University before being recruited by S.T.A.R. Labs to supervise their top-security Red Room in Detroit. This was a research repository for extraterrestrial, futuristic, and arcane technologies considered too dangerous for public knowledge. From his discoveries, Ivo developed the A-Maze Operating System, which resulted in the creation of machines able to mimic organic life down to the cellular level.

Ivo is terrified of dying and many of his discoveries stem from a determination to live forever. He emerged from the shadows after building the android Amazo to replicate the powers of the Justice League, subsequently devising a serum which greatly enhanced his lifespan. So great was his phobia that he cared little when it monstrously mutated his body such that he grew a second, near-impenetrable skin.

Fully embracing his evil side, he returned to constructing killer-androids and worked with the trans-dimensional Outsider to create the Secret Society of Super-Villains. **WW**

ON THE RECORD

In his first incarnation, Professor Ivo was one of the Justice League of America's most pernicious foes. His quest for immortality and expertise in creating robots and androids tested the heroes many times, and he was the man responsible for the JLA's biggest body-count.

When a stripped-down JLA relocated to Detroit, they were targeted by an army of Ivo's killer-droids, which murdered Vibe and Steel, and caused the despondent team to disband.

ETERNAL ENEMY
Ivo battled the JLA so often that he lost his mind and his humanity, until all that remained was hatred and madness.

PRINCESS PROJECTRA

DEBUT *Adventure Comics* #346 (Jul. 1966)
CURRENT VERSION *Legion of Super-Heroes* (Vol. 7) #12 (Oct. 2012)
REAL NAME Projectra
HEIGHT 5ft 6in **WEIGHT** 130 lbs
EYES Purple **HAIR** White
POWERS/ABILITIES Projections of three-dimensional illusions; strong sensory perceptions.
ALLIES Karate Kid
ENEMIES Nemesis Kid
AFFILIATIONS Legion of Super-Heroes

Scion of the royal family on her home world of Orando, Princess Projectra joined the Legion of Super-Heroes and gained fame because of her illusion-projecting abilities. She fell in love with teammate Karate Kid and they were married. When he was killed, she hunted down his murderer, Nemesis Kid, and eliminated him in revenge. Taking his life was a violation of the Legion's code, and she resigned from the group.

Princess Projectra later returned under the new moniker Sensor Girl, disguising her true identity from her teammates—though she was later unmasked by the Emerald Empress. She traveled with the Legion back to the 21st century, where they were separated until the combined efforts of the Justice League of America and the Justice Society of America brought them together. During the course of this mission, Sensor Girl helped bring back Wally West (the Flash) from an alternate reality at the same time Bart Allen appeared to have died. **AI**

ROYAL LEGIONNAIRE
Princess Projectra resigned following the murder of her husband Karate Kid, but she later returned to the Legion in the guise of Sensor Girl.

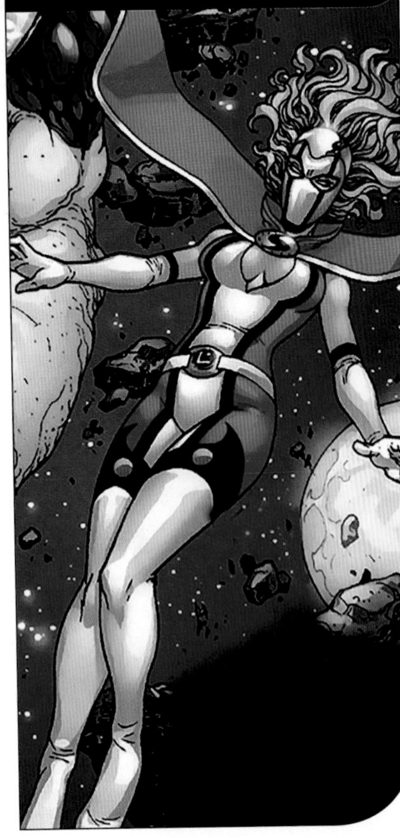

PROFESSOR PYG

DEBUT *Batman* #666 (Jul. 2007)
CURRENT VERSION *Batman* (Vol. 2) #1 (Nov. 2011)
REAL NAME Lazlo Valentin
BASE Gotham City
HEIGHT 5ft 11in **WEIGHT** 195 lbs
EYES Brown **HAIR** Brown
POWERS/ABILITIES Skilled at surgery.
ALLIES Scarecrow, Bane
ENEMIES Batman
AFFILIATIONS Circus of Strange, Secret Society of Super-Villains

Driven insane by his exposure to Doctor Dedalus' Spyral labyrinth, Lazlo Valentin became the pig mask-wearing Professor Pyg. He was committed to Arkham Asylum for his deranged medical experiments and was later prevented from escaping by Batman and Nightwing during a riot. Pyg, however, was freed to continue his exploits when the Crime Syndicate of America's attack drew attention away from Arkham.

Primarily, Pyg's work consisted of kidnapping unfortunate citizens of Gotham City and performing bizarre surgeries on them before adding doll-face masks that turned them into Dollotrons, his minions. In the lawless Gotham City created as Batman and other heroes were drawn into fighting the Crime Syndicate and the Secret Society of Super-Villains, Scarecrow struck a deal with Pyg to use his army of Dollotrons. Soon after, Bane slaughtered the Dollotrons and forced Pyg to work for him instead. **AI**

DRESSED TO KILL
In the pursuit of extreme medical breakthroughs, Professor Pyg didn't think twice about switching limbs on some of his unfortunate "patients."

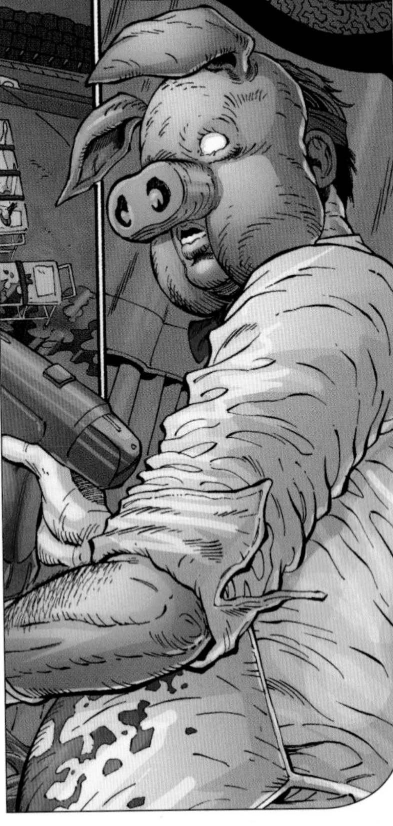

PROFESSOR ZOOM

DEBUT *The Flash* (Vol. 1) #139 (Sep. 1963)
CURRENT VERSION *The Flash* (Vol. 4) #40 (May 2015)
REAL NAME Eobard Thawne
BASE Central City; Keystone City in the year 2463
HEIGHT 5ft 11in **WEIGHT** 179 lbs
EYES Blue **HAIR** White
POWERS/ABILITIES Can control the passage of time around him to make him appear faster than everyone else; can affect the age of organic and inorganic matter.
ALLIES The Acolytes of Zoom
ENEMIES The Flash, Henry Allen, Magali

In the year 2463, young Eobard Thawne's father killed his mother and was jailed. A brilliant scientist fixated with the Super Hero the Flash (Barry Allen), Thawne went on to gain Speed Force powers similar to those of the Scarlet Speedster, and took the name Zoom. He used his newfound abilities to try to take over the Gem Cities (Central City and Keystone). However, inspired by the memory of the long-dead Flash, the people of these cities rose up against Thawne, who subsequently destroyed the Flash Museum in Central City during an intense fit of jealousy.

Thawne later acquired Rip Hunter's notes on time travel and built a new Cosmic Treadmill, using it to go back in time to kill Flash's mother—mirroring his own early life. Thawne believed that if Barry had the same bad start, he would not have become a hero. Zoom formed a group of acolytes with powers based on Speed Force energy to help defeat the Flash. However, when they realized Thawne was evil, they defeated the villain. **AI**

ON THE RECORD

In his first appearance, Thawne was also called the Reverse-Flash and for much of his career was known as Professor Zoom. Other pre-Flashpoint villains had also called themselves Zoom—each with a similar yellow costume that was a reverse of the Flash's; these included Citizen Abra, a time-traveler from the 64th century, and criminal profiler Hunter Zolomon.

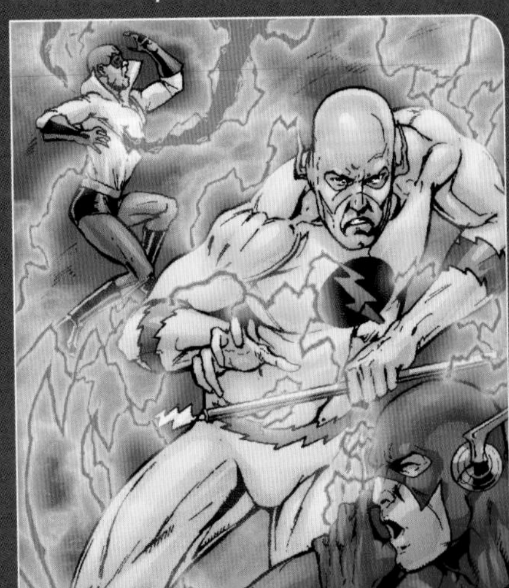

NEED FOR SPEED
Thawne was obsessed with the Speed Force, traversing timelines and dimensions to carry on his maniacal battle against all Flashes.

PROMETHEUS

DEBUT *Prometheus* #1 (Dec. 1997)
CURRENT VERSION *Midnighter* #1 (Aug. 2015)
BASE The Ghost Zone
HEIGHT 6ft 1in **WEIGHT** 180 lbs
EYES Brown **HAIR** White
POWERS/ABILITIES Genius intellect; technologically advanced armor and nightstick.
ENEMIES JLA
AFFILIATIONS Injustice Gang

All that is known of Prometheus' history is that he saw his criminal parents gunned down in a firefight with police, and devoted himself thereafter to destroying the forces of law and order any way he could.

He designed an armored suit with a cybernetic interface that made him an expert martial artist and set up camp in the Ghost Zone using the artifact known as the Cosmic Key. In the Zone, he built his headquarters, the Crooked House, which he utilized as a laboratory to develop his technological resources. He also used his House as a base from which to strike out at the Justice League of America. He saw the JLA as the ultimate law-enforcement organization, and therefore most in need of destruction. A psychotic devotee of violence, Prometheus has bested the JLA singlehandedly at times, but has also been defeated by Catwoman and Green Arrow—proving advanced technology is not the only way to win a battle. **AI**

TECHNOLOGICAL PROWESS
Prometheus continually refined his armor. His computerized helmet was Inked to his brain and he wielded an energized nightstick.

PSIONS, THE

DEBUT *The Witching Hour* #13 (Feb.–Mar. 1971)
CURRENT VERSION *Green Lantern Corps* (Vol. 3) #11 (Sep. 2012)
BASE Maltus
HEIGHT Variable **WEIGHT** Variable
EYES Yellow **HAIR** None
POWERS/ABILITIES Highly advanced technology.
ENEMIES Green Lantern Corps, Guardians
AFFILIATIONS Maltusian immortals

Created by the Oans from non-sentient reptilian life-forms on the planet Maltus, the Psions became ruthless experimenters just as their creators had been. The Psions traveled across the universe, searching out knowledge and stopping at nothing to pursue advancements in their technology. They viewed their experimental procedures on the native species of different planets as a gift and constantly strived to improve themselves through experimentation.

A group of Psions captured the Guardian Quaros and subjected him to brutal tests, melding his mind with the ship's command system. They also took possession of his Mother Box. Kyle Rayner and the New Guardians were tracking him, and when they found the Psions' ship, Quaros was able to free other imprisoned Guardians before causing the ship to self-destruct. Unfortunately, in so doing, Quaros killed the Psions, their long-suffering test subjects—and himself. **AI**

EXTRATERRESTRIAL TERROR
After discovering the experimental subjects, Kyle Rayner and Carol Ferris came face to face with the Psion menace.

PRYSM

DEBUT *Teen Titans* (Vol. 2) #1 (Oct. 1996)
REAL NAME Audrey Spears
HEIGHT 6ft 4in
POWERS/ABILITIES Invisibility; energy absorption and projection of light.
ALLIES Argent II, Hot Spot, Risk
ENEMIES Warlord, H'San Natall
AFFILIATIONS Teen Titans

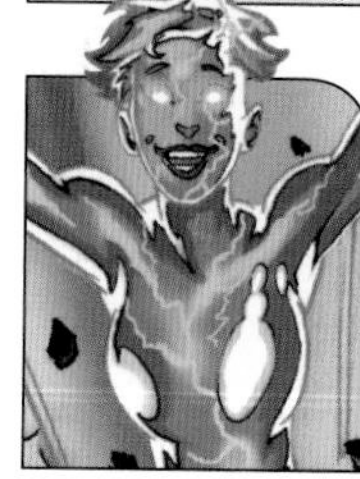

The alien H'San Natall created a human hybrid breeding program to install sleeper agents on Earth. One of these was Audrey Spears, who grew up inside a virtual fantasy world modeled on the popular shows of 1950s television. Escaping her artificial environment, she went to Earth with other hybrid teens Argent II, Hot Spot, and Risk, adopting the name Prysm for her ability to manipulate light. She later founded the post-Zero Hour Teen Titans.

Prysm hated the glassy appearance of her crystalline body structure, caused by the interaction of human and H'San Natall genomes. After meeting her true parents, she convinced the H'San Natall to stop their infiltration of Earth, and then remained with her parents in space, never feeling at home on Earth, nor with her hybrid teammates—particularly Risk, for whom she nursed unrequited romantic feelings. **AI**

PSIMON

DEBUT *New Teen Titans* (Vol. 1) #3 (Jan. 1981)
CURRENT VERSION *Forever Evil* #1 (Nov. 2013)
REAL NAME Simon Jones
HEIGHT 5ft 11in **WEIGHT** 145 lbs
EYES White **HAIR** None
POWERS/ABILITIES Immense telepathic and telekinetic powers; mind control.
ALLIES Trigon, Doctor Siva
ENEMIES Teen Titans, Outsiders
AFFILIATIONS Fearsome Five, Injustice League

During an experiment designed to breach the barriers between dimensions, physicist Simon Jones was struck by a beam of other-dimensional energy. Surviving the mishap, Jones discovered he had gained incredible psychic and psionic powers.

As Psimon, Jones joined villainous team the Fearsome Five and battled the New Teen Titans. One of its members, Raven, discovered Psimon was an agent of her father, the demon Trigon, who was also the source of Jones's power. After failing to defeat the Titans, Trigon banished Psimon to another dimension. After several further appearances, Psimon was exiled to a prison planet alongside other super-villains. He proposed starting a civilization there instead of trying to escape. The Joker, unamused by this idea, crushed his head with a rock. **AI**

PSYCHO-PIRATE

DEBUT *All-Star Comics* #23 (Winter 1944–1945) (Charley Halstead); *Showcase* #56 (May–Jun. 1995) (Roger Hayden)
CURRENT VERSION *Superboy* (Vol. 6) #23 (Oct. 2013)
REAL NAME Roger Hayden
HEIGHT 6ft 1in **WEIGHT** 180 lbs
EYES Green **HAIR** Red
POWERS/ABILITIES Medusa Mask conveys ability to control others' emotions.
ALLIES Anti-Monitor
ENEMIES Power Girl, Black Adam

Roger Hayden, better known as the Psycho-Pirate, was one of the Twenty, a group of otherwise unremarkable humans who Brainiac had infected with a virus that granted them psionic powers, but also destabilized them mentally.

Hayden believed the Medusa Mask would give him control over the virus. Escaping the H.I.V.E. Queen, who was draining the psychic energies of the Twenty, Psycho-Pirate tracked down Superman after learning his secret identity. He informed him that Brainiac was going to use the Twenty as hosts for the minds of people from Brainiac's destroyed home planet, and that the H.I.V.E. Queen planned to harvest psionic energy until she was powerful enough to enslave the entire world. He then attempted to drain Superman's psychic energy and use it to free his fellow psychics from the H.I.V.E. Queen's prison, but was defeated by a superpowered Lois Lane. **AI**

EMOTIONAL CATHARSIS
After the death of original Psycho-Pirate, Charles Halstead, Roger Hayden used a single Medusa Mask to control the whole emotional spectrum.

QUEEN BEE

DEBUT *Justice League of America* (Vol. 1) #23 **(Nov. 1963)**
CURRENT VERSION *Superman* #21 **(Aug. 2013)**
BASE Metropolis/The Swarm
HEIGHT 5ft 8in **WEIGHT** 135 lbs
EYES Brown **HAIR** Blonde
POWERS/ABILITIES Mind control; psychokinesis; psionic blasts; physical regeneration; creation of illusions.
ALLIES Brainiac
ENEMIES Superman, Hector Hammond, Psycho-Pirate
AFFILIATIONS H.I.V.E.

Queen Bee of H.I.V.E.—the Holistic Integration for Viral Equality—was one of the Twenty, humans abducted by Brainiac, the Collector of Worlds, and then returned after alien experimentation endowed them with considerable psychic powers. She controlled an army of agents devoted to her ultimate goal: spreading a mental virus to psychically dominate first Metropolis and then everyone on Earth. Her powers were enhanced by a substance called Techno-Plasmic Waste, purified from the emanations of negative emotions.

Both Hector Hammond and Superman fought her, but found her mind-control and telepathy powers difficult to overcome. She revealed that she was working on behalf of her "father," Brainiac, to protect the people of Earth by mentally enslaving them. As part of this plan, she hunted the rest of the Twenty and incarcerated psychics in a prison called the Swarm to tap their powers. The Psycho-Pirate, another of the Twenty, attacked her and she allied with Superman and Hector Hammond to defeat him break his control over the citizens of Metropolis. Along the way, she revealed her true appearance, and escaped to continue furthering Brainiac's machinations. **AI**

ON THE RECORD

Queen Bee and her swarms of Bee-Troopers joined Lex Luthor's Injustice Gang after making a deal that she would receive a portion of Earth's population as psychic slaves in return. She double-crossed Luthor and created her Royal Egg-Matrix in New York City, kicking off her eventual plan to turn all humans into her drones. Defeated, she later returned as a member of the Secret Society of Super-Villains and head of a criminal syndicate called H.I.V.E..

H.I.V.E. MIND
When Queen Bee threatened to turn the Earth's Super Heroes into mindless drones, she drew the attention of the New Gods, including Big Barda.

QUEEN, EMIKO

DEBUT *Green Arrow* #18 (May 2013)
HEIGHT 5ft 2in **WEIGHT** 100 lbs
EYES Brown **HAIR** Black
POWERS/ABILITIES Skilled archer; acrobat; and hand-to-hand combatant.
ALLIES Green Arrow
ENEMIES Komodo

The half-sister of Oliver Queen and daughter of archer and former assassin, Shado, Emiko Queen was kidnapped by Komodo as an infant and raised as one of the Outsiders, training as an archer. In her first battle as a member of the Outsiders, she wounded Green Arrow, unaware of their family ties. She had grown up believing that her parents were both dead and only realized the truth when she saw them at the Outsiders' Prague headquarters. Enraged, she turned on Komodo, and, in the ensuing battle, her father Robert Queen was killed. Emiko then killed Komodo and made her way to Seattle, finding her half-brother Oliver and helping him to fight the Longbow Hunters.

She then tried to claim the title of Green Arrow from him. Naturally he resisted this, and the two of them commenced an uneasy partnership, with Oliver training Emiko until she felt ready to strike out on her own heroic path. Recently, Emiko fought side-by-side with Green Arrow and Black Canary to take down the slave-trading Underground Men. Their triumph was short-lived, when Emiko reunited with her mother, Shado, to attack Oliver in his own home. **AI**

SIBLING RIVALRY
After first joining forces with her brother Oliver, Emiko fought him to be the next Green Arrow—until, like most siblings, they made their peace.

QUEEN OF FABLES

DEBUT *Justice League of America* #47 (Nov. 2000)
REAL NAME Tsaritsa
HEIGHT 5ft 10in **WEIGHT** 130 lbs
EYES Green **HAIR** Red
POWERS/ABILITIES Vast magical abilities, including rearranging reality.
ENEMIES Justice League of America

Centuries ago, Tsaritsa, the Queen of Fables arrived on Earth from another dimension, initiating a magical reign of terror, until her enemy Snow White trapped her in the Book of Fables. At the dawn of the 21st century, Tsaritsa escaped to sow chaos and calamity in New York City by conjuring a horde of ogres, witches, and goblins. The Justice League of America clashed with Tsaritsa when she attacked Wonder Woman, believing the Amazon to be the daughter of her old nemesis because of Diana's physical resemblance to Snow White.

With her unique brand of sorcery, the Queen drew the JLA into the realm of fairytales, where they faced monsters on an enchanted Manhattan Island. Eventually, Wonder Woman used her lasso to defeat Tsaritsa, imprisoning her inside a new book—the United States Tax Code. Within its dry, literal pages, the Queen of Fables was unlikely to find any magical elements to help her escape. However, she did free herself, later trying to seduce Superman and then turn a slanderous movie about Wonder Woman into the Amazon Queen's new reality. **AI**

SIMPLY FABULOUS
Mysteriously freeing herself from her tax code imprisonment, the Queen of Fables set her sights on winning her very own Prince Charming: Superman!

QUESTION, THE

DEBUT *Blue Beetle* (Vol. 3) #1 **(Jun. 1967)**
CURRENT VERSION *The New 52: Free Comic Book Day Special Edition* #1 **(Jun. 2012)**
BASE Mobile
HEIGHT 6ft 2in **WEIGHT** 185 lbs **EYES** Unknown **HAIR** Unknown
POWERS/ABILITIES Immortality, teleportation, shape-shifting, mental influence, other magical powers; use of the Spear of Inquisition.
ALLIES Doctor Thirteen, Phantom Stranger, Pandora
ENEMIES Phantom Stranger, Pandora
AFFILIATIONS Trinity of Sin

ON THE RECORD

Two people previously took on the role of the Question. Crusading reporter Vic Sage (the alter ego of Charles Victor Zsasz) was the first, tackling corruption and crime in Hub City. When he was stricken with the cancer that eventually killed him, Gotham City police detective Renee Montoya became the new Question. With extensive martial-arts training and her police experience, she battled threats from street crime to the Final Crisis, often in cooperation with Batman.

NEXT QUESTION
Intrepid Gotham City detective Renee Montoya is unable escape her strange destiny: to take on the role of the enigmatic Question.

The Question's true name and history are unknown. At some point in the distant past, he was called before the Council of Eternity to answer for his sins, along with Pandora and the man who would become the Phantom Stranger. Denying the Council's authority, he was punished by having his identity erased and his face magically disguised behind a blank visage.

In current times, he tried to take possession of Pandora's Box, hoping it would answer the question of his identity, but failed. He attempted to kill the Phantom Stranger, but later allied with him and Pandora; together they are known as the Trinity of Sin.

He was later tortured by the magical being Nimraa as part of her efforts to bring Dark Earth back into being, using the ritual power of the Trinity's sins. The Question betrayed Pandora and the Phantom Stranger, causing all of them to be imprisoned on Dark Earth. He atoned for that crime by leading the Trinity's escape and then attacked the other two to absorb their portions of Dark Earth's sin energy into himself. After this, he vanished, no one knows where. **AI**

TRINITY OF SIN
Phantom Stranger, Pandora, and the Question.

QUICK, JESSE

DEBUT ***Justice Society of America*** **(Vol. 2) #1 (Aug. 1992)**
REAL NAME Jesse Chambers
BASE Keystone City
HEIGHT 5ft 9in **WEIGHT** 142 lbs
EYES Blue **HAIR** Blond
POWERS/ABILITIES Super-speed; strength; flight.
ENEMIES Savitar

The daughter of World War II heroes Johnny Quick (not the Crime Syndicate villain of the same name) and Liberty Belle, Jesse Chambers inherited her parents' powers—notably her father's access to the Speed Force, which she could tap into by reciting the formula "3x2(9YZ)4A." Calling herself Jesse Quick, she fought alongside other speedsters, including the Flash (Wally West), Max Mercury, and Impulse.

She joined the Justice Society of America and the Teen Titans, juggling those responsibilities with her role as CEO of Quickstart Enterprises after her father was killed by speedster villain Savitar. Later she adopted her mother's role, becoming the new Liberty Belle and marrying JSA teammate Hourman. After the Teen Titans disbanded, Jesse maintained her heroic double duties by joining the JLA. **AI**

QUICK, JOHNNY

DEBUT ***More Fun Comics*** **#71 (Sep. 1941) (John Chambers);** ***Justice League of America*** **(Vol. 1) #29 (Aug. 1964) (Syndicate member)**
CURRENT VERSION ***Justice League*** **(Vol. 2) #23 (Oct. 2013)**
REAL NAME Jonathan Allen
BASE Earth-3
HEIGHT 5ft 11in **WEIGHT** 170 lbs
EYES Blue **HAIR** Blond
POWERS/ABILITIES Super-speed, concentrated and enhanced by a special helmet.

Earth-3 criminal Jonathan Allen and his girlfriend Rhonda Pineda were trapped at a S.T.A.R. Labs facility when lightning struck them. Allen gained superspeed and dubbed himself Johnny Quick, while Rhonda became size-changing Atomica.

When Earth-3 was endangered, they looked for an escape route, along with the rest of the Crime Syndicate of America. With the help of Earth-3's Alfred Pennyworth and Atomica, who had infiltrated the Justice League as the Atom, they found their way out. Attacking the Crime Syndicate's foes, Johnny sent the Teen Titans into the future and killed members of Doom Patrol. His luck ran out when he fell foul of a group of villains pitching in to save the world. Captain Cold froze Johnny Quick's leg and Alexander Luthor—as Mazahs—broke his neck. **AI**

R.E.B.E.L.S.

DEBUT *R.E.B.E.L.S.* (Vol. 1) #0 **(Oct. 1994)**
REAL NAME Revolutionary Elite Brigade to Eradicate L.E.G.I.O.N. Supremacy
BASE Rann
NOTABLE MEMBERS/POWERS Vril Dox II: Brilliant, cloned son of Brainiac; **Phase**: Can pass through solid matter; **Starfire**: Tamaranean powers; **Lobo**: Czarnian powers, expert combatant; **Tribulus**: Lightning generation and super-strength; **Adam Strange**: Tactical expert, planetary adventurer; **Captain Comet**: Pinnacle of human evolution with multiple superpowers; **Wildstar**: Genetically-altered human with superhuman abilities; **Strata** and **Garv**: Dryadan durability.

After surviving an invasion on a massive scale by the alien Dominators and their allies, Brainiac's son, Vril Dox II, decided to form his own universe-protection agency and called it L.E.G.I.O.N. However, when Vril's rebellious son, Lyrl Dox, opted to take over L.E.G.I.O.N., using his 12th-level intelligence to do so, Vril decided to form a new team comprised of L.E.G.I.O.N. members still loyal to him—the Revolutionary Elite Brigade to Eradicate L.E.G.I.O.N. Supremacy (R.E.B.E.L.S). Using his own impressive intellect and the efforts of his allies, Dox overcame his son before retiring for a time, and leaving L.E.G.I.O.N. in the safe hands of Captain Comet.

Dox's retirement did not last long, however. After being sent files on the Legion of Super-Heroes from his descendant, Legionnaire Brainiac 5, Dox decided to create a new team. He based his revamped R.E.B.E.L.S. on members of the Legion of Super-Heroes, and also recruited new teammates from the Legion's rogues gallery. Working with his old ally Strata, Vril Dox formed a formidable fighting force capable of defeating the starfish-like alien Starro, who was trying to take over the L.E.G.I.O.N. team and use its power to conquer the universe. In due course, other heroes, such as Starfire, Adam Strange, and Wildstar joined the R.E.B.E.L.S.' ranks. **MM**

STARSTRUCK
With Adam Strange failing as a leader and Lobo missing in action, the R.E.B.E.L.s faced a greater challenge when Vril Dox became Starro's mind-slave and led the alien conqueror's horde into battle.

R.E.B.E.L.S REFORMED
1 Vril Dox II
2 Adam Strange
3 Lobo
4 Captain Comet
5 Starfire
6 Tribulus

RAGDOLL

DEBUT *Villains United* #1 (Jul. 2005)
CURRENT VERSION *Resurrection Man* (Vol. 2) #6 (Apr. 2012)
REAL NAME Peter Merkel, Jr.
HEIGHT 5ft 11in **WEIGHT** 73 lbs
EYES Gray **HAIR** Red
POWERS/ABILITIES Superhumanly agile and triple-jointed.
ENEMIES Batgirl, the Riddler

While the original criminal Rag Doll (Peter Merkel) remains at large in Gotham City, his son, Ragdoll, has taken on his legacy with deranged gusto. Like his villainous father Ragdoll is an amazing contortionist, but he had to undergo multiple surgeries to achieve those abilities. He also needs a special ointment to stop his skin splitting from the strain his contortions put on it.

Ragdoll participated in a notorious riot at Blackgate Penitentiary caused by the criminal Bane, and later came up against Batgirl when her activist roommate was misled into performing an act of terrorism.

Shortly after, the Riddler coerced Ragdoll into fighting the Secret Six by withholding his skin ointment. Fortunately for him, the vigilante team defeated the Riddler, after which Ragdoll helped the Six and Scandal Savage protect his friend Black Alice from virtually the entire magical community. **MM**

RAGMAN

DEBUT *Ragman* (Vol. 1) #1 (Aug.–Sep. 1976)
CURRENT VERSION *Batman Eternal* #6 (Jul. 2014)
REAL NAME Rory Regan
BASE Gotham City
HEIGHT 5ft 11in **WEIGHT** 165 lbs
EYES Blue **HAIR** Brown
POWERS/ABILITIES Wears suit of rags made up of evil souls; superhuman agility.
ALLIES Batman, Batwoman, Clayface
ENEMIES Morgaine le Fey, Nocturna

Rory Regan inherited a suit made of rags from his grandfather. Little did Rory know that his suit was a golem of sorts, a costume created by an ancient council of Rabbis to protect the Jewish people. Able to absorb corrupt souls into its woven fabric and bestow their strengths and talents upon the wearer, the Ragman suit allowed Rory to transform into a Super Hero. The suit's single drawback was its vulnerability to fire.

Ragman assisted Batman from time to time, and also teamed with Batwoman to stop the resurrection of the evil sorceress Morgaine le Fey. Alongside the demon Etrigan, the temporarily amnesiac villain Clayface, and Batwoman's sister, Red Alice, Ragman became a founding member of the Unknowns, and successfully saved the Earth from le Fey's machinations. **MM**

RANKORR

DEBUT *Red Lanterns* #1 (Nov. 2011)
REAL NAME John (Jack) Moore
BASE Ysmault, Space Sector 666
HEIGHT 5ft 10in **WEIGHT** 166 lbs
EYES Green **HAIR** Red (formerly black)
POWERS/ABILITIES Possesses a rage-fueled Red Lantern power ring.
ALLIES Atrocitus, Bleez, Guy Gardner
ENEMIES Lobo, Mr. Baxter
AFFILIATIONS Red Lantern Corps

John Moore and his brother Ray were raised in the United Kingdom by their grandfather. The brothers reacted in very different ways when their grandfather was murdered by a street thug named Baxter. John tried to keep his grief to himself, while the more volatile Ray furiously claimed the police were covering up for the killer. John then witnessed the police beat his brother to death. This act released all the pent-up rage in John, and at that moment, a Red Lantern ring flew onto his finger and John became the Red Lantern Rankorr.

Rankorr tracked Baxter down, but before he could kill him, John was whisked away to Ysmault, the Red Lanterns' homeworld. As an Earthling, Rankorr had to fight hard to win the respect of Atrocitus and other Corps members. After serving bravely, he met his death at the hands of Lobo. **MM**

RAVAGERS, THE

DEBUT *The Ravagers* #1 (Jul. 2012)
BASE Los Angeles, California
NOTABLE MEMBERS/POWERS
Fairchild: Scientist, superhuman strength; **Terra:** Geokinesis, flight; **Beast Boy:** Can transform into any animal; **Thunder:** Creates sound-wave blasts; **Lightning:** Electrokinesis; **Ridge:** Super-strong and super-durable.
ALLIES Niles Caulder, Superboy, Teen Titans
ENEMIES Deathstroke, Harvest

While working for the demented super-villain Harvest, scientist Caitlin Fairchild's clone realized the error of her ways and helped a group of Harvest's prisoners escape. One of these was Ridge, a member of Harvest's elite personal army known as the Ravagers. In defiance at their incarceration, the young heroes adopted the name Ravagers and briefly set up shop at Dr. Niles Caulder's secret headquarters in Los Angeles.

Soon after, their makeshift home was invaded by Harvest's own Ravagers, Rose Wilson and Warblade, and the assassin-for-hire, Deathstroke. The heroes fought valiantly, but were overcome by Deathstroke who took them back to Harvest—except for Beast Boy, whom Deathstroke mistakenly believed to be dead. The rest of the team, aside from Terra, remained with Harvest until the villain's defeat by the Teen Titans. **MM**

RĀ'S AL GHŪL

DATA

DEBUT *Batman* (Vol. 1) #232 **(Jun. 1971)**
CURRENT VERSION *Batman, Incorporated* (Vol. 2) #2 **(Aug. 2012)**
BASE 'Eth Alth'eban
HEIGHT 6ft 5in **WEIGHT** 215 lbs
EYES Green **HAIR** Black with white streaks
POWERS/ABILITIES Expert swordsman and martial artist; extremely long lived thanks to his access to the age-retarding Lazarus Pits; genius-level intellect with a keen strategic skills; possesses an army of loyal assassins and many connections in nearly every nation on the globe.
ALLIES Talia al Ghūl
ENEMIES Batman, The Batman Family, Birds of Prey
AFFILIATIONS The League of Assassins

OUTLAW VS. OUTLAWS
Rā's al Ghūl clashed with Red Hood and the Outlaws after Jason Todd was briefly invited to join the League of Assassins.

LEGENDS CLASH
Batman and Rā's al Ghūl have battled each other many times. Their very first encounter led to a savage swordfight in the desert, with Talia al Ghūl looking on.

He is the legendary figure whose name roughly translates as "The Demon's Head." A villain who has earned that name a thousand times over, Rā's al Ghūl is one of the world's most infamous eco-terrorists and the leader of the League of Assassins, an ancient organization based in the mystical city of 'Eth Alth'eban. Rā's wants nothing more than to save the Earth by killing off the majority of the humans that "plague" it.

The stories of Rā's al Ghūl stretch back more than 700 years, making it nearly impossible to discern fact from fiction. Through the frequent use of the mystical Lazarus Pits and their life-renewing properties, Rā's has been able to survive for centuries. His reach is wide, with connections in most major governments, but he wasn't always so powerful. Having left his nomadic tribe to pursue a scientific career in the city, the man who would become Rā's al Ghūl found work as a humble physician to a great sultan. While attempting to save the life of the sultan's son, the doctor discovered the properties of the Lazarus Pits.

Resurrected from death, the sultan's son became deranged and ran amok, killing the physician's wife. The sultan refused to admit his son's guilt and imprisoned the doctor in a cage with her corpse, expecting him to die under the desert sun. However, he was rescued by local rebels, men he soon led back to the sultan's palace in an uprising that saw the doctor take the name Rā's al Ghūl. Rā's formed the League of Assassins, and embarked on an eco-terrorist mission to cull humanity and "save" the planet from over-population and pollution. He also fathered a daughter, Talia, with a woman named Melisande.

The villainous League of Assassins' Dr. Ebeneezer Darrk had a falling out with Rā's and kidnapped Talia. Batman rescued her, and Rā's decided that the Dark Knight would be the ideal son-in-law to take over his operations. Batman saw things differently, and the two became arch-enemies, united only by their mutual love for Talia, the "Daughter of the Demon." **MM**

ON THE RECORD

Rā's al Ghūl's origin and history have been revised more than once since his debut in the 1970s. Likewise, the Lazarus Pits that restore his vitality have changed markedly over the years.

At first, there was a single pit. Later, multiple green, bathtub-sized pools were linked to major ley lines of mystic energy, and each pit could only be used once. They soon evolved into a handful of large pools found around the world, including at the Batcave. Their properties remained the same, and they were responsible for resurrecting many characters, such as the Red Hood, the Riddler, Wonder Woman, and even Batman.

THE DEMON LAUGHS
The Joker once cheated death after a dip in the Lazarus Pits' life-giving waters. Unlike most people, who emerge violently deranged, the Joker 'enjoyed' a moment of calm sanity.

THE LAZARUS EFFECT
After immersing himself in the Lazarus Pits, Rā's al Ghūl is returned to the age and health of a man in his prime. The Pits' side-effect of brief madness may have altered Rā's outlook over time, making him ever more extreme in his tactics.

CLASSIC STORIES

***Batman* (Vol. 1) #232 (Jun. 1971)** Mentioned in an earlier story, Rā's al Ghūl finally makes his debut, fabricating a mystery just to test Batman's skills.

***Detective Comics* (Vol. 1) #444-448 (Jan.-Jun. 1975)** Rā's al Ghūl frames Batman for murder in a story told over five issues, a rarity for the time.

***Batman: Birth of the Demon* #1 (Dec. 1992)** Rā's is given an origin, exploring his tragic fall from an honorable physician to a corrupt terrorist leader.

***Detective Comics* (Vol. 1) #700-702, *Catwoman* (Vol. 2) #36, *Robin* (Vol. 4) #32-33, *Batman: Shadow of the Bat* #53-54, *Batman* (Vol. 1) #533-534 (Aug.-Oct. 1996)** In the Legacy storyline, Batman discovers that the evil mastermind behind the horrific "Clench" plague in Gotham City is none other than Rā's al Ghūl, aided and abetted by his new lackey, Bane.

R

RAVEN

DATA

DEBUT *DC Comics Presents* #26 **(Oct. 1980)**
CURRENT VERSION *Phantom Stranger* (Vol. 4) #1 **(Dec. 2012)**
REAL NAME Rachel Roth
BASE New York City
HEIGHT 5ft 10in **WEIGHT** 110 lbs **EYES** Blue **HAIR** Black
POWERS/ABILITIES Empathic sensitivity; manipulation of darkness; time travel; teleportation; projection of Soul-Self; other undefined magical powers.
ALLIES Beast Boy
ENEMIES Trigon
AFFILIATIONS Teen Titans

TEAM TITAN
With a demonic father and brothers, and an absent mother, young Raven felt that the Teen Titans were a proper family to her.

FATHER AND DAUGHTER
Raven was haunted by her father and struggled with her demonic nature and immense powers.

Sole daughter of the cosmic demon Trigon, Raven struggles to master the baser impulses she has inherited from him. While her father sees her as the key to his plans to consolidate his power, Raven uses her vast mystical and pyschic abilities to battle evil in all its forms alongside her adopted family, the Teen Titans.

Raven grew up in the realm of Azarath, protected by a mystical order of monks and taught to control the demonic influence of her father. Knowing Trigon would be hunting for her, she fled Azarath for her mother Arella's home planet, Earth, where she went into hiding. However, the Phantom Stranger found and captured her, turning her over to Trigon as part of a bargain to save Earth. Trigon made Raven ruler of the Under-Realms, and later brought her back to Earth, unleashing her as his "Black Bird of Terror" along with her demonic brothers, Belial, Rushkoff, and Suge.

Raven saved Beast Boy from Deathstroke and the Ravagers, but her allegiance remained in doubt despite the fact that she turned on her demonic brothers and helped save the rest of the Teen Titans. She was transported back in time when they fought Johnny Quick and Atomica. Raven later confronted Etrigan the demon, who wanted to kill her to weaken Trigon. Wonder Girl saved Raven and then helped her Soul-Self bring the rest of the Teen Titans back into the present after a journey through different futures where they tried to save Superboy from multiple versions of himself. Returned to the present, Raven was happy to discover that her projection through time had severed Trigon's control over her, and she struck the decisive blow against the villain Harvest, ending the Culling.

Now firmly a member of the Teen Titans family, Raven has all the support she needs to keep control over her powers. However, she remains fearful that her father Trigon will surely strike at her again when she least expects it. **AI**

ON THE RECORD

A touchstone of Raven's story has always been her relationship with Beast Boy. They became close immediately after she gathered the New Teen Titans, and their attachment blossomed into romance after her death and rebirth in a new body.

When her relationship with Beast Boy fell apart, and following the death of Kid Flash (Bart Allen) and the battle with Titans East, Raven left the team. She later returned seeking help after being attacked by Wyld, a demonic being she had inadvertently created. In so doing, she rekindled her relationship with Beast Boy after they had fought side-by-side to defeat the Legion of Doom and Superboy-Prime.

HER BEST BOY
Following a close call with Brother Blood, who had attempted to marry her, Raven began a relationship with fellow Teen Titan, Beast Boy, which continued on-and-off for several years.

CLASSIC STORIES

***New Teen Titans* (Vol. 1) #4–6 (Feb.–Apr. 1981)** Raven asks the JLA to help her fight against her father, but they refuse because Zatanna doesn't trust Raven. Desperate, she brings together the New Teen Titans, who imprison Trigon.

***New Titans* (Vol. 2) #121–130 (May 1995–Feb. 1996)** Surrendering to Trigon's influence, Raven implants the seeds of his dead children into new bodies, spreading evil. One of the seeds turns out to be the soul of her own good self.

***Teen Titans* (Vol. 3) #30–31 (Jan.–Feb.) 2006** After narrowly escaping marriage to Brother Blood and triggering armageddon, Raven joins the Teen Titans to combat Blood and his demonic army.

RAVERS, THE

DEBUT *Superboy and the Ravers* #1 (Sep. 1996)
BASE Event Horizon
MEMBERS/POWERS **Superboy:** flight, super-strength; **Kaliber:** Qwardian with shrinking and growing powers; **Aura:** powerful magnetic abilities; **Hero Cruz:** force-field generated from Achilles Vest, H-Dial allows transformation into a Super Hero identity; **Rex, the Wonder Dog:** enhanced intelligence; **Sparx:** wields electricity.
ALLIES Highfather
ENEMIES InterC.E.P.T., Darkseid

The Event Horizon was a mobile, intergalactic party frequented by cliques of teens invited by club owner Kindred Marx—the catch was that only those with superpowers could get in. The Ravers, led by Superboy, were the most outrageous of the club's regulars.

By touching their hand-stamps, team members could teleport to the Event Horizon from anywhere in the universe. The Ravers came into conflict with rival clique Red Shift and the interdimensional police force known as InterC.E.P.T. They also helped Highfather of New Genesis foil Darkseid's attempts to tap into the power of the Source.

After Raver Half-Life perished in a battle against the Qwardians of the Antimatter Universe, Kindred Marx closed down the Event Horizon, and most of the Ravers went their separate ways. **AI**

RAY

DEBUT *Smash Comics* #14 (Sep. 1940)
CURRENT VERSION *Ray* (Vol. 3) #1 (Feb. 2012)
REAL NAME Lucien Gates
BASE San Diego
HEIGHT 5ft 9in **WEIGHT** 165 lbs
EYES Brown **HAIR** Black
POWERS/ABILITIES Absorption and projection of light and electricity, flight, other light- and energy-derived powers.
ALLIES Chanti, Uncle Sam
ENEMIES Thaddeus Filmore
AFFILIATIONS Freedom Fighters

San Diego lifeguard Lucien Gates found himself transformed when he was hit by a particle beam fired from an experimental energy project in the Arizona desert. He discovered he could fly at any speed, but only in a straight line, requiring a reflective surface to change his flight path. He could also project light and create light constructs. One downside was that his clothes burned off, necessitating the constant maintenance of illusionary clothing.

Lucien's adoptive parents taught him to control his powers using yoga and meditation and he started to combat the other strange creations of the misfired beam. It emerged that many of these battles had been staged by the lunatic villain and filmmaker Thaddeus Filmore, who claimed to know the truth about Lucien's origins. Lucien defeated Filmore and remade his personality with light hypnotherapy. Filmore then made a movie about Lucien. Uncle Sam later recruited Lucien—along with Doll Man, the Human Bomb, and Phantom Lady—into a new hero team operating under the auspices of S.H.A.D.E. **AI**

ON THE RECORD

Lanford "Happy" Terrill, a reporter for the *New York Star*, became the first Ray after being deliberately exposed to a "light bomb" by scientist Dr. Dayzl.

Happy's son Joshua inherited his father's powers and became Ray's sidekick, Spitfire, before killing his mother in a tragic accident. Happy remarried and his second son Raymond also inherited the powers of the Ray. The youthful hero later exposed the third Ray, Stan Silver, as a traitor within the ranks of the Freedom Fighters.

NIGHT BOY
Before realizing he had light-based superpowers, Raymond Terrill was known as Night Boy because he only came out when it was dark.

ROBIN REDBREAST
Jason Todd wore a suit originally belonging to Nightwing, with a red-colored bat symbol on its chest.

RED HOOD

DEBUT *Detective Comics* #168 (Feb. 1951) (The Joker as Red Hood); *Batman* (Vol. 1) #357 (Mar. 1983) (Jason Todd)
CURRENT VERSION *Red Hood and the Outlaws* #1 (Nov. 2011)
REAL NAME Jason Todd
HEIGHT 6ft **WEIGHT** 225 lbs
EYES Blue **HAIR** Black
POWERS/ABILITIES Skilled acrobat and hand-to-hand combatant; some magical abilities due to immersion in Lazarus Pit.
ALLIES Batman, Starfire
ENEMIES Untitled, Rā's al Ghūl
AFFILIATIONS Outlaws, Batman Incorporated

Adopted by Batman before he could fall into a life of crime, Jason Todd trained as the second Robin. He discovered that this mother was still alive, and was lured by the Joker into a trap after their reunion. Killed in an explosion, Todd was resurrected in a Lazarus Pit by Talia al Ghūl, who sent him to train with the All-Caste. Plagued by fits of rage and a burning desire to get revenge on the Joker, he left the All-Caste for a short tour with the League of Assassins before starting his own mercenary team with Roy Harper and Starfire, called the Outlaws.

They battled the Untitled, who were killing off the All-Caste, and then Todd learned that the Joker had actually been manipulating him since his childhood. Traumatized, he had the All-Caste erase all painful memories from his mind and then fought with the League of Assassins against the Untitled—whose leader was revealed to be Rā's al Ghūl. Regaining his memories, Todd defeated Rā's and reunited the Outlaws before returning to Gotham City to assume a new role in Batman Incorporated. **AI**

REBIRTH

FACES OF EVIL
Since his death and resurrection, Jason Todd has always walked a fine line between heroism and villainy. Now fully embracing a new role, he becomes Batman's mole within Gotham City's underworld, dismantling this hierarchy of evil from within.

ON THE RECORD

Previous versions of the Red Hood intersect notably with the history of the Joker. The original Red Hood gang sent its members out on jobs each wearing the same hood, and one of them fell into a vat of toxic chemicals and emerged as the Joker. His identity remains unknown.

A later, more individualized, Red Hood appeared after the Joker murdered Jason Todd, the second Robin. Todd returned to life as Super Hero Red Hood following the Infinite Crisis storyline.

SEEING RED
Jason Todd started a vendetta against the Joker that triggered a city-wide gang war, before retiring the Red Hood identity and becoming Red Robin.

RED LANTERN CORPS

DEBUT *Green Lantern* (Vol. 4) #25 **(Jan. 2008)**
CURRENT VERSION *Red Lanterns* (Vol. 1) #1 **(Nov. 2011)**
BASE Styge Prime, Ysmault
MEMBERS All Corps members are able to vomit blazing bile; wearing Red Lantern rings affords flight, full environmental protection, intergalactic transportation, translation, violent energy projection, and hard-light constructs if the wielder can focus their thoughts. **Atrocitus:** Immortal magician; **Bleez:** Abused alien princess; **Rankorr:** Outraged Earthman; **Ratchett:** Tentacular Brain; **Vice:** Insectoid flesh-ripper; **Dex-Starr:** Incensed cat from Brooklyn; **Skallox:** Incinerated enhanced interrogator; **Zilius Zox:** Ball of fury; **Guy Gardner:** Undercover Emerald Warrior; **Kara Zor-El/Supergirl:** Constantly betrayed and marginalized Kryptonian.
ENEMIES Sinestro Corps, Green Lantern Corps, Blue Lantern Corps, Third Army, Volthoom, Relic, Guardians of the Universe, Black Lantern Corps, Krona, the Wheel
AFFILIATIONS Star Sapphire Corps

SEEING RED
Atrocitus assembled a fearsome force of ring bearers with a grudge.
1 Atrocitus
2 Bleez
3 Zilius Zox
4 Haggor
5 Ratchett
6 Skallox
7 Fury-6
8 Dex-Starr
9 Antipathy
10 Butcher (Rage entity)

Atrocitus is one of "Five Inversions" who survived the Massacre of Sector 666. Manhunter robots carried out the slaughter, but Atrocitus held their creators, the Guardians of the Universe, responsible. Imprisoned for billions of years on Ysmault as part of the Oans' furtive cover-up, Atrocitus eventually broke free and, through magic and the blood of his fellow captives, harnessed his boiling fury.

Building a Central Power Battery to tap the Emotional Spectrum's light of Rage, he dispatched red power rings to find beings similarly wronged and driven by a hunger for retribution. All across the universe, Red Lanterns began exacting fearful vengeance on those deemed to have escaped justice. Their rings constantly stoked their blazing fury.

Possession by a red power ring lasts a lifetime. The bonding is permanent, and the bearer dies in agony if it is removed. Like all Spectrum Warriors, Red Lanterns have their own oath to recite when recharging their rings: "With blood and rage of crimson red, Ripped from a corpse so freshly dead, Together with our hellish hate, We'll burn you all, that is your fate." **WW**

ON THE RECORD

In pre-Flashpoint reality, Atrocitus became concerned that Red Lanterns were usually too consumed with rage to conceive or form light constructs with their rings to solve the situations they encountered. Instead, they would strike with a boiling napalm spew of crimson bile generated from within their bodies. Atrocitus eventually devised a way to restore a degree of rationality to his furious fellows by immersing them in the blood-pool on Ysmault.

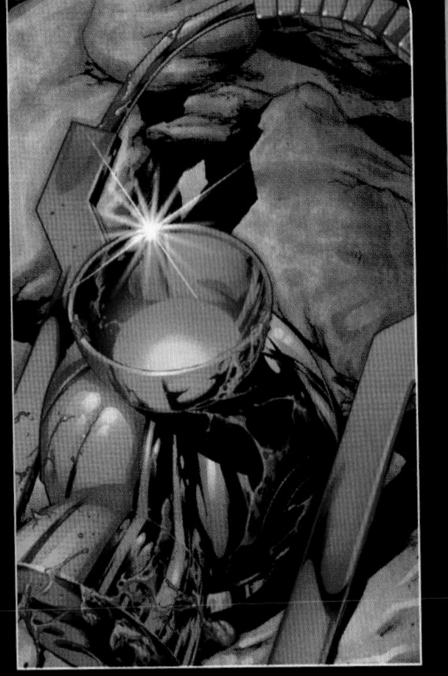

THERE WILL BE BLOOD
Atrocitus murdered his fellow Five Inversions and used their blood to power the Red Lanterns' Central Battery. Before long, Hal Jordan and the Green Lantern Corps would feel the wrath of the Red Lantern Corps.

RED BADGE OF COURAGE
Red Lanterns are utterly fearless. Hunger for bloody justice fills them with a fiery fury, blinding them to everything except their targets.

ALL THE RAGE
Even a truly dedicated warrior like Guy Gardner lost all composure when filled with the scalding scarlet fire of Rage.

RED STAR

DEBUT (As Starfire) *Teen Titans* (Vol. 1) #18 (Nov.–Dec. 1968)
REAL NAME Leonid Konstantinovitch Kovar
BASE Moscow, Russia
HEIGHT 5ft 10in **WEIGHT** 180 lbs
EYES Green **HAIR** Blond
POWERS/ABILITIES Super-strength, speed, endurance, flight and pyrokinesis; trained scientist and researcher.
ENEMIES Le Blanc, Hammer and Sickle, Doctor Light, Superboy-Prime

With his archaeologist father, young Russian Leonid Kovar was out exploring an extraterrestrial ship crashed in the Yenesi River when it exploded. Leonid somehow survived and, as a result of the energies released, developed superhuman powers. An ardent patriot, the boy offered his services to the State, and as Starfire became Russia's first official Super Hero.

While tracking international thief Le Blanc, he met the Teen Titans and subsequently changed his codename to Red Star. Some time later, Leonid left Russia to join the Titans. He formed a close relationship with were-woman Pantha and her foster-son, Baby Wildebeest.

Leonid returned to Russia and began fighting crime in his homeland, mostly over the objections of the Russian rulers. **WW**

REIGN

DEBUT *Supergirl* (Vol. 6) #5 (Mar. 2012)
EYES Black **HAIR** Red
POWERS/ABILITIES Superhuman strength, speed, and durability; highly advanced unarmed combat skills and swordsmanship, tactical and leadership training.
ALLIES Deimax, Perrilus, Flower of Heaven
ENEMIES Supergirl
AFFILIATIONS Worldkillers, Argo City

Reign was part of a clandestine Kryptonian experiment in which alien embryos were altered to create living weapons of vast power. They were designated Worldkillers after an ancient myth. Designed to fight and born to kill, five subjects were programmed with a hunger for destruction and gestated in a floating space laboratory. At some point, the scientists abandoned the project, leaving the subjects to grow to term in isolation. The newborns knew virtually nothing of their origins other than what could be gleaned from discarded datacores.

Reign, their leader, clashed with Supergirl in the ruins of Argo City when both went looking for answers. The Worldkiller quickly got the upper hand and Supergirl retreated to Earth. Reign followed, taking with her three companions, who wreaked havoc until Supergirl defeated them. Reign grudgingly withdrew, but swore to return. **WW**

RED TORNADO

DEBUT *All American Comics* (Vol. 1) #3 **(Jun. 1939)** (Ma Hunkel); *Justice League of America* (Vol. 1) #64 **(Aug. 1968)** (Android John Smith)
CURRENT VERSION *Worlds' Finest* #0 **(Nov. 2012)** (Android Lois Lane)
REAL NAME Lois Lane; Unit 1.3 **BASE** New Gotham City, Earth-2
POWERS/ABILITIES Android body containing Lois Lane's memories; enhanced senses; universal computer interface; enhanced strength, flight, and durability; can generate and manipulate wind blasts and super-speed vortexes.
ALLIES Kara Zor-El (Power Girl), Huntress, Val-Zod, Thomas Wayne (New Batman)
ENEMIES Brutaal, Superman clones, Darkseid, Ultra-Humanite, Steppenwolf

On Earth-2, Red Tornado is a robotic shell housing the personality of Lois Lane—Superman's wife and the foster-mother of Kara Zor-El. When Lois was killed by forces from Apokolips, her consciousness was uploaded to a mechanical frame capable of generating cyclonic winds—a secret weapon created to fight invading Parademons.

Reunited with her beloved foster-daughter Power Girl, Red Tornado spearheaded Earth-2's final fight against eradication, uniting other doomed heroes such as substitute Batman Thomas Wayne, his granddaughter Huntress, and lost Kryptonian Val-Zod. Their valiant efforts held the line against Darkseid long enough to allow humanity's last survivors to escape destruction and find temporary refuge in space arks. **WW**

WINDS OF CHANGE
Lois Lane lost everything—her husband, her daughter, even her body—but never stopped fighting to save her world.

ON THE RECORD

STORMING IN
The newly created Red Tornado gatecrashed a Justice Society meeting and insisted he was once a member of the team.

Red Tornado was constructed by futurist Thomas Oscar Morrow to counteract the Super Heroes who constantly interfered in his schemes. Unfortunately, the android's frame was possessed by a wandering wind elemental, and achieved a degree of power and sentience the mad doctor could never have imagined.

Joining the Justice League, "Reddy" experienced friendship and loyalty, and hungered for more. Adopting the human identity of John Smith, he married Kathy Sutton and adopted a young war orphan, Traya.

He has been destroyed and reconstructed many times—with varying degrees of success—leading to serious impairment of function and recall. He was barely articulate and operating on little more than instinct when co-opted into the mystic rapid response squad Primal Force. However, after being appointed overseer and guardian of the turbulent juvenile team Young Justice, Red Tonado grew to become a wise and tolerant mentor.

Reddy's greatest desire was to be human, but when his sympathetic comrades created an organic body for him, the complex mind-transfer process was subverted by Amazo and Professor Ivo. The result was murderous carnage and crushing disappointment.

SPIN CYCLE
The man-made hero was a caring champion who treasured a humanity he could never share.

RELIC

DEBUT *Green Lantern* (Vol. 5) #21 (Aug. 2013)
EYES White **HAIR** None
POWERS/ABILITIES Gigantic body, vast intellect, numerous technologies from another universe; manipulation and draining of all colors of Emotional Spectrum; powers of a New God.
ALLIES Highfather, Metron
ENEMIES Green Lantern Corps, White Lantern Kyle Rayner, Green Lantern Hal Jordan
AFFILIATIONS Lightsmiths, Black Lanterns

Relic is a survivor of the universe preceding the current one. A great scientist, he posited that the Emotional Spectrum was a finite resource being exhausted by the profligate Lightsmiths, who employed its colors as power sources. Ridiculed by his peers, he searched for the reservoir containing the emotional energies and found it in the Source Wall surrounding creation. The Lightsmiths went to war over the dwindling energies and his universe ended.

Relic was preserved in the Source and awoken by Kyle Rayner and the Templar Guardians. Seeing a new cosmos of beings making the same mistakes, Relic declared war on all Lantern Corps, resolved to save this universe. He destroyed Oa and then eradicated the Blue Lanterns before being trapped in the Source Wall, but was released by New Gods Highfather and Metron. **WW**

REPLICANT

DEBUT *The Flash Secret Files and Origins* (Vol. 1) #2 (Nov. 1999)
REAL NAME Anthony Gambi
BASE Keystone City
HEIGHT 7ft 5in **WEIGHT** 325 lbs
EYES Mirrored **HAIR** None
POWERS/ABILITIES Absorbs and replicates any technology or weaponry nearby.
ENEMIES Flash, Dark Flash (Walter West), Uncle Sam and the Freedom Fighters
AFFILIATIONS The Rogues, S.H.A.D.E.

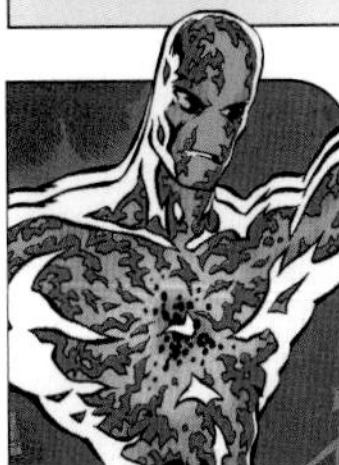

Anthony Gambi grew up around super-villains. With his mother dead and father in jail, Tony lived with his uncle Paul, a tailor-turned-armorer who created and repaired the costumes of the Flash's archfoes the Rogues. They spoiled the boy, and Tony viewed them as modern-day Robin Hoods.

When Captain Boomerang was crippled by a darker, more brutal Flash, Tony joined the Rogues. With powers provided by scientist T.O. Morrow, Tony could organically duplicate his idols' devices and weapons. As Replicant, Tony was soundly beaten by the Flash but escaped after discovering his newfound talent applied to any nearby technology. After allying with Abra Kadabra and inadvertently helping Wally West return, Replicant vanished. He was eventually captured by Father Time and S.H.A.D.E. **WW**

RESURRECTION MAN

DEBUT *Resurrection Man* (Vol. 1) #1 (May 1997)
CURRENT VERSION *Resurrection Man* (Vol. 2) #1 (Nov. 2011)
REAL NAME Mitchell Shelley
HEIGHT 6ft 1in **WEIGHT** 190 lbs
EYES Brown **HAIR** White
POWERS/ABILITIES Immortality and resurrection, various metahuman powers; Tektite enhancement, accelerated healing.
ENEMIES Suriel, Body Doubles, Hooker, Vandal Savage

Mitchell Shelley was a biologist working for a clandestine organization to create cutting-edge weapons and tech. His big project was Tektite nanites, intended to allow wounded US soldiers in Iraq to regenerate or at least survive major trauma. After many failures, a breakthrough arrived. Caught in a bomb blast, he lost an arm. To save his life, his staff injected him with Tektites. The procedure worked and his arm was reattached. However, Shelley then began growing a whole new arm and the reattached arm was removed. Incredibly, this arm grew into a clone of Shelley and escaped. Mitchell was desperate to track down his clone for further research.

Meanwhile, the clone, having few memories, searched for its past. Despite suffering from amnesia, it eventually realized it was being repeatedly killed and resurrected by unknown enemies. Each time it was brought back to life it possessed a different superpower. **WW**

DEATH BECOMES HIM
Mitch Shelley's clone died and was resurrected countless times, and on each occasion he found he had a new metahuman ability.

REVERSE-FLASH

DATA

DEBUT *The Flash* (Vol. 1) #139 **(Sep. 1963)**
CURRENT VERSION *The Flash* (Vol. 4) #0 **(Nov. 2012)** (Daniel West); *The Flash* (Vol. 4) #40 **(May 2015)** (Eobard Thawne)
REAL NAME Daniel West **BASE** Belle Reve Penitentiary
EYES Blue **HAIR** Brown
POWERS/ABILITIES Uses the extra-dimensional energy known as the Speed Force to travel back in time; costume acts like armor and includes part of the monorail he crashed into that was merged to his body by the Speed Force.
ALLIES Suicide Squad
ENEMIES The Flash, Rogues, League of Assassins
AFFILIATIONS Suicide Squad

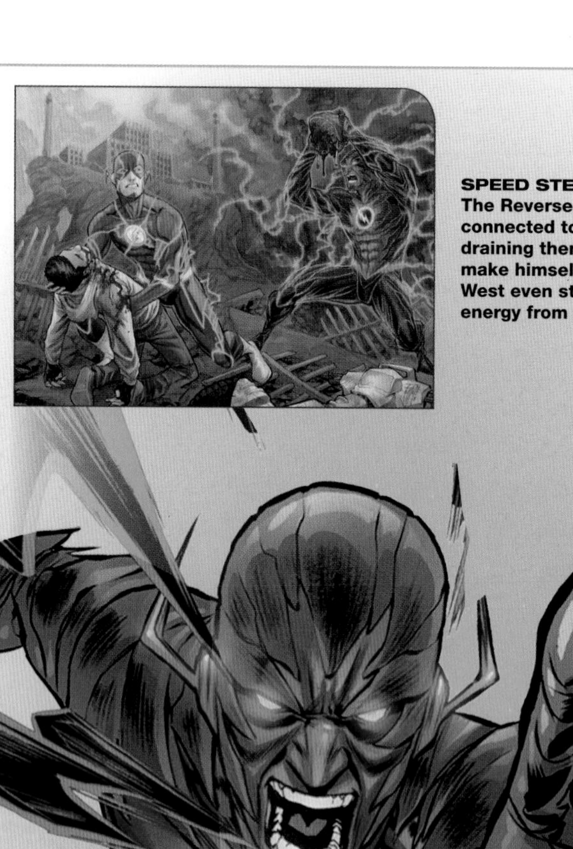

SPEED STEALER
The Reverse-Flash killed those connected to the Speed Force, draining them of their energy to make himself more powerful. West even stole Speed Force energy from the Flash himself.

Like the Flash, Daniel West gained his amazing powers of speed following an accident. However, unlike his nemesis, West became the Reverse-Flash, using his powers for his own selfish needs. The speedster cared little for those who had to die to help him accomplish his ultimate goal—to use the Speed Force to alter his own past.

SPECIAL BOND
The Speed Force allowed Daniel West to bond the metal from a monorail to his body. As Reverse-Flash, Daniel could manipulate it at will.

Daniel West's mother died giving birth to him. With his father a violent drunk, his sister Iris was his only friend. When Daniel's father killed some crickets the young boy had collected, Daniel snapped and pushed him down a staircase, injuring him. Terrified of being punished, he ran away, taking up a life of crime to survive. While acting as a getaway driver, he was captured by the Flash and jailed for five years. Shortly after Daniel's release, he got caught up in Gorilla Grodd's attack on Central City. Saved by the Rogues, he was trapped in their Mirror World base. Daniel escaped by stealing a car but crashed into a new monorail fitted with an experimental Speed Force battery. The accident threw Daniel back to Earth and imbued him with the Speed Force—fusing the remnants of the monorail to his body and showing him a vision of others connected to the Speed Force.

Daniel could now use the Speed Force to time travel, but needed more power to go back even further. He started killing those connected to the Speed Force; in time he gained enough energy to travel back to his own past, hoping to kill his father and repair his damaged relationship with Iris. When he tried to kill his father, the young Iris and Daniel, who witnessed the attempt, were terrified. The Flash arrived and Reverse-Flash allowed him to reabsorb the stolen Speed Force, returning them both to the present, where Daniel was again jailed. He joined Task Force X—the Suicide Squad—and is now presumed dead. **AC**

SPEED DEMON
The accident that turned Daniel West into Reverse-Flash created a distinctive red and metallic-gray suit.

ON THE RECORD

Several villains have taken on the role of Reverse-Flash over the years. Eobard Thawne was from the 25th century and a fan of the Flash. He even built his own version of the Flash's Cosmic Treadmill and traveled back in time to meet his hero. However, when Eobard learned that he was destined to become a villain and would die at the hands of the Flash, he went insane and became the Reverse-Flash. In later appearances, he called himself Professor Zoom.

When Wally West became the third Flash, he fought a new Reverse-Flash named Hunter Zolomon, who had once been Wally's friend. Zolomon also went by the name of Zoom.

YOU'RE NO BARRY ALLEN
The original Reverse-Flash, Eobard Thawne, was quickly driven mad by his fixation with the Flash (Barry Allen).

CLASSIC STORIES

***Flash Comics* #104 (Feb. 1949)**
Named "the Rival" at the time, the original Reverse-Flash fights the first Flash, Jay Garrick.

***The Flash* (Vol. 1) #139 (Sep. 1963)**
The Flash (Barry Allen) first encounters the menacing time-traveling Reverse-Flash from the 25th century.

***Flash: Rebirth* #1 (Jun. 2009)**
Eobard Thawne returns as the Reverse-Flash, aka Professor Zoom, while the Flash (Barry Allen) tries to escape from the Speed Force.

THE RIDDLER

DATA

DEBUT *Detective Comics* (Vol. 1) #140 **(Oct. 1948)**
CURRENT VERSION *Batman* (Vol. 2) #1 **(Nov. 2011)**
REAL NAME Edward Nygma **BASE** Gotham City
HEIGHT 6ft 1in **WEIGHT** 183 lbs **EYES** Blue **HAIR** Brown
POWERS/ABILITIES Expert at creating riddles and death traps; genius-level intellect; computer and electronics whiz; morally corrupt with a penchant for cheating; carries cane in the shape of a question mark from which he can fire electrical blasts or create holograms; makes use of exploding jigsaw puzzle pieces and crossword puzzle nets.
ALLIES Dr. Death
ENEMIES Batman, the Batman Family
AFFILIATIONS Arkham Asylum inmates

IN THE KNOW
A master of puzzles, the Riddler often knows more about Gotham City's mysteries than the Dark Knight himself. This has caused Batman to track down Nygma for information on more than one occasion.

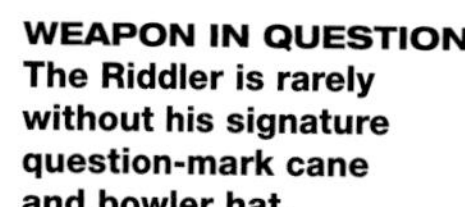

WEAPON IN QUESTION
The Riddler is rarely without his signature question-mark cane and bowler hat.

LASER FOCUS
The Riddler loves death traps, and Batman was forced to enter one in order to free Gotham City from the villain's hold.

The Riddler is a conflicted criminal. His dreams of wealth and prosperity are often at odds with his love of finding a worthy competitor—namely the Batman—to challenge to a game of mental and physical gymnastics.

Edward Nygma found his ticket to the big time as an employee of Wayne Enterprises. Gaining work as the advisor to Philip Kane—Bruce Wayne's uncle, who took over the Wayne corporation when Bruce left Gotham City to train to become the Batman—Nygma began plotting his takeover of the city. An expert strategist, with a genius-level knowledge of history, it was not long before the Riddler became a super-villain, employing the help of fellow criminal Dr. Death after he shut down power to all of Gotham City.

In the Riddler's twisted mind, he wanted to help evolution by forcing the citizens of Gotham City to either "get smart or die." As a super-storm hit the city, Riddler blew the retaining walls and grounded the city's blimps. With complete control of the electrical grid, Nygma created a dystopia of sorts with the city's tunnels flooded and its bridges rigged to explode. Using research stolen from Dr. Pamela Isley (later Poison Ivy), the Riddler reduced the city to a plant-covered wasteland, holding the entire population hostage. With the help of Lucius Fox and James Gordon, Batman took up the Riddler's challenge of wits, and even bested the super-villain before he could unleash total devastation on the city. Gotham City was freed, and the Riddler was banished to Arkham Asylum for his first stay of many. **MM**

ON THE RECORD

The Riddler debuted in the 1940s. His origin revealed that Edward Nigma (the "y" spelling was first used in 1992's *Batman: The Animated Series*) had always been amoral, acquiring an early love of games and puzzles after sneaking a peek at the solution to a classroom jigsaw puzzle assignment.

Later, while working as a carnival barker, the Riddler ultimately chose a life of crime, finding a worthy opponent in the form of Batman. This origin was left largely unchanged by the Crisis on Infinite Earths event, although it was later revealed that Edward's true birth name hadn't been Nigma at all, but Nashton.

REINTRODUCING THE RIDDLER
In the mid-1960s, the Riddler became a mainstay of Batman's Rogues Gallery. He eventually swapped the question-marked green jumpsuit for a suit and bowler hat.

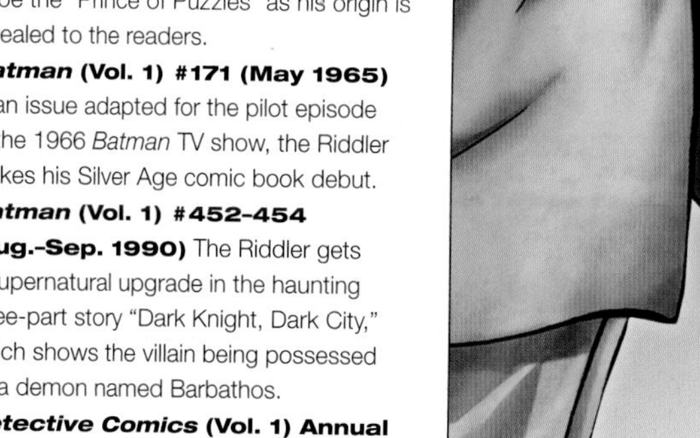

CLASSIC STORIES

***Detective Comics* #140 (Oct. 1948)** The Riddler debuts, proving himself to be the "Prince of Puzzles" as his origin is revealed to the readers.

***Batman* (Vol. 1) #171 (May 1965)** In an issue adapted for the pilot episode of the 1966 *Batman* TV show, the Riddler makes his Silver Age comic book debut.

***Batman* (Vol. 1) #452–454 (Aug.–Sep. 1990)** The Riddler gets a supernatural upgrade in the haunting three-part story "Dark Knight, Dark City," which shows the villain being possessed by a demon named Barbathos.

***Detective Comics* (Vol. 1) Annual #8 (1995)** The Riddler's origin is retold for the modern generation, introducing his two female sidekicks, Query and Echo.

RIOT

DEBUT *Superman: Man of Steel* #61 (Oct. 1996)
CURRENT VERSION *Green Team: Teen Trillionaires* #1 (Jul. 2013)
REAL NAME Mr. Murphy
POWERS/ABILITIES Instant generation of psychically linked clones with enhanced strength and speed.
ALLIES Temple Bellachek
ENEMIES "Commodore" Murphy, Green Team, Mohammed Qahtanii, J.P. Houston, Cecilia Sunbeam

The disgraced and exiled heir to the Murphy fortune began attacking his own son, "Commodore" Murphy, as masked marauder Riot after being medically altered by wealthy maniac Temple Bellachek. Faking his death, Riot then staged a series of brutal assaults hoping to regain the fortune his son had inherited. Unfortunately for Riot, Commodore had also inherited his father's fascination with metahuman improvement.

Young Murphy had surreptitiously purchased nanite-based armor, which he shared with his associates in the trillionaires-only social club the Green Team. These rich kids perpetually frustrated Riot's murderous attacks, defeating his clone army with ease and even toppling Temple Bellachek's empire. Riot apparently died in a final battle with his son. **WW**

RISK

DEBUT *Teen Titans* (Vol. 2) #1 (Oct. 1996)
REAL NAME Cody Driscoll
HEIGHT 5ft 11in **WEIGHT** 175 lbs
EYES Blue-green **HAIR** Blond
POWERS/ABILITIES Superhuman strength, speed, and reflexes; invulnerability; psychic powers.
ALLIES Loren Jupiter, Ray Palmer, Prysm
ENEMIES H'San Natall, the Veil, Haze, Deathstroke the Terminator, Sinestro Corps, Superboy-Prime

Cody Driscoll was abducted by aliens, the H'San Natall. Aboard their ship, he learned that he and other kidnapped kids were part of a breeding program—human/alien hybrids, designed to counter Earth's Super Hero defenders. As Risk, he and hero Ray Palmer joined a new Teen Titans group. When the volatile team broke up, Cody returned to his Colorado trailer-park home. His adrenaline-triggered powers made him a thrill addict, and he turned to petty crime. He redeemed himself by fighting valiantly during the Infinite Crisis, losing his right arm battling Superboy-Prime. Seeking no favors from his former friends, Risk vanished. But when the Sinestro Corps attacked Earth, Risk again tackled Superboy-Prime and had his left arm torn off. His whereabouts are unknown. **WW**

RO, KANJAR

DEBUT *Justice League of America* (Vol. 1) #3 (Feb.-Mar. 1961)
CURRENT VERSION *Green Lantern Corps* (Vol. 3) #24 (Dec. 2013)
REAL NAME Kanjar Ro
BASE Dhor, Thanagar, mobile
HEIGHT 5ft 7in **WEIGHT** 147 lbs
EYES Yellow **HAIR** Bald
POWERS/ABILITIES Cunning; tactical analysis; strategic planning; wide array of advanced technology and weapons taken in conquest.
ENEMIES The Durlans, Khunds, Hyathis of Alstair, Kromm of Mosteel, Sayyar of Larr, Green Lantern Corps, Guardians of the Universe, Metamorpho
AFFILIATIONS Thanagarian Ministry of Alien Affairs

CHAINS OF COMMAND
Despite his devious nature, Kanjar Ro's grand schemes frequently led to his being locked up beside his former possessions and chattels.

EYES ON THE PRIZE
Kanjar Ro is a consummate politician and pragmatist, eminently capable of turning any crisis to his personal advantage.

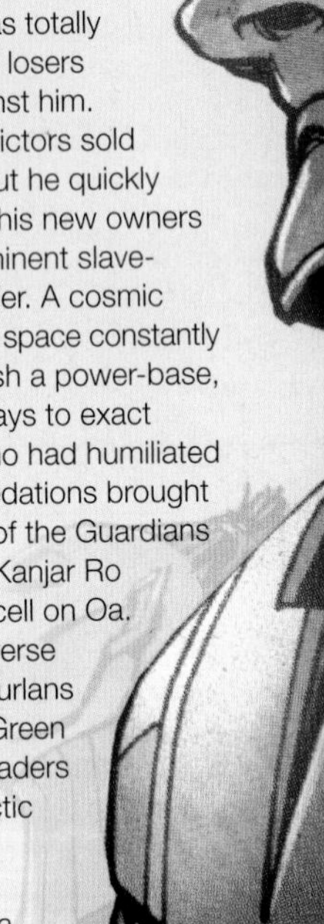

When a four-way war broke out in the Antares system, Dhorian dictator Kanjar Ro used cunning and duplicity to defeat his rivals. Imprisoning his foes, he luxuriated in the sybaritic joys of victory and was totally unprepared when the losers returned, united against him.

The unforgiving victors sold Kanjar into slavery, but he quickly turned the tables on his new owners and became a preeminent slave-trader and arms-dealer. A cosmic wanderer, he roamed space constantly seeking to re-establish a power-base, always looking for ways to exact revenge on those who had humiliated him. His brutal depredations brought him to the attention of the Guardians of the Universe and Kanjar Ro ended up in a Sciencell on Oa.

When the Guardians of the Universe died, an alliance of shape-shifting Durlans and barbaric Khunds attacked the Green Lantern Corps. These malignant invaders liberated Ro and several other galactic super-criminals, planning to press them into war service. Ro thus discovered that there was something he despised even more than groups of heroic do-gooders, and he led the Sciencell escapees in a coalition with the Green Lanterns against the invading alien alliance. **WW**

ON THE RECORD

The Silver Age Kanjar Ro was a quintessential alien evildoer. Ro was always hungry for conquest and used a variety of terrifying technologies. He was also small-minded and spiteful, obsessed with vengeance and with making the Justice League of America and Adam Strange his slaves.

Over time, however, Kanjar Ro evolved into an even more savage and bloodthirsty creature—a vile bureaucrat for the militaristic Thanagarians and later a petty dictator in conflict with Vril Dox II and his R.E.B.E.L.S.

SPACE INVADER
The dictator of Dhor traveled the universe accumulating incredible weapons just to avenge the insults inflicted upon him by so-called primitive humans.

ROBOTMAN

DEBUT *My Greatest Adventure* (Vol. 1) #80 **(Jun. 1963)**
CURRENT VERSION *My Greatest Adventure* (Vol. 2) #1 **(Dec. 2011)**
REAL NAME Clifford "Cliff" Steele
BASE Doom Patrol HQ, Midway City, Michigan; Las Vegas, Nevada; Los Angeles, California
HEIGHT 6ft 2in **WEIGHT** 295 lbs **EYES** Photocellular **HAIR** None
POWERS/ABILITIES Enhanced strength, speed, durability; electronically augmented senses; enhanced invulnerability; extendable limbs; heat generation.
ALLIES Dr. Will Magnus, Elasti-Girl, Negative Man
ENEMIES Dr. Niles Caulder, Brotherhood of Evil, Brotherhood of Dada
AFFILIATIONS Doom Patrol, Justice League United

Life seemed over for rugged sportsman and compulsive daredevil Cliff Steele when he died in a car crash. However, Cliff's brain was secretly preserved by radical scientist Dr. Niles Caulder and transplanted into a succession of mechanical bodies. Although the savant's motives seemed benevolent, Caulder was in reality a master manipulator who engineered catastrophes so that he could conduct unregulated experiments on human beings. His successes were then press-ganged into his private superteam, the Doom Patrol.

Initially bitter and hostile, Cliff Steele gradually adjusted to his condition and became the backbone of the unit: a hero in every sense of the word. As Robotman, he faced each incomprehensible danger with a wry wisecrack and every nasty shock life threw at him with unshakeable grit and determination. Eventually, Caulder's duplicity was exposed and Robotman became the Doom Patrol's moral compass. Seeing through the deranged genius' machinations, Robotman stayed with the team to limit the damage the fame-obsessed "Chief" might cause and to protect his more vulnerable friends on the squad.

Even this was not enough for the tireless, compassionate thrill-seeker. Robotman began operating as a substitute champion with Justice League United, and came to be regarded as a mentor and elder statesman for the next generation of Super Heroes. **WW**

ON THE RECORD

Cliff Steele was not DC Comics' first Robotman. In *Star-Spangled Comics* (Vol. 1) #7 (Apr. 1942), Robert Crane was killed by gangsters, and his best friend transplanted his brain into a marvel of mechanical engineering packed with crime-fighting gadgets. This prototype man of steel even had a faithful, talking robot dog, named Robbie, to help battle the bad guys. Robert Crane was later reimagined as a scientist in a rebuilt robotic body on Earth-2.

WARTIME HEROICS
Robotman stopped Commander Steel—brainwashed by Nazi Baron Blitzkrieg—from assassinating President Roosevelt, as the rest of the All-Star Squadron rushed to intervene.

ROCKET RED BRIGADE

DEBUT *Green Lantern Corps* (Vol. 1) #208 (Jan. 1987)
CURRENT VERSION *New Suicide Squad* (Vol. 1) #1 (Sep. 2014)
BASE Russia
POWERS/ABILITIES Classified
ENEMIES Commander Anatoli Knyazev, Task Force X, Suicide Squad
AFFILIATIONS Russian military high command

The impressive-looking Rocket Red Brigade was commissioned by Russia's rulers and military elite to act as an awe-inspiring terror weapon. Their purpose was not primarily offensive but symbolic: creating an atmosphere of fear among Russia's enemies—and allies—while evoking the old days of overwhelming military might poised to strike at a moment's notice. Rocket Reds are huge, complex but unwieldy mechanized war-suits piloted by extreme patriots willing to kill or die for their country.

The metal giants made their first public appearance when a cadre of America's Suicide Squad—on an assassination mission to curtail Russian expansion—infiltrated Moscow. In the aftermath of the invaders' assault on the Ministry of Foreign Affairs, Russian leaders were left scrambling to save face, going before the United Nations to officially deny any State connection to the Rocket Red Brigade. **WW**

IN THE RED
Rocket Reds looked impressive, but were expensive failures, often causing more damage than the threats they were deployed against.

ROSE AND THORN

DEBUT *Flash Comics* #89 (Nov. 1947)
CURRENT VERSION *National Comics: Rose and Thorn* #1 (Nov. 2012)
REAL NAME Rose Canton
EYES Green **HAIR** Brown
POWERS/ABILITIES Multiple personalities; relentless and remorseless drive to succeed.
ALLIES Aunty Cate, Melinda, Mister Mittens
ENEMIES Thorn, Mr. Varker

Teenager Rose Canton's world changed when she awoke with a rose tattoo and covered in someone else's blood. She couldn't remember anything and couldn't tell her Aunt Cate: It would only get Rose sent back to "the institution." More disturbingly, the popular girls who had tormented Rose at high school wanted to be friends now. Answers arrived as video messages on her phone from someone called Thorn, who looked like Rose.

Rose's father died when she was little. Now Thorn—a manic force of nature—was emerging from Rose's psyche to find out how and why, ripping her way through her dad's nasty old cronies before submerging back inside sweet, innocent Rose. Unless she wanted to return to the asylum, Rose had to let Thorn find out what they both needed to know. **WW**

REBEL WITH A CAUSE
Shy Rose just wanted to fit in at high school, but found acceptance as wild child Thorn. However, Thorn also had her own vengeful agenda.

ROSE BY ANOTHER NAME
Rose Forrest debuted in *Lois Lane* #105 (Oct. 1970). She developed a split personality after the murder of her police detective father and became a vigilante in Metropolis.

ROBIN

DATA

DEBUT *Batman: Son of the Demon* **(Sep. 1987)** (unnamed baby); *Batman* (Vol.1) #655 **(Sep. 2006)** (Damian Wayne)
CURRENT VERSION *Batman and Robin* (Vol. 2) #1 **(Nov. 2011)**
REAL NAME Damian Wayne **BASE** Gotham City
HEIGHT 4ft 6in **WEIGHT** 84 lbs **EYES** Blue **HAIR** Black
POWERS/ABILITIES Expert martial artist and assassin trained by the League of Assassins, Batman, and Dick Grayson; skilled detective and extremely intelligent; very athletic with some gymnastic training; briefly possessed Superman-like powers; weapons include armored suit with Utility Belt and access to the equipment in the Batcave.
ALLIES Batman, The Batman Family, Nobody II, Goliath
ENEMIES Rā's al Ghūl, League of Assassins, Nobody
AFFILIATIONS Batman, Inc., League of Assassins (formerly)

While Batman has been known to hide his feelings, Damian Wayne would be a hard son for even the most affectionate father to love. Headstrong, arrogant, and more than a little condescending to his fellow Super Heroes, Damian Wayne is the fifth and current Robin, and has managed to make enemies on both sides of the aisle despite his short tenure as a hero. The son of Bruce Wayne and the notorious League of Assassins leader, Talia al Ghūl, Damian was taught the ways of the League of Assassins by his mother. However, since joining his father, he has sided time and again with the Dark Knight's noble cause.

AT A GLANCE...

Assassin born
The son of Batman and criminal Talia al Ghūl, Damian Wayne was raised by his mother, constantly surrounded by the members of the notorious League of Assassins. With no qualms about killing those who got in his way, Damian didn't quite fit the mantle of a Robin when he first traveled to Gotham City to live with his father.

Like father, like son
After spending some time with Batman, Damian realized the nobility of the Dark Knight's cause, and wished to become more like the father he began to idolize. To that end, he did his best to put his killer instincts to one side and abide by Batman's uncompromising rules.

Attitude adjustment
Working with Dick Grayson—who had stepped up to be Batman—taught Damian Wayne a thing or two about true heroism and respecting his elders. However, Robin still maintained a trademark arrogance that could alienate his fellow Super Heroes.

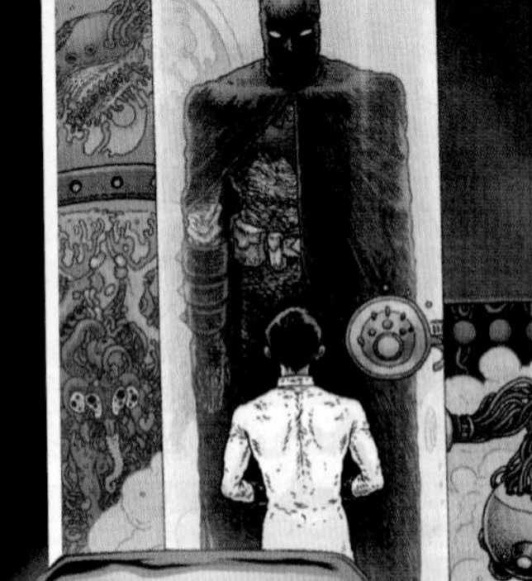

Batman and the international

terrorist named Rā's al Ghūl have battled for many years. While Rā's wants to "save the planet" by wiping out a huge percentage of the populace, Batman puts human life first and foremost, and has thwarted Rā's' plans on many occasions. However, despite the hostility shared between the Dark Knight Detective and the so-called Demon's Head, the two shared a common affection for Rā's daughter, Talia al Ghūl.

When one of Batman's romantic flings with Talia resulted in the birth of a son, the boy would become known as Damian Wayne. Accelerating the boy's growth through artificial means, Talia oversaw Damian's upbringing, training him in the many deadly arts known by Rā's al Ghūl's League of Assassins. Before he turned 10, Damian had mastered the violin, severed a tiger's head, harpooned a shark by hand, and killed humans and Man-Bats alike. He had become an assassin without remorse, one his mother was immensely proud of.

Knowing that her son could possibly be the heir to the al Ghūl empire, Talia presented the boy to Batman, hoping the Dark Knight could guide Damian to become more than the sum of what the masters of the League of Assassins could teach him. Rā's al Ghūl had long wanted Batman himself to take over his empire, but knowing that was impossible, instilling Damian with some of Bruce Wayne's qualities seemed to be the next best course of action for Talia to take.

While the Batman has faced many challenges in his life, taming Damian Wayne was probably among the most difficult. At first the boy seemed to be confused by Batman's ethics, in particular Batman's refusal to kill an opponent. But after seeing the Dark Knight in action, Damian was impressed by his father, and realized that he was a noble warrior.

Damian Wayne first officially adopted the mantle of Robin after Bruce Wayne was sent spiraling through time after a conflict with Darkseid. Realizing that Gotham City needed a Batman, Dick Grayson stepped up to the role and became the city's newest Dark Knight, with Damian Wayne as Robin by his side.

DADDY ISSUES
Young Damian Wayne was initially unimpressed with his birth father—not understanding why he refused to kill his enemies. But after spending time with him, Damian realized how heroic his father truly was.

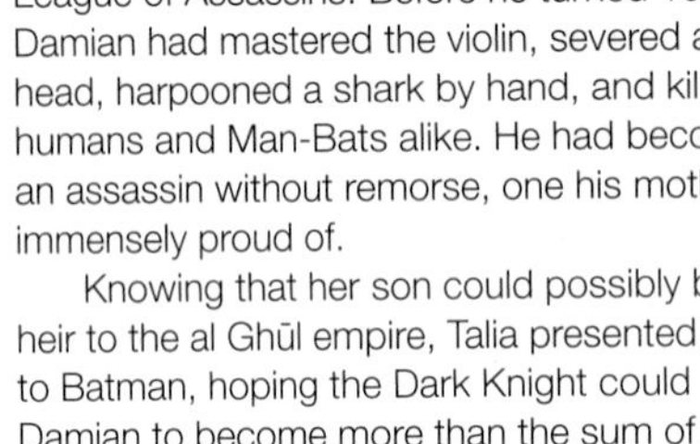

CLASSIC STORIES

***Batman: Son of the Demon* (Sep. 1987)** A romantic fling between Batman and Talia al Ghūl results in a child the Dark Knight knows nothing about: a boy who later becomes known as Damian.

***Batman* (Vol. 1) #655-658 (Sep.-Dec. 2006)** In "Batman and Son," Batman is introduced to his son, Damian, for the first time and attempts to curb the boy's ruthless form of vigilantism.

***Batman and Robin* (Vol. 1) #1 (Aug. 2009)** A new Batman and Robin are back in Gotham City: Dick Grayson as the Dark Knight and Damian Wayne as his youthful crime fighting partner.

***Batman, Inc.* (Vol. 2) #8 (Apr. 2013)** Damian Wayne meets his seemingly final fate as he valiantly fights his powerful "brother" clone, the Heretic.

THE DEATH OF ROBIN

After Batman returned from traveling through time, he was given a quick glimpse of a future threat called Leviathan. To battle this oncoming foe, Batman formed a global team of heroes called Batman, Inc., and later learned that Leviathan was headed by none other than Damian Wayne's mother, Talia al Ghūl. During a confrontation with Leviathan's forces and the villain Heretic, Robin was mortally wounded. It was a loss that Batman was unable to accept, and the Dark Knight began searching for a way to bring his son back to life.

DEATH IN THE FAMILY
Young Damian Wayne was killed battling the Heretic, an adult clone of himself who had been raised by Talia. Following Robin's death, Batman swore revenge, redoubling his efforts to take down Leviathan once and for all.

"Show me respect, father, and fight me!"

DAMIAN WAYNE

The two fought new villains such as Mr. Toad and Professor Pyg, until Bruce Wayne returned and reclaimed the Batman mantle.

Despite gaining true respect for Grayson during their tenure as partners in crime fighting, Damian was very excited to join his father as his partner. But besides fighting super-villains, Damian also found plenty of conflict within himself, especially when he felt forced to take another life, that of the criminal called Nobody. Despite his son's huge misstep, Batman refused to give up on Damian, and worked hard on strengthening their bond. When Damian was murdered by the villain Heretic, Bruce Wayne found himself not just without a partner, but without a son, a truly devastating moment in the Dark Knight's already tragic life.

Determined to see his son returned to him, Batman traveled to the planet Apokolips, where he eventually succeeded in resurrecting Damian. With a renewed lease on life, Robin then decided to venture out into the world on a globe-trotting adventure that saw him correct some of his past mistakes, committed while trying to prove himself to the League of Assassins. **MM**

ROBIN AND GOLIATH
While returning artifacts he had stolen from various cultures around the world, Robin employed the help of Goliath, a dragon-like bat creature he had adopted as a pet after slaying its family.

REBIRTH

LEADER OF THE GANG

Since his recent resurrection, Damian Wayne has become overbearingly ambitious. Assisting Nightwing in safeguarding Gotham City and teaming up with secret Superboy Jon Kent II, Robin has also convinced Starfire, Raven, Beast Boy, and the newest Kid Flash to join him in a campaign to destroy his immortal grandfather and would-be world conqueror Rā's Al-Ghūl.

Regrettably for Damian, although he arrogantly believes he has everything under control, he has no idea what his new allies think of him.

ROBIN "HOOD"
Damian's costume is slightly different from his predecessors', but keeps the trademark yellow cape as a badge of honor.

ROBIN RISES

Batman was willing to go to hell and back to see his son returned to the land of the living, and had to nearly do just that after the tyrant of the planet Apokolips, Darkseid, stole Damian's casket. It seems that years ago, Talia al Ghūl had discovered a fraction of a crystal called the Chaos Shard. The crystal had helped accelerate Damian's growth and seemed to be a source of renewable energy. Darkseid wanted the shard, and his people took Damian's body and the crystal back to Apokolips with them. Batman was forced to follow in his special Hellbat armor, and finally returned to Earth with his resurrected son.

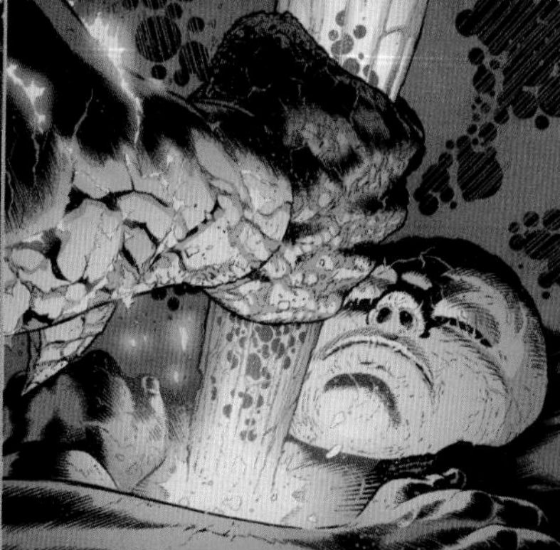

SECOND CHANCE
After returning to Earth, Batman resurrected his son by plunging the Chaos Shard into the boy's chest. It was a rebirth that briefly granted Damian powers akin to Superman's.

ON THE RECORD

After a brief appearance as a baby in 1987, Damian Wayne was reintroduced into the DC Universe again in 2006. With a relatively short career in comics before the dramatic Flashpoint event of 2011, Damian's backstory has barely altered despite the shifting landscape of the world around him.

Conflicting backstories

Originally, Damian Wayne was simply the unnamed child of Talia and Batman who was left on an orphanage's doorstep after their romance soured. All but forgotten, when Damian returned in the later continuity of 2006, his backstory was tweaked to reveal he had been raised in a lab, and had never in fact been abandoned by his mother.

Tackling the Titans

Joining the Teen Titans has been a time-honored tradition for Robins, starting with one of the team's founding members, Dick Grayson. While the second Robin, Jason Todd, only briefly served with the team, the third Boy Wonder, Tim Drake, helped found a new incarnation of the team that nearly reached the greatness of Grayson's era. Before the Flashpoint series significantly altered the Teen Titans' continuity—erasing almost all the stories that had come before—Damian Wayne had decided the Titans needed his particular skill set. While Dick Grayson volunteered Damian's services to the Teen Titans as a member—thinking the team dynamic would be good for Robin's social skills—Damian was angered that he was not immediately welcomed as team leader, and his tenure with them was relatively short.

Titan trouble

After leaving the Teen Titans, Damian Wayne was soon back operating with the Batman Family. But even that working relationship was a constant struggle for the headstrong teen.

WHAT CHILD IS THIS?
Damian's name was only revealed when he came into Batman's life as a troubled adolescent boy, placing in some doubt that the baby depicted in *Batman: Son of the Demon* and Damian Wayne were one and the same.

ROGUES, THE

DEBUT *The Flash* (Vol.1) #155 **(Sep. 1965)**
CURRENT VERSION *The Flash* (Vol. 4) #12 **(Oct. 2012)**
BASE Central City
MEMBERS/POWERS **Captain Cold** (Leonard Snart): Generates and controls ice; **Glider** (Lisa Snart): Astral projection, flight; **Mirror Master** (Sam Scudder): Access to the Mirror World; **Heat Wave** (Mick Rory): Fire projection; **Weather Wizard** (Marco Mardon): Weather manipulation; **Trickster** (Axel Walker): Gadgetry, cybernetic arm; **Pied Piper** (Hartley Rathaway): Sonic manipulation.
ENEMIES The Flash, Gorilla Grodd, Crime Syndicate
AFFILIATIONS Injustice League

HARD TARGETS
Having rejected the Crime Syndicate's offer to join them, the Rogues returned to a Central City devastated by Gorilla Grodd. Before long they were targeted by the Syndicate's Power Ring and Deathstorm.

The Rogues were low-level criminals united in their hatred of the Flash. They used hi-tech gadgetry and weapons to aid them in their crooked enterprises and in their attempts to outfox the Scarlet Speedster. The team abided by three rules that they viewed as a code of honor: not to kill unless necessary, not to use drugs, and not to fail in their crimes.

In his guise as the Flash, Barry Allen battled the Rogues on numerous occasions, each time doling out a bruising defeat. Eventually, the Rogues' leader, Leonard Snart, alias Captain Cold, grew tired of continually being bested by The Flash. He accepted an invitation from research scientist Dr. Darwin Elias, who had approached Snart claiming he could use his Genome Recoder to imbue the Rogues with the power of their weapons. However, something went wrong during the process; while each Rogue did gain superpowers, they came at a cost. Heat Wave was badly burned; Weather Wizard became emotionally linked to the weather he generated; and Mirror Master became trapped in the Mirror World. In addition, Snart's sister, Lisa, who was dating Mirror Master and was also present, found herself separated from her body in astral form.

As Glider, Lisa formed a new version of the Rogues, cutting Snart out of a heist and even going to war with him. Captain Cold rejoined in time to face an invasion of Central City by Grodd and his gorilla army, an episode that forced the Rogues to form an alliance with the Flash.

The team subsequently ran afoul of the Crime Syndicate, having resisted joining their ranks. After a series of skirmishes, the Rogues managed to banish Syndicate allies the Secret Society to the Mirror World. **NJ**

AT THE ROGUES' MERCY
In one of their earliest capers as a group, the Rogues teamed up to rob a department store. When the Flash (Barry Allen) arrived, the villains briefly thought they had disintegrated him with their weapons—only to find he had vibrated through the floor.

ON THE RECORD

Pre-Flashpoint, the Rogues were perennial thorns in the sides of not only Barry Allen but his successors as the Flash: Wally West and Bart Allen. Originally working separately, the Rogues gradually began to form partnerships, first as pairs, later as a larger group. Eventually, a number of the Rogues reformed, prompting a vicious Rogue War that came to an end only when Heat Wave and Trickster rejoined the fold. Arguably the Rogues greatest victory came when they murdered Bart Allen at the climax of the "Full Throttle" storyline. Shortly after, during Final Crisis, the Rogues rejected membership of Libra's Secret Society of Super-Villains. As a result, they were challenged by a new group of Rogues—each of whom was then killed by the originals.

PRISON PLANET
In the wake of the murder of the Flash (Bart Allen), the Rogues were rounded up by Amanda Waller and the Suicide Squad, deposited on a distant world, and left to fend for themselves.

ROSS, PETE

DEBUT *Superboy* (Vol. 1) #86 (Jan. 1961)
CURRENT VERSION *Action Comics* (Vol. 2) #6 (Apr. 2012)
BASE Smallville, Kansas
HEIGHT 5ft 11in **WEIGHT** 175 lbs
ALLIES Lana Lang, Clark Kent, Chief Parker, Kenny Braverman

Pete Ross may have been one of the select few who knew about Clark Kent's incredible abilities from early on, but, if he did, the future Superman didn't know it. As Clark's powers grew by leaps and bounds, he felt increasingly scared and alone. Pete kept him grounded and at ease with tension-breaking banter about what he'd do if he had superpowers. He also provided opportune distractions when Clark needed to act. Pete, Clark, and Lana Lang—the "Three Musketeers"—reunited one last time when Clark left Smallville. Pete wished his friend well in his journalism career, joking that, as he didn't have superpowers, he'd have to be a millionaire instead, or work in his dad's store.

Pre-Flashpoint, Pete, Clark, and Lana had also been the "Three Musketeers." When Pete became a Senator, he and Lana married and had a son, but after Pete accepted presidential candidate Lex Luthor's invitation to become his Vice President, the couple divorced. On Luthor's impeachement, Pete became President, returning to Smallville to open a general store when his term expired. **WW**

A STEADFAST FRIEND
After Clark Kent's parents died, Pete Ross helped his friend understand that his destiny lay in the wider world beyond Smallville.

ALL FOR ONE
The three Musketeers—Lana, Clark, and Pete—got together one final time as Clark prepared to leave Smallville for a new life in the Big Smoke, Metropolis.

ROULETTE

DEBUT *JSA Secret Files and Origins* (Vol. 1) #2 (Sep. 2001)
CURRENT VERSION *Catwoman* (Vol. 4) #30 (Jun. 2014)
REAL NAME Veronica Sinclair
HEIGHT 5ft 9ins **WEIGHT** 140 lbs
EYES Green **HAIR** Black
POWERS/ABILITIES Manipulator, martial artist; assessor of skills and abilities in others.
ENEMIES Catwoman, Golden Glider, Vice

Mystery woman Veronica Sinclair loved games and made vast profits compelling others to play them. As well as running numerous casinos—and less respectable gambling ventures—as Roulette, she was a devious and accomplished criminal.

Declaring herself the "Greatest Thief in the World," she challenged other high-profile crooks to prove her wrong. Selina Kyle was one of the underworld figures Roulette most wanted to compete against. As Selina had retired, Veronica forced Catwoman to join her "Race of Thieves" by claiming to have kidnapped children as hostages.

Grotesquely presenting a bag of kids' teeth, Roulette had Selina battle other robbery superstars in a global test, but soon came to regret her rash actions. Selina not only triumphed in style, but also uncovered Veronica's real motives for the rigged competition. Capitalizing on Roulette's crippling obsessive-compulsive disorder, Selina retaliated, punishing her, but also making a deadly enemy of the gambler. **WW**

CATFIGHT!
Roulette's rigging of the "Race of Thieves"—a test of the participants' deception, dexterity, and disguise—led to conflict with Catwoman.

ROYAL FLUSH GANG

DEBUT *Justice League of America* (Vol. 1) #43 (Mar. 1966)
CURRENT VERSION *Forever Evil* #1 (Nov. 2013)
BASE Atlantic City, New Jersey; mobile
MEMBERS/POWERS **Wild Card/Ace of Clubs** (Amos Fortune): Probability manipulation; **King of Spades** (Joseph Carny): Immortality; **Queen of Spades** (Mona Taylor): Ability to impersonate any woman; **Jack of Spades:** Energy weapons; **Ten of Spades** (Wanda Wayland): Skilled fighter; **Ace Android:** Robotic super-strength; **King of Clubs** (Kerry): Energy-charged playing cards; **Queen of Clubs:** Playing cards that influence behavior; **Jack of Clubs/ Hi-Jack:** Specially adapted playing cards.
ALLIES Hector Hammond
ENEMIES The Rogues, Justice League, Superman, Batman, the Joker
AFFILIATIONS Secret Society of Super-Villains

When they first showed their hand, the Royal Flush Gang were a quintet of outlandish thieves. They employed a variety of card-themed, reality-warping weapons and gadgets devised by crazy genius Amos Fortune. After the Justice League defeated them, the motif and concept were stolen by numerous crooks and masterminds. Eventually, the Gang became little more than a 52-man-strong mercenary unit riding flying card-sleds. The entire cadre was killed by the Joker in a feud with Alexander Luthor's Secret Society of Super-Villains, before Amos Fortune returned and franchised the Royal Flush concept throughout America's underworld.

The group's latest incarnation had no access to the advanced weaponry of the originals. No better than a pack of gun-toting thugs, this masked army of opportunistic killers traded off their predecessors' reputations. They rode flying cards while wearing card-suit masks.

After an invasion by Earth-3's Crime Syndicate, the extra-dimensional invaders placed a large bounty on the rebellious Central City Rogues for rejecting their rule. When the Royal Flush Gang attempted to collect the bounty, they proved no match for the Rogues, who wiped them out. **WW**

PURE BLUFF
The Royal Flush Gang rarely played with a full deck.
1 King of Spades
2 Jack of Spades
3 Ten of Spades
4 Ace of Spades
5 Queen of Spades

ON THE RECORD

Amos Fortune's Royal Flush Gang utilized arcane card lore and a selection of exotic weaponry. These devices were empowered by Fortune's discoveries in the manipulation of luck. The members were childhood friends from the same juvenile gang, and decked themselves out in costumes based on the suit of Clubs.

Much later, Hector Hammond revived the concept, gifting his squad with metahuman powers and weapons. For psychological impact and its connotations of death, he clad his team in Spades.

LUCK OF THE DRAW
The criminal card-sharps always proved that fortune favored the bold, even if they usually folded in the final reckoning.

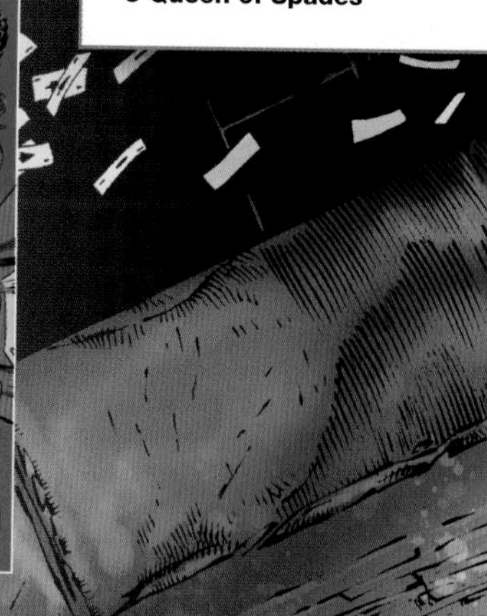

S.H.A.D.E.

DEBUT *Seven Soldiers: Frankenstein* (Vol. 1) #1 **(Jan. 2006)**
CURRENT VERSION *Frankenstein, Agent of S.H.A.D.E.* (Vol. 1) #1 **(Nov. 2011)**
REAL NAME Super-Human Advanced Defense Executive
BASE S.H.A.D.E. City, The Ant Farm, Manhattan (exact location highly classified)
NOTABLE MEMBERS **Father Time:** Director; **Ray Palmer:** Chief Science-Liaison; **Agent Belroy:** Psychic intelligence gatherer
ALLIES Frankenstein, the Bride, G.I. Robot Squadron
ENEMIES Army of Monsters, Humanids, Brother Eye, the Rot
AFFILIATIONS Justice League Dark, Creature Commandos, S.H.A.D.E. Net, Checkmate

The Super-Human Advanced Defense Executive (S.H.A.D.E.) was formed to counteract terrorism and contain all manner of supra-normal dangers to humanity. However, in recent years this ultra-secret government-sponsored group has concentrated exclusively on threats of a supernatural or paranormal nature and been officially re-designated a "Counter-Disaster Organization." Their remit is to quietly head off metahuman crises before they can seriously impact upon the American public. S.H.A.D.E. is led by immortal superhuman Father Time and utilizes arcane lore and advanced technologies, much of it confiscated from the monsters, aliens, and super-maniacs they have defeated over the decades.

S.H.A.D.E.'s current HQ is a miniaturized city-sized citadel. The Ant Farm is a vast, futuristic fortress inside an indestructible metal globe reduced to three inches in diameter and floating 2,000 feet above New York City. Although S.H.A.D.E. possesses its own highly trained paramilitary force, the bulk of its operations is carried out by specialist operatives, like Frankenstein and the Bride, or the Creature Commandos. They are equipped with extraordinary ordnance from the Toybox—a repository of impounded super-weapons, such as blockbusting Nazi War Wheels. **WW**

LEGION OF MONSTERS
Grim experience had proved that, for S.H.A.D.E., the best solution to fighting evil monsters was good ones, preferably carrying weapons.

ON THE RECORD

The original S.H.A.D.E. was a counter-intelligence operation created by President Lyndon B. Johnson in the mid-1960s. As metahumans began to proliferate, the power and influence of the unit dwindled, until it was almost forgotten.

S.H.A.D.E. was saved by the Infinite Crisis. With all Earth's heroes fully occupied, Father Time became aware of an imminent invasion by the time-rending Sheeda and orchestrated the government's counterstrike through his own recruits, the Atomic Knights and Freedom Fighters.

TOOLS OF THE TRADE
Father Time was content to let expendable agents do the dirty work, and use the power of the US Government to cover up his actions.

FUTURE PROOF
S.T.A.R. Labs is working on rational solutions to almost every physical problem facing mankind, but cannot ever escape its clandestine, conflict-tainted origins.

S.T.A.R. LABS

DEBUT *Superman* (Vol. 1) #246 **(Dec. 1971)**
CURRENT VERSION *Justice League* (Vol. 2) #2 **(Dec. 2012)**
REAL NAME Science and Technology Advanced Research Laboratories
BASE New York City
POWERS/MEMBERS **Josiah Power:** Exact role classified; **Manchester Black:** Head of Advanced Ideas Division; **Jensener:** Head of Artificial Intelligence Division; **Schmidt:** Head of Power Research Division.
ALLIES John Henry Irons
ENEMIES Lex Luthor, LexCorp, Algorithm
AFFILIATIONS The Teen Titans, Justice League, Superman, A.R.G.U.S.

S.T.A.R. Labs grew out of Operation Paperclip, by which the US Government put captured Nazi scientists to work on secret projects after World War II. Eventually, the organization declared its independence from government and was publicly launched as Earth's only cutting-edge, multi-disciplinary company specializing in "blue sky" science and employing radical thinkers unwilling to work for soulless corporations or the military-industrial complex. Their mandate covers all areas of scientific investigation, testing, exploration, and analysis.

S.T.A.R. Labs headquarters is a purpose-built skyscraper in downtown Manhattan, but they also maintain facilities worldwide. The company's most dangerous discoveries are archived in secure basement vaults. A separate facility was built on Governors Island, but this was destroyed soon after the company began an association with the Teen Titans.

Non-political and offering immense resources, S.T.A.R. Labs has become the first port of call for Super Heroes in need of technical assistance, medical aid, or advice in coping with the many metahuman menaces they contend with on a regular basis.

Over the years, S.T.A.R. Labs has fought off takeover bids from Lex Luthor's LexCorp and continues to deal daily with constantly multiplying dangers of alien or post-metahuman technologies and unchecked, fringe-science innovation. **WW**

ON THE RECORD

S.T.A.R. Labs quickly became a global mainstay of the pre-Flashpoint DC Universe, acting as a prison for metahuman menaces and a medical resource for injured or mysteriously afflicted Super Heroes. The company even briefly operated its own team. S.T.A.R. Corps featured old company alumnus Rampage and a squad of neophyte metahuman anomalies—Brainstorm, Deadzone, Fusion, Ndoki, and Trauma—all created by out-of-control Project Mindstorm, as it probed the mysteries of the human metagene.

PROOF OF CONCEPT
S.T.A.R. Labs' employment package included fun, thrills, good pay, rewarding work, a dental plan—and possible metahuman transformation.

SABBAC

DEBUT *Captain Marvel, Jr.* (Vol. 1) #4 (Feb. 1943) (Timothy Karnes); *The Outsiders.* (Vol. 3) #8 (Mar. 2004) (Ishmael Gregor)
REAL NAME Ishmael Gregor
BASE Mogo
EYES Black **HAIR** Black
POWERS/ABILITIES Demonically-fueled strength, speed, endurance, flight, fire breath.
ALLIES Dr. Sivana, High Priest of Bagdan
ENEMIES Shazam, Captain Marvel, Captain Marvel Jr., Superman, Nightwing, the Outsiders

Timothy Karnes was a huge disappointment to the Lords of Hell. Thanks to their infernal magic, he could transform into a monstrous engine of destruction whenever he shouted the acronym of their names; but as Sabbac, he was an ineffectual agent, easily defeated by Earth's Super Heroes. They were far happier when New York City mob-boss Ishmael Gregor murdered a bus full of people as a blood-sacrifice and stole the power from Timothy's expiring corpse.

Reveling in slaughter and chaos, the new Sabbac undertook a vicious campaign to amass wealth and bring about Hell on Earth. When he opened a portal and started recruiting demons from the Pit, he was routed by the Outsiders. Sabbac has returned many times, allying with coalitions of super-villains and the demon Neron. **WW**

SAINT WALKER

DEBUT *Final Crisis: Rage of the Red Lanterns* (Vol. 1) #1 (Dec. 2008)
CURRENT VERSION *Green Lantern: New Guardians* (Vol. 1) #2 (Dec. 2011)
REAL NAME Bro'Dee Walker
BASES Mogo, Odym, Astonia, Sector 1
EYES Black **HAIR** None
POWERS/ABILITIES Genius intellect, compassionate, and possesses indomitable willpower; commands a blue power ring to materialize hard-light constructs, translate languages, enable flight and protect against enemy attack. His power ring also boosts and hyper-charges all green power rings in immediate vicinity.
ALLIES Warth, Green Lantern Corps, Guy Gardner, Star Sapphires, Indigo Tribe
ENEMIES Sinestro, Larfleeze, the Reach, Relic
AFFILIATIONS Ganthet and Sayd, Blue Lantern Corps, New Guardians

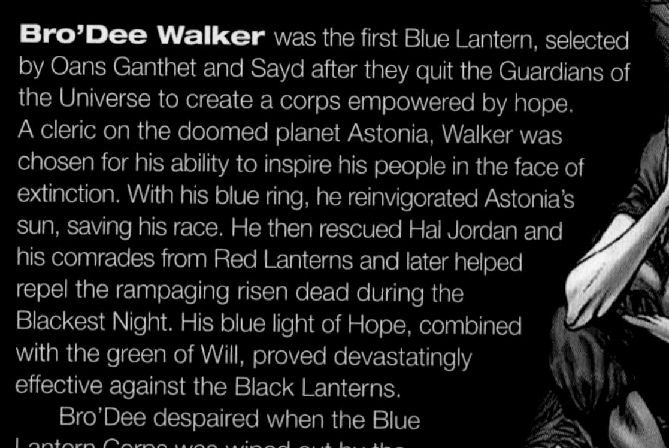

Bro'Dee Walker was the first Blue Lantern, selected by Oans Ganthet and Sayd after they quit the Guardians of the Universe to create a corps empowered by hope. A cleric on the doomed planet Astonia, Walker was chosen for his ability to inspire his people in the face of extinction. With his blue ring, he reinvigorated Astonia's sun, saving his race. He then rescued Hal Jordan and his comrades from Red Lanterns and later helped repel the rampaging risen dead during the Blackest Night. His blue light of Hope, combined with the green of Will, proved devastatingly effective against the Black Lanterns.

Bro'Dee despaired when the Blue Lantern Corps was wiped out by the fanatic Relic. His ring left him, but when his hope for the future finally returned, he regained the blue ring and set about spreading harmony throughout the cosmos once more. **WW**

ON THE RECORD

For tyrants and villains, Hope is the most dangerous hue of the Emotional Spectrum. A being possessing hope cannot be cowed or controlled, only killed. Despite the Guardian's misgivings and plans to destroy free will, Saint Walker became a trusted ally of the Green Lanterns and served with distinction in Kyle Rayner's multi-spectrum task force, the New Guardians. His assistance was crucial in crushing the Oans' oppressive Third Army.

AGAINST ALL HOPE
Although the Third Army was designed to eliminate Free Will in the universe, it would have just as readily eradicated the light of Hope.

SAIKO

DEBUT *Nightwing* (Vol. 3) #1 (Nov. 2011)
REAL NAME Raymond McCreary
EYES Brown **HAIR** Brown
POWERS/ABILITIES Highly trained acrobat, marksman and unarmed-combat fighter, employing hi-tech gadgets and weaponry, customized body-armor and wrist-blades.
ALLIES Raya Vestri, Zane, Bryan Haly
ENEMIES Court of Owls, C.C. Haly
AFFILIATIONS Haly's Circus

Raymond McCreary was always second-best. As a child at Haly's Circus, Dick Grayson was the star attraction, leaving his young companions in the shade. The circus had supplied the Court of Owls with high-potential children for years and, although Grayson was chosen to be their new Talon, the criminal cabal had to settle for Raymond after the bereaved orphan was unexpectedly adopted by Bruce Wayne.

Raymond endured torturous testing before being ultimately rejected by the Owls and left to die. He somehow survived and returned several years later as Saiko, a highly-proficient and savage contract killer, hell-bent on revenge. Allied with other disaffected children from the circus' past, he murdered the owner and sought to destroy Nightwing. Saiko knew that Nightwing was Dick Grayson, whom he blamed for his torment at the Court's hands.

Saiko perished in a cataclysmic conflagration he set off trying to destroy Haly's Circus and Nightwing. **WW**

CUT TO THE QUICK
A life of constant rejection turned Raymond McCreary into a murdering monster obsessed with revenge.

SALA

DEBUT *Green Lantern Annual* (Vol. 3) #9 (2000)
BASE Nabeul, Tunisia
HEIGHT 5ft 7in **WEIGHT** 138 lbs
EYES Green **HAIR** Brown
POWERS/ABILITIES Superhuman strength, speed, reflexes, durability, healing, energy-projection, combat skills, swordsmanship; divine empowerment from Ringstaff of Istar.
ALLIES Green Lantern Kyle Rayner, JLA
ENEMIES Ereskigal, Humbaba, Nergal, Pazuzu, Tiamat

Archaeologist Sala Nisaba saved artifacts endangered by Middle East conflicts. Arrested in Syria after uncovering Kurnugi, the Babylonian portal to Hell, she was rescued by Kyle Rayner. They were attacked by warlike Malthusians who had fled their birth world billions of years ago. Settling on Earth, the Malthusians were mistaken for gods and demons by the primitives of the Sumerian region. In the end they were defeated by one of their own, Istar, Lady of Battle, who banished her cruel comrades to another plane—until Sala resurrected them.

Grasping the goddess' Ringstaff while battling the resurgent monsters, Sala turned into a mighty warrior woman. Later, research revealed that she was Istar's descendant, and needed only a trigger to manifest her ancestor's powers and personality. **WW**

SALAAK

DEBUT *Green Lantern* (Vol. 2) #149 (Feb. 1982)
CURRENT VERSION *Green Lantern Corps* (Vol. 3) #1 (Nov. 2011)
BASE Mogo
HEIGHT 7ft 6in **WEIGHT** 207 lbs
EYES White **HAIR** None
POWERS/ABILITIES Skilled warrior and strategist; genius intellect; indomitable will enables command of a green power ring.
ENEMIES Sinestro, Guardians of the Universe, Parallax

Salaak of Slyggia was one of the most effective Green Lanterns the Guardians of the Universe had ever recruited. He served the Corps for years in many turbulent space sectors, and single-handedly defended those sectors from the Anti-Monitor during the Infinite Crisis.

When the Guardians reconstructed the Green Lantern Corps, he became protocol officer liaising between the Guardians and their agents. However, when the Guardians sought to replace their servants with a mindless Third Army, Salaak fought valiantly to thwart them. Painfully aware that many of his comrades still associated him with the treacherous Guardians, Salaak surrendered his post in Hal Jordan's new administration, and resolved to earn back the trust of his fellow Green Lanterns. **WW**

SAND

DEBUT *Adventure Comics* (Vol. 1) #69 **(Dec. 1941)**
REAL NAME Sanderson "Sandy" Hawkins
BASE Brooklyn, New York
HEIGHT 5ft 11in **WEIGHT** 162 lbs **EYES** Blue **HAIR** Blond
POWERS/ABILITIES Geokinesis, silicate transformation and phasing, extended lifespan, psychic affinity with the planet, precognitive dreams; skilled detective and criminologist, trained in combat.
ALLIES Wesley Dodds, Dian Belmont, John Law/Tarantula, Kendra Saunders, Rex Tyler
ENEMIES Johnny Sorrow, Mordru, Ian Karkull, Geomancer, Injustice Society, King of Tears
AFFILIATIONS Justice Society of America, All-Star Squadron, Young All-Stars

Sandy Hawkins started his adventurous life during World War II as sidekick to Sandman Wesley Dodds. A dynamic, acrobatic brawler, Hawkins learned all the crime-solving skills of a master detective from his brilliant senior partner before succumbing to a tragic accident. During a laboratory experiment to improve their crime-fighting arsenal, Sandy was accidentally transformed into a huge, raging silicoid monster. Not realizing what had happened to Sandy, Dodds tranquilized the inarticulate horror and kept it imprisoned and unconscious for decades. Sandy at last revived and escaped his confinement during an earthquake. It transpired that he had become attuned to the Earth's structure. Over time he learned to regain his human shape while retaining his geological sensitivities. His abilities included being able to turn into sand and travel through the planet's strata at incredible speeds, hence his new moniker—Sand.

With Dodds disabled by age and infirmity, Sandy adopted many of his tools and gimmicks, becoming the leader of a new, multi-generational iteration of the Justice Society of America. When he took his mentor's codename and inherited Wesley's awful power of prophetic dreaming, he stood down to become the team's covert intelligence-gatherer. **WW**

NO SLEEP FOR THE WICKED
No matter what form he took, Sand was a legacy hero who took his glittering heritage and evil-crushing duties seriously.

ON THE RECORD

Sandy the Golden Boy's Golden Age debut coincided with the Sandman's abrupt transformation from a moody, gas-masked mystery man into a bombastic masked acrobat, battling gangsters while haunting their dreams with two-fisted retribution. Years later, Sandy was reintroduced in a 1974 Justice League/Justice Society team up that revealed his decades of petrification and suspended animation. His restoration to human form in 1982 hinted that he may have gained powers from the experience, but it took the JSA's 21st-century revival to confirm it.

CRIME'S WORST NIGHTMARE
The Sandman and Sandy tirelessly pursued evildoers in their dreams and then dealt swiftly and forcefully with them in the real world.

SANDMAN

DEBUT *Adventure Comics* (Vol. 1) #40 **(Jul. 1939)**
CURRENT VERSION *Earth 2* (Vol. 1) #5 **(Dec. 2012)**
REAL NAME Wesley Dodds
HEIGHT 5ft 11in **WEIGHT** 172 lbs
POWERS/ABILITIES Able to teleport; expert in unarmed combat; weapons-master trained in all aspects of espionage and covert intelligence-gathering.
ALLIES Amar Khan, Al Pratt, Stormy Foster, Captain Steel, Red Arrow, Jay Garrick, Alan Scott, Dr. Fate, Red Tornado, Val-Zod
ENEMIES Steppenwolf, Parademons, Darkseid, Terry Sloan
AFFILIATIONS World Army, Red Files, the Sandmen, Arkham Base, Eight Wonders

When Earth-2 was attacked by the forces of Apokolips, the Superman, Batman, and Wonder Woman of that world bravely turned back the invasion at the cost of their lives. Despite their sacrifice, the planet was devastated and a World Army arose to unite and safeguard the remains of humanity while preparing for the next inevitable assault.

After five years of relative stability, the attack came and Commander Amar Khan marshaled all of his resources, including the legendary Canadian super-spy Wesley Dodds. The enigmatic and effective "Sandman" was considered near infallible—a combat-master particularly expert with gas weapons, Dodds could teleport to any destination he imagined and led a personally-trained cadre of black ops specialists. He deployed these Sandmen in numerous sorties against Darkseid's servants.

Despite valiant resistance, the Apokoliptian forces succeeded on every front. Dodds and his Sandmen sided with Khan when he rebelled against Earth's inept political leaders to take control of humanity's last-ditch resistance. When Earth-2 was finally consumed by Apokolips, Sandman was instrumental in securing a fleet of colony ships to ferry the last survivors of humanity away from their doomed world. **WW**

IN THE SHADOWS
Even in a doomed world, Sandman found what was necessary for humanity to survive.

ON THE RECORD

One of DC Comics' oldest heroes, Sandman was inspired by 1930s pulp-fiction stars. Sporting a suit, hat, cape, and gas-mask he employed his detective skills, sleeping gas, and other gimmicks against a legion of crooks.

During World War II, Sandman switched to gaudy tights and traded his gutsy girlfriend Dian Belmont for a boy sidekick. When revived in the 1960s, he had reverted to his moody original gear and methods.

THE SLEEP OF THE UNJUST
The Sandman punched heads and gassed goons, scattering sand calling-cards as a reminder to his targets to stay honest—or face the consequences.

SARGON THE SORCERER

DEBUT *All-American Comics* (Vol. 1) #26 (May 1941)
CURRENT VERSION *Constantine* (Vol. 1) #1 (May 2013)
REAL NAME Jaimini Sargent
BASE Temple of the Cold Flame
HEIGHT 5ft 10in **WEIGHT** 160 lbs
EYES Brown **HAIR** Black
POWERS/ABILITIES Highly skilled magician.
ENEMIES John Constantine, Justice League Dark, Frankenstein, S.H.A.D.E., Zatanna

Sargon the Sorcerer was John Sargent: one of the most powerful magicians of the 20th century; who used his miraculous Ruby of Life to battle the forces of injustice and supernatural menaces, such as the Blue Lama. He eventually retired, studying lost lore and creating the Cult of the Cold Flame with mages Mister E, Tannarak, and Zatara.

His daughter Jaimini claims to have killed him, stealing his power and twisting the cult's aims. She and John Constantine searched for Croydon's Compass, a mystic artifact of great power. Unsure whether she was attracted to him for himself or his mystic resources, Jaimini variously tried to seduce, enslave, and eradicate the trickster-magician, but in vain. Her goals remain clear: to amass enough knowledge and power to do anything she wants. **WW**

SATANUS

DEBUT *Action Comics* (Vol. 1) #527 (Jan. 1982)
CURRENT VERSION *Batman/Superman* (Vol. I) #13 (Oct. 2014)
REAL NAME Lord Satanus
BASE Hell
HEIGHT/WEIGHT Variable **EYES** Red
POWERS/ABILITIES Supernal physical prowess derived from a demonic nature; dimensional travel, reality alteration, flight.
ENEMIES Kaiyo, Batman, Superman, Catwoman, Lois Lane

Lord Satanus is supreme overlord of demonic underworld the Dark Realm. A creature of vast power and infinite life-span, Satanus lurks at the edges of reality looking for souls to torment and good lives to destroy. He has observed all aspects of human frailty, and occasional triumphs of virtue over adversity, which both amuse and repel him.

Though fiercely territorial over intrusions into his infernal realm, Satanus allowed Apokolips' trickster-demon Kaiyo to play her cruel games with Earth's greatest champions, Superman and Batman. She spitefully meddled with their lives and memories, drawing in Lois Lane, Catwoman and others, and providing Satanus with such great entertainment that the demon decided to imprison Kaiyo for the times that he craved further amusement. **WW**

SATURN QUEEN

DEBUT *Superman* (Vol. 1) #147 (Aug. 1961)
CURRENT VERSION *Legion of Super-Heroes* (Vol. 7) #14 (Jan. 2013)
REAL NAME Eve Aries
BASE 31st century, mobile
HEIGHT 5ft 5in **WEIGHT** 110 lbs
EYES Green **HAIR** Red
POWERS/ABILITIES Telepathy, hypnotism, mind-control.
ENEMIES Saturn Girl, Legion of Super-Heroes, Superman, Batman

Eve Aries grew up in the telepathic community of Titan, but suffered a radical personality shift after leaving the influence of Saturn's moon. On her world, wicked thoughts and anti-social behavior were practically unknown and deviant attitudes were easily detected and rapidly addressed. Once beyond her people's influence, Eve was gripped by criminal tendencies and started using her psionic gifts to dominate lesser minds. The further Eve strayed from Titan, the more evil she became.

Saturn Queen went on a spree of robbery and worse, teaming with Lightning Lord and Cosmic King. They formed a Legion of Super-Villains, battling their own era's heroes and, after stealing time-travel technology, attacking Superman in his own time in an attempt to remake history. **WW**

SAWYER, MAGGIE

DEBUT *Superman* (Vol. 2) #4 (Apr. 1987)
CURRENT VERSION *Batwoman* #1 (Nov. 2011)
REAL NAME Margaret Sawyer
BASE Metropolis
HEIGHT 5ft 10in **WEIGHT** 130 lbs
EYES Blue **HAIR** Light brown
POWERS/ABILITIES Skilled detective, trained in special weapons protocols.
ENEMIES The Weeping Woman, Medusa, Ceto, Mother of All Monsters, Nocturna

Maggie Sawyer spent most of her early life being punished by her religious father for being a tomboy. Years later, after her marriage ended, she quit the Metropolis Police Department and enlisted in the Gotham City force. While investigating the kidnapping killer Weeping Woman, Sawyer became romantically involved with Kate Kane. Kane later revealed that she was Batwoman while proposing to Maggie.

Maggie's career prospered and she was even tipped to succeed James Gordon as Commissioner. When he was framed for murder, the G.C.P.D. began sinking back into its old corrupt ways under interim Commissioner Jack Forbes. Sawyer secretly aligned with honest cops Jason Bard and Harvey Bullock to expose the criminal conspiracy and restore Gordon. **WW**

SATURN GIRL

DEBUT *Adventure Comics* (Vol. 1) #247 **(Apr. 1958)**
CURRENT VERSION *Legion: Secret Origin* #1 **(Dec. 2011)**
REAL NAME Imra Ardeen
BASE Legion of Super-Heroes HQ, 31st-century Metropolis
HEIGHT 5ft 7ins **WEIGHT** 130 lbs **EYES** Blue **HAIR** Blonde
POWERS/ABILITIES Wide array of psionic abilities including telepathy, mind-reading, thought-casting, mind-control, and illusion generation.
ALLIES Superman, Garth Ranzz, Rokk Krinn
ENEMIES Time Trapper, Legion of Super-Villains, Fatal Five, Dark Circle
AFFILIATIONS Legion of Super-Heroes

Imra Ardeen is a supremely powerful telepath, trained by elite mentalists on her birthplace, Saturn's moon, Titan. She planned to join the Science Police but en route to Earth she psychically "overheard" a plan to assassinate the hugely wealthy financier R.J. Brande. With fellow passengers Garth Ranzz and Rokk Krinn, she foiled the attempt and the grateful Brande offered his rescuers a chance to make a real difference to civilization. The multi-billionaire wanted to sponsor a Legion of Super-Heroes that could operate like Metropolis' legendary champion Superman. Imra realized that this was how she could best use her amazing psionic abilities.

When the Legion time-traveled to recruit Superboy, she became responsible for editing his memories to preserve the integrity of that particular timeline. As the team grew, she succeeded Rokk (Cosmic Boy) as leader, serving two successive terms and thereafter becoming advisor and "Elder Statesman" to later leaders.

Eventually she married Garth (Lightning Lad) and they had a son named Graym. The couple was unaware that their child had a twin whom Darkseid had supernaturally stolen and reshaped as the monstrous Validus. When the secret was finally revealed, Imra successfully convinced Darkseid to restore the child to human form. By this time, she and Garth were Legion Reservists, but they came to the aid of their teammates when the need arose. **WW**

ON THE RECORD

Saturn Girl was the first female comic book character to lead a team, though she initially won by using her telepathic powers to rig the election! A computer-projection revealed that a Legionnaire would die on duty, so she selflessly orchestrated events so that only she would be active at the time. Lightning Lad uncovered the plot and died instead, but she found a way to resurrect him and won a second leadership contest by popular acclaim.

THE TEAM COMES FIRST
Fiercely protective, Saturn Girl would go to any lengths and make any sacrifice to ensure the safety and wellbeing of her comrades.

SCARECROW

DATA

DEBUT *World's Finest Comics* (Vol. 1) #3 **(Fall 1941)**
CURRENT VERSION *Batman* (Vol. 2) #1 **(Nov. 2011)**
REAL NAME Dr. Jonathan Crane
BASE Gotham City
HEIGHT 6ft **WEIGHT** 140 lbs
EYES Green **HAIR** Brown
POWERS/ABILITIES Near genius intellect; brilliant chemist and psychiatrist; weapons include fear gas that causes victims to experience their worst nightmares.
ALLIES Professor Pyg, Merry-Maker, Harley Quinn, Mr. Freeze
ENEMIES Batman, the Batman Family
AFFILIATIONS The Secret Society of Super-Villains

WHO SCARES THE SCARECROW?
The Scarecrow has spent his life becoming a bogeyman to scare innocents. Unluckily for Crane, he often clashes with a creature of the night that frightens even him: Batman.

Dr. Jonathan Crane has spent as much time lurking in the dark corners of the human psyche as he has hiding in the shadowy parts of Gotham City. Obsessed with the idea of fear in its many forms, Crane has adopted the role of the Scarecrow, a living embodiment of things that go bump in the night. A career super-villain, Scarecrow lives to clash with the Batman, intent on making the Dark Knight cower in fear.

FEAR OF THE FATHER
Surrounded by skeletons and other horrors that would scare an adult, young Jonathan Crane grew up with fear, and would later embrace it.

SCARE TACTICS
From an early age, Jonathan Crane learned to turn his own fears into a weapon against those who dared to oppose him.

Jonathan Crane was born into a life of fear due to the terrible upbringing inflicted on him by his heartless scientist father. Jonathan's mother died when he was young and he was brought up by his father, who was obsessed with all aspects of terror—a grim passion he would pass on to his son. When Jonathan was a young boy, his father would hook him up to heart rate monitors and shove him beneath a trap door. The small, dark chamber beneath was stuffed full of macabre items more suited to the set of a Gothic horror movie. As soon as Jonathan was set free by his father, the terrified boy would run as fast as he could into a nearby cornfield, screaming and scaring away the birds.

A shy boy, mocked by his peers, young Jonathan focused on his studies. He became a professor of psychology, but his peculiar teaching methods terrified his students and he was fired. He then became a psychologist, but after attacking a patient, decided to accept his "true self" and adopted the name and costume of the scarecrow on his family farm. He embarked upon a criminal career that used his specially designed fear toxins to terrify victims, and after repeated clashes with Batman, even stitched his own mouth shut to closer resemble his namesake. **MM**

ON THE RECORD

While he is a key foe in Batman's modern-day Rogues Gallery, the Scarecrow's criminal career got off to a fairly slow start. Debuting in the 1940s, the villain only appeared once more before returning to commit new crimes in the 1960s.

The Scarecrow's ascendancy through Gotham City's criminal ranks continued in the following decades. His character grew darker and increasingly psychotic as he took on Batman and the Batman Family in such high-profile stories as *Batman: Dark Victory*, "Hush," "Knightfall," and even the cosmic saga "Blackest Night."

NATURE OF THE BEAST
Before Flashpoint altered reality, Scarecrow was given a power upgrade courtesy of a scheming Penguin, who transformed Crane into the hulking, super-powered Scarebeast.

CLASSIC STORIES

***World's Finest Comics* (Vol. 1) #3 (Fall 1941)** The Scarecrow debuts in Batman's chapter of this title, which stars both the Dark Knight and Superman in their own separate features.

***Batman* (Vol. 1) #189 (Feb. 1967)** Not glimpsed since the Golden Age, the Scarecrow returns to frighten a new generation of readers, armed with his signature fear gas.

***Batman* (Vol. 1) #457 (Dec. 1990)** Fledgling Robin Tim Drake proves his worth when he saves Batman from the Scarecrow and the villain's latest fear gas concoctions.

SCALPHUNTER

DEBUT *Weird Western Tales* #39 (Mar.–Apr. 1977)
CURRENT VERSION *Bizarro* #3 (Oct. 2015)
REAL NAME Brian Savage/Ke-Woh-No-Tay
BASE Opal City, 19th century
HEIGHT 6ft 1in **WEIGHT** 190 lbs
EYES Blue **HAIR** Black (later gray)
POWERS/ABILITIES Superb hand-to-hand fighter; excellent horseman; expert marksman.
ALLIES Bat Lash, Cinnamon, Jonah Hex, Shade
ENEMIES The Tuesday Club
AFFILIATIONS Rough Bunch, Black Lanterns

In the 1840s, the Kiowa tribe of Native Americans attacked the home of Matthew and Laurie Savage, kidnapping their young son Brian. Renamed Ke-Woh-No-Tay, meaning "He Who Is Less Than Human," Brian was raised by the Kiowa until he was captured during a raiding party and recognized. Sent to prison for a murder he did not commit, Brian escaped and caught the killers, procuring a pardon for himself in the process.

He became known as Scalphunter and befriended gambler Bat Lash, settling down in Opal City later in life. While only a ghost of Scalphunter has been glimpsed post-Flashpoint, he was resurrected during the Blackest Night event as a Black Lantern, joining forces with other Western icons. **MM**

SCARAB

DEBUT *Robin* #124 (May 2004)
REAL NAME Maat Shadid
BASE Gotham City
HEIGHT 5ft 4in **WEIGHT** 125 lbs
EYES Brown **HAIR** Black
POWERS/ABILITIES Hi-tech, armored suit allows flight, enhanced communication and durability; helmet provides night-vision; forearm-mounted blasters fire energy bolts.
ALLIES Fellow Scarabs
ENEMIES Red Robin, Spoiler, Batman
AFFILIATIONS Covenant of Ka

The killer for hire known as Scarab first arrived in Gotham City when she was hired by another villain, Johnny Warlock, to assassinate Robin (Tim Drake). However, Scarab took the contract during a time of great turmoil between Batman and Robin; Tim Drake had temporarily quit his position as the Dark Knight's closest ally, which resulted in Batman enlisting Stephanie Brown as a replacement Robin.

Nevertheless, Scarab began targeting boys who met Robin's description until she was defeated by Stephanie and Batman. When Tim Drake graduated to the position of Red Robin, he would clash with Scarab several more times, discovering she was just one of many assassin Scarabs working for the Covenant of Ka syndicate. **MM**

SCAVENGER

DEBUT *Aquaman* (Vol. 1) #37 (Jan.–Feb. 1968)
CURRENT VERSION *Justice League* (Vol. 2) #10 (Aug. 2012)
REAL NAME Peter Mortimer
HEIGHT 5ft 9in **WEIGHT** 176 lbs
EYES Brown **HAIR** Brown
POWERS/ABILITIES Underwater fighter; protective suit with air supply; Scorpion Ship.
ALLIES Black Manta
ENEMIES Aquaman, Tula, Mera
AFFILIATIONS Secret Society

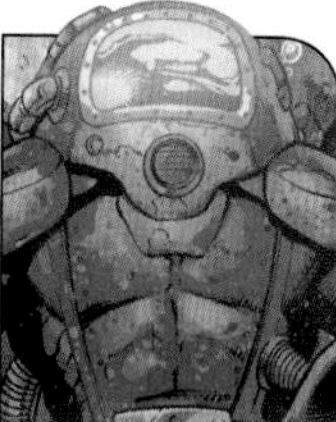

The super-villain called Scavenger has been a foe of Aquaman for many years. Indeed, he has earned a reputation as one of the Atlantean king's most steadfast enemies. When the super-villain Graves attempted to acquire knowledge about the Justice League, he interrogated Scavenger to learn more about Aquaman.

After Atlantis attacked the city of Boston, Scavenger was there to salvage from the ruins. Aquaman thought Scavenger was merely making off with stolen Atlantean weapons, but in reality the villain was preparing a surprise invasion of Atlantis—one that Aquaman barely managed to fight off. Scavenger was then recruited into the Secret Society of Super-Villains, and despite its apparent dissolution, Scavenger stayed on as one of the team's key members. **MM**

SEA DEVILS

DEBUT *Showcase* (Vol. 1) #27 (Jul.–Aug. 1960)
CURRENT VERSION *Aquaman* (Vol. 7) #17 (Apr. 2013)
BASE Mobile
NOTABLE MEMBERS Dane Dorrance, Judy Walton; Nick Walton
ENEMIES Captain Moller

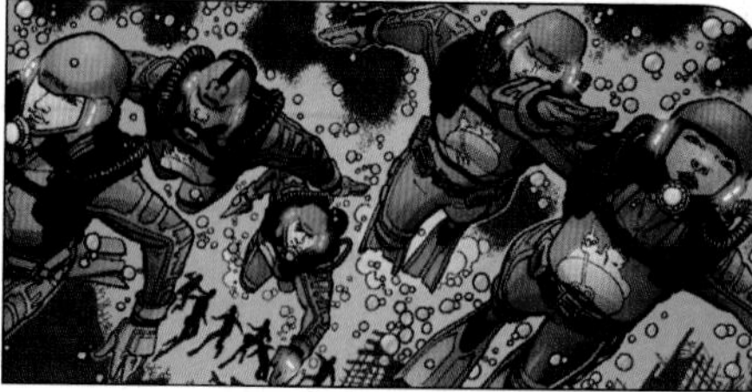

Seafaring vigilantes the Sea Devils are considered eco-terrorists by some and heroes by others. Led by activist Dane Dorrance, the team includes Judy and Nick Walton. The Sea Devils are reputedly responsible for bringing down an oil rig mid-construction, among other similar plots.

When the Sea Devils tracked the ship of Captain Moller, they found the corrupt skipper using stolen Atlantean weaponry to kill whales. As the captain turned his weapon on them, Aquaman came to their rescue. He introduced himself, only to find Dane suspicious of his nobility. Dane was angered that the Atlanteans had recently attacked the surface people because of the machinations of Aquaman's half-brother, Ocean Master. **MM**

SCANDAL

DEBUT *Villains United* #1 (Jul. 2005)
CURRENT VERSION *Secret Six* (Vol. 4) #2 (Apr. 2015)
REAL NAME Scandal Savage
HEIGHT 5ft 10in **WEIGHT** 143 lbs
EYES Brown **HAIR** Brown (with blue streak)
POWERS/ABILITIES Expert fighter, natural leader, intelligent; gauntlets with retractable blades.
ALLIES Ragdoll, Jeannette, Secret Six
ENEMIES Riddler

The daughter of infamous criminal Vandal Savage, Scandal hasn't quite followed in her dad's footsteps, but she hasn't led a civilian's life either. Blackmailed by the Riddler, who threatened to kill her two wives, Scandal was forced to do his bidding as the villain kidnapped Thomas Blake (the future Catman). Fearing for Blake's sanity, Scandal brought him a kitten to keep him company in his solitary jail cell.

Later—alongside two other mercenaries, Ragdoll and Jeannette—Scandal was forced to battle the Secret Six, Catman's allies. With neither team wanting to harm the other, they developed a mutual respect, especially when the Secret Six brought the Riddler to justice. Scandal offered to look after young member Black Alice, when she was being pursued by nearly every sorcerer in the world. **MM**

SCARLET

DEBUT *Batman and Robin* (Vol. 1) #1 (Aug. 2009)
CURRENT VERSION *Batman, Inc.* (Vol. 2) #3 (Sep. 2012)
REAL NAME Sasha (last name unknown)
BASE Gotham City
HEIGHT 4ft 6in **WEIGHT** 78 lbs
EYES Blue **HAIR** Red
POWERS/ABILITIES Adept hand-to-hand combatant trained by the Red Hood.
ALLIES Red Hood
ENEMIES Professor Pyg, Flamingo

A young girl named Sasha traveled to the US to start a new life with her father, Niko. When he was hired as a henchmen by the criminal Mr. Toad, Niko was lucky to escape his first encounter with Batman (Dick Grayson). Niko went to his apartment, but before he could escape with Sasha, the pair were ambushed by Professor Pyg, who placed a Dollotron mask on them both to control their minds. Freed by Robin, Sasha fought back against Pyg, setting the villain on fire.

After Sasha smothered her father in his hospital bed as a mercy killing, she was discovered by the Red Hood (Jason Todd) and became his vigilante partner, Scarlet. They fought foes including the Flamingo and the Menagerie, employing a deadlier brand of justice than Batman. **MM**

SCORN

DEBUT (Ceritak) *Superman* (Vol. 2) #122 (Apr. 1997); (Clyde Anderson) *Detective Comics* (Vol. 2) #22 (Sep. 2013)
BASE Metropolis, mobile
HEIGHT 12ft **WEIGHT** 975 lbs
EYES White **HAIR** White
POWERS/ABILITIES Superhuman strength and senses; flight; tracking vision.

The hulking creature known as Scorn is actually named Ceritak, a citizen of a bottled city created by the sorcerer Tolos. His father, Cerimul, was a Council Elder of the city, but Ceritak was a rebel, and escaped the confines of his bottled prison when Superman weakened the dimensional barrier between the city and the rest of the world.

Ceritak was dubbed Scorn by the media, despite only wanting to explore the world, often by the side of his love, Ashbury, daughter of *Daily Planet* writer Dirk Armstrong. Making Metropolis his home, Scorn did his best to protect the city during his short time there, fighting the likes of the Cyborg Superman.

After Flashpoint, small-time criminal Clyde Anderson used the name Scorn. Bearing a grudge against the G.C.P.D., Anderson teamed up with the super-villain Wrath, but when Scorn didn't reach his target number of kills, he was murdered by his partner. **MM**

BIG BLUE
Belying his threatening appearance, Scorn had a kind heart and helped to defend Metropolis.

THE WRATH OF WRATH
The new Scorn was Wrath's partner, until the villain murdered him for not eliminating enough police officers.

SCOTT, ALAN

DATA

DEBUT *All-American Comics* (Vol. 1) #16 **(Jul. 1940)**
UPDATE *Earth-2* (Vol. 1) #1 **(Jul. 2012)**
UNIVERSE Earth-2
EYES Green **HAIR** Blond
POWERS/ABILITIES An elemental conduit channeling Earth-2's life-energies through a Green Flame, providing super-strength, invulnerability, enhanced stamina, flight, mystic force generation, flaming construct manipulation, and enhanced senses.
ALLIES Hawkgirl, Jay Garrick, Dr. Fate, Power Girl, Val-Zod
ENEMIES The Grey, Solomon Grundy, Wotan, Parademons, Brutaal, Steppenwolf, Darkseid, Apokolips
AFFILIATIONS The Green, Eight Wonders, World Army

WONDERFUL WORLD
The "Wonders of the World" comprised the Super Heroes of Earth-2 who banded together to defend their planet from the malignant forces of Apokolips.

THE FIRE INSIDE
The power granted by the Green Flame enabled Alan to do almost anything, but it could not restore his fiancé Sam to life.

Alan Scott is the most powerful being on Earth-2. Resurrected, reborn, and rebuilt from the ashes of a dreadful disaster, he was fueled with the magic potency of the planet's collective life-force and tasked by an eerie green flame with the duty of defending the world. His powers are channeled through the engagement ring he had bought for his murdered beloved. Though the most imminent threat was the force of decay poisoning his wounded world, Scott's greatest challenge came when the planet was once more targeted by Darkseid.

Media tycoon Alan Scott was used to getting what he wanted. In the five years since humanity repelled an invasion from Apokolips, he had become one of the richest men alive. However, he lost what mattered most when his fiancé Sam Zhao was killed in a terrible train crash. The wreck should have killed Alan too, but he had been chosen by Earth-2's metaphysical life-spirit to battle imminent threats encroaching upon the embattled world. Fueled by anger, heartbreak, and blazing emerald fire, Scott accepted the job. The Green Knight soon clashed with the resurgent Avatar of Decay, Solomon Grundy, but was unable to finish the job without the aid of other metahumans who had arisen in this time of great need.

When Apokolips renewed its assault, determined to devour Earth-2, Scott grudgingly joined these "Wonders" and Earth-2's World Army in a ferocious war to save the world. Despite Herculean resistance, the heroes were continually defeated, even after Scott became the conduit for Earth-2's many elemental Parliaments working in unison. At that time he was reunited with his lost love after Sam's spirit was revealed as the latest Avatar of Earth-2's Air Elemental.

When Earth-2 was lost, the Green Knight battled Darkseid directly, buying time for humanity's remnants to flee the doomed world in colony ships. **WW**

FORCES OF WILL
Despite his greatest efforts as Earth-2's guardian, Alan's solo battles against Apokolips all failed until he united with the world's other defenders.

ON THE RECORD

Alan Scott was the original Green Lantern, debuting in 1940 to battle all forms of evil with a magic ring. He shone for over a decade as one of the brightest lights of the Golden Age before changing tastes benched him and many other costumed champions.

Scott returned in the 1960s as a hero from alternate Earth-2; an affable elder statesman sharing experiences and adventures with his science-based counterpart Hal Jordan and other heroes of the Justice Society of America. After *Crisis on Infinite Earths* rebooted continuity, Scott was given a new lease of life as the world's Sentinel.

CREATURE OF THE NIGHT
The earliest appearances of the Emerald Gladiator played up his mystical origins and uncanny power, as he terrorized crooks and killers.

CLASSIC STORIES

***Green Lantern Comics* (Vol. 1) #30 (Feb.-Mar. 1948)** Green Lantern gets a pet. Streak the Wonder Dog will push Green Lantern out of his own title and into retirement within two years.

***Green Lantern* (Vol. 2) #61 (Jun. 1968)** Fed up with fighting a never-ending battle, Scott orders his ring to banish all evil from Earth and is instantly the only human left on an empty planet.

***Green Lantern Corps Quarterly* (Vol. 1) #5-6 (Jun.-Sep. 1993)** Suddenly rejuvenated as Sentinel, Alan discovers his green flame is the Starheart, repository of ancient magic, bound by the Guardians of the Universe when the cosmos was young.

SERGEANT ROCK

DEBUT *Our Army at War* (Vol. 1) #81 **(Apr. 1959)**
CURRENT VERSION *Justice League United* #13 **(Nov. 2015)**
REAL NAME Franklin John Rock
BASE Various Operational Theaters of World War II
HEIGHT 6ft **WEIGHT** 183 lbs **EYES** Blue **HAIR** Auburn
POWERS/ABILITIES Excellent marksman and militarily trained combatant; peak human endurance, combat-honed instincts, overwhelming determination, leadership skills, and personal charisma.
ALLIES The Losers, Unknown Soldier, Jeb Stuart, Mlle. Marie
ENEMIES Nazi Germany, Iron Major, Japanese Empire, Vandal Savage
AFFILIATIONS United States Army, Easy Company, Suicide Squad, Justice League United

An indomitable fighting man, Sergeant Rock served in the US Army during World War II. Enlisting in 1941, he rose steadily in rank; soldiering from the burning sands of Africa to mainland Europe on D-Day. Leading from the front, he shepherded Easy Company from the beaches of Normandy into the heartland of Germany, always at the vanguard of the bloodiest battles.

Frank Rock was the quintessential soldier. He followed orders and got the job done swiftly and efficiently, witnessing extraordinary events during wartime, even the presence of super-powered beings on the battlefield. In later years, Frank most clearly recalls the horror of seeing men on both sides and an endless parade of greenhorns get maimed or killed. When hostilities ceased, Frank stayed a soldier, serving his country as both educator and clandestine agent.

His legacy lives on today through his grandson Joseph. Becoming a career soldier after a family tragedy, Joe joined other combat veterans in a radical enterprise started up by a private military contractor. He took charge of a new Easy Company that uses cutting-edge ordnance to provide an effective human response to metahuman or supernatural threats. **WW**

ON THE RECORD

In his civilian days, Frank Rock was a steelworker who boxed. He was certainly no champion, but he possessed one defining attribute. No matter how much punishment he took in the ring, he never fell down and never quit. This characteristic, along with his highly attuned combat instincts, made him the ideal leader for a hard-slogging squad of ordinary heroes like the unbeatable Easy Company, even against the most battle-hardened foes.

ROCK AND A HARD PLACE
Once Frank made his mind up, nothing the enemy could do would shift the implacable human barricade called The Rock.

SECRET SIX

DEBUT *Secret Six* (Vol. 1) #1 **(Apr.–May 1968)**
CURRENT VERSION *Secret Six* (Vol. 4) #1 **(Feb. 2015)**
BASE Gotham City, suburbia
MEMBERS/POWERS **Catman (Thomas Blake)** Feline strength, power, speed, agility, and reflexes; **Ventriloquist (Shauna Belzer)** Telekinesis, voice manipulation, ventriloquism; **Black Alice (Lori Zechlin)** Absorption of magical powers; **Porcelain (Kani)** Able to turn objects brittle and fragile; **Big Shot (Damon Wells/Ralph Dibny)** Transformation, super-strength, pliable body; **Strix (Mary Turner)** Former Talon, trained human weapon with exceptional proficiency in unarmed combat and acrobatics.
ENEMIES The Riddler, Agent Robbins, Punster, Susan Dibny, Felix Faust, Aquaman, Shiva Woosan

The Secret Six is the designation given to a succession of clandestine, non-governmental special ops teams: All have been characterized as being run by a leader dubbed Mockingbird who compels the services of his or her agents through coercion and blackmail.

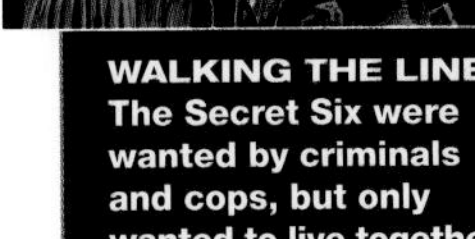

WALKING THE LINE
The Secret Six were wanted by criminals and cops, but only wanted to live together in peace and safety.

The most recent incarnation was created by the Riddler, who tested a disparate group of metahumans he believed had stolen a gem he craved. After a fruitless year of isolation and torture, the Riddler (aka Mockingbird) allowed his suspects to escape after planting a mole within their ranks.

On the run, the Secret Six retreated to suburbia to lay low and slowly forged close bonds of fellowship. Following several attacks by Mockingbird's hirelings and a final confrontation with the Prince of Puzzlers, they solved the mystery and exposed the infiltrator. Despite this betrayal, the fugitive oddities opted to stick together. Catman, Ventriloquist, Porcelain, and Big Shot became increasingly protective of the emotionally scarred Strix and especially Black Alice. The latter's predatory magical nature began manifesting, drawing the group into a universe-threatening conflict with the planet's supernatural community and the ancient League of Assassins. **WW**

ON THE RECORD

The first Secret Six were five exceptional humans used by scientist August Durant to remove terrorists and criminals beyond the law's reach. Actor King Savage, boxer Tiger Force, make-up artist Lili de Neuve, model Crimson Dawn and magician Carlo Di Rienzi worked beside Durant, but no-one could be sure which—if any of them—was pulling their strings as the mysterious Mockingbird.

When Durant and his teammates were murdered, Di Rienzi revived the project with new conscripts.

TRUST ISSUES
The team never trusted each other: they knew one of them was a manipulating blackmailer who held their lives in his or her hands.

THE SEEDER

DEBUT (As Woodrue) ***The Atom* #1 (Jun.–Jul. 1962)**
CURRENT VERSION (as Seeder) ***Swamp Thing Annual* (Vol. 5) #1 (Dec. 2012)**
REAL NAME Jason Woodrue
HEIGHT 6ft 2in **WEIGHT** 210 lbs
EYES Brown **HAIR** Black
POWERS/ABILITIES **As Seeder**: can manipulate the Green to grow fabulous plants; **As Avatar of the Green**: can control plant life around the world and draw power from the Green.

Jason Woodrue was a graduate student fascinated by the idea of using plants to create a world of peace and plenty. After years of searching, he finally made contact with the Parliament of Trees, custodians of the Green—the life-force of all plants on Earth. They offered him a deal: If he saved the life of their Avatar, Swamp Thing (Alec Holland), they would give him what he desired. Woodrue saved Alec from sorcerer Anton Arcane and, in return, received the ability to shape the Green.

He became the Seeder, wandering the Earth creating wondrous foliage, and the Parliament of Trees later chose him as their new Avatar. However, when Seeder used his new powers to try and kill all animal life on Earth, Alec took back the role. **WW**

SECRET SOCIETY OF SUPER-VILLAINS

DATA

DEBUT *Secret Society of Super-Villains* #1 **(May–Jun. 1976)**
CURRENT VERSION *Justice League* (Vol. 2) #6 **(Apr. 2012)**
NOTABLE CURRENT MEMBERS
BLACK MANTA: Expert in hand-to-hand combat; weapons master
BLACK ADAM: Divine powers; super-strength and speed; flight
BANE: Super-strength; advanced healing and stamina; high intellect
DESPERO: Astral projection; invulnerability; flight; reality manipulation
ROGUES: Blue-clollar criminals, including Captain Cold, Mirror Master, Weather Wizard, Trickster, and Heat Wave
CHEETAH: Cheetah-humanoid physiology; super-strength and speed
NOTABLE FORMER MEMBERS
LIBRA: Power absorption; super-strength and durability
DARKSEID: Immortality; Omega energy; super-strength; invulnerability
THE WIZARD: Magic; astral projection; illusion casting; hypnosis
ALEXANDER LUTHOR: Energy bursts; flight; shape-shifting
ULTRA-HUMANITE: Alien physiology; mind control; possession
ENEMIES Justice League
AFFILIATIONS Crime Syndicate of America

The villain team to end all villain teams, formed to pave the way for the arrival of Earth-3's Crime Syndicate of America. The Secret Society of Super-Villains (SSSV) is the brainchild of the Outsider, who found his way to Earth-1 during Darkseid's first attempt to breach the barrier between the dimensions.

AT A GLANCE...

The butler did it
The Outsider, leader of Earth-1's Secret Society, is Owlman's butler on Earth-3, Alfred Pennyworth. He raised an army of super-villains to help the Crime Syndicate take over Earth-1, but did not share their goal. When Black Manta found out, he defected from the group and put a permanent end to the Outsider and his machinations.

No honor among villains
Composed of power-hungry evildoers, The Secret Society has its share of competing agendas. Professor Ivo and the Outsider recruited the Society's members under false pretenses, telling them they would destroy the Justice League, without mentioning that they would then be subservient to the Crime Syndicate of America. Meanwhile Superwoman, Black Adam, and the Rogues all revealed themselves to be working at cross-purposes. Two of the defectors from the Society—Captain Cold and Black Manta—would play a decisive role in its defeat once they discovered the Outsider's true goal.

Assembled by Professor Ivo and the mysterious Outsider—shockingly revealed to be none other than Earth-3's Alfred Pennyworth—the Secret Society of Super-Villains was to be the Outsider's army on Earth-1, ready and waiting for the arrival of the Crime Syndicate of America following the opening of Pandora's Box. Hunting the box, the Outsider took steps to isolate Pandora from those who would protect her, manipulating the Justice League, Justice League of America (JLA), and Justice League Dark into a three-way battle in Kahndaq after the death of Black Adam. In addition to these preparations, the Outsider managed to place a mole inside the Justice League, with Earth-3's Atomica masquerading as the Atom until the Crime Syndicate could finally make their appearance.

WHAT'S IN THE BOX?
The Outsider understood that Pandora's Box was in fact a technological device that could open portals between alternate Earths.

The Justice League understood that the SSSV was forming and initiated a series of covert actions to discover the true nature of the threat. Green Arrow, under the alias Dark Hunter, infiltrated the group before being exposed and badly wounded. Catwoman was then sent on a similar mission. She was captured, interrogated, and murdered—whereupon it was revealed that she was actually the Martian Manhunter in disguise. The Manhunter briefly touched minds with the shadowy villain known as the Outsider, but was unable to discern his identity. The Outsider then destroyed the Justice League's Watchtower, using the ruins as his new base and holding Nightwing in a machine with a bomb wired to the beating of his heart. He also also held another prisoner, who turned out to be Alexander Luthor, the Shazam of Earth-3. The Justice League freed him and he went on a rampage, attacking hero and villain alike, but directing most of his rage and power at the members of the Crime Syndicate who had removed him from Earth-3. Because Alexander was Earth-3's version of Lex Luthor, their voices were the same, which allowed Lex to cry out "Mazahs!" and depower Alexander, after which Lex ruthlessly killed him.

Power Ring, Johnny Quick, Copperhead, and the Outsider all died in the climactic battle with the combined Justice League and JLA—along with defecting members of the Society, notably Deathstroke and Black Manta, who killed the Outsider. The Secret Society of Super-Villains was disbanded again and its membership scattered or imprisoned. Black Manta and a resurrected Black Adam rejected the Justice League's offer of amnesty and also disappeared, perhaps to sow the seeds of a new Secret Society. **AI**

CLASSIC STORIES

***Secret Society of Super-Villains* #1–15 (May–Jun. 1976 to Jun.–Jul. 1978)** The first Secret Society of Super-Villains rebels when it discovers Darkseid was behind the group's creation, but that doesn't stop them from battling the JLA and the Justice Society of America. The chain of command passes from Manhunter to Funky Flashman to Gorilla Grodd before the Wizard seizes control of the team.

***Justice League of America* #166–168 (May–Jul. 1979)** The Wizard's Society makes its last stand by invading the JLA's satellite stronghold, swapping bodies with the heroes and discovering their secret identities. Fighting back, the JLA defeats the Society and wipes their minds, an act that precipitates the later Identity Crisis event.

***Final Crisis* #1–7 (Jul. 2008–Mar. 2009)** Libra, leading a new Secret Society of Super-Villains, murders the Martian Manhunter and engineers a terrorist attack on the Daily Planet Building that nearly kills Lois Lane.

THE OUTSIDER
As the different Justice Leagues battled in Kahndaq, the Outsider finished gathering the new SSSV, capable of destroying the Justice League once and for all, in readiness for the arrival of the Crime Syndicate from Earth-3. He is a faithful servant of Earth-3's Owlman, completely dedicated—as any good butler should be.

STEADFAST LOYALTY
The Outsider humbles himself before Owlman, explaining how he brought the Secret Society together.

ALL HANDS ON DECK
The Secret Society of Super-Villains gathered to hear the Crime Syndicate's plans to finish off the Justice League. One notable absence—the Joker.

REBELLION
Led by Lex Luthor, a group rebelled when they found out the Crime Syndicate's ultimate goal was the subjugation of everyone on Earth.

DEFECTIONS

The Rogues—Captain Cold, Mirror Master, Heat Wave, Trickster, Weather Wizard, and Golden Glider—quit the Society before the Outsider's plot got underway. However, it was the defection of Deathstroke that caused real problems. Seeing that the Society was being used to further the goals of the Crime Syndicate, he turned on his fellow villains in the climactic battle, killing Copperhead and giving the Justice League time to free Alexander Luthor. After the Crime Syndicate's defeat, most of the Society scattered. Black Adam and Black Manta spurned the leniency offered them and went their own ways.

STRIKING OUT ON HIS OWN
Deathstroke, never a friend to the Justice League, liked the Crime Syndicate even less.

"All this time you were looking for who was behind this... as you say on your world... the butler did it."

THE OUTSIDER

ON THE RECORD

The first version of the Secret Society of Super-Villains was created by Darkseid to coordinate his efforts to rid Earth of all Super Heroes who would oppose his rule. A new assembly of evil, overseen by the Ultra-Humanite, targeted the JLA and JSA, before being banished to limbo.

Leadership changes

Despero awakened the memories of several former Society members and set them against the JLA just prior to Infinite Crisis. A fourth generation, the brainchild of Alexander Luthor, was known as Villains United. Control of the group's remaining members then passed first to the Wizard and then Calculator, bookending the Infinite Crisis event. Darkseid's prophet, Libra, then reformed the SSSV as Final Crisis loomed, before Cheetah took over and masterminded the creation of the post-Final Crisis version of the Society.

In syndication

While leaders of the Secret Society of Super-Villains come and go, the society's history with the Crime Syndicate of America stretches all the way back to the early 1960s, when a version of the Secret Society battled the original Crime Syndicate in one of the first cross-world "Crisis" stories. This story also established the conflict between the Crime Syndicate and the JLA, a touchstone for the "Forever Evil" crossover event.

VILLAINS UNITED
Deathstroke is central to Alexander Luthor's Villains United, hand-picked from the Secret Society to battle the splinter group called the Secret Six.

SERAFINA

DEBUT *Forever People* #1 (Feb.–Mar. 1971)
CURRENT VERSION *Infinity-Man and the Forever People* #1 (Aug. 2014)
REAL NAME Serafina Baldaur
BASE New Genesis
HEIGHT 5ft 7in **WEIGHT** 143 lbs
EYES Brown **HAIR** Brown
POWERS/ABILITIES Bio-bursts dazzle and disorient targets; other powers of the New Gods.
ALLIES Infinity-Man, Vikyn
ENEMIES: Mantis, Darkseid

Serafina Baldaur is one of the Forever People, a group of New Gods who can collectively become the mind of the Infinity-Man by tapping the powers of the Mother Box. Infinity Man forces this merger against their will as a way to direct them against dangers from New Genesis and Apokolips.

Infinity-Man meddled with the Forever People's first mission to Earth, which put them in conflict with the Lantern Corps. Despite Serafina's best efforts, this conflict broke out into a pitched battle between Infinity-Man and the Lanterns, who pooled their powers and faced him with Mecha Darkseid. Serafina and the rest of the Forever People then learned that Infinity-Man was the agent of the New God Highfather, fighting on his behalf against the resurgent threat of Darkseid himself. **AI**

SEVEN DEADLY SINS

DEBUT *Whiz Comics* #2 (Feb. 1940)
CURRENT VERSION *Justice League* #0 (Nov. 2012)
BASE Rock of Eternity
MEMBERS Pride, Gluttony, Sloth, Anger, Envy, Greed, Lust.
ALLIES Blight
ENEMIES The Wizard, Justice League Dark, Shazam, Captain Marvel

Also known as the Seven Deadly Enemies of Mankind, these entities embody the mortal sins that have been known since ancient times. Unleashed 10,000 years ago by the young Pandora, the Sins ravaged her village and began to corrupt the world. The wizards' council of the Rock of Eternity battled against their dire influence for millennia, while Pandora—condemned by that same council—learned magic in what became a quest to recapture them.

Pandora's Box was the key to containing the Sins. After the Trinity of Sin battled over possession of the box and the Blight was unleashed on the world—along with the Crime Syndicate of America and a resurgent Secret Society of Super-Villains—Pandora learned her true power and was able to dispel the Sins herself. **AI**

SEVEN SOLDIERS OF VICTORY

DEBUT *Leading Comics* #1 (Winter 1941–42)
BASE Mobile
CURRENT MEMBERS/POWERS **Bulleteer:** Invulnerable metal skin and enhanced strength **Spawn of Frankenstein:** Enhanced strength, injury-resistant undead body **Klarion the Witch Boy:** Spellcasting and monstrous transformations **Manhattan Guardian:** Peak physical condition, skilled fighter **Mister Miracle II:** One of the world's greatest escape artists **Shining Knight II:** Skilled fighter and excellent swordswoman **Zatanna:** Vast magical powers triggered by saying spells backward
ENEMIES Iron Hand, Injustice League, Darkseid
AFFILIATIONS Justice League of America, Justice Society of America, Super-Human Advanced Defense Executive.

LAWS' LEGIONNAIRES
Six of the original Seven Soldiers, before they had adopted their new team name. Only the Shining Knight remains a member of the team.

MAGNIFICENT SEVEN
The most recent incarnation of the Seven Soldiers, assembled for action against the Sheeda:
1 Klarion the Witch Boy
2 Shining Knight II
3 Zatanna
4 Spawn of Frankenstein
5 Guardian
6 Bulleteer
7 Mister Miracle II

Independently stopping the villainous agents of the Iron Hand, seven heroes joined together to become the Laws' Legionnaires, more commonly referred to as the Seven Soldiers of Victory. The team comprised: the Crimson Avenger, Billy Gunn; Shining Knight and his flying horse Winged Victory; Vigilante, the Spider; the Star-Spangled Kid; and Stripesy. The Crimson Avenger's aide, Wing, an unofficial eighth member, sacrificed his life in a battle against the Nebula Man in Tibet. The resulting temporal explosion scattered the group across the time stream. Before they reformed, Deadman organized a short-lived new incarnation of the team, including Adam Strange, Batgirl, Blackhawk, Mento, Metamorpho, and the Shining Knight. They defended the planet Rann from the Injustice League.

Two later versions of the Seven Solders fought the Sheeda, a powerful faerie race from the far future bent on the annihilation of humanity. The first group of Soldiers actually numbered only six, after the Bulleteer's last-minute refusal to join: Vigilante; I, Spyder; Gimmix; Boy Blue; Dyno-Mite Dan; and the Whip's granddaughter. The Sheeda defeated them and then faced a new team of Seven Soldiers who never actually met in person: Mister MiracleII ; the Spawn of Frankenstein; Zatanna; Clarion the Witch Boy; Shining Knight II; the Manhattan Guardian; and the returning Bulleteer, who struck the fatal blow against the malevolent Sheeda Queen. **AI**

THE SHADE

DEBUT *Flash Comics* #33 **(Sep. 1942)**
CURRENT VERSION *The Shade* (Vol. 2) #1 **(Dec. 2011)**
REAL NAME Richard Swift
BASE Opal City
HEIGHT 6ft 2in **WEIGHT** 170 lbs
EYES Gray **HAIR** Black
POWERS/ABILITIES Immortality; summoning of "shadowmatter" from the Dark Zone; manipulation of shadows.
ALLIES Starman
ENEMIES Simon Culp, Dudley Caldecott

In 1838, Richard Swift was transformed into yhe Shade, a near-immortal capable of manipulating shadowmatter, in an occult ceremony conducted by his evil, shadow-wielding counterpart, Simon Culp. He left his family behind and became a vigilante and seeker, battling both mystical threats and ordinary criminals. He and Culp became mortal enemies because of Culp's original subterfuge that trapped Swift in the shadowmatter ceremony.

Nearly 200 years after his creation, the Shade was attacked and killed by Deathstroke. He returned to life and embarked on a quest to discover who wanted him dead. The trail led to Caldecott Pharmaceuticals, a company that grew from a chemist's shop started by Shade's wife Elizabeth after he left the family, and through that connection, to Shade's descendant, Dudley Caldecott. Dudley and an ally had taken tenuous control of some Egyptian deities that bestowed him with good fortune in return for human sacrifice. The Shade turned the deities on Caldecott, but they escaped to London. Using a magical ceremony, the Shade learned the truth of their origin and dispelled them back to their home dimension—after which he reluctantly killed Dudley. **AI**

ON THE RECORD

Possibly due to the nature of shadowmatter, the Shade was one of the few people able to prevent a Black Lantern ring form attaching to him during Blackest Night. He also survived having his heart ripped out by Black Lantern David Knight. Sometimes a hero, sometimes a villain, The Shade was saved from a descent into villainy thanks to his long friendship with the hero Ted Knight, aka Starman.

DARK SHADOWS
Shadowmatter constructs take savage and lethal action without Richard Swift having to lift a finger.

SHADE, THE CHANGING MAN

DEBUT *Shade, The Changing Man* (Vol.1) #1 **(Jun.-Jul. 1977)**
CURRENT VERSION *Justice League Dark* #1 **(Nov. 2011)**
REAL NAME Rac Shade
HEIGHT 5ft 6in **WEIGHT** 108 lbs **EYES** Blue **HAIR** Red
POWERS/ABILITIES M-vest emits energy that distorts perception, projects force-fields, and enables flight and dimensional travel.
ENEMIES Cain
AFFILIATIONS Justice League Dark

Tormented to near-madness by the death of his lover Kathy, Rac Shade created a simulacrum of her using the reality-warping power of the M-Vest, a relic of his origin in the mysterious world of Meta. He consented to join the Justice League Dark at the request of Madame Xanadu after the Enchantress separated from June Moone, and played a critical role in the JLD's fight against resurgent occult powers. At the same time he fought an internal struggle against a malfunctioning M-Vest, which plagued him with visions of a deformed Kathy. The combination of the M-Vest's overwhelming powers and his terrible grief resulted in a mental breakdown, and Shade quit the team just as the final battle loomed with the vampire progenitor known as Cain.

Drawn into the Area of Madness by the M-Vest, Shade reunited with the Kathy simulacrum and told her he would not be returning to the team because the coming changes would leave no place for him there—or, he feared, anywhere. **AI**

CONFLICT RESOLUTION
Shade's conflicted relationship with the specter of Kathy culminated in an explosive rejection of her.

ON THE RECORD

Rac Shade was a secret agent on the other-dimensional world of Meta. He came into possession of the M-Vest to keep it from being utilized in a conspiracy to take over Earth, which was being hatched in a neighboring dimension. It later transpired that he had to occupy a different body when the M-Vest brought him to Earth, which led to his relationship with a traumatized Kathy George.

BALANCE OF POWER
As soon as Shade unleashed the powers of the M-Vest, he realized that that they would be difficult to control.

SHADOW CABINET

DEBUT *Shadow Cabinet* #0 (Jan. 1994)
CURRENT VERSION *Stormwatch* #4 (Feb. 2012)
BASE The Bleed
POWERS/ABILITIES Undisclosed
ENEMIES Daemonites, Hidden People, Kollective
AFFILIATIONS Stormwatch

Based in the interdimensional space The Bleed, which connects all realities of the multiverse, the mysterious Shadow Cabinet presides over the ancient alien defense organization Stormwatch. The four members, known as Shadow Lords, guided the group on its mission to defend Earth against both alien and paranormal threats, never revealing their identities or origins beyond the fact that they control technologies centuries in advance of anything available to humankind.

During the Martian Manhunter's membership in Stormwatch, the team clashed with the Shadow Lords over the Cabinet's manipulations. This led to a crisis that ended only when the time-controlling Kollective eradicated all traces of Stormwatch from the existing timeline. In the aftermath, the Shadow Lords formed a smaller, more clandestine team. They used a DNA sample from the Martian Manhunter to create Stormwatch's new leader, Forecaster. He mistrusted them, despite their promise to stop keeping secrets from the new team that might endanger their existence. **AI**

ON THE RECORD

The pre-Flashpoint version of the Shadow Cabinet was initially an ancient order of vigilante heroes based in the Shadowspire, and dedicated to protecting humanity from itself. Their leader, Dharma, maintained that they had to use controversial methods to achieve good ends. This brought them into conflict with other heroes.

ENDS JUSTIFY MEANS
The Shadow Cabinet stood as judge, jury, and executioner, believing hard choices were necessary to protect the common good.

SHARK

DEBUT *Green Lantern* (Vol. 2) #24 (Oct 1963)
BASE Mobile
HEIGHT 6ft 2in **WEIGHT** 243 lbs
EYES Black **HAIR** None
POWERS/ABILITIES Psionic manipulation of matter and energy; telepathy; flight.
ENEMIES Green Lantern, Aquaman
AFFILIATIONS Weaponers of Qward, the Society, Terrible Trio

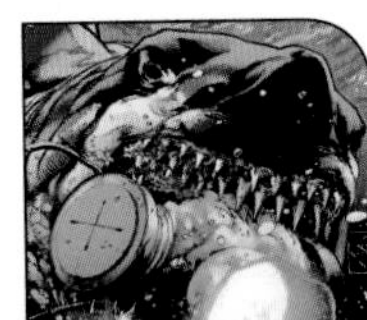

Radiation leaking from an oceanside nuclear power station transformed a tiger shark into a mutant humanoid monster. Imbued with greatly increased intelligence and psionic powers, the Shark now feasted on the psyches of his victims rather than their flesh. The Shark attacked Green Lantern Hal Jordan, hoping to consume his mind. However, Hal defeated the creature and devolved him to his original state.

The Shark regained his humanoid form on several occasions, battling both Green Lantern and Aquaman, briefly seizing the Throne of Atlantis and installing himself as Karshon. Later, the Shark was recruited by Green Lantern Guy Gardner to join a super-villain squad opposing the Qwardians. During Infinite Crisis, the Shark participated in a brutal attack on Atlantis, where he, allied with King Shark, apparently killed the mutant undersea hero Neptune Perkins. **AI**

SHADO

DEBUT *Green Arrow: The Longbow Hunters* #1 (Aug. 1987)
CURRENT VERSION *Green Arrow* (Vol. 5) #22 (Sep. 2013)
HEIGHT 5ft 3in **WEIGHT** 121 lbs
EYES Brown **HAIR** Black
POWERS/ABILITIES Unsurpassed skill with a bow and arrow; superior acrobat and martial artist.
ALLIES Green Arrow
ENEMIES Komodo, Count Vertigo

Raised as a Yakuza assassin, Shado was a superb archer who turned on her Yakuza master Ito when paid to kill him by Robert Queen and Simon Lacroix. She and Robert fell in love and had a daughter, Emiko. He then enlisted her in a search for a fabled artifact called the Green Arrow.

As the villainous Komodo, Lacroix kidnapped Emiko and turned her over to Count Vertigo, who held her captive for years because she refused to reveal the location of the Green Arrow—which she knew was not an artifact, but Robert's son, Oliver Queen. Oliver helped Emiko escape and Shado let the defeated Vertigo live so he could inform Lacroix/Komodo that she had the Green Arrow. During the escape, Shado also revealed to Oliver Queen that he had a half-sister: her daughter Emiko. **AI**

SHADOWPACT

DEBUT *Day of Vengeance* #1 (Jun. 2005)
BASE Oblivion Bar
MEMBERS/POWERS **Nightmaster**: Expert combatant with magical sword; **Blue Devil**: Enhanced strength, wields Trident of Lucifer; **Nightshade**: Teleportation, can form darkness into 3D shapes; **Ragman**: Absorbs sinners into his cloak and draws on their powers; **Detective Chimp**: Brilliant mind and can talk to animals; **Enchantress**: Vast magical abilities; **Zauriel**: Flight, enhanced strength, telepathy, sonic scream.
ENEMIES Spectre, Eclipso, Pentacle

According to legend, teams of mystics have called themselves the Shadowpact during struggles against dark sorcery. The most recent group assembled in the Oblivion Bar after an insane Spectre had teamed with Eclipso on a destructive rampage. Shadowpact survived the battle with help from Captain Marvel and Black Alice. The team later organized the cleanup after the destruction of the Rock of Eternity let loose the Seven Deadly Sins.

Following Infinite Crisis, Shadowpact spent a year battling and eventually defeating their evil opposites, the Pentacle, inside a sacrificial bubble of blood the villains had created around the town of Riverrock, Wyoming. The team returned to action against Doctor Gotham, and later welcomed Laurel, who took the Blue Devil's place. **AI**

AGAINST THE DARKNESS
The Shadowpact stands against occult and sorcerous threats, as it has for centuries and as it always will.
1 Blue Devil
2 Nightmaster
3 Nightshade
4 Ragman
5 Detective Chimp
6 Enchantress

SHAGGY MAN

DEBUT *Justice League of America* (Vol.1) #45 (Jun. 1966)
CURRENT VERSION *Justice League of America* (Vol. 3) #4 (Jul. 2013)
BASE Secret Society of Super-Villains mansion
HEIGHT 8ft 2in **WEIGHT** 550 lbs
EYES Red **HAIR** Brown
POWERS/ABILITIES Superhuman strength; near invulnerability; regeneration.
ALLIES Professor Ivo
ENEMIES Justice League of America

Shaggy Man was created by Professor Ivo as a genetic experiment that also involved the artificial synthesis of his tissue and fur. Recruited into the Secret Society of Super-Villains by his creator, Shaggy Man attacked the Justice League of America when they were infiltrating the Society's mansion headquarters to rescue Catwoman.

Proving himself invulnerable to the JLA's various powers, he singlehandedly subdued the entire team, except Hawkman. As he pursued Hawkman through the mansion, Stargirl freed the other members of the JLA, and they learned that the key to defeating Shaggy Man was cutting away his thick synthetic fur. Together Katana and Hawkman managed to do this, bringing the behemoth down and setting the stage for a mass breakout from the mansion. **AI**

SHAZAM JR.

DEBUT *Whiz Comics* (Vol. 1) #25 **(Dec. 1941)**
CURRENT VERSION *Justice League* (Vol. 2) #8 **(Jun. 2012)**
REAL NAME Freddy Freeman
BASE Philadelphia
HEIGHT 5ft 10in **WEIGHT** 164 lbs
EYES Blue **HAIR** Blond
POWERS/ABILITIES Possesses the powers and abilities of Shazam when Billy Batson shares them with his foster family.
ALLIES Shazam
ENEMIES Black Adam
AFFILIATIONS Shazam Family

Teenager Freddy Freeman was placed into foster care with the Vasquez family after both of his parents went to prison. A gregarious, likeable kid who saw himself as something of a fixer at his high school, he had a tendency to bend the rules—usually in harmless ways. In the Vasquez household, which was home to other foster children, Freddy made friends with the selfish and surly Billy Batson, a fellow foster kid. Freddy was the first of Billy's new friends to learn about his recently gained powers as Shazam.

At first, Freddy encouraged Billy to treat his magical powers as a lark—and a handy way of making some easy money. When Billy used his abilities to prevent an old woman being mugged, Freddy suggested that Billy should ask her for some money as a reward. Subsequently, Freddy started to take Billy's Shazam powers more seriously—which turned out to be a good thing when Black Adam attacked, bringing with him the threat of the Seven Deadly Sins. Billy shared the Shazam powers with Freddy and the rest of the Vasquez foster children and overpowered Black Adam. They then teamed up to defeat the demon Sabbac and counter the menace of the Seven Deadly Sins. **AI**

SHOCK AND AWESTRUCK
Freddy sees himself—and his foster sister Mary—transformed by the powers of Shazam for the first time.

ON THE RECORD

Freddy Freeman joined the Marvel Family just two years after the emergence of Captain Marvel. Crippled and orphaned by the sadistic Captain Nazi, young Freddy was granted access to the power of Shazam, which allowed him to walk again and even fly as Captain Marvel, Jr. After a series of trials that followed Infinite Crisis, Freddy Freeman became the new Captain Marvel (now calling himself Shazam), with Billy Batson assuming the Wizard's place overseeing the Rock of Eternity.

THE NEW CAPTAIN
As Captain Marvel, Jr., Freddy Freeman struggled with the temptation to exact revenge on Captain Nazi, the man who crippled him.

SHAZAM'S SQUADRON OF JUSTICE

DEBUT ***Justice League of America* #135 (Oct. 1976)**
MEMBERS/POWERS Bulletman and Bulletgirl: Married couple, each with a Gravity Helmet that turns them into projectiles; **Ibis the Invincible**: Magical powers granted by Thoth, focused in the Ibistick; **Mister Scarlet**: Acrobatics, various weapon proficiencies; **Pinky**: Acrobatics, various weapon proficiencies; **Spy Smasher**: Technical wizardry, unarmed combat expertise.
ENEMIES King Kull, Beastmen

Earth-S's Squadron of Justice was deputized by the god Mercury to counter an assault by king of the Beastmen, Kull, who plotted to destroy humanity and turn Earth-S over to the Beastmen. With the Shazam Family inactive because of Shazam's paralysis, the Squadron allied with the Justice League of America and the Justice Society of America to combat villains from three Earths: Earth-1 (JLA), Earth-2 (JSA), and Earth-S.

In a cataclysmic final battle with King Kull at the Rock of Eternity, Superman was driven into a murderous rage by red Kryptonite. The Squadron restored Shazam's powers and he broke the hold of the red Kryptonite, with help from several Green Lanterns. The Squadron then imprisoned Kull in magical chains, preserving the Rock of Eternity and thwarting the Beastmen's plot. **AI**

SHINING KNIGHT

DEBUT ***Adventure Comics* #66 (Sep. 1941)**
CURRENT VERSION ***Demon Knights* #1 (Nov. 2011)**
REAL NAME Ystin/Justin/Ystina
BASE Camelot
HEIGHT 6ft 2in **WEIGHT** 185 lbs
EYES Green **HAIR** Black
POWERS/ABILITIES Immortality; magical armor and weapons; control over animals.
ENEMIES Sheeda, Morgaine le Fay

The gender-fluid, immortal knight Ystin has been known as Ystina, Sir Justin, and the Shining Knight, and was present at Merlin's rebirth in Avalon as Adam One. As one of the Demon Knights—ancestors of Stormwatch—Ystina battled alien and demonic threats. Ystina was granted immortality after a sip from the Holy Grail during the fall of Camelot, but was cursed with an unquenchable desire to drink from the Grail again.

Ystin rode the winged horse Vanguard, fighting alongside such Demon Knights as Madame Xanadu and Jason Blood. He also wielded the sword known as Caliburn or Excalibur, marking him a champion of Camelot. Ystina fought with the Demon Knights against the vampire Cain and was bitten, fulfilling his vision of one day becoming undead. **AI**

SHRIEK

DEBUT ***Batman Beyond* (Vol. 2) #5 (Mar. 2000)**
REAL NAME Walter Shreeve
BASE Neo-Gotham, Earth-12
HEIGHT 5ft 10in **WEIGHT** 170 lbs
EYES Brown **HAIR** Brown
POWERS/ABILITIES Armored suit that generates destructive sound waves.
ENEMIES Batman

Walter Shreeve was a gifted audio engineer in Neo-Gotham. Unable to find a more legitimate way to profit from his advanced sound technologies, Shreeve fashioned a suit armed with sonic weaponry capable of destroying buildings. Hired to assassinate Batman, Shreeve almost succeeded but suffered hearing damage in the encounter and was imprisoned in Blackgate. While incarcerated he gained the trust of a prison doctor and began new research, developing earphones to restore his hearing and rebuilding his sonic technology.

Then he broke out, attacking Batman again and using low-frequency sound weapons to destroy buildings in Gotham City while he tried to steal power crystals to amplify his sound-projection weapons. He nearly unmasked Batman, but was buried in the collapse of a building he had weakened. Presumed dead, he survived and later plotted against Earth-12's Justice League. **AI**

SHRINKING VIOLET

DEBUT ***Action Comics* (Vol. 1) #276 (May 1961)**
CURRENT VERSION ***Legion of Super-Heroes* (Vol. 7) #1 (Nov. 2011)**
REAL NAME Salu Digby
HEIGHT 5ft 2in **WEIGHT** 105 lbs
EYES Violet **HAIR** Black
POWERS/ABILITIES Ability to alter size from subatomic to approx. 30ft tall, with proportionate change in mass and strength.
ENEMIES Fatal Five, Dominators, Daxamites

Like other natives of the planet Imsk, Salu Digby possessed size-changing abilities, making her a key member of the Legion of Super-Heroes' Espionage Squad. She learned unarmed combat after a highly traumatic period of captivity, which had consequences for her relationship with the team—particularly her lover, Lightning Lass.

Alongside the Legion, Shrinking Violet battled threats posed to 31st-century Legion Space by the Dominators, Daxamites, and Fatal Five. She was one of the Legionnaires catapulted back to the 21st century when the creation of Ultra the Multi-Alien destroyed their home timeline. Fighting alongside the Justice League United, Shrinking Violet helped to uncover the truth of Ultra's origins and save the Legion's future by preventing Ultra from becoming Infinitus. **AI**

SHAZAM!

DATA

DEBUT *Whiz Comics* (Vol. 1) #2 **(Feb. 1940)**
CURRENT VERSION *Justice League* (Vol. 2) #7 **(May 2012)**
REAL NAME William "Billy" Batson
BASE Philadelphia
HEIGHT 6ft 2in **WEIGHT** 110 lbs
EYES Black **HAIR** Black
POWERS/ABILITIES The Keeper of Magic; power over the Living Lightning; immense magical powers, including flight, speed, strength, and pyrokinesis; can share powers with others.
ALLIES The Wizard, Freddy Freeman
ENEMIES Black Adam
AFFILIATIONS Justice League

Possessing the powers of the Living Lightning, Billy Batson is an unlikely hero—a cocky delinquent foster child constantly grappling with the responsibilities that come with his immense powers as the Keeper of Magic. Billy is still a teenager, and Shazam is the idealized grown-up version of him. At times, the responsibility of being the last standard-bearer of the Council of Eternity can seem impossible to live up to. However, Billy's foster siblings always have his back, and after a rocky start to their relationship, so does the Justice League. What he lacks in experience he makes up for in courage, and soon becomes known as Earth's Mightiest Mortal.

AT A GLANCE...

S stands for...
Shazam's powers were originally granted by Solomon, Hercules, Atlas, Zeus, Achilles, and Mercury. But after the Darkseid War, new gods took over—S'ivaa, H'ronmeer, Anapel, Zonuz, Atë, and Mamaragan, the lightning wizard, who enlightened Shazam on his newfound abilities.

Family affair
Orphaned from an early age, troubled teenager Billy Batson found his family among his foster siblings. He can share his powers with them (and Tawky Tawny the tiger) in urgent situations, transforming them into the Shazam Family.

Say the magic word
By speaking the word "Shazam!" aloud, Billy Batson transforms himself and gains the use of the Living Lightning, the distilled essence of the powers bestowed by the six divine entities who empower him as the Keeper of Magic.

CLASSIC STORIES

***Whiz Comics* #2 (Feb. 1940)** Homeless newsboy Billy Batson is led into the tunnels beneath New York City, where the wizard Shazam grants him the powers to become Captain Marvel.

***Shazam: Monster Society of Evil* #1–4 (Apr.–Sep. 2007)** In this origin story, Billy Batson becomes a host for Captain Marvel, with whom he can merge by saying the word "Shazam!" They battle Doctor Sivana and an army of giant robots summoned by the Monster Society.

***The Trials of Shazam!* #1–12 (Oct. 2006–May 2008)** The aging Billy takes on the role of the Wizard, as new Captain Marvel Freddy Freeman strives to prove himself worthy of Shazam's powers.

Billy Batson became Shazam when the Wizard, the last surviving member of a magical council based at the Rock of Eternity, saw the need for a new Champion to meet the threat of a resurrected Black Adam. After rejecting a number of candidates, the Wizard tested Billy and found him too lacking in pure goodness. Billy argued that the Wizard's search for perfection would doom his quest to failure, and the Wizard realized that under Billy's rebellious exterior was a fundamentally good nature. Despite having serious misgivings, he made Billy the new Champion and Keeper of Magic.

Black Adam attacked Shazam and nearly overwhelmed him before Billy brought in the rest of his foster family and shared the Living Lightning with them. He also tried to change Tawky Tawny, a tiger at the Philadelphia Zoo, into a smilodon—but instead Tawny became a super-sized tiger fighting with the Shazam Family. Billy was unable to sustain the power sharing and only defeated Black Adam by challenging him to fight in mortal form. When Black Adam did this, he instantly suffered the effects of several centuries' aging… and collapsed into dust.

Trying to do the right thing, Billy returned Black Adam's ashes to his home in Kahndaq, inadvertently causing a diplomatic incident. The Justice League, Justice League Dark, and Justice League of America all converged on Kahndaq to try and defuse the situation, but instead a battle broke out with Shazam at its center. John Constantine drew Billy away from the battle, promising him knowledge of his true family, but instead stole his powers briefly so he could battle a demon. When Billy regained his

GATEWAY TO SHAZAM Billy discovers the way to the Rock of Eternity, where the Wizard—and Billy's destiny—await.

CLASH OF CHAMPIONS Billy came out on top in his first critical test as Shazam, but Black Adam was almost more than he could handle.

NEW ORIGIN
After Dr. Sivana frees ancient Black Adam from his tomb, the Wizard must create a new champion to oppose him, and chooses Billy Batson. Billy defeats Black Adam, first trying to reason with him, and then sharing his powers with his foster siblings—thereby passing the first test of the Wizard's faith in him.

TRINITY WAR/FOREVER EVIL
Billy inadvertently set off a battle among the three Justice Leagues after he tried to return Black Adam's remains to their rightful resting place. Then he became the fulcrum of a battle over Pandora's Box, before the Outsider tapped his power to fulfil his goal of bringing the Crime Syndicate to Earth.

NO GOOD DEED GOES UNPUNISHED?
Even bad guys deserve to be buried. But when Shazam tried to do the right thing by Black Adam it sparked an almighty fight with Superman.

powers, he joined the fight to capture and control Pandora's Box, then in Wonder Woman's possession. Billy touched the box and was overwhelmed by its powers, becoming a corrupted version of himself. Before his corruption could cause too much damage, the other members of the Justice League seized the box from him, but it had already used him to open a portal that allowed the Crime Syndicate to enter Earth. Deathstorm then trapped Billy within the Firestorm Matrix until Lex Luthor freed him. Luthor attempted to use Billy as leverage to gain membership of the Justice League, but the team rejected this ploy. They did admit Billy, however. Shazam began conducting missions with the League, developing a particularly close partnership with Cyborg.

Following Darkseid's invasion, the god-given pact granting the powers of Shazam was disrupted and the Wizard had to forge a new alliance. The new collective conferring the Living Lightning is now S'ivaa, Martian god H'ronmeer, Anapel, Darkseid's father Zonuz, Atë, and Mamaragan—the true name of the Wizard himself. **AI**

LIGHTNING LOAN
Constantine needed to borrow Shazam's power to take care of a little demon problem, but he gave it back.

SEARCH FOR THE RING
After Power Ring's former bearer was killed during the battle with the Crime Syndicate, it forced its new host, Jessica Cruz, on a rampage. Shazam and Cyborg hunted Power Ring down, fighting the Doom Patrol on the way. They finally located the ring and its unwilling host, who would later become a pawn of Darkseid.

CYBORG DOWN
Shazam warned Power Ring's new host, when she was unable to control its energies, and Cyborg paid the price.

ON THE RECORD

The wizard originally known as Shazam was one of Earth's first heroes, making his mark in ancient Canaan millennia ago. He bestowed his powers on a successor, Teth-Adam, who became Black Adam. Thousands of years later, Black Adam murdered the archeologist father of Billy Batson, and Shazam granted Billy his powers, transforming him into Captain Marvel.

Captain Marvel
Trapped in limbo for 20 years, Captain Marvel and his family returned without aging in the 1970s. Following 1985's *Crisis On Infinite Earths*, Cap's history was revised more than once, with the eventual revelation that Dr. Sivana and Black Adam bore responsibility for the deaths of Billy Batson's parents. After the wizard Shazam sacrificed his life to stop the Spectre's massacre of magicians, Captain Marvel assumed his place at the Rock of Eternity.
Now calling himself Shazam, Freddy Freeman continued the legacy on Earth until losing his powers during "Blackest Night." In the post-Flashpoint timeline, Billy Batson was once again the primary hero, but now used the name Shazam.

Other champions
Alexander Luthor is Mazahs, Earth-3's version of Shazam, who speaks the word to absorb the superpowers of other heroes and villains. Shazam also battles the Wizard's previous Champion, Black Adam, whose use of the word calls on the Egyptian gods Shu, Heru, Amon, Zehuti, Aton, and Mehen.

DAY OF VENGEANCE
Billy Batson—here as Captain Marvel—takes on the Spectre, who is out to destroy all magic and those who use it.

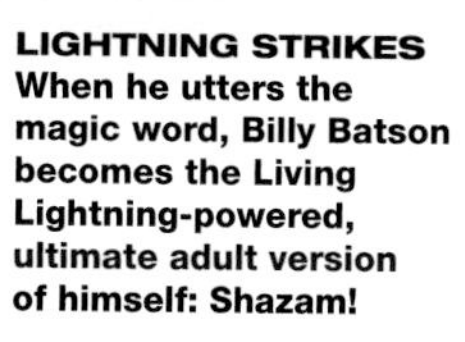

LIGHTNING STRIKES
When he utters the magic word, Billy Batson becomes the Living Lightning-powered, ultimate adult version of himself: Shazam!

"I'm not supposed to be Shazam. The Wizard said so himself."

SHAZAM

SHAZAM FAMILY

SIX OF THE BEST
It took the combined efforts of the Shazam Family to take down magic-wielding villain Black Adam, but they pulled together and got the job done.

DATA

DEBUT *Captain Marvel Adventures* (Vol. 1) #18 **(Dec. 1942)**
CURRENT VERSION *Justice League* (Vol. 2) #21 **(Dec. 2013)**
BASE Philadelphia
MEMBERS/POWERS **MARY BROMFIELD, EUGENE CHOI, DARLA DUDLEY, FREDDY FREEMAN, PEDRO PEÑA**
Each member of the group is able to share the magical powers of Shazam when Billy Batson calls upon them to do so.
ALLIES The Wizard
ENEMIES Black Adam, Seven Deadly Sins

STICKING TOGETHER
The kids who live in the Vasquez household have been through a lot, and they always have each other's backs.

The Shazam Family is a group of foster siblings who can each assume the powers of Shazam when Billy Batson grants them. None of them have a biological family link, but together they're as closely knit as any group of brothers and sisters can be.

Six foster siblings lived in the Vasquez family household in Philadelphia, all teenagers. One of them, Billy Batson, was granted the powers of Shazam, and shortly thereafter disclosed the secret to his foster brother, Freddy Freeman. The secret stayed between them until the super-villain Black Adam attacked, holding the rest of the siblings hostage and demanding Billy's powers. Billy tried to meet this demand, but accidentally bestowed the powers of Shazam on his six siblings, instead. They all battled Black Adam together, but were then surprised and nearly overwhelmed by the Seven Deadly Sins, who threatened the city of Philadelphia after being unleashed by Dr. Sivana. At the same time as Billy was fighting Black Adam in the zoo—where he granted Shazam's powers to Tawny the Tiger—his other siblings suddenly lost them.

During the battle, however, some of the members of this super-powered foster family discovered that they had variations on the powers of Shazam: Eugene displayed technopathic powers; Pedro even greater strength' and Darla incredible speed. Freddy, ever the joker, cracked that he wanted to be known as "King Marvel." This nickname didn't stick, but the Shazam Family is ready whenever Billy needs them. Knowing he can share his Shazam secret with them makes it easier for Billy to handle his new responsibilities. **AI**

CLASSIC STORIES

***Whiz Comics* #21 (Sep. 1941)** Billy Batson meets three namesakes, and shares the secret of Shazam with each of them—but they are reluctant to use it until the evil Sivana captures them. The original Billy sets out to rescue them, and all four become Captain Marvels. To avoid confusion, the three other Billies become the Lieutenants Marvel.

***Marvel Family Comics* #1 (Dec. 1945)** The family—now including Mary Marvel, Captain Marvel Jr., and Uncle Marvel—bands together to take on Black Adam for the first time as a group, setting the stage for a decades-long rivalry between Champions past and present.

ON THE RECORD

Originally known as the Marvel Family, when Shazam was going by the name Captain Marvel, the Shazam Family appeared under its current name after the death of the wizard Shazam and Captain Marvel assuming his name.

The Marvel Family dates back to the 1940s, and was part of the Fawcett stable of heroes brought into DC Comics after World War II. The pre-Flashpoint Marvel Family made an appearance in the prologue to the Darkseid War, during a flashback to *Crisis on Infinite Earths*.

Dr. Sivana and Black Adam are the Marvel/Shazam Family's oldest adversaries, both making their villainous debuts in the 1940s and posing a recurrent threat to Billy Batson and his loved ones (and namesakes) ever since.

The Marvel Family, gathered together for the first time, learned the secret of Black Adam from the Wizard.

MEET THE FAMILY
The Vasquez foster siblings become the Shazam Family for the first time.

1 Eugene Choi
2 Darla Dudley
3 Pedro Peña
4 Mary Bromfield
5 Freddy Freeman

SILVER SWAN

DEBUTS *Wonder Woman* (Vol.1) #288 (Feb. 1982) (Helen Alexandros); *Wonder Woman* (Vol. 2) #15 (Apr. 1988) (Valerie Beaudry); *Wonder Woman* (Vol. 2) #171 (Aug. 2001) (Vanessa Kapetelis)
POWERS/ABILITIES Flight, vocal sonic attacks.
ALLIES Mars, Circe, Dr. Psycho
ENEMIES Wonder Woman

JEALOUSY TAKES FLIGHT
The Silver Swan was driven to villainous acts by her jealousy of Wonder Woman's beauty and renown.

Three women have been known as the Silver Swan. The first, Helen Alexandros, was granted the powers of flight and sonic voice attack by Mars, and fought Wonder Woman at his behest before he withdrew her powers and she returned to normal life. The following two Silver Swans, Valerie Beaudry and Vanessa Kapatelis, achieved their powers by technological means, being altered by Henry Armbruster and Circe, respectively.

In each case, these women were manipulated using their jealousy of Wonder Woman's beauty and strength—Valerie because she had been deformed in the womb by nuclear testing, and Vanessa because Wonder Woman lived with her family in Boston for a while before being forced to leave after Dr. Psycho began manipulating Vanessa's mother. However, as they battled Wonder Woman, the Amazon Queen's virtue and strength made both Valerie and Vanessa realize the error of their ways. **AI**

SILVER BANSHEE

DEBUT *Action Comics* (Vol. 1) #595 (Dec. 1987)
CURRENT VERSION *Supergirl* (Vol. 6) #6 (Apr. 2012)
REAL NAME Siobhan Smythe
BASE New York City
HEIGHT 5ft 11in **WEIGHT** 140 lbs
EYES Blue **HAIR** White
POWERS/ABILITIES Sound manipulation; understanding of all languages; superhuman strength and endurance.
ALLIES Supergirl
ENEMIES Black Banshee

ARE WE STILL FRIENDS?
Supergirl gets a shock when she sees her friend Siobhan transformed into the Silver Banshee—and capable of understanding Kryptonian!

Leaving her past behind her, like so many other young people of Irish descent, Siobhan Smythe came to New York City after her mother's death to make a new life for herself. She encountered Supergirl shortly after settling in Queens, and helped Kara escape a potentially disastrous misunderstanding with the National Guard. The two young women became close friends and Kara stayed with Siobhan, getting used to Earth.

A talented musician, Siobhan was playing at a club when they were attacked by the Black Banshee—revealed to be Siobhan's father, whom she thought was long dead. This provoked the emergence of Siobhan's own alter ego, the powerful and frightening Silver Banshee. Together, she and Supergirl fought off the Black Banshee's attack and Siobhan began to grapple with the fact that her father was alive, while also trying to maintain her friendship with Supergirl. **AI**

SIN-EATER

DEBUT *JSA* (Vol. 1) #23 (Jun. 2001)
REAL NAME Onimar Synn
BASE Thanagar
HEIGHT 7ft 5in **WEIGHT** 480 lbs
EYES Yellow **HAIR** None
POWERS/ABILITIES Various powers derived from the suffering and fear of others; absorption of souls; creation of mindless thralls.
ENEMIES Hawkman, Hawkgirl, Justice Society of America
AFFILIATIONS Seven Devils

HUNGRY FOR SOULS
The Sin-Eater battles a resurrected Hawkman with the ultimate fate of Thanagar hanging in the balance.

Rumored to be one of the legendary Seven Devils of Thanagar, a race of demons that has plagued the planet since its birth, Onimar attempted to take over Thanagar and feed on the souls of its populace.
As Sin Eater, enslaved the population with Nth metal, an element found only on Thanagar, and killed thousands, feasting on their souls and transforming them into an undead army. Nth metal gave Onimar mastery over the four fundamental forces of the universe—strong, weak, gravitational, and electromagnetic.

Desperate to save the rest of their people, the high priests of Thanagar kidnapped Hawkgirl, who could summon Hawkman back from the dead through their divine connection. She succeeded, but it took the combined might of Hawkman, Hawkgirl, and the JSA to stop the Sin-Eater's undead warriors. Sin-Eater was apparently destroyed by the power of Hawkman and Hawkgirl's ancient love. **AI**

SILVERLOCK, OLIVE

DEBUT *Gotham Academy* #1 (Dec. 2014)
REAL NAME Olive Silverlock
BASE Gotham City
HEIGHT 5ft 3in **WEIGHT** Not telling
EYES Violet **HAIR** Silver
POWERS/ABILITIES Keen investigative instincts; determined disposition.
ALLIES Pomeline Fritch, Maps Mizoguchi, Kyle Mizoguchi, Colton Rivera
AFFILIATIONS Detective Club

ON THE CASE
Once Olive Silverlock uncovered mysterious goings-on in and around the halls of Gotham Academy, the Detective Club got serious.

Daughter of Sybil Silverlock (Calamity)—a comatose resident of Arkham Asylum—new kid at school Olive Silverlock began exploring Gotham Academy with one of her few friends, "Maps" Mizoguchi. She stumbled across a secret society at the school trying to contact a ghost—Millie Jane Cobblepot—whose journal Olive had in her possession. The ghost turned out to be fake, but their explorations uncovered tunnels that led under the abandoned and burned-out North Hall of the Academy...and beyond, possibly all the way to Arkham Asylum.

They also ran into Killer Croc hiding in the tunnels. He revealed that he knew Olive's mother, Sybil, and had promised to watch out for her. Olive then refused a request for Millie's journal from Batman, whom she blamed for her mother's imprisonment. She claimed that the journal had been burned in the North Hall fire, but Damian Wayne later stole it and gave it to Batman as Olive and her friends formalized their partnership as the Detective Club. **AI**

SINESTRO

DATA

DEBUT *Green Lantern* (Vol. 2) #7 **(Jul.-Aug. 1961)**
CURRENT VERSION *Green Lantern* (Vol. 5) #1 **(Nov. 2011)**
REAL NAME Thaal Sinestro **BASE** Ranx, Warworld, mobile
HEIGHT 6ft 7in **WEIGHT** 205 lbs **EYES** Yellow **HAIR** Black
POWERS/ABILITIES Indomitable will; mastery of fear and intimidation; mastery of unarmed combat; yellow power ring capable of generating light-constructs, flight, protection, energy-projection; when bonded with Parallax has the ability to manipulate time and reconfigure reality.
ALLIES Parallax, Lyssa Drak, Anti-Monitor, Lex Luthor, Black Adam
ENEMIES Hal Jordan, Guardians of the Universe, Red Lantern Corps, New Gods, the Paling
AFFILIATIONS Yellow Lantern Corps, Green Lantern Corps, New Guardians, White Lantern Corps, Indigo Tribe, Anti-Justice League

BROTHERS IN ARMS
Whenever or wherever Sinestro tried to advance his agenda against the Guardians, his old student Hal Jordan was there to thwart him.

Proud Thaal Sinestro of Korugar loved order. To preserve it, he pursued power in all its forms and became one of the most feared villains in the cosmos. He founded his own corps of cosmic terrorists and ultimately achieved his greatest desire by murdering the immortal Guardians of the Universe, who had treated him like a servant. By dominating and absorbing the cosmic entity Parallax, Sinestro became the Lord of Fear. He remains one of the most powerful beings in creation.

MIGHT IS RIGHT
On returning to the Green Lantern Corps, Sinestro realized that the Guardians adopted his ruthless methods for enforcing order.

Anthropologist Sinestro was reconstructing an ancient city when a wounded Green Lantern crashed at his feet. Prohl Gosgotha begged Sinestro to don his ring and defend them both from a Qwardian War-smith. Sinestro reveled in the ring's power and easily destroyed the invader. Prohl then asked Sinestro to return the ring, but he refused and left the Green Lantern to die of his wounds. The Guardians of Oa knew nothing of these events and welcomed Sinestro, who proved to be one of their most effective agents. His sector was the most peaceful of all, but only because he ruled it as dictator.

Sinestro was eventually banished to the anti-matter universe of Qward for his crimes. There the Qwardians tapped the power of the universal fear-entity to create their own power rings imbued with yellow energy, the only vulnerability of the Green Lanterns' rings. With his yellow ring, Sinestro struck remorselessly at the Guardians who had frustrated his dreams. Imprisoned within Oa's Central Power Battery, he freed the dormant fear-entity Parallax to possess Hal Jordan, thereby sowing the seeds of the universal War of Light.

Forcibly brought back into the Green Lantern Corps, Sinestro became the Guardians' pawn. As they sought to eradicate free will, he took his revenge by murdering them all. He now rules his Yellow Lantern Corps with godlike force and discipline. **WW**

UNTO A GOD
Sheer iron willpower allowed Sinestro to destroy all his enemies, dominate his troops, and overwhelm the cosmic personification of fear itself.

CLASSIC STORIES

***Green Lantern* (Vol. 2) #9 (Nov.-Dec. 1961)** In his second appearance, Sinestro debuts his deadly yellow power ring, trapping and impersonating Hal Jordan in a devious plan to destroy the Guardians of the Universe.

***Green Lantern* (Vol. 2) #52 (Apr. 1967)** Reduced to energy and possessing an ancient automobile, Sinestro springs his strangest trap on Green Lanterns Hal Jordan and Alan Scott.

***Green Lantern* (Vol. 3) #50 (Mar. 1994)** Released by the Guardians to battle a Parallax-possessed Hal Jordan, Sinestro is seemingly killed by Jordan, who then destroys the Central Battery of Power and de-powers the Green Lantern Corps.

FOND FATHER
The only softness in Sinestro's soul came from his sentimental but unshakable attachment to his estranged daughter, Green Lantern Soranik Natu.

SINGH, NAOMI

DEBUT *Green Arrow* Vol 5 #1 (Nov. 2011)
REAL NAME Naomi Singh
BASE Seattle, Washington State
EYES Brown **HAIR** Black
POWERS/ABILITIES Skilled computer hacker, business strategist, and tech specialist.
ALLIES Jax, Oliver Queen, John Diggle, Henry Fyff, Emiko
ENEMIES Richard Dragon, Killer Moth, Billy Tockman, Count Vertigo

After Oliver Queen broke with crime-fighting partners John Diggle and Roy Harper, he sought new allies. He needed dedicated individuals to help him run his business while still operating as Seattle's Super Hero Green Arrow. Brilliant computer programmer Naomi Singh became his most trusted assistant, running his innovations division Q-Core as a front and resource-provider for his secret crime-fighting life.

With assistants Henry Fyff and Jax, she provided intel and new weapons for Green Arrow. As the opposition grew increasingly dangerous, the team became embroiled in the actual fighting. After nearly being killed a number of times, Naomi dropped off the grid. Though she occasionally lends Team Arrow a hand, she prefers to stay hidden; her current whereabouts are unknown. **WW**

SIXPACK

DEBUT *Hitman* (Vol. 1) #9 (Dec. 1996)
CURRENT VERSION *Batman and Robin* (Vol. 2) #27 (Mar. 2014)
REAL NAME Sidney Speck
BASE Gotham City
EYES Bloodshot **HAIR** Brown
POWERS/ABILITIES Expert in unarmed combat and weapons handling; incredibly high tolerance for alcohol.
ENEMIES Bane, Many Angled Ones

Sidney Speck remains one of the world's strangest and most unsavory costumed champions. As Sixpack, he led a team of dissolute heroes, Section 8. With no abilities other than drunken bravado, he was always ready for a fight. His favorite weapon was a broken beer bottle.

A man of mystery, due to the damage booze had wrought on his memory, Sidney spent his days in Noonan's Bar regaling the clientele with tales of his Super Hero career. However, when Gotham City was invaded by demons, he led his men into battle and saw most of them die. After a prolonged period of sobriety, Sixpack began drinking again and revived Section 8, comprised of similarly delusional stalwarts Powertool, Bueno Excellente, Guts, the Grapplah, Dogwelder II, and Baytor. **WW**

SKEETS

DEBUT *Booster Gold* (Vol. 1) #1 (Feb. 1986)
CURRENT VERSION *Justice League International* (Vol. 3) #2 (Dec 2011)
BASE Vanishing Point
WEIGHT 5 lbs
POWERS/ABILITIES Flight; voice projection; historical records archive; numerous tools and weapons.
ALLIES Rip Hunter, Booster Gold, Will Magnus
ENEMIES Black Beetle, Per Degaton, Chronos, T.O. Morrow, Rex Hunter

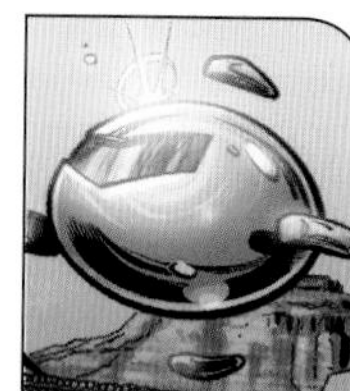

When disgraced sports star Michael Carter fled the 25th century, he stole technological artifacts from the museum where he worked and headed back four centuries to become Super Hero Booster Gold. He also took Skeets, a robotic museum tour-droid he had packed with historical data. With his personality growing, Skeets became a companion and friend, helping to curb some of Carter's wilder get-rich-quick schemes.

Moreover, when the fugitive from the future became the unheralded guardian of the timestream, Skeets was reconstructed and remodeled by Time Master Rip Hunter. He now functions as a sentient monitor and beacon allowing Booster Gold to travel the ever-fluctuating corridors of time and return safely to his starting point without wrecking the course of history. **WW**

SLEEZ

DEBUT *Action Comics* (Vol. 1) #592 (Sep. 1987)
REAL NAME Sleez
BASE Apokolips, Metropolis, mobile
HEIGHT 4ft 3in **WEIGHT** 181 lbs
EYES Black **HAIR** Bald
POWERS/ABILITIES Empathic nature; mind control; immortality; Apokoliptian strength and durability.
ENEMIES Mister Miracle, Superman, Big Barda, Newsboy Legion

Before Prince Uxas was transformed into Darkseid and became ruler of Apokolips, he was a typical spoiled aristocrat. He visited low-rent places with deviant hedonist Sleez as his guide and companion. Sleez soon became an embarrassment and Darkseid exiled him. Sleez found a home in the seamiest backwaters of Metropolis, using his psychic abilities to push humans into slaking their darkest hungers. His dire depredations were halted by Superman, Big Barda, and Mister Miracle. Sleez later played his sordid tricks on the staff of Project Cadmus. A tragic result of his meddling was the creation of a second cloned iteration of the Newsboy Legion.

Sleez was killed by the mysterious God Killer during the purge of the inhabitants of Apokolips and New Genesis. **WW**

SMOAK, FELICITY

DEBUT *The Fury of Firestorm* #23 (May 1984)
CURRENT VERSION *Green Arrow* (Vol. 5) #35 (Dec. 2014)
BASE Seattle, Washington State
EYES Blue **HAIR** Blond
POWERS/ABILITIES Brilliant computer technician, expert hacker, code-writer and breaker.
ALLIES Oliver Queen, John Diggle
ENEMIES The King, Zehra Darvish, the Cheetah
AFFILIATIONS Team Arrow, Mia Dearden, Steve Trevor, A.R.G.U.S.

Felicity Smoak is one of the world's greatest hackers: an infallible digital gun-for-hire. After successfully scrubbing her history from all records, she gained a peerless reputation among the wrong sort of people. For this reason she was hired by scheming billionaire John King to dismantle Queen Industries and assassinate Green Arrow.

King's problem with Green Arrow was that he considered him too weak and unfit to protect Seattle. However, though she was far from a saint, Felicity balked at murder and instead warned the hero, catapulting her into conflict with her vindictive former employer. For betraying him, King used his connections to have Felicity arrested for hacking government servers. He expected she would be killed within hours of arriving at Federal Supermax prison, as he had arranged for her to share a cell with the vicious super-villain Cheetah. This feral fury had harbored a grudge against Smoak ever since the hacker had exposed her family members to danger by publishing their addresses online.

Saved by Green Arrow, Felicity joined him, John Diggle, and a small army of heroes in stopping John King. Oliver Queen, knowing Felicity was considering an offer from Steve Trevor to work anonymously for top-secret government agency A.R.G.U.S., invited her to officially join Team Arrow. Although she initially stayed in contact with them, she has remained more than a little evasive on her final decision. **WW**

SMOKE AND MIRRORS
Felicity was clever, cunning, capricious, and capable of many things, but cold-blooded murder wasn't one of them.

ON THE RECORD

Entrepreneur Felicity Smoak was introduced in the mid-1980s, when computers were starting to be more commonplace. Her company was nearly ruined when Firestorm's negligence during a metahuman battle wiped out her proprietary software. It was the first of many unhappy and unlucky encounters with the Nuclear Man. These only grew more complicated when she married Ed Raymond, father of one of the two people who made up the composite Super Hero.

FIRESTORM AND FIREBRAND
Tech-company pioneer Felicity backed down for no man, least of all a bumbling junior super-freak who was more hazard than hero.

SOLOMON GRUNDY

DATA

DEBUT *All-American Comics* #61 **(Oct. 1944)**
CURRENT VERSION *Earth 2* #3 **(Sep. 2012)**
UNIVERSE Earth-2
BASE Slaughter Swamp
HEIGHT 7ft 5in **WEIGHT** 517 lbs **EYES** Black **HAIR** White
POWERS/ABILITIES Near-invulnerability due to undead nature; immense strength; elemental plant qualities, including regeneration; fatal touch and energy absorption through extrusion of life-draining vines.
ENEMIES Green Lantern, Batman, Justice Society of America
AFFILIATIONS Injustice Society

BATTLE OF THE CHAMPIONS
As champions of the Green and the Grey, Green Lantern and Solomon Grundy were destined to collide.

CLASSIC STORIES

***All-American Comics* #61 (Oct. 1944)** A shambling undead creature appears in a hobo encampment near Gotham City, unable to remember its origins. It is dubbed Solomon Grundy because one of its few memories is that it was "born on a Monday."

***All-Star Comics* #33 (Feb.–Mar. 1947)** Grundy's resistance to the Green Lantern's powers becomes established, and he is abandoned on the moon for the first time after a battle with the full JSA.

***Justice League of America* (Vol. 2) #1–6 (Oct. 2006–Mar. 2007)** Solomon Grundy realizes he has a shot at true immortality if he can possess Professor Ivo's undying essence. However, he will only be able to survive the process if he has the upgraded Red Tornado android as armor.

After more than a century lying dead in the occult muck of Slaughter Swamp, Solomon Grundy returned as the hulking, nearly invincible avatar of the Grey, the life-draining elemental force opposed to the life-giving Green. Pitted against the Green Lantern, he is a walking force of decay, who also packs a mighty punch.

BURIED ON SUNDAY
After murdering his boss, the anonymous butcher who would become Solomon Grundy also took his own life. His body descended into the depths of Slaughter Swamp, where he would be transformed into a different kind of monster.

The man who would become Solomon Grundy was a butcher driven to a murderous rage when his wife committed suicide after she was raped by his boss, Henry Pittance. He slaughtered Pittance and a number of his fellow workers before killing himself at the edge of Slaughter Swamp, behind the butcher shop. With his final breath he chanted the simple rhyme he used as a lullaby for his newborn child, as his body sank into the swamp… but Solomon Grundy's story was not yet over.

The elemental essence of the swamp would not let Grundy die completely, instead transforming him into an undead avatar of the Grey, the force that opposes life. Now a being of great elemental strength, Grundy was awakened when the Green anointed Green Lantern Alan Scott as its champion, and allied itself with him and the team called the Wonders of the World.

Grundy set out to battle the Green, attacking Washington, DC, to draw Scott's attention. With Hawkgirl, Flash, and the Atom, Scott answered the call. Grundy's plant-elemental nature made him largely immune to the power of the Green Lantern's ring, and his healing factor kept him in the fight even when Scott split his upper torso in half and Atom crushed his body to pulp. After Grundy defeated the rest of the Wonders, Alan Scott flew him up into space and stranded him on the moon, where there were no living things for the power of the Grey to attack. **AI**

ON THE RECORD

Solomon Grundy's name comes from a poem by Edwin Arlington Robinson, who won the first two Pulitzer Prizes for poetry.

Unlike the working-class butcher driven to madness, the Golden Age Solomon Grundy first appeared after rich man Cyrus Gold was murdered outside Gotham City and his body was dumped in Slaughter Swamp. This version also had a particular animosity for Green Lantern and the Justice Society of America. Grundy and the Green Lantern frequently squared off, with Grundy being abandoned on the moon at least twice.

BORN ON A MONDAY
Solomon Grundy's elemental powers made him a formidable opponent, even for the JSA.

SORROW, JOHNNY

DEBUT *Secret Origins of Super-Villains* #1 (Dec. 1999)
CURRENT VERSION *Earth 2: Society* #1 (Aug. 2015)
UNIVERSE Earth-2
HEIGHT 6ft 1in **WEIGHT** 192 lbs
POWERS/ABILITIES Uncovered face fatally shocks viewers; teleportation; intangibility.
ALLIES Despero, King of Tears
ENEMIES JSA
AFFILIATIONS Injustice Society

MAN BEHIND THE MASK
Remade in the hellish Subtle Realms, Johnny Sorrow acquired dangerous powers, a hunger for domination, and a face that nobody gets to see twice.

A silent-movie actor who couldn't make the transition to talkies, Johnny Sorrow stole a device called a Subspace Prototype, which malfunctioned, transporting him to another dimension—the Subtle Realms. The creatures who lived there made his visage so horrifying that anyone who saw it died from shock. They returned Sorrow to Earth to prepare the way for the godlike King of Tears, who was imprisoned by the Justice Society of America and the Spectre.

Decades later, Sorrow brought together a new Injustice Society to free the King of Tears, but it was defeated by the JSA, and Sorrow was sent back to the Subtle Realms. There he teamed with the alien Despero to unleash the Seven Deadly Sins against the combined JLA and JSA, but was defeated and banished, before returning to seize control of a new Injustice Society. **AI**

SPARK

DEBUT *Catwoman* (Vol. 4) #7 (May 2012)
BASE Gotham City
HEIGHT 6ft **WEIGHT** 190 lbs
POWERS/ABILITIES Control over various forms of electromagnetism.
ALLIES Catwoman

Spark's true identity is unknown. He made himself known to Catwoman when he saved her from arrest by creating a diversion and helping her escape. He then proposed that they should pool resources and talents, and start pulling heists together. She agreed and they worked on a plot targeting the Penguin and relieving him of a precious set of daggers in his possession. However, before they could complete the job, both of them became more interested in investigating a series of kidnappings of Gotham City prostitutes. It remains to be seen whether this is related to the Penguin, and whether the new partnership between Spark and Catwoman will survive.

Also known as Spark, Ayla Razz was from the planet Winath, and acquired the ability to cast lightning after crashing on the remote world of Korbal, where she was attacked by lightning beasts. She became a valuable member of the Legion of Super-Heroes, going under the moniker Lightning Lass. **AI**

SPARX

DEBUT *Adventures of Superman Annual* #5 (1993)
REAL NAME Donna Carol Force
BASE New York City
HEIGHT 5ft 5in **WEIGHT** 130 lbs
EYES Blue/white **HAIR** Brown/white
POWERS/ABILITIES Faster-than-light travel; lightning emission; flight.
ALLIES Superboy
AFFILIATIONS Canadian Force, Ravers

Donna Carol "D.C." Force was the only member of the Force Family without metahuman powers. This all changed when they discovered alien parasites in Metropolis whose bite triggered latent metahuman powers. In D.C.'s case, the parasites nearly killed her—but also bestowed upon her a number of powers, essentially transforming her into a living thunderbolt. Staying to fight alongside Superboy, D.C.—now known as Sparx—helped the New Bloods and the veteran heroes combat the alien horde.

Searching for her place in the world, D.C. discovered the Event Horizon, a never-ending rave party that floated from reality to reality, world to world. Soon after, Superboy was invited to the rave, and with Sparx, created a Super Hero team called the Ravers. Sparx was later considered for admission into the Teen Titans. **AI**

SPACE CABBY

DEBUT *Mystery in Space* #21 (Aug.–Sep. 1954)
CURRENT VERSION *Green Lantern: New Guardians Annual* (Vol. 1) #1 (Mar. 2013)
REAL NAME Rokko
HEIGHT 5ft 10in **WEIGHT** 175 lbs
ABILITIES Skilled pilot, navigator, engineer.

TAXI TO THE STARS... AND BEYOND
Space Cabby will get you where you need to go, whether it's around the block, through the galaxy... or even across time itself.

Orphaned as a child, the man know only as Space Cabby displayed an early talent for interstellar navigation, leading to distinguished service as a fighter pilot during the Bored Wars of 2146. After the war and a succession of truly forgettable jobs, he found his true calling as a cab driver behind the wheel of space cab #7433. Over the years, Space Cabby has seen more worlds then he can count and picked up a smattering of several alien languages. He has given lifts to a few 20th century heroes, such as Lobo, Starman, and even Superman, whom he transported across time streams when the Man of Steel was taken ill.

OUTTA SPACE
Rokko put Denise to the test and hyperjumped the Lanterns to safety.

Post-Flashpoint, Space Cabby got a name, Rokko, a smart-mouthed makeover, and a state-of-the-art cab called Denise. He reluctantly helped Lanterns Star Sapphire, Arkillo, and Saint Walker flee Tenebrian Space and a deadly glimmernet game show. **AI**

SPACE RANGER

DEBUT *Showcase* #15 (Jul.–Aug. 1958)
CURRENT VERSION *Threshold* #1 (Mar. 2013)
REAL NAME Rick Starr
BASE New York City; asteroid base near Mars
HEIGHT 6ft 2in **WEIGHT** 194 lbs
EYES Blue **HAIR** Black
ABILITIES Hand-to-hand combat; weapons expert.
ALLIES Myra Mason, Cryll, Hal Jordan
ENEMIES Gordanians, Jupiter's Jungle beasts

PATROLLING THE FINAL FRONTIER
Space Ranger and his shape-changing pal Cryll were armed and ever ready for all manner of alien threats.

Rick Starr was the 22nd-century's Space Ranger, patrolling Earth's solar system from his asteroid base near Jupiter. Often joined on his starship, *Solar King*, by his girlfriend Myra Mason, on one solo mission, Starr nearly died after being stranded on Pluto. He was saved by an alien shape-changer, Cryll, and the two became good friends. Starr later foiled a Gordanian invasion of Earth with the help of Green Lantern Hal Jordan.

PRIMETIME PREY
"Ric" Starr worked with Colonel T'omas T'morra to create blind spots during *The Hunted* games.

After Flashpoint, a new Rikane "Ric" Starr appeared on the scene. Having left the Space Rangers, Starr traveled to the planet Tolerance in the Tenebrian Dominion. Here he was branded a fugitive with a bounty on his head, and became an unwilling participant in the popular glimmernet gameshow, *The Hunted*. **SK**

SPECTRE

DATA

DEBUT *More Fun Comics* #52 **(Feb. 1940)**
CURRENT VERSION *Phantom Stranger* (Vol 4) #0 **(Nov. 2012)**
REAL NAME James Corrigan
BASE New York City
HEIGHT 6ft 1in **WEIGHT** 184 lbs
EYES Blue **HAIR** Red
POWERS/ABILITIES Magical and physical abilities, limited only by the need to bond with a host.
ENEMIES John Constantine, Phantom Stranger
AFFILIATIONS Gotham City Police Department, Detailed Task Force

DIVINE RETRIBUTION
The Spectre's powers can only be used while it has a human host, who takes on its frightening signature green-cloaked appearance.

James Corrigan is the latest in a long line of humans who have hosted the Spectre, the mystical embodiment of divine wrath. Torn between his desire for revenge and his destined role as an instrument of justice, Corrigan fights both the evils of the world and his own baser human impulses.

FATAL AMBUSH
The Phantom Stranger accidentally got Jim Corrigan killed, leading to his resurrection as the Spectre.

Gotham City police detective

Jim Corrigan found his kidnapped fiancée with the help of the Phantom Stranger, who had unknowingly led the detective into a trap. Corrigan and his girlfriend were killed by the kidnappers, but the omnipotent being known as "The Voice" then transformed him into the Spectre, and prevented him from taking out his vengeful rage on the Stranger. The Voice had chosen Corrigan to be its instrument of justice, granting him divine powers that the detective began using for revenge. The animosity between him and the Phantom Stranger flared up again when the Stranger believed Corrigan was responsible for kidnapping the Stranger's family. Again the Voice intervened (in the form of a talking terrier), correcting the Stranger and reminding Corrigan that he was meant to mete out justice, not simply vengeance.

Growing accustomed to his new existence, Corrigan helped Batman investigate supernatural events in Arkham Asylum, leading them to Deacon Blackfire and his demon army. He was then recruited to the Detailed Case Task Force, which undertook off-the-books investigations of supernatural phenomena. This did not prevent Corrigan from tangling with the Phantom Stranger once again, this time over how to prosecute the awakened powers of Chris Esperanza, who became a vessel for the Blight—the manifestation of all humanity's evils. Corrigan also sought John Constantine to punish him for his multitude of sins. Constantine convinced the Spectre that if allowed to live, he would remove more evil from the world than he would cause. The Spectre agreed, but vowed that he would claim Constantine's soul when he died. **AI**

TRUST ISSUES
Simmering tensions between the Spectre and the Phantom Stranger came to a boil during the Trinity of Sin crisis.

ON THE RECORD

Three men have hosted the Spectre. The first was James Corrigan, a classic 1940s noir cop who was killed by gangsters and rose from the dead to exact his revenge. Moderating his vengeful feelings, he became a charter member of the Golden Age JSA.

The Spectre's second host was Hal Jordan, the former Green Lantern who assumed the role after Corrigan refused. Jordan was chosen because the Spectre knew Hal was threatened with corruption by Parallax, and only the Spectre could purge Hal's soul.

After a period without a host, during which Eclipso turned the Spectre into a destructive force that wreaked havoc on Earth's magic users, the entity was forced into the recently deceased body of Crispus Allen. In this form he was killed by Eclipso, who brainwashed much of the Justice League to fight on his side.

SPECTRES THREE
Left to right: the original James Corrigan Spectre took no prisoners; Hal Jordan became the Spectre's reluctant host; the angry, vengeful third Spectre, Crispus Allen.

CLASSIC STORIES

***More Fun Comics* #52–53 (Feb.–Mar. 1940)** The Spectre makes his first dramatic appearance after tough cop Jim Corrigan is drowned in a cement-filled barrel, and returns soon after to take supernatural revenge on his killers.

***Crisis on Infinite Earths* #10 (Jan. 1986)** The only being on Earth capable of holding his own against the Anti-Monitor, the Spectre buys Earth's other heroes time to execute their ultimate plan to save creation.

SPELLBINDER I, II, AND III

DEBUT *Detective Comics* (Vol. 1) #358 **(Dec. 1966)** (Spellbinder I); *Justice League International* (Vol. 2) #65 **(Jun. 1994)** (Spellbinder II); *Detective Comics* (Vol. 1) #691 **(Nov. 1995)** (Spellbinder III)
REAL NAME Delbert Billings (Spellbinder I); Fay Moffit (Spellbinder III)
BASE Gotham City
HEIGHT 5ft 11in (Billings); 5ft 6in (Moffit)
WEIGHT 155 lbs (Billings); 137 lbs (Moffit)
EYES Brown (Billings); Pink (Moffit) **HAIR** Blue (Billings); Blue (Moffit)
POWERS/ABILITIES Can generate powerful illusions **ENEMIES** Batman

BEDAZZLED
The first Spellbinder, Delbert Billings, tested his hypnotic powers on Batman, who soon saw through the illusions.

Art forger Delbert Billings decided to embellish his criminal career by developing optical devices that would enable him to hypnotize others. As Spellbinder, Billings committed a rash of robberies, but was ultimately routed by Batman and Robin.

A second Spellbinder—mystically powered and unrelated to Delbert Billings—was briefly active during Billings' incarceration and battled the Justice League as a member of the government-sanctioned "Leaguebusters," before vanishing to parts unknown.

Upon his release from prison, Delbert Billings attempted a criminal comeback, but made the mistake of his life when he turned down the demon Neron's offer for enhanced powers in exchange for his soul. However, while Billings would not agree to Neron's offer, his moll, Fay Moffit, jumped at the chance and promptly shot Delbert in the head. Neron gave Moffit the ability to cast psychedelic illusions, and she became the third and most sinister Spellbinder. However, her power to alter others' perceptions of reality is directly tied to her own vision. Cover her eyes and she is rendered powerless. **AI**

COUP DE GRACE
Fay Moffit knew a good deal when she saw it and accepted Neron's offer to succeed Delbert Billings as the new Spellbinder.

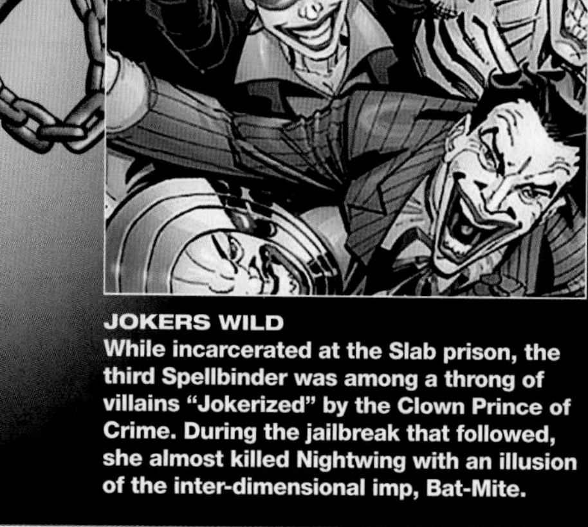

JOKERS WILD
While incarcerated at the Slab prison, the third Spellbinder was among a throng of villains "Jokerized" by the Clown Prince of Crime. During the jailbreak that followed, she almost killed Nightwing with an illusion of the inter-dimensional imp, Bat-Mite.

SPINNER, DOROTHY

DEBUT *Doom Patrol* (Vol. 2) #14 (Nov. 1988)
HEIGHT 5ft 3in **WEIGHT** 118 lbs
EYES Brown **HAIR** Brown
POWERS/ABILITIES Can bring imaginary friends and enemies to life for short periods.
ENEMIES Candlemaker
ALLIES Robotman, Beast Boy
AFFILIATIONS Doom Patrol

SAVAGE PSYCHE
Years of retreating from the real world and keeping her emotions in check were unleashed when Dorothy joined the Doom Patrol.

Dorothy's deformed simian-like features made her hide from the world, so she used her psychic ability to bring imaginary friends to life. When she met the Doom Patrol, she found equally strange friends who accepted her as one of their own. However, her time with the team also unleashed her innermost fears, giving life to the Candlemaker. The savage entity decapitated the Doom Patrol's leader, the Chief, and terrorized the team, but was eventually snuffed out by Dorothy.

Dorothy was then imprisoned within the other-dimensional Dream Country with other powerful children who were brought there to expand the region's power. She escaped and later unwittingly destroyed Robotman when he tried to reunite Dorothy with her mother. She created a new Robotman from her mind, but Beast Boy and Fever rebuilt the original and got Dorothy the psychiatric care she needed. **SK**

CANDLE KILLER
Dorothy's deepest fears, frustrations, and fury found all-too-real and terrifying form in the Candlemaker.

SPIVOT, PATTY

DEBUT *DC Special Series* # 1 (Sep. 1977)
CURRENT VERSION *The Flash* (Vol. 4) # 1 (Nov. 2011)
BASE Central City
HEIGHT 5ft 3in **WEIGHT** 133 lbs
EYES Blue **HAIR** Blonde
POWERS/ABILITIES Extremely intelligent forensic scientist with a real thirst for justice and seeing cases through to the end.
ALLIES Barry Allen, Solovar
ENEMIES Captain Cold, Gorilla Grodd
AFFILIATIONS Central City Police Department

GETTING SERIOUS
Despite a hesitant start, Patty Spivot knew that she and Barry Allen were destined to have a life together—even after he revealed he was the Flash.

Patty Spivot is the blood analysis specialist at the Centra City Police Department crime land, where she works with forensic scientist Barry Allen. After years of working together, Barry finally worked up the nerve to ask his colleague out on a date, and took her to a tech symposium, where their brief romantic moment was interrupted by an armed robbery.

Despite this shaky start they grew closer, but Patty soon realized she had a potential rival for Barry's affections. Reporter Iris West had a tendency to flirt with him while seeking leads for her articles.

After Barry was nearly killed in the line of duty, he and Patty took their blossoming relationship to the next level and officially became a couple. Patty then learned Barry was also the Flash, but moved in with him anyway. She eventually left Barry after a terrifying encounter with his future self tainted him in her eyes. **AI**

SPY SMASHER

DEBUT *Birds of Prey* (Vol. 1) #100 (Jan. 2007)
REAL NAME Katarina Armstrong
HEIGHT 5ft 11in **WEIGHT** 149 lbs
EYES Blue **HAIR** Blonde
POWERS/ABILITIES Intelligent and athletic; capable hand-to-hand fighter and markswoman; trained in espionage techniques.
ALLIES Covert operatives across the globe
ENEMIES Oracle (Barbara Gordon), Black Canary, Birds of Prey
AFFILIATIONS FBI, CIA, Checkmate, D.E.O.

Katarina Armstrong became the modern-day successor to World War II hero Spy Smasher. An old college rival of Barbara Gordon (Batgirl), Katarina shared Barbara's desire to be the best. Their rivalry spilled over onto the athletic track, where they became good friends—until Kat tripped Babs during a race.

After college, Katarina became a soldier. She then accepted the Spy Smasher name and, deducing Barbara was Oracle, tried to shut her down. In response, Oracle challenged Spy Smasher to an old-fashioned, hand-to-hand duel. Barbara won the fight, but Spy Smasher refused to back down on her threat to take over Oracle's operatives. However, when she tried to leave the premises, she was surrounded by the Birds of Prey and many of Oracle's other friends, and realized that this was one war she just couldn't win. **MM**

CLUB PRESIDENT
Like her rival Barbara Gordon, Spy Smasher tried to be the best at what she did. Her many, many credentials spoke for themselves.

ST. CLOUD, SILVER

DEBUT *Detective Comics* (Vol. 1) #470 (Jun. 1977)
REAL NAME Silver St. Cloud
BASE Gotham City
HEIGHT 5ft 5in **WEIGHT** 131 lbs
EYES Blue **HAIR** Silver
POWERS/ABILITIES Intelligent and witty; connections to Gotham City's elite social circles.
ALLIES Batman
ENEMIES Onomatopoeia, Rupert Thorne, the Joker, Deadshot

Bruce Wayne first met Silver St. Cloud at a party on his yacht, and they were very taken with one another. After Bruce left briefly to battle Dr. Phosphorous, he returned to the yacht only to have Silver touched his hair and realized it was wet. Suspicious of Bruce from then on, Silver nevertheless began to date him. But when she saw Batman in action and recognized Bruce beneath the cowl, she broke off their relationship, unable to deal with Bruce's nighttime activities.

Fate brought the couple back together, and Silver and Bruce became engaged. As a result, Batman began to let his guard down, revealing his secret identity to a vigilante calling himself Baphomet, and even bringing the young man back to the Batcave and introducing him to Silver. Bruce was appalled to discover that Baphomet was none other than the murderous villain Onomatopoeia, who slashed Silver's throat in front of his horrified eyes. **MM**

RELAXEZ-VOUS!
Silver was closer to Bruce Wayne than perhaps any of his previous girlfriends. She brought out his playful side, normally kept well under wraps.

SPOILER

DEBUT *Detective Comics* (Vol. 1) #647 (Aug. 1992)
CURRENT VERSION *Batman* (Vol. 2) #28 (Apr. 2014)
REAL NAME Stephanie Brown
BASE Gotham City
HEIGHT 5ft 5in **WEIGHT** 110 lbs
EYES Blue **HAIR** Blond
POWERS/ABILITIES Adept gymnast and fighter; fast on her feet with a matching quick wit; weapons include protective suit equipped with a myriad of offensive and defensive devices; skilled motorcyclist.
ALLIES Red Robin, Bluebird, Catwoman, Batman, the Batman Family
ENEMIES Cluemaster, Hush, Lincoln March

Teenager Stephanie Brown knew that her father was a little weird, but she had no idea that he was spending his nights as the third-rate costumed super-villain Cluemaster. But when she unintentionally walked in on her father's meeting with a bunch of other minor super-villains, including Firefly, Lock-Up, and Signalman, Stephanie found herself running for her life, as even her mother was in on the conspiracy.

Writing a blog called "Spoiler Alert" that told her story, Stephanie soon adopted the vigilante name of the Spoiler and a flamboyant purple costume, complete with a limited arsenal of weapons. Playing a lone hand, she used biking skills she had picked up from a rough-and-tumble childhood full of daring stunts to lure Cluemaster into a trap, ultimately resulting in his arrest. Even after her father was seemingly killed by his devious and dangerous former associate—Lincoln March from the Court of Owls—the Spoiler opted to continue her Super Hero career, imploring Catwoman to train her in fighting techniques, and constantly popping up in Batman's life. **MM**

TO THE VICTOR...
During a massive attack by the villain Mother, Spoiler helped protect Bluebird's brother, Cullen, and fight back against Mother with heroes including Red Robin and Midnighter.

ON THE RECORD

Before the Flashpoint event, Stephanie Brown was the only character to serve as both Robin and Batgirl. She debuted in the pages of *Detective Comics*, but soon became romantically involved with Tim Drake in his *Robin* title.

Having had a tumultuous life, including giving her baby up for adoption and troubles with her single mom, Spoiler eventually worked her way into Batman's good graces, briefly replacing Tim as Robin. Fired by the Dark Knight for not following his directions, she continued her crime-fighting career—with Barbara Gordon's blessing—adopting the name and costume of Batgirl.

HERO BY PROXY
As Batgirl, Stephanie fought crime on her college campus at Gotham University with the help of her own Oracle of sorts—computer expert Proxy. Thanks to a grant from Batman, Inc., Batgirl set up shop in her own Batcave-like hideout she called Firewall.

SPYRAL

DEBUT *Batman, Incorporated* (Vol. 1) #4 **(Apr. 2011)**
CURRENT VERSION *Batman, Incorporated* (Vol. 2) #1 **(Jul. 2012)**
BASE St. Hadrian's Finishing School for Girls, England
NOTABLE MEMBERS **Helena Bertinelli** (Matron, Current Director of Spyral); **Doctor Dedalus** (Agent Zero, Otto Netz); **Tiger** (Agent 1); **The Hood** (Agent 24, George Cross); **El Gaucho** (Agent 33, Santiago Vargas); **Dick Grayson** (Agent 37); **Mr. Minos** (Former Head of Spyral); **Elisabeth Netz** (Frau Netz); **Dr. Poppy Ashemore**
ENEMIES Batman, Dick Grayson, Tiger

The top-secret institution known as Spyral, led by the former "mafia princess" Helena Bertinelli, is a spy organization with a self-destructive streak, creating violence to beget more violence. Spyral was originally formed by Otto Netz, a Nazi scientist dubbed Doctor Dedalus when he began a career as a super-villain.

After Otto's death, the organization was briefly controlled by the corrupt and devious Mr. Minos. It then fell under the rule of his daughter, the mysterious Agent 0. Mr. Minos had been collecting information on the world's Super Heroes, and his efforts had attracted the attention of Batman. When Nightwing was publicly outed as Dick Grayson and then seemingly killed by the Crime Syndicate, Batman decided to exploit the situation to discover more about the mysterious organization: He persuaded Grayson to join Spyral as a undercover agent. All went smoothly for a while and Grayson worked with Spyral agent Bertinelli on several missions.

However, after Helena took over from the treacherous Mr. Minos as the institution's new head, Spyral's computer consciousness, an artificial intelligence called Spyder, ordered her to kill Grayson. As a result, Grayson and Agent 1, Tiger, turned against Spyral and began taking out their agents one by one. **MM**

SPY VS. SPY
Helena Bertinelli wanted to run Spyral along more principled lines, but found it near impossible thanks to Spyder, the organization's corrupt computer system.

ON THE RECORD

Spyral debuted shortly before the Flashpoint event. In the original version, Netz's daughter was not Agent 0, but the original Batwoman, Kathy Kane. She had a relationship with Batman, while also working for Spyral. This explained why the battle uniforms at St. Hadrian's Finishing School resembled the red and yellow of Batwoman's costume. After Flashpoint, Kathy Kane disappeared from the timeline, and Agent 0, Katarina "Luka" Netz, was introduced in her place.

SINS OF THE FATHER
The original Batwoman cut off her relationship with Batman after learning that Otto Netz was her father and that, years ago, she had been given up for adoption.

STALKER

DEBUT *Stalker* #1 (Jun.–Jul. 1975)
CURRENT VERSION *Sword of Sorcery* (Vol. 2) #4 (Mar. 2013)
HEIGHT 5ft 8in **WEIGHT** 145 lbs
EYES Red **HAIR** Black
POWERS/ABILITIES expert marksman, unparalleled hunting skills, magical knowledge; fires explosive blasts from hands; can create portals to other locations.
ALLIES Lyll'ana
ENEMIES Lucifer

A long time ago, young warrior king Stalker returned from battle to find his wife, Lyll'ana dying of fever. He prayed to his god to spare her life and that of his unborn child. He was visited by Lucifer, who made him a deal: a male soul of his bloodline for the health of his wife and child. His wife recovered, but died in childbirth. Stalker realized he was doomed to walk the Earth forever, presumably without a soul.

As a hitman in the modern world, Stalker was told by Lucifer to kill a woman, Clarissa Rowe. Stalker was shocked to find that she was pregnant and his descendant. He also realized that he had always had a soul, and that Lucifer was claiming this young boy as part of their deal. Realizing what a monster he had become Stalker drove Lucifer away from the infant. **MM**

STANLEY AND HIS MONSTER

DEBUT *The Fox & The Crow* #95 (Dec. 1965–Jan. 1966)
REAL NAME Stanley Dover, Jr.
BASE Star City
HEIGHT 3ft 2in **WEIGHT** 65 lbs
EYES Blue **HAIR** Blond
POWERS/ABILITIES Bound to a powerful 3,000-year-old demon.
ALLIES Spot, the monster
ENEMIES Stanley Dover, Sr. (aka Star City Slayer)

A dabbler in the dark arts, Stanley Dover, Sr. attempted to trap a demon using arcane magic, hoping he could transfer his soul into that of the powerful demon. During the summoning of the hell beast, Stanley's grandson, who happened to share Dover's name, was accidentally bound to the demon instead. The timid, kind-hearted monster, called Spot, hid in Stanley's closet and befriended the five-year-old boy, before the elder Dover discovered its existence.

Becoming a serial killer known as the Star City slayer, Stanley Sr. imprisoned his grandson and conducted rituals with his victims' blood, trying, and failing, to summon and capture Stanley's monster. The evil mage then crossed paths with Green Arrow Oliver Queen and, realizing that Queen was without a soul, set his sights on transferring his soul into Queen's body to catch Spot. Before Dover Sr. could complete the transfer, Green Arrow's soul was returned to him, and Stanley's monster then promptly devoured the warlock. **MM**

INNOCENCE LOST
When Stanley and his Monster found themselves embroiled in Green Arrow's troubling world, the boy's dark secret was revealed.

STAR BOY

DEBUT *Adventure Comics* #282 (Mar. 1961)
CURRENT VERSION *Legion of Super-Heroes* (Vol. 7) #1 (Nov. 2011)
REAL NAME Thom Kallor
BASE 31st-century Earth
HEIGHT 5ft 8in **WEIGHT** 160 lbs
EYES Brown **HAIR** Brown
POWERS/ABILITIES Can increase the weight of people or objects; Legion of Super-Heroes training and flight ring.
ENEMIES Infinitus, Dominators

Thom Kallor was born in a floating observatory to astronomer parents from the planet Xanthu, a unique situation that allowed him the power to borrow mass from stars. Unfortunately, young Thom used these abilities to destroy the observatory. His family moved back to Xanthu, and Thom underwent tests for his bizarre physical condition before running away from home.

After accidentally passing through a comet, he gained powers similar to Superman's, and joined the Legion of Super-Heroes as Star Boy. When his new powers faded, Thom continued Legion service, with a brief side mission for the Legion of Substitute Heroes. He recently traveled to the 21st century alongside other Legionnaires to stop the universe-annihilating threat of Infinitus. **MM**

STAR SAPPHIRE

DATA

DEBUT *Green Lantern* (Vol. 2) #16 **(Oct. 1962)**
CURRENT VERSION *Green Lantern* (Vol. 5) #7 **(May 2012)**
REAL NAME Carol Ferris
BASE Coast City, California
HEIGHT 5ft 7in **WEIGHT** 125 lbs **EYES** Blue **HAIR** Black
POWERS/ABILITIES Indomitable will and all-consuming love; capable of utilizing a violet gem or ring that affords flight, protection, energy projection and solid light-construct creation.
ALLIES Kyle Rayner, Hal Jordan, Hawkman, Hawkgirl
ENEMIES Sinestro, Larfleeze, Predator, Queen Shrike, Krona, Atrocitus, First Lantern, Third Army, Relic, Oblivion
AFFILIATIONS Star Sapphire Corps, Zamarons, Ferris Air/Ferris Aircraft, New Guardians

I SEE YOUR LOVE LIGHT SHINING Like everything in her life, Carol's relationships with teammates were always fraught with complications.

CLASSIC STORIES

***Green Lantern* (Vol. 2) #73–74 (Dec. 1969–Jan. 1970)** Carol's love for Hal together with Star Sapphire's increasing mental instability enable Sinestro to use her as a deadly weapon in an attack on their mutual foe—Green Lantern Hal Jordan.

***Superman* (Vol. 1) #261 (Feb. 1973)** Following a bizarre misunderstanding, the lethally protective but mentally muddled Star Sapphire attacks Superman, believing that the Man of Steel has harmed her chosen consort, Green Lantern.

***Action Comics* (Vol. 1) #601 (May 1988)** Under the influence of the ruthless Predator Entity, Star Sapphire kills Green Lantern Katma Tui to send a message to Hal.

EMOTIONAL ROLLERCOASTER Her time with the New Guardians showed Carol that love could not exist in an emotional vacuum.

Carol Ferris had no time for love, despite being torn between affection for test pilot Hal Jordan and being attracted to the hero Green Lantern. This emotional conflict led to mayhem after she was selected by warriors of an extraterrestrial matriarchy to wear the all-powerful Star Sapphire. With the gem, all Carol's subconscious desires could be realized and she repeatedly attacked the Green Lantern, determined to bend him to her will.

Carol became increasingly stressed by her life. Prolonged use of the violet gem—which, like a power ring, harnessed Love's violet light—affected her mind, creating a subconscious third personality, named Predator. "He" drove her to brutality and murder, and was later revealed as a physical manifestation of the Entity embodying the accumulation of universal love. Eventually she was cured, but when the War of Light brought all shades of the Emotional Spectrum into conflict, the alien Zamarons sought a new path to universal love, asking Carol to lead their Star Sapphire Corps. She thrived as a hero, battling against the marauding Sinestro Corps and the ghastly risen dead of the Black Lanterns. She even reformed the uncontrolled passions of the Predator Entity, creating a more benign and positive aspect of love.

Following valiant participation in the coming of the White Entity of Life on the Brightest Day and in the War of the Lanterns, Carol joined Kyle Rayner's multidenominational band of Spectrum Warriors as a New Guardian. Her long-held feelings for Hal Jordan began to wave, as she found herself increasingly drawn to Rayner. When Jordan was kidnapped by newly reinstated Green Lantern Sinestro, Carol returned to the New Guardians and found even greater purpose.

After it was learned that the Emotional Spectrum was a finite resource, the Green Lanterns decided to police all uses of the lights and Carol broke away from both Jordan and White Lantern Rayner to chart her own course. **WW**

ON THE RECORD

Golden Age Star Sapphire was an alien invader who fought the Flash. She was reinvented as Carol Ferris, and since then a number of women have worn the transformative gem.

Dela Pharon became the Zamarons' second choice for queen, while Deborah Camille Darnell—aka Remoni-Notra—just wanted power. Hal Jordan's old flame Jillian Pearlman was simply overwhelmed by the gem itself as it sought to discover which woman Hal loved the most.

LOVE IS A BATTLEFIELD The very first Star Sapphire loved only the thrill of battle and the allure of conquest.

STAR SAPPHIRE CORPS

DEBUT *Green Lantern* (Vol. 4) #20 **(Jun. 2007)**
CURRENT VERSION *Green Lantern: New Guardians* (Vol. 1) #1 **(Nov. 2011)**
REAL NAME Violet Lantern Corps
BASE Zamaron
CURRENT MEMBERS/POWERS **CAROL FERRIS, FATALITY, MIRI RIAM, QUEEN AGA'PO** Each member uses all-consuming love to power a violet power ring that affords flight, protection, energy projection, and solid light-construct creation.
ALLIES Blue Lantern Corps, Indigo Tribe, Green Lantern Corps
ENEMIES Guardians of the Universe, Sinestro Corps

A multi-species group of females empowered by love, the Star Sapphires were created by the immortal women of Maltus. Having broken away from their emotion-suppressing males in the wake of Krona's wounding of the cosmic fabric, the Zamarons sought to ease universal conflict, using love to soothe aggression. Initially they employed violet crystals, but these ultimately proved wild and attuned to love's darker side. Eventually they were equipped with power rings using the refined Light of Love broadcast from a Central Power Battery. The Star Sapphire Corps also use conversion crystals to envelop resistant or hostile targets, gradually reprogramming potential recruits to pursue the interests of love at all costs. Until recently all members were female, except for Guy Gardner, who briefly found love on his odyssey through the Emotional Spectrum.

The Star Sapphires have their own unique oath:
For hearts long lost and full of fright,
For those alone in blackest night,
Accept our ring and join our fight,
Love conquers all—with violet light! **WW**

ON THE RECORD

The Zamarons have been altered radically and often since their introduction in 1962. Initially super-scientific Amazons roaming the cosmos in search of a new ruler, their selection of Carol Ferris met with stiff resistance from the Green Lantern.

They were later revealed as the long-missing females of the Oan Guardians, complete with their own agenda for how creation should be run. Their return signaled a reconciliation of immortals and a new Millennium for the Universe.

TOGETHERNESS
Pooling their resources, a male and female immortal came to Earth with the intent of creating a group of transformative New Guardians.

STARLING

DEBUT *Birds of Prey* (Vol. 3) #1 (Nov. 2011)
REAL NAME Evelyn Crawford
BASE Gotham City
EYES Brown **HAIR** Brown
POWERS/ABILITIES Highly skilled unarmed combatant; skilled and aggressive vehicle driver; extremely proficient with firearms.
ALLIES Black Canary, Batgirl, Katana
ENEMIES The Penguin, Perrenials, Choke
AFFILIATIONS Birds of Prey, Amanda Waller

Starling is a wanted mercenary and master strategist. The covert surveillance operative and combat specialist met Black Canary when both were infiltrating the Penguin's operation in Gotham City. They decided to stick together after they were exposed, forming the Birds of Prey.

Starling repeatedly proved her worth in battle against terrorists such as Basilisk and metahuman maniacs like Choke and Talon, but she was not a team player, fighting with new members and acting with increasing ruthlessness. All the while, she was secretly supplying reports to Amanda Waller on Black Canary's sonic powers.

When the Birds finally learned of her treachery, working for Mr. Freeze and manipulating her teammates into going against the Court of Owls, she vanished. She remains a fugitive at large. **WW**

STARGIRL

DEBUT *Stars and S.T.R.I.P.E.* #0 **(Jul. 1999)**
CURRENT VERSION *Justice League of America* (Vol. 3) #1 **(Apr. 2013)**
REAL NAME Courtney Whitmore
BASE Moosonee, Ontario, Canada; Los Angeles, California
HEIGHT 5ft 5in **WEIGHT** 137 lbs **EYES** Blue **HAIR** Blond
POWERS/ABILITIES Trained martial artist and gymnast; carries a Cosmic Staff that increases strength, speed, and agility, and affords flight, force-field generation, gravity and electromagnetic manipulation, energy-construct creation, heat emission, and energy projection and absorption.
ALLIES Tuan, Supergirl, Miiyahbin, Green Arrow, Martian Manhunter, Alanna Strange
ENEMIES Shadow Thief, Despero, Cadmus, Secret Society of Super-Villains, Byth, Infinitus
AFFILIATIONS Justice League of America, Justice League United, Legion of Super-Heroes

Courtney Whitmore was a typical bratty kid until she found a costume and Cosmic Staff while snooping in her new stepfather's office. She discovered their incredible powers and was soon flying over Los Angeles. In a perfect "right place, right time" moment, she rescued citizens endangered by a fire and became a media sensation. Although he was furious, there was nothing her stepfather Pat Dugan could do except train her to use the gear properly. He also recognized that she had found her true calling: helping people.

Stargirl was asked to join A.R.G.U.S.'s Justice League of America project but quickly realized it was for publicity purposes and that it wouldn't help her fight or save people. She was unaware that Director Amanda Waller also intended her to be a counter to Justice Leaguer Cyborg, should he ever go rogue.

She played a major role in thwarting the Earth-3 Crime Syndicate's global invasion, even though her family were targeted and her little brother Ted murdered. She almost quit, but after her parents begged her, Courtney resumed her destiny, joining and eventually leading the fully independent Justice League United. **WW**

ON THE RECORD

On her debut, Courtney Whitmore was only allowed to be a Super Hero if her stepfather chaperoned her. Pat Dugan had been costumed crusader Stripesy in the 1940s and later turned his engineering genius to building the mechanical warsuit S.T.R.I.P.E. (Special Tactics Robotic Integrated Power Enhancer).

Unable to stop his wayward stepdaughter risking her life, he tagged along, but soon decided to let Stargirl go it alone.

STAR STRUCK
After months battling beside his stepdaughter, Pat realized Courtney was capable of handling any trouble as a solo star.

STARFIRE

DATA

DEBUT *DC Comics Presents* #26 **(Oct. 1981)**
CURRENT VERSION *Red Hood and the Outlaws* (Vol. 1) #1 **(Nov. 2011)**
REAL NAME Princess Koriand'r of Tamaran
BASE Key West, Florida
HEIGHT 6ft 1ins **WEIGHT** 210 lbs
EYES Green **HAIR** Red
POWERS/ABILITIES Converts ultraviolet radiation into energy, providing enhanced strength, speed, endurance, durability, gravity-repelling flight, and heat and energy projection; contact language assimilation; gladiatorial combat training.
ALLIES Orn of the Citadel, Dick Grayson, Jason Todd/Red Hood, Roy Harper, Atlee, Sheriff Stella Gomez
ENEMIES Komand'r, Simon Amal/Crux, Chida Monster, the Blight, Helspont
AFFILIATIONS The Dominators, Red Hood and the Outlaws, Teen Titans

CLASSIC STORIES

***New Teen Titans* (Vol. 1) #23-25; *New Teen Titans Annual* #1 (Sep.-Nov. 1982)** Starfire is recaptured by slavers and, with human allies, fights a climactic battle against her vicious usurping sister, Blackfire.

***New Teen Titans* (Vol. 2) #14-18 (Nov. 1985-Mar. 1986)** Koriand'r and the Titans visit Tamaran, where the Princess is compelled by her parents to enter into a state marriage to prevent civil war. The decision does not go down well with her boyfriend, Dick Grayson.

***New Titans* (Vol. 1) #109 (Mar. 1994)** After months of personal tragedy and escalating violence, Starfire undergoes a radical transformation and becomes a darker, meaner warrior woman.

SHINING STAR
Red Hood and Arsenal were fiercely protective of their alien ally Koriand'r, despite her staggering power and battle prowess.

YEARS A SLAVE
Imprisoned on the planet Takron, the young Koriand'r endured years of back-breaking hard labor and enforced drug-dependency.

An alien princess in exile, Koriand'r of Tamaran escaped a lifetime of brutality and betrayal as a slave and lab rat for the Citadel and Dominion. Years after manifesting incredible energy powers, she led a revolt and escaped to Earth in the commandeered slave spaceship S.S. *Starfire*. An engine of righteous fury, she fights to ensure no other beings have to endure the pain and indignity that ruined her life.

As a child, Princess Koriand'r of Tamaran was sold into slavery by her sister Komand'r to preserve their planet from invaders. Kori spent her early life in drudgery and as a subject of scientific experimentation. Drugged until she became an addict, her horrendous existence was lightened only by disgraced Citadel warrior Orn, who secretly taught her to fight and helped her get clean of the drugs.

After arriving on Earth, Kori spent some time fighting evil alongside a number of the planet's young heroes—most notably Dick Grayson. Eventually, however, she suffered damage to her memories, and retreated from human interaction. She was brought out of her shell by the resurrected vigilante Red Hood, who looked after her when she became a member his group, the Outlaws.

Following months of constant conflict on Earth, the Outlaws joined Starfire when she reunited with the slaves she had freed on a mission to occupied Tamaran. Her benighted homeworld was now under attack by the parasitic Blight. Though reluctant at first, Kori successfully liberated her people and reconciled with her sister, who now went by the codename Blackfire. Together they later repelled another invasion, this time by the monstrous Daemonite overlord Helspont.

With the situation resolved, Starfire returned to Earth and set up home in Key West, Florida. She largely turned her back on conflict and combat, and instead did her best to make a normal and contented life for herself. **WW**

ON THE RECORD

When Starfire was introduced in 1980, she was a naïve girl with staggering powers and a short temper. The alien princess trusted implicitly and always spoke her mind. Moreover, when she was in action with the New Teen Titans, she had to be constantly monitored because she had a tendency of going straight for the kill. After leaving the Titans, she served with distinction in the Justice League, the Outsiders, and interstellar peacekeeping force R.E.B.E.L.S.

GOLDEN GIRL
Though always confident and a little headstrong, Starfire was generally considered to be a team player, not a solo star.

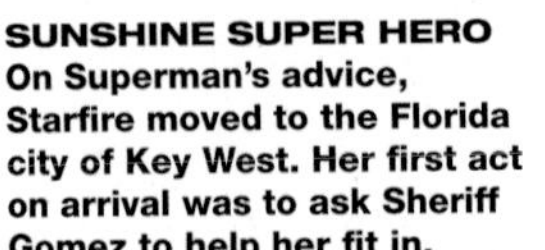

SUNSHINE SUPER HERO
On Superman's advice, Starfire moved to the Florida city of Key West. Her first act on arrival was to ask Sheriff Gomez to help her fit in.

STARMAN

DATA

DEBUT (Ted Knight) *Adventure Comics* (Vol. 1) #61 **(Apr. 1941)**
(Jack Knight) *Zero Hour* (Vol. 1) #1 **(Sep. 1994)**
REAL NAME Jack Knight
BASE Opal City
HEIGHT 6ft 1ins **WEIGHT** 165 lbs **EYES** Black **HAIR** Black
POWERS/ABILITIES Cosmic Staff enables flight, object-levitation, energy-projection, extreme heat production, and force-field generation.
ALLIES Ted Knight, Will Payton, Sadie Falk, O'Dare Family, the Shade, Jake "Bobo" Benetti, Phantom Lady, Mikaal Tomas, Solomon Grundy, Hamilton Drew, Black Condor, Charity, Ralph and Sue Dibny
ENEMIES Kyle, Bliss, Nash, the Mist, Culp, Rag Doll Cult, the Infernal Dr. Pip, Spider, Dr. Phosphorus
AFFILIATIONS Justice Society of America, Ralph and Sue Dibny

STARLIT KNIGHT
Jack Knight never let the astounding power in his hands overwhelm the wonder in his eyes or joy in his heart.

DEAD MAN TALKING
Deceased brother David would sometimes visit Jack in dreams. He offered advice and debate, brought the occasional guest-speaker, and proffered veiled warnings.

Jack Knight came from a dynasty of Super Heroes. His father was World War II mystery man Starman, and he was also related to the first Phantom Lady. However, he was content to let older brother David wield the Cosmic Rod as champion of Opal City. Jack preferred to pursue his love of history and popular culture. That all changed when David was assassinated.

Jack Knight became Starman only after David's murder was followed by an attempt on his own life. Using a prototype staff his father had discarded, Jack vanquished the killers and became the city's protector. Despite reservations, he was drawn to the life of adventure and exploration, although he steadfastly refused to wear a costume.

A born hero, Jack saved Opal City from numerous menaces, and even helped to revive the Justice Society of America for the modern age. He was truly unconventional. He turned super-villains like Bobo Bennetti, Solomon Grundy, and the Shade from the path of evil, and preferred to debate rather than fight. However, when necessity demanded, he pulled no punches. During an all-out battle for Opal, he led a coalition of unlikely champions against the savage forces of magical terrorist Culp.

Jack's greatest joy came from using his power to learn forgotten secrets. He once traveled through time and space to map the connection between all heroes who had ever called themselves Starman. Upon the birth of his daughter, Jack retired, giving the Cosmic Staff to teenage hero Courtney Whitmore, who carried on the legacy as Stargirl. **WW**

STARS IN THEIR EYES
The Astral Avenger crushed America's many enemies with his fists, backed up by the accumulated might and majesty of the heavens.

ON THE RECORD

Ted Knight became Starman after inventing a Gravity Rod that gathered and focused ambient energy from the stars. Ted refined and improved his creation until he devised the awesome Cosmic Rod, used by generations of champions who followed him. His career was interrupted by a nervous breakdown stemming from his contributions to the Manhattan Project, but upon recovery he resumed costumed crime-fighting until old age caught up with him. His eldest son, David, took over as Starman.

Other individuals to have held the mantle of Starman include Charles McNider—the hero Dr. Mid-Nite—who assumed the role during Ted Knight's breakdown. McNider was succeeded by David Knight, who was thrown back in time at the moment of his death, decades hence.

Mikaal Tomas, an alien would-be conqueror, rejected his species' plans to invade Earth and became Starman, Earth's guardian. Another alien, Prince Gavyn of the Crown Imperial, protected his domain as Starman until he died fighting Eclipso; his essence struck Earthman Will Payton, transforming him into Starman. Lastly, Farris Knight, a distant descendant of Jack Knight's, was the 853rd century's Starman.

Dr. Mid-Nite **Will Payton**

Mikaal Tomas

David Knight

Prince Gavyn

Farris Knight

CLASSIC STORIES

***Starman* (Vol. 2) #5 (Mar. 1995)** Jack has a painful discussion with his dead brother, resolving old fraternal concerns and setting the scene for years of sage advice to come.

***Starman* (Vol. 2) #30–33 (May–Aug. 1995)** Jack is saved from death by the ghost of buccaneer Jon Valor and helps the legendary pirate achieve eternal rest.

***Starman* (Vol. 2) #77–79 (May–Jul. 2001)** Jack discovers that when his brother David died, he traveled back in time and, in conjunction with Dr. Mid-Nite, fought crime as a new Starman, while Ted Knight was incapacitated.

CONQUEROR OF WORLDS When Cobi bonded with a Starro parasite, he became an almost unstoppable warrior who could take down armies by himself.

STARRO THE STAR CONQUEROR

DEBUT (Starro) *The Brave and the Bold* (Vol. 1) #28 **(Feb.-Mar. 1960)**; (Starro the Conqueror/Cobi) *R.E.B.E.L.S.* (Vol. 2) #5 **(Aug. 2009)**
CURRENT VERSION *Justice League* (Vol. 2) #6 **(Apr. 2012)**
REAL NAME *Cobi*
EYES Black **HAIR** Bald
POWERS/ABILITIES Immense strength and durability; controls trillions of beings through Starro parasites; can spawn spores from body.
ALLIES The High Vanguard **ENEMIES** R.E.B.E.L.S.

LEAGUE OF LEGENDS A Starro alien discovered Earth and attempted to conquer it with its mind-control powers. Fortunately, it was defeated by the Justice League on the team's first official mission.

Starros are a race of giant starfish-like aliens that use their parasitic spores to enslave other species. The immense Starro Motherstars ventured across intergalactic space, conquering and assimilating inhabited worlds with their spores as they went.

The Starros attacked the planet of Hatorei and began incorporating the inhabitants, but the psychic link shared by the Hatorei enabled some of the populace to fight back. A youth named Cobi tore the Starro spore from his head, and when an immature Motherstar spore attacked, it became latched to his chest. They bonded, but Cobi was now in charge and exerted control over all the Starro species. He became Starro the Star Conqueror, controlling nine galaxies and exercising indomitable psychic control over trillions of beings. Starro the Star Conqueror's commanders were the High Vanguard, who were allowed to retain some of their free will.

Starro's forces made several attempts to conquer Earth. The first incursion was met by a gathering of heroes who joined forces to defeat the invaders, thereby forming the Justice Society of America. Subsequent attacks launched by an undeterred Starro were thwarted by Vril Dox and L.E.G.I.O.N. **SW**

FACE-OFF When a spore forced him to kill his own brother, Cobi escaped its control and ripped it from his head.

STEEL II

DEBUT *Justice League of America Annual* (Vol. 1) #2 **(Oct. 1984)**
CURRENT VERSION *Convergence: JLA* (Vol. 1) #1 **(Jun. 2015)**
REAL NAME Henry "Hank" Heywood III
HEIGHT 5ft 11in **WEIGHT** 379 lbs
EYES Blue **HAIR** Red
POWERS/ABILITIES Cybernetic enhancements, alloyed skeleton, and armored suit provide prodigious strength, speed, and durability.
ALLIES Hank Heywood, Sr. (grandfather), Dale Gunn
ENEMIES Brotherhood of Evil, Despero, Professor Ivo,
AFFILIATIONS Justice League of America, Justice League Detroit, the Bunker

After Hank Heywood Jr. was killed in Vietnam, his son—Henry "Hank" Heywood III—was raised by his grandfather, Hank Sr. Obsessed with creating the perfect fighting machine, the old man inflicted years of suffering on young Hank, experimenting on and enhancing the boy in desperate attempts to create a cyborg super-soldier.

Hank Heywood, Sr. had joined the Marines in World War II, but was severely injured by a bomb. His college mentor Dr. Gilbert Giles rebuilt him with metal bones and micro-motors, creating the prototype Super Hero Steel. As Steel, Heywood saved Winston Churchill and was about to assassinate Hitler, when he was captured and brainwashed. On returning, he tried to kill Churchill, but was stopped by the All-Star Squadron. Seemingly deprogrammed, Heywood was eventually promoted to "Commander Steel" by President Roosevelt before joining the All-Star team. After the war, Heywood made a fortune designing munitions, obsessed with the idea that America needed better human weapons to safeguard it.

Young Hank rejected his grandfather's plans for him and, wishing to use his enhancements to help ordinary people, joined the Justice League as Steel II. In Detroit, he provided the League with a Bunker base and together they faced many incredible situations, including a "lost year" in an alternate universe. The latter culminated in a clash with rival metahumans from a tangential reality to save Gotham City.

A valiant, indomitable warrior, Steel II fell into a coma while battling Professor Ivo's android and was killed by Despero, who destroyed his life-support systems. His grandfather outlived him by a few years, emerging from long retirement as Citizen Steel, only to perish battling the cosmic villain Eclipso.

MECHANICAL SOLDIER Commander Steel's steel bones and micro-motor implants made him one of the first successful cyborgs.

BROTHERS IN ARMS The only family feeling and comradeship Steel II had ever known was with the Justice League. He was proud to stand, fight, or die with them.

STEEL

DATA

DEBUT *Steel, the Indestructible Man* #1 **(Mar. 1978)**
CURRENT VERSION *Action Comics* (Vol. 2) #2 **(Dec. 2011)**
REAL NAME John Henry Irons
BASE Steelworks
HEIGHT 6ft 7in **WEIGHT** 290 lbs **EYES** Brown **HAIR** Bald
POWERS/ABILITIES Genius inventor; armored suit boosts strength and allows flight via rocket boots.
ALLIES Superman, Wonder Woman, Batman, Animal Man, Lana Lang, Suicide Squad
ENEMIES Metallo, the Rot, Brainiac
AFFILIATIONS Infinity, Inc.

PROTECTIVE SUIT
Irons' organic steel armor can prevent him from succumbing to otherworldly infections. He can extend the liquid metal to protect others.

PIER SUPPORT
During Brainiac's attack on Metropolis, Steel used the power of his suit to stop a bridge collapsing.

John Henry Irons was named after a hammer-swinging American folk hero. He used his technical expertise to create a suit of power armor and became the heavy-hitting hero Steel. A close friend and ally of Superman, he stood by the Man of Steel's side during conflicts with Brainiac and Doomsday. Irons is also the owner of Steelworks, a tech start-up dedicated to building a better world through technology.

Engineer John Henry Irons worked for General Sam Lane of the US military and developed the advanced Metal-0 cybernetic interface system for the Steel Soldier armor program. However, after Irons saw a captured Superman being subjected to torture by Lane's consultant Lex Luthor, he quit in disgust.

Irons put on his experimental upgraded Steel Solider armor when Brainiac launched an attack on Earth. Steel then helped Superman fight the Brainiac-controlled Metallo and protect Metropolis' civilians. Inspired by Superman's heroism, Irons also started the Steelworks Company to promote ethical uses of technology. He helped Animal Man fight the encroaching Rot, and joined the Suicide Squad in their battle against O.M.A.C. when the Crime Syndicate invaded Earth.

When the monstrous Doomsday was released from the Negative Zone and went on the rampage on Earth, Steel fought him in Africa and was infected by a contagion which caused cellular degeneration. However, Irons developed an organic steel skin which halted the process. When Superman was also infected with the Doomsday virus and was slowly transformed into a Doomsday-like monster, Irons protected his friend from attacks by Metallo and the Atomic Skull.

Steel and Lana Lang journeyed into space when Brainiac's fleet entered the Solar System preparing to launch another invasion of Earth. Together they fought Brainiac's minion, Cyborg Superman, and when their ship was damaged, Irons used his organic steel to save Lana's life. After Superman joined them and routed Brainiac's invasion, Irons and Lang began dating. **SW**

ON THE RECORD

In the pre-Flashpoint universe, engineer John Henry Irons created the advanced Toastmaster weapon for AmerTek Industries, but quit when his invention fell into the wrong hands. While Irons was working in construction, Superman saved his life after he fell from a skyscraper.

When the Man of Steel died in "The Death of Superman," Irons built an armored suit and became the hero Steel, one of four new champions who emerged to continue Superman's legacy. Irons was killed in battle during *Our Worlds at War*, but returned to life after being placed in the Entropy Aegis armor. Unfortunately, the Aegis took control of him, and Superman had to save him again.

Irons retired and his niece Natasha became Steel. He did put on the armor once more, becoming leader of Infinity, Inc.

TITLE FIGHT
After the death of Superman, Steel encountered the Action Ace's other successors, including Superboy (Kon-El).

CLASSIC STORIES

***Superman: The Man of Steel* #22-26 (Jun.-Oct. 1993)** After the death of Superman, John Henry Irons builds the Steel armor and becomes a hero to continue the legacy of Metropolis' greatest champion.

***Superman Versus Darkseid: Apokolips Now!* (Vol. 1) #1 (Mar. 2003)** When John Henry Irons is taken over by the Aegis armor, Superman leads an invasion of Apokolips to get his good friend back.

***Infinity, Inc.* (Vol. 2) #1-12 (Nov. 2007-Oct. 2008)** Steel leads a new Infinity, Inc. team, which includes his niece Natasha (Starlight/Vaporlock)—but they ultimately come into conflict with the team's backer, Lex Luthor.

STEPPENWOLF

DEBUT *New Gods* (Vol. 1) #7 **(Feb.–Mar. 1972)**
CURRENT VERSION *Justice League* (Vol. 2) #6 **(Apr. 2012)**
REAL NAME Steppenwolf
BASE Apokolips
HEIGHT 6ft **WEIGHT** 203 lbs **EYES** Black **HAIR** Red
POWERS/ABILITIES Cable snare weapon fires energy beams, and entraps opponents; electro-ax; expert swordsman.
ALLIES Darkseid **ENEMIES** Wonders, Brutaal **AFFILIATIONS** Hunger Dogs

FEAR AND FURY Steppenwolf sought to carve out his own Earthly empire beside his savage Amazon daughter, Fury.

An Apokoliptian general and commander of the Hunger Dogs, Steppenwolf led an army against Earth with Desaad until Cyborg hacked their Boom Tubes and trapped them on Earth-2. Undaunted, he attempted to conquer that world in Darkseid's name, using an Anti-Life Generator for mass mind-control and unleashing an army of Parademons.

Steppenwolf killed Earth-2's Wonder Woman and Kal-L before Batman sacrificed himself to spread a virus among the Parademons, leaving Steppenwolf at the mercy of the World Army and the Wonders. Steppenwolf died at the hands of the Superman clone known as Brutaal, who murdered him on live television.

He was revived by unknown means and once again took up war on Darkseid's behalf against Mobius the Anti-Monitor, who had become the Anti-God. **AI**

ON THE RECORD

Steppenwolf's previous incarnation was as Darkseid's uncle and the ruler of Apokolips, following the reign of Heggra, Darkseid's mother and Steppenwolf's sister. Darkseid used him to start a war between Apokolips and New Genesis—a war which ended when Steppenwolf was killed by Izaya the Inheritor. Revived thanks to advanced Apokoliptian technology, Steppenwolf died once more during the Death of the New Gods event.

OLD SOLDIERS NEVER DIE Darkseid's uncle despised petty politics and double-dealing, living only for the addictive thrill of combat and butchery.

STOMPA

DEBUT *Mister Miracle* (Vol. 1) #6 (Jan.–Feb. 1972)
CURRENT VERSION *Justice League* (Vol. 2) #50 (Jul. 2016)
BASE Apokolips
HEIGHT 5ft 8in **WEIGHT** 330 lbs
POWERS/ABILITIES Heavy matter boots can pulverize even the densest material.
ENEMIES Supergirl, Superman

Reared on distant Apokolips and personally trained for terror by the vile Granny Goodness, Stompa is a member of the much-feared Female Furies, an elite squad of women warriors belonging to Darkseid's Special Powers Force. As her name implies, Stompa uses her considerable bulk to great advantage when crushing the enemies of Darkseid beneath her boot heels. She is stronger than a Parademon and just as mean.

She was among the Furies dispatched to Earth by Darkseid to capture Kara Zor-El, Superman's Kryptonian cousin, so that the dreaded lord of Apokolips could mold the young Supergirl to do his bidding. As expected, this mission brought Stompa and the Female Furies into direct conflict with the Earth's finest heroes, particularly Superman and Batman, as two worlds struggled for the soul of the young Kryptonian girl. **SB**

STEWART, JOHN

DEBUT *Green Lantern* (Vol. 2) #87 **(Dec. 1971–Jan. 1972)**
CURRENT VERSION *Green Lantern Corps* (Vol. 3) #1 **(Nov. 2011)**
REAL NAME John Stewart
BASE Mogo
HEIGHT 6ft 1in **WEIGHT** 201 lbs **EYES** Black **HAIR** Brown
POWERS/ABILITIES Green Lantern ring generates hard-light constructs, permits space travel, contains enormous database of information from across the universe, and grants its wearer near-invulnerability.
ALLIES Hal Jordan, Guy Gardner, Fatality
ENEMIES Guardians, First Lantern
AFFILIATIONS Green Lantern Corps

Detroit native John Stewart became an architect after serving in the Marine Corps. He was brought into the Green Lantern Corps as Hal Jordan's backup after successfully passing the Guardians of the Universe's test. Here he met fellow human Lanterns—Jordan, Kyle Rayner, and Guy Gardner—and took on more of a leadership role after both Jordan and Rayner left the Corps.

Alongside Gardner, Stewart investigated a threat to the Oan defense network and was forced to kill a vulnerable fellow Lantern. The Alpha Lanterns sentenced him to death, but Gardner helped Stewart escape, which was when they discovered that the Guardians were using the Alpha Lanterns to destroy the Green Lantern Corps. The Guardians then raised the Third Army, cloned from the DNA of the First Lantern, Volthoom. During this battle, the sentient planet Mogo reformed itself and rejoined the Green Lantern Corps before Volthoom and the Third Army were destroyed. In the aftermath, Stewart based himself on the reformed Mogo and began working out the complex relationship between him and the Star Sapphire known as Fatality. His distinguished service record with the Lanterns has granted him admission to the Oan Honor Guard. **AI**

ONCE A MARINE... Before he was a Green Lantern, John Stewart was a Marine. The Corps is always with him.

ON THE RECORD

A signature feature of John Stewart's career as a Green Lantern has always been the conflict between peaceful goals and violent means. He has suffered a great deal personally since first accepting a power ring, losing his wife Katma Tui and suffering the guilt of accidentally destroying the planet Xanshi. A somewhat brighter point in his life came when he had the chance to put his architect's training to work designing the new Justice League of America headquarters in Washington DC.

POWER RING John Stewart first feels the power of the Green Lantern ring after being deemed fit by the Guardians of the Universe.

STORMWATCH

DEBUT *Stormwatch* #1 **(Mar. 1993)**
CURRENT VERSION *Stormwatch* (Vol. 3) #1 **(Nov. 2011)**
BASE Eye of the Storm, Skywatch
CURRENT MEMBERS/POWERS **Apollo**: Photon-powered energy projection, flight, superhuman strength; **Jack Hawksmoor**: Alien technology grants superpowers in urban environments; **Jenny Quantum**: Teleportation, force-field projection; **Midnighter**: Cybernetically enhanced strength, speed, and senses, as well as advanced hand-to-hand combat skills; **Projectionist**: Perception of and control over electronic communications.
ALLIES Shadow Cabinet
ENEMIES Daemonites, Hidden People

The origins of Stormwatch reach back into the Middle Ages, when its members were known as Demon Knights. Among their first members were Artisan, Madame Xanadu, and Vandal Savage. They first became known as Stormwatch during the 14th century, when they battled the extraterrestrial Daemonites. The group was typically formed around a Century Baby—a person given powers by virtue of being born at the stroke of midnight as a new century dawned. Stormwatch revealed itself to the world's governments in the 18th century, which its ruling Shadow Council soon decided was a mistake. They worked to erase the group's existence from known history, and were successful by the beginning of the next century.

As the 21st century dawned, the group was in danger of losing its way, as its historical mission of combating alien threats now faced competition from the Justice League. Adam One (the avatar of Merlin, one of Stormwatch's original members) recruited a new Century Baby, Jenny Quantum, to maintain the group in the new era. Other core members included Jack Hawksmoor, Apollo, and the Midnighter, and briefly the Martian Manhunter. They battled the Daemonites, the Hidden People, and the Red Lanterns, among other threats, while keeping their existence and membership secret. **AI**

KEEPING WATCH
The core members of Stormwatch, maintain their vigil against threats from the vastness of space.
1 Midnighter
2 Jack Hawksmoor
3 Jenny Quantum
4 Projectionist
5 Apollo

ON THE RECORD

The original Stormwatch was formed in the wake of a disaster on board Monitor One, a UN space station. The event transformed the station's Team One into the dangerous Warguard, who were defeated and a new team—Stormwatch—recruited in its place. Its members were "Seedlings," humans who had been granted superpowers. Now based on an orbital platform called Skywatch, they monitored both terrestrial and alien threats.

THE PRICE OF VIGILANCE
Though no hostile force could long deter Earth's metahuman watchmen, internal dissent and hidden agendas would eventually tear the team apart.

STRANGE, ADAM

DEBUT *Showcase* #17 **(Nov.-Dec. 1958)**
CURRENT VERSION *Justice League United* #0 **(Jun. 2014)**
REAL NAME Adam Strange
BASE Rann
HEIGHT 6ft **WEIGHT** 175 lbs
EYES Blue **HAIR** Blond
POWERS/ABILITIES Expert pilot and multi-talented adventurer; uses advanced Rannian technology including guns and space suit.
ALLIES Alanna, Sardath
AFFILIATIONS Justice League United

Anthropologist Adam Strange was working a dig near James Bay in northern Ontario with his student Alanna Lewis when a strange beam made Alanna disappear. He later discovered a strange skeleton, which he showed to the heroes Animal Man and Star Girl. They investigated and came across what appeared to be a mass grave of aliens—and then a secret underground alien base. Fighting off an attack, Strange was knocked down into the base. Arming himself with a nearby jet-pack-powered space suit and a powerful ray gun, he rejoined the fight. He and the rest of the new Justice League United were then transported to Rann, where they learned that Byth Rok was responsible for Alanna's abduction.

The unpredictable Zeta Beam, which had transported them to Rann, then sent them back to Earth. Strange was reunited with Alanna as he and the JLU battled Ultra the Multi-Alien. Moving back and forth between Earth and Rann, Strange (now married to Alanna) fought Byth Rok with help from the time-displaced Legion of Super-Heroes. Strange and the JLU would later participate in the Justice League of America's counterattack against Vandal Savage when he besieged the JLA's Watchtower. **AI**

HAVE JET-PACK, WILL TRAVEL
Adam Strange experiments with the new technological wonders he found in the alien scientists' underground base.

ON THE RECORD

Adam Strange was introduced in 1958 in DC Comics' *Showcase* title, which also launched the career of the Silver Age Flash (Barry Allen). In his debut story, Adam was an anthropologist and adventurer, who was transported to Rann by a Zeta Beam experiment conducted on the scientifically advanced planet Rann. On his arrival, he fell for Alanna, daughter of the scientist Sardath, who had created the Zeta Beam.

More adventures followed, each limited to the fluctuating duration of the Zeta Beam's powers—which prolonged the blooming romance between Strange and Alanna. They were married on Rann, with the Justice League of America present.

BRAIN OVER BRAVADO
With every new threat he faced, Adam Strange became more famous for relying on his wits as much as his weaponry... and iconic wardrobe.

STRANGE, HUGO

DEBUT *Detective Comics* #36 **(Feb. 1940)**
CURRENT VERSION *Detective Comics* (Vol. 2) #5 **(Mar. 2012)**
BASE Gotham City **REAL NAME** Hugo Strange
HEIGHT 5ft 10in **WEIGHT** 170 lbs **EYES** Gray **HAIR** None
POWERS/ABILITIES Trained in psychology; brilliant deductive mind.
ENEMIES Batman

Psychologist Hugo Strange was recruited to Wayne Enterprises by acting CEO Philip Kane while Bruce Wayne was on extended leave following his parents' murder. Strange was tasked with researching the mysteries of the mind by exploring the overlap between the physiology and the psychology of the brain. After Bruce Wayne's return, Strange left Wayne Enterprises and established a new research lab at Arkham Asylum, studying the aberrant brains of its inmates and forming a working relationship with Harleen Quinzel. Strange also reconnected with his estranged son Eli, when Eli was caught cheating at cards by some Russian gangsters and narrowly avoided being killed. Strange brought Eli in on a plot to release the Scarecrow's Fear Gas over Gotham City.

While at Arkham, Strange was recruited into the Secret Society of Super-Villains by the Outsider, where his role was largely behind the scenes. He also continued his medical practice, working with Roy Harper, among others. This allowed him to involve the Outlaws in yet another scheme. **AI**

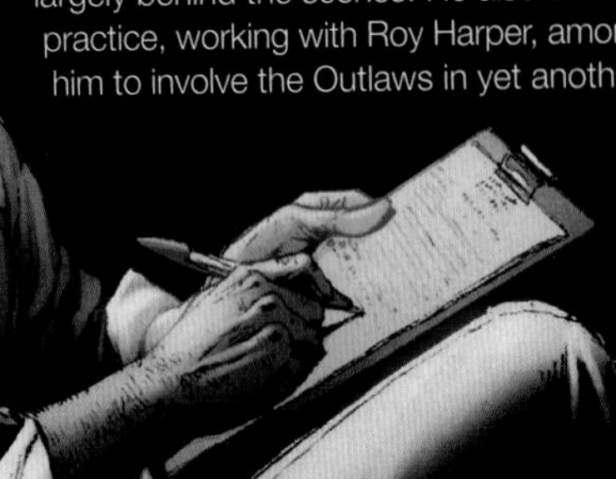

ALL IN THE MIND
As a professional psychologist, Hugo Strange was in a powerful position of authority to advance his own evil schemes.

ON THE RECORD

Hugo Strange was one of very few people who had deduced Batman's secret identity. He rose to fame as a psychological consultant on Gotham City talk shows, speculating on Batman's psyche and motivations. Fortunately for Batman, Strange's own psychological instability always made it difficult for him to remember what he knew for very long, so the Dark Knight avoided the danger of having his identity widely known.

MASKED MANIA
The master schemer was driven by a singular obsession with Batman.

STRIFE

DEBUT *Wonder Woman* **(Vol. 1) #183 (Jul.–Aug. 1969)**
CURRENT VERSION *Wonder Woman* **(Vol. 4) #2 (Dec. 2011)**
BASE Olympus
REAL NAME Eris
EYES Gold **HAIR** White
POWERS/ABILITIES Vast supernatural powers granted to Olympian Gods.
ENEMIES First Born
AFFILIATIONS Olympus

Sister to Ares, Strife was spiteful in an almost childlike way. It was her nature to disrupt any peace or alliance and she delighted in creating confusion among enemies and allies alike. This made her true allegiances extremely difficult to discern.

Strife saw the disappearance of Zeus from Olympus as a perfect chance to cause chaos among the Amazons, as well as on Mount Olympus. She appeared on Themyscira and carefully let slip the secret of her half-sister Wonder Woman's origin, causing Diana to leave Themyscira for a time, and revealing the Amazon Queen Hippolyta's dalliance with Zeus. At the same time, Strife fomented division among the Amazons, leading to the creation of Donna Troy and a civil war on Themyscira. This, in turn, resulted in the unprovoked massacre of the Sons of Hephaestus. **AI**

STRIPESY

DEBUT *Star-Spangled Comics* **#1 (Oct. 1941)**
CURRENT VERSION *Justice League of America* **(Vol. 3) #10 (Feb. 2014)**
BASE Blue Valley, Nebraska
REAL NAME Patrick Dugan
HEIGHT 6ft 1in **WEIGHT** 210 lbs
EYES Blue **HAIR** Red
POWERS/ABILITIES Great intellect and skill as a mechanic.

Pat Dugan was Sylvester Pemberton III's chauffeur when they respectively became Stripesy and the Star-Spangled Kid. After many World War II exploits, the duo joined the Seven Soldiers of Victory, and after one mission were briefly stranded in time. On Pat's return to the present he married and had a son, Michael. Sadly, Pat's exposure to the timestream caused Michael to rapidly age, a process that was only halted by the magical heroes of the JSA.

Pat later divorced and married Barbara Whitmore. When Pat's stepdaughter, Courtney Whitmore, laid claim to the Star-Spangled Kid's cosmic belt, Pat returned to Super Hero action in a robot battlesuit and the duo became Stargirl and S.T.R.I.P.E. The family moved to Metropolis to work with John Henry Irons' Steelworks, and later returned to Blue Valley. **AI**

STRIX

DEBUT *Batgirl* **(Vol. 4) #9 (Jul. 2012)**
BASE Gotham City
REAL NAME Mary Turner
HEIGHT 5ft 6in **WEIGHT** 125 lbs
EYES Brown **HAIR** Black
POWERS/ABILITIES Immortality; healing; acrobatics; martial arts; swordsmanship.
ALLIES Catwoman
ENEMIES Court of Owls
AFFILIATIONS Birds of Prey

Mary Turner suffered disfiguring burns during World War II when a Japanese fire balloon exploded in her Oregon hometown, killing her family. She was a circus acrobat before joining the Court of Owls, which gave her a Talon's powers of immortality and healing.

During the Court's war with the Batman Family, she fought Batgirl and Catwoman. She switched sides out of sympathy for Batgirl, who brought her into the Birds of Prey. With them, she fought agents of Basilisk and the Court of Owls.

Mr. Freeze forced Strix to take him to the lab where she had received her Talon powers by threatening to kill Birds of Prey agent Starling. Strix soon discovered she had walked into a trap—Starling had betrayed Strix and allied with Mr. Freeze. **AI**

SUPERMEN OF AMERICA

DEBUT *Supermen of America* **#1 (Mar. 1999)**
BASE Metropolis
MEMBERS/POWERS **Brahma** (Cal Usjak): Super-strength and invulnerability; **Loser** (Theo Storm): Possesses powerful dermal force field; **Maximum** (Max Williams): Channels bursts of superhuman energy; **Outburst** (Mitch Anderson): Manipulates magnetic fields; **Pyrogen** (Claudio Tielli): Flame-controlling pyrokinetic; **White Lotus** (Nona Lin): Martial artist; mystic aura generates a force field she can manipulate.
ALLIES Lex Luthor
ENEMIES O.M.A.C.

A heroic power vacuum left by Superman's brief departure from Metropolis to defend Earth gave rise to the Supermen of America. This team of teen heroes was unexpectedly sponsored by Superman's perennial opponent, Metropolis mogul Lex Luthor.

When Junior K-D, the lead singer of the band Crossfire, was gunned down during a benefit concert in Metropolis, the ensuing chaos forced teen hero Outburst into action. With Superman as his inspiration, Outburst eagerly accepted Lex Luthor's offer to recruit a force of young metahumans. He had soon gathered Brahma, Loser, Psilencer, Pyrogen, and White Lotus to serve as Supermen of America. The group helped to quell gang violence on Metropolis' streets and even tackled super-villains emboldened by Superman's temporary absence. When Psilencer was struck down by a gang member's bullet, he was replaced by the super-athletic Maximum. The Supermen of America eventually left Luthor's employ, later participating in the global fight against O.M.A.C.'s units prior to the Infinite Crisis, an event that left many of their members grievously injured. **AI**

HERE COME THE SUPERMEN!
1 Outburst **2 Brahma** **3 White Lotus** **4 Loser** **5 Pyrogen** **6 Maximum**

SWAMP THING

DATA

DEBUT *House of Secrets* #92 **(Jun.–Jul. 1971)**
CURRENT VERSION *Swamp Thing* (Vol. 5) #1 **(Nov. 2011)**
REAL NAME Alec Holland
BASE Houma, Louisiana
HEIGHT Variable **WEIGHT** Variable
EYES Red **HAIR** None
POWERS/ABILITIES Avatar of the Green, the cosmic energy that animates all plant life; can appear wherever there is life; can manipulate plant matter; travel in time; shape size and shape; possess prodigous strength and regenerative powers.
ALLIES Parliament of Trees
ENEMIES Anton Arcane, the Black
AFFILIATIONS The Green

AVATAR OF THE GREEN
The Swamp Thing is the living embodiment of the elemental force that animates all plant life in the known universe.

CLASSIC STORIES

***House of Secrets* #92 (Jul. 1971)** Swamp Thing's origin. Scientist Alec Holland is transformed into the elemental creature after being immersed in a chemically polluted swamp.

***Saga of Swamp Thing* #34 (Mar. 1985)** The mutual attraction between Swamp Thing and Abigail Cable, daughter of his nemesis Anton Arcane, blossoms into love.

***Swamp Thing* (Vol. 2) #37-50 (Jun. 1985–Jul. 1986)** John Constantine guides the Swamp Thing towards an understanding of his true powers as a member of the Parliament of Trees.

***Swamp Thing* (Vol. 2) #166–171 (May–Oct. 1996)** Having subsumed each of Earth's elemental Parliaments, The Swamp Thing takes his place in the Parliament of Worlds as its representative of the entire planet.

GREEN CHAMPION
Holland's bio-restorative formula was seen as a boon by the Green, but a threat by the Rot.

The Swamp Thing is the avatar of the Green: the mysterious force inherent in all plant life. Given physical form by botanist Alec Holland, he is the protector of the Parliament of Trees and the mortal enemy of anyone who threatens the natural balance of the Green.

Botanist Alec Holland, haunted by inexplicable memories of his own death—and visions of a life he had not lived—tried to find peace by leaving his scientific work and making a living as a carpenter. He soon found that destiny was not so easily avoided, however, when an emissary of the Green confirmed that he had in fact died. He was meant to have become Swamp Thing, but that fate did not come to pass when his death prevented his body from merging with the Green. Meeting Abigail Arcane, whom he recognized from those same fleeting memories, Alec was drawn into an elemental war between the Green and the force of death and decay called the Black, also known as the Rot.

Animal Man, avatar of the animal force called the Red, joined Alec in this fight between the forces of life and those of decay and death. When Alec was mortally injured by agents of the Rot, the Parliament of Trees—priomordial plant elementals—transformed him into Swamp Thing, and he saved Abby from becoming the horrific Black Queen, the Avatar of the Rot.

As Swamp Thing, Holland destroyed the soulless version of the creature that had existed before him. He fought the Rot, finally overcoming its new avatar, Anton Arcane, who had tried to seize control of the Rot. On the behest of the Parliament of Trees, Swamp Thing also fought a duel with Jason Woodrue—known as the Seeder—to determine which of them would become the champion of the Green. Woodrue briefly took up the mantle after Swamp Thing spared his life, but ultimately Swamp Thing triumphed and finally assumed his destined role as Avatar of the Green. **AI**

ON THE RECORD

There have always been Avatars of the Green, and three of them have had their Swamp Thing stories told: World War II pilot Albert Höllerer, Aaron Hayle, and Allan Hallman. From his origins in the pulp horror tradition, the character of the Swamp Thing has evolved over the years to become a way to explore environmental issues.

The 1972 Alec Holland origin story transformed him into the Swamp Thing after chemical exposure, engaging the emerging environmental consciousness of the time. Later the character came to represent the entire natural world, at war not just with individual villains, but with the human impulse to dominate and destroy nature.

NATURE'S REVENGE
The Swamp Thing has always been a warning of the dire consquences of polluting the natural world.

UNITED FRONT
Swamp Thing and Animal Man united the Green and the Red against the horde of Rotlings.

SUICIDE SQUAD

DATA

DEBUT *The Brave and the Bold* #25 **(Aug.-Sep. 1959)**
CURRENT VERSION *Suicide Squad* (Vol. 4) #1 **(Nov. 2011)**
REAL NAME Task Force X
BASE Belle Reve Penitentiary
ORIGINAL MEMBERS AND POWERS
AMANDA WALLER Highly trained soldier, covert operative
DEADSHOT (FLOYD LAWTON) Expert marksman
HARLEY QUINN (HARLEEN QUINZEL) Insane ex-psychiatrist
CAPTAIN BOOMERANG (GEORGE HARKNESS) Assassin
EL DIABLO (CHATO SANTANA) Pyrokinetic powers
BLACK SPIDER (DERRICK COE) Gotham City vigilante
KING SHARK (NANAUE) Humanoid shark, immense strength
VOLTAIC (VOLTAIC) Electrokinesis
FORMER MEMBERS
CHEETAH (BARBARA MINERVA) Catlike claws and teeth
REVERSE-FLASH (DANIEL WEST) Time travel
BLACK MANTA (BLACK MANTA) Expert combatant
JAMES GORDON, JR. Psychopath
THE UNKNOWN SOLDIER Arms expert
YO-YO (CHANG JIE-RU) Amazing elasticity
DEATHSTOKE (SLADE WILSON) Military tactician, mercenary
JOKER'S DAUGHTER (DUELA DENT) Psychotic, agile
ALLIES None
ENEMIES Basilisk, Crime Syndicate

The Suicide Squad is the nickname for Task Force X, a team of super-villains brought together by Amanda Waller to perform black ops missions of a highly dangerous nature. The members are among the most ruthless, craziest, and cold-blooded killers in the world—most sentenced to life-imprisonment in Belle Reve Penitentiary. The Squad has an ever-changing membership, but some villains—such as Harley Quinn and Deadshot—have survived several missions. If they stay alive, the squad members have their jail-time reduced or they can gain extra prison privileges.

When Amanda Waller became aware of the threat posed by the criminal Regulus and his Basilisk terror organization, she told the government she needed a new team to combat them. She wanted a squad made up of individuals who were easily expendable—super-villains. Waller tried out 37 potential candidates for the new group—all taken from the deadliest inmates of the notorious Belle Reve Penitentiary. The candidates were put through a lethal series of tests to see if they would break under pressure. Only six made it: Harley Quinn, Deadshot, Black Spider, El Diablo, King Shark, and Voltaic. They became the first members of Task Force X—nicknamed the Suicide Squad because of the high expected mortality rate.

RIGOROUS RECRUITMENT
The team was sent on a bogus mission and each person tortured to prove they were loyal and tough enough to join the squad.

Their first official mission was inside the Megadome in Mississippi, where 60,000 people had been infected with a technovirus that transformed them into zombie-like creatures. The group was tasked with terminating the infected and rescuing patient zero—who turned out to be a newborn baby that was immune to the virus. At the end of the mission, Deadshot killed teammate Voltaic, who was subsequently blamed for the outbreak.

Later missions for the team saw them take on Regulus and his Basilisk organization, and hunt one of their own when Harley Quinn went on the run after learning that the Joker—her ex-lover—was dead. Not all members survived their missions, with the dead quickly replaced by other super-villains. Yo-Yo and Captain Boomerang joined the team, replacing the deceased Voltaic and injured Black Spider. Some of the villains killed during missions were later resurrected using the Samsara serum that Waller had developed. Waller also introduced resident psychopath James Gordon Jr. to the team to act as their psychiatrist.

TERROR ATTACK
The Suicide Squad's second mission took the fight to the Basilisk terrorist network.

AT A GLANCE...

Loyalty insurance
Having survived the severe selection procedure, each criminal chosen by Amanda Waller had a nanite bomb injected into his or her neck. If they went rogue, the bomb would explode—a sure way to guarantee their loyalty to Amanda's cause.

Belle Reve
Amanda took her potential candidates from the notorious Belle Reve Penitentiary, which houses metahuman criminals and super-villains. Close to the Gulf of Mexico, the prison is surrounded by swampland.

CLASSIC STORIES

***The Brave and the Bold* #25 (Aug.-Sep. 1959)** The original Suicide Squad makes its first appearance as Colonel Rick Flag leads a team of scientists against a monster that terrorizes a seaside resort.
***Legends* #1 (Nov. 1986)** Amanda Waller and Rick Flag start Task Force X as an ancient evil threatens the world.
***Suicide Squad* (Vol. 1) #26 (Apr. 1989)** Rick Flag, the Squad's first team leader, is killed by a nuclear bomb.
***Suicide Squad* (Vol. 4) #1 (Sep. 2011)** Amanda Waller puts Deadshot and his fellow super-villains through a deadly fake mission to see if they are suitable for Task Force X.

DARK TRUTH
When the world learned that Clark Kent was Superman, the Suicide Squad was sent to test his abilities. The group drafted for the mission consisted of Deadshot, Harley Quinn, Reverse-Flash, Black Manta, and Captain Boomerang.

They faced a weakened Man of Steel whose powers had been taken by Vandal Savage, but with Wonder Woman fighting at Superman's side, Harley and Black Manta were soon taken out of action. When Superman and Wonder Woman sought answers for why the Squad had attacked, they were blasted by Deadshot with high-velocity armor-piercing shells. All the while, the fight was being watched by mysterious figures wanting information on Superman's impaired condition.

TEST OF STRENGTH
As Superman and Wonder Woman investigated the disappearance of people in Smallville, they were set upon by the Suicide Squad.

EVIL ATTACKS

After taking over the world, the Crime Syndicate tasked the Thinker with gaining control of a powerful O.M.A.C. (One Machine Attack Construct), one of the few weapons that could hurt the Syndicate. The Thinker had manipulated Power Girl, Unknown Soldier, Steel, and Warrant into fighting the Suicide Squad to help him with his plan. The heroes eventually realized they had been tricked, and joined the Suicide Squad to stop OMAC. Waller used special "bullets" to increase her team's strength, and with help from Kevin Kho, whose consciousness originally controlled OMAC, the Squad emerged victorious. Captain Boomerang then sent OMAC into the "toilet" (a gateway to places unknown) despite Kho having regained control of the construct.

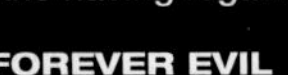

FOREVER EVIL
The Suicide Squad tried to stop the Crime Syndicate gaining control of OMAC.

REBIRTH

BUSINESS AS USUAL

With the world spiralling into even greater chaos than usual, Amanda Waller resurrects and redeems disgraced military legend Rick Flag, entrusting him with restoring Task Force X to full combat effectiveness.

Can the traumatized and disaffected veteran possibly be a match for Waller's rebellious and unwilling recruits, and the deadly modern menaces that she happily expends Suicide Squad against?

When the Crime Syndicate seized control of the world, Waller and the Suicide Squad tried to stop them acquiring a deadly O.M.A.C. unit. Following the Syndicate's defeat, Waller found her position undermined by government agent Vic Sage, who assembled a new Suicide Squad. In this line-up, Deadshot and Harley Quinn were joined by the Joker's Daughter, Black Manta, and Deathstroke—although the latter left the team during their first mission, and Harley Quinn beat the Joker's Daughter senseless to try and end her obsession with the Clown Prince of Crime. Reverse-Flash and Captain Boomerang were then drafted into the team and sent on a mission to destroy a Chinese base creating superpowered clones. Reverse-Flash was later killed in action during a mission in the Middle-East. When Vic Sage became involved with a corrupt corporation called the Pearl Group, he started to use the Suicide Squad to further the company's goals, something that brought him into further conflict with Amanda Waller. Not prepared to let Sage ruin what she had started and nurtured, Waller eventually regained complete control of Task Force X and had Sage arrested for his machinations. **AC**

"I want to use prisoners with nothing to lose and everything to gain. I want to create a Suicide Squad."

AMANDA WALLER

DEADLY FORCE
The Suicide Squad's members risk everything on their missions, with some not surviving.
1 Amanda Waller
2 Harley Quinn
3 Enchantress
4 Captain Boomerang
5 Parasite
6 Deadshot
7 Katana

ON THE RECORD

The Suicide Squad has changed a great deal since its first appearance in the *The Brave and the Bold*. The original Suicide Squad was a group of heroes led by Colonel Rick Flagg—the pilot of their base, the Flying Laboratory. The team also included chief medic Karin Grace, an astronomer Dr. Evans, and a physicist called Jess Bright. They investigated Fortean subject matter and often fought strange monsters and aliens.

Villainous legends
During the "Legends" miniseries, the modern Suicide Squad made their first dramatic appearance. This team was made up of imprisoned super-villains drafted into the Suicide Squad by Amanda Waller, a far different and more powerful looking woman in this incarnation. The team included villains such as Captain Boomerang and Deadshot, and their leader in the early missions was Rick Flagg, but he was eventually killed in action.

Task Force Omega
A later Suicide Squad—named Task Force Omega—was led by Sgt. Rock and originally included members who had once been part of the Injustice Society. Everyone except Major Disaster died on the team's first mission. Sgt. Rock recruited more villains for the team, bringing in the likes of Deadshot and Killer Frost. The team was eventually captured by a group called Onslaught. Some members were rescued by the Justice Society, who could only find a mask of Sgt. Rock in the cell where he was been held, implying their leader had been an imposter.

SUPERBOY

DATA

DEBUT *More Fun Comics* (Vol. 1) #101 **(Jan.-Feb. 1945)** (Superman as a boy); *Adventures of Superman* (Vol. 1) #500 **(Jun. 1993)** (Conner Kent, the clone)
CURRENT VERSION *Superboy* (Vol. 6) #1; *Teen Titans* (Vol. 4) #1 **(Nov. 2011)**
REAL NAME Kon-El
BASE New York City
HEIGHT 5ft 7in **WEIGHT** 150 lbs **EYES** Blue **HAIR** Black
POWERS/ABILITIES Limited telepathy; instinctive multilingualism; genius intellect; augmented recuperation; tactile telekinesis; limited level of physical powers such as flight, super-strength, invulnerability; and augmented senses deriving from partial Kryptonian genetic structure under a yellow sun.
ALLIES Superman, Caitlin Fairchild, Wonder Girl, Krypto, Red Robin, Bunker
ENEMIES Harvest, H'El, Jon Lane Kent, Rose Wilson, Zaniel Templar, Dr. Psycho, H.I.V.E., Psycho Pirate
AFFILIATIONS Teen Titans, N.O.W.H.E.R.E., Ravagers, Legion Lost, S.T.A.R. Labs

Some heroes are made, not born. A combination of human, Kryptonian, and unknown DNA, Superboy was an outsider from his inception. Grown in mere months by covert cabal N.O.W.H.E.R.E., he was being terminated as a failed experiment when he spontaneously achieved full consciousness. Displaying terrifying psionic abilities, he escaped. Over time, his powers matured into a unique combination of physical and mental abilities. His transition from emotionless tool to Super Hero took far longer, requiring constant struggle and the forging of true friendships in the fires of battle.

Constantly seeking his origins, Superboy at first believed he was designed to be a living weapon. After many battles with his creators, he eventually discovered his original purpose was to provide a cure for a genetically unstable human/Kryptonian boy, whose mixed heritage was slowly killing him. The fanatical, metahuman-hating time-traveler Harvest had cloned Superboy using genetic material from Jon Lane Kent, the son of an alternate-future Earth's Superman and Lois Lane.

The haunted hero, dubbed "Kon" by Supergirl, was the second such attempt create a "super boy." Somewhere there existed a predecessor, also cloned by N.O.W.H.E.R.E. for their sponsor Harvest. This one had inexplicably vanished from their labs and remained at large…

After escaping, Superboy was recaptured and reprogrammed by N.O.W.H.E.R.E.: re-purposed to capture the youngest and most malleable metahumans springing up all over the world. Finding that the ultimate purpose was to pit them against each other in death-matches and recruit the survivors to an army of killers, Kon shook off Harvest's influence began charting his own course.

THE CLONE COMES ALIVE
Superboy suddenly gained full awareness inside his mechanized gestation tank. Terrified, he escaped and became the world's most dangerous three-month-old fugitive.

This transition was guided by new-found allies, but the naive Kon made many mistakes—such as stealing from banks because they wouldn't miss the money. Eventually, however, he was set firmly on the right path.

At less than a year old, he was almost destroyed by H'El, a monster claiming kinship with the El family. H'El interrupted a grand scheme to restore Krypton just to attack the cloned abomination. He was ultimately foiled by a coalition of Superman's extended Earth family, the Justice League, and Kon and his Teen Titans comrades.

H'El later returned, using time itself as his weapon to strand Superman, Supergirl, and Superboy in different eras of Krypton's history. This inadvertently allowed Superboy to achieve his greatest triumph by lifting Argo City free of Krypton's immense gravity and allowing it—albeit briefly—to escape the doom that destroyed Krypton.

Time-travel once again brought trouble to Kon-El when the Teen Titans were projected into the future by Earth-3's Johnny Quick. While his teammates encountered the last heroes of a doomed Earth, Kon was attacked by his genetic donor Jon Lane Kent. Kon won the battle, but at the moment of victory was sucked into the timestream, and Jon seamlessly replaced him when the Titans returned to the era of their origin.

With the multiverse imperiled by chronal paradox, Jon, Kon, and multiple Superboy iterations clashed. Jon was erased from existence by his own better self, and reality righted itself, leaving a wiser, more composed Kon as Earth's one and only Superboy. **WW**

H'EL BENT
Determined to eradicate Earth and restore Krypton, H'El attempted to psionically separate hybrid clone Kon's human and Kryptonian halves.

AT A GLANCE...

Kon-El, the abomination"
When Superboy met Supergirl, his unpredictable abilities psionically linked them. He shared her memories of home and acquired her language, while she learned he was a clone and viciously attacked him. On Krypton, clones had fought a bloody war against their creators and been deemed monsters thereafter. Supergirl spitefully declared Superboy Kon-El—"abomination of the House of El"—predicting that he too would become a mindless killing machine.

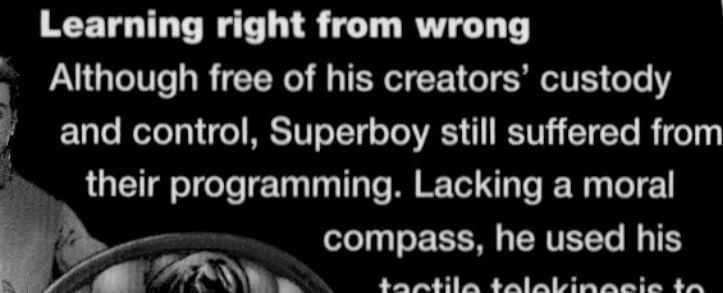

Titans together
Ordered by N.O.W.H.E.R.E.'s commander, Templar, to capture Wonder Girl, Superboy subsequently battled her comrades in the Teen Titans. From this violent clash of temperaments true friendships developed and Superboy eventually joined the team of like-minded, misunderstood youngsters, all looking for their place in the world.

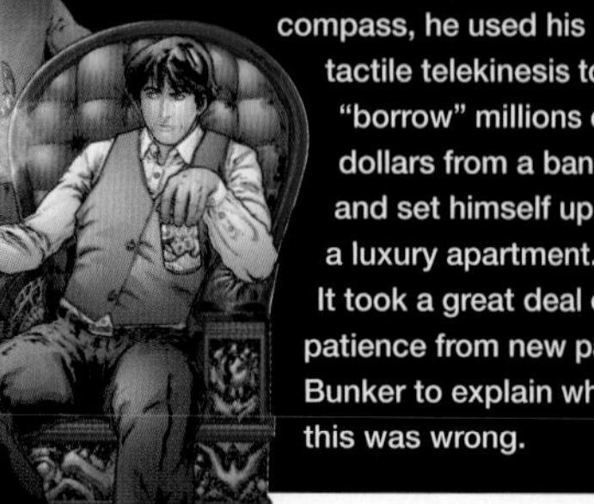

Learning right from wrong
Although free of his creators' custody and control, Superboy still suffered from their programming. Lacking a moral compass, he used his tactile telekinesis to "borrow" millions of dollars from a bank and set himself up in a luxury apartment. It took a great deal of patience from new pal Bunker to explain why this was wrong.

CLASSIC STORIES

***Adventure Comics* #210 (Mar. 1955)** One of Jor-El's lab specimens lands on Earth and Superboy has a euphoric reunion with his childhood pet, Krypto the Super-Dog.
***Superman* (Vol. 1) #97 (May 1955)** Superman wistfully recalls his last day in Smallville, an occasion that saw the entire population honor their native son before he left for Metropolis.
***Adventure Comics* (Vol. 1) #271 (Apr. 1960)** Superboy's great friendship with Lex Luthor ends badly when a lab accident destroys the boy genius' hair.
***DC Comics Presents* (Vol. 1) #87 (Nov. 1985)** As *Crisis on Infinite Earths* unfolds, a naïve and inexperienced new Superboy is introduced to the world.

DEFYING HIS ORIGINS
Although painfully aware he was cobbled together from other beings, Superboy was always ready to prove he was no cheap copy.

"This is my symbol, too... and I want people to know it."

SUPERBOY

REBIRTH

SUPER SON

Out of the blue, a new Superboy appears on the scene: a 10-year old youngster cautiously coming to terms with his daily growing arsenal of superpowers and tired of hiding out from the world.

Jonathan Kent II lives under the radar with his parents—the Superman and Lois Lane of a parallel world who have secretly made their home on Earth—where he learns to use his abilities for the benefit of humanity.

Living as "Jon White," Superboy has one friend who knows the truth: Damian Wayne, aka Robin, son of Batman, who is a reluctant partner in their ongoing heroic ventures.

ON THE RECORD

As first conceived, Superboy was a light-hearted look at "the adventures of Superman when he was a boy." These short tales were aimed at younger fans and geared for laughs rather than dramatic action. Superboy's adventures soon expanded into a secondary continuity, occurring 20 years prior to his adult incarnation's exploits.

A boy's life

The Silver Age Superboy provided years of family-oriented fun, blending action with intrigue, while slowly revealing many secrets of long-lost Krypton and how Superman became the World's Greatest Hero. When not foiling Lana Lang's attempts to prove that he was the Boy of Steel, Clark Kent was slowly gaining the experience needed for his future life. One particularly memorable moment came when the young hero learned to fly, thanks to Pa Kent and a large number of balloons.

BAD ATTITUDE
Conner may have looked like a young teen, but the new Metropolis Marvel always insisted: "Don't call me Super-BOY!"

A new kid on the block

Re-imagined in the 1990s, Superboy—later adopting the name Kon-El—was a cocky partial clone of Superman with telekinetic abilities mimicking, if not equaling, many of the Man of Steel's powers. Kon-El learned that, owing to his artificial origins, he would never age and was doomed to remain a minor for the rest of his life. Joining the Teen Titans, he carved out a stellar career as a true hero, gaining a selfless companion in Super-Dog Krypto and learning important life-lessons as Conner Kent, the latest foster-son of Jonathan and Martha Kent in Smallville, Kansas.

PRIMED FOR BATTLE
Though Conner Kent was completely out-powered by Superboy-Prime, the insane alternate had no answer to the clone's never-quit spirit.

Universally challenged

The most dramatic and shocking interpretation of Superboy came out of the Infinite Crisis. The boy of Steel from an alternate Earth where he was the only metahuman went mad after his entire universe was obliterated. Determined to change reality to fit his desires, this deranged Superboy-Prime went on to became one of the most ruthless and bloodthirsty monsters in comic book history.

KNOW THYSELF

While tumbling through time with the Teen Titans, Kon was replaced by his genetic forebear, Jon Lane Kent. Indoctrinated by Harvest, this murderous son of Superman and Lois Lane wanted to kill and consume all of Earth's metahumans; however, his psychic connection to Kon gradually weakened his resolve. Kon and Jon were eventually physically and psychically reconciled during a paradox-bending convocation of Superboys from every corner of the multiverse.

I AM LEGION
Kon-El was astounded by the apparently infinite number and bizarre variety of Superboys who populated virtually every aspect of creation.

SUPERGIRL

DATA

DEBUT *Action Comics* (Vol. 1) #252 **(May 1959)**
CURRENT VERSION *Supergirl* (Vol. 6) #1 **(Nov. 2011)**
REAL NAME Kara Zor-El
BASE New York City, Citadel Academy
HEIGHT 5ft 5in **WEIGHT** 135 lbs **EYES** Blue **HAIR** Blond
POWERS/ABILITIES Super-strength, speed, flight, invulnerability, enhanced senses, super-flare burst, regeneration, and rapid-healing fueled by direct and close exposure to solar energy from a yellow sun.
ALLIES Siobhan Smythe/Silver Banshee, Michael Harris, Superman, Superboy, Dr. Shay Veritas, Power Girl, Red Hood, Tsavo, Comet, Maxima, Preceptor Lys Amata
ENEMIES H'El, Simon Tycho, Reign, the Worldkillers, Cyborg-Superman, Lobo, Brainiac, Preceptor Korstus
AFFILIATIONS Red Lantern Corps, Crucible Academy, I'noxian Collective

When Supergirl crash-landed on Earth nobody—not even her cousin Superman—knew whether she would become one of its greatest defenders or most dangerous threats. Rocketed from Krypton and finding herself on a primitive world where every hand seemed raised against her, Kara Zor-El initially reacted with petulance and impatience. Moreover, she could barely control the incredible powers she manifested. Her new, superhuman strength and senses terrified her. Eventually, with the help of new friends, she adapted, abandoning anger, frustration, and loneliness to become a dedicated protector of life on Earth and across the cosmos.

AT A GLANCE...

Kara's best friend
Unable to understand human speech, Kara's first chance to truly communicate came after meeting Siobhan Smythe. Siobhan possessed the power to speak any language—the only advantage of being mortal host to the mystic predator Silver Banshee. Siobhan intervened when Kara was involved in a battle with the U.S. Army. She quickly became Supergirl's greatest confidante, and provided a vital window into the workings of Kara's new homeworld.

The girl who fell to Earth
When Earth's atmosphere was poisoned by Kryptonite, Supergirl was quickly overcome. She awoke in a lead-lined bomb-shelter, and met wheelchair-bound Michael Harris who nursed her back to health. His diligent care and the warmth of his parents finally opened Kara's eyes to the fact that her new world was not that different from Krypton.

The Sanctuary of Solitude
Kara eventually found her own underwater Kryptonian fortress, grown from programmed Sunstone crystals and complete with maternally-minded AI. However, when Kara's Earth-2 counterpart Power Girl visited, the house-systems incorrectly deduced Kara to be a clone and tried to destroy her as an "abomination."

Kara Zor-El never wanted to be a hero. Her greatest desire was to live in Krypton's Argo City, bringing honor to her family. With Krypton about to explode, her parents, Alura and Zor-El, forced her into a life-pod and sent her to the same world where Jor-El had sent her baby cousin, Kal-El. When she awoke on a strange world, she found that she had incredible strength, everyone was hostile, and Kal-El was twice her age. Somehow, Kara had arrived decades late, angry, confused, and with powers she could not control. Mystifyingly, she had arrived with her cells fully charged by yellow solar radiation, possessing similar abilities to Superman.

She was attacked by warriors babbling incoherently and lashed out at the only man who spoke Kryptonese. While Superman tried to calm her, her life-pod was stolen by genius industrialist Simon Tycho, who quickly learned to exploit the alien Sunstone technology and the scientific records of planet Krypton.

Wandering the planet, Kara clashed with Worldkillers from Krypton, her own adult counterparts from an alternate universe, as well as a hybrid clone of her cousin, Superman. She named this Superboy Kon-El—"abomination of the House of El."

Alienation and loneliness made her easy prey for the starfarer H'El, who needed her help to turn back time to save Krypton from destruction. At first she was passionately wedded to this cause; however, she could not stomach the obliteration of Earth and at last betrayed H'El.

This act almost killed her. After medical treatment by Dr. Shay Veritas, Kara left Earth

FATHER KNOWS BEST...
Kara had no idea that Zor-El had altered her physiology when she obeyed his wishes to escape Krypton's doom in his space pod.

FAMILY FEUD
Kara refused to believe that the obnoxious man known on Earth as Superman was the baby she had held on Krypton only days ago.

LOVE IS H'EL
When H'El, an interstellar outcast, arrived on Earth, Supergirl was swayed by his family connection to her lost homeworld and seduced by his promises to restore Krypton. She loved H'El deeply and even fought beside him against Earth's defenders. However, she came to oppose his murderous scheme to destroy the entire solar system and stabbed him with Kryptonite to stop him.

A MYSTERIOUS ATTRACTION
Kara could never be sure if her passion for H'El was real, triggered by homesickness for Krypton, or the result of H'El's psychic manipulations.

CLASSIC STORIES

***Action Comics* (Vol. 1) #252 (May 1959)** Superman's cousin arrives on Earth and, hidden in an orphanage under the name Linda Lee, immediately begins training as his secret weapon.

***Action Comics* (Vol. 1) #285 (Feb. 1962)** After years of operating in total secrecy, Supergirl publicly premieres to an adoring and astonished world and quickly becomes the world's favorite female hero.

***Crisis on Infinite Earths* (Vol. 1) #7 (Oct. 1986)** Supergirl's greatest triumph comes as, to save all reality, she sacrifices herself battling the Anti-Monitor.

***Supergirl* (Vol. 1) #10 (Oct. 1974)** A most unlikely team up occurs when the Girl of Steel saves teenage American President Prez Rickard from two assassination attempts by a witch.

SEEING RED
Due to Lobo's insufferable mind-games, Kara succumbed to blinding rage and was possessed by a fury-fueled Red Lantern Ring. She learned to temper her frustration and fury, and though removing the ring would cause agonizing death, decided to discard the ring inside Earth's sun. Unexpectedly, yellow solar energy boosted her power-levels and saved her life.

RED HOT
As the rage-maintaining ring pushed her to greater acts of insanity, Kara decided she was better off dead than Red.

to wander the stars, saving the I'noxian Collective from Brainiac and his herald, the Cyborg Superman. She never realized that this grotesque parody of her cousin was her own hideously reconstructed father, Zor-El.

Back on Earth, Kara clashed with alien assassin Lobo, who drove her into a fury that caused a Red Lantern ring to attach to her and stoke her rage. She rampaged through space, until captured by Green Lanterns and handed over to Guy Gardner's Red Lantern Corps.

Regaining some self-control, Kara realized that she would need to sacrifice her life to remove the ring, and decided to do so inside Earth's Sun. Unexpectedly surviving, she returned to Earth and was summoned to the Crucible Academy to train as a cosmic hero. She saved Kon-El from the school, and the school from war-mongering traitors, before going home to put into practice all she had learned: a true hero at last. **WW**

CRUCIBLE ACADEMY
Kara was surprisingly selected by the legendary intergalactic institution, dedicated to training young heroes. She gained new friends, learned how to become a true champion, and uncovered a plot to exploit Kon-El.

"All these sudden powers... and I can barely control them."

SUPERGIRL

LOOKING FOR A CAUSE
Supergirl Kara Zor-El is one of the mightiest beings in the universe, but struggles to find a heroic purpose to match her super powers.

REBIRTH

BACK FOR GOOD!
After tremendous transformation and the loss of her Kryptonian abilities, Supergirl turns to the Department of Extranormal Operations to restore her abilities. But can she trust them when their first attempt results in her having to battle a Werewolf from Krypton?

ON THE RECORD

There were numerous early attempts to create a female equivalent of the Man of Tomorrow. The particular prototype which clicked best with fans and prompted Kara Zor-El's official entry into the DC pantheon appeared in 1958 when Jimmy Olsen's wish for a female companion for his pal Superman came true.

Putty in His Hands
When the DC Comics continuity was rebooted in the 1980s, Supergirl was re-imagined as an artificial, protoplasmic life-form. Grown by a benevolent, alternate-world Lex Luthor, her psionic abilities mimicked Superman's powers. The shape-shifter Matrix migrated to Earth and chose Supergirl as her preferred form in the Man of Steel's team, Superman Squad. She alienated everyone by becoming the girlfriend of that Earth's Luthor, after the villain transplanted his brain into a younger, better-looking body.

Eventually, Supergirl merged her body and personality with troubled student Linda Danvers to save her from demonic possession. They ultimately evolved into a powerful supernatural entity known as the Earth Born Angel of Fire.

Supergirl's Dark Side
A tougher, rebellious Girl of Steel crashed to Earth in a reprise of her origin for the 2000s. More powerful than her cousin Kal-El, Kara caused a rift between Superman, Batman, and Wonder Woman. She also became a disciple of evil New God Darkseid before joining the right side.

OVERPOWERED
Darkseid looked on approvingly as Supergirl showed Superman who was boss.

Tomorrow's World
Believing that she was experiencing a prolonged dream, Supergirl joined the Legion of Super-Heroes. In a dystopian future, where teenagers were oppressed by adults throughout a vast federation of United Planets, Kara Zor-El led this rebellious group to triumph and glory.

SUPERMAN

DATA

DEBUT *Action Comics* (Vol. 1) #1 **(Jun. 1938)**
CURRENT VERSION *Justice League* (Vol. 2) #1 **(Nov. 2011)**
REAL NAME Kal-El; Clark Kent (adoptive name)
BASE Metropolis, USA
HEIGHT 6ft 3in **WEIGHT** 235 lbs **EYES** Blue **HAIR** Black
POWERS/ABILITIES Super-strength; super-speed; flight; invulnerability; numerous sense-based abilities; accelerated healing; self-sustenance (does not require food, sleep, or oxygen); super flare blast, all fueled by exposure to solar energy from a yellow sun.
ALLIES Batman, Dr. Shay Veritas, Wonder Woman, Steel
ENEMIES Lex Luthor, Brainiac, Zod, Vyndktvx, Helspont, Doomsday, Parasite, Nimrod, H'El, Phantom King Xa-Du, Erik Drekken, Wraith
AFFILIATIONS Justice League of America, Legion of Super-Heroes

Superman is the world's greatest hero. He is a tireless champion dedicated to protecting life and battling injustice not only in his city of Metropolis, but also all over his adopted world and across the universe. With his constantly developing array of powers and abilities, fueled by his alien cells—which hyper-efficiently process the solar energy of Earth's yellow sun—Superman is an unstoppable force for good and a steadfast punisher of evil. Perhaps the most powerful being on Earth, he is a founding member of the Justice League of America and, while still a teenager, spent many months as part of the 31st-century Legion of Super-Heroes.

AT A GLANCE...

Real and present dangers
The Man of Steel is not impervious to harm. He is weakened and will eventually die if exposed to Kryptonite—radioactive remnants of his old homeworld. He has no defense against magic and his mind will succumb to sufficient psionic assault, but his real vulnerability is his dependence on yellow solar radiation. Deprived of it, he becomes a mere mortal.

Fortress of Solitude
Even a Superman needs a place to hang his cape. After defeating the alien android known as the Collector of Worlds, he moved into the invader's vessel, turning it into an ark in space. When it was destroyed, Superman relocated to the Arctic. He now keeps his menagerie of alien creatures, advanced medical facilities, confiscated weapons, and other dangerous devices in a vast crystalline stronghold derived from recovered Kryptonian technologies.

Suited and booted
After saving Metropolis from the villainous Brainiac, Superman discovered an artifact from Krypton that transformed into a form-fitting, indestructible uniform sporting the crest of the House of El. Subtly enhancing his growing abilities, the Kryptonian battle armor is thought-activated and worn beneath Clark's ordinary clothes.

CLASSIC STORIES

***Action Comics* (Vol. 1) #1 (Jun. 1938)** A different kind of hero debuts with Superman creating a new literary genre and sparking a revolution in popular fiction.

***Superman* (Vol. 1) #423 & *Action Comics* (Vol. 1) #583 (Sep. 1986)** An era ends in tribute to 50 years of continuity as the Superman family retires to make way for a potent re-imagining of the characters.

***Superman* (Vol. 2) #75 (Jan. 1993)** After an epic storyline across multiple titles, a horrific pitched battle with Doomsday results in the "Death of Superman."

***Superman* (Vol. 1) #701-714 (Sep. 2010-Oct. 2011)** Following a mighty war against the people of New Krypton, which found him exiled from Earth, Superman reconnects with ordinary Americans by walking across the country.

Kal-El was born 27 light years from Earth, to Jor-El and Lara Lor-Van on the heavy-gravity world of Krypton, which circled the red sun Rao. The product of supremely evolved parents and a civilization at the apex of technological achievement, little Kal was hurriedly sent to Earth in a prototype starship. It was his father's last act of desperation and hope after Jor-El discovered their scientifically advanced world was doomed to explode from irreversible tectonic pressures.

Despite his greatest efforts, Jor-El could not convince his fellow Kryptonians to respond to the impending disaster. When his first plan—to seek refuge in the extra-dimensional Phantom Zone—was sabotaged by the Kryptonian criminals imprisoned there, he and Lara had no choice but to dispatch their precious son to safety in a hastily reprogrammed test rocket, aimed at a distant planet where Kal-El could survive.

When Kal-El's ship crashed on Earth it was spotted by Kansas farmers Jonathan and Martha Kent. A childless couple eager for a baby, they rescued the little star-child and, after shrewdly substituting a deformed stillborn calf for the occupant, handed over the downed vessel to the military authorities. Keeping Kal-El's extraordinary origins to themselves, the Kents named the precocious infant Clark and raised him as a perfectly normal little boy in their home town of Smallville.

However, as Clark grew older, foreboding hints of his true nature manifested themselves. His physical strength and speed grew exponentially. He was never sick, and as his teen years progressed, his senses became acutely sharper than those of his peers.

Clark learned early on that anyone in need had to be helped, and it was his duty to do the right thing. It was thanks to his parents' love, warmth, and social conscience that he grew up with the upright moral principles that shaped his later life.

LAST SON OF KRYPTON
Swaddled in his grandfather's red cape, baby Kal-El was sent to Earth and his destiny. He would be fully grown before he learned of his tragic origins.

CHILDHOOD'S END
Heartbroken, Clark left Smallville determined to live up to his foster-father's teachings, beliefs, and final words to "Never give up the fight to make this world a better place."

Jonathan and Martha also convinced Clark to keep his uncanny abilities secret—although father and son often indulged themselves by playing seemingly impossible pranks and practical jokes, usually on mean or petty-minded officials in Smallville. However, as Clark matured, he eventually shared the knowledge of his abilities with his closest friend, Lana Lang, a confidence she keeps to this day.

The mighty orphan grew up never knowing his true origins, often wondering whether he was a misplaced experiment or even a foundling from the future. Years of frustrating speculation would pass before he discovered the truth.

Clark learned a painful lesson on the night his adoptive parents died. They were victims of a road accident while he was at a school dance with Lana. Despite all his powers, there were some tragedies even he could not fix.

H'EL ON EARTH

When H'El, a mysterious survivor from Krypton, landed on Earth claiming to be a family associate of Jor-El and Lara, he tried to convince Superman and his cousin Supergirl that he could restore their destroyed homeworld. H'El neglected to mention that the energy needed to rearrange the timeline would come from detonating Earth's sun, and might well destroy the galaxy.

With Supergirl initially seduced to H'El's side, Superman needed the help of Superboy, the Teen Titans, and the Justice League to forestall the ultra-powerful zealot. Even Lex Luthor joined the alliance to save the world from destruction.

FAMILY FEUD
Combining native Kryptonian powers with an arsenal of psionic abilities, enigmatic invader H'El easily defeated Superboy, Supergirl, and Superman.

On moving to Metropolis to pursue a career in journalism, Clark began his battle against injustice by methodically dismantling the corrupt criminal empire of media tycoon Glen Glenmorgan. What the crusading junior journalist's news stories could not expose, an unstoppable human dynamo could destroy.

Wearing the indestructible blanket he was found in and a T-shirt printed with a distinctive S-symbol, Clark became a vigilante. His news stories exposed the guilty and his alter ego—who became known as Superman—dealt out summary justice to wrongdoers the police could not or would not touch. Superman saved the helpless from disaster and victimization, but also incurred suspicion and persecution from the authorities.

Superman's exploits made him a sensation, inspiring other metahumans and masked heroes to emerge from the shadows and work under the avid gaze of an adoring public—and that of the increasingly nervous military and federal authorities.

FASTER THAN A SPEEDING BULLET
An impatient Superman had no time for bad guys, compromised laws or cops who didn't do their jobs properly.

CHILDREN OF THE COMET

The decades-old mystery of the "Blake Farm Ghost"—a clandestine super-being performing miracles in Kansas—was finally exposed as the work of a psionic mutant, Adam Blake, aka Captain Comet. Blake returned to Earth to recruit Lois Lane's niece Susie—a fellow telepath—to his group, the Cometeers. Captain Comet didn't care that his efforts almost killed Lois or that his attack destroyed Superman's new secret identity of Johnny Clark. Thankfully, little Susie did care, rejecting Blake's invitation and staying on Earth to ensure her aunt was safe.

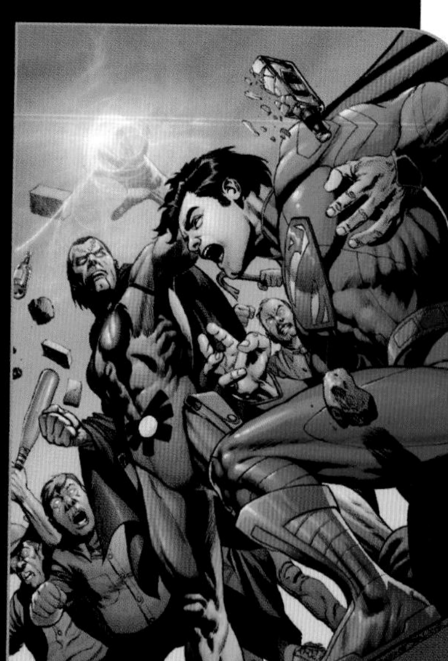

EVOLUTIONARY GAP
Captain Comet's mind control turned the people of Metropolis into a howling mob determined to stop Superman.

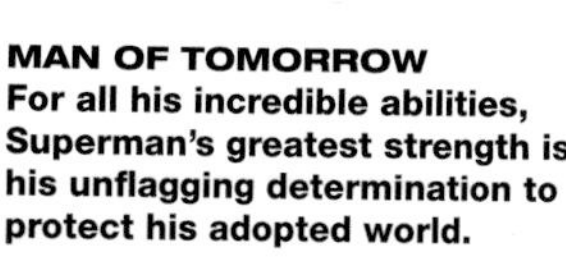

MAN OF TOMORROW
For all his incredible abilities, Superman's greatest strength is his unflagging determination to protect his adopted world.

"This is my fight to finish! This is a job for Superman!"

KAL-EL

SUPERMAN

COVER STORY
The *Daily Planet* offered Clark the opportunity to meet like-minded people and provided a platform for him to do some good as Superman.

Superman's activities boosted Clark Kent's career. His exposés for George Taylor's *Daily Star* won him a reputation as a dogged reporter, leading to his being hired by Perry White to work beside award-winning journalist Lois Lane on the *Daily Planet*, the greatest newspaper in the world.

For five years, Clark, Lois, and young photographer Jimmy Olsen made a fine team. Clark was heartbroken when media mogul Morgan Edge bought the *Planet* for his portfolio of "infotainment" concerns. He was appalled when Lois took a management job in Edge's new regime and started an independent online news service with fellow ex-*Planet* reporter, Cat Grant.

During these years, Superman became an acclaimed champion, his popularity soaring after he saved Earth from annihilation. He prevented Metropolis from being shrunk down and preserved in a bottle—a fate that had already befallen the last-remaining Kryptonian city of Kandor—by self-proclaimed savior of civilizations Brainiac, Collector of Worlds. While defeating this space marauder, Superman learned of his own cosmic legacy, took possession of Kandor, and gained a new uniform of Kryptonian battle armor.

REBIRTH

UPHOLDING THE LEGACY

While Superman battled an ever-growing number of threats, his extra-dimensional counterpart stayed in hiding, choosing to protect his wife, Lois, and super-son, Jonathan, under the anonymity of their assumed identities as the White family.

This Super Hero from another world only joined his namesake at the very last, coming to his aid against a deluded, supercharged foe, only to see Earth-0's Man of Steel give his life to save countless others.

However, after Lex Luthor appointed himself the new Superman of Metropolis, the alternate-Earth Man of Steel could no longer stomach the travesty. He launched himself into the public spotlight to honor the fallen hero through his own efforts, no matter what the cost and until Earth's true Superman returned.

HOSTAGE CRISIS
When scientist Lex Luthor and the army captured the Metropolis vigilante, they learned the limitations of their power—and the risks of antagonizing Superman.

Moreover, as his powers and reputation grew, so did his circle of enemies. Alexander Luthor had tortured the vigilante when the army first captured him and, convinced Superman was a threat to humanity, remade himself into a billionaire industrialist and obsessive archenemy. The Man of Steel was also targeted by an Anti-Superman Army of enhanced foes, all unknowingly acting for a hidden mastermind of immeasurable power—a malicious, imp-like murderer from the Fifth Dimension named Vyndktvx. Later, When Darkseid, the merciless ruler of Apokolips, attacked Earth, Superman found friends and allies—other heroes who rallied to help him fight off the attack. They decided to remain together and form the Justice League. He eventually began a turbulent relationship with Wonder Woman, but his unswerving dedication to justice remained undiminished.

After years of constant struggle, Superman's powers seemed to wane in the wake of battling Doomsday, Darkseid, Vandal Savage, Rao, and other powerful antagonists. Yet despite this and his identity being exposed, Superman continued to fight the good fight before apparently sacrificing himself to save his adopted world from a rampaging, solar-energized doppleganger. Many of the friends and comrades he left behind are sure he will return. **WW**

REBIRTH

SINO SUPER-MAN

During his final days, Superman's power waned. He was even attacked by Chinese superhumans seeking to steal his genetic material for their enigmatic leader, Dr. Omen. Soon after Kal-El's final battle, a new Chinese Super Hero debuted and it appeared that the Middle Kingdom had finally achieved the impossible dream of putting their own patriotic Super-Man onto the world stage. Kenji Kong, a brash young man, takes to this new role with great relish, determined to be China's Number One hero.

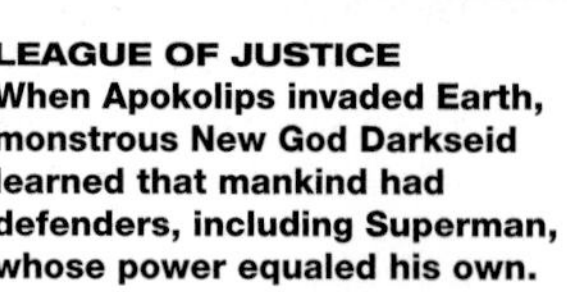

LEAGUE OF JUSTICE
When Apokolips invaded Earth, monstrous New God Darkseid learned that mankind had defenders, including Superman, whose power equaled his own.

ON THE RECORD

When Superman first appeared on the scene, he was as likely to go after greedy mine-owners and armaments manufacturers as mobsters and mad scientists. However, as he developed, the Man of Tomorrow specialized in battling monsters, crushing invasions, and tackling criminals no ordinary emergency services could handle. He became an accredited representative of the legal authorities.

Following a reordering of reality in *Crisis on Infinite Earths*, Superman was dramatically reimagined for a new generation. Much of his history was dialed back to parallel his earliest adventures, and his foster parents Jonathan and Martha Kent were resurrected to add a family element to the life of the interstellar orphan.

The Ultimate Sacrifice

When the alien beast Doomsday burst from the Earth on a destructive path to Metropolis, no force could stop it. After the creature smashed the Justice League and brutalized Superman, the city looked finished. However, its unyielding champion was determined to stop Doomsday at all costs. Despite his terrible injuries, Superman returned to the fray. He finally triumphed over the creature, but paid the ultimate price for victory with his life.

Superman's body was interred in Metropolis's Centennial Park. It was stolen by the military research group Cadmus for experimentation purposes, before being recovered by the fallen hero's friends and revived using Kryptonian technology. However, it was just an animated cadaver, as Superman's spirit was long gone.

It took the unfailing devotion of his Earth-born father to retrieve Clark from the afterlife. Grieving for his son, Jonathan Kent suffered a heart attack, and ascended to an eerie netherworld, from where he brought Clark back to stand at the forefront of Earth's champions.

DOOMSDAY SCENARIO
Despite being bloodied by attacks from the alien invader, Doomsday Superman fought to defend Metropolis.

Critical Condition

Superman's least likely archenemy, the Prankster, aka conman Harold Loomis, perhaps came closest to destroying the Man of Steel through ingenuity, patience and subtlety. Loomis hired minor sorceress La Encantadora to lose a fight with the Man of Steel and infect the hero with a Kryptonite nanovirus. Entering his system, the virus took months to debilitate his invulnerable body with Kryptonite cancer. In a last ditch effort to help the dying hero, the Atom miniaturized and injected Team Superman allies Steel, Superboy, and Supergirl into Superman's body to destroy the K-tumors by hand. However, their mission would have failed owing to the actions of a traitor on the team, if Superman's wife, Lois Lane, had not discovered the villain and taken charge of the situation.

THOROUGHLY GROUNDED
The Last Son of Krypton's resolute sense of justice is molded by the love, support, and good advice of his adoptive parents, Jonathan and Martha.

The Rise and Fall of New Krypton

The Man of Steel's uniqueness ended when citizens of the Bottled City of Kandor were restored to normal size. Under the leadership of Alura Zor-El and General Zod, legions of new supermen built a New Krypton. Before long, growing tensions and suspicions culminated in a "100 Minute War" against mankind, with Superman and Supergirl caught in the middle. With the help of Superboy and Nightwing, Zod was ultimately trapped in the Phantom Zone and Earth was safe once again.

WAR OF THE SUPERMEN
Superman and Zod clashed over the Kryptonian zealot's desire to turn Earth into a new Krypton.

TALIA AL GHŪL

DATA

DEBUT *Detective Comics* (Vol. 1) #411 **(May 1971)**
CURRENT VERSION *Batman and Robin* (Vol. 2) #2 **(Dec. 2011)**
HEIGHT 5ft 8in **WEIGHT** 120 lbs
EYES Brown **HAIR** Brown
POWERS/ABILITIES Accomplished fighter and assassin; adept in ballet and horseback riding; talented chemist; very intelligent and a cunning strategist; access to huge terrorist networks; charismatic leader.
ALLIES Rā's al Ghūl, Heretic, Red Hood
ENEMIES Batman, Batman Family, Batman, Inc.
AFFILIATIONS League of Assassins, Leviathan

DAMSEL CAUSING DISTRESS
She first met Batman when held captive by an enemy of Rā's al Ghūl. However, Talia has since become a threat in her own right as the head of the terrorist group Leviathan.

PARENTAL CONTROL
Rā's al Ghūl and Talia's relationship is complex. While he wants nothing more than total control over her, he was proud when she broke away and started Leviathan.

She is the daughter of the demon, the child of eco-terrorist Rā's al Ghūl, born into the world surrounded by the worst assassins known to man. She is the mother of Robin (Damian Wayne), and the estranged love of Batman. She is Talia al Ghūl, a conflicting mix of passion and apathy, compassion, and ruthlessness. And while the Dark Knight would wish to believe otherwise, at her core, Talia is truly her father's daughter.

When international terrorist Rā's al Ghūl met a young hippie named Melisande during one of his many travels, the two formed a close bond that Rā's hadn't shared with a woman in quite some time. As the founder of the League of Assassins and the infamous abuser of the life-extending properties of the fabled Lazarus Pits, Rā's al Ghūl had little time for love, despite having lived for centuries. Nevertheless, he and Melisande had a child, and named her Talia al Ghūl.

Talia was raised amongst brutal assassins and killers, but she doted on her father just the same. She soon followed in Rā's al Ghūl's footsteps, training in the many arts of fighting, and also mastering other skills such as chemistry, ballet, and horseback riding. Thanks to her father's vast wealth, she was provided with anything she wanted, and took advantage of that often. But it wasn't until she allowed herself to be kidnapped by Dr. Darrk that she finally met someone who truly interested her: Batman.

Despite her father's ongoing conflict with his nemesis, the Dark Knight, Talia and Batman shared a passionate romance and had a child named Damian. While Damian would later take his place by Batman's side as the new Robin, Talia felt shunned by the Dark Knight, and declared war against him, starting her own secret society called Leviathan. This led to her death at the hands of one of Batman's allies, but not before she ordered the death of her own son, simply to further harm Batman, her so-called "beloved." **MM**

MOMMIE DEAREST
Like her son, Damian, before her, Talia has been resurrected in the Lazarus Pits. However, Damian refused to return his mother's love when she tried to revive their relationship.

ON THE RECORD

First appearing in the 1970s, Talia al Ghūl matured into a formidable presence before the continuity-altering events of the *Flashpoint* miniseries. Breaking away from her father's influence in the 2000s, Talia took over LexCorp for Lex Luthor when he was elected to the position of President of the United States.

Going under the name Talia Head, she ran Luthor's company as its CEO. Having proved herself to be a shrewd businesswoman, she later purposely bankrupted LexCorp. Talia also served in the inner circle of both incarnations of the elite Secret Society of Super-Villains, working alongside Luthor and the likes of Black Adam, Deathstroke, Vandal Savage, and Gorilla Grodd.

SISTER, SISTER
In 2003, it was revealed that Talia had an older stepsister, Nyssa Raatko. Introduced in *Batman: Death and the Maidens*, Nyssa manipulated Talia into helping her murder their father.

CLASSIC STORIES

***Detective Comics* (Vol. 1) #411 (May 1971)** Batman meets Talia for the first time, but soon realizes that this strong woman needs little help rescuing herself.

***"The Lazarus Affair" Batman* (Vol. 1) #332-335 (Feb.–May 1981)** In a four-issue, multi-part tale rare for its time, Batman teams with Robin, Catwoman, and Talia to track down Rā's al Ghūl.

***Batman: Son of the Demon* (1987)** In this oversized special, Talia and Batman take their romance to the next level, resulting in the birth of a baby boy.

***Batman, Incorporated* (Vol. 2) #13 (Sep. 2013)** Talia al Ghūl is killed by former Batwoman Kathy Kane, in a showdown between Batman and Talia's Leviathan forces.

T

T.O. MORROW

DEBUT *The Flash* (Vol. 1) #143 **(Mar. 1964)**
CURRENT VERSION *Justice League* (Vol. 2) #3 **(Jan. 2012)**
REAL NAME Dr. Thomas Oscar Morrow
BASE Detroit, Michigan
HEIGHT 5ft 11in **WEIGHT** 187 lbs
EYES Blue **HAIR** Black
POWERS/ABILITIES Scientist with advanced knowledge of robotics and future studies; access to the highly classified Red Room at S.T.A.R. Labs.
ALLIES Dr. Silas Stone, Dr. Will Magnus, Sarah Charles
ENEMIES FBI
AFFILIATIONS Red Room, S.T.A.R. Labs

The brilliant scientist Dr. Thomas Morrow was interested in future technologies from an early age, having been influenced by science fiction, especially the works of H.G. Wells. He earned masters degrees from Harvard University in Emerging Technologies, Strategic Foresight, and Future Studies, before focusing on time travel. It was a field of scientific endeavor he was forced to give up after an accident nearly cost him his life.

Recruited by S.T.A.R. Labs in Detroit, Michigan, Morrow helped Dr. Silas Stone establish the clandestine Red Room facility. He was working in the lab when a Parademon attack caused extensive injuries to Silas' son, Victor Stone. This caused Dr. Stone to graft the experimental metal Promethium to Victor, using an equally experimental nanite technique for neural integration. The result was the hero Cyborg, who went on to become a founding member of the Justice League. T.O. Morrow continues his work at S.T.A.R. Labs to this day, working closely with Dr. Silas Stone and Cyborg. For unknown reasons, he is currently under investigation by the FBI. **MM**

ON THE RECORD

The quintessential mad scientist, T.O. Morrow was created in the 1960s and was a staunch enemy of the JLA. He created the android Red Tornado to use as a weapon against the League, until it rejected its programming and became a hero itself. After repeated clashes with the League, Morrow worked closely with fellow nutty Professor Ivo. Later, he set up shop on the scientific sanctuary of Oolong Island with a who's who of the world's most villainous scientists.

TOMORROW AND TOMORROW
T.O. Morrow worked with Professor Ivo, to create the android Tomorrow Woman (inset) to infiltrate and destroy the Justice League. However, Tomorrow Woman was too smart to play ball.

THE TAMARANEANS

DEBUT *The New Teen Titans* (Vol. 1) #3 (Jan. 1981)
CURRENT VERSION *Red Hood and the Outlaws* (Vol. 1) #3 (Jan. 2012)
BASE Tamaran
NOTABLE MEMBERS/POWERS
Starfire (Koriand'r): Energy projection, flight, language assimilation through touch; **Blackfire (Komand'r):** Firearms expertise, flight; **Sister Kala (Kaland'r):** Pyrokinesis, leadership, flight.

Long ago, the planet Tamaran was freed from its enemies by the goddess-like entity X'Hal. When X'Hal left Tamaran, so did some of her followers. They settled on a barren planet where Sister Kala (Kaland'r)—a future ally of White Lantern Kyle Rayner—was born. The rest of the Tamaraneans remained on Tamaran where, years later, princesses Koriand'r and her sister Komand'r were born.

When they were just young girls, the princesses' peaceful homeworld was invaded by the interstellar conquerors, the Citadel. In exchange for Koriand'r, the Citadel made Komand'r ruler of Tamaran. Koriand'r eventually escaped to Earth, becoming the hero Starfire. She later returned to Tamaran to help her people battle the malignant Blight. Komand'r took a different path, and united her people with demonic super-villain Helspont. **MM**

TAKION

DEBUT *Takion* #1 (Jun. 1996)
CURRENT VERSION *The Multiversity Guidebook* # 1 (Mar. 2015)
REAL NAME Joshua Sanders
BASE New Genesis
HEIGHT 6ft 2in **WEIGHT** Variable
EYES Red **HAIR** Flaming yellow
POWERS/ABILITIES Flight; energy blasts; matter manipulation; super-speed; super-strength; powered by the all-powerful Source;
ENEMIES Stayne, Darkseid, Infinity-Man

Blind from birth, psychologist Joshua Sanders was overcome with a tremendous surge of energy and suddenly knew everything there was to know. In that instant, he was whisked away to New Genesis, where his developing sight gazed upon Izaya, the New God's Highfather, who had chosen Joshua as his champion. Now known as Takion of the Source, he would take Izaya's place in the event of the latter's death.

Takion soon faced the threat of Stayne, created by Darkseid to counter the New Gods' existence. Despite frequent conflict, Takion's power grew, and he became the new Highfather for a time. Eventually, Takion was seemingly killed by the Infinity-Man, under direction from the Source. However, he has been glimpsed recently among the New Gods watching over Earth-51. **MM**

TALONS

DEBUT *Batman* (Vol. 2) #2 **(Dec. 2011)**
REAL NAME Talons
BASE Gotham City
POWERS/ABILITIES Brainwashed to be blindly loyal; highly trained in the use of various weapons as well as combat, assassination, stealth, and infiltration techniques; exceptionally fit and agile; ability to cheat death thanks to formula injected into their bloodstream by the Court of Owls.
ENEMIES Batman, Birds of Prey, the Batman Family, Talon (Calvin Rose), Mr. Freeze, Jonah Hex
AFFILIATIONS Court of Owls

A clandestine organization whispered about since the dawn of Gotham City itself, the Court of Owls is a powerful, well-connected cabal of Gotham society's elite. However, to bend an entire city to its will, the Court of Owls realized that they needed lethal enforcers, "invisible" assassins who could emerge in the dead of night, kill their target, and then vanish without trace. These enforcers were called Talons, and they served the Court of Owls after undergoing a series of demanding challenges, including physical and mental conditioning, which ensured they were loyal to their cause above all else.

To recruit Talons, the Court looked to Haly's Circus to find suitable candidates whose talents and skills they could develop. The best and brightest acts of each generation were abducted and forged into obedient, near-unstoppable killing machines. In recent years, the Court also developed a chemical formula that granted its Talons superhuman endurance and the ability to be reanimated from the dead. This allowed the Court to unleash several of their Talons at once to take on the Dark Knight and thwart his attempts to destroy the Court. **MM**

THE SECRET IS OUT
The upper echelons of the Court of Owls as well as many of their Talon enforcers know that Bruce is Batman.

TALON

DEBUT *Talon* #0 **(Nov. 2012)**
REAL NAME Calvin Rose
BASE Gotham City
HEIGHT 5ft 10in **WEIGHT** 174 lbs
EYES Brown **HAIR** Brown
POWERS/ABILITIES Expert escape artist; adept in several fighting styles; knowledge of electronics and security systems; expert assassin but now practices non-lethal crime fighting; access to funding and weaponry from Batman, Inc.; armored suit fires grappling line and darts; customized Utility Belt.
ALLIES Batman, the Batman Family, Strix, Casey Washington
ENEMIES Court of Owls, Bane, Lord Death Man, Sebastian Clark
AFFILIATIONS Batman Incorporated

TALON, INCORPORATED
Calvin Rose was later recruited into another society, this one on the side of the angels. He gladly accepted membership in Batman Incorporated.

CAGED BIRD
When his father abandoned him, Calvin made his first escape—awakening a deep interest in escapology.

DEFYING THE COURT
Unable to go through with the murder of Casey Washington, Calvin realized that the Court was no place for him.

Like all the Talons who were forged by the nefarious secret society called the Court of Owls, Calvin Rose lived a hard life. Calvin's father was abusive and, at only eight years of age, Calvin was locked and abandoned in an outdoor dog kennel. He waited for three days for his father to return and free him, but after the third night, he realized he was alone in the world. Calvin broke out of his cage, took to the road and was discovered by an escape artist who worked at the traveling Haly's Circus. In time, Calvin became the escape artist's successor—which was when he learned Haly's Circus' dark secret.

Every generation the Court of Owls trawled the circus looking for prospective new assassins, called Talons, who would be schooled and conditioned to do their bidding. Calvin was recruited, but after killing another Talon to complete the Court's rigorous and ruthless training, he realized he could not be one of their operatives and defected. He also saved the life of Casey Washington, a target he was supposed to eliminate. Armed with a modified Talon suit, Calvin set out to destroy the Court of Owls, later working alongside Batman. **MM**

TARANTULA II

DEBUT *Nightwing* **(Vol. 1) #71 (Sept. 2002)**
CURRENT VERSION *Green Arrow* **(Vol. 5) #44 (Nov. 2015)**
REAL NAME Catalina Flores
HEIGHT 5ft 7in **WEIGHT** 135 lbs
EYES Brown **HAIR** Black
POWERS/ABILITIES Adept hand-to-hand combatant; intelligent and well-traveled; weapons include gun that fires webbing-like netting and grappling lines.
ENEMIES Jefe

The heroine Tarantula made her public debut in Seattle to fight alongside Green Arrow. Arrow's dog George had been targeted by a cult of bone-obsessed killers called Skeletons, who managed to abduct the canine. Green Arrow and Tarantula teamed up, and traveled to her native Juarez in Mexico to retrieve his pet.

Green Arrow was unaware that Tarantula had sought him out to trade him for the life of her kidnapped cousin, a prisoner of the Skeletons' boss, Jefe. This became clear when they arrived at Tarantula's bar and were attacked by the villains. Despite double-crossing Green Arrow, Tarantula later headed back to Jefe's compound to save him. The heroes rescued George and bested Jefe, even as a romance sparked between them. **MM**

TATTOOED MAN

DEBUT *Green Lantern* **(Vol. 2) #23 (Sept. 1963)**
CURRENT VERSION *Justice League* **#30 (Jul. 2014)**
REAL NAME Abel Tarrant
HEIGHT 6ft **WEIGHT** 195 lbs
EYES Blue **HAIR** Brown
POWERS/ABILITIES Can bring to life any tattoo on his body and control it with his mind.
ALLIES Scavenger, Clayface, Dr. Alchemy
ENEMIES Green Lantern Hal Jordan, Justice League

The Tattooed Man is a member of a recent incarnation of the Secret Society of Super-Villains. He was present when the Justice League raided the team's hideout and incarcerated the members, thanks to the sharp-thinking leadership of then League member, Lex Luthor.

Before the Flashpoint event, however, the Tattooed Man was primarily a villain of Green Lantern Hal Jordan. With the ability to bring any of his tattoos to life and control them, he proved a powerful foe. After attempting to reform, Tarrant was killed by Mirror Master when he double-crossed the villain. Two other Tattooed Men emerged before Flashpoint: Titans member Mark Richards, and a man incarcerated with Tarrant, John Oakes. **MM**

EVERY PICTURE SPELLS DANGER
Using sheer willpower, Abel Tarrant, the Tattooed Man, brought to life the inked images on his skin, from weapons to fantasy creatures.

TATTOOED TOO
Mark Richards seemed more heroic than previous Tattooed Men. However, he was soon recruited by Deathstroke into an unscrupulous incarnation of the Titans.

TAWKY TAWNY

DEBUT *Captain Marvel Adventures* **#79 (Dec. 1947)**
CURRENT VERSION *Justice League* **#10 (Aug. 2012)**
BASE Philadelphia
HEIGHT 11ft 4in **WEIGHT** 480 lbs
EYES Yellow **HAIR** Orange, black, and white
POWERS/ABILITIES Temporarily given power of Shazam, he became super-strong, super-tough, and gained size.
ENEMIES Black Adam

Before the Flashpoint event, Tawky Tawny was a 6ft 2in tiger that walked and talked like a man, often helping Captain Marvel (Shazam) on his missions.

Post-Flashpoint, Tawny was a tiger at a zoo. For young orphan Billy Batson, visiting Tawny was the oldest memory that he had of his parents, and he would talk to the big cat and even feed him hamburgers. After Billy was given the mystical powers of Shazam, the similarly powered villain Black Adam began hunting him. Their fight led to the zoo, where Adam threw Shazam against Tawny's cage, freeing the animal. Tawny attacked Black Adam, but was swatted away, inspiring Shazam to give the big cat some of his powers. Larger and stronger than ever, Tawny attacked Black Adam, hurting the villain this time around. **MM**

TEAM 7

DEBUT *The Kindred* #3 (May 1994)
CURRENT VERSION *Team 7* (Vol. 1) #0 (Nov. 2012)
NOTABLE MEMBERS John Lynch; Canary (later Black Canary); Kurt Lance; Slade Wilson (later Deathstroke); Cole Cash (later Grifter); Captain Summer Ramos; James Bronson (later Majestic); Alex Fairchild; Amanda Waller; Dean Higgins (later Regulus); Steve Trevor
ENEMIES Eclipso

Over five years ago, an elite black-ops team was formed under the name Team 7 by John Lynch. He originally recruited Dinah Drake and Kurt Lance to choose only the very brightest and bravest (Kurt and Dinah would later be married, and Dinah would adopt the name Black Canary when Lynch augmented her abilities, sparking her famed Canary Cry).

The pair recruited mercenaries Slade Wilson and Alex Fairchild, as well as operatives James Bronson, pilot Captain Summer Ramos, ex-special forces soldier Cole Cash, NSA analyst Amanda Waller, and military intelligence agent Dean Higgins. Team 7 overcame the threat of Eclipso, yet Fairchild and Ramos were murdered battling the rogue Spartan programming. The team disbanded after Bronson transformed into the powerhouse Majestic. **MM**

TEMPEST

DEBUT *Adventure Comics* (Vol. 1) #269 (Feb. 1960)
CURRENT VERSION *Convergence Suicide Squad* #2 (Jul. 2015)
REAL NAME Garth
BASE Atlantis
HEIGHT 5ft 10in **WEIGHT** 235 lbs **EYES** Purple **HAIR** Black
POWERS/ABILITIES Can survive the great pressures and cold temperatures of the ocean, swim at fast speeds, and breathe underwater; superhuman strength, endurance, and durability; burning laser vision; intelligent and an adept hand-to-hand combatant; weapons include hi-tech trident.
ALLIES Aquaman, Mera
ENEMIES Mr. Whisper, Mammoth
AFFILIATIONS Atlanteans, Teen Titans

The Atlantean named Garth has yet to be called Tempest in current continuity, but if his modern incarnation is anything like his past versions, he's sure to adopt the name in future adventures. Much of Garth's history remains as mystifying as his memories of the Teen Titans, but, as he recently discovered, he used to fight crime as the hero Aqualad in his youth. However, not only did Garth forget that part of his past, but so did the rest of the world.

Garth later emerged in Atlantis on a strike force assembled by Mera to hunt Aquaman. He saw the error of his ways when he discovered that his orders weren't from his queen at all, but from an imposter paving the way for the invading Thule. Garth and Aquaman then turned the tide against the invaders.

Most recently, Garth used deadly force to stop a ring of organ smugglers dealing in Atlantean lungs. He soon found himself fighting Dick Grayson and Donna Troy, as if brought together by fate. When the three realized they knew each other from some forgotten past, they became uneasy allies, soon learning of their shared history as founding members of the first Teen Titans. **MM**

ON THE RECORD

Garth debuted in *Adventure Comics* as Aqualad, Aquaman's sidekick. An outcast from Atlantis due to his purple eyes, Garth found a friend in Arthur Curry, and more friends as he founded the Teen Titans alongside Robin, Wonder Girl, Kid Flash, and Speedy.

Aqualad went his own way when the Teen Titans became the New Teen Titans, but returned in a later incarnation called Titans after his transformation into the mage Tempest, a powerhouse player in any environment. Tempest was killed during Blackest Night.

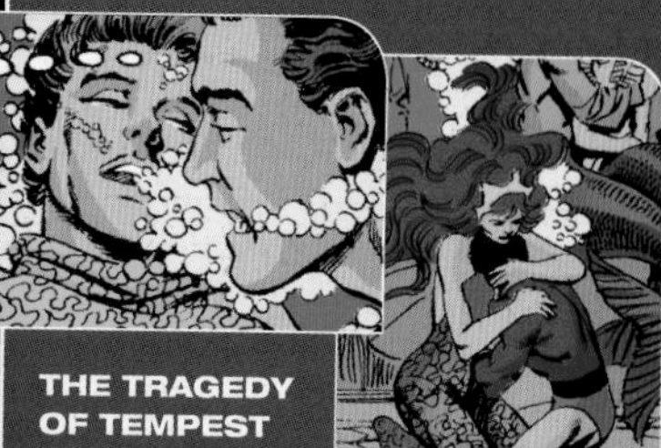

THE TRAGEDY OF TEMPEST While his first love, Tula, died during the original *Crisis on Infinite Earths*, Tempest was given another chance at love and married sometime hero Dolphin. They had a baby named Cerdian, but both Dolphin and Cerdian perished during the Infinite Crisis event.

TELOS

DEBUT *Warlord* #48 (Aug. 1981)
CURRENT VERSION *Convergence* #0 (Jun. 2015)
REAL NAME Arak
HEIGHT 6ft **WEIGHT** 190 lbs
EYES Purple **HAIR** None
POWERS/ABILITIES Extremely powerful entity with control of matter.
ALLIES Techne, K'rot, Stealth, Captain Comet
ENEMIES Computo, Validus, Brainiac

Arak's father was the king of his people, and forbade his son from fighting, despite Arak's aptitude for battle. Forced to study the ways of the Shaman, Arak gained the powers of his father and fought Brainiac when the villain appeared in his realm. Arak offered his life to Brainiac in exchange for the safety of his people and became Brainiac's servant, Telos.

Using his vast powers, Telos collected cities from many worlds in many dimensions and points of time. Brainiac intended to pit each city against each other and allow the victor to become the one, true reality in a great Convergence. When the heroes of the worlds rebelled, Telos helped Brainiac to see the error of his ways and realign the infinite Earths. Brainiac then set Telos free to search for his long-lost family. **MM**

TERRA

DEBUT *The New Teen Titans* (Vol. 1) #26 (Dec. 1982)
CURRENT VERSION *Superboy* (Vol. 5) #8 (Jun. 2012)
REAL NAME Tara Markov
HEIGHT 5ft 1in **WEIGHT** 98 lbs **EYES** Blue **HAIR** Blond
POWERS/ABILITIES Adept geokinetic, able to move earth and rocks; can fly by riding a levitating piece of rock or earth; can cause earthquakes and manipulate earth in a variety of ways, including raising lava.
ALLIES Beast Boy
ENEMIES Brother Blood, Deathstroke, Harvest
AFFILIATIONS Ravagers

Tara Markov's past remains a mystery, even to herself. While her last name suggests she might hail from the country Markovia and even be of royal blood, Tara's memories have all but been erased after being captured and experimented upon by the super-villain Harvest.

Forced to fight in Harvest's twisted Colony, in which teen "experiments" battled for survival to sharpen their skills, Terra befriended Beast Boy after saving his life. The two became close friends and stuck by each other when Caitlin Fairchild helped them escape to the outside world. There Terra joined forces with Fairchild, Beast Boy, and a group of young fellow survivors and formed the Ravagers, a short-lived team that was eventually defeated and brought back to Harvest by the mercenary Deathstroke. **MM**

ON THE RECORD

Tara Markov was the product of experiments by Dr. Helga Jace, responsible for giving Tara's brother, Geo-Force, his gravity-defying powers. Planted in the Teen Titans by Deathstroke, with whom she was having an affair, Terra went insane and died in battle. A Terra from an alternate reality took her place and became like a sister to Geo-Force, serving on the Team Titans before being killed by super-villain Black Adam.

A third Terra later emerged named Atlee, who had no relation to the original two, but also possessed rock-moving powers.

BROTHER MINE? The second Terra had a hard time accepting Geo-Force as her brother, and took a DNA test to make sure she wasn't the psychopathic original, brought mysteriously back to life.

TEEN TITANS

DATA

DEBUT *The Brave and the Bold* #54 **(Jun.–Jul. 1964)**
CURRENT VERSION *Teen Titans* (Vol. 4) #1 **(Nov. 2011)**
BASE New York City
NOTABLE MEMBERS/POWERS **ROBIN (DAMIAN WAYNE)** Formidable intellect, expert martial artist; **NEW KID FLASH (WALLY WEST)** Super-speed, accelerated healing; **STARFIRE (PRINCESS KORIAND'R)** Tamaranean physiology provides enhanced strength, speed, endurance, and flight; **RED ROBIN (TIM DRAKE)** Genius intellect, combat, Utility Belt; **RAVEN** Magical powers from demonic ancestry; **BEAST BOY (GARFIELD LOGAN)** Assumes the form of any animal; **WONDER GIRL (CASSIE SANDSMARK)** Silent Armor grants; powers of flight, force projection, and superhuman strength; **BUNKER (MIGUEL BARRAGAN)** Creates energy constructs; **POWER GIRL (TANYA SPEARS)** Scientific genius, superhuman strength, size alteration; **CHIMERA (RU'AT L'IWER)** Shape-shifting, power mimicry; **KID FLASH (BART ALLEN)** Super-speed, accelerated healing; **SKITTER (CELINE PATTERSON)** Transformation to arachnid gives superhuman speed and strength; **SOLSTICE (KIRAN SINGH)** Energy projection, flight, photokinesis; **SUPERBOY (KON-EL)** Partial Kryptonian super-strength, telekinesis.
ALLIES JLA, Legion Lost
ENEMIES N.O.W.H.E.R.E., Manchester Black

The Teen Titans banded together when Tim Drake—known as Red Robin—learned of a plot by the clandestine organization N.O.W.H.E.R.E. to capture adolescent metahumans and turn them to its own mysterious ends. But the group refused to be corrupted, survived the brutal gladiatorial combat known as the Culling, and unified against N.O.W.H.E.R.E.—all before they had even decided what to call themselves. United by their youth and shared sense of alienation, they became a media sensation, taking up the fight against evil as the next generation of heroes… and making many new enemies along the way.

After a series of running battles with agents of N.O.W.H.E.R.E., the teenage team ran into the organization's greatest success and secret weapon: Superboy. A bruising battle ensued, after which the Teen Titans (so named by Kid Flash) convinced Superboy to join them in the fight against N.O.W.H.E.R.E.. Infuriated by this setback, the organization's leader Harvest stepped in and, after capturing the ragtag team, brought them to N.O.W.H.E.R.E.'s hidden facility, the Colony.

Here, Harvest's assistant Omen tried to break the spirits of the Teen Titans individually, focusing on Red Robin. Harvest believed that if he could drive Red Robin to kill, the rest of the team would follow and Harvest would have his next generation of Ravagers, as he called the metahuman teams that survived the Culling. However, the Teen Titans escaped and put together a plan of attack with the recently time-displaced 31st-century Legion Lost.

N.O.W.H.E.R.E. MAN
Harvest had big plans for the Teen Titans—if they survived the Culling.

After destroying the Colony, the Legion Lost disappeared in their Time Bubble and the Teen Titans returned to New York, where they came under attack—from Wonder Girl. When Superboy removed Wonder Girl's Silent Armor, it was stolen by her former ally Diesel, who planned to use it to bring about the end of the world. The team recovered the armor, but was unable to prevent Superboy from being kidnapped by the Kryptonian clone H'El. Before he returned, Superboy and the rest of the Super-Family battled for the fate of the solar system against H'El, who planned to drain the sun's energy as part of an elaborate plan to save Krypton from destruction. At the same time, the Joker planned to get rid of the Teen Titans, hoping their demise would break Red Robin's spirit and isolate Batman. Amanda Waller, deciding she needed to rein in the Titans' activities, sent the Suicide Squad to bring them in for a little conversation. Nobody, in short, would leave them alone.

After his harrowing experiences, Superboy rejoined the team and the Titans fought off the corrupting demonic influence of Raven and Trigon, as the demon attempted to take over Earth. Raven turned against her father and joined the Teen Titans, as did Beast Boy, and two new heroes—Bunker and Skitter. Kid Flash's origin was revealed during the course of the Titans' adventures with the Legion Lost, and he then returned to his native 31st century to serve out a criminal sentence for acts he had no memory of committing. Solstice, unwilling to face life without him, committed a crime so that she could accompany him. Red Robin made the decision to disband the team,

TRIGON
Driven to conquer Earth because his daughter Raven's mother was human, Trigon made his move, sending Raven ahead to weaken the Teen Titans. However, she ultimately turned against him and joined the Teen Titans instead, rejecting the darker side of herself to find a home within the group.

WAYWARD DAUGHTER
Raven turned against her father Trigon when he wanted her to bring together all the worlds he ruled—and add Earth.

AT A GLANCE...

Teen spirit
The Teen Titans take both parts of their group's name seriously. They're a formidable fighting force, but they don't handle things the same way as other groups, because they're the next generation—headstrong, idealistic, and prone to lots of arguing.

Red Robin—leading the way
The glue holding the Titans together is Red Robin, who has the leadership qualities to keep such a disparate gang together—usually. He also has the necessary cynicism to keep the team suitably suspicious of the adult forces that want to use the Titans for their own ends.

Surrogate family
The Teen Titans tend to come from difficult backgrounds, and the team represents a surrogate family, with all that entails. They argue, they bicker, they occasionally make each other miserable… but when the chips are down, they're always there for each other.

CLASSIC STORIES

***New Teen Titans* (Vol. 2) #1–5 (Aug. 1984–Feb. 1985)** In "The Terror of Trigon," the group are forced to confront their darkest alternate selves as Raven's demonic father attempts to enslave and destroy the Earth.

***Teen Titans* (Vol. 3) #1–7 (Sep. 2003–Mar. 2004)** Reeling from the deaths of Donna Troy and Omen, the group try to figure out where it fits in, juggling adolescent problems and the new responsibilities of being the Teen Titans—and brawling with the JLA along the way.

***Tales of the Teen Titans* #42–44, *Tales of the Teen Titans Annual* #3 (May 1984–Jul. 1984)** The Titans face down H.I.V.E. and Deathstroke in "The Judas Contract," which features the first appearance of Dick Grayson as Nightwing.

leaving open the possibility of bringing them back together in the future, but he was under no illusion that the loss of Kid Flash and Solstice had done more damage than could be easily repaired.

In time, a reconstituted Teen Titans was approached by the mysterious Manchester Black with a tempting offer: ally with Black and have all the technological wherewithal of S.T.A.R. Labs at their disposal. Suspicious of Black's motives, Red Robin believed they needed to know more before making a decision. Meanwhile, the Titans were also finding their newfound fame was bringing its own tensions, and could become an unnecessary distraction. They did manage to prevent a renegade group of scientists from stealing dangerous technology sequestered in S.T.A.R. Labs, but then Manchester Black showed his true colors. He unveiled a new antihero team named the Elite, planning to wrest Superboy away from the Teen Titans. To make matters worse, former Titans Wonder Girl, Power Girl, and Kid Flash had become Elite members. However, the Teen Titans reunited with their past teammates when it became clear that Black was the real enemy. After defeating Black and contending with numerous challenges, including the loss and stormy return of Superboy, wavering public support, and personal crises and disputes, Red Robin once more called it a day for the tumultuous Teen Titans, and the heroes went their separate ways.

But not for long. Beast Boy and Raven were later joined by Starfire and a new Kid Flash in a revamped Teen Titans led by bad boy Damian Wayne, aka Robin, in time to face Damian's megalomaniac grandfather, Rās al Ghūl. **AI**

KRYPTONIAN FURY
The team (plus a returned Kid Flash) have their hands full with a raging Superboy.

"...We might be good or evil, black or white, man or woman, straight or gay. But one thing you can count on... we are very, very dangerous."

BUNKER

ROGUE TARGETS

After being kidnapped by H'El, Superboy was accused of crimes in the future, and the Teen Titans were implicated. They broke into a metahuman prison and were caught inside by Alpha Centurion and the Pax Galactica cosmic knights, looking to bring them all to future justice.

CAGED ROBIN
Red Robin experienced the penal system of the future, but they didn't hold him for long.

ON THE RECORD

In their initial incarnation, the Teen Titans were assembled from existing sidekicks and new junior versions of established heroes. Aqualad, Kid Flash, and Robin teamed up to defeat Mister Twister, and later recruited Donna Troy—then Wonder Woman's younger sister—into the team, completing their original lineup. From the Titans Lair they embarked on a series of teen-themed adventures against villains such as Ding Dong Daddy and the Mad Mod, giving the series a defining youth-culture flavor that continued in later iterations.

Infiltrations and manipulations

With the introduction of the telepath Raven in 1980, a new Teen Titans team was formed, featuring three existing members—Kid Flash, Wonder Girl, and Robin—and new additions Cyborg, Starfire, and Changeling (formerly Beast Boy). Raven manipulated the team into joining forces against her demonic father Trigon, after which they stayed together to face Deathstroke the Terminator and his protégé Terra, who had infiltrated the Titans.

Graduation day

The next epochal shake-up in the Teen Titans' lineup came after the (no longer Teen) Titans and Young Justice resisted interference from the secretive Optitron Corporation. They then tangled with a Superman robot that killed both Omen and Donna Troy. In the aftermath, both teams disbanded, with some members forming a new Teen Titans and others joining the Outsiders. Donna Troy, who had been resurrected after *Crisis on Infinite Earths*, would rejoin briefly but then leave to pursue membership in the Justice League of America.

Growing pains

The following years saw further upheaval—leadership shake-ups and a changing roster. Cyborg and Starfire left for the JLA, and Damian Wayne took on a leadership role, teaming up with Red Robin before a clash between them led to Damian's exit. With Red Robin in charge, the Teen Titans battled Superboy-Prime in a story that prefigured their post-Flashpoint debut.

FINAL MOMENT
Donna Troy thought she had the Cyborg Superman down, but that proved to be a fatal mistake.

TITANS, GO!
Robin (Damian Wayne) takes charge of the new Teen Titans.
1 Robin
2 Kid Flash
3 Starfire
4 Beast Boy
5 Raven

REBIRTH

KIDS' STUFF

Every incarnation of the Teen Titans has been beset by headstrong natures and internal strife. That's bad enough against ordinary super villains, but when Damian Wayne gathers Starfire, Raven, Beast Boy, and the newest Kid Flash to battle his grandfather Rā's Al-Ghūl, is the arrogant little bully leading the kids to their inevitable doom?

THANAGARIANS, THE

DEBUT *The Brave and the Bold* (Vol. 1) #34 (Mar. 1961)
CURRENT VERSION *Savage Hawkman* (Vol. 1) #1 (Nov. 2010)
BASE Thanagar
POWERS/ABILITIES Great strength and speed; long-lived and fast-healing with enhanced resistance to temperature extremes and acute hearing, sight, and sense of smell.
ALLIES Justice League United, Legion of Super-Heroes, Rann

Thanagarians are an ancient warlike race who built a civilization using a wonder element. Thanagar is situated in the over-crowded Polaris star-system, and is the only known planet with naturally occurring Nth metal.

The abundance of the ore—a psycho-reactive mineral with supernatural properties—allowed Thanagarians to perfect anti-gravity technologies. This enabled them to fly at incredible speeds using wings, armor, and their own muscular physiques.

Thanagar is a militaristic culture that adopted the motif of avian predators, with soldiers and law keepers patterned on feathered raptors. It is often referred to as "Hawkworld". Recently its moon Thalsalla was taken over by immortal criminal Byth. He used advanced science and the genetic hybrid Ultra the Multi-Alien to try and dominate reality. As a result of his world-shattering scheme, Thanagar and its people had to be moved into a binary orbit with ancient rival world Rann. **WW**

WINGED VICTORIES
Thanagarians possess an unshakable air of martial superiority, considering themselves apex predators at the top of the interstellar food chain.

THIRST

DEBUT *Aquaman* (Vol. 6) #5 (Jun. 2003)
BASE Secret Sea
HEIGHT 6ft 8in **WEIGHT** Variable
EYES Black **HAIR** None
POWERS/ABILITIES Life energy absorption, water and moisture absorption, creation of zombie slaves.
ALLIES Hagen, Black Manta
ENEMIES Aquaman, the Waterbearer, Lady of the Lake, Sentinels of Magic

The Thirst is a mystical construct derived from river mud; an antithetical being who hunted the sorcerous deities who guarded the Secret Sea. This vast metaphysical ocean was comprised of the communal imagination of humanity and underpinned the health of the planet's watery arteries and ultimately the life of mankind.

The Thirst was reawakened when Aquaman used his mystic water-hand to perform evil acts. It stalked the sea king while scheming to drain all life on Earth. Anything the Thirst drained would be reborn as a withered husk subservient to its will.

After numerous battles with Aquaman, the arid atrocity was tricked into merging with its Atlantean adversary. Knowing that he could defeat the Thirst from within, Aquaman surrendered their combined totality to the spiritual perfection of the Secret Sea. **WW**

THIRD ARMY

DEBUT *Green Lantern Annual* (Vol. 5) #1 (Oct. 2012)
POWERS/ABILITIES Superhuman strength; can survive vacuum, extreme cold, and radiation of space; communal mind link—they multiply by converting victims into versions of themselves.
ENEMIES White Lantern Kyle Rayner, Guy Gardner, Green Lantern Corps, Red Lantern Corps, Zamarons, Star Sapphire Corps
AFFILIATIONS Guardians of the Universe

The Third Army were a mind-linked bio-weapon designed by the Guardians of the Universe, and activated using the power of Volthoom, the First Lantern. The Army was released after the immortals decided that true order was only possible if free will was eradicated from the cosmos.

The Third Army were programmed to assimilate all life into their ranks. Though possession of a power ring from any Spectrum Corps offered protection from conversion, the drones were strong enough to dismember Lanterns and remove the rings.

Despite intense resistance from assorted color Corps, the creatures were on the verge of total triumph. However, protracted battles forced the Guardians to tap more of Volthoom's power, awakening their captive. He reclaimed his power and the Third Army disintegrated. **WW**

THAROK

DEBUT *Adventure Comics* (Vol. 1) #352 (Jan. 1967)
CURRENT VERSION *Legion of Super-Heroes* (Vol. 7) #15 (Apr. 2013)
BASE 31st-century Zadron, mobile
HEIGHT 6ft 4in **WEIGHT** 225 lbs
EYES Black **HAIR** None
POWERS/ABILITIES Cybernetically amplified intellect and limited mind control; enhanced strength and strategic competence.
ENEMIES Legion of Super-Heroes, Polar Boy

Tharok was a thief until a caper went terribly wrong and half his body disintegrated. A robotic frame was hastily constructed to replace the missing skeleton, but it also unexpectedly amplified Tharok's intelligence.

When Tharok and four other super-criminals were captured, they were offered amnesty by the sorely-stretched Legion of Super-Heroes if they would help battle a Sun-eater menacing Earth's solar system. Tharok convinced his criminal confederates to team up as a Fatal Five whose combined power could control the universe.

Many Fatal Five schemes involved ways to restore Tharok's human appearance while maintaining his computer-enhanced mind. After tapping the power of the Promethean Giants and ascending to a higher form, he was finally contained; frozen by Polar Boy. **WW**

THINKER

DEBUT *All Flash* #12 (Fall 1943)
CURRENT VERSION *Suicide Squad* (Vol. 4) #24 (Dec. 2013)
BASE Cell Nine, Belle Reve Penitentiary, Louisiana
POWERS/ABILITIES Hyper-intelligence
ALLIES James Gordon Jr., Harley Quinn
ENEMIES Amanda Waller, O.M.A.C., Suicide Squad, Unknown Soldier, Kevin Kho

Anonymous career criminal the Thinker had a great knack for extrapolating foolproof plans from scant data. He correctly predicted an invasion by super-villains from another reality and set himself up to benefit from their victory. From his cell in Belle Reve prison, the Thinker manipulated the inmates to build satellite technology in advance of the Crime Syndicate's arrival.

However, the Thinker's cerebral gifts came at a terrible price: his mental exertions drew energy from his body, so although he was only 25 years old, he had the body of a frail old man. When the Crime Syndicate triumphed, Thinker installed his wondrous mind in the possibly immortal body of O.M.A.C.. However, he had underestimated the resistance of incumbent personality Kevin Kho and the stubbornness of Amanda Waller's Suicide Squad, and was banished to another dimension. **WW**

THOMAS, DUKE

DEBUT *Batman* (Vol. 2) #21 (Aug. 2013)
BASE Gotham City
EYES Yellow **HAIR** Black
POWERS/ABILITIES Keen intellect; basic unarmed combat training; advanced puzzle-solving capabilities.
ALLIES Leslie Thompkins, DaxAtax, Dre-B-Robbin, R-Iko, Robina
ENEMIES The Joker, Riddler, Johnny Bender Jr., the Preacher, the Nest, the Talon
AFFILIATIONS We Are Robin, Batman

When he was young, Duke Thomas saw Gotham City blacked out and in total chaos. The Riddler was behind the city-wide panic, demanding that Gotham City residents "get smart" or die by natural selection. Duke immediately began training his mind with puzzles and conundrums to challenge the villain. When Duke's family saved Bruce Wayne from Hurricane Rene, another link was forged in a strengthening chain of destiny between the boy and the Bat.

Some years later the Joker—aware of the link—attacked Duke's family and Batman was only able to save the boy. While living in foster care, Duke joined the underground youth movement "We Are Robin:" a band of teenage vigilantes who came together to help Gotham City as grass-roots anti-crime crusaders proudly wearing the symbol of Batman's famous assistant.

Duke recently had to up his game as Batman offered him a possible front-line crime-fighting role and costume. **WW**

PART OF THE SOLUTION
Duke was convinced that crime and disaster were simply problems to be solved by enough good people making a concerted effort.

THOMPKINS, DR. LESLIE

DEBUT *Detective Comics* (Vol. 1) #457 **(Mar. 1976)**
CURRENT VERSION *Red Hood and the Outlaws* Vol. 1 #0 **(Nov. 2012)**
BASE The East End, Gotham City
HEIGHT 5ft 7in **WEIGHT** 130 lbs **EYES** Blue **HAIR** Gray
POWERS/ABILITIES Trained doctor and psychologist, with extensive experience in trauma injuries and drug dependency.
ALLIES Alfred Pennyworth, Bruce Wayne, Stephanie Brown, James Gordon, Jason Todd
ENEMIES Black Mask Society, Killer Croc
AFFILIATIONS Duke Thomas, Gotham City Child Services

Leslie Thompkins was a colleague of Dr. Thomas Wayne before he and his wife were gunned down in front of their son Bruce. With family retainer Alfred Pennyworth, she acted as surrogate parent to the traumatized orphan in the years following the murder, but as Bruce grew older and more distant she lost touch with him.

A skilled clinician and deeply compassionate, Leslie forsook private practice to work in medical centers for Gotham City's less fortunate citizens. In one of these she first met Jason Todd. The kid was living on the streets and stealing to survive, but hadn't been quick enough on his latest score. She tended to him diligently for a week until he healed, but in the end Jason vanished, swiping prescription drugs on the way out. When Batman caught the boy, Leslie ferociously defended him and instead of Todd being sent to a juvenile detention center or worse, to prison, Jason moved into Wayne Manor and finally began turning his life around.

Detesting violence and always willing to give people a second chance, the good Dr. Thompkins also spends time finding homes for orphans and runaways in Gotham City's Child Protection system. Her altruistic actions have consequently brought her into contact with many of the City's most conflicted characters such as Duke Thomas and Catwoman.

Despite the inherent and ever present dangers of her calling, Leslie is driven to help whenever and however she can. **WW**

HEART AND SOUL
Leslie Thompkins' greatest regret was that she was unable to persuade Batman's "family" to adopt less violent methods to keep Gotham City's monsters at bay.

ON THE RECORD

Leslie Thompkins was introduced in the classic Batman story "There is No Hope in Crime Alley." Here Batman was shown to visit a sordid backstreet of Gotham City on a particular night every year. This time, however, he saves a gentle old lady from muggers and a flashback reveals how that gentle stranger once reached out to the terrified young Bruce Wayne after the murder of his parents. Leslie offered love and comfort during the most horrific moment of his life.

ANGEL OF HOPE
Leslie Thompkins always knew that orphaned little Bruce would grow to be a most remarkable man.

THUNDER III

DEBUT *Outsiders* **(Vol. 3) #1 (Aug. 2003)**
REAL NAME Anissa Pierce
BASE Brooklyn, New York; New Orleans, Louisiana
HEIGHT 5ft 7in **WEIGHT** 119 lbs
EYES Brown **HAIR** Black
POWERS/ABILITIES Ability to increase mass and density; super-strength and invulnerability; can create shock waves by striking the ground.
ENEMIES Sabbac, Simon Hurt, Brother Blood

The daughter of Super Hero Black Lightning, Anissa Piece followed her father's wishes and went to college before starting her own crime-busting career. However, on the day she qualified as a doctor, she donned a costume for the first time and began helping people in a more unique way as the Super Hero Thunder. Her sister Jennifer later took up costumed crime-fighting as Lightning.

Just after her solo debut, Anissa accepted a place with the Outsiders, reasoning that the best place to learn was with seasoned professionals. Soon she was tackling some of the most terrifying villains around, like Simon Hurt and Brother Blood, and also started a relationship with teammate Grace.

As the battles became more intense, Anissa was gravely wounded many times. Once, after triggering a booby trap, she was in a coma for months, and later went into semi-retirement. **WW**

THUNDER, JONNI

DEBUT *Jonni Thunder* **(Vol. 1) #1 (Feb. 1985)**
BASE Los Angeles, California
HEIGHT 5ft 6in **WEIGHT** 130 lbs
EYES Green **HAIR** Blond
POWERS/ABILITIES Partially controlled ability to possess a high-voltage electrical entity.
ALLIES Harry Trump, Shamus, Skyman
ENEMIES Clarence "Slim" Chance, Red Nails
AFFILIATIONS : J. Thunder Detective Agency, Infinity Incorporated

Jonni Thunder was a tough-as-nails Los Angeles private eye. She gained accidental control of a magical thunderbolt, which lived in an old lamp belonging to her father, a former cop. His former partner Slim Chance desperately sought the artifact, eventually attempting to kill Jonni for it.

After Jonni brought Chance to justice, she remained on the fringe of the LA metahuman community. She was always reluctant to acknowledge her powers, but she did work closely with millionaire hero Sylvester Pemberton in his roles as Skyman and founder of Infinity Incorporated.

An alternate Jonni Thunder recently appeared on Earth-2, liberated from World Army incarceration by John Constantine. She joined Brainwave in trying to enslave the last survivors of humanity, and it is not known if she survived the planet's annihilation. **WW**

THUNDER, JOHNNY

DEBUT *Flash Comics* **(Vol. 1) #1 (Jan. 1940)**
CURRENT VERSION *DC Universe: Rebirth* **#1 (May 2016)**
REAL NAME Jonathan L. Thunder
BASE New York City; Gotham City; Fifth Dimension
HEIGHT 5ft 8in **WEIGHT** 125 lbs
EYES Blue **HAIR** Blond
POWERS/ABILITIES Absolute control of wish-granting "Thunderbolt" Genie—actually an energy being employing Fifth Dimensional science.

Johnny Thunder was the seventh son of a seventh son born under mystical circumstances. As an infant, he was taken by cultists from Bahdnisia, and through arcane rites was bonded to a powerful wishing genie. Under fortuitous circumstances—luck always favored Johnny—he was rescued before his seventh birthday and returned to his family in Brooklyn. For years, he never realized the phrase "Cei U" (say you) activated Yz, his invisible wish-granting Thunderbolt, for an "hour of power." An honest, decent soul, Johnny became an unlikely hero helping those in need through his "luck."

Johnny served the JSA with implausible distinction for many decades. He was murdered by the Ultra-Humanite, but his personality was absorbed by Yz. They now abide in the Fifth Dimension. **WW**

THUNDER, JAKEEM

DEBUT *The Flash* **(Vol. 2) #134 (Feb. 1998)**
REAL NAME Jakeem Johnny Williams
BASE Keystone City; New York City
HEIGHT 5ft 7in **WEIGHT** 130 lbs
EYES Brown **HAIR** Black
POWERS/ABILITIES Inherited control of "Thunderbolt" Genie from the original Yz/Johnny Thunder to deploy Fifth Dimensional science.
ALLIES Yz/Johnny Thunder, Stargirl
ENEMIES Triumph, Solomon Grundy, Mordru

After meeting the first Flash, orphan Jakeem Williams kept the pen Jay Garrick had used to sign autographs. Nobody realized that it housed elderly Johnny Thunder's Fifth Dimensional companion, Yz. The Thunderbolt bonded with Jakeem, and when a malign sprite from Yz's dimension invaded Earth, Yz and Jakeem were instrumental in helping the JSA defeat it. To accomplish the feat, Yz had to merge with fellow thunderbolt Lkz into a whole new entity—Yzlkz—activated whenever Jakeem clicked the pen and uttered the phrase, "So Cûl" (so cool).

An orphaned street kid, Jakeem was initially reluctant to join the JSA, but soon made friends with younger members such as Stargirl. As one of the team's "legacy heroes" he became an invaluable member of both the JSA and its First Strike component the All-Star Squadron. **WW**

THUNDER AND LIGHTNING

DEBUT *New Teen Titans* (Vol. 1) #32 (Jun. 1983)
CURRENT VERSION *Teen Titans Annual* (Vol. 4) #1 (Jul. 2012)
REAL NAMES Alexei and Ayla
EYES Black (Alexei); Brown (Ayla)
HAIR Brown (Alexei); Blonde (Ayla)
POWERS/ABILITIES **Alexei:** Able to generate destructive sonic wave-fronts by clapping his hands together; **Alya:** Can absorb energy and generate electrical blasts.
ENEMIES Harvest, N.O.W.H.E.R.E., Brother Blood, Niles Caulder

Metahuman siblings Alexei and Ayla don't know who they are or where they come from. Their earliest memories are of being experimented upon by N.O.W.H.E.R.E. technicians, who sought to boost their powers and make them the most potent living weapons possible.

As victors of the brutal gladiatorial contests known as the Culling, Thunder and Lightning were expected to join Harvest's murderous elite kill-squads. However, they were rescued by undercover operative Caitlin Fairchild, the Teen Titans, and a few time-displaced Legionnaires. Alexei and Ayla joined Fairchild's fugitive band of Ravagers but could find no peace. On the run from time-traveling tyrant Harvest, the twins stumbled from one battle to another and have since gone into hiding. **SW**

TIME MASTERS

DEBUT (As Rip Hunter and Crew) *Showcase* #20 (May–Jun. 1959); (As Time Masters team) *Time Masters* #1 (Feb. 1990)
CURRENT VERSION *Convergence* #1 (Jun. 2015)
BASE Vanishing Point, Rip Hunter Time Lab, Arizona Lab, Arizona
MEMBERS Rip Hunter, Dan Hunter, Tony, Bonnie Baxter, Corky Baxter, Jeff Smith, Booster Gold, Superman, Green Lantern Hal Jordan
ALLIES Starfire II, Claw the Unconquered, Skeets
ENEMIES Illuminati, Vandal Savage, Gog, Black Beetle, Per Degaton, Despero

The Time Masters are a loose affiliation of explorers and heroes assembled by scientist Rip Hunter to unearth the secret history of Earth and preserve the sanctity of the time-line. After being trapped in a dystopian 25th century, time-traveler Hunter deduced that an ancient cabal called the Illuminati would be responsible for a devastating global conflict, and resolved to stop it.

Hunter convened a second team to rescue Batman after he was cast adrift in the time-stream by Darkseid. Superman, Green Lantern, and Booster Gold tracked the Dark Knight from era to era, but Batman returned to his original time through his own efforts.

A later iteration of the team, consisting of Hunter, Booster Gold, and his sister Michelle Carter currently act as clandestine custodians of the time-stream; protecting reality from villains seeking to bend history to their desires. **SW**

TIME TRAPPER

DEBUT *Adventure Comics* (Vol. 1) #318 (Mar. 1964)
BASE The End of Time
POWERS/ABILITIES Immortality, transformation, manipulation of the time-stream.
ALLIES Glorith
ENEMIES Mordru, Legion of Super Heroes, Superman, Parallax

The Time Trapper is a sentient force resident at the end of space/time. An aspect of cosmic entropy, it easily weathers the dramatic changes wrought by reality-revisions such as the Infinite Crisis and Zero Hour. Each time the multiverse has changed or shifted, the Trapper has been personified by a new being. Previous examples have included: Cosmic Man, Rokk Krinn; Time Witch, Glorith; a Malthusian Controller, Lori Morning; and even the psychotic Superboy-Prime.

The Trapper has spent much of his attention challenging the 31st-century Legion of Super-Heroes and claims to have been instrumental in their creation as a weapon against his true enemy, Mordru. However, having complete control over the future, his ultimate goal remains constant—to bring about the dissolution of Creation in preparation for a new Big Bang. **SW**

TOMAHAWK

DEBUT *Star-Spangled Comics* (Vol. 1) #69 (Jun. 1947)
CURRENT VERSION *All-Star Western* (Vol. 3) #13 (Dec. 2012)
POWERS/ABILITIES Advanced unarmed combat skills; proficiency with knife, spear, bow and arrows, and throwing hatchet.
ALLIES Blue Jacket, Tecumseh, the Prophet
ENEMIES General Anthony Wayne, General George Washington, General Arthur St. Clair
AFFILIATIONS Iroquois Tribe, Shawnee Tribe

Born of Iroquois and Shawnee blood, Tomahawk was a mighty warrior among the Indian nations. He battled long and hard against the white invaders who were inexorably swallowing up their land.

When George Washington ordered ruthless General Anthony Wayne to wipe out every Indian settlement in the territory, Tomahawk's family were killed and he swore vengeance on all Americans. He had allies among the British forces occupying the colonies, but when he sought their help, he was betrayed as the white men worked together to force the Indians out.

Tomahawk's braves won another battle against the united invaders, and he took revenge on the man who killed his kin, but he realized his people would never know peace and security again. **SW**

TIMBER WOLF

DEBUT *Adventure Comics* (Vol. 1) #327 (Dec. 1964)
CURRENT VERSION *Legion Lost* (Vol. 2) #1 (Nov. 2011)
REAL NAME Brin Londo
BASE 31st-century Metropolis; 21st century New Orleans
EYES Brown/Golden **HAIR** Brown
POWERS/ABILITIES Human/wolf hybrid; enhanced senses, strength, speed, and agility.
ENEMIES Lord Vykor, Tor, Alastor Faud, Hypersapiens, Black Razors, Templar, Harvest

Brin Londo gained animalistic powers from a serum his father created from the genetic material of Timber Wolves. When Lord Vykor killed Brin's parents, Brin escaped to live on the streets. He became a savage vigilante, eventually bringing Vykor to justice. Science Police officer Captain Adym was impressed with Brin and recommended him to the Legion of Super-Heroes. Before long, the lone wolf had graduated from the Legion Academy and, despite his feral nature, became a valued team member.

On one mission, Brin and other Legion members were trapped a thousand years in the past. Brin's prior experience of rough living came to the fore helping them survive in this primitive age, before Brainiac 5 brought them back to their original era. **SW**

TIME WARP
The Time Masters traveled through time thanks to a time machine built by Rip Hunter, and were fully aware of the risks of changing the time-stream.

FRIENDS FIRST
The Time Masters team was made up of Rip Hunter's friends and family members.
1 Tony
2 Dan Hunter
3 Corky Baxter
4 Jeff Smith
5 Rip Hunter
6 Bonnie Baxter

TITANS OF MYTH

DEBUT *New Teen Titans* (Vol. 1) #11 (Sep. 1981)
BASE Tartarus
MEMBERS **Oceanus and Tethys**: Can control the oceans and all sea creatures; **Hyperion and Thia**: Can project devastating sunfire; **Coeus and Phoebe**: Can project nighttime darkness; **Cronus and Rhea**: Can manipulate earth and vegetation; **Crius and Mnemosyne**: Pre- and postcognitive powers and possess the universe's memories; **Iapetus and Themis**: Arbiters of law.
ENEMIES Gods of Olympus, Teen Titans, Wonder Woman, Hindu Gods

The Titans are a primordial group of very powerful extra-dimensional entities who dominated parts of Earth in mythic pre-history. They were the paired offspring of primeval sky-god Ouranos and Earth-mother Gaea, but supplanted their parents' rule after Cronus murdered their father. Attaching themselves to the tribes of what is now Greece, they fed off the fearful worship and enforced adoration of mortals, and were in turn ousted by Cronus' son Zeus.

Zeus exiled the Titans to Tartarus and created his own pantheon: the Gods of Greece. At some point, Thia escaped and hid amongst the mortals of Earth. When she clashed with the Teen Titans, her kindred were also released and Cronus spawned a newer, deadlier family, employing them to attack Olympus. They were defeated by Gaea, Wonder Woman, and the Greek and Hindu pantheons, and all the Titans were returned to Tartarus. **SW**

ALL IN THE FAMILY
The Titans of Myth are pairs of siblings who each control specific elements of the World. Their children will become the Olympian gods and goddesses.

TWINNED TITANS
1 Oceanus, 2 Tethys (Titans of the Seas)
3 Cronus, 4 Rhea (Titans of the Moon)
5 Thia, 6 Hyperion (Titans of the Sun)
7 Phoebe, 8 Coeus (Titans of the Earth)
9 Crius, 10 Mnemosyne (Titans of Memory)
11 Iapetus, 12 Themis (Arbiters of Law)

TOMAR-RE

DEBUT *Green Lantern* (Vol. 2) #6 **(May–Jun. 1961)**
CURRENT VERSION *Green Lantern* (Vol. 5) #14 **(Jan. 2013)**
BASE Xudar, Space Sector 2813
HEIGHT 6ft 2in **WEIGHT** 210 lbs **EYES** Red **HAIR** No hair, orange fins
POWERS/ABILITIES Brilliant research scientist and engineer; skilled diplomat commanding a power ring able to materialize hard-light constructs, translate languages, generate in-planet and intergalactic flight, and protect against hostile environments and enemy attack.
ALLIES Hal Jordan, John Stewart, Arisia of Graxos, Katma Tui, Stel of Grenda, Tomar-Tu
ENEMIES Atomic Changeling, Goldface, Sinestro, Nekron, Black Hand, Anti-Monitor
AFFILIATIONS Green Lantern Corps, Green Lantern Honor Guard

Tomar-Re was the Green Lantern assigned to the space sector nearest Earth. The Xudarian became a lifelong friend to Hal Jordan when the human took over from Abin Sur. Hal and Tomar worked together often, despite the Guardians' rules about fraternization between active agents.

A great scientist and warrior, Tomar-Re served for many years and was eventually rewarded with elevation to the elite Green Lantern Honor Guard. His service ended when he was killed by Goldface in the anti-matter universe during the *Crisis on Infinite Earths*. However, even after death Tomar-Re worked with living Lanterns on two further missions. He rallied thousands of deceased Green Lanterns to attack Nekron, the Lord of Death, after he attempted to invade the living universe. Tomar later acted as a guide and advisor to Hal Jordan and Sinestro when Black Hand trapped them in Nekron's dire Dead Zone. His sector was inherited by his son Tomar-Tu who carries on his tradition of superlative service to the universe. **SW**

ON THE RECORD

Though lauded as one of the greatest Green Lanterns of åall, Tomar-Re's most significant achievement was actually his greatest failure. Urgently dispatched by the Guardians to stop a planet from being destroyed by geological pressures, he was the victim of a fateful accident which temporarily blinded him. Unable to prevent Krypton's demise, Tomar had no idea that his momentary affliction was instrumental in the creation of the universe's most momentous hero—Superman.

LANTERN CALLING
Tomar-Re used his power ring to contact Hal Jordan and request his his help in saving the planet Aku.

TOYMAN

DEBUT **(As Winslow Schott)** ***Action Comics*** **(Vol. 1) #64 (Sep. 1943); (As Hiro Okamura)** ***Superman*** **(Vol. 2) #177 (Feb. 2002)**
CURRENT VERSION ***Batman/Superman*** **(Vol. 1) #5 (Jan. 2014)**
REAL NAME Hiro Okamura
BASE Toymaster Gameshop, Gotham City
EYES Brown **HAIR** Black
POWERS/ABILITIES Genius polymath, brilliant in many scientific disciplines.
ENEMIES Mongul, Joker, Lex Luthor

Many men have claimed the title of Toyman, transforming toys into weapons in search of profit. Most used their innovations for criminal endeavors rather than simply market the fruits of their genius.

Though still a teenager, Hiro Okamura was one of the smartest people on Earth. Driven to challenge himself and have fun, Hiro built fantastic robots and designed complex and engaging computer games. Although his motives may have been pure, he often got carried away, such as when his massive multiplayer online game grew large and authentic enough to allow alien invader Mongul to endanger Batman and Superman in the real world. After helping the heroes beat Mongul, Hiro became their technical advisor and information resource, allowing them to keep him occupied and out of trouble. **SW**

TOMORROW, TOMMY

DEBUT ***Real Fact Comics*** **#6 (Jan. 1947)**
CURRENT VERSION ***Threshold*** **# 2 (Apr. 2013)**
REAL NAME T'omas T'Marra
BASE Tolerance, Tenebrian Dominion
EYES Blue **HAIR** Blond
POWERS/ABILITIES Cunning planner and problem-solver with advanced combat skills.
ALLIES Brent Wood, Tuftan the Tiger Prince
ENEMIES Jediah Caul, Star Sapphire, Stealth, Rikane Starr, Knights of the Galaxy

Tommy Tomorrow's most consistent history is as a valiant explorer, peace-keeper, and an agent of the Planeteers. In another time and dimension he was Kamandi, the Last Boy on Earth, struggling to re-establish humanity on a planet teeming with intelligent and aggressive animals. In yet another reality, Major Thomas Tomorrow is a military martinet with a secret agenda.

His most recent transformation took him to the Tenebrian Dominion as Colonel T'omas T'Marra: a double-dealing opportunist secretly running the galaxy's most popular entertainment. Glimmernet sensation *The Hunted* is a gameshow where viewers can win big prizes simply by catching and killing the featured stars. Naturally, T'Marra has more than one reason to keep the runners running and the pursuers confused. **SW**

TRACI 13

DEBUT ***Superman*** **(Vol. 2) #189 (Feb. 2003)**
BASE Metropolis
HEIGHT 5ft 5in **WEIGHT** 127 lbs
EYES Brown **HAIR** Black
POWERS/ABILITIES Urban magic; able to tap into the spiritual energy of cities to cast spells.
ALLIES Leroy, Blue Beetle, Kid Eternity, Zatanna
ENEMIES: Heartbreakers, Eclipso, Brother Blood, the Futuresmith

Traci Thirteen and her father never saw eye to eye. Dr. Terence Thirteen was a magic-debunking scientist, while his daughter was a magic-using witch. Traci … power from her mother—a member of the human sub-species Homo Magi—and when Mrs. Thirteen died, Traci's dad blamed her and forbade her from ever using her gifts. When he suddenly vanished, Traci began accruing mystical knowledge, eventually she moved on, basing herself in Metropolis as freelance supernatural problem-solver Girl 13, aka Traci 13.

After helping Superman defeat an infestation of Heartbreaker demons, Traci was reunited with her father, who had been possessed by one of the horrors after her mother died. Since then she has operated on the fringes of the Super Hero community, offering mystical aid to mortal heroes. **SW**

TRENCH

DEBUT ***Aquaman*** **(Vol. 7) #1 (Nov. 2011)**
BASE Marianas Trench, Pacific Ocean
EYES Black **HAIR** None
POWERS/ABILITIES Water-breathing; immense strength; able to withstand tremendous pressure; neuro-toxic secretions; mimicry; bio-luminescence; steel-rending teeth and claws; ability to weave cocoons to transport prey.
ENEMIES Aquaman, Mera
AFFILIATIONS King Atlan, Dead King's Sceptre, Atlantis, Xebel

The Trench are cannibalistic sea-dwellers subsisting at the bottom of the deepest ocean chasm on Earth. Millennia ago they formed one of the seven kingdoms that survived the catastrophic sinking of the Atlantean continent caused by King Atlan.

Mutated into beings capable of surviving beneath the sea, they seemingly lost all rationality, becoming primitive and bestial. The ravenous creatures subsisted in darkness at the bottom of the Marianas Trench for eons, unsuspected and forgotten by the sub-sea empire of Atlantis, which had developed in shallower regions. In recent times, shifts in sea floor geology allowed the Trench to rise from the depths, where they discovered waters and land teeming with sustenance.

They were eventually turned back by Aquaman and Mera, who found that the beasts were actually gathering food to feed their next generation. **SW**

FROM THE DEPTHS
Aquaman and Mera were investigating the disappearance of people from Beachrock, when they were attacked by the hungry Trench.

TREVOR, STEVE

DEBUT *All-Star Comics* (Vol. 1) #8 (Dec. 1941–Jan. 1942)
CURRENT VERSION *Justice League* (Vol. 2) #3 (Jan. 2012)
REAL NAME Steven Rockwell Trevor
HEIGHT 6ft 1in **WEIGHT** 195 lbs **EYES** Blue **HAIR** Blond
POWERS/ABILITIES Expert pilot and military tactician.
ALLIES Amanda Waller, Wonder Woman, Etta Candy
ENEMIES David Graves, Cheetah, Menagerie, Crime Syndicate of America
AFFILIATIONS A.R.G.U.S., Justice League of America

A.R.G.U.S. ORIGINS
The President personally asked Trevor to become the founder and acting director of A.R.G.U.S.

Decorated pilot and respected command officer Steve Trevor was one of Wonder Woman's first friends when she appeared in the world beyond Themyscira. He argued on her behalf with Amanda Waller, who considered Wonder Woman and the Amazons a significant security threat. Trevor became the government's liaison to Wonder Woman and the Amazons, and also fell in love with her. His feelings were not reciprocated and they became leverage for Waller when she needed Trevor to help form a new hero team to counterbalance the potential threat of the Justice League. Waller showed him a picture of Diana kissing Superman to point out that metahumans were different from normal humans and needed oversight—specifically, an A.R.G.U.S.-controlled Justice League of America.

Trevor agreed to put this team together, and the newly-formed JLA saw its first action in the fight for Pandora's Box in Kahndaq. He took to the field himself, notably fighting the Cheetah and her Menagerie in Central Park and recapturing Wonder Woman's Lasso of Truth from the feline villain in the run-up to the final devastating confrontation between the merged Justice Leagues and the Crime Syndicate of America. **AI**

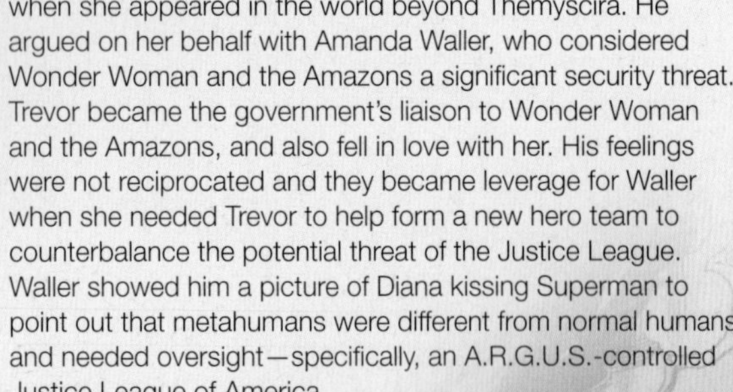

DARKSEID INVASION
Steve Trevor was at Wonder Woman's side when Darkseid unleashed his terrifying Parademons on Earth.

ON THE RECORD

Over the years, Steve Trevor has been Wonder Woman's guide, friend, confidant, lover, and husband. Throughout it all, his loyalty to her and her ideals has remained constant. In his 1987 origin story, he was connected with the Amazons even before he was born. He was the son of Diana Trevor, who sacrificed her life to save the women of Paradise Island from the demon Cottus and posthumously lent her name to the newly born girl who would later become Wonder Woman.

REJECTED PROPOSAL
When Wonder Woman saved Steve from a plane crash, he gratefully asked her to marry him. Diana respectfully declined, explaining that she had to focus on her duty fighting evil.

TRIAD

DEBUT *Action Comics* (Vol. 1) #276 (May 1961)
CURRENT VERSION *Legion: Secret Origin* #1 (Dec. 2011)
REAL NAME Luornu Durgo
BASE Legion Space
HEIGHT 5ft 7in **WEIGHT** 136 lbs
EYES Orange/violet **HAIR** Auburn
POWERS/ABILITIES Can divide into three or more different bodies; martial-arts training takes advantage of fighting with multiple bodies.
ENEMIES: Dominators, Fatal Five

Also known at various times as Triplicate Girl or Duplicate Girl, Luornu Durgo was born on the planet Cargg in the latter half of the 30th century, where the triple sun gave native Carggites the power to split into identical duplicates. Unlike other Carggites, however, Luornu's three duplicates manifested their own individual personalities, and she was forced to spend time in a mental institution for this unusual aberration.

She was inducted into the Legion of Super-Heroes and became a key part of their espionage activities as they battled the Dominators and other threats to Legion Space. Along the way she honed her powers until she could to create a nearly limitless number of duplicates. After the Legion was disbanded following the shattering battle against the Fatal Five, Triad appeared again with the reunited team on 21st-century Earth to combat Byth Rokk's plot to create the universe-destroying entity called Infinitus. **AI**

ME, MYSELF, AND I
When Luornu splits herself, her duplicate bodies each have distinct personalities and sets of abilities.

TRICKSTER

DEBUT *The Flash* (Vol. 2) #183 **(Apr. 2002)**
CURRENT VERSION *The Flash* (Vol. 4) #3 **(Jan. 2012)**
REAL NAME Axel Walker
BASE Central City
HEIGHT 5ft 7in **WEIGHT** 150 lbs **EYES** Blue **HAIR** Blond
POWERS/ABILITIES Possesses various gadgets including anti-gravity boots, and a cybernetic arm.
ALLIES Captain Cold, Mirror Master, Weather Wizard, Heat Wave
ENEMIES Flash, Johnny Quick
AFFILIATIONS Secret Society of Super-Villains, Rogues

As a young man, the Trickster was recruited into the Rogues and then kicked out again for making too many mistakes that endangered the team. He tried to ingratiate himself with Gorilla Grodd, but had his arm torn off for his trouble. With a brand-new cybernetic arm, he was imprisoned after being framed for a heist, then broken out to rejoin the Rogues. They traveled to Happy Harbor and learned that the Crime Syndicate's Johnny Quick had broken them out, and they were offered a chance to join the Syndicate.

Trickster and the Rogues couldn't stomach the Syndicate's violence, so they went on the run, with Deathstorm and Power Ring on their trail. A trip through Mirror World landed them in Gotham City, where Poison Ivy poisoned Trickster to force him to get Weather Wizard to bring sunlight back to her flowers. Trickster then hot-wired a G.C.P.D. vehicle to get the team out of Gotham City, but Johnny Quick and Grid were in close pursuit. Mirror Master saved Trickster and the rest of the Rogues by trapping their pursuers in Mirror World while the Injustice League defeated the Crime Syndicate, returning things to their villainous status quo. **AI**

EASY MONEY
The Trickster puts his anti-gravity footwear to good use, escaping from the scenes of his crimes.

ON THE RECORD

The first Trickster was James Jesse, the stage name of Giovanni Giuseppe, a trapeze artist with a fear of heights who invented a pair of "air walker shoes" that allowed him to perform safely. Eventually he turned to crime, before turning FBI informant and retiring.

Sometime later, the villain Blacksmith wanted someone with similar skills in her new gang and selected wayward teenager Axel Walker, giving him upgraded versions of the Trickster's tools.

JOINING FORCES
In the pre-Flashpoint continuity, the Trickster and Captain Cold teamed up after robbing the *Picture News* costume ball. They were defeated by the combined efforts of the two Flashes.

TRIGON

DEBUT *New Teen Titans* (Vol. 1) #2 **(Dec. 1980)**
CURRENT VERSION *Phantom Stranger* (Vol. 4) #1 **(Dec. 2012)**
BASE Azarath
HEIGHT Variable **WEIGHT** Variable **EYES** Yellow **HAIR** Black
POWERS/ABILITIES Demonic powers including draining souls, unleashing energies, transmutation of elements, destroying planets.
ENEMIES Teen Titans

An ancient trinity of cosmic entities known as the Divine attempted to eradicate evil from the universe. Punishing the brutal conqueror of a world, they sentenced him to be consumed by the Heart of Darkness, but he fought back and instead fed on the Heart of Darkness, assimilating the evils of a billion worlds and transforming into the all-powerful demon, Trigon.

He became the ruler of the Under-Realms, and fathered children to spread his evil. One of those children was the human girl Raven, whom Trigon believed would unify all dimensions under his rule. When she fled to Earth, Trigon made a bargain with the Phantom Stranger that he would spare Earth from destruction if the Stranger would capture and return Raven—now with the Teen Titans—to him, which he duly did.

Later, alerted to the presence of the mystical Silent Armor on Earth, Trigon unsuccessfully tried to take it from its new host, Cassie Sandsmark (Wonder Girl). He also attempted to destroy the Teen Titans from within, but even Trigon's immense powers could not overcome the Titans' unity and they repelled him even after he briefly possessed their minds. Once Trigon was forced back to Azarath, Raven rejoined the teen Titans, trying to break free of her father's malign influence. **AI**

ON THE RECORD

Trigon's home dimension of Azarath was once said to be a place of peace, overseen by powerful sorcerers who raised Raven under their protection when she rejected her father's evil, and fought to prevent Trigon from breaching the barriers between their dimension and Earth's.

Trigon finally succeeded and Raven, seeing no other choice, agreed to rule with him if he spared Earth. Knowing he wouldn't keep his side of the bargain, she gathered the New Teen Titans to fight against his coming invasion. Their defeat of Trigon was their signature achievement.

RAVEN'S SACRIFICE
Facing Trigon in the Temple of Azarath, the Titans were easily defeated. Raven realized that the only way to save Earth was to join her father. Together they vanished in a cloud of smoke.

TROY, DONNA

DEBUT *The Brave and the Bold* (Vol. 1) #60 **(Jun.–Jul. 1965)**
CURRENT VERSION *Wonder Woman* (Vol. 4) #37 **(Feb. 2015)**
REAL NAME Donna Troy
BASE Themyscira
HEIGHT 5ft 9in **WEIGHT** 135 lbs
EYES Brown **HAIR** Black
POWERS/ABILITIES Superhuman strength, endurance, agility, and durability; healing factor; expert fighter; weapons include Amazon armor and swords.
ALLIES Dick Grayson, Arsenal, Wonder Woman
ENEMIES Mr. Twister, Aegeus
AFFILIATIONS The Titans, Amazons

When Donna Troy emerged on Themyscira, Wonder Woman was busier than ever. Torn between life as Themyscira's queen, her duties as the newly appointed God of War, and as a Justice League member, Wonder Woman was subjected to much critique from her Amazon people.

One of these critics was an old woman named Derinoe, who saw weakness in Diana. Using black magic and the clay remains of Wonder Woman's mother, Hippolyta, Derinoe created a so-called perfect Amazon, Donna Troy. Donna challenged Diana's claim to the throne, leading her army to murder dozens of Amazon men. Using her Lasso of Truth, Diana showed Donna the error of her ways. Donna regretted believing Derinoe's lies, and Wonder Woman imprisoned her for a time. Donna was later turned to stone by an arrow shot by Aegeus and seemingly killed. She returned to life, thanks to Zeus, reborn as Fate itself. **MM**

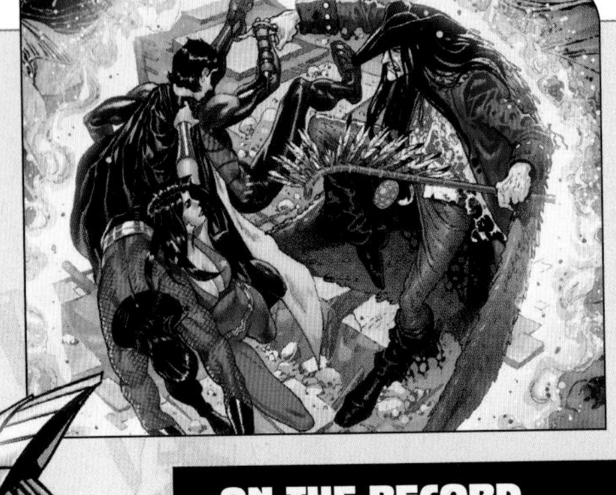

FORGOTTEN TITANS
When Donna Troy discovered she had mysterious shared memories with other heroes, including Dick Grayson and Arsenal, she teamed up with these so-called Titans and came into conflict with the dastardly Mr. Twister.

ON THE RECORD

Donna Troy's backstory has been an ever-evolving one, nearly from the time of her creation. Originally conceived as Wonder Girl, Donna was meant to be a teenage version of Wonder Woman as a founding member of the newly formed Teen Titans. She became one of the team's mainstays, taking the independent name Donna Troy, and appearing only once in a Wonder Woman story during the Bronze Age.

Continuity was altered in the 1980s to recreate Donna as a girl chosen for training by the Titans of Myth, during which she adopted the name Troia. In the 1990s, Donna was reestablished once more, but this time as a magical doppelganger of Wonder Woman brought to life, while Diana was out of action for a while.

THE RETURN
Donna Troy's history was somewhat streamlined after she was killed by a rogue Superman robot. She came back as a combination of all her past selves, but relied primarily on her Titans of Myth origin.

TUI, KATMA

DEBUT *Green Lantern* (Vol. 2) #30 (Jul. 1964)
CURRENT VERSION *Green Lantern* (Vol. 5) #37 (Feb. 2015)
BASE Coast City
HEIGHT 5ft 11in **WEIGHT** 131 lbs
EYES Blue **HAIR** Black
POWERS/ABILITIES Green Lantern ring allows flight, force-fields, and space travel.
ALLIES Green Lanterns: John Stewart, Hal Jordan, and Kilowog
ENEMIES Sinestro, Star Sapphire

Born on the planet Korugar, Katma Tui became the Green Lantern for Space Sector 1417, replacing the corrupt Lantern-turned-super-villain, Sinestro. Despite a difficult start, with the Korugarans distrusting the Green Lanterns and regarding their new protector as "Katma Tui the Lost," Katma went on to prove herself many times over.

After several successful missions, she was assigned to train another Green Lantern, John Stewart, and, after a rocky start to their relationship, they fell in love. She eventually journeyed to Earth with John to help form Earth's own Green Lantern Corps, and the two married. Some time later, during a home invasion by Star Sapphire, Katma was viciously killed. John never fully recovered from the loss, haunted by her death for years after.

Katma would see life in a fashion one last time when resurrected as part of the Black Lantern Corps. However, this evil, undead version of the once well-respected hero was ultimately destroyed. **MM**

NOTHING SINISTER
Though from the same planet as Sinestro, the only other trait Katma Tui shared with the corrupt Green Lantern was her skill with a power ring.

TULA

DEBUT *Aquaman* (Vol. 1) #33 (May–Jun. 1967)
CURRENT VERSION *Aquaman* (Vol. 7) #14 (Jan. 2013)
BASE Atlantis
HEIGHT 5ft 5in **WEIGHT** 119 lbs
EYES Blue **HAIR** Brown
POWERS/ABILITIES Ability to breathe underwater and swim at extreme speeds.
ALLIES Murk, Garth, Swatt, Ocean Master, Mera, Aquaman
ENEMIES Scavenger
AFFILIATIONS The Drift

The Atlantean named Tula first became known to the surface world when Ocean Master, Aquaman's half-brother Orm, led an invasion against the US and the surface world. After Aquaman defeated Orm and reclaimed his role as the King of Atlantis, he met with Tula who commanded the Drift, a faction of the Atlantean army.

What Aquaman did not know was that Tula had her own allegiances. As Orm's sister, she was determined to break her brother out of Belle Reve prison with the help of Ocean Master loyalists such as Murk and Swatt. However, when Atlantis was attacked by the Scavenger, Tula and her allies went home.

Tula later proved her loyalties towards Mera, accepting her as her queen for the sake of peace. She also grew to accept Aquaman when Arthur revealed to Tula that she had been following the orders of a Mera impersonator who had secretly taken the true Atlantean queen's place. **MM**

EASILY MISGUIDED
In her relatively short career as commander of the Drift, Tula has mistakenly followed a corrupt Mera imposter and the villain Ocean Master.

T

TWO-FACE

DATA

DEBUT *Detective Comics* (Vol. 1) #66 **(Aug. 1942)**
CURRENT VERSION *Batman* (Vol. 2) #1 **(Nov. 2011)**
REAL NAME Harvey Dent
BASE Gotham City
HEIGHT 6ft **WEIGHT** 182 lbs
EYES Blue **HAIR** Brown
POWERS/ABILITIES Dangerous split personality makes him unpredictable; expert knowledge of law and police procedure; extremely intelligent and a brilliant strategist; relies on lucky coin to make decisions.
ALLIES Gilda Dent (deceased), Bruce Wayne (formerly)
ENEMIES Batman, Batman Family, Erin McKillen
AFFILIATIONS The Secret Society of Super-Villains

CLASSIC STORIES

***Batman* (Vol. 1) #234 (Aug. 1971)** Two-Face is reintroduced to Bronze Age comic readers in a classic tale that saw the villain seek gold hidden aboard an old ship.

***Batman* (Vol. 1) Annual #14 (Dec. 1990)** Two-Face is given an updated origin that ties neatly into "Batman: Year One" and deals with his fractured psyche.

***Batman: The Long Halloween* #1-13 (Dec. 1996-Jan. 1998)** Harvey Dent's wholesale descent into madness is chronicled month-by-month as the mysterious Holiday serial killer strikes in Gotham City.

***Detective Comics* (Vol. 1) #817-820 and *Batman* (Vol. 1) #651-654 (May-Aug. 2006)** In the "Face-to-Face" storyline, a healed Harvey Dent attempts to follow in Batman's footsteps as a hero in Gotham City, only to be reborn as Two-Face.

BIRTH OF TWO-FACE
In a violent, life-changing act of revenge, criminal Erin McKillen tied DA Harvey Dent to his desk and poured acid on his face, claiming that the world could now see how two-faced he truly was.

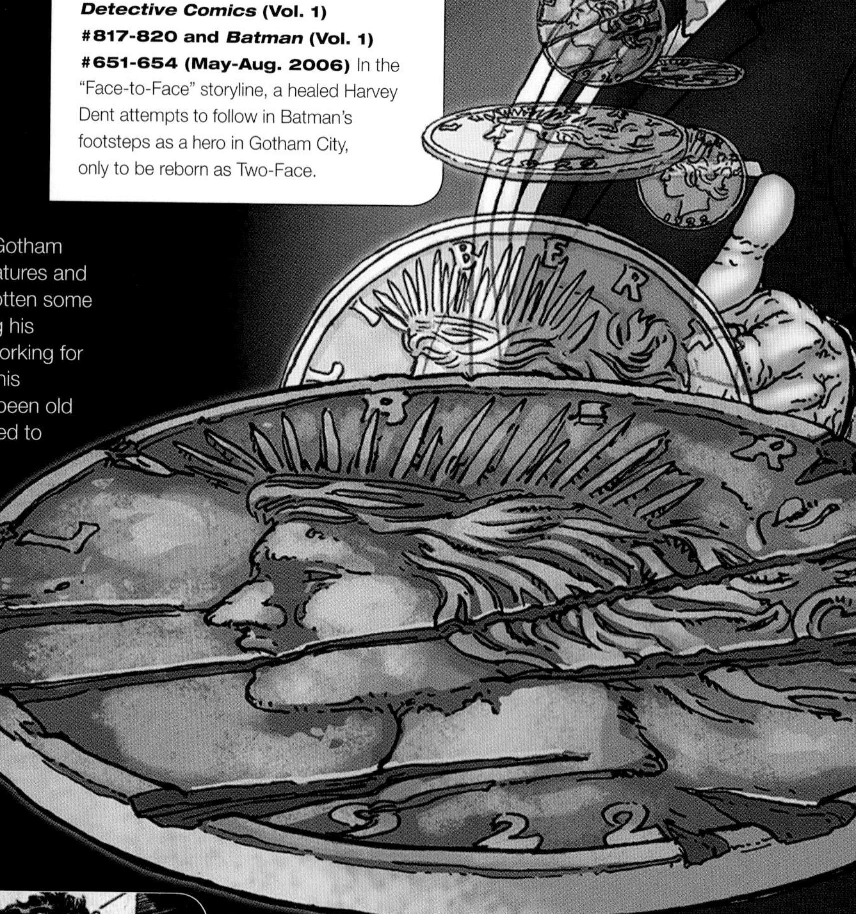

Harvey Dent has led a deeply conflicted life. Possessing a split personality that veers between two extremes—good and evil—Dent goes by the name of Two-Face. It is an apt description of his physical appearance. Scarred by acid into outwardly becoming the monster he once hid away from the world, Two-Face has become a tragic figure and one of Batman's most unpredictable and dangerous opponents.

Harvey Dent lived an enviable life in Gotham City. As a premier defense attorney with handsome features and a beautiful wife named Gilda, he had it all. Dent had gotten some of the city's worst criminals back on the street by using his knowledge of the law's technicalities. However, after working for the notorious McKillen Clan he was starting to rethink his priorities. Twin sisters Shannon and Erin McKillen had been old friends of Bruce Wayne since childhood, but both turned to crime in later years, even going as far as hiring a hit on Commissioner James Gordon. It was after this failed assassination attempt that Dent was approached by his old friend Bruce Wayne. Wayne admired Dent's legal skill and wanted him to run for District Attorney, turning his expertise towards putting criminals away rather than setting them free. Dent agreed to run for office, and soon he found himself partnering with both Jim Gordon and the Batman, setting his sights on the McKillen sisters.

After the McKillen twins were jailed, thanks in part to Harvey Dent's exemplary work as District Attorney, Shannon McKillen killed herself to give Erin a chance to break out. One of Erin's first stops was to Dent's office where she set about enacting savage revenge on the double-crossing lawyer she held responsible for her sister's death. She stabbed and killed Gilda, then knocked Harvey unconscious. When Harvey awoke, he was tied to his office desk, and Erin was pouring acid on his face, scarring him for life. It was on that day that Harvey Dent adopted the name Two-Face. He soon showed his talent as a cunning, if psychotic, master criminal who relies on a scarred coin to make his decisions for him, forever torn between his old, noble self and his dark side. **MM**

ON THE RECORD

One of Batman's oldest enemies, Two-Face first debuted in the 1940s, his original alias being Harvey Kent. With his last name being perhaps a little too close to the alter ego of a certain Kryptonian Super Hero, Harvey's surname was changed to "Dent" as he continued to be a thorn in Batman's side over the decades.

After the *Crisis on Infinite Earths* event, Harvey Dent was reintroduced during "Batman: Year One" as Gotham City's golden boy, a white knight in the city's crusade against crime. Through several different origin stories that followed, it was disclosed that Harvey had always struggled with a dark dual personality. His true split self only emerged fully when the over-zealous District Attorney's face was irreparably scarred by gangster Sal Maroni.

A MAN DIVIDED
Harvey Dent's modern origin revealed that he had been abused by his father, a traumatic event that split his personality years before Two-Face was born. Later, even after plastic surgery to fix his face, Harvey couldn't let go of his dark past.

TWO OF A KIND
Batman and Two-Face share a long history. It was Bruce Wayne who introduced Harvey Dent to his future wife, Gilda. Despite Harvey's past crimes, Batman wants nothing more than to restore the sanity of his old friend.

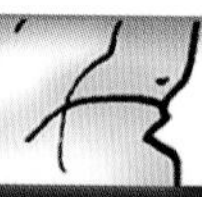

ULTRA-HUMANITE

DEBUT *Action Comics* (Vol. 1) #13 **(Jun. 1939)**
CURRENT VERSION *Action Comics* (Vol. 2) #36 **(Jan. 2015)**
BASE Phantom Zone
POWERS/ABILITIES Telepathy, teleportation, fear-projection, illusion-casting, mind control, possession, soul corruption, unchecked growth fueled by the absorption of his victims' terror.
ENEMIES Superman, Steel, Toymaster, Lana Lang
AFFILIATIONS Eight Wonders of the World, Michael Holt

Ultra-Humanite has been trapped in the Phantom Zone for eons: long enough to have forgotten his name and how and why he was imprisoned there. He briefly escaped to Earth when schoolboy Clark Kent felt great fear during a crop fire in Smallville. However, Clark's emotional strength was too intense and the psychic parasite retreated into the timeless dungeon dimension.

Twenty years later, when the Phantom Zone was ruptured by Superman's battle against Doomsday and Brainiac, the predator broke out again. Possessing many Smallville residents, Ultra-Humanite again attempted to amplify Superman's fears and feed on them. Aided by Lana Lang, Steel, Toymaster and a group of telepathic Smallville elders, Superman chased Ultra-Humanite back into the Phantom Zone, where the hungry horror again tried to absorb his fear. As Superman drew the monster's attention away from its corrupted pawns, he also absorbed all their fears, forcing the beast to focus solely upon him. Just as in their first encounter, Superman's raw emotions were too much, and Ultra-Humanite explosively released all his victims and retreated to the most remote regions of the Phantom Zone. **AI**

ON THE RECORD

Ultra-Humanite was DC Comics' original mad scientist and first recurring villain. He fought Superman many times, evading justice by transplanting his brain into new bodies, ranging from a movie actress to a giant insect. As a mutated albino ape, he led the Secret Society of Super-Villains and battled the Justice Society of America.

Constantly increasing his powers, he killed the Crimson Avenger and Johnny Thunder. However, after usurping the magic of Thunder's Thunderbolt, he was shot dead by a new Crimson Avenger.

BRAWN OVER BRAINS
Despite his impressive intellect, Ultra-Humanite was obsessed with making each new body stronger than the last.

ULTRA BOY

DEBUT *Superboy* #98 (Jul. 1962)
CURRENT VERSION *Legion of Super-Heroes* (Vol. 7) #1 (Nov. 2011)
REAL NAME Jo Nah
BASE Legion Headquarters
HEIGHT 6ft **WEIGHT** 190 lbs
EYES Brown **HAIR** Brown
POWERS/ABILITIES Vast strength, speed, invulnerability, flight, vision like Superman—but can only use one power at a time.
ENEMIES Daxamites, Dominators, Fatal Five

Growing up on the planet Rimbor, Jo Nah was a troublemaker who ran with the Emerald Dragons gang. After a monstrous creature ate him alive, he was freed by the Galactic Patrol before he could be digested. However, he was affected by the monster's radiation and discovered he had multiple superpowers—although he could only use one of them at a time.

As Ultra Boy, Jo Nah became a core member of the Legion of Super-Heroes, battling the Daxamites and the Dominators, before the entire Legion took on the Fatal Five with the fate of the universe at stake. He was also with the Legionnaires who traveled back to the 21st century to fight alongside Justice League United against Byth Rok and Ultra the Multi-Alien before Ultra could grow into Infinitus and destroy the Legion's future. **AI**

UNCLE SAM

DEBUT *National Comics* (Vol. 1) #1 **(Jul. 1940)**
CURRENT VERSION *The Ray* (Vol. 3) #4 **(May. 2012)**
HEIGHT 6ft 5in; variable **WEIGHT** 140 lbs **EYES** Blue **HAIR** White
POWERS/ABILITIES Super-strength, speed, invulnerability, immortality; enhanced senses, charisma, and reflexes; clairvoyance; ability to alter size; interdimensional teleportation; all sustained by the American people's belief in the ideals of Liberty and Democracy.
ALLIES The Ray, Phantom Lady, Doll Man, Human Bomb, Firebrand, the Spectre, Superman, Justice League of America
ENEMIES Secret Society of Super-Villains, Imperiex, Black Adam, Sinestro, Deathstroke
AFFILIATIONS S.H.A.D.E.

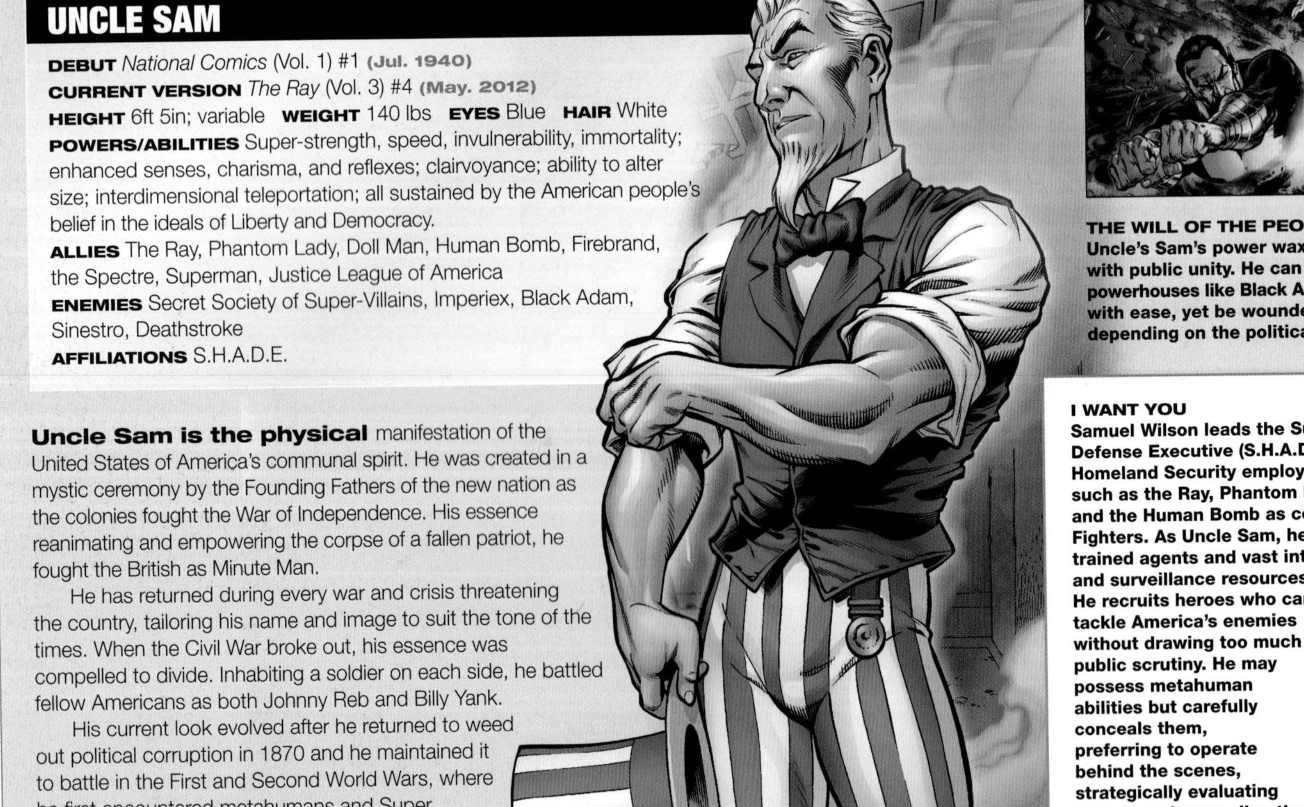

Uncle Sam is the physical manifestation of the United States of America's communal spirit. He was created in a mystic ceremony by the Founding Fathers of the new nation as the colonies fought the War of Independence. His essence reanimating and empowering the corpse of a fallen patriot, he fought the British as Minute Man.

He has returned during every war and crisis threatening the country, tailoring his name and image to suit the tone of the times. When the Civil War broke out, his essence was compelled to divide. Inhabiting a soldier on each side, he battled fellow Americans as both Johnny Reb and Billy Yank.

His current look evolved after he returned to weed out political corruption in 1870 and he maintained it to battle in the First and Second World Wars, where he first encountered metahumans and Super Heroes. In recent times, with the will of the people increasingly divided, his power levels have fluctuated wildly so he increasingly works with allies such as the Freedom Fighters to defeat America's foes. **WW**

THE WILL OF THE PEOPLE
Uncle's Sam's power waxes and wanes with public unity. He can tackle real powerhouses like Black Adam or Sinestro with ease, yet be wounded by bullets, depending on the political mood.

I WANT YOU
Samuel Wilson leads the Super Human Advanced Defense Executive (S.H.A.D.E.), a branch of Homeland Security employing metahumans such as the Ray, Phantom Lady, Doll Man and the Human Bomb as covert Freedom Fighters. As Uncle Sam, he commands trained agents and vast intelligence and surveillance resources. He recruits heroes who can tackle America's enemies without drawing too much public scrutiny. He may possess metahuman abilities but carefully conceals them, preferring to operate behind the scenes, strategically evaluating threats and expending the assets of S.H.A.D.E. to "defend the 21st century."

THE UNTITLED

DEBUT *Red Hood and the Outlaws* #4 (Feb. 2012)
POWERS/ABILITIES Virtually immortal beings of pure evil; intangibility; darkness manipulation; shape-shifting.
ENEMIES All-Caste, Jason Todd (Red Hood), Outlaws (Starfire, Arsenal), Essence

Eons ago, before "the sun began to cast shadows over the Earth," a clan of nine brothers and sisters—the Untitled—discovered the waters of Absolute Evil. One by one, they drank deep of the flowing waters, which conferred dark and unspeakable powers, as well as immortality. One sister, Ducra, resisted the evil. She formed the All-Caste, a mystical and martial arts clan. The bitter antagonism between the Untitled and the All-Caste lasted for thousands of years. Eventually the Untitled tracked the All-Caste to their secret Himalayan base and all-but wiped them out.

The Untitled's brutal actions incurred the enmity of former Robin Jason Todd, who had been cared for and trained by the All-Caste after being gravely injured by the Joker. Todd had even fallen in love with Ducra's daughter, Essence, so had an additional reason for hating the Untitled.

As Red Hood, Jason continued to track down the Untitled along with his Outlaws team. All he knew was that the remaining dozen or so members usually hid in positions of authority to cover their tracks. **AI**

DARK EVOLUTION
The tainted black waters imparted great power and immortality, but could only corrupt those lacking the moral strength to resist its temptations.

UNKNOWN SOLDIER

DEBUT *Our Army at War* (Vol. 1) #168 **(Jun 1966)**
CURRENT VERSION *G.I. Combat* (Vol. 3) #1 **(Jul. 2012)**
HEIGHT 5ft 9in **WEIGHT** 155 lbs **EYES** Black **HAIR** None
POWERS/ABILITIES Expertise with all forms of military ordnance and most unarmed combat disciplines; master of disguise with excellent strategic and tactical skills and an uncontrollable ability to tap into the memories of soldiers throughout history.
ALLIES Amanda Waller, Komal Akbari
ENEMIES Al-Isri, Ali "Ollie" Hassan, Roman, Crime Syndicate

CAREER SUICIDE
Running roughshod over a squad of government-sanctioned criminal maniacs was a new challenge for the "Immortal G.I."

The Unknown Soldier joined the Army after his family was killed in London during a terrorist attack. Disfigured in combat in Afghanistan, he was retrained as a clandestine operative, carrying out black-ops missions all over the world for the covert organization Advanced Medical Military Operations.

Wounded again in Dubai, during his recuperation he learned he was the latest in a line of Unknown Soldiers stretching back to the Middle Ages—and perhaps beyond. He also began suffering flashbacks and hallucinations, possibly caused by nanites A.M.M.O. had implanted to track him while he was in the field.

Rebelling against his increasingly untrustworthy A.M.M.O. bosses, he tried disappearing and taking up civilian life, but war and conflict seemed to seek him out. After his return from Afghanistan, A.R.G.U.S. chief Amanda Waller brought him into the Suicide Squad, placing him in charge of a detachment dubbed the Reverse Squad.

Their first mission was to hunt down O.M.A.C. and capture those members of the Crime Syndicate who had survived the final battle with the Justice League. It is assumed he is still working with A.R.G.U.S.. **AI**

ON THE RECORD

The original Unknown Soldier was a World War II infantryman whose face was obliterated by the same grenade that killed his brother. He was intensively retrained, mastered disguise skills, and became the Allies greatest intelligence agent. After the war he was biologically augmented, extending his operational usefulness by decades.

The Unknown Soldier was radically re-imagined in 2008 as a Ugandan doctor, Moses Lwanga. Caught up in an insurgency, the good doctor learned that his personality and memories were fabricated by the previous Unknown Soldier. His predecessor had attempted to transfer his persona and skills to Lwanga to create peace instead of perpetuating war.

THE KNOWN UNKNOWN
The Unknown Soldier strides into battle, his face bandaged to both hide his disfigurement and protect his identity.

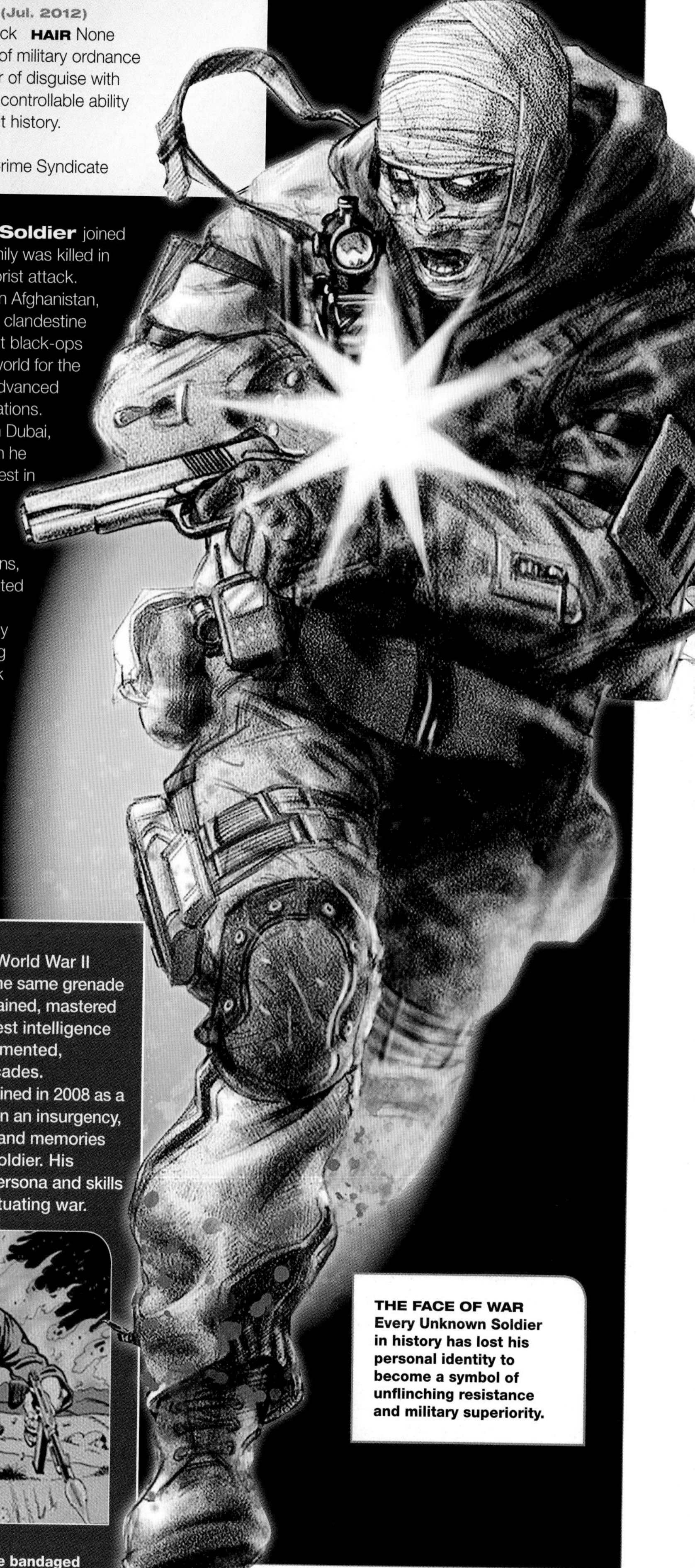

THE FACE OF WAR
Every Unknown Soldier in history has lost his personal identity to become a symbol of unflinching resistance and military superiority.

VALE, VICKI

DEBUT *Batman* (Vol. 1) #49 (Oct.-Nov. 1948)
CURRENT VERSION *Batman* (Vol. 2) #1 (Nov. 2011)
BASE Gotham City
HEIGHT 5ft 8in **WEIGHT** 115 lbs
EYES Red **HAIR** Green
POWERS/ABILITIES Ace reporter; extremely intelligent; adept at self-defense.
ALLIES Bruce Wayne, Jason Bard
ENEMIES The Penguin, Carmine Falcone

Vicki Vale is a star reporter for *The Gotham Gazette*, and a member of Gotham City's elite. Thanks to her busy social life, Vale knows Bruce Wayne personally, and grew better acquainted with the notorious bachelor when he helped take the *Gazette* online.

Although used to vetting her sources, Vale was duped when she began a romance with Jason Bard. While Bard quickly ascended the ranks of the Gotham City Police Department, eventually becoming commissioner, Vicki helped his rise, publicizing his heroic deeds. She didn't realize that Bard had a vendetta against the Batman, and was using his power to stop the Dark Knight once and for all. Vale finally discovered the truth, and Bard eventually turned over a new leaf, offering her an exclusive confession for the *Gazette* to get back in Vicki's good graces. **MM**

VANGUARD

DEBUT *The New Teen Titans* (Vol. 2) Annual #1 (1985)
BASE Mobile
NOTABLE MEMBERS Anti-Matterman, Black Nebula, Drone, Scanner, Solaar, White Dwarf.
ENEMIES Brainiac

The Vanguard is a team of superpowered beings that roams the universe in their sentient starship, Drone, helping worlds that have need of their astonishing cosmic powers. Mistaking Superman for a threat, the Vanguard journeyed to Earth, and tried to capture the Man of Steel. The Teen Titans came to Superman's aid, but quickly realized that this Man of Steel was merely a robot duplicate. The real Superman had been captured by Brainiac to be used as an organic power source for his interstellar war machines. Brainiac had also killed Vanguard member Black Nebula when she tried to stop him.

The Teen Titans joined forces with the remaining Vanguard members: the anti-matter universe siphoning Anti-Matterman; the psychically superior Scanner; the gravity and density controlling White Dwarf; and the energy manipulating Solaar, to take on Brainiac. Their united strength eventually saw off the cybernetic villain, allowing the Vanguard to return to the stars. **MM**

VANDAL SAVAGE

DEBUT *Green Lantern* (Vol. 1) #10 **(Winter 1943)**
CURRENT VERSION Demon Knights #1 **(Nov. 2011)**
REAL NAME Vandar Adg
BASE Mobile
HEIGHT 5ft 10in **WEIGHT** 176 lbs **EYES** Brown **HAIR** Black
POWERS/ABILITIES Immortal due to ancient blood rituals; cannot be killed through traditional means; wounds heal regardless of severity; incredibly intelligent with ancient connections throughout the world; briefly possessed superhuman strength, endurance, durability, and flight when supercharged by the returning comet that gave him his powers.
ALLIES Signalman, Giganta, Madame Xanadu, Jason Blood, Shining Knight
ENEMIES Agent Kassidy Sage, Superman, Wonder Woman, Swan-Killer, Pandora, Mordru, Scandal Savage
AFFILIATIONS Demon Knights, Justice League United, the House of Savage

The man known as Vandal Savage has been plaguing the Earth for millennia. According to Vandal, he has remained alive due to the blood sacrifice rituals he makes every so often to forgotten gods who opt to grant him immortality. More than 16 years ago, Savage was known as Jonathan Savage, the Cherry Blossom Killer, when he abandoned his wife and daughter to fulfill his blood ritual to ancient gods. Over 1,000 years ago, he served as a member of the Demon Knights, a fractious team of early superhumans and immortals that he founded—more by accident than design—to fight the sorcerer Mordru. More than 40,000 years ago, Vandal Savage was a Neanderthal caveman called Vandar Adg, who, during a battle with a Cro-Magnon tribe, stumbled upon a fragment of a comet that is now recognized to be the true source of his power and immortality.

In recent years, Vandal Savage joined the Secret Society, battled the legendary mystic warrior Pandora, and even reluctantly joined a mission with Justice League United. All the while, he had been biding his time for the return of his precious comet to Earth. To this end, Vandal conspired against Superman, draining the Man of Steel's powers to draw the comet closer to the planet. However, despite the asteroid re-energizing Savage, Superman still brought the villain to justice. **MM**

STAYING ALIVE
Vandal Savage believed that slaughtering Superman—even a powerless one—would extend his life for centuries to come.

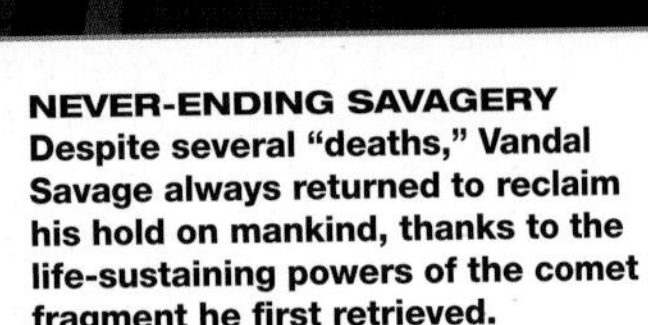

NEVER-ENDING SAVAGERY
Despite several "deaths," Vandal Savage always returned to reclaim his hold on mankind, thanks to the life-sustaining powers of the comet fragment he first retrieved.

ON THE RECORD

Vandal Savage originally debuted in the Golden Age of Comics in the pages of *Green Lantern*. He fought the first Green Lantern Alan Scott, and over the years would come to face nearly every major character in the DC Comics stable.

Before *Crisis on Infinite Earths* altered continuity, Vandal was an Earth-2 resident and battled the Justice Society of America. After the Crisis, he became the prime adversary of the Flash (Wally West), before emerging as the arch-nemesis of the youthful hero Damage, the long-lived Resurrection Man, and even the time-traveling hero Rip Hunter.

THE MAN WHO WANTED THE WORLD!
In his 1943 debut, Vandal Savage fought Earth-2 Green Lantern Alan Scott and his doughty sidekick "Doiby" Dickles. Savage would go onto become a recurring JSA foe in his early comic book exploits.

VENTRILOQUIST AND SCARFACE

DEBUT *Detective Comics* (Vol. 1) #583 **(Feb. 1988)**
CURRENT VERSION *Batgirl* (Vol. 4) #20 **(Jul. 2013)**
REAL NAME Shauna Belzer (Ventriloquist)
BASE Gotham City
HEIGHT 5ft 11in **WEIGHT** 115 lbs
EYES Brown **HAIR** Grayish black
POWERS/ABILITIES Telekinesis; often uses her abilities to control the bodies of others as well as her ventriloquist dummy named Ferdie; dangerously insane; weapons include Ferdie, her puppet, who is equipped with drill hands.
ALLIES "Ferdie"
ENEMIES Batman, Batgirl, the Riddler
AFFILIATIONS The Secret Six

The woman currently boasting the title of the Ventriloquist is Shauna Belzer, a demented super-villain who grew up in the shadow of her gifted twin brother, Ferdie. Shauna's brother was a child star, popular with his classmates and favored by their parents. Meanwhile, Shauna bore the cruel nickname of "Shabby Shauna" and grew to resent Ferdie's success. When she discovered that she had telekinetic powers, Shauna used them to force one of her teasing classmates to step in front of an approaching car. She then forced her brother to swing so hard on a swing set that the chain snapped and he was killed.

Shauna then started to use her powers more overtly, forcing her parents to follow her every command. When, at a friend's birthday party, Shauna encountered a ventriloquist, she became immediately infatuated with his wooden dummy. She forced the ventriloquist to slit his own throat, and then kept the dummy for her own, naming him after her brother, Ferdie, and forming a twisted relationship with the inanimate puppet. Shauna often uses Ferdie to give vent to her dark side, using him to murder anyone who dares to cross her. **MM**

DEADLY DOUBLE ACT
Shauna and Ferdie constantly bickered, but it was always other people who paid the ultimate price.

ON THE RECORD

The original Ventriloquist, before Flashpoint altered the status-quo, was the mild-mannered murderer, Arnold Wesker, the right-hand man to his gangster boss Scarface, a ventriloquist's dummy.

After facing Batman several times and becoming known as one of Gotham City's most notorious crime bosses, Wesker was killed. Scarface was adopted by the equally unbalanced Peyton Riley, who acted out the role of Scarface's moll, using the dummy's reputation to earn a place for herself in the underworld.

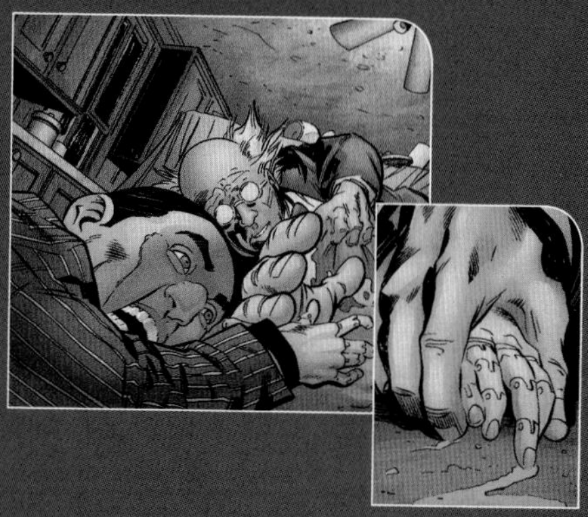

END OF A BEAUTIFUL RELATIONSHIP
When Arnold Wesker was murdered by the insane criminal the Great White Shark, Scarface also died. He was later resurrected by Peyton Riley, the next Ventriloquist.

VERTITAS, SHAY

DEBUT *Superman* (Vol. 3) #13 (Dec. 2012)
REAL NAME Dr. Shay Veritas
BASE The Block (near the Earth's core)
HEIGHT 5ft 5in **WEIGHT** 109 lbs
EYES Brown **HAIR** Purple
ABILITIES Genius-level intelligence; access to advanced scientific equipment.
ALLIES Superman, Supergirl
ENEMIES Doomsday, Lobo

Dr. Shay Veritas is an eminent omniologist, who studied virtually everything under the sun and worked at the Block—an advanced research facility near the Earth's core. Equipped with an array of advanced equipment, Dr. Veritas became the perfect ally for Superman, who would often visit her to assess the range and magnitude of his powers. For Shay, it was a unique opportunity to run experiments on his superhuman form.

Their friendship apparently began when Superman saved the center from a stream of destructive maelstroms. A flirtation ensued, and although it never developed into a romance, Veritas is the only person on the planet who the Man of Steel trusts with sensitive information about his physiology and his abilities. While Veritas remains at the Block at all times, she sends out a holographic projection to communicate with the surface world. **MM**

VIBE

DEBUT *Justice League of America Annual* (Vol. 1) #2 **(1984)**
CURRENT VERSION *The New 52: Free Comic Book Day* Special Edition #1 **(Jun. 2012)**
REAL NAME Francisco "Cisco" Ramon
BASE Detroit, Michigan
HEIGHT 5ft 7in **WEIGHT** 145 lbs **EYES** Brown **HAIR** Black
POWERS/ABILITIES Taps into the vibrational strands that hold reality together, allowing him to project vibrations at others; can see objects vibrating at unique frequencies.
ALLIES Dale Gunn, Breacher, Gypsy
ENEMIES Suicide Squad, Rupture, Parademons
AFFILIATIONS Justice League of America

Cisco Ramon gained his powers unknowingly, when the event horizon of a Boom Tube opened in front of him, killing his brother. After the incident, Cisco was studied for years, without his knowledge, by the government agency A.R.G.U.S.. When A.R.G.U.S. agent Dale Gunn tested his powers, Cisco passed with flying colors. Gunn then outfitted him with a special suit developed by his agency, and Cisco became Vibe. Not only that, Cisco was told that starting the following day, he would become a member of a new team called the Justice League of America. **MM**

GOOD VIBRATIONS
Cisco's powers allowed him to pinpoint incursions by extradimensional "Breachers" into Earth's reality—and he was trained to deal with them if they proved hostile.

ON THE RECORD

Vibe originally debuted in the mid-1980s, before the *Crisis on Infinite Earths*. He was one of four new recruits into the Justice League of America, later nicknamed "Justice League Detroit" when the title began showcasing new characters. Alongside Gypsy, Steel, and Vixen, Vibe became a valued member of the League, but would be killed by one of Professor Ivo's androids only a few years after his debut. His undead body later returned as a Black Lantern during the Blackest Night event.

FEELIN' THE VIBE
Breakdancer Paco Ramone said he was too cool to join a team of old super dudes, but realized he needed them as much as they needed Vibe.

VIXEN

DEBUT *Action Comics* (Vol. 1) #521 **(Jul. 1981)**
CURRENT VERSION *Justice League International* (Vol. 3) #1 **(Nov. 2011)**
REAL NAME Mari Jiwe McCabe
HEIGHT 5ft 9in **WEIGHT** 140 lbs **EYES** Amber **HAIR** Brown
POWERS/ABILITIES Uses the power of the Tantu Totem to take on the abilities of any animal, allowing her to gain massive strength, fly, dig rapidly, or perform many other feats.
ALLIES Justice League
ENEMIES Peraxxus, Ocean Master
AFFILIATIONS Justice League International

Mari McCabe is a Super Hero and fashion model from the African nation of Zambesi. As bearer of the Tantu Totem, she can take on the abilities of any animal by tapping into the Red, the morphogenetic field of all life on Earth. As Vixen, Mari was recruited into the United Nations' Justice League International team, led by Booster Gold. She took part in their first mission, to defeat the planet-plundering alien Peraxxus and his Signal Masters. However, she was later seriously injured in a bomb attack at the UN and had to quit the team while she recuperated.

By the time Ocean Master and his Atlanteans attacked Boston and took key members of the Justice League captive, Vixen was once more ready for action. She was drafted into the Justice League as a temporary member and used her powers to help drive back the Atlantean tide.

In the aftermath of the attack, she was considered for full Justice League membership. She and other potential candidates were invited to the Watchtower and, when Platinum went out of control, Vixen used gorilla-strength to help subdue her. However, despite her quick thinking and demonstration of her powers, Vixen was not chosen to join the team. **SW**

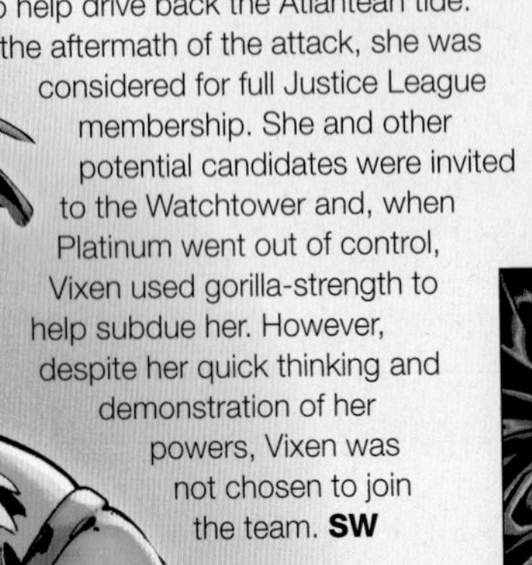

PRIMAL FURY
The Tantu Totem allows Vixen to channel the abilities of any animal, making her a formidable opponent.

FACING PERAXXUS
In Peraxxus, Vixen faced an enemy of enormous power. Even so, she managed to land some telling blows before he escaped.

LEAGUE CASUALTIES
The bombing of the Justice League's ceremony at the UN killed League member Gavril Ivanovich and severely injured Vixen.

ON THE RECORD

The pre-Flashpoint Vixen served as a member of many teams, including the Suicide Squad, Justice League of America, Birds of Prey, and Justice League Task Force. On one memorable adventure she faced the African trickster-god Anansi within the Tantu Totem itself. She also returned to Africa and came to terms with her past by facing her mother's murderer—Aku Kwesi, a warlord who was taking control of local villages with help from Intergang.

WRATH OF THE VIXEN
Mari returned to Zambesi to avenge her mother and put an end to Intergang's schemes. But her enemy was far stronger than she realized, and the battle was not an easy one.

VIGILANTE

DEBUT *New Teen Titans Annual* (Vol. 1) #2 (Aug. 1983)
REAL NAME Adrian Chase
BASE New York City
HEIGHT 6ft 2in **WEIGHT** 197 lbs
EYES Blue **HAIR** Blond
POWERS/ABILITIES Superb athlete; expert with knives and firearms; master of multiple martial arts; meditates to heal injuries.
ALLIES Teen Titans, Nightwing
ENEMIES New York Mafia, Electrocutioner, Saber, Cannon, Peacemaker

Adrian Chase was once a crusading District Attorney in New York City, using the legal system to take on the Mob. However, after a vengeful gang boss killed his wife and children in a bombing, the lawyer was contacted by a mysterious group dedicated to fighting evil from outside the law. They trained him in the martial arts and meditation, and on returning to New York he embarked on a crime-fighting career as Vigilante.

Despite his noble intentions, Adrian found himself sliding toward darkness as his war against crime progressed. When he tried to retire, his friend Alan Welles and then his court bailiff Dave Winston took up the mantle—but both were killed in action. Adrian finally decided to become Vigilante once again, but could not deal with the stress and took his own life. The identity was later taken up by rogue police officer Pat Trayce; the mysterious Justin Powell; and then Adrian's own brother, Dorian Chase. **SW**

VIOLENT METHODS
Despite initially trying to use non-lethal techniques, Adrian's descent into darkness resulted in him killing without hesitation.

VIKING PRINCE

DEBUT *The Brave and the Bold* (Vol. 1) #1 (Aug.–Sep. 1955)
REAL NAME Jon Haraldson
HEIGHT 5ft 11in **WEIGHT** 171 lbs
EYES Blue **HAIR** Blond
POWERS/ABILITIES Skilled warrior and great narrator; cannot be harmed by fire, water, wood, or metal.
ALLIES Sgt. Rock, Black Canary
ENEMIES Krogg the Red

Many legends are told of the mysterious time-lost warrior called the Viking Prince. According to some tales, he crossed the Atlantic to find Vinland; in others, he fell in love with a Valkyrie and wished to die to be with her, but was cursed by Odin so that fire, water, wood, and metal could not slay him.

As well as sailing across the seas and battling monsters and other mighty foes, he was transported through time on several occasions. The Lord of Time forced the Viking Prince to join the Five Warriors From Forever to face the Justice League of America. He was stranded with other temporal exiles on Dinosaur Island, and later, in World War II, fought beside Sgt. Rock of Easy Company. Killed by explosives while battling the Nazis, perhaps the Viking Prince finally beat Odin's curse and achieved the death he long desired. **SW**

VOODOO

DEBUT *W.I.L.D. Cats* (Vol. 1) #1 (Aug. 1992)
CURRENT VERSION *Voodoo* (Vol. 2) #1 (Nov. 2011)
BASE Dead City of the Daemonites, Europa
EYES Brown **HAIR** Brown
POWERS/ABILITIES Shape-shifting; mimicry; telepathy; poison quills; life support; can extrude wings or claws from body.
ENEMIES Black Razors, Black Jack, Green Lantern (Kyle Rayner)

Priscilla Kitaen was an exotic dancer with the stage name "Voodoo," who was captured by the alien Daemonites. They subjected her to procedures that transformed her into a shape-changing human/alien hybrid, but when she escaped, the Daemonites used her DNA to create another hybrid: Voodoo.

Voodoo took over Priscilla's old identity (and even her job) to blend in and gather data on Earth's superhuman population, but she was found by the alien-hunting Black Razors. She took refuge in a safehouse, but Green Lantern (Kyle Rayner) tracked her down, forcing her to return to the Daemonite mothership. Voodoo was furious when a Daemonite commander explained that she was just a genetic experiment, but agreed to work with them after being offered command of all hybrids on Earth. Voodoo set out to kill Priscilla and faced her on Jupiter's moon, Europa. However, Priscilla convinced her that she didn't have to follow the Daemonites, and could choose her own destiny. **SW**

HYBRID ABILITIES
Voodoo's wings and razor-sharp claws made her formidable in close combat, while her shape-shifting made her highly suited for espionage.

VUNDABAR, VIRMAN

DEBUT *Mister Miracle* (Vol. 1) #5 (Nov.–Dec. 1971)
BASE Apokolips
HEIGHT 5ft 2in **WEIGHT** 103 lbs
EYES Blue **HAIR** Black
POWERS/ABILITIES As a New God, Virman is immortal and has superhuman physical attributes; a relatively skilled strategist.
ENEMIES Mister Miracle, Big Barda, Justice League International

A product of one of Granny Goodness' infamous orphanages, Virman Vundabar was a member of Darkseid's inner circle. He was obsessed with military discipline and devoted to Granny, but despite his best efforts he repeatedly failed to capture Mister Miracle for her.

When Darkseid was lost in the Source Wall, Virman sided with Granny as the dark lord's henchmen jockeyed for influence. When Darkseid returned, Vundabar made a foolhardy grab for power by trying to assassinate his lord, and was destroyed by Darkseid's Omega-Beams. He was later resurrected by Darkseid, only to be killed again by the Infinity-Man. Reborn on Earth, Vundabar ran the Dark Side Club's gladiatorial competitions. He finally suffered the ignominy of being beheaded by the Clock King, one of the club's fighters. **SW**

VILLAINS UNITED (THE SOCIETY)

DEBUT *Villains United* #1 (Jul. 2005)
CORE MEMBERS **Lex Luthor** (actually Earth-3's Alexander Luthor, Jr.) Ring Leader; **Talia al Ghūl**: Trained assassin; **The Calculator**: Master schemer; **Black Adam**: Channels the powers of the Egyptian pantheon of gods; **Doctor Psycho**: Mind-warping telepath; **Deathstroke**: Combat expert with augmented physical and metal capabilities.
ENEMIES Secret Six, Freedom Fighters, the Joker, the real Lex Luthor, Vandal Savage

After Earth-3's Alexander Luthor Jr. escaped the pocket dimension to which he had been exiled following the *Crisis on Infinite Earths*, he impersonated Earth-0's Lex Luthor and used his resources to found a new villainous group. Under the leadership of an inner circle consisting of Talia al Ghūl, Doctor Psycho, Black Adam, the Calculator, and Deathstroke, Luthor recruited more than 200 members of the super-villain community. Known as The Society, the clandestine group also went by the moniker Villains United.

Luthor, Jr. offered these super bad guys protection from an increasingly ruthless Justice League, making it abundantly clear that the penalties for refusal would be severe. However, a shady figure called Mockingbird (actually the real Lex Luthor in disguise) formed the Secret Six to battle the Society. The Society moved quickly against these renegades, but the Six survived the ensuing battle after Vandal Savage threatened to kill Alexander Luthor, Jr.. Meanwhile, the Joker was disgruntled about not being asked to join the Society and began a terror campaign against them.

During the Infinite Crisis, Alexander Luthor, Jr. led the Society in the Battle of Metropolis, but they were ultimately defeated. When he was later killed by Lex Luthor and the Joker, the Society was effectively dismantled, though new groups would continue its legacy, notably Libra's Secret Society of Super-Villains. **SW**

HERE COME THE BAD GUYS
Alexander Luthor Jr. assembled some of the worst villains around to take on an increasingly violent Justice League.
1 Talia al Ghūl
2 Black Adam
3 Alexander Luthor Jr.
4 Deathstroke
5 Doctor Psycho
6 The Calculator

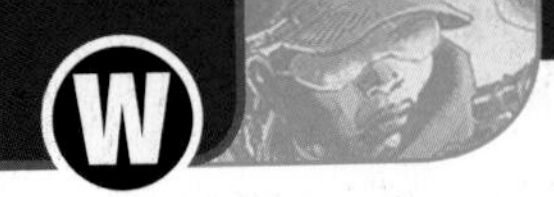

WALLER, AMANDA

DEBUT *Legends* #1 **(Nov. 1986)**
CURRENT VERSION *Suicide Squad* (Vol. 4) #1 **(Nov. 2011)**
REAL NAME Amanda Waller
BASE Belle Reve Penitentiary
EYES Brown **HAIR** Black
POWERS/ABILITIES A wealth of experience with superpowered beings; superb leader and analyst with military epertise.
ALLIES James Gordon, Jr.
ENEMIES Black Spider, Basilisk, Regulus, Crime Syndicate, O.M.A.C.
AFFILIATIONS Suicide Squad, Team 7, NSA, A.R.G.U.S.

MEAN TEAM
Amanda Waller came to prominence as part of Team 7, countering the emerging metahuman threat alongside Steve Trevor, Deathstroke, Grifter, and others.

Amanda Waller was a brilliant NSA analyst who served in the elite Team 7 special ops unit. Her intelligence, management skills, and willingness to make hard decisions then landed her a job as head of A.R.G.U.S. and director of Task Force X, alias Suicide Squad, a secret team made up of convicted super-villains.

Maintaining control over a team comprised of ruthless superpowered criminals required someone equally ruthless. Waller demonstrated she was willing to have potential candidates tortured and killed in training, use nerve gas on rioting prisoners, and order the deaths of thousands of innocent civilians if deemed necessary.

Waller may have been in control at Belle Reve, but she was caught off guard when Squad member Black Spider turned traitor and held her and her beloved Nana hostage. Amanda fought Black Spider with skill and determination, but was unable to prevent Nana from being killed.

During the Crime Syndicate's invasion of Earth, their henchmen attacked Belle Reve and sent O.M.A.C. rampaging through the prison. Though Suicide Squad was able to contain the menace, the institution was wrecked. In the aftermath of the attack, Waller set about forming a new and improved Suicide Squad. **SW**

ON THE RECORD

Pre-Flashpoint, Amanda Waller was an abrasive and controversial figure who frequently ignored the rules—and paid the price. She was found guilty of unauthorized deployment of Suicide Squad against the occult Loa cartel, and later jailed for other offences by President Lex Luthor.

She was subsequently freed and assigned a position in UN agency Checkmate, but was forced to resign after it was discovered that she had illegally deported super-villains to the hostile planet of Salvation.

PUSHY ATTITUDE
Amanda "the Wall" Waller's arrogance earned her few friends in the Super Hero community. Wallers's relationship with Batman was especially fraught.

KEYBOARD WARRIOR
Director Waller currently does most of her work in front of a monitor or a congressional committee, but she is also a combat veteran.

SUICIDAL TENDENCIES
Amanda Waller handpicked the members of Task Force X—the Suicide Squad—including King Shark, El Diablo, Black Spider, Deadshot, and Harley Quinn.

THE WANDERERS

DEBUT *Adventure Comics* **(Vol. 1) #375 (Dec. 1968)**
CURRENT VERSION *Action Comics* **(Vol. 2) #18 (May 2013)**
MEMBERS/POWERS Aviax (formerly Ornitho): Winged, changes into any flying animal; **Dartalon** (formerly Dartag): Changes into quilled form and fires spikes; **Re-Animage** (formerly Immorto): Can heal or resurrect beings; **Elvar** (formerly Elvo): Wields emotion-powered energy sword; **Psyche:** Can manipulate emotions or fire bolts of mental energy; **Quantum Queen:** Ability to transform any energy on the electromagnetic spectrum; **Celebrand** (original team leader): Brilliant tactician.
ALLIES Legion of Super-Heroes
ENEMIES Controllers, Darkseid

The Wanderers were a celebrated Super Hero team from the 30th century. Allies of the Legion of Super-Heroes, the two teams befriended each other during their first encounter. However, things changed when the Wanderers flew their ship through the Nefar Nebula, which altered their personalities and turned them into criminals.

However, when the Wanderers stole the Seven Stones of Alactos, the Legion sprang into action to save their friends and recover the stones. The Wanderers were also one of several groups to join the Legion in battling Darkseid and his army of Daxamites.

Some time later, the Wanderers were found dead under mysterious circumstances. However, the Controller Clonus cloned new bodies for them (except for their leader Celebrand, whose duplication failed), and some members took new names to match their new forms. They then worked as agents for the United Planets, but disappeared when exploring a strange anomaly in space. Their whereabouts remains unknown. **SW**

WANDERING STARS
The ultimate fate of the Wanderers was one of the most confounding mysteries of the 30th century.
1 Aviax, 2 Quantum Queen, 3 Elvar, 4 Dartalon, 5 Psyche, 6 Re-Animage

THE WATCHMEN

DATA

DEBUT *Watchmen* #1 **(Sep. 1986)**
MEMBERS/POWERS **OZYMANDIAS** (Adrian Veidt): Genius, polymath, tycoon, and master martial artist; **SILK SPECTRE** (Laurie Juspeczyk): Skilled hand-to-hand fighter; **NITE OWL** (Daniel Dreiberg): Gadgeteer and inventor, owner of flying Owlship; **COMEDIAN** (Edward Blake): Combat veteran and firearms expert; **RORSCHACH** (Walter Kovacs): Investigator and brawler; **DOCTOR MANHATTAN** (Dr. Jon Osterman): Ability to control and manipulate matter at a quantum level.
ALLIES The Minutemen
ENEMIES Moloch the Mystic, Big Figure, Lady Sin
AFFILIATIONS The Crimebusters

BEFORE WATCHMEN
The Minutemen were America's original costumed crime-fighters. Operating throughout the 1940s, it was Captain Metropolis who instigated the team when he approached Silk Spectre and her manager, Laurence Schexnayder, to suggest joining forces. The team comprised:
1 Silk Spectre (Sally Juspeczyk)
2 Nite Owl (Hollis Mason)
3 The Comedian (Edward Blake)
4 Mothman (Byron Lewis)
5 Cpt. Metropolis (Nelson Gardner)
6 Hooded Justice (Unknown)
7 Dollar Bill (William Brady)
8 Silhouette (Ursula Zandt)

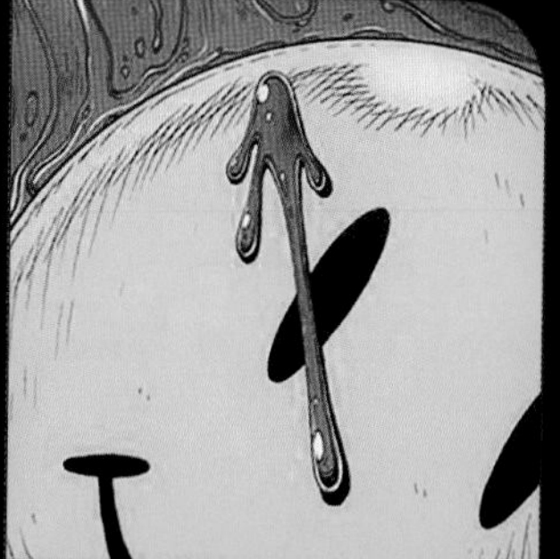

NO LAUGHING MATTER
Investigating a routine homicide, Rorschach found a bloodstained badge—his first clue that the victim, Edward Blake, was none other than the Comedian.

Though never refered to as the Watchmen at the time, this team of mighty costumed adventurers were once America's most celebrated heroes. However, a public backlash against vigilante violence forced them to go their separate ways in the 1970s. In 1985, as Cold War tensions between America and the Soviets escalated, one of these feted heroes was found murdered. Investigating the crime, his old teammates were forced to deal with issues from their past, and uncovered evidence of a conspiracy with far-reaching ramifications.

On the Earth of the Watchmen, the emergence of costumed heroes in the late 1930s changed the course of world history. In the 1940s, these colorful adventurers teamed up as the crime-fighting Minutemen. They were succeeded by a new generation of heroes who initially banded together as the Crimebusters, but over time developed a reputation as the Watchmen. Among this second generation were: Rorschach; the second Nite Owl; the second Silk Spectre; Ozymandias; Minutemen veteran the Comedian; and Doctor Manhattan. Created in a lab accident in the 1960s, Doctor Manhattan was the only hero on Earth with superhuman powers. His extraordinary ability to control quantum forces made him a living nuclear deterrent, and his very existence altered the balance of power between the USA and the USSR.

In the 1960s and 1970s, the tide of public opinion turned against costumed vigilantes. Following rioting and a police strike, the Keene Act was passed in 1977, banning vigilante activity. The Watchmen were forced into retirement, except for Doctor Manhattan and the Comedian, who worked for the government, and Rorschach, who refused to give up his personal war on crime.

When the Comedian was found murdered in 1985, Rorschach suspected that former heroes were being targeted. This appeared to be born out when Adrian Veidt—Ozymandias—was almost assassinated. To compound matters, Doctor Manhattan was then accused of being the cause of cancer in some of his former associates. Manhattan responded by going into exile on Mars, leading to increased tensions with the USSR. As the world edged ever closer to nuclear conflict, Rorschach and Nite Owl uncovered evidence of a bizarre plot that would kill millions—and the mastermind appeared to be one of their fellow adventurers. **SW**

WHO WATCHES THE WATCHMEN?
1 Ozymandias, 2 Silk Spectre, 3 Doctor Manhattan, 4 Comedian, 5 Nite Owl, 6 Rorschach

CLASSIC STORIES

***Watchmen* #1–12 (Sep. 1986–Oct. 1987)** Arguably the defining comic of its decade, *Watchmen* recounts a dark and disturbing tale of murder and conspiracy in a world on the brink of nuclear annihilation.

***Before Watchmen: Minutemen* #1–6 (Aug. 2012–Mar. 2013)** A prequel that explores the history of the Watchmen's predecessors from the perspective of the original Nite Owl, as chronicled in his book *Under the Hood*.

***Before Watchmen: Ozymandias* #1–6 (Sep. 2012–May 2013)** Ozymandias is perhaps the most distant and mysterious character in *Watchmen*. This miniseries looks at his early adventures and first encounters with the other *Watchmen* characters.

LIFE ON MARS
Accused of being a cause of cancer, Doctor Manhattan retreated to Mars—to think, to remember, and to build.

WAYNE, THOMAS AND MARTHA

DEBUT *Detective Comics* (Vol. 1) #33 **(Nov. 1939)**
CURRENT VERSION *Batman* (Vol. 2) #9 **(Jul. 2012)**
REAL NAME Thomas Wayne, Martha Wayne
BASE Gotham City
HEIGHT 6ft 2in (Thomas); 5ft 4in (Martha)
WEIGHT 210 lbs (Thomas); 108 lbs (Martha)
EYES Blue (Thomas and Martha); **HAIR** Black (Thomas); Brown (Martha)
POWERS/ABILITIES Gotham City power couple with connections in the city's elite social circles and business world; charitable and intelligent with an eye for philanthropy; loving parents; Thomas Wayne was also a skilled surgeon.
ALLIES Bruce Wayne, Lucius Fox, Alfred and Jarvis Pennyworth
ENEMIES Joe Chill, Court of Owls

Thomas Wayne was heir to the Wayne family fortune. He was the latest member of a proud dynasty, including one of the city's most influential figures, Alan Wayne—that dated back to the founding of Gotham City itself. Although he did not need to work, Thomas was an extremely intelligent man and, in addition to working closely with the family business, Wayne Enterprises, he became a surgeon. He also found another stimulating challenge in his courtship with the equally brilliant Martha Kane. Hailing from another of Gotham City's first families, Martha was renowned in the most elite social circles for her kind heart and keen philanthropy. She and Thomas were married, and had a son named Bruce.

After a young Bruce got in trouble for sneaking into Gotham City to see the film *The Mark of Zorro*, Thomas Wayne decided a family outing was in order, and the three went to see the movie later that night. In a random act of violence, perpetrated by a small-time crook named Joe Chill, Thomas and Martha were shot and killed in an alley near the Monarch Theater. Bruce was left an orphan, and the cruel and senseless murder of his parents would later inspire him to create his alter ego, Batman, sworn to protect the innocent in crime-infested Gotham City. **MM**

ON THE RECORD

While their famous son, Batman, debuted in *Detective Comics* #27 (May 1939), his origin was not related until November of that year. In a famous two-page introduction, Thomas and Martha Wayne first appeared, with only Thomas given a first name.

In later years, Batman's origin was fleshed out, particularly in *Batman* #47 (Jun.–Jul. 1948); Martha was given her first name, as was the Wayne's killer, Joe Chill.

In 1956, it was revealed that Thomas Wayne had actually worn a Batsuit to a costume party that served as inspiration to a young Bruce, in a story that provided an employer for Joe Chill—organized criminal Lew Moxon—on that fateful night.

BATMAN SR.
Long before the Flashpoint event, Thomas Wayne tried on the original Batsuit. During Flashpoint, in a alternate universe, Thomas served as that world's Batman.

WARP

DEBUT *The New Teen Titans* #14 (Dec. 1981)
CURRENT VERSION *Blue Beetle* (Vol. 3) #1 (Nov. 2011)
REAL NAME Emil LaSalle
HEIGHT 5ft 8in **WEIGHT** 134 lbs
EYES Brown **HAIR** Brown
POWERS/ABILITIES Flight; able to open a hole in space to teleport.
ALLIES Phobia, Plasmus, Brain, Monsieur Mallah
ENEMIES Blue Beetle, Brutale, La Dama, Rompe-Huesos, Coyote

Before Flashpoint, the Frenchman Warp was a major foe of the Teen Titans. Subsequently, he became a more universal player, teaming with both the Brotherhood of Evil and the Secret Society. A mercenary, Warp worked with Phobia and Plasmus to recover an ancient artifact called the Blue Beetle. Unfortunately for these Brotherhood of Evil members, a crime boss named La Dama also had her eye on the Beetle, and sent her lackeys Brutale, Rompe-Huesos, and Coyote to retrieve it.

As fate would have it, the Blue Beetle came into the possession of a teen named Jaime Reyes, and merged with him, changing him into the Super Hero known also as the Blue Beetle. With that mission failed, Warp joined the Outsider's Secret Society, and helped recruit Cheetah into the fold. **MM**

WARLORD

DEBUT *First Issue Special* #8 (Nov. 1975)
REAL NAME Travis Morgan
BASE Skartaris
HEIGHT 6ft **WEIGHT** 188 lbs
EYES Blue **HAIR** White
POWERS/ABILITIES Brilliant strategist; natural leader; expert hand-to-hand combatant; extraordinary swordsman; extremely athletic.
ALLIES Shakira, Jennifer Morgan, Machiste
ENEMIES Deimos

On June 16, 1969, Air Force pilot Lieutenant Colonel Travis Morgan was flying an SR-71 Blackbird at 80,000ft on a spy mission over Russia when he was shot down and sent spiraling to Earth. Bailing out and expecting to freeze to death in chilling water, Morgan instead parachuted into Skartaris, a land of eternal sunlight where mythical creatures and prehistoric beasts roamed. There he became known as Warlord, a warrior who battled and eventually killed Skartaris' corrupt mage, Deimos.

While he ventured from Skartaris a few times, including a memorable visit to Seattle to partner with Green Arrow, Warlord found a home in this land hidden inside the Earth. He died in a duel with his own son, Joshua Morgan. Joshua later honored his father's legacy by taking up the Warlord mantle. **MM**

WAVERIDER

DEBUT *Armageddon 2001* #1 (May 1991)
CURRENT VERSION *Convergence: Booster Gold* #2 (July 2015)
REAL NAME Michael Jon Carter
BASE The Vanishing Point
HEIGHT 6ft 5in **WEIGHT** 215 lbs
EYES Blue **HAIR** Blond
POWERS/ABILITIES Can see the future of any individual; one with the time-stream, allowing time-travel; superhuman strength, durability.
ENEMIES Monarch

The original Waverider was Matthew Ryder, a scientist from a future reality in the year 2030 ruled by the tyrant Monarch. Resolved to stop Monarch's iron rule before it got started, he became Waverider. Knowing only that Monarch was a former Super Hero, Waverider went back in time to investigate possible futures for many heroes and discovered that Hawk was destined to become the super-villain in question.

The first Waverider was killed in the line of duty. However, during the Convergence event, an aged Booster Gold from an alternate Earth became the new Waverider when he was fed into the time-stream by Earth-0's Booster Gold. This Waverider took on a career in the multiverse, first helping Telos and various Super Heroes convince Brainiac to realign the multiverse. **MM**

WE ARE ROBIN

DEBUT *Convergence: World's Finest* #2 (Jul. 2015)
BASE Gotham City
NOTABLE MEMBERS **Duke Thomas**; **Daxton Chill** (DaxAtax); **Anre "Dre" Cipriani** (Dre-b-Robbin); **Isabella Ortiz** (Robina); **Troy Walker** (The Troy Wonder); **Riko Sheridan** (R-iko)
ALLIES Alfred Pennyworth, the real Robins
ENEMIES Court of Owls

The Robin movement began at a time when Batman was thought dead after a brutal battle with the Joker below Gotham City. To fill the void as best they could, former Commissioner James Gordon took over the role of Batman and Alfred Pennyworth recruited heroic teens as Robins. Alfred sent them on missions via text messages from the secrecy of "the Nest." Due to past run-ins with the original Batman, Duke Thomas was recruited to join the movement. Shortly after, a Robin named Troy Walker was killed during a Robin-related mission.

As the We Are Robin movement began to grow in infamy, so did it swell in numbers. The nefarious Court of Owls turned public opinion against it, and caught and caged the teens. The real Robins (Damian Wayne, Dick Grayson, Red Hood, and Red Robin) saved the kids from the Court's clutches and helped them fight back. **MM**

WEATHER WIZARD

DEBUT *The Flash* (Vol. 1) #110 **(Dec. 1959–Jan. 1960)**
CURRENT VERSION *The Flash* (Vol. 4) #9 **(Jul. 2012)**
REAL NAME Marco Mardon
BASE Central City
HEIGHT 6ft 1in **WEIGHT** 184 lbs **EYES** Blue **HAIR** Black
POWERS/ABILITIES Able to manipulate the weather and call down storms, lightning, tornados, and other weather phenomena; weather powers affect his mood; can manipulate wind in order to fly.
ALLIES Captain Cold, Mirror Master, Heatwave, Glider, Trickster
ENEMIES The Flash, Elsa Mardon
AFFILIATIONS The Mardon Family, the Rogues

Over two years ago in Central City, Claudio Mardon, the 22-year-old leader of the Mardon crime family, realized he was in over his head. He had jumped into the business when his father died, wanting to make a name for himself and prove himself worthy of the Mardon name. His brother Marco, on the other hand, wanted nothing to do with organized crime, and left that tainted legacy for his brother. While in Central City, Claudio was shot and killed, but not by the rival crime family he was in town to do business with. Instead, his wife Elsa had arranged the hit, worrying that Claudio was going to give away too much of the family's territory in the name of peace.

Hearing of his brother's death, Marco returned to the family, just as Elsa had planned. After the Flash debuted in Central City, Marco opted to take on the name and mantle of Weather Wizard, and the two metahumans became sworn enemies. Weather Wizard even joined the Rogues, the infamous team of super-villains that often challenge the Scarlet Speedster. **MM**

ON THE RECORD

Before Flashpoint and *Crisis on Infinite Earths*, criminal Mark Mardon became the Weather Wizard thanks to the ingenuity of his brother, Clyde, a scientist of weather conditions. When Clyde died of an apparent heart attack after discovering how to control weather, Mark escaped his prison guards and went to Clyde's home. Using his brother's notes, he crafted a weather wand and became the Weather Wizard. He later joined the Rogues and became a recurring foe for the Flash and Kid Flash.

STORMY WEATHER
Tired of facing the Flash (and certain defeat) at one point Weather Wizard tried his luck in Gotham City where he met and was bested by the team of Batman and Robin.

WEAPONERS OF QWARD

DEBUT *Green Lantern* (Vol. 2) #2 **(Sep.–Oct. 1960)**
CURRENT VERSION *Justice League of America's Vibe* #1 **(Apr. 2013)**
BASE Qward, anti-matter universe
NOTABLE MEMBERS Kramen; Drik; Chomin; Kiman; Yokal the Atrocious; General Fabrikant.

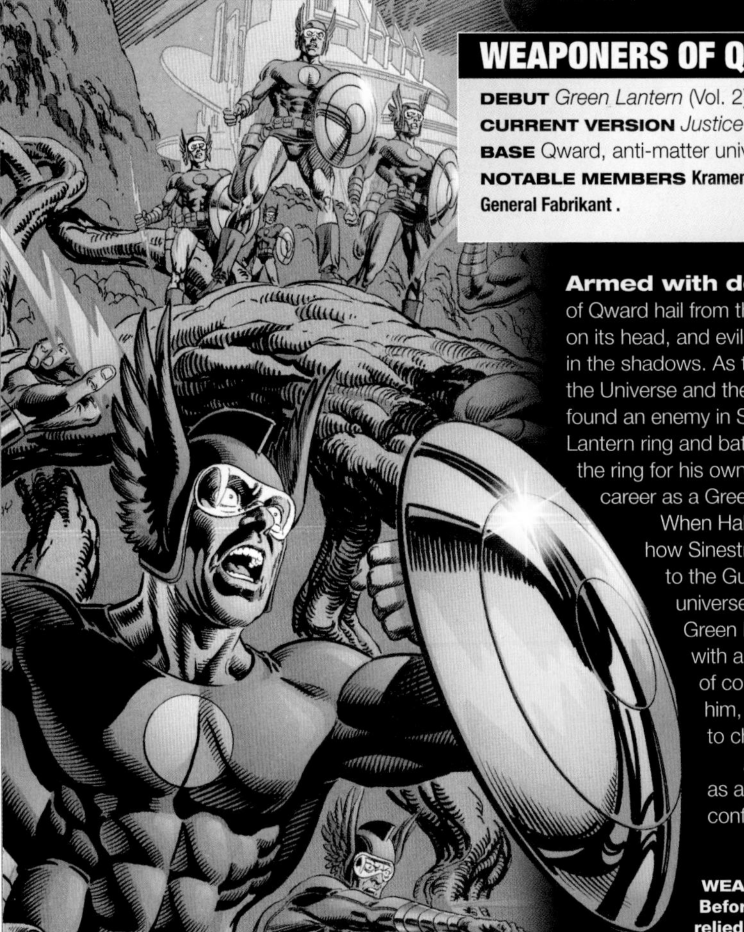

Armed with devastating Qwa-bolts, the Weaponers of Qward hail from the anti-matter universe, where morality is flipped on its head, and evil rules, with the few good citizens forced to hide in the shadows. As the equal and opposite power to the Guardians of the Universe and their Green Lantern Corps, the Weaponers originally found an enemy in Sinestro. The future super-villain discovered a Green Lantern ring and battled an attacking Weaponer, who wished to have the ring for his own. Sinestro killed the Qwardian, starting his own career as a Green Lantern.

When Hal Jordan also became a Green Lantern and saw how Sinestro's own people feared him, he reported this problem to the Guardians, who banished Sinestro to the anti-matter universe of Qward, effectively ending Sinestro's tenure as a Green Lantern. The Weaponers soon equipped Sinestro with a yellow power ring in order to take their message of corruption back to the positive matter universe with him, and Sinestro later recruited his own Sinestro Corps to challenge his former allies.

A lone Weaponer of Qward was recently spied as a captive at an A.R.G.U.S. facility, nearly escaping confinement during a mass breakout. **MM**

WEAPON MASTERS
Before the Flashpoint event, the Weaponers relied heavily on their yellow shields and lightning-bolt weapons.

ON THE RECORD

In *Green Lantern* (Vol. 2) #2, Hal Jordan met Telle-Teg, a refugee from Qward who was one of the few people on his planet rebelling against the evil Weaponers. When a Destroyer from Qward followed Telle-Teg, Green Lantern fought the villain, and eventually made his way to Qward as well.

There he learned the Weaponers had designs on taking all the power batteries in the universe. They soon managed to steal Hal's power battery and bring it to their capital city, Qwar-Deen. In the second part of this first adventure, Green Lantern was able to steal back his battery and stop the two Qwardians on Earth, who were posing as door-to-door salespeople.

BOLT OF DESTRUCTION
Telle-Teg tried to protect Green Lantern as his ring was powerless against the golden Qwa-bolts. Telle-Teg died, but Hal found a way to defeat the Weaponers of Qward.

WEST, IRIS

DEBUT *Showcase* #4 **(Sep.-Oct. 1956)**
CURRENT VERSION *The Flash* (Vol. 4) #1 **(Nov. 2011)**
BASE Central City
HEIGHT 5ft 6in **WEIGHT** 130 lbs
EYES Blue **HAIR** Brown
POWERS/ABILITIES Trained journalist with a suspicious nature, dogged determination and the instincts of a detective.
ALLIES Barry Allen, Daniel West (formerly), Hartley Rathaway
ENEMIES Reverse-Flash/Daniel West
AFFILIATIONS Gotham Gazette, Speed Force

Iris West grew up handling trouble. Her brother Daniel ran away from home after crippling their abusive father, leaving her to care for him. Daniel West soon turned to crime and was caught by a new Super Hero on the streets, the Flash. Despite her family burdens, Iris went to college in Keystone City and after getting her journalism degree, interned at the *Gotham Gazette*. While there, she met the easy-going Barry Allen.

Years later, she met him again when he was working as a forensic scientist for the Central City Police Department. The Flash had just begun protecting the Gem Cities and soon Barry realized Iris was either using him to get inside information on the Scarlet Speedster or to secure information on her brother's case. Although their relationship stalled they stayed friends.

When Iris gained powers from contact with the Speed Force, the Flash gave Iris a special outfit to protect her from the Reverse-Flash who was targeting the Flash's associates. When the super-speed psychopath was revealed as her own brother, Daniel, she sacrificed her powers to save the Flash and regretfully helped him put Daniel back behind bars at Iron Heights Prison. **WW**

ON THE RECORD

Iris West debuted as Barry Allen's girlfriend in the very first Silver Age comic story. A sharp, go-getting reporter for *Picture News*, she spent much of her time berating the seemingly hapless Barry for his constant tardiness.

When they married, he agonized for a year over whether to reveal his Super Hero identity to her. When he came clean she just laughed. She'd known from their first night together, because the Flash talked in his sleep!

FLEET OF FOOT
No matter how fast the Flash was or carefully Barry worked, his wife Iris was always two steps ahead of him.

WHITE MARTIANS

DEBUT *Justice League* (Vol. 1) #71 (May 1969)
CURRENT VERSION *Martian Manhunter* (Vol. 4) #1 (Aug. 2015)
EYES Red **HAIR** None
POWERS/ABILITIES Telepathy, telekinesis, flight, enhanced senses, and shape-shifting.
ALLIES Ma'alefa'ak, Phobos
ENEMIES J'onn J'onzz, Earth's Super Heroes
AFFILIATIONS The Epiphany, Martian Manhunter, Martian Man-Eater, Red Rising

A race of telepathic shape-shifters who had mastered all arts and sciences, White Martians were the sole inhabitants of the Red Planet for eons. However, when their ancient world began to die, they abandoned philosophy for dark blood-magic in their quest for survival.

The White Martians crafted a biological super-weapon—J'onn J'onzz—and sent it to infiltrate a younger neighboring planet. They bided their time as they had no desire to invade or occupy Earth. Using dark sorceries and the power of their hungry moon Phobos, they would steal Earth's life-force and recreate Mars in all its early glory.

However, they had underestimated the vaulting ambition of the blood-magic priest Ma'alefa'ak and failed to consider that J'onn J'onzz might defy his programming and side with the humans. **WW**

WHITE LANTERN CORPS

DEBUT *Blackest Night* (Vol. 1) #7 **(Apr. 2010)**
CURRENT VERSION *Green Lantern: New Guardians* (Vol. 1) #1 **(Nov. 2011)**
CURRENT MEMBERS/POWERS Kyle Rayner, Swamp Thing. All resurrected ring-wearers are able to fly, generate white energy blasts, force fields and light-constructs.
NOTABLE PREVIOUS MEMBERS Hal Jordan, Thaal Sinestro, Simon Baz, Maxwell Lord, Deadman, Hank Hall, Superman, Kid Flash, Firestorm, Aquaman, Martian Manhunter, Captain Boomerang, Jade, Professor Zoom, Green Arrow, Donna Troy, Hawkman, Hawkgirl, Ice, Osiris, Animal Man.
ALLIES Green Lantern Corps, Blue Lantern Corps, Indigo Tribe
ENEMIES Nekron, Black Lantern Corps, Black Hand

DEATH IS NOT THE END
Alive or dead, Life's greatest defenders could not resist the urgent siren call of the mysterious White Entity.

The White Entity is the most enigmatic of all beings embodying aspects of the Emotional Spectrum. It only appears in times of ultimate cosmic peril and seemingly chooses its agents for specific purposes and missions. The White Entity can wholly resurrect the dead rather than merely reanimate corpses like Nekron.

The White Lantern Corps began when Hal Jordan merged with the Entity which had lain dormant and hidden for millennia on Earth. As the Blackest Night ended, Hal brought Nekron's avatar—Black Hand—back to true life, forcing the Death Lord to retreat to his dolorous Dead Zone while reducing his Black Lantern Corps zombies to dust.

In recent times, Kyle Rayner mastered all seven colors of the Emotional Spectrum and became the White Lantern, wandering the universe and preserving life from forces beyond the power of reality's regular champions. **WW**

ON THE RECORD

As epilogue to the Blackest Night, the unholy cosmic terror was followed by a Brightest Day.

A dozen deceased heroes and villains returned, each with a mysterious mission to fulfill. Closely observed by revived revenant Boston Brand, the White Lanterns pursued their ascribed goals, searching for fulfillment.

Their efforts eventually led to the return of Earth's elemental protector, as Alec Holland once again took up the mantle of Swamp Thing—avatar of The Green.

RENEWAL AND REBIRTH
The White energies of the Brightest Day were used to purge Swamp Thing of Nekron's pestilent influence and revive the guardian of Earth's ecology.

WHITE WITCH

DEBUT *Adventure Comics* (Vol. 1) #350 (Nov. 1966)
CURRENT VERSION *Legion of Super-Heroes* (Vol. 7) #5 (Mar. 2012)
REAL NAME Mysa Nal
BASE 31st-century Legion HQ; Naltor; Zerox
HEIGHT 5ft 8in **WEIGHT** 118 lbs
EYES Blue/white/red **HAIR** White
POWERS/ABILITIES Skilled magic-user.
ALLIES Blok, Nura Nal/Dream Girl
ENEMIES Mordru, Evillo, Byth, Infinitus
AFFILIATIONS Legion of Super-Heroes

Mysa Nal is the sister of Legion of Super-Heroes' leader Dream Girl. She was born lacking her people's native talent to see the future and grew up a troubled outcast. Running away to the Sorcerers' world, Zerox, Mysa intensively studied the mystic arts—her aptitude becoming such that arch mage Mordru grew envious and wary.

Eventually, Mysa left Zerox to join her sister as a Legionnaire. As her power grew, her hair lightened and skin paled, but after defeating Mordru, Mysa was physically and spiritually transformed into a Black Witch after she absorbed the Dark Lord's power.

Mysa recently cleansed her spirit and returned to her albino appearance and benevolent disposition, rejoining the Legion and battling Infinitus. **WW**

WHITE, PERRY

DEBUT *Superman* (Vol. 1) #7 **(Nov.-Dec. 1940)**
CURRENT VERSION *Superman* (Vol. 3) #1 **(Nov. 2011)**
REAL NAME Perry White
BASE Daily Planet, Metropolis
HEIGHT 5ft 10in **WEIGHT** 200 lbs **EYES** Blue **HAIR** Brown
POWERS/ABILITIES Incisive mind, keen journalistic instincts, deductive reasoning, organizational and logistics expertise, inspirational leader and mentor with great personal charisma.
ALLIES Lois Lane, Jimmy Olsen, Clark Kent, Ron Troupe, Miko Ogawa, Heather Kelly
ENEMIES Morgan Edge, Izzy Izquierdo, Glen Glenmorgan, Lex Luthor
AFFILIATIONS *Daily Planet*, Cat Grant, George Taylor

WORDS OF WISDOM Perry White could juggle 10 stories at once and still be ready with a dozen fresh angles and an idea for the next big thing.

Perry White was a crusading, prize-winning journalist with the Metropolis-based *Daily Planet* for decades before taking a desk job. Once installed in an office, however, Perry surprised himself, and others, by proving to be an even greater editor than he was a roving news hound. An old-fashioned two-fisted reporter, Perry covered wars and political scandals, gang wars and murders, always aware that the public has a right to know and journalists have a sworn duty to root out the truth and tell their loyal readership.

As Editor and Editor-in-Chief, he made his own ironclad ethics and standards the yardstick by which all staff had to measure themselves. His is an increasingly difficult job in a multimedia world where integrity loses out to sensationalism every day. Perry's greatest role is as a mentor; teaching the next generation how to balance story against personal interest and how, in the end, journalism is a business not entertainment or a soapbox.

Recently, working for the *Daily Planet* has become one of the most dangerous jobs in the business, drawing Perry and his team into regular contact with aliens, monsters, and superpowered madmen. However, his uncanny ability to discover and train great reporters like Lois Lane, Clark Kent, and Ron Troupe—and get the best out of them—is legendary throughout the industry. He has also resisted every effort to lure him away from his beloved *Daily Planet*. **WW**

ON THE RECORD

An irreplaceable part of the "Superman Family," Perry White is one of the most iconic supporting characters in the history of comics. However, he was actually created for the *Superman Radio Show* in February 1940 and only introduced on the printed page at the year's end.

Before White's appearance, Clark Kent had jumped to the barked orders of Editor George Taylor and the great Metropolitan newspaper they worked for was the called the *Daily Star*.

HOLD THE PRESSES! Hard-bitten, hard-boiled, and beefy, Perry knew that to get good stories you had to make your reporters hustle, but when things got tough you could trust them with your life.

WILDCAT

DEBUT *Sensation Comics* (Vol. 1) #1 **(Jan. 1942)**
CURRENT VERSION *Earth 2: World's End* (Vol. 1) #6 **(Jan. 2015)**
REAL NAME Ted Grant
HEIGHT 6ft 5in **WEIGHT** 250 lbs **EYES** Blue **HAIR** Bald
POWERS/ABILITIES Boxer and mixed martial arts fighter in peak physical condition.
ALLIES Dick Grayson, Barbara Grayson, Johnny Grayson, Red Arrow, Batman
ENEMIES Brainwave, Jonni Thunder, Obsidian, forces of Apokolips
AFFILIATIONS Wonders of the World II, World Army

In 1941, boxer Ted Grant was framed for murder and on the run when a comic book inspired him to don a costume and track down the real killer. As Wildcat, Ted cleared his name and, loving the double life, kept going. Specializing in sports-related crimes, he sometimes helped his manager, Stretch Skinner, with the latter's detective agency.

During World War II, Wildcat served with the Justice Society of America and All-Star Squadron. Cursed by the Spirit King, Ted was saved by magical ally Zatara who altered the spell, granting him nine lives. Wildcat spent them carefully, but no matter how many times he died, he always seemed to have nine lives left. Ted scarcely aged, but he saw almost everyone he loved pass away. He found renewed purpose training JSA recruits in combat.

After Flashpoint, a different Ted Grant appeared on Earth-2. He never wore a costume, but was a hero nonetheless. A fight-coach at the Wildcat Gym, this Ted Grant protected Dick Grayson and his family as they joined thousands of refugees fleeing a second invasion from Apokolips. Grant trained and guarded them until the survivors could escape. He then assisted the remaining heroes, such as Red Arrow and a new Batman. **WW**

GENTLE GIANT Ted Grant could stop most fights with a glance, but if that failed he could fall back on sheer muscle. Which came in handy when he scooped up Dick Grayson and took him to safety during Apokolips' second invasion of Earth-2.

WILDCAT II

DEBUT *Infinity, Inc.* (Vol. 1) #12 (Mar. 1985)
CURRENT VERSION *Earth 2: World's End* #13 (Feb. 2015)
REAL NAME Yolanda Maria Dorothea Lucia Montez **BASE** Central City
HEIGHT 5ft 8in **WEIGHT** 123 lbs
EYES Blue **HAIR** Brown
POWERS/ABILITIES Superhuman strength and speed, cat-like reflexes and agility; claws.
ALLIES Ted Grant, Nuklon, Alexander Montez
ENEMIES Dr. Benjamin Love, Psycho Pirate

Before Yolanda Montez was born, her mother was given experimental drugs by deranged doctor Benjamin Love. His experimentation resulted in a number of children being born with mutant abilities.

Yolanda kept her cat-like powers hidden until her godfather—the original Wildcat—was crippled during the *Crisis on Infinite Earths*. She then took over his Super Hero identity as the new crime-busting Wildcat.

She served with West Coast super-team Infinity, Inc. and later joined a covert team invading the nation of Parador to battle Eclipso. She was personally executed by the vengeful monster.

A new Yolanda Montez appeared during the final days of Earth-2. As Avatar of the Red, she could tap into the life-force of Earth's fauna. **WW**

WILDFIRE

DEBUT *Superboy* (Vol. 1) #195 (Jun. 1973)
CURRENT VERSION *Legion Lost* (Vol. 2) #1 (Nov. 2011)
REAL NAME Drake Burroughs
HEIGHT 6ft 2in **WEIGHT** Variable
POWERS/ABILITIES Composed of antimatter; can project and absorb energy across the electromagnetic spectrum; flight.
AFFILIATIONS Legion of Super-Heroes

Drake Burroughs was testing an antimatter propulsion system when he was engulfed by an energy release that should have killed him. Instead, he became a being of antimatter energy, requiring a containment suit to keep himself from dispersing. Wanting to put his misfortune and new powers to good use, he joined the Legion of Super-Heroes as Wildfire.

Wildfire and members of the Legion of Super-Heroes were hunting the time-traveling terrorist Alastor, when they were stranded in the 21st century; their Legion flight rings malfunctioned and Alastor destroyed their Time Bubble. While struggling not to affect the future to which he hoped to return, Wildfire wrestled with his feelings for Dawnstar. Any romance was doomed, however, because he had no physical body. He was later said to have joined, and then left, the Justice League. **AI**

WIZARD

DEBUT *All-Star Comics* #34 (Apr.–May 1947)
REAL NAME William Asmodeus Zard
HEIGHT 6ft **WEIGHT** 182 lbs
EYES Blue **HAIR** Black
POWERS/ABILITIES Magical powers include casting of illusions, hypnotism, and projection into the astral plane.
ENEMIES Justice Society of America, Justice League of America
AFFILIATIONS Injustice Society

A career criminal from a young age, William Zard was in and out of prison all through the 1930s. Deciding to refashion his criminal life, he left the US and traveled to a Tibetan monastery. Here he studied with a master lama and learned hypnotism and astral projection, before using those newfound skills to murder his teacher.

Zard then became the Wizard, returning to post-war USA and offering his services to the Justice Society of America in the mistaken belief that they were a criminal organization just pretending to be heroes. They, of course, refused, provoking Zard's lasting enmity and causing him to form the Injustice Society as a villainous counterpart to the JSA. They clashed numerous times as Zard increased his magical knowledge and expanded his list of enemies to include the Justice League of America. **AI**

THE WIZARD (SHAZAM'S WIZARD)

DEBUT *Whiz Comics* #2 (Feb. 1940)
CURRENT VERSION *Justice League* (Vol. 2) #7 (May 2012)
REAL NAME Mamargan
BASE Rock of Eternity
HEIGHT 6ft **WEIGHT** 175 lbs
EYES Blue **HAIR** White
POWERS/ABILITIES Vast magical powers.
ALLIES Shazam
ENEMIES Black Adam, Seven Deadly Sins

The last survivor of the Council of Wizards, the Wizard bestowed the powers of Shazam on Billy Batson after initially rejecting him for the role of his champion on the grounds that he was not perfectly good.

The Wizard was also responsible for the creation of Black Adam, an ancient champion who was a frightened orphan just like Billy, but who later killed the other members of the Council and would eventually become Billy's nemesis. The Wizard revealed to Pandora that he finally accepted Billy because he anticipated his own end and needed a successor. He also apologized to Pandora for her wrongful conviction by the Council of Wizards millennia in the past, when they made her part of the Trinity of Sin along with the Phantom Stranger and the Question.

The Wizard was later revealed to be the physical form of the god Mamargan, and lent his name to the new SHAZAM acronym that gave Billy Batson his powers—and his new heroic name. **AI**

ANCIENT GUARDIAN
The Wizard was one with the mysterious Rock of Eternity and the last survivor of the once-mighty Council of Wizards.

WRATH

DEBUT *Batman Special* #1 (Jun. 1984)
CURRENT VERSION *Detective Comics* (Vol. 2) #22 (Sep. 2013)
REAL NAME Elliot Caldwell
BASE Gotham City
HEIGHT 6ft 2in **WEIGHT** 205 lbs **EYES** Blue **HAIR** Black
POWERS/ABILITIES Suit and device technology mirroring Batman's; trained combatant, both unarmed and with a variety of firearms; brilliant mind.
ALLIES Emperor Blackgate
ENEMIES Batman
AFFILIATIONS Scorn

Caldwell Tech's namesake CEO, E.D. Caldwell, was a business magnate who first came to Batman's notice when he attempted to buy Wayne Enterprises. Bruce Wayne refused knowing that Caldwell Tech was a weapons company and would turn Wayne Enterprises' research to violent ends. At the same time, a series of murders targeting policemen drew Batman's attention and he uncovered the truth about Caldwell: he was a killer calling himself Wrath, modeling his appearance after Batman and using Caldwell Tech as a front to destroy the Gotham City Police Department and create an army of his own, using both Caldwell and Wayne technologies.

Caldwell captured Alfred Pennyworth, who revealed more of the CEO's story to Batman after his rescue: Caldwell's hatred of the police began after his father was murdered during a diamond heist by corrupt police officers. With this knowledge, Batman was able to confront and defeat Wrath, imprisoning him in Blackgate—where he began a villainous partnership with the criminal Emperor Blackgate, whose ultimate goals remain unknown. **AI**

ON THE RECORD

The original Wrath also modeled himself after Batman, and focused his obsession on destroying those he blamed for the deaths of his parents—law enforcement officers.

After years as an assassin for hire, he returned to Gotham City and plotted to assassinate Commissioner James Gordon. However, he died in a fall from the roof of a building where he was fighting Batman. His adopted son, trained to be the Robin to Wrath's Batman, later adopted the Wrath's name and mission as well, before being caught by Batman and Nightwing.

WRATHFUL OBSESSION
The first Wrath was haunted and inspired by Batman—and determined to destroy him.

WONDER GIRL

DATA

DEBUT *Wonder Woman* (Vol. 2) #105 **(Feb. 1996)**
CURRENT VERSION *Teen Titans* (Vol. 4) #1 **(Nov. 2011)**
REAL NAME Cassandra "Cassie" Sandsmark
BASE New York City
HEIGHT 5ft 3in **WEIGHT** 124 lbs **EYES** Blue **HAIR** Blond
POWERS/ABILITIES Silent Armor and War Bracelets convey powers of light, super-strength, and force-field projection; carries magical lasso.
ALLIES Superboy, Red Robin
ENEMIES Trigon
AFFILIATIONS Teen Titans

STAR-CROSSED
Fighting Superboy during N.O.W.H.E.R.E.'s kidnapping operation, Cassie had no idea she and Kon-El would one day fall in love.

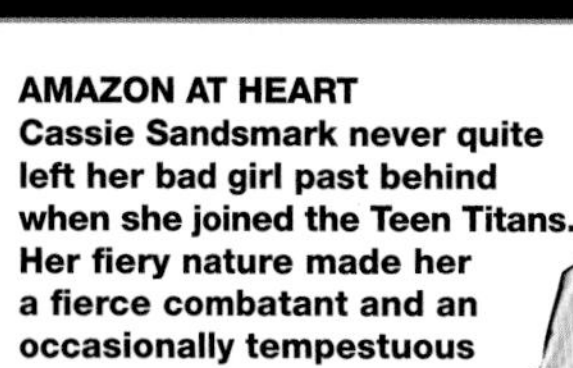

AMAZON AT HEART
Cassie Sandsmark never quite left her bad girl past behind when she joined the Teen Titans. Her fiery nature made her a fierce combatant and an occasionally tempestuous teammate.

WONDER BIRTH
The alien Silent Armor binds itself to the young Cassie Sandsmark, and Wonder Girl is born.

The daughter of archaeologist Helena Sandsmark and the demigod Lennox, Cassie Sandsmark was destined for great adventure. She began to find it after a brief teenage criminal career led her to the discovery of the mysterious Silent Armor—and then to membership in the Teen Titans as Wonder Girl. Despite her name, she has no relationship to Wonder Woman, and bristles whenever the topic comes up.

Growing up with her single mother after her father—whom she barely remembered—left them, Cassie Sandsmark traveled the world to different archaeological digs. Frustrated and lonely, she began stealing art and artifacts, coming under the sway of an older thief, the charismatic Diesel. He and the teenage Cassie were exploring a temple near a Cambodian dig site when Diesel was attacked by a seemingly sentient being of liquid metal. A stunned Cassie was able to control it using a pair of bracelets that she found nearby. The bracelets were part of the Silent Armor, an alien parasite that enabled superpowers, but also constantly tried to subvert Cassie's will.

Cassie continued her life of crime until the villain Harvest swept her up in his Culling project to train a new generation of metahumans under his control. There she met Superboy, as well as the other young heroes who would form the Teen Titans. Her battle to control the Silent Armor culminated when Diesel took it from her and she was forced to use the Armor's magical lasso on him to get it back. He died, and the Armor attracted the attention of the demon Trigon, who taunted Cassie by telling her he knew the identity of her father. Before she could pursue Trigon, the Teen Titans had to face the Crime Syndicate—including Johnny Quick and Atomica. The Teen Titans were catapulted through several timelines and Cassie was heartbroken when Superboy remained in a future time.

Cassie, now in a leadership role, returned from these adventures with the rest of the Teen Titans. They defeated the Crime Syndicate and rode a wave of popularity—a group of young women, inspired by Wonder Girl, even went on a vigilante campaign against criminals who targeted women. Meanwhile, Cassie's mother tried to re-establish her relationship with Cassie after the pair had long been estranged. **AI**

ON THE RECORD

The previous version of Cassie Sandsmark was not at all reluctant to be associated with Wonder Woman, having seized the mantle of a hero when Wonder Woman came to Cassie's hometown of Gateway City. Temporarily "borrowing" the Amazing Amazon's Sandals of Hermes and Gauntlet of Atlas, Cassie gained prodigious strength and the ability to fly—superpowers she used to help smash a clone of Doomsday.

Later, taking on the name Wonder Girl—an identity used before her by Donna Troy—she helped Wonder Woman defeat a manifestation of entropy called Decay.

AMAZONIAN ALLIANCE
As the symbol on her costume suggested, Wonder Girl was closely allied to Wonder Woman and the Amazons.

CLASSIC STORIES

Young Justice **(Vol. 1) #4 (Jan. 1999)**
Cassie Sandsmark, wearing a black wig and goggles to mimic the appearance of her idol Donna Troy, joins up with Young Justice as Wonder Girl.

Teen Titans **(Vol. 3) #1 (Sep. 2003)**
The new Teen Titans are formed, with Wonder Girl as one of the founding members, just as the previous Wonder Girl, Donna Troy, helped found the first Teen Titans. Romance with Superboy looms, and she discovers the truth about her father's identity.

WONDER WOMAN

DATA

DEBUT *All Star Comics* #8 **(Dec. 1941–Jan. 1942)**
CURRENT VERSION *Wonder Woman* (Vol. 4) #1 **(Nov. 2011)**
REAL NAME Diana
BASE New York City; London; Themyscira
HEIGHT 6ft **WEIGHT** 165lbs **EYES** Blue **HAIR** Black
POWERS/ABILITIES Divinely bestowed strength and durability matching the Olympian gods; expertise in all forms of armed and unarmed combat; flight; Lasso of Truth compels those in its coils to tell the truth; Bracelets of Victory contain and channel her powers.
ALLIES Batman, Superman
ENEMIES First Born, Donna Troy
AFFILIATIONS Justice League of America, Amazons

Wise as Athena, stronger than Hercules, swift as Hermes, and beautiful as Aphrodite, Wonder Woman is Diana, daughter of Zeus. She's also the God of War, Queen of the Amazons, and a founding member of the Justice League. After a childhood learning the arts of war on the island of Themyscira, she ventured into the world of mortals as the Amazons' ambassador of peace and became a powerful ally of Superman. Diana abides by a strict ethical code that forbids the killing of other human beings. Her goal is peace and harmony between women and men, but she knows there's a very long way to go before this can be achieved.

AT A GLANCE...

Amazon Queen
The Amazons of Themyscira were created thousands of years ago by a group of Greek goddesses, who combined their powers to give new life to the spirits of women killed by men. After their first home was destroyed by Hercules, they retreated to a hidden island, where they were charged with guarding Pandora's Box.

Aegis bracelets
Wonder Woman's bracelets were forged from the fragments of Athena's shield, Aegis. They are both an indestructible defense and a source of power—Diana can use them to create weapons and to channel Zeus's lightning. They also keep her true powers, which equal those of Zeus, in check.

Roping them in
Wonder Woman's Lasso of Truth is made from the girdle of the primordial Earth goddess Gaea. Whoever is caught in the Lasso is compelled to tell the full truth. Its also virtually unbreakable.

CLASSIC STORIES

***Wonder Woman* (Vol. 1) #212–222 (Jun.–Jul. 1974 to Feb.–Mar. 1976)** After losing her powers, Diana has to perform 12 labors to earn her way back into the Justice League—and Hercules can't help her.

***Wonder Woman* (Vol. 2) #1–6 (Feb.–Jul 1987)** Introduces Wonder Woman's modern history and her mission as an ambassador of peace, along with the now-classic origin of her powers as gifts from various Greek gods.

***Wonder Woman* (Vol. 2) #90–93, #0 (Sep. 1994–Jan. 1995)** Angry at Diana for the perceived failures of her mission in the outside world, Hippolyta declares a contest to determine a new Wonder Woman. This is won by the Amazon Artemis, who briefly claims Diana's title.

***Wonder Woman* (Vol. 2) #219 (Sep. 2005)** Faced with an impossible choice, Wonder Woman kills Maxwell Lord, freeing Superman of his mind control, but leaving her future with the Justice League in doubt.

Diana was the daughter of Zeus and Queen Hippolyta. However, her origins were hidden for decades to protect her from the wrath of Zeus' wife Hera, who was known to hunt down and kill her husband's illegitimate children. This gave rise to the legend that Hippolyta had sculpted Diana from clay. The Amazons believed this to be true until the facts were revealed by Strife, sister of the God of War, Ares, after Diana had grown to womanhood. As a child she was tutored by Ares in the arts of war, but her training was cut short when he deemed her a failure because of her belief in mercy and compassion. This would become a cornerstone of her principles when she reached adulthood and ventured out into the world.

Diana discovered the truth of her parentage after saving a young mortal woman named Zola from centaurs. Returning with the girl to her island home, she met Strife, who told her that Zola was carrying Zeus' child—who would be Diana's sibling. Shocked, Diana confronted her mother, who admitted the truth. Furious and betrayed, Diana left Themyscira. When she returned—after connecting with the Justice League—she found Hera had changed her mother into a clay statue and the rest of the Amazons into stone.

LEARNING FROM THE MASTER
Diana was instructed in the arts of war by Ares, the God of War, who considered her his most promising student.

Diana's brother Apollo learned from his oracles that Zeus had disappeared, leaving an empty throne for the taking—and Apollo wanted it. Among the other gods, Ares was not interested in the throne, though Poseidon coveted it, and perhaps Hades, too. Living in London with Zola and the messenger god Hermes, Diana concocted a plan with the mysterious Lennox. They would stir up the gods against each other to help protect Zola and figure out where Zeus, whom she was still adjusting to thinking of as her father, had really gone.

The scheme worked, and also drew Hera down from Olympus. Diana used Hermes' staff to transport herself there instantly, destroying Hera's Scrying Pool with one of the candles from Hades' head. When Diana returned to Earth, Hades turned the tables, taking Zola hostage to force Wonder Woman to honor her deal that he and Poseidon share the throne.

Shortly afterward, Wonder Woman discovered that a brutal war was coming, as Zeus' oldest son—known as First Born—had returned from millennia of exile, with revenge and Zeus' throne on his mind. In her initial confrontation with First Born, inside Westminster Abbey in London, Wonder Woman killed Ares and became the new God of War, to prevent First Born from assuming that power for himself.

THE MINOTAUR
During her training with Ares, the adolescent Diana had to prove herself on a number of occasions. As the moment approached when Ares would decide whether she had completed her training, he sent her into the legendary Labyrinth, where she encountered the Minotaur. She defeated it, and Ares demanded that she kill the creature. Diana refused to do so, demonstrating the compassion and mercy that have always defined her character. Ares then cut off her training, considering her his greatest failure. Later, however, this act of mercy would save her life, when the Minotaur returned the favor and refused First Born's order to kill her.

IN THE LABYRINTH
Diana's training ended when she learned that true strength sometimes comes through mercy.

"You know who I am. Who the world needs me to be. I'm Wonder Woman."

WONDER WOMAN

WARRIOR FOR THEMYSCIRA
Diana refuses to kill humankind, but she's more than willing and able to bloody her sword in brutal battle against First Born's supernatural armies.

SCORNED
Even though they're half siblings, First Born doesn't take it well when Diana refuses his marriage proposal.

The New Gods, including Orion and Milan, became involved in the succession war as First Born put his final plan in motion. He killed Apollo and Hades, and Hera resurrected the Amazons—but not their Queen, Hippolyta. The Amazons weren't pleased to be fighting for a baby boy (Zola's child, Zeke), and they liked it even less when Hephaestus rallied an army of men from his forges to fight alongside them at Themyscira.

First Born's armies attacked Themyscira, and he captured Diana, taking her to Olympus and demanding that she marry him to begin a new Olympian dynasty and complete First Born's revenge on their father Zeus. She refused and scorned him, after which he stabbed her and left her to die.

As First Born's assault on Themyscira continued, Baby Zeke's powers began to manifest. He resurrected Hippolyta, who took charge of the Amazons against First Born's army. Wonder Woman, who had rallied thanks to the spiteful encouragement of Strife, returned to join the battle, but realized she had an opportunity to thwart First Born's plan. Hermes took her, with Zola and Zeke, to Olympus, where she planned to place the baby boy on the throne—the throne First Born had desired for 7,000 years.

However, during their absence, Poseidon had claimed the throne, and he tried to kill Zeke, but Zola fought him, unexpectedly revealing new powers and a latent divinity. Wonder Woman joined the fight against Poseidon. First Born arrived and captured Zeke and Zola, whereupon Wonder Woman cast her bracelets to the ground, declared herself God of War and daughter of Zeus and Hippolyta, and challenged First Born to a final battle.

GOD OF WAR
With the fate of Olympus hanging in the balance, Wonder Woman assumes the mantle of the dead Ares, becoming the new God of War.

THE AMAZO VIRUS

Lex Luthor's organic virus version of the Amazo android operating system transformed Dr. Armen Ikarus into Patient Zero. The virus gave him the uncanny ability to mimic any superpower he encountered. In the event, Wonder Woman subdued him long enough for Batman to get a sample of the virus to begin ascertaining its origin. One of the few heroes who was immune to the virus, Wonder Woman then convinced Superman to work with Lex Luthor to discover a cure. Diana was also the one who figured out that Patient Zero could not mimic cold powers, laying the groundwork for Superman to neutralize the threat with his freeze breath, while Lex Luthor began distributing the vaccine.

PATIENT ZERO
He could mimic almost any superpower after being infected with the Amazo virus, but even Patient Zero was not able to simply shrug off the Lasso of Truth.

WONDER WOMAN

In answer, First Born cast Zola and Zeke into the void surrounding the pinnacle of Olympus. Hermes teleported down to save them, while Wonder Woman caught First Born in the Lasso of Truth. With First Born held fast, Hermes took mother and child to the summit of Olympus and placed the boy on the throne—revealing that baby Zeke was Zeus brought back to life, and Zola was possessed by the divine essence of Athena. The upheaval caused by the return of Zeus shook Olympus, nearly throwing Wonder Woman and First Born into the void. When he reached out to take her hand, she made the choice to save Olympus and threw him off the precipice.

HIPPOLYTA DIES
Transformed into a clay statue by the vindictive Hera, resurrected, and then returned once more to clay, Hippolyta melted while Diana was on Olympus.

She then had to plead for Zola's life with Athena, who was about to shed the last trappings of her humanity. Wonder Woman's compassionate plea convinced Athena, who let Zola live and flew away in the shape of an owl. However, at this moment of victory, personal tragedy struck Diana. Back on Themyscira, her mother Hippolyta—reverted to clay statue form during the war over Zeus' throne—melted away in a torrential rainstorm.

In Diana's absence, rebellious Amazons performed a sacrificial ritual using Hippolyta's remains to create a rival for Wonder Woman: Donna Troy. Keeping her presence a secret, they pressured Diana to retreat from the outside world and assume the throne of Themyscira, as was her birthright. While Diana was away from Themyscira on another mission with the Justice League, Hippolyta's former lover Derinoe presented Donna Troy to the Amazon council. Derinoe pronounced Donna to be the perfect Amazon—born of no man—and proposed her as fitter than Diana to lead the warrior women.

Taking Derinoe's cue, Donna Troy led the rebellious Amazons to massacre the men of Hephaestus's army still living on Themyscira. Diana returned and fought Donna Troy after discovering that Hippolyta had now become part of the island, a spirit presence to guide her. Once Donna Troy was defeated, Diana claimed the title of Queen and sent Donna to a prison on Olympus.

Sobered by these experiences, and by the knowledge that becoming War had brought her a terrible burden, Wonder Woman continued to balance her responsibilities to the Justice League and the people of Themyscira. **AI**

DIVIDED LOYALTIES

Drawn away from Themyscira again, Wonder Woman partnered with Superman, with whom she had just begun a romantic relationship, to thwart Zod's plot to extract Doomsday from the Phantom Zone. In a last-ditch move, she split an atom with her sword to destroy the Phantom Zone Gate. But the more time Diana spent with the Justice League away from her home, the more dissent developed among the Amazons.

STAR-CROSSED LOVERS?
Wonder Woman's relationship with Superman caused some tension in the Justice League—and indirectly led to the creation of Amanda Waller's competing Justice League of America.

DONNA TROY
Magically created from Hippolyta's remains, Donna Troy was a pitiless killer, designed by a rebellious Amazon faction to replace Diana.

REBIRTH

TRUTH SEEKER

Transformed by the power of the New Gods in the Darkseid War, Diana returns to Earth and discovers that her memories, her godly attributes, and even her mystic Lasso of Truth, are all broken.

Simultaneously recalling starkly different memories of her origins and those of her immortal sister Amazons, Wonder Woman undertakes a sacred quest. She hopes to establish the actual facts of her existence and destined place in the modern world, even though the gods, unknown enemies, and old foes like the Cheetah all bar her path to knowledge.

ON THE RECORD

From the outset, Wonder Woman has been portrayed as a complex amalgamation of feminist icon and glamorous heroine. Over the years, the character has been a vital touchstone for comics' portrayal of women. She has also generally been known for her ability to find nonlethal solutions, even in the midst of bloody battles.

THEMYSCIRA'S CHAMPION
A strong believer in Amazonian ideals, Wonder Woman tried to spread a message of peace and mercy in the wider world.

Changing With the Times

With her character established in comics' Golden Age, Wonder Woman transformed during the Silver Age, becoming reborn for the feminist era. A 1959 origin story was the first to trace her powers to the blessings of the Olympian gods. Demeter granted her strength, Athena wisdom, Artemis the Eyes of the Hunter, Hestia control over the Fires of Truth, Aphrodite beauty, and Hermes the power of flight. Surrendering her powers from 1968 to 1972, the now-mortal Diana Prince trained in martial arts with the blind master I Ching and wore mod fashions in a series of adventures taking her around the globe.

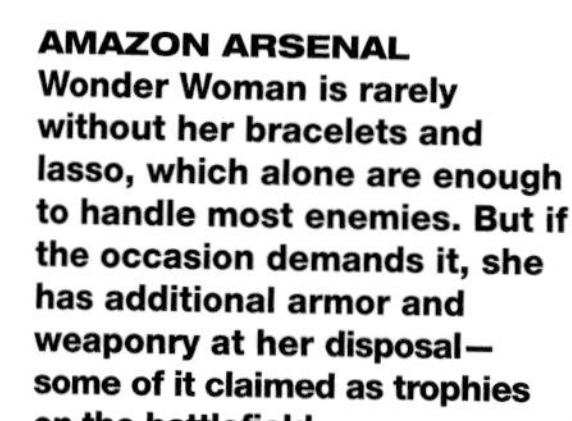

AMAZON ARSENAL
Wonder Woman is rarely without her bracelets and lasso, which alone are enough to handle most enemies. But if the occasion demands it, she has additional armor and weaponry at her disposal—some of it claimed as trophies on the battlefield.

Keeping the Peace

Following *Crisis on Infinite Earths*, Wonder Woman was recreated as an emissary bringing a message of peace to "Patriarch's World" from Themyscira—the new name for Paradise Island, with a new history to go with it. The romance aspects of her character, diminishing since the 1960s, almost completely disappeared, and new layers were added to the original story of Hippolyta forming her from clay.

Battle Royale

Diana's role and obligations in the outside world caused tensions back at home on Themyscira, eventually leading to all-out war between the different factions of Amazons on Themyscira and in the desert kingdom of Bana-Mighdall. This epic conflict destroyed Themyscira and led to the abolition of the Amazon royal family, however, Themyscira was later rebuilt as an archipelago of floating islands.

PARADISE LOST
When war came to Themiscyra, Wonder Woman put her life on the line without compromising her ideals.

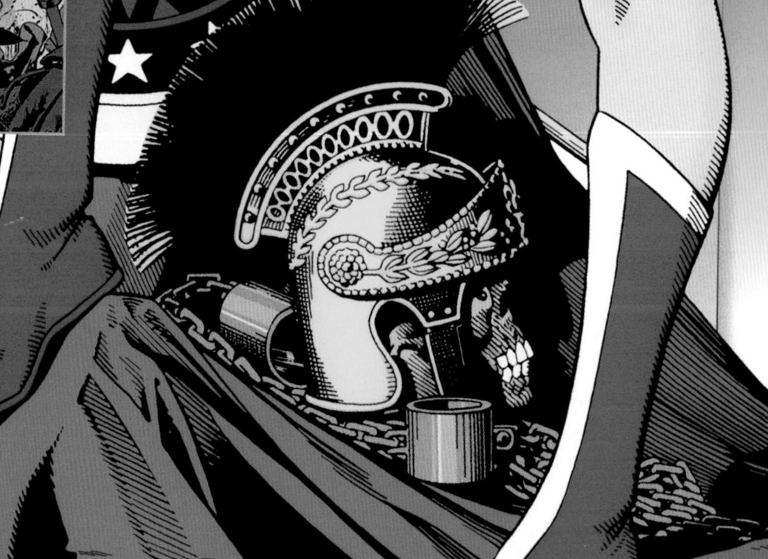

Fatal Consequences

The most notable exception to Wonder Woman's commitment to nonlethal combat was her necessary killing of Maxwell Lord, who had seized control of Superman's mind. This choice had devastating consequences, alienating her from Batman and Superman—both of whom condemned her actions, but without suggesting what else she might have done—and laying the groundwork for the multiverse-shattering event known as Infinite Crisis.

THE HARDEST CHOICE
Seeing no other way to protect the world from Superman, Wonder Woman broke her own cardinal rule and killed Maxwell Lord.

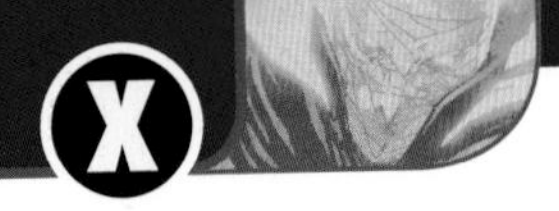

XYLON

DEBUT *R.E.B.E.L.S.* (Vol. 2) #4 (Jul. 2009)
POWERS/ABILITIES Telepathy, exemplary marksmanship.
ALLIES R.E.B.E.L.S., L.E.G.I.O.N.
ENEMIES Starro the Conqueror, Kanjar Ro

Xylon was a member of the alien race known as the Dominators, a highly advanced and violent civilization that lived at the edge of the universe in a strict caste society. Each Dominator's position in society was determined by the size of a red dot that appeared on their forehead.

After serving as the Fleet Admiral of the Xylon Expanse, and later as Warrior Caste Commander, he became the first Dominator to take an individual name. Now calling himself Xylon, he joined Vril Dox's R.E.B.E.L.S. (Revolutionary Elite Brigade to Eradicate L.E.G.I.O.N. Supremacy), the splinter group of the intergalactic peacekeeping force L.E.G.I.O.N. (Licensed Extra-Governmental Interstellar Operatives Network). Working alongside his newfound allies they were able to defeat Starro the Conqueror.

Soon after this first battle, and in defiance of the Dominator caste system, the rebellious Xylon replaced the telltale red dot on his forehead with the L.E.G.I.O.N. symbol. **SK**

STATUS SYMBOL
The large red dot on the forehead of the Fleet Admiral of the Xylon Expanse denotes his high social ranking within the Dominators.

CASTE AWAY
When the R.E.B.E.L.S. transitioned into a reformed L.E.G.I.O.N., Xylon took its symbol as his own.

XS

DEBUT *Legionnaires* #0 (Oct.1994)
REAL NAME Jenni Ognats
BASE 30th-century Earth
EYES Brown **HAIR** Black
POWERS/ABILITIES Super-speed
ALLIES Legion of Super-Heroes
ENEMIES Tangleweb, Savitar

Jenni Ognats was born in the 30th century on the planet Aarok. She was the granddaughter of Barry Allen, the second hero known as the Flash. When Jenni was a teenager, she discovered that she had inherited the family's power of super-speed. She could run close to the speed of light and even vibrate through solid matter by altering the molecules of her body. At first Jenni found it difficult to coordinate her movements while traveling at maximum velocity, but in time she gained control and became the hero XS.

As XS, Jenni was accepted into the Legion of Super-Heroes and gained the power of flight, thanks to her Legion flight ring. On one of her first Legion missions, she traveled back to the 20th century and teamed up with her cousin Bart Allen, then known as the hero Impulse. Together, the two heroes allied with Superboy to fight the villainous speedster Savitar, who was intent on eradicating his super-fast rivals. After that, Jenni journeyed to the 100th century and for a while was trapped at the end of time. The Time Trapper intervened, and Jenni was able to return to the 30th century. **SK**

TESTING THE LIMITS
In addition to superspeed, XS could fly thanks to her Legion flight ring, but she was not prepared for the time-travel she would do on the Legion's behalf.

XA-DU

DEBUT *Adventure Comics* (Vol. 2) #283 (Apr. 1961)
CURRENT VERSION *Action Comics* (Vol. 2) #5 (Mar. 2012)
POWERS/ABILITIES Multiple superpowers, including flight, heat vision, super-strength.
ALLIES Mr. Mxyzptlk, Brainiac, Little Man
ENEMIES Superman, Batman, Wonder Woman

Xa-Du was a doctor on the planet Krypton who conducted experiments in the forbidden area of suspended animation, turning some of his patients into virtual zombies. For this crime, Xa-Du was the first prisoner to be dematerialized and banished to the interdimensional realm known as the Phantom Zone. Before he was dispatched, Xa-Du swore revenge on the man who had discovered the Zone—fellow scientist Jor-El—and all his kin.

After Krypton exploded, Xa-Du built an ecto-suit that allowed him to escape from his confinement and travel to Superman's Fortress of Solitude. While there, he used a Phantom Zone Projector to send the Man of Steel himself into the dreaded Zone. Luckily, Superman was able to disable Xa-Du's ecto-suit and sent the villain back to his incorporeal prison. Using the alias of the Phantom King, Xa-Du would return to Earth several times, teaming up with Mr. Mxyzptlk, Brainiac, and Little Man to combat their mutual enemy. As Xa-Du possesses many of the same powers as Superman, he is an especially formidable opponent. **SK**

PATH OF REVENGE
Protected by his ecto-suit, Kryptonian sociopath and Phantom Zone fugitive Xa-Du would not rest until he had eliminated the House of El.

XERO

DEBUT *Xer0* #1 (May 1997)
REAL NAME Coltrane Walker
BASE National City
POWERS/ABILITIES Can fire laser blasts; able to phase; master of unarmed combat.
ALLIES Frank Decker
ENEMIES Doctor Polaris, targets of Xer0's agency

Coltrane "Trane" Walker was an African-American athlete who played for the National City Vipers basketball team. He was also a technologically enhanced secret agent and assassin for a covert government agency, who disguised himself as a blond and blue-eyed Caucasian. He was renowned for his ruthless efficiency in cleaning up after espionage operations, including eliminating any witnesses.

Walker was killed on his very first mission, but he was resurrected through the use of an experimental X-enzyme. His physical health was restored, but the new drug drained Walker of all emotions. This not only made him a star basketball player, but also a remorseless killer, and he became known in the business as Xer0, aka the "closer." Walker died again in a test of his capabilities set up up by his superior, Frank Decker, and was once again brought back to life. This time, though, Walker's rebirth left him seriously brain damaged. It remains to be seen whether his agency will attempt to return Walker to his role as Xer0. **SK**

CLOSE TO DEATH
Famed as the ultimate "closer," Xer0 was ambushed during his final mission and suffered chronic brain damage.

YA'WARA

DEBUT *Aquaman* (Vol. 7) #7 (May 2012)
BASE Brazil
EYES Blue **HAIR** Black
POWERS/ABILITIES Telepathic communication with animals; uses magic pendant to teleport.
ALLIES Aquaman, the Others
ENEMIES Black Manta, Madame Xan, Mayhem

Ya'Wara is a powerful warrior of the Tapirape, an indigenous Brazilian tribe that lives deep in the Amazon rainforest. An Amazon deity granted her the power to communicate telepathically with animals, which she uses as a fierce protector of wildlife and the Earth's fragile environments. She is a skilled fighter, equally good at hand-to-hand combat and wielding her twin daggers. If that fails, her loyal pet jaguars are never far from her side.

Ya'Wara also possesses a pendant that allows her to teleport almost anywhere, including to the moon. This pendant was one of seven ancient magical relics that were created by Atlan, the first king of Atlantis. The relic also brought her in touch with Aquaman, with whom she also shared a telepathic connection. Together, they briefly joined forces with the team known as the Others, to search for the other relics.

During a fight with Black Manta and his cohorts, who were also looking for Atlan's mystical artifacts, one of Ya'Wara's jaguars was killed. She responded by slaughtering the hunters, much to Aquaman's horror. In a final confrontation, Manta stole Ya'Wara's pendant and used it to escape. **SK**

ANIMAL INSTINCTS
Believing Stephen Shin had betrayed The Others to Black Manta, Ya'Wara was set to kill him, when Aquaman and Mera intervened.

YO-YO

DEBUT *Flashpoint* (Vol. 2) #1 (Jul. 2011)
CURRENT VERSION *Suicide Squad* #3 (Nov. 2011)
REAL NAME Chang Jie-Ru
EYES Brown **HAIR** Black
POWERS/ABILITIES Shape-shifting
ALLIES Suicide Squad, Harley Quinn
ENEMIES Basilisk, Red Orchid

Chang Jie-Ru was a convict at the Belle Reve prison for metahumans. He had the ability to increase or decrease his body mass, and volunteered to join the Suicide Squad to shorten his prison sentence. During a prison riot, he was swallowed whole by fellow Suicide Squad member King Shark. Yo-Yo managed to survive that ordeal by living inside King Shark's stomach. This convinced Suicide Squad leader Amanda Waller that Yo-Yo was virtually invulnerable.

Yo-Yo temporarily lost his powers when he battled the terrorist group Basilisk and his sister, the crime-boss known as Red Orchid. After regaining his shape-shifting powers, Yo-Yo chose to sacrifice his life by stretching his neck around his sister and pleading with Deadshot to detonate a nanobomb that was implanted beneath his skin. Deadshot triggered the bomb, and both Yo-Yo and Red Orchid were killed. **SK**

YEUNG, EDGAR FULLERTON

DEBUT *Wonder Woman* (Vol. 1) #157 (Oct. 1965)
CURRENT VERSION *Harley Quinn Annual* (Vol. 2) #1 (Dec. 2014)
POWERS/ABILITIES Self-designed robotic bodies provide mobility, articulated limbs, and weapons systems to his limbless, egg-like form.
ENEMIES Cap'n Horatio Strong

The brilliant, egg-bodied being Edgar Yeung has a weird origin that involves the Great Ten, Chinese sleeper agents, extra-strong glue, and a giant bird's nest. When he was evicted from his SoHo apartment and could not find a new place because of his odd appearance, he hatched a desperate plan: kidnap Poison Ivy so that she could brew a potion to make people like him. Ivy's friend Harley Quinn went one better, and offered him a room in her apartment. "Eggy" moved in, got a job at the sideshow downstairs, and joined in Harley's wacky adventures. He also did the housework, renovations, and the training of Quinn's "Gang of Harleys" team.

Pre-Flashpoint, the egg-shaped role was taken by evil genius Chang Tzu who, with his Science Squad, created the dread Four Horsemen of Apokolips. He was killed in succession by Will Magnus and his mini-Metal Men, Wonder Woman, and Power Girl, only to rise again in a new cyborg body. **SK**

YAT, SODAM

DEBUT *Tales of the Green Lantern Corps Annual* (Vol. 1) #2 (Sep. 1986)
CURRENT VERSION *Green Lantern Corps* (Vol. 3) #31 (Jul. 2014)
BASE Sector 1760
EYES Green **HAIR** Greyish black
POWERS/ABILITIES Daxamite superpowers and a Green Lantern power ring that generates hard-light constructs and enables flight and travel through space.
ALLIES Green Lantern Corps
ENEMIES Mongul, Sinestro, Durlans

As a boy on his home planet of Daxam, Sodam Yat dreamed of traveling through outer space. After an alien spaceship crashed near his home, he helped to nurse the pilot, Tessog, back to health. However, his outraged Daxamite parents killed the extraterrestrial and brainwashed Yat into thinking the alien was part of an invasion force. Sometime later, Yat saw the stuffed body of Tessog in a museum diorama, which reawakened his memories and he became horrified by his race's extreme xenophobia. He devoted himself to rebuilding the Tessog's spaceship so that he could escape, and just as he was about to leave Daxam, he was chosen as a new Green Lantern and acquired his own power ring. The Guardians chose not to tell Yat of the twin prophecies that he would become the ultimate Green Lantern and was also destined to be the last surviving member of the Lantern Corps.

Yat fought bravely to defend the planet Mogo during the Sinestro Corps War. The Guardians then empowered Yat with the Ion Force, the living embodiment of willpower, and he brought glory to the Corps in many subsequent battles. Most recently, Yat suffered a rare defeat when he was captured by the Durlans, who removed his ring and experimented upon him. With the help of the Green Lantern Corps, Yat escaped and defended his home planet against the Durlans. **SK**

SODAM'S RETURN
After he was captured by the Durlans, Sodam Yat was held on the planet Corona Seven. He was harshly interrogated but later freed by the Green Lantern Corps.

ON THE RECORD

Sodam Yat has repeatedly lived up to the prophecy declaring him the ultimate Green Lantern. He has challenged some of the most fearsome villains in the universe, including Mongul, Darkseid, and even the Anti-Monitor. In *Green Lantern Corps* (Vol. 2) #17 (2007), Yat came close to death from lead poisoning, after being exposed to the metal during a fight with Superboy-Prime. He battled courageously, but as a result of that incident Yat will die within minutes if he ever removes his ring.

ION FORCE
Sodam Yat is able to access and generate the green willpower energy of the symbiotic Ion Force, which bestows him with immense power.

YELLOW LANTERN CORPS

DATA

DEBUT *Green Lantern* (Vol. 4) #10 **(May 2006)**
CURRENT VERSION *Green Lantern* (Vol. 5) #1 **(Nov. 2011)**
REAL NAME Sinestro Corps **BASE** Qward, anti-matter universe
MEMBERS/POWERS **SINESTRO** Guiding Light/host and master of Parallax; **ANTI-MONITOR** Conceiver/sponsor; **ARKILLO** Deputy leader/drill sergeant; **LYSSA DRAK** Guardian of the Book of Parallax; **WEAPONER OF QWARD** Armorer; **KARU-SIL** Reared by beasts; **DEVILDOG** Mechanoid assassin; **MURR THE MELTING MAN** Flesh-dissolving ravager; **SLUSHH** Sentient bag of acids; **TRI-EYE** Subterranean ambush-predator; **SKIVOR** Psionic persuader who kills through proxies; **SETAG RETSS** Aquatic assassin; **AMPA NNN** Serial killer and organ collector; **ROMAT-RU** Mass-murderer of children; **MAASH** Three brains constantly at war with each other; **SCHLAGG-MAN** Petty thug with killer bite; **LOW** Blood-sucking parasite; **TEKIK** Renegade robot.
All members are capable of instilling great terror, operating yellow power rings that channel the part of the Emotional Spectrum that draws on universal fear.
ALLIES Green Lantern Corps, Weaponers of Qward, Manhunters
ENEMIES Guardians of the Universe, Red Lantern Corps, Justice League, Alpha Lantern Corps, Star Sapphire Corps, Blue Lantern Corps, Indigo Tribe
AFFILIATIONS Parallax, the Fear Lodges, Book of Parallax, Sinestro

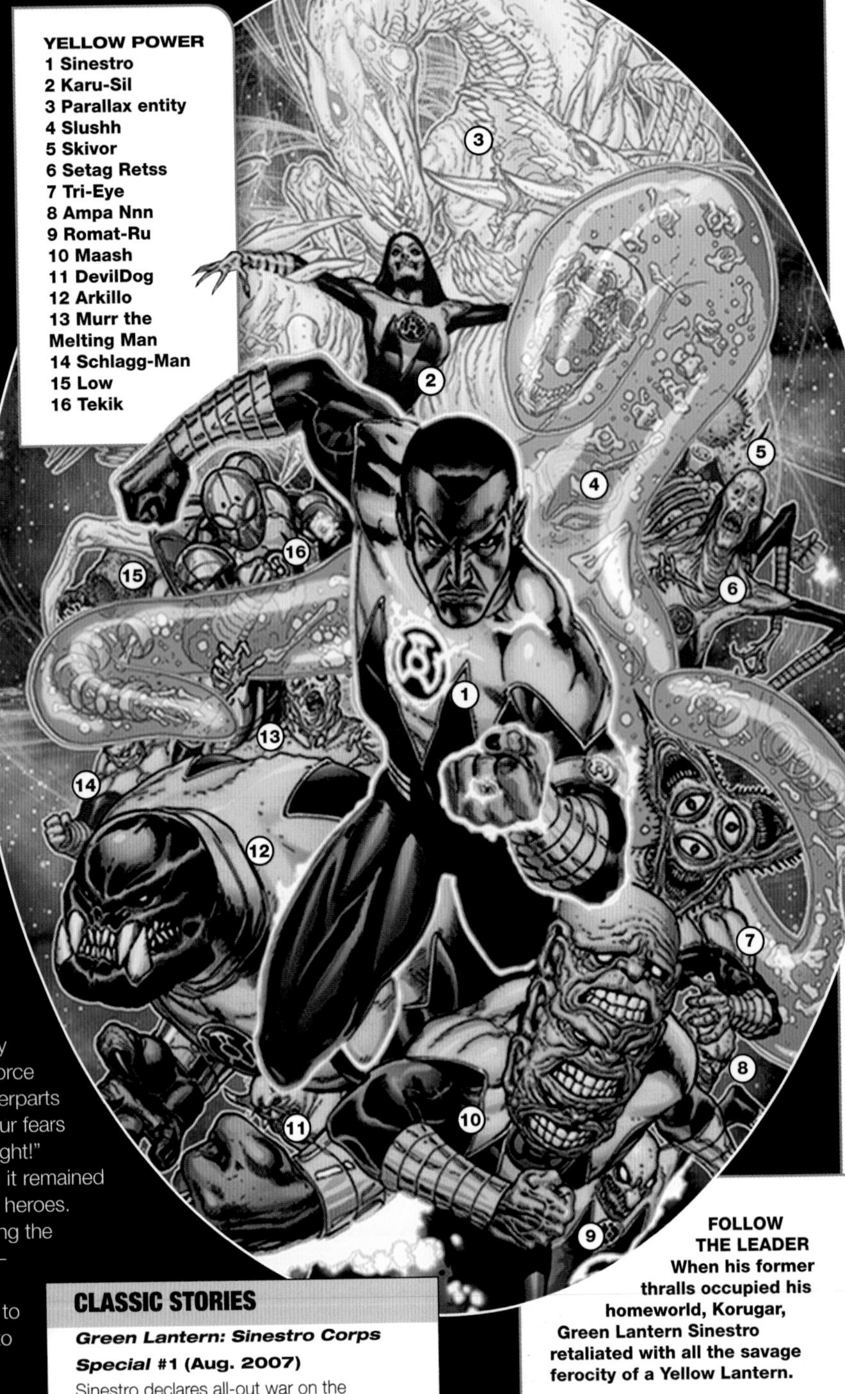

YELLOW POWER
1 Sinestro
2 Karu-Sil
3 Parallax entity
4 Slushh
5 Skivor
6 Setag Retss
7 Tri-Eye
8 Ampa Nnn
9 Romat-Ru
10 Maash
11 DevilDog
12 Arkillo
13 Murr the Melting Man
14 Schlagg-Man
15 Low
16 Tekik

The Anti-Monitor devised Yellow Lanterns to facilitate his consumption of the positive matter universe. He caused angry arch-renegade Sinestro to create an army able to counter the Guardians of the Universe and kill their agents, inducing the arrogant Korugarian to name the group after himself. Channeling creation's primal emotion of Fear, the Sinestro Corps launched itself upon unsuspecting civilizations, eradicating Green Lanterns, destroying worlds, and making sentient beings everywhere understand the true meaning of fear.

SILENCE IS GOLDEN
Mongul seized control of the Yellow Lantern Corps and stifled all dissent by publicly ripping out the tongue of his rival Arkillo.

Sinestro's Corps comprised the worst monsters in creation, filled with a hunger to hurt and the ability to "instill great fear"—and now possessing the power to realize their destructive desires. Their murderous drives were harnessed by charismatic Sinestro, who marshaled them into a disciplined force and had them launch a concerted attack on their green counterparts and Earth, while chanting their chilling oath: "In blackest day, in brightest night / beware your fears made into light / Let those who try to stop what's right / burn like his power... Sinestro's might!"

Sinestro divined Earth was supremely important to the Guardians of the Universe and it remained his focus even after his defeat at the hands of the Green Lanterns and Earth's assembled heroes. The Yellow Lanterns carried on his dream under a succession of brutal usurpers, precipitating the long-prophesied War of Light and Darkest Night. In the aftermath, the existence of an eighth—White—entity was revealed, and the Yellow Lanterns struck a tenuous truce with the Green Lantern Corps. When the Guardians forced Sinestro to rejoin their Corps, Arkillo was unable to maintain discipline and Yellow Lanterns ravaged Korugar. Following the Guardians' attempt to replace the universe's population with their Third Army, Sinestro absorbed and mastered the Parallax entity, taking control of his Corps once more. **WW**

FOLLOW THE LEADER
When his former thralls occupied his homeworld, Korugar, Green Lantern Sinestro retaliated with all the savage ferocity of a Yellow Lantern.

ON THE RECORD

Sinestro's yellow power ring was created by the evil Weaponers of Qward during the Korugarian's exile to the anti-matter universe. Its function and origins were never fully explained, but it remained a constant threat to Hal Jordan and other Green Lanterns for decades.

Before the terror weapons were mass produced for the Yellow Lantern Corps, Guy Gardner briefly used Sinestro's yellow power ring to facilitate his new career as an independent, maverick hero.

WAY OF THE WARRIOR
When Guy Gardner was kicked out of the Green Lanterns, his search for new powers made him a problem for his erstwhile allies.

CLASSIC STORIES

***Green Lantern: Sinestro Corps Special* #1 (Aug. 2007)** Sinestro declares all-out war on the Guardians, the Green Lantern Corps, the entire universe, and Earth's Super Heroes in particular. To conduct his campaign of terror, he recruits many of the worst menaces in the universe to his unholy cause.

***Green Lantern* (Vol. 4) #59–60 (Dec. 2010–Jan. 2011)** During the Brightest Day event, Parallax possesses Barry Allen, and Green Lantern Hal Jordan is forced to offer himself up as a host to save his best friend.

***Forever Evil* (Vol. 1) #4 (Feb. 2014)** Batman briefly becomes the Sinestro Corps operative for Space Sector 2814 after donning a yellow ring to battle Power Ring, the deranged Green Lantern antithesis from Earth-3.

YOUNG ALL-STARS

DEBUT *Young All-Stars* (Vol. 1) #1 (Jun. 1987)
MEMBERS/POWERS **Iron Munro** (Arnold Munro): Chemically created Superman; **Dan the Dyna-Mite** (Danny Dunbar): Atomic-charged tiny titan; **Flying Fox**: Canadian First Nations mystic; **Fury** (Helena Kosmatos): Amazon warrior, fueled by the anger of the mythic Furies; **Neptune Perkins**: Aquatic adventurer; **Sandy the Golden Boy** (Sanderson Hawkins): Acrobatic detective; **Tigress** (Paula Brooks): Martial artist, weapons master, tracker and manhunter; **Tsunami** (Miya Shimada): Controller of tidal forces; **Nisei** (Japanese-American): Sub-sea storm bringer.
ALLIES Justice Society of America, All-Star Squadron
ENEMIES Ultra-Humanite, Axis Amerika, Baron Blitzkrieg, Mekanique, Black Circle, Per Degaton, Hugo Danner, Bedlam, Darkseid
AFFILIATIONS Justice Society of America

During World War II, a wave of metahumans and mystery men arose to battle the forces of fascism. Many of these costumed heroes had juvenile sidekicks and, as the conflict intensified, felt increasingly unhappy about subjecting them to the horrors that were unfolding on a daily basis.

In 1942, the Young All-Stars was created as a youth auxiliary to the All-Star Squadron. Here the frustrated kids and a number of new champions were usefully kept away from the action to appear at Bond Drives and publicity appearances, raising funds for the war effort. However, they were targeted by Nazi super-squad Axis Amerika and soon found themselves undertaking a non-stop crusade against evil every bit as deadly as anything the adult heroes faced on the battlefront.

The Young All-Stars broke up due to personality conflicts before the war ended, although many of the team continued as individual heroes—and villains—in the postwar years. **WW**

KID COMMANDOS
The world's first superpowered teen team eventually joined the ranks of the adult All-Star Squadron.
1 Neptune Perkins
2 Flying Fox
3 Iron Munro
4 Fury I
5 Dan the Dyna-Mite
6 Tsunami

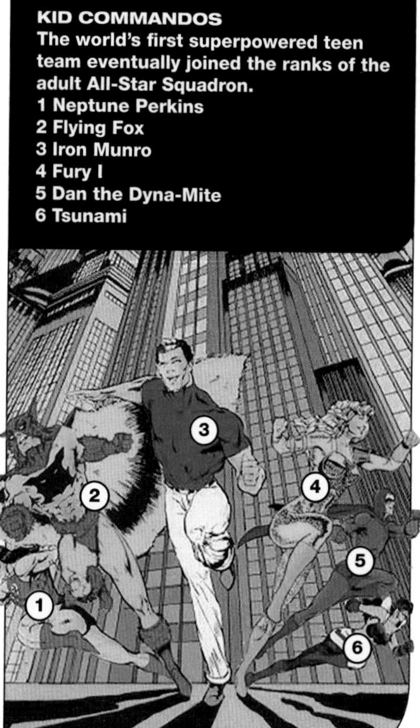

YOUNG JUSTICE

DEBUT *Young Justice: The Secret* (Vol. 1) #1 (Jun. 1998)
BASE Secret Sanctuary, Happy Harbor, Rhode Island
MEMBERS/POWERS **Robin** (Tim Drake): Genius, computer expert, martial artist, acrobat; **Superboy** (Kon-El/Connor Kent): Limited Kryptonian powers; **Impulse** (Bart Allen): Super-speed; **Red Tornado** (John Smith): Android with wind powers; **Secret** (Greta "Suzie" Hayes): Ghostly powers; **Arrowette** (Bonnie King): Archer; **Empress** (Anita Fite): Acrobat, martial arts; **Wonder Girl** (Cassie Sandsmark): Super-strength, speed, invulnerability, flight; **Batgirl** (Cassandra Cain): Martial arts, acrobat; **Slobo**: Super-strength, durability; **Ray Terril**: Light manipulation
ALLIES Snapper Carr, Donald Fite, Forever People
ENEMIES Agenda, Klarion, Harm, Buzz, Mr. Mxyzptlk, D.E.O., Bedlam, Darkseid

JUST KIDDING
The junior sidekicks all had a lot to prove and didn't need adults holding their hands or holding them back.

Young Justice was formed after a magic spell transported all Earth's adults to another world, leaving only the planet's sidekicks to conquer the threat of the magic-possessed kid Bedlam and restore the status quo. Crisis averted, Robin, Impulse, and Superboy decided to hang out and have fun without adult supervision. A loose affiliation—but certainly not a bona fide team—was born.

After they rescued the disembodied girl Secret from a clandestine Department of Extranormal Operations holding center, the teenagers decided to stick together and keep doing good. As their membership grew, the adults started taking notice, and when Young Justice were installed in the JLA's old mountain headquarters, they had to accept the android Red Tornado as a live-in guardian. Eventually the team became a beacon for every young hero in the business.

However, after many frantic months of nonstop adventure and mayhem, the team were forcibly disbanded by Nightwing after Troia and Omen were killed by Brainiac-controlled super-robots. The bitter remnants of the team renamed themselves Teen Titans and continued under the supervision of wiser heads—Cyborg, Starfire, Beast Boy, and Raven. **WW**

JUNIOR JUSTICE LEAGUE
1 Superboy
2 Secret
3 Robin
4 Wonder Girl
5 Empress
6 Impulse

ALL TOGETHER NOW
From an accidental start, Young Justice attracted many young heroes into its ranks and, for a time, became a formidable fighting force.

ZATANNA

DATA

DEBUT *Hawkman* (Vol. 1) #4 **(Oct.–Nov. 1964)**
CURRENT VERSION *Justice League Dark* #1 **(Nov. 2011)**
REAL NAME Zatanna Zatara
BASE The House of Mystery **EYES** Blue **HAIR** Black
POWERS/ABILITIES Expert magician with knowledge of innumerable spells, which she can use to teleport, create mystic barriers, fire energy bolts, control the elements, heal bodies, and manipulate minds; generally casts an enchantment by reciting a word backward, but can also cast a spell by other means.
ALLIES John Constantine, Giovanni Zatara
ENEMIES Nick Necro, Enchantress, Felix Faust, Blackbriar Thorn
AFFILIATIONS Justice League Dark

ZATARA BURNS
Zatanna is plagued by the memory of her father being burned alive in a magic ritual that went terribly wrong, and blames Constantine for his death.

MISTRESS OF MAGIC
As one of the sorcerous *Homo magi*, Zatanna possesses mastery over mystical and cosmic forces.

HAT TRICKS
Zatanna enchanted audiences with her stage magic routine—but they were unaware she was capable of real sorcery.

Zatanna Zatara is one of the most powerful magicians in the world, able to alter reality with a single word. As a member of Justice League Dark she helps defend the Earth from supernatural threats. However, this mighty sorceress has learned to her cost that magical power can be a curse as well as a blessing.

Zatanna Zatara is the daughter of famed magician Giovanni Zatara. She became a stage magician like her father, but then learned that both she and Giovanni were members of the *Homo magi*—a subspecies of human with a gift for real magic. She began a relationship with the mage Nick Necro, who taught her sorcery, but when Necro became obsessed with his hunt for the Books of Magic and embraced evil, Zatanna turned to the British street magician John Constantine. Together, they vanquished Necro, but tragedy later struck when a ritual led by Constantine went awry and burned Zatanna's father alive.

Several years later, the world was threatened by the malevolent Enchantress and the Super Heroes of the Justice League proved helpless against her witchcraft. Realizing that the world needed a new, specialized Justice League to fight supernatural threats, Madame Xanadu recruited Zatanna, John Constantine, Deadman, and Shade the Changing Man into a new team: Justice League Dark. After vanquishing the Enchantress, the team regrouped to take on the newly awakened vampire lord Cain, and later disbanded.

The government agency A.R.G.U.S. then asked the Justice League Dark to reunite to recover a map to the Books of Magic, and Zatanna agreed so that she could retrieve her father's trademark top hat, which was held in A.R.G.U.S.'s secret Black Room. After locating the map, the team soon found itself locked in a battle for the Books of Magic with several mystic foes, and discovered that the creation of Justice League Dark had been orchestrated by Nick Necro, who wanted revenge on Zatanna and John Constantine. Necro was defeated once more, and after a detour through Timepoint, the dimension of Epoch, Zatanna returned to serve in Justice League Dark. **SW**

ON THE RECORD

The pre-Flashpoint version of Zatanna is also haunted by the death of her father, and obsessed with bringing him back from Hell. She joined the JLA, playing a key role in the Identity Crisis event. After Doctor Light molested Sue Dibny and threatened the Justice League's loved ones, Zatanna used her magic to alter his mind. The debate about the ethics of this caused a schism in the JLA—especially when it was revealed that Zatanna had also altered the memories of her teammates.

MIND BENDING
Zatanna employs controversial, mind-altering magic to neutralize the threat of super-villain Doctor Light.

CLASSIC STORIES

***Seven Soldiers: Zatanna* #1-4 (Jun.–Dec. 2005)**
After Zatanna loses her magical powers in a clash with the magical entity Gwydion, the intrepid enchantress and her apprentice Misty Kilgore embark on a quest to recover them.

***Justice League* (Vol. 2) #39-40 (Jan.–Feb. 2010)** During Blackest Night, Zatanna battles her undead father in a dramatic sorcerous duel. In the aftermath, she quits the Justice League.

***Bloodspell* (TPB) (2014)**
When Black Canary tangles with a magic-wielding gang, she goes looking for magical help—which leads her to her first encounter with her future friend Zatanna.

ZATARA

DEBUT *Action Comics* (Vol. 1) #1 **(Jun. 1938)**
CURRENT VERSION *Justice League Dark* #12 **(Oct. 2012)**
REAL NAME Giovanni "John" Zatara
HEIGHT 5ft 11in **WEIGHT** 170 lbs **EYES** Blue **HAIR** Black
POWERS/ABILITIES: Can cast a wide variety of magic spells by speaking a word or phrase backward; excellent stage showman and a master of prestidigitation.
ENEMIES King Inferno, Allura, Lobo
AFFILIATIONS Cult of the Cold Flame, All-Star Squadron

Giovanni 'John' Zatara learned the ways of stage conjuring as a child, after his uncle gave him a magic kit. However, while performing on stage he instinctively cast a spell to put out a fire and discovered that he could do real sorcery. He became a magician of considerable power—a member of the *Homo magi*, a subspecies of humanity that could wield genuine magic—and fell in love with a woman named Sindella. They had a daughter named Zatanna who inherited her father's gift for magic.

LOVE WILL TEAR US APART
Zatara loved his daughter Zatanna so much that he sacrificed himself to save her—and was damned in the process.

Shortly after Zatanna turned 18, Zatara fought the evil elemental Allura and managed to subdue her, but not before she placed a curse on him declaring that any contact with his kin would end in death for all concerned. Zatanna eventually found a way to break the curse, but Zatara later sacrificed himself to protect his daughter during a ritual that went horribly wrong and was damned to Hell. Zatanna was determined to rescue her beloved father and later, during the Reign in Hell conflict, she saved him from endless torment by sending him to oblivion in the Abyss.

Zatara was briefly raised from the dead as an undead member of the Black Lantern Corps during the Blackest Night. **SW**

SPELLBOUND
Zatara would do anything to protect his young daughter Zatanna—as puppeteer and criminal Oscar Hempel discovered. Zatara turned Oscar into a living puppet! Something that would come back to haunt Zatanna in later life.

ZAURIEL

DEBUT *JLA* (Vol. 1) #6 (Jun. 1997)
CURRENT VERSION *Trinity of Sin: Phantom Stranger* #10 (Sep. 2013)
REAL NAME Zauriel
BASE Heaven
EYES Glowing white **HAIR** Bald
POWERS/ABILITIES Angel physiology; changes form; casts spells; uses wings to fly.
ENEMIES Sin Eater, Felix Faust, the Blight, Nick Necro

Zauriel is an angel who has protected the tormented hero Phantom Stranger for more than two millennia. He helped the Stranger against the Question when he betrayed him and fellow 'sinner' Pandora. He has also been forced to intervene on many occasions when the Stranger attempted to re-enter heaven in violation of a divine edict.

In one of these encounters, Zauriel was lured into the House of Mystery and trapped in a magic circle by John Constantine, one of the Stranger's teammates in Justice League Dark, who wanted the angel's help in a looming supernatural battle. Motivated by his love for the Phantom Stranger, Zauriel joined the group in their fight against the Blight, Nick Necro, and Felix Faust. Ultimately, Justice League Dark triumphed, but the conflict took its toll on Zauriel and he weakened and died. However, the Phantom Stranger confronted his own demons and God himself to bring about Zauriel's resurrection, and the angel returned in a new female form. **SW**

GUARDIAN ANGEL
As a member of the angelic host, Zauriel has watched over the Phantom Stranger for thousands of years, appearing in many guises.

ZEUS, MAXIE

DEBUT *Detective Comics* (Vol. 1) #483 (Apr.–May 1979)
CURRENT VERSION *Batman Eternal* #6 (Jul. 2014)
REAL NAME Maximillian Zeus
BASE Arkham Asylum
EYES Brown **HAIR** Brown
POWERS/ABILITIES Despite delusions of divinity, Maxie Zeus has no powers, though he is a cunning gang leader.
ENEMIES Batman

Maximilian Zeus was a history professor until the death of his beloved wife, which drove him insane. Maximilian's obsession with Classical mythology led him to believe that he was actually an incarnation of the Greek god Zeus, and he embarked upon a career as a crime lord in Gotham City.

After committing a brazen series of mythologically inspired crimes, he was arrested by Batman and incarcerated in Arkham Asylum. However, crazed cultists devoted to deceased villain Deacon Blackfire chose Maxie's muscled body as the vessel for the spirit of their leader. Blackfire then performed a ritual intended to merge Gotham City with Hell, but the Spectre intervened and exorcised Blackfire from Zeus' body. In the aftermath of the conflict Maxie's body was found by Detective Jim Corrigan, who took him to safety. Zeus recovered, but he still believed that he was an immortal Olympian god, and remained incarcerated in Arkham Asylum. **SW**

DIVINE DELUSION
Maxie Zeus believed he was a Greek god and dressed and bulked up accordingly. Little did he know he was just Deacon Blackfire's puppet.

ROLL CALL

The DC Comics Universe (DCU) is populated with a myriad of memorable characters. The *DC Comics Encyclopedia* presents as many of these as possible, and Roll Call spotlights some of the more notable players who round out that rich and diverse DCU.

Text: Steve Korte

ABRA KADABRA
DEBUT *Flash* #128 (May 1962)
REAL NAME Citizen Abra **BASE** Keystone City
ALLIES Injustice Gang, Secret Society of Super-Villains
ENEMIES The Flash
BACKGROUND Abra Kadabra came from the 64th century and used technology from that era to create a new identity and masquerade as a magician. He later made a deal with the demon Neron and became a true sorcerer, able to cast spells and fire energy bolts. He used real magic to battle the Flash.

AGENT LIBERTY II
DEBUT *Superman* #691 (Oct. 2009)
BASE Washington, D.C.
ENEMIES Ursa
BACKGROUND It was never revealed whether the second Agent Liberty was related to the murdered Benjamin Lockwood, the first Agent Liberty, or the paramilitary group the Sons of Liberty. Agent Liberty II served as a bodyguard to the then president of the United States, Martin Suarez, and lost her life when the Kryptonian villain Ursa attacked the White House.

AIR WAVE II
DEBUT *Green Lantern* #100 (Jan. 1978)
REAL NAME Harold "Hal" Lawrence Jordan
BASE Dallas
ALLIES Justice Society of America **ENEMIES** Kobra, Lex Luthor
BACKGROUND Harold Jordan, named after Hal Jordan of the Green Lantern Corps, is the son of Air Wave I. He inherited his father's helmet, which allowed him to change his molecular structure and fly at super-speed. He perished during the Infinite Crisis but was reanimated as a member of the Black Lantern Corps.

AMAZING GRACE
DEBUT *Superman* #3 (Mar. 1987)
BASE Apokolips
ALLIES Darkseid **ENEMIES** Superman
BACKGROUND The sister of Darkseid's star propagandist, Glorious Godfrey, Amazing Grace was able to manipulate the will of others with her beauty and persuasive powers. She was a master of mind control who lived in the slums of Apokolips. She located resistance groups and beguiled their leaders, drawing them out long enough for Darkseid to annihilate them.

ANANSA THE SPIDER QUEEN
DEBUT *Animal Man* #81 (Mar. 1995)
BASE Montana
ALLIES Her children **ENEMIES** Animal Man
BACKGROUND Anansa was a giant humanoid spider with the power to read minds. Prepared to do whatever it took to protect her offspring, she harvested human bodies to feed them. Her spider-children soon learned how to abduct and cocoon humans so that Anansa could feed off their dreams. The Spider Queen eventually abducted Animal Man and his son.

ANDROMEDA
DEBUT *Legion of Super-Heroes* #6 (Apr. 1990)
REAL NAME Laurel Gand
ALLIES Legion of Super-Heroes
ENEMIES Composite Man, Superboy-Prime
BACKGROUND Gand came from the planet Daxam in the 30th century. She was a member of the Legion of Super-Heroes where she represented her home planet. Gand possessed similar powers to Superman, including super-strength, heat-vision, and the ability to fly. However, she was hypersensitive to the element lead.

ANGLE MAN
DEBUT *Wonder Woman* #70 (Nov. 1954)
CURRENT VERSION *Forever Evil* #1 (Nov. 2013)
REAL NAME Angelo Bend
BASE Milan
ALLIES Devastation, Circe **ENEMIES** Cheetah, Catwoman
BACKGROUND Angle Man was a master thief who used a magical weapon called an Angler. It allowed him to teleport, bend space, alter gravity, and warp perception. He worked alone and also with the Secret Society of Super-Villains.

ANIMA
DEBUT *New Titans Annual* #9 (Jul. 1993)
REAL NAME Courtney Mason
ALLIES Cyborg, Superboy, Hawkman
ENEMIES The Nameless One
BACKGROUND Courtney Mason's body contained the Animus, a shadow being that possessed powerful abilities such as super-strength, flight, and shape-changing powers. It gave Courtney the power to leech bio-energy from both living and non-living things. She died in a battle with the villain Prometheus.

ANTITHESIS
DEBUT *Teen Titans* #53 (Feb. 1978)
BASE Limbo
ALLIES Bromwell Stikk **ENEMIES** Teen Titans
BACKGROUND The vile creature known as the Antithesis used its powers of telepathy and mental manipulation against the Justice League of America. It hypnotized them by absorbing their negative emotions, and forced them to commit crimes, until they were stopped by the Teen Titans. The heroes Nightwing and the Herald defeated the Antithesis and exiled the creature to Limbo.

APPARITION
DEBUT *Action Comics* #276 (May 1961)
REAL NAME Tinya Wazzo
BASE Legion World, U.P. Space
ALLIES Saturn Girl, Timber Wolf **ENEMIES** Princess Projectra
BACKGROUND Apparition was a native of the planet Bgztl. Also known as Phantom Girl, Apparition had the ability to phase all or any part of her body into an intangible or phantom state and, hence could not be harmed by conventional methods of attack. She fought alongside the Legion of Super-Heroes.

AQUAWOMAN
DEBUT *Earth 2* #18 (Feb. 2014)
REAL NAME Marella
UNIVERSE Earth-2 **BASE** Atlantis
ALLIES Batman **ENEMIES** Darkseid
BACKGROUND Aquawoman was the female ruler of Atlantis on Earth-2 and was skilled at hydrokinesis. After being imprisoned by the World Army in the Black Basement beneath Arkham Asylum, she was freed by Batman and joined him in a battle against Darkseid. Marella disliked being called "Aquawoman."

ARGENT II
DEBUT *Teen Titans* #1 (Oct. 1996)
REAL NAME Antonia Louise "Toni" Monetti
BASE New Jersey
ALLIES Teen Titans **ENEMIES** H'San Natall
BACKGROUND Teenager Toni Monetti was abducted by aliens and given the superpower to generate silver plasma and shape it to whatever form she desires. Her ability to control bursts of silver plasma energy earned her the codename "Argent." Toni was an on-and-off member of the Teen Titans.

ARGUS
DEBUT *The Flash Annual* #6 (1993)
REAL NAME Nicholas Kovak (aka Nick Kelly)
BASE Keystone City
ALLIES The Flash III **ENEMIES** Keystone's mobsters
BACKGROUND Kovak was working as an FBI agent when he was attacked by a space alien. The attack altered Kovak's body chemistry, allowing him to become virtually invisible in shadows and see beyond the normal spectrum. As the Super Hero Argus, he often teamed up with the Flash—although he preferred to operate alone.

ARRAKHAT
DEBUT *Robin* #78 (Jul. 2000)
BASE O'salla Ben Duuram
ALLIES Arghulian, Tapeworm **ENEMIES** Robin, Connor Hawke
BACKGROUND The demon Arrakhat was an evil djinn from the O'salla Ben Duuram, which translates as "Oasis of the Damned," one of the descending circles of Hell. He manifested as an armored demon wielding a flaming scimitar. Arrakhat's formidable powers were mystical in nature. When summoned, Arrakhat had the ability to grant three deaths instead of three wishes.

ARTEMIS III
DEBUT *Suicide Squad* #35 (Nov. 1989)
BASE Apokolips
ALLIES Darkseid's Female Furies **ENEMIES** Superboy, Supergirl
BACKGROUND Also known as Artemiz, this skilled archer was recruited by Granny Goodness to become one of Darkseid's Female Furies. She commanded a pack of cybernetic warhounds who helped her to hunt down enemies. Although highly skilled in hand-to-hand combat, her main role in the Female Furies was that of a huntress. Artemiz battled the Suicide Squad, Supergirl, and Superboy.

ARYAN BRIGADE
DEBUT *Justice League Task Force* #10 (Mar. 1994)
BASE Pine Heights, Nebraska
ALLIES Aryan Nation, the Cadre **ENEMIES** Justice League Task Force
BACKGROUND The Aryan Brigade was a team of white supremacist terrorists that created a virus to destroy non-white human DNA. This fanatical team would have exterminated most of the globe's population if it had not been stopped by the Justice League. The five metahumans who made up the group were Backlash, Blind Faith, Golden Eagle II, Heatmonger, and Iron Cross.

ASMODEL
DEBUT *JLA* #7 (Jul. 1997)
BASE Heaven
ALLIES Neron **ENEMIES** Zauriel, Justice League of America
BACKGROUND Asmodel was once the commander of the Angel Army of Heaven, but he rebelled and was consigned to Hell. There he obtained the rank of Archfiend and became a servant of the demon Neron. Asmodel wielded a flaming staff and had few rivals as a military commander. He was immortal and invulnerable, with vast super-strength, super-speed, acidic blood, and the power of flight.

ATMOS

DEBUT *Legion of Super-Heroes* #32 (Mar. 1987)
REAL NAME Marak Russen
BASE Planet Xanthu in the 31st century
ALLIES Uncanny Amazers **ENEMIES** The Blight
BACKGROUND Atmos was a member of the Uncanny Amazers, the planet Xanthu's counterpart to the Earth-based Legion of Super-Heroes. A living nuclear reactor, Russen's powers included super-strength, speed, and flight. He could generate a protective force field and survive unaided in the vacuum of space.

AUCTIONEER, THE

DEBUT *Action Comics* #841 (Sep. 2006)
BACKGROUND The Auctioneer was a powerful, giant alien passionate about collecting and reselling items from across the cosmos. His starship was large enough to house entire buildings. He took an interest in Earth and pocketed monuments like the Eiffel Tower and the Golden Gate Bridge. He even captured Superman and other metahumans to sell at auction, but the Man of Steel, allied with Nightwing, Aquaman, and others, escaped. When Superman vowed to release the Auctioneer's private database, the alien withdrew.

AZAZEL

DEBUT *Sandman* #4 (Apr. 1989)
BASE Hell
ALLIES Lucifer **ENEMIES** John Constantine, Morpheus
BACKGROUND Azazel is one of the most powerful demons in Hell, ruling alongside Lucifer and Beelzebub. When Lucifer closed Hell for a time, Azazel tried to claim it for his own and failed. He was then trapped by Morpheus, the Dream King, and locked away in a jar. However, he is not to be underestimated. Azazel commands mystic and eldritch forces that allow him to eradicate a demon from existence.

BAD SAMARITAN

DEBUT *The Outsiders* #3 (Jan. 1986)
REAL NAME Zviad Baazovi
ENEMIES The Outsiders
BACKGROUND Baazovi is a spy-for-hire, a terrorist, or an insurrectionist, depending on who pays his fees. He is loyal to no organization, or country. He is also a ruthless assassin and a master of disguise. Baazovi always wears dark glasses—his trademark—as his eyes are sensitive to bright light, or so he claims. In all his encounters with the Outsiders, he has escaped and remains at large.

BALLOON BUSTER

DEBUT *All-American Men of War* #112 (Nov.–Dec. 1965)
REAL NAME Steven Henry Savage, Jr.
BASE France
BACKGROUND The son of legendary cowboy Brian "Scalphunter" Savage, Steve Savage, Jr. was a matchless marksman and a skilled biplane pilot. He fought fearlessly in World War I and earned the nickname "Balloon Buster", after using his exceptional flying skills to down several German attack balloons. He disappeared in South East Asia in 1924.

BAT-QUEEN

DEBUT *Detective Comics* #402 (Aug. 1970)
CURRENT VERSION *Detective Comics #19* (Jun. 2013)
REAL NAME Francine Lee **BASE** Gotham City
ALLIES Wrath **ENEMIES** Man-Bat, Batman, G.C.P.D.
BACKGROUND Lee was a scientist who married Dr. Kirk Langstrom, the monstrous Man-Bat. Forced to ingest the Man-Bat serum made by her husband she became a feral She-Bat, calling herself Bat-Queen. A deranged Lee terrorized Gotham City with a string of killings and was eventually defeated by Langstrom.

BAYTOR

DEBUT *The Demon* #43 (Jan. 1994)
BASE Gotham City
ALLIES Tommy Monaghan **ENEMIES** Etrigan
BACKGROUND Baytor was a minor demon who briefly proclaimed himself the ruler of Hell. After his attempted coup failed, he fled to Earth and settled in crime-torn Gotham City. He worked as a bartender in Noonan's Bar where he met Tommy Monaghan and joined his gang of criminals and mercenaries. Baytor could project a liquid onto his enemies; when it dried, it caused them to shatter.

BEEFEATER

DEBUT *Justice League Europe* #20 (Nov. 1990)
REAL NAME Michael Morice
BASE Ipswich, England
ALLIES Justice League International **ENEMIES** The Auctioneer
BACKGROUND Morice first became a liaison to Justice League International and later a costumed hero in charge of Basement 101, Britain's prison facility for meta-villains. Morice inherited his father's collapsible battle rod, which projected force blasts. However, his inept use of it left a lot to be desired.

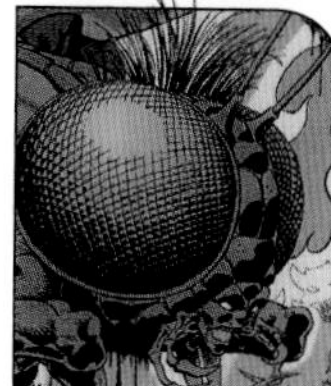

BEELZEBUB

DEBUT *Sandman* #4 (Apr. 1989)
BASE Hell
ALLIES Azazel, Lucifer **ENEMIES** Supergirl
BACKGROUND Beelzebub is one of the three rulers of Hell. Also called the Lord of the Flies, he has vast demonic powers and can take the form of a giant fly. Beelzebub has dominion over decay and decomposition and has existed since the creation of death. He has crossed paths with the Earth-based heroes Kid Eternity and Supergirl, and continues to spread his evil throughout the universe.

BEK, GARRYN

DEBUT *Invasion* #1 (Jan. 1989)
BASE Cairn
ALLIES Vril Dox II **ENEMIES** Kanis-Biz
BACKGROUND Bek was a police administrator on the drug-trafficking planet of Cairn and an exceptional coordinator and a starship pilot. Imprisoned by the alien team Alliance, which was bent on destroying Earth, Bek escaped along with his cell mate, Vril Dox II. He then transformed Cairn's entire police force into a peacekeeping agency known as L.E.G.I.O.N.

BELIAL

DEBUT *Captain Marvel, Jr.* #4 (Feb. 13, 1943)
CURRENT VERSION *Phantom Stranger* #2 (Jan. 2013)
BASE Hell
ALLIES Sabbac **ENEMIES** Captain Marvel, Jr.
BACKGROUND The eldest son of Trigon, Belial was one of the most ambitious demons in Hell. He used arcane dark arts and his intellect to make up for his relative lack of demonic strength. He also ran the Lucky Devil casino in Las Vegas. Belial's schemes on Earth were usually thwarted by Captain Marvel, Jr.

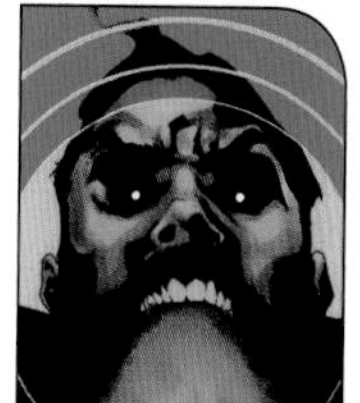

BLACK BANSHEE

DEBUT *Supergirl* #8 (Jun. 2012)
REAL NAME Garrett Smythe
BASE Dublin
ENEMIES Supergirl, Silver Banshee
BACKGROUND As the Black Banshee, Smythe was a skilled master of the magical arts. He possessed superhuman strength and was able to emit an incredibly destructive hypersonic scream. He traveled to Earth to battle his daughter Siobhan, the Silver Banshee, and also Supergirl.

BLACK BISON

DEBUT *The Fury of Firestorm* #1 (Jun. 1982)
CURRENT VERSION *Fury of Firestorm: The Nuclear Men #18* (May. 2013)
REAL NAME John Ravenhair, Black-Cloud-In-Morning **BASE** New York City
BACKGROUND Seeking to right the wrongs that had been done to his Native American ancestors, Ravenhair donned a traditional tribal costume and launched a crime spree that included a battle with Firestorm. Black Bison became a member of the Secret Society of Super-Villains, and used a tribal coup stick to control the weather and to animate objects.

BLACK CONDOR II

DEBUT *Black Condor* #1 (Jun. 1992)
REAL NAME Ryan Kendall **BASE** Opal City
ALLIES Primal Force **ENEMIES** The Shark, Sky Pirate
BACKGROUND As the second Black Condor, Kendall used telekinesis and was an expert knife-thrower. Acquiring his powers from a monstrous radiation experiment conducted by his grandfather, Kendall was recruited to his new role by the first Black Condor, Richard Grey—the high-flying 1940s Freedom Fighter. Kendall served in the JLA, but later died during the Infinite Crisis.

BLACK PIRATE

DEBUT *Action Comics* #23 (Apr. 1940)
REAL NAME Jon Valor
ALLIES Bruce Wayne **ENEMIES** Blackbeard
BACKGROUND The legend of the Black Pirate began in 1588 when British nobleman Jon Valor donned a pirate's costume and sailed the high seas in the cause of justice. Over three centuries later, his grandson Jack was inspired by Batman to fight crime as the new Black Pirate. Yet Jack Valor's spirit couldn't rest until his name was cleared, which it was with the help of the Jack Knight, Ralph Dinby and Hamilton Drew.

BLACK ZERO

DEBUT *Superboy* #61 (Apr. 1999)
REAL NAME Kon-El
BASE Metropolis
ALLIES Doomsday **ENEMIES** Earth's Superboy
BACKGROUND An evil clone of Superman from an alternate Earth, Black Zero possessed nearly all of the Man of Steel's powers. He had superhuman strength and speed, was invulnerable, and possessed psionic vision, similar to heat-vision. Black Zero invaded our planet, only to be destroyed by Earth's Superboy.

BLOOD PACK, THE

DEBUT *Showcase '94* #12 (Dec. 1994)
ALLIES New Bloods **ENEMIES** Quorum
BACKGROUND When parasites invaded Earth during the Bloodlines crisis, several teenagers acquired superpowers, including Ballistic, a super-strong weapons expert; Geist, who could turn invisible; Sparx, who controlled electrical energy; Nightblade, with enhanced regenerative powers; and Loria, a steel-skinned warrior. Led by established heroine Jade, the team got corporate support and formed the Blood Pack team. Several members were killed by Superboy-Prime during the Infinite Crisis.

BODY DOUBLES

DEBUT *Resurrection Man* #1 (Mar. 1996)
REAL NAMES Bonny Hoffman and Carmen Leno
ALLIES Secret Society of Super-Villains **ENEMIES** Resurrection Man
BACKGROUND The Body Doubles were hired killers who worked for the Requiem, Inc. Assassination Agency. They were martial arts experts and employed the latest hi-tech weaponry, including deadly gadgets hidden in their makeup cases. They often came into conflict with the hero Resurrection Man and even tried to take on Catwoman, but the Princess of Plunder soon put them in their place.

BOLPHUNGA
DEBUT *Green Lantern* (Vol. 2) #188 (May 1985)
CURRENT VERSION *Green Lantern #20* (Jul. 2013)
ALLIES Burlls, Fatality, Quade **ENEMIES** Green Lanterns
BACKGROUND Known as "Bolphunga the Unrelenting" for his tenacious pursuit of enemies and fugitives, this intergalactic warrior earned a fierce reputation as a bounty hunter who was obsessed with violence. Although of low intelligence, Bolphunga possessed superhuman strength and stamina. Green Lantern Guy Gardner was a frequent target.

BOY COMMANDOS
DEBUT *Detective Comics* #64 (Jun. 1942)
BASE Metropolis, mobile
ALLIES The Guardian, Newsboy Legion **ENEMIES** Agent Axis
BACKGROUND In 1942, Captain Eric "Rip" Carter led four brave orphaned boys—Alfy Twidgett, Andre Chavard, Daniel "Brooklyn" Turpin, Jan Haasan—on missions throughout war-torn Europe, as the Boy Commandos. Percy Clearweather and Tex joined after the war ended. As adults, the individual team members still fought injustice, with Turpin joining Metropolis' Special Crimes Unit.

BRAINSTORM
DEBUT *Mister Terrific* #2 (Dec. 2011)
REAL NAME Dominic Lanse
BASE California
BACKGROUND Dominic Lanse was a scientist studying mind-control and artificial intelligence in machines. He eventually acquired the ability to influence the minds of others. His mind-manipulating powers also indirectly caused the death of Paula Holt, Mr. Terrific's wife. An enraged Mr. Terrific beats Lanse to an inch of his life, a shocking act of violent that was witnessed by many people on television.

BREACHER
DEBUT *Justice League of America's Vibe* #3 (Jun. 2013)
REAL NAME Quell Mordeth
BASE Piradell
ALLIES Gypsy, Vibe **ENEMIES** Rupture
BACKGROUND After being exposed to massive amounts of energy, Mordeth acquired the power to expel energy from his body and teleport between dimensions. He traveled from another reality to warn Earth about Darkseid's invasion. Mordeth became a freedom fighter who fought for his people against the villainous Rupture.

BROTHER POWER
DEBUT *Brother Power the Geek* #1 (Sep.–Oct. 1968)
ENEMIES Lord Sliderule
BACKGROUND Strauck by a lightning bolt a store mannequin was brought to life as Brother Power, the Geek. The Earth's only "puppet elemental," the pacifist Brother Power will do anything to avoid hand-to-hand combat. He has superhuman durability and strength, and is highly pliable and resistant to injury. Brother Power ran for Congress, was imprisoned as a circus freak, and enslaved on an assembly line by the villain Lord Sliderule. He has also crossed paths with Batman and the Phantom Stranger.

BROTHERHOOD OF DADA, THE
DEBUT *Doom Patrol* (Vol. 2) #25 (Aug. 1989)
NOTABLE MEMBERS Mr. Nobody, Sleepwalk, Frenzy, the Fog, the Quiz, Number None, Love Glove, Alias the Blur, the Toy **ENEMIES** The Doom Patrol
BACKGROUND Rejected by The Brotherhood of Evil, Mr. Nobody assembled a group of outcasts dedicated to the absurdity of life: The Brotherhood of Dada. The team included Sleepwalk, whose super-strength only manifested while asleep; the Fog, a psychedelic cloud; and the Quiz, who had "every superpower you haven't thought of yet." But they were no match for the almost equally bizarre heroes of the Doom Patrol.

BRUTALE
DEBUT *Nightwing* #22 (Jul. 1998)
CURRENT VERSION *Blue Beetle #1* (Nov. 2011)
REAL NAME Guillermo Barrera **BASE** Hascaragua
ALLIES La Dama, Coyote, Rompe-Huesos **ENEMIES** Blue Beetle
BACKGROUND A master of knives, Barrera is quite formidable with this weapon of choice. He was an assassin from South America who moved to the United States and donned a gargoyle costume to became the deadly Brutale. He later became a member of the Secret Society of Super-Villains.

BULLETGIRL II (WINDSHEAR)
DEBUT *The Power of Shazam!* #32 (Nov. 1997)
REAL NAME Deanna Barr
BASE Fawcett City
ALLIES Captain Marvel **ENEMIES** Chain Lightning
BACKGROUND Deanna Barr was the daughter of the original Bulletgirl, Susan Kent. Deanna's anti-gravity helmet enables her to fly and create an invisible electromagnetic field. With the help of her father, Jim Barr, she used her newfound abilities to rescue the depowered Marvel Family from the clutches of Chain Lightning.

BUSHMASTER
DEBUT *Super Friends* #8 (Nov. 1977)
REAL NAME Bernal Rojas
BASE The Dome
ALLIES Justice League International **ENEMIES** Queen Bee of Bialya
BACKGROUND Rojas was a herpetologist who created a cybernetic costume that allowed him to duplicate certain reptile abilities. He donned this garish suit that was equipped with a venom gun and heat sensors to become a Super Hero. He became a member of the Global Guardians, but was shot and killed by bank robbers.

CADRE, THE
DEBUT *Justice League of America* #235 (Feb. 1985)
ALLIES Aryan Brigade, New Extremists
ENEMIES Justice League Detroit
BACKGROUND The Cadre was a group of superpowered villains that received their powers from an alien known as the Overmaster. The team existed in many forms. The original members included Black Mass, Crowbar, Fastball, Nightfall, Shatterfist, and Shrike. Over time, the group lost several members, which were replaced by newly empowered recruits.

CALCULATOR
DEBUT *Detective Comics* #463 (Sep. 1976)
REAL NAME Noah Kuttler
ALLIES Doctor Psycho, Doctor Light, Deathstroke **ENEMIES** Oracle
BACKGROUND After a failed career as a costumed villain, Kuttler, with his genius level intellect, reinvented himself as a computer expert and became a member of the Secret Society of Super-Villains. He eventually converted from a costumed crook to an information-broker for villains.

CAPTAIN COMPASS
DEBUT *Star-Spangled Comics* #83 (Aug. 1948)
REAL NAME Mark Compass
BASE The High Seas
ALLIES Penny Steamship Lines
BACKGROUND A skilled fighter with a keen deductive mind, Mark Compass served as a frogman in the US Navy, and later commanded his own vessels. After leaving the Navy, he joined Penny Steamship Lines as a roving nautical detective, solving mysteries and preventing crimes aboard the *S.S. Nautilus*.

CAPTAIN FEAR
DEBUT *Adventure Comics* #425 (Dec. 1972–Jan. 1973)
REAL NAME Fero
BASE The Caribbean
ALLIES His crew of pirates **ENEMIES** Baron Hemlocke
BACKGROUND When a young Fero was taken captive in a Spanish raid, he vowed to extract vengeance from all Spaniards. He became Captain Fear and sailed across the Caribbean in the 16th century, protecting his countrymen. He and his crew were later killed by demonic forces, who doomed them to wander the seas as spirits.

CAPTAIN STINGAREE
DEBUT *Detective Comics* #460 (Jun. 1976)
REAL NAME Karl Courtney
BASE Gotham City
ALLIES Cavalier, Captain Cold **ENEMIES** Batman, Secret Six
BACKGROUND Courtney was obsessed with pirates and donned pirate garb to launch his criminal career. He was an expert swordsman, but not a successful villain. He joined the Secret Society of Super-Villains and died fighting the Secret Six alongside his secret lover, Cavalier, and other super-villains.

CAPTAIN STORM
DEBUT *Capt. Storm* #1 (May–Jun. 1964)
REAL NAME William Storm
BASE Europe and the South Pacific
BACKGROUND Storm was a skipper on a patrol boat during World War II. He lost his ship, crew, and one of his legs during the war. Courageous and patriotic, Storm was determined to stay in the US Navy. He was eventually recommissioned, after which he joined a band of military misfits known as the Losers. He led them to many victories, but died alongside his comrades during the Crisis event.

CAPTAIN X
DEBUT *Star Spangled Comics* #1 (Oct. 1941)
REAL NAME Richard "Buck" Dare
ALLIES The Group **ENEMIES** KGB, Stalnoivolk
BACKGROUND Richard Dare was a pilot during World War II and flew top-secret missions in a special aircraft called *Jenny*. It was an experimental plastic plane that was virtually invisible and used Uranium-235 as its atomic fuel source. Captain X remained active during the Cold War until he was killed by KGB agent Stalnoivolk. Dare is the grandfather of Ronnie Raymond (Firestorm the Nuclear Man).

CAPTAIN TRIUMPH
DEBUT *Uncle Sam and the Freedom Fighters* #3 (Nov. 2006)
ALLIES Magno **ENEMIES** Freedom Fighters, Red Bee
BACKGROUND When Chemo attacked Blüdhaven, a young woman's meta-gene was activated, giving her superhuman abilities. She became Captain Triumph and was forced by government agency S.H.A.D.E. to join the Crusaders. The heroes thwarted an alien Bee invasion of Earth, but at great cost—the deaths of Triumph's teammates Citizen X and Libertine. Soon after, Captain Triumph broke away from S.H.A.D.E and fought crime alongside Magno.

CAPUCINE
DEBUT *Swamp Thing* #20 (Jul. 2013)
ALLIES Swamp Thing **ENEMIES** Etrigan
BACKGROUND Capucine was a French warrior from the 12th century who was granted 1000 years of immortality. She was a lethal fighter who honed her skills over centuries of combat. She had superhuman abilities and was skilled at hand-to-hand combat. She enlisted Swamp Thing to help her fight the demon Etrigan, who had come for her soul. After defeating Etrigan and at the end of her long life, Swamp Thing placed her in the Green, where she could exist for eternity.

CAVALIER
DEBUT *Detective Comics* #81 (Nov. 1943)
CURRENT VERSION *Batman: The Dark Knight* (Vol. 2) #2 (Dec. 2011)
REAL NAME Mortimer Drake **BASE** Gotham City
ALLIES Captain Stingaree, Black Lightning **ENEMIES** Secret Six
BACKGROUND Drake was a minor villain obsessed with antiquated costumes and weaponry. A skilled swordsman who carried a stash of weapons, he was one of the Secret Society of Super-Villains who battled the Secret Six. During the brawl, Bane performed a "Backbreaker" on Drake and broke his back.

CELESTE
DEBUT *Legion of Super-Heroes* #6 (Apr. 1990)
REAL NAME Celeste McCauley
ALLIES Legion of Super-Heroes **ENEMIES** The Dominators
BACKGROUND Celeste was a member of the 30th-century Legion of Super-Heroes. During a fight with Glorith the Sorceress, Celeste became a being of pure energy. Later, she was caught in the blast of a dead Green Lantern's exploding power ring and became the living embodiment of Green Lantern energy. Celeste had an indomitable will, and could fly and become invisible.

CELSIUS
DEBUT *Showcase* #94 (Aug.–Sept. 1977)
CURRENT VERSION *Justice League Vol 2 #24* (Dec. 2013)
REAL NAME Arani Desai Caulder **BASE** Kansas City
ALLIES The Chief **ENEMIES** General Immortus
BACKGROUND Possessing a formidable intellect, Arani was an Indian woman given the gift of immortality by her husband, Niles Caulder. She found she could now also project rays of intense heat or cold. She joined the Doom Patrol, but died during an alien invasion of Earth and was later reanimated as a Black Lantern.

CHEMICAL KING
DEBUT *Adventure Comics* #371 (Aug. 1968)
REAL NAME Condo Arlik
ALLIES Legion of Super-Heroes **ENEMIES** Dark Circle
BACKGROUND Arlik left his planet Phlon to join the 30th century Legion of Super-Heroes and became one of the Legion Academy's first members. His mutant abilities enabled him to act as a "human catalyst" to slow down or speed up chemical reactions. On an undercover mission to Australia with Timber Wolf, he sacrificed his life to prevent Deregon, a Dark Circle agent from starting World War VII.

CH'P
DEBUT *Green Lantern* #148 (Jan. 1982)
BASE H'lven
ALLIES Lantern Salaak **ENEMIES** Doctor Ub'x and his Crabster Army
BACKGROUND As the Green Lantern of Sector 2014, Ch'p defeated an invasion of his homeworld by Ub'x and his army. He was run over by a truck and died on Oa. Like many other deceased Green Lanterns, he was later resurrected as a Black Lantern, who then began attacking the still-living Green Lanterns. The Black Lantern Central Power Battery was eventually destroyed and Ch'p died once again.

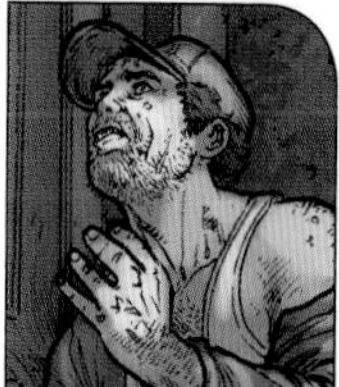

CHILL, JOE
DEBUT *Detective Comics* #33 (Nov. 1939)
CURRENT VERSION *Batman: The Dark Knight #0* (Nov. 2012)
REAL NAME Joseph Chilton **BASE** Gotham City
BACKGROUND Chill was a low-level criminal whose actions created one of the greatest Super Heroes of all. On one fateful night, Chill robbed Bruce Wayne's parents and then killed them. Before he became Batman, Bruce tracked him down, demanding to know why. Bruce was prepared to murder Chill in revenge, but when the thug begged for his life, Bruce relented and spared him.

CHRIS KL-99
DEBUT *Strange Adventures* #1 (Aug.–Sep. 1950)
REAL NAME Christopher Ambler
BACKGROUND Born in the 21st century, Chris KL-99 was a brilliant scientist, astronaut, and astronomer. He piloted an interplanetary vessel named *The Pioneer* and explored new worlds in search of his parents' graves. Occasionally traveling with the Martian adventurer Halk and the Venusian scientist Jero, Chris discovered more inhabited planets than anyone in history. During the *Crisis on Infinite Earths*, Chris helped build a time-travel conduit to send heroes back to the dawn of mankind.

CICADA
DEBUT *Flash* #170 (Mar. 2001)
REAL NAME David Hersch **BASE** Keystone City
ALLIES Magenta **ENEMIES** The Flash
BACKGROUND Cicada was an insane megalomaniac who, after being struck by lightning, could achieve immortality by consuming the life forces of others. He was a villain who believed that the Flash (Wally West) was a fellow "brother of the lightning." He kidnapped him, but the Flash emerged triumphant. After a stint in prison, Cicada joined the Secret Society of Super-Villains during the Infinite Crisis.

CINNAMON
DEBUT *Weird Western Tales* #48 (Sep.–Oct. 1978)
CURRENT VERSION *All-Star Western* #6 (Apr. 2012)
REAL NAME Katherine Manser
ALLIES Nighthawk **ENEMIES** August 7
BACKGROUND When her father was gunned down, young Katherine Manser was sent to a cruel orphanage where she was nicknamed Cinnamon. She escaped and became a superb markswoman and a savage fighter for justice. Teaming up with the gunslinger Nighthawk, the two became legendary outlaw hunters during the late 1800s.

CLAY, JOSHUA
DEBUT *Showcase* #94 (Aug.–Sep. 1977)
CURRENT VERSION *Justice League #24* (Dec. 2013)
BASE Happy Harbor, Rhode Island
ALLIES Negative Woman, Robotman **ENEMIES** Niles Caulder
BACKGROUND Clay was a Vietnam Vet able to project powerful bolts of energy from his hands. He deserted his military unit, took the name Tempest, and joined the Doom Patrol. Clay was murdered by the Chief, but later reanimated as one of the Black Lantern Corps, with the power to control the weather, creating tornadoes and lightning.

CLOUD, JOHNNY
DEBUT *All-American Men of War* #82 (Nov.–Dec. 1960)
REAL NAME Flying Cloud
BASE Europe **ALLIES** The Losers **ENEMIES** Nazis
BACKGROUND Flying "Johnny" Cloud was a Navajo US Air Force pilot who fought bravely during World War II, leading the "Happy Braves" air patrol. He was later recruited by PT-boat commander Captain Storm to join the military misfits known as the Losers. He saved Sergeant Rock's Easy Company from a battery of Nazi artillery, but was killed by an enemy fighter plane.

CONGORILLA
DEBUT *Action Comics* #248 (Jan. 1959)
REAL NAME Congo Bill
BASE Africa
ALLIES Mikaal Thomas **ENEMIES** Prometheus
BACKGROUND Congo Bill was an explorer and naturalist in Africa who obtained a magical Golden Gorilla ring that allowed him to transform into a giant ape known as Congorilla. The transformation eventually became permanent, and he used his powers as a crime fighter, teaming up with members of the Justice League.

CONTESSA, THE
DEBUT *Superman: The Man of Tomorrow* #1 (June 1995)
REAL NAME Erica Alexandra del Portenza
ALLIES Klarion the Witch Boy
ENEMIES Lex Luthor
BACKGROUND The mysterious Contessa del Portenza was the former wife of Lex Luthor and the mother of his daughter, Lena. She was the head of the criminal genetics group known as the Agenda, and rumored to be immortal. It was unknown whether she survived an assassination attempt authorized by Lex Luthor.

CORONA
DEBUT *Aquaman: Time and Tide* #3 (Feb. 1994)
REAL NAME Kako
BASE Alaska
ALLIES Aquaman **ENEMIES** Ocean Master
BACKGROUND Aquaman met a young Inuit girl named Kako in Alaska, and returned to Atlantis, unaware that Kako was pregnant with his son. Years later, she was murdered by the Deep Six and then resurrected as a fire elemental called Corona. In her new guise, she acquired the powers of pyrokinesis and flight.

CRIMSON FOX
DEBUT *Justice League Europe* #6 (Sep. 1989)
REAL NAMES Vivian and Constance D'Aramis **BASE** Paris
ALLIES Justice League Europe **ENEMIES** Maurice Puanteur, Mist
BACKGROUND Vivian and Constance D'Aramis were twin sisters whose mother died at the hands of a corporation owned by their father. Vowing to avenge her, they ruined his business by setting up the rival Revson Corporation. They then created shared identities that would allow one to run the business and the other to fight crime as Le Renarde Rousse, the Crimson Fox.

DAANUTH, GARN
DEBUT *Warlord* #59 (Jul. 1982)
ALLIES Majistra
ENEMIES Justice League of America, Warlord
BACKGROUND Daanuth was a powerful sorcerer and master of dark magic who tried to destroy his home, Atlantis. He possessed powers of flight and astral projection and was able to control the minds of others. Although he died in a fight with the Justice League, his evil legacy lived on in the form of Bedlam, a being created by an artifact suffused with Daanuth's magical power.

DANNY THE STREET
DEBUT *Doom Patrol* #35 (Aug. 1990)
CURRENT VERSION *Teen Titans* #2 (Dec. 2011)
ALLIES Red Robin **ENEMIES** N.O.W.H.E.R.E.
BACKGROUND An ally of the Teen Titans, Danny the Street was a living, sentient, transvestite street who could experience feelings. He communicated through signs and billboards, but could not speak. He caould alter his form, change the buildings within his street, and even travel to a different city, to bring happiness to its citizens. Among his aliases were Danny the Alley and Danny the Brick.

DARK NEMESIS
DEBUT *Teen Titans* #7 (Apr. 1997)
BASE Metropolis **ALLIES** Pylon, the Veil **ENEMIES** Teen Titans
BACKGROUND Dark Nemesis was a team of mercenary superpowered villains—Axis, Blizzard, Carom, and Scorcher—hired to battle human/alien hybrids. When Scorcher was revealed to be one of these hybrids, she was killed by Axis. A new Scorcher was recruited, before Dark Nemesis took on a mission for the Veil to capture the Teen Titans. They almost succeeded, but the Atom's last-minute intervention turned the tide, and Dark Nemesis was defeated and incarcerated in Slabside Penitentiary.

DEATHBLOW
DEBUT *Grifter* (Vol. 3) #9 (July 2012)
REAL NAME Michael Cray
ALLIES Sister Mary, Sigma
ENEMIES Black Angel, Damocles
BACKGROUND Cray was a Navy SEAL who was recruited to join the newly formed Team 7. The team was exposed to the Gen-Factor, which gave them superpowers, but it took years until Cray discovered that he had the power to regenerate his body parts. After he was killed, he even managed to return to life.

DEATHSTORM
DEBUT *Brightest Day* #10 (Nov. 2010)
CURRENT VERSION *Justice League #23* (Oct. 2013)
REAL NAME Martin Stein **UNIVERSE** Earth-3
ALLIES Power Ring **ENEMIES** Members of the Justice League
BACKGROUND When Pandora's Box was opened during the Trinity War, the Earth-3 creature Deathstorm emerged along with his fellow Crime Syndicate team members and attacked the Justice League. Deathstorm was originally Martin Stein, who harnessed the powers of the Firestorm Matrix for his evil plans.

DEMONS THREE
DEBUT *Justice League of America* #10 (March 1962)
CURRENT VERSION *Justice League Dark* #10 (Aug. 2012)
BASE The Inferno **ALLIES** Felix Faust **ENEMIES** Timeless Ones, JLA
BACKGROUND The deadly trio of Abnegazar, Rath, and Ghast, also known as Demons Three, ruled the galaxy a billion years ago, but they were banished to Hell. They have returned to Earth several times, often summoned by the sorcerer Felix Faust to battle the Justice League of America. Their powers include the ability to travel through time and space, give life to inanimate objects, and fire bolts of energy.

DOCTOR ALCHEMY
DEBUT *Showcase* #13 (Mar.–Apr. 1958)
REAL NAME Albert Desmond **BASE** Central City
ALLIES Captain Cold, Mirror Master, Trickster **ENEMIES** The Flash
BACKGROUND Albert Desmond suffered from dissociative identity disorder; his evil side used his chemistry knowledge to become Dr. Alchemy and battle the Flash. He came into possession of the magical Philosopher's Stone, which created a twin construct named Alvin who briefly became Dr. Alchemy. When the construct was eventually destroyed, Albert resumed his criminal identity.

DOCTOR DEATH
DEBUT *Detective Comics* #29 (Jul. 1939)
CURRENT VERSION *Batman* #25 (Jan. 2014)
REAL NAME Karl Helfern **BASE** Gotham City
ALLIES The Riddler **ENEMIES** Batman
BACKGROUND Karl Helfern was a brilliant scientist who worked at Wayne Enterprises, trying to create a serum to strengthen human bones. After he lost his job and suffered a mental breakdown, he took the name Doctor Death and started working for the Riddler. Their plan failed when Doctor Death lost his life in a battle with Batman.

DOCTOR IMPOSSIBLE
DEBUT *Earth 2* #18 (Feb. 2014)
REAL NAME Jimmy Olsen
UNIVERSE Earth-2
ALLIES Thomas Wayne, Red Tornado **ENEMIES** Terry Sloane
BACKGROUND On Earth-2, Jimmy Olsen was a computer hacker known as Accountable. He was captured by the World Army and imprisoned at Arkham Asylum. After he was freed by Batman, Olsen acquired the powers of a New God and took the name Doctor Impossible. He was now able to fly and project energy.

DOCTOR MIST
DEBUT *Super Friends* #12 (Jun.–Jul. 1978)
CURRENT VERSION *Justice League Dark* #9 (Jul. 2012)
REAL NAME Nommo Balewa **BASE** South Africa
ALLIES Felix Faust, Nick Necro **ENEMIES** Amethyst, Frankenstein
BACKGROUND African wizard Nommo Balewa gained immortality and magical powers thousands of years ago to become Doctor Mist. He was a member of the magical division of A.R.G.U.S., the military team that supported the Justice League, but betrayed them in order to obtain the Books of Magic.

DOCTOR OCCULT
DEBUT *New Fun* #6 (Oct. 1935)
CURRENT VERSION *Justice League Dark* #12 (Oct. 2012)
REAL NAME Richard Occult **BASE** New York City
ALLIES Rose Psychic, JSA **ENEMIES** Nick Necro
BACKGROUND Doctor Occult and his partner/lover Rose Psychic ran a detective agency that specialized in supernatural crimes. During World War II, he joined the All-Star Squadron. Occult and Rose Psychic later merged into a single being, and helped the JSA with mystic crises. He was murdered by the sorcerer Nick Necro.

DOMINUS
DEBUT *Action Comics* #747 (Aug. 1998)
REAL NAME Tuoni
ALLIES Kem-L
ENEMIES Kismet, Superman
BACKGROUND Tuoni was once a priest who was incinerated and exiled to the Phantom Zone after he attacked his former lover, Kismet. Kryptonian technology resurrected him, and he became the powerful super-villain Dominus, able to create multiple realities based on his opponents' worst fears.

DOUBLE, JONNY
DEBUT *Showcase* #78 (Nov. 1968)
REAL NAME Jonathan Sebastian Double
BASE San Francisco
ALLIES Wonder Woman **ENEMIES** Kobra, Doctor Tzin-Tzin
BACKGROUND Jonny Double was a former police detective who formed his own detective agency, working alongside a waitress, Crystal Cross, and a pool shark known as Fish-Eye. Although Double mostly worked on local crimes, he counted Supergirl and Wonder Woman as allies and fought the super-terrorist Kobra.

DOUBLE DARE
DEBUT *Nightwing* #32 (June 1999)
REAL NAME Margo and Aliki Marceau
ALLIES Cheshire, Calculator, Deathstroke
ENEMIES Blockbuster, Secret Six
BACKGROUND The Marceau sisters were acclaimed circus acrobats who led secret lives as the costumed thieves Double Dare. While in Blüdhaven, the sisters made an enemy of crime boss Blockbuster and also competed for the affections of Nightwing. Double Dare later joined the Secret Society of Super-Villains.

DRAGON KING
DEBUT *All-Star Squadron* #4 (Dec. 1981)
ALLIES His daughter Shiv **ENEMIES** All-Star Squadron, Shining Knight
BACKGROUND The Dragon King was a brilliant Japanese scientist who created a nerve gas during World War II. However, his biggest achievement was devising a mystical energy field around Axis countries that stymied any magically powered beings that came within its zone of influence. After the war, he experimented on himself, transforming into a deadly human/reptile hybrid. He seemingly perished during a fight with Star-Spangled Kid, S.T.R.I.P.E., and the Shining Knight.

DREAMSLAYER
DEBUT *Justice League Europe* #15 (Jun. 1990)
ALLIES The Extremists **ENEMIES** Justice League Europe
BACKGROUND Dreamslayer was a powerful sorcerer who could manipulate matter, read minds, teleport between dimensions, and fly. He led the terrorist group known as the Extremists and was responsible for annihilating the planet Angor. Finding his way to Earth, he came up against Justice League Europe, killing the Silver Sorceress, but not before she dispatched him to the astral plane. He escaped and tried to steal the Overmaster's powers, but was banished to the dimension of terrors.

DUSK, NATHANIEL
DEBUT *Nathaniel Dusk* #1 (Feb. 1984)
BASE New York City
ALLIES Amanda Cooper **ENEMIES** Joseph Costilino, Valentine Cooper
BACKGROUND A veteran of World War I, ex-soldier and pilot Nathaniel Dusk worked in New York City as a policeman in the 1930s. Disgusted with the seemingly endemic corruption in the police force, he left to open his own detective agency. Courageous, intelligent, and driven, Dusk was good in a fight and handy with a gun. He was also completely incorruptible and never gave up on a case.

EKRON
DEBUT *Adventure Comics* #352 (Jan. 1967)
ENEMIES Lobo, Lady Styx
BACKGROUND Ekron is a mysterious ancient construct, though it is believed to have been built by the Guardians. Its eyes can fire energy beams and manipulate the minds of others. Following the Infinite Crisis, the bounty hunter Lobo obtained one of the eyes, leaving Ekron (and its operator, the Green Lantern of Vengar) defenseless against Lady Styx's invading army. Ekron's pursuit of its eye brought it into conflict with Lobo and the outer-space exiles Animal Man, Adam Strange, and Starfire.

EL GAUCHO
DEBUT *Detective Comics* #215 (Jan. 1955)
CURRENT VERSION *Batman Incorporated* #1 (Jul. 2012)
REAL NAME Santiago Vargas **BASE** Buenos Aires
ALLIES Batman, Club of Heroes **ENEMIES** Club of Villains
BACKGROUND Inspired by Batman's heroic exploits, Vargas became a costumed crime fighter in Argentina, notably opposing powerful drug cartels. He joined Wingman, Freight Train, Looker, Batwing, Halo, and the Hood to form the Dead Heroes Club, a division of Batman Incorporated.

EL MUERTO
DEBUT *Superman Annual* #12 (Aug. 2000)
REAL NAME Pablo Valdez **BASE** Mexico City
ALLIES Iman, Acrata, Superman **ENEMIES** Duran
BACKGROUND Valdez idolized Superman but lacked superpowers. After Valdez died fighting crime, he was resurrected through mysticism and became the undead Super Hero El Muerto. This time, however, he hated Superman for not being there to prevent his death. El Muerto teamed up with fellow heroes Acrata and Iman to defend Mexico city from the sorcerer Duran and eventually reconciled with the Man of Steel.

ELIAS, DARWIN
DEBUT *The Flash* #1 (Nov. 2011)
REAL NAME Dr. Darwin Elias
BASE Central City
ALLIES The Flash **ENEMIES** Rogues
BACKGROUND Dr. Darwin Elias was a wealthy, intelligent, and dedicated scientist who helped the Flash utilize all aspects of the energy source known as the Speed Force. When the Flash temporarily disappeared from Central City, Elias tried to take control of the Speed Force himself, but was defeated by the Flash.

EMINENCE OF BLADES, THE
DEBUT *Stormwatch* #1 (Nov. 2011)
REAL NAME Harry Tanner
ALLIES The Engineer **ENEMIES** Scourge of Worlds
BACKGROUND Tanner was a member of Stormwatch; he was also thought to be centuries old. One of the best swordsmen on Earth, he could imbue his blades with energy. He also possessed a unique form of telepathy that masked a deceptive and persuasive nature and rightfully earned him the title "The Prince of Lies." He would betray his teammates if he felt it was in his best interests to do so.

EMPEROR PENGUIN
DEBUT *Detective Comics* #13 (Dec. 2012)
REAL NAME Ignatius Ogilvy **BASE** Gotham City
ALLIES Poison Ivy, Bane **ENEMIES** Batman, the Penguin
BACKGROUND Ignatius Ogilvy was a common street thug when he joined the Penguin's gang, but he was smart and eventually became the group's second-in-command. He then betrayed the Penguin and took over the gang as "Emperor Penguin." Later, he ingested a concoction of several drugs, including Man-Bat serum and Venom, that gave him superpowers and a monstrous appearance.

EMPRESS
DEBUT *Young Justice* #16 (Jan. 2000)
REAL NAME Anita Fite
ALLIES Arrowette
ENEMIES Agua Sin Gaaz
BACKGROUND Anita Fite inherited mystical powers from her grandmother, who was a powerful voodoo priestess. Fite was inspired by Arrowette and battled crime as Empress, often fighting alongside Young Justice. She possessed mind control powers and the ability to teleport, as well as being skilled at hand-to-hand combat.

ENCANTADORA
DEBUT *Action Comics* #760 (Dec. 1999)
REAL NAME Lourdes Lucero **BASE** Metropolis
ALLIES General Zod **ENEMIES** Etrigan, Rā's al Ghūl, Superman
BACKGROUND Lucero was the daughter of an archaeologist who discovered the magical Mists of Ibella. She used the Mists to become La Encantadora and spent her life trying to defeat Superman, despite the Man of Steel invariably coming to her rescue when her plans went awry. She once almost killed him by releasing a cell-destroying nanobot into his body with a kiss, but immediately regretted the act.

ESSENCE
DEBUT *Red Hood and the Outlaws* #1 (Nov. 2011)
BASE Himalayas
BACKGROUND Essence was the daughter of Ducra, the leader of an ancient group of warrior monks known as the All-Caste. After the All-Caste was slaughtered by their enemy, the Untitled, Ducra's mystical powers were transferred to Essence. Now, she was seemingly immortal and could manipulate darkness, enabling her to disappear into shadows. Essence had trained with Jason Todd while he was with the All-Caste and Todd mistakenly believed that she had betrayed them to the Untitled.

EVIL STAR
DEBUT *Green Lantern* #37 (June 1965)
BASE Planet Aoran
ALLIES Legion of Doom **ENEMIES** Green Lantern
BACKGROUND Evil Star was a scientist who attempted to achieve immortality by inventing the Starband, which harnessed the energy of stars. It also gave him the power to fly, create force blasts, and control the Starlings—miniature versions of himself. Having destroyed his own world when it dared to turn against him, Evil Star tried to overthrow the Guardians of the Universe, but was defeated.

FAIRCHILD, VESPER
DEBUT *Batman* #540 (March 1997)
BASE Gotham City
ALLIES Bruce Wayne **ENEMIES** Lex Luthor
BACKGROUND Nighttime radio talk show host and investigative journalist Vesper Fairchild was romantically involved with Bruce Wayne for a short period. She was murdered at Wayne Manor and Bruce was charged with her death and forced to become a fugitive in order to find the real killer. He finally managed to clear his name and prove that Lex Luthor had hired the assassin David Cain to eliminate her.

FASTBAK
DEBUT *The New Gods* #5 (Oct.–Nov. 1971)
BASE New Genesis
ALLIES Highfather **ENEMIES** Darkseid
BACKGROUND Fastbak was one of the youngest of the New Gods on the planet New Genesis and was renowned for his ability to fly at high speeds, thanks to the aeropads in his boots. His body was resistant to friction heat, even through the upper atmosphere. Fastbak died during the Death of the New Gods event, when his soul was tragically ripped from his body.

FASTBALL
DEBUT *Justice League of America* #234 (Jan. 1985)
REAL NAME John Malone
BASE Detroit
ALLIES The Cadre **ENEMIES** Justice League, the Power Company
BACKGROUND Malone was recruited by the Overmaster to join the Cadre. As Fastball, he had super-fast reflexes and specialized in throwing explosive spheres. After the Justice League defeated him, he joined Doctor Polaris but was defeated again by the Power Company. Fastball died at the hands of an O.M.A.C. unit.

FEVER
DEBUT *Doom Patrol* #1 (Dec. 2001)
REAL NAME Shyleen Lao
BASE New York City
ALLIES Thayer Jost **ENEMIES** Virman Vundabar
BACKGROUND Lao could generate intense heat over short distances, allowing her to soften metal and other substances. As Fever, she became the youngest member of the newly reformed Doom Patrol, even though she had not completely mastered her powers. Fever was murdered by a member of the Dark Side Club.

FILM FREAK
DEBUT *Batman* #395 (May 1986)
REAL NAME Burt Weston, aka "Edison"
BASE Gotham City
ALLIES Angle Man **ENEMIES** Catwoman
BACKGROUND A failed movie actor, Weston became a criminal and committed many thefts that were inspired by scenes from classic movies. He stole a nuclear bomb, placed it in a movie theater, and took over a TV studio so that he could broadcast his nuclear threat. Catwoman defeated him and defused the bomb.

FIREBIRD
DEBUT *Firestorm, The Nuclear Man* #69 (March 1988)
REAL NAME Serafina Arkadina
BASE Russian Federation
ALLIES Ronnie Raymond **ENEMIES** Aliens
BACKGROUND Arkadina had psychic abilities, including telekinesis, telepathy, and the power to hypnotize people. As Firebird, she joined other superpowered Russian teenagers to form a team called Soyuz. The government initially opposed the team, but eventually sanctioned Soyuz after they bravely fought off an alien invasion.

FIREBRAND I
DEBUT *Police Comics* #1 (Aug. 1941)
REAL NAME Rod Reilly
BASE New York City
ALLIES Slugger Dunn **ENEMIES** Secret Society of Super-Villains
BACKGROUND Bored millionaire Rod Reilly decided to improve his athletic skills. He trained with an ex-heavyweight boxer, and then donned a red and pink costume to fight crime as Firebrand in New York City. Reilly served as a sailor during World War II and eventually joined Uncle Sam's Freedom Fighters to battle the Nazis.

FIREBRAND III
DEBUT *Firebrand* #1 (Feb. 1996)
REAL NAME Alexander "Alex" Sanchez **BASE** New York City
ALLIES Noah Hightower **ENEMIES** Checkmate
BACKGROUND Sanchez was a policeman who lost the use of his legs after a criminal bombed his apartment. His life was turned around when philanthropist Noah Hightower provided him with robotic legs and hi-tech armor that could shoot energy bolts, thus creating Firebrand III. He was later killed by the villain Checkmate-Knight in a gladiatorial contest rigged by Roulette.

FIREBUG
DEBUT *Deadshot* #1 (Feb. 2005)
BASE Gotham City **ENEMIES** Deadshot, Batman
BACKGROUND Little is known about the third villain to use the name Firebug, who, like his predecessors, specialized in arson-based crimes. Firebug wore an outfit containing a dangerous napalm derivative, and he projected the intensely flammable liquid from flamethrowers in the fingertips of his gloves. Deadshot defeated the villain when he shot Firebug and ignited the deadly liquid in his costume, encasing the arsonist in flames.

FIREHAIR
DEBUT *Showcase* #85 (Sep. 1969)
BASE Great Western Plains
ALLIES Hawk **ENEMIES** Wise Owl
BACKGROUND Firehair was an infant when he became the sole survivor of a wagon train massacre by a tribe of Blackfoot Indians in the early 1800s. His life was spared by the chief, Grey Cloud, and he grew up to be a great warrior and expert horseman. Firehair left the tribe to discover his true heritage and joined forces with the young gunslinger Hawk, son of Tomahawk.

FIREHAWK
DEBUT *The Fury of Firestorm: The Nuclear Men* #1 (Nov. 2011)
REAL NAME Therese **BASE** France
ALLIES Justice League International **ENEMIES** Scorn, Candace Zither
BACKGROUND Firehawk's origins and identity were a mystery, other than the fact that she was known as Therese. As the French Firestorm, she joined Firestorm Jason Rusch to prevent a rogue Firestorm from destroying the Eiffel Tower. She also fought alongside Justice League International. Her current whereabouts remain unknown.

FLYING FOX
DEBUT *Young All-Stars* #1 (June 1987)
ALLIES Iron Munro, Fury
ENEMIES Axis Amerika, the Nazis
BACKGROUND Flying Fox was a member of the First Nations tribe in Canada. After he was murdered by the Nazis, he was magically brought back to life and given a special mask and cape that gave him the powers of flight and invisibility. He also possessed the ability to cast fire from his hands. Flying Fox traveled to America, where he joined the All-Star Squadron and fought the Nazis.

FOLDED MAN

DEBUT *The Flash* #153 (Oct. 1999)
REAL NAME Edwin Gauss **BASE** Central City
ALLIES Secret Society of Super-Villains **ENEMIES** The Flash
BACKGROUND Gauss was a physicist who created a special suit that allowed him to transform his body and teleport between dimensions. He became the Folded Man, capable of flattening into a 2D form or expanding to a 4D state. A recurring Flash (Wally West) foe, he was often able to escape Scarlet Speedster with his multi-dimensional powers.

FREEDOM BEAST

DEBUT *Animal Man* #13 (Jul. 1989)
REAL NAME Dominic Mndawe **BASE** Capetown
ALLIES Animal Man, Global Guardians **ENEMIES** Prometheus
BACKGROUND After Mndawe was chosen to inherit the duties of B'Wana Beast, he acquired a magic elixir and helmet that enabled him to control minds and merge animals into hybrid creatures. Renaming himself Freedom Beast, he used his new powers to fight crime in Africa, often with his friend and ally, Animal Man. Mndawe later joined the Global Guardians and was killed while fighting alongside Congorilla.

FRINGE

DEBUT *Teen Titans* #4 (Jan. 1997)
BASE H'San Natall empire, deep space
ALLIES Teen Titans **ENEMIES** Pylon, the Veil
BACKGROUND A half-human, half-alien hybrid, Fringe was abandoned by his parents because of his appearance and superhuman strength. He was found by a mysterious magical being known as the Entity, who granted him psychic powers. Hunted and captured by the villains Pylon and the Veil because of his alien genetics, he was rescued by the Teen Titans and later joined the team.

G.I. ROBOT

DEBUT *Weird War Tales* #101 (Jul. 1981)
REAL NAME J.A.K.E. 2 **BASE** Pacific Islands
BACKGROUND US scientists developed the super-strong G.I. Robot during World War II. The first model, J.A.K.E., developed artificial intelligence and sacrificed itself to save an American fleet. The next model, J.A.K.E. 2, was more powerful, being able to spray bullets from its fingers and shoot flames from its mouth. It fought with the Creature Commandos during the war and the military created an army of J.A.K.E. 2s. During Final Crisis, G.I. Robot was enlisted to fight Justifiers and other anti-life drones.

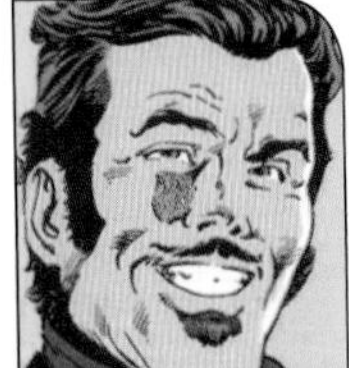

GAMBLER

DEBUT *New Titans* #68 (Jul. 1990)
REAL NAME Steven Montgomery Sharpe V
BASE Gotham City **ENEMIES** Titans, Justice Society of America
BACKGROUND The first Gambler, Steven Sharpe III, was a master of disguises, a skilled thief, and handy with a Derringer; he frequently battled the first Green Lantern, Alan Scott. After the Gambler lost his fortune in a casino, he committed suicide. His grandson, Steven Sharpe V, took over his identity and plotted to defeat the Justice Society of America, but first he had to deal with the Teen Titans.

GAMEMNAE

DEBUT *JLA* #70 (Oct. 2002)
BASE Poseidonis, Atlantis
ALLIES League of Ancients **ENEMIES** Justice League
BACKGROUND A powerful sorceress, Gamemnae was cast out of Atlantis 3,000 years ago. She enslaved Aquaman and transported Atlantis to 1,004 BCE. Her ultimate plan to conquer the universe was thwarted by the Justice League, which rescued Aquaman and restored Atlantis to its proper place. Gamemnae died in a battle with Manitou Raven, one of the Ancients who had originally helped her.

GANGBUSTER

DEBUT *Adventures of Superman* #428 (May 1987)
REAL NAME José Delgado
BASE Suicide Slum, Metropolis
ALLIES Hawkman, Dr. Light **ENEMIES** Street gangs, Bizarro Supergirl
BACKGROUND Delgado grew up fighting in the streets of Suicide Slum and later became a Golden Gloves boxing champion. He returned to his neighborhood to fight crime as Gangbuster, but suffered a spinal cord injury while fighting Combattor. An implant allowed him to patrol the streets of Metropolis once again.

GATES

DEBUT *Legion of Super-Heroes* #66 (Mar. 1995)
REAL NAME Ti'julk Mr'asz **BASE** Vyrga
ALLIES Legion of Super-Heroes **ENEMIES** Superboy-Prime, Alastor
BACKGROUND Mr'asz was an outspoken radical on the planet Vyrga, and was one of the few members of his race with the power to create portals and travel through outer space. Much to his dismay, he was drafted as a member of the Legion of Super-Heroes in the 30th century, a group he had labeled "fascists." Even so, he acquitted himself well against the villainous likes of Mantis, Validus, and Rās al Ghūl.

GENERAL GLORY

DEBUT *Justice League of America* #46 (Jan. 1991)
REAL NAME Joseph Jones
ALLIES Justice League of America **ENEMIES** Captain Schmidt
BACKGROUND American soldier Joseph Jones was mystically bestowed with superpowers by Lady Liberty during World War II. He became General Glory and was joined in his fight against the Third Reich by a young partner Ernest, E. Earnest, alias Ernie. General Glory also worked alongside his UK counterpart Beefeater and a time-traveling Booster Gold, out to stop a Nazi scientist from creating a time machine.

GENERAL ZAHL

DEBUT *Doom Patrol* #121 (Sep.–Oct. 1968)
ALLIES Brotherhood of Evil **ENEMIES** Doom Patrol, Robotman
BACKGROUND During World War II, Zahl was the ruthless commander of a Nazi U-boat, achieving one of the highest kill rates in the German fleet. After the war, he fled to Argentina to work as a mercenary, where he came into conflict with Niles Caulder, head of the Doom Patrol. Zahl later joined forces with Madame Rouge from the Brotherhood of Evil to ambush the Doom Patrol and destroy their island base. He died in a gun battle with Robotman.

GENIUS JONES

DEBUT *Adventure Comics* #77 (Aug. 1942)
REAL NAME Johnny Jones
UNIVERSE Earth-2 **BASE** New York City
ALLIES I, Vampire, Doctor Thirteen, Anthro **ENEMIES** Black Manta
BACKGROUND Stranded on a desert island, Johnny Jones burned 734 books to attract the attention of a passing ship, but not before he absorbed every bit of knowledge from the books. After he returned home, he took the name Genius Jones and offered to answer any question for a fee.

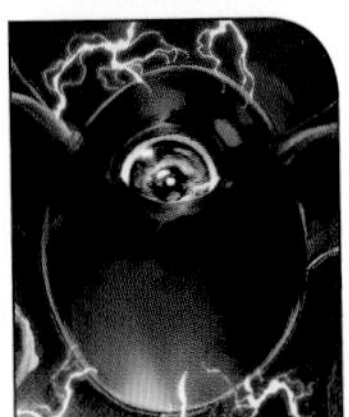

GENTRY, THE

DEBUT *The Multiversity* #1 (Oct. 2014)
ALLIES Mr. Stubbs, the Dark Monitor **ENEMIES** Society of Super-Heroes
BACKGROUND Intellectron, Dame Merciless, Demogorgunn, Hellmachine, and Lord Broken were five enormously powerful alien forces known as the Gentry. Capable of warping the laws of physics, they came to destroy Earth-7 and then moved on to corrupting other worlds with the aid of the Dark Monitor. Each member of the Gentry was the personification of a cultural fear or bad thought, and their goal was to take control of every mind in existence.

GHOST PATROL, THE

DEBUT *Flash Comics* #29 (May 1942)
BASE France
ALLIES Shadowpact **ENEMIES** The Nazis
BACKGROUND Among the unsung heroes of World War II, the Ghost Patrol was three deceased members of the French Foreign Legion. Slim, Fred, and Pedro returned from beyond the grave to join the fight against Nazi Germany. With the ability to control their ectoplasm, changing from solid to insubstantial, the spectral trio proved effective soldiers, especially on clandestine sabotage missions.

GIRDER

DEBUT *The Flash: Iron Heights* (Aug. 2001)
CURRENT VERSION *Flash #5* (March 2012)
REAL NAME Tony Woodward **BASE** Central City
ALLIES Chroma, Tar Pit **ENEMIES** The Flash
BACKGROUND Steelworker Woodward fell into a vat of molten steel that also contained debris from a S.T.A.R. Labs experimental project. He survived and emerged with a body of living steel. Taking the name Girder, he started a life of crime. Girder possessed a virtually indestructible metal body and superhuman strength.

GLOSS

DEBUT *Millennium* #2 (Jan. 1988)
REAL NAME Xiang Po
ALLIES Tasmanian-Devil, Crimson Fox III, Jet **ENEMIES** Prometheus
BACKGROUND Chinese-born Xiang Po was one of 10 humans chosen to become one of the immortal Guardians of the Universe. She acquired the ability to control the Dragon Lines of Power, energy fields that coursed through the Earth. With this power, Gloss could create force fields, duplicate herself, and teleport. She joined the Global Guardians but was seemingly killed by the super-villain Prometheus.

GOLDEN ARROW

DEBUT *Whiz Comics* #2 (Feb. 1940)
REAL NAME Roger Parsons
ALLIES Nugget Ned **ENEMIES** Brand Braddock
BACKGROUND Roger was the son of Paul Parsons, inventor of a new gas for balloon transportation. When his father was killed by rival Brand Braddock, Roger was raised by a prospector, Nugget Ned. He grew up to become a fearless fighter and a skilled archer. Dipping his homemade arrows in gold, he took the name Golden Arrow and set out to avenge his father's death and fight for justice on the western frontier.

GOLDFACE

DEBUT *Green Lantern* #38 (Jul. 1965)
REAL NAME Keith Kenyon **BASE** Keystone City
ALLIES The Flash (Wally West) **ENEMIES** Green Lantern, Blacksmith
BACKGROUND Kenyon discovered a chest of gold, the molecular structure of which had been altered by chemical waste. It gave his body a gold-plated tone. He took the name Goldface and embarked on a life of crime, often clashing with Green Lantern. After serving a prison sentence, Kenyon reformed, became a union leader, and helped the Flash (Wally West) bring the villain Blacksmith to justice.

GOLEM

DEBUT *Suicide Squad* #45 (Sep. 1990)
REAL NAME Moyshe Nakhman
BASE Jerusalem
ALLIES Hayoth group **ENEMIES** Kobra
BACKGROUND Golem is a 300lb monster that can alter the chemical composition of his body and take on the nature of any substance near him, including metal, water, and sand. He fought as a member of the Hayoth group and captured the terrorist Kobra in Israel. He later battled Superman and the Suicide Squad.

GRAIL
DEBUT *Justice League* #40 (Jun. 2015)
ALLIES Anti-Monitor **ENEMIES** Justice League, Green Lantern
BACKGROUND Grail was the daughter of Darkseid and the Amazonian assassin Myrina. It was prophesied at her birth that Grail would cause great destruction in the universe. As a hybrid Amazon/New God, Grail possessed almost limitless powers, including great strength, will corruption, and immortality. She allied herself with the Anti-Monitor and declared war on her father. During the cataclysmic conflict that ensued, she came very close to destroying the Justice League.

GRAVES, DAVID
DEBUT *Justice League* #6 (Apr. 2012)
ALLIES Several demonic entities **ENEMIES** Justice League
BACKGROUND David Graves was an author and historian who blamed the Justice League for the death of his family after they were exposed to a virus from Apokolips. He traveled to Asia and sought help from demons; he then stole the mystical Orb of Ra from A.R.G.U.S. Horribly disfigured, Graves tried to destroy the Justice League but was defeated. While incarcerated in Belle Reve prison, warden Amanda Waller suggested Graves write a book entitled *How to Defeat the Justice League*.

GREEN MAN
DEBUT *Green Lantern* #164 (May 1983)
BASE Space Sector 2828
ALLIES Alpha Lantern Corps, Omega Men **ENEMIES** Superboy-Prime
BACKGROUND Green Man came from the watery planet Uxor and was a Green Lantern for many years. He disobeyed the Guardians of the Universe to destroy the Spider Guild, left the Green Lantern Corps, and joined the Omega Men. After he was killed by the Durlans, a second Green Man was chosen from Uxor, and he became a member of the elite Alpha Lantern Corps.

GRETEL
DEBUT *Batgirl* #5 (Mar. 2012)
REAL NAME Lisly Bonner **BASE** Gotham City
ENEMIES Boss Whittaker, Batman, Batgirl
BACKGROUND Lisly was an investigative reporter for the *Gotham Flame* who was shot in the head by gangster Boss Whittaker. She survived and discovered that she had acquired hypnotic powers. Taking the name Gretel, she murdered Whittaker and his family, and began a life of crime in Gotham City. When she tried to kill Bruce Wayne, she came up against Batman and Batgirl and was soundly defeated.

GRID
DEBUT *Justice League* #23 (Oct. 2013)
ALLIES Crime Syndicate **ENEMIES** Justice League
BACKGROUND Grid was a software program that gathered information for Cyborg. The program grew and evolved into a living computer virus. In its new, malevolent form, this sentient form of artificial intelligence attacked the Justice League, forming an alliance with Earth-3's Crime Syndicate. For its invaluable services, Grid demanded two things: a body, culled from the robotic prostheses of Cyborg, and emotions, which was its ultimate goal.

HACKER, THE
DEBUT *The Hacker Files* #1 (Aug. 1992)
REAL NAME Jack Marshall
BASE Raleigh
ALLIES Sarge Steel, Speed Metal Kids **ENEMIES** Walter Sutcliffe
BACKGROUND Marshall worked for Digitronix, where he created a top-selling computer. After he was fired for requesting a share of the company's profits, he took the username Hacker and stole back his data. He allied with the Speed Metal Kids, a group that solved computer-related problems around the world.

HARJAVTI, RUMAAN, AND SUMAAN
DEBUT *Justice League* #2 (Jun. 1987)
BASE Bialya
ALLIES The Joker **ENEMIES** Queen of H.I.V.E., Justice League International
BACKGROUND Rumaan Harjavti was a dictator in the African nation of Bialya. He joined forces with the Joker in an attempt to defeat the Justice League, and later teamed with the villain Queen Bee (Queen of H.I.V.E.) to fight the Global Guardians. After Harjavti was murdered by Queen Bee, his identical twin brother Sumaan assumed his identity and became ruler of Bialya.

HARRIGAN, HOP
DEBUT *All-American Comics* #1 (Apr. 1939)
ALLIES All-Star Squadron, Prop Wash **ENEMIES** Silas Crane, the Nazis
BACKGROUND Hop Harrigan had no formal training as a fighter. Even then he was one of the top flying heroes of World War II. He flew secret missions for the US Army Corps, fighting Nazis in South America, and Japanese forces throughout the Pacific. He occasionally used the alias Guardian Angel and sometimes joined forces with the All-Star Squadron. After the war, Harrigan fought crime for a brief period under the name Black Lamp.

HAYOTH, THE
DEBUT *Suicide Squad* #45 (Sep. 1990)
BASE Israel
ALLIES Doctor Simon LaGrieve **ENEMIES** Kobra
BACKGROUND The Hayoth was a quartet of superpowered soldiers who acted as a strike force for the Israeli military. Dybbuk was a sentient form of artificial intelligence, Golem was a shape-shifter, Judith was a skilled martial arts warrior, and Ramban was a magician. The team came into conflict with the Suicide Squad, Superman, and Atom, and was also active in Israel.

HECKLER
DEBUT *The Heckler* #1 (Sep. 1992)
REAL NAME Stuart Moseley **BASE** Delta City
ALLIES Ledge, Mr. Dude **ENEMIES** Boss Glitter, John Doe, Cosmic Clown
BACKGROUND Stuart Moseley was leading a quiet life running a Skid Row diner in Delta City when he heard a voice telling him to don the yellow and orange tights of the Heckler and fight crime. Armed with sarcastic wit but no superpowers, the Heckler was remarkably resilient and recovered quickly from physical damage. He was known to hang out with fellow zany heroes Plastic Man and Ambush Bug.

HELLHOUND
DEBUT *Catwoman Annual* #2 (July 1995)
REAL NAME Kai **BASE** Gotham City
ENEMIES Black Canary, Catwoman
BACKGROUND Kai was the top martial arts student at a secret dojo in Gotham City until Catwoman joined the facility and bested him. Filled with jealous rage, he vowed to top Catwoman in her crime sprees. He became Hellhound, a mercenary with a penchant for knives and daggers. When he died, his identity and legacy were bought by Jack Chifford, who joined the Secret Society of Super-Villains.

HERO HOTLINE
DEBUT *Action Comics Weekly* #637 (Jan. 31, 1989)
BASE New York City
BACKGROUND Not every problem requires the help of a superpowered hero. Tex Thomson set up a hotline phone number (1-800-555-HERO), known as the Hero Hotline, so that the public could summon lesser-powered heroes to handle routine emergencies. Members included Stretch, Hotshot, Diamondette, Microwavabelle, Private Eyes, Marie the Psychic Turtle, Rainbow Man, Mr. Muscle, Voice Over, and Zeep the Living Sponge.

HORSEWOMAN
DEBUT *Demon Knights* #1 (Nov. 2011)
REAL NAME Clytemnestra **BASE** Avalon
ALLIES Demon Knights **ENEMIES** Questing Queen
BACKGROUND Horsewoman was a mysterious figure who occasionally joined the Demon Knights during medieval times and was always seen riding a horse. A skilled archer, she could also communicate telepathically with horses, thought to be her way of tapping into the animal life force the Red. Although a paraplegic, she used a magical saddle and rope to mount her horses.

HOT SPOT
DEBUT *Teen Titans* (Vol. 2) #1 (Oct. 1996)
REAL NAME Isaiah Crockett **BASE** Ivy University, Rhode Island
BACKGROUND Aged 16, Crockett was on his first day of college when he was abducted by the alien race known as the H'San Nattal. He learned that he was not fully human, but an alien-human hybrid with thermokinetic powers created by the H'San Natall to assist their conquest of Earth. Isaiah escaped with fellow hybrid abductees Toni and Cody Moretti (Argent and Risk) and Audrey Spears (Prysm). Together, they became Super Heroes, banding together as a new incarnation of the Teen Titans.

HOUNGAN
DEBUT *The New Teen Titans* #14 (Dec. 1981)
REAL NAME Jean-Louis Droo **BASE** Paris
ALLIES Brotherhood of Evil **ENEMIES** New Teen Titans
BACKGROUND Houngan, a voodoo priest, convinced Droo, a computer scientist, to merge his computer skills with dark voodoo arts. Droo created a computerized voodoo doll and electronic needle stylus that could inflict terrible pain and bring death to his victims. Taking on the name Houngan, he joined the New Brotherhood of Evil and became a loyal follower of the Brain.

HUMAN BOMB
DEBUT *Battle for Blüdhaven* #1 (Jun. 2006)
CURRENT VERSION *Human Bomb #1* (Feb. 2013)
REAL NAME Michael Taylor **BASE** New York City
BACKGROUND During the Battle for Blüdhaven, Michael Taylor was one of several US Marines experimented upon by an organization called C.R.O.W.N. and turned into human bombs. Turner disobeyed the group's ruthless order to self-detonate and joined forces with S.H.A.D.E. to save other innocent soldiers from becoming unwitting suicide bombers.

HUMPTY DUMPTY
DEBUT *Arkham Asylum: Living Hell* #2 (Aug. 2003)
REAL NAME Humphry Dumpler **BASE** Gotham City
ALLIES Warren White, Black Mask **ENEMIES** Death Rattle, Two-Face
BACKGROUND Dumpler suffered from an unfortunate name, an egg-shaped head, and a compulsive desire to repair broken items. This led him to derail a subway train and damage a clocktower, killing a dozen people. Committed to Arkham Asylum, he joined Black Mask's new group when the villain destroyed the asylum, and later became a member of the Secret Society of Super-Villains.

HUNTERS THREE
DEBUT *Animal Man* #1 (Nov. 2011)
ALLIES The Rot **ENEMIES** Animal Man
BACKGROUND The Hunters Three were once men and women who were members of the Red, the life force that connects all animal life in the universe. The Red also gave Animal Man his superpowers. After they died, the Hunters Three became agents of the Rot, the force associated with death and decay. The group then took the form of hideous monsters and became relentless in their deadly pursuit of Animal Man and his family.

HURRICANE

DEBUT *Fury of Firestorm: The Nuclear Men* #8 (Jun. 2012)
BASE London, England
ALLIES Firehawk **ENEMIES** The Rogues, Pozhar
BACKGROUND Hurricane was created by Zithertech, and became Britain's officially sanctioned Firestorm. He could generate energy blasts and create constructs. Hurricane fought bravely alongside the French Firestorm, Firehawk, against rogue Firestorms; he died battling the energy-transforming monster Pozhar, when his Zithertech creators activated a kill switch in his suit.

HURT, SIMON

DEBUT *Batman* #673 (Jun. 2008)
REAL NAME Thomas Wayne **BASE** Gotham City
ALLIES Black Glove Organization **ENEMIES** The Joker
BACKGROUND Hurt had many aliases, including Doctor Death, El Penitente, and Jack the Ripper. He was one of Bruce Wayne's distant ancestors, and a devil-worshipper. After gaining immortality, Hunt co-founded the mysterious Black Glove organization that menaced Bruce and his family. After one of his many attempts to kill Batman failed, he escaped, but was drugged and buried alive by the Joker.

HYBRID, THE

DEBUT *The New Teen Titans* #24 (Oct. 1986)
ALLIES Dayton **ENEMIES** Teen Titans, Blue Beetle
BACKGROUND Following the *Crisis on Infinite Earths*, a deranged Mento formed a new version of the Doom Patrol. He gathered together injured people from around the world and infused their bodies with the metal alloy Prometheum to give them superpowers. The result was a team of hapless villains that included Pteradon, Gorgon, Harpi, Behemoth, Sirocco, Prometheus, and Touch-N-Go. The team fell into disarray when Mento was cured of his madness by the Teen Titans' Raven.

I-CHING

DEBUT *Wonder Woman* #179 (Nov.–Dec. 1968)
ALLIES Batman, Robin, Nightwing **ENEMIES** Rā's al Ghūl
BACKGROUND I-Ching was a monk and the last surviving member of an ancient sect that practiced mystical arts and believed that science and magic were inextricably linked. I-Ching was also a master martial artist and helped Wonder Woman hone her fighting skills after she temporarily lost her powers. I-Ching later teamed with Batman, Nightwing and Robin, using a unique combination of meditation and violence to bring down Rās al Ghūl at the very edge of a Lazarus Pit.

IMAN

DEBUT *Superman Annual* #12 (Aug. 2000)
REAL NAME Diego Irigoyen **BASE** Mexico City
ALLIES El Muerto, Acrata, Superman **ENEMIES** Duran, Darkseid
BACKGROUND Irigoyen was a renowned Mexican scientist who became a S.T.A.R. Labs astronaut. While he was on a mission in outer space, his mother was kidnapped and murdered. Upon his return, a grieving Irigoyen designed a superpowered, metallic battle suit that allowed him to fight crime in Mexico as the hero Iman. Diego also teamed up with his hero Superman and fellow local heroes El Muerto and Acrata.

INDIGO

DEBUT *Titans/Young Justice: Graduation Day* #1 (Jul. 2003)
ENEMIES The Outsiders, Teen Titans
BACKGROUND A robotic being from the future, Brainiac 8 (a descendant of the original Brainiac) traveled back in time to pose as the naïve hero Indigo. By 'accidentally' unleashing a defective Superman robot, Indigo triggered the death of Donna Troy. Indigo subsequently joined the Outsiders, but it later was revealed that Indigo had killed Donna to ensure the future of the Computer Tyrants of Colu. The Outsiders and the Teen Titans teamed up to defeat her.

INSECT QUEEN

DEBUT *Legion of Super-Heroes* #82 (Jul. 1996)
REAL NAME Lonna Leing **BASE** Xanthu
ALLIES Legion of Super-Heroes **ENEMIES** Khunds, Robotica
BACKGROUND Leing came from the planet Xanthu in the 31st century. She possessed the ability to transform into an insect and use its powers. As a member of the Uncanny Amazers, a group of super beings created to counter Khunds incursions, she came into conflict with the Legion of Super-Heroes. However, she formed an alliance with them when the cyborg world Robotica invaded Xanthu.

INVICTUS

DEBUT *Green Lantern: New Guardians* #5 (Mar. 2012)
BASE Orrery
ALLIES Angels of Vega **ENEMIES** Larfleeze
BACKGROUND Invictus was the leader of the Angels of Vega, a peaceful race that existed millions of years ago and was destroyed by Larfleeze. He emerged from the destruction with mighty powers, such as the ability to project blasts of energy from his body. He broke the barrier between dimensions and constructed the Orrery, his own recreation of the Vega system.

I, SPYDER

DEBUT *Seven Soldiers* #0 (Apr. 2005)
REAL NAME Thomas Ludlow Dalt **BASE** Keystone City
ALLIES Seven Soldiers of Victory **ENEMIES** Sheeda
BACKGROUND Dalt was the son of the first villainous Spider, Tom Ludlow Hallaway. He was a skilled fighter and archer, who killed his brother Lucas, the second Spider, to become the one and only "I, Spyder." After the Seven Unknown Men granted him immortality and heightened his abilities, Dalt joined the Seven Soldiers of Victory to fight against the Sheeda, a malevolent race of faeries and deadly foes of humanity.

JANE DOE

DEBUT *Arkham Asylum: Living Hell* #1 (Jul. 2003)
BASE Gotham City
ALLIES Black Mask, Mr. Zsasz, Firefly **ENEMIES** Great White Shark, Batman
BACKGROUND Jane Doe was the alias used by a serial killer who studied the personalities of her victims, killed them, and then perfectly assumed their identities, male or female. She had an uncanny ability to mimic body language and speech patterns, and in one incident, even donned the skin of a police officer to break into the G.C.P.D. to murder Gotham City's DA and shoot James Gordon.

JANISSARY

DEBUT *JLA Annual* #4 (Aug. 2000)
REAL NAME Selma Tolon **BASE** Bursa
ALLIES JLA, Wonder Woman **ENEMIES** Circe
BACKGROUND Tolon was a medical student who returned home to Turkey and discovered the scimitar of Sultan Suleiman the Great, and the spell-casting Eternity Book of Merlin the Magician. These mystical items empowered her with flight and super-strength, and she became the Super Hero Janissary. She used her powers to defend her homeland but also to aid Wonder Woman when Circe attacked New York.

JAX-UR

DEBUT *Adventure Comics* #289 (Oct.1961)
CURRENT VERSION *Action Comics* #13 (Dec. 2012)
ALLIES General Zod **ENEMIES** Nightwing, Flamebird
BACKGROUND Jax-Ur was a brilliant, but deranged scientist on Krypton who conducted an infamous experiment that destroyed Wegthor, one of the planet's inhabited moons. He was banished to the Phantom Zone for this crime, and was later freed by General Zod and traveled to Earth. There he adopted the alias of Dr. Phillings and began conducting despicable experiments at S.T.A.R. Labs.

JESTER, THE

DEBUT *Freedom Fighters* #3 (Jan. 2011)
REAL NAME Charles Lane II
ENEMIES Arcadian Order, Freedom Fighters
BACKGROUND Charles Lane II was the grandson of Chuck Lane, the masked vigilante from the All-Star Squadron who fought the Nazis. After helping his retired grandfather avenge his father's death at the hands of the secretive Arcadian Order, the younger Lane became the new Jester and took to a life of crime. He fought Uncle Sam's Freedom Fighters and once even kidnapped the US Vice-President and his wife.

KHAN, RAMA

DEBUT *JLA* #62 (Mar. 2002)
BASE Jarhanpur
ALLIES Gamemnae **ENEMIES** Justice League of America
BACKGROUND Khan, a great magician, possessed the powers of immortality and super-strength. In a battle with Wonder Woman, he shattered the hitherto unbreakable Lasso of Truth; this unraveled reality, as existence became defined by belief rather than truth. The elemental defender of Jarhanpur, Khan fought the Justice League several times, including the mighty battle that took place in 1,004 BCE.

KING FARADAY

DEBUT *Danger Trail* #1 (Jul.–Aug. 1950)
CURRENT VERSION *Infinity May and the Forever People # 6* (Feb. 2015)
ALLIES Helena Bertinelli, Infinity Man **ENEMIES** Dick Grayson, Agent 1
BACKGROUND Given the codename I-Spy, King Faraday was a government agent who led the Central Bureau of Intelligence. The New God Infinity Man saved Faraday's life after he was injured in an explosion. Faraday also worked closely with the clandestine government agency known as Spyral, agreeing to help Helena Bertinelli bring in a rogue agent, Dick Grayson.

KINGDOM, THE

DEBUT *Batwing* #1 (Nov. 2011)
BASE Democratic Republic of the Congo
ALLIES Batwing **ENEMIES** Massacre
BACKGROUND The Kingdom were comprised of Dawnfire, Deity, Earth Strike, Josiah Kone, Razorwire, Staff, Steelback, and Thunder Fall. They fought to bring freedom to the Democratic Republic of the Congo and then disappeared. Batwing later discovered that Massacre had murdered three of the group's members. The others were scattered across the globe, leaving the team in limbo.

KISMET

DEBUT *Adventures of Superman* #494 (Sep. 1992)
REAL NAME Ahti
ALLIES Eternity, Superman **ENEMIES** Dominus, Krona
BACKGROUND Kismet was a cosmic entity and a Lord of Order. Wielding powers such as astral projection, time travel, and reality manipulation, she was charged with protecting the universe from evil. Ahti's rise to the role of Kismet created an eternal enemy of Dominus, who craved the position for himself. She frequently helped Superman and played a crucial role in ending the Imperiex War.

KOLE

DEBUT *Crisis on Infinite Earths* #3 (Jun. 1985)
REAL NAME Kole Weathers **BASE** New York City
ALLIES Team Titans **ENEMIES** Thia
BACKGROUND As a teenager, Kole became a victim of her father's flawed scientific experiments. An ensuing nuclear explosion triggered her meta-gene, enabling her to project crystal forms. She joined the Teen Titans and fought bravely until she seemingly lost her life during the *Crisis on Infinite Earths* while trying to protect Earth-2's Robin and the Huntress from the Anti-Monitor's shadow demons.

KORDAX

DEBUT *Atlantis Chronicles* #4 (Jun. 1990)
BASE Atlantis
ALLIES Koryak **ENEMIES** Poseidonians, Aquaman
BACKGROUND Born of Atlantean royalty Kordax was sent away because of his ugly appearance. As a royal scion of Atlantis, he possessed super-strength and marine telepathy, and returned as an adult, leading an army of sharks in a failed attempt to steal the throne of Atlantis. His punishments included the loss of his hand and banishment. He was later defeated by Aquaman, and chose to kill himself.

KORYAK

DEBUT *Aquaman* #5 (Jan. 1995)
BASE Atlantis
ALLIES Aquagirl **ENEMIES** Anton Geist, Spectre
BACKGROUND Koryak was the son of Aquaman and Kako. He grew up unaware of his father's identity or the truth of his royal heritage. Later, Koryak moved to Atlantis and rebelled against his father's wishes. He journeyed to the tunnels below the city of Poseidonis and accidentally freed the evil Kordax, which led to a devastating war. Koryak was later killed when the Spectre attacked Atlantis.

LAB RATS

DEBUT *Lab Rats* #1 (Apr. 2002)
BASE The Campus
ALLIES Abigail Gooss **ENEMIES** Robert Quinlan
BACKGROUND The Lab Rats was a group of teenagers who became test subjects for a mysterious experiment in virtual-reality combat. Alex, Dana, Gia, Isaac, Trilby, Wu, and Poe went to a secret training ground, the Campus, where they were subjected to virtual dangers. Gia was the first to die. Her six remaining teammates escaped, but later lost their lives in the real world.

LADY FLASH

DEBUT *Flash* #7 (Dec. 1987)
REAL NAME Ivana Christina Borodin Molotova
ALLIES Blue Trinity **ENEMIES** The Flash
BACKGROUND Two boys and a young girl named Christina were entrusted to the care of a Soviet scientist, who created a serum, Velocity 9, that could duplicate the Flash's power of super-speed. The three of them often battled the Flash. After Christina ingested this drug, she donned a Flash costume and became Lady Flash, allying herself with one of the Flash's oldest enemies, Vandal Savage.

LADY OF THE LAKE

DEBUT *Aquaman* #1 (Feb. 2003)
REAL NAME Vivienne
BASE The Secret Sea
BACKGROUND The Lady of the Lake was a water spirit of seemingly limitless powers who aided both Aquaman and Britain's King Arthur. She was immortal and oversaw the Secret Sea, an enchanted realm that was also known as the Waters of Truth. When Aquaman lost his hand, she replaced it with a hand composed of magical water that received its powers from the Lady.

LADY VIC

DEBUT *Nightwing* #4 (Jan. 1997)
CURRENT VERSION *Batwing #23* (Oct. 2013)
REAL NAME Lady Elaine Marsh-Morton **BASE** England
ALLIES Double Dare, Bane **ENEMIES** Deadshot, Nightwing
BACKGROUND Lady Vic was a true-blue aristocrat, a skilled martial artist, a superb athlete, and a ruthless killer-for-hire, fond of wielding her family's heirloom weapons. She was captured by the Suicide Squad, but later escaped to Gotham City, where she tried to blow up Wayne Enterprises. She was defeated by Batwing.

LADY WEEDS

DEBUT *Swamp Thing Annual* #2 (Dec. 2013)
BASE Servus, Arctic Circle
ENEMIES Swamp Thing
BACKGROUND "Born" in the 19th century, Lady Weeds was a powerful avatar of the Green, the elemental force that connects all forms of plant life on Earth. Her cruel nature led her to break away from the Green and betray Swamp Thing. As a result, she was paralyzed and lost her powers. She later became an avatar of the Machine Kingdom with a new body composed entirely of metal.

LADY ZAND

DEBUT *Young Justice* #50 (Dec. 2002)
BASE Zandia
ENEMIES Young Justice, Solstice, Wonder Girl
BACKGROUND Lady Zand possessed many elemental powers, including the ability to command the soil of her homeland and transform into a towering giant composed of rock and earth. She was the cruel and quick-tempered ruler of Zandia, a Baltic island and secret haven for fugitive super-villains. It was also the headquarters for the worldwide Church of Blood.

LANCE, KURT

DEBUT *Teen Titans* #8 (Jun. 2012)
BASE Gotham City
ALLIES Amanda Waller **ENEMIES** Black Canary
BACKGROUND Little is known about the early years of Lance before he became a member of a group of heroes known as Team 7. Equally mysterious were the events surrounding his alleged death after he married Dinah Drake, the Black Canary. Drake believed that she had killed him with her Canary Cry, but Lance was in fact alive and working with Amanda Waller to track down the Teen Titans.

LEATHER

DEBUT *Nightwing* #62 (Dec. 2001)
REAL NAME Mary Kay Tanner **BASE** Peckinpah, Texas
ALLIES The Joker **ENEMIES** Nightwing
BACKGROUND Mary was born with metahuman powers as a result of her mother's use of illegal, experimental narcotics, which gave her leathery skin and razor-sharp claws. In her teens, she joined a gang that smuggled illegal immigrants between Mexico and the US. Her psychotic temper and deadly barbed whips made her a formidable opponent. She was imprisoned, but later freed by the Joker.

LEVIATHAN ORGANIZATION

DEBUT *Batman: The Return* #1 (Jan. 2011)
BASE Gotham City
ALLIES League of Assassins **ENEMIES** Batman Incorporated
BACKGROUND Leviathan was a mysterious group of terrorists that worked to create an army of surgically altered metahumans. The group was headed by Talia al Ghūl, and other agents included Nazi superspy Doctor Dedalus, Son of Pyg, Goatboy, and the Heretic. Leviathan provided drugs to Gotham City's poor to try to enslave them and also worked to control Gotham City's children.

LIBERTY BELLE

DEBUT *Boy Commandos* #1 (Dec. 1942)
REAL NAME Elizabeth "Libby" Lawrence-Chambers **BASE** New York City
ALLIES All-Star Squadron **ENEMIES** Baron Blitzkrieg, Captain Nazi
BACKGROUND A descendant of the Revolutionary War heroine Miss Liberty, Libby gained superpowers through a mystic link to the Liberty Bell and became Liberty Belle, a founder member of the All-Star Squadron. After being irradiated by Baron Blitzkrieg, Libby gained the ability to manipulate sound. Decades after the war, Libby donned her costume once more to fight with the JSA during Infinite Crisis.

LIGHTNING LORD

DEBUT *Superman* #147 (Aug. 1961)
REAL NAME Mekt Ranzz **BASE** Winath
ALLIES Legion of Super-Villains
ENEMIES Legion of Super-Heroes
BACKGROUND When Mekt Ranzz and his siblings were attacked by lightning beasts on Korbal, they gained the power to absorb electricity and project powerful energy bolts. Mekt's siblings joined the Legion of Super-Heroes, but he decided to use his powers for evil under the name Lightning Lord.

LIONHEART

DEBUT *Justice League International Annual* #4 (Summer 1993)
REAL NAME Richard Plante **BASE** London, England
ALLIES Justice League International **ENEMIES** Alien Parasites
BACKGROUND Plante, a direct descendant of King Richard I, was a former dockworker who donned a hi-tech battle suit that gave him enhanced strength and the ability to fly. As the hero Lionheart, he wielded an energy-sword and fought crime, occasionally working with the Justice League International. His first mission was to prevent an invasion of alien parasites from wreaking hell on his home turf.

LITTLE MERMAID

DEBUT *Super Friends* #9 (Dec. 1977)
REAL NAME Ulla Paske **BASE** Denmark
ALLIES Global Guardians, JLE **ENEMIES** Jack O'Lantern, Queen Bee, Bialya
BACKGROUND An Atlantean hybrid, Ulla Paske possessed mutant powers that allowed her to fly, breathe underwater, and transform her legs into fins. As the Little Mermaid, she became a founding member of the Global Guardians and also worked alongside the Justice League. In the battle for Bialya, Paske was apparently killed by the villain Jack O'Lantern, but she was later seen in action with the Guardians.

LODESTONE

DEBUT *Doom Patrol* #3 (Dec. 1987)
REAL NAME Rhea Jones **BASE** Kansas City
ALLIES Arani Desai **ENEMIES** Geomancers
BACKGROUND Rhea Jones was exposed to an overdose of electromagnetic radiation as a teenager. Due to this, she acquired super-strength, the power of flight, and the ability to attract or repel metallic objects. She was recruited to become a member of the Doom Patrol. She underwent a metamorphosis that heightened her powers and altered her looks, before teaming up with a Superboy clone.

LONAR

DEBUT *Forever People* #5 (Oct.–Nov. 1971)
CURRENT VERSION *Threshold* #3 (May 2013)
BASE New Genesis **ALLIES** Blue Beetle **ENEMIES** Darkseid
BACKGROUND Lonar was one of the New Gods, renowned for his bravery and fighting skills as he rode into battle astride his flying steed Thunderer. He defended New Genesis from invasions by Darkseid, and never hesitated to protect other lands from the Dark Lord. He formed an unlikely alliance with Blue Beetle on the planet Tolerance during a bounty-hunting game show known as *The Hunted*.

LOOSE CANNON

DEBUT *Action Comics Annual* #5 (1993)
CURRENT VERSION *Teen Titans* #11 (Sep. 2012) and also *Bloodlines* #1 (Apr. 2016)
REAL NAME Eddie Walker **BASE** Metropolis
ALLIES Maggie Sawyer, Eradicator **ENEMIES** Lissik, Glonth, Pritor
BACKGROUND Eddie was a police detective who was attacked by alien parasites and gained the power to transform into a giant, blue monster. He became the super-strong Loose Cannon and joined the Teen Titans, but betrayed the group.

LORD DEATH MAN
DEBUT *Batman* #180 (May 1966)
BASE Japan
ENEMIES Batman, the Outsiders, Mr. Unknown
BACKGROUND Lord Death Man was a mysterious crime boss who could return from the dead. In one gruesome incident, he came back to life mid-autopsy and slaughtered several people in a hospital. Lord Death Man also had superhuman strength and stamina, which he used to battle Batman, the Outsiders, and Talon. Rās al Ghūl even sought to siphon the regenerative fluids from Lord Death Man's body.

LORD SOLOVAR
DEBUT *Flash* #106 (Apr.–May 1959)
CURRENT VERSION *Flash* (Vol. 4) #9 (Jul. 2012)
BASE Gorilla City
ALLIES The Flash **ENEMIES** Gorilla Grodd
BACKGROUND Solovar was the king of the superpowered apes in Gorilla City. One of his duties was to absorb the calm, positive thoughts of his subjects. Solovar was a gifted telepath and a benevolent ruler. When Gorilla Grodd threatened to usurp his throne, Solovar sought the help of the second Flash, Barry Allen.

LUMP
DEBUT *Mister Miracle* #7 (Mar.–Apr. 1972)
BASE Apokolips
ALLIES Granny Goodness **ENEMIES** Mister Miracle, Batman
BACKGROUND The Lump was a monster on Apokolips that had the power to mold his body into any form he desired. He used this ability to lure enemies into the Arena of the Gods, a realm that existed inside the Lump's own mind. The New God Mister Miracle fought a battle within the creature's mind-world and triumphed by driving the Lump insane. The Lump later lost his life in a battle with Batman.

LYNX
DEBUT *Robin* #1 (Jan. 1991)
REAL NAME Ling **BASE** Gotham City
ALLIES Ghost Dragons, King Snake, the Penguin **ENEMIES** Robin, Batgirl
BACKGROUND Ling, a formidable martial artist and a ruthless killer, started out as a thief on the streets of China, working for King Snake and his Ghost Dragons gang. She later took the name Lynx and became a hired assassin for the Penguin in Gotham City, eventually returning to Hong Kong, deposing King Snake, and taking over the Ghost Dragons. Ling died while extending her operations into Gotham City.

MADAME .44
DEBUT *All Star Western* #117 (Feb.–Mar. 1961)
CURRENT VERSION *All-Star Western #30* (Jun. 2014)
REAL NAME Jeanne Walker **BASE** Mesa City
BACKGROUND Walker's father was killed when thieves bombed his gold mine. She was trapped inside and, as she dug her way out, she wandered into a mysterious land with two moons. Walker defeated Kerberos, the demonic ruler of this strange world and, newly emboldened, emerged from the mine as the pistol-toting hero Madame .44, determined to seek justice for her father's murder.

MADEMOISELLE MARIE
DEBUT *Star-Spangled War Stories* #84 (Aug. 1959)
CURRENT VERSION *Checkmate #5* (Oct. 2006)
REAL NAME Josephine Tautin **BASE** The Castle, Switzerland
BACKGROUND Many brave French women have fought for justice using the name Mademoiselle Marie. One of the most famous operated behind enemy lines in occupied France during World War II, working as a saboteur, spy, and soldier for the French underground. Fearless and deadly, she frequently fought alongside Sgt. Rock. Josephine Tautin was the latest hero to take the name Mademoiselle Marie.

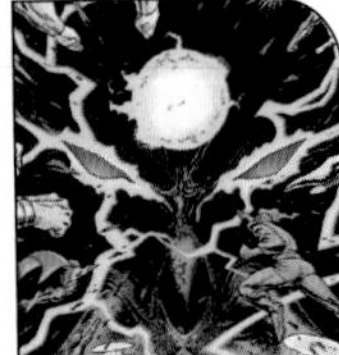

MAGEDDON
DEBUT *JLA* #37 (Jan. 2000)
ENEMIES Orion, Justice League
BACKGROUND Mageddon was created by the Old Gods as a sentient war machine. A living doomsday device, it could project lethal energy blasts and take control of anyone's mind, changing any species into warlike savages. It traveled the universe and eventually targeted Earth, where it battled Orion and the Justice League. After the Mexican Super Hero Aztek sacrificed himself to weaken Mageddon, Superman was able to absorb its energy and disable the machine.

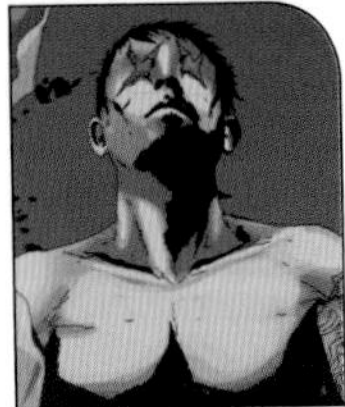

MAGUS
DEBUT *Green Arrow* #17 (Apr. 2013)
BASE Prague
BACKGROUND The mysterious Magus could teleport and transform his body at will and was also believed to be immortal. Despite being blind, he was highly adept at unarmed combat, and could also expel a dangerous red smoke from his body that could disorient or even kill opponents. Magus was a member of secret society the Outsiders and also an ally of Green Arrow. On one occasion, he disguised himself as the Super Hero.

MAN-OF-BATS
DEBUT *Batman* #86 (Sep. 1954)
CURRENT VERSION *Batman Incorporated #0* (Nov. 2012)
REAL NAME William "Bill" Great Eagle **BASE** South Dakota
ALLIES Raven Red, Batman Inc. **ENEMIES** Leviathan, Dr. Hurt
BACKGROUND Native American Eagle was so inspired by Batman that he gave up his career as a doctor and became Man-of-Bats, a vigilante crime fighter. His son became Red Raven and they joined the Club of Heroes and later Batman Inc. together. They both became valuable allies to Bruce Wayne and helped defeat the Leviathan.

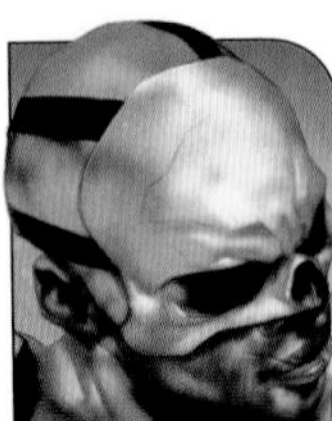

MASSACRE
DEBUT *Batwing* #1 (Nov. 2011)
REAL NAME Isaac Zavimbe **BASE** Africa
ENEMIES Batwing, The Kingdom
BACKGROUND Trained to become a human killing machine, Zavimbe was a ferocious child soldier in Africa. He systematically set about assassinating each member of African Super Hero team the Kingdom. Massacre murdered several Kingdom members, and then almost succeeded in killing Batwing, until the latter got the upper hand and unmasked the villain as his own brother, Issac.

MATSUDA, SHIHAN
DEBUT *Detective Comics* #0 (Nov. 2012)
BASE The Himalayas
ALLIES Bruce Wayne **ENEMIES** Mio
BACKGROUND After the death of his parents, Bruce Wayne traveled to a remote monastery in the Himalayas, where he trained with the legendary monk warrior Shihan Matsuda. A master of mind-control, Matsuda told Wayne that he was destined to soar like a god, and he trained the young man in combat and the use of weapons. Matsuda was murdered by his daughter, Mio.

MAWZIR
DEBUT *Hitman* #1 (April 1996)
BASE Hell
ALLIES Arkannone **ENEMIES** Tommy Monaghan, Catwoman
BACKGROUND In the last days of World War II, five Nazi soldiers were hanged as war criminals. Their souls went to Hell, where the Arkannone, the Lords of the Gun, transformed them into a ten-armed demon called Mawzir. This monster frequently clashed with Catwoman and Tommy Monaghan. After Monaghan destroyed the Mawzir, the Arkannone brought the creature back to life.

MAYA
DEBUT *Justice League Europe* #47 (Feb. 1993)
REAL NAME Chandi Gupta **BASE** India
ALLIES Justice League Europe **ENEMIES** Overmaster, Sonar
BACKGROUND As a teenager, Gupta acquired an array of elemental powers from the deity Maya. She was able to control and emit fire and water, and used her powers to fight crime, firing mystic arrows composed of those two elements. She allied with the Justice League to stop the villain Sonar from conquering Europe, and later, with the JLE's help, thwarted the alien Overmaster's plan to annihilate Earth.

MAZURSKY, NINA
DEBUT *Flashpoint: Frankenstein and the Creatures of the Unknown* #1 (Aug. 2011)
CURRENT VERSION *Frankenstein, Agent of S.H.A.D.E.* #1 (Nov. 2011)
ALLIES Creature Commandos **ENEMIES** Humanids
BACKGROUND Mazursky was a scientist who worked for S.H.A.D.E., creating stronger strains of human genetics. Her first subjects were the dangerous monsters who became known as the Creature Commandos. Mazursky developed a second, more successful generation of Creature Commandos, but thanks to her experiments, she was transformed into a human/amphibian hybrid herself.

MEKANIQUE
DEBUT *Infinity Inc.* #19 (Oct. 1985)
ALLIES Per Degaton, Professor Malachi Zee **ENEMIES** All-Star Squadron
BACKGROUND Mekanique was a robot from the 23rd century that was sent back in time to alter history and prevent a slave rebellion from occurring. The robot arrived in 1942 and used its powerful energy blasts to battle the All-Star Squadron. It later joined forces with Commander Steel to fight his grandson, Steel, Infinity Inc., and the Justice League. After it lost that battle, Mekanique vanished, but a lookalike, golden-plated robot called Matrix was later spotted on Earth-2.

MERCENARIES, THE
DEBUT *G.I. Combat* #242 (Jun. 1982)
ENEMIES Colonel Q
BACKGROUND The Mercenaries were three men who had deserted the French Foreign Legion to become successful soldiers of fortune. The group consisted of the American Gordon, the British Philip "Prince" Edwards, and the German Horst Brenner. Together, they traveled the world fighting for any army that would pay them. The three were masters of armed and unarmed combat and showed great loyalty to their paying employers.

MERRY, GIRL OF 1,000 GIMMICKS
DEBUT *Star Spangled Comics* #81 (June 1948)
REAL NAME Merry Pemberton King **BASE** Civic City
ALLIES Star-Spangled Kid, Stripesy **ENEMIES** Brainwave
BACKGROUND Pemberton was quick-witted and a superb athlete. The adoptive sister of the Star-Spangled Kid, she became Gimmick Girl, using a variety of crime-fighting gadgets. She stood in for Stripesy when he was injured and in her later years helped form a team of senior heroes known as Old Justice. She was the mother of the super-villain Brainwave and the ill-fated hero Gimmix.

METALEK
DEBUT *Action Comics* #11 (Sep. 2012)
ENEMIES The Multitude, Superman
BACKGROUND The Metaleks were aliens who traveled to Earth after their own planet was destroyed by the Multitude. Taking the form of sentient heavy-duty construction equipment, such as giant ditch diggers and plows, the Metaleks tried to alter their new world to suit their needs. However, they soon came into conflict with the people of Earth. Some Metaleks were captured by the British government, and others were defeated by Superman.

MINION
DEBUT *New Titans* #114 (Sep. 1994)
REAL NAME Jarras Minion
ALLIES Teen Titans, Cyborg **ENEMIES** Raven
BACKGROUND Minion escaped the destruction of his home planet Talyn by donning a powerful, cybernetically bonded suit of armor, the Omegadrome. He traveled to Earth, where he teamed with the Teen Titans to defeat Psimon, the villain he learned was responsible for Talyn's destruction. Minion joined the New Teen Titans, helping them defeat the evil Raven, and eventually gave his armor to Cyborg.

MIRAGE
DEBUT *The New Titans Annual* #7 (1991)
REAL NAME Miriam Delgado **BASE** New York City
ALLIES New Titans **ENEMIES** Lord Chaos
BACKGROUND Delgado could disguise herself as another person by creating psychic illusions around her body. She became Mirage and joined the Team Titans, who traveled back in time to prevent the birth of the godlike villain Lord Chaos, the son of Donna Troy. Their mission only succeeded with the aid of the Teen Titans, and Mirage later fell in love with Nightwing, disguising herself as his girlfriend, Starfire.

MIST I AND II
DEBUT *Adventure Comics* #67 (Oct. 1941) (Mist I); *Starman* #0 (Oct. 1994) (Mist II)
REAL NAME Nash (last name unknown) **BASE** Opal City
ALLIES Kyle, Mary Marvel **ENEMIES** Jack Knight (second Starman)
BACKGROUND The first Mist was a scientist who created a device to transform objects and living things into a thin mist, making them invisible. Mist passed his hatred of the Knight family on to his son Kyle—killed by Starman Jack Knight—and to his granddaughter, Nash, who became the second, far deadlier Mist.

MISTER BLOOM
DEBUT *Batman* #43 (Oct. 2015)
BASE Gotham City
BACKGROUND Likened to a noxious weed, spreading his evil seeds across Gotham City, Mister Bloom was both a super-villain and a power broker. His seeds were deadly Man-Bat-based implants that granted superpowers to a new wave of criminals, such as Precious Precious, Gee Gee Heung, and Qi Tsu. Mister Bloom used those same implants to transform himself into a super-strong killer with sharp claws and the ability to stretch his body to an extraordinary lengths.

MISTER COMBUSTIBLE
DEBUT *Detective Comics* #6 (Apr. 2012)
BASE Gotham City
ALLIES The Penguin **ENEMIES** Batman
BACKGROUND Mister Combustible was a small-time criminal with a knack for explosives. As a trainee mobster, he joined the Penguin's gang, and for a while became one of Bane's foot soldiers after the Crime Syndicate let the inmates of Arkham Asylum loose on Gotham City. During the ensuing Arkham War, his unique, glass-shaped head was shattered by the Ventriloquist's living puppet, Ferdie.

MISTER TOXIC
DEBUT *Detective Comics* #6 (Apr. 2012)
REAL NAME Hugh Marder **BASE** Gotham City
ALLIES The Penguin **ENEMIES** Batman
BACKGROUND Marder was the CEO of the Wayne Enterprises affiliate Mecha-North Corporation by day, and the Gas Man by night. He later appeared as Mister Toxic, with the power to emit a deadly gas and energy bolts at will. In a battle with Batman at the Mecha-North laboratory, it was revealed that Marder had died in a radiation accident, and Mister Toxic was his clone.

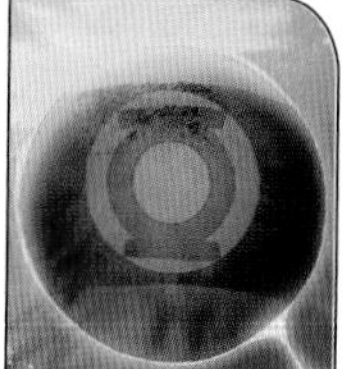

MOGO
DEBUT *Green Lantern* #188 (May 1985)
CURRENT VERSION *Green Lantern Corps* #13 (Dec. 1912)
BASE Sector 2261
ALLIES Kyle Rayner, Green Lantern Corps **ENEMIES** Despotellis
BACKGROUND Mogo was a living, sentient planet that became the Green Lantern of Sector 2261. It was responsible for the crucial tracking system of the power rings, guiding the rings to new Green Lanterns. The planet played an important role in the battle against Superboy-Prime.

MONGREL
DEBUT *Hawkman Annual* #1 (Sep. 1993)
REAL NAME Josh Xan
ALLIES Hawkman, Quorum **ENEMIES** Solomon Grundy, Superboy-Prime
BACKGROUND Alien parasites gave Vietnamese African-American Xan the power to fire deadly bolts of "darkforce" energy from his hands. He took the name Mongrel and used his superpower to assist Hawkman during the Bloodlines crisis. He then joined other teenagers who had acquired powers from the aliens to fight crime as the Blood Pack. He was killed alongside his teammates by Superboy-Prime

MONOCLE, THE
DEBUT *Flash Comics* #64 (May 1945)
CURRENT VERSION *Forever Evil* #1 (Nov. 2013)
REAL NAME Jonathan Cheval **BASE** New York City
ALLIES Merlyn, Deadshot **ENEMIES** Hawkman, JSA
BACKGROUND Cheval was an optician who turned to crime after he lost all his money. He used his optic skills to become the Monocle and fashion lens-based weapons that could project light, heat, lasers, and cosmic rays. He became a member of the Secret Society of Super-Villains, but was later eliminated by the Manhunter.

MORTALLA
DEBUT *Orion* #6 (Nov. 2000)
BASE Apokolips
ALLIES Darkseid **ENEMIES** Orion
BACKGROUND It was unclear whether Mortalla was the wife or mistress of Darkseid, but no one doubted her deadly powers—She could kill opponents with a single touch. Her preference, however, was to use fear as a weapon to defeat her enemies. After Darkseid's apparent death and Orion's assumption of the Dark Lord's throne, Mortalla seduced Orion. She was later killed by an unknown assassin.

MRS NYXLY
DEBUT *Action Comics* #1 (Nov. 2011)
REAL NAME Nyxlygsptlnz **BASE** Metropolis
ALLIES Mr. Mxyzptlk, Superman **ENEMIES** Vyndktvx
BACKGROUND Mrs. Nyxly's real name was Nyxlygsptlnz. A powerful imp from the fifth dimension, she was the daughter of King Brpxz and the wife of Superman's foe, Mr. Mxyzptlk. Nyxlygsptlnz was hiding in Metropolis from her husband's jealous rival, Vyndktvx, who had killed her father and seriously hurt her husband. She came to the Man of Steel's aid when he confronted Vyndktvx and the Anti-Superman Army.

MURK
DEBUT *Aquaman* #17 (Apr. 2013)
BASE Atlantis
ALLIES Orm **ENEMIES** Scavenger
BACKGROUND Murk was a fierce soldier, dedicated to protecting Atlantis from the "evils of man." Incredibly strong and ruthless, Murk was trained in the fire pits, and led the elite army known as the Men-of-War. He fought bravely for King Orm, battling the Fire-Trolls and the Deep Six, but after Aquaman returned to the throne, Murk rebelled against his new king's tolerant attitude toward humans.

MUSKETEER
DEBUT *Detective Comics* #215 (Jan. 1955)
CURRENT VERSION *Batman Incorporated #0* (Nov. 2012)
REAL NAME Jean-Marie (last name unknown)
ALLIES Batman, Club of Heroes **ENEMIES** Black Glove
BACKGROUND Mysterious Frenchman the Musketeer was inspired by the exploits of Batman to commence a career as a costumed crime fighter. He was one of the founding members of the Global Guardians and later answered the call of his idol to join Batman Inc. in the fight against the Back Glove.

NAIAD
DEBUT *Firestorm the Nuclear Man* #90 (Oct. 1989)
REAL NAME Mai Miyazaki
ENEMIES Shogun Oil Company
BACKGROUND Japanese-born Mai Miyazaki was a passionate environmental activist who piloted her boat Naiad near a leaking oil rig in the Pacific Ocean. The rig's captain set fire to the oily waters, engulfing Miyazaki in flames. She was rescued by the Earth spirit Maya and granted powers to become the planet's Water Elemental. In her new role as Naiad, she could control water in all its forms.

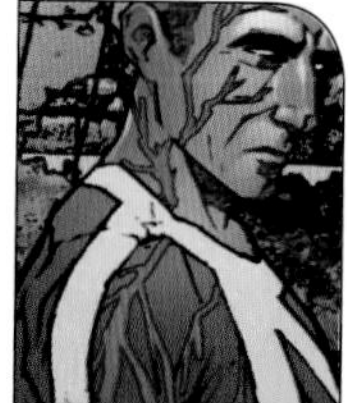

NEON THE UNKNOWN
DEBUT *Hit Comics* #1 (Jul. 1940)
REAL NAME Tom Corbett, Langford Terrill **UNIVERSE** Earth-2
ALLIES Uncle Sam and the Freedom Fighters **ENEMIES** The Axis forces
BACKGROUND Tom Corbett became the first Neon the Unknown after he drank from a lake of magic waters and gained the powers to fly and project powerful energy bolts from his hands. He joined the Freedom Fighters and fought during World War II. He disappeared after the war and was later found by Langford Terrill, the original Ray. Terrill drank from the same lake waters and became the second Neon.

NERGAL
DEBUT *Green Lantern Annual* #9 (Sep. 2000)
BASE Kurnugi
ENEMIES Ninurta, Justice League of America
BACKGROUND Nergal was an immortal alien with almost unlimited powers who left the planet Oa and traveled the universe for millennia before settling on Earth. Nergal became a tyrannical god to the Mesopotamians, but was defeated by one of Earth's first Green Lanterns and sent to the portion of Hell known as Kurnugi. Nergal escaped and was defeated again, this time by the Justice League of America.

NIGHTBLADE
DEBUT *Green Lantern Annual* #2 (1993)
REAL NAME Nik Mayak
ALLIES Blood Pack **ENEMIES** Solomon Grundy, Superboy-Prime
BACKGROUND An automobile accident cost Nik Mayak the use of his legs, but he worked hard in the hospital to train his upper body and practiced knife-throwing. After alien parasites attacked the hospital and drank Mayak's spinal fluid, he gained the power to regenerate his damaged legs. Newly healed, he fought crime as Nightblade and became a member of the Super Hero team Blood Pack.

NIGHTHAWK
DEBUT *Western Comics* #5 (Sep.–Oct. 1948)
CURRENT VERSION *All-Star Western* #6 (Apr. 2012)
REAL NAME Hannibal Hawkes **BASE** The Old West
BACKGROUND Hawkes was a boy when he set sail on a whaling ship in 1861. After the ship's captain was murdered, Hawkes vowed to fight injustice in the world. Years later, he teamed up with another gunslinger, Cinnamon, and the pair became the most feared outlaw hunters in the West. Both heroes used a special medallion, found at an Indian burial site, which gave them enhanced strength and healing abilities.

NIGHTRUNNER

DEBUT *Detective Comics Annual* #12 (Feb. 2011)
REAL NAME Bilal Asselah **BASE** Clichy-Sous-Bois, France
ALLIES Batman, Robin
BACKGROUND Bilal Asselah was a superb athlete and a college student in Paris, France. Spurred on by the death of his best friend in a race riot, Bilal became Nightrunner and fought to prevent civil war erupting in his city. Batman and Robin recruited him as the French member of Batman Incorporated, and they defeated a child slavery ring. Despite initial misgivings, Bilal became the protector of Paris.

NOCTURNA

DEBUT *Detective Comics* #529 (Aug. 1983)
CURRENT VERSION *Detective Comics #9* (Jul. 2012)
REAL NAME Natalia Mitternacht **BASE** Gotham City
ALLIES Secret Society of Super-Villains **ENEMIES** Batwoman
BACKGROUND Natalia Mitternacht was sentenced to Arkham Asylum for killing her husband. She escaped and stalked the streets of Gotham City as Nocturna, exhibiting many of the traits of vampirism, including hypnosis and enhanced strength. She later became a member of the Secret Society of Super Villains.

NUCLEAR FAMILY

DEBUT *The Outsiders* #1 (Nov. 1985)
BASE California
ALLIES Secret Society of Super-Villains **ENEMIES** The Outsiders
BACKGROUND The Nuclear Family was a family of androids named Dad, Mom, Bigg, Sis, Brat, and Dog. A deranged scientist named Eric Shanner created the group, and gave each member lethal superpowers, including the ability to emit nuclear radiation and intense heat. The Nuclear Family was subsequently destroyed during a battle with the Outsiders.

ORACLE

DEBUT *Supergirl* (Vol. 6) #16 (Mar. 2013)
BACKGROUND The enigmatic, all-powerful cosmic being known as the Oracle awoke when the Kryptonian clone H'El journeyed to Earth, determined to destroy it in a mad quest to save Krypton, his long-dead planet. Since the dawn of time, the Oracle had had the same role: To both serve as a witness to every dying world and also to warn of a planet's imminent destruction. After Supergirl saved Earth from H'El's machinations, the Oracle faded away. He later reappeared for the destruction of Earth-2, as well as during the Convergence event.

ODD MAN

DEBUT *Detective Comics* #487 (Dec. 1979–Jan. 1980)
REAL NAME Clayton "Clay" Stoner **BASE** River City
ENEMIES Pharaoh, Queen of the Nile **AFFILIATION** Hero Hotline
BACKGROUND River City's sole champion, the Odd Man lived up to his name. His clownish garb, concealed gimmicks and wacky weapons, proved surprisingly effective in disorienting and defeating opponents. He made fools of hardened criminals, took down jewel thieves posing as the reincarnated Nile Queen and her Pharaoh, and found further gigs with the Super Hero agency Hero Hotline.

O.S.S. SPIES AT WAR

DEBUT *G.I. Combat* #192 (Jul. 1976)
BASE Washington, D.C.
ALLIES Blackhawk squadron
BACKGROUND When World War II began, the US government assembled a group of men and women to form the Office of Strategic Services. The O.S.S. operated as spies, working as liaisons to the Blackhawk squadron and undertaking dangerous covert missions. The team members used codenames, including Falcon, Shadow, Sprinter, and Mongoose. After the war, the group was absorbed into the CIA.

PAPA MIDNITE

DEBUT *Hellblazer* #1 (Jan. 1988)
CURRENT VERSION *Constantine #4* (Aug. 2013)
REAL NAME Linton Midnite **BASE** Club Midnite, NYC
ENEMIES John Constantine, Neron
BACKGROUND Linton Midnite was a voodoo priest from Haiti and a nightclub owner. The demon Neron took over his club and Papa Midnite tricked his old foe, occult sleuth John Constantine, into helping him get it back. Neron sent them both to Hell, but Constantine escaped, leaving Papa Midnite to his fate.

PERIL, JOHNNY

DEBUT *Comic Cavalcade* #19 (Feb.–Mar. 1947)
CURRENT VERSION *Justice League Dark* #11 (Sept. 2012)
BACKGROUND Johnny Peril's past was shrouded in mystery, and his name was almost certainly an alias. His occupations included reporter, soldier-of-fortune, and private detective specializing in the occult. It was in this last capacity that he became involved in supernatural incidents, working alongside psychic Heather Storm. As Dr. John Peril, he worked as a scientist at US agency A.R.G.U.S., using his knowledge of biology and technology to combat malign magical forces.

PERKINS, NEPTUNE

DEBUT *Flash Comics* #66 (Aug.–Sep. 1945)
BASE Hawaii
ALLIES Young All-Stars **ENEMIES** Secret Society of Super-Villains
BACKGROUND Neptune Perkins was a human/dolphin hybrid who could hold his breath underwater for seven minutes. His webbed hands and feet made him an exceptionally powerful swimmer, and he could also communicate with sea creatures. He became a member of the Young All-Stars and fought with them during World War II. Years later, Perkins died defending Atlantis during the Infinite Crisis.

PERSUADER

DEBUT *Adventure Comics* #352 (Jan. 1967)
CURRENT VERSION *Legion of Super-Heroes* #17 (Apr. 2013)
ALLIES Fatal Five **ENEMIES** Legion of Super-Heroes, Batman, Blue Beetle
BACKGROUND Several villains were known as the Persuader, but all of them used an "atomic axe" that could cut through anything. The alien Nyeun Chun Ti was the first Persuader and joined the Fatal Five. A second Persuader, Cole Parker, was a member of the Suicide Squad. Elise Kimble, allegedly an ancestor of Nyeun Chun Ti, later became the Persuader as an assassin-for-hire and member of the Terror Titans.

PERUN

DEBUT *Firestorm* #70 (Apr. 1988)
REAL NAME Ilya Trepliov **BASE** Russian Federation
ALLIES Firestorm **ENEMIES** Imperiex
BACKGROUND Ilya Trepliov began his career as the Super Hero Perun when he was only 17. Named after a Russian God of Thunder, Perun possessed the power to mentally control electricity and channel it in any way he desired. He joined the Russian team of superpowered heroes known as Soyuz, and together they protected Earth from the alien invader Imperiex.

PHANTASM

DEBUT *The New Titans Annual* (Vol.2) #3 (1987)
REAL NAME Danny Chase **ENEMIES** Wildebeest Society
BACKGROUND Danny Chase possessed the power of telekinesis and was a member of the Teen Titans. After several Titans were murdered by the Wildebeest Society, Chase faked his death. He then donned a mask and costume to become Phantasm. In a battle with the Wildebeest Society, his powers became linked with the hero Raven and her mother, Arella. Chase and Arella died, but their essences united to form an even more powerful Phantasm.

PLUNDER

DEBUT *Flash* #165 (Oct. 2000)
BASE Mirror image dimension
ALLIES Mirror Master, Captain Cold **ENEMIES** The Flash, Professor Zoom
BACKGROUND Plunder was a bounty hunter and deadly marksman from another dimension who worked for the Thinker and teamed up with Mirror Master and Captain Cold to invade Keystone City. He later murdered police detective Jared Morillo and assumed his identity, before being exposed. He was defeated by Professor Zoom and sent back to his dimension.

POW-WOW SMITH

DEBUT *Detective Comics* #151 (Sep. 1949)
REAL NAME Ohiyesa **BASE** Elkhorn **ALLIES** Hank Brown (deputy)
BACKGROUND The frontier town of Elkhorn was plagued by armed gangs until Ohiyesa (sarcastically nicknamed Pow-Wow Smith), the only Indian lawman in the west, rescued them. An expert marksman and horseman, Smith was also a great detective. In the 1940s, a descendant of Ohiyesa's adopted the name Pow-Wow Smith and became a detective; his son later took up the mantle, fighting alongside Robin, Huntress, and Nighthawk to bring the latest version of the Trigger Twins to justice.

POZHAR

DEBUT *The Fury of Firestorm* #62 (Aug. 1987)
CURRENT VERSION *Fury of Firestorm: The Nuclear Men* #4 (Feb. 2012)
REAL NAME Mikhail Arkadin **BASE** Moscow, Russia
BACKGROUND Professor Mikhail Arkadin was the Russian Firestorm Pozhar. He claimed to have worked with Martin Stein to invent the protocols that created the original Firestorm program. After manipulating Firestorm Ronnie Raymond, he combined with him to become the monstrous energy being Scorn. He died in a cataclysmic clash with Firestorms Jason Rusch, Firehawk, Hurricane, and Rakshasi.

PRANKSTER

DEBUT *Action Comics* #51 (Aug. 1942)
CURRENT VERSION *Nightwing* #19 (Jun. 2013)
REAL NAME Oswald Loomis **BASE** Chicago
BACKGROUND As a boy, Loomis watched William and Wallace Cole murder his father. One brother went to jail, while the other became mayor of Chicago. Determined to fight such injustices, Loomis became a cyber-thief, using the name "Prankster." His pranks, though, soon turned serious, and he kidnapped a Chicago politician. The Prankster almost killed Nightwing, but was defeated and sent to prison.

PSYBA-RATS

DEBUT *Robin Annual* #2 (Sep. 1993)
BASE Gotham City **ALLIES** Robin **ENEMIES** The Collector
BACKGROUND Hired by the Collector to break into Wayne Enterprises, the Psyba-Rats was a team of five teenagers who operated as techno-thieves. After the Collector killed two members of the group, the three remaining—Sharp, Hackman, and Channel—were attacked by an alien and gained superpowers. Taking the names Razorsharp, Channelman, and Hackrat, they sought revenge on the Collector. The hero Robin joined them, and the team made him an honorary Psyba-Rat.

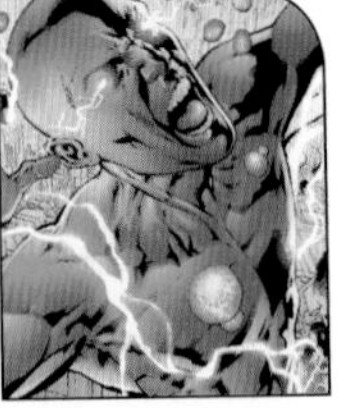

QUANTUM MECHANICS

DEBUT *JLA: Heaven's Ladder* (Nov. 2000)
BACKGROUND Born in the wake of the Big Bang, the Quantum Mechanics were ancient, almost godlike beings, who roamed the universe in search of divine enlightenment. Aware that their race was finally dying out, they decided to create a perfect afterlife and started collecting planets in order to build a ladder to their version of Heaven. One of the planets was Earth, which brought them into conflict with the Justice League of America. Eventually, the JLA was able to save Earth and also help the Quantum Mechanics to ascend to their afterlife.

QWSP

DEBUT *Aquaman* #1 (Jan.–Feb. 1962)
BASE The Fifth Dimension
ALLIES Aquaman, Aqualad (when good) **ENEMIES** JLA (when bad)
BACKGROUND Qwsp was an imp from the Fifth Dimension who traveled to Earth, where he could reshape reality, and manipulate time and matter. Formerly a friend to Aquaman, Qwsp turned evil when the sea king became a grim warrior and teamed up with the evil genie Lkz to battle the JLA. For his crimes, the rulers of his dimension sentenced Qwsp to one million infinities in an eight-dimensional maze.

RAJAK, COLONEL

DEBUT *Adventures of Superman* #590 (May 2001)
REAL NAME Ehad Rajak **BASE** Bialya
BACKGROUND The African country of Bialya has seen its share of iron-fisted leaders come and go. After Colonel Rajak took control he perpetuated the anti-American stance for which the nation had become well known. President Luthor asked Superman to help rescue the *Newstime* journalist Andrew Finch from the country, hoping to avoid direct military intervention. Finch, however, was actually a C.I.A. assassin working under Luthor's orders. Superman rescued Finch but prevented him eliminating Rajak.

RAMULUS

DEBUT *World's Finest* #21 (Summer 1942)
ENEMIES The Sandman, Sandy the Golden Boy
BACKGROUND Originally known as the villain Nightshade, Ramulus created mechanized plants to terrorize his victims. When the Sandman (Wesley Dodds) and his protégé, Sandy, fought him, Nightshade lost control over his plants and was seemingly killed by them. Somehow surviving, Nightshade was found by the Aztec priestess Nyola. Given greater control over his techno-flora, and the ability to manipulate living vegetation, Nightshade became Ramulus and joined Nyola's Monster Society of Evil.

RATCATCHER

DEBUT *Detective Comics* #585 (Apr. 1988)
CURRENT VERSION *Batwing* #27 (Mar. 2014)
REAL NAME Otis Flannegan **BASE** Gotham City
ALLIES Menace **ENEMIES** Batwing
BACKGROUND A spell in Blackgate prison turned rat exterminator Otis into a hardened criminal. After his release, he declared war on the citizens of Gotham City and became the Ratcatcher, using deadly poisonous gases and leading an army of sewer rats. He later teamed up with the villain Menace to battle Batwing.

RAVEN RED

DEBUT *Batman* #86 (Sep. 1954)
CURRENT VERSION *Batman Incorporated* #9 (May 2013)
REAL NAME Charles Great Eagle **BASE** South Dakota
ALLIES Man-of-Bats, Batman **ENEMIES** Leviathan, Black Glove
BACKGROUND Charles Eagle was the son of William Eagle, aka Man-of-Bats, who fought for his fellow Native Americans' rights. Charles became Raven Red and also fought crime, but unlike his father, he longed to take on international villains. Both father and son joined Batman Inc. to battle the crime organizations Leviathan and Black Glove.

RAYMOND, ROY—TV DETECTIVE

DEBUT *Detective Comics* #153 (Nov. 1949)
BASE Metropolis
BACKGROUND Roy Raymond found fame as the host of the TV show *Impossible—But True!,* in which he showcased strange and exotic items. Describing himself as a "TV Detective," Raymond traveled around the world with his assistant Karen Colby debunking hoaxes and exposing fraudulent claims; Raymond even created hoaxes himself to help the police trap criminals. His son, Roy Raymond, Jr., continued his father's work and later fought crime as the costumed hero Owlman.

REAPER

DEBUT *Batman* #237 (Dec. 1971)
BASE Gotham City **ENEMIES** Batman
BACKGROUND At least three villains have taken the identity of the Reaper to terrorize Gotham City and battle Batman. The first Reaper was a World War II concentration camp survivor named Benjamin Gruener, while a later incarnation was the vigilante Judson Caspian. Joe Chill, Jr. saw his father murdered by the Reaper and later took the identity of the villain himself. No one knew for sure if Chill was the latest Reaper to stalk the streets of Gotham City.

RED BEE

DEBUT *Uncle Sam and the Freedom Fighters* #5 (Jan. 2007)
REAL NAME Jenna Raleigh
ALLIES Freedom Fighters, S.H.A.D.E. **ENEMIES** S.H.A.D.E. (under Father Time)
BACKGROUND Richard Raleigh was the first Red Bee, a World War II hero brandishing a special stinger gun. He was aided in his fight against crime by trained bees. After his death, his grandniece Jenna became Red Bee, wearing a battle suit that simulated a bee's sting. She was mutated by an alien insect colony and transformed into a human/insect hybrid with super-strength and the power of flight.

RED DART

DEBUT *World's Finest* #95 (Aug. 1958)
CURRENT VERSION *Green Arrow* #31 (Jul. 2014)
ALLIES Longbow Hunters **ENEMIES** Green Arrow, Green Lantern
BACKGROUND At least three villains have been Red Dart. The first was Green Arrow foe John "Midas" Mallory; followed by an unknown thief who stole Kyle Rayner's Green Lantern power ring. The current Red Dart is a member of Richard Dragon's Longbow Hunters. With a penchant for trick darts, she teamed up with Brick and Killer Moth to collect a bounty on Green Arrow's life. The Emerald Archer defeated all three.

RED PANZER

DEBUT *Wonder Woman* #228 (Feb. 1977)
ENEMIES Wonder Woman, Titans
BACKGROUND The first villain known as Red Panzer was the former Nazi general Helmut Streicher, who donned a crimson battle suit that fired energy blasts. After his death, three criminals were inspired to continue as Red Panzer—a neo-Nazi and a teenager who became a member of Vandal Savage's villainous team, Tartarus. The most recent Red Panzer was recruited from Tartarus by Savage and lived on the island nation of Zandia, when he was not striking at his constant foe, Troia.

RED TORPEDO

DEBUT *Crack Comics* #1 (May 1940)
REAL NAME James Lockhart **ALLIES** the Freedom Fighters
BACKGROUND The first, most famous Red Torpedo was former US Navy Captain Jim Lockhart, whose submarine, the Torpedo, could travel to the bottom of the ocean and also fly. Lockhart donned a costume and fought as Red Torpedo alongside the Freedom Fighters. A later Red Torpedo—a female android possessing hydrokinesis, flight, and super-strength—was created and later abandoned in the ocean by super-villain scientist T.O. Morrow; she was later rescued by Red Tornado.

REGULUS

DEBUT *Team 7* #0 (Nov. 2012)
REAL NAME Dean Higgins **ENEMIES** Team 7, Birds of Prey, Suicide Squad
BACKGROUND Dean Higgins was working for US Military Intelligence when he was recruited by John Lynch to join the metahuman specialists known as Team 7. His final mission with the group was to secure Pandora's Box, but a freak accident caused his brain to meld with the brain of world terrorist Kaizen Gamorra. Higgins called himself Regulus and assumed control of the Basilisk terrorist network. His stated goal was to control or destroy every metahuman on Earth.

RELATIVE HEROES

DEBUT *Relative Heroes* #1 (Mar. 2000)
ALLIES Impulse, Young Justice **ENEMIES** D.E.O., Girth, Napalm, Kittyhawk
BACKGROUND After their parents died in a car crash, the Weinberg children united to form Relative Heroes. While team leader Houston had no superpowers, his siblings did: Temper could control electricity; Allure possessed magical persuasive abilities; Blindside had the power of invisibility; and Omni could imitate the powers of those around him. Pursued and captured by the D.E.O., the group learned that Omni was an alien, but they convinced the residents of his world to let Omni remain on Earth.

REX, THE WONDER DOG

DEBUT *The Adventures of Rex, The Wonder Dog* #1 (Jan.–Feb. 1952)
ALLIES Danny Daniels
BACKGROUND Rex, the Wonder Dog was an ordinary puppy that was transformed into a super-strong dog by a scientific experiment. Rex fought bravely during World War II and the Korean War as part of the elite K-9 Corps, taking part in many combat parachute jumps. He was later adopted by a young man named Danny Daniels and the pair's adventures took them around the world. The resourceful Rex eventually joined the US government's Bureau of Amplified Animals.

RISING SUN

DEBUT *Super Friends* #8 (Nov. 1977)
REAL NAME Isumi Yasunari **BASE** Tokyo, Japan
BACKGROUND Several members of the Yasunari family developed cancer as a result of the atom bomb that destroyed Nagasaki, Japan, during World War II. As a young man, Isumi Yasunari discovered he could absorb solar radiation. He became the hero Rising Sun and used his newfound power to project intense heat and flames from his body as he defended Japan from evildoers. Rising Sun became a member of the Global Guardians and fought alongside them for many years.

ROVING RANGER

DEBUT *All Star Western* #58 (Apr.–May 1951)
REAL NAME Jeff Graham **BASE** Mid-19th century Texas
BACKGROUND A captain in the Confederate army, Jeff Graham joined the Texas Rangers after the Civil War ended. As a Ranger, he brought lawbreakers to justice, including the infamous bandit El Dorado, in reality Bud Huston, a former fellow Confederate officer whom Graham convinced to give up his criminal ways. Along with other "History's Heroes," the Roving Ranger was transported to the present and helped prevent the Ultra-Humanite from stealing a space shuttle from Cape Canaveral.

SARGE STEEL

DEBUT *Sarge Steel* #1 (Dec. 1964)
CURRENT VERSION *O.M.A.C.* Vol.4 #2 (Dec. 2011)
BACKGROUND The mysterious espionage agent known only as Sarge Steel held many jobs, including a stint leading the Central Bureau of Intelligence and working with the government combat team Checkmate. Project Cadmus hired Steel to investigate O.M.A.C. attacks, and he led a team of agents, including Maribel and Little Knipper. Steel lost a hand during a battle with O.M.A.C., but grew even more formidable with a replacement hand made of solid steel.

SAVAGE, MATT: TRAIL BOSS

DEBUT *Western Comics* #77 (Sep.–Oct. 1959)
BASE The Texas Trail
BACKGROUND Matt Savage was a legendary trail boss on the Dogiron trail in Texas during the 1860s. He led 2,000 steers and his seven-man Dogiron Crew through flood and drought, Indian attacks, and thundering stampedes. Savage possessed a keen sense of fair play, but he never hesitated to use his fast guns or quick fists to battle cattle rustlers and outlaws. Jebediah Kent, an ancestor of Clark Kent's adoptive father, Jonathan, briefly worked for Savage's team.

SAVANT
DEBUT *Birds of Prey* #56 (Aug. 2003)
CURRENT VERSION *Suicide Squad* #1 (Nov. 2011)
REAL NAME Brian Durlin **BASE** Gotham City
ENEMIES Batman, Black Canary
BACKGROUND Durlin suffered from a chemical imbalance that gave him sporadic amnesia. After his father disinherited him, he took the name Savant and turned to a life of crime, often blackmailing his victims. After he kidnapped Black Canary, Savant was arrested; he then joined the Suicide Squad.

SAVITAR
DEBUT *The Flash* #108 (Dec. 1995)
BASE Tibet **ENEMIES** The Flash (Wally West), The Flash (Barry Allen)
BACKGROUND Savitar was a former Eastern bloc military pilot who was able to tap into the Speed Force. This allowed him to move his body at near light speed and absorb motion from other objects and people. He believed that his super-speed was a divine gift and named himself after Savitar, the Hindu god of motion. Over time, he became obsessed with stripping the Speed Force from other heroes, but was ultimately absorbed into the energy field, where he was trapped.

SCORCH
DEBUT *Adventures of Superman* #582 (Sep. 2000)
REAL NAME Aubrey Sparks **BASE** Pisboe, Virginia
ALLIES Joker **ENEMIES** Superman
BACKGROUND Aubrey Sparks was transformed into the super-villain Scorch when the Joker briefly gained Mr. Mxyzptlk's cosmic powers. The Joker recruited her for his Joker League of Anarchy team. Scorch went on to battle Superman and later fell in love with the Martian Manhunter. Tormented with memories of her human self, she came under the supervision of the Department of Extranormal Operations.

SECRET
DEBUT *Young Justice: The Secret* #1 (Jun. 1998)
REAL NAME Greta Hayes **ALLIES** Young Justice
BACKGROUND Greta Hayes was an ordinary teenager who became Secret, a mysterious phantom girl able to take a ghost-like form. This allowed her to pass through solid objects and create psychic manifestations. She joined Robin, Superboy, and Impulse to form the team Young Justice. Secret was later corrupted by Darkseid, which caused her to turn on her teammates. After Robin saved her, Darkseid punished Secret by restoring her humanity—which suited her perfectly.

SECTION EIGHT
DEBUT *Hitman* #18 (Sep. 1997)
BASE Gotham City **ALLIES** Hitman, Batman
BACKGROUND Section Eight was a mostly befuddled team of semi-heroes with a headquarters in the sewers beneath Gotham City. The team's name was taken from the US military designation "section eight," meaning "mentally unfit for duty." The tubby leader of the team was Sixpack, who gathered various misfits together to stumble into crime scenes alongside Hitman and Batman. Three of the longest-serving members were Bueno Excellente, Baytor, and Dogwelder.

SENSOR
DEBUT *Legionnaires* #43 (Dec. 1996)
REAL NAME Jeka Wynzorr
ALLIES Legion of Super-Heroes **ENEMIES** Universo
BACKGROUND Sensor was a snake-shaped member of the Legion of Super-Heroes who used her illusion-casting power to disguise herself as a human being. Originally a princess from the planet Orando, a world ruled by large snakes, she renounced her heritage to travel the universe. After joining the Legion, Sensor helped to build the artificial planetoid Legion World and later defeated the super-villain Universo.

SETHE
DEBUT *Swamp Thing* #1 (Nov. 2011)
ENEMIES Swamp Thing, Abigail Arcane
BACKGROUND Sethe was the overwhelming presence of death and decay on Earth. As the Avatar of the Rot, he stood in terrifying opposition to the forces of life known as the Red and the Green. Responsible for all the plagues that have ravaged humankind, he could control the elements and bring death to anything he touched. Sethe battled Swamp Thing, the champion of the Green, but it was Abigail Arcane who ultimately defeated the vile villain.

SHADOW LASS
DEBUT *Adventure Comics* #365 (Feb. 1968)
REAL NAME Tasmia Mallor **BASE** Talok VIII
BACKGROUND Tasmia Mallor could connect with the source of all darkness in the universe. She could project darkness over large areas of space, trapping enemies who would become disoriented and fearful. Tasmia was also a superb athlete and her homeworld's hand-to-hand combat champion. When her planet was invaded by the Fatal Five, she joined the Legion of Super-Heroes and helped to defeat the invaders. She also fought under the name Umbra.

SHIFT
DEBUT *Titans/Young Justice: Graduation Day* (Vol. 1) #3 (Aug. 2003)
BACKGROUND When Metamorpho fell to Earth following the destruction of the JLA's satellite, a fragment of him broke loose and formed its own consciousness. Unaware of his origin, this clone became Shift and later joined the Outsiders. Shift's unstable molecular structure allowed him to transform himself and other objects into chemical compounds. After he accidentally killed a number of people during Black Lightning's escape from Iron Heights Penitentiary, the grief-stricken Shift chose to re-integrate his body with Metamorpho.

SHIMMER
DEBUT *The New Teen Titans* (Vol. 1) #3 (Jan. 1981)
REAL NAME Selinda Flinders **ENEMIES** Teen Titans, Psimon
BACKGROUND Selinda Flinders and her brother Baran were born with superpowers, with Selinda able to transform one element or compound into another. Both siblings were recruited by Doctor Light for his Fearsome Five team: Selinda took the name Shimmer and her brother became Mammoth. They battled the Teen Titans and were imprisoned several times, but Shimmer was ultimately betrayed and killed by her own teammate, Psimon. Later, Doctor Sivana resurrected her for his new Fearsome Five.

SILVER MONKEY
DEBUT *Detective Comics* #685 (Mar. 1995)
BASE Asia **ENEMIES** Batman, Robin, Nightwing
BACKGROUND Silver Monkey was the codename of the mysterious mercenary and deadly martial artist who was hired by crime lord General Tsu to murder King Snake during a gang war in Asia's Golden Triangle. Batman, Robin, and Nightwing joined the battle when it moved to Gotham City, barely preventing Silver Monkey from killing King Snake. Silver Monkey surfaced years later on the eve of another Gotham City gang war; he was believed to have been killed by Scarface.

SKITTER
DEBUT *Teen Titans* #2 (Dec. 2011)
REAL NAME Celine Patterson **ENEMIES** Grymm
BACKGROUND Celine Patterson was a young girl when she underwent a metamorphosis and emerged from a cocoon as a metahuman with the powers and appearance of a spider. She possessed superhuman strength and could project webs and a corrosive substance from her body. When N.Y.P.D. officers ambushed the Teen Titans, Skitter rescued them by spinning webs around the cops. In honor of her bravery, she became a member of the Teen Titans.

SKORPIO
DEBUT *Steel* (Vol. 2) #37 (Apr. 1997)
REAL NAME Dennis Samuel Ellis **BASE** New Jersey
BACKGROUND Dennis "Sam" Ellis was a resident at the Garden State Medical Center when he was recruited to work for gang boss Arthur Villain. Ellis wore a reptile-like suit with concealed weapons and became Skorpio. After his criminal activities brought him into conflict with Steel, Ellis lost his medical license and was arrested. Skorpio joined Alexander Luthor's Secret Society of Super-Villains and was one of the first criminals to be sent to the prison-planet Salvation.

SKYROCKET
DEBUT *JLA* #61 (Feb. 2002)
REAL NAME Celia Forrestal **BASE** San Francisco, California
BACKGROUND US Navy aviation instructor Celia Forrestal was the daughter of two Argo Industries scientists. Her parents invented the Argo Harness, which could absorb, convert, and redirect energy. The terrorist group Scorpio, attempting to steal the device, killed her parents. Celia donned the Argo Harness, became the hero Skyrocket, and joined the Power Company. She also aided rescue efforts during the Infinite Crisis and was part of an all-female team created by Wonder Woman.

SLATE GANG
DEBUT *Static Shock* #1 (Nov. 2011)
BASE New York City **ENEMIES** Static
BACKGROUND The Slate Gang consisted of Cole Brick, Jann Jon, Kaitlin Stone, Kim Dagar, Nico Patrollus, and Trey Uhuru. This powerful syndicate specialized in technology theft and illegal surveillance, but their unlawful businesses were disrupted by the arrival of the hero Static. The team ordered the monster Virule—a killing machine composed of a living virus—to assassinate Static. After Virule failed in its mission, the team lost much of its prestige and influence.

SOBEK
DEBUT *52* #26 (Nov. 2006)
REAL NAME Yurrd **ENEMIES** Black Adam, Batman, Superman
BACKGROUND The giant crocodile Sobek has been known as Famine, one of the Four Horsemen of the Apokolips. He was bioengineered by the villain Doctor Sivana to become a ravenous murderer, and one of his first crimes was to devour the unsuspecting Osiris. Black Adam slaughtered Sobek in revenge, but the crocodile's spirit returned, along with the other Horsemen, to the wastelands of Bialya to feed on the misery of the nation's refugees and later battle Batman and Superman.

SOLARIS II
DEBUT *DC One Million* #1 (Nov. 1998)
ENEMIES Superman dynasty
BACKGROUND The first Solaris was a NASA engineer named Clifton Lacey, who created the deadly Heliotron and died in a battle with Kobra. The second Solaris was a man-made tyrant sun from the 853rd century that tried to destroy several planets with a techno-virus. Solaris first battled Superman-Prime in the 853rd century, and then traveled through time to combat members of the Superman dynasty. Solaris exerted its gravitational pull to wrench planets into its own orbit.

SON OF VULCAN
DEBUT *Son of Vulcan* (Vol. 2) #1 (Aug. 2005)
REAL NAME Miguel Devante **BASE** Derby Youth Home, Charlton's Point
BACKGROUND Miguel "Mikey" Devante was a 14-year-old metahuman orphan. When the Floronic Man took Mikey and others hostage, the hero Vulcan came to their rescue. However, it was Mikey who saved the day by chopping off Floronic Man's arm. Vulcan chose the boy as his successor, Son of Vulcan. After his mentor's death, Miguel took the name Vulcan and fought alongside the Teen Titans, battling the likes of Bork of the Power Company and Trigon, the latter seriously injuring him.

SONAR
DEBUT *Green Lantern* (Vol. 2) #14 (Jul. 1962)
CURRENT VERSION *Green Lantern (Vol. 5) #46* (Jan. 2016)
REAL NAME Bito Wladon **BASE** Balkan country of Modora
ENEMIES Green Lantern
BACKGROUND The first Sonar was a sonic-altering alien monarch who battled Green Lantern. The newest Sonar was Bito Wladon, a terrorist from war-torn Modora. He exploded bombs in Coast City to draw attention to his country's plight. Green Lantern stopped him destroying the United Nations building, but Sonar escaped.

SOYUZ
DEBUT *Firestorm, the Nuclear Man* (Vol. 2) #70 (Apr. 1988)
BASE Russia **ALLIES** Firestorm **ENEMIES** Zuggernaut
BACKGROUND This team of superpowered Russian teens came together to rescue the family of Mikhail Arkadin, the Russian Firestorm. Calling themselves Soyuz, Arkadin's niece, Serafina, a telepath, became Firebird and based her teammates' names on Russian mythology. They included Morozko, Perun, Rusalka, and Vikhor, and among their powers were the abilities to control electricity, water, and cold weather. They have remained active fighting crime in Eastern Europe.

SPEED SAUNDERS
DEBUT *Detective Comics* #1 (Mar. 1937)
REAL NAME Cyril Saunders **ALLIES** Justice Society of America
BACKGROUND As a young man, Cyril Saunders traveled the world in search of adventure, becoming an expert explorer, tracker, climber, and survivalist. It was strongly rumored that he founded the World War II spy agency known as the Office of Strategic Services, and he also teamed up with the Justice Society of America during the 1940s. He became the guardian of his granddaughter, Shiera Saunders, and trained her to become the new Hawkgirl.

SPLIT
DEBUT *Steel* #6 (Jul. 1994)
BASE Metropolis **ALLIES** Hazard **ENEMIES** Steel
BACKGROUND Split was a member of a short-lived black ops organization led by Hazard (Manuel Cabral). Hazard called Split one of the team's most valuable assets, as he had the power to teleport himself and others. Hazard was far less keen on Split's casual attitude. When Split teleported Hazard's assassins from a crime scene, they crossed paths with Steel (John Henry Irons). Steel forced Split to teleport him out of Hazard's bunker, and later took him out with a blow from his hammer.

STALNOIVOLK
DEBUT *Firestorm the Nuclear Man* #67 (Jan. 1988)
REAL NAME Ivan Illyich Gort **BASE** Moscow, Russia
BACKGROUND Ivan Illyich Gort was given the name Stalnoivolk and transformed by the Soviet government into a superpowered agent to fight the Nazis during World War II. His aging was also slowed, and he became immune to pain and injury. He remained loyal to dictator Josef Stalin after the war and was an active participant in the government's bloody purges. Decades later, he traveled to the US to work as a KGB agent against Firestorm and eventually joined the Suicide Squad.

STAR HAWKINS
DEBUT *Strange Adventures* #114 (Mar. 1960)
CURRENT VERSION *Threshold* #1 (Mar. 2013)
BASE Tolerance, Tenebrian Dominion
BACKGROUND Down-at-heel private eye Star Hawkins was hired to investigate the identity of the Legend, the longest-surviving member of the bounty-hunting game show *The Hunted*. After Hawkins discovered that said Legend was none other than Lady Styx, the ruthless ruler of the Tenebrian Dominion, his faithful robot assistant Ilda activated an internal bomb that allowed him to escape.

STAR ROVERS, THE
DEBUT *Mystery in Space* (Vol. 1) #66 (Mar. 1961); *Green Lantern: New Guardians Annual* #1 (Mar. 2013)
BACKGROUND The Star Rovers were a group of mercenary smugglers led by Homer Gint, comprising Chuddu, Karel Sorensen, and Rick Purvis. One of their earliest jobs was smuggling Carol Ferris, Arkillo, and Saint Walker into the Tenebrian Dominion. Instead, the Star Rovers sold them to agents searching for contestants in *The Hunted* game show. Later, the group was hired by Larfleeze to recover valuable stolen items, including his Orange Lantern Power Battery.

STRATA
DEBUT *Invasion!* #2 (Feb. 1989)
BASE The planet Cairn **ALLIES** L.E.G.I.O.N., R.E.B.E.L.S., InterC.E.P.T.
BACKGROUND Strata came from the planet Dryad, where the inhabitants were virtually invulnerable, rock-like humanoids. Strata teamed with Vril Dox to become a founding member of interstellar law-enforcement agency L.E.G.I.O.N. In an altercation with the bounty hunter Lobo, Strata's skin shattered, revealing that Strata was female. She served as chief training officer of L.E.G.I.O.N. and married team member and fellow Drayd, Garv. She later worked for the R.E.B.E.L.S. and InterC.E.P.T.

STRIKER Z
DEBUT *JLA* #61 (Feb. 2002)
REAL NAME Danny Tsang **BASE** San Francisco
BACKGROUND Stuntman Danny Tsang fell into a vat of experimental fuel-cell plasma. The liquid transformed him into a human battery, capable of fueling the high-tech devices and flight jacket designed by his friend, a former S.T.A.R. Labs engineer named Charlie Lau. While wearing the jacket, Danny could generate sonic energy and shoot cannon blasts. As Striker Z, he worked for superpowered legal firm Power Company, and was badly hurt in a fight with Doctor Impossible.

SUN BOY
DEBUT *Action Comics* #276 (May 1961)
CURRENT VERSION *Legion of Super-Heroes* #1 (Nov. 2011)
REAL NAME Dirk Morgna **ENEMIES** Dr. Regulus, Superboy-Prime
BACKGROUND Dirk Morgna could generate and manipulate solar energy, and was invited to join the Legion of Super-Heroes as Sun Boy. He was captured and plugged into a machine that used his energy power to transform Earth's sun from yellow to red. After he escaped, Sun Boy died when his Legion cruiser crashed on a remote planet. The planet's inhabitants cooked and ate him.

SUMO, SONNY
DEBUT *Forever People* (Vol. 1) #4 (Aug.–Sep. 1971)
ALLIES New Gods, Super Young Team **ENEMIES** Darkseid, Megayakuza
BACKGROUND Noble, super-strong prize fighter Sonny Sumo was unaware his brain held a portion of the Anti-Life Equation, which gave him power to defeat even almighty Darkseid. After freeing the Forever People, Darkseid blasted Sonny back to Feudal Japan. During Final Crisis, Sonny reappeared at a metahuman nightclub, where he swiftly dispatched a drunken cyborg called Megayakuza before joining Mister Miracle and the Super Young Team to oppose an Apokoliptian invasion of Earth.

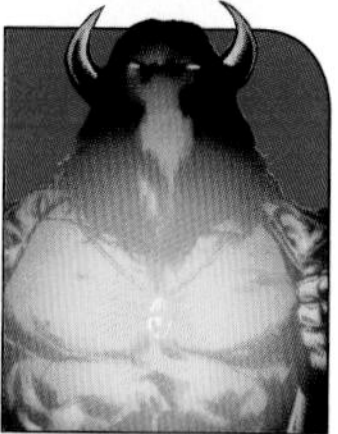

SUPER-CHIEF II
DEBUT *All-Star Western* #117 (Feb.–Mar. 1961)
REAL NAME Jon Standing Bear **BASE** North America
BACKGROUND Jon Standing Bear descended from Flying Stag, the greatest warrior of the Wolf Clan in the 1400s, who became the Supreme Chief of the Iroquois Nations. But none of that mattered to the jaded ex-con and war veteran until, at his father's funeral, he was given the Moon Stone, a family heirloom that bestowed longevity, super-strength, super-speed, and flight. Like his ancestor, Jon became Super Chief; he also helped found a new JLA with Firestorm, Firehawk, and Ambush Bug.

SUPER MALON
DEBUT *The Flash Annual* #13 (Sep. 2000)
BASE Buenos Aires, Argentina **ALLIES** The Flash **ENEMIES** Gualicho
BACKGROUND Following in the footsteps of the Gaucho, a 1950s Argentinean hero, a team of metahumans came together to fight crime as Super Malon. Led by the sorceress Salamanca, the team included superspeedster El Yaguarette, swashbuckling Cimarron, wolf-like El Lobizon, wind-surfing Pampero, horse-like El Bagual, bird-like Cachiru, and master-thief Vizacacha. They joined the Flash to fight the wizard Gualicho, and helped Wonder Woman defeat Cheetah.

SWATT
DEBUT *Aquaman* (Vol. 7) #19 (Jun. 2013)
BASE Atlantis
BACKGROUND Swatt was perhaps the only resident of Atlantis unable to breathe underwater. When in Atlantis, he wore a pressure suit that allowed him to do this, even in the deepest parts of the ocean. His physiology led Swatt to spend a lot of time on the surface world, an activity that King Orm had forbidden. Like all Atlanteans, Swatt was super-strong; he also possessed the unique ability to control and discharge electricity, allowing him to harm enemies—or start a vehicle.

SYONIDE
DEBUT *Batman and the Outsiders* #19 (Mar. 1985)
ALLIES Tobias Whale, Fauna **ENEMIES** The Outsiders
BACKGROUND The first Syonide was a bounty hunter who worked for mob kingpin Tobias Whale. Wracked with guilt, he committed suicide. Whale recruited a mysterious, cold-hearted, hitwoman to become the new Syonide and his personal bodyguard, but she died in a battle with the original Outsiders. A third Syonide joined Lady Eve's Strike Force Kobra, working with the villainess Fauna. She seemingly died fighting a reformed Outsiders, but was later seen as part of Queen Bee's team.

TANNARAK
DEBUT *Phantom Stranger* (Vol. 2) #10 (Nov.–Dec. 1970)
CURRENT VERSION *Constantine* #1 (May 2013)
BASE New York City **ENEMIES** John Constantine
BACKGROUND Born over a century ago, Tannarak was an immortal and powerful sorcerer, able to project magical energy blasts from his hands. He was also a master of alchemy. He owned the interdimensional Bewitched nightclub in San Francisco, but he lost it to Brother Night. He was one of the founding members of the occult group, the Cold Flame, which often clashed with John Constantine.

TARANTULA
DEBUT *Star-Spangled Comics* #1 (Oct. 1941)
REAL NAME Jonathan Law **BASE** Blüdhaven
BACKGROUND Jon Law was a crime novelist in the 1930s who wrote about Super Heroes and longed to become one himself. He began fighting crime as Tarantula, his name and weapons being inspired by his pet spider. His equipment included a web-gun that shot sticky webbing. A skilled acrobat, he joined the wartime heroes known as the All-Star Squadron. Decades later, he moved to Blüdhaven, where he was murdered by Blockbuster (Roland Desmond).

TAR PIT
DEBUT *Flash* #174 (Jul. 2001)
CURRENT VERSION *The Flash* #5 (Mar. 2012)
REAL NAME Joseph "Joey" Monteleone **BASE** Keystone City
ENEMIES The Flash
BACKGROUND Armed robber Joey was in Iron Heights Penitentiary when he found he could transfer his consciousness outside the prison. His astral form became stuck in a vat of hot tar, turning him into Tar Pit, a large, sticky monster. As his human body sank into a coma, Tar Pit roamed Keystone City, causing trouble for the Flash.

TARTARUS

DEBUT *Teen Titans* #6 (Aug. 1999)
BASE Scotland **ENEMIES** The Titans, Omen, Deathstroke
BACKGROUND The team known as Tartarus was formed when Vandal Savage kidnapped former Teen Titan member Omen, forcing her to use her telepathy to create the perfect team to defeat the Titans. She undermined his plans by choosing five villains who would never work well together: Gorilla Grodd, Siren, Red Panzer, Cheshire, and Lady Vic. The Titans teamed with Deathstroke to fight the team, and Red Panzer died in battle. After the Titans invaded the villains' home base, Tartarus disbanded.

TASMANIAN DEVIL

DEBUT *Super Friends* #9 (Dec. 1977)
REAL NAME Hugh Dawkins **BASE** Sydney, Australia
ALLIES Global Guardians, Infinity Inc., JLA **ENEMIES** Prometheus
BACKGROUND Hugh Dawkins claimed his mother was a werewoman who was worshipped by his father in a Tasmanian devil cult. As a teenager, Hugh discovered that he had inherited his mother's powers and was able to transform into the hulking, super-strong Tasmanian Devil. He became a crime fighter in Australia, helping form the Global Guardians and, later, the Justice League of America.

TECHNOCRAT

DEBUT *Outsiders* #1 (Nov. 1993)
REAL NAME Geoffrey Barron
ALLIES Outsiders, Geo-Force **ENEMIES** Faust, Sanction
BACKGROUND Barron invented the Technocrat 2000 battle armor, which enabled flight and housed high-tech weaponry. While demonstrating the suit in Markovia, Barron was attacked by the sorcerer Faust, who changed Barron's assistant, Charlie Wylde, into a bear-like beast. Barron became the hero Technocrat and, with Wylde, formed a new Outsiders team. After they disbanded, Technocrat joined Geo-Force.

TEMPLAR GUARDIANS

DEBUT *Green Lantern Annual* #1 (Oct. 2012)
ALLIES Green Lantern Corps **ENEMIES** Guardians of the Universe
BACKGROUND The Templar Guardians were Reegal, Gurion, Paalko, Quaros, Yekop, and Zalla, a group of Oans who were members of the Guardians of the Universe. Their duty was to guard the crazed First Lantern, who had been sealed within the Chamber of Secrets to keep the universe safe. Reegal died in a battle with the Guardians of the Universe when they tried to free the First Lantern. The Templar Guardians were later elevated to the role of Guardians of the Green Lantern Corps.

TEZUMAK

DEBUT *JLA* #66 (Jul. 2002)
BASE South America
ALLIES Justice League of America **ENEMIES** Gamemnae
BACKGROUND Tezumak was a pre-Aztec Mexican monk, whose suit of armor—oiled with sacrificial blood— enhanced his strength and endurance. He joined the sorceress Gamemnae to fight the Justice League of America, who had traveled back in time to search for Aquaman. When Tezumak learned that Gamemnae's real aim was to achieve power and exterminate the JLA, he sacrificed his life to defeat her.

THREE WITCHES, THE

DEBUT *The Witching Hour* #1 (Feb.–Mar. 1969)
BACKGROUND The Three Witches were immortal goddesses who appeared in various guises. Possessing unlimited supernatural powers, they were aware of every event on the physical and metaphysical planes. They represented three aspects of one being: the mother (Mildred), the crone (Mordred), and the maiden (Cynthia). Their magical powers were strongest at midnight, and they would answer any three questions if asked as part of a ritual. During the Imperiex War, the Three Witches assumed the roles of the Greek Fates to destroy Themyscira.

TIG

DEBUT *I, Vampire* #3 (Jan. 2012)
REAL NAME Tig Rafelson
ALLIES Andrew Bennett **ENEMIES** Mary, Queen of Blood
BACKGROUND Tig was a 16-year-old vampire hunter when she met vampire Andrew Bennett, who, with his friend John Troughton, was searching for Mary, Queen of Blood and her gang. Tig attacked Bennett and, although she learned he was not dangerous, remained distrustful. Despite her skepticism, Tig joined the hunt for Mary. She later revealed that her father, who had become a vampire, had tried to kill her.

TIME COMMANDER

DEBUT *The Brave and the Bold* #59 (Apr.–May 1965)
REAL NAME John Starr **BASE** Gotham City
ALLIES Time Foes **ENEMIES** Batman, Green Lantern, Team Titans
BACKGROUND Starr developed a time-shifting hourglass, which he used, unsuccessfully, to battle Batman and Green Lantern. He later joined other time-themed villains—Chronos, Clock King, and Calendar Man—to form the Time Foes. He died fighting a teen team from the future. Starr's protégé, Sterling Fry, became the new Time Commander and fought Hourman to obtain the tachyon particles in the hero's hourglass.

TNT & DAN THE DYNA-MITE

DEBUT *Star-Spangled Comics* #7 (Apr. 1942)
REAL NAMES Thomas "Tex" N. Thomas (TNT); Daniel Dunbar (Dyna-Mite)
ALLIES All-Star Squadron, Old Justice **ENEMIES** Nazi forces
BACKGROUND After an experiment went awry, science teacher Thomas and his star pupil Dan became TNT and Dan the Dyna-Mite, atomic-powered heroes able to hurl energy bolts from their hands. They joined the All-Star Squadron during World War II and fought together until TNT was killed by Nazi saboteurs. Dan later joined the Young All-Stars and, decades after the war, resurfaced as a member of Old Justice.

TOMORROW WOMAN

DEBUT *JLA* #5 (May 1997)
REAL NAME Clara Kendall **BASE** JLA Watchtower
ALLIES JLA, Hourman **ENEMIES** Professor Ivo, T.O. Morrow, Taint
BACKGROUND Tomorrow Woman was an android created by Professor Ivo and T.O. Morrow to infiltrate the Justice League of America. With superpowers including telekinesis and telepathy, she soon became invaluable to the team. Instead of destroying the JLA, she developed a conscience, disobeyed her creators, and sacrificed herself. A statue in her memory was erected in the JLA's Garden of Heroes.

TOP, THE

DEBUT *Flash* #122 (Aug. 1961)
CURRENT VERSION *The Flash* #41 (Aug. 2015)
REAL NAME Roscoe Dillon **BASE** Central City/Keystone City
ALLIES Mirror Master **ENEMIES** The Flash
BACKGROUND Claiming his powers came from the Speed Force, the criminal the Top could generate and control centrifugal force, spinning at great speeds. He could also lift or smash objects with his spinning powers. He became an enemy of the Flash and joined other super-villains to form the Rogues criminal gang.

TORQUE

DEBUT *Nightwing* #1 (Oct. 1996)
REAL NAME Dudley Soames **BASE** Blüdhaven
ALLIES Blockbuster **ENEMIES** Nightwing
BACKGROUND Soames was one of Blüdhaven's most corrupt cops, working secretly for the mobster Blockbuster. After Blockbuster broke Soames' neck, twisting it right around, Soames vowed revenge and became the villain Torque. Defeated by Nightwing, he was sent to prison, where he enlisted the aid of the vigilante Nite-Wing to escape. Soames planned to kill his new partner, but instead Nite-Wing murdered Torque.

TRIGGER TWINS

DEBUT *All-Star Western* #58 (Apr.–May 1951)
REAL NAME Walter and Wayne Trigger **BASE** Rocky City
BACKGROUND Walt and Wayne Trigger were identical twin brothers who fought for law and order in the Old West. Walt was Rocky City's sheriff, and Wayne ran the general store. When needed, Wayne secretly took Walt's identity and even rode a twin of his horse. Two modern-day Trigger Twins, Tom and Tad Trigger, were Gotham City criminals who fought Batman, Robin, and Nighthawk, before joining an army of villains to attack Metropolis. They were killed in action by Vigilante and Wild Dog.

TRIUMPH

DEBUT *Justice League America* #91 (Aug. 1994)
REAL NAME William MacIntyre **BASE** JLA Watchtower
BACKGROUND Triumph was a Super Hero who controlled the electromagnetic spectrum. He joined the JLA to battle the alien Plasma-Man, directing all his energy at Plasma's spacecraft. The resulting power surge damaged the space/time continuum, and Triumph disappeared, irrevocably altering history. He reemerged a decade later and sold his soul to the demon Neron to regain his lost time. He then came under the influence of an evil Thunderbolt named Lkz and died in a battle with the Justice League.

TSUNAMI

DEBUT *All-Star Squadron* #33 (May 1984)
REAL NAME Miya Shimada **BASE** San Francisco, California
ALLIES Young All-Stars, Aquaman **ENEMIES** Axis forces, Rhombus
BACKGROUND Shimada was a Japanese American who could control water. Disgusted by the prejudice she faced in the US during World War II, she became Tsunami and helped the Japanese Navy. After several battles against the All-Star Squadron, she switched sides and joined the Young All-Stars to fight the Japanese military. After the war, she and the sorcerer Atlan had a daughter who became the aquatic hero Deep Blue.

TURBINE

DEBUT *Flash* #7 (May 2012)
REAL NAME Roscoe Hynes **BASE** Keystone City
ALLIES The Rogues **ENEMIES** Gorilla Grodd
BACKGROUND Hynes was a World War II Tuskegee Airman who became trapped in the Speed Force for seven decades. He tried to use his new speed powers to help him return to the real world, but it was the Flash's arrival in the Speed Force that pulled Hynes to present-day Keystone City. Taking the name Turbine, he fought alongside the Rogues during the gorilla invasion of the city and has since joined the team.

TWEEDLEDEE AND TWEEDLEDUM

DEBUT *Detective Comics* #74 (Apr. 1943)
REAL NAMES Deever and Dumfree Tweed
BASE Gotham City
ALLIES Mad Hatter, Secret Society of Super Villains **ENEMIES** Batman
BACKGROUND The rotund, super-strong villains Tweedledee and Tweedledum began as thieves. After a stint with the Secret Society of Super Villains, they joined the Wonderland Gang, working with the Mad Hatter. Most believed the Mad Hatter was in charge, but the Tweeds controlled him, using one of his own mind-control devices.

ULTRAA

DEBUT *Justice League of America* #153 (Apr. 1978)
CURRENT VERSION *The Multiversity: Ultra Comics* #1 (Mar. 2015)
ALLIES Queen Maxima **ENEMIES** Captain Atom, Ultra
BACKGROUND A warlord from the planet Almerac, Ultraa arrived on Earth in search of his consort Lady Maxima. When she bestowed her favors on Captain Atom instead, a brutal battle ensued that Ultraa appeared to win. Despite this, he was rejected by Maxima and sent home. During the recent Multiversity Crisis, Ultraa was defeated by Ultra, a lab-created Super Hero designed to fight the Gentry.

ULTRA THE MULTI-ALIEN

DEBUT *Mystery in Space* #103 (Nov. 1965)
CURRENT VERSION *Justice League United* #1 (Jul. 2014)
BASE The Moon of Thalsalla
BACKGROUND Ultra the Multi-Alien was created by Lord Byth, who spliced together DNA from many prisoners to form one creature—Ultra the Multi-Alien. Byth prophesied that the child would become the world-devouring Infinitus. However, a battle to control Ultra developed between Byth and some of the Justice League United, forcing the Martian Manhunter to wipe Ultra's mind. Byth later fell into a black hole.

VALDA

DEBUT *Arak, Son of Thunder* #3 (Nov. 1981)
BASE Aix-le-Chapelle, Frankland, 8th century
ALLIES Arak **ENEMIES** Baledor, Angelica
BACKGROUND Valda, aka Iron Maiden, was one of the bravest knights in 8th-century Europe. After her mother's death, she was tutored by the sorcerer Malagigi and trained in swordfighting by the ghost of Amadis of Gaul. Knighted after defeating her uncle, Rinaldo, Valda teamed up with Arak, Son of Thunder, with whom she fell in love. Valda later traveled to the present and joined Shadowpact to fight the Spectre.

VETERAN

DEBUT *Robin* #138 (Jul. 2005)
REAL NAME Nathan Howe
ALLIES US Military, Superman, Robin **ENEMIES** The Auctioneer
BACKGROUND The Veteran was a legendary (and seemingly indestructible) Super Hero, rumored to have fought in all of America's wars, and earning the rank of General in Operation Desert Storm. A superb combatant, marksman, and strategist, the Veteran commanded his own elite squad of solders to handle everything from street crime to metahuman threats. He also fought alongside Robin and Superman.

VIGILANTE I

DEBUT *Action Comics* #42 (Nov. 1941)
REAL NAME Greg Sanders **BASE** New York City
ALLIES Stuff, the Chinatown Kid, El Diablo **ENEMIES** The Dummy, Sheeda
BACKGROUND When Greg Sanders' father was killed by bandits, he left a career as "the Prairie Troubadour" to become the crime fighter Vigilante. Moving to New York, he partnered with young marital artist Stuff, the Chinatown Kid, and even teamed with Superman to track down a werewolf. He later formed a new Seven Soldiers of Victory team to fight the far-future Sheeda, but they were massacred in the battle.

VON GUNTHER, BARONESS PAULA

DEBUT *Sensation Comics* #4 (Apr. 1942)
ALLIES Nazi forces (formerly), Amazons
ENEMIES JSA, Wonder Woman
BACKGROUND During World War II, von Gunther was Adolf Hitler's assistant and a practitioner of dark magic. She summoned the ancient spirit Dark Angel, who took over her body and empowered her to attack the Justice Society of America. Hippolyta defeated von Gunther and separated her from Dark Angel's spirit. Paula then renounced her Nazi ties and relocated to Themyscira, where she became a scientist.

VOSTOK-X

DEBUT *Aquaman* #7 (May 2012)
ALLIES The Others, Aquaman **ENEMIES** KGBeast, Black Manta
BACKGROUND Vostok was a Russian cosmonaut-trainee who spent years in an isolation chamber preparing for space travel. When Russia's space program was shelved, Vostok fled to Siberia and joined Aquaman in a battle against Black Manta. Vostok later donned an Atlantean helmet created by the first king of Atlantis, which granted him great powers, including the ability to survive without food, sleep, oxygen, or water. He became the hero Vostok-X and joined Aquaman and the Others to fight the KGBeast.

VYKIN BALDAUR

DEBUT *Forever People* #1 (Feb.–Mar. 1971)
CURRENT VERSION *Wonder Woman* #131 (Mar. 1988)
ALLIES Forever People, Highfather **ENEMIES** Darkseid, Mantis, Guy Gardner
BACKGROUND Vykin was a Warrior Class 7 New God, raised on New Genesis with his twin sister Serafina. A highly skilled combatant, he also possessed super-strength and could control his density. Vykin traveled to Earth to fight alongside the heroic Forever People. Though Vykin had a somewhat testy relationship with some members of the team, he eagerly joined the battle against the Red Lantern Guy Gardner.

VYNDKTVX

DEBUT *Action Comics* #1 (Nov. 2011)
ALLIES Anti-Superman Army **ENEMIES** Superman, Mr. Mxyzptlk
BACKGROUND Vyndktvx was an imp in the 5th Dimension and the court magician of King Brpxz. When the king chose Mr. Mxyzptlk as his favorite and permitted him to marry his daughter, Vyndktvx flew into a rage and vowed to kill his rival. He killed the king by mistake and trapped Mr. Mxyzptlk in a glass coffin. Vyndktvx then attacked Superman several times, gathering super-villains to form an Anti-Superman Army. He failed and was banished to a 5th Dimension prison for eternity.

WEIRD, THE

DEBUT *The Weird* #1 (Apr. 1988)
CURRENT VERSION *Stormwatch #19* (Jun. 2013)
ALLIES Stormwatch, Justice League **ENEMIES** Macrolatts
BACKGROUND The Weird came from an alternate dimension inhabited by Zarolatts, a race of largely passive energy beings. When their tyrannical overlords, the Macrolatts, decided to attack Earth, the Weird intervened and animated a human corpse, enabling the Weird to alter his own molecular density and that of anything he touched. He later joined heroes like the Engineer and Hellstrike to form the team Stormwatch.

WHIP, THE

DEBUT *Flash Comics* #1 (January 1940)
REAL NAME Rodney Elwood Gaynor **BASE** Seguro, New Mexico; NYC
BACKGROUND In 1939, millionaire Rod Gaynor was inspired by the legend of Don Fernando Suarez, the 19th century hero El Castigo, "the Whip," and became an expert bullwhip handler and equestrian. As the new Whip, astride his stallion Diablo, he fought crime in New Mexico, defending Mexican immigrants. During World War II, the Whip served in the All-Star Squadron. Decades later, Rod's granddaughter Shelly joined the Seven Soldiers of Victory as the latest Whip, but died fighting the Sheeda.

WHITE RABBIT

DEBUT *Batman: The Dark Knight* #1 (Nov. 2011)
REAL NAME Jaina Hudson **BASE** Gotham City
ALLIES Clayface, Bane **ENEMIES** Batman
BACKGROUND Jaina Hudson was a prominent Gotham City socialite who dated Bruce Wayne. She was also the mysterious White Rabbit, and seemed to be able to physically separate her two personas. Batman first encountered White Rabbit when she freed inmates from Arkham Asylum. He discovered she was working with the villain Clayface, and she almost managed to inject the Dark Knight with a dangerous toxin.

WILD DOG

DEBUT *Wild Dog* #1 (Sep. 1987)
REAL NAME Jack Wheeler **BASE** Quad Cities, Iowa
BACKGROUND Jack Wheeler faced several tragedies, first when his fellow US Marine troops were killed by a terrorist bomb in Beirut and, later, when a mobster murdered his girlfriend. Returning to his hometown of Quad Cities, Wheeler donned a hockey mask and a State U. college shirt. Armed with machine guns and taser-shooting gloves, he became the hero Wild Dog. The Quad Cities police were not happy about Wild Dog's vigilante crime-fighting methods, but he soon became a local hero.

WILDEBEEST

DEBUT *The New Teen Titans* #36 (Oct. 1987)
BASE Science City, Russia
ALLIES New Titans, Cyborg **ENEMIES** Superboy-Prime
BACKGROUND The Wildebeest Society was a group of super-strong villains; each one operated under the name Wildebeest to make it seem that there was only one. The Teen Titan Jericho took control after he was possessed by a demon, and initiated the creation of human/animal hybrids as hosts for the group. The Society was destroyed, but one member, Baby Wildebeest, survived and joined the New Titans.

WINDFALL

DEBUT *Batman and the Outsiders* #9 (Apr. 1984)
REAL NAME Wendy Jones **BASE** Los Angeles, California
ALLIES The Outsiders, Suicide Squad **ENEMIES** Kobra
BACKGROUND Wendy Jones was a metahuman able to generate and control winds, from breezes to tornadoes. Unlike her sister, the water-wielding villain New Wave, Wendy fought for justice with the Outsiders. Duped into joining Strike Force Kobra, Windfall eventually realized her mistake and rejoined the Outsiders. She was later recruited to the Suicide Squad and died in action in the Middle East.

WING

DEBUT *Detective Comics* #20 (Oct. 1938)
ALLIES Crimson Avenger, Seven Soldiers of Victory **ENEMIES** Nebula Man
BACKGROUND Wing was a Chinese immigrant to the US in the 1930s, who worked for ace reporter Lee Travis, secretly the crime-fighting Crimson Avenger. Donning his own costume, Wing and Travis joined the All-Star Squadron during World War II, and Wing became the unofficial eighth member of the heroic team known as the Seven Soldiers of Victory. In a battle with the cosmic being Nebula Man, Wing sacrificed his life to save the Seven Soldiers, who were scattered across time.

WITCHFIRE

DEBUT *JLA* #61 (Feb. 2002)
REAL NAME Rebecca Carstairs **BASE** San Francisco, California
ALLIES Power Company **ENEMIES** Nekron, Seven Deadly Sins
BACKGROUND Rebecca found a book of spells as a youngster, inspiring her to dabble in magic. As an adult, she took the name Witchfire, launching her career as a singer, actress, and motorcycle daredevil. After she accidentally summoned a demon, Witchfire vowed to refine her abilities. She joined the Super Hero team Power Company, but soon discovered she was a homunculus, a magically created artificial being.

ZILIUS ZOX

DEBUT *Final Crisis: Rage of the Red Lanterns* #1 (Dec. 2008)
ALLIES Red Lanterns **ENEMIES** Sinestro
BACKGROUND The Red Lantern of Sector 3544 was Zilius Zox, a savage, hate-filled creature who pledged allegiance to Atrocitus and swore revenge against Sinestro and the Sinestro Corps. Zox notoriously murdered the Sinestro Corps Soldier of Sector 2332 by crushing him within his giant mouth and then seemingly swallowing parts of his body. He possessed superstrength and super-speed, and his Red Lantern Ring gave him the rage-fueled powers of flight and energy projection.

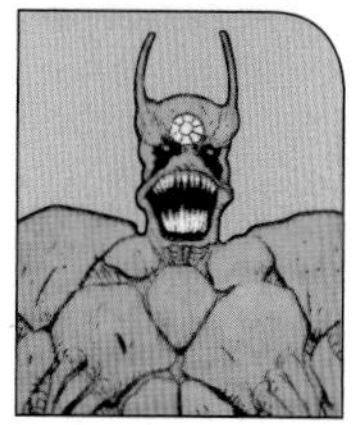

ZUGGERNAUT

DEBUT *Firestorm the Nuclear Man* #66 (Dec. 1987)
ENEMIES Firestorm, Soyuz
BACKGROUND Zuggernaut was a shape-shifting, symbiotic alien that crash-landed in Russia and then merged its monstrous body with a small-time criminal, Matvei Rodor. Zuggernaut tried to kill one of Rodor's enemies, a prosecutor named Soliony, but was thwarted by the American hero Firestorm. Zuggernaut returned to battle the Russian Super Hero team Soyuz, but was again defeated by Firestorm, who used the creature's own explosive energies to defeat it.

INDEX

Page numbers in **bold** refer to main entries

C

M

N

T

W

Y

Z

ACKNOWLEDGMENTS

Dusty Abell, Jerry Acerno, Daniel Acuña, Vincenzo Acunzo, Art Adams, Neal Adams, Dan Adkins, Charlie Adlard, Jack Adler, Kalman Adrasofsky, Ian Akin, Christian Alamy, Gerry Alanguilan, Oclair Albert, Jeff Albrecht, Rafael Albuquerque, Alfredo Alcala, Alcatena, Pascal Alixe, Roy Allan Martinez, Michael Allred, Bob Almond, Marlo Alquiza, Sal Amendola, Brad Anderson, Brent Anderson, Murphy Anderson, Kalman Andrasofszky, Ross Andru, Jim Aparo, Sergio Aragones, Renato Arlem, Paolo Armitano, Jason Armstrong, Ulises Arreola, Tom Artis, Stan Asch, Mahmud Asrar, Derec Aucoin, Terry Austin, Brandon Badeaux, Mark Badger, Mark Bagley, Bernard Baily, Michael Bair, Kyle Baker, Jim Balent, Ryan Banjamin, Darryl Banks, Matt Banning, Carlo Barberi, David Baron, Dell Barras, Mike Barreiro, Eduardo Barreto, Al Barrionuevo, Eddy Barrows, Sy Barry, Hilary Barta, Sami Basri, Chris Batista, Eric Battle, John Beatty, Terry Beatty, David Beaty, C.C. Beck, Howard Bender, Scott Benefield, Ed Benes, Mariah Benes, Joe Benitez, Ryan Benjamin, Joe Bennett, Lee Bermejo, Ramon Bernado, Ian Bertram, Simone Bianchi, Jack Binder, Jerry Bingham, J.J. Birch, Steve Bird, Simon Bisley, Stephen Bissette, Bit, Tex Blaisdell, Fernando Blanco, Bret Blevins, Greg Blocks, Will Blyberg, Jon Bogdanove, Brian Bolland, Henry Boltinoff, John Bolton, Philip Bond, Roger Bonet, Richard Bonk, Brett Booth, Alisson Borges, Geraldo Borges, Wayne Boring, Ron Boyd, Belardin Brabo, Ken Branch, Craig Brasfield, Brett Breeding, Ryan Breeding, Jeff Brennan, Andrei Bressan, Norm Breyfogle, Mark Bright, June Brightman, June Brigman, Pat Broderick, Greg Brooks, Bob Brown, Daniel Brown, Garry Brown, Reilly Brown, Jimmy Broxton, Joe Brozowski, D. Bruce Berry, Al Bryant, Rick Bryant, Rebecca Buchman, Mark Buckingham, Rich Buckler, Danny Bulanadi, Rick Burchett, Chris Burnham, Ray Burnley, Jack Burnley, Sal Buscema, Buzz, Mitch Byrd, John Byrne, Ralph Cabrera, Jim Calafiore, Talent Caldwell, Ben Caldwell, Dennis Calero, Ignacio Calero, Robert Campanella, Marc Campos, Giuseppe Camuncoli, Eric Canete, Zander Cannon, Greg Capullo, W.C. Carani, Nick Cardy, Sergio Cariello, Joe Carta, Richard Case, John Cassaday, Marco Castiello, Anthony Castrillo, John Cebollero, Joe Certa, Gary Chaloner, Keith Champagne, Ernie Chan, Bernard Chang, Kiki Chansamone, Travis Charest, Howard Chaykin, Michael Chen, Sean Chen, Jim Cheung, Cliff Chiang, Tom Chiu, Michael Choi, Nick Choles, Bert Christman, Andrew Chul, Ian Churchill, Vicente Cifuentes, Yidiray Cinar, Yildiray Cinar, Matthew Clark, Mike Clark, Scott Clark, Andy Clarke, Becky Cloonan, Martin Coccolo, Dave Cockrum, Andre Coelho, Olivier Coipel, Gene Colan, Jack Cole, Simon Coleby, Hector Collazo, Vince Colletta, Bill Collins, Mike Collins, Ernie Colon, Amanda Conner, Kevin Conrad, Will Conrad, Darwyn Cooke, Dave Cooper, Pete Costanza, Denys Cowan, Jeromy Cox, P. Craig Russell, Clayton Crain, Dennis Cramer, Reed Crandall, Saleem Crawford, Steve Crespo, Jake Crippen, Chris Cross, Charles Cuidera, Paris Cullins, Bruce D. Patterson, Fernando Dagnino, Federico Dallocchio, Rodolfo Damaggio, Antonio Daniel, Alan Davis, Dan Davis, Ed Davis, Shane Davis, Sam De La Rosa, Randy Deburke, Mike Decarlo, Nelson Decastro, Marc Deering, Nuzio Defilippis, Adam Dekraker, Luciana Del Negro, Jose Delbo, John Dell, Jesse Delperdang, J.m. Dematteis, Mike Deodato Jr., Tom Derenick, Hi-Fi Design, Johnny Desjardins, Stephen Destefano, Tony Dezuniga, Netho Diaz, Dick Dillin, Steve Dillon, Steve Ditko, Rachel Dodson, Terry Dodson, Derec Donovan, Colleen Doran, Evan Dorkin, Les Dorscheid, Alberto Dose, Bob Downs, Mike Dringenberg, Victor Drujiniu, Christian Duce, Armando Durruthy, Michal Dutkiewicz, Jan Duursema, Bob Dvorak, Kieron Dwyer, Joshua Dysart, Everett E. Hibbard, Freddie E. Williams Ii, Dale Eaglesham, Scot Eaton, Neil Edwards, Marty Egeland, Martin Egeland, Lee Elias, Chris Eliopulos, Randy Eliott, Lee Ellas, Gabe Eltaeb, Will Ely, Randy Emberlin, Tan Eng Huat, Steve Epting, Gary Erskine, Steve Erwin, Mike Esposito, Ric Estrada, George Evans, Nathan Eyring, Rich Faber, Jason Fabok, Nathan Fairbairn, Mark Farmer, Wayne Faucher, Duncan Fegredo, Tom Feister, Norman Felchie, Jim Fern, Raúl Fernández, Javi Fernandez, Eber Ferreira, Julio Ferreira, Pascual Ferry, David Finch, Fabrizio Fiorentino, John Fischetti, Creig Flessel, Sandu Florea, John Floyd, Max Flumara, John Ford, Travel Foreman, John Forte, Tom Fowler, Ramona Fradon, Francesco Francavilla, Gary Frank, Frank Frazetta, Fred Fredericks, George Freeman, Ron Frenz, Paul Fricke, Derek Fridolfs, Richard Friend, Danis Frietas, Jenny Frison, James Fry, Harry G. Peter, Anderson Gabrych, Kerry Gammill, Lee Garbett, German Garcia, Manuel Garcia, Alex Garner, Ron Garney, Brian Garvey, Roy Garvey, Ale Garza, Gabrynch Garza, Carlos Garzón, Phil Gascoine, Stefano Gaudiano, Drew Geraci, Frank Giacoia, Vince Giarrano, Dave Gibbons, Ian Gibson, Joe Giella, Keith Giffen, Craig Gilmore, Dick Giordano, Sam Glanzman, Jonathan Glapion, Patrick Gleason, Frank Gomez, Fernando Gonzales, Adrian Gonzales, Nei Googe, Neil Googe, Julius Gopez, Jason Gorder, Al Gordon, Chris Gordon, Sam Grainger, Jerry Grandenetti, Jerry Grandinetti, Mick Gray, Dan Green, Timothy Green II, Sid Greene, Mike Grell, Al Grenet, Tom Grindberg, Peter Gross, Tom Grummett, Ig Guara, Fred Guardineer, Renato Guedes, R.M. Guera, Gianluca Gugliotta, Jackson Guice, Yvel Guichet, Andres Guinaldo, Paul Guinan, Mike Gustovich, J. H. Williams III, Gene Ha, Matt Haley, Jim Hall, Craig Hamilton, Cully Hamner, Scott Hampton, Scott Hanna, Ed Hannigan, Chad Hardin, Chard Hardin, Fred Harper, Ron Harris, Tony Harris, James Harvey, Irwin Hasen, Jeremy Haun, Mike Hawthorne, Rob Hayes, Fred Haynes, Doug Hazlewood, Daniel HDR, Russ Heath, Don Heck, Marc Hempel, Andrew Hennessy, Daniel Henriques, Scott Hepburn, Phil Hester, Bryan Hitch, Rick Hoberg, James Hodgkins, Josh Hood, Ken Hooper, Dave Hoover, Sandra Hope, Sarah Hope, Alex Horley, Greg Horn, Richard Howell, Corin Howell, Mike Huddleston, Jeff Huet, Adam Hughes, Dave Hunt, Rob Hunter, Victor Ibanez, Jamal Igle, Stuart Immonen, Carmine Infantino, Frazer Irving, Mark Irwin, Geof Isherwood, Chris Ivy, Kevin J. West, Jack Jadson, Mikel Janín, Dennis Janke, Klaus Janson, Georges Jeanty, Dennis Jensen, Oscar Jimenez, Phil Jimenez, Jorge Jiménez, Dave Johnson, Drew Johnson, Staz Johnson, Jeff Johnson, Arvell Jones, Casey Jones, J.G. Jones, Kelley Jones, Robert Jones, Malcolm Jones III, Arnie Jorgensen, Ruy José, Juan José Ryp, Dan Jurgens, Justiano, John K. Snyder Iii, Barbara Kaalberg, John Kalisz, Michael Kaluta, Viktor Kalvachev, Bob Kane, Gil Kane, Kano, Rafael Kayanan, Stan Kaye, Joe Kelly, A.j. Kent, Dale Keown, Karl Kerschl, Karl Kesel, Loh Kin Sun, Kinsun, Jack Kirby, J.J. Kirby, Leonard Kirk, Tyler Kirkham, Barry Kitson, George Klein, Scott Koblish, Irene Koh, Scott Kolins, Tony Kordos, Don Kramer, Peter Krause, Ray Kryssing, Adam Kubert, Andy Kubert, Joe Kubert, Aaron Kuder, Szymon Kudranski, Andy Kuhn, Alan Kupperberg, Michel Lacombe, José Ladrönn, David Lafuente, Harry Lampert, Greg Land, Justin Land, Stefano Landini, Andy Lanning, David Lapham, Serge Lapointe, Michael Lark, Greg Larocque, Bud Larosa, Salvador Larroca, Erik Larsen, Ken Lashley, Stanley Lau, Bob Layton, Bob Le Rose, Rob Lea, Garry Leach, Rob Lean, Jim Lee, Norman Lee, Paul Lee, Alvin Lee, Jae Lee, Alex Lei, Steve Leialoha, Rob Leigh, Jay Leisten, Rick Leonardi, Bob Lewis, Mark Lewis, Steve Lieber, Rob Liefeld, Sonny Liew, Steve Lightle, Ron Lim, Mark Lipka, John Livesay, Victor Llamas, Beni Lobel, Don Lomax, Alvaro Lopez, David Lopez, Aaron Lopresti, John Lowe, Jorge Lucas, José Luis Garcia-Lopez, Emanuela Lupacchino, Daniel Luvisi, Greg Luzniak, Tom Lyle, Howard M. Shum, Mike Machlan, Dev Madan, Wilson Magalháes, Kevin Maguire, Rick Magyar, Larry Mahlstedt, Doug Mahnke, Alex Maleev, Marcelo Malolo, Francis Manapul, Leonardo Manco, Tom Mandrake, Mike Manley, Lou Manna, Guillem March, Pablo Marcos, Marvin Mariano, Bill Marimon, Álvaro Martínez, Cindy Martin, Cynthia Martin, Gary Martin, Marcos Martin, Shawn Martinbrough, Kenny Martinez, Allen Martinez, Marcos Marz, José Marzan Jr., Nathan Massengill, Jason Masters, Steve Mattsson, J.p. Mayer, Sheldon Mayer, Mike Mayhew, Rick Mays, Dave Mazzucchelli, Trevor Mccarthy, Ray Mccarthy, Aaron Mcclennan, Tom McCraw, John Mccrea, Scott McDaniel, Luke Mcdonnell, Todd Mcfarlane, Tom Mcgraw, Ed Mcguinness, Dave Mckean, Mark Mckenna, Mike Mckone, Frank Mclaughlin, Bob Mcleod, Shawn Mcmanus, Lan Medina, Paco Medina, Linda Medley, Carlos Meglia, David Meikis, Adriana Melo, Jaime Mendoza, Jesus Merino, Mort Meskin, William Messner-Loebs, J.D. Mettler, Jonboy Meyers, Pop Mhan, Joshua Middleton, Grant Miehm, Rodolfo Migliari, Mike Mignola, Danny Miki, Al Milgrom, Frank Miller, Steve Mitchell, Lee Moder, Sheldon Moldoff, Romano Molenaar, Jorge Molina, Karl Moline, Shawn Moll, Steve Montano, Jim Mooney, Jerome Moore, Travis Moore, Marcio Morais, Mark Morales, Rags Morales, Ruben Moreira, Tomeu Morey, Gabriel Morrissette, Gray Morrow, Win Mortimer, Ibrahim Moustafa, Jeffrey Moy, Phil Moy, Sean Murphy, Brian Murray, Todd Nauck, Paul Neary, Rudy Nebres, Mark Nelson, Diogenes Neves, Fabiano Neves, Denis Neville, Don Newton, Dustin Nguyen, Tom Nguyen, Peter Nguyen, Art Nichols, Troy Nixey, Martin Nodell, Graham Nolan, Cary Nord, Irv Novick, Leo Nowak, Kevin Nowlan, John Nyberg, Michael O'Hare, Sonia Oback, Bob Oksner, Patrick Oliffe, Ben Oliver, Ariel Olivetti, Patrick Olliffe, Jerry Ordway, Joe Orlando, Guillermo Ortego, Andy Owens, Richard Pace, Carlos Pacheco, Carlo Pagulayan, Mark Pajarillo, Tom Palmer, Jimmy Palmiotti, Peter Palmiotti, Dan Panosian, Eduardo Pansica, Pete Pantazis, Pete Panzatis, George Papp, Yanick Paquette, Charles Paris, Ande Parks, Mike Parobeck, Francisco Paronzini, Sean Parsons, Fernando Pasarin, James Pascoe, Chuck Patten, Bruce Patterson, Chuck Patton, Jason Paz, Jason Pearson, Paul Pelletier, Mark Pennington, Andrew Pepoy, Mike Perkins, Rich Perrotta, Frank Perry, Bob Petrecca, Hugo Petrus, Joe Phillips, Javier Piña, Wendy Pini, Fco Plascencia, Al Plastino, Kilian Plunkett, Keith Pollard, Adam Pollina, Alberto Ponticelli, Francis Portela, Howard Porter, Howie Post, Eric Powell, Joe Prado, Miguelanxo Prado, Hendry Prasetya, Bruno Premiani, Mark Propst, Steve Pugh, Javier Pulido, Jack Purcell, George Perez, Joe Quesada, Frank Quitely, Mac Raboy, Pablo Raimondi, Elton Ramalho, Humberto Ramos, Rodney Ramos, Ron Randall, Khary Randolph, Tom Raney, Rich Rankin, Norm Rapmund, Fred Ray, Brian Reber, Frank Redondo, Sal Regia, Ivan Reis, Rod Reis, Paul Renaud, Cliff Richards, Roy Richardson, Robin Riggs, Eduardo Risso, Paul Rivoche, Trina Robbins, Jeremy Roberts, Clem Robins, Andrew Robinson, Jerry Robinson, Roger Robinson, Kenneth Rocafort, Robson Rocha, Denis Rodier, Carlos Rodiguez, Anibal Rodriguez, Danny Rodriguez, Jasen Rodriguez, Rodin Rodriguez, Noel Rodriguez, Francisco Rodriguez De La Fuente, Marshall Rogers, Prentis Rollins, T.G. Rollins, John Romita Jr., William Rosado, John Rosenberger, Alex Ross, Dave Ross, Luke Ross, Riley Rossmo, Duncan Rouleau, Craig Rousseau, George Roussos, Stephane Roux, Stephane Roux, Jim Royal, Mike Royer, Josef Rubinstein, Steve Rude, Marco Rudy, Nei Ruffino, Felix Ruiz, Vince Russell, Paul Ryan, Matt Ryan, Tony S. Daniel, Mike S. Miller, Jesœs Sa's, Jesœs Sa'z, Bernard Sachs, Stephen Sadowski, Jesus Saiz, Edgar Salazar, Tim Sale, Javier Saltares, Chris Samnee, Daniel Sampere, Jose Sanchez, Medina Sanchez, Alex Sanchez, Rafa Sandoval, Derlis Santacruz, Mateus Santolouco, Clement Sauve Jr., Alex Saviuk, Kurt Schaffenberger, Mitch Schauer, Christie Scheele, Ira Schnapp, Mark Schultz, Damion Scott, Nicola Scott, Trevor Scott, Bart Sears, Stephen Segovia, Mike Sekowsky, Mike Sellers, Val Semeiks, Miguel Sepulveda, Declan Shalvey, Eric Shanower, Hal Sharp, Liam Sharp, Kevin Sharpe, Howard Sherman, Pen Shumaker, Joe Shuster, Jon Sibal, Bill Sienkiewicz, R.B. Silva, Emanuel Simeon, Tom Simmons, Joe Simon, Dave Simons, Walt Simonson, Howard Simpson, Alex Sinclair, Paulo Siqueira, Steve Skroce, Steven Skroce, Louis Small Jr., Andy Smith, Bob Smith, Cam Smith, Dietrich Smith, Jeff Smith, Tod Smith, Peter Snejbjerg, Ray Snyder, Ryan Sook, Andrea Sorrentino, Aaron Sowd, Dexter Soy, Jack Sparling, Dan Spiegle, Dick Sprang, Frank Springer, Chris Sprouse, Claude St. Aubin, Cat Staggs, John Stanisci, Fiona Staples, Jim Starlin, Arne Starr, Leonard Starr, Rick Stasi, John Statema, Joe Staton, Ken Steacy, Marvin Stein, Brian Stelfreeze, N. Steven Harris, Dave Stevens, Cameron Stewart, Roger Stewart, John Stokes, Kevin Stokes, Karl Story, Larry Stroman, Larry Stucker, Rob Stull, Robert Stull, Michael Suayan, Goran Sudzuka, Tom Sutton, Curt Swan, Ardian Syaf, Michael T. Gilbert, Marcio Takara, Bryan Talbot, Billy Tan, Philip Tan, Romeo Tanghal, Babs Tarr, Jordi Tarragona, Christopher Taylor, Ty Templeton, Jason Temujin Minor, Greg Theakston, Art Thibert, Stephen Thompson, Frank Thorne, John Timms, Marcus To, Alex Toth, Julian Totino Tedesco, John Totleben, Tim Townsend, Jonas Trindade, Tim Truman, Chaz Truog, Koi Turnball, Dwayne Turner, Michael Turner, George Tuska, John Tyler Christopher, Angel Unzueta, Carlos Urbano, Alina Urusov, Juan Valasco, Ethan Van Sciver, Brad Vancata, Rick Veitch, Sal Velluto, Charles Vess, Al Vey, Carlos Villagran, Ricardo Villagran, José Villarrubia, Dexter Vines, Alessandro Vitti, Juan Vlasco, Trevor Von Eeden, Wade Von Grawbadger, Matt Wagner, Ron Wagner, Brad Walker, Kev Walker, Chip Wallace, John Watson, Lee Weeks, Joe Weems, Alan Weiss, Chris Weston, Doug Wheatley, Mark Wheatley, Glenn Whitmore, Bob Wiacek, Mike Wieringo, Aron Wiesenfeld, Admira Wijaya, Anthony Williams, Scott Williams, J.H. Williams III, Bill Willingham, Ryan Winn, Phil Winslade, Chuck Wojtkiewicz, Walden Wong, Wally Wood, Pete Woods, John Workman, Moe Worthman, Chris Wozniak, Bill Wray, Jason Wright, Berni Wrightson, Annie Wu, Kelly Yates, Tom Yeates, Steve Yeowell, Leinil Francis Yu, Patrick Zircher.

The publishers have made every effort to identify and acknowledge the artists whose work appears in this Encyclopedia.